World War II
in the Pacific

World War II in the Pacific
An Encyclopedia

Stanley Sandler
Editor

Garland Publishing, Inc.
New York & London
2001

Published in 2001 by
Garland Publishing, Inc.
29 West 35th Street
New York, NY 10001

Published in Great Britain by
Garland Publishing, Inc.
11 New Fetter Lane
London EC4P 4EE

Garland is an imprint of the Taylor & Francis Group

Production Editor:	Jeanne Shu
Copyeditors:	Ingrid Sterner, Bob Weber, Beth Wilson
Indexer:	Leoni Z. McVey
Photo Researcher:	Martin Levick
Composition:	Impressions Book and Journal Services, Inc.
Development Manager:	Richard Steins
Publishing Director, Reference:	Sylvia K. Miller

10 9 8 7 6 5 4 3 2 1

Library of Congress Cataloging-in-Publication data is available from the Library of Congress.

World War II in the Pacific : an encyclopedia / Stanley Sandler, editor.
    p. cm.
  Includes bibliographical references and index.
  ISBN 0-8153-1883-9 (alk. paper)
    1. World War, 1939–1945—Campaigns—Pacific Ocean—Encyclopedias. I. Sandler, Stanley, 1937–
D767.W68 2000
940.54′25′03—dc21   00-061773

Printed on acid-free, 250-year-life paper
Manufactured in the United States of America

Contents

Introduction

From the Japanese point of view at the time, war with the United States was almost entirely unprovoked. For they knew that it was the Americans who had despised Japanese immigrants and insultingly segregated them in West Coast schools. It was the Americans who had gone on about the "Yellow Peril." It was the United States which had imposed a state of naval inferiority on Japan at the Washington Naval Conference of 1922. And it was the United States government which, for its own imperialistic purposes, objected to Japan's attempts to bring order (from Japan's point of view) to a "decadent" and "corrupt" Nationalist China.

In the war games played out on the polished floors of the U.S. Naval War College, Japan was the most likely enemy. These war games, of course, assumed that the U.S. Navy was by far Nippon's most worrisome opponent; both nations fortified their Pacific island territories against each other. Yet the Japanese had never, certainly in public, brandished their swords against the Americans and their Pacific possessions, although they inveighed against European and American colonialism in Asia. Up to 1931 the provocation and the inflammatory rhetoric was almost entirely American.

This one-sided animosity actually intensified after 1931, and for far more tangible reasons than any vague worries about the "Yellow Peril." The Japanese invasion of Manchuria in 1931 was an act of unmitigated aggression. Even so, it was certainly not directed against the United States and in no way tangibly affected American interests. But it did give a focus to the previously amorphous anti-Japanese feeling among many Americans. Six years later, the launching of full-scale warfare against China, for which Americans felt a sort of proprietary sympathy, sharply intensified that focus. The owner of the enormously influential *Time, Life,* and *Fortune* magazines, Henry Luce, the offspring of American missionaries to China, made sure that Japanese atrocities against the Chinese people were vividly documented. These atrocities were well-documented tales of medieval-like savagery, with entire cities put to the sword, and with women raped and people burned and buried alive in literal orgies of wanton cruelty. Millions of Chinese would die before the Japanese were finally evicted. This savagery seemed all the more incomprehensible in that the Japanese were not reacting to any Chinese aggression against their own nation. Although the Chinese had a contempt for the Japanese as "barbarians," the history of modern China had been one of Chinese resistance to Japanese aggression, never the other way around. The popular author Pearl Buck, like Luce the child of American missionaries to China, wrote movingly of the noble, patient spirit of resistance to the Japanese invaders. (It must be remembered that of the 22 million deaths in the Pacific War, some 19 million were civilian, and most of those deaths were directly caused by the Japanese army.)

The conflict between Japan and the United States was no war over markets or colonies, either. The United States was in the process of shedding its Philippine territory (which had achieved commonwealth status and was scheduled for independence in 1946), while the Japanese preached their own anticolonial rhetoric, although they were at the same time most interested in the resources of those European and American Pacific colonies. U.S. investments in Asia were minuscule compared to those of the European colonial powers.

Rather, World War II in the Pacific was the result of a clash of political goals: the Japanese calling for "Asia for the Asiatics" (always under Japanese dominion, of course), the Americans demanding an "open door" policy in China (which might open the way for future U.S. investments) and preparing increasingly to resist any further Japanese expansion. The Japanese, with their war goals restricted to dominance in Asia, were thus the only major belligerent of World War II with basically limited aims. Numerous Japanese statesmen and diplomats (as well as a few Americans) endeavored to the very eve of the Japanese attack on Pearl Harbor (1941) to work out some modus vivendi between these two nations that had so little reason for conflict. The Americans after Pearl Harbor, of course, fought for nothing less than Japan's unconditional surrender.

For Americans, World War II began and ended in the Pacific. And from the attack on Pearl Harbor to Japan's signing of the instrument of unconditional surrender aboard the American battleship *Missouri* in Tokyo Bay on September 2, 1945, the Pacific war was essentially an American-Japanese war. The United States basically had only two serious allies in the Pacific war—Great Britain and China. The contribution of the British Empire/Commonwealth was but grudgingly tolerated by the Americans, while China could be generally considered more of a victim of than an ally against Japan. The British eventually reconquered Burma, but the contributions of America's allies (except for the Australians) consisted primarily of tying down large enemy formations.

Americans had no such reluctance in accepting any aid the Australians could give. Hailing from a land with a small population and with most of its militarized young male population on the other side of the globe in the Middle East, the Australians nonetheless earned wholehearted American respect as tough and resourceful fighters. The Australians paid a bitterly high price for their participation in the Pacific war: some 50,000 POWs from the early disasters in Malaya and Singapore were held in nearly unspeakable conditions by the Japanese for most of the war's duration. All carried permanent marks of this captivity for the rest of their lives. In addition, the rather ignominious British defeats early in the Pacific war reoriented Australia's defense allegiance from the British Empire to the United States.

The United States did not enter World War II in response to any treaty commitments or as the result of any geopolitical or strategic considerations, but solely because of the Japanese attack on Pearl Harbor. Even then, the United States did not declare war on Japan's ally, Germany, but rather Hitler declared war on the United States in a decision that in its inexplicable folly was only matched by his invasion of the Soviet Union six months earlier.

Even though Americans felt more personal animosity toward Japanese than toward the Germans, the fact remains that throughout World War II the American war effort was directed primarily against Germany; it was always "Germany First." Only about 15 percent of U.S. industrial capacity went toward the war in the Pacific. In their island-hopping campaigns, the Americans faced primarily naval garrison troops and overall only about 10 to 15 percent of the Japanese army. Only in the Philippines and in the South Pacific did U.S. ground forces fight a mass continental-style campaign, and only at sea did the United States devote the bulk of its military resources against the Japanese, as did the Australians.

Oddly, the Japanese themselves were also not oriented primarily toward the Pacific. The Japanese army concentrated on Southeast Asia and the China-Manchuria-Korea theater. Even at the very end of the war, the Soviet armies found themselves facing some 20 percent of the Japanese army. As with the Americans, the Japanese devoted the bulk of naval forces only to the Pacific, while army and other ground and air forces were assigned elsewhere.

The war with Japan was more often than not a grudge match, and "Remember Pearl Harbor" was no empty home front propaganda slogan. Americans knew that those who fell into Japanese hands were often subjected to barbaric treatment. The news of the Bataan death march (1942), coming after the fall of the Philippines, the greatest defeat in American military history, inflamed those feelings, as did the execution of some captured airmen from the famous Doolittle raid on Tokyo in early 1942.

U.S. troops responded in a cold rage, often shooting down the few surrendering Japanese soldiers, mutilating enemy dead, using their skulls for souvenirs, and cheering wildly on news of the atomic bombing of Japanese cities in August 1945. It is illustrative that the worst single fire raid in terms of civilian casualties was not on Berlin, Hamburg, or Dresden, but on Tokyo in March 1945, after which it was claimed that a broad-based pyramid 100-feet high could have been constructed with the bodies of children killed in that assault. Americans also used fire on the Pacific battlefields. The horrific napalm and flamethrowers turned Japanese soldiers into human torches and were justified as the only way to get the "fanatical" enemy out of his bunkers. The argument was not without purely military merit, considering the minuscule Japanese surrender rate. Fire, however, was rarely used against the Germans.

Judging by casualties inflicted compared to casualties suffered, the U.S. Army Air Forces' B-29 strategic heavy bomber was the world's most efficient killing machine, and, again, it was used only against the Japanese. The U.S. Navy, in turn, came far closer than Germany ever had in starving an enemy into submission through unrestricted submarine warfare. (It was America's righteous horror at

Imperial Germany's use of just such a campaign had led to its entrance into World War I.) And yet, the same U.S. military then turned to the mundane tasks of military occupation of defeated Japan and gave that crushed nation an most enlightened, even benign military government that could only be equalled by the Western Allies' military occupation of postwar Germany.

In the Japanese, the Allies found for the first time on any large scale an enemy that was quite likely actually to fight to the hackneyed "last round of the last man." Adolf Hitler could exhort his troops to such sacrifice, but the Soviets captured some 100,000 German troops at Stalingrad (1943) and the Americans and British bagged a similar number at Tunis at the close of the North African fighting in 1943. But in the Pacific fighting, most of the Japanese who wound up as POWs were more likely those knocked unconscious or who were in some other way incapable of resistance—or of suicide. This "never surrender" Japanese attitude was the main cause of the Japanese brutal treatment of enemy soldiers who were unfortunate to fall into their hands. To the Japanese, prisoners of war had disgraced themselves and were fit for little more than slave labor on starvation rations as permanent "guests of the Emperor." For those enemies who did fight to the death, the Japanese could on occasion spare some sympathy. Japanese aircraft dropped wreaths over the underwater wrecks of the British navy's *Prince of Wales* and *Repulse* the day after sending them to the bottom; their crews had fought bravely until their warships had sunk under them, and they were thus (in Japanese eyes) entitled to the honors of war. That said, it could be pointed out that the Chinese had resisted bravely at Nanking, and the infuriated Japanese went on on a six-week drunken orgy of mass killing, rape, beheading, and torture. The Americans and Filipinos had fought well at Bataan and were subjected to the Bataan death march. Japan had not signed the Geneva Convention of 1929, but nonetheless assured Allied POWs that they would be treated in accordance "with the tenants of bushido," small comfort indeed in light of the Japanese record of almost unrelieved brutality toward their prisoners.

When dealing with the Japanese military in the Pacific war, the word "mindless" comes up perhaps too readily. But when one examines the inane decision to provoke the "sleeping giant" into war with the attack on Pearl Harbor, the assumption that such an attack would so demoralize the "soft" Americans that they would sue for peace, the belief that mass terror and murder would subdue the Chinese people, and the unexamined conviction toward the end of the conflict that "our spirit will prevail against their steel," it is not too difficult to apply the term.

For all its unremitting ferocity, the Pacific war was a conflict without a prime villain. Half a century after Hitler's ignominious death in Berlin, the outpouring of books about him shows no signs of abating. But those few works on Japan's warlord Hideiki Tojo are basically those of scholars writing for scholars. Unlike Hitler, Tojo was not the master of some dark ideology incomprehensible to any "right-thinking" American. Tojo lived by the precepts of bushido, a value system that by definition was reserved to the Japanese. Americans had no worries that its sinister message would appeal to any citizen—except supposedly to Japanese-Americans. Even well-informed Americans of the World War II generation would be hard pressed to recollect Hideiki Tojo's exact fate. (He was hanged three years after the war.)

About the only thing that both Axis leaders had in common as far as Americans were concerned was that both were often portrayed as ridiculous figures of fun, but even here Hitler had the edge. Cartoons and caricatures of Tojo and of the rest of the Japanese nation were rooted in the racist stereotypes of the times. Tojo was usually portrayed as a dull-witted, buck-toothed, near-blind blunderer. But Hitler, with his Charlie Chaplain mustache, his platform posturing during his incomprehensible speeches, his absurd salute, always provided far more vivid copy for mimics, satirists, and comics. (One of the most popular songs of the war years was the manic American band leader Spike Jones' "Right in Der Fuhrer's Face!" There was no Tojo equivalent.) In sum, what determined Americans to "gain the inevitable victory, so help us God" (in President Roosevelt's words) was pure rage and hatred over the bombing of Pearl Harbor, not any one Japanese villain or Japanese ideology.

Although the Pacific war threw up no personal icon of enemy evil, "Remember Pearl Harbor" served just as well. There may not have been an arch villain in the Pacific war, but this was nonetheless a war of hatred, and usually to the death. Like the Nazis, the Japanese committed mass murder, and their name to this day is anathema in those lands unfortunate to have been occupied by the Imperial Japanese Army. The "Rape of Nanking" has not been forgotten by the Chinese more than sixty years later. And yet, the Japanese did not practice genocide, if by that term one means the *systematic* extermination of entire peoples. The Japanese, infuriated by Chinese resistance, still did not intend to exterminate the Chinese people. The same could be said about the Japanese occupation of the Philippines. And where the population more or less acquiesced to the Japanese, as in Burma and Malaya, Japanese occupation laid burdens on their conquests that were fairly light, considering that they were fighting a major war. At least on paper, most of Japan's conquests were given "independence," and were to be treated as "Asian brothers" in the great struggle against imperialism. "Asia for the Asiatics" resonated strongly throughout the Pacific (except, from the start, in the Philippines) until the Japanese occupiers tightened the screws as they began to lose the war.

World War II in the Pacific was a juxtaposition of the ancient and modern. The modern saw vast oceanic distances conquered by modern fleet resupply and management methods. It opened with two great naval battles, Coral Sea and Midway, where surface ships never spotted each other but fought it out through air power and submarines. The first and only use of nuclear weapons in war and an unrelenting submarine blockade brought about the unprecedented unconditional surrender of a major power even though its main army was still intact and its home territory uninvaded.

The "ancient" Pacific War can be seen in the brutal beach and jungle battles by lightly armed soldiers that would not have been out of place in earlier wars. It can also be seen in the medieval bushido code of the Japanese warrior, with its beheadings of captives, contempt for technology, and its ancestor and emperor veneration. Many times, desperate Japanese soldiers would stage a banzai charge, officers waving swords and lightly armed soldiers screaming, against American troops who took some gratification in dispatching them to the last man (or "to their ancestors", as U.S. troops often laconically put it). Entire cities could be given over to rape and pillage as a reward to the troops and as a lesson in terror—a tactic of Genghis Khan. American and Australian troops on occasion collected Japanese skulls, mounting them on tanks or mailing them home to girlfriends, something almost unknown in the European theater. Although German cities, like their Japanese counterparts, could be burned out in an evening by Allied incendiary bombing, the use of the flame thrower and the horrific napalm jellied petrol bomb on the battlefield was reserved for the Pacific theater.

This tremendous conflict altered the Pacific Basin in ways that could not be imagined in 1941 (see "Epilogue: Results of the Great Pacific War"). In presenting World War II in the Pacific, we have attempted to provide as comprehensive a coverage of events from the late 1930s to the Japanese surrender in 1945. Included are articles that describe military campaigns, weaponry, diplomacy, politics, and the social effects of the war. Articles on major personalities are also included. Because of space limitations, we have not provided separate entries on all of the numerous players in the war. However, our index reveals that the roles of all major figures are discussed throughout the volume, even if they are not singled out in individual biographies.

We have also attempted to portray in an even-handed manner the Japanese perspectives and expectations on the war. The articles on Japanese logistics and U.S. logistics, for example, reveal how cultural differences affected not only how armies performed but the very ways they were supplied during the course of the conflict. The article on stereotypes reveals racial and cultural attitudes that affected how each side viewed the enemy—points of view that hardened as the war progressed and the brutality of combat increased.

Finally, we hope that the articles can be enjoyed for the lively and accessible writing that will make military subjects interesting for the nonspecialist. Military history is more than a chronicle of aircraft carriers, battles, and generals and admirals. It is also about ordinary people caught up, in this case, in one of history's most cataclysmic moments.

Stanley Sandler

Contributors

Agoratus, Steven

Belpedio, James R.

Bielakowski, Alexander M.

Birdseye, James

Blewett, Daniel K.

Bloom, James

Boyd, Carl

Brown, D. Clayton

Browne, Blaine T.

Bunker, Robert J.

Cahow, Richard

Cardwell, Thomas A.

Carlson, Eric D.

Chapman, Roger

Coffey, David

Cordier, Sherwood

Deutsch, James T.

Clarkin, Thomas

Cranston, John

Crosswell, Daniel

Curtis, George H.

Cyr, Arthur I.

Dean, Camille

DeHart, Bruce J.

Deutsch, James T.

Donnelly, William M.

Dougherty, Kevin

Dreyer, Philip H.

Elleman, Bruce A.

Farrell, Brian P.

Fisher, Mike

Fitzgerald, Gerald J.

Ford, Bonnie L.

Ford, Jonathan

Friedman, Hal M.

Gibbon, Philip

Gonzales, Monica

Gray, Robert

Green, David M.

Grey, Jeffrey

Griffith, Thomas E., Jr.

Harrington, Peter

Hart, Russell A.

Hawk, Alan

Huston, James A.

Isemann, James L.

Jordine, Melissa R.

Kaminski, Theresa

Kinard, Jeff

Kiras, James D.

Kirchubel, Robert

Lansford, Tom

Laurie, Clayton D.

Leary, William M.

Leitich, Keith A.

Liestman, Daniel D.

Luconi, Stefano

Macina, Mark A.

Malkasian, Carter

Mays, Thomas D.

McGowen, Stanley S.

McMullen, Tom

McNabb, James

Melnyk, Les A.

Millard, Kenneth A.

Miller, Roger

Morden, Bettie J.

Moser, John E.

Motohashi, Hirotake

Ohl, John Kennedy

Osborne, Eric W.

Pacer, Matthew

Page, Edward C.

Parshall, Jon

Parillo, Mark P.

Perry, James

Peterson, Barbara

Ricketts, Travis

Roberts, Priscilla

Rogers, William

Ross, Rodney J.

Ryan, James G.

Sandler, Stanley

Sarantakes, Nicholas E.

Schafer, Elizabeth D.

Schliffer, John

Schumacher, F.

Schuster, Carl O.

Seligman, Matthew

Shoptaugh, Terry L.

Sinisi, Kyle S.

Snead, David L.

Steins, Richard

Stone, David

Sugita, Yone

Sunderam, Chandar

Swedin, Eric

Taaffe, Stephen R.

Tucker, Spencer C.

Ulbrich, David

Valone, Stephen J.

Vance, Jonathan F.

Walker, Michael C.

Weber, Michael

Whitman, John W.

Willbanks, James H.

Wintermute, Bobby A.

Wood, Laura Matysek

Wright, David C.

Zabecki, David T.

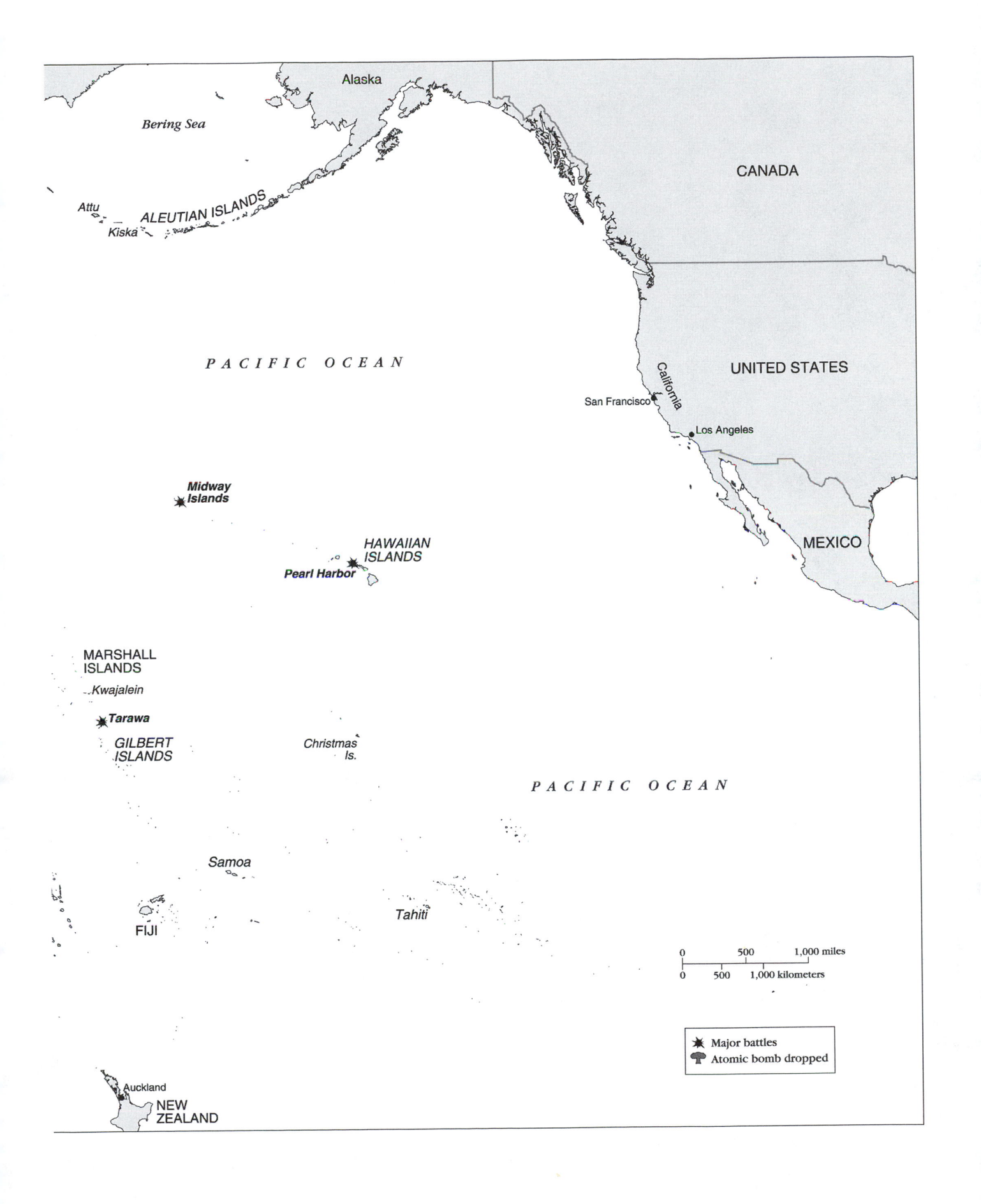

Alaska

Bering Sea

Attu
ALEUTIAN ISLANDS
Kiska

CANADA

PACIFIC OCEAN

UNITED STATES

California

San Francisco

Los Angeles

Midway
Islands

HAWAIIAN
ISLANDS

Pearl Harbor

MEXICO

MARSHALL
ISLANDS

Kwajalein

Tarawa

GILBERT
ISLANDS

Christmas
Is.

PACIFIC OCEAN

Samoa

Tahiti

FIJI

0		500		1,000 miles
0	500		1,000 kilometers	

Auckland

NEW
ZEALAND

Major battles
Atomic bomb dropped

World War II
in the Pacific

ABDA Command

ABDA Command was the first effort on the part of the Allied powers (in this case, the United States, Great Britain, the Netherlands, and Australia) to establish a joint command for the defense of Southeast Asia. The decision to create ABDA Command came during the Anglo-American Arcadia Conference of late December 1941, that is, after the eruption of war in the Pacific. At that conference both U.S. President Franklin Roosevelt and British Prime Minister Winston Churchill reaffirmed their earlier agreement that the defeat of Hitler's Germany would take precedence over Pacific affairs. At the same time, the British rankled at U.S. insistence on having Supreme Allied Commanders in all theaters, because they feared that U.S. generals and admirals would be chosen for all these positions. Still, both sides recognized that some attempt had to be made to present, in the face of the rapidly advancing Japanese army and navy, a united Allied front.

ABDA was viewed as a means of providing such a front, as well as assuaging Churchill's fears about Supreme Allied Commanders, since it was decided that a British general, Sir Archibald Wavell (who was also commander in chief in India), would be overall commander of ABDA. All Allied forces in Burma, Malaya, the Dutch East Indies, western New Guinea, and the north and northwest coasts of Australia were placed under his command. These forces included some sizable military contingents, including a formidable Dutch squadron and the U.S. Asiatic Fleet, but because there was no intention on the part of either the British or the Americans to reinforce ABDA, Wavell was expected to do no more than to delay the Japanese advance while the main Allied military might concentrated on Germany.

It soon became clear, however, that ABDA could not even meet these relatively modest expectations, for the organization was hampered from the start by its multinational command structure and was in almost every way but numbers of troops inferior to the Japanese. Under Wavell, Dutch Lieutenant General Hein ter Poorten was in command of the ground forces; British Air Chief Marshall Sir Richard E. C. Pierce had responsibility for the air contingents; and Admiral Thomas C. Hart, commander of the U.S. Asiatic Fleet, was placed in command of the combined naval forces. Although there had been some preliminary discussions of mutual defense early in 1941, few details had been worked out. The four nationalities had practically no experience in working together; in fact, they did not even have a common code. Not surprisingly, there were also serious disagreements over how best to defend the 2,000-mile front for which ABDA had responsibility. The Americans were mainly concerned with their Philippines possessions, while the Dutch were preoccupied with defending the Dutch East Indies. The Australians were concerned about their own defense, which was understandable, given that most of the Royal Australian Army was fighting in North Africa at the time. Wavell and the British, meanwhile, wanted to emphasize the empire's possessions of Burma and Malaya; indeed, although ABDA headquarters was located at Batavia in the Dutch East Indies, Wavell absented himself to inspect the defenses at Singapore and Rangoon.

Nevertheless, ABDA's first engagement with the enemy, off Balikpapan in the Dutch East Indies on January 24, 1942, met with gratifying success. Four destroyers under the command of Rear Admiral R. A. Glassford managed to sink four Japanese transports and a patrol boat in the Makassar Strait, although this victory did not delay Japanese landings on Balikpapan by more than a day. Further efforts, moreover, were far less successful. When the ABDA fleet sortied in mid-February to prevent the Japanese from landing on Bali, the Allied ships fell under heavy air and surface attack, which cost the Allied command several destroyers and did serious damage to U.S. cruisers *Marblehead* and *Houston.* The fleet was then humiliated at Bandung Strait on the night of February 20, when two aggressive Japanese destroyers managed to hold off three Dutch cruisers and a dozen Dutch and U.S. destroyers.

The catastrophic fall of Singapore on February 15, 1942, provoked a serious crisis within ABDA's command structure. Wavell infuriated the Dutch by claiming that further defense of the Dutch East Indies was probably hopeless. The Dutch claimed that the problem lay in Hart's naval command and demanded that the East Indies be defended to the last. Although Hart could hardly be held accountable for ABDA's naval setbacks, the British and Americans concluded that multinational command was simply not working. Hart was recalled, ostensibly for health reasons, and overall command of naval forces was turned over to Dutch Vice Admiral Conrad E. H. Helfrich. Wavell, meanwhile, returned to India with most of ABDA's air contingents. It was the Dutch who would preside over ABDA's final destruction.

On February 27, 1942, the Allied fleet moved to intercept a large Japanese convoy near the island of Bawean in the Java Sea. It encountered a Japanese force of similar size and in the ensuing battle—the largest naval surface action since Jutland in 1916—lost two cruisers and four destroyers. Most of the remaining ships were sunk by Japanese aircraft or ships while trying to escape to the Indian Ocean. The invasion of the Dutch East Indies, meanwhile, moved along on schedule. The Japanese landed on Java on March 1, and Batavia fell on the following day. General Ter Poorten led his men in a valiant defense of the island's oil fields, but to no avail. Within the next week the remaining Dutch forces on the island surrendered. ABDA was dissolved, but it was reconstituted in March as the Southwest Pacific Command, headquartered in Australia and placed under the command of General Douglas MacArthur.

Although ABDA's multinational character was certainly a hindrance, it would not be accurate to place all the blame for its disastrous defeat on this single factor. There was probably no way that the 2,000-mile front could have been defended for long in the face of the sustained Japanese advance of early 1942. A more creative, aggressive strategy might have been more successful in slowing down the enemy, but such an approach was unlikely to be implemented. Though the forces at ABDA's disposal were considerable, the realization that reinforcements were unavailable, and that losses could not be replaced, dictated a conservative defensive strategy which

merely attempted to parry Japanese thrusts. ABDA also faced a Japanese navy armed with far superior torpedoes and a high level of training for night combat, and the command's air units were never strong enough to mount a serious challenge to Japan's control of the skies. Finally, ABDA suffered from lack of support from the highest echelons of command in Washington. Allied planning throughout the first half of 1942 suffered from a persistent unwillingness to believe that the Japanese were capable of inflicting much harm. As a result ABDA was assigned such a low priority that it was wholly unprepared even to delay, let alone stop, the Japanese advance.

FURTHER READINGS
Costello, John. *The Pacific War* (1981).
Spector, Ronald H. *Eagle against the Sun: The American War with Japan* (1985).
Winslow, W. G. *The Fleet the Gods Forgot: The U.S. Asiatic Fleet in World War II* (1982).

John E. Moser

SEE ALSO Navy, U.S.; Dutch East Indies

Aerial Resupply

The China-Burma-India (CBI) theater saw the first extensive use of aerial resupply in modern warfare. The chief recipients of this innovation were the 2,997 men of the officially designated 5307th Composite Unit (Provisional), more popularly known as "Merrill's Marauders" after their commander, Brigadier General Frank D. Merrill.

The unit's mission was to conduct long-range penetrations behind enemy lines in Japanese-held Burma. The terrain of northern Burma presented major difficulties for the Marauders. In the far north, the Himalayas are virtually impassable, with peaks rising to 20,000 feet. On the Indian frontier, a continuous range runs southwest from the Himalayas along the Assam border in parallel ridges reaching heights of 10,000 feet. On the Chinese border, the Himalayas curve south to complete the three-sided isolation of the region. This rugged hill country is further divided into two compartments by the north–south Kumon Range, with elevations in excess of 10,000 feet. Additionally, Burma experiences a wet season from June to the end of September, which causes lowlands to be flooded to the extent that movement is greatly restricted. Add all this to the fact that northern Burma in 1944 was almost void of roads. Native footpaths and cart tracks provided the only means of communication in most of the area, and the only road suitable for motor traffic was itself unusable in the wet season.

These environmental considerations rendered normal methods of resupply impractical for a highly mobile dismounted unit operating behind enemy lines, such as were Merrill's Marauders. One innovative measure was to provide the force with 700 animals to be used as pack transport, but the ultimate source of the Marauder's strategic mobility was aerial resupply. This technique had been used with success in 1943 by British Major General Orde C. Wingate's 77th Infantry Brigade under similar circumstances, and the Marauders would take advantage of several lessons learned. Among the prerequisites were the need for detailed planning, excellent radio communications, trained pilots, careful packaging of loads, and rapid response to requests. Air and ground forces would have to attain the closest of cooperation, and pilots would have to be willing to fly under almost all conditions. The Marauder's need for food and ammunition could not always wait for good weather.

In recognition of the importance of this type of resupply, Merrill established an aerial resupply section under the supervision of Major Edward T. Hancock. From his warehouses in Dinjan, Hancock was able to monitor all radio traffic to Merrill's command headquarters 32 miles away at Ledo. Hancock prepared standard units of each category of supply based on estimated requirements for one day. These packages were always ready for delivery and could easily be adapted for specific needs.

Initially, the 2d Troop Carrier Squadron and later the 1st Troop Carrier Squadron would fly the missions. Ammunition, medical supplies, and food were dropped by parachute from an altitude of 200 feet. Clothing and grain were dropped without parachute from 150 feet. The air force performed superbly, flying in all types of weather. In March 1944 alone, it flew seventeen missions and dropped 376 tons of supplies.

The Marauders tried to plan their route so that they would be near a flat, open area suitable for a drop zone whenever a resupply was scheduled. This measure had two advantages: It saved the troops from the heavy labor of clearing a drop zone, and it enabled pilots to use aerial photographs and maps to identify destinations.

The resupply packages came in easily manhandled bundles ranging from 115 to 125 pounds. From the drop zone, the bundles were loaded on mules and removed to a secure area for breakdown and distribution. Rations and ammunition were packaged for individual issue, and each man would file by to pick up his share.

The standard procedure was to send back radio requests in the evening for supplies to be delivered the next

afternoon. Major Hancock maintained a situation map to keep abreast of anticipated requirements, and his men were so responsive that ammunition was kept uploaded on trucks ready to dash to the airfield on a moment's notice. Hancock's performance zenith occurred on May 6, 1945, when a C-47 reached the drop area, 128 miles from Dinjan, just two hours and twenty-two minutes after the message had been filed in the field.

The success of Merrill's Marauders would have been impossible without the smooth operation of the aerial resupply network. There was close cooperation between the tacticians and the logisticians, and the latter were always responsive to the former's needs. Hancock was capable of monitoring Merrill's command communications, and he remained abreast of the situation on the ground. Packages were configured in standard loads, and the activities of the resupply party emphasized speed and security. For Merrill's Marauders, aerial resupply was the only available means of logistical support, and their execution of this phase of their operation was nearly flawless.

FURTHER READINGS

Dougherty, Kevin. "Supplying Merrill's Marauders." *Army Logistian* (May–June 1992).

Hogan, David. *U.S. Army Special Operations in World War II.* U.S. Army Center of Military History (1992).

Shelton, George C. "The Alamo Scouts." *Armor* (September–October 1982).

U.S. Army Military Intelligence Division. *Merrill's Marauders* (February–May 1944).

Kevin Dougherty

SEE ALSO Merrill's Marauders (Galahad)

African American Troops

There were two African American infantry divisions in World War II, the 92d and 93d. The 92d Infantry Division was deployed to the European theater, while the 93d eventually was sent to the Pacific. The 93d is not a unit that brings to mind the glory (or horror) of war. It is a division that suffered from cultural atmospherics: definitions of courage, intelligence, cowardice, and how a soldier should look and act. Even so, the 93d operated efficiently and effectively in the monotonous and thankless assignments given it in World War II. A study of the record reveals that the performance of the 93d was satisfactory, probably even more so because of the generally unappealing assignments given it. The nature of these tasks dictated the morale and amount of publicity, positive and negative, that the unit received.

When Congress passed the Selective Service Act of 1940, it forced an increase in the number of African American units. This legislation called for 4,595 additional African American soldiers immediately, doubling their number in the U.S. Army. This was the first time since the 1920s that African Americans in some cities had been allowed to enlist in the armed forces. The Selective Service Act of 1940 also instructed the armed forces that there would be no discrimination based on race, creed, or religion. However, Section 3 of this act provided a loophole. If an individual recruiter harbored prejudices, he could deem the prospective recruit to be unacceptable according to his own standards. An additional provision stipulated that no man should be drafted unless suitable food, shelter, and sanitary services were provided. This furnished another opportunity to declare that there were not suitable (which in this case meant segregated and as isolated as possible from white population centers) accommodations for African American troops.

Mobilization for war played a large role in overcoming the barriers that had denied African American an opportunity to serve their country in the armed forces. An unexpected, rapid escalation of the admission of African American recruits occurred. On June 15, 1942, the editors of *Life* magazine published an article claiming, "The U.S. Army is getting rid of its old prejudices against the African-American and is putting him where he will do the most good—in the front ranks of its fighting men." However, despite the positive outlook of this article, some in the army refused to believe that African Americans could be used effectively as combat troops. Much of their more reflective thinking was based on a series of studies carried out by Army War College students in the early 1920s which concluded that African Americans (or "Negroes") were for the most part innately unfit for combat but could prove valuable behind the lines, in small, segregated units, if led by white officers.

In 1941 the army projected that thirty-two divisions would be formed and that four of them would be African American. Yet, because of prejudice among senior officers, only two, the 93d and 92d, were activated. Lieutenant General Leslie J. McNair recommended using African Americans by attaching battalions where they were needed, because "a colored division is too great a concentration of Negroes to be effective." A former commanding general of the 92d was quoted as advising that "no Negro units larger than a regiment be formed in the future."

With the large increase in the number of African American troops, the army now had to find places to station them. According to an official history of the U.S. Army, in 1940 the people of Arizona were not opposed to the stationing of African American troops in their state. Therefore, in January 1942, Army G-2 (intelligence) recommended that African Americans be stationed in units not larger than a brigade in the continental United States, except in Fort Huachuca, Arizona, which could accommodate an African American division.

In mid-April 1942, Major General C. P. Hall and his staff arrived at Fort Huachuca to prepare for the arrival of the 93d, which was to be activated on May 15, 1942. At its activation, the division was composed of the 25th Infantry Regiment (which had been originally activated in 1866), the 368th Infantry Regiment (which had been activated March 1, 1941), the 369th Infantry Regiment, Field Artillery Battalions 593–596, the Division Artillery Headquarters, the 93d Quartermaster Battalion, the 793d Light Maintenance Ordnance Company, the 93d Signal Company, the 318th Combat Engineer Battalion, the 318th Medical Battalion, and the 93d Cavalry Reconnaissance Troop—all courtesy of the Selective Service. The 93d had, in its 16,000 men, all the elements necessary to operate as an independent division. Any decision to divide it up could not have hinged on claims that it did not have the necessary units to operate as a separate entity.

The activation of the 93d signaled an important step for the African American soldier. Not only was it the first African American division activated in World War II, but the activation of other African American units would theoretically depend on the availability of cadre. Since cadre came from units that had been activated before the unit under consideration, the limited number of cadre available restricted the speed of future activations.

Initially, the insignia of the 93d was the blue French helmet that the 369th Infantry Regiment had used in World War I during action in France. This regiment had since become the 369th Anti-Aircraft Regiment and had no relation to the current 369th Infantry Regiment serving with the 93d. Consequently, according to the division's files, the 93d decided that the helmet insignia had no bearing on the current 93d and received permission to change the insignia. The men of the 93d submitted at least twenty-eight possible symbolic insignias ranging from rattlesnakes to the state of Arizona. After much excitement and considerable bickering, the black panther design (incidentally the favorite of Assistant Division Commander Brigadier General Allison J. Barnett, who served on the committee) emerged as the victor in the contest. Before the new insignia became official, this decision was overturned by the War Department. The reasons given for the rejection of the black panther insignia were "the historical significance of the blue helmet, the cost of the change, and the desire of the War Department to retain all possible World War I insignia." The historical significance of the blue helmet for many of those units of the 93d was irrelevant; it was likely that prejudice, not history, was the determining factor in the decision.

Basic training, delayed because of the staggered arrival of the enlisted men, began on June 8, 1942, and lasted for seventeen weeks. On November 11, 1942, for the first time in twenty-five years, a commander reviewed an African American division. During the period March 14–25, 1943, the 93d trained in its divisional ("D") exercises in southwest Arizona. From there, the division proceeded to the Louisiana Maneuvers, where its adversary was the 85th Division. For three months the two units engaged in mock battle, marking the first time an African American division trained against a white division. The prominent African American periodical *The Crisis* titled its column on the event "Maneuvers Show 93d Is Ready." In two articles (May and June 1943), it had nothing but praise for the efficiency of the 93d and the willingness and enthusiasm of the commanding general and the Fort Huachuca commander in working with the African American troops. The 93d had preformed "better than expected," but this praise was premature, as the 93d in the end received an unsatisfactory rating.

The 93d Division, now known as the Maneuvers Division because of its continual exercise, then returned to Fort Huachuca briefly before undergoing desert training at Camp Clipper and Camp Young in California. Again, the African American troops were barred from local establishments because of prejudice.

Before the rapid mobilization, white officers commanding African American troops had generally been West Point graduates. These officers usually were sufficiently professional to accept African Americans as soldiers. With the expansion of manpower in the army, all 93d Division warrant officers were supposed to be African Americans, although many of the units did not comply. Most other African American officers were chaplains or medical officers. The 93d, however, was unique. When formed, one-fourth of its officers were African American, most had college degrees, and all were limited to junior officer positions.

The 93d Division suffered from numerous misconceptions because of race. A much publicized issue was the matter of providing African American officers for African American troops. While some of the brass, such as Colonel Edmund M. Barnum of the 92d, supported allowing competent African Americans to lead African American troops in combat, most believed that African Americans did not have enough education and suffered from a pas-

sive psyche. Therefore, they reasoned that African American officers should be restricted to a noncombat role. The troops were aware of such sentiment, and in March 1943 rumors ran rampant that the War Department had ordered Major General Fred Miller, the commander of the 93d, to restrict African American officers to the rank of first lieutenant. As noted in the African American newspaper the *Pittsburgh Courier* on March 4, 1943, Secretary of War Henry L. Stimson denied that he gave such an order, even citing evidence to the contrary, showing that as of December 31, 1942, there were 2,200 African American officers in the armed forces. Stimson did not mention how insignificant such a number was, given that African American troops in the army alone at that time numbered 467,000.

The rotation system proved to be another problem for the 93d. Beginning in 1943, white officers who had been in service with African American troops for eighteen months and had been rated "very satisfactory" could be transferred, and many were. Hence, the 93d found itself left with the worst of the white officers. This loss was made somewhat more palatable by the increase up to 575 in the number of black officers in the division by December 1943.

Also hindering the esprit de corps of the 93d was that many in the government viewed the African American soldiers as an extension of the Public Works Administration. Units in Seattle and Richmond were forced to shovel snow, although no white troops worked at the same task. The governor of Arizona asked for soldiers to pick cotton, claiming that it was "vital to the war effort." Even though the African American soldiers and press objected to their being subject to tasks that white soldiers were not, the army ordered the 93d to pick the cotton. The order was later rescinded when it became public knowledge that the cotton producers had refused workers supplied by the Farm Security Administration and simply wanted free African American labor. This type of nonsense served to erode further the morale of the 93d.

The 93d also suffered from imposed solitude brought on by a hostile regional populace. The isolated Arizona location of Fort Huachuca was considered an asset in obtaining it as a training camp for the 93d, but the location also had its drawbacks. The closest sizable town, Bisbee, was 35 miles away; when it learned the makeup of the 93d, the town declared itself "off-limits to non-resident Fort Huachuca personnel." Five theaters and several churches had to be built on the post. Fry, a small camplike reversion to the days of camp followers, supplied the men at Huachuca with prostitutes. Consequently, venereal disease in the 93d reached epidemic proportions—

three times the incidence in comparable white divisions. In an attempt to solve the problem, authorities moved the known prostitutes into a wire enclosure adjacent to the post known as "The Hook." According to the press clippings of the 93d housed at Eisenhower Library, "hundreds of solders" daily passed the military police and prophylactic station at the gate to the Hook.

Like the conditions at the fort, the equipment supplied for use by the 93d was often substandard. First Lieutenant George Looney described some of the secondhand equipment given to the soldiers because of their race, saying, "White soldiers trained with trucks marked 'tanks'; we trained with horses and wagons marked 'trucks.'" Physically deficient and poorly educated soldiers also slowed the progress of the 93d. In the first year of duty, 3,790 men were discharged for physical disabilities. The Army General Classification Test showed that members of the 93d also had less "intelligence." The army divided the scores for the test into five categories, with Class I being the brightest and Class V having supposedly the least capacity for intellectual prowess. In the 93d, only 0.1 percent qualified for Class I, and 45 percent qualified for Class V. In white divisions, the averages were 6.6 percent for Class I and only 8.5 percent for Class V. Although the test was probably culturally biased, some African Americans did manage to score well. Most of these were officers, who were sent where their training could not be used efficiently. For example, the twenty-two African Americans sent to Officers' Candidate School found themselves guarding an airfield in Texas until mid-1943. Thus, the most intelligent African Americans in the 93d were not training troops—they were guarding airplanes, a job for privates.

Large segments of the African American public as well as "liberal" whites in 1942 and 1943 expressed disappointment that neither of the African American divisions had been deployed overseas. *Life* ran an article in 1942 entitled "Negroes at War: All They Want Is a Fair Chance to Fight." A few members of Congress also objected that African American troops were not being utilized. For example, Representative Hamilton Fish (R-N.Y.) emphasized that Russians and Japanese with little or no education were war heroes. As a result of this public pressure, stateside training for the 93d finally came to an end, and the division was sent overseas. Despite the controversy about the 93d being kept out of combat, it proceeded overseas at approximately the same time as two white divisions, the 84th and 85th, that had been activated at about the same time in the spring of 1942.

The destination of the 93d perplexed the army's Operations branch. In October 1943, G-3 (Assistant Chief of Staff, Operations) recommended the Mediterranean theater for the 93d. However, the chief of staff of Allied Force Headquarters informed G-3 that the 93d would probably not see action if deployed in the Mediterranean. The next probable destination of the 93d was Hawaii. It appeared to the men of the 93d that this would indeed be the case, because the unit was being stripped of men to fill service units. If sent to Hawaii, they would continue with what they perceived to be the cyclic training that they had so far endured. The men in the 93d had come to doubt whether they would ever be sent into combat. When word came that Lieutenant General Millard F. Harmon, army commander in the South Pacific, had requested a white division but would accept an African American division if necessary, morale and discipline soared. On January 2, 1944, word came that the 93d was not bound for Hawaii and more monotonous training but would go to the South Pacific, where it would indeed see action.

The 93d left its staging area, Camp Stoneman, California, in five groups, with the first leaving January 10, 1944. The division sailed out of San Francisco on troopships *West Point, John Pope, Lureline, Holbrook,* and *Torrence.* The division band was the last unit to arrive on Guadalcanal, on March 5, 1944. According to the military police files, at this time "the moral [*sic*] was exceptionally high." The divisional files at Eisenhower Library indicate that, because of the refusal of high command to permit the 93d to enter combat as a division, this staggered arrival in the Solomons marked the last time the 93d operated as a unit until the end of the war.

One day after the arrival of the divisional band, Secretary of War Stimson cabled Lieutenant General Harmon and directed that some of the 93d be introduced into combat immediately. The rest were to get extensive training—even more training. The 25th Infantry Regiment, composed mainly of raw recruits, provided the bulk of the forces that went to Bougainville in the southwest Pacific. It arrived on March 28, 1944, along with elements of the Military Police Platoon, 93d Cavalry Reconnaissance Troops, and 593d Field Artillery Battalion. Soon after, the 25th Infantry entered combat, marking the first taste of battle for a part of the division. While on Bougainville, battalions of the 25th accompanied veteran battalions of the Americal Division on patrol. Under these circumstances, they fared well. However, in another instance, 3d Battalion, Company K, went on patrol with a single veteran. The Japanese ambushed Company K, and records indicate that a lack of leadership and discipline contributed to the chaos. Ten men were killed and twenty wounded in the ensuing firefight; many of the casualties were probably caused by friendly fire. Company K's failure was something that could have been expected of green troops, especially troops that had been trained to fight in the desert, not the jungle. It should also be noted that the white commander of Company K was the first to appear running out of the jungle toward friendly lines, an indication of the quality of some of the division's white officers.

General George C. Marshall, army chief of staff and principal military adviser to President Franklin D. Roosevelt, chose to overlook the circumstances surrounding the incident. Although a genius as a logistics manager, he suffered from the bigotry which ran rampant in the U.S. Army during World War II. As General Marshall remembered in 1949, the 93d on Bougainville "wouldn't fight—couldn't get them out of the caves to fight." Secretary Stimson at the time said that the 25th had performed reasonably well, but he voiced reservations, saying: "I do not believe they can be turned into really effective combat troops without all officers being white." According to "Tan Yanks Come Through" in *Negro Digest* (July 1943), five soldiers from the 93d found themselves trapped behind enemy lines. The article credited their escape to resourcefulness; one of the soldiers credited prayer. Also noted in this article was a statement by Major General Raymond G. Lehman, the commander of the 93d, who said, "They have the same courage, the same fear and fighting spunk as any other soldiers. They are quick to learn and eager to perform. They . . . are about the best disciplined men in the Army."

This article and another in *Time* both commended the 25th for beating off frontal attacks and infiltrators. The 25th Regiment, noted *Time* on May 29, 1944, can be said to have "fought and acquitted themselves with honor." The Silver Star and several Bronze Stars awarded attested to that. However, the Japanese had exhausted themselves with suicidal onslaughts by the time the men from the 93d arrived. What action they saw occurred mainly on patrols. It should be noted that the 593d Field Artillery Battalion received a commendation from Brigadier General W. C. Dunckel of the Americal Division for construction of position areas and accuracy of fire. Although some news such as the commendation from General Dunckel painted a flattering picture regarding the 93d, in the rest of the southwest Pacific the outlook was not so positive.

While the 25th Regiment engaged the enemy on Bougainville, the rest of the 93d, which according to the wisdom of the day could not fight effectively as a unit, was scattered across the southwest Pacific. The Russell Islands, New Georgia Islands, Guadalcanal, Hollandia, and Vella Lavella all saw units of the 93d. These troops were supposed to be training in jungle warfare. However, the Southwest Pacific Command needed service troops. White infantry divisions were seldom employed as service troops, and when emergencies dictated such an assignment, it did not last long. The mission of the 93d on these islands, by contrast, was to serve as occupation troops, to patrol and guard the islands, to load and unload ships, and to train when time permitted.

On June 8, 1944, the 25th Regiment moved toward Japan in mop-up operations by occupying the Green and then the Treasury Islands. According to the division files, the other units of the 93d became warehouse, motor-pool, and fatigue-duty workers on Biak, Munda, Emiru, Middleburg, Noemfoor, and the Stirling Islands.

By early April 1945, many elements of the division started to arrive on the island of Morotai, located between New Guinea and the Philippines. This assignment probably marked the 93d's greatest contribution to the war effort. For the next several months, Morotai was on the cutting edge of the Allied advance. The official purpose of the 93d here was to relieve the 31st Infantry Division and to destroy the 500 to 600 remaining Japanese on the island. For assistance, the 93d could call upon the 80th Wing of the Royal Australian Air Force (RAAF) and Naval Unit 701.2 (motor-torpedo boats). After the Australians injured nine men of the 369th Regiment during bombing practice, not much cooperation remained between these two units. Cooperation with the motor-torpedo boats, however, did prove invaluable in preventing Japanese reinforcements and supplies from arriving by barge and canoe from Halmahera.

By June, most of the 93d were on the busy island. In addition to patrols undertaken in cooperation with the Netherlands Indies Civil Affairs Organization (NICA), the invasion of Borneo was staged from Morotai. As a supplement to their regular duties, the men of the 93d again became truck drivers and laborers. Nevertheless, units of the 93d were engaged in combat and, as shown in the following table that summarizes the daily after-actions reports, by the beginning of August they had exacted a heavy toll from the Japanese:

KIA (killed in action)	324
POW (prisoner of war)	59
Found dead	86

Occasionally, the soldiers of the 93d received fire from Japanese using mortars and machine guns, but snipers were the greatest threat. Many of the Japanese who were killed and captured were armed with only knives or bayonets, and some had no weapons at all. Therefore, according to divisional files, casualties suffered by the 93d were very light, even rare. Several of the casualties resulted from booby traps such as the "Jap Remote Control Rifle."

Propaganda played a major role in trying to convince the Japanese to surrender. The 93d used motor-torpedo boats to make broadcasts, and within one week aircraft dropped 150,000 leaflets on Morotai. At times, divisional officers released prisoners to encourage other Japanese to surrender.

The high point of the occupation of Morotai, and of the time overseas for that matter, had to be the capture of Colonel Ouchi. Members of the 369th Regiment seized him as he went to a stream to bathe with nine of his men. This was a rare accomplishment in that he was one of the highest-ranking Japanese officers captured in the Pacific fighting.

Through propaganda, cooperation with naval units, and patrols, the 93d killed approximately four hundred Japanese and captured sixty on Morotai. Ironically, after the surrender of Japan, more than six hundred Japanese troops came forward and surrendered on this island. When the 93d first arrived on Morotai in April 1945, intelligence reports indicated that fewer than six hundred Japanese remained on the island. While engaging in routine patrols, the 93d usually had troops working on the docks and in the warehouses, guarding prisoners, and training. There are numerous commendations in the division files complimenting the 93d for its logistical efforts.

In October 1945, after the surrender of Japan, the 93d moved to Mindanao in the Philippines. There they worked shipping out supplies, prisoners, and U.S. troops. Ironically, it was there that they almost went into "combat" as a division. It started with a conflict over Philippine women. The 93d occupied one side of a road, and the Dixie Division was on the other side. Both divisions stood with fixed bayonets and live ammunition. Only the frantic efforts of officers on both sides prevented massive bloodshed.

Eventually, the men of the 93d were shipped out of Leyte, and in January 1946 only six hundred remained in the division. By the end of February, the last remnants of the 93d arrived in San Francisco for deactivation and to be greeted by a society that did not respect them for their sacrifices. The 93d Division in World War II never had a chance to develop a positive reputation. It accomplished the missions assigned to it, and the division usually received accolades for the quality and efficiency of its work. It was, however, continuously discriminated against and misused. The U.S. Army did not train infantry divisions to operate as stevedores, fatigue cleaners, and drivers. Nor

were divisions organized to be divided and parceled out to different areas. Divisions and the components within them were designed and trained to fight as a unit. The 93d Infantry Division was not given that right.

FURTHER READINGS
Lee, Ulysses. *The Employment of Negro Troops* (1966).
MacGregor, Morris J., Jr. *Integration of the Armed Forces, 1940–1965* (1981).
Motley, Mary Pennick, ed. *The Invisible Soldier: The Experience of the Black Soldier, World War II* (1975).
Official Files, 93d Infantry Division History, Eisenhower Library, Abilene, Kans.

Travis Ricketts

SEE ALSO Army Ground Forces, U.S.

A-Go Plan

In early 1944, the Japanese navy developed a plan to stop the Allied advance in the central Pacific by annihilating the U.S. Pacific Fleet in one decisive battle. A-Go Plan called for an air and sea battle in the area of the Palaus or the western Carolines, close to Japanese fuel supplies and within range of Japanese land-based air forces. The land-based air power was important because the Japanese knew they would be outnumbered by the U.S. carriers and counted on the island-based planes to even the odds.

The task of fighting the "decisive" battle was given to Vice Admiral Jisaburo Ozawa, commander of the First Mobile Fleet, which made up at least 90 percent of the surface part of the Japanese navy (nine carriers with 430 combat aircraft, five battleships, thirteen cruisers, and twenty-eight destroyers). By mid-May, the preponderance of Ozawa's force lay at Tawi-Tawi in the Sulu Archipelago, awaiting developments. There they were well located for a sortie to the north, east, or southeast. Ozawa convinced Combined Fleet Headquarters to allow him to move his forces to Cebu in the central Philippines, which was better suited to training Ozawa's carrier groups.

Meanwhile, the Allies had invaded the Mariana Islands, and although A-Go originally called for Ozawa's force to strike the navy supporting General Douglas MacArthur's struggling on Biak, the Japanese had to react to an immediate threat to Saipan, the loss of which would make Japan itself subject to the pounding of U.S. long-range bombers. On June 15, as the Allies landed on the beaches at Saipan, Ozawa received orders to "activate the A-Go Operation for decisive battle." Ozawa was told to find and annihilate the U.S. fleet in the Philippine Sea west of the island. The decisive battle would be much farther north and east than the Japanese strategic planners desired, but battles must be fought where the opportunity presents itself, and Japan had to stop the Allies from taking Saipan and the adjacent islands.

In accordance with his orders, Ozawa steamed north. His force now numbered 222 fighters and about 200 dive-bombers and torpedo bombers embarked in nine carriers. The U.S. force he was trying to lure into battle included almost 500 fighters and over 400 dive-bombers and torpedo bombers in fifteen carriers. Ozawa was in an inferior position: He was outnumbered in airplanes, and most of his veteran pilots had died in the Solomon Islands battles. The majority of his fliers had only two to six months' training, and few had seen combat. Nevertheless, Ozawa was confident. Since his planes were more lightly armored, they had a greater range than that of the Americans (by 210 miles) and could stay beyond reach of U.S. carrier planes while launching their own strike. Ozawa also counted on the reported 90 to 100 Japanese land-based planes at Guam, Rota, and Yap to even the odds, and he expected to use Guam to rearm and refuel his own aircraft after striking the Americans. Thus, Ozawa's planes could hit the U.S. carriers, which would already have been damaged by the land planes; land at Guam to refuel and rearm; and strike the U.S. carriers a second time on the way back to the Japanese carriers.

It was a sound plan, but reality would reveal two fatal flaws in its execution. Vice Admiral Kakuta Kakuji, who commanded the land-based aircraft, had misled Ozawa about his actual strength, and the land-based warplanes failed to damage the U.S. fleet as planned. Ozawa would get very little help from that quarter. Additionally, U.S. planes had destroyed most of the aircraft that would have supported Ozawa's operation from the fields of Saipan, Guam, and Tinian. The battle would be fought between carrier aircraft only (which Ozawa would not know until the battle was over).

During the impending battle, Vice Admiral Marc A. Mitscher, commander of Task Force 58 (TF 58), was in tactical command of the U.S. forces, but the major decisions were made, or concurred in, by Admiral Raymond A. Spruance, commander of the Fifth Fleet. While Ozawa maneuvered for the decisive battle wherever it might come, Spruance's primary worry was to cover and protect the U.S. invasion of Saipan, and this tied him fairly closely to the immediate area of the Marianas.

The approach of the Japanese warships became known to Spruance when two of his submarines spotted the vessels in Philippine waters. On the evening of June 15, Ozawa's force—as it left the San Bernardino Strait—was observed by U.S. submarine *Flying Fish*. Around mid-

night on June 17, U.S. submarine *Cavalla* reported a Japanese task force 800 miles west–southwest of Saipan, and closing. On the following morning, *Cavalla* reported that the Japanese fleet was continuing on the same course. It was apparent that the Japanese were looking for a fight. Although the U.S. commander knew from his submarines the general position of Ozawa's fleet, Spruance did not know the exact location of the Japanese ships. Mitscher wanted to steam southwest at high speed to close on the contact, but Spruance, who feared a Japanese diversion, wanted to keep TF 58 in position to cover Saipan against all eventualities. He did not want the Japanese to try an "end run" to get at the amphibious forces spearheading the invasion. Spruance ordered the transports unloading troops at Saipan to run eastward to safety, and he sent Mitscher and TF 58 into the waters 180 miles west of Tinian to block the Japanese advance.

Ozawa's search planes located Mitscher's ships on the afternoon of June 18. Rear Admiral Obayashi Sueo, one of Ozawa's carrier-division commanders, wanted to strike the task force immediately, but Ozawa told him to wait until morning. Ozawa was unsure of the condition of the fields on Guam and did not want his returning pilots to have to land there in the dark. Accordingly, the Japanese lost an excellent opportunity to catch the U.S. forces by surprise, in that the Americans did not know the whereabouts of the Japanese fleet at that time.

By 0730 hours on June 19, Ozawa's scout planes had found the U.S. task force. About an hour after receiving this report, Ozawa launched the first of four heavy raids against Mitscher's carriers. When the incoming Japanese planes were spotted, Mitscher launched his F6F Hellcat naval fighters, which swarmed over the attackers. The veteran U.S. pilots, flying superior aircraft, quickly shot down at least two dozen Japanese aircraft; only one U.S. warplane was lost during this first Japanese attack. The Japanese fighters that made it through the line of Hellcats were taken under fire 15 miles in front of the U.S. carriers. The battleships and their escorts downed another dozen of the Japanese planes. Only one enemy aircraft scored a hit, which did some minor damage to battleship *South Dakota*.

The second Japanese raid, with more than 125 aircraft, suffered even greater losses, and only a few aircraft made it through the fighters and the battle line to attack the carriers—none of which received any damage. Only thirty-one Japanese planes survived this attack. Ozawa was struck an additional blow when heavy carrier *Taisho*, which was Admiral Ozawa's flagship and the newest carrier in the dwindling Japanese fleet, was torpedoed by U.S. submarine *Albacore*. Later that morning, submarine

Cavalla put four torpedoes into heavy carrier *Shokaku*, setting it afire. By nightfall, both carriers had sunk, with heavy loss of life on both ships.

Despite his losses and still believing that the Japanese land-based aircraft were in the fight, Ozawa launched a third wave of Japanese planes at 1000 hours. Many of these aircraft became separated and never attacked TF 58, but were intercepted and shot down while trying to land on Guam. Ozawa launched a fourth attack of more than eighty fighters and dive-bombers at 1130 hours. These too were badly misdirected, very few found their target, and they suffered the same fate as the earlier attackers when they tried to reach Guam. Only 19 of them made the field, and most of them were shot up by strafing carrier planes.

The attack had been a disaster for the Japanese. In all, fewer than a hundred of Ozawa's 373 planes managed to return to the Japanese carriers. Additionally, 50 Guam-based Japanese aircraft were shot down. The Americans lost only 29 planes, in what became known as "The Great Marianas Turkey Shoot."

As Ozawa tried to rally his forces, Mitscher continued to look for Ozawa's fleet, but could not find it. Finally, at 1600 hours on the following day, June 20, a plane from carrier *Enterprise* sighted Ozawa's fleet about 275 miles from TF 58. Despite the long range and other difficulties, Mitscher launched his aircraft (seventy-seven dive-bombers, fifty-four torpedo bombers, and eighty-five fighters). The U.S. flyers knew they were operating at the end of their aircrafts' range, but they flew on and eventually caught up with the Japanese, sinking carrier *Hiyo*, badly damaging three other carriers, and sinking two accompanying oilers. The three other carriers escaped unhurt, and the damaged ones returned to Japan for repairs. Sixty-five more Japanese planes were shot down. The U.S. planes turned for their carriers, but about eighty aircraft were lost because they ran out of fuel or had landing accidents in the dark. All but sixteen pilots and thirty-three crewmen were picked up by patrolling warships and seaplanes.

The Japanese had gotten their decisive battle, but it had not turned out the way their naval planners had hoped. Ozawa did not get the land-based aircraft he had been promised, and his outmatched fleet and inexperienced pilots were unable to carry out A-Go Plan. The Japanese lost nearly four hundred aircraft and three carriers. Numerous other ships were severely damaged. The two-day battle had cost the Americans 130 planes and seventy-six airmen and had clearly been a U.S. victory. Despite this, the Battle of the Philippine Sea—as the action on June 19 and 20 came to be known—left a bitter

taste among U.S. naval commanders, who were disturbed that the enemy had escaped total destruction. Nevertheless, the battle broke the back of Japan's naval air force, and never again would its carriers do battle on a major scale.

FURTHER READINGS

Belote, James H., and William M. Belote. *Titans of the Seas: The Development and Operations of Japanese and American Carrier Task Forces during World War II* (1975).

Dull, Paul A. *A Battle History of the Imperial Japanese Navy (1941–1945)* (1978).

Morison, Samuel Eliot. *The Two-Ocean War* (1963).

Spector, Ronald H. *Eagle against the Sun* (1985).

James H. Willbanks

SEE ALSO Navy Japanese; Navy, U.S.

Air Force, Royal

The Royal Air Force (RAF) in the Pacific theater during World War II is often referred to as the "forgotten air force." Nonetheless, the RAF proved to be an effective and competent match to its Japanese counterparts. Initially vastly outnumbered and outfought by the Japanese—and forced to use inferior equipment—the RAF in the Pacific was dramatically reorganized and resupplied during the war to become an integral part of the Allied success in the Pacific theater.

Before the outbreak of war, the RAF presence in the Pacific was minuscule. Plans were drawn up in the 1930s for the expansion of air defenses to protect such key British colonies as Singapore and Hong Kong, but with the attention of the British high command focused on the war in Europe, scant resources remained to be shifted to the Far East. As a result, it was October 1941 before the RAF began seriously to prepare for war in the Pacific. When the Japanese attacked at Kota Bahru on December 8, 1941, the RAF was still unprepared.

The RAF had only 181 aircraft in Southeast Asia at the beginning of the war and used only nine of twenty-seven planned airfields in the region. The Japanese, on the other hand, could put some two thousand aircraft in the skies. Great Britain's Air Ministry had decided not to send any of its main fighter aircraft—the Hurricane—to the Far East. Shipments originally intended for Singapore went, instead, to Russia to stop the German advance, and so the only fighters available to the RAF were seventy-nine obsolete Buffaloes. The Buffalo was slower, had a much poorer climb rate, and was less maneuverable than the main Japanese fighter, the Zero. (In fact the Brewster Buffalo always has pride of place in any listing of "The

World's Worst Aircraft.") The RAF's bombers and reconnaissance aircraft were also obsolete in comparison with their Japanese counterparts.

The RAF did possess one notable advantage over the Japanese: radar. At the start of the war, the British had two coastal radar sites and a number of mobile radars. The radar units did not cover the entire range of the British Far East positions, but major areas such as Singapore could receive at least thirty minutes warning in case of air attack. The ground-to-air links through VHF communication were limited, however, and information could be passed to British aircraft for a distance of only about twenty miles. This weak link severely limited the ability of the radar units to convey information to the airborne units and to coordinate attacks.

RAF reconnaissance aircraft spotted a Japanese convey bound for the Malay Peninsula on December 6, 1941, but bad weather hampered British efforts to shadow the Japanese movement. On December 8, the Japanese attacked British defenses at Kota Bahru, and the Pacific war began for Great Britain. The British responded quickly to the Japanese landings at Kota Bahru, where eight Hudson bombers flew seventeen sorties in just three hours, sinking one Japanese merchant ship and twenty-four landing barges and damaging numerous other vessels. In all some three thousand Japanese troops were killed in the bombing attacks. But by day's end, the Japanese had established a beachhead and had begun to advance inland. The bombings at Kota Bahru proved to be the only major success for the RAF (or any other British military arm) in the opening of the war in the Pacific.

The Japanese launched continuous air attacks on Singapore and on British positions in northern Malaya. By December 9, the Japanese had destroyed over half the RAF's aircraft and had established clear air superiority. The RAF was unable to prevent the Japanese aerial torpedo attacks, which sank the new British battleship *Prince of Wales* and old battle-cruiser *Repulse* on December 10, and were unable to provide air support for British ground forces in northern Malaya. As the Japanese ground troops swiftly advanced, the RAF evacuated its northern bases and concentrated on the defense of Singapore.

The British attempted to reinforce the air defenses of Singapore by diverting aircraft from the Middle East and Australia—including Hurricane fighters for the first time—but these reinforcements arrived too late and in far too few numbers to make a decisive impact on the Japanese advance. By March 1942, Hong Kong, Singapore, Java, and Rangoon had all fallen to the Japanese, and the RAF had lost almost all its air strength. Elements of the famed American Volunteer Group ("The Flying Tigers")

were diverted to defend Burma and to share their experience in air combat with the RAF. But the British refused to take any advice from the "inexperienced" Americans—particularly the lesson that was most needed: how to fight the lightweight Japanese Zero and win. The heavy Hurricanes attempted to engage the Zeros in dogfights, using the tactics of the Battle of Britain, and were shot out of the sky. The planes that survived were evacuated to India, where the Far East RAF was reorganized with its headquarters at Bengal, under the command of Air Marshall Sir Richard Peirse.

In April 1942, the Allies divided the Pacific theater into zones of responsibility. The British operational theater included India, Burma, Malaya, and Sumatra; everything farther east, including Australia and New Zealand, was under U.S. command. Japanese gains in Burma essentially closed the overland supply routes to China, so the transport of Allied supplies to China had to be by air. Only the United States had the necessary airlift capabilities to accomplish this feat. Hence, the U.S. Army Tenth Air Force was stationed in India, but this group and the majority of subsequent American reinforcements were concentrated in supporting the Chinese. With this division, however, Peirse was able to concentrate the resources of the RAF against the Japanese in Burma, as part of the larger British effort to protect India.

Peirse built up the resources and facilities of the RAF in India. With the Japanese threatening the Indian subcontinent, and even bombing Bengal and Calcutta, an immense quantity of supplies and materiel had to be sent to bolster British defenses.

By November 1943, the RAF had 140 airfields operational in the theater and had also established a radar system with fifty-two stations supported by nine communications centers. New aircraft streamed into India. By year's end, there were more than fifty squadrons with close to seven hundred operational aircraft and some eighty thousand men (approximately 10 percent of the RAF's total strength). These numbers included squadrons that were beginning to be equipped with modern versions of Spitfire fighters and Beaufighter attack warplanes. The replacement of obsolete fighters allowed the RAF to engage Japanese Zeros on a more than equal basis.

There remained deficiencies in the RAF's capabilities. The strategic bombing campaign against Germany made London reluctant to spare any heavy bombers. Consequently, until 1944, the RAF had only one squadron of heavy bombers, and its warplanes were U.S. B-24 Liberators. To augment the RAF's bombing capacity, Peirse ordered three squadrons of American-built Vengeance light bombers and had five squadrons of Hurricanes converted into fighter bombers. Nonetheless, it was 1944 before the RAF could conduct significant bombing raids against the Japanese.

Another major constraint on the RAF was transport aircraft. As with bombers, the RAF was initially critically short of air transport and had to rely on U.S. aircraft. There were only five transport squadrons—all flying either Hudson or C-47 Dakota aircraft (both U.S.-built)—to service the entire theater throughout 1943 and into 1944. In fact, the average mileage of the RAF transports grew from 5,000 miles per week in 1942 to 37,000 per week within a year.

In the first months of 1943, the Japanese conducted limited air strikes, involving from ten to twenty aircraft, against British air bases and ground positions in India. Although these raids formed the main thrust of the continuing Japanese air offensive, they did little significant damage. By June, when the monsoon season effectively ended most aerial missions, the RAF had lost fourteen fighters, with twelve damaged, and the Japanese had lost twenty-three aircraft, with another twenty probably destroyed.

Throughout 1943 and into 1944, the role of the RAF was essentially one of support for the ground offensives aimed at recapturing Burma. During the first Arakan campaign, the RAF provided reconnaissance and interdiction for the ground troops, culminating in the RAF's first major bombing campaign in the Far East, in May 1943. Major air strikes were carried out by the RAF with the support of U.S. Army Air Forces (USAAF) B-17 Flying Fortresses in an effort to cut the main Japanese supply routes through central Burma. Although the offensive failed, it demonstrated the potential for joint air and ground assaults and led to the creation of Army Air Support Control (AASC) teams, which were assigned to British ground units to coordinate close air support. The offensive also demonstrated the hard-hitting power of the Beaufighter in close air support, with its four 20-mm cannon and six .303-caliber machine guns.

The RAF also provided the main support for the "Chindit" guerrilla campaigns behind Japanese lines. Each Chindit unit had an RAF section to coordinate air support and supply. During the first Chindit campaign, in February 1943, the RAF dropped some three hundred tons of supplies and flew eight air strikes and even evacuated wounded on several occasions from improvised landing strips. The relative success of this expedition led to a second, in March 1944. During this second Chindit operation the guerrillas had their own air force of seconded USAAF planes supported by RAF fighters (the RAF again supplied the ground sections). RAF resupply

and air support proved even more critical during the second expedition.

Throughout 1943 and 1944, the main strategic priority for the RAF was to establish clear air superiority in the theater. This became particularly important because the Japanese launched major offensives which isolated the British IV Corps at Imphal and at a British garrison at Kohima. These two key positions had to be resupplied by air for a period of months. In addition, for the first time in history, an entire division was airlifted from one front, in Arakan, several hundred miles away to another front, Imphal. The RAF undertook a vigorous campaign against Japanese air bases in order to protect the air supply routes. Still handicapped by a lack of heavy bombers, the RAF was able to use its Beaufighters and newly arrived Mosquitos and U.S.-built P-47 Thunderbolts to conduct extremely effective air strikes against Japanese positions.

The increased number and quality of RAF and U.S. aircraft, and the Japanese withdrawal of aircraft to combat the American offensives elsewhere in the Pacific, gave the RAF clear air superiority over Burma and the Malay Peninsula by the fall of 1944. In addition, increasing numbers of USAAF aircraft were being used to support British operations after both the RAF and the USAAF were integrated into a single command, the Air Command South-East Asia (ACSEA). ACSEA was initially commanded by Peirse and later by USAAF General George E. Stratemeyer. ACSEA increased the capabilities of the RAF by bringing in U.S. heavy bombers (including the futuristic B-29s) and transport and supply craft to support RAF operations. By 1945, the Americans provided almost 70 percent of the aircraft needed to supply the advancing British forces, although the main focus of the USAAF in Southeast Asia remained China.

By 1945, ACSEA had over fifteen hundred aircraft, compared with only three hundred Japanese. The Allies had enjoyed air superiority from 1943 on. The British were able to relieve both Imphal and Kohima and to launch a major offensive in February 1945. The RAF conducted aerial mine-laying and bombing attacks on the sea-lanes to cut off Japanese resupply efforts. By May 1945 both Rangoon and Mandalay had been recaptured, although Japanese air units had begun to conduct kamikaze "suicide" attacks against Allied forces.

By June, the RAF had its own bombing capabilities, so USAAF bombers were transferred to aid in the bombing of Japan. As the RAF prepared to transfer two squadrons of bombers to Okinawa to support strategic U.S. bombing operations in August, the dropping of the atomic bombs caused the Japanese to accept the Allied surrender terms on August 15, 1945.

Despite the war's end, the RAF continued to carry out a number of operations. Because of isolation and a disbelief in the surrender by some Japanese units, sporadic fighting continued, and the RAF carried out combat operations for another week after the official end of the war. The RAF dropped some 18 million leaflets over Southeast Asia announcing the Japanese surrender; it also dropped supplies to the 100,000 Allied prisoners held by the Japanese, and it evacuated some three thousand POWs.

Although it never came near to matching the strength of the USAAF, the RAF carried out essential missions ranging from air supply and transport to air defense and air support for ground operations. In doing so, it allowed the Americans to concentrate resources elsewhere, and the British to recover from early Japanese successes. Despite its austere beginnings, by the later stages of the war the RAF had become an integral element in the Allied campaigns in the Pacific.

FURTHER READINGS

Allen, Louis. *Burma: The Longest War* (1984).

Dean, Maurice. *The RAF and Two World Wars* (1979).

Innes, David J. *Beaufighters over Burma* (1985).

Probert, Henry. *The Forgotten Air Force* (1995).

Tom Lansford

SEE ALSO Aircraft: Japanese, U.S., and British; Army Air Corps/Air Forces, U.S.; China-Burma-India Theater of Operations

Air Force, Royal Australian

The Royal Australian Air Force (RAAF) was established as an independent service in March 1921, but military aviation in Australia predated World War I, and the four squadrons of the Australian Flying Corps had fought on the Western Front and in the Middle East from 1914 to 1918. In the interwar period the air force made do with limited resources; it successfully resisted attempts by the army and the navy to divide it between themselves, and it concentrated on local defense capabilities and the pioneering of civil aviation infrastructure. In 1939 Australia signed the agreement which set up the Empire Air Training Scheme (also known as the Commonwealth Air Training Plan) to provide aircrew for the Royal Air Force (RAF) in Europe, and this was to have severe long-term implications for the RAAF in Australia. Thousands of Australians served in Europe throughout World War II, and the British government demonstrated a marked reluctance to release them for return to Australia even when, in the latter part of the war, many of them were surplus to requirements.

At the beginning of the Pacific war the RAAF was small in size, suffered from a lack of training, and was equipped with obsolescent aircraft. Four squadrons were deployed to Malaya, and these were the first RAAF units to see action against the Japanese. Nos. 1 and 8 Squadrons flew Hudson bombers, while Nos. 21 and 453 Squadrons were equipped with Brewster Buffalos—and both were outclassed by the Japanese in a campaign that established the enemy's early dominance in the air. In Australia itself there was as yet no integrated air defense system, and when the Japanese bombed Darwin in the first of a series of heavy air raids on February 19, 1942, numerous Australian and U.S. aircraft were destroyed on the ground.

When General Douglas MacArthur arrived in Australia in April 1942, he assumed control over all forces in the Southwest Pacific Command. With the arrival of General George C. Kenney in August to take command of the Allied Air Force (AAF), he established separate command and control systems for the RAAF and the U.S. Army Air Forces (USAAF), creating RAAF Command and the Fifth Air Force. On a personal level Kenney respected his Australian counterparts and generally enjoyed good relations with the senior officers of that service. The great weakness in the RAAF was of the Australians' own making. At the beginning of the Pacific war the chief of the Air Staff had been a British officer on detached service, Air Chief Marshal Sir Charles Burnett. When he retired in May 1942, he was succeeded by Air Vice Marshal George Jones—not by Air Vice Marshal W. D. Bostock, who had been Burnett's choice; Jones was junior in rank not only to Bostock but also to seven other senior officers on the air force list. Bostock became air officer commanding RAAF Command and was responsible to Kenney for RAAF operations in the Southwest Pacific Command, while Jones had administrative responsibility for the air force. Relations between the two were poisonous, and the corrosive effect this had on the RAAF as a whole played itself out for the remainder of the war. But ill will among senior officers had been a feature of the interwar air force as well.

As a result of the divisions at the top, the RAAF generally failed to develop a strategic doctrine acceptable to the United States, which in turn prejudiced attempts to acquire frontline aircraft for the RAAF from the Americans, which in its turn meant that Australian squadrons were relegated to lower-priority roles and tasks. Senior command postings to No. 9 Operational Group in 1943 reflected the feuding in the high command and further undermined U.S. confidence in the RAAF's capabilities.

The Australian government was aware of the problem but lacked sufficient resolve to do anything about it. This high-level rancor and the far smaller size of the RAAF meant that the air service was fated to play a subordinate role in the Pacific war. Nonetheless, the RAAF expanded to impressive size and strength: At its peak in August 1944 it numbered 182,000 personnel, which by war's end had declined to 132,000 as the government partly demobilized in response to the manpower crisis. In August 1945 the RAAF fielded fifty squadrons and some six thousand aircraft (3,200 operational and the rest trainers).

In June 1944 the air forces in the theater were reorganized, with Kenney announcing the formation of the Far East Air Force comprising the Fifth and Thirteenth Air Forces, both American. This meant that the Allied Air Force, of which he retained command, henceforth comprised only Australian, New Zealand, and Dutch East Indies squadrons, although U.S. squadrons could be attached to the AAF for specific tasks. The AAF, like its army counterparts, was assigned "mopping-up" duties against bypassed enemy forces in the islands to Australia's north while the U.S. forces proceeded to the reconquest of the Philippines and the contemplated invasion of the Japanese home islands.

First Tactical Air Force (1st TAF) was formed in October 1944 from No. 10 Operational Group and began operations against Japanese positions from bases on Morotai in November. Dissatisfaction with their role grew among the squadrons, and in April 1945 a group of eight senior officers attempted to resign in protest. The "Morotai mutiny" prompted the removal of the commander of the 1st TAF and an inquiry which confirmed that decision. When Jones threatened disciplinary action against the eight, Kenney—who had spoken to the officers concerned and concluded that they had acted in good faith—declared that he would appear in their defense in any court martial.

In June 1945 with a strength of 21,893, of all ranks, the 1st TAF supported the Australian landings in Borneo and continued to fly against Japanese targets elsewhere in the Dutch East Indies until the war's end. In the war against Japan the RAAF suffered some two thousand casualties—killed, wounded, and prisoners of war.

The performance of the RAAF in the Pacific war was disappointing, in that it failed to conduct a leading role in the Southwest Pacific Command, its primary theater in the defense of Australia. The weakness in senior command explains much of this failure, and blame both for creating and then for sustaining this situation must lie with the government of the day. On the other hand, by 1945 the RAAF had grown into a large and capable or-

ganization, with many combat-experienced aircrew and officers who had held senior command and staff positions. Although aircraft acquisition had been a difficult problem in the first half of the war because of competing priorities elsewhere, by 1945 the RAAF possessed large numbers of modern aircraft and the capability to support them. The failures at the top were not matched by a lack of performance elsewhere in the organization.

FURTHER READINGS

Gillison, Douglas. *Royal Australian Air Force 1939–1942* (1962).

Odgers, George. *Air War against Japan 1943–45* (1957).

Stephens, Alan. *Power Plus Attitude: Ideas, Strategy and Doctrine in the Royal Australian Air Force 1921–1991* (1992).

Jeffrey Grey

SEE ALSO Australia

Air Offensive, Japan

The officially recognized campaign "Air Offensive, Japan" extended from April 17, 1942, the day before the Doolittle raid on Tokyo, to September 2, 1945, the day the war ended. Although the Doolittle raid—a small raid by later standards, but a tremendous psychological shock to the Japanese—opened the air offensive, no more attacks on Japan occurred until 1944. Part of an overall effort intended to prepare for the invasion of Japan scheduled for November 1945, the air offensive against Japan was conducted by B-29 Superfortress long-range heavy bombers of the U.S. Army Air Forces (USAAF) 20th and 21st Bomber Commands from June 5, 1944, to the end of the war. The air offensive, which the Japanese could not effectively contest, devastated Japan through destruction of arms and armament factories, widespread incendiary bombardment of cities and urban areas, and the mining of Japanese waters. Culminating finally in the loosing of two atomic bombs, the air offensive contributed greatly to the surrender ending World War II.

Conducted at first from bases in India, and later from the Mariana Islands in the Pacific, the air offensive featured a number of innovations. Originally intended to be conducted according to the theory of high-altitude daylight precision strategic bombardment developed by senior USAAF officers before the war, the air offensive evolved as it encountered problems of a type and scope never before experienced in aerial warfare. The immense distances of the theater of operations in which the B-29 fought placed a premium on aircraft—and aircrew—

performance. The B-29s had to climb over the highest mountains in the world, the Himalayas. High-speed, high-altitude "jetstream" winds over Japan blew planes and bombs off course. Frequent poor weather prevented precision bombardment.

The B-29 Superfortress represented a challenge in and of itself. Based on cutting-edge technology, the B-29 featured the most powerful engines, (Wright R-3350 radials of 2,200 horsepower each, yet adapted for any production bomber); an innovative, centrally controlled defensive machine-gun fire system; and a pressurized cabin. Rushed into production, the plane brought to combat technical problems that normally would have been worked out during a prolonged testing and development period. Among other problems, the B-29's engines were fireprone, and its clear plastic gun-sighting blisters often blew out.

USAAF officers, both in the field and back in Washington, created solutions to which the B-29 and its aircrews proved remarkably adaptable. Thousands of technical fixes were made; new maintenance methods were introduced; and bombing altitudes were lowered to get away from the jetstream. Night area incendiary bombardment of Japanese cities—less affected by bad weather than daylight precision bombardment—increased the air offensive's effect.

The idea of a bombing offensive against Japan extended as far back as the beginnings of the U.S. rivalry with Japan early in the century. Both the Japanese and the Americans realized that Japanese urban areas, built largely of wood, were vulnerable to bombardment, whether from aircraft or ship. As prewar discussions evolved into strategies and tactics on how to fight a possible war with Japan, the idea of a long-range heavy bomber grew. A number of U.S. Army Air Corps career officers advocated strategic bombardment to reduce or even eliminate an enemy's warmaking capacity through destruction of arms and munitions factories. As war clouds gathered, the United States began arming itself for a role in the fighting in Europe as well as against Japan. Although a number of state-of-the-art bombing planes were under development, the chief of the Army Air Corps, General H. H. Arnold, solicited bids from aircraft manufacturers that called for an aircraft to redefine that state.

Two serious prototypes were considered: Boeing's B-29 and Consolidated Aircraft's B-32. Eventually settling on the B-29, Arnold, a strategic bombardment proponent, ordered the aircraft while it was still in blueprints—a highly unusual move for an industry accustomed to careful testing of new designs. This caused the B-29, and Arnold, many headaches in the days ahead. Nonetheless,

he felt he could not afford to wait for normal development to wend its way to completion; the enemy certainly would not. (The B-32 was placed in limited production as a backup in case the B-29's problems became overwhelming.) Arnold pushed the program, although there were setbacks. On February 18, 1943, famed Boeing test pilot Eddie Allen was killed when his B-29 crashed into downtown Seattle as a result of engine fires.

In early 1943, after much discussion reflecting interservice and theater rivalries, Arnold ordered 20th Bomber Command (20 BC) activated. To avoid intratheater rivalries over command and control of the B-29 bombing force, the Joint Chiefs of Staff agreed that the 20th would be under their direct control, with General Arnold as their "executive agent." This unusual arrangement was another innovation by the pragmatic Arnold to overcome obstacles and objections and to ensure the success of U.S. airpower. Arnold in turn appointed General K. B. Wolfe, who had been heading up B-29 development, to command the 20th.

Determining that Germany was already practically defeated, Allied leadership at the Trident Conference in Washington (May 12–27, 1943) earmarked the B-29 for use against the Japanese. Initial plans called for the planes to be based in China to reinforce the alliance with Chiang Kai-shek. Lack of success in the ground war in China meant that bases were not available in range of seaports which could supply the vast amounts of fuel, bombs, and parts needed by the B-29s. General Joseph Stilwell, the theater commander, suggested basing the B-29s in India—far out of the planes' range of Japan—instead of China. The planes would shuttle through airfields in the Cheng-tu area of China, which was held by friendly forces, and then refuel and take off for Japan. Far from roads or seaports, these airfields would have to be supplied entirely by air. Inasmuch as competing demands such as the Fourteenth Air Force, based in the Cheng-tu area, stretched air transport resources razor thin, the B-29s themselves would have to fly in the gasoline they needed to refuel for the long flight to Japan. Although any such operations would be difficult at best, the Joint Chiefs eventually approved this method, and General Arnold in September 1943 directed General Wolfe to work up a plan— Operation Matterhorn—for bombing Japan from bases in India, after shuttling through China. General Wolfe ordered that bases be constructed in India and China.

Concurrently, USAAF planners—General Heywood S. Hansell, in particular—noticed that B-29 operations out of India would never be easy and recommended that the Mariana Islands be seized from the Japanese. Consisting of three principal islands (Guam, Tinian, and Saipan), the Marianas were located in the central Pacific ocean within B-29 range of Japan. They enjoyed good weather and could be supplied easily. A longtime U.S. possession, Guam had been garrisoned by marines before the war. The navy, which viewed the islands as important bases for the invasion of Japan, concurred. The nascent bombardment campaign received further impetus in November when General Hansell managed to convince the Joint Chiefs of Staff to issue a position paper at the Sextant Conference in Cairo, admitting the possibility that heavy bombardment and sea mining might win the war without the necessity of an invasion.

Logistics, command, the war itself, and such local difficulties as labor and weather delayed completion of the B-29 bases in India and China. Finding no progress as late as January 1944, General Wolfe borrowed the 853d Engineer Aviation Battalion and the 382d Engineer Construction Battalion from Stilwell's Ledo Road project, and he also drafted civilians. After two months, 6,000 U.S. troops and 27,000 Indian laborers had the bases in India ready for B-29s. In China, civilians pulled large rollers by hand to tamp down B-29 runways.

Pushing aside studies telling him that the B-29 force might not see action until 1947, and under pressure to reinforce the alliance with Chiang Kai-shek, Arnold ordered that the first group of B-29s fly to India by April 1944. To make the deadline, he pulled mechanics from Boeing's Wichita assembly line to help ready the first 100 bombers, which he found awaiting repair during a March 9–10 personal inspection at Smoky Hill Army Airfield, near Wichita, Kansas. Working around the clock in cold and snow, mechanics readied enough planes that they could begin leaving for India on March 26, barely three weeks later. Flying over Africa and the Mideast, the first B-29 landed at Kharagpur, about seventy miles west of Calcutta, India, on April 2, 1944. By May 8, there were 130 planes in India; two days later, the bases in China were deemed ready.

The 20th's first mission was not to Japan but from India directly to Japanese-held Thailand, on June 5, 1944, to give the new crews some experience. Sixteen of the hundred bombers scheduled for the mission turned back or were lost because of mechanical problems; clouds prevented formation flying and also forced some forty-eight of the seventy-seven planes that hit the target area to bomb by radar. Bombing results were poor. Although the mission was deemed an "operational success," the 20th soon learned that problems experienced on this first B-29 operation would characterize later missions.

Impatient with such "training" missions, General Arnold insisted that Wolfe bomb Japan itself. Tactically, he wanted Wolfe to assist Chiang Kai-shek, by taking the heat off Japan's offensive in China, and to cover an "important operation in the Pacific": the invasion of Saipan. Wolfe planned a mission to the Imperial Iron and Steel Works at Yawata in northern Kyushu. The B-29s began stocking Chengtu-area shuttle airfields with fuel, flying over the Himalayas and dodging bad weather and Japanese interceptors—a routine they soon termed "flying the Hump." Each B-29 had to complete roughly six flights over the Hump to accumulate enough fuel in China to fly a bombing mission over Japan. The task complete, on June 15, U.S. forces invaded Saipan; the 20th flew to the Imperial Iron and Steel Works.

Arnold had wanted the mission to fit U.S. bombing doctrine by being flown at high altitude, by daylight, in tight formation. Believing this took more experience than his crews had, Wolfe won a concession from Arnold: The mission would fly at night, with no formations, from medium altitudes of 8,000 to 18,000 feet. Sixty-eight planes of the original ninety-two made it over Japan, and the rest were turned back by mechanical problems. Bombing accuracy was poor. Despite positive stories in the press, General Arnold made some changes.

On July 4, 1944, Arnold promoted Wolfe to head B-29 development and production at USAAF Materiel Command. He replaced him with the Eighth Air Force's General Curtis E. LeMay. Innovative and imaginative, LeMay did everything he could—in all facets of a unit, from the quality of the food, to aircraft maintenance, to training, to formation flying—to obtain the optimal results from each bombing mission, at first as the head of the famed 305 BG (H) and later of the 3d Air Division, with the Eighth Air Force in England. Operation Matterhorn's difficulties were tailor-made for his talents. Arriving on August 29, LeMay instituted his training, maintenance, and formation systems. Performance improved but was still short of General Arnold's expectations. Just weeks before LeMay's arrival, Guam and Tinian fell to U.S. forces, and Seabee bulldozers began the massive airfields needed for the huge B-29 forces.

Limited success on repeated missions to Anshan on September 8 (the 20th's first mission since LeMay's arrival) and on September 26 generated pressure in Washington for the USAAF to try different tactics. Arnold's strategists tinkered with the target mixture, concentrating less on steel than on aircraft assembly plants; and in response to repeated suggestions by naval officers they ordered the B-29s to mine waters in Japanese-held areas. Eventually the 58th Bomb Wing dropped 987 mines between August 1944 and March 1945. Discussions also returned to the firebombing of urban areas, rather than the high-explosive precision bombardment of industrial targets.

October and November 1944 saw heartening if limited progress on a number of fronts. Ranging from Formosa to Japan, the 20th's bombing improved, as LeMay's crews concentrated on his tactics of formation flying, fuel economy, the "lead crew" concept he had brought from Europe, and "synchronous" bombing (in which the radar operator and the bombardier, with his optical bombsight, worked together to increase bombing accuracy even if clouds hid the target). On November 5, fifty B-29s flew 4,000 miles round trip from India to put the King George VI graving docks out of commission for three months at the Japanese-occupied naval base at Singapore. Ground crews took advantage of maintenance methods brought by LeMay, such as the sharing of technical specialties among units. Modifications to the R-3350 engine increased its reliability. The number of bombers that had to drop out of missions with mechanical problems decreased.

The 73d Bomb Wing of the 21st Bomber Command established the air offensive in the Marianas with the first B-29—flown by 21st commander, Brigadier General Hansell, the strategist who had recommended taking the Marianas—arriving at newly constructed airfields on Saipan on October 12. The primary targets would be aircraft and engine assembly plants centered in Tokyo, Nagoya, and Osaka. After briefly training on a few such nearby targets as the great Japanese base on Truk, the 21st, under pressure to produce results, sent 110 bombers to the Mushashino engine plant in Tokyo on November 24. The mission was flown at high altitude, according to precision daylight bombing doctrine, but unexpected high winds and clouds arose. Only twenty-four bombers accurately hit the target, seventeen aborted because of mechanical failures, and six others did not bomb. The 21st Bomber Command had expected more than five hundred Japanese aircraft to oppose the B-29s; about a hundred actually did, bringing down a single B-29 and damaging eight others. Nonetheless, conditions encountered by the 21st on its first mission characterized, and frustrated, its operations for the next month. The B-29 and the air offensive were not living up to their promise. General Arnold decided once again to make changes to improve the B-29's effectiveness.

In January, Arnold returned General Hansell to Washington; LeMay replaced him as head of 21 BC. LeMay privately thought, as did Hansell, that the B-29s could end the war without landings in Japan, although he continued the official strategy of preparation for an invasion. Despite the improvements in aircraft dependability and aircrew proficiency that had begun under Hansell and were continued by LeMay's techniques, high winds and clouds continued to hamper accurate high-altitude daylight precision bombing on the sixteen missions LeMay sent to Japan after taking command of 20 BC. Trying to avoid winds and clouds, LeMay noted that Arnold's strategists had once again turned to area incendiary attacks. Theoretically, area incendiary attacks would encounter the same problems as daylight precision attacks. Soon it became apparent to him, and to the strategists advising General Arnold and the Joint Chiefs of Staff, that success would mean changes to hallowed daylight precision strategic bombardment doctrine.

While LeMay pondered changes to 21 BC's techniques, B-29 units continued to arrive. Under Brigadier General Thomas S. Power, 314 BW arrived in Guam in February. Iwo Jima, a volcanic island between the Marianas and Japan, was invaded on February 19, to eliminate Japanese fighter interceptions of B-29s from there, and to provide an emergency landing strip for combat-damaged B-29s. Taking of the tiny island would result in fewer ditchings and fewer men lost at sea.

Pushing aside concerns, Arnold ordered a maximum-effort mission to Tokyo for February 25, experimenting with the new firebomb technique. Bad weather forced the B-29s to bomb from 25,000 feet, about 5,000 feet lower than usual; of the 231 aircraft which flew, clouds covering the target forced 172 to bomb by radar. Despite high hopes, results did not measurably improve. However, mulling over reconnaissance photographs revealing a square mile of the city burned out, LeMay hypothesized that the slightly lower bombing altitude helped to concentrate the firebombs in that area. Consulting with Washington, he changed the air offensive's direction, discarding long-held tenets of daylight precision strategic bombardment. Navigating and sighting by radar, B-29s would drop firebombs on cities at night, from low altitude. The wind would not blow away planes and bombs; engines would not burn out; weather would not hide targets; and range would increase, increasing the B-29's bomb load. It took considerable courage for the strategists in Washington to discard the tenets of their own doctrine. Auspiciously, the first B-29 landed on Iwo Jima on March 4. Area destruction was to replace "precision" bombing, and over the next several months several hundred thousand Japanese civilians were about to be incinerated.

Although Washington and 21 BC developed the new tactics in concert, General LeMay took responsibility for their success or failure. Expecting little or no fighter opposition on low-altitude night missions, he ordered all but the tail guns removed from the heavily armed B-29s. The planes would fly singly, instead of in formation, to avoid collisions. With careful training, LeMay taught even the least adept radar navigators how to get to the target. On March 9, 1945, the first firebomb mission went to Tokyo, where 325 planes bombed from 4,900 to 9,200 feet. After so many months of futile attempts and incremental improvement, the results were astounding: 15.8 square miles were burned out in the center of the city, including 25 percent of the city's buildings. Official figures listed 83,793 people killed and 40,918 injured—many horribly burned. The Tokyo fire raid remains the worst single aerial bombardment in history. Only fourteen USAAF aircraft were lost.

Capitalizing on this success, 21 BC flew five more such missions in ten days, going on March 11 to Nagoya and on March 13 to Osaka, where 8 square miles were burned out. On March 16 Kobe was the target, and on March 19 it was Nagoya once again—exhausting the supply of firebombs in the Marianas and temporarily ending the incendiary offensive. The results of this week's work were deemed, finally, successful. Almost sixteen hundred bomber flights had delivered 9,373 tons of bombs, which had burned out almost thirty-two square miles of Japanese cities. Washington prepared a list of thirty-three urban areas which had a concentration of heavy industry. Other types of bombing would continue; nighttime low-level area attacks would be mounted in weather not suitable for daylight precision bombardment.

While LeMay instituted a war-winning strategy in the Pacific, General Ramey's 58 BW wrapped up Operation Matterhorn with a night attack on a oil-tank farm on Bakum Island, near Singapore, on March 29, and prepared to move to the Marianas. Despite the experience gained in operating the B-29 and working out some of its problems, and despite the support given to the Chinese and their pathfinding role in the air offensive against Japan, the official air force history deemed Matterhorn's ten-month efforts a failure. If there were any successes, they were expensive.

Aerial mining of Japanese waters began as well, after much persistence by both U.S. Navy and USAAF proponents. Drawing on the experiences of 58 BW, the specially trained and equipped 313 BW, commanded by Brigadier General John J. Davies, flew the mining missions. The first mission, on March 27, 1945, mined the key bottleneck Shimonoseki Strait between Honshu and Kyushu. Soon, combined with submarine warfare, the mining caused imports of desperately needed food and supplies to drop tremendously.

On April 13, the B-29s, loaded with incendiary bombs straight from newly arrived cargo ships, burned out an-

other 11 square miles of Tokyo in the first firebomb raid since March 19. Kawasaki and Yokohoma were hit on April 15. At that point, despite misgivings of USAAF leadership, the 21st ceased strategic bombardment in favor of tactical support of the invasion of Okinawa. The navy credited B-29 poundings of kamikaze airfields with abatement of that danger to the fleet.

With 58 BW's arrival in the Marianas, Arnold pulled together 20 BC and 21 BC under the Twentieth Air Force, with LeMay in charge as before. On May 14 and 16, released from Okinawa support, the 20th flew daylight incendiary precision attacks to the Mitsubishi engine factory in Nagoya. The bombers firebombed Tokyo on May 23 and again, for the last time, on May 25. The last raid, by more than five hundred B-29s, burned out 16 square miles. A growing Japanese antiaircraft capability brought down twenty-six B-29s and damaged another hundred. At the end of May, P-51 Mustang fighter planes, based on Iwo Jima, began escorting the B-29s. Ominously, 509 Composite BG under the command of Lieutenant Colonel Paul Tibbetts Jr., began moving into North Field, on Tinian.

After mid-June, LeMay's photo interpreters reported all of Japan's larger cities burned out (except for those "reserved" for the atomic bomb, or for other reasons). While daylight precision strikes continued against industrial targets during clear weather, the B-29s firebombed some fifty smaller cities between June 17 and August 14. The 20th completed its growth, with 315 BW flying its first mission on June 26. Commanded by General Frank Armstrong of European theater Eight Air Force fame, the B-29s of the 315th were equipped with Eagle radar, developed specifically for bombardment. The 315th's mission was night bombardment of petroleum industry targets. Throughout the summer it dropped 9,000 tons of high explosives, losing just four aircraft, and completed the destruction of the already critical industry.

Portentous developments characterized July 1945. Scientists successfully test-detonated the atomic bomb at Alamogordo, New Mexico, on July 16. The Potsdam Conference on July 26 called for unconditional surrender of Japan; the alternative was "prompt and utter destruction." To demonstrate to the Japanese their helplessness to prevent bombing, General LeMay began dropping warning leaflets—actually giving the date of the attack—on targets before sending B-29s.

As invasion preparations stepped up, Fifth and Seventh Air Forces fighters and bombers which had fought their way up the southwest and central Pacific theaters, respectively, joined the air offensive in early July. Flying from newly captured Okinawa, by the end of the war they had dropped 7,100 tons of bombs on airfields, railroads, bridges, and industrial and urban targets.

August 1945 brought into clear focus the massive strategic and tactical forces being brought to bear on Japan in preparation for the November invasion, Operation Olympic. General Spaatz officially assumed command of the U.S. Strategic Air Forces, Pacific. LeMay became his chief of staff; Lieutenant General Nathan F. Twining, late of the Fifteenth Air Force in Italy, assumed command of the Twentieth Air Force. Under Lieutenant General James H. Doolittle, the mighty Eighth Air Force began moving from England to Okinawa. The air offensive continued as B-29s wiped out 99.5 percent of Toyama on August 1. A week later, on August 6, the 509th dropped the first atomic bomb—code-named Little Boy—on Hiroshima.

Spaatz sent incendiary-filled bombers to Yawata and Fukuyama on August 8, as Fat Man, the second atomic bomb, took shape on Tinian. On August 9, Fat Man was detonated over Nagasaki. Giving the Japanese a chance to surrender, the 20th waited until August 14 before firebombing Kumagaya and Isezaki. Aircraft similarly loaded were recalled the next day upon word of Japan's surrender. The air offensive came to an end, without an invasion of Japan.

Although the air offensive forestalled an invasion that would have been costly to both sides, it also left a troubling legacy. While night area incendiary bombardment helped to cripple Japanese military and industrial capabilities, it also took the lives of many noncombatant civilians. The bombardment of cities and the use of nuclear weapons have been surrounded by controversy ever since the fateful days of their use over Japan in August 1945.

FURTHER READINGS

Birdsall, Steve. *Superfortress: The Boeing B-29* (1980).

Coffey, Thomas M. *Hap: The Story of the U.S. Air Force and the Man Who Built It, General Henry H. "Hap" Arnold* (1982).

Craven, Wesley F., and James Lea Cate, eds. *The Army Air Forces in World War II*, vol. 5, *The Pacific: Matterhorn to Nagasaki, June 1944 to August 1945* (1953); vol. 6, *Men and Planes* (1955).

Hallion, Richard P. "Prelude to Armageddon," *Air Power History* 42 (1995).

Jablonski, Edward. *Air War: An Illustrated History of Air Power in the Second World War*, vol. 2, *Outraged Skies/ Wings of Fire* (1971).

LeMay, Curtis E., with MacKinlay Kantor. *Mission with Lemay: My Story* (1965).

Maurer, Maurer. *World War II Combat Squadrons of the United States Air Force: The Official Military Record of Every Active Squadron* (1969).

Wheeler, Keith. *Bombers over Japan: World War II* (1982).

Werrell, Kenneth P. *Blankets of Fire: U.S. Bombers over Japan during World War II* (1992).

Steven Agoratus

SEE ALSO Aircraft: Japanese, U.S., and British; Army Air Corps/Air Forces, U.S.

Aircraft: Japanese, U.S., and British

At the beginning of the Pacific war neither Japan nor the United States possessed large numbers of warplanes, despite unprecedented programs of prewar aircraft development and production. Thus, early Pacific war air operations on both sides were undertaken with what were small forces compared with those engaged in Europe. Most British aircraft were, of course, in Europe, although there were air assets in Asia, in such places as Singapore, and Commonwealth air forces in Australia and New Zealand.

With long lead times in aircraft production from inception to production—up to four years for airframes and more than that for engines—timing and strategic decisions were extremely important. Both Germany and Japan caught aircraft modernization at the right time, that is, during the decade of the 1930s, when aircraft technology changed faster and more profoundly than at any time before or since. Furthermore, Japan's penchant for secrecy enabled that country to keep the West unaware of what it had accomplished. Washington discounted reliable reports about the quality of Japanese aircraft, including reports from Claire Chennault, then supervising the Chinese air force.

Even though the Japanese air force was superbly equipped and trained at the outset of the conflict, it was in fact too small for world war. In December 1941 Japan had fewer than 3,000 combat-ready aircraft (the army had about 1,500 planes and the navy another 1,400). The vast majority of these were, however, of modern design (although several models with fixed, "spatted" landing gear gave a deceptively obsolete appearance) and were well suited for long-range operations. Japan emphasized maneuverability and long range in its fighters, and long range and bomb capacity in its bombers.

The weak design point of Japanese aircraft was their engines, in large part because of materials shortages, inferior lubricants, and inadequate quality control. Japan also continued to rely on prewar aircraft designs. Its basic design types—the Zero, the Betty, and the Val—all flew throughout the war. And Japan largely ignored defensive aircraft.

Japan wanted a strike force capable of carrying out long-distance missions and inflicting maximum damage. Japanese pilots were superbly trained and had gained extensive combat experience against the Russians and the Chinese in the late 1930s, but Japan lost air supremacy in the great land-sea battles of 1942. Midway cost the navy four carriers and the lives of hundreds of experienced airmen. Guadalcanal was even more expensive; it became a "meat grinder" battle, in which Japan lost perhaps nine hundred aircraft, and, because Japanese bombers had relatively large crews (the Betty required seven men), it lost some twenty-four hundred trained pilots and aircrew. After Guadalcanal the United States launched many more carriers and vastly more aircraft (many of which were newer types), while the Japanese were forced for the most part to make do with updated versions of earlier aircraft, without veteran pilots to fly them.

Japan's major effort at aircraft production came too late: Production rose from 1,500 aircraft in 1937 to 4,467 in 1939, and then it leveled off to 4,768 aircraft in 1940 and 5,088 in 1941. Japan produced 8,861 planes in 1942; 16,693 in 1943; 28,180 in 1944; and 11,066 in the first eight months of 1945. This production included only limited numbers of new types.

In December 1941 the United States outnumbered Japan 2 to 1 in terms of numbers of aircraft: 3,305 combat-ready aircraft for the army and 3,300 for the navy. Few of these were capable of contesting one-on-one with their Japanese counterparts, but the United States was first among the warring powers to recognize the necessity of producing vast numbers of aircraft. It built aircraft not only for itself but also for other Allied powers. The United States constructed 6,028 aircraft in 1940 and 19,445 in 1941. In 1942, U.S. production was 47,836 planes; in 1943 it was 85,898; in 1944 (the peak year) it rose to 96,318; and in 1945 it fell back to 47,714. In all, from 1941 to 1945 the United States built 297,199 combat aircraft, including 99,742 fighters and 97,592 bombers.

Great Britain had only some 3,700 frontline aircraft in September 1939 at the start of the war. It produced 7,000 in 1939; 15,000 in 1940; 20,100 in 1941; 23,671 in 1942; 26,263 in 1942; and 28,189 in 1944. At the end of the war Great Britain had built 125,254 aircraft of all types.

Australia also manufactured aircraft, including the Tiger Moth trainer and its own Commonwealth CA-3 Wirraway trainer, the Bristol Beaufort and its own Commonwealth CA-12 Boomerang fighter, and the Commonwealth CA-11 Woomera bomber. Great Britain and the other Commonwealth nations in the Pacific war flew not only British aircraft but also such U.S. planes as

the Brewster Buffalo and P-40 Kittyhawk fighters, the Consolidated PBY Catalina amphibious patrol bomber/reconnaissance aircraft, and the Lockheed A-28 Hudson reconnaissance aircraft.

By 1943 the United States gained the qualitative edge. Its F4U Corsair, P-38 Lightning, and F6F Hellcat outclassed Japanese aircraft in speed, range, armor, armament, and—in the case of the Hellcat at least—maneuverability. U.S. air advances also included refinements in equipment, such as lightweight radar, better armament, and improved radio and lifesaving equipment. U.S. troops also learned quickly in combat and set up the logistics base and training facilities that enabled them to win the air war.

Great Britain also had a number of aircraft in the Pacific theater of war. The Royal Air Force was, of course, the world's first independent air force, and the Royal Navy had pioneered many naval air procedures and practices.

Changes in aircraft design during the war may be seen in the following descriptions and discussion of the principal types deployed by Japan, the United States, and Great Britain. (All speeds given are maximums.)

Japanese Fighters

Japanese fighters were light, fast, and highly maneuverable. The *Mitsubishi A5M* navy interceptor (code-named Claude and Sandy in the 1942 U.S. identification system) went into production in 1936 (in various models 1,094 were produced). A transitional fighter, it was the predecessor of the A6M Zero. An open-cockpit fighter with fixed landing gear, the A5M had a speed of 270 mph and a range of 746 miles, and it was armed with only two machine guns and 132 pounds of bombs. A5Ms dominated the skies over China until the beginning of World War II.

The *Nakajima Ki-27* (3,399 produced; known as Abdul and Nate) entered service in 1939. Another transitional fighter with fixed landing gear, it led to the Nakajima Ki-43 Hayabusa (see below). The Hayabusa had a speed of 292 mph and a 1,060-mile range, and it carried (still) only two machine guns and 220 pounds of bombs.

By far the best and most famous Japanese fighter of the Pacific war was the *Mitsubishi A6M Reisen* (Zero, known as Zeke to the Americans but generally called Zero by all nations—eventually even by the Japanese, who nicknamed it Zero-sen). An excellent original design, it entered service in 1940. More Zeros (10,449) were built during the war than any other Japanese warplane. The A6M2 model that led the attack at Pearl Harbor had a speed of 332 mph and the exceptional range of 1,930 miles. It was exceptionally light; the fuselage was skinned with almost-paper-thin duralumin, and there was no seat armor; nor were its gas tanks self-sealing. At 6,264 pounds loaded, the A6M was almost half a ton lighter than the F4F Wildcat. It was also as maneuverable as any fighter of the war. The Zero had a surprisingly heavy armament—two 7.7-mm machine guns in the upper fuselage and two wing-mounted slow-firing 20-mm cannon. It could also carry 264 pounds of bombs. It was, however, deficient in structural strength.

Based on bitter experience, U.S. pilots developed tactics to defeat the Zeros. Pairs of F4Fs, using the "Thach weave," could handle four or five Zeros. The Zero went through a succession of models. The final (1945) A6M8 model had a 1,560-hp engine—60 percent more powerful than the engine in the A6M2—and could achieve 356 mph.

The *Nakajima A6M2-N* (Rufe) was a float-plane fighter. Introduced in 1942, it was essentially a Zero with a center pontoon and two wing floats. The Rufe was developed to provide air support to the many small Japanese island bases. It had a speed of 270 mph and a range of 1,207 miles, and it carried two 20-mm cannon, two machine guns, and 264 pounds of bombs. Fast and maneuverable despite its large floats, it was no match for the later U.S. fighters. Between 1941 and 1943, Japan produced 327 A6M2-Ns.

The *Nakajima Ki-43 Hayabusa* (Peregrine Falcon, known as Jim and Oscar to the Allies) entered service in 1940. The Japanese army's counterpart to the Zero, the Oscar was often confused with it. The Oscar had a speed of 308 mph and a range of 745 miles and was armed with two machine guns and 66 pounds of bombs. It went through a succession of models and was in production the entire war. In fact, the Imperial Japanese Army produced more Ki-43s (5,919) than any other fighter. The 1942 version had a more powerful engine, a speed of 329 mph, and a range of 1,095 miles; it carried the same armament but a heavier bomb load (1,102 pounds). Like the Zero, the Oscar was fast and maneuverable, but it had no armor protection or self-sealing gasoline tanks, and its armament was too light.

Entering service in 1943, the *Nakajima Ki-44 Shoki* (Tojo) was a second-generation aircraft; 1,225 were produced. A fast, heavily armed fighter, it reversed the Zero's design formula in being structurally strong and fast but not maneuverable. Specifically designed as an interceptor, the Tojo was effective against U.S. bombers. It had a speed of 376 mph and a range of 1,050 miles. It was armed with four machine guns.

The *Kawasaki Ki-45 Toryu* (Dragon Slayer, known as Nick) entered service in 1942; a total of 1,701 were produced. With a speed of 340 mph and a range of 1,404 miles, it was armed with one 20-mm cannon and three machine guns, and it carried 1,100 pounds of bombs. It enjoyed success only at the end of the war, in a night-fighter role against U.S. bombers.

The *Kawasaki Ki-61 Hien* (Swallow, code-named Tony) was another second-generation Japanese fighter; it entered service in 1943, and 3,078 were produced during the war. It and the J2M Raiden (see below) were the principal adversaries of the B-29 bomber in the last months of the war. The only wartime Japanese fighter powered by a liquid-cooled (1,175-hp) engine, the Tony had a speed of 368 mph and a range of 684 miles. It had armor protection, self-sealing fuel tanks, and as many as four 12.7-mm machine guns. Well-liked by its pilots, the Tony was, however, difficult to maintain, and its engine was unreliable.

The *Nakajima Ki-84 Hayate* (Gale, code-named Frank) entered service in 1943, and 3,514 were produced. It had a speed of 392 mph and a range of 1,347 miles. A small aircraft, the Ki-84 was highly maneuverable and rugged; it was equipped with armor and self-sealing tanks and armed with two 20-mm cannon, two 12.7-mm machine guns, and 1,202 pounds of bombs. Used mainly in the defense of Japan, the Frank registered some successes against U.S. bombers, but it suffered from numerous mechanical problems.

The *Mitsubishi Ki-83* entered service in 1944. Powered by two 2,200-hp engines, it had a speed of 438 mph and a range of 2,175 miles, and it was armed with two 30-mm cannon and two 20-mm cannon. It could carry 220 pounds of bombs and had a crew of two. Intended as a long-range escort fighter, the Ki-83 was as maneuverable as its single-engined rivals.

The *Kawanishi N1K1-J Shiden* (Violet Lightning, code-named George) was a navy fighter that entered service at about the same time as the Frank. With a speed of 363 mph, it was 30 mph faster than the Zero and almost as maneuverable. Its range was 890 miles. Armed with four 20-mm cannon and two machine guns, the George could carry 264 pounds of bombs.

The *Kawanishi N1K12-J Shiden-kai* (George-21) was an improved version of the N1K1-J. It entered service in 1944 and was as fine a fighter as any in the Pacific theater; both it and the original George were capable of competing with such U.S. planes as the F6F Hellcat and the F4U Corsair. With a speed of 369 mph and a range of 1,293 miles, the George-21 had an armament of four 20-mm cannon and carried 1,102 pounds of bombs. It was, however, also plagued with mechanical problems. Japan produced a total of 1,435 planes of these last two types.

The *Kawanishi N1K1 Kyofu* was a single-engined float-plane fighter designed to replace the Zero. It had a speed of 304 mph, a range of 1,036 miles, and armament of two 20-mm cannon and two machine guns; it carried 264 pounds of bombs.

The *Mitsubishi J2M Raiden* (Jack) entered service in 1943. After its problems had been ironed out, it replaced the Zeke as the Japanese navy's chief fighter. Introduced as an interceptor, the Jack was powered by an 1,800-hp radial engine and could achieve 363 mph and a range of 1,180 miles. It had four 20-mm cannon and could carry 264 pounds of bombs. Only 476 Jacks were produced.

The *Kawasaki Ki-102* (Randy) entered service in 1944. A two-engined fighter with a crew of two, it had a speed of 360 mph and a range of 1,240 miles and was armed with one 37-mm cannon, two 20-mm cannon, and one machine gun. Only 208 were produced.

The last prototypes of Japanese fighters in the war—all introduced in 1945—were the *Kyushu J7W Shinden*, an unusual pusher-design, very high speed interceptor with elevators at the front of the fuselage; the *Kawasaki Ki-100*; the *Mitsubishi A7M Reppu* (Sam), which was to have replaced the Zeke; and the *Mitsubishi J8M Shusui* (a direct copy of a German design). The J8M was a rocket aircraft (another copy—this one of the very dangerous [to its pilots] German ME-163) that developed 2,307 pounds of thrust but had an endurance of only five minutes and thirty seconds. It was armed with two 30-mm cannon. Only seven J8M prototypes were built by the end of the war; only one of these flew, and it—like many of its Luftwaffe progenitors—exploded.

U.S. Fighters

When Japan attacked Pearl Harbor on December 7, 1941, most U.S. fighters were hopelessly obsolete. Typical were the Boeing P-26 (the Peashooter), still in service at Pearl Harbor, and the Seversky P-35 (also at Pearl Harbor), dating from 1937. The *Boeing P-26*, introduced in 1934, was a low-winged, fixed-undercarriage, open-cockpit aircraft that was the Army Air Corps' first all-metal monoplane, armed with two machine guns and 110 pounds of bombs. It had a maximum speed of 234 mph and a range of 620 miles and was, by the time of World War II, hopelessly obsolete.

The *Seversky P-35* had originally been sold to Sweden, but in October 1940 Washington requisitioned sixty of these planes. The U.S. Army Air Corps' first cantilevered monoplane with retractable landing gear, it was powered by a Pratt & Whitney R-1830-9 air-cooled 950-hp en-

gine. It had a maximum speed of 281 mph and a range of 1,150 miles. It was armed with two machine guns and 300 pounds of bombs. The P-35 lacked both the armor and the armament for air combat, and its major contribution was that it led to the Republic P-47 Thunderbolt (see below).

The *Curtiss P-36* (also at Pearl Harbor) entered service in 1937 and was also obsolete in December 1941. Powered by a Pratt & Whitney R-1830-49 air-cooled 1,200-hp engine, it was capable of 311 mph and had a range of 825 miles. It was armed with two machine guns.

The *Republic P-43A Lancer*, another obsolete design, joined the army in 1941. Powered by a Pratt & Whitney R-1830-49 air-cooled 1,200-hp engine, it had a maximum speed of 356 mph and a range of 800 miles. It was armed with four machine guns and carried 200 pounds of bombs.

The main U.S. opponents of the Zero early in World War II were the army P-39 Airacobra and P-40 Warhawk and the navy/marine F4F Wildcat. The *Bell P-39 Airacobra* entered service in 1941. Its design centered on its unique armament—a 37-mm cannon firing through the middle of the nose cone—which dictated the entire structure of the aircraft. The engine was mounted in the center of the fuselage, behind the pilot, and the driveshaft to the propeller did double duty as a 37-mm cannon! The P-39 also had retractable tricycle landing gear positioned under its nose—the first such arrangement in a fighter. At 8,300 pounds, it was significantly heavier than the Zero, although its speed of 385 mph was faster. It had a range of 650 miles. The P-39 had one 37-mm cannon, four machine guns, and 500 pounds of bombs. No match for the Zero in one-on-one combat, the P-39 excelled in ground support operations. Of 9,558 P-39s produced during the war, fully half went to the Soviet Union for tactical support.

The *P-40 Warhawk* (known as the Tomahawk or Kittyhawk in its British versions and as the Lafayette in the Free French version) was the most important fighter during the United States' first two years of the war. It entered service in 1940. The P-40s (actually Tomahawks diverted from a British contract) gained popular acclaim in service with the American Volunteer Group (Chennault's Flying Tigers) in China. The P-40B, at 7,600 pounds, was far heavier than the Zero; but its 352-mph speed made it marginally faster, and it was much more solidly built. It had a range of 940 miles and was armed with four machine guns. The P-40N, armed with six machine guns and 500 pounds of bombs, had a more powerful engine, a speed of 378 mph, and a range of 240 miles. A total of 13,733 P-40s in ten models were produced during the war (undoubtedly too many for a design that was already obsolete in 1941). Chennault insisted that his P-40 pilots fly in pairs and use hit-and-run tactics to attack Japanese bombers and capitalize on the fighter's heavy firepower and superior speed and diving capability.

The *Brewster F2A Buffalo* was the first monoplane ordered by the U.S. Navy. A fighter-bomber that became operational in 1941, it participated in the Battle of Midway. It had a speed of 321 mph and the impressive range of 965 miles. Armament included four machine guns and 220 pounds of bombs. The F2A's disappointing design, which actually led to a congressional investigation and the winding-up of the Brewster Aeronautical Company, soon disappeared from U.S. service; the bulk of the 507 completed planes went to Great Britain and the Netherlands, where they also fared badly. This seemingly disastrous aircraft somehow redeemed itself in Finnish service, amassing an impressive score against Soviet aircraft. (Either the Finns were among the world's best pilots, or the Soviets were among the world's worst.)

The *Grumman F4F Wildcat* entered service in December 1940. Powered with a 1,200-hp air-cooled engine, it was, at 7,000 pounds, only slightly heavier than the Zero and as fast as it (331 mph), but not nearly as maneuverable. Its range was 845 miles, and it was armed with six machine guns and 200 pounds of bombs. The F4F-4 (1941) had a speed of 318 mph and a range of 770 miles. The Wildcat was also quite strong. Although the Zero could easily outmaneuver the P-40 and F4F, U.S. Navy and Marine pilots developed tactics enabling them to utilize their heavy (.50-caliber) machine guns to cut the Zeros apart. The Wildcat was also faster than the Zero in a turning dive. The F4F remained in manufacture (8,000 produced) through the end of the war for service on escort carriers.

The *Grumman F6F Hellcat* entered service in 1943. A myth persists that the Hellcat was based on secrets discovered by examining a Japanese Zero taken intact in July 1942 on Akutan Island in the Aleutians. The problem with that theory is the fact that the F6F had first flown the month before. One of the design triumphs of the war, the F6F went from drawing board to production in only slightly more than two years. It used the Pratt & Whitney R-2800 Double Wasp 2,000-hp engine and was built specifically to counter the Zero. The F6F-3 had a speed of 376 mph and a range of 1,090 miles and was armed with six machine guns. The F6F-5 had a maximum speed of 380 mph and a range of 1,040 miles and was armed with six machine guns and 2,000 pounds of bombs. The Hellcat was both extremely rugged and maneuverable. Its five models registered nearly 75 percent of the navy's aerial

victories: 5,000 Japanese aircraft against about 250 losses. A total of 12,272 Hellcats were produced.

The *Vought F4U Corsair,* known to the Japanese as "Whistling Death," entered service in 1943. Conceived in 1938, its gull-winged design was built around the same Double Wasp 2,000-hp engine that powered the Hellcat. The F4U had a speed of 417 mph and a range of 1,015 miles. The 1944 F4U-1D had a speed of 425 mph. It was armed with six machine guns and 2,000 pounds of bombs. Extraordinarily rugged and versatile, the Corsair could carry a large ordnance load and deliver it on target. It was the first U.S. fighter to surpass 400 mph in level flight and the piston-engine fighter longest and last in U.S. production (from 1942 to 1954). A total of 12,681 were built. The Corsair had an 11-to-1 kill ratio against Japanese fighters. Some Japanese pilots felt that it was the best fighter aircraft they faced, and some aviation historians have termed it the best fighter of World War II. Later, it performed well in the Korean War and in Indochina.

The *Lockheed P-38 Lightning* (9,923 produced) entered service in 1942. With its second-engine insurance and long range the P-38 was a workhorse in the Pacific theater; it was also one of the top fighters of the war. The first twin-engined single-seated fighter ever in mass production, it was highly versatile and was used for long-range escort, photographic reconnaissance, night fighting, and ground support. P-38s shot down more Japanese aircraft than any other U.S. warplane. Their successes included the surgical strike of April 1943 to down the Betty bomber carrying Admiral Yamamoto. The P-38 had a speed of 395 mph and a range of 1,425 miles. Its armament was one 20-mm cannon, four machine guns, and 2,000 pounds of bombs. The J version (1943) had a speed of 414 mph and a range of 2,260 miles. It had the same armament, with the exception of a heavier bomb load—3,200 pounds. The last version was the M model, a radar-equipped night fighter; its operator sat in an extra cockpit behind that of the pilot.

The *Republic P-47 Thunderbolt*—the largest single-seated piston-engined fighter ever built (15,683 produced)—became operational in 1943. Powered by the Double Wasp 2,000-hp radial engine, the C model boasted a speed of 433 mph and a range of 550 miles and was armed with eight machine guns and 500 pounds of bombs. The D model had a more powerful 2,535-hp engine, a speed of 428 mph, and a range of 475 miles. It was armed with eight machine guns and carried 2,500 pounds of bombs. The P-47 may have been the best single-engined heavy fighter of the war. It was extremely useful both as an escort aircraft and a fighter-bomber for ground support. It continued after the war in the air forces of a dozen countries.

The *North American P-51* became operational in 1943. Perhaps the top fighter aircraft of the entire war, it was powered with a 1,200-hp engine. It had a speed of 390 mph and a range of 750 miles, was armed with four machine guns, and carried 1,000 pounds of bombs. The first prototype was constructed for the British in just 117 days. The P-51 owed its success in large part to its British Rolls Royce Merlin 61 engine, built in the United States under license by the Packard Motor Company. Its 1944 (D) version had a 1,510-hp engine, a speed of 437 mph, and a range of 950 miles. It was armed with six machine guns and carried 2,000 pounds of bombs. The H model—delivered in time to take part in the final operations against Japan—was capable of 487 mph. A total of 15,686 P-51s were produced. The P-51 also flew extensively in the Korean War.

The *Northrop P-61 Black Widow* (700 produced) became operational in 1944. A twin-engined night fighter with a crew of three, it was powered by two 2,000-hp engines and had a maximum speed of 366 mph and a range of 3,000 miles. It was armed with four 20-mm cannon and four machine guns, and it carried 6,400 pounds of bombs.

British Fighters

Two of the most famous aircraft of the entire war were the British Hawker Hurricane and the Supermarine Spitfire.

The Hurricane went through a number of models during the war. The *Hurricane Mark I* appeared in 1937 as a fighter and bore the brunt of the Battle of Britain in 1940. It was powered by a 1,030-hp Rolls-Royce Merlin II air-cooled engine. The Hurricane had a maximum speed of 320 mph and a range of 460 miles. It was armed with eight .303-caliber machine guns.

The *Hurricane Mark II* was a fighter-bomber, produced beginning in 1941. Powered by the Rolls-Royce Merlin XX liquid-cooled engine, it developed 1,280 hp and had a maximum speed of 329 mph and a range of 460 miles. It was armed with four 20-mm cannon and 1,000 pounds of bombs. A total of 14,233 Hurricanes of all types were produced.

The Spitfire went through even more models than the Hurricane—as many as twenty-one. The *Spitfire Mark I,* which first appeared in 1938, was powered by a Rolls-Royce Merlin II liquid-cooled engine that developed 1,030 hp. It had a speed of 344 mph and a range of 500 miles. It was armed with eight .303-caliber machine guns. The *Spitfire Mark XIV,* introduced in 1944, had a Rolls-

Royce Griffin 65 engine that developed 2,050 hp—nearly double that of the Mark I. It produced a maximum speed of 448 mph and a range of 448 miles. It was armed with two 20-mm cannon, four .303-caliber machine guns, and 1,000 pounds of bombs. A total of 20,351 Spitfires of all types were produced.

The *Supermarine Seafire* was the naval version of the Spitfire and went through four production models. The *Seafire Mark IIC* had a Rolls-Royce Merlin liquid-cooled engine developing 1,340 hp. It had a maximum speed of 333 mph and a range of 755 miles. Armament consisted of two 20-mm cannon and four .303-caliber machine guns. A total of 2,089 were produced.

Other early British fighters of the war included the Blackburn Roc, Fairey Fulmar, Boulton Paul Defiant, and Bristol Beaufighter. The *Blackburn Roc* went into service in 1940 and served both with the RAF and the Fleet Air Arm. Awkward in appearance, it was nonetheless an effective fighter. Powered by a Bristol Perseus XII air-cooled engine of 890 hp, it had a maximum speed of 223 mph and a range of 810 miles. It was armed with four .303-caliber machine guns and had a crew of two.

The *Fairey Fulmar* also entered service in 1940. Powered by a Rolls-Royce Merlin VIII 1,080-hp air-cooled engine, it had a maximum speed of 280 mph and a range of 800 miles. Flown by a crew of two, it was armed with eight .303-caliber machine guns. A total of 602 were produced.

The *Boulton Paul Defiant* entered service in 1940. Inferior and outclassed, its Rolls-Royce Merlin III liquid-cooled engines delivered 1,030 hp. It had a maximum speed of 303 mph and a range of 465 miles. All its armament was concentrated in a dorsal turret with four manually worked .303-caliber machine guns. It was flown by a crew of two. A total of 1,064 were produced.

The twin-engined *Bristol Beaufighter* (also referred to as the "Beau") entered service in 1940; 5,562 were produced. Powered by two Bristol Hercules XI air-cooled radial engines of 1,400 hp each, it had a maximum speed of 321 mph and a range of 1,170 miles. Flown by a crew of two, it was armed with four 20-mm cannon and six .303-caliber machine guns. A total of 5,562 were produced.

The twin-engined *De Haviland D.H. 98 Mosquito* was one of the finest aircraft of World War II; it too filled a variety of roles, including reconnaissance, night fighting, and precision bombing. De Haviland had to overcome great opposition to the plane, principally because it was constructed of wood, pressed and bonded into smooth curving shapes. The prototype first flew in November 1940; the Mosquito first entered service as a fighter in

May 1941. The most numerous model was the fighter-bomber version. In all, 6,439 were produced, including 200 in Australia. Powered by two Rolls-Royce Merlin engines, it developed 1,230 hp (1,690 hp in its later version), and its maximum speed was 370 mph (425 in the later version); its range was 1,860 miles with small drop tanks and 3,500 miles with large drop tanks. It had a crew of two men. The fighter version was armed with four 20-mm cannon and four .303-caliber machine guns. The fighter-bomber version was armed with four 20-mm cannon and four .303-caliber machine guns. It could carry 500 pounds of bombs internally, plus 1,000 pounds of bombs externally, along with eight 60-pound rockets under its wings.

The *Fairey Firefly* entered service in 1943. A total of 638 were produced. It had a Rolls-Royce Griffin liquid-cooled engine developing 1,730 hp. With a maximum speed of 316 mph, it had a range of 1,300 miles and was armed with four 20-mm cannon. It had a crew of two.

The British produced some of the best fighter-bombers. These included the *Westland Whirlwind,* first delivered in 1940. The first twin-engined single-seated fighter to go into production in Britain, it was powered by two Rolls-Royce Peregrine liquid-cooled 885-hp engines and had a maximum speed of 360 mph. It was armed with four 20-mm cannon and 1,000 pounds of bombs. Introduced as a fighter, it was too underpowered and by 1942 was used as a fighter-bomber.

The best British fighter-bombers were the Hawker Typhoon and Tempest. The first *Hawker Typhoon* came on line in 1940. Powered by a Napier Sabre IIA liquid-cooled 2,189-hp engine, it had a maximum speed of 412 mph and a range of 980 miles. It was armed with four 20-mm cannon and 2,000 pounds of bombs. A total of 3,300 were produced.

The *Hawker Tempest* went into service in 1944. Powerful and fast, it was a fine fighter. Powered by a Napier Sabre II liquid-cooled 2,180-hp engine, it had a maximum speed of 427 mph, a range of 1,530 miles, and was armed with four 20-mm cannon and 2,000 pounds of bombs. Just under 800 Tempests were produced.

The Australians manufactured their own *Commonwealth CA-12 Boomerang* fighter. It entered service in 1943. Powered by a Pratt & Whitney R-1830 air-cooled 1,200-hp engine, it had a maximum speed of 302 mph and a range of 930 miles. It was armed with two 20-mm cannon, four machine guns, and 500 pounds of bombs.

Japanese Bombers

The Japanese bomber force was well prepared for World War II, the war with China being particularly useful as a proving ground. The *Mitsubishi Type 96* bomber (later designated G3M, code-named Nell) was a modern twin-engined bomber with the longest range of any bomber in the world when it was introduced in 1937. On August 14, 1937, the Japanese navy used Nells in the world's first transoceanic bombing raids, to fly some 1,250 miles over water from Formosa to hit targets in China and return. The Nell was the backbone of navy bomber units and was largely responsible for sinking the British capital ships *Prince of Wales* and *Repulse.* This lean, twin-engined bomber had a speed of 232 mph and a range of 2,722 miles, and it was armed with one 20-mm cannon and four machine guns. It carried 1,764 pounds of bombs and had a crew of seven. Later versions were given more powerful engines and increased fuel capacity. They served throughout the war, and 1,048 were produced.

The *Mitsubishi G4M* (Betty) twin-engined navy bomber entered service in 1941. It was Japan's best medium bomber of the war. More Bettys were produced (2,446) than any other Japanese bomber. A handsome, somewhat rotund aircraft, it had 266-mph speed and the amazing range of 3,748 miles. Quite maneuverable for its size and weight, the Betty was a near-ideal medium bomber, except for its limited bomb load of 1,765 pounds. Although more heavily armed than most Japanese bombers (one 20-mm tail cannon and four 7.7-mm machine guns), it was quite vulnerable to attack (to save weight, early models had no armor or fire-resistant fuel tanks). The Betty's propensity to burst into flame earned it the nickname of "Flying Lighter." It had a crew of seven.

The Japanese army's counterpart to the Nell and the Betty was the *Mitsubishi Ki-21* (Sally), introduced in 1941. A total of 2,064 of these twin-engined bombers were produced in the war, making them second only to the Betty among Japanese bombers. The K-21-IIb had a speed of 302 mph and a range of 1,680 miles. It was armed with six machine guns and 2,205 pounds of bombs. The crew was five to seven men. The K-21 remained in service to V-J Day.

The *Kawasaki Ki-32* (Mary; 854 produced) light bomber was introduced in 1938. It was powered with a single liquid-cooled engine (one of the few Japanese aircraft to have one) and had a speed of 263 mph, a range of 1,218 miles, and armament of two machine guns. It carried 992 pounds of bombs and had a crew of two.

The *Aichi D3A* (Val) dive-bomber entered service in 1940. In many ways similar to the German JU-87 Stuka, it was Japan's top naval dive-bomber of the war and the most successful Axis warplane against Allied ships. An all-metal, low-winged monoplane with fixed landing gear, it was comparable to but somewhat lighter (at 8,047 pounds) than the Douglas SBD Dauntless of the United States (see below). The D3A (1,495 produced) was capable of 240 mph and a range of 915 miles. It was armed with three machine guns and carried one 551-pound bomb under the fuselage and two 132-pound bombs under the wings. A total of 126 Vals took part in the Pearl Harbor strike. Vals served throughout the war and were used at war's end as kamikaze aircraft.

The *Yokosuka D4Y Suisei* (Comet, code-named Dot and Judy) was a modern navy dive-bomber that entered service in 1943. It was quite small (only about the size of a Zero) with excellent maneuverability. With 343-mph speed (more than 100 mph faster than the Val) and a range of 978 miles, it was armed with three machine guns and carried 683 pounds of bombs. Flown by a crew of two, it had neither armor protection nor self-sealing fuel tanks—surprisingly, for a second-generation aircraft. Yokosuka produced 2,038 D4Ys.

The two principal adversaries in the Pacific theater were aware of the potential of aircraft specifically designed to attack shipping. When the *Nakajima B5N* (Kate) took part in the Pearl Harbor attack, it was the world's most advanced torpedo bomber—vastly superior to its counterpart, the Douglas TBD Devastator (see below). Introduced in 1940, the Kate (1,149 produced) was a low-winged, all-metal, single-engined aircraft. With a speed of 235 mph and a range of 1,237 miles, it was armed with one machine gun. With a crew of three men, it carried one 1,764-pound torpedo or three 550-pound bombs. At Pearl Harbor some Kates had 1,800-pound armor-piercing bombs converted from battleship shells. B5Ns served throughout the war and were wholly or partly responsible for sinking U.S. carriers *Yorktown*, *Lexington*, *Wasp*, and *Hornet*.

The *Nakajima B6N Tenzan* (Heavenly Mountain, code-named Jill) entered service in 1943. Essentially a more powerful version of the Kate, it was faster (299 mph) and had a longer range (1,892 miles), but it was also plagued with engine problems and was difficult to handle on a carrier. Armed with two machine guns, it carried 1,764 pounds of bombs and had a crew of three. A total of 1,268 Tenzans were built, and they flew to the end of the war.

In 1942 the Japanese introduced other new bombers, but many were in fact inferior to those they were designed to replace. The *Kawasaki Ki-48* (Lily) was a twin-engined light bomber entering service in 1942. Inspired by the Russian Tupolev SB-2, it resembled the U.S.-made Martin Maryland. The Lily had 314-mph speed but could carry only 1,764 pounds of bombs. With a range of 1,491

miles, it was armed with three machine guns and had a crew of four. A total of 2,038 Lilys were produced during the war.

The *Nakajima Ki-49 Donryu* (Helen; 819 produced) also entered service in 1942. It had a speed of 306 mph and a range of 1,833 miles and was armed with one 20-mm cannon and five machine guns. It carried 2,205 pounds of bombs and had a crew of eight.

The *Mitsubishi Ki-67 Hiryu* (Peggy; 698 produced during the war) was a twin-engined bomber that entered service in 1944 and was used by both the army and the navy. Designed to replace the Ki-49, it was capable of 334-mph speed and a range of 2,360 miles. It was armed with one 20-mm cannon and four machine guns. The Peggy carried 1,764 pounds of bombs and had a crew of six to eight.

The *Nakajima G8N Renzan* (Rita) was Japan's four-engined bomber. It appeared at the end of 1944. With a speed of 368 mph, an incredible range of 4,639 miles, and armament of six 20-mm cannon and four machine guns, it carried 8,818 pounds of bombs and had a crew of ten. Although Tokyo planned to build vast numbers of these aircraft, the G8N remained in the prototype stage; only four Renzans were built.

Japan introduced four additional bombers in 1945. The *Yokosuka P1Y Ginga* (Frances; 1,096 produced) was a modern twin-engined bomber with a speed of 340 mph, a range of 3,338 miles, and armament of two 20-mm cannon. Intended as a land-based navy bomber, it was in some ways the best such Japanese bomber of the war. Highly versatile, the Frances was even used as a torpedo bomber and a night fighter. It carried 2,205 pounds of bombs and had a crew of three.

The *Aichi B7A Ryusei* (Grace) was a single-engined 1945 bomber. It had a speed of 352 mph, a range of 1,888 miles, and armament of two 20-mm cannon and one machine gun. It carried 1,896 pounds of bombs or one 1,764-pound torpedo and had a crew of two.

The Japanese navy also developed a twin-engined jet fighter-bomber, based on German technology and closely resembling the Me.262A. The one-man *Nakajima Kikka* had two 1,047-pound thrust engines, a speed of 443 mph, a range of 586 miles, and armament of 1,764 pounds of bombs.

The *Yokosuka MXY7 Ohka* (Cherry Blossom, derisively code-named Baka—"fool"—by the Americans) was a rocket-powered kamikaze designed to attack carriers and battleships. Carrying a 2,646-pound warhead, it had a 17-foot wingspan and a speed of 403 mph and was built mostly of wood. With a range of only 20 miles, the Ohka was carried to its target area beneath the G4M2 Betty bomber. It first saw combat on March 21, 1945, in the Battle for the Philippines. Encountered 60 miles from their target by U.S. Hellcats, the Bettys immediately launched the Ohkas—all of which fell into the sea—and the mother ships were all shot down. Japan produced only 852 Ohkas, and few saw action.

U.S. Bombers

U.S. industry made its mark in the production of bombers. The *Douglas A-20 Havoc* (7,385 produced) entered service at the end of 1941. Twelve were at Pearl Harbor on December 7, 1941. A short-range, handsome, twin-engined light bomber, the A-20 saw service in New Guinea in May 1942. With a speed of 339 mph and a range of 1,090 miles, it carried 4,000 pounds of bombs. The A-20 was initially armed with four forward-firing .30-caliber machine guns, but in New Guinea Major Paul Gunn added four nose-mounted .50-caliber machine guns and two fuel tanks in the bomb bay. These changes made the A-20 a useful long-range aircraft that helped secure air mastery in the campaign. It had a crew of three.

The *Boeing B-17 Flying Fortress* four-engined strategic bomber (8,685 produced) first flew in 1935 and went into production in 1938. Its maximum speed and range were 317 mph and 3,000 miles. Armed with ten to thirteen machine guns, it carried 17,600 pounds of bombs. It had a crew of nine. In the Battle of Midway B-17s were sent to bomb ships, but they registered no hits. (This is somewhat ironic in that the B-17 was sold to an isolationist-minded U.S. Congress in the guise of a coast defense weapon, not as a strategic bomber.) Extraordinarily sturdy, the B-17 could fly with major components badly damaged. Nonetheless, there is no evidence that level-bombing sank even one Japanese warship. The Flying Fortress made its reputation in European skies.

The *North American B-25 Mitchell* was the U.S. counterpart to the Betty. First flown in August 1940, it was more strongly built, faster, and heavier, and it carried more bombs—but for shorter distances—than its Japanese counterpart: 3,000 pounds of bombs for 1,350 miles. The B-25 went through a variety of models. The A model had a speed of 315 mph. The B-25 had armor and self-sealing fuel tanks and a variety of armament packages ranging from two power-operated turrets, each with two .50-caliber machine guns, to a solid nose with eight forward-firing .50-caliber machine guns (the work of Major Gunn). Its heavy armament enabled the B-25 to suppress most ship antiaircraft fire and made it a highly successful merchant-ship killer in the Pacific theater. Some later models had no less than twelve .50-caliber machine

guns and a 75-mm cannon. The B-25 had a crew of five. A total of 11,000 were produced.

The *Martin B-26 Marauder* entered service in 1942. A fast, efficient medium bomber, its early problems earned it the nickname of "Widow Maker" or "The Baltimore Whore" ("No visible means of support"). These problems, however, were overcome by properly trained pilots. The B-26B's maximum speed and range were 317 mph and 1,150 miles. It was armed with six machine guns, carried 3,000 pounds of bombs, and had a crew of seven. A total of 5,157 were produced.

The *Consolidated B-24 Liberator* entered service in 1942. Intended as a complement to the B-17, its design was begun only in 1939. The B-24 was a remarkable aircraft, but many air force personnel preferred the older but tested-and-tried B-17 (whose wings were much less likely to come off in combat). A total of 18,188 B-24s were produced—more than any other bomber of World War II. With its exceptionally long range, the B-24 played a key role in antisubmarine combat in the Atlantic, but by the end of 1944 the USAAF was operating more than six thousand B-24s in the Pacific theater. Equipped with lightweight radar that enabled its crews to detect vessels through overcast skies, the B-24 was an effective ship killer. The J Model (introduced in 1943) had a speed of 300 mph and a range of 2,100 miles. It was armed with ten machine guns and carried 8,800 pounds of bombs and a crew of eight to twelve men.

The *Douglas A-26 Invader* (2,446 produced) entered service in 1944. It had a speed of 355 mph and a range of 1,800 miles. It was armed with ten machine guns, carried 4,000 pounds of bombs, and had a crew of three.

The U.S. Navy attached great importance to the dive-bomber. The first and most famous of these was the *Douglas SBD Dauntless,* which entered service at the beginning of 1941. A single-engined monoplane with a two-man crew, its speed was 250 mph, and its range was 1,345 miles. It had four machine guns and carried 1,200 pounds of bombs. Comparable to the Japanese Val (see above), it was somewhat stronger and heavier. Easy to fly and maintain, the Dauntless played a decisive role in the Battle of Midway, sinking three Japanese carriers. A total of 5,936 were produced during the war.

The Dauntless's successor was the *Curtiss SB2C Helldiver.* It entered service in 1943 but was difficult to handle, and its mechanical problems earned it the name of "the Beast." It had a two-man crew, could attain a speed of 281 mph, and carried two 20-mm cannon, two machine guns, and a 2,000-pound bomb load. Despite these characteristics superior to its predecessor, the SB2C-4 was never a popular aircraft. Most pilots preferred the Dauntless. A total of 7,002 SB2Cs were produced.

The *Douglas TBD Devastator* torpedo bomber carried a three-man crew and was armed with two machine guns. Introduced as long ago as 1937, it was the U.S. Navy's first carrier-based torpedo bomber and low-winged all-metal service monoplane. With a range of 716 miles and maximum speed of 206 mph (it was barely able to make 115 mph when carrying a torpedo), the Devastator was no match for Japanese fighters and was itself devastated in the Battle of Midway. Of the forty-one planes that took part in attacks on Japanese ships in that battle, thirty-six were shot down.

The *Grumman TBF Avenger* entered service in 1942 and replaced the Devastator—much to the relief of U.S. torpedo bomber crews. Although five of six Avengers that participated in the Battle of Midway were shot down, this three-seated torpedo bomber soon became the best of its type in the war and was a major scourge to Japanese shipping. It had a maximum speed of 271 mph and a range of 1,215 miles. Armament consisted of three .50-caliber machine guns—two wing-mounted and one in the dorsal turret—and one .30-caliber machine gun in the ventral tunnel. It carried one 22-inch torpedo or 1,600 pounds of bombs. A total of 9,836 Avengers were produced (the Royal Navy received 958, and the Royal New Zealand Air Force secured 60, and they flew for the French in the first Indochina war).

The *Boeing B-29 Superfortress* was the most sophisticated aircraft yet built and the best heavy bomber of the war; nothing similar was even on the drawing boards of the other major aviation powers. (The RAF, for example, skipped this final stage of the piston-engined heavy bomber and went directly from the modified Lancaster-Lincoln to the V-bomber all-jet force.) First conceived of in 1939, the B-29 entered production in 1943 and began arriving at bases in India and China in 1944. It had pressurized cabin areas, turbo-charged engines, and remote-controlled guns which employed an early type of computerized control from a central station, except for the tail gun. The B-29 was quite fast (358 mph unloaded and 258 mph loaded) and had a ceiling of 35,000 feet—above most Japanese fighters. Its range was 4,100 miles. The B-29 was capable of carrying a 10-ton bomb load, although the usual load for long distances was 4 to 6 tons. It was armed with one 20-mm cannon and ten machine guns and had a crew of ten to twelve men. In addition to strategic bombing of the Japanese home islands, B-29s were used with great effectiveness to lay mines. In May and June 1945, mines laid by B-29s sank an estimated half million tons of Japanese shipping. In all, 3,970

Superfortresses were produced. The appalling death toll of Japanese civilians, that the B-29 exacted in its conventional firebombing of Tokyo (history's worst air raid) and its nuclear bombings of Hiroshima and Nagasaki give the B-29 the dubious distinction of having killed more civilians than any other weapon in history.

In addition, the United States manufactured aircraft for the Allies. The British used the single-engined dive-bomber *Vultee A-35 Vengeance* ("Vultee Vibrator"; 1,528 produced) in Burma until the end of the war. There were two twin-engined bombers: the *Martin Baltimore* (1,575 constructed; mainly used in the Mediterranean) and the *Douglas Boston* (also in service until the end of the war).

British Bombers

The British *Fairey Swordfish* was already approaching peacetime obsolescence when the war began. It first flew in 1934 and filled a variety of roles with the fleet as a trainer and as a carrier-borne spotter and reconnaissance aircraft. It also operated as a convoy protection aircraft, flying from escort carriers, and as a land-based minelayer. It was also an excellent torpedo bomber and was most active particularly early in the war. Swordfish aircraft, for example, carried out the daring British attack on Taranto that so heavily influenced Japanese planning for the attack on Pearl Harbor. The last of the fully operational biplanes, the Swordfish served throughout the five years of war and was taken out of production only in 1944. A total of 2,391 were produced.

The *Bristol Beaufort* was a torpedo bomber that entered service in 1939. Powered by two Bristol Taurus VI air-cooled 1,130-hp engines, it had a maximum speed of 265 mph and a range of 1,600 miles. The Beaufort was armed with four machine guns and one 1,605-pound torpedo. It had a crew of four. A total of 1,121 were produced.

Another torpedo bomber, the *Fairey Albacore*, entered service in 1940. Powered by two Bristol Taurus II air-cooled 1,065-hp engines, it had a maximum speed of 161 mph and a range of 930 miles. It was armed with three machine guns and one 1,610-pound torpedo. It had a crew of three. A total of 800 were produced.

In 1943, the *Fairey Barracuda* was introduced. Powered by one Rolls-Royce Merlin 32 liquid-cooled 1,640-hp engine, it had a maximum speed of 288 mph and a range of 686 miles. It was armed with two machine guns and carried one 1,620-pound torpedo. It had a crew of three. A total of 2,572 were produced.

The *Fairey Battle*, a twin-engined bomber, was in service beginning in 1937. Powered by a single Rolls-Royce Merlin Mark I 1,030-hp liquid-cooled engine, it had a maximum speed of 241 mph and a range of 1,050 miles.

It was armed with two machine guns and could carry 1,000 pounds of bombs. It had a crew of three men. A total of 2,185 were produced.

The *Vickers Wellesley* was another British bomber in service at the outbreak of the war. Introduced in 1937, it was powered by a single Bristol Pegasus XX air-cooled engine and had a maximum speed of 228 mph and a range of 1,100 miles. It was armed with two machine guns and could carry 2,000 pounds of bombs. It had a crew of two.

The bomber version of the *De Haviland D.H. 98 Mosquito* (discussed under fighters) could carry a 2,000-pound internal bomb load. The Mark IX was modified to carry a 4,000-pound bomb in a bulged bay.

The *Bristol Blenheim* joined the RAF in 1937. Some of these bombers were actually rebuilt as fighters with four fixed-belly machine guns. They were the first in the world to go into service as night fighters with rudimentary airborne radar. After 1941 Blenheims were being replaced in Great Britain and saw increasing service overseas, including in India, Burma, Singapore, and Australia. Powered by two Bristol Mercury engines, each developing 840 hp (later 950 hp), the Blenheim had a maximum speed of 283 mph. Its range with bombs—depending on type of aircraft—was between 1,125 and 1,660 miles. It could carry 1,000 pounds of bombs and had a fixed .303-caliber machine gun in the nose and another one in a dorsal turret. The later versions had two machine guns in the dorsal turret as well as two in an added chin turret. A total of 5,213 Blenheims were produced.

The British bomber that was produced in the largest numbers during the war was the *Vickers Wellington*. Entering service in 1938, it was powered by two Bristol Pegasus XVIII air-cooled 1,000-hp engines, and it had a maximum speed of 235 mph and a range of 2,200 miles. It was armed with six .303-caliber machine guns and could carry 4,500 pounds of bombs. It had a crew of six. A total of 11,461 Wellingtons were produced. Only the German Junkers Ju-88 (14,980) and the U.S. Consolidated B-24 Liberator (18,188) were produced in greater numbers.

The *Short Stirling* was a four-engined bomber. Powered by Bristol Hercules XI air-cooled engines of 1,590 hp each, its maximum speed was 260 mph with a range of 2,330 miles. It was armed with eight .303-caliber machine guns and carried 14,000 pounds of bombs. It had a crew of seven or eight men. A total of 2,371 were produced.

The *Handley Page Halifax* entered production in 1944. It had four Bristol Hercules XVI air-cooled engines, each developing 1,615 hp for a maximum speed of 281 mph and a range of 1,077 miles. It was armed with nine machine guns, could carry 13,000 pounds of bombs, and had a crew of seven. A total of 6,176 were produced.

The British *Avro Lancaster* was one of the best bombers of the war. It was by far the easiest British bomber to build and maintain. Its chief problem was the lack of protection on its vital underside. Easily distinguished by a line of small windows along the side of the fuselage, the Lancaster saw extensive service in the European theater but also in the Pacific. It had a nine-man crew. Powered by four 1,460-hp Rolls-Royce Merlin XX liquid-cooled engines, the Lancaster had a typical maximum speed with full bomb load of 287 mph. Its range was 1,660 miles with a full bomb load of 22,000 pounds. Its defensive armament consisted of ten .303-caliber machine guns. A total of 7,366 were produced.

Australia also produced a bomber: The *Commonwealth CA-11 Woomera* (A23). Powered by two Pratt & Whitney R-1830 air-cooled engines of 1,200 hp each, it had a maximum speed of 282 mph and a range of 2,200 miles. It was armed with two 20-mm cannon and seven machine guns and could carry 3,200 pounds of bombs. It had a crew of three.

Patrol and Reconnaissance Aircraft

As an oceanic maritime power, Japan necessarily emphasized reconnaissance and thus had superior aircraft for this work. As a result, the Japanese navy invariably located U.S. ships first. The *Mitsubishi C5M2* (Babs), a single-engined aircraft with a 691-mile range, was introduced in 1940. The *Aichi E13A* (Jake), introduced in 1941, was a handsome twin-float monoplane. Manned by a pilot and two crewmen, it had a slow speed (120 mph cruising) but an endurance of fifteen hours. The *Nakajima E8N2* (Dave) was another patrol aircraft. The *Kawanishi H6K* flying boat (Mavis), introduced in 1940, was a sleek four-engined aircraft used as both a patrol plane and a bomber. Another four-engined flying boat, the *Kawanishi H8K* (Emily), introduced in 1942, was one of the best patrol bombers of the war; during March 4–5, 1942, two bombed Oahu. The H8K was both heavily armed and difficult to shoot down. One of the last of the Japanese reconnaissance aircraft, the single-engined *Nakajima C6N1 Saiun,* had a range of 3,300 miles.

Of U.S. reconnaissance aircraft, the twin-engined army *Lockheed A-28 Hudson* was introduced in 1939. The navy flew the *Vought OS2U Kingfisher,* a float plane introduced in 1940. The *U.S. Consolidated PBY Catalina* flying boat patrol bomber, in service by 1941, was one of the finest such aircraft of the war. It had a speed of 189 mph and a range of 2,990 miles. Armed with four machine guns, it could carry up to 4,000 pounds of bombs, two torpedoes, or four 325-pound depth charges. More PBYs (3,290) were produced than any other reconnaissance aircraft of the war. The four-engined *Consolidated PB2Y* flying boat, introduced in 1941, could carry 12,000 pounds of bombs. Other reconnaissance aircraft were the *Curtiss SO3C Sea Mew,* the *Lockheed PV-1 Ventura,* the *Lockheed PV-2 Harpoon,* the *Curtiss SC-1 Seahawk* float plane, and two flying boats: the twin-engined *Martin PBM Mariner* and the four-engined *Consolidated PB4Y-2 Privateer.* The *F-13* was the reconnaissance version of the B-29.

The British *Fairey Swordfish* filled a variety of roles, including reconnaissance missions with the fleet. The *De Haviland Mosquito* was also used as a reconnaissance aircraft. The Bristol Blenheim bomber was also reconfigured as the *Bolingbroke* for reconnaissance purposes.

The British also had two flying boats. The first was the *Supermarine Walrus,* introduced in 1936. Powered by a Bristol Pegasus 11.M.2 air-cooled 775-hp engine, it had a maximum speed of only 135 mph and a range of 600 miles. It was armed with two or three machine guns and had a crew of four. A total of 744 were produced.

The *Short Sunderland* was introduced in 1938. This large, four-engined flying boat was powered by four Bristol Pegasus XXII air-cooled 1,010-hp engines. It had a maximum speed of 210 mph and a range of 2,980 miles. Defended by seven machine guns, it could carry 2,000 pounds of bombs. It had a crew of thirteen men. A total of 741 were produced.

As in the European theater, the aircraft of both Axis and Allied air powers in the Pacific went through enormous changes in the forced crucible of war. The cycle of development and production turned against the Axis by 1943, however, and despite their introduction of some outstanding models with pioneering technology, they could not turn the tide.

FURTHER READINGS

Anderson, David. *A History of the U.S. Air Force* (1989).
Angelucci, Enzo. *The Rand McNally Encyclopedia of Military Aircraft, 1914–1980* (1983).
Boyne, Walter J. *Clash of Wings: Air Power in World War II* (1994).
Brown, Captain Eric M., RN. *Duels in the Sky: World War II Naval Aircraft in Combat* (1988).
Campbell, Christy. *Air War Pacific* (1990).
Day, David. *The Great Betrayal: Britain, Australia and the Onset of the Pacific War, 1939–42* (1988).
Francillon, René. *Japanese Aircraft of the Pacific War* (1988).
Lazarus, Allan M. "The Hellcat Myth," *Naval History* (Summer 1989).
Mayer, S. L., ed. *The Rise and Fall of Imperial Japan* (1984).
Swanborough, Gordon, and Peter Bowers. *United States Military Aircraft since 1909* (1989).
———. *United States Naval Aircraft since 1911* (1968).
Spencer C. Tucker

SEE ALSO Army Air Corps/Air Forces, U.S.; Army Air Force, Japanese

Aircraft Carrier Raids, U.S. Navy (1942)

In early 1942, U.S. Navy Pacific Fleet aircraft carriers conducted a number of raids, the best known of which is the April 18, 1942, strike on Tokyo. These served to dispel some of the overall gloom of the period and led the Japanese to make strategic dispositions that helped bring about their ultimate defeat.

Fortunately for the United States, its carriers had not been at Pearl Harbor on December 7, 1941, but the loss of the Pacific Fleet battleships in that attack meant that for a long time the sole U.S. riposte possible in the Pacific would be by carriers and submarines.

Soon after the Pearl Harbor attack the United States increased its carrier strength in the Pacific to three, when *Saratoga* arrived from San Diego to join *Lexington* and *Enterprise* in patrols. *Saratoga* was then sent to ferry Marine Corps fighter aircraft to Wake Island. On December 22 it was nearing the launch point when Vice Admiral W. S. Pye, who had temporarily relieved Admiral Husband E. Kimmel as Pacific Fleet commander, ordered the mission scrubbed. Pye knew that Japanese carrier planes had attacked Wake and was fearful that *Saratoga* might run into a superior enemy force. Despite this precaution, *Saratoga* was lost for five months beginning on January 11, 1942, when it was damaged by a torpedo from a Japanese submarine and had to be sent to Puget Sound for repairs.

On December 31, 1941, Admiral Chester W. Nimitz became commander of the Pacific Fleet, and Admiral Ernest J. King became chief of naval operations. King and Nimitz realized that for the indefinite future the United States would have to remain on the defensive. Determined to hold Midway and keep open lines of communication from Hawaii to Australia, in late January Nimitz ordered Admiral William F. Halsey to attack Japanese bases in the Marshall Islands, some two thousand miles from Hawaii.

Halsey's Task Force 8 was centered on *Enterprise* and the carrier *Yorktown,* which had just arrived from the Atlantic. Ignorant of Japanese defenses, Halsey divided his force into three groups in order to try to hit all enemy targets simultaneously. *Enterprise* and three destroyers were to attack Wotje, Taroa Island in Maloelap Atoll, and Roi and Kwajalein islands in Kwajalein Atoll. Rear Admiral Raymond A. Spruance would take heavy cruisers *Northampton* and *Salt Lake City* to bombard Wotje. Cruiser *Chester* would shell Maloelap, while Rear Admiral Frank Jack Fletcher would take *Yorktown*, cruisers *Louisville* and *St. Louis,* and four destroyers to attack Jaluit and Mili in the southern Marshalls and newly occupied Makin Island in the Gilberts.

Enterprise and *Saratoga* sailed in company from Samoa, but on January 31 they separated for their 500-mile runs to the different targets. The raid took place the next day, February 1, 1942. *Lexington's* SBD Dauntless dive-bombers attacked Roi airfield, while TBD Devastators struck the seaplane base and naval anchorage at Kwajalein. F4F Wildcat fighters hit known airfields at Wotje, which turned out not to be operational, and Taroa Airfield on Maloelap. In the Kwajalein attack the Japanese lost the subchaser *Shonan Maru No. 10,* and two transports were heavily damaged, as were a submarine and a minelayer. Several other ships were hit, and both sides lost aircraft. The Wildcats encountered heavy enemy opposition over Maloelap, and *Chester* was damaged by a Japanese bomb but remained fully operational.

Aircraft from *Yorktown,* meanwhile, hit the southern Marshalls and Makin. Fletcher planned simultaneous attacks at Jaluit, Mili, and Makin, but bad weather broke up the approach flights and forced planes to ditch on their return flights. Plane losses from the two carriers were about the same, but all those from *Yorktown* succumbed to bad weather. The attackers destroyed several four-engined Japanese Mavis flying boats.

During its withdrawal *Enterprise* came under attack from Japanese Nell bombers but escaped serious damage. *Yorktown* retired without incident. In the February 1 raids the Americans sank one enemy ship, damaged others, and destroyed nine Japanese planes on the ground and three in the air. The United States lost twelve planes, and one ship, *Chester,* was damaged.

Fleet Admiral Isoroku Yamamoto responded by sending four carriers, two fast battleships, three cruisers, and nine destroyers against Darwin in Australia. On February 19 a total of 188 Japanese aircraft struck the city and port and sank a four-stack destroyer, *Peary,* and a number of transports. The Americans and Australians also lost eleven P-40s, six Hudsons, a Waterway, and three PBYs. Two hundred civilians died.

At the same time the Japanese were running wild in the Indian Ocean south of Java. Neither Nimitz nor King dared send U.S. carriers into the Indian Ocean, but the Marshall Islands raid had shown the feasibility of utilizing them elsewhere. Thus while the Japanese were hitting Darwin, another carrier task force was steaming toward the main Japanese base of Rabaul in the Solomon Sea. Commanded by Vice Admiral Wilson Brown, this task force was centered on *Lexington.* Nimitz hoped that Brown's raid would divert the Japanese from attacking Port Moresby on the south coast of New Guinea, which radio intercepts had revealed as a Japanese objective.

Lexington was about four hundred miles from Rabaul when its radar detected an approaching aircraft, which turned out to be a Japanese Mavis flying boat. Although the plane was promptly shot down, its crew or another aircraft reported the U.S. presence, and *Lexington* promptly came under attack by two flights of Betty bombers. That day the Americans shot down thirteen of seventeen attacking Bettys and three Mavises. Lieutenant Edward H. "Butch" O'Hare singlehandedly shot down five of the Bettys and was later awarded the Congressional Medal of Honor. The Japanese claimed ten Wildcats shot down, but the Americans actually lost only two. The Japanese pilots had, however, saved Rabaul from attack.

The abortive U.S. raid did convince the Japanese command on Truk that landings scheduled for Port Moresby and Tulagi for March would be too risky and would have to await the arrival of carriers sent by Admiral Yamamoto. This would not be until the end of April 1942, and it led to the Battle of the Coral Sea.

While *Lexington* was returning from the raid on Rabaul, Halsey and *Enterprise* were steaming for Wake Island. His plan called for SBD Dauntless dive-bombers and TBD Devastator torpedo bombers, protected by F4F Wildcats, to attack the island early on the morning of February 24, after which cruisers and destroyers would bring it under bombardment. Bad weather delayed the launch and reversed the order of attack. Good targets were scarce, although the attackers destroyed three Mavis flying boats. *Enterprise* was retiring toward Midway Island when Nimitz radioed Halsey to strike Marcus Island. Located about halfway between Wake Island and Iwo Jima near the Japanese Bonin Islands, Marcus is only about a thousand miles from Tokyo. After refueling off Midway, *Enterprise* steamed toward Marcus. Bad weather slowed the destroyers, which were unable to keep up. Halsey, demonstrating his nickname of "Bull," left them behind and charged ahead with only cruisers *Salt Lake City* and *Northhampton.* Even the presence of two Japanese submarines, which the Americans detected and attacked, did not deter Halsey. Early on March 4, thirty-two Dauntlesses and four Wildcats struck Marcus. Halsey kept the slow Devastators aboard the carrier, preferring one quick strike and hasty withdrawal. U.S. aircraft inflicted little damage at the cost of one Dauntless shot down. But word of the attack brought a blackout in Tokyo. The U.S. task force then returned safely to Pearl Harbor.

March 10 brought another U.S. carrier raid, at Lae and Salamaua on the north coast of Papua. Because the direct approach to Rabaul had been detected earlier, the Americans decided to attack Japanese forces about to land on New Guinea. Instead of sailing close to Rabaul and subjecting themselves to attack from numerous Japanese land-based planes there, they would send planes across the Owen Stanley Range from the Coral Sea off Port Moresby. To ensure maximum firepower Admiral Brown's two carriers, *Lexington* and *Saratoga,* would operate together. The attack was set for March 10, by which date it was believed the Japanese would already have landed on New Guinea. The Japanese landings had indeed begun on March 8, at Lae and Salamaua, north of Port Moresby. The Japanese intended to turn them into outposts to protect Rabaul from the south. The attack on the morning of March 10 was the heaviest mounted by the Americans thus far—sixty-one SBD Dauntlesses, twenty-five TBD Devastators, and eighteen Wildcats for cover. The pilots claimed to have sunk two cruisers, but actually they destroyed two transports and damaged cruiser *Yubari,* two destroyers, a minelayer, a tender, a seaplane tender, and two converted minesweepers. One U.S. plane was lost.

On April 18, 1942, the United States carried out its most spectacular carrier raid thus far, against Tokyo. Although it was the least successful of these raids in military terms, its propaganda value and strategic effect were spectacular.

The early 1942 carrier raids provided a great boost to U.S. morale and the first "payback" for Pearl Harbor. They also provided valuable experience for the personnel involved and revealed equipment and tactical shortcomings, such as the need for delayed-action fuzes to allow bombs to penetrate below decks before exploding. More important, the raids caused the Japanese high command to draw their air assets to defend Tokyo and to take the disastrous step of expanding their defensive ring.

FURTHER READINGS

Belote, James H., and William M. Belote. *Titans of the Seas: The Development and Operations of Japanese and American Carrier Task Forces during World War II* (1975).

Merrill, James M. *A Sailor's Admiral: A Biography of William F. Halsey* (1976).

Morrison, Samuel Eliot. *History of United States Naval Operations in World War II* (1961).

Spencer C. Tucker

SEE ALSO Aircraft Carriers: Japanese, U.S., and British; Darwin, Japanese Bombing of; Doolittle (Tokyo) Raid

Aircraft Carriers: Japanese, U.S., and British

Aircraft carriers are warships designed to carry aircraft that can be both launched and recovered on board. Originally intended only to scout for and provide a defensive "air umbrella" over vessels of the battle line, the performance of the aircraft carrier during World War II revolutionized naval warfare. Its ability to project fire power at ranges far greater than that of even the largest shipborne gun caused the aircraft carrier to supplant the battleship well before the end of World War II as the nucleus of the modern naval striking force.

Carriers developed along three distinct lines during the war: strike, escort, and transport. Japanese doctrine initially emphasized the mass strike by carriers grouped into large task forces; there was little regard for either convoy protection or aircraft transport. Later in the war, heavy losses of both carriers and (just as important) trained aircrew fostered a tendency toward dispersal in order to reduce the chances of several carriers' being damaged or sunk simultaneously. (After the Battle of Midway, in June 1942, no fleet lost more than one carrier at a time.) Convoy protection and aircraft transport—although they assumed growing importance as the westward advance in the Pacific lengthened resupply routes—were also less pressing for the United States. The mass air strike, therefore, was the principal doctrine of U.S. carriers as well, especially from 1943 on. The large-scale production of carriers and their aircraft eventually allowed the U.S. Navy to mount overwhelming offenses with multiple task groups and hundreds of planes. Royal Navy carriers performed all three tasks: fleet carriers performed strike duties; escort carriers protected convoys and acted as semi-independent units against submarines; and transport carriers moved aircraft reinforcements to threatened areas.

A few of the earliest carriers were armed with antiship (AS) guns: Japan's *Akagi* and *Kaga* with ten 8-inch (203-mm) guns apiece, and *Hosho* with four 5.5-inch (140-mm) guns; the U.S. giants *Lexington* and *Saratoga* with eight 8-inch guns each; and Great Britain's *Hermes* with six 5.5-inch guns. The gradual realization, however, that gun battles would never take place between aircraft carriers and battleships or cruisers soon caused the near complete disappearance of AS armament from aircraft carriers and their replacement by rapid-fire dual-purpose air-defense guns. Indeed, no aircraft carrier built by any nation after 1930 was equipped with AS armament.

All carrier designers realized the need for antiaircraft (AA) weapons, however. The most popular AA weapon on Japanese carriers was the 5-inch (127-mm) gun, though 4.7-inch (120-mm), 3.9-inch (100-mm), 3.2-inch (80-mm), and 3-inch (76-mm) guns appeared as well. U.S. carriers likewise employed 5-inch guns, while British carriers used 4.7-inch and 4.5-inch guns. All were mounted in either twin or single turrets. Carrier air defense was further supplemented by increasingly large numbers of heavy machine guns (MGs)—usually 1-inch (25-mm) guns on Japanese ships and 1.5-inch (40-mm) and 0.7-inch (20-mm) guns on U.S. and British ships. They were mounted in groupings of two, three, or four to give the greatest possible concentration of firepower. Indeed, ships of all navies fairly bristled with heavy machine guns by 1944; any free space offering a clear arc of fire was adapted for the purpose. (Note that all figures for MGs that follow are initial ships' totals, not improved complements. Similarly, all tonnage figures are standard.)

Japanese Aircraft Carriers

Although slightly slower as a rule than their U.S. counterparts (but faster than British ships), Japanese aircraft carriers were generally excellent ships. They were well equipped and ably crewed, and their crew proved capable of operating their aircraft efficiently even when pilot training standards declined disastrously. The Imperial Japanese Navy possessed ten aircraft carriers on December 7, 1941—more than any other nation (the United States had eight, split evenly between the Atlantic and the Pacific). Before the war was over, Japan listed at one time or another no less than thirty ships classifiable as aircraft carriers: thirteen large, or "fleet," carriers; seven midsized, or "light," carriers; five small, or "escort," carriers; two "merchant" carriers; and three amphibious support, or "auxiliary," carriers. Only four of the thirty survived the war. Additionally, nine more Japanese ships served intermittently as seaplane carriers, either built as such or converted from other vessels ranging in size from small merchantmen to battleships.

Japan entered the war with six fleet carriers. The first, *Akagi,* was commissioned on March 25, 1927, and was constructed on the uncompleted hull of a battle cruiser. Initially displacing 30,074 tons, *Akagi* had a top speed of 28.5 knots, carried a crew complement of 1,600 men and sixty planes, and was armed with ten 8-inch AA guns, twelve 4.7-inch AA guns, and twenty-two 25-mm MGs.

Akagi was originally built with three stepped flight decks—the bottom two being half-decks set forward with the top deck extending only three-quarters the length of the ship—and two lifts. Modifications from 1935 to 1938 removed the two lower half-decks, extended the upper flight deck and hangar the length of the ship, increased the total aircraft to ninety-one, reduced the AS armament from ten to six 8-inch guns, and added six more 25-mm MGs to the AA armament. After modernization, the ship displaced 36,500 tons, had three lifts, and was capable of 31.2 knots. *Akagi* served in the Sino-Japanese War in 1937 and was the flagship of the task force that attacked Pearl Harbor on December 7, 1941. It also participated in operations against Rabaul and Port Darwin and in the Indian Ocean before being sunk on June 5, 1942, at the Battle of Midway.

Fleet carrier *Kaga* was built on the uncompleted hull of an battleship. Commissioned on March 31, 1928, it originally displaced 30,074 tons, had a top speed of 23 knots, carried a complement of 1,340 men and sixty planes, and had the same armament as sister ship *Akagi*. *Kaga,* too, initially had three stepped flight decks and two lifts. Modernization in 1935–1936 provided a single full-length flight deck, a hangar, and a third lift and upgraded the AA armament by replacing twelve 4.7-inch guns with sixteen 5-inch guns. These modifications increased the ship's displacement to 38,200 tons, its top speed to 28.3 knots, and its total aircraft to ninety. *Kaga* served in the Sino-Japanese War in 1932 and in 1939 and participated in the attacks on Pearl Harbor, Port Darwin, and Rabaul before also being sunk at the Battle of Midway, on June 4, 1942.

Fleet carrier *Soryu* was commissioned on January 29, 1937. It displaced 16,154 tons, had a top speed of 34.5 knots, carried a complement of 1,100 men and sixty-three to seventy-one aircraft, had three lifts, and was armed with twelve 5-inch AA guns and twenty-eight 25-mm MGs. Despite differences in size, displacement, and design, *Soryu* was regarded as belonging to the same class as *Hiryu*. This arrangement was made because the two ships formed a "central rectangle," working in tandem with flight decks abreast. Commissioned on July 5, 1939, *Hiryu* displaced 17,300 tons and was capable of 34.3 knots. It was crewed by 1,101 men, carried sixty-four to seventy-three planes, had three lifts, and was armed with twelve 5-inch AA guns and thirty-one 25-mm MGs. Throughout their careers, both ships served together in the same actions. They took part in operations against the Chinese in 1939, in the Pearl Harbor attack, at Wake Island, in the East Indies, at Port Darwin, and in the

Indian Ocean. And both were sunk at the Battle of Midway; *Soryu* on June 4 and *Hiryu* on the day following.

Fleet carriers *Shokaku* and *Zuikaku* also formed a class. *Shokaku* was commissioned on August 8, 1941; *Zuikaku*, on September 25, 1941. They were the first Japanese fleet carriers built as such from the keel up. Each ship displaced 26,086 tons, had a top speed of 34.2 knots, carried a crew complement of 1,660 men and seventy-two to eighty-four aircraft, had three lifts, and was armed with sixteen 5-inch AA guns and thirty-six 25-mm machine guns. *Shokaku* served in the Pearl Harbor attack and carried out raids on New Guinea before being seriously damaged in the Battle of Coral Sea. It was damaged again in the Battle of Eastern Solomons and nearly destroyed in the Battle of Santa Cruz Islands, sustaining six direct bomb hits. It was finally sunk by a U.S. submarine on June 19, 1944, in the Battle of the Philippine Sea. The career of *Zuikaku* paralleled that of its sister-ship for the first six months of the war. After the Battle of Coral Sea, it served in the Aleutian Islands campaign and was seriously mauled in the Battle of the Philippine Sea before being sunk on October 25, 1944, in the battle off Cape Engano.

The Japanese built an additional seven fleet carriers after the war began. *Junyo* and *Hiyo*—commissioned respectively on May 5 and July 31, 1942—formed a class. They each displaced 24,526 tons, had a top speed of 25.5 knots and a crew of 1,200 men, carried fifty-three planes, had two lifts, and were armed with twelve 5-inch AA guns and twenty-four 25-mm MGs. *Junyo* took part in the Aleutian Islands campaign and the Battle of Santa Cruz Islands before being seriously damaged in the Battle of the Philippine Sea. *Junyo* was never repaired; was surrendered on September 2, 1945; and was scrapped in 1947. *Hiyo* was sunk by U.S. carrier planes on June 20, 1944, in the Battle of the Philippine Sea.

Taiho, commissioned on March 7, 1944, was the first Japanese carrier built with an armored flight deck, following Royal Navy practice. Displacing 29,769 tons and with a top speed of 33.3 knots, it carried a crew of 1,751 men and fifty-three to eighty-four aircraft, had two lifts, and was armed with twelve 3.9-inch AA guns and seventy-one 25-mm MGs. After only three months of service, *Taiho* was torpedoed by a U.S. submarine and sank on June 19, 1944, in the Battle of the Philippine Sea.

Fleet carriers *Unryu*, *Amagi*, and *Katsuragi* were the only units finished of a class that was to have totaled sixteen when complete. Three others of this class—*Aso*, *Kasagi*, and *Ikoma*—were all launched in 1944 but never commissioned. *Unryu*, commissioned on August 6, 1944, displaced 17,424 tons; *Amagi*, commissioned on August 10, 1944, displaced 17,460 tons; and *Katsuragi*, launched in 1944 but never formally commissioned, displaced 17,260 tons. Each had a top speed of 34 knots, was crewed by 1,595 men, was designed for fifty-three to sixty-five planes, had two lifts, and was armed with twelve 5-inch AA guns and fifty-one 25-mm MGs. None of the three was ever used in action because of shortages of aircraft and fuel. *Unryu* was sunk by a U.S. submarine off Shanghai on December 19, 1944, after only five months of service. *Amagi* was bombed, and capsized, at Kure on July 24, 1945. *Katsuragi* was surrendered on September 2, 1945, and was broken up.

Japan's last fleet carrier was *Shinano*, the largest aircraft carrier of the war, with a displacement of 65,837 tons, two lifts, a top speed of 27 knots, and a minimal crew complement of 2,400 men. Although designed to carry up to 120 planes, only 40 to 50 made up the air group; the balance were intended as replacement aircraft for other fleet carriers and forward land bases. *Shinano* had two lifts and was armed with sixteen 5-inch AA guns, 145 MGs (25-mm), and 336 rocket launchers. Built on the hull of the unfinished third battleship of *Yamato* class, this carrier was armored and compartmentalized so completely that it was regarded by the Japanese as unsinkable. Launched on October 8, 1944, *Shinano* was never commissioned. It was torpedoed and sank on November 29, 1944, during its maiden cruise between Tokyo and Kobe—giving it the dubious distinction of being the shortest-lived "unsinkable" large warship in modern naval history.

Of the seven Japanese light carriers that served during the war, four were commissioned before the Pearl Harbor attack. Japan's first aircraft carrier built from the keel up (and, incidentally, its longest-lived) was *Hosho*. Commissioned on December 27, 1922, it displaced 7,590 tons and had a top speed of 25 knots. It had a complement of 550 men, two lifts, and a full-length flight deck with a hangar for twenty-one to twenty-six aircraft, and it was armed with four 5.5-inch AS guns, two 3-inch AA guns, and two 25-mm MGs. After a great deal of pioneering and experimental work during the 1920s, *Hosho* had been relegated to secondary roles by the end of 1933 but returned to active service after the attack on Pearl Harbor and served in the Combined Fleet at Midway. It then reverted to its role as a pilot-training ship; was surrendered on September 2, 1945; and was finally scrapped in 1947.

Ryujo was commissioned on May 9, 1933. Displacing 8,128 tons and with a top speed of 29 knots, it was crewed by 600 men, carried thirty-seven to forty-eight planes, had two lifts, and was armed with eight 5-inch AA guns and twenty-two 25-mm MGs. During the first six months of the war, *Ryujo* covered landings in the Philippines and the East Indies and participated in the Aleutian Islands campaign. It was sunk on August 24, 1942, in the Battle of Eastern Solomons.

Shoho and *Zuiho* formed a class. Converted from submarine tenders, they displaced 11,442 tons apiece and had a top speed of 28.5 knots. Each was crewed by 785 men, carried thirty aircraft, had two lifts, and was armed with eight 5-inch AA guns and eight 25-mm MGs. *Shoho*—commissioned on January 26, 1942—was sunk on May 7 in the Battle of Coral Sea. This was the first and the shortest-lived Japanese carrier lost in the war. *Zuiho* was commissioned on December 27, 1940, and provided air cover for the invasion of the East Indies before suffering serious damage in the Battle of the Santa Cruz Islands. After repairs, it served in the Battle of the Philippine Sea. *Zuiho* was sunk in the battle off Cape Engano on October 25, 1944.

Ryuho, commissioned on November 28, 1942, was also converted from a submarine tender. When completed, the ship displaced 13,574 tons, had a top speed of 26.5 knots, carried 989 men and thirty-one planes, had two lifts, and was armed with eight 5-inch AA guns and thirty-eight 25-mm MGs. *Ryuho* was employed mainly as a training ship during the war. Damaged at anchor by an air raid on March 19, 1945, it was never repaired; the ship was surrendered on September 2, 1945, and was broken up in 1946.

The last two Japanese light carriers—sister ships *Chiyoda* and *Chitose*—were originally seaplane tenders of the same name, commissioned in 1938 on December 15 and July 25, respectively. Both were converted to conventional aircraft carriers between 1942 and 1944. After conversion, each of them displaced 11,190 tons, had a top speed of 29 knots, was crewed by 800 men, carried twenty-four to thirty planes, had two lifts, and was armed with eight 5-inch AA guns and thirty 25-mm MGs. *Chitose* helped cover Japanese landings in the Philippines and East Indies and on the Gilbert Islands before being damaged in the Battle of Eastern Solomons. *Chiyoda* was part of Admiral Yamamoto's reserve at Midway but took no part in the battle. Both ships were sunk on October 25, 1944, in the battle off Cape Engano.

Japan had five ships classified as escort carriers: *Taiyo, Unyo, Chuyo, Kaiyo,* and *Shinyo.* The first three—commissioned respectively on September 15, 1941; May 31, 1942; and November 25, 1942—formed a class. Originally cargo steamers, they displaced 18,115 tons apiece and were capable of a top speed of 21 knots. Each had a complement of 747 men, carried twenty-seven aircraft, had two lifts, and was armed with six 4.7-inch AA guns and eight 25-mm MGs. All three ships were used mainly for transport and training duties throughout their careers, although *Taiyo* served in a supporting role during the Battle of Eastern Solomons. All were torpedoed and sunk by U.S. submarines: *Taiyo,* in the South China Sea on August 18, 1944; *Unyo,* off Hong Kong on September 16, 1944; and *Chuyo,* off Yokosuka on December 4, 1943.

Kaiyo was the smallest of the Japanese escort carriers. Converted from a passenger ship, it displaced only 13,818 tons and was capable of 24 knots. It carried twenty-four planes, had two lifts, and was armed with eight 5-inch AA guns and twenty-four 25-mm MGs. Commissioned as a carrier on November 23, 1943, *Kaiyo* was used as an aircraft transport until mid-1944 and for pilot training afterward. It was disabled by British carrier planes off Kyushu on July 24, 1945, and was scrapped after the war.

The last unit, *Shinyo,* was converted from a German liner stranded in Japan in 1939. Commissioned on December 15, 1943, this carrier displaced 17,780 tons and had a top speed of 22 knots; it was crewed by 942 men, carried thirty-three planes, had two lifts, and was armed with eight 5-inch AA guns and thirty 25-mm MGs. *Shinyo* was used primarily for training. It was sunk by a U.S. submarine off Shanghai on November 17, 1944.

A sixth Japanese escort carrier, *Ibuki,* is said to have been converted from the hull of a *Mogami*-type cruiser at Sasebo. Details are somewhat hazy. It supposedly displaced 12,700 tons, was to have a top speed of 29 knots, and was to be crewed by 1,015 men; it was designed for twenty-seven aircraft, had two lifts, and was to be armed with four 3-inch AA guns, forty-eight 25-mm MGs, and 168 rocket launchers. Although listed as being commissioned on May 21, 1943, *Ibuki* was never actually completed and was broken up after the war.

The Japanese navy possessed several more small ships with flight decks that were loosely classified as "merchant" aircraft carriers. The only two completed, *Otakisan-Maru* and *Shimane-Maru,* were converted from tankers. They had small forward hangars, single lifts for twelve aircraft, and displaced 11,989 tons apiece; with a top speed of 18.5 knots, they were armed with two 4.7-inch AA guns and fifty-two 25-mm MGs. *Otakisan-Maru* was never commissioned. It drifted onto a mine at Kobe soon after the war ended and was later scrapped. *Shimane-Maru* was commissioned on February 28, 1945, and was sunk on July 24 by U.S. aircraft off Shikoku. The others in the class, *Daykyu-Maru* and *Taisha-Maru,* were never finished. Two more units with neither hangars nor lifts, *Chigusa-Maru* and *Yamashio-Maru,* were on the stocks at the end of the war.

The navy was not the only Japanese service to operate carriers during the war. The army also possessed five amphibious assault ships loosely classified as "auxiliary" carriers. Converted from merchantmen, they had short flight decks from which planes could take off (but not land) for the rapid establishment of land-based air defense. The first two, *Akitsu-Maru* and *Nigitsu-Maru,* formed a class. Each displaced 11,989 tons, was capable of 20 knots, had one lift, carried twenty planes (or, alternatively, twenty landing craft), and was armed with two 3-inch AA guns and ten 3-inch army-type ex-field guns (presumably for shore bombardment). The details of their service are not known. Commissioned on January 30, 1942, *Akitsu-Maru* was sunk by a U.S. submarine off Kyushu on November 15, 1944. *Nigitsu-Maru* was commissioned in March 1943 and was sunk by a U.S. submarine on January 12, 1944, east of Formosa. The third unit, *Kumanu-Maru,* was commissioned in March 1945. It displaced approximately 10,500 tons, had a single lift, was capable of carrying thirty-seven aircraft at a top speed of 19 knots, and was armed with eight 3-inch guns and six 25-mm MGs. This unit never saw action and was reconverted into a merchant ship in 1947.

The Japanese army also converted two tankers into escort carriers in 1944: *Yamashiro-Maru* and *Chigusa-Maru.* Equipped with army aircraft, their purpose was to provide air defense for troop convoys. Each displaced about 10,000 tons, had a top speed of 13 knots, was crewed by 221 men, carried eight planes, and was armed with sixteen 25-mm MGs. Because they had neither hangars nor lifts, their aircraft were spotted aft for takeoff and were manhandled back along the flight deck after landing. *Yamashiro-Maru* was commissioned on January 27, 1945, and was sunk by U.S. aircraft at Yokosuka on February 17. *Chigusa-Maru* was never completed as a carrier and was reconverted into a tanker after the war.

The Japanese navy also had ten seaplane carriers during the war—ships without flight decks but equipped with either catapults or derricks to launch seaplanes and cranes to retrieve them. Two oil tankers, *Notoro* and *Tsurumi,* were converted into seaplane carriers cum transports in 1924. Each displaced 14,275 tons, was capable of 12 knots, carried ten planes, and was armed with two 4.7-inch and two 3.2-inch AA guns. They served until 1942, when they were reconverted into tankers. *Notoro* served in the Sino-Japanese War in 1937, after which it was used as a floating depot. It survived the war and was broken up in 1947. *Tsurumi* was reconverted into a tanker in 1931 and was torpedoed and sank in August 1942. Another oiler, the U.S.-built *Kamoi,* was converted into a seaplane carrier in 1932–1933. Displacing 17,272 tons

and capable of 15 knots, it housed twelve planes and was armed with two 5.5-inch and two 3.2-inch AA guns. *Kamoi* was reconverted into a tanker in 1943 and was sunk in an air attack at Hong Kong (date uncertain).

Mizuho and *Nisshin* were fast seaplane carriers, very similar to *Chitose* and *Chiyoda* before their conversion into aircraft carriers. Commissioned on February 25, 1939, the 11,104-ton *Mizuho* had four catapults and one lift; it was capable of 22 knots, carried twenty-four planes, and was armed with six 5-inch AA guns and twelve 25-mm machine MGs. The ship was also equipped with a dozen midget submarines, which could be floated out through a special hatch in the stern. *Mizuho* helped cover Japanese landings in the Philippines and on Ambon before being sunk by a U.S. submarine on May 2, 1942, off southern Honshu. *Nisshin*—launched in 1939 and commissioned on February 27, 1942—displaced 11,498 tons, had two catapults, was capable of 28 knots, carried twenty-five planes, and had the same armament and midget submarine capability as *Mizuho*. *Nisshin* was sunk on July 22, 1943, by U.S. aircraft in the Bougainville Strait. Two improved *Nisshin*s were planned in 1942 but were never begun.

The last three Japanese seaplane carriers were the converted battleships *Ise* and *Hyuga* and the cruiser *Mogami*. Both battleships had their stern armament replaced in 1943 by two catapults, one lift, and hangars for twenty-two planes. *Mogami* finished a similar conversion in November 1943. None of the three ships ever saw action as a seaplane carrier. *Ise* and *Hyuga* had their catapults removed in 1944 to resume their true roles as battleships. Both were sunk by air raids in port at Kure in July 1945. *Mogami,* serving as a cruiser, was sunk on October 25, 1944, by a Japanese destroyer after being hopelessly damaged in battle in the Surigao Strait.

U.S. Aircraft Carriers

Although the U.S. Navy began the war in the Pacific with less than half the number of carriers possessed by Japan, the United States ultimately produced no less than 111 ships during the war that were classifiable as aircraft carriers: 25 fleet carriers (CVs), 9 light carriers (CVLs), and 77 escort carriers (CVEs). Most of these served in the Pacific theater at one time or another, and—in marked contrast to the near destruction of Japan's carrier forces—only twelve U.S. carriers were lost in action: five fleet, one light, and six escort carriers. American carriers had excellent speed and aircraft-handling characteristics, although the latter was achieved in some cases (most notably, that of the CVLs) only after reducing the size of air groups to more manageable numbers.

The United States commissioned eight carriers before the war. The first was *Langley* (CV-1), commissioned on March 20, 1922. Converted from a collier, it displaced 12,903 tons and had a top speed of 14 knots. *Langley* had a crew of 350 men, carried thirty-four aircraft, and was armed with four 5-inch AA guns. Although it had a full-length flush deck, there was no hangar or lift; planes were stored in four holds and had to be hauled onto the flight deck by cranes. Despite being the pioneer carrier of the U.S. Navy (and, indeed, the only one for five years), *Langley* was too slow to be usefully employed with the battle fleet. It was converted into a seaplane tender and aircraft transport ship (redesignated A-3) in 1937. Its career during the war was brief; it was attacked and sunk by Japanese bombers south of Tjilatjap on February 27, 1942, while trying to deliver aircraft to Java. Although far too small to be a true fleet carrier, especially in light of the ships that followed, *Langley* nonetheless is honorably remembered by the designation CV-1 on U.S. Navy rolls to this day.

The first two U.S. carriers built as a class were *Lexington* (CV-2) and *Saratoga* (CV-3). Commissioned in 1927 on December 14 and November 16, respectively, they were constructed on uncompleted battle-cruiser hulls. They displaced 39,116 tons apiece and were capable of 33.25 knots. Each had crew complements of 2,122 men, carried sixty-three to eighty planes, had two lifts, and was armed with eight 8-inch AS guns, twelve 5-inch AA guns, and forty-eight 20-mm MGs. After the attack on Pearl Harbor, *Lexington* conducted offensive patrols out of Hawaii and skirmished with the Japanese off Rabaul and New Guinea before being sunk on May 8, 1942, in the Battle of the Coral Sea. *Saratoga* had a rather varied career. During patrols following the Pearl Harbor attack, it was torpedoed twice by Japanese submarines—first in January and again on August 31, 1942. Through most of 1943 it conducted land strikes and attacks on Japanese shipping in the southwest Pacific, and during the first half of 1944 it operated with the British Pacific Fleet in the Indian Ocean. In February 1945 *Saratoga* was crippled by Japanese kamikazes off Iwo Jima and, seriously strained by many injuries, trained pilots for the rest of the war and was finally expended as a target ship in the Bikini atomic bomb experiments on July 25, 1946.

Although *Ranger* (CV-4) was the first U.S. aircraft carrier designed as such, it proved a disappointment in carrier design, in effect being a replica of *Langley* except that planes were kept in a below-deck hangar rather than in four holds. Commissioned on July 4, 1934, it displaced 14,224 tons, had a top speed of 29 knots, and—uniquely, for U.S. carriers—had no island. Carrying a crew complement of 1,788 men and seventy-six aircraft, the ship had two lifts and was armed with eight 5-inch AA and forty "smaller" guns. Shortcomings as a fleet carrier relegated the ship mainly to aircraft transport duties in the Atlantic from 1941 to 1943, and in 1944 it was used as a training ship before being posted to the Pacific that August. *Ranger* was decommissioned on October 18, 1946 and was sold for scrap in January 1947.

Yorktown (CV-5) and *Enterprise* (CV-6) formed a class. Commissioned respectively on September 30, 1937, and May 12, 1938, they displaced 20,190 tons apiece and had a top speed of 32.5 knots. Each had a crew complement of 1,890 men, carried eighty to ninety-six planes, had three lifts, and was armed with eight 5-inch AA guns and thirty-two MGs (sixteen 40-mm and sixteen 20-mm). Stationed at Norfolk when Pearl Harbor was attacked, *Yorktown* immediately transited to the Pacific and attacked Japanese shore installations and shipping off New Guinea in early 1942 before being heavily damaged in the Battle of the Coral Sea. Hastily repaired, *Yorktown* was hit by three bombs and two torpedoes on June 4, 1942, in the Battle of Midway and was sunk two days later by a Japanese submarine. *Enterprise* fought in the Battles of Midway, Guadalcanal, and the Santa Cruz Islands. Following a major refit during the second half of 1943, it conducted strikes against Japanese targets on Pacific islands until a kamikaze hit in May 1945 put it out of action for the rest of the war. The ship was decommissioned on February 17, 1947, and—despite strenuous efforts to preserve it as a memorial—was sold for scrap on July 1, 1958.

Wasp (CV-7) was commissioned on April 25, 1940. Displacing 14,935 tons, it had a top speed of 29.5 knots and carried 1,889 men and seventy-six to eighty-four aircraft; it had three lifts and was armed with eight 5-inch AA guns and forty MGs (sixteen 40-mm and twenty-four 20-mm). *Wasp* served with the Atlantic Fleet in 1941 before transferring to the Pacific in June 1942. It was torpedoed and sunk by a Japanese submarine on September 15, 1942, following the Battle of the Eastern Solomons.

The last prewar U.S. carrier was *Hornet* (CV-8). Commissioned on October 20, 1941, its design was mainly a repeat of *Yorktown* except for a wider flight deck, some two hundred tons more in displacement, differences in the island detail, and a slightly heavier AA armament. Indeed, it was similar enough to *Enterprise* and *Yorktown* for some authorities to consider all three ships as belonging to the same class. *Hornet* lasted in service barely more than a year. After launching the famous Doolittle raid in April 1942, it served in the Battles of Midway and the Santa Cruz Islands, where it was sunk on October 27, 1942.

Of the twenty-four units of the *Essex*-class fleet carriers, seventeen were commissioned before the end of the war. This class was divided into two groups: short hull and long hull (the former having a pointed bow extending beyond the flight deck; otherwise, the two were identical). Displacing 27,635 tons and capable of 32.7 knots, these ships had a crew complement of 2,682 men and carried 82 to 103 aircraft. They had three lifts each and were armed with twelve 5-inch AA guns (later models had only ten) and seventy-eight MGs (thirty-two 40-mm and forty-six 20-mm). *Essex* (CV-9), *Yorktown II* (CV-10), *Intrepid* (CV-11), *Hornet II* (CV-12), *Franklin* (CV-13), *Lexington II* (CV-16), *Bunker Hill* (CV-17), *Wasp II* (CV-18), *Bennington* (CV-20), and *Bon Homme Richard* (CV-31) were short-hull ships; *Ticonderoga* (CV-14), *Randolph* (CV-15), *Hancock* (CV-19), *Boxer* (CV-21), *Antietam* (CV-36), *Shangri-La* (CV-38), and *Lake Champlain* (CV-39) were long hulls. *Essex* was commissioned first, on December 31, 1942; and *Lake Champlain* came last, on June 3, 1945. All but *Boxer* and *Lake Champlain* saw action in the Pacific, and not one was lost. (Although the majority of these warships were named for ships or victorious battles of the American Revolution, it is obvious that considerations of Anglo-American amity did not bulk large in the christening process.)

The nine units of *Independence*-class light carriers commissioned by the United States during the war were built by converting hulls of light cruisers already under construction. They displaced 10,833 tons apiece and had a top speed of 31 knots. Each had two lifts and carried 1,569 men, forty-five planes (reduced to thirty-two in May 1944, to improve aircraft-handling abilities), and was armed with two 5-inch AA guns and twenty-six MGs (sixteen 40-mm and ten 20-mm). The ships in the class were *Independence* (CVL-22), *Princeton* (CVL-23), *Belleau Wood* (CVL-24), *Cowpens* (CVL-25), *Monterey* (CVL-26), *Cabot* (CVL-27), *Langley II* (CVL-28), *Bataan* (CVL-29), and *San Jacinto* (CVL-30). All were commissioned in 1943: *Independence* first, on January 14; *San Jacinto* last, on December 15. All served in the Pacific, and of the nine only *Princeton* was lost, sunk on October 24, 1944, in the Battle of Leyte Gulf.

The first U.S. escort carrier (or "Jeep" carrier, in U.S. Navy slang) was *Long Island* (CVE-1), converted from a merchantman and commissioned on June 2, 1941, and the first U.S. Navy carrier since *Langley* not to be named for a battle. It displaced 8,012 tons and was capable of 16 knots carrying a crew complement of 970 men and sixteen to twenty-one planes; it had one lift and was armed with one 4-inch and two 3-inch AA guns and four 20-mm MGs. After early service in the Atlantic, *Long Island* was transferred to the Pacific, where it delivered the first U.S. Marine Corps fighters to Henderson Field on August 20, 1942. It then became a training carrier.

Four more ships were converted from merchantmen in the spring and summer of 1942—three of which were delivered to the Royal Navy as *Avenger*-class carriers. The sole unit retained by the United States was *Charger* (CVE-30), commissioned on March 3, 1942. It displaced 11,989 tons and was capable of 17 knots. Crewed by 856 men, it carried twenty-one to thirty-six planes, had one lift, and was armed with three 4-inch AA guns and ten 20-mm MGs. *Charger* was not used in combat and spent the war training pilots for the Royal Navy.

In early 1942 another twenty-six ships were bought for conversion into escort carriers. Of the total, eleven composed the U.S. *Bogue* class, eleven more were delivered to Great Britain as the *Attacker* class, and the remaining four made up the U.S. *Sangamon* class. The eleven ships of the *Bogue* class displaced 8,524 tons apiece and had a top speed of 18 knots; each was crewed by 890 men, carried twenty-one to twenty-eight planes, had two lifts, and was armed with two 5-inch AA guns and ten 20-mm MGs. All were commissioned between August 20, 1942, and June 15, 1943. Six of the class served in the Pacific, either as aircraft transports or convoy escorts: *Copahee* (CVE-12), *Nassau* (CVE-16), *Altamaha* (CVE-18), *Barnes* (CVE-20), *Breton* (CVE-23), and *Prince William* (CVE-31). *Block Island* (CVE-21), which served in the Atlantic, was torpedoed and sunk by a German U-boat in May 1944—one of only six U.S. escort carriers lost in action during the war.

The four units of the *Sangamon* class were built on the hulls of steam-powered oil tankers. Similar to the ships of the *Bogue* class in appearance, they displaced 10,668 tons and were capable of 18 knots. Each was crewed by 1,080 men, carried thirty or thirty-one aircraft, had two lifts, and was armed with two 5-inch AA guns and twenty MGs (eight 40-mm and twelve 20-mm). All four ships were commissioned in 1942: *Santee* (CVE-29), on August 24; *Sangamon* (CVE-26), on August 25; *Chenango* (CVE-28), on September 19; and *Suwannee* (CVE-27), on September 24. After participating in Operation Torch (the Allied invasion of North Africa in November 1942), they transferred to the Pacific, where all but *Chenango* saw combat.

The fifty units of the *Casablanca* class (CVE-55 to CVE-104) were the first purpose-built U.S. escort carriers, and they once again were named after battles. All were commissioned in the remarkably short time span of 314 days; the first, *Coral Sea* (CVE-57)—later renamed *Anzio*—on August 27, 1943; and the last, *Munda*

(CVE-104), on July 8, 1944. Displacing 8,331 tons apiece, they were capable of 19 knots. Each was crewed by 860 men, carried twenty-seven or twenty-eight planes, had one lift, and was armed with one 5-inch AA gun and twenty MGs (eight 40-mm and twelve 20-mm). Nearly all served in the Pacific theater at one time or another, and five were sunk in action: *Liscombe Bay* (CVE-56), on November 24, 1943, by a Japanese submarine off the Gilbert Islands; *St. Lo* (CVE-63), on October 25, 1944, by a kamikaze at Leyte; *Gambier Bay* (CVE-73), on October 25, 1944, by gunfire from Japanese cruisers; *Ommaney Bay* (CVE-79), in early January 1945, by a kamikaze while en route for Lingayen Gulf; and *Bismarck Sea* (CVE-95), on February 21, 1945, by a kamikaze off Iwo Jima.

The last U.S. escort carriers were the nineteen ships of the *Commencement Bay* class, eleven of which (CVE-105 to CVE-115) were completed before the end of the war. They displaced 19,211 tons apiece and had a top speed of 19 knots. Each had a crew complement of 1,066 men, carried thirty to thirty-four aircraft, had two lifts, and was armed with two 5-inch AA guns and fifty-six MGs (thirty-six 40-mm and twenty 20-mm). All were commissioned between November 27, 1944, and July 16, 1945, but only five of the ships saw service, in the Pacific, before the end of the war. The number of U.S. Navy aircraft carriers constructed during the war was truly remarkable.

British Aircraft Carriers

British aircraft carriers were generally more heavily armored than their Japanese or U.S. counterparts, allowing them to take more damage without being disabled. As a consequence, however, they carried fewer planes (as well as a higher proportion of fighters to attack aircraft) and were not as effective as strike ships. In some significant ways, it could be said that the Royal Navy built its carriers like battleships. Great Britain possessed eighty-four aircraft carriers of all types at one time or another during the war. Of the total, thirty-two (plus another four that arrived too late) served against Japan, and only those will be treated here.

The light carrier *Hermes* was the first British aircraft carrier to be designed and built without using the hull of another ship. Commissioned in July 1923, it displaced 11,024 tons and had a top speed of 25 knots. The crew complement was 664 men. *Hermes* carried twenty planes, had one lift, and was armed with six 5.5-inch AS guns and three 4-inch AA guns. Although it served mainly on the China Station throughout its career, it spent much of 1939–1940 hunting raiders in the Atlantic and attacking German positions and shipping in East Africa and the

Middle East. It was sunk by Japanese carrier aircraft on April 9, 1942, off Ceylon.

The four fleet carriers of the *Illustrious* class were *Illustrious, Formidable, Victorious,* and *Indomitable.* Begun in the years immediately preceding the war, they displaced 23,368 tons apiece and were capable of 30.5 knots. Each had a crew complement of 1,200 men, carried a mere thirty-six aircraft, had two lifts, and was armed with sixteen 4.5-inch AA guns and forty-eight 2-pounder (2-pdr) MGs. *Formidable* was commissioned on November 24, 1940, and served mainly in the Mediterranean until transferring to the Far East in the autumn of 1944. Placed on reserve in 1947, it was scrapped in 1956. *Illustrious,* commissioned on May 25, 1940, moved to the Pacific in early 1944; it became a trials carrier after the war, was placed on reserve in 1954, and was broken up in 1956. *Victorious* was commissioned on May 15, 1941, and transferred to the Far East in July 1944. Refitted in 1960 and again in 1967, it was finally sold and broken up in 1969. *Indomitable,* commissioned on October 10, 1941, joined British forces in the Far East in July 1944, continued in service after the war, and was sold for scrap in 1953. Although all four ships were damaged by kamikazes in 1945, only *Victorious* was disabled for any length of time.

Unicorn was commissioned on March 12, 1943. Displacing 16,794 tons, it had a top speed of 24 knots, was crewed by 1,094 men, carried thirty-six aircraft, had two lifts, and was armed with eight 4-inch AA guns and twenty-nine MGs (sixteen 2-pdr and thirteen 20-mm). *Unicorn* deployed to the Pacific in time to participate in the invasion of Okinawa. In reserve from 1946 to 1949, it was recommissioned as a transport carrier for the Korean War and then returned to reserve in 1953; it was sold for scrap in 1959.

The last British fleet carriers to see action against Japan were the two ships of the *Implacable* class: *Indefatigable* and *Implacable.* They were Britain's largest wartime aircraft carriers. Each displaced 23,825 tons and was capable of 32 knots. They had a crew complement of 1,400 men, carried fifty-four aircraft, had two lifts, and were armed with sixteen 4.5-inch AA guns and eighty-five MGs (forty-eight 2-pdr and thirty-seven 20-mm). *Indefatigable* was commissioned on May 3, 1944, and served in the Pacific theater from August 1944 to the end of the war, when it suffered superficial damage from a kamikaze hit. In reserve from 1946 to 1949, it served again as a training ship from 1950 to 1954 and was sold for scrap in 1956. *Implacable,* commissioned on August 28, 1944, joined the British Pacific Fleet near the end of the war. Refitted in 1948–1949, it served as a training ship from 1952 to mid-1954, after which it was sold in 1955 and broken up.

Four fleet carriers of the ten-ship *Colossus* class—*Colossus, Glory, Venerable,* and *Vengeance*—arrived in the Pacific too late to see action but performed mopping-up duties after the Japanese surrender. *Colossus* was commissioned on December 16, 1944; the others, respectively, on April 2, January 17, and January 15, 1945. Each displaced 13,401 tons, was capable of 25 knots, had a crew complement of 1,300 men, carried forty-eight planes, had two lifts, and was armed with fifty-six machine guns (twenty-four 2-pdr and thirty-two 20-mm). *Colossus* was purchased by France in 1951; *Glory* served in the Korean War and against Malayan communists from 1951 to 1953, was stricken in the late 1950s, and was sold for scrap in 1961.

Finally, twenty-four British escort carriers served in the Pacific during the war: seven from the eleven-ship *Attacker* class and seventeen from the twenty-three-ship *Ameer* class. Attackers—commissioned between October 11, 1942, and June 14, 1943—displaced 10,363 tons apiece and were capable of 18.5 knots. They had a crew complement of 646 men, carried twenty planes, had two lifts, and were armed with two 4-inch AA guns and fourteen 20-mm MGs. Ameers were commissioned between August 1, 1943, and February 21, 1944. They displaced 11,582 tons and had a top speed of 18 knots. They had a crew of 646 men, carried twenty aircraft, had two lifts, and were armed with two 5-inch AA guns and thirty-six MGs (sixteen 40-mm and twenty 20-mm). The ships of both classes served mostly as aircraft transports, convoy escorts, and fighter support ships.

World War II in the Pacific was the only conflict in naval history which saw carrier-to-carrier battles in which neither side's ships sighted each other; rather, their aircraft fought it out, attacking enemy "flattops," as did submarines, or defending their own. It was a type of naval warfare not likely to be repeated.

FURTHER READINGS

Brown, David. *Warship Losses of World War Two* (1990).

Chesneau, Roger. *Aircraft Carriers of the World, 1914 to the Present: An Illustrated Encyclopedia* (1984).

D'Albas, Andriew. *Death of a Navy: Japanese Naval Action in World War II* (1957).

Dull, Paul. *A Battle History of the Imperial Japanese Navy (1941–1945)* (1978).

Galuppini, Gino. *Warships of the World: An Illustrated Encyclopedia* (1989).

Jane's Fighting Ships of World War II (1989).

Morison, Samuel Eliot. *Supplement and General Index: History of United States Naval Operations in World War II,* vol. XV (1962).

———. *The Two-Ocean War: A Short History of the United States Navy in the Second World War* (1963).

Rohwer, J., and G. Hummelchen. *Chronology of the War at Sea 1939–1945: The Naval History of World War Two* (1992).

Edward C. Page

SEE ALSO Aircraft: Japanese, U.S., and British; Coral Sea, Battle of the; Midway, Battle of; Navy, Japanese; Navy, U.S.

Alamo Scouts

The Alamo Scouts, officially known as the Sixth Army Special Reconnaissance Unit, were formed because Lieutenant General Walter Krueger needed accurate and timely information as he prepared to invade New Guinea. Krueger had access to general information gleaned from captured documents, prisoner-of-war interrogations, missionaries, aerial observation, and Australia's Coastwatchers, but he lacked the specific information needed to plan a major offensive. It was for this purpose that Krueger developed the Alamo Scouts, named in honor of the heroic defenders of the Alamo in San Antonio, Texas.

Krueger modeled the organization after such other elite World War II units as the 1st Special Service Force, the Rangers, and the Naval Amphibious Scouts. He established the first Alamo Scout Training Center (ASTC) on December 3, 1943, under the command of Lieutenant Colonel Frederick Bradshaw. In order to keep the Scouts near his headquarters, where they could receive instructions from his G-2 (intelligence), Krueger had the ASTC located on Ferguson Island, approximately forty miles north of the tail of New Guinea, at the village of Kalo Kalo. This was the first of six such centers that followed the Sixth Army's advance to the Philippines. After Bradshaw, Major Homer Williams and then Major Gibson Niles commanded the Scouts.

Selection for the Scouts was demanding. Volunteers were drawn from throughout the Sixth Army after rigorous screening at the company, battalion, regiment, and division levels. Candidates had to be good swimmers in excellent physical condition and could not wear glasses.

After being admitted to the program, candidates underwent six weeks of training at the ASTC. The course included scouting and patrolling, infiltration and exfiltration techniques, intelligence collection, rubber-boat handling, communications, land navigation, rudimentary language and native customs, jungle survival, Allied and enemy weapons familiarization, first aid, and self-defense.

Throughout the course, the cadre emphasized working in small teams.

During the final week, each enlisted man was asked on a secret ballot to name the three officers, in order of preference, he would be most willing to follow on a mission. He was also asked to name the five enlisted men with whom he would not hesitate to work on a mission. The officers were also asked to name those soldiers with whom they would not hesitate to go on a mission. The staff officers then added their own recommendations, and the total votes were tallied. This selection process remained in place for the duration of the ASTC's existence.

Class size ranged from 40 to 100 candidates, with attrition as high as 40 percent during the first two weeks. Throughout the war, the ASTCs produced eight classes and graduated 250 enlisted men and 75 officers. Of these, only 117 enlisted men and 21 officers were retained. Those who were retained were placed on teams consisting of an officer and five or six enlisted men, and the team assumed the last name of the ranking officer. Those graduates who were not retained were released to their unit, where Kreuger hoped they would be used for scout work. Officially, the Alamo Scout organization and its missions were to be kept secret.

The Scouts' first mission began on February 27, 1944. A team led by Lieutenant John McGowen landed from a Catalina flying boat near the southwest tip of Los Negros Island in the Admiralties to determine whether the Japanese had evacuated a key area as had been reported earlier. The Scouts learned that the enemy had not evacuated, and they reported this information after being picked up the next morning. Subsequently, almost every Sixth Army amphibious operation was preceeded by Alamo Scout reconnaissance.

Another notable Scout mission involved a joint effort with the U.S. Navy and the Army Air Forces to reconnoiter the Cape Sansapor area of the Vogelkop Peninsula in June 1944. The Vogelkop was the last Japanese stronghold in New Guinea as well as being General Douglas MacArthur's springboard into the Philippines. The reconnaissance effort provided Allied planners with detailed hydrographic, terrain, and enemy troop information. The beaches around the Sansapor area were found to be capable of supporting all types of landing craft, and an area previously believed to be a partially cleared airstrip was identified as a native garden.

Perhaps the best known of the Alamo Scouts' missions was the part the unit played in the raid on the Cabantuan prison on Luzon—an operation that the Sixth Army's weekly G-2 report described as "an almost perfect example of prior reconnaissance and planning." The 6th Ranger Battalion conducted the raid itself, but the bulk of the reconnaissance effort was accomplished by two teams of the Alamo Scouts.

On January 27, 1945, both teams left the Rangers' base camp at Calasiao and marched to a guerrilla headquarters at Guimba, where they linked up with native guides. From there, the Scouts moved to Platero, three miles north of the objective, where they contacted local guerrillas. From that point on, the Scouts kept the objective under surveillance. Their mission was to determine how many Japanese troops were in the area, who the guards were, and what their routines were like, and then to pass this information on to the Rangers. On January 29, the Rangers made a rendezvous with Lieutenants Thomas Rounsaville and William Nellist of the Scouts at Balincarin, about five miles northeast of the objective. The Rangers had hoped to conduct the operation that night, but when they learned that the Scouts had not completed their reconnaissance, they decided to wait twenty-four hours. The Scouts had already observed that there were large numbers of Japanese in the area and that the highway in front of the camp had been heavily traveled by withdrawing Japanese during the previous twenty-four hours. Additionally, 200 to 300 Japanese were bivouacked on Cabu Creek, a mile north of the compound.

As the Rangers moved up to Platero, the Scouts continued their reconnaissance, which included verifying maps and aerial photographs and selecting tentative firing positions. The information they uncovered was highly detailed and allowed the Rangers to complete their plan.

What the Scouts had found was that the compound was on the south side of the Cabanatuan City–Cabu highway and that it measured 600 by 800 yards. It was enclosed by three barbed-wire fences about 4 feet apart and 6 to 8 feet high. Other less impressive barbed-wire fences further subdivided the camp into several compartments. The main entrance was blocked by a locked 8-foot-high gate and was guarded by one sentry in a well-protected shelter. There were also three manned 12-foot-high guard towers and one pillbox occupied by four heavily armed guards. The Scouts believed that one building inside the compound contained four tanks and two trucks.

The Scouts counted 73 Japanese on guard at the stockade, but some 150 others had entered the compound, apparently to rest. Most of the heavy force that had been in the area the previous day had left, and traffic on the highway was light. The closest possible reaction force was 800 Japanese with tanks and trucks at Cabu. The prisoners were housed in buildings in the northwest corner of the compound. Everything appeared normal.

Armed with this excellent report, the Rangers launched their attack at dusk. Right up to the initiation of the raid, the Scouts kept the stockade under continuous surveillance. They employed civilian runners to carry periodic intelligence updates to the Ranger commander at Platero.

Largely because of the reconnaissance efforts of the Alamo Scouts, the Rangers enjoyed great success. They liberated 511 U.S. and Allied POWs and killed or wounded an estimated 523 Japanese. As the G-2 report continued, the operation demonstrated "what patrols can accomplish in enemy territory by following the basic principles of scouting and patrolling, 'sneaking and peeping.' . . . "

Throughout the war, the Alamo Scouts accumulated an impressive record of 103 known reconnaissance and raid missions, including two prison-camp liberations. In all these operations, the Scouts did not lose a single man. During campaigns in the Bismarck Archipelago and New Guinea, they performed thirty-six missions and were credited with eighty-four confirmed kills, twenty-four prisoner-of-war captures, and approximately 550 civilian rescues. From February to October 1944, the Scouts earned nineteen Silver Stars, eighteen Bronze Stars, and four Soldier's Medals.

The unit was disbanded without ceremony in late November 1945 in Kyoto, Japan. In 1988, the Alamo Scouts veterans were awarded the Special Forces Tab by the army at the behest of the John F. Kennedy Special Warfare Center and School—a recognition that placed them among the forerunners of the modern Special Forces.

FURTHER READINGS

King, Michael. *Rangers: Selected Combat Operations in World War II,* Leavenworth Paper No. 11 (Combat Studies Institute, Fort Leavenworth, Kans., 1985).

Zedric, Lance. "Prelude to Victory: The Alamo Scouts," *Army* (July 1994).

Kevin Dougherty

SEE ALSO Office of Strategic Services, Detachment 101

Aleutian Islands Campaign

Although considered by many to be an insignificant sideshow in the Pacific war, military operations in the Aleutian Islands from June 1942 into August 1943 significantly influenced events in World War II. The Aleutian Islands chain reaches over 1,100 miles into the North Pacific from the Alaska mainland. Only 650 miles from the Japanese Kurile Islands, the end of the Aleutians offered an inviting invasion route both westward into

northern Japan and eastward into Alaska. From Alaska, Seattle and its bomber plants could be reached by long-range Japanese aircraft, and Japanese planners took great interest in controlling the islands after U.S. bombers attacked Tokyo in the April 1942 Doolittle raid. Some imperial military planners even thought that the raid originated from a secret base in the Aleutians.

Under a plan created by Admiral Isoroku Yamamoto, Japanese naval and army units sought to capture strategic islands in the Aleutian chain along with Midway Island on the western end of the Hawaiian chain. These islands would provide bases for Japan's defense of the northern and central Pacific. Yamamoto also planned to use the islands as bait to draw out and destroy the U.S. Pacific Fleet. He believed that he could annihilate the American forces by a surprise attack when they sailed from Pearl Harbor in reaction to a diversionary attack in the Aleutians.

As part of this plan, Vice Admiral Boshiro Hosogaya sailed from Japan with two carriers (*Junyo* and *Ryujo*), three heavy cruisers, twelve destroyers, and several troop transports loaded with soldiers to occupy Adak, Attu, and Kiska Islands in the Aleutians. He was also to conduct air attacks on the U.S. bases around Dutch Harbor on Unalaska Island. On June 3–4 Hosogaya struck installations around Dutch Harbor with carrier aircraft. The sudden appearance of U.S. fighter planes and intense antiaircraft defenses surprised the Japanese pilots, who expected little resistance; but this was to be no Pearl Harbor.

The United States, for once with some foresight, had begun preparing defenses in Alaska in 1939. Construction on naval installations at Dutch Harbor and on Kodiak Island began that year. In 1940 Colonel (later Lieutenant General) Simon Bolivar Buckner Jr. took command of army defenses in the Alaska region. He aggressively built airfields and expanded fortifications with any means at his disposal. As a result of his efforts several P-40 fighters and a few B-17s and LB-30s (radar-equipped export versions of the B-24) replaced the obsolescent P-26s (!) and B-18s of Alaska's Eleventh Air Force. Buckner also provided installations with additional antiaircraft batteries. U.S. intelligence read Japan's naval messages. Thus the Americans were on alert when Hosogaya began his attacks.

To prepare for the Japanese assault, Admiral Chester W. Nimitz, commander of the central and northern Pacific, placed Rear Admiral Robert A. Theobald in command of Alaska's naval and air defenses. Nimitz split his meager forces and placed Task Force 8—consisting of five cruisers, fourteen destroyers, six submarines, and auxiliaries—under Theobald's command. Theobald established his headquarters on Kodiak Island but, far from the action, refused to confront the Japanese until their two carriers had been put out of action. His reluctance and Buckner's aggressiveness caused conflict in U.S. operations until Theobald was relieved of command in January 1943.

After Yamamoto's defeat at Midway, he ordered Hosogaya to continue with landings in the Aleutian chain. On June 6–7, 1942, Japanese troops occupied Kiska and Attu. An American teacher, Charles F. Jones, was the only casualty of the landings; he died of wounds sustained while trying to escape the invading soldiers. Japanese leaders believed that after the Midway debacle a success in the Aleutians would boost Japanese morale. (In retrospect, Hosogaya's presence at Midway might have changed the outcome of that battle.) Occupation of the Aleutians would also prevent a U.S. invasion of the Kurile Islands of northern Japan. Additionally, the islands could provide forward bases to move toward the Alaskan mainland or into the Soviet Union's maritime provinces. Japan's military strategists never really considered either of these options and for fourteen months attempted only to maintain a hold on Kiska and Attu.

For both sides weather was the worst impediment to operations in the region. Dense fog, sleet, snow, and sudden storms with violent winds and high seas constantly plagued any stratagem. Airmen searched vainly for enemy shipping over the vast North Pacific, while naval commanders hid in the fog and storm fronts and groped for the contact that would lead to a decisive engagement and rid the seas of their adversaries. In this contest U.S. ships and bombers enjoyed an advantage because some were equipped with radar, but it was not foolproof. On several occasions both aircraft and warships attacked islands that radar operators mistakenly thought to be enemy vessels.

Only by superhuman efforts could the weather and terrain be conquered. The islands consisted of volcanic ash covered with muskeg that moved under foot. If a vehicle broke through the surface crust, it became hopelessly mired. Only tracked vehicles traversed the cold morasses of the islands, and these did so with difficulty. To add to the misery sudden storms called "williwaws" blasted the region with winds strong enough to crash aircraft and beach small ships.

Japanese, U.S., and Canadian soldiers created construction miracles during the campaign. U.S. and Canadian troops had the advantage of heavy construction equipment, and through heroic efforts they achieved astounding results. From March to November 1942 they completed over seventeen hundred miles of the Alaskan Highway—from Dawson Creek, Canada, to Fairbanks,

Alaska. The road provided a protected supply line to Alaska from the lower United States.

On August 30, 1942, U.S. troops landed on Adak, and within two weeks bombers flew off a hastily constructed airfield there to attack Japanese forces farther west in the Aleutians. Several battalions of African American and Mexican American engineers labored on the road and airfields. These troops, unaccustomed to the intense cold, suffered terribly but never faltered.

From August 1942 until May 1943 both the Japanese and the Americans continued slowly to build up forces along the Aleutian chain. Efforts of both sides received low priorities as operations in the Solomon Islands took precedence. Japan did, however, manage to send over eight thousand men to reinforce its Aleutian garrisons. It also sent several float planes. The Nakajima Rufe proved equal to most Allied fighters and succeeded in blunting bombing attacks, until the Rufes were lost in combat.

In mid-January 1943 Vice Admiral Thomas C. Kinkaid replaced Theobald. He moved immediately to attack Japanese forces. Under his direction, more forward air bases were built, and additional naval forces arrived to support planned landings on the Japanese-held islands. Both Kinkaid and Buckner requested additional land forces to conduct landings on Kiska. The army provided the 7th Infantry Division. This unit, trained as a motorized division destined for North Africa, required amphibious training and new equipment for cold-weather combat. Unfortunately, planners on Kodiak Island did not realize the extremes of cold and wet weather in the Aleutians. As a result many soldiers entered combat improperly equipped. Hundreds of men went into the harsh climate wearing only field jackets and leather combat boots. Hundreds suffered trench foot and other cold-weather injuries, reducing the division's combat effectiveness. Japan also tried to strengthen its hold in the Aleutians by sending more troops and equipment into the theater, but submarines and smaller ships were unable to elude U.S. blockaders, and supplies slowed to a trickle. Hosogaya decided that a bold move with large forces could break the blockade. He assembled a force of two heavy cruisers, two light cruisers, several destroyers, and a convoy of armed transports to sail to Kiska. On March 26 U.S. naval forces commanded by Rear Admiral Charles Horatio McMorris intercepted this task force in what became known as the Battle of the Komandorski Islands.

With only heavy cruiser *Salt Lake City*, light cruiser *Richmond*, and four destroyers, McMorris's force was heavily outnumbered. Engaging in World War II's largest day surface action without aircraft participation, McMorris's brilliant retiring action, utilizing a smoke screen, frustrated Japanese hopes of major reinforcement. Their tenacity and threat of land-based bombers caused Hosogaya to return to the Kurile Islands—despite the fact that *Salt Lake City,* through an engine-room misadventure, went dead in the water for a short period.

Initially, Kinkaid planned to recapture Kiska and then move on to Attu. Updated intelligence indicated that the Japanese had over six thousand troops on Kiska. Attention then shifted to Attu, where the Americans thought there were only five hundred enemy soldiers. After some scrutiny of the island, however, estimates tripled. Nonetheless, with the forces available, Kinkaid and Buckner believed they could retake the island in three days. By occupying Attu at the end of the chain, they would cut off Kiska from Japan, easing its capture after the defenders ran out of supplies.

To support the invasion, Kinkaid received additional naval support. No fewer than three battleships—*Nevada, Pennsylvania,* and *Idaho* (the first two, survivors of Pearl Harbor)—along with escort carrier *Nassau* arrived, commanded by Vice Admiral Francis W. "Skinny" Rockwell. Kinkaid immediately ordered this heavy naval force and the Eleventh Air Force to begin concentrated attacks on both Kiska and Attu to soften up Japanese defenses. During a naval bombardment of Attu, American sailors reported several torpedo wakes. When cautioned of the danger to his battleships, Rockwell quipped, "Screw the torpedoes. Slow speed ahead!"

U.S. strategists developed five plans for the invasion of Attu, and on May 11, 1943, elements of Major General Arthur Brown's 7th Division landed on the island. Two major landings occurred on the north and south shorelines of the island, along with two supplementary landings on other parts of the island. The major invasion force landed on the south beach in Massacre Bay, a name which undoubtedly did little to raise U.S. troop morale. Colonel Edward P. Earle commanded the latter force, which consisted of two battalions of the 17th Infantry Regiment and another of the 32d Infantry Regiment. These units were supported by three batteries of 105-mm artillery and other auxiliary troops. Earle's mission required his units to drive up Massacre Valley along both sides of a hogback ridge and to link up with the northern landing force on the high ground near the center of the island. From there both forces would attack down the passes toward the main Japanese installations around Chichagof Harbor. Because of inclement weather this force did not land until 1620—several hours later than planned. The men struggled up the frozen, snow-clad hills until 1900, when they came under intense Japanese fire that pinned them down in the rocky terrain.

Lieutenant Colonel Albert V. Hartl commanded the small invasion force which landed on the north side of the island. His command comprised one battalion of the 17th Infantry Regiment, reinforced by a battery of artillery and support troops. These units landed to the west of Holtz Bay, intending to take a dominant terrain feature called Hill X and then to advance to the interior to meet the southern force. A provisional battalion consisting of the 7th Scout Company and a reconnaissance platoon landed farther east to add additional strength to the northern forces' drive inland. Although his men had to scale a 250-foot cliff and came under fire from Japanese 75-mm dual-purpose guns, Hartl moved quickly to capture his objective. A fierce Japanese nighttime counterattack failed to dislodge the Americans from Hill X.

The defenders took every advantage of terrain afforded them. Their commander, Colonel Yasuyo Yamasaki, used his time on the island to construct mutually supporting automatic weapons positions that covered the major approaches into Holtz Bay and Chichagof Harbor. Japanese troops also found the weather to their advantage. Ice-covered slopes and thick fog made any rapid American movement impossible. The fog shrouded the high ridges, obscuring the Japanese but allowing them to observe their aggressors. As a result of determined resistance, weather, and terrain, U.S. commanders found that the battle for Attu demanded much more effort than they planned.

Skillfully placed mortar and artillery positions exacerbated the Americans' difficulties and forced them to commit their reserve, including Buckner's tough 4th Infantry Regiment from Alaska. GIs required five days of intense combat to link up near the enemy's positions on Holtz Bay. Because of the slow progress, poor communications, and a misconception of actual circumstances, on March 16 Kinkaid replaced Brown with Major General Eugene M. Landrum, who assumed command just as American attacks forced Japanese soldiers to withdraw toward Chichagof Harbor. Several more days of brutal fighting were required to secure Attu, however.

As American soldiers forced the Japanese into a smaller perimeter, Yamasaki decided on a bold venture. On the night of June 29 he assembled between 750 and 1,000 of his remaining soldiers and prepared for a last-ditch banzai charge. If the attack went well, his men could break through the U.S. lines into supply areas and artillery positions. Yamasaki did not believe he could hold Attu, but he intended to inflict maximum casualties on the enemy. He silently moved his force toward the entrenched U.S. troops.

When the screaming Japanese soldiers attacked, their main thrust hit a company that was being pulled off the line for a hot meal. As a result the banzai charge broke into the American rear areas and had to be stopped by engineers, artillerymen, and service troops. The heavy casualties suffered by Japanese troops in this attack virtually ended the battle for the island. On June 30 Japan announced the loss of Attu. Americans counted over 2,300 Japanese dead and estimated the total at more than 2,500. Only twenty-nine prisoners were captured. To avoid surrender as many as five hundred Japanese committed suicide. Out of a U.S. force totaling about 15,000, 549 were killed; 1,148 were wounded; and over 2,100 suffered from cold-weather injuries. Attu cost the United States the second-highest casualty ratio of the Pacific war.

Because of the landing difficulties on Attu, U.S. commanders conducted intensive amphibious training and planned for a coordinated attack on Kiska. However, intelligence reports in early August indicated that few enemy troops remained there. Admiral Kinkaid decided to continue with the invasion. If the Japanese were gone, the landings would be an excellent training exercise. On August 15, 1943, U.S. and Canadian troops stormed ashore on Kiska and indeed met no resistance. For three days they vainly searched for the enemy. Later it was learned that on July 28 Vice Admiral Shiro Kawase had sent a surface fleet to Kiska and, in less than an hour, under cover of a fog-laden sea, had evacuated almost six thousand men. Embarrassment proved to be the smallest calamity of the landing. Mines, booby traps, and friendly fire on Kiska killed or wounded no fewer than 313 Allied troops.

The campaign to recapture the Aleutian Islands had served several purposes. The islands provided bases from which to bomb the northern islands of Japan. This threat forced the Japanese to keep one-sixth of their fighter aircraft on the Kuriles to protect the home islands—aircraft that could have been better used elsewhere. Because of Japan's Aleutian requirements Allied landings at Rendova resulted in light Allied casualties. In addition to the psychological advantage of sweeping the enemy from U.S.-held territory, the Allied presence in the Aleutians protected the neutral Soviet Union's maritime provinces and the Kamchatka Peninsula. Additionally, Japan no longer threatened the Lend-Lease route through Alaska to the Soviets.

Operations in the Aleutians also provided the Allies with several tactical lessons. A Zero fighter, captured virtually intact, gave U.S. flyers insight into the enemy plane's capabilities, although it is a myth that the U.S. Hellcat was based on secrets discovered from this Zero. The several landings tested new amphibious landing techniques and equipment. Marine Corps Major General Holland M. "Howlin' Mad" Smith participated as a trainer and observer during the landings and was later able to apply knowledge gained at Tarawa and Iwo Jima. The Eleventh Air Force began adapting techniques for radar bombing and forward air control that other air force units adopted and employed in both Europe and the Pacific. For a "sideshow," the Aleutians afforded valuable contributions to the Allied military war effort.

FURTHER READINGS

Conn, S., R. Engelman, and B. Fairchild. *Guarding the United States and Its Outposts* (1964).

Morison, Samuel Eliot. *Aleutians, Gilberts, and Marshalls, June 1942–April 1944* (1964).

Craven, Wesley F., and James L. Cate, eds. *The Pacific: Guadalcanal to Saipan, August 1942 to July 1944* (1950).

"The Capture of Attu as Told by the Men Who Fought There." *Infantry Journal* eds. (1944).

Garfield, Brian Garfield. *The Thousand-Mile War: World War II in Alaska and the Aleutians* (1969).

Carter, Worrall Reed. *Beans, Bullets, and Black Oil* (1952).

Stanley S. McGowen

Americal Division

The Americal Division, an infantry division of the U.S. Army, and the Philippine Division were the only such units never to have had a numerical designation. The Americal was formed from the units assigned to Task Force 6814, which had arrived on New Caledonia on March 12, 1942, and had then garrisoned and defended both New Caledonia and the New Hebrides Islands. The division was activated on May 27, 1942, and included the 132d Infantry Regiment (Illinois National Guard), the 164th Infantry Regiment (North Dakota National Guard), and the 182d Infantry Regiment (Massachusetts National Guard). Because U.S. troops had received such a warm welcome in New Caledonia, the new division was named Americal (*America-Cale*donia), in honor of the island.

The division first saw combat as the 164th Infantry arrived at Guadalcanal under Japanese air attack on October 13, 1942. The 164th Infantry defended Henderson Field against a major Japanese counterattack on October 24 and was then joined on Guadalcanal by the 182d Infantry on November 12. The divisional headquarters and the 132d Infantry reached Guadalcanal on December 8, 1942. The division was heavily engaged from its arrival until January 9, 1943, when it was relieved by the 25th Infantry Division.

The American Division was then moved by echelon to the Fiji Islands between March 1 and April 10, 1943. In the Fiji Islands, the division was reorganized and reequipped—several units which were originally part of Task Force 6814 were disbanded or reassigned, while other new units were now attached to or integrated into the division. The division was then moved again by echelon to Bougainville Island between December 17, 1943, and January 12, 1944. Beginning on January 2, portions of the division were engaged in combat, even before the remainder of the division had arrived. The American was engaged in almost continuous combat from January 2 until December 10, 1944, when the division was relieved by the Australian 3d Infantry Division.

Between December 11, 1944, and January 7, 1945, the American Division conducted amphibious warfare training and prepared for movement to the Philippine Islands. The division was moved by echelon to the Philippines between December 8 and 28, 1945. In the Philippines, the division relieved the 77th Infantry Division on Leyte Island. The 132d and 164th Infantry Regiments conducted operations on Leyte between February 5 and March 10, 1945, when they finished the encirclement and mopping up of Japanese forces on the island. At the same time, the 1st Battalion, 182d Infantry, assaulted Samar Island on February 19, 1945, while the remainder of the regiment assaulted Biri Island on February 20. The 1st Battalion, 132d Infantry, assaulted Burias and Ticao Islands on March 3 and had eliminated Japanese forces by March 10. The 132d and 182d Infantry Regiments then assaulted Cebu Island on March 26. These regiments were joined by the 1st and 2d Battalions, 164th Infantry, which arrived at Cebu on April 10. Meanwhile; the 3d Battalion, 164th Infantry, assaulted Bohol Island on April 11 and had eliminated Japanese resistance by April 25. The entire 164th Infantry Regiment then assaulted Negros Occidental on April 26, 1945, and had eliminated Japanese resistance by June 12. The division was then reassembled on Cebu Island and was engaged in training for the projected invasion of the Japanese home islands from June 21, 1945, until the end of the war.

The American Division had five different commanders during World War II. The division's first commander was Major General Alexander M. Patch (USMA 1913), who commanded the division from May 1942 to December 1942, when he became commander of the III Corps. The division's second commander was Brigadier General Edmund B. Sebree (USMA 1917), who had served as the assistant division commander from May 1942 to Decem-

ber 1942 and then commanded the division from January 1943 to April 1943. Sebree then became the assistant division commander of first the 35th Infantry Division and then the 28th Infantry Division for the remainder of the war. The division's third commander was Major General John R. Hodge, who had served as the assistant division commander of the 25th Infantry Division from June 1942 to April 1943. Hodge commanded the American Division from May 1943 to March 1944, after which he commanded the XXIV Corps, and in 1945 he became military governor of South Korea. The division's fourth commander was Major General Robert B. McClure (ex-USNA 1920), who commanded the division from April 1944 to October 1944, when he became the chief of staff of U.S. Forces in the China theater. The division's last wartime commander was Major General William H. Arnold (USMA 1924), who served as the chief of staff of the XIV Corps from April 1943 to November 1944. Arnold then commanded the American Division from November 1944 until the end of the war.

During World War II, the American Division lost 981 men killed in action; another 3,052 were wounded in action, and 176 died of wounds. The division's campaign streamers include Guadalcanal, Northern Solomons, Leyte, and Southern Philippines (with arrowhead). The division was awarded a Presidential Unit Citation (Navy) for its service on Guadalcanal and a Philippine Presidential Unit Citation for service in the Philippines. When the division was reactivated for service in Vietnam on September 25, 1967, it was redesignated the 23d Infantry Division (Americal).

FURTHER READINGS

Cronin, Francis D. *Under the Southern Cross: The Saga of the Americal Division* (1951).

Eichelberger, Robert L., and Milton MacKaye. *Our Jungle Road to Tokyo* (1950).

Krueger, Walter. *From Down Under to Nippon: The Story of the Sixth Army in World War II* (1953).

Stanton, Shelby L. *Order of Battle: U.S. Army, World War II* (1984).

Wilson, John B., ed. *Armies, Corps, Divisions, and Separate Brigades* (1987).

Alexander M. Bielakowski and James H. Willbanks

SEE ALSO Army Ground Forces, U.S.; Island-Hopping and Leapfrogging, U.S. Strategies

American Volunteer Group

Few military units have captured the attention of the U.S. public as did the American Volunteer Group (AVG), better known to admirers as the Flying Tigers. Brought together by maverick fighter-aircraft aviator Claire Chennault, AVG pilots challenged Japanese dominance of the skies over China and Burma in 1941–1942. Though operational as a combat unit for less than a year, the Flying Tigers gave hope to the beleaguered Chinese and provided Americans with a sense of heroic accomplishment during a period in which defeats far outnumbered victories in the Pacific theater. Before disbandment in summer 1942 and absorption by the U.S. Army Air Forces, the AVG accounted for the destruction of nearly three hundred Japanese aircraft.

The AVG owed its genesis to two individuals: Chiang Kai-shek, president of Nationalist China, and Claire Chennault, an Army Air Corps officer who had retired from U.S. service in spring 1937. Chennault had a well-established reputation for challenging orthodox opinion about aerial strategy when he accepted an offer from Chiang's government to conduct a survey of the Chinese air force in April 1937. Chennault arrived in China as the Sino-Japanese War was turning into a major conflict and, because of U.S. neutrality laws, was officially employed by T. V. Soong's Bank of China. Soong was among the most influential of the familial clique that governed China, and he was brother to Madame Chiang, the president's wife. Like many Americans, Chennault was drawn to the eloquent and graceful Madame Chiang, whose persuasive abilities were rapidly becoming a significant factor in Sino-U.S. relations.

Arriving at Nanking, Chennault quickly realized that the Chinese air force existed in name only. China had no air force whatsoever until the early 1930s, when Japanese aggression in Manchuria and Shanghai drove Chinese officials to approach the United States about organizing such a force. A group under Colonel John. H. Jouett spent about two years attempting to create a rudimentary Chinese air arm, but the effort was ultimately deterred by obsolete equipment, graft, and corruption. The mission succeeded, however, in training several hundred Chinese pilots, and in the mid-1930s this foundation was built up by an Italian mission headed by Count Galeazzo Ciano, son-in-law of Italian dictator Benito Mussolini. The Italians proceeded to organize a flying school and sold the Chinese government millions of dollars worth of obsolete aircraft. Bowing to Chinese social conventions, Italian instructors graduated any Chinese student-pilot who survived flight training, to avoid causing any loss of face. To make matters worse, the Italians perpetuated a phantom air force by keeping on the active roster even aircraft that had crashed. This was the hollow force that Chennault inherited.

In July 1937, as China went to war with Japan, Chennault offered Chiang his services and was directed to take charge of combat training for Chinese aviators. Chennault quickly judged the Italian-trained pilots as incompetent and impossible to deal with. The Chinese pilots rejected training flights and practice missions, seeing them as a challenge to their competency. Western concepts of an ongoing regimen of training and proficiency exercises were rejected out of hand. The consequences were predictable; within months, China's ill-equipped and poorly disciplined air force was virtually nonexistent, the victim of accidents and crashes as much as of Japanese air power. Although the Chinese pilots scored some successes against Japanese bombers flying against undefended Chinese cities, they were too few in number to affect the direction of air war. An effort to form an "international squadron" comprising U.S. and European flight leaders foundered when most of Chinese aircraft were destroyed in Japanese air raids. However, the worsening circumstances of the European war in spring 1940 afforded Chiang's government an opportunity to press the United States for direct aid; out of these circumstances the AVG was born.

In fall 1940 Chennault journeyed to Washington, D.C., to help Soong press a Chinese request for more than five hundred aircraft—the majority of which were to be fighters—from the Roosevelt administration. Soong also hoped to convince Secretary of the Treasury Henry Morgenthau to include a number of B-17 bombers, which, it was proposed, could be used to reduce Japan's cities to ashes—a good example of the utopian dreams of prewar airpower theorists. (If the Japanese had been unable to burn undefended Chinese cities like Chungking to the ground, what basis was there for believing that Japanese cities, on the other hand, could be devastated by a few B-17s?) The bomber request foundered on the doubts of General George C. Marshall and Secretary of War Henry Stimson. Considering the problems in training Chinese fighter pilots, the obstacles to assembling competent four-engine bomber crews beggared description; the best that Chiang's government might hope for immediately was a mere one hundred fighter aircraft. This agreement was reached, and Soong next pressed for U.S. volunteer pilots. By spring 1941 the "special air unit" was being recruited by the Central Aircraft Manufacturing Company (CAMCO), which had been responsible for assembling much of the Chinese air force to that date. CAMCO ultimately enlisted 100 pilots, all detached for duty from the U.S. Navy, Marine Corp, or Army. Most were offered monthly pay of $600 and vague hints of $500 bonuses for each downed Japanese aircraft. About two hundred ground personnel were also hired, and by summer both groups were literally on a slow boat to China.

The first training base utilized by the special air unit was actually at Kyedaw airfield in southern Burma—most of China being unsecured. The base, leased from the British, was a depressing nightmare of ramshackle huts, mud, and legions of repulsive tropical insects. Nonetheless, the American Volunteer Group—officially designated as such by Chiang on August 1, 1941—proceeded to get organized. Among the first tasks was the assembly of the group's primary fighter aircraft, the Curtiss P-40 Tomahawk (British designation). Designed for infantry support and coastal defense, the sleek, low-winged fighter was powered by a 1,000-hp in-line (liquid-cooled) General Motors Allison engine and was built for toughness rather than maneuverability. Given the absence of a supercharger the plane performed best at altitudes under 20,000 feet. Against Japan's most formidable fighter, the Mitsubishi A6M Zero, the P-40's main disadvantage was in turning. Distinct advantages, however, were the Tomahawk's pilot armor and self-sealing fuel tanks. Added to the plane's durability and rapid acceleration in a dive, these factors made the U.S. craft a viable if not superior opponent of the Zero. As Chennault set about readying aircraft and pilots for action, members of the AVG busied themselves establishing a collective reputation for being undisciplined. Individuals like Greg "Pappy" Boyington contributed greatly to the rapidly spreading tales of brawling, drinking, womanizing, and general hell-raising that would follow the AVG throughout its existence.

The months before outbreak of war in December 1941 were trying in a variety of ways. Assembly and organization of the squadron proceeded in fits and starts. Training and ferry flights produced several accidents, costly in terms of both aircraft and pilots. Assembling and adequately equipping the aircraft brought constant frustration. The squadron lacked such basic items as aviator sunglasses and proper gun sights. Chennault aide Joseph Alsop once visited Rangoon with a supply list of over one thousand different items needed by the AVG. Morale was the obvious casualty of such circumstances, and even as the final contingent of pilots arrived in late November the men were anxious to be done with preliminaries. The same month, Chennault won approval for the creation of the 2d American Volunteer Group, a bomber unit which, it was hoped, would be capable of carrying the air offensive to the Japanese. Authorization for a third group of fighters was also gained, along with commitment of the necessary aircraft. Chennault's ceaseless campaign for airpower in south Asia culminated with the release of a flood of badly needed supplies that same month.

The outbreak of war in early December 1941 found the AVG approaching readiness with a roster of eighty airmen. Chennault's pilots were soon left to their own devices as the U.S. position in the Pacific deteriorated. Wartime exigencies brought about a redeployment of the group, with the first thought being to defend the increasingly important Burma Road. With their P-40 nose cones now bearing the soon-to-be-famous shark's mouth (an affectation copied from a photo of Australian-flown Tomahawks in North Africa), one squadron was sent to Rangoon, while remaining forces moved to Kunming (China). First blood was drawn on December 20 as the air warning net reported ten Japanese bombers flying out of Indochina over Yunnan province, with Kunming as the likely target. The sixteen P-40s of 1st Squadron which rose to meet the Japanese raiders accounted for four of the surprised bombers in the course of a wild aerial melee. The returning AVG pilots were greeted at Wu Chia Ba airfield by a crowd of thousands of grateful Chinese.

The events of that day prefigured the reputation that the AVG would soon gain at home: outnumbered but courageous U.S. pilots flying against a cruel enemy in defense of helpless Chinese. Even as the AVG's first wartime exploits made the pages of *Time* magazine, the genesis of the Flying Tiger name and symbol was proceeding apace. The AVG's Washington support staff had initially approached Walt Disney studios with a request to design a flying-dragon emblem, not knowing that the AVG pilots had already adopted a shark's face as its group insignia. Adding to the confusion were concerns about whether dragons and tigers were omens of good or ill in Chinese and Japanese symbolism. Though the origins of the Flying Tiger are somewhat uncertain, a compelling anecdote has T. V. Soong rejecting the dragon as being a symbol of archaic China and recalling a proverb about "giving wings to the tiger." Whatever its origin, the Flying Tiger shark/tiger insignia—ably stylized by the Disney studio—rapidly gained national and international recognition as a symbol of determination and courage against unfavorable odds. In 1942, Hollywood immortalized the emblem and the AVG in the film *The Flying Tigers,* starring, of course, John Wayne.

Between December 1941 and July 1942, the AVG doggedly confronted a numerically superior enemy, dwindling supplies, and an increasingly precarious Allied position in Asia. Despite these obstacles, the accomplishments of the group were not insignificant. On February 25, 1942, a Japanese bomber force of 166 aircraft attacking Rangoon was opposed by a mere nine P-40s whose pilots succeeded in knocking down twenty-four Japanese aircraft with a loss of only three AVG fighters. When 200

Japanese bombers attacked the following day, nineteen of the raiders fell, with no loss to the AVG. However, the success of the AVG was always at least partly contingent on the course of the ground war, which went distinctly in Japan's favor during the first half of 1942. As much as the AVG pilots might harass Japanese airfields and interdict Japanese bombers, they could not stem the Imperial Japanese Army's momentum toward Burma. Further, Royal Air Force commanders in Burma refused to adopt Chennault's tactics even though their Hawker Hurricanes were in significant ways superior to the P-40s (after all, what could the Americans teach the victors of the Battle of Britain?), and so they were shot out of the sky. Rangoon's fall on March 7 forced Chennault to withdraw his forces to China, from where the Flying Tigers could continue their aerial defense of western Chinese cities, conduct raids into Japanese-held Burma, and offer air cover to convoys attempting to travel the Burma Road.

Whatever its successes, the AVG was ultimately an organizational anomaly, a product of an era in which a non-belligerent United States hoped to stem the Japanese tide in China by fighting a limited proxy war. Chennault's Flying Tigers were bound to fall victim to the strategic and command struggles that a more formal conflict brought. Consequently, Chennault announced to his men that on July 4, 1942, the AVG would be disbanded and absorbed into a regular Army Air Forces unit. Though there was some disillusionment over the terms of induction, many pilots and technicians made the transition into the 23d Fighter Group, part of the China Air Task Force and thus still something of an anomaly. While Chennault retained immediate command, he was made subordinate to both USAAF General Clayton Bissell and U.S. Army General "Vinegar" Joe Stilwell, both of whom disapproved of Chennault's strategies for the Asian air war. The now-defunct AVG left behind an impressive record. Though historians and official records differ somewhat about its record, the unit appears to have destroyed about 299 enemy aircraft, with claims to 153 probables. Only four AVG pilots were killed in aerial combat; the other twenty-one pilot deaths occurred as a result of accidents or ground fire. On the other hand, one historian credits the AVG with inflicting about four hundred combat casualties on Japanese forces, at a cost of eighty-six aircraft to all causes. Historians still debate the ultimate contribution of the AVG to the Allied cause in the China-Burma-India theater. At the very least, the Flying Tigers successfully challenged theretofore uncontested Japanese air power over south Asia, slowed the Japanese advance, and gave heart to both beleaguered Chinese and victory-starved Americans at a very grim point in the Pacific war.

FURTHER READINGS
Chennault, Anna. *Chennault and the Flying Tigers* (1963).
Ford, Daniel. *Flying Tigers: Claire Chennault and the American Volunteer Group* (1991).
Schultz, Duane. *The Maverick War: Chennault and the Flying Tigers* (1987).
Toland, John. *The Flying Tigers* (1963).
Tuchman, Barbara. *Stilwell and the American Experience in China, 1911–1945* (1971).

Blaine T. Browne

SEE ALSO Aircraft, Japanese, U.S., and British; Army Air Corps/Air Forces, U.S.; Chiang Kai-shek; Chennault, Claire Lee; Chinese Communists versus Nationalists

Amphibious Operations

Amphibious operations generally refers to the seaborne transport of troops for their insertion onto a hostile land objective. The particular shore for landing may or may not be defended by enemy positions. However, if troops are landed under direct enemy fire, that action is more commonly referred to as an *amphibious assault*. In sum, not all amphibious operations require an amphibious assault, but all such assaults fall under the general description of amphibious operations.

For example, U.S. strategy during the Pacific war had forces under General MacArthur moving offensively by late 1942 into the southwest Pacific sector to secure lines of communication to Australia. This area contained sufficiently large landmasses to allow for options when deciding on landing areas. With this capability, commanders were able to put forces ashore in regions less heavily defended. Hence, amphibious operations were conducted where assaults were not always required. In contrast, the central Pacific area was a great expanse of ocean dotted with relatively small islands and atolls. When Pacific Fleet and U.S. Army units attacked under Admiral Nimitz in this area, the targets were usually small, heavily defended, and awaiting attack. In consequence, amphibious operations in the central Pacific campaign were nearly always amphibious assaults.

Inasmuch as the United States and its Allies were conducting operations in the wide expanses of the Pacific Ocean and generally were involved with the transport of troops to eject Japanese soldiers from defensive positions, particularly by late 1942 to the late summer of 1945 nearly every campaign during the Pacific war had amphibious operations characteristics.

The United States had been developing its amphibious doctrine since the early 1920s. Two events (one in 1920 and one during 1921–1922) motivated the U.S. Marine Corps to carefully study amphibious operations. On October 1, 1920, the U.S. Office of Naval Intelligence published a confidential document compiling the combined thinking of a group of officers then attached to the Plans Division, Office of Naval Operations. The report, "The Conduct of an Overseas Naval Campaign," stipulated that in the case of a war between two maritime nations located at opposite ends of an ocean, a strategy aimed only at attacking each other's ships and commerce would prove indecisive. The analysis went on to state that in order to exert decisive pressure on a nation, it had usually been necessary to occupy important sectors of territory and to defeat armed forces. Based on this supposition, the paper concluded that in every war between two naval powers separated by an ocean, one of the two nations must, if decisive pressure is to be exerted, prosecute an overseas naval campaign and be prepared to transport and land troops to force a capitulation.

The second factor providing motivation for the evolution of amphibious doctrine was the Washington Conference of 1921–1922, which ensured the Japanese navy a chance to expand its power in Far East waters by setting an arms control ratio on the building of naval vessels in the United States and Great Britain. Based on these two intersecting events, for the two decades preceding World War II the U.S. Marine Corps transformed itself from fleet sentry duty to a specialization in amphibious operations and assault. Further, the corps was ready in 1940 with a cadre of officers well versed in the strategy and tactics and the geography of the Pacific area. At the outset of hostilities they were able immediately to move to training army troops in amphibious operations.

Moving soldiers by water and inserting them ashore for military operations had been conducted for centuries. The objective of these maneuvers, however, had been to avoid well-defended beaches and shoreline and simply to ferry land forces to disembark, form up, and engage the enemy in land operations away from the water. U.S. Marine Corps doctrine transcended the ferry approach and conceived of an amphibious operations and assault as a ship-to-shore tactical movement. This basic doctrine was set forth by the marines in 1934 and was officially accepted by the navy in 1938.

One week after the German army invaded Poland in September 1939, U.S. President Franklin D. Roosevelt declared a limited national emergency, and included in the proceeding measures were directions to the Navy Department to accelerate the mobilization, organization, equipping, and training of amphibious forces. At this time the total strength of the Fleet Marine Force, the amphibious warriors, was 4,525 officers and men. This number was doubled in 1940 and tripled in 1941. By the summer of 1942, two army infantry divisions and two marine divisions had been trained and were combat-ready for amphibious operations. As early as the summer of 1941, the 2d and 3d Marine Battalions had been deployed to Samoa in the Pacific.

The reinforced marine division which formed the core of landing-force organization, particularly in central Pacific operations, consisted of three regimental combat teams (RCTs), each containing three battalion landing teams (BLTs). Each infantry battalion was reinforced with artillery, tank, engineer, and service units. The choice of equipment for amphibious operations was based on the mission assigned and the particular capability of the transports.

The marines had developed the technique of unit combat loading, which stipulated that amphibious forces tailor their weapons and tactical units to fit aboard ship. This technique included the planned stowage of equipment and supplies in accordance with the anticipated situation ashore, given the critical necessity of speed in unloading in the sequence needed. Materiel needed immediately was loaded last. U.S. amphibious forces were constantly reviewing and redesigning characteristics of transport and landing craft. In terms of the tactical ship-to-shore movement, three distinctive pieces of equipment evolved and were widely deployed, particularly in the final months of the war.

The first wave of the movement to shore, particularly in assault actions, came to rely on the tracked amphibian (amphtrac) armored vehicle, which could drive out of the surf and take its occupants across the beach before debarking. The second wave utilized the larger "Higgins" beaching boat equipped with a front ramp that dropped, so that troops and equipment debarked at or near the shoreline. The third type of vehicle was the larger seagoing vessels that, in different variations, had the capacity to beach and land heavy armor, including tanks. These were landing ship tanks (LSTs), and by the end of the Pacific conflict the United States had produced more than one thousand. No other nation built such large landing ships. There were many variations on the three main landing platforms, and the U.S. Coast Guard manned many of the marine's landing craft.

In addition to the landing craft, large attack transports were developed on which landing troops and craft were embarked and which had the ability to match the speed of destroyers and carriers of an amphibious task force.

Amphibious operations command ships were also developed from which admirals and generals could jointly coordinate operations.

Beyond the large amphibious surface campaigns, the U.S. Navy also conducted smaller specialized operations during the Pacific war. For example, the 2d Marine Raider Battalion (225 officers and men) disembarked at 0300 hours on August 17, 1942, from the large submarines *Nautilus* and *Argonaut* and landed in rubber boats in an assault against Makin Island. The marines destroyed the Japanese garrison of 150 troops but suffered a 30 percent casualty rate. This action was the navy's first combat operation involving a submarine-borne landing force. By war's end the United States had conducted more than six hundred amphibious operations, ranging from small riverine operations to division-sized amphibious assaults.

In a large-scale surface amphibious operation the naval or joint attack force generally consisted of seven major components: a transport group, containing the assault transports and cargo vessels; a fire support group, consisting of ships deployed to deliver gunfire support to the landing force; an air group, encompassing the requirement for air superiority and close ground support and bombardment; a mine group, tasked with sweeping the transport and fire support areas; a screening group, charged with protecting vessels and craft engaged in the transport and landing of troops; a salvage group, responsible for the salvage and maintenance of small craft; and, finally, a landing force, organized as a self-sufficient and mobile combat strike force.

There were two prerequisites for a successful amphibious operation in the Pacific theater: (1) command of the sea and air around the objective and (2) secure sea lines of communication from rear bases into the zone of conflict. As the war progressed through 1942, U.S. forces increasingly commanded the sea and air in and around all amphibious operations. By late 1944, with the infusion of large numbers of new carriers from the United States, Pacific Fleet forces could attack and destroy any island or atoll target they chose. This sea and air superiority allowed Nimitz's central Pacific forces to conduct what became known as an "island-hopping" strategy, which recognized that certain Japanese island garrisons—after being cut off from their own sea lines of communication and without air or sea assets—were militarily useless and could be bypassed by U.S. forces in their march to Japan's home islands.

The U.S. Joint Chiefs of Staff had recognized that the quickest way to defeat Japan was to seize bases in the central Pacific from which Japanese sea and air power could be engaged decisively so that Japan's industrial capacity to make war could be bombarded and its overseas commerce strangled. To take these bases with the necessary conditions of air and sea superiority and secure sea lines of communication, the first requirement was to cripple the Japanese fleet and keep it on the defensive. After these conditions were achieved, the amphibious operations that aimed at seizing forward bases could be undertaken successfully. By the fall of 1943 a series of encounters with the U.S. Navy had seriously degraded the Japanese capability to interdict U.S. amphibious operations. With the U.S. victory at the Battle of Leyte Gulf the Imperial Japanese Navy ceased to possess the capability to fight a major naval action.

The amphibious tactics that were employed to carry out the strategic plan for defeating Japan and Germany were similar and were based on the navy-marine amphibious doctrine which had evolved in the two decades before the outbreak of World War II. By the end of the conflict all major combatant nations, except Russia, had adopted the basic U.S. amphibious doctrine. The difference in the two applications in the European and Pacific theaters was the landing on continents as opposed to atolls. In the Pacific there were also the two campaigns of MacArthur in the southwest and of Nimitz in the central Pacific. The southwest campaign was more similar to European amphibious operations; as stated earlier, the forces under Nimitz were largely involved with specialized amphibious assault.

In the central Pacific, the mission of gaining and holding command of the air and sea was primarily borne by navy surface warfare assets and carrier air power, while land-based air forces in the southwest sector played a substantial role in MacArthur's efforts. However, General MacArthur also relied on carriers to increase the range of his advances. These included operations at Hollandia in Dutch New Guinea and on Leyte and the Luzon Islands in the Philippines.

During the Pacific war amphibious warfare was conducted in a series of tactical stages, commonly referred to as the "pattern of attack," starting with aerial reconnaissance for the selection of an adequate landing area. The goals were the presence of beach terrain suitable for vehicular maneuverability, with as hard and flat a surface as possible, and tide conditions favorable to the attack. The ideal site would provide access inland and also be close to the operational objective. Reconnaissance methods improved throughout the war, but in the early stages the lack of sophistication proved costly to amphibious troops. On November 20, 1943, elements of the 2d Marine Division, 5th Amphibious Corps, U.S. Navy Fifth Fleet, assaulted Tarawa Atoll as part of Operation Galvanic in the Gilbert Islands. The assault force, particularly units with the assignment to capture Betio Island, suffered heavy casualties—more than a thousand dead and two thousand wounded during the three-day fight. A majority of the losses came in response to the need for the troops to cross 700 yards of shallows leading to the assigned beachheads. Although the first wave of amphtracs were able to get quickly to the beach, a large reef obstructed the ability of the standard flat-bottomed landing craft to negotiate successfully to shore. The marines exited the stalled craft and were forced to assault the beach under continuous machine-gun and artillery fire. Five hundred perished the first day. The following day LSTs landed tanks behind Japanese lines, and eventually U.S. forces secured the island.

Preceding landing-area selection and reconnaissance came the first bombardment, either by long-range ground-based air power or by carrier aircraft. After the amphibious task force had moved into place for the attack, a second bombardment took place, with surface ships joining the pounding of enemy defensive positions. The new *Iowa*-class battleships with their 16-inch guns were particularly well suited for ship-to-shore bombardment. Dive-bombers also proved to be effective in preassault bombardments, with their ability to hit targets on the shoreline with precision.

During these periods of preassault bombardment, covering operations by fleet units on many occasions involved naval actions to prevent intervention by Japan's fleet. These covering actions eventually took their toll on the Japanese navy. The many engagements during the Guadalcanal action, the Battle of the Philippine Sea, during amphibious operations at Saipan, and the Battle of Leyte Gulf were in large measure responsible for the destruction of Japan's fleet.

The preassault bombardment was a critical step in amphibious operations, and how well it achieved its objectives was closely linked to the number of casualties among the landing force. Late in the war, in operations against Iwo Jima, the original battle plan called for a ten-day preassault bombardment; instead it was conducted for only four days. With a substantial portion of Japan's emplacements still intact and operational, in February 1945 two marine divisions assaulted Iwo Jima. By the time the island was secured in March, 6,821 U.S. troops had been killed, and 20,000 were wounded. The Japanese fought nearly to the last man, and 21,000 soldiers died.

Before the actual launch of the invasion landing craft in an amphibious assault, the preassault bombardment rose to an intensity which came to be known as "Dog Day bombardment." At the target area, transports an-chored offshore and disembarked their troops and supplies in the landing craft, which were combat-loaded and allowed the carrying of small troop units intact to the beach or close to the shoreline. At a designated time these craft approached a line of departure parallel to the landing beaches, marked off by control vessels. The landing craft on signal then sprinted for the beach.

In a multiwave assault typical of most large Pacific theater operations, the first wave of assault infantry would be reinforced by an engineering complement to clear emplaced obstacles, including minefields. In many instances tanks were brought in to reinforce the first wave of infantry. The amphtrac, or armored vehicle capable of moving from the sea onto land, became the landing craft of choice for assault operations. Follow-on waves would insert artillery, equipment, and infantry reinforcements. A primary first objective was to land artillery at the earliest possible moment and open fire. In general, the initial objective was not the beach itself but a dry inland area, and then the seizure of the high ground surrounding the beach or shoreline itself. After this was achieved, the next stage was to provide for a quick buildup of supplies ashore and to transform the undertaking as quickly as possible from an amphibious operation to a land battle. The water and the beach were considered a no-man's land, because troops in these zones were most vulnerable to attack. As a result, commanders attempted to move their forces through these zones as quickly as circumstances allowed.

In large assaults, such as the massive operation at Okinawa, a division was assigned 1,500 yards of shoreline. Generally, individual beaches were assigned to separate and distinct commands. After troops were ashore, the ground offensive was scheduled to commence on or beyond the enemy's first defensive line. When the transformation from amphibious to land warfare was assured, there would be continued logistical and tactical support from the amphibious task force until the island or objective had been secured. The final phase involved garrison logistics and the development of a naval or air base.

The mutually supporting drives in the southwest and central sectors kept the Japanese operating in the Pacific theater at risk from two directions and from two types of threats: carrier- and land-based attack. When army and navy assault forces landed in the Mariannas at Saipan in June 1944 under Admiral Nimitz, Japan's home islands came within range of U.S. strategic bombers. In late 1944, B-29s began operations from Saipan against targets in Japan. In order to provide an emergency landing strip for these aircraft, an amphibious assault was conducted against Iwo Jima in February 1945. The difficulty in taking Saipan, and the high casualty rate, foretold the story of the last amphibious assault in the Pacific: Okinawa.

At Okinawa, the Japanese had over 100,000 soldiers prepared to defend against the coming attack. This force was the largest that the United States had faced in an amphibious assault during the Pacific war. The preassault bombardment at Okinawa lasted seven days and rained more than 30,000 heavy-caliber shells onto Japanese positions. The United States attacked the island with 81 battleships, 40 carriers, and 200 destroyers. A total of 1,800 ships were involved in the Okinawa assault. The first assault phase was conducted against the island without the expected substantial U.S. casualties. The ensuing fighting, however, was the bloodiest of the war. The United States suffered 12,000 dead and more than 30,000 wounded. Japan's casualties exceeded 100,000, with an enormous amount of loss of life among the civilian islanders.

In the summer of 1945, after Okinawa fell and before the atomic bomb was dropped on Hiroshima, six marine divisions were being prepared for the first assault on Japan's home islands at Kyushu and Honshu. This enterprise, the greatest amphibious assault of all time, was code-named Operation Olympic and was planned to be launched on November 1, 1945. Olympic was to be twice the size of the D-Day landings in Europe. But the unconditional surrender of Japan in August 1945 precluded the necessity of further amphibious Pacific war operations.

FURTHER READINGS

Barbey, Daniel E. *MacArthur's Amphibious Navy: Seventh Amphibious Force Operations 1943–1945* (1969).

Frost, H. H. *Office of Naval Intelligence: The Conduct of an Overseas Naval Campaign* (1920).

Hittle, James D. "Jomini and Amphibious Thought," *Marine Corps Gazette* (May 1946).

Isley, Jeter Allen. *The U.S. Marines and Amphibious War: Its Theory and Its Practice in the Pacific* (1951).

Smith, Holland M. *The Development of Amphibious Tactics in the U.S. Navy* (History and Museums Divisions, Headquarters, U.S. Marine Corps, 1992).

James McNabb

SEE ALSO Island-Hopping and Leapfrogging, U.S. Strategies; Marine Corps, U.S.; Navy, U.S.

Armor, U.S.

Armor played a strong supporting role in the Pacific. Inasmuch as tanks were an essential element of combat on the European front, U.S. commanders in the Pacific justly felt that the armor allotted to their forces was puny in comparison. Commanders from mid-1942 onward, however, consistently improved the use of whatever armor they possessed. The Japanese also made good use of the armor they had, adapting to new strategies with every battle.

At the beginning of the war, in December 1941, the U.S. Army had the grand total of two battalions of light tanks for each of two corps and two battalions of light tanks in the Philippines.

The first tank-to-tank battle involving U.S. forces took place during the doomed defense of the Philippines, but these were small engagements with light tanks on both sides and had little effect on the outcome—although U.S. artillery mounted on halftracks gave a very good account of itself and was feared by the Japanese invaders.

By late 1942, however, Allied forces were able to mount a successful series of offensive actions against Japan. After U.S. landings in New Guinea in November 1942, seven Stuart light tanks worked with three infantry battalions to overcome early heavy resistance. Four U.S. tanks then assisted the 1st Battalion, 126th Infantry Regiment, in taking the main airfield (Old Strip) on December 29, 1942, in probably the first U.S. tank victory of the Pacific war.

On Guadalcanal in the Solomon Islands, 600 miles northeast of New Guinea, the U.S. Marines occupied Henderson Field on August 7, 1942, taking the enemy by surprise. On August 21, a light tank platoon supported three marine battalions across a sandbar in the Ilu River against an estimated 930 soldiers of the Ichiki Force. Only 130 of the enemy survived.

Command shifted from marines to army on December 9, 1942. On January 22, 1943, sixteen soldiers from 2d Battalion of the 132d Infantry Regiment, supported by a single light tank, penetrated 200 yards into an enemy line surrounding the fortress called the Gifu. The fortress was cleared soon afterward, with all of Guadalcanal falling to the combined marine-army force on February 9, 1943.

By the end of 1943, the Joint Chiefs of Staff had planned an advance through the Philippines via the Gilbert Islands, with the army in the Makin and the marines in the Tarawa Atoll operations. The Makin operations (November 20–23, 1943) went according to plan with the 165th Infantry Regiment, supported by light tanks from the 193d Tank Battalion, landing at Red and Yellow Beaches. The waterproofed tanks and supporting infantry reached land without major mishap and knocked out enemy tanks which had been sealed into pillbox positions. Twelve medium tanks from Yellow Beach accompanied an infantry battalion through the western tank barrier, while tank crews accompanied another battalion through the eastern tank barrier.

Communications among infantry, armor, and field artillery consistently improved by the time the operation ended on November 23. The battle of Tarawa (November 20–24) proved much tougher. Seven tanks supported marines on each of two flanks. The Japanese had spent a year fortifying the island. The U.S. tanks—the new, medium M4 Shermans, armed with flamethrowers—proved essential for knocking out enemy bunkers. At Red Beach 1, only two of the seven tanks, supporting a marine battalion, survived the first day. At Red Beach 2, two marine battalions, aided by field artillery, took the airfield on the second day; 1st Battalion of the 6th Marine Regimental Combat Team (RCT), supported by an armor platoon, took Green Beach on the opposite side of the island on the same day, essentially cutting the enemy's forces in two. The fearsome flamethrowing Shermans enabled infantry forces to break through 4-foot sea walls and to rout Japanese soldiers from their pillboxes and bunkers.

In July 1943, the marines assaulted Munda Field, on New Georgia Island in the Solomons, north of Guadalacanal. The 10th Marine Defense Battalion found that tanks could proceed well on the open roads and by August, having taken the hills around Munda Field, requested more tanks.

Marines landed on December 26, on New Britain Island, with tanks from Company A, 1st Tank Battalion, supporting the 1st Marines in taking Cape Gloucester's airfield on that day. On March 13, 1944, a single tank crew assisted a reconnaissance platoon in leading three cavalry companies from 2d Squadron, 7th Cavalry Regiment, in taking the island of Hauwei by surprise. On Lugos Mission, in the Admiralty Islands, northwest of New Britain, a single tank working with B Troop, 1st Squadron, 8th Cavalry Regiment, on March 15–16 wiped out three pillboxes which had guarded the airstrip. On Bougainville—the largest and northernmost island in the Solomons—on March 12, 1944, 1st Platoon of Company C, 754th Tank Battalion, was called on to assist company G, 129th Infantry Regiment, in reducing five stubborn pillboxes. The tankers, having almost exhausted their ammunition, were relieved by 2d Platoon at day's end; the pillboxes were destroyed with no loss of life in the combined tank-infantry assault.

Tanks also accompanied infantry to Leyte in the Philippines. The initial day of the landing went well, with 7th Infantry Division and 776th Amphibious Tank Battalion breaking through from the beaches with particular effectiveness, only to bog down on the island itself. Other divisions used tanks in the initial barrages. The 382d Infantry Regiment, with Company B, 763d Tank Battalion, went through Hindang on October 24, 1944, using flamethrowers. M8 armored cars, tanks, and field artillery provided support in the first (south valley) phase. In the second phase, toward the north valley, infantry battalions tended to work well with tank platoons. In the third phase, on November 11, tanks and infantry made a breakthrough. In an attack on Breakneck Ridge, 1st Battalion, 21st Infantry Regiment, with Company A, 44th Tank Battalion, proceeded up the last 300 yards south of the crest of the ridge, moved down the reverse slope, and destroyed an estimated twenty-five enemy positions. One tank went off the edge of the road, but the crew was rescued by another vehicle. On November 12, 3d Battalion, 21st Infantry Regiment, with six tanks and a tank destroyer platoon assisted in consolidating positions. By November 16, Breakneck Ridge lay in Allied hands. Each Japanese position had to be eliminated in a yard-by-yard conquest. By teaming tank companies with infantry battalions, the Americans were improving their coordination and opening the way to the final conquest of the island.

In a dramatic change of policy, a 77th Infantry Division landing behind enemy lines at Ormuc made possible the final December 1944 battle for conquest. Company A, 776th Tank Battalion, led the invasion of Ormuc itself. The use of tanks inland was delayed only because of logistical problems. The armored bulldozers and tank destroyers led the initial attack, shelling and leveling enemy blockhouses. By December 14, four tanks had assisted the 307th Infantry Regiment in securing its perimeter. Company A of the 776th, with the 305th Infantry Regiment, secured Palompan in a battle from December 22 to 31 and helped to clear Leyte by year's end.

The battle for the island of Luzon, including Manila, the capital city, lasted from January through June 1945. General Douglas MacArthur decided against using air bombardment on his Philippine allies; thus, tanks assumed singular importance. In the initial phases, the Japanese lost two tanks penetrating the lines in their first counterattack (January 12–16). Eight tanks of the 716th Tank Battalion assisted the 169th Infantry Regiment in taking Mount Alava in the battle from January 20 to 24. Within Manila itself, a few U.S. tanks often sufficed, inasmuch as the soldiers possessed accurate prewar road maps and could easily navigate, with support from the city's inhabitants. At Santo Tomas University, one tank from the 44th Tank Battalion broke down the wall so that 2/8 Cavalry Regiment troops on February 3, 1945, could occupy the university's compound. One company from the 44th Tank Battalion in early February led the way into the suburbs, with two platoons of tanks working with the 145th Infantry in a long and bitter fight to take the new police station. In the Philippines, tanks—often directed by guerrilla forces—performed best in the urban environment.

The Battle of Iwo Jima, from February 19 through March 26, 1945, included reducing 1,500 dug-in Japanese emplacements. Many of the Sherman tanks stalled in water during the landing. However, in the battles for the so-called Hill, the Amphitheater, and the Turkey Knob, the flamethrower tank proved essential to the three marine regiments, especially at Turkey Knob. On March 7, a single tank crew rescued the last five soldiers of Company F, 9th Marine Regiment, by dragging an officer and four troopers through the escape hatch after thirty-six hours of brutal fighting had devastated the unit. On March 20, tanks followed marines of the 5th Division against the Japanese 145th Infantry Regiment in the gorge to the south of Kitano Point. Tank-bulldozers blazed open a trail, with the Shermans joining with foot-soldiers in the final attack. By March 25, one day before the formal end of the battle, Lieutenant General Tadimachi Kuribyashi committed ritual suicide.

Iwo Jima was but a dress rehearsal for the final Battle for Okinawa. For a year, enemy forces had dug into three mountain "rings" in Machinato, Shuri Castle, and the final southwest corner of the island. General Mitsuru Ushijima hoped to launch a counteroffensive from the first of the rings after U.S. forces had landed. Tanks with 96th Infantry Division forces failed on April 9–10 to take Kakazu Ridge in the outermost ring, facing unexpectedly heavy Japanese fire. However, from April 16 to 21, U.S. tanks did assist 77th Infantry Division soldiers in taking the neighboring island of Ie Shima, which was vital for fighter aircraft assaults on mainland Japan. Infantry/armor forces surrounded the northern and southern sides of the "Pinnacle" mountain and subdued the enemy in a deadly battle of attrition, cave by cave.

Back on Okinawa, however, the 27th Infantry Division forces to the west (right) of the 96th failed to bypass the Kakazu Ridge on April 19, losing no fewer than twenty-two of thirty tanks in the engagement. Finally, to the far east (left), by April 23—in field artillery, tank, and infantry coordination—soldiers of 1st Battalion, 17th Infantry Regiment, managed to penetrate Rocky Crags, making the initial penetration in the first of the three rings. On April 23, Company B, 763d Tank Battalion, preceded by an armored bulldozer, crossed at a gap in the Nishibaru Ridge and then took Tanabaru Escarpment under direct attack. Also on April 23, infantry/tank forces consolidated at the Kakazu Ridge and by the end of the day had penetrated the first enemy ring. From April 27 to 29, the 763d Tank Battalion assisted three regiments of the 77th Infantry Division in taking the Maeda Escarpment, forward of the Nishibaru Ridge. On May 4, General Ushijima launched a counteroffensive which failed and which deprived him of vital reserves. U.S. forces now prepared to attack the second ring at the Shuri Line, with marines from III Amphibious Corps joining in the assault to the east of the XXIV Corps.

The marines at Sugar Loaf encountered a new opposing strategy, whereby Japanese forces drew attackers over the summits of the ridges, only to throw them back from concealed positions on reverse slopes. But after four fruitless days of fighting, Company D, 29th Marine Regiment, with three tanks subdued enemy forces on the reverse slope. A Japanese counterattack failed. By May 21, elements of the 1st Marine Division were attacking Shuri Ridge, the last obstacle to taking the castle itself. To their extreme east, or left, the 383d Infantry Regiment of the 96th Infantry Division, supported by the 763d Tank Battalion, took Conical Hill on May 13. Then, three regiments of the 77th Infantry Division advanced from the Maeda Escarpment, supported by tanks, and on May 21 took Chocolate Drop and then Flattop Hills, once again using flamethrower tanks to seal enemy-held caves.

On May 21, General Ushijima withdrew his forces from the Shuri Line to make a final, four-week stand in the island's southwest corner. Tanks carried casualties from Kunishi Ridge on June 13, losing twenty-one of their number in the effort. In a final battle from June 13 to 17, the 769th Tank Battalion used flamethrowers to take Hill 89, advancing across a final long plateau—ironically the best tank-fighting territory in the entire battle.

The Pacific war had seen no great tank-to-tank clashes, as was the case on both the eastern and the western fronts in Europe. Rather, U.S. tanks, deployed in limited numbers, had provided essential support to the infantry. In the Philippines, armor had excelled in urban terrain. On Iwo Jima, tanks had provided support in the yard-by-yard battle which followed the initial landing. At Okinawa, borrowing on lessons learned from Iwo Jima, tank commanders had worked with armored bulldozers in forging the way through mountainous terrain.

U.S. armor forces were indeed fortunate that the Japanese fielded no medium or heavy tank of their own in any numbers. Unlike the situation in Europe, where U.S. tankers often found themselves qualitatively outmatched by German armor, the Americans could consistently count on armor supremacy in each of their offensives against the Japanese.

FURTHER READINGS

Appleman, Roy, et al. *Okinawa: The Last Battle: U.S. Army in World War II* (1948).

Crow, Duncan, and Robert J. Icks. *Encyclopedia of Armoured Cars and Halftracks* (1976).

Baily, C. *Faint Praise: American Tanks and Tank Destroyers during World War II* (1983).

Ellis, Chris. *Tanks of World War II* (1981).

Hogg, Ian. *Armour in Conflict: The Design and Tactics of Armoured Fighting Vehicles* (1980).

Hunnicutt, R. P. *Sherman: History of the American Medium Tank* (1978).

John Cranston

SEE ALSO Army, Japanese; Army Ground Forces, U.S.

Army, Japanese

The Japanese soldier in World War II fought from as far north as the Aleutians to as far south as Guadalcanal. He sailed close to Midway and penetrated into India. He guarded Manchukuo from the ever-dangerous Soviets and rampaged through central and south China. From frostbite to heatstroke, from continental mountain ranges to coral lagoons, the Japanese soldier saw every kind of combat.

Throughout the Pacific war, the Japanese soldier proved tough, tenacious, and disciplined—a man who would fight to the death rather than surrender. He knew that he would be dishonored if taken prisoner, and his family would not receive a pension. If he died in battle, his ashes would be sent to the national shrine of Yasukuni, his family would receive a pension, and his memory would be honored. Japanese units fought on in circumstances and under conditions where a Western army would surrender. With no option to surrender, the Japanese soldier glorified death in battle.

Most Japanese soldiers were peasant conscripts and were comfortable with a frugal, hard life on the farm. Stocky and well built, 19 to 45 years old, they had carried 200-pound loads of rice seedlings on their backs during planting season, and so the army load was no problem at all. Unpleasant conditions, fleas, lice, and flies were a natural part of life. The Japanese soldier could make incredible marches on scanty rations. He feared his seniors considerably more than any enemy. Throughout his life, the Japanese government had praised the heroism and noble calling of the warrior. Soldiering was not only honorable; it was inevitable.

The Japanese issued forty thousand pamphlets entitled *Read This Alone—and the War Can Be Won*. The pamphlet's author compared the U.S., British, and Dutch armies with the Chinese army. He determined that because their officers were Europeans and their noncommissioned officers were usually natives, the spiritual unity throughout enemy armies was zero. Their tanks, airplanes, and guns were far superior to the Chinese army's, but their equipment was old, and their crews were poor soldiers.

According to this pamphlet, Westerners considered themselves superior to the Japanese. Actually, Westerners were inferior to the Japanese—effeminate and cowardly, afraid to fight in rain or mist or at night. The pamphlet encouraged each soldier to regard the enemy as his own father's murderer: "Here before you is the man whose death will lighten your heart of its burden of brooding anger. If you fail to destroy him utterly you can never rest at peace." It was up to each soldier to demonstrate to the world the true worth of Japanese manhood. Such sentiments led directly to the deaths of tens of thousands of the emperor's soldiers.

Japanese soldiers were the product of a hard system. Recruit training capitalized on traditional Japanese customs, on emperor worship, and on physical assaults. Face slappings, beatings, and rough training toughened the recruit. A soldier's highest duty was to die for the emperor. Peer pressure was intense. Emperor Meiji's Imperial Rescript of 1873 had founded the modern Japanese army and delineated its conduct. "Five Words (Five Principles of the Soldier)" guided officers and soldiers alike, and they took the principles seriously. "Five Words" filled three pages of small type but can be boiled down to:

1. A soldier must do his duty to his country. "Remember that the protection of the state and the maintenance of its power depend upon the strength of its arms. . . . Bear in mind that duty is weightier than a mountain, while death is lighter than a feather."
2. A soldier must be courteous. "Inferiors should regard the orders of their superiors as issuing directly from Us" (the emperor).
3. A soldier must show courage in war. "Never to despise an inferior enemy, or to fear a superior, but to do one's duty as a soldier or sailor—that is true valor."
4. A soldier must keep his word. "Faithfulness implies the keeping of one's word, and righteousness the fulfillment of one's duty."
5. A soldier lives simply. "If you do not make simplicity your aim, you will become effeminate or frivolous and acquire fondness for luxurious and extravagant ways."

Unfortunately for the Japanese common soldier, he did not receive the strategic or tactical leadership, the material, and the logistics that his obvious bravery deserved. Senior officers began the war without a clear or realistic vision of how to conclude it. Japanese leaders believed that the Pacific war was to be but an extension of the China war. Only by defeating the West could Japan cut the flow of supplies to China and win that debilitating, demoralizing, brutal war. Planners realized that the Pacific had become of primary importance only when the U.S. Guadalcanal offensive began. Generals, from Tojo on down, knew that the war was lost by late 1942 and early 1943, and yet they drove their men through three more years of useless combat.

At lower levels, officers who might advocate a prudent approach to a battle were treated like cowards or were transferred out of their units, whereas foolhardy officers were never punished for their failures. Officer losses in China and at Nomonhan (in fighting against the Soviets, bringing Japan its first military defeat in modern times) as well as army expansion led to an influx of new officers—many promoted from the ranks, ill-trained and holding positions above their grades. Low-quality officers meant poor-quality staff work, especially in logistics.

Japan employed the Imperial Japanese Army to seize resource-rich lands and then defend them from Allied counterattack. Japan planned to bleed white the U.S. counteroffensive and gain favorable terms at a peace settlement. Its conquest of the Philippines, Netherlands East Indies, Malaya, and Burma seemed to validate the decision for war and the army's prowess in land warfare.

Yet Japan's military masters had an imperfect, unbalanced instrument with which to conduct this war, regardless of initial successes. The poor showing of the Japanese army in battles with the Soviets at Nomonhan in 1939 opened a debate within army circles. Should the army undergo a thorough reorganization or just upgrade artillery and reinforce the current structure? The Japanese knew they had out-of-date equipment. But partly because of industrial constraints, partly because the navy and air forces consumed so many assets, and partly because of the mystic belief in the superiority of Japanese spirit (particularly in hand-to-hand fighting with the bayonet), the army chose the second course of action. As an answer to the enemy's firepower, the army placed its trust in its spirit, its will, and its advanced infantry tactics. It would enter the Pacific war badly outgunned and outsupported by its opponents.

The Japanese army grew from a strength of 1.7 million in December 1941 to a peak of more than 5 million. Division strength had grown from 24 divisions in 1937,

to 39 in 1939, to 51 in 1941—with another 59 brigade-size units. Japan would continue to mobilize divisions and separate brigades/regiments in a flurry of activity throughout the war, ending with 175. The rapid growth diluted the quality of soldiers by bringing in older men and lower-quality recruits. By mid-1941, 185,000 Japanese soldiers had died in China, and manpower was already a problem. Basic training suffered from a flood of recruits and a shortage of qualified trainers.

The Japanese army began the war with five major army commands (groups of armies): the Japan Defense Army in the home islands, the Kwantung Army in Manchukuo, the China Expeditionary Army, the Korea Army, and the Southern Army in Taiwan and Indochina. Corps, in the Western sense, did not exist. In December 1941, for example, the Southern Army commanded four "armies": the 14th, scheduled to invade the Philippines; the 15th, going to Thailand; the 16th, tasked to take the East Indies; and the 25th, targetted at Malaya and Singapore. Although the 25th and the other armies in the Southern Army were called armies, they were actually corps in Western terms and had combat and service support troops similar to a Western corps. In 1942, Japan began activating geographical armies called "area armies." The Southern Army became the Southern Area Army. The 14th Army, for example, became the 14th Area Army with the 35th Army and other elements under its command.

Japanese divisions varied greatly in strength and were often organized to fit the mission and available resources. A standard division might have 20,000 or fewer men in three infantry regiments, a field artillery regiment, and other supporting arms. Divisions were not mechanized or motorized in the Western sense. Horses played an important part, for a standard division depended on 16,000 horses to move its guns, ammunition, and supplies. Japan did not have elite, jungle-wise, tropical-trained units at the beginning of the war, contrary to some opinion in the West. They were, instead, regular cold-weather divisions hastily converted for tropical service. They were no more inherently capable of operating in jungles than anyone else. (Japan has no jungle.) But they had practiced and trained on a far larger and more intense scale than had their enemies.

Division artillery most often consisted of three battalions totaling thirty-six 75-mm guns and 2,000 horses. This organization was badly outgunned by Western armies, in particular by a U.S. division's artillery, with three battalions of thirty-six 105-mm and one battalion of twelve 155-mm, all towed by trucks. The Japanese had a deadly flaw in their field artillery. Doctrine stressed employment of guns (not cannon) well forward in a direct-fire role. Japanese guns were designed to be light and mobile in order to accompany the fast-moving infantry. Therefore, their ranges were relatively short, and shell killing power was limited. Doctrine called for short preparations just before an infantry assault. Insufficient transportation existed to feed masses of shells to these guns, so they could not duel or suppress enemy artillery or inflict large numbers of casualties over a sustained period.

Fire control was managed through telephone wire much more often than over radio. Artillerymen had to fire slowly when registering, and the guns became vulnerable to air and artillery attack during the process. So batteries were displaced after a few rounds, and they started the process all over again. It was not a procedure to win battles. The Japanese attempt to disrupt Henderson Field on Guadalcanal with a battery of long-range 150-mm guns failed when they could manage to fire only 800 rounds throughout the entire campaign. The mass and precision of U.S. artillery fire in the forlorn defense of the Bataan Peninsula came as an unpleasant surprise to the Japanese invaders.

The lack of mass and of ammunition turned Japanese artillery into an annoyance rather than a serious part of a combined arms team. Because Japanese artillery could not suppress opposing artillery, their infantry had the nearly impossible task of attacking through uninhibited U.S. artillery defensive fires. In later defensive battles, individual Japanese pieces that were deeply dug in and camouflaged were deadly, but only once (in the Bataan campaign of April 1942) did Japanese artillery determine the course of a battle. In most armies, artillery is the deadliest arm. But the Japanese had too few medium- and large-caliber weapons and could not keep them supplied with ammunition. Mortars are ideal for light infantry—much easier to produce by industry and more easily supplied with ammunition over bad terrain than field artillery is. The Japanese were quite good with mortars. But mortars lacked the punch or the range of artillery, and they could not suppress distant enemy artillery.

The Japanese were fond of forming mixed brigades and regiments, organized and equipped for specific roles. They had three to six infantry battalions with only small artillery, engineer, and signal support. Independent mixed regiments defended many Pacific islands and were supported or subsumed by airmen and navy detachments.

Division medical service was extensive, at least in manpower. The goal was to keep wounded men as close to the front as possible in order to expedite their return to combat. Division medical battalions were, however, short of drugs and all types of medicine and medical supplies. They had no prophylactic injections to prevent tetanus,

and penicillin never reached more than a fraction of the troops. When conditions deteriorated, medics were known to practice "grenade medicine"; that is, they killed the seriously wounded.

Japanese armor in the Pacific was poor. The Japanese never developed either the doctrine or the equipment for large-scale tank warfare. Their tanks were lightweight, thin skinned, lightly armed, and cramped. Experience in China had given Japan no reason to change, so the fight at Nomonhan was a shock. By then, it was too late to change, nor could industry support a change. The size and organization of Japanese tank regiments varied. Although they had set a goal of ten armored divisions after their defeat at Nomonhan, and although they grouped some tank regiments together with their supply and maintenance, they did not create a true tank division until 1943. Tanks continued to support infantry, to operate as mobile pillboxes, and to act as dug-in artillery.

Japan's use of two-tank regiments (actually battalions in size if not title) on Luzon in 1941–1942 was cautious, uninspired, and uncoordinated with either infantry or artillery. Their use of four-tank regiments in Malaya was more effective, especially because so few Indian troops had ever before even seen a tank and especially because few British had expected them to be used here. Even in Malaya, however, the tanks fought on a very narrow front and were often stopped by antitank fire. The Japanese use of tanks on Guadalcanal and subsequent island battles was hardly worthy of note.

Each infantry division had an engineer regiment, generally of three field companies and a stores company (or a materiel platoon). These men were equipped with shovels, axes, wire cutters, and saws and had none of the motorized or power equipment common to Western divisional engineers. Separate organizations such as shipping engineer regiments existed to operate barges and support landing operations.

The Japanese army never developed close air support as did Western armies—a near-fatal flaw. The nation's limited industrial base concentrated output to support the navy's one decisive battle. So ships and naval aircraft took priority over aircraft for close air support. Once war began, the Japanese did not have sufficient aircraft to protect their own airfields and lines of communications and could hardly spare any for close support of their infantry. Furthermore, a shortage of communications gear would have hindered close air support, even had aircraft appeared in sufficient numbers.

Japanese military schools taught that the infantry was the backbone of the army. True enough, but the schools then neglected logistics, science, and technology—areas necessary to create the effective combined arms team. A poor industrial base meant that engineer equipment would be in short supply. Antiaircraft guns were outmoded. The high cost of manufacturing artillery meant that mortars too often replaced normal rifled artillery. The weak (then) Japanese electronics industry meant that the large numbers of radios needed to tie infantry, artillery, and supporting forces together would not exist. Radar came late to the armed forces and in insufficient quantities.

As discussed, the Japanese army was a flawed tool sent on an impossible mission. The Pacific, China, Burma, the Netherlands East Indies, and India were simply too overwhelmingly large for the Japanese army to conquer and defend. Yet that is exactly what Imperial General Headquarters sent the army to do. Imperial General Headquarters did not recognize the limits of its offensive capabilities. Japan's limited industrial output meant that the Japanese rifleman went into battle poorly supported by artillery, air, signal, engineer, transportation, and supply forces. It is a measure of just how poor were the Allied armies in the Pacific that the Japanese soldier was successful everywhere in the first months of the war.

There was a startling degree of self-deception, almost mindlessness, within the Japanese army. It had suffered a severe reversal based on firepower at Nomonhan, yet it kept the results of those battles secret from its own men. It had even failed to overrun the recently recruited, ill-equipped Filipino army on Bataan in 1942 and required a second campaign to complete the job. It fixated on the easy and amazing successes in Malaya, Burma, and the Netherlands East Indies and ignored the failures. There was a surprising inclination in 1942 to relax and enjoy the fruits of victory. The military authorities assumed, on no evidence, that the democratic United States would not be able to attack for eighteen to twenty-four months after Pearl Harbor and that its citizens could not stomach heavy losses. The army considered itself undefeatable and failed to take prudent, long-term actions to prepare for the inevitable U.S. counteroffensive.

This "victory disease" meant that Japan launched invasions of the Solomon Islands and New Guinea without adequate thought, without a hardheaded assessment of what the Allies could do, and without massing sufficient forces and logistics in either their lead elements or their reserves. Sufficient air and ground forces existed. But the army did not bring them to the potential battlefields. Army priorities were concentrated in China and against the Soviet threat. So even when the army held the initiative, in early 1942, it failed to exploit it.

Officers within the army did not highly value the intelligence field. The best and brightest officers of the general staff gravitated to the Operations Bureau. Officers did not see intelligence or logistics work as career-enhancing; neither field had any of the characteristics that a Japanese officer held honorable. In particular, intelligence called for caution, patience, and plodding long-term effort. Japanese mathematicians were not up to Western standards, nor did Japan have the resources in men and equipment to apply to codebreaking.

The Japanese had been closely scrutinizing the wrong enemy—the Soviets—and were ignorant of U.S. military capabilities and potentialities. The army's Operations Bureau believed that the United States could not mount a counteroffensive until 1943 (U.S. Marines landed on Guadalcanal on August 7, 1942), and the Operations Bureau assumed that only minor U.S. forces would enter the Pacific, because of American priorities in Europe. These same officers focused all their attention on the armies in the field and showed little interest in international relations, the economy, or their own civilians.

Even at lower echelons, there was little appreciation for intelligence. The Southern Army united its intelligence section with the operations section after it had completed its conquests. Its officers reasoned that, having accomplished the mission, the intelligence section had lost its raison d'etre. Imperial General Headquarters approved the merger, and the Southern Army did not reverse its action until February 1944. The Japanese must have assumed there would be no Allied threat—a most contemptuous attitude to take. The absence of a separate intelligence section hobbled the Southern Army's ability to forecast Allied offenses.

Underestimating the enemy was rampant within Japanese army circles. It started in China, where Japanese officers developed disdain for their enemies. They underestimated the prowess and firepower of the Soviets before Nomonhan. This error continued in the Philippines, where officers estimated MacArthur's 1942 Bataan Filamerican army at 20,000 men when there were actually 80,000 on the peninsula. They estimated British forces on Singapore at 30,000 when there were 85,000. They estimated U.S. Marines on Guadalcanal at 2,000 when there were more than 10,000 and at 10,000 when there were 20,000. They underestimated by half the U.S. forces holding the Empress Augusta Bay perimeter on Bougainville.

Nor did the Japanese know their potential battlefields very well (with the exception of well-mapped Manchuria). They knew less about New Guinea than did the Americans. They had few maps of the areas in which they were to operate. After the initial burst of conquest, the army was singularly unsuccessful in gathering tactical information about U.S. forces. In contrast, Japanese radios and prisoners hemorrhaged information. Japanese soldiers had not been trained on how to act if captured, because it was unthinkable to be captured. Ill-handled classified documents revealed order-of-battle and operations plans. The time and location of Japanese attacks were sometimes posted on the bulletin boards of U.S. units.

Japanese army-navy cooperation during World War II was incredibly bad, making the traditional U.S. Army-Navy rivalry seem little more than football competition by comparison. The Imperial Japanese Army and Navy refused to share research data and refused to cooperate on production, and each ran its own separate atomic weapons programs—again in contrast to the successful unified U.S. effort. Rivalry between the Japanese services hindered strategy and tactical planning. Army and navy procurement agencies fought with one another over aircraft production. Only in November 1943, when the Ministry of Munitions was established, was there serious coordination between army, navy, and civilian supply systems.

The Japanese army did not know that the navy was building an airbase on Guadalcanal until the Americans landed. The navy concealed its own losses, grossly magnified enemy losses, and left the army to plan its strategy on false assumptions of friendly and enemy naval strength. It is difficult to maintain interservice harmony in the face of defeat, but the Japanese set a new level in interservice hostility.

The Japanese army placed great emphasis on offensive actions, surprise, and rapidity of movement—all of which were well suited for the open lands of Manchuria. Commanders and staffs operated well forward, where they could keep in touch with the fighting. Officers lived under the same conditions as their men and ate the same food. Surprise was an ever-present element in their planning, and they planned for it and counted on it even when there was no chance of surprise.

Encirclement, turning movements, and infiltration were their means of avoiding frontal attacks. Lightly equipped and sparsely supplied infantry marched at a breakneck pace. Infantrymen carried their own food and were not, in the short run, tied to roads. Their speedy march down Malaya to Singapore and their rout of British forces from Burma were the ultimate expressions of Japanese light-infantry maneuver, encirclement, and disruptive roadblocks. Their overland march against Port Moresby became one of their first failures.

When favored maneuver options were foreclosed, Japanese commanders had trouble acknowledging that their original plan had failed. The Japanese army launched frontal night attacks with enthusiasm and often with great stupidity. Frontal attacks worked against shaken, uncertain, and demoralized enemies—especially in the first six months, when Japan could mass power wherever it wished and while the army was fresh and healthy. But when a frontal attack failed, the results were disastrous. Many commanders continued their attacks knowing full well that their resources were inadequate for success. The piecemeal commitment of troops to retake Guadalcanal and the repeated understrength assaults showed both a shocking contempt of U.S. troops as well as a failure to properly support the campaign logistically.

Time and again, Japanese officers lacked either the courage or the tactical knowledge to order a retreat or even to plan for the future. Some Japanese generals could not physically bring themselves to say that retreat was in order. A myopic fixation on the attack, and the emotional certainty that Japanese esprit could overcome terrain and firepower, froze officers' judgment. Commanders would choose attack when, to any Western officer versed in orthodox tactics, something else was needed. During island battles, the Japanese preferred a desperate assault into U.S. firepower over a more militarily sound, if still doomed, defense. Occasionally, Japanese commanders made the wise choice, enforced their decision on their men, and fought skillful defensive actions; Yamashita in north Luzon, Kuribayashi on Iwo Jima, and Ushijima on Okinawa come to mind.

Doctrine called for a simple plan to be executed with power, determination, and speed of movement. Despite this admonition toward simple plans, many Japanese actions required multiple columns to take multiple paths over bad terrain against multiple objectives. Such plans looked good on paper and showed proper esprit, yet once again there was a flaw. Japanese military teachings had placed little emphasis on time and space factors. Japanese officers were generally unable to concentrate their efforts and bring all supporting arms together at the key point at the same time. The attacks against the Henderson Field perimeter on Guadalcanal are perfect examples of their deviation from the doctrine of simplicity, of their piecemeal commitment of troops, and of their failure with time and space.

Despite many years of experience, Japanese officers repeatedly violated fundamental principles of tactics. They failed to mass, they neglected security, and they ignored enemy firepower. They were slow to learn how to avoid artillery. They were burdened with a racist attitude and an ideological disdain for their enemies. They had fought the Chinese too long. Soldiers had been taught that they were morally superior to their enemies and that Japan's culture stood above the cultures of "lesser" nations. The Japanese failed to credit their opponents with good judgment, with a fighting spirit equal to their own, and with equal or better military efficiency. Army units would attack at strength ratios well short of Western standards and would trust to their innate spiritual strength over Western materiel and firepower.

The first failure of Japanese offensive doctrine (and of the spiritual superiority of will over firepower) occurred in the Philippines in January 1942. Japanese officers on Bataan launched battalions against divisions and even against corps. They failed. Only when fresh troops and siege artillery came in, and only when the U.S.-Filipino Bataan army was collapsing from disease and starvation, did their offensive operations succeed. In this case, they combined tanks, infantry, artillery, and air support in a traditional "Western-style" combined arms attack. And it succeeded.

Their march on Port Moresby failed, as did offensive operations on Guadalcanal, partly because Australians and Americans were grasping the one-dimensional Japanese tactics. Once the Western armies decided to fight rather than retreat, or when they found themselves unable to retreat, the shock and terror of the screaming banzai charge lost much of its effectiveness. In the blink of an eye, all the Japanese army's culture, training, and doctrine had disintegrated into failure.

It had to have been a disconcerting moment, for the Japanese had nothing with which to replace their offensive doctrine—no tactical close air support to act as mobile artillery like the German Stuka, no strategic air power to cut Allied lines of communications, no tanks and mechanized infantry for maneuver, no masses of artillery or the requisite ammunition to blow holes in the enemy line, no technological breakthroughs in weapons efficiency, and no subtle misdirection or intelligence coups. And almost immediately there were no longer even masses of infantry, for Allied control of the air and sea began to isolate each battlefield from reinforcements.

All the Japanese could do was fall back on the unique strength of the infantry—its willingness to die to no purpose. In this, the army proved unequalled. Japanese soldiers gained renown for the doggedness and tenacity of their defensive battles. They were faced with overwhelming naval gunnery, land artillery, and tactical air strength, and so they naturally went to ground. They dug as had no Western army in all of World War II.

From the bogs of Buna to the coral atolls of the central Pacific to the mountains of Luzon and Okinawa, Japanese engineers and common soldiers showed initiative in creating camouflaged bombproofs and defenses worthy of great praise. Resilient coconut-log above-ground bunkers protected soldiers on low-lying Pacific islands. Deep mountain tunnels hid artillery and supplies on larger land masses. The army's field engineering talents were excellent.

Japanese soldiers gained experience in each island battle, but that experience availed them little in the face of the lavish, overwhelming, industrial warfare waged by the West. They defended the beaches and were crushed by naval gunfire. They launched strong counterattacks and were mowed down by infantry. They abandoned the beaches and built defenses inland, only to be pried out by direct fire, flamethrowers, and determined infantry. Nothing they did worked. The Japanese Army never won a battle after the fall of the U.S. forces on Corregidor in the spring of 1942. The Allies learned that any Japanese position could be taken. It would cost men and materiel, but the West had solved the tactical problem of defeating the Japanese army.

Great praise is due the average Japanese soldier for his endurance, determination, and dedication to duty. Yet even greater censure is due him for his barbaric and murderous treatment of civilians and prisoners of war. This was a distinct change from the Russo-Japanese War and World War I, in which Japanese soldiers were under perfect discipline and control. Yet in World War II examples of rape, savagery, and murder in every country occupied by the Japanese are legion. A few commanders tried to restrain their men, but it was for naught. The famed General Yamashita wrote in his diary, "I want my troops to behave with dignity, but most of them do not seem to have the ability to do so." It is not evident whether Yamashita did anything about his troops' flouting of his commands, and for that he would die on the gallows after the war.

The Japanese had initiated a policy of humiliation of the white man. Their code of Bushido withheld the option of surrender, and so a military prisoner was more a contemptible criminal with no honor or shame than he was a fellow soldier due honorable treatment. Japanese government and army policies were deliberately directed toward brutality, exploitation, and murder. The Bataan death march, the death of 16,000 British and 60,000 Asians while building the Thailand-Burma railroad, massacres beyond count in China, prison-camp starvation and disease, and the prisoner-of-war "hell ships" out of the Philippines were but peaks in years of daily butchery.

The army's treatment of civilians ranged from barbarous to murderous to simply ill-disciplined—from 200,000 Chinese murdered at Nanking to ten killed here and thirty killed there. The army was little more tender to its own civilians. Japanese civilians on Saipan were considered no different from the military. The army ordered civilians to arm themselves with bamboo spears for a final attack against the Americans. Nearly 22,000 Japanese civilians thus died.

The army prepared home-island civilians to fight to the death even as discipline in the army itself began to break down. The suffering of the civilian populace was a secondary consideration in repulsing the Americans. More and more officers looked to drink and personal pleasure and neglected their men. Disorderly soldiers swarmed through towns and villages. The army competed with industry for the last dregs of the manpower pool. Officers encouraged their men to develop a "metaphysical spirit" to overcome U.S. materiel superiority: "Our spirit against their steel!" In Manchuria and the home islands, the army mobilized new divisions that it could not equip, as though the number of divisions alone would stave off defeat.

The Japanese army had entered World War II improperly equipped and inadequately supplied for warfare with the West. Its officers used tactics dependent on will overcoming firepower. They were unable to replace either their equipment or their tactics with something that worked. Like the Japanese navy, whose excellence in night surface actions became an obsolescent form of warfare, the army's competence in speed marches followed by night shock-action infantry assaults no longer fit the situation. Had the Japanese army been armed, trained, and supplied in a Western manner (which was impossible given Japan's weak economy), the quality of its soldiers would have made it a most formidable foe indeed.

FURTHER READINGS

Barker, A. J. *Japanese Army Handbook 1939–1945* (1979).
Bergamini, David. *Japan's Imperial Conspiracy* (1971).
Drea, Edward J. "In the Army Barracks of Imperial Japan," *Armed Forces and Society*, vol. 15, no. 3 (spring 1989).
Harries, Meirion, and Susie Harries. *Soldiers of the Sun: The Rise and Fall of the Imperial Japanese Army* (1991).
Hayashi Saburo. *Kogun: The Japanese Army in the Pacific War* (1959).

John W. Whitman

SEE ALSO Navy, Japanese

Army, U.S.-Filipino

The United States began World War II with a partly mobilized, inadequately trained, and poorly equipped *overseas* army. General Douglas MacArthur's relatively unknown Philippine army—an army that was doomed from the moment MacArthur conceived of it—was a force of Americans and Filipinos that had its origins in prewar planning and late 1941 mobilization.

The Joint Board in Washington began developing five war plans in 1939, one for each of five scenarios. The plans focused on Europe, South America, and the Pacific. Rainbow Five set conditions that came closest to what happened. The main effort would be made against Germany. While fighting a strategic defense in the Pacific, the United States would quickly send forces to the eastern Atlantic and to Africa and Europe to act against Germany and Italy.

The Joint Board adopted Rainbow Five in May 1941. Although the Asiatic fleet had the mission of supporting the army in the Philippines, the fleet's principal units (its cruisers and destroyers) would sail to the relative safety of the Indian Ocean, there to wait for the Pacific Fleet to fight its way to the Philippines. From southern bases they would help Allied naval forces defend the Malay Barrier.

The United States planned to defend the Philippines using the army's War Plan Orange 3 (WPO-3), a derivative of War Plan Orange. The United States was blue, and Japan was orange. The plan described how the United States would defeat Japan, and planners used it as their touchstone for discussions of supporting plans.

Army planners in the Philippines had completed their most recent revision of plans for war with Japan in April 1941. Regular army forces on the island of Luzon would fight the Japanese at their landing site. The Philippine army would mobilize and relieve the regulars. If forced to withdraw, the army would delay the enemy's advance as long as the defense of the Bataan Peninsula were not jeopardized. No attempt would be made to defend all the islands, nor even all of Luzon; instead, planners would hold only central Luzon. Manila Bay, in particular, with its harbor and transportation facilities, was the key to Luzon. If the worst were to happen, the army would hold the Bataan Peninsula and the fortress island of Corregidor to the last extremity.

Planners hoped that the Philippines could hold for six months. By that time, the navy would have fought its way across the Pacific with reinforcements. But no knowledgeable planner really believed that the navy could fight its way back to the Philippines in six months, and prewar plans were mute over what would happen if Bataan and Corregidor fell. Contingency plans did not exist for concentrating men and equipment on the U.S. west coast for a relief effort. Planners hoped that something could be done when the time came. Because there were not enough forces successfully to defend all the islands, or even Luzon, Washington faced two unenviable choices: either the pain and humiliation of losing the islands and the garrison or the need to send an unprepared, under equipped relief expedition.

MacArthur had been in the Philippines since 1935 and had developed his own plan for national defense. There would be five Filipino reserve divisions on Luzon as well as the U.S. Army's Philippine Division. MacArthur would divide his Luzon army into three parts: a northern force, a southern force, and a general reserve. Three divisions would compose a Visayan-Mindanao force to prevent small Japanese forces from seizing airstrips for operations against Luzon.

When U.S. air power on Luzon and the southern islands grew strong enough, it could cut Japanese supply lines to the south. This, in particular, had been Army Chief of Staff General George C. Marshall's hope. If the army could defend the Philippines with heavy bombers and pursuit aircraft, the United States could block a Japanese southward advance. Everything depended on operating heavy bombers from the Philippines. At this time, the U.S. Army Air Corps had great faith in its B-17 "Flying Fortress" a four-engined heavy bomber.

As early as February 1941, MacArthur had proposed to Washington that war plans be changed. In his view, all the Philippines should be defended, not just the entrance to Manila Bay. When the new Rainbow Five plan reached Manila, MacArthur saw that it still addressed solely the defense of Manila Bay, not the entire archipelago. The plan implicitly accepted the loss of the Philippines. No reinforcements would be sent, either before or after war started.

MacArthur sent a strong letter to the War Department on October 1. He argued that his Philippine army would number about 200,000 men by early April 1942. If an enemy could establish air bases on the southern islands—islands undefended in current war plans—that enemy could threaten a local Manila Bay defense. All the islands had to be defended in order to protect Manila Bay, and MacArthur believed that the U.S. and Filipino forces projected for the Philippines would be capable of such a mission. Marshall answered on October 18, informing MacArthur that the Joint Board would approve his plan within the next ten days.

Then, in a letter dated October 28 (written and sent before Marshall's October 18 response arrived), MacArthur optimistically outlined the Philippine military situation to Marshall. Rather than follow the current plan, which he considered defeatist—to wit, an understrength beach defense with regulars, a withdrawal to Bataan, and

a defense of Bataan—MacArthur favored defending Luzon and the other major islands at the beaches.

MacArthur could, as commander of U.S. Army Forces in the Far East (USAFFE), write and execute any sort of plan he wanted, as long as it met the War Department's broad guidlines. But his desire to defend the beaches required assets he did not have. To get those assets from Washington, he had to convince Marshall that a beach defense could work. So MacArthur pressed his plan to defend all the land and sea areas needed to protect the Philippine Archipelago, rather than just Manila Bay.

Admiral Thomas C. Hart, commander of the small, antiquated Asiatic fleet, was enthusiastic about MacArthur's plan. Hart proposed to the Navy Department that the current naval plan for Philippine defense be changed. Rather than sending his ships south when hostilities were imminent, Hart wanted to concentrate them in Manila Bay. Assuming that the army could provide reasonable harbor security, Hart believed that the fleet would be more effective if employed from Manila Bay. He also believed that MacArthur's growing air force would be sufficient to defend fleet units in the bay and that MacArthur's P-40 pursuit air strength had become so strong that even if some enemy bombers got through, there would be no sustained bombing. Finally, Hart pointed out that the United States had a moral obligation to defend its territory and its citizens. So little progress had been made on combined war plans with other nations that a move of the fleet to southern waters might prove worse than useless.

Hart's proposals were significant, and the Navy Department took some time to answer them. But Secretary of the Navy Frank Knox finally said "no." This answer posed a problem for Hart, for he had expected concurrence and had shelved plans to move his ships out of Manila Bay. As a result, some of the ships and supplies that would have been safely tucked away when war started would now be caught in Manila Bay. On receipt of the Navy Department's message, Hart started his ships on their way south. He decided, however, to keep his submarine tenders in Manila Bay; Hart's twenty-nine submarines were his strongest arm, and they needed all the support the tenders could provide.

The Joint Board concurred with MacArthur's plans on November 21. Here was a most amazing inconsistency. The Joint Board said to MacArthur: "Yes, you may defend the islands as you propose. You may form your Filipino army, and we will equip it. Maybe the B-17s will deter the Japanese. If not, maybe a large U.S. and native army will deter them from invading. If they do invade, maybe enough arms and men will have arrived from the States to repulse the Japanese." But MacArthur's wide-area defense implied the necessity for open lines of communications. The three-corps army that MacArthur proposed and was then mobilizing required frequent supplies from the United States. Yet the Joint Board's own minutes stated that MacArthur's changes did not revise the fundamentals of Rainbow Five!

Yes, defend Luzon and the major islands at the beaches. Yes, we will send significant air and ground reinforcements. But no, naval support will not be increased, no reinforcements will be sent when war begins, and there will be no changes to the navy's mission. Other theaters would receive quick reinforcements after war began, but not the Philippines. The navy would still go south. The Pacific Fleet would adhere to its plan to draw enemy strength away from the Malay Barrier.

MacArthur started implementing his plan. He formally established three major commands: North Luzon Force, South Luzon Force, and the Visayan-Mindanao Force. (They had already existed unofficially for several months.) The defense of Luzon would require seven reserve divisions, so USAFFE ordered two divisions up from the Visayan-Mindanao Force to join the five reserve divisions already on Luzon.

Little time remained to implement the new strategy, nor was the mobilizing Philippine army ready for the expanded mission. If any of MacArthur's commanders or staff raised doubts, MacArthur ignored them. And if MacArthur noticed the glaring conflict between the Joint Board's decision and Rainbow Five, he ignored it as well. Under WPO-3, stocks of supplies were to be cached on the Bataan Peninsula. Now, under MacArthur's new plan, these supplies were moved to various camps, motorheads, railheads, and divisional areas in order to be available at the beaches.

Part of the reason MacArthur put his men on the beaches rather than withdrawing them to Bataan when war began concerned air power. MacArthur said that the Japanese had studied German use of air power and would copy it. He expected that the Japanese would attack his airfields and transportation assets. Air attacks on lines of communications and on populated areas would inhibit movement of supplies and choke roads with refugees. If MacArthur's Filipino troops dug in on the beaches, they would not have to move under Japanese air attack. Positioning supplies close to Filipino units would give them the capacity to fight on their own, despite air attacks.

And, of course, MacArthur had to protect his growing air force. It made little sense to build air bases and develop the largest aerial striking force the U.S. military had if these assets were not protected by a field army. Nor would

it be easy politically to mobilize the Filipinos and then abandon the fortified islands and all of Luzon except the minor province of Bataan.

Another reason for the beach defense plan was the propaganda and boasting that justified and buttressed the existence of the new army. Misleading progress reports had so distorted the actual condition of the army that it was a shock to learn its true condition. Even the men grinding out the glowing reports came to believe them. MacArthur believed that the Filipinos could defend the beaches. He had spent years acting as the Philippine army's chief spokesman. After lobbying for money, men, and equipment—after years of envisioning what the defense establishment would ultimately look like, and after years of being ridiculed as a comic field marshal of a toy army—MacArthur believed that he was near the goal.

MacArthur had been living in the future for so long that the present had lost some of its reality. He had struggled daily with Filipino and Commonwealth officials who were disillusioned and defeatist about a national defense. MacArthur's positive, repeated, and long-term affirmations that he and the Philippine army could defend all the islands made it impossible for him to admit he might be wrong. He had expended great political capital and had come close to being sacked by Philippine President Manuel Quezon—all during his struggle to form and fund the Philippine army.

His optimism had infected even the War Department. On November 28, Marshall responded to an enthusiastic report from MacArthur by replying, "The Secretary of War and I were highly pleased to receive your report that your command is ready for any eventuality." Yet in all the history of U.S. prewar planning, there was no sadder self-delusion than that concerning army defense of the Philippines.

The War Department's efforts to reinforce the Philippines involved numerous ships and thousands of men. On August 16, Marshall directed that the Philippines be given the highest priority for equipment. Many of the reasons for not reinforcing the Philippines earlier—no men, no money, no equipment—were not as valid as they had once been. Funds were available, strategy had changed, and requests from MacArthur over the next three months were almost instantly approved. Reinforcements would be limited solely by the availability of shipping. The United States would defend the Philippines but would not so extend itself as to jeopardize major efforts—then in progress and expected—in the Atlantic.

Claims that Washington wrote off the Philippines and abandoned its garrison are unjustified, at least in dealing with the period after 1940. MacArthur had convinced

Secretary of War Henry L. Stimson and Army Chief of Staff Marshall that the islands could be defended. MacArthur's plan did, in fact, offer a better chance of fending off the Japanese than did the current strategy. Unfortunately, no one ever married Rainbow Five's provisions of "Europe First" to the Philippine reinforcement effort.

If Washington had accepted the inevitability of the islands' loss, the reinforcement effort that began in August never would have started. The exceptional efforts to rush aircraft to the Philippines would not have occurred. In hindsight, the decision to reinforce MacArthur came too late. Mobilization of the Philippine army also began too late. Most significant was the gap between the army's trying to hold out for six months and the navy's opinion that a return to the Philippines would take two years. Regardless of that strategic blind spot, there was no stinting of efforts in Washington to reinforce the garrison.

No matter how much the leaders in Washington tried, however, a hard logistical fact was that it took about forty-five days for the average cargo ship to sail from New York to Manila, and a fast passenger ship needed nineteen days to come in from San Francisco. Manila is 5,000 miles from Honolulu and 7,000 miles from San Francisco. Hampered by these facts, the flow of men and materiel into the islands began in earnest. *President Pierce* departed San Francisco on August 28 and arrived in Manila on September 16. It carried the New Mexican 1st Battalion, 200th Coast Artillery Regiment—part of an antiaircraft regiment evaluated as the best available, regular army or National Guard.

The next big ship was *President Coolidge,* a luxury liner used as a troop transport. It arrived in Manila on September 26 after an eighteen-day voyage from San Francisco and landed the 194th Tank Battalion, the remainder of the 200th Artillery, the 17th Ordnance Company, and numerous officer and enlisted casuals. The ship unloaded quickly and headed back to the United States.

The 194th Tank Battalion was the first of two battalions of light tanks to reach the Philippines. They carried with them equipment they had picked up on the docks at San Francisco—equipment so new that the men were unfamiliar with it. About 35 percent of the tankers were recent draftees and new to any kind of armor. More than half the company commanders were lieutenants rather than captains.

Handling of ships at Manila's docks had taken on a new urgency. Ships arrived under blackout conditions and were escorted by U.S. Navy cruisers. Passengers disembarked with stories of blackouts at sea, escorting warships, and convoy procedures. Dockworkers unloaded cargo quickly, and the ships departed. Warships entered Manila Bay with their charges and were out again before the next morning. The arrival in late summer and early fall of even the grand ships had turned from an event worthy of celebration into just another big job requiring new storage space, transportation, and billets.

Two troopships then arrived, *Tasker H. Bliss* and *Willard A. Holbrook,* both escorted into Manila by heavy cruiser USS *Chester. Bliss* carried the 803d Engineer Battalion—with its big tractors, steamrollers, and graders—as well as unassigned personnel. Sixteen hundred enlisted men had been billeted on *Bliss* and had slept on canvas bunks stacked four tall. There was just enough room to sleep flat on one's back or stomach. When a man turned over, he bumped the men above and below.

The two ships and their 2,261 men entered Manila Bay on October 24. Grim-faced soldiers waited to get the men and equipment off the ships as quickly as possible. They unloaded the engineers, the casuals, Headquarters and Headquarters Squadron of the 19th Bomb Group, the 30th and 93d Bomb Squadrons, the 7th Materiel Squadron, four ordnance companies, and a few smaller units.

The last two troop ships to reach the Philippines arrived on November 20. *Hugh L. Scott* carried the 192d Tank Battalion. MacArthur now had two light tank battalions. These National Guardsmen and draftees were ordered to draw their weapons; the islands were on alert! War could be expected with Japan at any moment. The second ship, *President Coolidge,* arrived packed with major formations: Headquarters and Headquarters Squadron of the 27th Bombardment Group (light); 16th, 17th, and 91st Bomb Squadrons; 48th Materiel Squadron; 5th Air Base Group; 21st and 34th Pursuit Squadrons; and the 454th Ordnance Company. Pilots and ground crews made up the bulk of the passengers.

Reinforcements from the United States would give MacArthur only a part of his army. The rest he had to raise in place. So in August 1941, MacArthur issued orders calling ten infantry regiments into service by September 1—one regiment for each of the reserve divisions. MacArthur's mobilization affected ten divisions: the 11th, 21st, 31st, 41st, 51st, 61st, 71st, 81st, 91st, and 101st. USAFFE inducted units and personnel into the armed forces of the United States. Cadres of other divisional elements were also called to the colors.

USAFFE began revising the Philippine army's tables of organization and equipment. The old tables had been based on the equipment available. Newer gear was soon to arrive in quantities larger than ever before seen. Staff officers completed the new tables, mimeographed them, and distributed them in early September. By December

8, the Philippine army would total 120,000 men, of whom 76,750 would be on Luzon, the island fated to serve as the decisive theater.

In bits and pieces, the first regiments mobilized. Young U.S. engineer lieutenants bought building materials for the new camps, often purchasing and expending supplies whose value exceeded $500,000. Construction went slowly at first, but progress increased as supervisors, workers, and suppliers learned their jobs. Camps were basic in the extreme—bamboo or sawed framework nailed or tied together, floors two feet off the ground made of split bamboo strips, 4-foot tall walls of woven leaves or broadleaf grass open to the eaves, and roofs of thatch.

USAFFE realized in late October that sufficient space would be ready by mid-November to mobilize another infantry regiment for each division. In early November, USAFFE mobilized the second infantry regiment to each division and several of the artillery regiments. When USAFFE later called up 90,000 inductees to report to ten mobilization centers, MacArthur's staff crossed their fingers, for it was a real guess whether or not the cadre would be ready to receive them.

The shortest period required to raise and train a division in the United States was longer than a year, and this assumed that the necessary equipment, training areas, and instructors were available. But even at home, where mobilizing soldiers stood next door to factories and depots, assets were spread terribly thin. In the Philippines, infantry divisions were brought forth in haste, fielded in confusion, and sent into battle in less than four months.

Philippine army divisions were, by necessity, light divisions and never received the equipment standard to U.S. infantry divisions. As equipment became available from U.S. stocks, it was shipped to the islands. In this fashion, old equipment being used by the Filipinos was to be replaced with more modern items. The artillery situation was especially bad. Divisional artillery regiments and field artillery training centers needed 160 2.95-inch mountain howitzers, but only 98 were available. USAFFE needed 240 75-mm guns for the ten divisions and thirty-six for the training centers. Ultimately, 114 would become available, 63 of which were the old British Model 1917s—steel-tired, wooden-wheeled, short-ranged, inaccurate, and hard to maneuver. Corps- and army-level artillery was likewise inadequate in numbers and range.

MacArthur would ultimately form three new artillery units from scratch. First, the Americans split the 200th Artillery Regiment in two, pulled extra guns from warehouses and men from other units, and fielded a complete regiment in forty-eight hours. Second, field artillerymen organized a new regiment by manning twenty-four 155-mm guns that had been in storage. Third, by using men from a variety of units, USAFFE formed a provisional artillery group of three battalions of 75-mm self-propelled mounts.

The most visible characteristic of the Philippine army was its incompleteness. For instance, prewar plans had called for engineer mobilization to conclude in October 1942 with each divisional engineer battalion carrying 500 officers and men. But as of December 1, not one battalion had been completely equipped, and all were at about 80 percent strength. Even token organization of these divisional engineers was impractical, considering the untrained personnel and shortages of equipment. Corps and army engineers did not exist.

Time did not allow completion of either mobilization or modernization, and never would a Philippine division reach half the strength of a U.S. division. The Philippine army retained its own national character, uniforms, pay scale, promotion lists, rations, and military law, but as time passed, it took on the appearance of the American army. Most significant was the influence exerted by the hundreds of U.S. officers and enlisted instructors.

MacArthur had mobilized his army and called the Filipinos to the colors. He now had to train them. The training program was supposed to prepare Filipino officers and sergeants to command their own units. Americans were to instruct the Filipinos through native Filipino leaders. MacArthur hoped simultaneously to instruct the Filipino leaders, develop their self-confidence, and gain the trust of the private soldiers. Wherever possible, Filipino leaders would instruct. All too often, however, even the U.S. officers did not know what was going on.

MacArthur's training cadre were U.S. Army regulars, native Filipino scouts and constabulary, and a few Philippine army regulars. The average Filipino draftee did not want to be in the army. He wanted to be back with his family growing rice as his ancestors had been doing for hundreds of years. Yet the Filipinos would work under conditions that U.S. soldiers would not even dream of, living in the open in the rain and mud and cheerfully accepting all manner of hardships. If they were mistreated, however, they never openly rebelled. Rather, they stopped their U.S. instructor cold by passive failure to do anything when his back was turned.

Filipino recruits had to learn about wearing shoes, proper sanitation, and weapons—all with inadequate supplies of clothing, equipment, and weapons. Only the most rudimentary of military skills could be taught. Living conditions were spartan in the extreme. In many camps, a fifteen-minute warning was adequate to alert everyone to leave with all his personal and military gear. Soldiers wore canvas helmets, short-sleeved khaki shirts, short khaki trousers, and rubber-soled canvas shoes. Normal field garb was blue denim trousers without leggings and short-sleeved blue denim shirts. The officers and men were young, of medium size, lean, and attentive.

Language difficulties among the diverse Filipino recruits were acute. The languages of business and social affairs were English and Spanish, and of the hundreds of dialects in the Philippines only two were used extensively: Tagalog on Luzon and Visayan on the southern islands. Except in some regiments formed from Manila citizens, there was a language problem that had to be experienced to be believed. Sergeants could not talk to their corporals, and corporals could neither talk to nor understand their men. People and dialects were thrown together, and babel ensued.

Many U.S. officers had serious doubts about forming an effective army with Filipino draftees, whom some judged as being simple and physically soft, lacking vigor and individualism, fearing the supernatural, and being unwilling to seek responsibility. The farther a recruit lived from a major city, the less was his sense of nationhood and patriotism. Recruits' lives centered on their families, and they evidenced little interest in assuming the responsibilities that came with soldiering.

Headquarters personnel often had no special qualifications and were assigned by lot. Although these men were expected to organize, equip, and train the new formations, they were in no better shape than their subordinate units. A large percentage were illiterate. Tactical training in the infantry regiments had hardly begun. Leadership abilities were sadly lacking, particularly in the absence of trained personnel.

Newly commissioned Filipino third lieutenants commanded some of the mobilizing battalions. Filipino officers had received more training than their men, but it still seemed a pale reflection of what was considered minimal. Key Filipino officers went to the local Command and General Staff School for a six-week course and were then expected to handle division-level training, administration, and logistics. Staff officers were new to their jobs. Most had never before held a staff position.

Trainers faced two big problems: a lack of training manuals and an absence of rifle ranges. Many camps did not have rifle ranges, even though marksmanship was one of the first items on training schedules. Only three Browning automatic rifles were issued to each company, and the only antitank armament available were vintage .50-caliber water-cooled Colt machine guns so old that none of the Americans were familiar with them. There were problems even with the water-cooled .30-caliber ma-

chine guns. Old and badly worn barrels made overhead fire dangerous, inaccurate, and impractical. No steel helmets or pistols were ever procured. Yet through all these hardships, the Filipinos remained cheerful, and morale was excellent.

December 8 came all too soon. Units had not completed training, equipment was desperately short, and Japanese naval and aerial superiority doomed any hopes of reinforcements from the United States. Units deployed to their beach defenses and continued to train. Commanders tried to do everything at once—dig in, incorporate untrained men and unfamiliar equipment, and train. With only two weeks before the main Japanese landing, it proved an impossible task.

Yet without MacArthur's immense effort to mobilize and train this army, the Japanese would have conquered the Philippines with ease. The Filipino army and a small nucleus of Americans delayed the Japanese near the beaches, fought them during the withdrawal down central Luzon, and stopped them on the Bataan Peninsula, which fell from starvation. Then the Japanese stormed Corregidor. For the Americans and Filipinos—from general officer to private soldier—it was a worthy, brave, and honorable effort.

FURTHER READINGS
Meixsel, Richard B. "George Grunert, WPO-3, and the Philippine Army." *Journal of Military History* (April 1995).
Miller, Edward S. *War Plan Orange: The U.S. Strategy to Defeat Japan, 1897–1945* (1991).
Morison, Samuel Eliot. *History of United States Naval Operations in World War II*, vol. III, *The Rising Sun in the Pacific, 1931–April 1942* (1948).
Morton, Louis. *United States Army in World War II: The War in the Pacific. Strategy and Command: The First Two Years.* Office of the Chief of Military History (1962).
Whitman, John W. *Bataan: Our Last Ditch. The Bataan Campaign, 1942* (1990).

John W. Whitman

SEE ALSO MacArthur, Douglas; Philippines, Fall of the; Quezon, Manuel

Army Air Corps/Air Forces, U.S.

To understand fully the U.S. Army Air Corps/Air Forces in the Pacific during World War II, one must look at the development of the country's air forces before its involvement in the war in Asia and the Pacific. The acquisition in the nineteenth century of the Midway Islands, Alaska, the Hawaiian Islands, the Philippine Islands, and Somas supported the maritime policy of the United States at the time and accented the need for a military presence in the area. These acquisitions made the United States a major power in the Pacific Ocean region.

For Japanese and U.S. naval and military leaders—who also fielded their air forces—the problems associated with the central Pacific intensified after World War I. U.S. planners, becoming more and more concerned about the strategic positioning of the Philippines, argued for many years about whether the islands should, or could, be held. Both army and navy officers knew that defending the islands would be nearly impossible if Japan were to move against them. And if war were to break out in this region, the U.S. military could only hope that the Philippines could be retained until reinforcements arrived. Yet with the Caroline, the Mariana, and the Marshall Islands controlled by the Japanese, inserting reinforcements would be more difficult and more dangerous. At the same time Japanese strategists appreciated the value of their island possessions and recognized the problems created by having a major U.S. military base within their own sphere of influence.

As the world situation grew more unstable in the 1930s, war seemed inevitable—and not only in Europe. In 1940 Japan signed the Tripartite Alliance and openly joined the Axis, setting the stage for war in the Pacific.

The development of U.S. armed forces in the 1930s and early 1940s was marked by much discussion about how to organize. There were two independent armed services—the army and the navy; the Army Air Corps/Air Forces would not become a separate service until 1947. Therefore the air force was part of the U.S. Army. It was called the Army Air Corps in 1935 and then the Army Air Forces in 1941.

During the interwar years the Army Air Corps/Air Forces demanded independence. Additionally, there was increased pressure from outside the military establishment for an independent air arm with cabinet representation. The threat of war made the proposal seem so radical that it was not seriously considered. Nonetheless, General George C. Marshall, the army chief of staff, had become very sympathetic toward the airman's point of view in 1939. He preferred an evolutionary as opposed to a revolutionary approach to effecting needed changes in the chain of command. Not surprisingly, General Henry H. "Hap" Arnold, who had been appointed chief of the Army Air Corps in the previous year, favored a more rapid transition. Although he had a different point of view, he worked very closely, and loyally, with General Marshall.

A compromise solution that was reached in 1940 proved very disappointing and was scrapped on June 20, 1941.

Several reorganizations took place between 1920 and 1941, with the last prewar reorganization occurring just six months before the Japanese attacked Pearl Harbor on December 7, 1941. The new Army Air Forces took control of General Headquarters (GHQ) Air Force and the Office of the Chief of the Air Corps. GHQ became the combatant arm of the air force, and the Office of the Chief of the Air Corps became the administrative, support, service, and training arm. General Arnold remained the air commander for the duration of the war. Army Regulation 95-5 (June 20, 1941) established the Army Air Corps and the organization that was in place at the start of the Pacific war.

The Munich Crisis and the obvious importance of the Luftwaffe in Adolf Hitler's diplomatic victory persuaded President Franklin Roosevelt of the need for an immediate and vast expansion of U.S. air power. His successful request in the winter of 1939 for a large defense apportionment provided the necessary means, but it appeared that Roosevelt was more interested in accelerating aircraft production than in organizational issues.

The Army Air Corps at this time played a more prominent role in the procurement and training of men than in the production of aircraft. Extensive use was made for the first time of civilian facilities for turning out aircrews and technicians to man and support the large number of aircraft that were being built, and for the first time provision was made for the training of African American combat aviators, at Tuskegee Army Airfield, Alabama.

From 1926 until 1942 the Army Air Corps' logistical responsibilities were vested in the Office, Chief of the Air Corps (OCAC) Material Division, which was headquartered at Wright Field in Ohio and had four major depots distributed across the United States. A more unified structure was established in 1941 with the restructuring of the Material Division and the creation of the Air Service Command. This provided for clearer lines of authority. To help in the war effort and to supervise the shipment of supplies overseas, the Air Service Command maintained both the Atlantic and the Pacific Overseas Service Commands.

Not only did the newly developed Army Air Corps desire an independent air arm, but it also wanted to develop an air doctrine that evolved around use of heavy bombers for strategic bombardment. Brigadier General "Billy" Mitchell led this fight in the interwar years.

The Army Air Corps Tactical School at Maxwell Field, Alabama, taught the official doctrine for air power. It was during this period that the air theorists began to discuss how best to fight a war not only in Europe but also in the Pacific. What General Mitchell and the other air theorists (most prominently, Italy's General Jilio Douhet) taught was the theory of strategic bombardment. In general, this doctrine stated that air power could strike across great distances against an enemy's national structure. It was offensive as opposed to defensive in nature. This firepower was directed against the enemy's industrial base to destroy its ability to wage war. Strategic bombardment ignored other forms of air power such as fighter escort for the bombers, interceptors, close support of ground forces, and air transport designed to supply deployed forces and to drop paratroopers. The army, on the other hand, understandably felt that the proper role of air power was transport and close support of the ground forces, not strategic bombing.

It should be noted that strategic bombardment was only a theory until Boeing Aircraft Company built the long-range B-17 bomber in 1935. The B-17 seemed to legitimize the concept and provided its proponents with a strong practical argument for their theory. But the army was interested only in direct support of its land forces, or close air support as it was called. With the development of the P-39 and P-40 the army had low-level fighters designed to provide this, so the doctrinal discussion was temporarily suspended. All factions were more or less satisfied, at least for the time being.

The Army Air Corps training program was expanded to accommodate the rapid increase in aircraft, growing from 20,196 trainees in 1938 to 2,372,293 by 1944. The Air Service made up 11 percent of the army's strength in 1938 and 31 percent in 1944.

Traditionally, pilot training had been divided into primary, basic, and advanced courses, which were conducted at Randolph Field, Texas. Then each pilot took a transitional combat-training course for the type of aircraft to which he was assigned. Faced with the problem of gearing up to train the expanding force in 1938, many thought the best way was to reproduce "Randolph Fields" at many locations. But General Arnold had accepted the idea of "mass pilot production," and he advocated using civilian schools to provide primary and technical training. In 1939 he secured nine civilian schools to conduct primary flight training. By the time Pearl Harbor was attacked, civilian schools numbered forty-one, and they increased by May 1943 to fifty-six. During the same period the length of pilot training at civilian schools was reduced, from twelve weeks in 1939 to nine weeks in 1943. A major problem facing the Army Air Corps was the recruitment and retention of civilian instructors. This was

mitigated by using British and U.S. Army air force officers who had served in the Battle of Britain.

Before the 1941 attack on Pearl Harbor, both German and Japanese pilots were receiving more training before unit assignment than were American pilots. But by the end of the war in 1945, U.S. pilots were averaging 360 flying hours to the German Luftwaffe average of about 110 hours; during the same period the Japanese were committing kamikaze pilots (planned or unplanned) to combat with as little as seventy hours of flying time. The discrepancy was even greater when it came to training in combat models.

The use of civilians for the technical training of Army Air Corps nonpilots was a little slower to develop. In 1939 seven civilian schools were under contract, and by the war's start only fifteen were engaged in technical training. In 1941 there were four students per instructor, and expansion came rapidly as the newly established U.S. Army Air Forces (USAAF) turned to universities, airline companies, and aircraft factories for technical training of officer candidates. Most training was still provided by the USAAF and related to such roles as bombardier, navigator, and gunner.

As the world's political situation in the late 1930s deteriorated, a slowly rearming United States was oriented more toward preparing for war in Europe than toward protecting U.S. interests in the Pacific. Then, as war broke out and intensified in Europe, Germany's attack on Russia in June 1941 served as a catalyst for Japan to increase its belligerence. Although in 1937 Japan was engaged in an undeclared war with China, war with the West did not come until four years later. When it did come—Japanese style, and totally unexpectedly—war swept like a scythe through the Far East and the Pacific in 1941 and 1942.

As the Pacific war loomed, the United States flew strategic bombers into the Philippine Islands, which caused Japanese apprehensions to grow and led them to develop overwhelming odds in preparing for war. The Japanese armed forces were divided into five powerful agencies including the Inspectorate of Aviation, which trained and supervised the army's air forces. To support their land campaigns, the army assigned about 430 planes to General Yamashita and about 150 planes to General Homma.

In contrast, in mid-1940 the U.S. Army had only 26 obsolete fighters in Luzon to defend the Philippine Islands. By October 1940 the first P-40s arrived, along with older fighter-bombers. More aircraft were ordered to support the Philippines—265 B-17s and 240 newer models of the P-40—but by war's start only 35 B-17s and 107 P-40s, of various models, were on hand.

As constituted in 1939, the U.S. aircraft industry did not have the capacity to produce within acceptable time limits the planes needed by foreign nations and by the U.S. Army and Navy. Before 1938, M-Day plans for mobilizing the aircraft industry were concerned only with preventing competition among U.S. military agencies. Reflecting contemporary concepts of the air mission, those plans were hopelessly inadequate to provide guidance for President Roosevelt's startling demands. In 1939 some effort was made to educate the arms industry as a means to encourage expansion of munitions factories, but the real incentive to expand came from foreign orders. Before the start of the war, industry leaders were often criticized as being "merchants of death" who actually provoked conflicts, and this made expansion difficult. But under the impetus of the war in Europe, public opinion in the United States began to change. The government and private industry agreed that aircraft production would be expanded by the industry itself. But because profits were limited by the Vinson-Trammell Act, the U.S. aircraft industry preferred to sell to Great Britain and other foreign nations, where no profit limits were imposed. Nonetheless, the industry rose to the occasion and produced aircraft in record numbers for both the domestic and the Allied markets.

Increased emphasis on heavy bomber production came in the autumn of 1940. Because of the size and complexity of these aircraft, current methods of production seemed inadequate. The solution to this problem came in the pooling of resources by several large firms. Consolidated, Douglas, and Ford first tried it when they cooperated in the production of the B-24. The program was expanded to the B-17 program, with Douglas and Vega aiding Boeing. Pooling of assets of Boeing, Douglas, and Vega likewise mass-produced the B-29. Further expansion of this program came in the Victory Program of 1941. Some of the factories were located inland to lessen the dangers of an air attack on the two seaboards. (The production of fighter aircraft was less complicated and therefore did not present similar problems. In fact, one naval fighter producer, Brewster, was forced out of business by the government because its products were hopelessly obsolete and the company itself was mired in corruption.)

None of the new factories was in production when the war began, and some were not in full production until as late as 1943. The start of hostilities seemed to be the impetus to expansion as larger firms made greater use of smaller firms. By the end of 1942 most of the factory space for airframes had been built, and even some excess capacity existed. Aircraft engine and accessory plants continued to expand after 1942.

Shortly after their attack on Pearl Harbor the Japanese struck Luzon, the chief island of the Philippines, destroying the vast majority of the newly formed U.S. Army Air Forces—a debacle similar to Pearl Harbor and even more inexcusable. Next fell Guam (December 8, 1941) and then Wake Island (attacked first on December 10 and finally on December 23). The collapse of Great Britain's defense of Malaya and the fall of the Philippines were the worst military catastrophes in modern British and U.S. history. The Japanese were successful in all these attacks, and it appeared that the Allied responses were ineffectual.

The Japanese "Basic Plan for the Greater East Asia War" called for (1) the seizure of the southern areas; (2) the attack on the U.S. Fleet in Hawaii; (3) the establishment of a perimeter around the southern areas and Japan's home islands (a line that joined the Kuriles, the Marshalls, Wake, the Bismarcks, Timor, Java, Sumatra, Malaya, and Burma); (4) the consolidation and strengthening of the defensive perimeter; and (5) the interception and destruction of any attacking strength which might threaten the defensive perimeter. Intending to destroy the United States's will to fight, the Japanese put their "Basic Plan" into effect on December 7, 1941, and began the first of three major phases: a centrifugal offensive, a period of consolidation, and a defensive phase.

In January 1942 the U.S. Joint Chiefs of Staff and President Roosevelt discussed ways to strike back at Japan. The use of naval air power was dismissed because it was felt that launching aircraft from carriers would put both at fatal risk. They decided to use long-range strategic bombers. General Arnold, in his book *Global Mission,* said that he expected to have two heavy-bombardment groups—about eighty warplanes in four pursuit groups, or 320 aircraft, and one dive-bomber group of fifty-two airplanes—in the Far East by March 1942. President Roosevelt then discussed aircraft production and requested that it be stepped up to meet demands not in the Far East but in the European theater. On April 2, to meet the strategic-bombardment requirements approved by President Roosevelt for the Pacific theater, a mere sixteen B-25 bombers under the command of Colonel James Doolittle left San Francisco harbor aboard USS *Hornet* to conduct the famous Doolittle bombing raid on Tokyo. After being sighted by Japanese picket boats, Admiral Halsey decided to launch the bombers when they were within 650 miles of Tokyo. The B-25s were at the extreme limits of their endurance, and the mission was chancy at best. Thirteen bombers dropped their payloads on Tokyo and three other targets. Only five bombers landed safely, and all were abandoned. The raid might be seen as insignificant were it not for its impact on the Japanese high command: The strategic bombing threatened the home islands themselves.

General Arnold later wrote that there were those who favored immediate bombing of Japan by establishing bases in northern China and in the Aleutian Islands. Inasmuch as the military action in the Far East was an Allied operation, the discussions centered on the representatives of the United States, Great Britain, Australia, the Netherlands, and Russia. And like any discussion of Allied military action, the issues of command and control came up. One of the most difficult problems to resolve was joint operations of army and naval forces in the Pacific, or the combined operations of the Americans, the British, the Dutch, and the Australians. In Southeast Asia the issue of unity of command was resolved by creating the ABDA (American-British-Dutch-Australian) Command. But the issue was never fully resolved for the Pacific as a whole, where only the U.S. Army and the U.S. Navy were involved. (In Europe unity of command was resolved with General Dwight Eisenhower in command of all Allied operations.) The Japanese had a great advantage in this regard because they had one commander in the theater, which allowed him to send air, land, or naval troops in any direction he wanted. The Allies, and particularly the United States, always had two or even three commanders whose operating responsibilities overlapped.

Unity of command aside, General Arnold's USAAF operated under the following fundamental principles:

1. The main objective of the Air Force is bombardment; large formations of bombardment planes must hit the enemy before the enemy hits us. [Just how the enemy could hit the continental United States in any significant numbers with the short-range aircraft of the time was left unanswered.] In short, the best defense is an attack.

2. Our planes must be able to function under all climatic conditions from the North Pole to the tropics.

3. Daylight operations, including daylight bombing, are essential to success for it is the only way to get precision bombing. We must operate with precision bombsight—and by daylight—realizing full well that we will have to come to decisive combat with the enemy Air Force.

4. We must have highly developed, highly trained crews working together as a team—on ground for maintenance and in the air for combat.

5. In order to bring the war home to Germany and Japan, and deprive them of the things that are essential for their war operations, we must carry our strategic precision bombing to key targets, deep in the enemy plants, submarine pens, Navy yards, etc.

6. In addition to our strategic bombing, we must carry out tactical operations in cooperation with ground troops. For that purpose we must have fighters, dive-bombers, and light bombers for attacking enemy airfields, communications centers, motor convoys, and troops. All types of bombing operations must be protected by fighter airplanes. This was proved to be essential in the Battle of Britain, and prior to that our own exercises with bombers and fighters indicate that bombers alone could not elude modern pursuit, no matter how fast the bombers traveled.

7. Our Air Force must be ready for combined operations with ground forces, and with the Navy.

8. We must maintain our research and development programs in order to have the latest equipment it was possible to get, as soon as it was possible to get it.

9. Air power is not made up of airplanes alone. Air power is a composite of airplanes, air crews, maintenance crews, air bases, air supply, and sufficient replacements in both planes and crews to maintain a constant fighting strength, regardless of what losses may be inflicted by the enemy. In addition to that, we must have the backing of a large aircraft industry in the United States to provide all kinds of equipment, and a large training establishment that can furnish the personnel when called upon.

At the height of the Japanese war expansion in the summer of 1942 the Japanese empire controlled nearly 40 million miles of ocean and landmass. To respond to Japan's lopsided dominance in the Pacific, the USAAF formed six self-contained air forces that were charged with defending specific areas: the Eleventh Air Force defended Alaska as well as Attu and Kiska (the Japanese had taken a toehold in these two areas of the Aleutians); the Tenth (commanded by World War I air ace Major General Clayton L. Bissell) and Fourteenth Air Forces operated in the China-Burma-India theater (the Fourteenth, led by General Claire L. Chennault, included the units known as the Flying Tigers); and the Fifth (under the command of Lieutenant General George C. Kenney), Seventh, and Thirteenth Air Forces were charged with waging war in the southern and central Pacific.

By the latter part of 1942 the Allied forces had seized the initiative in accordance with the "Europe First" decision, which gave the war in Europe priority over the war with Japan. This created problems for military planners in the Pacific, but so did the sheer size of the theater and the logistical challenges they faced. Fortunately, successes by General Douglas MacArthur and Admiral Chester Nimitz gave encouragement that the Allied forces in the Pacific would eventually also be victorious.

After the Allied seizure of the Marianas brought the B-29 heavy strategic bomber into range of Japan's home islands, the USAAF could begin what it felt was the main air effort: the bombardment of those islands' infrastructure. Engineers began the development of airfields on the Marianas for use by the B-29s. It should be noted that this offensive, like the Combined Bomber Offensive against Germany in the European theater, was no more than an adjunct to other plans for the defeat of Japan.

When the B-29 offensive was launched in 1942, no final strategy for the defeat of Japan had been developed. Two plans were advocated. One was that General MacArthur's forces—mainly U.S. Army—would advance northward from New Guinea, by way of the Philippines, toward Japan. Proponents of this strategy pressed for a decision to concentrate U.S. resources, including air power, on this line of attack. Advocates of the second strategy favored a drive, under the leadership of Admiral Nimitz, that would concentrate air and sea resources on the China coast as preliminary to an attack on Japan's home islands. By the summer of 1944 the Joint Chiefs of Staff resolved the debate by determining that for the time being there were advantages in keeping the Japanese forces under the pressure of a double attack. Thus both "strategies" were left in place. Meanwhile, the strategy of island hopping allowed engineers to develop airfields for the USAAF to use in support of the air campaign in the Pacific. Between October and December 1944, many air and naval battles had the objective of securing the islands.

One battle in particular, the Battle of Leyte Gulf in the Philippines, proved one of the principles of air operations in reverse. The principle is that, to be successful, air operations must be able to assert and maintain superiority in the area of battle. The Leyte operation, however, was a risk—but one that seemed worth taking. The operation also violated a cardinal principle of the Pacific strategy: to keep each forward move within reach of the land-based air forces. Admiral Nimitz assured all that he could provide sea-based protection until General Kenny could move his air garrisons forward.

Allied naval and air forces eased the landing on Leyte by means of preinvasion bombardment. The Japanese had anticipated the invasion and had positioned their forces to resist these initial landings in the Philippines. But the daring of the U.S. fleet forces, assisted by the air assets (and blunders by the Japanese), saved the beachhead from the intended assault by the main body of the Japanese fleet.

General Kenny reacted promptly to the emergency request for help at Leyte, immediately dispatching warplanes. When these air assets were in place, they created a lucrative target for the enemy, because crowded conditions clustered the P-38s together. The Japanese sent more than a thousand sorties against Leyte over a period of sixty-five days. Fortunately, U.S. defense forces proved superior, and losses were relatively low.

In October 1944, the Far East Air Forces used both heavy-bombardment groups of the Thirteenth Air Force to fly sorties on Philippine targets. The groups were brought forward to the island of Morotai. By November 7 the USAAF's heavy-bombardment group, the 494th, added weight to the attack. The heavy bombardment by the naval and air forces began to count, and U.S. air forces began to gain air superiority over the region.

Fortunately, given time, the U.S. Command had more than enough resources to make good the gamble at Leyte; fortunately, too, the leaders showed continued willingness to count on the declining power of the Japanese. The U.S. Command stepped up the timetable of operations. With success in the Philippines the Joints Chief of Staff resolved the strategy debate in October 1944 by agreeing with General MacArthur that his advance should be through the island of Mindoro; he then was to stand ready to assist Admiral Nimitz in a later occupation of Okinawa. Mindoro was to serve as an advanced air base for cover of the landings by MacArthur's forces on the island of Luzon. The rapid development of the Philippine campaign allowed U.S. forces not only to overrun Luzon but also to retake the entire Philippine Archipelago by the summer of 1945.

The U.S. Army Air Forces demonstrated an extraordinary versatility both in the fulfillment of its primary responsibility and also in the support of the other services. In the Philippines, as earlier in New Guinea and Midway, USAAF planes struck ahead of land and amphibious forces to clear the way and to protect convoys and other troop movements. The USAAF not only found the resolve to assist the Australians in the reconquest of Borneo but also assumed responsibility for the defense of Formosa (Taiwan) and aided the naval forces on Okinawa. When kamikaze attacks seriously endangered U.S. operations supporting the Okinawa operations in April 1945, the USAAF stepped up its attacks on suspected kamikaze bases on the islands of Kyushu and Formosa. One of the lessons learned by the kamikaze attacks was that air supremacy can never be assumed as an absolute.

When the war had ended, USAAF units flying from the hard-won bases of Okinawa had already brought Kyushu—the southernmost of Japan's home islands—under attack in a preparatory move to assist in a scheduled amphibious landing in November 1945. Earlier assumptions that the assault on Japan would require the establishment of some sort of lodgment or base on the Chinese mainland had been abandoned.

As mentioned above, the issue of command in the Pacific complicated agreeing on a strategy for the defeat of Japan. That was resolved when General MacArthur was given command of all army units and Admiral Nimitz was assigned all naval forces. The two commanders were to cooperate in joint operations. The Far East Air Force—enlarged by the addition of the Seventh Air Force redeployed to Okinawa—was to operate as MacArthur's air command. A new command, the U.S. Army Strategic Air Forces in the Pacific, would control XXI Bomber Command and the Eighth Air Force when redeployed from the European theater. It too would be stationed on Okinawa, after being established on Guam under General Carl Spaatz in preparation for invading Japan.

The decision to mount the attack from island bases without the benefit of a lodgment on the east coast of China meant that the war would end with no real connection between the Pacific theater and the China-Burma-India (CBI) theater. The CBI was plagued by personal animosities and the divergent interests of the three Allied powers. It lay at the extreme end of the supply lines from the United States, and it was accorded a low priority in the assignment of combat forces. The Tenth Air Force was committed in the summer of 1944 to a campaign in northern Burma with dual objectives to open a road into China and to secure bases for a route over "the Hump" (the route from India to free China). After the Burma campaign, the Tenth was moving into China to unite with the Fourteenth Air Force under the leadership of General Claire Chennault. He developed tactics that were so successful that his warplanes were able to support Chinese ground forces and strike at shipping from advance bases in eastern China while still protecting the northern end of the route.

The CBI command structure was made more complicated by the deployment of XX Bomber Command, which, equipped with B-29s, was dedicated to strategic bombardment. The B-29, developed during the expansion of the Army Air Corps/Air Forces from 1939 on, was made combat-ready by 1944 only by the Air Service staff's willingness to take shortcuts in testing and procurement.

XX Bomber Command was really more an air force than a command. It was put together in a hurry, and its mission in the CBI was to provide shakedown experience for the B-29 and the organization. The Joint Chiefs of Staff established the Twentieth Air Force under its own command with General Henry "Hap" Arnold, Air Service chief of staff, as "executive agent." This meant that whichever theater commander whose area of operation had B-29s stationed would be charged with administrative and logistical responsibilities but would not have operational control. That would remain with Army Air Forces headquarters in Washington. This system of divided responsibilities was tested most severely in the CBI.

Although the B-29 was originally designed to be used in the European theater against the Germans, by the summer of 1943 it was felt that the plane could be better used against the Japanese (the B-17 and B-24 were beginning to succeed in the air war over Germany). The B-29 was now seen as a strategic bomber to be used against Japanese industry and population centers. But it would take months before bases would be seized and expanded to accept the B-29s in the Pacific. In the meantime, in order to bolster flagging Chinese morale, and with the concurrence of President Roosevelt, the B-29 was sent to the CBI.

Air support of the Pacific operations was designed to prevent Japan from reinforcing its air garrisons during the invasion of the Philippines. When XX Bomber Command finally began operations in the Pacific, from its newly won bases on the Mariana Islands, it shifted its attention from the steel-industry missions it had been flying from the CBI, without much success, to aircraft factories, repair shops, and staging bases in Formosa and Manchuria and to factories in Japan itself.

From the end of November 1944 to mid-March 1945 most of the air missions were directed against the aircraft industry. The B-29 assault began on November 24, 1944, with a strike against Nakajima's Musashino aircraft plant in Tokyo. The B-25 medium bomber also played an important role in the Pacific theater. In March 1943, a squadron of B-25s under the command of General George Kenney destroyed an entire convoy of more than six thousand Japanese reinforcements aboard seven transports with attending escorts headed for the port of Lae in northern New Guinea.

The first mass bomber raid on Tokyo was undertaken on March 9, 1945, when 325 B-29s departed from bases in Saipan, Tinian, and Guam for the 6-hour flight to Tokyo. This was a low-level incendiary attack against a city constructed primarily of wood. The results exceeded all expectations: 16 square miles of Tokyo were burned out completely, and about 85,000 Japanese, mostly civilians, perished in the worst nonnuclear air raid in history.

Thus opened XXI Bomber Command's incendiary attacks against urban areas, which changed the nature of bombing campaigns. Now both industrial targets and urban centers were being hit. Future U.S. air attacks against cities, as against Pyongyang and Sinuiju during the Korean War, would basically aim to burn them down. Additionally, Japan's home islands were subjected to heavy bombardment by U.S. Navy and Army Air Forces fighter aircraft, which now could range almost unopposed. The air attacks appeared to be taking their toll on the enemy's war resolve, and it was hoped that they would bring Japan to the peace table. But there was no official word from the Japanese government—only resolutions to carry on the struggle.

Undoubtedly the greatest single contribution of the Army Air Forces was the delivery of the atomic bomb. At 8:15 on the morning of August 6, 1945, the *Enola Gay,* a B-29 from the specialized 509th Composite Group, dropped a single uranium nuclear bomb—"Little Boy"— on Hiroshima, releasing the power of 20,000 tons of TNT in a millisecond. This mission was the culmination of over four years of development by the United States and Great Britain (which helped mostly in the difficult initial stages) at a cost of some $2 billion. The new weapon was first tested near Alamogordo, New Mexico, on July 16, just twenty-one days before the bomb was dropped. President Harry S. Truman personally and specifically authorized its use if Japan refused to accept the Allies' terms of surrender in the Potsdam Declaration.

At 11:01 on the morning of August 9, another B-29 dropped a second bomb—the plutonium "Fat Man"— over Nagasaki. In addition, the razing of Japan by conventional air strikes continued until August 15, 1945, when the Japanese government, after much internal struggle, finally accepted the Potsdam Declaration's terms. Thousands of American servicemen and Japanese civilians would not have to die in the projected invasion of Japan, the greatest U.S. military operation ever planned. For the first time, a major nation had been defeated without the enemy's landing on its soil.

FURTHER READINGS

Arnold, H. H. *Global Mission* (1949).
Blakeney. "The Japanese High Command." *Military Affairs* IX (summer 1945).
The Campaigns of the Pacific War. United States Strategic Bombing Survey—Pacific (1946).
Cardwell, Thomas A. III. *Command Structure for Theater Warfare* (1984, 1992).
Craven, Wesley F., and James Lea Cate, eds. *The Army Air Forces in World War II,* vol. 5, *The Pacific: Matterhorn to Nagasaki, June 1944 to August 1945* (1953); vol. 6, *The Pacific: Men and Planes* (1955).
Goldberg, Alfred, ed. *A History of the United States Air Force, 1907–1957* (1957).
Momyer, William W. *Air Power in Three Wars* (1978).
Mason, Herbert Mollory Jr. *The United States Air Force: A Turbulent History* (1976).

Thomas A. Cardwell

SEE ALSO Aircraft: Japanese, U.S., and British; Air Offensive, Japan; Kenney, George C.; LeMay, Curtis

Army Air Force, Japanese

Unlike their German and British counterparts, the Japanese did not create a separate aviation arm but maintained a Naval Aviation Force, which included float, carrier-based, and ground-based elements and an Army Air Force of ground-based air forces. The Japanese Army Air Force consisted primarily of observation, air superiority (fighter), and bomber aircraft, and the supporting logistics, maintenance, ground support, and administrative units with the command structures to direct and lead them. The Imperial Army Air Force, however, lacked a strategic mission or the heavy forces needed to carry out such a mission. The absence of strategic industrial targets in the theater of operations among potential adversaries and the distances involved, along with the cost of required units, precluded the development of the strategy and forces needed. The army's forces were tied to the mission of supporting the army and its ground operations. A medium bomber force was developed and proved very effective in China and the Pacific.

The Japanese Army Air Force was created in the years before World War I (1914–1918). Japanese aviation units took part in the operations against the Germans in China and supported the army with observation missions. In the interwar years Japanese youth caught aviation fever like the rest of the world, and like the rest of the world aviators found themselves at odds with conservative leaders of the army. However, the Japanese ground commanders in Manchuria and later in China found air support useful, and the lack of a strategic force meant that air power was seen as a helpful addition to the army rather than its replacement.

The Japanese Army Air Force was organized in a manner similar to its Western counterparts. Although the emperor was in nominal control, the Imperial Army Headquarters exercised real control through the Aviation Inspectorate General with approval of the chief of staff and the War Department. Although the General Headquarters Air Force was created in 1936, the independence and prestige of the Army Air Force increased significantly after 1938. The Aviation Inspectorate General had control over aircraft acquisition and training, although deployment and tactical operations fell under the War Department and the field commanders. Several wings were created in 1936. They were located in as follows: the First Wing in Kagamigahara, Japan; the Second Wing in Kainie, Korea; and the Third Wing in Kagi, Formosa. The wing commanders were responsible for training, maintenance, and operations within their wings. The wings themselves consisted of a number of administrative and support units as well as one or more air divisions, each of which was made up of regiments of similar aircraft with similar missions. In turn, the air regiments were made up of squadrons of between eight and sixteen aircraft with administrative and maintenance elements as organic ground support.

The design and procurement of aircraft was divided between the services (army and navy), with the designs being shared and modified to meet the needs of each service. Army designs focused multi-engine aircraft for a variety of missions and later on single-engine aircraft for defense of the homeland. This process produced a number of successful designs, although there tended to be a focus on maneuverability and range over crew and vital component (engines, avionics, and fuel) protection. In 1937, the army had 540 first-line aircraft, adding 200 or so a year. By December 8, 1941, the day after the Japanese attack on the U.S. naval base at Pearl Harbor, Hawaii, it had close to 1,500 first-line planes. There were 550 fighters, 660 bombers (two-engine tactical) and 290 observation and reconnaissance aircraft when the war started. Production increased slowly during the war and by 1945, the Imperial Army was adding 3,000 aircraft a year, which, however, was not enough to keep up with losses.

The training of pilots was time consuming and wasteful in both men and material. Pilot cadets were selected from a pool of highly qualified candidates and then placed in a rigorous flight-training program. The training consisted of avionics, aerodynamics, and ground, flight, and formation training. Numerous candidates were lost to accidents and washouts in the two-year program. (The American training program lasted six months and was shortened during the war to produce the pilots needed for combat; a number of training requirements were completed once the new pilots arrived at their units.) Al-

though the graduates were well-trained, the flight schools only produced a trickle of new pilots that never seemed to meet the operational needs of the Army Air Force, even before the pressures of sustained combat operations. The constant attrition in China and later expansion into the Pacific and the increased combat losses meant that experienced pilots stayed in combat much longer than their counterparts on the Allied side. Despite the need for more pilots in the field, the schools opposed lower standards; this opposition received some support from the military hierarchy until late in the war, when it became evident that the pilot shortage was crippling air operations. Also contributing to the decision to shorten the training program was a shortage of fuel for training. The decision to resist reform in pilot-training programs ultimately led to a collapse of the training system by 1943, with new pilot graduates being wholly unprepared for combat and the numbers of veterans so reduced as to be unable to even provide cadre for the new units and mentors for the new pilots being fielded by 1944. The extreme swing from an intense training program to virtually no real training proved disastrous for the units in the field and the entire force.

By the time the army accepted the use of the suicide kamikaze attacks during the Philippines campaign, pilot training had reached such a low level that even that one-way flight was a challenge for many of the young men who flew the missions. Life expectancy for young pilots on normal nonkamikaze missions was so low that there appeared to be little difference between the two.

The operational control of Japanese Army Air Force units in theater was nominally under the ground commander and his staff, but in practice the air units conducted their own campaigns. This was a result of two factors: (1) limited experience with air operations on the part of ground commanders leading to a tendency to defer operational control to the air commanders, and (2) the desire of the air commanders themselves to have control over their own operations. Despite these drawbacks, the Japanese ground operations were often well-supported by air units in China and in the early stages of the Pacific war. Air observation especially proved effective and forward control by air of the artillery fire missions and counter battery fire often gave the Japanese the upper hand on the battlefield.

Army air units participated in the southern expansion and provided the bulk of the air units for the Chinese campaign. This campaign proved to be an excellent opportunity for experimentation in equipment and tactics as well as providing hands-on maintenance and logistics training for ground-support units. The Japanese also applied the prevailing theory of terror bombing on a number of Chinese cities including Nanking and later Shanghai.

Japanese Army air units participated to some degree in every campaign in the Pacific war. During the war, the Army Air Force maintained sizable units in China and Manchuria. Army air units operated in the Burma theater and the Southwest Pacific campaigns in New Guinea, the Philippines, and the Solomons. Normally, the army found its units in a defensive role after 1942.

The Japanese Army Air Force also played a significant role in the defense of the homeland once the Allies began their strategic bombing campaign. The Army Air Force used a number of new types of aircraft including rocket propelled and specially designed kamikaze planes designed to be flown into enemy bomber formations. But the small number of experienced pilots, overwhelming numbers of enemy bombers, lack of an effective early-warning system, and aggressive U.S. fighter escorts prevented the defenders from achieving any significant results.

FURTHER READINGS

Barker, A. J. *Japanese Army Handbook, 1939–1945* (1979).

Reports of General MacArthur: Japanese Operations in the Southwest Pacific Area. Vol. II, Parts I and II, U.S. Government Printing Office (1966).

Maver, S. L., ed. *The Japanese War Machine* (1976).

James Birdseye

SEE ALSO Aircraft: Japanese, U.S., and British

Army Ground Forces, U.S.

U.S. Army ground forces in the Pacific saw every type of combat imaginable: retreats and defeats in the steamy Philippines, cold-weather operations in Alaska and the Aleutians, and slow advances and torturous fights for small patches of swamps. There were land marches, ship-to-shore and shore-to-shore operations, amphibious landings, airborne drops, airlift movements, tank battles, atoll warfare, island warfare, jungle warfare, mountain warfare, and city combat.

Starting in late 1942, the American soldier bested the Japanese in an unbroken string of victories. The U.S. Army soldier was tactically flexible and responded to every obstacle placed in his path—from rugged terrain to debilitating weather to a tough, disciplined enemy. Battalions and regiments started the trek to Tokyo and were followed by corps and armies. The American soldier's

bravery and determination wore down and buried the Japanese beneath a landslide of U.S. production as well as a sizable numerical superiority.

The army has traditionally been the nation's main killing punch. Its strategy has been one of raw power and annihilation. In the Pacific, however, it had a slightly different role. With the significant exception of General MacArthur in the Philippines in 1944–1945, the army fought not to seize land masses, or to capture cities and resources, or even to destroy the enemy's armed forces in the field—long the touchstone of the American principles of war.

Rather, in the Pacific the U.S. Army fought to establish air bases, naval bases, and anchorages. It fought to extend the air umbrella and logistics bases as steps toward the Japanese home islands and the goal of all U.S. troops: Tokyo—and then home. It had to fight its way into a position from which it could launch its traditional decisive blow. The army bypassed enemy resistance where it could and focused its power against targets that had to be attacked. Army and navy campaigns along different axes supported one another, allowed the use of the nation's vast industrial output, and kept the Japanese constantly under pressure and usually off balance.

The army seized and secured air bases and logistical staging points to support the next hop forward. An aircraft's radius of action helped determine subsequent targets. Once close enough to the home islands, submarines cut supply lines, and B-29s began the conventional and atomic bombings that directly attacked Japan's war-making ability. Bombardment and blockade—the airplane and the submarine—were the decisive tools in the Pacific war. Yet without the army ground forces to seize the bases for land-based aircraft and ships and hold them against counterattack, there would have been no victory in the Pacific.

The biggest problem for the army in the Pacific would prove not to be of strategy, or tactics, or even combat with the Japanese—although the last was obviously the deadliest, for the Japanese may well have been the best large-scale light infantry force in modern history. The biggest problem lay with resource prioritization both within the Pacific theater (army versus navy, southwest Pacific versus central Pacific) and without (Europe, Mediterranean, and China-Burma-India versus the Pacific). "Germany first" was the plan, and so it would be. The European Theater of Operations (ETO) had a priority over the Pacific theater that, for the entire war, dominated U.S. Army fighting and supply efforts.

The U.S. War Department decided early to allocate forces to the Pacific at a level sufficient for safety and for offensive action but insufficient for swift conquest. In particular, army air strength was dispatched only reluctantly to the Pacific. Later, when the army began deploying huge numbers of troops and amounts of equipment, ETO priorities still strictly conditioned Pacific efforts. Army service forces in the Pacific—actually the shortage thereof—also limited how quickly air and ground forces could be committed to combat.

Only 23 percent of the army's divisions went to the Pacific—twenty-one divisions (Americal, 1st Cavalry, 11th Airborne, 6th, 7th, 24th, 25th, 27th, 31st, 32d, 33d, 37th, 38th, 40th, 41st, 43d, 77th, 81st, 93d, 96th, and 98th Infantry) versus sixty-eight in Europe and the Mediterranean. On the other hand, most of the navy's strength went to the Pacific, including all six of its marine corps divisions. For the U.S. Army and Army Air Forces a feeling would grow that "the big war" was in Europe while the Pacific was secondary. Even so, by the end of the war 1,804,408 army personnel were deployed throughout the Pacific.

The Joint Chiefs of Staff—America's supreme military authority except for the president himself—also decided to forgo unity of command. In the navy's view, the war in the Pacific would be primarily a naval war and would thus require naval leadership. That service refused to put its forces under General MacArthur. The navy's choice for the Pacific Command was Admiral Chester W. Nimitz, but he was too junior (in length of service) to MacArthur and too unknown to be placed over MacArthur. The army, likewise, did not want to work under the navy. The Joint Chiefs therefore divided the Pacific into the Southwest Pacific Area Command (under MacArthur) and, to the north and east, the Pacific Ocean Areas Command (under Nimitz).

The issue of who should command in the Pacific—MacArthur or Nimitz—surfaced periodically. Yet the command problem had little impact on the prosecution of the war. Divisions and corps fought under both army and navy command. "Jointness," that is, different military services operating together, succeeded. In particular, the farther forward one traveled and the closer one came to actual fighting, the better were joint operations and the will of the services to cooperate. Turf battles seemed to be the sport of rear-echelon types.

War is wasteful. And the Pacific war was a war of attrition. Although there were big battles, the army and navy ground down the Japanese principally through daily skirmishes and deaths. There were no thundering mechanized double envelopments, no corps-level thrusts deep into enemy territory, no destructive headline-grabbing surrender of armies and capture of cities. Instead, it was

one damned island after another—one ship sunk, one airplane shot down, men killed here, men bypassed and starved there. But it all added up. The Japanese could not replace their losses, rebuild shattered forces, or even repulse American attacks. By the fall of 1943, U.S. forces were generally stronger than the Japanese. By mid-1944, U.S. ground, air, and sea superiority moved toward the overwhelming.

Getting the combat arms—the "shooters"—into place has always been the easiest part of a war. Getting the support structure there to keep the shooters active has been the hardest part. There were two principal considerations for the army in the Pacific: (1) the vast distances and lack of infrastructure and (2) the weighty drag of ETO priority. Fortunately, the United States had enough resources that adequate supplies reached the Pacific front. Destruction and wearing out of equipment in the combat zones was to be expected. Frontline troops were none too concerned about fastidiously maintaining what they had: Use it up; wear it out; abandon the remains. As war correspondent Ernie Pyle wrote, "At the front there just isn't time to be economical." (Or as the "soldiers' cartoonist" Bill Mauldin had a British trooper remark to a U.S. soldier amid war's debris in Italy, "You Yanks certainly leave a messy battlefield.")

What was disturbing was the waste in the rear areas. A lack of trained quartermaster troops and materiel-handling equipment, an absence of warehousing facilities, and delays in movement of supplies over inadequate roads routinely damaged goods. Trucks hauling supplies off beaches broke down from sand and salt. Insufficient engines and spare parts were being forwarded. Despite all that, more and more supplies and more and more soldiers arrived.

Shipping tonnage handcuffed strategy and tactics throughout the war. There were never enough ships. The shipping shortage was so severe in mid-1944 that cargo bound for the Pacific stacked up on the West Coast. The lack of modern unloading equipment in the western Pacific areas and the absence of warehouses, trucks, and labor meant that ships could not unload quickly. The ships often served as floating warehouses—their crews useless and numb from boredom—and could not recycle back to the United States as planned. That then threw into confusion the entire supply effort.

Aggravating the supply problem was the weather. Pacific heat, rain, and mold ravaged poorly stored supplies of all kinds. Hard handling at U.S. ports started the deterioration. Rough seas, poor storage in ships' holds, and hasty unloading weakened and destroyed packaging. Troops handling the flow of goods through the pipeline siphoned off their share and ensured that their footlockers were packed before supplies continued forward.

Then the wet, hot Pacific weather rotted, broke, and spoiled up to 25 percent of all food sent there. Leather dissolved. Metal rusted. Ammunition corroded. Canvas rotted. In 1944, soldiers staging on New Guinea lived under canvas that normally would have been condemned and discarded. Men lived in primitive conditions and ate field rations for extended periods. Clothing shortages in the United States resulted in a warning to the Pacific armies to make exceptional efforts to salvage and reuse damaged uniforms. In short: wash off the blood, sew up the holes, and put the uniform back on.

The United States deployed a citizen army to the Pacific, mainly volunteers and draftees. In 1940, there were only two regular divisions in the army strong enough and well enough equipped to be dignified with the title "division." The regulars were scattered across the country, beginning the early stages of mobilization. At the height of the war, only 3.5 percent of the army ground forces were regulars, 2.6 percent of the army service forces, and 1.3 percent of the army air forces. The vast majority of the fifty-four officers per 1,000 enlisted men (the highest ratio of any serious army in the world) were guardsmen, reservists, or newly commissioned.

By December 7, 1941, the army had mobilized sixteen regular army divisions, fifteen National Guard divisions, and two Army of the United States (draftee) divisions. All were poorly equipped and in need of training. The army was extremely fortunate that it had time and space to absorb the Japanese attack while it trained its divisions. However, that time and space had come at a cost. Lost in the Philippines were the regular army's excellent Philippine Division as well as twelve recently mobilized, understrength, poorly equipped Filipino divisions. There were also U.S. Navy and British, Australian, and Dutch losses throughout the Pacific.

Of the twenty-one Pacific divisions deployed out of the United States and Hawaii, fourteen had been in existence before December 7. The nine National Guard divisions had averaged thirteen months to organize and train in federal service before war began. Eleven months of war passed before the 32d Division made first contact with Japanese at Buna in New Guinea, and another month elapsed before the first U.S. Army contact at division strength with the Japanese on Guadalcanal. Only five divisions were fighting as late as March 1943, and they had averaged over sixteen months of post–December 7 training before commitment to combat.

It took time for U.S. air and naval forces to beat down their Japanese opposite numbers. Only then could army divisions reach terrain on which they could fight. By December 1942, nine army divisions were in the Pacific theater (Hawaiian Islands or farther west), of which only two were in combat contact. By December 1943, fifteen divisions were in the Pacific, but still only two were fighting. Six more arrived in 1944, so that by the end of that year all twenty-one were present. Of that number, about eight were in serious contact with the enemy by December 1944. Because it took so long to reach battlefields large enough to accommodate significant numbers of troops, U.S. divisions averaged more than twenty-four months of post–December 7 training time before entering combat.

The War Department made a prewar decision that saved many lives when it determined to remove many National Guard officers from their division command and staff positions based on their poor performance during 1940 and 1941 maneuvers. These officers had often achieved their positions through state political connections or by able World War I service. Many were overage for their duties. They could not now perform at the required pace, and out they went. A similar purge of regular army officers prevented too great a cry of anti-Guard discrimination.

The Pacific's exceptionally long lines of communications created another manpower problem. Vast quantities of supplies and tens of thousands of men were always awaiting transportation or were en route. And large numbers of troops were tied up in serving them. Theater commanders and the War Department disagreed over how many men and supplies were actually available. The War Department had shipped x men and supplies, but the theater commanders were fighting the war with y—almost always a figure significantly lower than x. Much of the difference was flowing through the pipeline. Pacific commanders wanted more, and they had little use for Washington's bookkeeping.

Enormous logistics efforts accompanied the troops. The army service forces ran those logistics, and Australia became the first great army supply base. The army staged through and drew its supplies from Australia for nearly two years. Australia served as a zone of the interior in a manner similar to the continental United States for all overseas theaters. Only in 1944 did New Guinea become the army's chief logistical base. That base staged forward into the Philippines in 1945. Although there was occasional logistics chaos and confusion, the simplest verdict on the army service forces was, "It worked, didn't it?"

The army overcame all the organizational, logistics, weather, distance, and terrain obstacles; ate mediocre food and endured disease; and still found time—when teamed with their navy, marine, and army air forces comrades—

to kill or starve Japanese at astounding enemy-friendly ratios: 4 to 1 on Attu in the Aleutians, 15 to 1 at Guadalcanal, 19 to 1 during the approach to the Philippines, 18 to 1 at Leyte, 25 to 1 in the Philippines, and a disturbing drop to 9 to 1 on Okinawa. These ratios admittedly decline dramatically when friendly wounded are added to U.S. totals.

Massive firepower, battlefields isolated by the navy and by the army air forces from Japanese relief, and U.S. strategic and battlefield mobility left few of the campaigns in doubt. Time and again, the army ground forces, the navy, the army air forces, and the marines proved that they could take any ground they wanted. There was always a price, but nowhere could the Japanese stop the advance.

European combat—especially long, multiple-month campaigns—cut heavily into army manpower. Replacing combat losses was never accomplished in an efficient manner or in the necessary quantities in that theater. The situation was somewhat different in the Pacific. Campaigns were usually relatively short and isolated in time and space, with obvious exceptions like New Guinea and Luzon. There was a physical limit to the size of Pacific battlefields and the numbers of men who could be employed. Battalions and regiments, not divisions and corps, were often the key maneuver units.

Infantry losses were far higher than expected. On Luzon, infantry suffered 90 percent of all casualties. European combat had taught that divisions should not be left in the line for more than thirty to forty days. Otherwise, men got tired and careless. Fatigue and anxiety reduced the will to fight. Sick rates and casualties rose. For most Pacific units, although combat losses might be heavy, they were usually incurred over relatively limited periods. And until 1945, there were generally long periods between campaigns to rest, refit, and bring in replacements. In fact, the out-of-action time of Pacific divisions is astounding. Only in 1945 did the average division spend more time in combat than it did in moving, training, resting, and rehabilitating.

The army of World War II had been tailored for mobility at the expense of power. Officers who wrote tables of organization and equipment had looked to Europe and to the principle of maneuver when they designed the triangular division—a division inferior in infantry and staying power to the World War I square division. Yet army strategy harkened back to Ulysses S. Grant and John J. Pershing—to wit: overwhelming attacks with overwhelming strength. The World War II triangular divisions had too few infantry for a battle of attrition, yet that is where the losses would occur. Nor could these divisions often exploit their mobility advantage. Only in the march down Luzon's central plain and the approach to Manila in 1945 could the army flex its overwhelming mobility advantage.

The ETO soldier lived better in matters of health, food, and housing than did his Pacific comrade. Disease was more challenging in the Pacific than in Europe and seriously reduced U.S. fighting strength. Doctors generally understood and could treat European diseases. Exotic Pacific diseases, however, took time to isolate, understand, and treat. On Guadalcanal, 65 percent of hospitalized soldiers were felled by disease. Luzon probably saw the highest U.S. Army nonbattle casualty rate experienced in World War II (excluding the 1941–1942 Bataan–Corregidor campaign). The army admitted 86,950 sick soldiers to hospitals (which included a growing number of psychiatric cases) versus 47,000 battle casualties. Okinawa was a slightly more temperate island than many farther south, yet hospitalized nonbattle casualties cost 15,613 soldiers, while the Japanese more directly killed 4,582 and wounded 18,099.

The unique Pacific problems were debilitating weather, disease, the long pipeline that gobbled up replacements, and (in the absence of an infrastructure) the requirement for an unusually large number of service troops. The Pacific did not receive forces of sufficient size—especially army air and service forces—to destroy the Japanese swiftly. Commanders knew the restorative value of even a few days out of the front line to shave, wash, eat, and sleep. But commanders were also always tempted to put what they had into the line. Like the ETO, the Pacific theater had too few divisions to allow regular and frequent rotation during a given campaign. In fact, two divisions that had been scheduled for the Pacific, the 86th and 97th, were diverted to Europe in March 1945 because of losses at the Battle of the Bulge and a shortfall in infantry. Nonetheless, the Pacific did receive enough ground, air, and service forces to keep advancing—slowly, and not without desperate and costly fighting that was more expensive than it should have been.

Combat wears on the spirit as well as the body. By the time of the Luzon invasion in January 1945, all Sixth Army's divisions had fought through one campaign, and most had been in two. A third of the officers and men had been overseas three years—a long time to be exposed to harsh climates, poor food, and the uncertainties of war (although some Commonwealth/Empire troops could claim to have been in combat since 1939). The men had learned that no matter how good a soldier might be, no matter how well-trained and dedicated and no matter how hard he tried, bad luck and the laws of probability would someday get him. There is a thin line between battle-tested and battle-weary, between blooded and bloodied.

Units were already short of personnel, and replacements from the United States could hardly keep pace with battle casualties, let alone nonbattle losses. The lean, no-frills, 14,253-man triangular divisions of 1943 had already had the "fat" wrung out of their prewar square structures—organizations that had carried 22,000 men. World War II divisions could not absorb casualties and then reorganize internally. A flow of replacements from the United States was mandatory. But the flow did not flow well.

One U.S. source of manpower, African American troops, never developed to its full potential. One combat regiment (24th Infantry) and one division (93d) deployed to the Pacific. The 24th Infantry cleaned up diehard Japanese on Saipan and Tinian, and the 93d Division skirmished with the enemy on Bougainville. Unfortunately, rumors that defamed the 93d Division were so damaging that the division never got a chance to disprove them. The men spent 1944–1945 relieving other divisions, cleaning out Japanese stragglers, and unloading and loading ships. These were useful and essential duties, but not what a division was designed to do. African American troops most in demand were engineer and quartermaster outfits. Port and amphibious truck companies participated at Saipan, Tinian, Iwo Jima, and Okinawa.

The return to the Philippines and the march beyond began in Australia. Engineers arrived to find everything there strange, from the rocks and trees, to the soil and weather, to even the stars themselves. They had trouble finding local manpower, for the Australians were already heavily committed to their war in Europe. Simply reconnoitering the country took an immense amount of time. One of the biggest engineering problems was a shortage of construction equipment. Graders and bulldozers were more important in the Pacific than tanks. Whereas from the first day of the war in Europe the army had called on the resources and infrastructure of an advanced industrial society, such infrastructure did not exist in the Pacific. The engineers had to build it.

The army's first fight on the road to Tokyo occurred on Guadalcanal. Units were committed piecemeal—a regiment here, a battalion there. It was not until November 1942 that a division organization was established (the American Division) and as late as January 1943 before the first corps offensive (by XIV Corps with the American and 25th Divisions) kicked off. Even then, XIV Corps lacked traditional service units and organic corps artillery.

Experiences on Guadalcanal proved that army doctrine and tactics were basically sound and flexible enough to respond to unusual circumstances. The Japanese were impressed at how quickly the Americans adapted to Japanese tactics and how quickly they replaced unsuccessful tactics with effective ones. U.S. Army weapons proved their worth—especially the M-1 rifle, machine guns, and 105-mm and 155-mm artillery.

On Guadalcanal and early in New Guinea, the army started to develop the tactics and techniques necessary to reduce a dug-in enemy. Leaders learned lessons in amphibious warfare and combined operations. The technique of seizing important but weakly defended areas and of bypassing fortified harbors and airfields (Rabaul as a prime example of the latter) developed during the march along New Georgia, Bougainville, the Bismarck Archipelago, and the Admiralty Islands. The army supported the navy's central Pacific drive into the Gilberts, the Marshalls, and the Marianas.

The army in the Pacific did not execute its first multiple-corps operation until it landed at Leyte on October 20, 1944. Sixth Army put ashore 200,000 men in two corps (X and XXIV) led by seasoned corps commanders with three veteran divisions (1st Cavalry and 7th and 24th Infantry) and one well-trained but untested division (96th). Two more divisions were in reserve—the combat-hardened 32d and the 77th, a veteran of Guam.

Next came the January 1945 landings on Luzon, the largest ground operation of the Pacific war. More army ground and service forces fought here than in the landings and operations in North Africa, Italy, or southern France. The Luzon campaign included forces larger than the entire Allied commitment to Sicily and allowed the employment of mass and maneuver on a scale exceeded only by the army's drive across northern France into Germany. Three corps fought here (I, XI, and XIV), of which two (I and XIV) landed abreast at Lingayen Gulf with four divisions. By the time the Luzon campaign had concluded, it had used two armies (Sixth and Eighth), three corps, ten divisions, five regimental combat teams, and more armored units than a standard armored division.

The U.S. Navy launched the invasion of Okinawa. Tenth Army commanded the ground component, which consisted of XXIV Corps (7th, 27th, 77th, 96th Divisions) and III Amphibious Corps (1st, 2d, 6th Marine Divisions). Tenth Army as a headquarters had no combat history, but its personnel did. It included navy and marines in its staff, and XXIV Corps had gained experience on Leyte. Tenth Army went ashore at Okinawa with two corps abreast, each corps with two divisions abreast; in all, 190,000 soldiers would fight here. The Okinawa campaign saw the use of propaganda drops (8 million leaflets) and the deployment of loudspeaker teams to its greatest extent to date. Both were used to induce trapped soldiers and civilians to surrender. By this time in the Japanese army's destruction, such appeals were more and more effective in at least lowering Japanese morale, if not in snaring prisoners on any large scale.

Corps staffs had trained in the United States and then shipped to the Pacific. XIV Corps, for instance, had originally been Headquarters and Headquarters Company, VIII Corps, until shipped overseas to become XIV Corps. It was the first corps headquarters to reach the Pacific. Subsequent corps headquarters would have between two and four years to organize, train, and exercise in the United States before deploying—a luxury that few if any U.S. Allies could enjoy. Only XXIV Corps was activated in theater, on Oahu, and it had but five months to get ready before entering combat.

Two schools that would have produced officers trained in corps- and army-level staff work—the Army War College and the Army Industrial College—had been closed in 1940 so that their cadre and students could help mobilize the army. The short courses at Fort Leavenworth's Command and General Staff School qualified officers only up to division level. Not surprisingly, corps, army, and theater staffs had trouble finding men trained in high-level staff work. The staff work required for each invasion grew until it became nearly unmanageable.

Despite trouble staffing echelons above division, the army ultimately fielded six corps to the Pacific (I, IX, X, XI, XIV, and XXIV). From late 1944 through 1945, adequate corps and army troops existed. Corps and army artillery, engineer, antiaircraft, and all supporting branches were available in impressive numbers. Divisions, too, wielded much more firepower and service support than had been available in the 1942–1943 division structure.

Multiple corps required army headquarters. Sixth Army opened in Australia in February 1943 using key members transferred out of the U.S.-based Third Army. When MacArthur asked for another army headquarters, the War Department picked Headquarters and Headquarters Company, Second Army—250 officers and 750 men who had been training in the United States for two years. It became Eighth Army when it arrived in the Pacific in September 1944. A third army, Tenth Army headquarters, activated in the United States in June 1944 and then deployed to Oahu. MacArthur planned to keep all three armies directly under his command for the invasion of the Japanese home islands. He did not activate or bring in an army group headquarters as was common in Europe. His general headquarters would act as an army group headquarters.

As the size of army forces in the Pacific grew, the flexibility inherent in small-division and single-corps operations declined. A beachhead or small island campaign allowed a quick response to terrain problems and to enemy threats. As campaigns grew larger, in particular on Luzon and Okinawa, multiple-corps operations had to be more tightly controlled. The same tactics and techniques the army had developed for waging Continental warfare came into play on Luzon and Okinawa. Large troop movements and their coordination with air support and logistics called for a more deliberate approach than earlier campaigns. Luzon was only the second multiple-corps operation in the Pacific, and army commanders were learning their job, as were corps commanders who now had to work with an army headquarters and an adjacent corps.

Especially annoying to soldiers in the Pacific was that while they were still fighting there, the U.S. war effort was actually declining. The end of the war in the ETO began army demobilization—at the very moment that the army's "in contact" rate in the Pacific peaked, with eighteen of its twenty-one divisions actively campaigning. Yet ETO soldiers were being discharged under a point system unless they possessed special skills necessary for the war against Japan, or unless their unit was being shipped so quickly to the Pacific that they could not be replaced.

In the midst of corps and army operations, the Philippines presented the army with ideal conditions to initiate, encourage, and direct guerrilla warfare. Of course, many guerrilla forces, often U.S.-led, had been operating with increasing efficiency since the fall of the islands to the Japanese in 1942. Everything was new: the mission, organization, supply procedures, communications, propaganda, training, insertion, and which information should be solicited from agents. The army established communication and intelligence networks, countered Japanese propaganda, and built guerrilla units capable of striking Japanese rear areas. It developed the southern island of Mindanao into a supply base for guerrilla operations on the other islands. Ultimately, six guerrilla "divisions" operated on Mindanao alone. By the end of the war, 21,000 Filipino guerrillas supported U.S. forces in northern Luzon; 22,000 operated elsewhere on Luzon; and about 75,000 men and women were fighting in the southern islands.

Had the submarine war and the conventional and atomic bombings not ended the Japanese aggression, the army ground forces would have returned to their traditional role, that of destroying the enemy's army in the field and destroying the will to resist. The army would have invaded the home islands. Two divisions (86th and

97th) had just arrived from Europe, and the Europe-wise XIII Corps with the 13th and 20th Armored Divisions were en route. Four corps headquarters and twelve divisions (2d, 4th, 5th, 8th, 28th, 35th, 44th, 86th, 87th, 91st, 95th, 104th) would come in over the next eight months. The veteran, workhorse First Army headquarters would arrive from Europe, and Fourth Army headquarters would come in from the United States. A huge air and logistics force would accompany these reinforcements. It would have been the greatest—and the bloodiest—military operation in U.S. history.

The sudden, unexpected end to the Pacific war threw personnel procedures into turmoil. The army was executing a massive redeployment of men and equipment from Europe to the Pacific. MacArthur had received the task of preparing bases to stage twenty-two divisions in the Philippines by November 1945 and eleven more by February 1946. The remaining divisions would stage in the Ryukus, Saipan, and Hawaii.

Executing the surrender required a spectacular airlift of occupying forces into Japan. The Air Transport Command provided the army with an organization that was greatly superior in quality and quantity to all enemies and allies. It peaked at 200,000 men and 3,700 aircraft in July 1945, when it carried 275,000 passengers and 100,000 tons of cargo world wide. Here was a feat comparable to building and operating six airlines with branch and feeder lines. Military Air Transport Command now went to work ferrying troops into the home islands.

The 11th Airborne Division led U.S. occupation troops into the islands. Air landings began on August 28, when soldiers arrived in thirty-six 4-engine C-54s. By August 30, aircraft were landing at a rate of one transport every three minutes. Soon the 27th Division landed, then the 1st Cavalry Division, and then the 6th Marine Division. Army air forces were also active in the search for Allied prisoners of war. B-29s flew out to drop medicine, food, and supplies into 154 camps in Japan, China, and Korea.

In raw numbers, the Pacific war was the third-largest theater-level effort ever waged by the U.S. Army, inferior only to northwest Europe in World War II (sixty-one divisions, 3 million men) and Europe in World War I (thirty divisions, 2 million men). The Pacific war covered greater distances, mounted more amphibious operations, and included more army-navy coordination than any other campaign. It was the first campaign ever fought where, for most of the war, the enemy's armed forces in the field were not the army's principal objective. Only after Okinawa did the army revert to its traditional role and prepare for a classic invasion of the home islands.

Credit for the victory must go to the citizen-soldier, trained and led by the small cadre of regulars. And by no means can the army ground forces' war in the Pacific be understood without acknowledging the decisive roles played by air, naval, and service forces. It was a team effort.

FURTHER READINGS

Army, U.S. *U.S. Army in World War II* (numerous volumes covering the war in the Pacific).

Craven, Wesley Frank, and James Lea Cate, eds. *The Army Air Forces in World War II*, 7 vols. (1948–1958).

James, D. Clayton. *The Years of MacArthur*, 3 vols. (1970–1985).

Kreidberg, Marvin A., and Merton G. Henry. *History of Military Mobilization in the United States Army 1775–1945*. Department of the Army Pamphlet No. 20-212 (1955).

John W. Whitman

SEE ALSO Army Air Corps/Air Forces, U.S.; MacArthur, Douglas; Marine Corps, U.S.; Navy, U.S.

Arnold, Henry Harley ("Hap") (1886–1950)

U.S. Army five-star general and Air Service officer and "Father of the U.S. Air Force," Henry Harley "Hap" Arnold was born on June 25, 1886, in Gladwyne, Pennsylvania. He graduated from the U.S. Military Academy in 1907 and was assigned as a second lieutenant to the 29th Infantry Regiment in the Philippines (1907–1909) and then to Governor's Island, New York (1909–1911). In April 1911 he transferred to the aeronautical section of the Signal Corps, received his flight training from the Wright brothers in Dayton, Ohio, and obtained his pilot's license in June—and was thus one of the first U.S. military aviators. Subsequently assigned as an instructor at College Park, Maryland, he set a world altitude record and was awarded the first Mackay Trophy in 1912. After being involved in and witnessing a series of air crashes in 1912, First Lieutenant Arnold was sent back to the infantry in the Philippines (1913–1916). He returned to the air in 1916 as a captain at the aviation school at Rockwell Field, San Diego. In 1917 Arnold commanded the 7th Air Squadron in Panama.

When the United States entered World War I in April 1917, Arnold headed the information office of the aviation section of the Signal Corps. From August 1917 to May 1918, with a wartime promotion to colonel, he served as assistant director of military aeronautics with responsibility for training and acquisitions at aviation bases. Arnold did not see combat duty during the war, arriving in Europe only in time for the Armistice (November 11, 1918). He returned to the rank of captain at the end of the war but made major in 1921.

After holding a variety of postings at aviation bases in California, Arnold returned to Washington to attend the Army Industrial College and serve as information officer of the Air Service (1925–1926). In 1926 Arnold was assigned to Fort Riley, Kansas—he claimed, as part of his "exile" for testifying favorably at the court-martial of Brigadier General Billy Mitchell. He attended the Army Command and General Staff School at Fort Leavenworth (1928–1929) and briefly held command posts at Fairfield and Wright Fields in Ohio. As a lieutenant colonel in 1931 he was reassigned to March Field in Riverside, California, with orders to transform it from solely a training to an operational base. He intensified training for aircrews, experimented with materials and tactics, increased the scope of maneuvers, and worked closely with scientists from the California Institute of Technology. In March 1933 he became commander of 1st Fighter Wing while also supervising thirty camps for the Civilian Conservation Corps. He received a Distinguished Flying Cross and his second Mackay Trophy in 1934 for commanding a flight of ten modern Martin B-10 bombers that flew from Washington to Alaska and back. Promoted to brigadier general in early 1935, he became commander 1st Wing, General Headquarters Air Force, at March Field.

Recalled to Washington in 1936, Arnold served as assistant chief of the U.S. Army Air Corps until his promotion to major general and chief of the corps in September 1938. In essence he remained as head of the Air Service Command from 1938 to his retirement in 1946. As head of the Army Air Corps, Arnold strove to increase its capabilities and combat readiness. He encouraged President Franklin Roosevelt to expand the corps and convinced business leaders to make needed changes in technology for the building of more aircraft. He also pushed private flying schools to accelerate the training of pilots. In October 1940 he became deputy chief of the army for air matters and, upon its creation in 1941, chief of the U.S. Army Air Forces (USAAF). He convinced Congress in 1941 to approve more than $2.1 billion for aircraft production. He attended the Atlantic Charter Conference in August 1941 with the president (he would attend almost all the wartime conferences), and because of his close work with British air leaders, he became a member of the British-U.S. Combined Chiefs of Staff (CCS) and the U.S. Joint Chiefs of Staff (JCS) in the fall of that year and was promoted to lieutenant general.

Although he desired an independent air service, Arnold deferred this struggle until after the war. In March 1942 the army was reorganized and divided into three components—ground, service, and air—with Arnold in command of the latter. In the army chain of command, he served as a deputy to General George C. Marshall, but in the JCS and CCS he sat as an equal, and his large and capable staff became a serious rival.

He became a full (four-star) general in March 1943 but suffered serious heart problems in May. Arnold finally received combat duty in April 1944 as commanding general of the Twentieth Air Force in the Pacific. Although Arnold maintained his headquarters in the Pentagon, he personally directed the Twentieth's strategic B-29 bombing campaign and traveled frequently to its bases. In December 1944 Arnold was promoted to general of the army (five stars), a recognition of the significance of air power. He missed the important wartime conference at Yalta in early 1945 because of a heart attack that required extensive hospitalization, but World War II ended with the dropping of the atomic bombs from the B-29s of his USAAF.

Arnold was a true believer in the Douhet-Mitchell-Trenchard doctrine of victory through strategic bombardment, and he insisted that such a campaign against Japan's cities would win the war. It would also go far with Congress toward establishing the U.S. Air Force as a separate and equal service with the U.S. Army and U.S. Navy. Thus, Arnold opposed the use of the atomic bomb and was, in fact, the only high-ranking military officer to do so.

In early 1946 Arnold retired and turned over command of the USAAF to General Carl A. Spaatz, one of his European theater commanders. He continued to write extensively and argue for a strong air defense. He was named permanent general of the newly created and independent U.S. Air Force in May 1949. He died on January 15, 1950, in Sonoma, California, and was buried in Arlington National Cemetery in a ceremony attended by President Truman. All three of his sons graduated from the U.S. Military Academy.

Arnold was a man of ability and vision who quickly grasped the importance that air power would play in the future. His September 1941 war plan proved to be an accurate forecast of World War II air war strategy and logistics, and he helped plan the strategic bombing campaigns against Germany and Japan. Starting with only a handful of aircraft, he built the greatest air force in the world during the war. Arnold also worked hard to create a cadre of capable officers to lead the air service in the postwar world. He understood the value of technology and worked directly with scientists to speed innovation in aviation. In fact, he oversaw the transition from the fabric-covered, open-cockpit, fixed-landing-gear aircraft of the early 1930s—which were not much of an advance over the warplanes of World War I—to the enclosed, retractable-landing-gear, all-metal aircraft configuration that began to come on line later in the same decade and which prevails to this day. As did most of the high-ranking officers of the U.S. military air service, he held a greatly exaggerated opinion of the abilities of long-range heavy-bombardment aircraft, believing that the heavily armed B-17 could make its way unescorted to an enemy target and wreak destruction by "pinpoint" bombardment—and suffer few losses. Combat soon would demonstrate otherwise. Friendly, dedicated, at times volatile, "Hap" Arnold, more than any other man, worked to create the U.S. Air Force.

FURTHER READINGS

Arnold, H. H. *Global Mission* (1949).

Coffey, T. *Hap: General of the Air Force Henry Arnold* (1982).

DuPre, F. *Hap Arnold: Architect of American Air Power* (1972).

Laura Matysek Wood

SEE ALSO Aircraft: Japanese, U.S., and British; Air Offensive, Japan; Army Air Corps/Air Forces, U.S.

Artillery, Japanese

Before the start of World War II, Japanese artillery was not organized to provide command and control at the higher echelons. Japanese tacticians saw artillery almost exclusively as a forward infantry-support weapon. Artillery in small units was allocated directly to infantry control, which often left inadequate artillery assets under centralized divisional control.

By early 1944 this organizational concept had undergone significant change, leading to the introduction of both field-army artillery headquarters and artillery groups. Army Artillery Headquarters was commanded by a lieutenant general or a major general; it exercised unified control over all the artillery within the field army as well as the artillery of subordinate divisions. Artillery Group Headquarters was commanded by a major general or a colonel; it exercised control over all the artillery of a division and coordinated the artillery of the division's constituent regiments.

The standard artillery component of a triangular Japanese infantry division was a regiment of thirty-six guns using 75-mm field artillery—or, in some cases, mountain artillery. Throughout the war the Japanese used both horse-drawn and motorized artillery units. The horse-drawn regiments required some two thousand horses. The artillery regiments were commanded by colonels and were organized into three battalions. Each battalion was further organized into three gun batteries plus a battalion train. A gun battery had four guns and 183 soldiers and officers. Some divisions had mixed artillery regiments, which were armed with twelve 75-mm field guns and twenty-four 105-mm howitzers.

As opposed to the standard Japanese triangular-type division, the strengthened division was supported by an artillery group. The artillery group consisted of a headquarters, (usually) a mixed artillery regiment, and a medium artillery battalion. The medium artillery battalions were armed with twelve 150-mm howitzers, organized into three batteries. Some strengthened divisions had motorized medium artillery battalions, but most were horse-drawn, requiring almost eight hundred horses. The artillery group also controlled any additional independent artillery units that might be attached to the division for specific missions. These might include antitank and antiaircraft artillery units.

At the higher echelons the Japanese army had special heavy artillery regiments. Many of these units were fixed, but mobile heavy regiments began to appear after 1937. These regiments usually were organized into two battalions of four-gun batteries. The mobile regiments were armed with either 150-mm or 240-mm howitzers. The fixed regiments were armed with 240-mm or 300-mm howitzers.

Higher-level artillery assets also included observation regiments—what generally are now called target acquisition units. Before the war, Japanese observation equipment and techniques were generally inferior to those of most Western armies, and in the U.S. artillery of the Bataan campaign they almost met their match. By the end of the war the observation regiments were capable of fairly sophisticated sound ranging, flash ranging, and well-coordinated aerial observation. The 675-man regiments also provided survey, meteorological, and photographic services.

Fire Support Doctrine and Tactics

Japanese army commanders believed that the primary function of field artillery was the immediate and close support of the infantry assault. They did recognize, of course, other important artillery missions. These included destroying the enemy's infantry and supporting weapons; the destruction of obstacles that impeded the advance of

Japanese Artillery of World War II

Model	Year in Service	Caliber (mm)	Weight in Action (pounds)	Weight of Projectile (pounds)	Muzzle Velocity (feet/second)	Range (meters) (ceiling)
Field Artillery						
Model 38 gun	1905	75	2,501	14.5	1,640	11,960
Model 90 gun	1930	75	3,085	14.3	2,296	14,950
Model 95 gun	1935	75	2,438	14.3	1,640	10,950
Model 94 mountain gun	1934	75	1,181	14.3	1,165	8,300
Model 91 howitzer	1931	105	3,306	34.8	1,790	10,760
Model 92 gun	1932	105	8,220	34.8	2,493	18,250
Heavy Artillery						
Model 96 howitzer	1936	150	9,108	68.6	2,657	11,850
Model 89 gun	1929	150	22,928	100.8	2,250	19,900
Model 45 howitzer	1912	240	83,909	298.2	1,205	10,340
Antiaircraft Artillery						
Model 88 gun	1928	75	5,390	14.3	2,360	8,850
Antitank Artillery						
Model 94 gun	1934	37	814	1.5	2,310	4,600
Model 01 gun	1941	47	1,660	2.3	2,740	7,680

the Japanese infantry; the disruption of enemy rear areas and lines of communication; and—to a lesser degree—counterbattery fire. In practice, however, direct support of the infantry tended to be emphasized at the expense of all other missions.

Japanese doctrine laid heavy emphasis on keeping artillery well forward. Firing positions were sited within a few hundred yards of the enemy's leading positions. Command posts were positioned right beside the guns so that fires could be controlled by voice command.

Jungle fighting had its own special set of problems for artillery. The extension of close fire support was more complicated because of the difficulty in tracking friendly infantry. The jungle terrain also made it necessary to fire over trees, which often had the effect of placing the fire too far ahead of the friendly infantry. In the jungle, therefore, Japanese doctrine required placing the artillery on the flanks of the friendly infantry. This technique had the advantage of simplifying the computations of the firing solutions. It also allowed the guns to place their fire immediately in front of the advancing infantry, without exposing the troops to potential premature overhead detonations caused by the heavy foliage.

Before an attack, the Japanese artillery fired a preparation of one to two hours duration. The preparations were divided into three roughly equal phases, focusing on (1) ranging, (2) the elimination of obstacles, and (3) the

enemy's leading infantry positions. With the start of the attack, the mission of the artillery became one of support, with special emphasis on enveloping the enemy's flank. The usual basic load of ammunition maintained at the guns was three days of fire, with one day of fire computed at 300 rounds.

Overconfidence in the inherent superiority of their infantry often caused the Japanese to attack an objective without adequate artillery preparation. Night attacks in particular relied heavily on infiltration and surprise, rather than on fire preparation. Japanese doctrine recognized the requirement for the enemy's artillery to be neutralized as a prerequisite for a successful attack, but the principle was seldom observed. Rather than counterbattery fire, the Japanese relied more heavily on the infiltration of artillery-destroying raiding parties. As the war progressed, however, the Japanese came to emphasize longer and more methodical preparations—even for night attacks.

Japanese offensive doctrine held that difficult terrain should not be permitted to inhibit operations. Quite the contrary, the Japanese saw rugged terrain as an asset. By passing through what appeared to be impenetrable terrain, they believed they could take their enemy by surprise and attack where defenses might be weakened by reliance on terrain obstacles. Japanese artillery also aggressively followed this doctrine.

During the advance on Port Moresby, Japanese artillery units dragged guns through dense jungles and up the steep slopes of the Owen Stanley Range. In the fighting on Bougainville, where difficult terrain normally would have made artillery support impossible, the Japanese nonetheless hauled their artillery pieces over narrow mountain trails and through dense rain forests to place them in position overlooking the Allied perimeter.

Japanese tactical doctrine was overwhelmingly offensive in nature. The defense was seen as merely a temporary situation with the primary mission of inflicting as much damage as possible on the enemy before resuming the offensive. In such defensive situations, the bulk of Japanese artillery was echeloned from 1,700 to 2,000 meters behind the main line of resistance. As the enemy's infantry massed for the attack, the defending artillery was to bring down counterpreparation fires. During the actual attack, the mission of the artillery was to break up the enemy's formations with series of standing barrages.

Given the island topography of the fighting in the Pacific, the Japanese often used field artillery in a coastal defense role. Again, coastal defense was seen as primarily offensive in nature, since its purpose was to destroy the enemy before a landing could be effected. On Attu, the Japanese positioned field batteries to concentrate their fire on landing craft and to deliver antipersonnel fire against troops already on the beach. In the Marshalls and Gilberts, the guns were sited to bring flat trajectory fire on landing craft and vehicles. The guns were positioned well forward, not in depth, and were fired by direct laying. Batteries maintained local fire control, with two or three guns controlled from observation towers at the gun positions. On Saipan, single guns were sited to fire directly on landing craft, while batteries were positioned to place concentrated fire on the channels through which the boats had to pass.

Weapons

The Japanese entered the artillery arena later than almost any other modern nation. Most Japanese had never even seen a cannon before the arrival of Perry in 1853. Even for many years afterward, Bushido doctrine militated against modern armaments, considering them cowardly and dishonorable. With the restoration of the emperors in 1867, the Japanese lacked modern firearms as well as the know-how and industrial facilities to make them. For many years, all Japanese artillery was imported from Western firms, principally Krupp.

The Japanese started their own artillery manufacturing program only in 1905—some thirty-eight years into the Meiji reign. That year the Oksaka Arsenal produced its first modern piece of artillery, a mountain gun of French design. Through the end of World War I, most Japanese-

produced artillery was based on European designs. In 1918, Oksaka started manufacturing its own designs, which were still heavily influenced by European models. Eventually Oksaka produced a complete line of artillery weapons, ranging from pack howitzers to heavy coastal defense guns.

While the U.S. Army and most European armies moved to 105 mm as the standard caliber for divisional artillery, the Japanese stayed with 75 mm throughout the war. The standard direct support gun during the war was the 75-mm Model 90. Introduced in 1930, it replaced the older Model 38, which still saw service throughout the war. The Model 90's relatively high muzzle velocity of 2,296 f/s (feet per second) made it especially effective in an antitank role. The Model 90 was produced in two versions, one with artillery wheels for horse draft, and one with pneumatic tires and disk wheels for tractor or truck draft. The slightly more modern Model 95 was introduced in 1935, but with a muzzle velocity of only 1,640 f/s it was not nearly as effective against armor.

The 75-mm Model 88 antiaircraft gun was one of the most widely encountered guns of the Pacific island fighting. Its flat trajectory and very high muzzle velocity of 2,360 f/s made it very effective against armor. The Japanese used it in a dual role to defend airfields against both ground and air attack. Its main disadvantage was limited mobility. It was a very effective weapon when fired from ambush, but it could not move and fight simultaneously very well.

The 75-mm Model 94 mountain gun was the standard weapon of the pack artillery, especially in dense jungle. It could be assembled and laid for firing in about ten minutes, and disassembled in three to five minutes. The entire gun could be carried by eighteen men—although on Bougainville forty-one troops were assigned to carry each gun because of the extremely rough terrain.

The standard 105-mm guns were the Model 91 howitzer and the Model 92. With a maximum range of 18,250 meters, the Model 92 could throw a 35-pound projectile farther than almost any other 105-mm artillery piece of World War II.

Japanese field artillery came to be characterized by its long range and light weight compared with European designs of similar caliber. Projectile weights were approximately the same as those of corresponding calibers of the Western armies. The major exception was the 150-mm family of guns and howitzers, whose projectiles averaged about 15 pounds lighter.

During World War II, lack of ruggedness was the principal shortcoming of Japanese field guns. Japanese designers achieved weight savings by making fairly drastic reductions in the weight of the tube, the equilibrators, and especially the recoil system and trails. The light weight of these components led to fairly high failure rates with the heavy firing that came with sustained combat conditions.

With their primary doctrinal focus on infantry, the Japanese entered World War II without adequate industrial facilities for large-scale artillery production and maintenance. They lacked tooling for both standardization and mass production. In 1944, Lieutenant General Katsuzo Kosuda, chief of the Ordnance Administration Headquarters, admitted that little study had been given to production problems before the war. As a result, the Japanese army was always chronically short of artillery and had great difficulty maintaining what they did have because of poor interchangeability of parts.

FURTHER READINGS

Bailey, Jonathan B. A. *Field Artillery and Firepower* (1989).

Hogg, Ian V. *The Illustrated Encyclopedia of Artillery* (1987).

Huber, Thomas M. *Japan's Battle of Okinawa, April–June 1945* (1982).

McLean, Donald B., compiler. *Japanese Artillery: Weapons and Tactics* (1973).

U.S. War Department, Military Intelligence Division. *Japanese Field Artillery* (1944).

David T. Zabecki

SEE ALSO Army, Japanese; Artillery, U.S.

Artillery, U.S.

During World War II the U.S. Army employed four broad categories of artillery: field artillery (FA), coastal artillery (CA), antiaircraft artillery (AAA), and antitank artillery (AT).

The mission of the FA then, as now, was to provide fire support to the ground-gaining forces. The mission of the CA was to provide land-based defense for naval bases and harbors, coastal cities, and other important installations, such as the Panama Canal and Manila Bay. As such, CA played only a very limited tactical or operational role in World War II. The CA of the Corregidor forts sealed off Manila Bay from the Japanese invaders for the first five months of the war. In fact, the giant 12-inch cannon of Fort Drum ("The Army's Concrete Battleship") throughout those early months were the heaviest weapons by far employed against the Axis forces. Fort Drum itself was never taken but surrendered with the overall U.S. capitulation in the Philippines.

By far, the most significant contribution by the coastal artillery corps was provided by its AAA units. Initially started as a logical extension of the coastal defense role, AAA units quickly grew in numbers to provide air defense capabilities to all major army units operating in the field. AAAs were also widely used by the navy, and to a very limited extent there was some cooperation between the two services in AAA procurement.

AT artillery units—which were designated tank destroyer (TD)—had the mission of destroying enemy tanks by direct gunfire. When not engaged in their primary mission, these units often performed a secondary mission as reinforcing artillery.

Over the course of World War II, the U.S. Army raised a total of 727 field artillery battalions (including divisional and nondivisional). Of that number, 149 saw service in the Pacific, including 2 battalions that were stationed in Kunming, China. The coastal artillery corps had a total of 121 coastal defense battalions and 583 AAA battalions. Thirty-six coastal and 121 AAA battalions, respectively, served in the Pacific. Of the 107 TD battalions raised during the war, only nine saw service in the war against Japan—an indication of the relative weakness of Japanese armor.

Field Artillery (FA)

Although the United States had suffered the least of any of the major combatants of World War I, a sense of war weariness and the resultant keen desire to cut military budgets produced an overwhelming postwar popular sentiment to eliminate as much of the U.S. military as possible. In 1920, the U.S. Army carried 174 FA batteries in the active force. By the start of 1935, the active army was down to ninety-eight batteries, 40 percent of them still horse-drawn. Between 1926 and 1930 more than a thousand FA enlisted men were involuntarily transferred to the fledgling U.S. Army Air Corps. In 1934, the Knox Trophy for the best-firing battery in the U.S. Army could not be awarded because there was not enough ammunition for all eligible batteries to take part in the competition.

By the mid-1920s, the U.S. Army started to abandon many of the hard-learned artillery lessons of World War I. Lack of mobility and the resulting inability to mass rapidly had been the real causes of the stagnation that resulted in trench warfare. Many Western military thinkers, however, incorrectly concluded that the massive firepower of World War I was the cause of that deadlock. At the same time, the proponents of air power in the United States and Great Britain were making exaggerated and widely publicized claims for their arm. Yet, airmen in both

Towed Field Artillery

Model	Caliber	Type	Year	Max Range	Typical Service (meters)
M1A1	75-mm	pack howitzer	1927	8,650	14
M2a1	105-mm	howitzer	1940	10,980	33
M1918	155-mm	howitzer	1918	11,160	95
M1a1	155-mm	howitzer	1941	14,700	95
M1	155-mm	gun	1938	22,860	95
M2	8-inch	howitzer	1940	16,660	200
M1	240-mm	howitzer	1943	14,760	345

Self-Propelled Field Artillery

Model	Gun Caliber	Gun Model	Chassis	Year in Service	Crew Size
M7	105-mm	M2A1	M3A1 tank	1941	7
M7B1	105-mm	M2A1	M4A3 tank	1943	7
M37	105-mm	M2A1	M24 tank	1945	6
M41	155-mm	M1A1	M24 tank	1944	6
M12	155-mm	M1 gun	M3A1 tank	1941	6
M40	155-mm	M1 gun	M4A3 tank	1945	6

Towed Antitank Guns

Model	Caliber	Year in Service	Max Range (meters)	Muzzle Velocity at 500 Meters (feet/sec)	Penetration (mm)
M3A1	37-mm	1939	11,560	2,900	61
M1	57-mm	1941	9,230	2,800	82
M1	76-mm	1943	9,000	2,700	110
M5	3-inch	1941	14,490	2,600	135
M3	90-mm	1944	19,260	2,800	140

Self-Propelled Antitank Guns

Model	Gun Caliber	Gun Model	Chassis	Year in Service	Crew Size
M10 (Wolverine)	3-inch	M5	M4A2 tank	1942	5
M18 (Hellcat)	76-mm	M1	GMC T70	1943	5
M36	90-mm	M3	M4A3 tank	1944	5

Antiaircraft Guns: Army

Model	Caliber (meters)	Year in Service	Max Horizontal Range (feet)	Max Altitude	Sustained Rate of Fire (rounds/min)
M55 (Quad MG)	0.50-inch	1942	1,500	1,000	320
M1A1	37-mm	1939	8,000	10,500	120
M5	40-mm	1940	9,800	11,000	120
Bofors M3	3-inch	1928	13,300	31,500	18
M51	75-mm	1945	13,000	30,000	45
M2	90-mm	1941	17,600	33,800	25
M3	105-mm	1940	18,000	37,000	15
M1	120-mm	1940	24,800	47,400	12

Antiaircraft Guns: Navy

Model	Caliber (meters)	Year in Service	Max Horizontal Range (feet)	Max Altitude	Sustained Rate of Fire (rounds/min)
Bofors	20-mm	1940	5,000	5,000	240
Bofors	40-mm	1941	9,000	11,200	120
M14	3-inch	1927	14,000	32,300	18
M24	3-inch	1945	14,000	32,300	30
M25	5-inch	1935	17,000	23,100	12

countries (but, significantly, not in Germany) strongly resisted the idea of using their aircraft for direct support of ground troops. The result was a retarded development of close air support. In the U.S. Army, the focus of ground tactics shifted back to an infantry-centered world.

Right up to the start of World War II, the U.S. Army neglected corps-level artillery and ignored the requirements of artillery command and control above the divisional level. What corps-level artillery there was formed little more than a holding pool for firepower assets. In theory, counterbattery fire was the responsibility of the corps. In 1938, Lieutenant Colonel (later Major General) John S. Wood noted in an article published in *Field Artillery Journal,* "Since . . . corps artillery exist[s] only in the imagination, counterbattery training is equally imaginary."

Fortunately, the U.S. Army did not go quite as far as the British, French, or even the Germans in abandoning the artillery lessons of World War I. The characteristic American propensity for technical applications prevailed, and the Field Artillery School at Fort Sill continued to experiment with all forms of fire control techniques, including aerial observation.

From the late 1920s right until the eve of World War II, despite lean budgets, the Gunnery Department at Fort Sill—under the successive leadership of Major (later General) Jacob Devers, Major Carlos Brewer, and Major Orlando Ward—developed and refined a flexible and quick method of massing large numbers of firing units. In 1934, they introduced the first battalion Fire Direction Center. In 1940, they developed the Graphical Firing Table (a specialized artillery slide rule), which made the calculation of the firing solution much faster. In April 1941, Fort Sill demonstrated for Army Chief of Staff General George Marshall a divisional shoot, by massing the fires of four separate battalions.

When this process started at Fort Sill, the assistant commandant of the school was Brigadier General Lesley J. McNair, who had commanded a field artillery brigade in France during World War I. During the U.S. buildup of 1940–1941, McNair became one of the chief architects of the military machine as commander of U.S. Army ground forces. A strong believer in flexible massed fires, McNair continually pushed for the development of longer-range guns and supported all initiatives to centralize artillery command and control systems. Under his direction, nondivisional medium and heavy FA units grew from 135 battalions for a planned 100-division army in November 1942 to 257 battalions for an actual 89-division army in July 1944.

The U.S. Army, then, entered World War II with the unsurpassed ability to mass widely dispersed fire units. This led to an unprecedented level of coordination between infantry and artillery. American fire support capability exceeded that of the Japanese and the Germans throughout the war. The system was not perfect, however. The U.S. Army continued to have difficulty coordinating above divisional level and even between divisions.

U.S. Army doctrine specified two principal combat roles for FA units in World War II: (1) supporting the ground-gaining units (infantry, cavalry, armored) by fire, neutralizing or destroying those targets that presented the most danger to the supported arms; and (2) giving depth to combat by counterbattery fire, by fire on enemy reserves, by restricting movement in enemy rear areas, and by disrupting enemy command and control systems.

In combat, all U.S. FA units were assigned one of three basic tactical missions. Direct support meant that an artillery unit was assigned to provide fires for a specific maneuver unit. An FA unit in direct support established liaison and signal communications with the supported unit and moved with it whenever necessary to ensure that its guns were always within range. Normally, an FA battalion provided the direct support for an infantry regiment. A unit with a general support mission was responsible for providing fires for a larger unit, the subunits of which often had their own direct support artillery.

A unit with a reinforcing mission was assigned to deliver fires to reinforce those of another artillery unit. General support and reinforcing artillery units were among the primary means by which divisional and higher-level commanders directly influenced the battle.

During World War II, the divisional artillery of a typical infantry division consisted of four battalions of three batteries each. Each battery had four guns, for a divisional total of forty-eight. Three of the battalions were armed with towed 105-mm howitzers, and each generally was assigned to provide direct support for one of the division's infantry regiments. The fourth battalion was armed with towed 155-mm howitzers and had the general support mission for the division.

U.S. armored divisions were organized somewhat differently. The armored divisional artillery had only three battalions of three batteries, but each battery had six self-propelled 105-mm howitzers. This gave the armored division a total of fifty-four guns. Two of the battalions were placed in direct support of the division's two combat commands, with the third battalion held in general support.

Almost all artillery above divisional level came under the corps artillery. The primary functions of corps artillery were counterbattery fire and long-range interdiction.

Corps units generally had the tactical missions of either general support to the corps or the reinforcing to the artillery of a specific division. This latter mission usually was assigned for very specific situations, for example, when that particular division was designated to make the main effort of a corps attack.

Corps artillery organizations were flexible, usually consisting of two or more artillery groups of two or more artillery battalions each. Artillery groups routinely were transferred from corps to corps as the tactical and operational situations required. In the final years of World War II, a typical corps artillery had an average of thirteen battalions controlled by an appropriate number of groups. Almost all corps artillery units were armed with guns of 155-mm and larger caliber.

The U.S. Army classified FA guns and howitzers into three basic categories based on their weight: light, medium, and heavy. Light guns usually were found only in divisional artillery. The airborne divisions were armed with the 75-mm M1A1 howitzer, also called a pack howitzer. It was designed for easy disassembly, which allowed it to be air-dropped or transported by mules. The 75-mm pack howitzer saw extensive service in the jungles of the Pacific, where its ease of transport made it very popular.

The workhorse of most infantry divisional artillery was the 105-mm M2A1 howitzer. Next to the World War I–era French 75-mm field gun, the American 105-mm was probably the most successful artillery piece in history. It was accurate, reliable, and could withstand an incredible amount of punishment and mishandling. Design work began on this weapon immediately following World War I, and originally it was intended to be towed by a team of six horses. In March 1940, the design was standardized as the M2A1, towed by a 2½-ton truck (a go-anywhere vehicle that was itself the most successful motor truck in military history) which also carried the gun's basic load of ammunition. Armored divisions used the same gun in a self-propelled mount; either the M7B1 mounted on a Sherman tank chassis or, after 1945, the M37 mounted on a Chaffee tank chassis.

After World War II, the M2A1 was modified very slightly and became the M101A1. That version remained in service with the U.S. Army through the Korean and Vietnam Wars. Between 1940 and 1953, some 10,200 M2A1s and M101A1s were built and supplied to at least forty-five different countries. The M101A1 was still in service with U.S. Army reserve units as late as 1990. The M101A1 undoubtedly will remain in service in some countries well into the twenty-first century.

The standard U.S. medium artillery piece was the 155-mm M1A1 towed howitzer. Most of the general support battalions in the infantry divisions were armed with this piece. A self-propelled version, the M41, was mounted on the Chaffee tank chassis, but only a hundred or so were ever built. The towed version was successful and popular, even though it was heavy and somewhat difficult to handle. After World War II, it too was modified very slightly and became the M114A1. That version was supplied to twenty-eight countries and remained in service with some NATO armies through the late-1990s. The cannoneers on the gun crews called these weapons "pigs"—short for pig iron.

The most widely used U.S. heavy gun was the 155-mm M1 towed gun—not to be confused with the 155-mm M1A1 towed howitzer. The 155-mm gun was 2½ times as heavy as the 155-mm howitzer and could shoot a shell of the same weight (95 pounds) 60 percent farther. Being a gun, it had a very long barrel in relation to the size of its bore; and it shot its shell at a very high velocity but with a relatively flat trajectory. The 155-mm gun's 19-foot barrel gave it its nickname, Long Tom. Two self-propelled versions existed: the M12, based on a Grant tank chassis; and the M40, based on the Sherman tank chassis.

The 8-inch M2 towed howitzer used the same carriage as the 155-mm M1 towed gun. While the bore sizes of all other U.S. artillery pieces were designated in millimeters, this one was designated in inches because it originally was adopted from a British design. The 8-inch had the reputation of being the most accurate artillery piece ever invented. After World War II it was fitted to a self-propelled (SP) mount. Newer SP mounts were introduced in the 1950s, and a nuclear shell was introduced. The 8-inch underwent various modifications and improvements and saw service in Korea, Vietnam, and the Gulf War. It was retired from U.S. service in 1992.

The heaviest U.S. artillery battalions were armed with the 240-mm M1 towed howitzer, called the Black Dragon. It was towed by an M6 38-ton tractor, which gave it surprisingly good mobility for a gun weighing almost 21 tons. It took about two hours to bring the piece into action. The 240-mm howitzer remained in U.S. and British service until the late 1950s.

Antitank (AT) Artillery

In 1939, the U.S. Army's primary AT weapon was the light, towed 37-mm M3. Its design was based closely on the German PAK 35/36. In studying the Polish and French campaigns of 1939 and 1940, U.S. planners quickly recognized the inadequacy of the M3 against modern armor. As part of the Lend Lease package of agreements, the United States in 1941 acquired the design for the British 6-pounder (6pdr) AT gun. With very few modifications, the gun was copied and produced in mass as the 57-mm M1.

As newer tanks were developed with thicker armor, the M1 became obsolete very quickly. In fact, even before the M1 was fully fielded, work began in its successor, the 3-inch M5. Because of the time and economic pressures of wartime, the M5 was a composite design, consisting of a 105-mm howitzer carriage, a 3-inch antiaircraft gun tube, and a 105-mm breechblock. For all its mixed lineage, it was a very successful weapon. In 1942, the M5 gun was mounted on the M4A2 tank chassis to produce the M10 Wolverine tank destroyer, one of the most widely used self-propelled AT weapons of the war.

In 1943, the United States introduced a 76-mm variant of the M5. Designated the M1, it had a shorter tube and a specifically designed carriage. The towed version never progressed far beyond the prototype stage, but the gun itself became the main armament for the self-propelled M18 Hellcat. The M18 was unique in that its GMC T70 chassis was originally designed to be a tank destroyer (TD), rather than being modified from a standard tank chassis—as were most other U.S. self-propelled armored vehicles of the war.

In the last year of the war, the United States introduced the M36, a self-propelled TD mounting the 90-mm M3 gun. No TD units armed with the M36 saw action in the Pacific.

As the name "tank destroyer" indicated, the U.S. Army's tactical doctrine called for self-propelled AT guns to hunt enemy tanks aggressively rather than waiting in defensive positions for them to approach. In the early years of the war, a great variety of weapon and chassis combinations were produced. Early models included the 37-mm M3 gun on a Dodge truck; the 75-mm M1897 (a World War I field gun) on a M3 GMC (gun motor carriage) half-track; and the 57-mm M1 gun, also on a half-track. Though their mobility was clearly an advantage and they enjoyed some success in the doomed Philippine defense, by the time any of them saw action the gun was too light for the job.

Initially all AT ammunition was solid shot, but technological advances led to new types of AT rounds as the war progressed. Using tungsten cores obtained from Britain, a round with an armor-piercing discarding sabot (sleeve) was developed for the 90-mm. In service, however, it became apparent that the rifling of the tube and the round's discarding sleeve were not compatible. More successful was the composite rigid-shot round, its ultrahard tungsten core being encased in a light alloy casing that was not discarded. This combination produced very high muzzle velocities—an essential attribute for an AT gun—and consequently great penetration, especially at shorter ranges.

Antiaircraft Artillery (AAA)

When the United States entered World War II, it had a wide variety but relatively low numbers of AAA in service. The army and navy used different weapons until both services finally adopted the same license-built Bofors 20-mm and 40-mm light AAA. Both services fared somewhat better in their efforts to develop medium and heavy AAA. The navy's dual-purpose 5-inch guns proved particularly outstanding weapons. More important, both services eventually fielded precise fire control radars and proximity fuses, which significantly contributed to the effectiveness of the weapons systems.

In the 1930s, both services conducted extensive research into light, medium, and heavy AAA, but the resulting light weapons proved a disappointment. Those designs were either unreliable or had too slow a rate of fire. The navy originally negotiated with the Swedish armament firm Bofors in 1937, but the discussions broke down. In 1939, the navy asked the army to approach the company. The army at the time had been developing its own 37-mm gun similar to the Bofors 40-mm, but the superiority of the Bofors design led to its selection for both services in 1940.

The Bofors 40-mm became the most popular of the army's light AAA. Despite its popularity, however, the Bofors never completely replaced the 37-mm in army service during the war, but it did become the navy's principal light AAA. Only the Bofors 20-mm gun served in greater numbers in the fleet. The army also fielded a self-propelled twin-Bofors gun system mounted on a light tank chassis. Called the Duster, the weapon was still in service during the early years of Vietnam as a ground defense weapon.

The best U.S.-made AAA were the medium and heavy designs. By 1945, a fully automatic 75-mm gun entered service to replace both the earlier semiautomatic weapons and the 90-mm gun that entered service in 1940. That weapon also saw service in the U.S. Navy from 1947 to 1992. Although a 105-mm AAA gun entered service in 1940, only a few were built—all stationed in the Panama Canal Zone. The heavier 120-mm gun introduced the same year was built in larger numbers but was rarely deployed overseas.

The U.S. Army, like the German Army, based its heavy tank guns on antiaircraft guns. The Pershing tank of 1945 used a modified version of the M2 90-mm AAA gun. This mirrored the broader tactical situation late in the war.

After 1943, Allied air supremacy was so complete that many AAA units either were converted to infantry or employed their weapons in a ground support role. The U.S. Navy, on the other hand, found its light AAA essential to the survival of its forces in the Pacific and installed increasing numbers of them on its ships as the war progressed. In all, the United States fielded artillery weapons that were fully the equal of its enemies and Allies and in many cases superior.

FURTHER READINGS

Bailey, J. B. A. *Field Artillery and Firepower* (1989).

Dastrup, Boyd. "Travails of Peace and War: Field Artillery in the 1930s and Early 1940s." *The U.S. Army and World War II: Selected Papers from the Army's Commemorative Conferences.* Washington: U.S. Army Center of Military History (1998).

Hogg, Ian V. *The Guns, 1939–45* (1970).

Hogg, Ian V. *British and American Artillery of World War II* (1978).

Zabecki, D. *Steel Wind: Colonel Georg Bruchmüller and the Birth of Modern Artillery* (1994).

David T. Zabecki

SEE ALSO Army Ground Forces, U.S.; Artillery, Japanese

Atomic Bomb, Decision to Use against Japan

Only one nation has used nuclear weapons on another nation: the United States, against Japan in August 1945 during World War II. The decisive impact of the bombings of Hiroshima and Nagasaki in bringing about the surrender of Japan, the resulting redefinition of global international relations, and the profound moral questions raised by such vastly destructive weapons all make this one of the most important topics among the many relating to the Pacific theater of that war. Moreover, the enormous destructive capacity of nuclear weapons, their proliferation among nations, and their diversification in type since World War II argue for continuing emphasis on the facts and implications of the U.S. decision to actually use such a weapon in armed conflict.

The U.S. atomic bomb program was approved by President Franklin D. Roosevelt even before the Japanese attack on Pearl Harbor in Hawaii on December 7, 1941. The devastation of the U.S. Pacific Fleet (and coordinated Japanese attacks on the Philippines) compelled the United States to declare war on Japan and even inspired Hitler to declare war on the United States. The atomic project had begun two months earlier, however. On October 9, 1941, in profound secrecy, FDR accepted a recommendation from Vannever Bush, the head of defense research in the administration, to explore whether an atomic bomb could in fact be created. Roosevelt for long had strongly opposed the Axis powers, especially Germany. An undeclared naval war was already being fought in the Atlantic, and rapidly deteriorating relations with Japan fueled growing speculation about a Pacific war as well.

Roosevelt's political style almost invariably involved ambiguity. He maintained as many options as possible, and he postponed decisions whenever possible. These attributes were reflected in his reaction to Bush's recommendation. There was approval of a research and development effort, but no detailed follow-up. This approval, however, was the genesis of the Manhattan Project to construct an atomic bomb.

Even earlier, on October 11, 1939, FDR had received a letter from Albert Einstein, the scientist whose theory of relativity formed the conceptual "core" of the atomic weapons program which was to come. The letter was delivered to Roosevelt by Alexander Sachs of the Lehman Corporation, who supplemented the presentation with two memos of his own. The letter later became the centerpiece of popular discussion about the genesis of the atomic bomb. McGeorge Bundy—in his classic study of the nuclear age, *Danger and Survival: Choices about the Bomb during the First Fifty Years*—argues persuasively that the letter's impact is almost certainly exaggerated. Einstein provided few specifics beyond prediction of a "powerful chain reaction," and Sachs was not a technician. Moreover, the evidence indicates that there was no follow-up by Washington.

More generally, however, the pressures of expanding war in Europe and Asia led to steadily increasing contacts between scientists and government, including the migration during this time of Bush—a strong and politically sophisticated organizer—from the Massachusetts Institute of Technology to Washington. After FDR's decision in 1941 Bush was able to assemble and press ahead with atomic weapons development, reporting back to the president occasionally. The effort also brought about close early cooperation between the Americans and the British, the latter having brought together their national atomic effort under an umbrella entitled the Maud Committee. All this was in contrast to the impressive technical innovations but lack of fundamental strategic breakthroughs by Germany's scientific community, which was generally segregated from the Nazi government.

One of the most striking features of the development of the atomic bomb is that an enterprise which ultimately became so massive was nevertheless successfully carried out in secrecy. Richard Rhodes in *The Making of the Atomic Bomb* notes that FDR insisted that policy discussion be restricted to a total of six people—no more. His preoccupation with secrecy was no doubt crucial to keeping the effort hidden from the enemy. One inexcusable consequence, however, was that when Roosevelt died on April 12, 1945, Vice President Harry Truman became president with no knowledge whatsoever of this war-winning and historic project.

The principal motivation for using the bomb against Japan was the strong desire to shorten the war. By the middle of 1945, when the weapon became available, Germany had surrendered, but fighting in the Pacific still raged as ferociously as before. Contrary to historical experience that a nation's will to fight erodes as defeat nears, the Japanese military seemed to be fighting ever harder as U.S. forces approached the home islands of Japan. On April 1, 1945, the battle of Okinawa opened. The struggle would last three months; deaths included 12,000 U.S. troops, 110,000 of the enemy, and 75,000 Japanese civilians. The introduction of kamikaze "suicide pilots" added to the deep U.S. concern about losses to come. An overwhelming desire to end the fighting was paramount in Washington. At the same time, no doubt, hatred which included a racial component further encouraged using the bomb once available. The attacks on Pearl Harbor and the Philippines and the brutal treatment of U.S. prisoners of war—especially in the Bataan death march in 1942—made the determination to punish Japan especially strong.

However, arguments that the use of the bomb was motivated primarily by racial hatred of the Japanese do not stand up to evidence or reason. Fear that Germany would develop an atomic weapon was from the start the main spur for the Manhattan Project. Leslie A. Groves, who directed the project, stated explicitly in his memoirs that Roosevelt planned to use the bomb against Germany.

When Truman became president, he immediately iterated established war policy. His first statement in office as chief executive was a brief, direct declaration on the need to end the war as quickly as possible: "The world may be sure that we will prosecute the war on both fronts, east and west, with all the vigor we possess to a successful conclusion." His declaration to Congress and the country—"Every day peace is delayed costs a terrible toll"—fitly summarized U.S. public opinion at the time.

On April 25, Truman met with Groves and Secretary of War Henry Stimson for his first briefing on the atomic bomb project. The record indicates there was no discussion whatsoever about whether the weapon should be used—only when. A test was planned for New Mexico in July, and Japan could be bombed by August. A special air delivery team was in training and already in place in the Pacific. Truman clearly raised no question or objection to the assumption of those already engaged in the project that the bomb would be used as early as possible.

The more general planning for the final stages of the war strongly reinforced this sense of urgency. In overall strategic matters, Roosevelt and then Truman, Stimson, Chief of Staff George C. Marshall, and others relied on the Operations Division (OPD) of the Department of War's general staff. The OPD had a strong reputation for effectiveness, reliability, and *accuracy*. The point was made very consistently from this source that the United States confronted the prospect of broad, long-term ground fighting on the Japanese home islands and possibly on the mainland of Asia unless the enemy could be defeated by other means. By the time the bomb was ready, this perception was fully accepted throughout the government. Moreover, by 1945 devastating bombing of cities and massive killing of civilians was an accepted part of war strategy. At the same time, of course, unrelenting and unrestricted U.S. Navy submarine warfare was slowly starving the Japanese population—the same type of warfare denounced by Americans of a previous generation as "barbaric" when used by Germany against Great Britain in World War I. Fleets of modern B-29 heavy bombers were laying waste Japanese cities and exacting a heavy toll from civilians, who were burned alive by the tens of thousands in great fire raids. By the summer of 1945 there were indeed few restraints on the conduct of the Pacific war by any belligerent party.

Recognizing the momentousness of what was unfolding, a special Interim Committee was formed in May to deal with atomic weapons and related policies after the war. The committee had a broad range of concerns, from how to handle public reactions to the use of the new weapon on Japan to long-term international regulation and control of this very new power. This body included men at the very top of the physics profession centrally involved in the development of the weapon: Arthur Compton, Enrico Fermi, Ernest Lawrence, and J. Robert Oppenheimer. Although a complete record of their meetings is not available, clearly there were detailed discussions of options for using the bomb and an explicit statement against any purely "technical demonstration." A separate report by leading scientist James Franck did argue for the alternative of exploding a test bomb in a desert or barren island environment, to be observed by members of the United Nations. But the test bomb might not work; the shock effect on the enemy of actual use on a Japanese city could not be guaranteed from just a demonstration. Furthermore, the number of bombs was too limited to expend more than even one in a test after the initial experimental explosion. Another senior scientist, Leo Szilard, made the case that Japan was already beaten and that therefore a political end to the war should be sought. The counter to this argument was that although the United States knew that Japan was indeed practically beaten by every objective measure, the Japanese leaders did not seem to be aware of that fact. None of these minority sentiments was persuasive to the majority.

The bomb was tested in July in Alamagordo, New Mexico. While theoretically the event could have been staged as a public demonstration, the chance of failure of the bomb was seen as too great to risk. The spectacular success of the test could not be foreseen in advance—that was the purpose of the test. McGeorge Bundy writes of the impact of the blast on the observers: "The first official account, written by Groves, remains persuasively terrifying even now: the blinding flash of light, the enormous ball of fire, the mushroom cloud, the steel test tower vaporized, and the estimated yield in excess of 15,000 to 20,000 tons" (*Danger and Survival,* p. 72).

Only one member of the Interim Committee, Ralph Bard, considered changing the agreed policy of using the bomb against Japan without warning. Although originally he had concurred in the agreed policy, on reflection he had doubts. A combination of concern about U.S. humanitarian and fair-play traditions weighed heavily on his mind. He argued for giving Japan two or three days warning, through private contacts with Japanese government representatives following the Potsdam Conference of Western Allies. He felt sufficiently strong about this to press the case with President Truman, who responded that the matter had already been thoroughly considered.

During a meeting on June 18, 1945, among President Truman and his top advisers to discuss the invasion plans for Japan, there was more detailed consideration of the atomic bomb. John McCloy, an influential voice specifically consulted by Truman, argued strenuously for an effort at political settlement of the war before invasion of Japan, to include both explicit guarantees that the role of the Japanese emperor would be maintained and some warning about the new weapon. Secretary of War Henry Stimson had a similar view, though James F. Byrnes—very soon to be secretary of state—and others disagreed. In evaluating the merits of the various proposals, it is difficult to imagine the Japanese leaders surrendering their empire on the mere warning of a "terrible new weapon." After all, they had endured the Tokyo fire raid in March,

the worst bombing raid in history, with little if any observable weakening of determination. Stimson did not have a very significant influence in target selection, although he was able to remove from the list Kyoto, ancient capital and an artistic center of Japan.

There was no overall, comprehensive internal debate on the use of the new atomic bomb. Truman, rightly famous for very orderly procedures in the definition and implementation of policy, did not follow such a course in this instance because of various factors. First, there was the overall momentum of a process already in place. The decision to use the fearsome new weapon had already been made long before the new president took charge. The assumption of use was well ingrained by the time the new weapon finally was completed, just after Truman's installation in office. Since the attack on Pearl Harbor, the overriding assumption of the leadership of the government was that the war would be prosecuted as aggressively as possible, with maximum emphasis on achieving total victory and sustained effort to minimize U.S. casualties. Second, and closely related, was that military necessity included maintenance of secrecy across the board. This worked against any open discussion of the new weapon within the administration. Finally, the successful completion of the Manhattan Project was also closely related to secrecy. These dimensions directly reinforced the primary war aim of defeating Japan as quickly as possible.

At the Potsdam Conference of Allied leaders in July 1945, a final warning was issued to Japan to surrender. There was no explicit mention of the new atomic weapon, though vague ominous warnings were communicated. Truman's journal entries during this time indicate that he persuaded himself that Hiroshima and Nagasaki, the cities selected for atomic attack, were primarily military targets, in contrast to the civilian character of Tokyo. Truman in his diary noted that "women and children" would not be targets. This distinction existed only in his mind; there were plenty of civilians in both targeted cities. Also at Potsdam, the Soviets iterated a pledge made at the earlier Yalta Conference to enter the war against Japan. The United States, following the successful atomic test in New Mexico, felt less urgency about Soviet military participation in the war. Characteristically, the Soviets emphasized the importance of secrecy regarding their move. This was also a time of contacts between representatives of the Japanese and Soviet governments, with the former requesting the latter to mediate peace on their behalf. The effort, orchestrated by Japanese foreign minister Togo Shigenori, emphasized a solution which would stop short of "unconditional surrender." The United States had intercepts of these messages at Potsdam but did not know that the

Japanese initiative was focused on the priority importance of maintenance of the emperor. Stalin had nothing to gain by a foreshortened war which would see him absent from the victors' table, and thus he spun out useless but tempting negotiations until he was ready with his totally unprovoked declaration of war.

On August 6, 1945, Hiroshima was devastated by an atomic bomb. The Japanese cabinet, apprised of the total destruction of the city and enormous casualties of approximately one hundred thirty thousand people, nevertheless divided evenly on the issue of surrender. The emperor asserted himself to tilt the balance to ending the war on Washington's terms. The announcement did not come soon enough, however, to stop the second U.S. atomic bombing, of Nagasaki on August 9. The Japanese propaganda machine simply told the public of a "new and terrible weapon used by the enemy" and publicized detailed and rather useless means by which civilians could avoid becoming casualties.

In later years, Harry Truman always spoke forcefully, sometimes emotionally, and sometimes very bluntly about the decision to use the bomb. He indicated that he never lost any sleep over this move, dictated by the necessities of war. His personal library indicates a more thoughtful approach and includes a very extensive collection of literature on the use of this terribly destructive weapon which changed forever the nature of warfare and international relations. The debate on the wisdom and the morality of the awesome twin atomic bombings of Hiroshima and Nagasaki shows few if any signs of abating in the United States even as the bombings themselves recede further into history.

It should also be noted that, like the Germans, the Japanese had their own atomic weapons program (perhaps in advance of the Germans). The evidence is strong that, along with biological warfare, the Japanese themselves were fully prepared to use atomic and biological warfare against their enemies.

FURTHER READINGS

Bundy, McGeorge. *Danger and Survival: Choices about the Bomb during the First Fifty Years* (1988).

Ferrell, Robert H. *Off the Record: The Private Papers of Harry S. Truman* (1980).

Pacific War Research Society. *The Day Man Lost* (1972).

Rhodes, Richard. *The Making of the Atomic Bomb* (1986).

Wilcox, Robert K. *Japan's Secret War* (1985).

Arthur I. Cyr

SEE ALSO Atomic Bomb Program, Japanese; Truman, Harry S.

Atomic Bomb Program, Japanese

Japan could claim some of the world's leading nuclear physicists before the war—men who had been closely associated with those who would later head the U.S. atomic bomb project, Niels Bohr and Albert Einstein. Moreover, Japan had military leaders who understood atomic power's potential, both as a weapon and as an energy source. They had followed the course of prewar atomic research and by 1940 had successfully convinced their government to initiate an atomic power program of its own. Concerned about Japan's dependence on energy imports and the disparity between its own resources and those of its most likely opponents in the war—the United States and the Soviet Union—they saw nuclear power and weapons as a solution to both problems. Lacking the financial resources and raw materials of Germany and the Western Allies, the Japanese program progressed slowly and was further inhibited by excessive secrecy, divisions between the two services' separate projects, and the lack of reasonable-grade uranium ores. Forced by U.S. bombing to move to the Korean Peninsula in 1945, Japan's atomic bomb program failed to achieve fission, but its Korean facilities were removed to Russia by Soviet troops in 1946 and may have contributed to the Soviet Union's successful postwar atomic weapons development.

Although the Japanese navy was the first service to concern itself with atomic research, it was the army which funded the first effort, beginning in July 1941. Its program had its roots in a study ordered by Lieutenant General Takeo Yasuda in April 1940. Yasuda had noticed that the Americans had ceased to publicize their atomic research efforts. More important, he noticed an increasing level of security around all U.S. research, which, of course, was influenced by growing tensions between the United States and Japan. His study was completed in October 1940. It concluded that an atomic bomb was not only possible but that the United States probably was working on one and had the potential to build it. Still, Yasuda's superiors were not convinced of Japan's need for a bomb until the spring of 1941. The army approved funding for development of a *Genzai Bakuda,* or atomic bomb, just before the United States froze all Japanese assets inside its borders on July 26, 1941.

The army program was originally centered in the Japanese industrial city of Nagoya under one of Japan's leading scientists, Dr. Yoshio Nishina, who was also a close friend and associate of the famous Danish nuclear physicist Niels Bohr. Nishina's team was headquartered in Japan's Institute of Physical and Chemical Research, or RIKKEN. At the time, the institute had Japan's only working cyclotron, a recently invented device which greatly facilitated atomic research. Other scientists assisting him included Dr. Ryokichi Sugane, Tameichi Yazuki, and Hidehiko Tamaki. Funding was limited, and the scientists had very little uranium or other radioactive materials with which to work. Nonetheless, they were hopeful. The Japanese Foreign Ministry and the army's materiel division were actively working to gather uranium ores and other materials from Japan's conquered territories and Axis allies. They also established a spy network in the United States, with German and Spanish assistance. Among the intelligence requirements laid on those networks was one to determine the extent of U.S. progress in nuclear research.

The Spanish, or "TO," network under Alcazar de Velasco was the core of this network. Dispatching agents up through Mexico and down from Canada, it discovered the U.S. Manhattan Project but underestimated its progress. As a result, the Japanese may actually have felt that they were ahead of the Americans. More important, they never gained any insights into U.S. failures or technical developments before their network was crippled by FBI raids and diplomatic restrictions in late 1943.

The Japanese navy entered the nuclear race later than the army. Following the U.S. seizure of Japanese assets, navy Captain Yoji Ito contacted an old friend, Dr. Tsunesaburo Asada at the University of Osaka, with his concerns about overseas nuclear research. Dr. Asada had urged the development of atomic power, including a bomb, as early as 1938, and he was able to convince Captain Ito of the strategic imperative. The navy gathered its scientists, including the army's Dr. Nishina, in October 1941. Interestingly, Dr. Nishina did not reveal that he was already working on the same program for the army. Moreover, the navy decided not to inform the army of its nuclear program. Although he must have been very conflicted, Dr. Nishina adhered to that decision. As a result, the two services' programs continued separately in competition for the same resources until the war's final months, despite the fact that both programs often employed the same scientists. The navy designated its program as Project F-go. It was directed by Dr. Bunsaku Arakatsu beginning in July 1942.

Dr. Arakatsui was uniquely qualified for the position. A close friend of Albert Einstein and the father of modern Japanese physics, he had studied nuclear physics under Einstein in the late 1920s, at Cambridge and in Switzerland, and he spoke English and German fluently. He was assisted by Dr. Hideki Yukawa, who would later become the first Japanese scientist to earn the Nobel Prize for Physics (in 1949). The navy's program started with an allocation of 600,000 yen a year at a time when the army was funding its program at 100,000 yen annually.

Both programs had similar problems. Japan had only one cyclotron and only one other under construction. More significantly, acquiring quantities of suitable uranium ore proved to be a major challenge. The army reported having 800 kilograms of uranium oxide in Shanghai, and both services had access to several mines in Korea (near today's North Korean cities of Pyongyang and Hungnam) that yielded small quantities of fergusite and permagtites—low-grade uranium ores. The supply was not enough for both services, but it might have been enough if they had pooled their resources. The army's efforts to acquire the higher-grade pitchblende from Germany were initially rebuffed, but several hundred pounds were delivered by submarine in 1944.

The second major problem Japanese scientists faced was the separating of the fissionable U-235 from the more abundant U-238. Dr. Takeuchi favored gas separation, whereby vaporization enabled the lighter U-235 to be skimmed off and condensed into a more enriched material. This proved to be a slow process that produced inadequate quantities, and so he also settled on thermal diffusion as an second, supplemental method. Thermal diffusion used a hot inner tube to vaporize the uranium and a cold outer tube to condense it. Thermal diffusion caused the heavier U-238 to cling to the cold outer tube, while U-235 had a tendency to coalesce around the inner tube. Dr. Takeuchi successfully employed the thermal diffusion method for the first time in July 1943 but was not able to complete a practical production facility until September 1944.

None of this solved the problem, however, because Japan still lacked adequate quantities of high-grade ore to produce the amounts of fissionable material required. Still, progress was being made, albeit very slowly. By March 1944, the researchers had settled on carbon as a better moderator than heavy water. That same month, the army increased its funding to 20 million yen (about $5 million in 1940 dollars), allowed its air component to lead the project under General Hatsuzo Taniguchi, and assigned the 8th Technical Laboratory in support. Seven months later, the navy had lost interest in developing an atomic reactor and, with its fleet all but destroyed, agreed formally to cooperate with the army on development of an atomic bomb. Japan's nuclear program was now consolidated, but Allied bombing precluded any advantage from being gained. The bombing came just as the additional cyclotrons came on line and reasonable quantities of U-235 were being produced. The Nagoya facility was bombed in November 1944, and bombing was also interfering with the transport of critical materials. Meanwhile, Allied submarines were wreaking havoc with Japanese imports. Ore and other critical materials simply never arrived.

Despite these problems, the scientists began testing samples of "enriched uranium" in March 1945. The eight "separators" were ordered to work around the clock, but ore deliveries were becoming intermittent. Facing increasing devastation by Allied bombing, Japan's military authorities evacuated the facilities and project to Konan, Korea. That placed it closer to its primary sources of ore and other materials, as well as in an area so far ignored by Allied bombing. Konan, which lay near the port of Hungnam, was home to a massive industrial complex which produced heavy water, synthetic fuel, and more electrical power than was generated in all of Japan. Japan's military leaders hoped the nuclear program facility would be fully operational by August 1945, the month when in actuality Japan surrendered. Although the war ended before Japan's physicists achieved fission or detonated a bomb, navy leaders felt they were within weeks of success.

Interestingly, Japanese troops defending the Konan complex fought on against Soviet troops for at least two months after the war officially ended. Records and some facilities and equipment were destroyed. Nonetheless, the Soviets were able to recover much material and remove it and many scientists and technicians to the Soviet Union in 1946. The Konan complex and its nearby hydroelectric facilities figured prominently in the later Korean War. South Korean troops reported the discovery of a vast "underground complex" including a large "uranium-producing facility" there as they advanced northward in September 1950. Unfortunately, the Chinese offensive of later that year drove all United Nations forces away in the famous Battle of the Chosin Reservoir. The facility's full story has never been exposed. (A USAAF B-29 on a POW relief mission was shot down by Soviet fighters near Konan just after the end of the World War II. Although the pilots attempted to strafe all survivors, only one USAAF crewman was lost, and the Soviets attributed the whole episode to a "misunderstanding.")

Japan's atomic bomb project is one of the last secrets to come out of World War II. It was a disjointed effort conducted within almost total secrecy and, before 1944, with very limited resources. Most of the records and equipment were destroyed either during the war's final weeks or during the early days of the U.S. and Soviet occupations of Japan and North Korea, respectively. However, the information acquired was not lost to the Japanese. The scientists involved in the World War II program became key figures in Japan's postwar scientific and economic revival. It remains to be seen whether Japan could have achieved its goals of several such weapons in time to destroy the expected Allied invasion fleet, but there is no doubt that Japan would have used them had any such weapons been available.

FURTHER READINGS
Coffey, Thomas M. *Imperial Tragedy* (1970).
Pacific War Research Society. *The Day Man Lost* (1972).
Wilcox, Robert K. *Japan's Secret War* (1985).

Carl O. Schuster

SEE ALSO Atomic Bomb, Decision to Use against Japan

Australia

As part of the self-governing British Commonwealth and empire, Australia had been one of the first nations to enter the war against Germany in September 1939, and its ground, air, and naval forces had been deployed to the Mediterranean theater. There they took part in the early fighting against the Italians, and subsequently the Germans, in North Africa; in the disastrous campaigns in Greece and Crete; and against the Vichy French in Syria. Two divisions of the 2d Australian Imperial Force (AIF), the 6th and 7th, were returned to Australia at the beginning of 1942 following Japan's entry into the war; the third division in the Middle East, the 9th, remained as part of General Bernard Montgomery's Eighth Army and was repatriated to Australia after El Alamein at the end of that year. The majority of Australia's naval units likewise returned to the Pacific, but a sizable proportion of the air force remained in Great Britain under the terms of the Empire Air Training Scheme.

Japan had been identified as Australia's most likely future enemy by senior military planners as early as 1920, and events in northeast Asia in the 1930s had heightened Australian apprehensions of Japan's likely future intentions. As in Great Britain and elsewhere in the Commonwealth, however, the Australian government began to rearm only after 1937, and by the outbreak of the war in Europe the Australian armed forces were still inadequately trained, and their equipment was often obsolescent. This was especially true of the air force, which in 1939 possessed no modern frontline fighter aircraft, and of the army, which in 1939 was still training on World War I artillery pieces. The navy possessed a number of modern cruisers, but some of these suffered from inadequate weaponry (especially a lack of high-angle armament for defense against aircraft), while the fleet itself was unbalanced and incapable of independent action, being both too small and designed to fit into a larger, British organization. The defense industry was in a similarly underdeveloped state. In 1939 there were just five government munitions factories supplying small arms, ammunition, and the lesser scale of equipment to the ground forces, and by the beginning of the Pacific war this number had risen to just seven; some indication of the Pacific war's impact may be gauged from the fact that by June 1942 this had increased to seventeen, and by mid-1943 it had risen again, to thirty-two. But Australia had no indigenous automobile industry before the war, while the Commonwealth Aircraft Corporation had been founded only in 1936 and had produced a limited range of foreign designs under license.

The Australian government did take steps to meet the potential Japanese threat, especially in the course of 1941. The 8th Division, raised in 1940, was kept back from the Middle East, and in May 1941 the government despatched two of its brigades under the command of Major General Henry Gordon Bennett to reinforce Malaya; the third brigade was held back to be distributed in battalion groups on Ambon and Timor and at Rabaul, where they were easily overcome by superior Japanese forces in the opening weeks of the war. The combined British, Indian, and Australian forces in Malaya were unevenly trained, sometimes poorly equipped, and badly led in general; their efforts were further hampered by surrendering the strategic initiative to the Japanese, who concentrated their invasion force in southern Indochina and "neutral" Thailand. The key to success in the Malayan campaign was air superiority, and the Japanese quickly established this through the destruction of the outnumbered and mostly outclassed squadrons available to the British. By the time the Australians were brought into the fighting, in southern Johore in early January, the Japanese had taken most of Malaya and thus largely neutralized the defenses of Johore and, by extension, of Singapore itself. The defenders withdrew into Singapore on January 31, followed by a Japanese amphibious assault on the night of February 8–9. The surrender of the city and garrison on February 15 was the greatest reverse in British military history and saw some 80,000 troops—more than fifteen thousand of them Australian—go into captivity.

The loss of "impregnable" Singapore was received with profound shock in Australia. For twenty years the country's defense had been predicated on a navalist strategy with the Singapore base at its heart. The rapid Japanese advance and string of seemingly inexorable victories, coupled with the loss of a complete division within a matter of weeks of the war's beginning, were profoundly unsettling to a nation which increasingly looked to be on the front line—an impression strengthened by the first large-scale Japanese air raid on the northern port city of Darwin, on February 19. In fact, the Japanese never intended to invade Australia but, appreciating its strategic position as a base of operations against their newly acquired Southern Resources Zone in southeast Asia, sought to neutralize it by creating a barrier running through New Guinea and the islands of the South Pacific.

The United States likewise appreciated Australia's potential as a strategic base from which to mount operations against the Japanese, although initially this plan was conceived fairly narrowly, in terms of providing support for General MacArthur's increasingly beleaguered forces in the Philippines. Following the Arcadia Conference, Roosevelt and Churchill agreed that the Southwest Pacific Area (SWPA) should become an American responsibility, utilizing Australia as a base, and in March MacArthur was ordered to leave the Philippines to take command of the new theater. He was greeted as a savior on his arrival, and the Australian government, which had little experience of either military affairs or government generally (having come into office only in October the previous year), ceded control of much of the Australian war effort to MacArthur in a manner which they were to regret later.

Contrary to prevailing myth, Australia was saved from the Japanese in 1942 largely by Australian efforts, although the naval victory in the Coral Sea on May 7–8, 1942, was won by U.S. naval forces with elements of the Royal Australian Navy (RAN) attached. Two U.S. National Guard divisions, the 32d and 41st, were sent to MacArthur's command in April–May 1942, but their state of training and equipping was such that they were of little immediate use, and they were to perform poorly in their first battles in New Guinea. Ultimately there would be 800,000 U.S. personnel in SWPA, but even by September 1943 there were still only 120,000 Americans in the U.S. Army Forces in Australia (USAFIA). In April 1942, as the critical fighting for Papua was about to begin, the frontline units engaging the Japanese were Australian: 46,000 in the AIF returned from the Middle East; 63,000 AIF men who had completed their training in Australia; 280,000 militia for home defense (which included Papua but not New Guinea); and 33,000 Americans from all services. The command arrangements, however, were overwhelmingly American. There was no attempt to create a combined staff, no Australian or Dutch officers were appointed to the staff branches of the supreme commander's headquarters, and although the commander in chief of the Australian Military Forces, General Sir Thomas Blamey, was made commander of Allied land forces, MacArthur ensured that he did not exercise command over U.S. ground formations.

Japanese attempts at a seaborne landing near Port Moresby were frustrated by the carrier engagement in the Coral Sea, and after a further and more disastrous defeat at Midway in June the Japanese decided on a landward advance across country from bases around Lae. Moresby received initial reinforcements in May, but MacArthur's intended move toward Buna was now frustrated by the Japanese landings there and at Gona on July 21–22. Militia units in the area were forced to retreat, although a Japanese attempt in late August to move around their flanks with an amphibious landing at Milne Bay was defeated after heavy fighting which saw most of the Japanese force destroyed. The Japanese made extensive gains in their advance along the Kokoda Track, opposed by poorly equipped and mostly young soldiers from the militia who nonetheless put up a stiff resistance and slowed the advance. New Guinea Force continued to receive reinforcements, the Japanese were at the end of long supply lines in very difficult terrain, and with the reverses suffered at Guadalcanal these factors now combined to force the Japanese onto the defensive; in mid-September they began to withdraw back to the coast. By November they were in positions around Buna, Gona, and Sanananda facing the Australians and American units of the 32d Division. The Japanese defended vigorously from numerous pillboxes and strong points, and casualties on both sides were high. The survivors of the Japanese forces were evacuated by sea or broke out overland in January 1943; 13,000 of a force of 20,000 were killed in the fighting for Papua, while the Australians lost 2,165 killed and 3,533 wounded, and the Americans suffered about 3,000 casualties as well.

In January 1943 the 9th Division returned to Australia, having played a key role in the Allied victory at El Alamein the previous October. By 1943 the Australian government was faced with a manpower crisis, and the needs of industry, agriculture, and the armed forces could not all continue to be met from a total population base of less than 7 million. In addition, with Papua cleared of the Japanese the army faced a problem in that the provisions of the Defense Act did not permit militia soldiers to serve in New Guinea or anywhere else outside Australian territory unless they volunteered specifically for service there. In February 1943 the act was amended for the duration to extend the areas in which the militia could be deployed, but in fact volunteers remained the mainstay of the army outside Australia for the rest of the war. To meet its manpower difficulties, the government increased the use of women in nontraditional areas of employment

but also began a partial demobilization of the army; some units and formations in Australia were disbanded, and in May 1944 the Volunteer Defense Corps (the Australian equivalent of the British Home Guard) was reduced in strength substantially.

The operational focus now shifted to the Australian-mandated territory of New Guinea. Following their disastrous defeat in the Solomon Islands, the Japanese resumed the offensive in New Guinea and attempted to capture Wau with a reinforced division based at Lae in January 1943. This attempt was defeated by Australian troops of the 17th Brigade who were airlifted to Wau, while in early March a Japanese troop convoy attempting to land at Lae was destroyed by Allied aircraft in the Battle of the Bismarck Sea. The Australians and Americans in SWPA now went over to the offensive themselves following the decisions reached at the Quadrant Conference in Quebec in August 1943. The intention was to neutralize and isolate the major Japanese position at Rabaul through a series of coordinated airborne and amphibious operations designed to clear New Guinea of the Japanese from east to west. U.S. forces from General Walter Krueger's Sixth Army staged a series of amphibious landings while Allied air power coordinated by Kenney's Fifth Air Force destroyed large numbers of enemy aircraft in August. Lae and Salamaua fell in September, and Finschhafen was captured at the beginning of October, but the Australians made slow progress in the fighting for Sattelberg, while the Shaggy Ridge positions in the Ramu Valley were not cleared until January 1944. On February 10 Australian units linked up with the Americans on the coast at Saidor.

The conditions imposed by climate and terrain were appalling, but the Australians and Americans were increasingly in a better position to withstand the remorseless demands of the campaign than were the Japanese, whose strength was ground down relentlessly while their strategic position became increasingly hopeless. The Americans landed in New Britain at the end of 1943 and captured the Admiralty Islands in February 1944. MacArthur then bypassed the Japanese forces at Wewak and Hansa Bay with an amphibious operation against Hollandia and Aitape, followed by further landings at Biak. The Japanese could still respond strongly on occasion, as at the Driniumor River, but the Hollandia operation signaled the beginning of the end of the New Guinea campaign and the total defeat of the Japanese there.

MacArthur's focus had always been on a return to the Philippines, and increasingly Australian and American strategic interests began to diverge. The reconquest of the Philippines (a U.S. possession) was to be an American undertaking, and MacArthur ordered the Australian commander in chief, Blamey, to relieve U.S. forces at Aitape-Wewak and on New Britain and Bougainville; Blamey had intended to relieve the 6½ U.S. divisions involved with seven brigades, but he was ordered to increase the size of the force to twelve brigades. These mopping-up operations have proved controversial ever since. On Bougainville the Australians suffered 516 dead while inflicting 8,500 Japanese casualties, with the latter suffering a further 9,800 deaths from disease; 23,500 enemy personnel surrendered at the end of the war. On New Britain 93,000 Japanese from Imamura's Eighth Area Army were contained by numerically much smaller Australian forces at a cost of seventy-four Australian dead. In the Aitape-Wewak area the remains of Adachi's Eighteenth Army, about 35,000 strong, were contained and reduced by the Australian 6th Division, which lost 442 killed and 1,141 wounded; the Japanese lost more than 9,000 killed in action and 14,000 from disease and starvation. Impressive though these results may have been, many at the time were convinced that the losses involved were unnecessary and did nothing to shorten the war.

The final Australian campaign in the war against Japan took place in the Dutch and British territories on the island of Borneo. These campaigns were MacArthur's idea and were undertaken despite the misgivings of both Blamey and the Australian government. The idea was to deny the oil resources of the territory to the Japanese, who by this stage of the war were incapable of exploiting them in any case, and to secure bases for a further advance into the Netherlands East Indies in order to restore Dutch colonial rule. The plan's strategic value was basically nil. Australian forces landed at Tarakan on May 1, at Labuan and Brunei Bay on June 10, and at Balikpapan on July 1. The Australians lost 225 killed at Tarakan, 229 at Balikpapan, and a further 114 at Labuan. Like the mopping-up operations in New Guinea, this campaign was regarded as futile at the time and has proved controversial since.

Blamey represented Australia on the deck of USS *Missouri* in Tokyo Bay on September 2, and Australians presided over numerous local surrender ceremonies throughout SWPA. The traumatic process of reclaiming those prisoners of the Japanese who had survived incarceration and Japanese cruelty was expedited, although for some—like the 2,500 murdered at Sandakan and Ranau between May and August 1945—the end of the war just came too late. The Australians prosecuted their own war crimes trials in their areas of responsibility; these lasted until 1951. Although sometimes regarded as more harsh than trials conducted by other Allied governments, there is little evidence for the proposition that the Australians were motivated more by vengeance than by justice.

World War II was the greatest war in Australian history, and its impact on Australia was long term. It produced a more complex economy and increased the importance of the manufacturing sector within it. After 1945 the country opened itself to great waves of non-British migration. Women had moved into the paid workforce in ways which had not occurred from 1914 to 1918, and although many of them moved out again in the immediate aftermath of the war, ideas about women's employment had changed fundamentally. Finally, the great influx of Americans from 1942 to 1945 opened Australian society to new influences not previously experienced, and although Australia was to remain a narrowly British society in many respects until the 1960s and 1970s, the effect of the American "invasion" in breaking down Australian social provincialism should not be underestimated. Australia's defense system was realigned from orientation to Great Britain to a close relationship with the United States—a relationship that continued through the cold war. Finally, the Pacific war saw Australians fighting in direct defense of Australia for the first and only time in their history, and the memory of this and the shock which it had induced were to influence the direction of Australian defense and foreign policy in powerful ways during the cold war which quickly followed the peace.

FURTHER READINGS
Beaumont, Joan, ed. *Australia's War 1939–45* (1996).
Robertson, John Robertson. *Australia at War 1939–1945* (1981).

Jeffrey Grey

SEE ALSO Air Force, Royal Australian; MacArthur, Douglas

Franklin Delano Roosevelt, 32d president of the United States, as he appeared in the 1940s. © *Bettmann/CORBIS*.

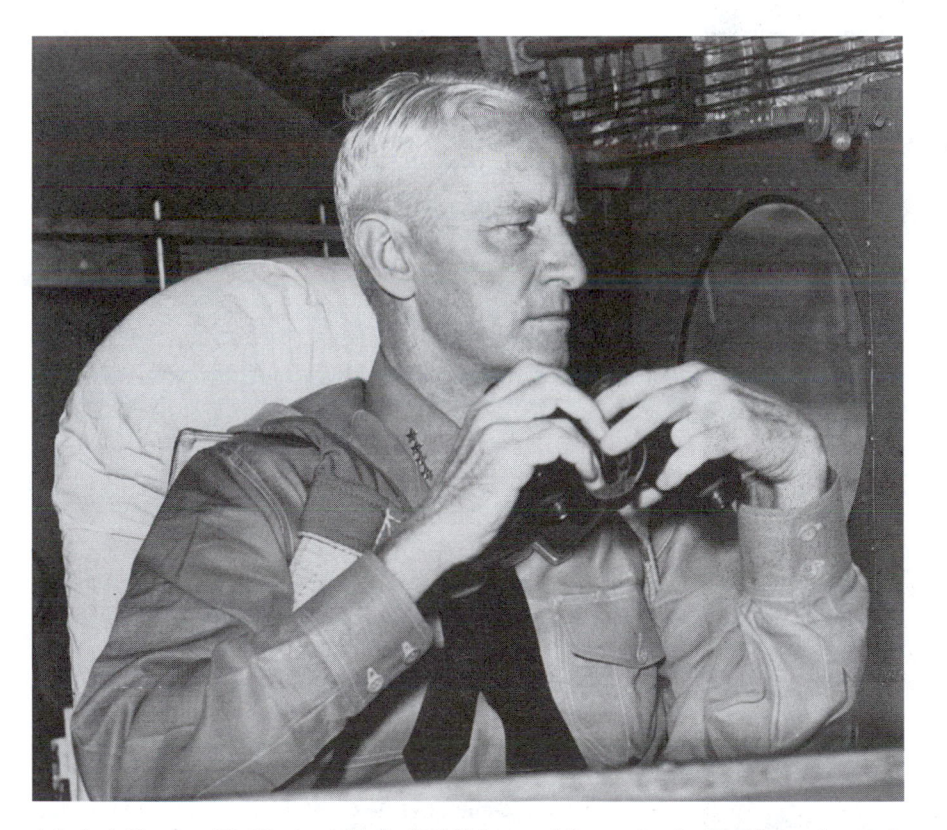

Admiral Chester W. Nimitz, chief of all U.S. naval forces in the Pacific and grand strategist of the island-hopping campaign. © *Bettmann/CORBIS*.

Vice Admiral Raymond A. Spruance, one of the most influential U.S. naval leaders in the Pacific during World War II, as he appeared in February 1944. © *Corbis/Bettmann-UPI.*

General Henry Harley "Hap" Arnold, the first general of the U.S. Air Force, as he appeared in 1940. *American Stock/Archive Photos.*

Britain's Major General Orde C. Wingate, shortly before the departure of glider formations for infiltrations behind Japanese lines in Burma, May 1, 1944. *Popperfoto/Archive Photos.*

Japanese troops entering Shanghai, China, 1932. © *Hulton-Deutsch Collection/CORBIS.*

Japanese soldiers on the march in Asia. © *Hulton-Deutsch Collection/CORBIS.*

Japan's most famous fighter, the Mitsubishi Zero. © *Museum of Flight/CORBIS.*

Stunned American sailors watch as balls of fire rise up from burning U.S. planes during the Japanese attack on Pearl Harbor, December 7, 1941. *Archive Photos.*

American and Filipino troops surrendering to the Japanese at Corregidor, May 6, 1942. *Archive Photos.*

The Bataan death march, 1942. Thousands of Filipinos and Americans died on the forced march. In this photograph, the dead and injured are carried in litters by those still able to walk. © *Bettmann/CORBIS.*

The aircraft carrier USS *Yorktown* takes a hit from Japanese fighters at the Battle of Midway, June 1942. Severely damaged, the *Yorktown* sank after a valiant effort on the part of her crew to save her. © *CORBIS.*

On board the USS *Hornet,* April 1942. A B-25 bomber prepares to take off for the first U.S. bombing raid against Tokyo. Led by Colonel James Doolittle, the raid caused little damage but was a devastating psychological blow to the Japanese, who believed that U.S. air power could never reach their shores. *Archive Photos.*

U.S. citizens of Japanese ancestry lining up as they enter an internment camp, 1942. © *Seattle Post-Intelligencer Collection/CORBIS.*

African American troops during the Pacific war. © *Bettmann/CORBIS.*

During the war, women entered the workforce in great numbers. Here, they assemble a bomber at an aircraft factory. *Anthony Potter Collection/Archive Photos.*

Members of the first WAC unit in overseas service leave for their assignment in North Africa, 1943. *Archive Photos.*

A naval convoy crossing the Pacific. © *CORBIS*

U.S. Marines loading material into landing boats on the beach at Guadalcanal. The naval battles in and around the Solomon Islands began in mid-1942 and lasted for several months. *Archive Photos.*

A squadron of Douglas Devastator torpedo bombers unfold their wings for takeoff from the USS *Enterprise* during the Battle of Midway, June 1942. The Japanese lost four aircraft carriers, a devastating blow to their navy and the end of their expansion in the central Pacific. *UPI/Bettmann.*

Dive-bombers waved for the takeoff from a carrier, November 1943. *UPI/Corbis-Bettmann.*

Sober-faced pilots walk across the carrier deck to their planes, poised for a raid on Truk, March 1944. *UPI/Bettmann Newsphotos.*

Looking back. A fighter clears the deck of the USS *Saratoga*, February 1944.
© *Bettmann/CORBIS*.

A squadron of fighters banks to the left and prepares to circle before landing on the carrier deck. *UPI/Corbis-Bettmann*.

Admiral Marc A. Mitscher, carrier force commander, watches as planes launch from the carrier deck to strike Hollandia, in Dutch New Guinea, 1944. *UPI/Bettmann Newsphotos.*

Admiral William F. Halsey, on board the USS *New Jersey* en route to the Philippines, 1944. *Archive Photos.*

Outlined against the sky, Grumman F6F Hellcats are spotted forward on the flight deck of the Essex-class carrier USS *Hancock* as it rides at anchor in the Pacific, April 1945. *UPI/Corbis-Bettmann.*

Ships of Task Force 38 moving in line of bearing prior to their entry into Ulithi anchorage, where they received supplies and ammunition. In the foreground is the USS *Langley.* Next is the big Essex-class carrier USS *Ticonderoga.* In the background are the masts of the battleships *North Carolina, Washington,* and *South Dakota. UPI/Corbis-Bettmann.*

The aftermath of a kamikaze attack on the USS *Intrepid.* © *CORBIS.*

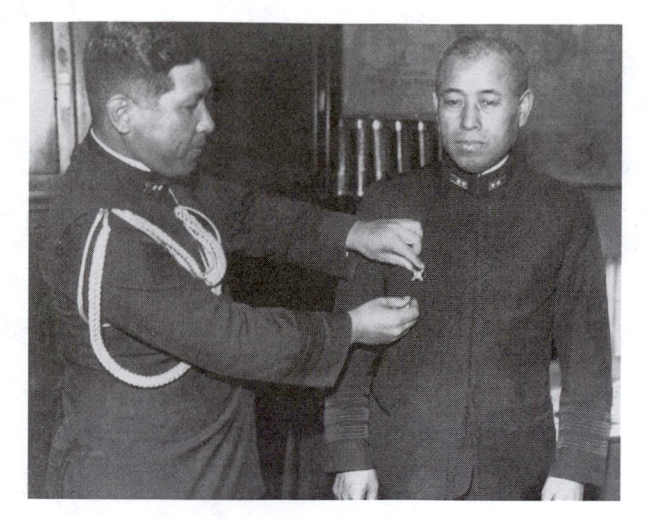

Admiral Isoroku Yamamoto (right) receiving a medal for his service in China, 1938. Yamamoto, Japan's great strategist and wartime leader, was killed when his airplane was shot down over New Guinea by U.S. forces in 1943. © *Bettmann/CORBIS.*

General Tomoyuki Yamashita, conqueror of Malaya and Singapore. A brilliant general, he paid the ultimate price after the war when he was hanged—many believe unjustly—for atrocities that were committed without his knowledge in Manila. *Archive Photos.*

Admiral Kichisaburo Namura, naval leader and Japan's ambassador to Washington in 1941. A personal acquaintance of President Franklin D. Roosevelt, Nomura possessed a better understanding of the United States than did his superiors in Tokyo. © *CORBIS.*

General Douglas MacArthur returns to the Philippines, 1944. © *CORBIS*.

Prisoners of war assemble behind the barbed wire surrounding their camp shortly after their liberation, 1945. © *Bettmann/CORBIS*.

Iva Toguri D'Aquino, the mythical "Tokyo Rose," as she appeared in 1945. She was convicted of treason, but she was also only one of a number of women who broadcasted for the Japanese and were labeled as "Tokyo Rose." *Archive Photos.*

"Little Boy," the atomic bomb dropped on Hiroshima, Japan, on August 6, 1945. *Archive Photos.*

USS *Missouri,* the battleship on which the surrender of Japan was accepted in Tokyo Bay, September 2, 1945.

Bataan Death March

One of the most infamous atrocities of the Pacific during World War II was the Bataan death march, in which thousands of American and Filipino prisoners of war (POWs) died either directly at the hands of the Japanese or because of the grueling pace and the conditions of the march. Despite the horrific nature of the event and the resultant casualties, the death march was not a deliberate act by the Japanese army but rather the result of poor planning and miscalculations, combined with the Japanese military's disdain for soldiers who surrendered.

The death march itself was an attempt by the Japanese Fourteenth Army on the Bataan Peninsula, under the command of Lieutenant General Masaharu Homma, to move some seventy-eight thousand American and Filipino POWs out of the immediate theater of operation as the Japanese forces prepared to besiege Corregidor. For three months the Fourteenth Army had blockaded and bombarded the U.S.-Filipino forces on Bataan—men who were additionally weakened by disease and malnutrition. On April 3, 1942, Homma launched an offensive which completely shattered the lines and led to the surrender of U.S. and Filipino forces by Major General Edward King on April 9.

Homma wanted to move the POWs out of southern Bataan for several reasons. The large number of POWs would place unwanted burdens on the Japanese logistics system as it moved weapons and materiel closer to the coast to build up the invasion force. In addition, Homma wanted to lull the American defenders of Corregidor into believing that he intended to conquer the island forts through a combination of blockade and bombardment; he did not want American POWs in the vicinity as his troops practiced amphibious landings. Finally, if the POWs and their guards remained on Bataan, they would be subject to U.S. artillery bombardment from Corregidor.

Because the Japanese believed that the Americans would fight for at least a month longer, they were unprepared for the sudden collapse. (Even so, the U.S.-Filipino forces on Bataan had withstood the Japanese for almost two months longer than had the British at Malaya and Singapore, who had outnumbered their Japanese conquerors by almost 3 to 1.) The plans for the evacuation of POWs had not been designed to accommodate their sheer numbers and were to proceed in two phases. First the prisoners would be sent to a single collection point; after this movement was completed, the second phase involved moving them, en masse, to a permanent POW camp in the north.

Specifically, the plan called for all prisoners to be concentrated at Balanga, about 5 miles from the original front line of the battle. Balanga was chosen because it was centrally located and no POWs would have to move more than 25 miles to get there. The Japanese army was not a highly motorized force, and there were few vehicles which could be spared to transport prisoners. This and the absence of rail lines in southern Bataan meant that marching the captured prisoners was really the only means of moving them. After the majority of the POWs were at Balanga, they would be marched 31 miles north to the village of San Fernando, which was on a major rail spur. From San Fernando, the prisoners would travel 25 miles by rail to Capas and then march 9 miles to a former Philippine army post, Camp O'Donnell.

The Japanese plan made several other miscalculations about the American POWs. Most important, they underestimated the number of prisoners they would capture, presuming that only about 25,000 troops would surrender. A distance of 25 miles was considered a normal day's march for the Japanese army, and so Japanese planners expected to be able to concentrate all POWs at Balanga within a day. They failed to take into account that U.S.

troops usually covered only 15 to 20 miles a day—under the best conditions. Worn and battered after five days' heavy fighting and rapid retreating, many captured soldiers could not maintain even this normal pace. Another miscalculation concerned the physical condition of the POWs. The Japanese were unaware that the U.S. and Filipino forces had been on reduced rations for some time and that diseases, such as malaria and dysentery, had taken a heavy toll on the health of many troops. Because the Japanese expected to consolidate all the POWs within a day, they made no provisions to distribute food until reaching Balanga, after which they had established three points along the route to feed the prisoners. And although there were plans to establish two field hospitals—one at Balanga and one at San Fernando—these were designed to care for only about a thousand patients each.

The quickness of the U.S. surrender also had major consequences for the treatment of POWs. The Japanese had not expected a surrender until the end of April, and so resources to care for the POWs would not be ready until April 20. The Fourteenth Army itself numbered some 81,000 men; with the surrender of the 78,000 Americans and Filipinos, the demands on the Japanese supply and medical systems increased by 100 percent. At the beginning of April, Homma's command was already critically short of medical supplies, but the general had expected to be able to build up his stocks by the end of the month. However, the rapid collapse of the U.S.-Filipino forces caught the Japanese almost completely unprepared for the coming influx of prisoners.

The Japanese plans quickly unraveled, and tragedy began to stalk the POWs. As word of General King's surrender spread, U.S. and Filipino troops surrendered to the Japanese in both large and small groups. Any hopes of an organized surrender ended almost immediately. It became obvious that the Japanese troops were not sure what to do with the POWs, and so the treatment of prisoners varied greatly. Some were simply relieved of their weapons and were told to march themselves to Balanga. Others were stripped of anything of value—watches, rings, fountain pens—and beaten. All the POWs were separated by race. The first glaring atrocity occurred when 350 to 400 Filipino officers and noncommissioned officers of the 91st Division were summarily executed by their Japanese captors after surrendering.

Meanwhile, the Japanese evacuation plans broke down almost immediately. The U.S. forces were deployed in two units, I Corps and II Corps. Although General King's surrender on April 9 included all U.S. and Filipino troops and although most of II Corps surrendered immediately, most of the troops of I Corps in western Bataan did not

surrender until April 10 or 11. Consequently, instead of being able to collect the POWs at Balanga within a day, the Japanese were still bringing prisoners to Balanga a week after the surrender. The troops of I Corps were sent first to Mariveles and then were marched in columns to Balanga. Because there were no preparations to supply prisoners with food or water as they were marched to the collection point, many perished along the way from heat and exhaustion. In addition, the Japanese often bayoneted any POWs who fell behind or who were unable to march. At Balanga, conditions improved little, if at all. The Japanese failed to set up the planned hospital, and so medical care was provided by U.S. medical personnel, with few or no supplies. Furthermore, the crowded conditions and inadequate sanitation at Balanga spread dysentery and other diseases rapidly. The situation was worsened by the lack of food and water, which were distributed sporadically; some POWs received rice and water daily, while others went without any food until they left Balanga.

After the majority of POWs had been concentrated at Balanga, phase 1 of the evacuation plan ended, and phase 2—the move to San Fernando—began. Major General Yoshikata Kawane was assigned to oversee the second phase, and he had originally planned to transport about one-quarter of the POWs to San Fernando by truck. But this was based on the assumption that only 25,000 troops would surrender. Ultimately, several thousand POWs did make the journey to San Fernando by truck, but the overwhelming majority were forced to walk the 31 miles. Kawane moved the POWs in groups of 100, departing with little time between groups.

The columns of POWs were marched to Orani, about 8 miles north of Balanga. Most stayed there overnight, although some remained for twenty-four or even forty-eight hours. Although Orani was intended to serve as the first feeding point north of Balanga, shortages of supplies meant that most POWs were fed only one serving of rice; some received no food at all and were given one cup of water from the single faucet which serviced the compound.

From Orani, the columns were marched 15 miles to Lubao, the next feeding point on the march. There they were housed in an abandoned warehouse with a single water spigot and no sanitation facilities. Conditions steadily deteriorated as corpses and raw sewage were left uncovered. Although the Japanese permitted three American doctors to set up a first-aid station in the yard of the warehouse, they provided no medical supplies. They did allow the most seriously injured and sick to remain in Lubao for some time, and even those with severe blisters were given only three or four days' rest. Prisoners again were fed only a single serving of rice per day, but on several occasions the Japanese allowed Filipino civilians to give food to the POWs.

After staying a day or so at Lubao, the prisoners were marched the remaining 8 miles to San Fernando. Although shorter than the 15-mile trek from Orani to Lubao, this segment of the march was the most difficult for many. The POWs were starving and physically drained, and many suffered from dysentery or malaria; yet anyone who fell behind was shot or bayoneted. The Japanese guards also committed random acts of brutality throughout the march, often striking or bayoneting the passing prisoners.

In San Fernando the POWs were kept at a number of small assembly points and near two large buildings: the schoolhouse and the municipal center. Now they were fed twice daily and had their first hot meal. They were also given better access to water, and the Philippine Red Cross was allowed to care for a very small number of prisoners.

From San Fernando, the prisoners next were transported by train, which entailed new hardships. A hundred or more prisoners were crammed into each sealed boxcar, spending an average of four hours in stifling, unventilated heat without sanitation facilities. Disease and exhaustion continued to take their toll. And when the trains finally reached Caspas, the POWs once again were formed into columns and were marched the remaining 9 miles to Camp O'Donnell, their final destination. In all, it took the Japanese almost three weeks to move the POWs, and even toward the end of May some prisoners were still struggling along the route.

Determining how many POWs died on the Bataan death march is impossible, because no one knows how many U.S. and Filipino troops were killed in the final Japanese offensive. Complicating matters is the fact that at least several thousand Filipinos and several hundred Americans were able to escape during the march, although many of these were subsequently killed. Of 11,796 Americans on the Bataan Peninsula when General King surrendered, approximately 650 died on the death march; and of 66,304 Filipino troops, it is estimated that 5,000 to 10,000 perished.

FURTHER READINGS

Falk, Stanley. *Bataan: The March of Death* (1962).
Kerr, E. Bartlett. *Surrender and Survival* (1985).
Knox, Donald. *Death March* (1981).

Tom Lansford

SEE ALSO Homma Masaharu; Philippines, Fall of the

Battleships

The principal naval weapon for the first forty years of the twentieth century, battleships reached their apogee of technology and performance during World War II. However, in Pacific war combat they played a less important role than did aircraft carriers.

Although early battles demonstrated the potential of carrier-launched aircraft to sink battleships, neither U.S. nor Japanese naval leaders easily surrendered long-held beliefs in the sovereignty of big-gun capital ships. Even as aircraft carriers demonstrated the superiority of air power, each navy repeatedly attempted to engage the other's battleships in a long-anticipated decisive surface engagement.

The intensity of Pacific war combat created new roles for battleships. Equipped with large numbers of anti-aircraft guns, battleships helped protect aircraft carriers from enemy air attacks. They also bombarded enemy positions on land, and shore bombardment evolved to a science during the island-hopping amphibious campaigns. But because of the supremacy of aircraft carriers, most battleships were mothballed or scrapped after the war.

The Washington Naval Treaty of 1922 (also known as the Five Power Naval Treaty) strongly influenced the number and type of U.S. and Japanese battleships that were available to fight in the Pacific War. After World War I a major naval construction contest of potentially great expense ensued among the major world powers: the United States, Great Britain, France, Japan, and Italy. The United States alone in 1919 was building or planned to build twelve hulls, six each of battleships and battle-cruisers. In 1920 the United States suggested a naval treaty restricting the number and size of capital ships.

Signed in 1921, this treaty, through complex formulas, halted battleship construction for ten years, restricted the number of such ships each signatory country would be permitted, and restricted the improvements each country could make on them. It limited the size of battleships to 35,000 tons and their gun bores to sixteen inches. The treaty assigned a different numbers of battleships to each country: the United States and Great Britain were allowed fifteen battleships each, but Japan only nine. The Japanese resented this apparent relegation to second-class power status, pointing out with some logic that their island nation and its empire were, if anything, as dependent on maritime trade and its protection as was Great Britain.

In the meantime, admirals on both sides of the Pacific planned for the "decisive surface battle" that they were sure someday would ensue, matching the capabilities and skills of their ships and crews against those of the other side. Naval doctrine of the time called for battleships to operate in a classic "battle line," meeting the enemy's battleships in a high-stakes contest for naval—and international—supremacy. The Japanese and the Americans each developed doctrines and techniques they thought would give them an advantage over the other.

The Japanese brought optically–sighted and directed gunnery to a fine art, installing high foremasts with gun direction platforms on their ships. They also developed proficiency in night fighting, training gun director crews to work with searchlights. During the 1930s the United States took advantage of the rapidly increasing capability of aircraft spotting to develop the "indirect method" of firing at targets that were over the horizon or that were otherwise obscured from the ship's line of vision. Skills learned in gun aiming with this indirect method benefited the fleet when the rapidly developing technology of radar was installed on U.S. Navy ships. By October 1942, 198 radar sets were in operation. The Japanese developed radar also, but they did not take advantage of the technology to the extent that Americans did. Japanese reliance on optics long after the American Navy had turned to radar was to affect the outcome of a number of battles in the Pacific war. The development of the aircraft carrier affected battleship design as well.

The treaty of 1921 permitted each country to convert two battleship hulls under construction to aircraft carriers, and it allotted a certain tonnage of aircraft carrier construction thereafter. Despite the inevitable tension between advocates of battleships and supporters of aircraft carriers, naval practice evolved during the 1920s and 1930s to include carrier air power. Aircraft could scout out the enemy fleet, drive off opposing planes, and soften up the enemy's battleships with bombs and aerial torpedoes; battleships then could finish off the enemy with big guns. Yet despite the potential of aircraft against ships that was clearly demonstrated in a number of tests and exercises in the 1920s and 1930s, many naval planners did not believe that warplanes could seriously damage a battleship. Battleships represented a country's international standing and will. It was under this philosophy that the senior naval leaders on both sides in the Pacific war—future carrier as well as battleship admirals—developed as junior officers.

The 1930 London treaty extended the Washington treaty's naval building "holiday" another five years, although Japan, its overseas ambitions growing, secretly exceeded treaty limits on improvements to some of its battleships. The 1936 London naval treaty included an "escalator" clause that permitted members to match tonnage and armament increases by nonmembers. By this time, however, Japan's imperial aspirations caused it to

give the required two-year notice to drop out of the treaty, and in doing so, a naval construction race ensued.

After Japan abrogated the treaty, the United States began to design and build new battleships, but it continued to follow treaty limits on tonnage and size of guns. Despite the urgency with which construction started in 1937, battleships, among the largest and most complex of capital ships, took an average of three to four years to build. Thus, at the start of hostilities in 1941 both the United States and Japan had a majority of battleships that were at least twenty years old.

At the entry of the United States into the Pacific war the U.S. fleet contained fifteen "old" battleships that predated the Washington naval treaty of 1921, and two "new" battleships, built under treaty terms in the late 1930s. Twenty-one additional battleships and "large cruisers" were under construction or on order.

The "old" battleships were built between 1910 and 1921. Consisting of the Oklahoma, Pennsylvania, New Mexico, California, and Maryland classes, they displaced from 26,000 to 32,300 tons and had an average speed of 21 knots. Fourteen-inch 45- and 50-caliber naval guns, the primary purpose for their existence, armed nine of the "old" battleships. The newest three classes, Maryland, West Virginia, and Colorado had 16-inch/45 caliber weapons. These warships were built to the British *Dreadnought* model of a heavily armored ship that sacrificed speed for durability. Those built after the Pennsylvania class featured a turbo-electrical propulsion system, in which the ships' turbines turned generators that powered electric motors, which, in turn, rotated the propellors. The system offered many advantages, but was heavier, more dangerous, and more likely to be knocked out of operation. No other navy adopted electric propulsion, and the U.S. Navy itself did not utilize it in battleship designs of the late 1930s. Modernized under treaty terms in the 1920s and 1930s, these later-designed battleships were converted from coal to oil fuel, equipped with gunfire spotting platforms, or "tops," and given additional armor plate from ships scrapped under the treaty. At the time, they represented the zenith of naval technology.

In the early 1920s, the *Dreadnought* model of battleship construction competed with the "battlecruiser" concept. The battlecruiser was a fast—over 25 knotspeed—heavily armed, but less heavily armored ship. It could operate on its own, accomplishing such missions as scouting and commerce raiding, which the slower, more heavily armored battleships could not perform. Ships of both types were under construction in U.S. shipyards at the time of the 1921 treaty. Soon the "battlecruiser" concept evolved into the "fast battleship," a vessel that would have the speed of a battlecruiser but would not sacrifice protection for speed. The "fast battleship" could fight as part of a battle line as the *Dreadnought* class ships or range afield on its own.

As aircraft carriers joined both the American and Japanese fleets during the 1920s, it was discovered in naval exercises that fast battleships, which could keep up with aircraft carriers, could perform as part of a newly devised fast carrier task force. The carrier task force's combination of aircraft carriers and battleships could use bombs, aerial torpedoes, and gunfire to master an enemy's battleline.

The United States planned six new battleships under provisions of the 1921 treaty. Known as the North Carolina class ships (*North Carolina, Washington*), they were designed as fast battleships. Although their speed was 27 knots, their 35,000-ton displacement conformed to treaty restrictions. Designers originally intended the North Carolinas to be equipped with a 14-inch/50 caliber gun and accordingly equipped the ships with armor sufficient to protect them against enemy shells of an equal caliber. Later, the armament was changed to the sixteen-inch 45 caliber gun.

While construction started on the first two ships of the class, naval engineers modified the designs to protect the ships against sixteen-inch shells. The result was the South Dakota class of four 35,000 ton ships: *South Dakota, Indiana, Massachusetts,* and *Alabama.* At 680 feet in overall length, these ships were shorter than those in the North Carolina class, which were at 728 feet in overall length; designers used tonnage saved in length to add armor. As fast as the North Carolinas, their unique combination of hull design and weight distribution made the South Dakotas among the most maneuverable of U.S. battleships.

When Japan anounced that it would drop out of the naval armaments limitation treaties, the United States exercised the London naval treaty tonnage "escalator" clause to increase displacement to 45,000 tons. The result was the Iowa class of six ships (only the *Iowa, New Jersey, Missouri,* and *Wisconsin* were completed). Although 887 feet long overall, the Iowas had a beam of 108 feet—the same as the far shorter South Dakotas—and were one foot narrower than the Panama canal locks. Considered a faster South Dakota design, the Iowas made 33 knots and were armed with nine 16-inch 50 calibers.

Engineering considerations limited to 27 knots the speed of the succeeding 60,000-ton Montana class. The first battleships designed after the onset of war, the Montana design sported twelve 16-inch 50 calibers and had a length of 925 feet overall and a beam of 121 feet. Once completed, all seventeen ships of the four classes would effectively double the U.S. battlefleet. The Montanas and

the last two Iowas (*Illinois, Kentucky*) were canceled because of the rapidly evolving combat situation.

The battle cruiser advocates were not silenced during these years. The Alaska class, known as "large cruisers," was equipped with nine 12-inch 50 caliber guns. These ships, 808 feet long and with a 91-foot beam, had a top speed of 33 knots and displaced 27,000 tons. They were armored to protect against German pocket battleships and Japanese battle cruisers of similar performance and armament, but not against battleship fire. Two ships of a projected six were completed, the only "battlecruisers" ever completed for the U.S. Navy. (Many contemporary naval authorities profess not to understand what possible purpose these warships could serve.)

The Imperial Japanese Navy entered the war with ten pretreaty battleships of four classes. The treaty had allowed nine, but the Japanese had secretly re-equipped one ship of the Kongo class, *Hiei,* that had been disarmed under treaty terms. Reflecting contemporary discussions in naval circles, the oldest class of ships were originally the battlecruiser Kongo class. Built between 1912 and 1915, the four-ship class boasted eight 14-inch naval rifles apiece, displaced 27,500 tons, and were 704 feet long, with a beam of 92 feet. Modernized in the 1920s and 1930s, they were redesignated fast battleships as speed increases brought them to 27 knots. The two-ship Fuso class vessels were battleship versions of the Kongo design. Built between 1914 and 1917, they displaced 30,600 tons and had twelve 14-inch guns. They made 22 knots, were 665 feet long, and had a beam of 94 feet. Both were lost in Surigao Strait during the battle of Leyte Gulf in October 1944, their only major engagement. Similarly equipped with twelve 14-inch weapons, *Ise* and *Hyuga* were improved Fusos. Displacing 31,260 tons, they were 675 feet long and 94 feet abeam, but they made only 22 knots. Equipped during the war with flight decks astern, these Leyte Gulf survivors were out of fuel at Kure when sunk in shallow water by U.S. aircraft in 1945. The final pretreaty battleships were the *Nagato* and the *Mutsu.* Armed with eight 16-inch naval rifles, they were built between 1919 and 1921 just as the treaty took effect and were the Imperial Navy's only ships thus armed. Arguably the first 16-inch armed battleships in the world, these Nagato class ships were fine examples of battleship design, making 26 knots on a hull of 700 feet overall length, 95 feet of beam, and displacing 33,800 tons. *Mutsu* sank in the Inland Sea in 1943 probably as a result of a magazine explosion. *Nagato* was found tied up at Kure, out of fuel and going nowhere, at the war's end in 1945.

The Japanese realized they did not have the industrial or economic ability to outbuild the United States in battleships. They chose instead to build just a few large battleships of superior capability, the Yamato class. This class displaced 69,500 tons, was 862 feet long overall, had a beam of 121 feet, and made 27 knots. The ships featured nine 18-inch guns, larger than those of U.S. ships. Measures to keep secret the Yamatos' true capabilities from the United States—so that the Japanese would not again find themselves outbuilt—were so successful that the United States did not know of them until after World War II. As foreign policy goals collided with the realities of building schedules, the Japanese Navy found itself going to war with ten old and two new battleships.

The Royal Navy's attack on the Italian fleet at Taranto, Italy, in 1940 was one of the first signals that the age of the battleship was over. The Japanese attack on Pearl Harbor in December 1941, in which carrier-launched aircraft crippled the U.S. Pacific fleet's battleships at their berths, bought time for the Japanese to expand their empire without effective U.S. interference. The sinking of British battleship *Prince of Wales* and battlecruiser *Repulse* at sea off Malaya on December 10, 1941, was another clear sign of the vulnerability of battleships to aircraft. Coral Sea (May 1942) was the first battle fought entirely between aircraft, and Midway (June 1942) revealed the changing, secondary, role of battleships. Although carrier-borne aircraft played a primary role at Midway, the Japanese had still planned to send battleships to finish off the remnants of the U.S. fleet after their carrier planes had crippled it. The two fast battleships, *Haruna* and *Kirishima* that accompanied the carrier formation—and absorbed some U.S. attacks—showed the potential of battleships to provide anti-aircraft escort to carriers.

The battles around the Solomon Islands from August to November 1943 demonstrated a number of emerging tendencies. USS *North Carolina,* providing anti-aircraft support, again demonstrated the possibilities of battleship escort of carriers in the Battle of the Eastern Solomons on August 24, 1942. An even more convincing example was provided by the *South Dakota* a few weeks later. Trailing carrier *Enterprise* by a thousand yards in the Battle of Santa Cruz on October 25–27, 1942, the *South Dakota* shot down twenty-six attacking Japanese planes.

In the fall of 1942, a shortage of carriers and the limited room for maneuver in the seas in and around the Solomons permitted, at least temporarily, a return to the battleship's speciality of surface warfare. On November 12, 1942, as Japan and the United States escalated the stakes at sea in the battle for Guadalcanal, a Japanese task force led by fast battleships *Hiei* and *Kirishima* sank two U.S. light cruisers and four destroyers in a searing night action known as the first battle of Guadalcanal. U.S.

cruisers did manage to severely damage *Hiei,* leaving it to be finished off by planes from the *Enterprise* the next day. The two sides came together again on the night of the November 14, as USS *Washington,* firing by radar, sank the *Kirishima* in the second battle of Guadalcanal. *South Dakota,* participating in the same battle, absorbed one 14-inch and twenty-six 8-, 6-, and 5-inch shell hits from *Kirishima* and two accompanying cruisers. *South Dakota* suffered only superficial damage structurally, but its fire control, communications, and radar systems were damaged.

The battle of the Philippine Sea revealed both the inability on the part of naval people to drop the prewar idea that carrier airpower prepared the field for battleships, and the newly emerged task of carrier escort for battleships. The Japanese commander, Vice Admiral Jisaburo Ozawa, arranged his battleships and carriers as carrier task forces, with *Yamato, Musashi, Haruna, Kongo,* and *Nagato* as part of the anti-aircraft screen around the carriers. They would furnish protection for the carriers until their planes had crippled the enemy fleet, then sortie as a battle line to finish off the remnants. The Japanese battleships filled the sky with salvos of anti-aircraft fire during the famous U.S. evening attack on the fleet. U.S. pilots shot down so many Japanese planes that the battle was dubbed the "Marianas Turkey Shoot." Ozawa considered, but did not go ahead with, a battleship night surface engagement with the enemy fleet. The United States deployed battleships under Admiral Willis A. Lee ahead of the carriers on the night of June 19 in the event that Ozawa went ahead with the idea.

The last big-gun surface engagement in history, the battle of Leyte Gulf (October 20–24, 1944) finished the Imperial Japanese Navy as a fighting force and in the process demonstrated how aircraft had influenced the role of battleships. Rear Admiral Jesse Oldendorf's surviving battleships from Pearl Harbor, the "old" battleships so carefully husbanded and matched against their Japanese counterparts for twenty years, caught Vice Admiral Shoji Nishimura in the Surigao Strait on the night of October 24. By executing the classic naval manuever of crossing the enemy's "T".—rehearsed for some twenty years in these same ships—Oldendorf's force, firing by radar, sank the battleships *Fuso* and *Yamashiro.* This major surface engagement was as close to the "decisive surface battle" as the Japanese or American battleship admirals would ever get.

The next morning, Vice Admiral Takeo Kurita steamed through the San Bernardino strait with the battleships *Yamato, Nagato,* and *Haruna.* Falling upon Rear Admiral Clifton A. Sprague's escort carriers, Kurita's force sank light carrier *Gambier Bay* and two destroyers in a dramatic chase that became known as the battle of Samar. Various recriminations were heard because the U.S. fast battleship force, chasing Ozawa's carriers with Task Force 38, missed Kurita's force off Samar, the only opportunity they would have had for their own classic line-of-battle engagement.

The battles of the Philippine Sea and Leyte Gulf also demonstrated the innate toughness of battleships. On June 19, USS *South Dakota* was hit in the superstructure by a bomb, and USS *Indiana* absorbed a torpedo. Both ships suffered only minor damage. Halsey's aviators, in turn, sank *Musashi* on November 24, 1944, but took seventeen bombs and almost twenty torpedoes to do so. *Yamato* shrugged off a direct bomb hit while retreating through San Bernardino Strait on November 25. Operating with Ozawa's decoy force, *Ise* and *Hyuga* suffered numerous near misses. Later in the war, *Yamato* absorbed six bombs and thirteen torpedoes from U.S. carrier aircraft on April 7, 1945, before sinking. Just a few days later, battleship *Missouri* suffered only minor damage after being struck by kamikazes on April 11 and 16, 1945.

Shore bombardment on behalf of troops operating on land evolved in importance and sophistication as island-hopping in the southwest and central Pacific got underway. Although *Hiei* and *Kirishima* bombarded U.S. forces operating on Guadalcanal, the commander of the fleet, Admiral Isoroku Yamamoto, did not believe in using battleships as shore-bombardment weapons. Therefore, Japanese battleships did not shell Midway during the great battle of 1942, nor, despite specially developed bombardment ammunition, did they even attempt in their bombardments of Guadalcanal's Henderson field to reach the precision later achieved by U.S. forces.

U.S. battleship and amphibious force commanders soon developed shore bombardment—what later would be termed "naval surface fire support"—to a science. They learned what was necessary to demolish enemy positions from such early invasions as Tarawa in November 1943. Careful training and teamwork among amphibious force planners, gun directors and crews, and air spotter planes was emphasized. Pinpoint aiming, appropriate types of shells, after-fire checks of targets, and repeated refiring as necessary were all used to ensure a successful shore bombardment.

Although all types of ships participated, battleships were particularly valued for the ability of big naval guns to reach the most deeply dug enemy fortifications. Experience and training meant everything; the new "fast" battleships wasted ammunition in a pre-invasion bom-

bardment of Saipan in June 1944, because they did not have the appropriate knowledge of shore bombardment.

The Royal Navy's elderly *Renown, Queen Elizabeth,* and *Valiant,* joined by the more modern French *Richelieu,* grasped the concept of shore bombardment early as well and shelled Sabang in the Celebes and Surabaya, Java, to draw Japanese attention off U.S. amphibious operations in New Guinea.

The Royal Navy's carriers, two of the fast 29-knot King George V class battleships and the French *Richelieu*—which at 32 knots was almost as fast as an Iowa class ship—participated as Task Force 57. U.S. carriers, with unarmored decks, suffered grievously when hit; battleships, although not prime targets, were better able to absorb severe attacks.

The Japanese also understood the potential of carrier escort by battleships, with two and sometimes all four of the fast Kongo class battleships accompanying Admiral Chuichi Nagumo's mobile fleet of carriers during the successful sweep across the Far East after Pearl Harbor. Despite the urgings of some officers, however, the Japanese did not install thickets of anti-aircraft guns on their ships or deploy them in carrier screens until much too late in the war.

The evolution of anti-aircraft technology made a difference as well in the Pacific war. By 1943 American shells contained proximity fuses, which made them explode and scatter shrapnel in the vicinity of enemy aircraft. The Japanese did not have proximity fuse technology. Gun crews continued to use pre-fused shells before firing. Such shells exploded in different colors of smoke to permit the crews to spot and correct their shot. Pre-fused shells were a far less effective technology than were proximity fusing, and they limited the effectiveness of the battleships function as an anti-aircraft escort in such engagements as Midway, the Philippine Sea, and Leyte Gulf. The Japanese did, uniquely, equip their main battleship guns with main battery anti-aircraft shells.

The Pacific war saw the eclipse of the battleship as the prime maritime weapon in the arsenal of most navies. Although their usefulness as anti-aircraft escorts and naval surface fire support vessels, and their ability to absorb damage was unquestioned, battleships were too expensive for most navies to operate. Most U.S. battleships were mothballed after the war and finally scrapped or donated as war memorials in the early 1960s. The four newest ships of the Iowa class were reactivated for the Korean War and again in the 1980s, and they saw active service in the Gulf War in 1991. *New Jersey* also gave valued service as a fire support vessel in Vietnam in 1968 and 1969. By the turn of the twenty-first century, however, all four of the Iowas had been transformed into museums. The battleships of the other Pacific war belligerents have all been scrapped, leaving the United States as the only nation where one can walk the teakwood decks of a *Dreadnought*-type battleship.

FURTHER READINGS

Belote, James H., and William M. Belote. *Titans of the Seas: The Development and Operations of Japanese and American Carrier Task Forces during World War II* (1975).

Davidson, Joel R. *The Unsinkable Fleet: The Politics of U.S. Navy Expansion in World War II* (1996).

Garzke, William H., Jr., and Robert O. Dulin, Jr. *Battleships: United States Battleships, 1935–1992* (1995).

Hagan, Kenneth J. *This People's Navy: The Making of American Seapower* (1991).

Hamer, David. *Bombers versus Battleships: The Struggle Between Ships and Aircraft for Control of the Surface of the Sea* (1998).

Ireland, Bernard. *Jane's Battleships of the Twentieth Century* (1996).

King, R. W., ed. *Naval Engineering and American Sea Power* (1989).

Prange, Gordon W. *Miracle at Midway* (1982).

Sturton, Ian, ed. *All the World's Battleships, 1906 to the Present* (1996).

Sumrall, Robert. *Iowa Class Battleships: Their Design, Weapons and Equipment* (1988).

Van der Vat, Dan. *The Pacific Campaign: The U.S.-Japanese Naval War, 1941–1945* (1991).

Steven Agoratus

SEE ALSO Aircraft carriers: Japanese, U.S., and British; Navy, Japanese; Navy, Royal; Navy, U.S.

Bengal Famine

During 1943–1944 as many as 3.8 million people died in Bengal province in northeast Bengal, India, as a result of food shortages caused by a combination of tragic circumstances. While the Japanese conquest of Burma was the initiating cause, natural disasters along with British wartime policies conspired to produce the Bengal famine.

The quick advance of Japanese forces in the months after the 1941 attack at Pearl Harbor set the stage for the Bengal famine; the fall of Burma in May 1942 was critical. During the preceding two generations, Burma had become the primary supplier of cheap rice for much of South Asia. Although Bengal continued to export higher grades of rice, by 1930 more rice was imported than exported.

Magnifying the loss of Burmese rice, which provided about 5 percent of the yearly amount consumed in Bengal, were several other war-related factors. Refugees and the additional troops to defend against an expected Japanese invasion added hundreds of thousands of mouths to feed, while governmental purchases of land for bases and camps further reduced native food production.

Nature conspired against Bengal as well, when in October 1942 a cyclone and tidal wave devastated the western coast. All told, over fourteen thousand persons died during or immediately after the storm, and about 2.5 million Bengalis had their property destroyed or damaged. Not only did the storm kill much of the maturing winter rice, but a crop disease swept through the affected regions and ruined much of the remaining paddy. It is estimated that the net effect of the loss of the Burma market, the cyclone, and crop disease reduced the supply of rice and paddy in 1942 to about 90 percent of usual. While certainly this situation was serious—particularly given the many rigors imposed by wartime conditions—it was not so grave as to cause the enormous loss of life associated with the Bengal famine. For a full explanation, British policies, as well as the popular response to them, must be considered.

In the spring of 1942, faced with the apparently unstoppable Japanese onslaught and the imminent fall of Burma, British officials had to prepare for the possible invasion of India. In that context, denying possible resources to the enemy made sense militarily despite the long-term economic repercussions involved. Fearing an invasion through the lower Bengal Delta, some 66,500 boats large enough to carry at least ten people were removed from use and/or destroyed to prevent their falling into enemy hands. As a result, economic life in the delta was severely dislocated for almost a year as hundreds of thousands of peasants lost their livelihoods.

A similar plan was devised to prevent rice from feeding advancing Japanese troops by having the government purchase large quantities of the staple. The subsequent scarcity of this critical commodity helped to double its prewar price by June 1942. The authorities responded by imposing price controls on rice. Unfortunately, the primary result was that most suppliers either withheld their stock from the marketplace or sold it on a thriving black market. Fearing the impact of a food shortage in Calcutta, authorities confiscated stores of rice to feed the capital— only to encourage more hoarding by merchants and farmers. Price controls were removed by the spring of 1943, but that caused the price of rice to increase to seven times its prewar amount, making it virtually impossible for the impoverished masses to purchase food. A renewed crackdown against hoarders did little to improve the market supply of rice. Relief efforts, particularly in rural areas, were unable to avert a tragedy for millions. While a record harvest of rice in the fall of 1943 did ultimately lead to an end to the famine, diseases subsequently ravaged the weakened population such that mortality rates did not fall to normal levels until 1946. The Bengal famine was one more reason that increasing numbers of Indians became alienated from British rule and began to demand independence ever more stridently.

FURTHER READINGS

Greenough, Paul. *Prosperity and Misery in Modern Bengal* (1982).

Sen, Amartya. "Famine Mortality: A Study of the Bengal Famine of 1943." In *Peasants in History: Essays in Honor of Daniel Thorner*, ed. E. Hobsbawm (1981).

Stephen J. Valone

SEE ALSO Burma; India

Biak, Battle for

The 1944 Allied seizure of the Island of Biak (May 27–July 29) was an important step toward reconquest of the Philippines. On March 12, 1944, the U.S. Joint Chiefs of Staff issued a directive calling for an accelerated drive in the Pacific, to take place that spring and summer. This amounted to a blueprint for interdiction of Japanese forces along the northern coast of New Guinea.

On April 22, U.S. Army forces under the command of General Douglas MacArthur landed at Hollandia and Aitape. These operations went smoothly, despite an abortive Japanese counterattack against Aitape. With land-based air cover from Hollandia, and following a landing on New Guinea opposite Wakde Island, U.S. forces landed on Wakde, which lies 125 miles northwest of Hollandia.

The final step in the movement along the northern coast of New Guinea was the island of Biak. Situated some 180 miles northwest of Wakde, it lies astride the opening to Geelvink Bay. A coral island, Biak is covered with dense rain forest and jungle undergrowth. Mangrove swamps along its shore were a potential problem for amphibious landings. Also, the island's coral absorbs the rainfall, making drinking-water supply a problem.

The Japanese had planned five airfields on Biak, but they had only completed three by the time of the Allied landing. Nevertheless, they placed 11,000 troops on the island, commanded by Lieutenant Colonel Kuzume Na-

oyuki. It was these scratch troops who held off Lieutenant General Fuller's 41st Infantry Division for nearly two months.

On May 27, 1944, Fuller's forces landed on Biak. Against no Japanese opposition they immediately moved inland toward the main airfield. On reaching it, U.S. troops came under fire from caves and pillboxes situated in the surrounding high ground. Although the troops soon captured the airfield, no aircraft could land there because of enemy fire.

The Japanese saw the loss of Biak as a threat to their position on the southernmost Philippine island of Mindinao and to their hopes for a decisive engagement against the U.S. Navy in this area of the Pacific. To counter the threat, they tried to reinforce the island and sent in troops of the 2d Amphibious Brigade of their Southern Army's strategic reserve from Mindinao via the "Tokyo Express." This operation, which they dubbed "Kon," was to be covered by warships and air reinforcements from the Philippines, the Marianas, and Japan.

The first two Japanese attempts to reinforce their garrison on Biak met with only marginal success; U.S. land-based planes from New Guinea, Hollandia, and Wakde harassed their warships. Only about a thousand Japanese made it to Biak to strengthen the defense. But just as the Japanese sent their third and most formidable reinforcement steaming toward Biak, they learned that the U.S. Fifth Fleet was in the vicinity of the Mariana Islands. This information caused the Japanese to turn their fleet northwestward to engage the Americans in what would become the Battle of the Philippine Sea.

The last-ditch defense of Biak by Naoyuki's troops took place around two caves that commanded the main airfield. On June 28 the Japanese abandoned the eastern cave following relentless U.S. bombing and flamethrower assaults. Shortly thereafter, Naoyuki ordered his colors burned, and he committed suicide. Japanese defenders at the western cave remarkably held on for another month; a hundred wounded Japanese soldiers give their lives in a final stand. The battle for Biak officially ended on July 29, 1944.

Japanese casualties in the battle were estimated at 6,000 dead and 460 captured. U.S. losses were 438 dead and 2,400 wounded; there were many more casualties from tropical intestinal diseases.

Until the battle for Biak the Japanese had followed a pattern of contesting U.S. landings and then holding out for final suicidal banzai charges. Naoyuki's new tactics were a grim foreshadowing of what was to come as U.S. forces moved ever closer to Japan. Tokyo did not accept fighting on to the end from caves and pillboxes as doctrine until late 1944. However, major bloodlettings such as Iwo Jima and Okinawa burned into the minds of U.S. commanders the importance of the lessons learned at Biak.

FURTHER READINGS

Manchester, William. *Goodbye, Darkness: A Memoir of the Pacific* (1980).

van der Vat, Dan. *The Pacific Campaign: World War II, the U.S.-Japanese Naval War, 1941–1945*. (1991).

Mark A. Macina

SEE ALSO MacArthur, Douglas

Bismarck Sea, Battle of the

A B-24's chance discovery of a sixteen-ship Japanese convoy on March 1, 1943, set off a three-day running battle (March 3–5) between Japanese and Allied forces in the Bismarck Sea. On the one hand was a very determined Japanese convoy escort of eight destroyers commanded by Rear Admiral Masatomi Kimura, who intended to deliver the 51st Imperial Infantry Division and over thirty thousand tons of critical fuel, ammunition, and other supplies to the beleaguered Japanese forces in New Guinea. He was supported by Admiral Kusaka's Eleventh Naval Air Fleet. Their opponents were General Kenney with his Fifth Air Force and a small squadron of PT boats. Coming at a crucial point in the New Guinea campaign, the outcome in the Bismarck Sea would have a direct and decisive affect on the campaign ashore.

The convoy run had been ordered by the Japanese commanders in Rabaul. General Okabe's failure to seize the port of Wau had jeopardized Japan's overland campaign to capture Port Moresby. Logistics were the key. Both Japanese and Allied forces were at the end of their logistical tether. Japanese army and naval air squadrons desperately needed fuel and spare parts, while the ground forces needed food, ammunition, and fresh troops. The convoy's merchant ships and oilers would deliver the required material, while two troop transports would carry the 51st Division; its nearly seven thousand troops could tip the balance ashore. Recognizing the Allied air threat, Admiral Kusaka ordered daily combat air patrols and provided eight destroyers with strong antiaircraft batteries to protect the convoy. Admiral Kimura also expected to encounter U.S. submarines, but he could do little except order additional lookouts. Few of his destroyers had active sonar, but it was their lack of radar and air cover which would prove decisive in the coming battle. The submarine threat never materialized.

The convoy departed Rabaul on February 28 and was detected late in the afternoon of the next day. A rainstorm hindered Allied efforts to shadow the convoy, and it was lost at sundown, before any air strikes could be launched. It was rediscovered the next morning, and seven B-17s forged through the bad weather to press home their attacks. Three attacked from high altitude and missed, but four struck from below 6,000 feet, sinking one transport and damaging two others. Later attacks were less successful, their efforts hampered by bad weather, aggressive Japanese fighter patrols, and the bombers' limited numbers. Sunset brought the Japanese a reprieve, but the next day would see both sides redouble their efforts. Two destroyers picked up survivors and delivered them to Lae overnight, returning to rejoin the convoy in the early morning.

General Kenney ordered a maximum effort for the next day, including all available Australian as well as U.S. aircraft. The resulting 137 bombers with supporting fighter escorts overwhelmed the forty-two Japanese naval Zeros protecting the convoy. Lacking radar to vector their fighters to the bombers, the Zeros became embroiled with the Allied fighter escorts while the heavy and medium bombers punched through unscathed to strike the convoy. The American A-20s and B-25s employed the new "skip-bombing" technique and recently installed forward firing armaments to devastating effect. Every ship suffered some damage—several, seriously.

Two destroyers, including flagship *Shirayuki*, and a transport were sunk. Another destroyer and three merchant ships were knocked dead in the water. Several ships were burning. The next wave of Allied aircraft nearly finished the convoy off, critically damaging one destroyer and sinking the previously crippled destroyer and two more cargo ships. The surviving transports were immobilized, and the water was littered with struggling seamen and soldiers. The Japanese sent dozens of fighters to provide air cover and despatched two submarines to pick up survivors. Two destroyers fled to Rabaul packed with 2,700 survivors. Two others, *Yukikaze* and *Asaguma*, remained behind to pick up the remainder and fled during the night. The one surviving crippled cargo vessel, *Oigawa Maru*, and the two remaining disabled destroyers were finished off by American PT boats that night and by American bombers the next morning, respectively. Another transport went down that night. The Japanese submarines *I-17* and *I-26* marked the last moments of the battle by fishing more than two hundred survivors from the water during the evening of March 4. American PT boats unsuccessfully attacked the latter submarine as it was finishing its mission. The Battle of the Bismarck Sea, a disaster for the Japanese, was over.

The Japanese lost more than four thousand men and nearly thirty thousand tons of supplies in the battle. This devastating defeat ended Japan's strong efforts to reinforce its forces on New Guinea. The combination of deadly Allied air power by day and PT boat patrols by night all but strangled the Japanese forces in New Guinea. All future Japanese logistics support would come by submarine and would never approach the quantities needed to support effective ground operations. In effect, the Allied victory in the Battle of the Bismarck Sea both demonstrated air power's dominance in naval warfare and also ensured the ultimate Allied victory ashore.

FURTHER READINGS

Hoyt, Edwin P. *The Jungles of New Guinea* (1989).

Morison, Samuel Eliot. *History of United States Naval Operations in World War II,* vol. VI (1968).

Salmaggi, Cesare, and Alfredo Pallavisini. *2194 Days of War* (1977).

Carl O. Schuster

SEE ALSO Navy, Japanese; Navy, U.S.; New Guinea

Bliuhker, Vasilii Konstantinovich (1890–1938)

Soviet Red Army comander in the Far East in the late 1920s and 1930s, Vasilii Konstantinovich Bliuhker was a peasant's son, drafted into the Russian army during World War I. Wounded and decorated several times for bravery, Bliuhker nevertheless joined Lenin's Bolshevik Party in 1916, and soon after Russia's 1917 October Revolution he led a Red Guards unit, a Bolshevik paramilitary group. After this irregular service with the Red Guards and a term as a partisan commander, Bliuhker rose rapidly in Soviet Russia's Red Army during the civil war against the anti-Communist White Russian forces, winning renown as a skilled officer and becoming first a division commander and later an army commander. In 1921–1922 he served as military minister and commander in chief of the armed forces of the short-lived Far Eastern Republic, a buffer state set up in Siberia by the Soviet government to head off war with Japan.

When the Russian civil war wound down, Bliuhker occupied various conventional posts in the Soviet Army, but he also served in China during the mid-1920s as a military adviser to Chiang Kai-shek's Kuomintang Party. Under the cover name "Galin" Bliuhker helped to found the Whampoa Military Academy and mold the Kuomintang's army into an effective fighting force. When Chiang turned against his Chinese Communist allies in

1927, his Soviet advisers were forced to flee back home, ending the collaboration.

Following his work in China, Bliuhker was sent to Siberia to command Soviet forces in the Far East. Through 1929 tensions on the Manchurian-Soviet border sharply increased. The semi-independent Manchurian government of the Chinese warlord, Zhang Xueliang, began harassing Russian employees of the Chinese Eastern Railway, jointly owned by the Chinese and the Soviets, and border violations by both sides raised tensions still further. As a result, on August 6, 1929, the Soviet high command created the Special Far-Eastern Army under Bliuhker.

A show of force by Soviet troops and river flotillas on October 12 and 30–31 did not sufficiently intimidate Zhang's forces, so on November 17, 1929, the Special Far-Eastern Army sent its Transbaikal group into Manchuria in a strike intended to be both punitive and preventative. The blow aimed to destroy Chinese military potential in Manchuria, rendering further Chinese provocations impossible. It also punished Zhang for violating the Soviet border, tacitly supporting anti-Soviet White Russians and attempting to squeeze the Soviets out of the Chinese Eastern Railway. The Soviets claimed from the beginning of their operation that they had no intention of carrying out territorial acquisitions; their purpose instead was to devastate Chinese forces in Manchuria. In a lightning campaign, Bliuhker's multipronged assault using well-coordinated infantry, cavalry, and air attacks, as well as some of the first Soviet tanks, completely broke Chinese resistance in less than two weeks.

On December 22, 1929, Chinese and Soviet representatives signed the Khabarovsk protocol, ending hostilities and marking the Soviet Union's near-complete victory. All of Bliuhker's troops were withdrawn from Manchuria by December 25, and his Special Far-Eastern Army was in honor of its whirlwind victory awarded a new name: the Special Red-Banner Far-Eastern Army. Bliuhker himself grew increasingly powerful, thanks to his continuing presence in the Far East, becoming a kind of regional satrap. In 1935, he became one of five officers awarded the new rank of marshal of the Soviet Union.

Bliuhker was still at his post in the Far East when new tensions arose with the Japanese around Lake Khasan. Soviet border troops, unknown to Bliuhker, had crossed the border into the Japanese puppet state of Manchukuo, leading to border skirmishes with Japanese troops assigned to protect the region. Stalin, informed by his spy Richard Sorge in Tokyo that the Japanese government had no intention of starting a war with the Soviet Union at this point, ordered Bliuhker to take a firm stand against any Japanese incursions. Small-scale skirmishes with Japanese forces escalated into more serious fighting in late July, lasting until a cease-fire on August 10, 1938. Bliuhker's halfhearted performance here—compared with his impressive successes in 1929—sent exactly the wrong message at this time of increasing paranoia in the Soviet Union, as Stalin's Great Purges, which included the mass arrests of army officers, gathered speed. Bliuhker's successor in the Far East, Grigorii Shtern, would receive credit for Soviet successes, while he was accused of cowardice.

Bliuhker had served on the military tribunal that sentenced Mikhail Tukhachevskii and other prominent Soviet generals to death on trumped-up charges of treason in June 1937, and he himself soon fell under suspicion. Purges against Bliuhker's own subordinates followed, and in the fall of 1938 he was recalled to Moscow in disgrace. He was relieved of command in September 1938, was arrested in October, and died under torture on November 9, 1938. Once again, the revolution had devoured another of its own.

FURTHER READINGS

Haslam, Jonathan. *The Soviet Union and the Threat from the East, 1933–1941* (1992).

Lensen, George A. *The Damned Inheritance: The Soviet Union and the Manchurian Crises, 1924–1935* (1974).

Stephan, John. *The Russian Far East: A History* (1994).

Wilbur, C. Martin, and Julie Lien-ying How. *Documents on Communism, Nationalism, and Soviet Advisers in China, 1918–1927* (1956).

David Stone

Bomb Balloons, Japanese

The Japanese bomb balloons were the result of Project FU-GO (wind weapon), an attempt to strike at targets on the North American continent from long range. In 1933, the Japanese military began experimenting with large, free-floating balloons designed to utilize prevailing wind currents. The project did not receive high priority, however, until after James Doolittle's raid on Tokyo in April 1942. Then, provided with greater resources, Japanese military and civilian scientists developed effective long-range balloons that were capable of being carried by the jet stream across the northern Pacific at a height of 30,000 feet. The balloons were inflated with hydrogen and equipped with devices to regulate each balloon's altitude. They also had mechanisms to drop ballast at timed intervals and release incendiary bombs after the balloon was, it was hoped, over North America. An explosive device to destroy the balloon after it had released the incendiaries was included.

FU-GO launched its first bomb-laden balloons from the coast of Honshu in November 1944. The object was to ignite forest fires in the American Northwest, produce panic among the civilian population, and force the United States to redirect air and ground forces from the Pacific campaign. By the end April 1945, FU-GO had launched more than nine thousand balloons into the jet stream. Several hundred reached North America.

The U.S. military became aware of the threat when a patrol craft found the remains of a balloon in the ocean off California. Examining this and the recovered wreckage of other balloons, analysts determined the balloons' functions and intended use. Naval and army air force units established patrols along the West Coast to spot and destroy balloons before they made shore. Antiaircraft batteries on the coast were strengthened. These brought down few balloons, if any. To prevent public hysteria, the U.S. government at first prevented all but a few news stories about the balloons from being released.

This silence may have contributed to the only fatalities caused by the bomb balloons. On May 5, 1945, five children and a woman were killed near Bly, Oregon, after finding the wreckage of a balloon and accidentally triggering the explosive charge. The husband escaped, unscathed. The government thereafter lifted the veil of silence, and publications warned people about the bombs. Other bomb balloon landings caused property damage, and one may have set a small forest fire. The only military damage from the balloons occurred when a balloon crashed on a power line near Hanford, Washington, cutting off electricity to the nation's first nuclear reactor facility. The interruption of plutonium production for the Manhattan Project lasted three days. The Japanese were completely unaware of the moderate damage they had caused to the facility that would help bring the apocalypse to them.

Project FU-GO launched its last balloons in April 1945. Wind currents had changed, and U.S. B-29s had destroyed the hydrogen production facilities. The bomb campaign thus failed. But, however inaccurate, the balloons did carry bombs across an ocean, to a distant enemy.

FURTHER READINGS

Hidagi, Yasushi. "Attack Against the U.S. Heartland." *Aerospace Historian* (summer 1981).

Mikesh, Robert C. *Japan's World War II Balloon Bomb Attacks on North America* (1973).

United States, Department of the Army. *Documents and Studies on the Japanese Free Balloons of World War II* (1976). (microfilm)

Webber, Bert. *Retaliation* (1975).

Terry L. Shoptaugh

Bombing of Civilians

Both sides in World War II in the Pacific (as in Europe) knowingly bombed heavily populated areas, causing great loss of life. Especially damaging to civilian populations were incendiary bombs. The United States used them with devastating effect against Japanese cities, and the Japanese had earlier employed them in China. And, of course, the United States destroyed two Japanese cities, Hiroshima and Nagasaki, with atomic bombs.

Japanese Attacks

As war between China and Japan escalated in 1937, Japan heavily bombed Nanking and Shanghai, using both explosive and incendiary bombs. Large sections of both cities were leveled. The bombings were widely reported around the world, and the publicity contributed greatly to arousing Western public opinion against Japan. A photograph, widely distributed by the Associated Press, of a battered child sitting amid the bodies and rubble at the Shanghai railroad station became a symbol of the horrors of Japan's aggressive war in China. U.S. Secretary of State Cordell Hull condemned the "large number of instances" of attacks on "places near which there were no military establishments or organizations" and "the use of incendiary bombs which inevitably and ruthlessly jeopardize non-military persons and property."

After Pearl Harbor, as Japan mounted offensive operations against U.S. and British possessions, Japanese airplanes on several occasions bombed cities. When Japan invaded the Philippines on December 8, 1941, Manila, the capital, was a major objective. As fighting approached the city, the U.S. commander, General Douglas MacArthur, declared Manila an "open city" on December 27. In international law, this meant the city would be undefended and free from attack and bombardment. The Japanese, however, ignored MacArthur's declaration, and two days later Japanese planes began heavy bombing of Manila's port and the *Intramuros*—the Walled City that was the site of the original Spanish settlement and the location of many churches.

Singapore was devastated by Japanese bombing in late 1941 and early 1942. The attacks destroyed the city's water system and also hampered the efforts of civilians to evacuate. The British surrendered Singapore on February 15, 1942. A few days later, on February 19, a Japanese air raid on Allied ships in port at Darwin, Australia, left much of that city in ruins.

In 1944–1945, Japan launched thousands of bomb-carrying paper balloons against the United States and Canada. They were first observed in the United States in November 1944. There was great concern that the balloons might contain biological agents, which American intelligence knew the Japanese had developed. (Biological weapons were used by the Japanese in China.) In fact, the balloons carried incendiary bombs intended to burn North American forests. They were easily shot down, however, and had virtually no effect. (An Oregon woman and five children were killed while they were fishing on May 5, 1945, when they came upon a balloon bomb and tried to examine it; they were the only casualties of the war on the American mainland.) Some two hundred balloon bombs were found in the United States and Canada, one as far east as Grand Rapids, Michigan.

U.S. Attacks

Despite the no doubt sincere detestation American leaders expressed for the Japanese attacks on civilian targets, the United States conducted similar but even more intense attacks on Japan. Even before Pearl Harbor, American and Chinese leaders had discussed plans for bombing Japanese cities from Chinese bases. The first U.S. raid against Japan, however, was the carrier-based bombing attack led by Colonel James Doolittle on April 18, 1942. Sixteen B-25s carrying explosive and incendiary bombs bombed Kobe, Nagoya, Yokohama, Yokosuka, and Tokyo. Docks and factories were targeted, but houses were also hit and civilians killed. Of little military significance, the raid was important mainly—and indeed was planned at President Franklin D. Roosevelt's urging—as a morale booster for Americans.

More intensive bombing of Japanese cities began in June 1944. Like the British and American attacks in Europe, this campaign intended to destroy industrial, transportation, and communications targets. When daylight "precision" or "pinpoint" attacks proved unsuccessful because of weather difficulties and the enemy's defenses, "area bombing" of cities with incendiary weapons was undertaken. The Americans were well aware that Japanese cities, with their many wood and paper buildings, were highly vulnerable to incendiary bombs. Tests conducted against Japanese-style buildings constructed in the Utah desert confirmed this. The revulsion Hull and others had earlier expressed over Japanese incendiary attacks was now forgotten. An army air force report in January 1945 stated that Japanese cities "are a valid and eventually important military objective . . . because of the heavy dispersal of industry within the cities and within the most congested parts of them." That civilians would become casualties was also expected, and accepted. Few high-ranking leaders—Secretary of War Henry Stimson was a notable exception—questioned the morality of such bombing. The general feeling was that the Japanese "had it coming to them" for their earlier aggression.

New, huge B-29 bombers, at first based in China, carried out the attacks. Later the B-29s took off from bases in the Mariana Islands, which were captured in mid-1944. Ironically the very first large-scale attack by B-29s carrying incendiary bombs was against a target in China—the Japanese-controlled city of Hankow, in late fall 1944. The Hankow raid was targeted against docks but killed many civilians. In this and later raids, a new kind of incendiary bomb was used; it was filled with napalm, a gelatinous form of gasoline that created streams of flame on the ground.

In early 1945, General Curtis LeMay, a veteran of the bombing of Germany, took charge of the bombing campaign against Japan's cities. LeMay sent the B-29s out in masses of hundreds, at night, flying at very low altitudes. In the massive firebombing raid on Tokyo of the night of March 9–10, more than fifteen square miles were completely burned out and about one half of the city destroyed. More than 83,000 people were killed and over 100,000 injured. This was probably the largest number of casualties in a single action in the entire war—in Europe and the Pacific—and most of the victims were civilians. LeMay was well pleased with the results. "We have them cold," he commented. Fearing adverse public reaction in the United States to the fearsome destruction, the army instructed LeMay to stress in his press releases that the purpose of the attacks "was *not* to indiscriminately bomb civilian populations. The objective *was* to destroy the *industrial and strategic targets* concentrated in the urban areas."

Over the next several months, Tokyo was hit again, and Nagoya, Kobe, Osaka, Yokohama, and Kawasaki—Japan's leading industrial centers—as well as scores of smaller cities were also devastated. With their planes now virtually unchallenged in the skies over Japan, the Americans dropped leaflets urging inhabitants to flee targeted cities. Whether this indicated some anguish on the Americans' part over the civilian casualties they knew they were inflicting is conjectural.

Bombing attacks causing civilian casualties continued until the very end of the war. They included, of course, the dropping of atomic bombs on Hiroshima and Nagasaki. The U.S. atomic bombs were developed in what was first thought of as a race with Germany to build a new kind of weapon with unprecedented destructive capacity. Had the new bombs been ready earlier—or had the war in Europe lasted longer—there is little doubt that they would have been dropped on German cities. When the weapons did become ready in early summer 1945, their use against Japan was approved in the hope that they would hasten the end of the war. Other motives for their use—to strengthen the American hand in postwar negotiations and the postwar era, and to deter future wars—were present but clearly secondary. President Harry Truman accepted the recommendations of the Interim Committee, a civilian group appointed to advise him on the political, military, and scientific issues associated with use of the atomic bomb. The weapons would be used as soon as possible against targets that contained both sites of military importance and concentrations of population. Truman wrote privately that the decision was a terribly difficult one. Yet in another frame of mind, after the Nagasaki attack, he said, "When you deal with a beast you have to treat him as a beast."

Both Hiroshima and Nagasaki were considered important military targets. Hiroshima had many military installations, including the largest army base in western Japan. Nagasaki was a shipbuilding and repair center, and the torpedoes used against Pearl Harbor had been manufactured there.

As a result of the explosion over Hiroshima on August 6, 1945, 71,379 people died, according to the official Japanese account. A nearly equal number is thought to have died later from radiation poisoning. More than 90 percent of the structures in the city were damaged or destroyed. In the Nagasaki attack on August 9, the Japanese concluded, 25,680 people died and another 45,000 succumbed later to radiation. About 44 percent of the city was destroyed.

Evaluation

The Japanese attacks on Chinese cities seem indefensible today, as indeed they did to many in 1937. Whether the even more horrendous civilian casualties inflicted on Japan by the U.S. bombing in 1944 and 1945 were justified is a matter for debate and necessarily involves very difficult hindsight judgments, both military and moral. The Japanese estimated that the U.S. bombing as a whole killed 241,000 people, injured 313,000, and destroyed 2.3 million homes. The U.S. Strategic Bombing Survey gave even higher estimates. It seems clear that the Tokyo and other firebombings certainly shattered the morale of the Japanese population and in that sense perhaps contributed to shortening the war. The same was undoubtedly true of the atomic attacks.

Does that justify the immense human carnage? The battle of Okinawa, which ended in early July, had cost thousands of American casualties. Japanese losses were much higher—about 110,000 soldiers and sailors plus many thousands of civilians dead. Had the war continued, and the planned invasion of the Japanese home islands taken place, those numbers undoubtedly would have been multiplied many times. Yet the Strategic Bombing Survey concluded that "certainly prior to 31 December 1945, and in all probability prior to 1 November 1945, Japan would have surrendered even if the atomic bombs had not been dropped. . . . " Clearly, however, a dispassionate conclusion reached in peacetime is quite a different thing from decisions made after years of bitter war by leaders working under great pressure amid news of ghastly battle losses.

FURTHER READINGS

Hoyt, Edwin P. *Japan's War: The Great Pacific Conflict* (1986).

Werrell, Kenneth P. *Blankets of Fire: U.S. Bombing over Japan during World War II* (1996).

Michael Weber

SEE ALSO Atomic Bomb, Decision to Use against Japan; Doolittle (Tokyo) Raid; LeMay, Curtis; Manila, Fall of; Singapore, Fall of; Tokyo Fire Raid

Borneo, Allied Operations against

One of the lesser-known campaigns of the Pacific war was the Allied invasion of Borneo. With the recapture of the Philippines, the ongoing battle for Okinawa, and the collapse of Germany, there was little attention focused on the Allied efforts against Borneo, but the capture of the territory denied the Japanese a significant source for raw materials such as rubber and oil. In addition, the island of Tarakan had been used by the Japanese fleet to refit after several battles.

Borneo fell within the Southwest Pacific Command of General Douglas MacArthur. MacArthur believed the capture of the Borneo oil fields to be extremely important, but the British and the Australians considered the ongoing offensive in Mandalay (Burma) to be the more pivotal. Nonetheless, MacArthur secured permission to launch a campaign in May 1945. The general's plan involved three separate landings. The first was to be on the oil-rich island of Tarakan, some 150 miles northwest

of Borneo; the second was to be at Brunei Bay on the northwest coast of Borneo itself; and the third was to be at Balikpapan, in the southwest. One early obstacle encountered by the Allies was the enormous number of mines sown by the Allies themselves to disrupt Japanese naval traffic and by the Japanese to defend against invasion. Minesweeping efforts were further complicated by uncharted waters and strong currents. Allied minesweepers were so effective, however, that only one Allied ship, destroyer *Jenkins,* was damaged in the initial invasion.

On April 30, 1945, Allied commandos seized the small island of Sadau, just west of Tarakan, and an artillery battalion was then moved onto the island to support the invasion. Japanese positions on Tarakan were attacked by air and sea, and on May 1, the 13,000 men of the Australian 2d Brigade landed on the island. The Japanese initially offered only brief resistance, and by May 5 Tarakan town and the island's airfield had been captured. As the Australians moved deeper into the island, Japanese resistance stiffened, and it took another month to clear the island. The Allies lost 225 men killed and some 669 wounded while the entire 1,540 men of the Japanese garrison were killed. MacArthur had hoped to use the island's airfield to support further operations, but the field was so damaged during the fighting that it could not be repaired in time for the other invasions.

Brunei Bay was the next Allied target. Site of an excellent natural harbor, the area was also the most heavily populated area of Borneo. For this phase of the campaign, the Allies could count on significant aid and intelligence from a well-established guerrilla network on the island. There were four separate, major insurgent units led by British officers which were operating near the site of the invasion. The guerrillas had even managed to construct a small airfield and were well supplied by the Allies. But before the Allies could invade the coastal areas of the bay, they had to take a series of small islands which stretched across the mouth of the 30-mile-wide bay. The main Allied objectives of this stage of the invasion were the island of Labuan, the town of Brunei itself, and the oilfields at Seria and Miva.

While there were only 1,500 Japanese troops defending the invasion site, the Allied commanders were concerned about the possibility of a Japanese naval raid during the actual invasion. To counter this threat, a squadron of heavy cruisers was stationed between Brunei Bay and Singapore (the possibility of a surprise enemy sortie was dramatically reduced when a British submarine sank one of the two Japanese cruisers remaining in the South China Sea).

On June 10, the hundred ships of the Allied invasion fleet sailed into Brunei Bay, conducted an intense shelling of the coast, and landed the veteran 9th Australian Division of Tobruk fame at three points: on Labuan Island, on Maura Island and on the west coast of Brunei Bay. Resistance was light at all three beaches. Only a single Japanese bomber made a futile bombing run against the invasion fleet, and the only casualties suffered by the Allied naval forces came when a minesweeper struck a mine. MacArthur himself came ashore two hours after the landings to view the progress of the assault. Within two days, tanks moved into the three landing sites to exploit the beachheads. Maura Island was quickly overwhelmed, and by June 13 the Australians had captured Brunei town and moved 17 miles into the interior. Most of Labuan Island including the main town of Victoria was under Allied control within four days, but one pocket of Japanese held out and eventually had to be subjected to air and sea bombardment for two days before they were overrun. Engineer units moved onto Labuan, and by the end of July they had constructed a wharf, ten oil storage tanks, and an airfield.

On Borneo itself, the Japanese steadily retreated into the interior, pursued by the Australian troops. The Australians were able to capture the oil fields at Miva intact, but the retreating Japanese set fire to thirty-seven oil wells at Seria, and it would be three months before the Allies were able to extinguish the last fire. By July, it was clear that the Japanese had conceded Brunei Bay and immediate coastal areas. The Australian commander, Major General George Wooten, decided to avoid pursuing the enemy into the dense jungle of Borneo and instead used patrols and guerrilla raids to keep the Japanese forces bottled up. British civil affairs officials moved into Brunei with the troops and began the process of rebuilding the area and caring for both the seven thousand civilians and the several hundred POWs from the Indian army who had been confined in Brunei since 1942.

The third phase of the Allied operation against Borneo called for the invasion of Balikpapan in the former Dutch colonial area. After the Combined Chiefs of the Allies canceled plans to invade Java, many senior Allied commanders felt that the final phase of the Borneo campaign was unnecessary and that resources could be better used elsewhere; however, MacArthur was adamant and ordered the final landings to proceed.

The Japanese had approximately fifty-five hundred men and a significant number of coastal artillery emplacements and antiaircraft guns to defend Balikpapan. In addition, this section of the Borneo coastline contained the heaviest concentration of minefields and would require significant minesweeping activity before landings could occur.

The invasion was spearheaded by the 33,000 troops of the 7th Australian Division, complete with three squadrons of tanks (including a squadron of flamethrowing tanks). Before the invasion, eight Allied cruisers and nine destroyers bombarded the beaches, while B-25 and B-24 bombers conducted saturation bombings and fighters from three aircraft carriers strafed the beaches. To give the Dutch a presence during the operation on their former colony, one of the cruisers was a Dutch vessel, *Tromp*. The sixteen-day naval bombardment proved to be the lengthiest of the war. The Japanese tried to respond to the Allied air onslaught with a surprise air attack of their own on June 25. Six Japanese torpedo planes made runs against the Allied fleet but did no damage and in fact lost three of their planes.

On July 1, the Australians landed at three beaches along the coast. Even though Allied minesweepers had begun clearing lanes fifteen days before the invasion, mines proved to be the main obstacle to the invading forces, inasmuch as four of the five landing craft sunk during the invasion were victims of mines (twelve other landing craft were damaged by either mines or enemy fire during the assault). Once on the beaches the Australians encountered only minor resistance. Allied troops entered Balikpapan on the first day of the invasion, and by July 3 the entire city had been taken. The invaders had also captured Klandasan, the other major city on the coast, and had overrun both major airfields.

Heavy resistance was encountered on July 5, as the Australians moved along the two main highways leading north and east. The naval task force and the air units continued to provide support, and most of the defender's fortified bunkers that had not been damaged by the pre-invasion bombardment were destroyed by close air support. The defense soon became unorganized and fleeting. The flamethrowing tanks of the Australians, supported by artillery and air units, advanced quickly, and by July 9 all the Allies' objectives had been taken. The Japanese defenders then tried to conduct a fighting withdrawal to pull the Australians into the jungle. Major General E. J. Milford, the Australian commander, decided not to advance into the interior but to follow the pattern that had been established at Brunei, where regular patrols and guerrilla activity were used to contain the remaining Japanese troops. A number of small skirmishes followed, the last being on August 9, just one week before the Japanese national surrender.

FURTHER READINGS

Gailey, Harry. *The War in the Pacific: From Pearl Harbor to Tokyo Bay* (1995).

Karig, Walter, Russell Harris, and Frank Manson. *Battle Report: Victory in the Pacific* (1949).

Morrison, Samuel. *The Liberation of the Philippines: Luzon, Mindanao, the Visayas.* In *History of the United States Naval Operations in World War II* (1975).

Tom Lansford

SEE ALSO Australia

Bose, Subhas Chandra (1897–1945)

Subhas Chandra Bose, an anti-British Indian nationalist, led the pro-Japanese Provisional Government of Free India and the Indian National Army against Allied forces in Burma during World War II.

A career politician from Bengal, Subhas Bose, like many Indian nationalists in the prewar period, was repeatedly jailed by British authorities for his activities advocating Indian independence from the Crown. In 1938–1939 Bose served as the president of the Indian National Congress Party under the slogan "Give me blood and I promise you freedom." Bose favored a more militant stance than most of his colleagues and proposed violent resistance to British rule to gain independence. Soon after the start of World War II in Europe, Bose resigned the presidency of the Indian National Congress and broke off relations with Mohandas Gandhi and his followers who refused to use the opportunity provided by the war to start organizing violent opposition in India against a weakened Great Britain. Bose's advocacy of violence put him outside the mainstream of Indian nationalist thought at the time and in direct opposition to Gandhi, who favored a program of nonviolent civil disobedience. Bose's militant opposition to British rule lead to his arrest and imprisonment as a dangerous dissident in 1940.

Subhas Bose soon escaped from prison in India, however, fleeing first to Afghanistan and then to Nazi Germany. Arriving in Berlin in January 1941, Bose would spend nearly two years in the Nazi capital. During his time in Germany Bose was attracted to Nazi ideology and imitated Adolf Hitler by adopting the title *Netaji*, or "leader." His efforts to gain support for Indian independence, however, produced little in the way of concrete action by the Nazis, although his presence in Germany did generate a great deal of propaganda capital for the Axis. On the suggestion of the Germans, Bose did organize a small group of volunteers known as the Indian Legion who fought alongside the Wehrmacht against the Western Allies. This volunteer force was recruited from among the sizable pool of Indians captured while serving with British Commonwealth forces in North Africa between 1940 and 1942.

Following Japan's entry into the war in December 1941, and after their early military successes throughout Asia, Subhas Bose returned to the Far East at Japan's invitation to lead a Free India movement. He traveled by German U-boat, first landing in Malaya in February 1943 before going on to Tokyo in a Japanese submarine, arriving in June. Once in Tokyo, he became the much publicized leader of the Indian Independence League. Bose's aspirations for India fitted neatly with Japanese propaganda promoting the Greater East Asia Co-Prosperity Sphere and independence for colonial peoples of the region. On October 23, after prompting by Japan, Bose declared war on both the United States and Great Britain on behalf of the newly created Provisional Government of Free India, which he was to lead for almost two years. The next month, at the Japanese-sponsored Greater East Asian Conference, the Indian provisional government was given control of the Andaman and Nicobar Islands in the Indian Ocean off the coast of Malaya, although Bose based his government in Singapore and, from January 1944 to April 1945, in Rangoon.

In order to fulfill plans to liberate Indian from British rule, Bose recruited the Indian National Army (the Azad Hukumat-e-Azad-Hind) consisting of three divisions totaling approximately thirteen thousand men. This force, like the earlier Indian Legion, consisted of volunteers recruited from among British Indian army troops captured during the 1942 Malaya campaign, who, by late 1943, were slowly starving to death in disease-ridden Japanese prisoner-of-war camps throughout Southeast Asia.

Perhaps believing Japanese propaganda about the depth of anti-British and anti-European feeling in Asia, Bose thought that a popular revolution would instantly follow any invasion of India spearheaded by his army. In general, however, the soldiers of the Indian National Army were treated as inferiors by the Japanese, and most units were chronically under strength and poorly supplied. One division did take part in the ill-fated Imphal-Kohima operation—the Japanese invasion of India launched from Burma in March 1944. The unit, however, suffered repeated defeats, along with their Japanese allies, and utterly failed to convince Indians at home to rise up against the British as planned. After the disastrous Japanese defeat in Burma in 1945, Bose's increasingly ineffective Indian National Army rapidly disintegrated as its ranks began surrendering en mass to British forces, who treated the surrendering Indians relatively well considering their recent allegedly treasonous activities. Although Bose wanted to stay and fight on in Rangoon, Burma, after April 1945, the Japanese persuaded him to flee to Bangkok, Thailand. Here he conducted anti-British propaganda broadcasts, before fleeing once more to Saigon, French Indochina.

Even after the Japanese surrender, Bose was determined to carry on the Free India movement and planned to return to the Subcontinent, despite his renegade status among the British. But on August 18, 1945, the airplane carrying him from Dairen, Manchukuo, to India crashed on takeoff from an airfield on Formosa, and Bose was killed. Allegedly, his last words were, "I believe India will soon be free. Nobody can hold India captive now." Rumors persisted as late as 1956 that Bose had survived and was living incognito in Japan, but an Indian government mission that same year established the falsehood of such claims. To many Indian nationalists Subhas Chandra Bose and the members of the Indian National Army remain heros today for their wartime exploits.

FURTHER READINGS

Bose, Sisir K. *The Flaming Sword Forever Unsheathed: A Concise Biography of Netaji Subhas Chandra Bose* (1986).

Corr, Gerald H. *The War of the Springing Tigers* (1975).

Gordon, Leonard. *Brothers against the Raj: A Biography of Indian Nationalists Sarat and Subhas Chandra Bose* (1990).

Lebra, Joyce C. *Jungle Alliance: Japan and the Indian National Army* (1972).

Pandit, H. N. *Netaji Subhas Chandra Bose: From Kabul to Imphal* (1988).

Sareen, T. R. *Japan and the Indian National Army* (1986).

Clayton D. Laurie

SEE ALSO India; Indian National Army

Bougainville, U.S. Operations against

By the fall of 1943 the Allies were entering the final phase of Operation Cartwheel, the operation to envelop and neutralize the major Japanese base at Rabaul on New Britain Island. In the South Pacific, plans called for Admiral William Halsey, the area commander, to land forces on Bougainville, an island in the northern Solomons around November 1, 1943, and construct airfields so that Allied fighters and medium bombers could bring Rabaul under sustained bombardment. Because the Japanese forces on Bougainville and nearby islands numbered approximately 40,000 troops and 20,000 naval personnel, and because of the island's rugged and swampy terrain, it was decided that the capture of the entire island would be too costly.

Instead, Halsey would seize a section where the Japanese had few troops, establish a defensive perimeter, and build airfields for raids against Rabaul.

During the weeks before the invasion, U.S. Fifth Air Force bombers flying from New Guinea pounded Rabaul, while Air Command Solomons forces attacked Japanese air bases on Bougainville, rendering them inoperative by invasion day. The ground campaign began on October 27 when New Zealand and U.S. troops captured the Treasury Islands, just south of Bougainville, and a U.S. Marine battalion, in a feint, landed on Choiseul Island to the southeast of Bougainville to convince the Japanese that the invasion of Bougainville would come on the east coast of the island. The actual invasion began on November 1 when the 3d Marine Division of Lieutenant General Alexander A. Vandergrift's I Marine Amphibious Corps came ashore at Empress Augusta Bay about midway up the west coast of Bougainville. This area was isolated from the major Japanese bases on the southern and eastern coasts of the island, and despite opposition from a small, well dug-in garrison, the marines were able to place 14,000 men ashore by the end of the day and carve out a narrow lodgement about one mile deep and several miles in length.

Lieutenant General Harukichi Hyakutake, commander of the Seventeenth Japanese Army, which was charged with the defense of Bougainville, reacted slowly to the landing, for he was certain that it was only a ruse and that the main assault would come elsewhere. Even if Hyakutake had not misjudged U.S. intentions, the weather and the island's terrain and lack of roads would have prevented him from concentrating forces for an early counterattack. Japanese naval and air forces, however, reacted quickly. During the night of November 1–2, a Japanese task force attempted to attack the landing force, but in the Battle of Empress Augusta Bay it was turned back with the loss of a cruiser and a destroyer by a U.S. task force commanded by Rear Admiral A. Stanton Merrill. On November 2 Japanese air attacks from Rabaul tried to knock out Merrill's ships and isolate the beachhead, but they were stymied by American air units from New Georgia Island. Over the next days U.S. carrier-based aircraft and Fifth Air Force bombers steadily hammered Rabaul, while Allied air units gained air supremacy over Bougainville. Together, these operations reduced to a nuisance the Japanese air threat to the Empress Augusta Bay perimeter and ended any serious threat from the Japanese navy. Later that month U.S. destroyers intercepted a Japanese task force bringing reinforcements to nearby Buka Island, and in the Battle of Cape St. George they sank two destroyers and a destroyer-transport.

Meanwhile, the marines were expanding their perimeter at Empress Augusta Bay to the ridges overlooking the beachhead, and during the next weeks—now commanded by Major General Roy S. Geiger and joined by the army's 37th Division—they endured air raids and artillery shelling and repulsed a Japanese counterattack. By the middle of December they had established strong defensive positions along a perimeter about 10,000 yards deep and 23,000 yards long. At the same time, construction units built an airfield at Cape Torokina, and on December 10 the field was ready to participate in the defense of the perimeter and in raids against Rabaul. Two other airfields were completed shortly afterward. In December the army's Americal Division arrived on Bougainville to replace the 3d Marine Division, and on December 15 Major General Oscar Griswold, commander of the army's XIV Corps, assumed command of all forces on Bougainville.

For three months after their failed counterattack in November, the Japanese contented themselves with minor attacks along the perimeter, providing Griswold with ample opportunity to strengthen his defenses. Hyakutake was determined to drive the Americans into the sea, however, and by March 1944 he had assembled a force of 15,000 men to hurl at them. The Japanese initiated their attack on March 8, and over the next two weeks fierce fighting raged, especially at Hill 700 in the middle of the perimeter line and at Hill 260 on the east side. But the U.S. positions were too strong, and by March 27 the Japanese were in full retreat, having lost 5,000 killed and another 5,000 wounded. American losses were 263 killed.

By April 1944 the Bougainville lodgement was securely in American hands. Even more importantly, Allied operations had neutralized Rabaul as a strategic base for the Japanese, and the Bougainville campaign, which had aided in this victory by providing vital air bases, was thereafter rapidly reduced to a backwater affair. Over the next months there was sporadic fighting along the perimeter, and in one of these engagements the 1st Battalion of the 24th Infantry Regiment became the first African American infantry unit to see action in World War II. Griswold continued to strengthen the perimeter and engaged in aggressive patrolling to keep the Japanese off balance. However, U.S. commanders saw no need to undertake an offensive to seize the entire island as long as the perimeter was secure. The Japanese, moreover, were now cut off from outside aid, and, suffering terribly from food shortages, they too adopted a defensive posture. In October 1944 Australian units started to arrive on Bougainville to replace the Americans, and in November Lieutenant General Sir Stanley Savige, commander of the Australian II Corps, assumed control of the Allied forces. Except for some service troops, all U.S. units were withdrawn by February 1945.

The Australian commanders, unwilling to see their troops relegated to little more than a garrison force, adopted a strategy counter to that of the Americans and launched a major offensive in early 1945 to destroy the remaining 42,000 Japanese on Bougainville. The Japanese were severely handicapped by disease, starvation, and shortages of supplies and munitions. But they resisted fanatically in sustained fighting that lasted until the end of the war and cost the Australians 516 killed and 1,572 wounded in this demonstration of aggressiveness; the Japanese lost 18,000 dead from combat, illness, and starvation. Of the 60,000 Japanese on Bougainville and the nearby islands when the Americans landed in November 1943, only 21,000 were still alive to surrender on August 21, 1945.

FURTHER READINGS

Gailey, Harry. *Bougainville, 1943–1945: The Forgotten Campaign* (1991).

Hoyt, Edwin P. *The Glory of the Solomons* (1983).

Lofgren, S. J. *Northern Solomons* (1993).

Miller, John, Jr. *Cartwheel: The Reduction of Rabaul* (1959).

Morison, Samuel E. *History of United States Naval Operations in World War II,* vol. 6, *Breaking the Bismarks Barrier* (1950).

Morton, Louis. *Strategy and Command: The First Two Years* (1962).

Rentz, John N. *Bougainville and the Northern Solomons* (1948).

John Kennedy Ohl

SEE ALSO Australia; Marine Corps, U.S.; Navy, U.S.

Brown, Wilson (1882–1957)

Naval aide to four U.S. presidents and naval commander during World War II in the Pacific, Wilson Brown was born on April 27, 1882, in Philadelphia, Pennsylvania. Brown graduated in the lower half of his class from the U.S. Naval Academy at Annapolis in 1902 and was commissioned an ensign. After service with the fleet, he became an instructor at the academy in 1907–1908. More shipboard service was then followed by two years as an aide to the commandant of the New York Navy Yard from 1911 to 1913. During World War I, Brown served as a staff officer with Admiral William S. Sims in London, and he then commanded destroyer USS *Parker.*

After World War I, Brown commanded destroyer USS *Blakeley* in 1919–1920, before completing the course at the Naval War College, at Newport, Rhode Island, in 1921. He then served as the executive officer of battleship USS *Colorado,* before becoming an aide to the commander of the Destroyer Squadrons, U.S. Navy Battle Fleet, from 1924 to 1926. Brown then began the service for which he has become most famous, that of naval aide to the president of the United States.

In all, he would serve as the naval aide to four presidents from both political parties. His first efforts in this role was serving, in succession, as the naval aide to both Presidents Calvin Coolidge and Herbert Hoover.

After duty as the naval aide to Presidents Coolidge and Hoover, Brown became commander of the New London, Connecticut, Submarine Base, at which the U.S. Navy trained their submarines. He then became the commanding officer of battleship USS *California* in 1932–1933, which was followed by service as the chief of staff at the Naval War College, in 1933–1934. Then Brown again served as the president's naval aide, this time to President Franklin D. Roosevelt. After two years in this position, he was rewarded by a promotion to the rank of rear admiral and the position of commander of the Training Squadron, Scouting Force (the nucleus of the Atlantic Fleet), a command which he held from May 1936 to February 1938.

After commanding the Training Squadron, Scouting Force, Brown became the superintendent of the U.S. Naval Academy from 1938 to 1941. He then advanced to the rank of vice admiral and assumed command of the Scouting Force, Pacific Fleet, a command he held from February 1941 to April 1942. On December 7, 1941, when the Japanese attacked Pearl Harbor, Brown was aboard heavy cruiser USS *Indianapolis* (later sunk by a Japanese submarine with great loss of life), leading a task force that had just completed a simulated bombardment and landing exercise at Johnson Island. Returning to Pearl Harbor, he was given command of Task Force (TF) 11, with aircraft carrier USS *Lexington* as his flagship. TF 11 was one of three formed in what would ultimately be an abortive attempt to reinforce naval and marine personnel on Wake Island. TF 11 was to execute a diversionary raid on Jaluit Atoll in the hope of pinning down enemy forces in the Marshall Islands. TF 8, under the command of Vice Admiral William F. Halsey Jr. and with aircraft carrier USS *Enterprise* as his flagship, was to operate to the west of Johnson Island in order to cover the Hawaiian Islands and support the main strike if necessary. TF 14, with the main group built around aircraft carrier USS *Saratoga* and under the command of Rear Admiral Frank

Jack Fletcher, was to advance toward Wake Island in hopes of relieving the Japanese siege it was then under. Through a combination of bad luck and poor command decisions, the efforts to relieve Wake Island were unsuccessful, and the three task forces returned to Pearl Harbor.

After the failure of the Wake Island reinforcement effort, Brown's task force (which now consisted of aircraft carrier USS *Lexington,* four heavy cruisers, and ten destroyers) was sent to the southwest Pacific to operate under the command of Australian Admiral Leary as part of the ANZAC Force. Brown suggested using USS *Lexington* to launch an air strike on Rabaul, and Leary gladly accepted the suggestion. Unfortunately, Brown's force was detected by Japanese aircraft before they were able to launch their strike on Rabaul. During the ensuing air battle, approximately twenty Japanese planes were shot down with the loss of only one U.S. pilot and two planes. The loss of the element of surprise, however, caused Brown to call off the attack.

Following the attempt to attack Rabaul, Brown advised the CINCPAC (commander in chief, Pacific), Admiral Chester Nimitz, that any such future raids should be undertaken by no less than two aircraft carriers. Nimitz agreed and released aircraft carrier USS *Yorktown* to Brown's command. On March 8, 1942, the Japanese captured the islands of Lae and Salamaua in the Bismarck Sea, which seemed to add additional weigh to the threat of a possible Japanese invasion of Australia.

By an attack on these islands, Brown saw the opportunity both to hit the Japanese before they had had the chance to fortify their positions and to halt the Japanese advance on Australia. He thus ordered an attack by 104 planes of both carriers, which flew over the Owen Stanley Range of New Guinea in order to reach the Bismarck Sea. The naval aviators found many merchant and combat ships and managed to sink a minesweeper, a transport, and a light cruiser, with the loss of only one pilot and one plane.

After returning with his force to Pearl Harbor, Brown served as the commandant of the First Naval District from April 1942 to February 1943. He then accepted a voluntary reduction in rank to rear admiral in order to serve again as the naval aide to President Roosevelt. In December 1944, Brown was retired for age, but was immediately brought back on active duty. He continued to serve as the president's naval aide, continuing such duty under President Harry S. Truman, the fourth president he served in that capacity. Finally retiring with the rank of vice admiral, Brown, whose decorations included the Navy Cross and the Distinguished Service Medal (Navy), died at the

New Haven Naval Hospital in Connecticut on January 2, 1957.

FURTHER READINGS

Goodwin, Doris K. *No Ordinary Time: Franklin and Eleanor Roosevelt—The Home Front in World War II* (1994).

Larrabee, Eric. *Commander in Chief: Franklin Delano Roosevelt, His Lieutenants, and Their War* (1987).

Loewenheim, Francis L., Harold D. Langley, and Manfred Jonas, eds. *Roosevelt and Churchill: Their Secret Wartime Correspondence* (1975).

Morison, Samuel E. *History of United States Naval Operations in World War II*, vol. III, *The Rising Sun in the Pacific, 1931–April 1942* (1949).

Roosevelt, Elliott, ed. *F.D.R.: His Personal Letters, 1928–1945* (1950).

Alexander M. Bielakowski

SEE ALSO Navy, U.S.

Buck, Pearl S. (1892–1973)

It could be argued that no individual did more to shape popular images of Asia in the twentieth century than did the American author Pearl S. Buck. Daughter of missionaries to China, Buck lived there long enough to develop a fascination and love for that nation's people, languages, and traditions. These sentiments found expression in Buck's prodigious writings, both fiction and nonfiction. Through her periodical articles and best-selling novels such as *The Good Earth* (1931), Pearl Buck familiarized Westerners with a distant and seemingly alien people, portraying the Chinese as industrious, honorable, and long-suffering. Inasmuch as her most famous works were published in the 1930s and 1940s, she played a signal role in shaping perceptions of Asia and Asian peoples just as the United States was being drawn inextricably into the widening conflict between China and Japan.

Pearl Sydenstricker Buck was born in West Virginia on June 26, 1892, to Absalom and Caroline Sydenstricker, a missionary couple on leave from their post in China. They soon returned there with their infant daughter, and Pearl grew up in a world far removed from her birthplace. She learned to speak Chinese before English, and her early education was overseen by a Confucian scholar who familiarized her with Chinese history and philosophy. During the Boxer Rebellion of 1900, the Sydenstricker family was forced to flee from the interior to Shanghai, where Pearl's education continued at a mission school and a girl's school, whose headmistress introduced her to the myriad social and economic problems faced by the Chinese masses. With this background established, Pearl returned to the United States in 1910 to attend Randolph-Macon Woman's College, where her literary proclivities developed alongside her realization that her Asian experiences separated her from most of her fellow students. After graduation, Pearl taught briefly at the college before heading back to China to nurse her sick mother and teach English to Chinese students. Even as her study of China intensified, she met and married John L. Buck, an agricultural expert serving the Presbyterian Mission Board. Her husband's work led the couple to the remote Anhwei province, where the daily struggles of the ordinary Chinese peasant were manifest. After a five-year stay, the couple moved to Nanking and accepted teaching posts. In relatively cosmopolitan Nanking, the disruptive impact of change and Western ideas was apparent to Buck, who had grown familiar with the apparently timeless cycles which governed the lives of isolated peasants. In 1925, Pearl returned to the United States to take a master's degree in English at Cornell. Back in China in 1927, Buck found the country in political turmoil and barely escaped a revolutionary assault on Nanking.

Few Americans were as intimately familiar with and attached to China as was Pearl Buck in 1930, the year in which her first major publication, *East Wind; West Wind,* appeared. The novel prefigured much of her more famous work. Told from the perspective of a young Chinese woman, it was an examination of the clash of tradition and change in Chinese society, and it tended toward sentimentalism. Though fairly popular, the novel was largely a prelude to what was arguably Buck's most famous work, *The Good Earth* (1931). The obvious product of Buck's empathy with the ever-struggling Chinese peasant, the latter novel is the story of Wang Lung and his family, hard-working farmers whose lives are inextricably bound to the grudging soil that they work. The Wang clan are not the "heathen Chinee" that most Westerners had come to know in the late nineteenth century, thanks to such writers as Rudyard Kipling. Instead, they are depicted as honorable, morally centered, and patient—accepting the incredible burdens of their lives with the admirable stoicism innate in a timeless society. *The Good Earth* is a celebration of China's common people, who supposedly bore many of the positive qualities of the Jeffersonian yeoman.

Ironically, the novel became a best-seller at the moment when China was descending into war, famine, and chaos, brought on in part by the Japanese invasion and annexation of Manchuria in 1931. Later Japanese attacks on Shanghai and the conquest of Jehol in 1933 brought little effective official response from the United States, but public sympathy was clearly on the side of the beleaguered Chinese. *The Good Earth* undoubtedly played a role in determining the attitudes of many Americans, few of whom had any clear idea of Chinese life other than that conveyed through popular literature. In 1937 Buck's novel was made into a feature-length film by MGM. Five years in the making, the film was described by studio publicists as an effort to provide an accurate picture of Chinese society. Reviews were overwhelmingly favorable—despite unlikely casting, which gave the central roles to two Caucasians, Paul Muni and Luise Rainer(!). As testimony to the importance given the film by the Nationalist Chinese government, MGM agreed to subject it to approval by Chinese censors. The timing of the film's release could not have been more propitious; the outbreak of the Sino-Japanese war ensured that Americans would see the film in order to gain some understanding of a people now under siege. In general, the release of the film *The Good Earth* coincided with a period in which Americans were increasingly willing to view the Chinese in a positive light while seeing the Japanese as dangerous.

During the prewar decade Buck produced a number of other works which dealt with China as she knew it. She intended *The Good Earth* as part of a trilogy called *House of Earth.* The other two parts were *Sons* (1932) and *A House Divided* (1935), which completed Buck's study of the generational history of a Chinese family. Yet another novel with a Chinese theme was *The Mother,* published in 1934. *The Patriot,* published in 1939, was an examination of the revolutionary movement in Shanghai in the 1920s. Though these latter novels did not influence Western opinion to the same degree as had *The Good Earth,* they collectively affirmed Buck's portrayal of the Chinese as an admirable people. Most of the criticism of Buck's fictional China came from Chinese scholars, who maintained that many of her depictions of Chinese customs and traditions were inaccurate or grounded in the biased perspective of a Christian missionary. By 1937, however, China faced all-out war with Japan, and so the Nationalist government was more willing to overlook such academic criticisms and instead build a reservoir of public sympathy for China by whatever means.

In 1938, Pearl Buck was awarded the Noble Prize in literature—surprisingly, not for her novels about China but rather for two biographies of her parents, *The Exile* and *Fighting Angel,* both published in 1936. Yet most Americans would continue to associate Pearl Buck with China, with Asia, and, increasingly, with the conflict burgeoning in the Pacific. After the United States went to war against the Axis powers, Buck devoted much of her energy to promoting the Allied cause and international understanding that might lead to the acceptance of the equality of all peoples. Buck wrote a series of six radio plays for the Office of War Information, which, despite low ownership of radio receivers in war-torn, impoverished China, was broadcast as "America Speaks to China." Additionally, she wrote plays for United China Relief and founded the East and West Association, a group committed to studying characteristics of all nations as a prelude to international harmony. A widely disseminated essay, "Tinder for Tomorrow," addressed the question of racial equality for Asian peoples and was meant to challenge the most troublesome of Japan's propaganda issues in the Far East: anticolonialism and racial equality.

Buck also pursued a theme which undergirded much of her writing—her contention that the Americans and Chinese peoples had much in common. In her article "Understanding the Chinese," which appeared in *Rotarian,* Buck maintained, with somewhat circuitous logic, that "Americans and Chinese should best understand each other because temperamentally they are extremely alike." In her book *What America Means to Me* (1942), Buck asserted that, like Americans, the Chinese believed in "the worth of the common man" and "are a strong, brave, superior people" possessed of a "fundamentally democratic character." (Buck didn't delve into who would have to be the "inferior" peoples to the "superior" Chinese.) Many of these assertions were evident in Buck's wartime novel *Dragon Seed* (1942). The novel centers on the family of Ling Tan, a farmer who is swept up by the currents of war as the Japanese invade his country and wreak havoc. Buck's Japanese behave as utter barbarians in the most fundamental sense of the word—raping, torturing, and killing—while the Chinese resist heroically against great odds. It is a compelling if not always realistic story, and it found its way to the screen in 1944, once again featuring Caucasians in the main roles: Katharine Hepburn and Walter Huston. (Did Hollywood not have any Asiatic actors who could escape such stereotypical dialogue as "We have ways to make you talk"?) *Dragon Seed* garnered somewhat mixed reviews but was generally lauded as a valiant effort to depict Japan's savage war in China. A sequel to the novel, entitled *The Promise* (1943), followed the same Chinese family as the war extends to Burma.

The end of World War II also brought an end to Japanese depredations in China, but nothing like the stability or renewal for which Pearl Buck and the Chinese people hoped. Instead, the final phase of the Chinese revolution began in 1946 as Chiang Kai-shek's Nationalists battled Mao Tse-tung's Communists for control of the country.

Once again, China deteriorated into chaos, culminating in the Communist victory in October 1949. Many Americans were stunned, wondering how their vision of a democratic, pro-Western China could have proved so inaccurate. Pearl Buck was foremost among those who argued that the "real" Chinese would ultimately prevail. In an article entitled "Still the Good Earth," published in *Saturday Review* in 1949, Buck asserted that "the people of China are the same as they have ever been" and that they would refuse the role that the Communists intended for them, because of their "inner wholesomeness, this basic peace, which has led the Chinese to be a peaceable people." Eventually, she predicted, the Chinese would reject Maoist tyranny because they naturally gravitated to a "basic and popular democracy" and disliked forceful leadership. Buck, like most Americans, had difficulty coming to grips with the realization that the monumental forces reshaping China after 1949 had little in common with the idyllic and sentimental vision of that nation which Buck had done much to popularize. As the cold war intensified, images of the "Good Earth" receded as China was rapidly redefined in the Western mind as a threatening and unpredictable "Red Menace."

Pearl Buck's literary career continued into the 1970s with a variety of works including children's books, novels, and books dealing with Korea, Japan, and Asia in general. None, however, had as much impact on public opinion about Asia as her earlier publications had. Without question, Pearl Buck's fiction helped define China and to a lesser extent Asia for many Westerners in the 1930s and 1940s. In particular, her portrayal of the Chinese people was central to the positive image of China that predominated in the United States before 1949. Pearl Buck died of lung cancer on March 6, 1973.

FURTHER READINGS

Conn, Peter. *Pearl S. Buck: A Cultural Biography* (1996).
Doyle, Paul A. *Pearl S. Buck* (1980).
Harris, Theodore F. *Pearl S. Buck: A Biography* (1969).
Spencer, Cornelia. *The Exile's Daughter: A Biography of Pearl S. Buck* (1944).

Blaine T. Browne

SEE ALSO Chinese Communists versus Nationalists

Buckner, Simon Bolivar, Jr. (1886–1945)

Commander, Alaskan Defense Force, 1940–1944; commander, U.S. Tenth Army, 1944–1945; killed in action June 18, 1945. The son of a Civil War lieutenant general, Buckner attended Virginia Military Institute (1902–1904) before entering the U.S. Military Academy. From his graduation there in 1908 to 1919 Buckner saw numerous field assignments in both the United States and the Philippines, including a stint with the army air service. He gained slow but steady promotion, making first lieutenant in 1914 and captain three years later.

Buckner's continued military education and his recognized teaching ability kept him out of World War I and directed his career during the interwar period. From 1919 to 1923 he taught infantry tactics at West Point. In 1924 he completed the advanced infantry course at Fort Benning, Georgia. The following year he attended the Command and General Staff School at Fort Leavenworth, Kansas, where he remained as an instructor until 1928. Buckner spent the next four years as a student and instructor at the Army War College in Washington, D.C., before returning to West Point. After a year as instructor of tactics, Buckner served as commandant of cadets (1933–1936).

Promoted to major in 1920 and lieutenant colonel in 1932, Buckner was elevated to colonel in 1937. After a brief assignment with the 66th Infantry Regiment he assumed command of Fort McClellan, Alabama, encompassing the 22d Infantry Regiment and District D, Civilian Conservation Corps. In 1939 he became chief of staff, 6th Division. In 1940 Buckner was selected to head the Alaskan Defense Force. His promotion to brigadier general followed shortly thereafter.

General Buckner approached his new command with zeal. Playing on concerns of Soviet aggression created by the Nazi-Soviet pact, he brought Alaska to the attention of the Joint Chiefs. While this threat dissipated, the Japanese attack on Pearl Harbor emphasized the strategic importance of Buckner's command. Promoted to major general (1941), he directed the buildup of Alaska's defenses and military usefulness that included the construction of the Alcan Highway linking Alaska to the continental United States. Before much could be accomplished, in June 1942 Japanese forces, in concert with operations at Midway, evaded U.S. Navy units and occupied the U.S. islands of Kiska and Attu in the Aleutian chain.

Although this occupation posed little threat to U.S. security, the symbolic effect of Japanese troops on U.S. soil brought a response. In May 1943 Buckner's significantly enlarged command joined Rear Admiral Thomas Kinkaid's naval forces in an effort to reclaim the islands. Bypassing Kiska, their amphibious assault fell on Attu on May 11. After eighteen days of bitter and costly fighting Attu was secured. In August another amphibious landing on Kiska found the island evacuated. The Aleutians campaign afforded the U.S. Army its first experience at amphibious assault on an enemy-held island and offered tangible evidence of Japanese military fanaticism—their garrison on Attu fought almost to the last man. This also provided valuable experience for Buckner, who earned promotion to lieutenant general.

In the summer of 1944 General Buckner was further rewarded when he was selected to command the newly created Tenth Army. Tenth Army contained the four army divisions of Lieutenant General John H. Hodge's XXIV Corps and the three marine divisions of Major General Roy Geiger's 3d Amphibious Corps. Buckner's new command provided the ground troops for the last major offensive of the war, the assault on the Japanese island of Okinawa.

On April 1, 1945, elements of Tenth Army landed on Okinawa to begin one of the largest land-air-sea battles in history. Buckner's slow frontal advance brought criticism from the navy and marines, but he maintained his conservative, grinding offensive for most of three months. He rejected calls for a second amphibious landing in the Japanese rear, doubting the ability to maintain two fronts against such determined opposition. Although extremely costly, Buckner's relentless advance continued, and by mid-June victory was imminent.

On June 18, 1945, Buckner, who habitually maintained close contact with the front, moved to a marine observation post to view the closing action. Five rounds from one of the last serviceable Japanese artillery pieces struck nearby. Shards of rock, coral, and metal ripped Buckner's chest and abdomen. He died minutes later, the highest-ranking U.S. officer (and one of only two general officers) killed by enemy fire during the war. The conquest of Okinawa was completed three days later.

Known as one of the army's finest scholars and instructors, Buckner also enjoyed great popularity with his men. Although a strict disciplinarian, he had a warm and humorous disposition. Criticism of his methods on Okinawa notwithstanding, Buckner worked effectively with officers and men of the other services.

FURTHER READINGS

Block, Maxine, ed. *Current Biography* (1942).
Feifer, George. *Tennozan: The Battle of Okinawa and the Atomic Bomb* (1992).
Mason, David. *Who's Who in World War II* (1978).
Perret, Geoffrey. *There's a War to Be Won: The United States Army in World War II* (1991).

David Coffey

SEE ALSO Aleutian Islands Campaign; Army Ground Forces, U.S.; Marine Corps, U.S.; Navy, U.S.

Bulkeley, John Duncan (1911–1996)

U.S. Navy officer and patrol torpedo (PT) boat commander in World War II, John D. Bulkeley graduated from the U.S. Naval Academy in 1933, but the Depression delayed his commissioning until 1934. He became an Army Air Corps flying cadet during this hiatus but washed out of the course. Back in the navy, he ultimately joined PT boats in February 1941, participated in their sea trials, and proved that they could stand the pounding of long, open-ocean trips.

He headed for the Philippines in August 1941 as commander of Motor Torpedo Boat Squadron 3, with six 77-foot-long boats, each carrying four torpedoes, two twin-.50-caliber machine guns in power turrets, and two .30-caliber guns on fixed mounts. He offloaded his boats in Manila Bay and stashed nine spare engines in private garages throughout Manila rather than at Cavite Navy Yard—a thoroughly prescient precaution considering what was to come.

Japan attacked the Philippines on December 8, 1941, and two days later Bulkeley's PT boats actively engaged Japanese Zeros over Manila Bay, claiming three fighters shot down. Japanese horizontal bombers hit Cavite with a severe bombing that would have destroyed Bulkeley's spare engines had he not secreted them in Manila.

Bulkeley's boats began a series of successful and daring raids on Japanese shipping in Subic Bay. The squadron's boats crept into Subic twice and each time torpedoed a Japanese ship. Because the U.S. public had little to cheer about during these dark days, the press hailed Bulkeley's exploits.

On the night of January 22, 1942, the 30-year-old Bulkeley was aboard PT-34 as it engaged two Japanese troop barges off Bataan's west coast. PT-34 fired into the vulnerable flank of the first landing boat until it sank. Bulkeley sighted a second barge, overtook it, and opened fire. A couple of well-thrown hand grenades took the fight out of the Japanese, and Bulkeley boarded the enemy barge; he was collecting documents and prisoners when it sank. He tread water and kept his two wounded prisoners afloat until the sailors on PT-34 fished them out.

In March, Bulkeley and his four remaining PT boats were ordered to ferry General Douglas MacArthur and members of his staff through the Japanese blockade. They departed Corregidor the evening of March 11. Despite 600 miles of largely uncharted waters, heavy seas, and storms, Bulkeley landed his twenty-two passengers on Mindanao right on schedule.

A most unusual mission then arose. MacArthur feared that Philippine President Manuel Quezon, in danger of capture by the Japanese, might decide to cooperate with the enemy. So he sent Bulkeley by PT boat to the island of Negros to bring Quezon back using whatever means were necessary, "whether he likes it or not." Bulkeley arrived at night at Quezon's front door to "rescue" him. Bulkeley was a frightening apparition, exhausted from the trip, dirty, bearded, and heavily and ostentatiously armed. With his long hair tied back with a bandanna, he looked like a pirate and had to use stern, unyielding diplomacy three times to convince the reluctant Quezon to come with him—once at the house, once more at the dock, and yet again when at sea.

When MacArthur flew to Australia, Bulkeley stayed in the islands. MacArthur, however, remained true to his PT boat crews. He ordered Bulkeley and the remaining crewmen—who were now completely out of boats—to Australia. MacArthur wanted veteran sailors to form new PT boat squadrons, return to the southwest Pacific, and work for him.

Bulkeley traveled to the United States, where he received a hero's welcome. He was the daring skipper who had raided Subic Bay. He was the blockade runner, the man who had saved MacArthur. Bulkeley was feted at huge parades, he spoke to crowds, and he encouraged factory workers to buy war bonds and increase their production efforts. He recruited new PT boat skippers from Ivy League universities. President Roosevelt awarded him the Medal of Honor (he already had the Navy Cross, two Distinguished Service Crosses, and an Army Silver Star). Bulkeley even gave a detailed report on the Philippine situation to Roosevelt.

Bulkeley disliked the speaking circuit. He had seen Japanese atrocities in China before the war, he hated the Japanese, and he wanted to fight them. Promoted to lieutenant commander, he took command of Motor Torpedo Squadron 7 in early October 1942, deployed to Australia in January 1943, and fought with his squadron of PT boats at the Battle of the Bismarck Sea and along the coast of New Guinea.

Bulkeley was high-strung, temperamental, and brave. His energy and desire for combat seemed limitless. He went out on patrol every chance he got, and his men held him in awe. Bulkeley threw himself into the fights, boarded another Japanese barge with drawn pistol, and personally shot an enemy soldier. He wreaked fierce vengeance on the Japanese until malaria felled him and sent him back to the United States in September 1943. The rest of his war would be in Europe.

John D. Bulkeley remained in the navy, retiring in 1975 as a vice admiral.

FURTHER READINGS

Breuer, W. *Sea Wolf: A Biography of John D. Bulkeley* (1989).

White, W. *They Were Expendable* (1972).

John W. Whitman

SEE ALSO Philippines, Fall of

Buna, Operations at

During the summer of 1942 both the Japanese and the Allies looked to occupy the northern coast of Papua, the Australian protectorate that made up the eastern part of New Guinea. The Japanese planned to seize Buna, site of an Australian government mission, and then send troops south along the Kokoda Trail, which wound over the rugged Owen Stanley Range, to capture the Allied base at Port Moresby on the southern coast of Papua. From there they could threaten Australia. The Allies, meanwhile, planned to build a base near Buna to support operations against the Japanese strongholds at Lae and Salamaua farther west along the coast as part of their strategic design to seize the Japanese base at Rabaul on the island of New Britain.

The Japanese won the race when, on July 22, troops from the South Seas Detachment landed at Buna. Over the next weeks Japanese forces snaked their way across the Owen Stanleys, continually outflanking Australian defensive positions. But the jungle took its toll, leaving many of their men sick and hungry, and with their supply line under steady attack from Major General George Kenney's well-run U.S. Fifth Air Force and Australian resistance stiffening as they neared Port Moresby, the Japanese began a retreat (one of their first of the war) to Buna on September 18, reaching it on November 7. There they carved out a narrow fortified zone, approximately sixteen miles long and several miles deep, along the coast. Within it the Japanese had strongpoints at Gona Village, the western anchor; Sanananda Point, in the center; Buna Village; Buna Mission; and Duropa Plantation, the eastern anchor.

In the meantime, General Douglas MacArthur, commander of the Southwest Pacific Area, launched an operation to capture the Buna-Gona zone, utilizing the Australian 7th Division and the American 32d Division, a National Guard division that had yet to see any action or even receive proper jungle training. The Australians pushed north along the Kokoda Trail in pursuit of the retreating Japanese, while a battalion from the 126th Infantry Regiment of the 32d Division crossed the Owen Stanleys on a parallel trail to the southeast. The remaining battalions of the 126th Infantry and the 128th Infantry Regiment were airlifted from Port Moresby to an airstrip about sixty miles southeast of Buna. From there they made their way by land and sea to the Buna sector. By the middle of November both the Australians and the Americans were in place for their final drive to push the Japanese into the sea.

MacArthur, persuaded by intelligence reports that the remaining Japanese in Papua were exhausted and not very numerous, expected an easy victory. In fact, he was in for a tough fight. Rather than the two thousand Japanese estimated to be in the Buna-Gona zone, there were approximately eight thousand. Their defensive positions, consisting of well-camouflaged bunkers and trenches, could be approached only by narrow trails through jungle and swamps. No assault from the sea was possible because of a lack of landing craft and because Vice Admiral Arthur Carpender, MacArthur's naval commander, would not risk his heavy ships in the waters off Buna out of fear of air attack and the treacherous reefs. To make matters worse, supply shortages, high humidity and temperatures, and jungle diseases quickly caused the morale of the inexperienced Americans to plunge.

If these problems were not enough, Major General Edwin F. Harding, commander of the 32d Division, had only one heavy artillery piece and no tanks, because MacArthur's staff had decided it would be too difficult to bring them to Buna and keep them supplied and because Kenney had boasted that his planes could substitute for artillery. Kenney had too few planes, however, and his pilots lacked the expertise to provide effective direct support where troops were close to the Japanese. For fire support Harding had to rely on light guns and mortars whose shells bounced off the log walls of the Japanese bunkers, forcing his men to try to knock them out by getting within a few yards of them and lobbing in hand grenades.

The Allied attack began on November 16. After meeting no serious opposition for two days, the Australians ran into heavy machine-gun fire and stalled at the outskirts of Gona. Another Australian thrust at Sanananda also fell short. At Buna, where the Japanese defensive position occupied an area about three and one-half miles long and three-quarters mile deep and contained about 3,450 naval troops, Harding faced a tactical nightmare. Because the sea made the Japanese flanks unapproachable, Harding had to send the 128th Infantry (his only force available, because the 126th Infantry had been sent to reinforce the Australians) in a frontal assault down two trails that were separated by impassable swamps and jungle. Encountering heavy machine-gun fire on November 19 from cleverly concealed networks of bunkers, both of his attacking forces—dubbed Urbana and Warren—made little headway.

MacArthur, lacking personal knowledge of conditions at Buna, ordered Harding to attack again and take Buna at once "regardless of cost." Given back a battalion of the 126th Infantry, Harding launched the attack on November 23. Units from the 126th Infantry got within 300 yards of Buna Village, but the 128th Infantry got nowhere. Short of supplies and with little to show for his efforts, Harding now became reluctant to order more assaults unless they had a good chance of success. Instead, he asked MacArthur for howitzers, tanks, and the division's third infantry regiment, the 127th Infantry. Under renewed pressure from MacArthur, Harding sent his forces forward in another attack on November 30; however, it was easily repulsed.

Even before the failure of Harding' latest attack, MacArthur had become agitated by the lack of progress at Buna. Australians, to his embarrassment, were making disparaging remarks about the morale and discipline of the 32d Division, and his difficulties in New Guinea contrasted sharply with the recent U.S. triumphs at Guadalcanal. At the end of November, MacArthur sent staff officers to look into the situation at Buna. They did not go to the front to see firsthand the conditions the troops faced and saw instead only the wounded, demoralized, and frustrated men in the rear, which led them to report that the officers of the 32d Division were unaggressive and that the men lacked the will to fight. Major General Richard K. Sutherland, MacArthur' chief of staff, advised Harding to make changes in the division's leadership, but Harding refused, apparently ready to take the heat for his subordinates.

The reports of his staff convinced MacArthur that the trouble at Buna was not the strength of the Japanese position and the 32d Division' need for proper weapons and reinforcements but Harding's leadership. As a result, on November 30 he sent Lieutenant General Robert Eichelberger, commander of the I Corps, to Buna, telling him, "Take Buna or don't come back alive." Arriving at Buna on December 1, Eichelberger, after a quick tour of the front, judged that the division was awash in inertia and combat avoidance. Following a bitter exchange with Harding over the division's leadership, Eichelberger relieved him, fired most of his regimental- and battalion-level officers, and made plans for a new attack.

In Eichelberger, MacArthur had a hard-nosed leader who understood that he was to "do something" and not be overly concerned about the "butcher's bill"—one of Harding's principal failings in MacArthur's eyes. Initially, however, when Eichelberger launched his own offensive on December 5, he had no more success than had Harding. But after a week of bloody fighting, a platoon from the 126th Infantry reached the sea, driving a wedge between Buna village and the mission, and on December 14 Americans overran the village. The Australians, meanwhile, captured Gona village on December 9.

Eichelberger's battlefield success was matched by an improving supply and manpower situation. Food supplies were now arriving in sufficient quantities, greatly boosting morale, and the tanks that Harding had requested also began to arrive. At the same time, there was an injection of fresh troops, including the 127th Infantry and two Australian infantry battalions, to reinforce the depleted 128th Infantry.

On December 18 Eichelberger launched another attack. Using tanks to envelop the Japanese bunkers and aided by the growing weariness and hunger of the defenders, U.S. and Australian infantry on the Warren front gradually pushed the Japanese back and seized Duropa Plantation. On the Urbana front, where the terrain could not support tanks, the infantry advanced slowly, fighting from tree to tree and bunker to bunker. Finally, the two forces linked up on December 28, and between December 31 and January 2, 1943, they flushed out the last Japanese from Buna mission and the surrounding jungle. Fighting concluded on January 22, when Australian and U.S. units—augmented by a recently arrived regiment from the 41st Division—wiped out the last Japanese pocket at Sanananda.

The elimination of the Buna–Gona stronghold ended the Papua campaign. During its five months the Japanese lost nearly 12,000 men. The Australians had 2,000 dead and wounded, and the 32d Division had 690 dead and 1,700 wounded. Another 2,900 men from the 32d Division were hospitalized suffering from tropical diseases. For the Allies the campaign was a significant victory. MacArthur now had airfields from which Kenney could cover future offensives, and the Americans had learned much about jungle combat and Japanese tactics that served them in good stead. Also, the campaign greatly influenced MacArthur's thinking. Mortified by the heavy Allied casualties, he concluded that similar battles should be avoided in the future. Thereafter, with "No more Bunas" as his watchword, he would try to avoid well-defended Japanese strongpoints and let them wither on the vine as he fought his way toward the Philippine Islands.

FURTHER READINGS

Anders, Leslie. *Gentle Knight: The Life and Times of Major General Edwin Forrest Harding* (1985).

Chwialkowski, Paul. *In Caesar's Shadow* (1993).

Doherty, Tom. "Buna: The Red Arrow Division's Heart of Darkness." *Wisconsin Magazine of History* (1993–1994).

James, D. Clayton. *The Years of MacArthur*, vol. 2 (1975).

Luvaas, Jay. "Buna, 19 November 1942–2 January 1943: A Leavenworth Nightmare." *America's First Battles, 1776–1965*, ed. Charles E. Eller and William A. Stofft (1986).

Mayo, Linda. *Bloody Buna* (1974).

Milner, Samuel. *Victory in Papua* (1957).

John Kennedy Ohl

SEE ALSO Eichelberger, Robert Lawrence; MacArthur, Douglas; New Guinea

Burma

The Japanese turned their eyes to Burma at the start of the Pacific war, for through that country flowed the supplies that were sustaining the Nationalist Chinese in their long war with the Japanese. Thus, a major reason for Japan's decision to go to war was to conclude the ongoing and interminable China War, so cutting those very lines of communications made Burma a priority target. The Japanese planned to turn Burma into the northern stronghold of their Southern Resources Area.

Japanese Conquest

Great Britain's major strategic objective was to hold as much of Burma as possible so as to keep open lines of communications north to Mandalay and China. The British desired to hold Burma if for no other reason than to keep Japanese aircraft out of range of Calcutta and northeast India. In addition, the loss of Burma would also encourage Indian nationalists to strengthen their demands to "Quit India!" Furthermore, Burma was something of the "rice basket" of that part of Asia, and its loss would seriously deplete food stocks in India, a nation subject at times to severe famine. And Burma also had large reserves of petroleum. Although reinforcements were required to hold the country, the British were slow to bring them in. They did not believe that Malaya would fall. They were also slow to accept Chinese aid because they did not think Chinese troops were needed. Numerous changes soon to occur in the British command structure meant differing views and troublesome communications at the top.

Lieutenant General Tom J. Hutton assumed command of Burma on December 27, 1941. Chiang Kai-shek considered the defense of Burma as the defense of China and promised troops for the country's defense. He tapped his Fifth and Sixth Armies for the mission. The British would never actually command these Chinese troops, for Chinese commanders took orders only from Chungking. The

British needed to gain time to bring in the Chinese troops from the north as well as British reinforcements through Rangoon. Unfortunately, British troops dispatched for Burma were diverted to Malaya as the situation there deteriorated.

The Japanese Southern Army had area responsibility for Burma. Lieutenant General Shojiro Iida's 35,440-man strong Fifteenth Army with the 33d and 55th Divisions and the 10th Air Brigade had the mission of seizing Burma. Fifteenth Army had served as the right flank guard to Yamashita's Twenty-Fifth Army as it drove into Malaya. Fifteenth Army entered Bangkok on December 8. The first Japanese incursion into Burma, on a small scale, occurred on December 11 when they seized the British air base at Victoria Point.

Fifteenth Army began its air campaign on December 23 with a major attack against Rangoon's airfield and dock area, as yet unprotected by antiaircraft guns. The Royal Air Force and the American Volunteer Group ("Flying Tigers") intercepted them and inflicted some casualties. The Japanese attack served a purpose, however, for it drove off large numbers of dock and city workers, sent many Indian residents of Rangoon on a desperate hike toward India, and left the port short of labor.

The Japanese continued their air operations into late January and through late February 1942 but suffered such heavy losses that they finally abandoned attempts to shut down Rangoon's port. (This Allied air success was in distinct contrast to the skies over Malaya/Singapore, where the Japanese ruled supreme.) This was important. Burma had no land link with India, and all supplies sent into Burma's interior came through Rangoon. The city was the base through which the British supported the defense of Burma. General Hutton was concerned about the possible loss of Rangoon, so he ordered the evacuation of Rangoon's reserve stocks 260 miles north to the Mandalay area.

While the air battles raged, Fifteenth Army concentrated its ground forces, converted much of its wheeled transport to horse and cattle, and improved roads (with the enthusiastic support of the Thais) to the frontier. Large-scale ground operations began on January 20 when the 55th Division attacked. Speed for the Japanese would be critical, for Fifteenth Army support and transportation troops were ridiculously few and totally inadequate to meet the logistical demands of an army. The men would have to conquer quickly before they ran out of food and ammunition.

The 16th Brigade of Major General John Smyth's 17th Indian Division (with few experienced officers, a high number of recruits, and new weapons on which they had not yet trained) absorbed the Japanese attack, lost most of its transport, and fell back. None of the division's three Indian brigades had trained at brigade level, nor had the division trained as a division. Tactically, the British would have been better off to have concentrated their men, but strategically they needed to engage the Japanese as far forward as possible so as to gain time. Strategy took precedence over tactics.

The Japanese seized the first major town, Moulmain, east of Rangoon across the Gulf of Martaban, on January 30–31, 1942. It was a hard and costly fight for the Japanese. The 2d Burma Brigade of the 1st Burma Division defended the town, inflicted numerous casualties on the Japanese, and then spirited away 75 percent of its men by river steamers as the Japanese entered. The 17th Indian Division then deployed to hold the Salween River (95 miles due east of Rangoon), but the long river had many crossing points. The Japanese crossed on February 9. Gurkha counterattacks broke up the first roadblock the Japanese established, but additional crossings soon had the two Japanese divisions across the river. The 17th Indian Division, fighting without antitank guns and field artillery, withdrew.

The first major fight, however, would take place at the Bilin River, 75 miles northeast of Rangoon. Once again, however, the river was fordable almost everywhere. The Japanese were marching cross-country so swiftly that their lead elements got across the Bilin before the motorized British could set up behind the river! British counterattacks on February 17 failed to budge the Japanese. More Japanese crossed on February 18 despite British counterattacks. The British decided to withdraw.

The 17th Indian Division broke contact and moved 17 miles to the large Sittang River, 65 miles northeast of Rangoon, a city normally holding a half million people. Withdrawing to the Sittang meant that the line of communications to China would be cut, for the road and railroad north out of Rangoon would come under Japanese artillery fire. Rangoon's air defenders would have to withdraw west into eastern India, for air warning would be too short to continue to use the field.

The 17th Division began to funnel its transport across the single-lane bridge over the broad, unfordable Sittang the night of February 21–22, 1942, but a vehicle jammed on the bridge and delayed movement. The Japanese had in the meantime been engaged in a heroic cross-country foot march that lasted fifty-six hours and placed them near the Sittang. On the morning of February 22, Japanese forces attacked the east bank defenses out of the northeast. Additional attacks continued into the night.

Although the Indian troops were holding, confusion was so great that the soldiers in charge of bridge demolition believed most of the division had crossed the river. Fearful of losing the bridge to the Japanese, the demolition party on the west bank blew the bridge at 0530 hours on February 23. Loss of the bridge trapped most of the 17th Division on the east bank. The 17th Division troops abandoned their equipment and weapons and swam or rafted across the mile-wide river.

The situation stabilized for the moment. The Japanese had learned that British reinforcements continued to arrive at Rangoon's port and that Chinese armies were moving south into Burma. Speed was important, but so were supplies and river-crossing equipment. Their attack into Burma had been accomplished without a supply line. Everything they used had been carried or captured. Fifteenth Army now had to reestablish contact with its base.

Both the 33d and 55th Divisions crossed the Sittang on March 3 against negligible resistance. Small British counterattacks made no impression on the Japanese. Retreating is a hard habit to break, and the British succumbed to the urge once again. But Lieutenant General Harold Alexander arrived on March 5 and stopped that process. He wanted to hold Rangoon. He ordered the 63d Indian Brigade and the recently arrived 7th Armored Brigade to counterattack. Bitter fighting resulted, and there were some British successes. But the overall situation did not change. Rangoon was doomed.

The Rangoon denial scheme went into effect on March 7. General Hutton had wanted to begin demolitions on February 27, but General Archibald Wavell, Supreme Commander of ABDA, had resisted. Rangoon must be held. So now, on March 7, it was too late to do everything that should have been done. In the midst of civilian looting and large-scale arson, military engineers blew up or set fire to refineries and oil storage tanks, power stations, and public buildings. Shipping berths and storage sheds in the dock area went up in flames, and men smashed wharf equipment. They could not get it all, and many warehouses and jetties remained intact. Hundreds of river craft remained afloat. Large stocks of military stores, timber, coal, steel rails, and bridging materiel were abandoned. In fact, the port remained sufficiently intact that the Japanese would supply all the divisions they ever deployed in Burma and India through Rangoon's facilities.

The Japanese had already slipped men behind the British line of retreat and established one of their patented roadblocks. Attacks on March 7 by the 17th Indian Division and 7th Armored Brigade failed to reduce it, and it looked as though the entire British force might be trapped. Just before the British launched an all-out attack the next morning, the Japanese unexpectedly withdrew.

The Japanese had turned south toward Rangoon. They expected that the British would fight for Rangoon and were afraid that their activities on the road north out of the city would compromise their plan to outflank the city from the north. So they withdrew their men and marched south toward Rangoon even as the British retreated north. The Japanese took Rangoon on March 8, realized the British had withdrawn, and quickly pursued. But even the hard-marching Japanese infantry could not regain contact.

The fall of Rangoon cut China off from Western aid; deprived the Allies of Burma's rice, oil, timber, and minerals; and cut off the British Burma Army from all seaborne supplies. Japan could reinforce and resupply its Burma army by sea rather than over the difficult land trek. The British hoped to hold Mandalay in central Burma, protect the supplies they had evacuated before the fall of Rangoon, and hold the road into China. Only two weak British divisions, 150 aircraft, and two Chinese armies (each equivalent to a British division) faced the Japanese.

The Japanese began to exploit the advantages of sea lines of communications. The 7th and 12th Air Brigades and the 56th and 18th Divisions were en route. Additional forces included two tank regiments, two heavy field artillery regiments, two independent engineer regiments, and antitank, antiaircraft, signal, and line-of-communications troops. Burma's southern airfields were available to support Japanese air operations. With this disparity in forces, all the British and Chinese could do in central and upper Burma was to delay their enemy as much as possible.

U.S. Lieutenant General Joseph W. Stilwell's Chinese forces (nine divisions operated in Burma) fought magnificently in some cases, but Stilwell was hamstrung by the command setup, which required Chiang Kai-shek's approval before Chinese commanders would obey him. His men retreated into China between May 11 and 30.

Japanese attacks in mid-April inflicted heavy casualties on the 1st Burma Division and cost it much of its transport. The British Burma Corps (Burcorps) with 1st Burma Division, 17th Indian Division, and 7th Armored Brigade began its withdrawal to the Irrawaddy River on the night of April 25–26. The British abandoned burnt-out Mandalay on April 29. Burcorps' fighting retreat back to India concluded the longest such action in British history. Britain's new strategic objective was the protection of northeast India. Building the logistics to support that defense was now a top priority.

The Japanese had driven the British out of Burma through superior light infantry tactics (as in Malaya/Singapore, the British forces had outnumbered their opponents), had inflicted 13,463 British casualties and had suffered 4,957 of their own. The Japanese had left their heavy artillery behind, marched and fought thirty-four battles and skirmishes, and covered 1,500 miles of rugged ground. The most that could be said of the Allied defense of Burma—aside from acknowledging personal heroism—was that they had made a better fight than had their compatriots in the defence of Malaya/Singapore. With the loss of Burma, Allied strategy here would be directed toward recapturing enough of the country to secure an air route to China and to reopen the ground route. But it would be a long march for the Allies.

FURTHER READINGS

Hattori, Takushiro. *The Complete History of the Greater East Asia War,* vol. 2 (1953).
Kirby, S. Woodburn. *The War against Japan,* vol. II, *India's Most Dangerous Hour* (1958).

John W. Whitman

SEE ALSO Army, Japanese; Malaya, Japanese Conquest of

British Reconquest

Having gained their envisaged defensive perimeter, the Japanese went over to the defensive along the northeastern frontier of India. Fearing a Japanese invasion of India or the severing of communications with Chiang Kai-shek's beleaguered Nationalist forces in China, the Allies planned counteroffensive operations to improve communications with China and regain coastal airfields and ports. But more pressing strategic priorities elsewhere denuded the CBI (China-Burma-India) theater of resources, especially amphibious assault capacity. Ill-supported Allied forces were, therefore, capable only of very limited counteroffensive operations during 1942–1943.

The only major Allied initiatives carried out during the 1942–1943 dry season was an attack on Akyab and long-range penetration operations by Chindit irregular forces across the Chindwin River. The Arakan campaign, as the attack toward Akyab became known, ended in failure. At the same time, the Chindits, entirely resupplied by air, advanced well into the enemy rear to cut the Mandalay-Myitkyina railroad and harass enemy rearward control and communications. After initial success, however, the Japanese closed in on the Chindits, who were forced to disperse and make their way back to India in small groups. With heavy loss in troops and equipment and consider-able expenditure of precious supplies and aerial resources, the Chindit operation failed to achieve a great deal tangibly. However, news of even their limited success helped to boost morale generally and largely offset the disappointment of the failure of the Arakan expedition.

Reorganization of British command during the summer of 1943 placed the talented Lieutenant General William J. Slim, a man of lower-middle-class origins who had advanced from the ranks during the World War I, in charge of a new Fourteenth Army tasked with recapturing Burma. Slim immediately and energetically set about refitting his army for offensive operations to be carried out during the spring of 1944 before the summer monsoon arrived. He developed a good understanding of Japanese offensive doctrine and sought to retrain and to prepare his troops with the logical counters to the enemy's techniques. He emphasized that his forces should stand and fight if the enemy cut their rearward communications, rather than adopt the demoralizing withdrawals of previous campaigns. He also pledged to resupply any such isolated units by air and to prepare relief measures to rescue the trapped troops. To uphold these promises, Slim required good ground-to-air coordination and set about forging a close accord with the Third Tactical Air Force. In addition, he stressed that Fourteenth Army must utilize deception and surprise to compensate for its numerical and material deficiencies.

In November 1943 Slim appreciated that the Japanese intended to launch their own offensive across the Chindwin, and he launched a preemptive strike with a renewed attack by his XV Corps into the Arakan in order to gain a firm hold of the high ground in front of his lateral lines of communication, as well as to protect his right flank and airfields in East Bengal. By late January 1944 Slim had achieved most of his limited objectives; his success forced the Japanese to launch prematurely and piecemeal their planned offensive as a counterattack.

The new Japanese offensive operations did, however, disrupt Slim's preparations for more substantial counteroffensive operations during the spring of 1944. The two British attacks into the Arakan had demonstrated the vulnerability of the Japanese front, and thus in late January 1944 the Japanese Fifteenth Army struck across the Chindwin in force in an attempt to seize the Imphal plain and to establish a more defensible line in Assam. Slim quickly and correctly read the enemy's intentions and decided to fight with IV Corps on the Imphal plain, which enhanced his aerial superiority and marginal advantage in armor. Nevertheless, Slim's forces were still outnumbered, and the Japanese advance managed to surround the 7th Indian Division along with elements of the 5th Indian Division.

In accordance with his previous instructions, Slim ordered these formations to hold fast. At the same time, he activated his plan for air resupply and organized a relief force made up of 26th and 36th Indian Divisions to restore the situation. As a result, the Japanese Fifteenth Army was badly mauled between the counterattack forces and the determined resistance of the beleaguered Indian divisions. The remnants of the Japanese invasion force was compelled to disperse and to retreat in fragments through the jungle. This success convinced even skeptics of the validity of Slim's approach and boosted troop morale.

The Japanese responded to this setback by reinforcing their Burma Area Command and again striking across the Chindwin in strength on March 12, 1944, in a renewed attempt to gain a better defensive front by capturing the important communications center of Imphal. This unexpected renewal of offensive action by the Japanese compelled the 17th and 20th Indian Divisions to make a fighting withdrawal. While the latter successfully retired and beat off all Japanese attacks, the enemy managed to isolate the 17th Division north of Tiddim, and a relief force had to rescue the formation before it could retire and take up defensive positions outside Imphal on April 5. A new Japanese push toward the important rail junction of Kohima then threatened Slim's communications and forced him to rush reinforcements, including the fresh XXXIII Corps from India, to the Imphal sector.

Between April and May 1944 IV Corps ably supported by the Third Tactical Air Force fought a protracted battle of attrition with the enemy, who continued to advance on Imphal. By mid-May Fourteenth Army had ground the Japanese offensive to a halt, and Slim then assumed the offensive. By June 22 he had badly beaten the Japanese amid the difficult conditions of jungle fighting and laid the preconditions for an advance into Burma.

After his victory at Imphal, Slim realized that to operate effectively in the 1944–1945 dry season he must immediately exploit his success by gaining control of the crossings over the Chindwin. Despite atrocious monsoon conditions, he advanced through difficult terrain, to seize the Chindwin crossings at Sittang and Kalewa. He then organized lines of communication via Tamu through the Kalew Valley to Kalewa. During the late summer of 1944 Slim prepared to engage and to destroy the enemy on the Shwebo Plain in December via a pincer movement on Mandalay, but growing evidence of Japanese preparations for a general withdrawal behind the formidable obstacle of the Irrawaddy River forced him to revise his plans.

Instead, he now decided to make a deep strike for Meiktila, the base and communications center on which the Japanese defense of both Mandalay and the Irrawaddy depended. This daring 300-mile advance through the jungle could succeed only if Slim could deceive the enemy regarding his intentions. Aided by wireless deception and air superiority, he secretly redeployed IV Corps from Tamu to Pokokku on the Irrawaddy within striking distance of Meiktila. In the meantime XXXIII Corps launched a frontal assault across the Irrawaddy on Mandalay, which drew Japanese reserves to this sector. Once the Japanese reserves were fully committed, IV Corps struck across the Irrawaddy and captured Meiktila on March 3, 1945. The Japanese were thrown off balance by this daring and lightning strike, and Mandalay also fell, on March 20. From March 15 to 30, Japanese troops fiercely but futilely counterattacked to regain Meiktila but suffered such heavy losses in the process that the Japanese Fifteenth Army was effectively neutralized.

While the fighting for Mandalay-Meiktila was still going on, Slim was already preparing the way for an advance on Rangoon.

He again relied heavily on air resupply as his forces dashed for the city before the monsoon arrived. In a combined assault, Rangoon fell on May 2, 1945, as the first monsoon rains began to fall. Thus, in a remarkable feat, operating with very limited resources and with an army that had been previously badly beaten, Slim overcame a powerful opponent to regain Burma with only marginal superiority in the air as well as on the ground. His success was based on correct appreciation of Japanese methods and intentions and vigorous retraining of the troops under his command with techniques—deception, aerial resupply, and holding fast—that ultimately vanquished the enemy. With all this in mind, some authorities have claimed that William Slim (later Viscount Slim of Burma) was likely the best commander produced by Great Britain throughout World War II, and certainly one of the best of any belligerent in the Pacific war.

FURTHER READINGS
Allen, L. *Burma, the Longest War 1941–1945* (1984).
Bidwell, S. *The Chindit War: Stilwell, Wingate, and the Campaign in Burma* (1980).
Liang, C. *General Stilwell in China, 1942–44: The Full Story* (1972).
Romanus, Charles, and R. Sunderland. *Stilwell's Mission to China*, U.S. Army in World War II (1953).
——— and ———. *Stilwell's Command Problems*, U.S. Army in World War II (1956).
——— and ———. *Time Runs Out in CBI*, U.S. Army in World War II (1959).
Slim, W. Viscount. *Defeat into Victory* (1956).

Spector, Ronald H. *Eagle against the Sun: The American War with Japan* (1985).

Stilwell, Joseph W. *The Stilwell Papers,* ed. Theodore H. White (1948).

Tuchman, Barbara W. *Stilwell and the American Experience in China, 1911–45* (1971).

White, Theodore H., and Annalee Jacoby, *Thunder out of China* (1946).

Russell A. Hart

SEE ALSO Bose, Subhas Chandra; Burma Road

Burma Road

A motor road constructed by the Chinese Nationalist government to provide an avenue for outside aid in the war against Japan, and that later figured prominently in Allied strategic planning, the Burma Road was a marvelous feat of ingenuity and persistence. It stretched more than 700 miles from Kunming, China, westward to Lashio in Burma, where materials and munitions arrived by rail and road from the port of Rangoon. This "back door to China" was closed in the spring of 1942 by the Japanese conquest of Burma and was not reopened until January 1945. By then, Allied successes elsewhere had greatly reduced the significance of the road in the plans to defeat Japan.

Hard pressed by battlefield successes of the Imperial Japanese Army in the opening stages invasion of China in 1937, the government of Chaing Kai-shek (Jiang Jieshi) removed to Nanking and finally to Chunking, atop the impregnable bluffs of the Yangtze River. The invaders soon captured all of the coast, severing Chiang's sea routes to outside assistance; the Gobi Desert to the northwest and the Himalayas to the southwest rendered overland aid all but impossible. To secure a lifeline to Western sympathizers, the Nationalist government ordered construction of a drivable road through the mountain passes of Yunnan province into the uplands of the British colony of Burma, over which cargo might continue to enter China.

Construction of the Burma Road, which began in December 1937, was a monumental achievement in several ways. First, the route traversed 600 miles of some of the most inhospitable terrain in China, if not the world, with a further 116 miles of arduous construction in upland Burma. Approximately two-thirds of the route in China had trails and some roadbed upon which to build, but 280 miles of completely new construction was required, some of it across unstable soils, steep mountains, and rivers with swift currents. One mountain required five months of effort by three thousand workers for the roadbed to be cut. About 250 miles of the route traversed solid rock; the most difficult stretch was near the Salween River, where the highway ascended 4,800 feet in 18 miles. Nevertheless, surveying was completed in seven months instead of the two years normally required, and construction was completed in less than a year. The lack of heavy machinery and the impossibility of acquiring any until the road was opened presented the second significant obstacle to completing the project. The British were able to build the Burmese segment of the road with modern machinery, but the Chinese lacked such equipment. Using only crude tools powered by human muscles, laborers in China removed 36 million cubic yards of earth and cut through 3,860,000 yards of rock, then surfaced the entire length of the road with 1-inch stones, set by hand. A hundred limestone rollers, each weighing 3 to 5 tons and pulled by dozens of men, substituted for machinery, though at the cost of many deaths and injuries, especially on the steep grades of the road's westernmost portions. The scarcity of dynamite led to further casualties because the Chinese resorted to thousands of smaller, fuse-lit detonations of gunpowder each day.

More than two hundred engineers and 160,000 laborers built the Chinese portion of the road almost literally by hand, with never fewer than 20,000 workers toiling on the project at any one time. Because the highway snaked through some of the least populated areas of China, thousands of laborers had to be transported to the road, some from as far as 200 miles away. Moving these swarms of workers and then supporting them with the bare necessities of life were prodigious logistic feats in themselves.

Though the straight-line distance from Kunming to Lashio is 320 miles, the Burma Road stretched 716 miles through the rugged countryside. The roadbed was 23 feet wide for much of its length, the middle 10 feet covered with gravel. The road crossed more than 4,500 culverts, many originally of bamboo, and nearly 500 bridges. Because of the swift currents and solid limestone river bottoms of the Salween, Mekong, and Yangpi rivers, the Chinese had to bridge these waterways with single-span suspension designs, the longest of which was 410 feet. Materials for these engineering marvels were hauled 300 miles from Lashio to the bridge sites by mules and humans.

Traffic on the Burma Road commenced in late 1938, though the primitive nature of the surface, the steep grades, a relative paucity of motor vehicles, and the problems of maintaining the artery under trying weather and terrain conditions kept deliveries light. Construction crews, now with American technical advisers, continued to improve the road's quality by reducing grades and turn radii, replacing wooden and bamboo structures with metal constructions, removing outcroppings prone to landslides, and adding backup bridges across the three great rivers. Thousands of workers and, in emergencies, conscripted villagers labored to keep the Burma Road open in the face of bridge washouts, mudslides, and intermittent Japanese air attacks. As many as a hundred landslides occurred in a 20-mile stretch of the road; and one of the worst, in October 1941, halted seven hundred trucks near Kunming until makeshift maintenance crews removed 120,000 cubic feet of earth in seventy-two hours of continuous effort. Even when it was open, the condition of the highway limited trucks to a top speed of 12 miles per hour. A one-way trip over the Burma Road normally took six days, and trucks wore out after two or three round trips.

Before 1941, the average number of trucks on the road at any given time was a hundred, with perhaps a few passenger vehicles, except during the May through October rainy season, when traffic dwindled by as much as 85 percent. In 1941, more trucks arrived from the United States and Great Britain, and deliveries to China rose to between 10,000 and 15,000 tons per month. Cargo included vitally needed raw materials, machinery and equipment, munitions, and other supplies to support China's war effort. For instance, in April 1941 the war materiel sent to China by the United States via the Burma Road amounted to 710 tons of TNT and other explosives, 117 cases of aircraft parts, eighty machine guns, and four cases of machine gun accessories. Great Britain, Italy, and Germany also sent military equipment and ammunition to the Chinese, along with cement, steel, motor vehicles, copper wire, machine tools, and petroleum products. On the return trips, the trucks brought out tungsten, antimony, wolfram, tung oil, silk, and other items to alleviate Nationalist China's surging trade deficit. Though the bulk of the carriers were under contract to Chiang's government and operated by Chinese drivers, smuggling and black market trading were rampant.

In July 1940, under intense diplomatic pressure from Japan and harried by the recent defeat of France and the prospect of an invasion of the British Isles, an embattled Great Britain agreed to close the Burma Road for three months. Prime Minister Winston Churchill announced the reopening of the road on October 8, and there were no serious interruptions of traffic again until the Japanese captured Lashio, the road's western terminus, in late April 1942, during their conquest of Burma. The Chinese then tore up the first 15 miles of the road inside their borders to deny the route for any Japanese offensive uses.

Now isolated from outside aid, Chiang's government faced perhaps its severest crisis of the war. U.S. planners quickly initiated a dangerous air route over the Himalayas to keep some assistance coming to the beleaguered Chinese, but the ultimate capacity of these flights "over the Hump" was strictly limited. Allied planners were confronted by the grave possibility that Chiang's China might make a separate peace with the invaders, freeing up major Japanese military assets and denying the Allies the use of Chinese territory as a base for the eventual assault on the Japanese home islands. For the Allies, reopening the Burma Road was thus an issue bound up with judgments about the value of the Chinese military effort and the optimum routes by which the Japanese empire might be penetrated and defeated.

Claire Chennault, commander of U.S. air forces in China and an influential adviser to Chiang, advised expanding the aerial supply route in order to sustain his air offensive against the Japanese, which he predicted would be sufficient to end the war, at minimal cost. This strategic vision was opposed by U.S. Army General Joseph Stilwell, Chiang's chief of staff and commanding general of the Chinese field forces in the Burma area, who argued that only an overland route could supply the large-scale land operations necessary to save China and establish a base for the final offensives against Japan itself. With the backing of Army Chief of Staff George C. Marshall, Stilwell's view prevailed. On their return flights from China, "Hump" transport aircraft began carrying recruits to India to be trained into an army to recapture northern Burma from the Japanese. In late 1942, American engineers began building a road from Ledo, in the northeastern Indian province of Assam, toward the Burma Road north of Lashio, at Mongyu, 478 miles away through the trackless, monsoon-ravaged, and heavily overgrown hills of northern Burma. Construction of the Ledo Road, as this new approach to the Burma Road was called, was another feat of remarkable engineering skill and perseverance.

The Ledo Road reached Mongyu in January 1945, just behind the advancing Chinese armies. The combined Burma and Ledo roads now stretched 1,079 miles from Ledo to Kunming, and the entire route was designated the Stilwell Road in honor of its chief advocate. A convoy of cargo trucks, prime movers towing artillery pieces, weapons carriers, jeeps, and maintenance vehicles departed from Ledo on January 12 and, delayed twice by fighting along the way, reached Kunming seventeen days later. Regular convoy service commenced on February 1. Original plans called for the employment of Chinese drivers, but their lack of training resulted in inordinate losses of vehicles and cargo. When emergency training programs failed to correct this deficiency, the problem was solved by hiring Indian operators for the segments of the Stilwell Road in Burma, freeing up American truck drivers, many of them African Americans who volunteered to drive to Kunming, for the portions in China.

From January 1945 until the Japanese surrender in August, the Allies delivered 25,000 vehicles and 120,000 tons of cargo to Kunming over the Stilwell Road. American engineers had built dual pipelines along the route that ultimately became more valuable than the highway itself. The route's capacity could have been multiplied severalfold with asphalt paving and other improvements to the roadbed, as called for in earlier plans, but by the time land communications with China were reopened in early 1945, events elsewhere had robbed the road of much of its strategic meaning. Cargo reaching China over the Stilwell Road in 1945 amounted to less than half of what was flown in by the expanded "Hump" operation in the same period, and U.S. advances in the Pacific obviated the necessity for Chinese bases for the final assault on Japan. The subject of intense controversy and the object of enormous expenditures of material and engineering skill, the Burma Road, in the end, proved to be a strategic dead end.

FURTHER READINGS

Anders, Leslie. *The Ledo Road* (1965).
Fischer, Edward. *The Chancy War* (1991).
Stilwell, Joseph W. *Stilwell's Personal File—China, Burma, India, 1942–1944* (1976).
Tarling, Nicholas. *Britain, Southeast Asia and the Onset of the Pacific War* (1996).
Tuchman, Barbara W. *Stilwell and the American Experience in China, 1911–1945* (1970).

Mark P. Parillo

SEE ALSO Chiang Kai-shek; Chennault, Claire Lee; Stilwell, Joseph Warren

Bushido

Bushido was originally a code of conduct for the samurai, the warrior class of feudal Japan. The term literally means "the way [do] of the warrior [bushi]." Basic principles of Bushido developed during and in the centuries of warfare before the Kamakura Shogunate (1192–1333). The term came into normal usage during the stable Tokugawa Shogunate (1603–1867), when the samurai were subordinated to the will of the state and the literary classic *Hagakure* (1716) was written.

This warrior code was based on concepts of Zen Buddhism, which provided its martial or warlike nature, and later of Confucianism, which instilled social responsibility. Yet it required loyalty to one's feudal lord (daimyo) above all else. Major principles of Bushido were based on honor, duty, courage, and a willingness to sacrifice one's self in battle or in ritual suicide. Possession of a warrior spirit and mastery of the horse, bow, and sword represented other attributes of this ethical code.

With the Meiji Restoration in 1868 and abolition of the samurai class and the feudal structure on which it was based, Bushido was for a time subordinated to Western concepts of modernization. This subordination was short-lived, and by the late nineteenth century Bushido was deliberately both revived and revised so that it could be used to infuse Japanese of all social classes with its martial and ethical teachings. These principles were elaborated to Westerners in Inazo Nitobe's influential *Bushido: The Soul of Japan,* which was translated into English in 1900.

Bushido had a pronounced influence on the modernized Japanese military system of the early to middle twentieth century. At the Battle of Tsushima in 1904, Admiral Togo, on the bridge of battleship *Mikasa,* proved his "warrior spirit" in a famed incident. During a critical part of the battle, his second in command was given permission to take in his hand the admiral's testicles, which, not being seized up, showed the admiral's bravery. This incident was followed by the seppuku (ritual suicide) of General Maresuke, a Russo-Japanese War (1904–1905) hero, who on hearing of the death of the Meiji emperor in 1912 took part in a practice known as junshi as a statement of extreme loyalty to his fallen lord.

Before World War II, the philosophy of Bushido was taught to Japanese schoolchildren. With Japan militarizing in the 1930s, the more martial attributes of this warrior code began to be stressed, among all civilians. (A possibly apocryphal story tells of the Japanese locomotive engineer who, shamed by bringing in a new train on its inaugural run a trifling few minutes late, committed seppuku on the Tokyo station platform: His Imperial Majesty, the emperor, had been on board.) Instances where conscripts took copies of the *Hagakure* or Nitobe's *Bushido* with them to the front became common. In the Pacific conflict Bushido thus came to help define the spirit and actions of the Japanese armed forces.

Following the teachings of this code, no provision was made for the surrender of Japanese military forces. Furthermore, the code's promotion of sacrificial death served to explain the suicide charges undertaken by defeated Japanese infantry forces, whose sword-wielding officers and men preferred death to the dishonor of being captured.

The willingness of kamikaze pilots and kaitan submarine crews—who also engaged in suicide attacks on Allied warships toward the end of the war—becomes clear.

For all these noble examples of self-sacrifice and duty, a darker side to Bushido also existed. Because this warrior code lacked notions of humility which were found in such Western concepts as the chivalric code, social inferiors and nonwarriors were generally held in contempt. As an outcome of this lack of sympathy, numerous atrocities took place against both prisoners of war and conquered civil populations during World War II. Such atrocities included the rape of Nanking, the Bataan death march, and the sack of Manila, which resulted in the deaths of hundreds of thousands of innocent people and, in the process, brought lasting dishonor to this warrior code. With this in mind, the Japanese could count themselves fortunate that, despite their fears, the U.S. military occupiers of postwar Japan did not abide by any such code of Bushido.

FURTHER READINGS

Collcutt, Martin C. "Bushido." *Kodansha Encyclopedia of Japan,* vol. 1 (1983).

Inazo, Nitobe. *Bushido: The Soul of Japan; An Exposition of Japanese Thought* (1970; reprint of 1905 edition).

Newman, John. *Bushido: The Way of the Warrior; A New Perspective on the Japanese Military Tradition* (1989).

Wilson, William Scott, trans. *Hagakure: The Book of the Samurai* (1979).

Yamamoto Tsunetomo. *Hagakure* (1716).

Robert J. Bunker

SEE ALSO Army, Japanese

Cabanatuan Raid

In December 1941, Japanese forces invaded the Philippine Islands. On the main island of Luzon, the Japanese moved quickly toward the capital city of Manila. In a short time, American and Filipino military forces retreated into the Bataan Peninsula, west of Manila and across Manila Bay. After several months of bitter fighting, the ill-supplied troops surrendered. Sick and injured American and Filipino soldiers were gathered up and forced to walk 65 miles to railway transfer points. Along this trail, thousands of prisoners perished under inhumane treatment at the hands of the Japanese. This was the Bataan death march. Many of the captured were interned in the Philippines; however, some were shipped out to other prisoner of war camps throughout the Japanese Empire in the Western Pacific. Over the next three years, thousands of American and Filipino prisoners died from abuse, malnutrition, and disease. By 1945, only a remnant of the defeated U.S. and Philippine armies remained alive on Luzon.

On January 9, 1945, U.S. Army forces landed on Luzon. The U.S. Sixth Army, consisting of the I Corps and XIV Corps, landed unopposed at Lingayen Gulf. As U.S. soldiers moved toward Manila, Japanese resistance stiffened. In late January, Filipino guerilla leaders reported to Sixth Army officials that up to five hundred American prisoners of war were being held 5 miles from Cabanatuan City. The prison camp was only 25 miles from the front lines of the U.S. 6th Infantry Division, which was rapidly approaching the vicinity. General Douglas MacArthur and Sixth Army commander General Walter Krueger feared that Japanese prison guards might kill the captives as U.S. forces neared the camp. Because time was of the essence, General Krueger called for a raid to rescue the remaining survivors of the Bataan death march.

For the rescue mission, Krueger tapped the U.S. Sixth Ranger Battalion, commanded by Lieutenant Colonel Henry C. Mucci. Previously, the battalion had been used in only a limited fashion throughout the Southwest Pacific; the raid would be the first major test of their combat skills. On January 27, Colonel Mucci met with army intelligence (G-2) officers who gave him the most recent information available on enemy troop concentrations. According to G-2 officers, there were approximately eight hundred Japanese near Cabanatuan City. Local roads were of little use because they swarmed with troops and armor attempting to block advancing American units. One issue that army intelligence officers stressed during their meeting with Mucci was surprise. If the Japanese were alerted of the impending raid, they would kill the prisoners before the rescue took place. An Alamo Scout team was sent out to reconnoiter and gather intelligence on the camp. Colonel Mucci also arranged for a P-61 Black Widow night fighter warplane to provide air cover and for the assistance of local Filipino guerilla units during the raid. Quickly, Mucci returned to the Rangers encampment to prepare for the upcoming attack.

Sixth Army gave Colonel Mucci complete authority to plan the tactical aspects of the raid. Overall planning for the raid took almost eight hours and was updated when new information arrived from the Alamo Scouts. The rescue force consisted of 128 Rangers, Alamo Scouts, and Filipino guerillas. The Rangers carried rations, trench knifes, rifles, machine guns, and bazookas. The next morning the Ranger force left by truck to Guimba. From Guimba the Rangers moved to the village of Balincarin, 5 miles from the prison site. Over the next day and a half, Alamo Scouts continued to observe the camp and continued information on troop numbers and perimeter strength. On January 29, by coincidence, more than two hundred Japanese soldiers reinforced the camp's 223 man guard detail. Despite this setback, the raid was planned for the following evening.

At nightfall on January 30, the rescue force assembled 700 yards away from the camp. As dusk turned into night, the Rangers walked at first, and then crawled toward the camp. Overhead a P-61 buzzed the camp drawing attention from the approaching Rangers. At 1944 hours the attack began. Dozens of Rangers rushed the camp, killing the outside guards. Once inside the camp, one-half of the Rangers eliminated the remaining guards, while the others searched for prisoners. When gunfire erupted, prisoners in the barracks feared the worst—that the Japanese were summarily killing prisoners. Rangers yelled for the prisoners to move toward the front gate. Most captives were in a state of shock, and many of the sick or injured needed assistance. By 2115 the attack had ended. The Ranger force and 512 prisoners prepared to return to American lines.

The mission, however, was far from over. As the group of Rangers and prisoners left the area, a Japanese relief force quickly advanced toward the campsite. Filipino guerillas held off these intruders, while the rescue team left. A major problem was the prisoners' condition. After three years of captivity, many were too sick to make the long 25 mile night march. Along the way, the Rangers appropriated large carts to carry the sick and the wounded. Colonel Mucci tried to raise the U.S. Sixth Army by radio, but contact was never established. After hours of marching in the jungles the group of exhausted Rangers and prisoners reached Sibul, where they were able to contact the U.S. Sixth Army for relief. Soon trucks and ambulances arrived and transported them back to American lines. Though hastily planned, the Cabanatuan raid was a tremendous success. It was a textbook case of the use of tactical surprise and security. Hundreds of prisoners were saved with the loss of only two Rangers. The Japanese losses were staggering—more than two hundred were killed in the attack.

FURTHER READINGS

Breuer, William. *Retaking the Philippines: America's Return to Corregidor and Bataan, October 1944–March 1945* (1986).

Krueger, Walter. *From Down Under to Nippon: The Story of the Sixth Army in World War II* (1953).

McRaven, William H. *Spec Ops Case Studies in Special Operations Warfare: Theory and Practice* (1995).

Erik D. Carlson

SEE ALSO Alamo Scouts

Canada

Canada's participation in World War II was even more extensive than in World War I. Most of Canada's attention and resources were focused on the European, Mediterranean, and Atlantic theaters of operations, where the United Kingdom was under the greatest threat. Canada's participation in the Pacific war was correspondingly limited, and less has been written on it.

The United States was naturally concerned that its northern neighbor could be threatened by other countries, which would in turn affect U.S. security. President Franklin Roosevelt had promised U.S. aid in 1938 in case Canada was invaded by a foreign power, and in August 1940 a Permanent Joint Board on Defense was established to coordinate military policies between the two nations. (Canadian officers were enjoined from pointing out to their U.S. counterparts that the only time Canada had ever been threatened and actually invaded by "a foreign power" was by the United States—and on several occasions.) At Hyde Park, New York, on April 20, 1941, the two countries signed a cooperative war production agreement.

Because the main Canadian effort was directed toward Europe and the Atlantic, only small Canadian naval and aerial forces were available to help in the Pacific theater. Two infantry battalions, from the Winnipeg Grenadiers and the Royal Rifles of Canada, took part in the doomed defense of Hong Kong, and over 40 percent were killed or wounded. Considerable bitterness remained long after the war among the survivors, who knew that the Canadian government had understood that they were doomed and that their mission had been more political than military. The U.S. territory of Alaska was the natural focus of Canadian interest, because it bordered Canada, was relatively accessible, and was an obvious target for Japanese planners. The Royal Canadian Air Force (RCAF) provided fighters for defense in 1942, when U.S. forces were still very weak. These were removed by early 1944, because the Japanese threat had been ended. But by the summer of 1943 there were some 34,000 Canadian troops stationed in Alaska and in the Canadian northwest. The multilingual 5,300-man 13th Infantry Brigade ("Greenlight Force") took part in the invasion of Kiska Island, in the Aleutian Islands, in August 1943. Major General George R. Pearkes, the commander in chief of the Canadian Pacific Command, was on hand to lead his troops. Many Canadian officers wanted to mount an invasion of the Japanese home island of Hokkaido from Alaska, which would have included more Canadian troops and led to greater recognition of Canada's involvement. But this absurd option was rejected by the United

States and instead was used only as a ruse to worry the Japanese, who may not have taken it too seriously.

The U.S. high command was concerned about joint Canadian-U.S. operations because of equipment incompatibility, different tactical doctrines, and the natural desire for independent Canadian commands. There was also some concern about how many troops Canada could supply, since conscription for overseas duty was an extremely sensitive domestic political issue. After much negotiation, particularly at the Second Quebec Conference (September 1944), a Canadian division (the 6th) was slotted to participate in the planned 1946 invasion of the main Japanese island of Honshu (Operation Coronet). The RCAF would be deployed to operate with the Royal Air Force (RAF), and the warships would sail with the British Royal Navy. But with no troops readily available in September 1945, Canada did not even participate in the Allied occupation of Japan.

Japanese Canadians in western Canada were treated like their counterparts in the United States; in 1942 more than twenty-three hundred eventually were forcibly moved away from the west coast and big cities to camps farther inland. Canada was also hit by the Japanese balloon bomb campaign late in the war (Operation Fugo), but little damage was suffered.

Although Canadian fighting forces did not weigh heavily in the calculations for the Pacific war, the country proved to be a vital partner in Allied logistical operations. Canada's scientific and industrial capacity supported the Allies before the United States was fully mobilized, and Canada closely coordinated its production with the United States and the United Kingdom. The Commonwealth Air Training Program graduated thousands of Allied pilots; many U.S. airmen gained valuable experience before Pearl Harbor was attacked by serving with the Canadian forces.

The Canadian northwest was used as a transportation corridor for U.S. military services in the North Pacific theater and for Lend-Lease supplies moving to the Soviet Union via Alaska and Siberia. For a long time the United States had wanted to improve its military and civilian communications with Alaska, and the war gave this opportunity. Airfields, railroads, and bases were expanded or established. Many new military bases were constructed. An oil pipeline, called "Canol," was laid from oil fields near the Mackenzie River to the Alaskan port of Waterways.

The best-known project was the Alaska-Canada Highway, popularly known as the "Alcan Highway." It stretched more than 1,500 miles from the railhead at Dawson Creek, British Columbia, to Big Delta, 100 miles from Fairbanks, Alaska. Construction took place between the spring of 1942 and October. More than sixteen hundred Canadian and eleven hundred U.S. engineers and civilians—many of them African Americans—labored under extreme environmental conditions to complete the highway. Brigadier General William H. Hoge directed this $138 million project, which officially opened to traffic on November 20, 1942.

Under the direction of its National Research Council, Canada also made major contributions to Allied atomic programs. Britain moved its scientists to Canada to keep them safe from German attacks. And Canada was the only secure source of uranium ore for the Allies, because the Belgian Congo was too distant. The deposits at Great Bear Lake in the Northwest Territories were important, but they turned into a source of controversy between the United States and the United Kingdom. Outside the U.S. and British governments, only the top Canadian leadership knew when and where the U.S. atomic bombs were to be used. The development of radar and proximity fuses also benefited from Canadian scientific efforts.

Although U.S.-Canadian relations were very close during the Pacific war, the Canadian government had little say in strategic decisions. There were many jurisdictional issues regarding U.S. and Canadian forces operating on each other's soil, but these were ironed out. Mackenzie King, leader of the Liberal Party and prime minister since 1936, had a good personal relationship with President Roosevelt. But many Canadians feared domination by their powerful southern neighbor, and Canada made sure that all U.S. bases were returned to Ottawa's control after the war. The successful and fruitful partnership of Canada and the United States during the Pacific war is a prime example of two countries cooperating completely to achieve a common goal.

FURTHER READINGS

Avery, Donald H. *Science of War: Canadian Scientists and Allied Military Technology during the Second World War* (1998).

Barry, P. S. *The Canol Project: An Adventure of the U.S. War Department in Canada's Northwest* (1985).

Coates, Kenneth S., and William R. Morrison. *The Alaska Highway in World War II: The U.S. Army of Occupation in Canada's Northwest* (1992).

Daniels, Roger. *Concentration Camps: North American Japanese in the United States and Canada during World War II* (1993).

Dziuban, Stanley W. *Military Relations between the United States and Canada, 1939–1945*, History of the United

States Army in World War II, U.S. Army Chief of Military History (1959).

Eggleston, Wilfrid. *Canada's Nuclear Story* (1965).

Granatstein, J. L. *Canada's War: The Politics of the Mackenzie King Government, 1939–1945,* 2d ed. (1975).

Stacey, Charles P. *Arms, Men and Governments: The War Policies of Canada, 1939–1945* (1970).

———. *Six Years at War: The Army in Canada, Britain and the Pacific,* Official History of the Canadian Army in the Second World War, vol. I (1955).

Daniel K. Blewett

SEE ALSO Aleutian Islands Campaign

Carrier Raids

See Aircraft Carrier Raids, U.S. Navy (1942).

Carriers

See Aircraft Carriers: Japanese, U.S., and British.

Cavite

The capital of the province of Cavite and the site of a major U.S. naval station, which was bombed and then captured by the Japanese during World War II, Cavite is located on the island of Luzon, Philippines, on a forked tongue of land in Manila Bay approximately 8 miles south of Manila. A native town was already in existence when the Spaniards took control of the area after their occupation of Manila in 1571–1572. Despite competition from, and attacks by, the Dutch and British, the Spanish retained control of the Philippines, and thus Cavite, until 1898.

Hostilities erupted between the United States and Spain after the explosion of battleship *Maine* under suspicious circumstances in Havana harbor on February 15, 1898. On May 1, 1898, Commodore George Dewey of the U.S. Navy commanded a force that overcame the Spanish fleet and captured Cavite. After the conclusion of this conflict, the United States established a presence in the Philippines. From 1898 until 1941, Cavite served as one of the chief naval bases and coaling stations of the U.S. Asiatic Fleet (the coaling docks were at Sangley Point, in the north end of the municipality).

The importance of such stations throughout the Pacific became apparent in the 1930s, when the deterioration of relations between the United States and Japan became a cause of increasing concern. One result of worsening relations was the intensification of efforts to crack

several of the Japanese codes. A code-breaking unit for the Pacific, established at Cavite, was called Cast, a prewar phonetic designation for C or Cavite. Redfield Mason, a Japanese-language officer who served as intelligence officer on the staff of the commander in chief of the Asiatic Fleet, organized and put this unit into operation. The value of this unit, however, as well as of the listening post to intercept Japanese radio traffic that operated from Cavite, was limited by the fact that much of the information gathered was not shared with other U.S. intelligence organizations because of "security" issues. The navy commander used the high-frequency transmitters located at Cavite to contact submarines at night when they surfaced to charge their batteries.

By 1940, the U.S. Navy was assessing the preparedness of its facilities in the Pacific to support the fleet in the event of war with Japan. That summer, Admiral Thomas Hart was appointed to command the Asiatic Fleet; he arrived in Manila in October 1940. Hart believed that a Japanese attack on the Philippines was imminent, and he inspected all facilities in the area. According to Hart, "the various machine shops and shipyard facilities at Cavite and elsewhere were 'inadequate' for the maintaining of the Asiatic Fleet in a combat worthy state." (Some steps were taken to strengthen the U.S. defenses at Cavite, and elsewhere, in the months prior to the Japanese attack on Pearl Harbor in December 1941, but the U.S. stations in the Philippines could not be held in the face of a multi-faceted Japanese assault.)

The Japanese surprise attack on Cavite on December 8, 1941, was part of a complex plan that called for the simultaneous assault on several power plants, the supply office, and the torpedo repair shop. The result was a disastrous series of fires encompassing most of the navy yard and a third of the town. The fires raging in the navy yard were designated as beyond control, in part because of a strong wind. The naval ammunition depot, however, had not sustained a direct hit and contained much-needed powder and ammunition. This powder and ammunition and some spare parts that had been stored in casements were all that could be salvaged. These items were transferred to tunnels on Corregidor. The flag officers responsible for the salvage operation also decided that the radio station and fuel depot at Sangley Point should be maintained as long as possible. (It should be noted that in the two-day interval between the bombing of Clark Field and the bombing of Cavite, no additional measures, such as the removal of *Sealion* and *Seadragon* or the placing of additional loose gear in casements or tunnels, was carried out.) One of the most significant losses was the stock of torpedoes that had been completely destroyed. The failure of the U.S. Navy to stockpile a large number before war broke out, as well as losses from other Japanese attacks, meant that submarine torpedoes were a precious commodity practically from the outbreak of hostilities.

As a result of the Japanese attacks that culminated with the destruction of the navy yard at Cavite, the U.S. Navy lost control of the waters and air surrounding Luzon; consequently, no supplies or reinforcements could reach MacArthur's army. After these and additional devastating air attacks, the Japanese were able to land in the Philippines with only limited resistance from the remaining ships and planes of the Asiatic Fleet. The Japanese did face strong opposition during their Philippines campaign of 1941–1942—from the U.S. Army. The Japanese commander, General Homma Masaharu, put his troops ashore on Luzon on December 10 and began to advance toward the capital. This was followed by another large-scale landing close to the capital. MacArthur's forces fell back into a strong position on the Bataan Peninsula, including the island forts of Corregidor. The fall of Corregidor on May 6, 1942, marked the Japanese conquest of the whole of the Philippines. The Japanese held Cavite until 1945, when it was recaptured by the United States. Negotiations provided for the continued use of the base at Cavite, with certain limitations, after the Philippines became independent.

FURTHER READINGS

Blair, Clay, *Silent Victory: The U.S. Submarine War Against Japan* (1975).

Costello, John. *The Pacific War* (1981).

Deacon, Richard. *The Silent War: A History of Western Naval Intelligence* (1988).

Morison, Samuel Eliot. *History of the United States Naval Operations in World War II.* Vol. 3, *The Rising Sun in the Pacific 1931–April 1942* (1948).

———. *The Two-Ocean War: A Short History of the United States Navy in the Second World War* (1963).

Toland, John. *Infamy: Pearl Harbor and Its Aftermath* (1982).

Van der Vat, Dan. *The Pacific Campaign: World War II, the U.S.–Japanese Naval War, 1941–1945* (1991).

Melissa R. Jordine

SEE ALSO Philippines, Fall of

Ceylon

This island and British colony off the southeast tip of India was most significant during the Pacific war because of Japanese raids on and near it in April 1942. These raids accomplished little tactically or operationally; what they failed to do, however, was of critical strategic importance.

Following the rampage which took the Imperial Japanese Navy from Pearl Harbor to the South Pacific, the Japanese naval general staff cast about for new operations. Hawaii had been alerted by the attack on Pearl Harbor and promised to be a tough fight. Australia was too large, and New Zealand was too far away. Therefore, the general staff leaned toward a move into the Indian Ocean. This option gained impetus on January 19, 1942, when Japan signed the Tripartite Pact with Germany and Italy.

Admiral Yamamoto decided on a major strike west for a number of reasons: (1) The Royal Navy had been rebuilding its forces in the Indian Ocean after the sinking of HMS *Prince of Wales* and *Repulse*. Always looking for another 1904-style decisive battle, the Japanese wanted to "Pearl Harbor" the British as well. (2) The Japanese thought that India might be ready to fall if Great Britain suffered one more major defeat. (3) The Japanese hoped to link up with Hitler's forces, which were moving through Egypt and soon would be heading into the Caucasus region of the Soviet Union. (4) The Japanese hoped to get Madagascar with the help of German pressure on the Vichy French. (5) Japan wanted to disrupt Allied shipping in the Indian Ocean, Red Sea, and Persian Gulf.

Now that Japan's initial moves were nearing completion, cooperation between the Japanese army and navy became strained. The army wouldn't provide the requested two divisions to occupy Ceylon, although these forces were currently nearby. (Six British, Australian, or East African brigades defended Ceylon, but without sizable air support.) The operation was also scaled down in duration. Prophetically, the naval staff wanted the fleet near Japan in case of U.S. carrier strikes against the home islands. The final plan, called Operation C, (not much of a "cover" code name) consisted of a limited attack toward Ceylon and the Bay of Bengal.

Vice Admiral Nobutake Kondo commanded the Southern Area Force, which was divided into two parts. His force consisted of five attack and one light carrier deploying 300 aircraft, four *Kongo*-era fast battleships, one light and two heavy cruisers, eight destroyers, and seven submarines. A larger force would make for Ceylon. This was Vice Admiral Chuichi Nagumo's 1st Carrier Striking Force, consisting of *Akagi, Hiryu, Shokaku, Soryu, Zuikaku* (the other Pearl Harbor veteran, *Kaga*, returned to Japan with engine problems), and escorts. A third, smaller force, centered on *Ryujo* under Vice Admiral Jisaburo Ozawa, would attack shipping in the Bay of Bengal. Aboard *Akagi*, Kondo slipped out of Staring Bay in the Celebes Islands on the morning of March 26.

The British Eastern Fleet under Admiral James Somerville was made up of the modern fleet carriers HMS *Formidable* and *Indomitable* and light carrier *Hermes* (among the world's oldest carriers) with 100 aircraft total, five battleships, two heavy and five light (including one Dutch) cruisers, sixteen destroyers, and seven submarines (two Dutch). As a humiliating sign of British weakness, the entire fleet was to *avoid* the Japanese. Instead, Somerville skirted Kondo, looking for the unlikely chance to fight a small portion of the Japanese force at favorable odds. British intelligence had informed Somerville of the Japanese departure from the Celebes, so he kept his fleet at a safe distance at Addu Atoll in the Maldives from March 30 to April 2. When the Japanese failed to materialize, he assumed either that his intelligence was bad or that the enemy's operation had been canceled. He therefore sent *Hermes,* destroyer *Vampire,* and heavy cruisers *Cornwall* and *Dorsetshire* back to Ceylon for repairs. This proved to be fatal for all four warships.

Alerted of a pending attack on the port of Colombo on April 5, the two cruisers put to sea. They were spotted by Japanese reconnaissance aircraft 200 miles south of the island. Fifty-three Val dive-bombers promptly attacked, coming in from 12,000 feet. Both ships sank in less than half an hour, taking down 422 sailors without loss to the Japanese. However, Nagumo failed to follow up his victory by searching in the direction that the British ships were steaming. If he had looked southwest of the cruisers' position and course, he very well could have found the rest of Somerville's fleet.

Using radar to keep out of enemy search range, Somerville patrolled to the southwest. Four days later Nagumo's planes attacked Trincomalee. They spotted *Hermes* and *Vampire,* which had left the harbor the night before. Attacking at 1030 hours, seventy Vals scored forty hits on *Hermes* in ten minutes (by British estimate) while fifteen Vals attacked *Vampire,* sinking both and causing an additional 315 deaths. Shore facilities on Ceylon were smashed, and thirty-seven British aircraft were destroyed.

Meanwhile Ozawa's group sent twenty-three merchantmen totaling over 112,000 tons to the bottom, using old Type 96 biplane torpedo bombers. He also attacked Indian shore installations and disrupted coastal traffic for weeks. Japanese submarines destroyed an additional 32,000 tons of shipping.

Somerville utterly failed to hinder the Japanese thrust, and his fleet retreated to East Africa for a year and a half. Total materiel cost to Kondo for Operation C was twenty-nine aircraft. By April 13, Kondo, low on fuel, cleared Singapore on his way back to Japan, unknowingly marking the high-water mark of the Greater East Asia Co-Prosperity Sphere.

However, on April 18, as the Japanese fleet moved past the northern tip of Luzon, radios aboard *Akagi* received word of Doolittle's raid on Tokyo—another operation with small materiel impact but huge strategic implications. Operation C was a half-measure and accordingly achieved only partial results. Kondo had not caused India to topple into revolt. He had not interrupted Allied shipping to Egypt even for a few months. Nor had he cut supplies to the Soviet Union. (Far greater amounts of Western Allied supplies were sent to Stalin through Iran from 1942 to 1944 than were channeled through the Arctic.) The dreaded linkup of Japanese and German forces was still a pipe dream. In fact, Axis failure to act in a coordinated manner condemned them to defeat.

Among all major combatants Japan was still the odd man out, having only limited objectives for the war. But while Kondo was chasing after the Royal Navy 3,000 miles away in the Indian Ocean, the United States had sneaked up and bombed his homeland. Nagumo's carriers couldn't be in two places at the same time. The Japanese navy, charged with defending Japan's home islands, could not do that and operate on the empire's boundaries as long as the U.S. Navy was intact, had freedom of action, and was intent on taking the war to Japan proper.

FURTHER READINGS

Wilmot, H. P. "Empires in the Balance." *United States Naval Institute Proceedings* (19??).

Robert Kirchubel

SEE ALSO India; Navy, Japanese; Navy, Royal

Chaplains, U.S. Army

Approximately nine thousand U.S. Army chaplains ministered to servicemen's religious and morale needs during World War II. Many of these chaplains served in the South Pacific theater, tending to the unique interests and problems of soldiers stationed there—particularly cultural differences and extreme climates and conditions. Chaplains in the Pacific also shared common concerns with chaplains on the European and North African fronts, mainly helping soldiers during a period of personal upheaval and crisis while setting moral and spiritual standards. Basically, chaplains bolstered soldiers' faith as well as their determination to serve their country and their fellow soldiers.

Army chaplains all volunteered to serve in the Pacific; such service was not compulsory, for the Selective Service

Act exempted ordained ministers. But many of those who elected to minister to troops had some previous military experience, most often in the military reserves or the National Guard.

Army chaplains had ministered to troops since the American Revolution and had served in every major military conflict after that. The thousands of World War II army chaplains agreed to serve for the duration of the emergency plus six months after the war ended. General William A. Arnold was U.S. Army Chief of Chaplains during World War II—the first army chaplain to achieve the rank of general. Throughout the war, General Arnold presided over the largest military chaplaincy in history.

Prospective army chaplains underwent a review process to be accepted into service. They had to present an ecclesiastical endorsement from their denomination and had to have completed appropriate college and seminary training. Each chaplain had to pass the same physical tests as line officers, to weed out those who might have physical disabilities that would prevent them from serving effectively in a war zone. Those selected then were sent to chaplain school to learn military protocol and procedures as well as how to adapt the ministry to military service.

The U.S. Army Chaplain School opened in March 1942 at Fort Benjamin Harrison, in Indiana. By August of that year, it was moved to Harvard University, where chaplains trained through August 1944, when the school was transferred to Fort Devens, in Massachusetts. After fingerprinting, the students were immersed into a five-week basic course to orient them to the military before they reached the battlefield. The army chaplains studied military law, customs, administration, and map reading. They also rehearsed for such duties as first aid and graves registration. Outside the classroom, drills and physical training prepared them for amphibious landings and defense against chemical warfare. Chaplains who had been overseas before the school was established were sent back to reinforce their skills and to advise the new chaplains about the realities of Pacific service.

Chaplains were assigned to troop camps before embarking to the Pacific, and they accompanied soldiers on transport ships across the Pacific Ocean. Every American serving in the Pacific had been given a pocket Bible with a message from President Franklin D. Roosevelt: "As Commander-in-Chief I take pleasure in commending the reading of the Bible to all who serve in the armed forces of the United States." Army chaplains led Bible study groups aboard transports, hoping that the "words of wisdom, counsel and inspiration" could provide "a fountain of strength" and "an aid in attaining the highest aspirations of the human soul."

Army chaplains served all major denominations. Historians estimate that at least fifty religious groups were represented, proportional to troop demographics. Chaplains were expected to respect each soldier's religious choices and denominational needs and not to force their personal beliefs on the troops. Protestant chaplains thus heard confessions and granted absolution, just as Catholic and Jewish chaplains respected Protestant religious traditions. Chaplains were not permitted to proselytize or attack other faiths—an injunction that the overwhelming majority cheerfully acknowledged, despite their own often strong denominational or doctrinal convictions.

Each army infantry regiment was assigned three chaplains—one Catholic and two Protestant—a ratio determined according to soldier populations. A Jewish chaplain served larger army units, and more chaplains were assigned when possible as troop size increased. Remote, isolated conditions in the Pacific, however, often interfered with military planning. Sometimes only one chaplain was available to serve in an area, and he provided general religious services to the extent possible.

The chaplains' first duty most often was helping soldiers adjust to the difficulties they encountered in wartime. Army chaplains interviewed recruits about religious matters. Soldiers were often homesick and uncomfortable at being crowded into camps with strangers, and they often exhibited a variety of anxieties. Chaplains influenced the men by setting an example and encouraging teamwork and providing spiritual strength to survive suffering and hardships. They prepared the men to deal with aspects of military service, including killing enemy troops and preparing to die or to see comrades die. They attempted to strengthen soldiers' ability to resist such temptations as alcohol abuse and prostitution as well as to bolster their faith.

This service placed demanding expectations on chaplains, who daily faced conflicts between the tenets of their religious calling and the restrictions of military duty. Committed to serve for the war's duration, army chaplains sometimes tired of hiding their own fears and doubts. They often missed the normal routine of their civilian churches and congregations, feeling isolated and lonely. Some chaplains questioned their usefulness. Others battled with moral issues that conflicted with their beliefs, such as the Allied bombing of civilians.

Chaplains mediated between servicemen and officers but often argued with officers about authority issues; although the chaplain was under military jurisdiction, he was the only commissioned officer to whom soldiers could talk without fear of being disciplined. The men often complained to chaplains about officers and combat worries and asked for passes or furloughs. The officers and chaplains differed in opinion about the chaplains' role in the Pacific. James L. McBride wrote: "Chaplains are not in the army because government is primarily interested in the saving of men's souls. The chaplain shares the mission of all other arms of the service to strengthen the will to victory." McBride emphasized that "religion can and does make souls strong for battle." Chaplain Alfred G. Belles countered that "chaplains are not in uniform to preach and teach religious and moral values to insure military triumph. I am primarily interested in the saving of men's souls."

Many of the younger soldiers were not church members or had rarely contemplated spiritual matters before being sent to the Pacific. Army chaplains baptized men who asked, sending certificates to their families and contacting their local ministers. Chaplains also performed marriage ceremonies, administered sacraments, gave Holy Communion, and celebrated religious holidays. They observed Jewish dietary laws to help soldiers observe the Passover Festival and Hanukkah. Chaplains also ensured that holiday goodwill packages were distributed.

Chapels in the Pacific theater represented the chaplains' ingenuity. Soldiers helped construct chapels wherever possible in camp, often using indigenous materials, including coral, palm leaves, and bamboo; khaki cloth could be stretched across fuel drums to build an altar and pulpit. Floors usually were covered with sawdust, and benches might simply be coconut logs. Parachutes were used to make altar cloths, and antiaircraft shells were transformed into chimes. Many of the army chapels in the Pacific were intended as memorials to soldiers killed in action. One of the first photographs released from the Bataan showed a mass that was performed in a jungle chapel known as the "Catholic chapel of Lourdes."

Chaplains conducted daily sermons and devotions, with occasional liturgies in Latin. Most services were brief, affirming through prayer the existence of a higher power and the men's military duty. The chaplains prepared the troops spiritually for wartime dangers, listened to confessions, and granted absolution before battles. In the field, a jeep's hood could be pressed into service as a makeshift altar, and tent chapels were often surrounded by foxholes so the men could take cover in case of enemy fire during the service. Native peoples also attended services, and Japanese soldiers occasionally listened from nearby caves—although to what effect has never been determined. Pacific Command officers reported that the troops displayed an unparalled interest in religious and spiritual matters, with six times more religious attendance than in any other theater of war.

Chaplains were also responsible for informing men about family emergencies, coordinating with the Red Cross and other relief societies. On the Bataan Peninsula, chaplains secured shortwave radios so servicemen could contact their families. Army chaplains visited sick, wounded, and dying soldiers to comfort and pray with them. They assisted medical personnel, reassured soldiers, and aided those in rehabilitation who had lost limbs. Chaplains wrote and sent messages for servicemen and counseled those in need of assistance; many soldiers admitted their loss of faith or confided remorse for killing enemy soldiers.

Undoubtedly, U.S. Army chaplains' most trying duties involved giving last rites, identifying the dead, and overseeing burials. Chaplains marked graves and registered deceased soldiers' names, notifying relatives by telegram and sending personal effects—primarily wedding bands and watches—home with condolence letters. They also sought information about men missing in action. On the Pacific islands, the chaplains often said a mass in tribute to the dead and marked the graves with palm fronds before the troops departed. Others counseled soldiers arrested for offenses, and several had perhaps the most unpleasant duty of all, ministering to a U.S. soldier before his military execution.

Despite their noncombat status, army chaplains often risked the battlefields to rescue soldiers and minister to the wounded. Wearing a white cross on their helmets, chaplains moved from trench to trench to pray with the troops. Some aggressively sought out wounded soldiers, carrying pistols to defend themselves. Many remained with wounded men who could not be moved, knowing that they risked capture. During the foredoomed U.S. defense of the Philippines, Chaplains John Curran, Joseph V. LaFleur, and Ralph Brown helped transport wounded to the hospital. After the bloody Battle of Tarawa, Chaplain Joseph Wieber stated, "If God had not given me His Special protection I would have been wounded or killed at least a dozen times." He and other chaplains were under heavy enemy fire as they hit the beaches in landing craft. On the beach, the chaplains sorted body parts under sniper fire.

Some chaplains were captured by the Japanese. Several made the Bataan death march, and others were held in prison camps, where they comforted fellow prisoners. Guards sometimes stole religious articles, such as rosaries, and were seen torturing and killing chaplains. Whether imprisoned or free, chaplains suffered weight losses and diseases, insect and snake bites, high humidity, torrential rains, and seemingly insurmountable terrain. Japanese snipers indiscriminately fired at them, sometimes even during a burial service.

Twenty army chaplains died just in the campaign to liberate the Philippines. One, Chaplain Aquinas T. Colgan, was revered by the GIs because of the risks he took plunging into a thicket to retrieve wounded. The 124th Regimental Combat Team named Colgan Woods in his honor. At least one "miracle" was associated with a chaplain: James Deasy was buried alive by the fallout of a 700-pound mortar shell; but his helmet fell over his face, trapping sufficient oxygen, and he managed to wriggle his fingers to be seen above ground and was rescued. Religion also inspired men to achieve what seemed impossible. Chaplain Charles Suver promised soldiers a mass on top of Mount Suribachi if they could raise the flag there.

Approximately forty army chaplains had been killed in action by 1945. Another forty-seven had died in service, 105 were wounded, thirty-eight were held by the enemy, and one was missing in action. Legions of Merit and letters of commendation for religious services under fire were presented, and at least 384 army chaplains were decorated with awards including the Purple Heart, Distinguished Service Cross, and Silver Star.

When the war ended, chaplains led prayers and masses of thanksgiving. But their duties did not end with the gunfire. They accompanied occupation units into Japan and helped repair bombed churches and finance orphanages. Believing that religion could reinforce democracy in Japan, chaplains formed an association organized by Eighth Army Chaplain Yandell S. Beans, dedicated to assist the Japanese toward that goal. Several army chaplains, including DeWitt C. Clemens and Francis P. Scott, even ministered to Japanese war criminals at the Sugamo military prison.

Before the army chaplains returned home to their congregations, they established a foundation for postwar religion. They urged soldiers to attend hometown churches and wrote ministers letters asking them to help returning soldiers adapt to civilian life. Most army chaplains experienced some difficulty in readjusting to civilian religious needs. Many churches supported former chaplains while they recuperated, and the Army-Navy Chaplains' Association also helped with educational materials to advance them professionally.

In 1948, the U.S. Postal Service issued a three-cent stamp honoring World War II chaplains, and Chaplains' Memorial stands in Arlington National Cemetery.

FURTHER READINGS

Crosby, Donald, S.J. *Battlefield Chaplains: Catholic Priests in World War II* (1994).
Gushwa, Robert L. *The Best and Worst of Times: The United States Chaplaincy, 1920–1945* (1977).
Honeywell, Roy J. *Chaplains of the United States Army* (1958).
U.S. Army Office of the Chief of Chaplains Records, U.S. National Archives, Suitland, Maryland.
Venzke, Rodger R. *Confidence in Battle, Inspiration in Peace: The United States Army Chaplaincy 1945–1975* (1977).

Elizabeth D. Schafer

Chennault, Claire Lee (1893–1958)

Air power advocate and military aviation ally of the Nationalist Chinese, Claire Lee Chennault was born on September 6, 1893, in Commerce, Texas, the son of a farmer. Chennault grew up in northeast Louisiana and briefly attended Louisiana State University (1909–1910). He applied to both the U.S. Military Academy (West Point) and the U.S. Naval Academy (Annapolis) but was rejected by both. Chennault then went to the State Normal School of Natchitoches, received his teaching certificate in 1910, and then taught school. He married Nell Thompson in December 1911, and the couple would have eight children.

During World War I Chennault repeatedly applied for flight training but was denied. He instead attended Officer Training Camp in Indiana and was commissioned a first lieutenant in the Infantry Reserve in November 1917. While stationed at Kelly Field in San Antonio, Texas, Chennault learned to fly on his own. He then transferred to the Aviation Section of the Signal Corp and became a pilot and flight instructor. He achieved his rating as a fighter pilot in 1919, but the war had ended. In April 1920 he was discharged from the army and briefly returned to farming in Louisiana. But on September 24, 1920, he was commissioned as a first lieutenant in the U.S. Army Air Service. He served as a member of the 94th Fighter Squadron at Ellington Field, Texas (1920–1923), and then commanded the 19th Pursuit Squadron at Wheeler Field, Hawaii (1923–1926). Stationed at the U.S. Air Corps Training Center (1926–1930), Chennault served as instructor, operations officer, and director of training; he also worked with paratroopers during this time. After his promotion to captain in 1929, Chennault was stationed at the Air Corps Tactical School at Langley Field, Virginia, and later at Montgomery, Alabama, (1930–1936), where he was first a student and then an instructor. While at the Tactical School, he organized and led the Air Corps aerobatic exhibition team, known as "Three Men on the Flying Trapeze"—forerunner of the

U.S. Air Force Thunderbirds. He also began to develop air tactics that would serve him so well during World War II, such as team combat and paratroop techniques. He consolidated his tactical and strategic concepts into a book, *The Role of Defensive Pursuit,* published in 1935, in which he challenged the prevalent ideas about strategic bombers. Chennault also pushed hard for improvements in fighter aircraft, particularly regarding their range and firepower. In 1936 Chennault commanded the 20th Pursuit Group at Barksdale Field, Louisiana. In April 1937 Lieutenant Colonel Chennault retired from the Air Corps because of physical disabilities, which included chronic bronchitis and partial deafness.

Three days after retirement, Chennault left for China and destiny with an invitation from Madame Chiang Kaishek to survey the Chinese air force. In July 1937 he became the personal adviser to Generalissimo Chiang Kai-shek and supervised training of the Chinese air force by U.S. instructors. In late 1940 Chiang Kai-shek sent Chennault back to the United States to procure support, manpower, and equipment for a U.S. air unit to fight in China; General Hap Arnold opposed this idea. China had friends, however, including President Franklin Roosevelt, and Chennault was able to recruit a hundred pilots and purchase as many Curtis-Wright P-40B fighters. Chennault returned to China to command the American Volunteer Group (AVG), nicknamed "Flying Tigers" because of the tiger teeth painted on their aircraft. The AVG trained at Toungoo Royal Air Force Base in Burma and then moved to Kunming, in southern Yunnan, China. It was Chennault's personality, determination, decisiveness, and teaching skills that transformed a ragtag group of mercenaries into a first-class fighting unit; he gained his men's respect and affection with his thoroughness and caring. From mid-December 1941 to July 1942 the AVG compiled a great record, shooting down nine Japanese planes for every one they lost. Chennault taught pilots to fight in pairs, using hit-and-run tactics combined with accurate gunnery, rapid refueling, and an elaborate Chinese air-raid warning system. Along with the Royal Air Force, the AVG helped keep the Burma Road open and thwarted an invasion of Yunnan province; in the process the AVG lost four pilots in combat, along with only twenty-six airplanes, while demolishing at least 299 Japanese aircraft. Chennault loved the freedom he had to mold the AVG—without what he saw as the confining structures of regular military discipline and command—and he encouraged individualism within the AVG. Unfortunately, he had trouble handling the administrative side of the job, lacked interpersonal skills, and often refused to share credit for successes.

In April 1942 Chennault was recalled to active duty in the U.S. Army Air Corps with the rank of colonel, although he had protested this action. In July 1942 the AVG was incorporated into the U.S. Army as the 23d Fighter Squadron, and Chennault became chief of U.S. Army Air Forces (USAAF) in China and director of tactical air operations for the China-Burma-India (CBI) theater. In March 1943 Chennault was promoted to major general, and his command became the Fourteenth Air Force. From 1942 to 1945 Chennault's forces destroyed 2,600 enemy aircraft (with another 1,500 probable); sank 2,300,000 tons of shipping; and killed 66,700 enemy troops while losing only 500 aircraft. Unfortunately, Chennault and his CBI commander, Lieutenant General Joe Stilwell, hated each other, but Chiang Kai-shek (the true object of Stilwell's contempt) supported Chennault, which gave him some protection. Stilwell and Chennault also disagreed on tactics to be used in this remote area. Chennault had convinced President Roosevelt in 1942 that with only a small air force he could bomb and cripple Japan, thus helping to relieve pressure on other areas. Stilwell and most other army leaders believed that the Japanese would simply overrun Chennault's bases in eastern China. Roosevelt gave Chennault permission to try these tactics in May 1943 and provided him with supplies. In 1944 the Japanese launched an offensive and easily overran Chennault's eastern bases as predicted, but Chennault continued to operate out of bases farther west. Chennault's plan had been overambitious and unrealistic, given the supply problems that faced the forces in Southeast Asia and China, and by going straight to the president, Chennault had angered other commanders, such as Stilwell, who then felt vindicated by Chennault's setbacks.

By the spring of 1945 China was no longer an area of great significance, and Chennault's opponents—particularly Army Chief of Staff General George Marshall and USAAF Chief of Staff General "Hap" Arnold—forced him out of his command in August 1945. Chennault retired from the army in October 1945 as a major general. He received China's highest decoration, the Order of White Sun and Blue Sky.

Chennault did not fade away, however. He divorced Nell Thompson in 1946 and in late 1947 married Anna Chen, a young Chinese journalist. He became an outspoken critic and opponent of Communism in the Far East. In 1946 he organized a civilian airline in China, which airlifted supplies to Nationalist forces fighting in the interior until the end of the civil war. The airline was reorganized in 1948 as the Civil Air Transport (CAT), one of the largest air-cargo carriers in the world. This airline would become the Central Intelligence Agency's first "proprietary" enterprise and played a covert role in the Korean War, Indochina, North Vietnam, Laos, and Tibet as well as at Dien Bien Phu in 1954.

On July 27, 1958, Chennault died in New Orleans, Louisiana. That same month he was given the rank of lieutenant general by an act of the U.S. Congress. Chennault was a great proponent of air power, a brilliant tactician, and a superb organizer, but he had an inflated belief in the effectiveness and decisiveness of air power. His personal doubts about himself drove him to excessive competitiveness and often pettiness; he was a loner, defiant and stubborn—a problem often compounded by his deafness.

FURTHER READINGS

Archibald, Joseph. *Commander of the Flying Tigers: Claire Lee Chennault* (1949).

Byrd, Martha. *Chennault: Giving Wings to the Tiger* (1987).

Ford, Daniel. *Flying Tiger: Claire Chennault and the American Volunteer Group* (1959).

Schultz, Duane. *The Maverick War: Chennault and the Flying Tigers* (1987).

Scott, Robert Lee. *Flying Tiger* (1959).

Laura Matysek Wood

SEE ALSO Army Air Corps/Air Forces, U.S.

Chiang Kai-shek (1887–1975)

Chinese political and military leader, headed the Nationalist government in China and on the island of Taiwan. Chiang Kai-shek (jee-ahng' ky-shek) was born on October 31, 1887, in Zhejiang (Chekiang) province. Raised by his widowed mother, he early decided on a military career, attending military schools in northern China and Japan. In 1908 Chiang joined a revolutionary organization devoted to the overthrow of the Qing (Cawing or Manchu) dynasty, an effort that was ultimately successful in 1911–1912.

After 1920, Chiang allied himself with Sun Yat-sen, who built up the Kuomintang (Nationalist Party) at Guangzhou (Canton) with Soviet aid. He was made commandant (1924) of the party's Whampoa Military Academy, and his power as a military leader grew rapidly after Sun's death in 1925. In the Northern Expedition of 1926–1927, Chiang secured the backing of the Shanghai business community, whereupon he suppressed the labor movement, purged Communist influence, forced out the Russian advisers, and brought numerous warlords to heel or into the Nationalist fold. In December 1927, Chiang married Soong Me-ling of the wealthy Christian Soong family.

From 1928, Chiang headed a new Nationalist government at Nanking (Nanking), giving first priority to the elimination of the Chinese Communists; he ineffectually resisted the Japanese occupation of Manchuria in 1931. In 1937, when the Japanese invasion of China launched the second Sino-Japanese war, Chiang was compelled to form a united front with the Communists. He led the war from Chonguing (Chungking) in southwestern China.

Japan's invasion seizure of Manchuria and its subsequent full-scale assault against China brought expressions of disapproval from the U.S. government and from influential segments of the American media, particularly from Henry Luce, owner of *Time, Life,* and *Fortune* magazines. With public opinion strongly isolationist, however, Franklin Roosevelt's administration could not act to halt Japanese expansionism. Not until the outbreak of World War II in Europe and the escalation of Japanese aggression did the United States respond more strongly.

In 1940, Nazi Germany's march into western Europe opened opportunities for Japan to consolidate its position in China and penetrate Southeast Asia, thereby advancing the Japanese goal of dominating a "Greater East Asia Co-Prosperity Sphere." After the fall of France, the Vichy government accepted (August 1940) Japanese demands that aid through French Indochina to the Chinese Nationalists be cut off and that Japan be allowed to use air bases in Indochina. In September, Japanese troops moved into northern Indochina, and Japan joined the Axis. Meanwhile, with Great Britain fighting for its life and with the Netherlands under Nazi occupation, Japan pressured the British to close the Burma Road to supplies bound for China and called for the Dutch East Indies to make economic and political concessions. In July 1941, Japan occupied southern Indochina—an obvious prelude to further expansion in Southeast Asia, which was a rich source of rubber, tin, oil, quinine, lumber, foodstuffs, and other vital raw materials.

Japanese prime minister Prince Konoe Fumimaro hoped that the United States would accept Japan's actions, but in September 1940 President Roosevelt imposed an embargo on U.S. exports of scrap iron and steel to Japan. In July 1941 (in the wake of the French capitulation to Japan's demands on Indochina) he froze all Japanese assets in the United States. This action virtually ended U.S.-Japanese trade, depriving Japan of vital oil imports.

On September 6, 1941, an imperial conference met in Tokyo to consider the worsening relations with the

United States. Emperor Hirohito and Prime Minister Konoe favored a continuation of negotiations in Washington, D.C. The war minister, General Tojo Hideki, however, believed that the United States was determined to throttle Japan, that war was inevitable, and that it would be preferable to begin the conflict sooner rather than later. Tojo's views had wide support within the Japanese military, which generally believed that the Americans were "too soft" to put up much of a fight, anyway.

On November 26, Secretary of State Cordell Hull formally iterated the U.S. position: Japan must withdraw from China and Indochina, recognize the Chiang Kai-shek regime in China, renounce territorial expansion, and accept the Open Door policy of equal commercial access to Asia. An imperial conference on December 1 set the Japanese war machine in motion.

After the outbreak of World War II one of the most controversial and colorful of U.S. generals, Joseph W. Stilwell, became the Chief of Staff and commander of U.S. troops in the China-Burma-India theater. His Chinese troops were defeated by the Japanese and driven out of Burma in 1942; with the remnants of his forces, however, he made his way through most difficult terrain to India. He spent the rest of the war attempting to regain Burma, which the Allies finally accomplished in 1945. The controversy around Stilwell arose chiefly from his intense antipathy to Chiang and from his public criticisms of the Chinese leader. Because of this controversy, he was relieved of his command in 1944.

Chiang got along much better with Stilwell's successor, U.S. Air Force General Clair Chennault. Chennault had been Chiang's air adviser from 1937 to 1941 and had gained fame as the leader of the very successful American Volunteer Group (AVG, the "Flying Tigers"), whose U.S. fighter pilots had scored so heavily against the Japanese (about the only Allied air unit to enjoy any success at the time). Chennault's unrealistic (some said cockamamie) scheme to defeat the Japanese with only a small force of bombers appealed to Chiang, who was shepherding his best units to fight against the Communists at the end of the war. Even Chennault's scheme to bomb Japan from Chinese air bases fell apart when Japanese land forces simply took the bases, inflicting large-scale miseries on the Chinese population.

Chiang became increasingly dependent on the United States, while the morale of his own forces declined and corruption became rampant. After the Japanese surrender in 1945, Nationalist–Communist hostilities were renewed. The Nationalists lost the civil war (1945–1949), and in 1949 remnants of the Kuomintang fled to the island of Taiwan, where Chiang ruled until his death on April 5, 1975.

Chiang's power was exercised through a variety of posts—party leader, chairman of the Supreme National Defense Council, and president of the Republic of China. Intellectually Chiang Kai-shek was a conservative who admired the authoritarian aspects of Confucianism, which he revived as a state cult. In *China's Destiny* (1943; English translation, 1947), he rejected equally the revolutionary Marxist doctrines and the liberal-democratic ideas that had gained vogue in China since 1911.

FURTHER READINGS
Chiang Kai-shek. *Soviet Russia in China* (1957).
Crozier, Brian. *The Man Who Lost China: The First Full Biography of Chiang Kai-shek* (1976).
H Pu-y. *The Military Exploits and Deeds of President Chiang Kai-shek* (1971).
Lo, Pecan. *The Early Chiang Kai-shek* (1971).

Bruce A. Elleman

SEE ALSO Chennault, Claire Lee; China-Burma-India Theater of Operations; Stilwell, Joseph Warren

China-Burma-India Theater of Operations

The China-Burma-India (CBI) theater was formed in the spring of 1942, when General George C. Marshall, U.S. Army Chief of Staff, gave Lieutenant General Joseph Stilwell the command. Chinese Nationalist Generalissimo Chiang Kai-shek had asked that an American serve as the chief of staff of the Combined Forces in the theater, and Marshall reluctantly gave Stilwell the assignment. Stilwell was his best corps commander, and although Marshall had planned to give him the command of U.S. troops in Europe, the chief of staff could think of no other general qualified to serve in China. Stilwell had several previous assignments in the country, spoke the language, and had a healthy respect for the capabilities of the people. In many other, more important ways, however, Stilwell was the wrong choice for this assignment. While a brilliant field commander and trainer of troops, Stilwell had neither the personality nor the temperament for either the political or the diplomatic work that his new assignment would entail. Impatient, direct, and indiscreet, he rarely suffered fools and was with good reason known as "Vinegar Joe." Stilwell was the only commander of this theater, and its fortunes waxed and waned with those of the general.

The difficulties that would plague the CBI command during the war years, however, had less to do with Stilwell's personality than with the fact that the Americans, British, and Chinese had no common objectives. The United States believed that the Imperial Japanese Army had overextended itself in China. As a result, the key to defeating Japan was to keep its army occupied on the Asian continent while U.S. forces advanced through the Pacific theater toward the home islands. Stilwell's mission was to train and equip the Chinese army so that it could actively engage the Japanese in active combat and to direct U.S. Lend-Lease supplies to the Chinese so that they could prosecute the war. Believing in the potential of the individual Chinese soldier, Stilwell wanted to initiate ground-combat operations against the Japanese before their strength increased, using aggressive tactics. President Franklin Roosevelt expected that postwar China, with its huge manpower, would be one of the four great powers that would police international affairs. He was well aware of China's shortcomings and viewed this role as a prospect of long-term development, rather than an immediate probability.

Chiang had a different set of plans, designed above all else to preserve his political power. The Chinese army was not a strong, unified, or viable force. It was really an amalgamation of the old warlord armies, and many units owed their loyalty to their immediate commanders rather than to the national government. The strength and loyalty of the divisions that were directly under Chiang's control were the basis of his hold on power. As a result, officers received their commands more on the basis of their loyalty than ability. Chiang was far more concerned with preserving his strength, thwarting domestic political rivals, and preparing for a showdown with the Communists than he was with fighting the Japanese. (He supposedly said that the "the Japanese were a disease of the body, the Communists a disease of the soul.") His personal strategy was to allow the Americans to fight and defeat the Japanese. Chinese units would adopt cautious tactics, attacking only when they had clear numerical superiority. In his diary, Stilwell called Chiang's views "amateur tactics," and he soon began referring to the Chinese leader in his diary and letters home as "Peanut" and the "Peanut dictator." Chiang viewed Lend-Lease as his due as a U.S. ally, which he hoarded in preparation for the postwar confrontation. With these considerations in mind, Chiang understandably found the air-power ideas of U.S. Army Air Forces Brigadier General Claire Chennault more to his liking than the land-based strategy of Stilwell. Chennault had organized the American Volunteer Group (AVG; better known as the Flying Tigers) and argued, without much

evidence, that air power alone could defeat the Japanese in China. Chiang favored this idea because the planes, pilots, and materiel would all come from the United States; he would not have to expend much of his precious resources. Meanwhile, Stilwell had called Chennault a "pain in the neck." Needless to say, a huge dispute about strategy developed between the two U.S. commanders.

The main goal of the British was to preserve their colonial administrations in Burma and India. Accordingly, the English saw the Americans and the Chinese as posing as much of a political threat to their interests as the Japanese posed militarily. When the Allies agreed to make Chiang commander in chief of the China theater, the British opposed efforts to give him authority in the eastern provinces of Burma. The British also turned down his offer of Chinese soldiers for the defense of the colony, fearing that it would be difficult to remove the Chinese and reestablish their authority and administration at war's end.

As Stilwell traveled to his new command, the Japanese launched a spring offensive in Southeast Asia, quickly taking Singapore and defeating the Allied navies in the Battle of the Java Sea, which exposed Australia to attack. The Japanese advanced into Burma and threatened to cut off China from its allies. British imperial forces temporarily blocked the advance but were quickly driven back. The British decided that they would accept the service of the Chinese army in the defense of Burma. When Stilwell arrived, he discovered that he had no real authority over the Chinese divisions under his command and that Chiang bypassed him, sending orders directly to unit commanders. Some of these divisions fought well, but British imperial forces collapsed under Japanese assault and exposed the flank of the Chinese. While the same Chinese and British imperial units retreated into India, the Japanese attacked and cut off the Chinese escape route back into China. With his back against the jungle-covered mountains of northern Burma, Stilwell was trapped, but he marched his staff into the wilderness and hiked 140 miles to Imphal, India. Every one of the 114 people who had left Burma with him three weeks before made it to India alive. His honest and direct comments about the defeat ("I say we took a hell of a beating") turned him into a media hero.

The loss of Burma effectively cut off China from its allies. Washington responded in two ways to supply Chiang and keep China in the war. First, the United States sent supplies through air transport. Although the distance between the airfields in India and China was less than 1,000 miles, the planes had to travel over the Himalayas; the high altitude limited the amount of materiel the planes could carry. In fact, flying supplies over the mountains ("The Hump") was basically a futile effort, because the Air Transport Command consumed a gallon of fuel for every gallon it delivered. The second U.S. response was the construction of a road from Ledo, India, through the jungles of northern Burma to southern China. Construction took two and a half years, and by the time the road was finished, the Allies had driven the Japanese out of Burma. Now planes could fly a more direct route that avoided the Himalayas and allowed them to carry more supplies.

Despite these logistical efforts, Stilwell believed the key to supplying China was to retake Burma, and he proposed an immediate counteroffensive to push the Japanese out. His plan called for a two-pronged offensive. Nationalist units from southern China would attack one Japanese flank while a task force of Chinese and British imperial divisions would attack the other flank from India. The general figured that simultaneous operations from both the west and the east would make it difficult for the Japanese to counter either. Chiang reluctantly agreed to this plan, providing that the British played an active role and that the Allies had an effective air force. He also agreed to allow Stilwell to set up a training center at Ramagarh in eastern India. Inasmuch as Lend-Lease supplies were stockpiling in India, Chiang had little choice if he wanted to keep the British from taking materiel that he believed belonged to him. The transport planes flying supplies from Ramagarh to China returned with Chinese soldiers, often stripped of all clothing, for training.

Under strong pressure from the United States, the British reluctantly agreed to launch an offensive in Burma. The plan was soon shelved, much to the joy of Chiang. President Roosevelt liked Chennault's ideas more than Stilwell's, and British Prime Minister Winston Churchill believed that the jungles of Burma were about the last place in the world where the Allies should fight the Japanese. Chennault received command of the new Fourteenth Air Force and promotion to the rank of major general. He failed, however, to deliver on his projections of success; his planes did little damage to Japanese supply lines and were unable to secure air superiority.

In the late summer of 1943, the British, in an effort to prove that they were committed to an offensive in East Asia, proposed the creation of the Southeast Asia Command. The commander would be the aristocratic Vice Admiral Lord Louis Mountbatten. The Combined Chiefs assigned Stilwell to serve as his deputy, which complicated command organizations, since some officers who also had double assignments were his subordinates in one theater and his superiors in the other. Although

Stilwell and Mountbatten were agreeable and polite in public, they feuded in private. The admiral supported Chinese efforts to have Stilwell relieved of his command, thus increasing the American's dislike of the "limeys." Mountbatten initially proposed a multioperation offensive code-named Tarzan and Buccaneer. The Tarzan plan called for a combined land and airborne operation in central Burma, while Buccaneer was an amphibious assault on the Andaman Islands in the Bay of Bengal. Mountbatten's proposal met Chiang's requirements that the British contribute to an attack to retake Burma, but the Combined Chiefs of Staff rejected the plan, seeing no advantage in taking the islands and finding that amphibious assault craft were needed to launch the invasion of France. Mountbatten then proposed Operation Axiom—basically, to abandon plans to retake northern Burma and finish the Ledo Road and, instead, to retake the British colony of Malaya. Stilwell's opposition to Axiom was instant and intense. The British and U.S. Chiefs of Staff backed either Mountbatten or Stilwell, respectively, which resulted in stalemate until events on the battlefield took over.

In late December 1943, Stilwell initiated an offensive to retake northern Burma and thus forced a resolution of the debate on strategy, hoping that other Allied commands would take supportive action once he was committed in the field. He also decided to accompany the troops into the field, so he could prod reluctant Chinese units into action. Except for a few quick trips to his headquarters, he remained in the jungles of Burma until July 1944. Stilwell's forces had local air superiority and outnumbered the Japanese. Although slow and not as aggressive as Stilwell might have liked, the Chinese defeated the Japanese in their first engagement. Stilwell also deployed the 5307th Provisional Regiment, better known as Merrill's Marauders, a commando unit that was designed to conduct long-range patrols and raids well behind enemy lines, disrupting communications and supply efforts. Stilwell intended to use the Marauders as the spearhead to his attack, and they did their job well; but the jungle and Japanese opposition whittled them down to half their strength. Using the fast-moving Americans and the slower Chinese divisions as a hammer and anvil, Stilwell marched through northern Burma toward the town of Myitkyina, a critical road junction. The Marauders quickly took the airfield on May 17, but they lacked the strength to drive the Japanese garrison from the town itself. The Japanese rushed reinforcements to the town, but they overestimated the strength of the Allies and made no effort to drive out the force controlling the airfield. The heavy rains of monsoon season turned the battle for control of Myitkyina into a siege that lasted until August 3.

While this battle went on, the Japanese launched two offensives in the spring; one posed a direct threat to Stilwell's military position, and the other eventually destroyed his political standing. The first attack came in March, with the Japanese attempt to invade India along its boarder with Burma. The attack surprised the British, who thought the jungles of Burma were a natural defensive barrier. The Japanese quickly surrounded garrisons along the boarder, which had the potential not only of opening up India to Japanese occupation but also of cutting off and isolating Stilwell in Burma. British imperial forces, however, held out, supplied through air drops. The struggle soon turned into a bloody battle of attrition. The Japanese had long, weak supply lines and were at a disadvantage. In July their invasion force withdrew, having suffered casualty rates of 50 percent.

A month after attacking India, the Japanese launched Operation Ichigo, a plan to advance deep into central China and seize U.S. airfields in order to end raids on Japanese supply lines. The Fourteenth Air Force could only hamper and slow down the advance, which appeared to have the real potential to knock China out of the war. Chennault demanded more supplies, but Marshall refused, believing that air power alone could not stop the Japanese. During this period of crisis, the United States decided to make some low-level contacts with the Communist forces in northeast China. The U.S. officials and journalists accompanying them were favorably impressed with the Communists' energy, willingness to fight, and direct manner, which seemed so different from the corruption and weakness of Chiang's Nationalist regime. The observers recommended that the United States provide the Communists with Lend-Lease supplies. Stilwell was receptive to the proposal but was soon removed from command, and the new U.S. ambassador adamantly opposed the idea. Little came from the mission.

In July 1944, officials in Washington considered the situation in the CBI theater desperate. The Japanese were advancing at will, limited only by their ability to keep supply lines in contact with troops. Believing that the situation required drastic action to prevent the collapse of China, President Roosevelt sent a sharp note calling on Chiang to give Stilwell command of all Allied forces in the country, including the Communists. To make the request more tolerable, Roosevelt promoted Stilwell to the rank of general. Chiang stalled. He agreed in principle to put Stilwell in command but asked for a U.S. representative to resolve differences between himself and the general. The tactic worked, delaying resolution of the crisis as a representative traveled to China.

Another crisis, however, forced an ultimate showdown between Chiang and Stilwell. Fearing the Japanese advances, Chiang threatened to withdraw the Chinese units fighting for Myitkyina so they could defend the portion of southeast China that he still controlled. General Marshall responded with a second note from President Roosevelt to Chiang, insisting that he give command of his army to Stilwell. When the message arrived in China, Stilwell insisted on delivering it personally. Americans who watched Chiang read the note said that he reacted as though he had taken a blow to the stomach. "I understand," was his only reply. But he refused to bend to the U.S. pressure and brazenly demanded Stilwell's removal instead. He couched the terms of his refusal in matters of national sovereignty, saying that he no longer had confidence in Stilwell and that, as chief of state, he had the authority to insist on the removal of an officer whom he found wanting. Roosevelt agreed to recall the general, believing that the dispute was largely a clash of personalities and that his choice was between either Chiang or Stilwell.

On October 19, 1944, Stilwell received word that he was being recalled and that he had only forty-eight hours to leave. The China-Burma-India Command dissolved with the end of Stilwell's tenure. Lieutenant General Daniel Sultan became the commander of the Burma-India theater, while Major General Albert Wedemeyer replaced Stilwell as chief of staff to Chiang and commander of U.S. forces in China. Stilwell's last position, as deputy commander of the Southeast Asia Command, went to Lieutenant General Raymond Wheeler. Stilwell left his command with a mixed record. His efforts to retake Burma were successful, and he had also shown that the Chinese soldier could be an excellent fighter. But he had made no progress in initiating institutional reforms in the Chinese army to make it an effective fighting force, and he had not turned the China theater into an important arena of combat operations.

FURTHER READINGS

Anders, L. *The Ledo Road: General Joseph W. Stilwell's Highway to China* (1965).

Romanus, Charles, and Riley Sunderland. *Stilwell's Mission to China* (1953).

———— and ————. *Stilwell's Command Problems* (1956).

———— and ————. *Time Runs Out in CBI* (1959).

———— and ————. *Stilwell's Personal File: China, Burma, India, 1942–1944,* 5 vols. (1976).

Tuchman, Barbara. *Stilwell and the American Experience in China, 1911–1945* (1971).

White, T., ed. *The Stilwell Papers* (1948).

Ziegler, P. *Mountbatten* (1985).

———, ed. *Personal Diary of Admiral the Lord Louis Mountbatten, Supreme Commander, South East Asia, 1943–1946* (1988).

Papers of General Joseph W. Stilwell. Hoover Institute, Stanford University, California.

Nicholas E. Sarantakes

SEE ALSO Chiang Kai-shek; Merrill's Marauders (Galahad); Mountbatten, Louis; Office of Strategic Services in the Pacific; Stilwell, Joseph Warren

Chindits

Name given to the long-range penetration groups (LRPGs) employed by the British army in Burma during World War II. The term "Chindits" was derived from the "Chinthe" lion statues that guard the entrances to Burmese pagodas, and was coined by the journalist Alaric Jacob, of the *Daily Express* of London, in May 1943.

When Japan overran Burma in March 1942, the British commander, General Archibald Wavell, asked the eccentric Brigadier Orde Wingate to organize a special force to operate behind Japanese lines. The year before, Wingate had successfully led Ethiopian guerrillas during Wavell's campaign in Italian East Africa.

By July 1942, Wingate was training 77th Indian Infantry Brigade, using his ideas on jungle warfare and air supply. The 77th Brigade comprised two, rather than the usual three, battalions but did include the 142d Commando Unit, Burmese Rifles troops, Royal Air Force personnel, and signals specialists. It was organized into eight columns for infiltration into Burma. The Chindits' first campaign commenced on February 14, 1943, when they crossed the India–Burma border in two groups. The northern group, with 2,200 troops and 850 mules, crossed the Chindwin River at Tonhe; the southern group, with 1,000 troops and 250 mules, crossed at Auktaung. They first clashed with the Japanese at Mainyaung on February 18. The Chindits destroyed rail lines and bridges, then crossed the Irrawaddy River on March 9. Lack of water in the area between the Irrawaddy and Scweli rivers and increasing Japanese opposition led Wingate to begin evacuating his force on March 27. Only 2,182 malaria- and dysentery-racked survivors, of whom only 600 were fit for further service, reached India. But the Chindits had marched 1,500 miles in six weeks and had proved that air drops could keep them supplied while operating behind Japanese lines. That the Chindits had not been destroyed by the Japanese was hailed as a victory at a time when other British troops had been soundly defeated in their first Arakan offensive in Burma. Thus the Chindits provided a great morale boost to the British in the Pacific.

As a result Wingate became a favorite of British Prime Minister Winston Churchill, who was attracted to unconventional warfare. Wingate attended the Quebec Conference of August 1943, where he impressed U.S. President Franklin Roosevelt.

Wingate gained permission to expand the Chindits into six long-range penetration group (LRPG) brigades and was promised U.S. air support, the 1st U.S. Air Commando. This unit, commanded by Colonel Philip ("Flip") Cochrane (inspiration for the very popular comic strip of the time, "Terry and the Pirates"), comprised 12 C-47 transports, 225 WACO gliders, 100 L-5 light planes, 12 B-25 bombers, 30 P-51 fighters, and 6 helicopters. With these resources at his disposal, Wingate modified his tactics. Each LRPG brigade would be landed at a suitable site, deep inside Burma, where it would construct defended bases. From there each brigade would fan out and attack Japanese lines of communication.

During 1944, the Chindits conducted their second campaign, code-named "Thursday," which planned to insert three LRPG brigades supported by the Air Commando. The remaining three LRPG brigades would be flown in later as reinforcements. The purpose of "Thursday" was to assist U.S. General Joseph Stilwell, who, with three Chinese divisions and the 5307th U.S. Composite Regiment (Merrill's Marauders), was moving against Myitkyina and Mogaung in northern Burma. One Chindit column would move overland to attack Indaw, and two Chindit brigades would be dropped near Mawlu and Mohniyn. From there they could sit astride Japanese road, rail, and river traffic routes, blocking any supplies and reinforcements from reaching the Japanese opposing Stilwell. At the time that "Thursday" was launched, the Japanese began their drive on India that culminated in the battles of Kohima and Imphal. This offensive was conducted partly because the Japanese commander in Burma, General Mutaguchi, believed that he needed to strike the British before they conducted another Chindit operation in the Japanese rear areas.

"Thursday" commenced on February 5, 1944, when Brigadier Bernard Ferguson's 16th Brigade left Ledo, India, to march into Burma. By March 1, the brigade was well inside Burma, having crossed the Chindwin. Brigadier Mike Calvert's 77th Brigade was meant to seize three landing grounds, Piccadilly, Broadway, and Chowringhee.

But on March 5, as Calvert's brigade was about to enplane, air reconnaissance revealed that Piccadilly was covered in tree obstructions. Therefore the entire 77th Brigade landed at Broadway. Calvert used accompanying U.S. engineers to clear an airstrip for subsequent landings. Within a few days, antiaircraft guns and artillery were delivered, together with other heavy equipment and reinforcements. On March 9, Morrisforce landed at Chowringhee. It marched to the Kachin Hills and recruited Kachin guerrillas to harass the Myitkyina–Bhamo road. By March 11, Brigadier W. D. A. Lentaigne's 111th Brigade had arrived at Broadway and Chowringhee. The day before, the 16th Brigade established Aberdeen base, 27 miles northwest of Indaw.

After establishing Broadway, Calvert's brigade moved westward toward the railway. One column blew up the railway bridge at Mawhun while another destroyed road convoys near Pinwe. A third column headed south to Shwegu on the Irrawaddy, where they blocked river traffic. The bulk of Calvert's brigade established a base just north of Mawlu. This was White City, so called because of the supply parachutes festooning the trees there (and also named in memory of a popular London stadium). On March 21, Japanese forces made their first assault on White City. Wingate flew to Broadway, White City, and Aberdeen to assess the situation; he died in an air crash while en route to India on March 24. Command of the Chindits passed to Lentaigne, and that of the 111th Brigade to Major John Masters (later a successful novelist).

With the British Fourteenth Army facing encirclement on the Indian border, its commander, General William Slim, retained use of the Chindits' 23d Brigade and the Air Commando's C-47s; he released the 14th Brigade and 3d West African Brigade for use at Aberdeen. Brigadier Tom Brodie's 14th Brigade began arriving on March 24. Wingate had ordered Ferguson to strike from Aberdeen and take Indaw, but lack of C-47s prevented the 14th Brigade from reinforcing Ferguson in time. When Ferguson attacked on March 26, the Japanese had entrenched three battalions around Indaw. After four days of fighting, the 16th Brigade retreated to Aberdeen.

On March 26, the Japanese made their major assault on Broadway. With air support, they were able to breach the perimeter defenses but were ejected by March 31. Meanwhile, the 77th Brigade had expanded White City by capturing Mawlu. Calvert now controlled 40 miles of railway and blocked river traffic on the Irrawaddy, so White City was a major threat to Japanese communications. From April 6 to April 12, the Japanese employed six battalions, aircraft, tanks and a 3-inch siege mortar to attack White City. After the 3d West African Brigade sent reinforcements overland from Aberdeen, Calvert counterattacked on April 7. By April 15 the siege of White City was lifted.

Slim then ordered the Chindits to abandon their bases and move farther north along the railway. His concern was that the imminent monsoon would make the airstrips at Aberdeen, Broadway, and White City unusable, thereby rendering air supply of the Chindits impossible. Slim's solution was to establish a new base, close to Indawgyi Lake, from which flying boats could operate. Lentaigne ordered the air evacuation of the exhausted 16th Brigade to India, beginning April 27, thus closing Aberdeen. Chowringhee was already deserted, White City was abandoned on May 8, and Broadway was vacated on May 13. Three days later, operational control of the Chindits passed from Slim to the prickly Stilwell.

The 111th Brigade began establishing a new base, Blackpool, on May 9. When Stilwell captured Myitkyina's airfield on May 17, the Japanese sent their 53d Division north from Indaw to relieve their encircled garrison in Myitkyina town. Blackpool was meant to block such reinforcements but suffered Japanese attacks before its defenses were completed. Heavy rain denied Masters air support, and he received little help from the other Chindit brigades. The West African and 14th brigades were protecting the route to Indawgyi Lake. Stilwell, pressing on against Mogaung, had ordered the 77th Brigade to assist him. On May 14, the Japanese attacked Blackpool. The 111th Brigade stalled them until May 25, when Masters ordered a retreat to Mokso.

Morrisforce had closed the Myitkyina–Bhamo road when Stilwell ordered Brigadier Morris to participate in Myitikyina's encirclement. Direct assaults on Waingmaw and Maigna decimated Morris's small unit, which was evacuated on July 14. Meanwhile, the 77th Brigade reached Mogaung on May 31. Calvert's troops fought their way into Mogaung but were exhausted by June 13. The Chinese 114th Regiment's arrival on June 18 helped Calvert renew the attack. Mogaung fell to the Chindits on June 26. The decimated 111th and 77th brigades were evacuated in early July. During June–July, the remaining Chindit brigades campaigned around Taugni. The 14th Brigade was evacuated on August 17; the West African Brigade, on August 26.

"Thursday" cost the Chindits 3,628 battle casualties, with many more ill. Such heavy losses, plus Wingate's death, sealed the Chindits' fate. Slim ordered their disbandment in late 1944. Nonetheless, the Chindits had helped defeat the Japanese invasion of India by distracting the equivalent of two Japanese divisions that otherwise would have been available at Kohima or Imphal.

FURTHER READINGS

Calvert, Michael. *The Chindits* (1974).

Rooney, David. *Burma Victory* (1992).

Shaw, James. *The March Out* (1956).

Slim, Field Marshal the Viscount William. *Defeat into Victory* (1956).

Jonathan Ford

SEE ALSO China-Burma-India Theater of Operations; Slim, William Joseph; Stilwell, Joseph Warren; Wingate, Orde C.

Chinese Communists versus Nationalists

China's Kuomintang (Nationalist Party) was the 1912 successor of Sun Yat-sen's T'ungmenghui Party, founded in 1905. Sun soon became the sole leader of the Kuomintang, which founded an anti-Beijing (Peking) opposition government in Canton in 1917. In January 1923, Sun signed an agreement with the Soviet official Adolf Joffe, establishing the so-called United Front policy.

The Chinese Communist Party (founded in 1921) was an unwilling member of the United Front. In fact, recent research has shown that the Soviet Union ordered the Chinese Communists to enter the United Front with the Kuomintang in order to pressure Beijing into acceding to its diplomatic demands that Outer Mongolia and the Chinese Eastern Railway in Manchuria remain under Russian control. This policy produced tensions in the first United Front that contributed to its eventual demise.

Under Soviet influence, in 1924 the Kuomintang held its first party congress, which included Communists, and accepted Sun's "Three Principles of the People," which called for nationalism, democracy, and "People's livelihood" (similar to, but not exactly compatible with, socialism). When Sun died in 1925, his successor, Chiang Kai-shek assumed control. After completing the Kuomintang's 1926–1927 northern expedition against Beijing, Chiang dismissed his Russian advisers and violently purged the Chinese Communist Party from the United Front. In 1928 the Kuomintang founded a central Chinese government at Nanking.

After 1927, the Kuomintang continued its efforts to destroy the Chinese Communists, who concentrated their forces in south Jiangxi province. During the course of five major "bandit suppression campaigns," beginning in December 1930 and lasting until 1935, the Kuomintang attempted to exterminate the Communists. The fifth, and final, campaign forced the Chinese Communists from their base in southern China. In 1934–1935, under the leadership of Mao Tse-tung, the Chinese Communists undertook the Long March and relocated to northwestern China.

In 1931, Japan occupied Manchuria and created the puppet state of Manchukuo. Four years later, the Communists once again proposed a United Front with the Kuomintang. In December 1936, Chang Hsueh-liang, the former warlord of Manchuria, kidnapped Chiang and pressured him to ally with the Communists. Although no formal agreement was signed, on December 25, 1936, Chiang returned to Nanking with Chang, who was placed under house arrest. After the so-called Xian incident, Chou En-lai held talks with Chiang and other Kuomintang officials, and the Chinese Communists and the Kuomintang soon established a second United Front. The civil war abated, and both parties turned their attention to Japan.

On July 7, 1937, full-scale war with Japan erupted after the Marco Polo Bridge incident. During 1937–1938, the Nanking government allowed the Chinese Communist Army to be reorganized as the Eighth Route Army. The Eighth Route Army garrisoned the northwestern border regions, which included the former Communist areas. In return, during the first three years the Communist forces received money and ammunition from the Nationalist government. In addition, Chou En-lai was selected as a member of the presidium of the Extraordinary National Congress of the Kuomintang in March 1938 and was appointed Vice Minister of the Political Training Board of the National Military Council, a position he held until 1940.

In late 1938, relations between the Kuomintang and the Chinese Communist Party deteriorated, as the Kuomintang outlawed Communist-sponsored mass organizations and criticized the Communists for not allowing the Nationalist government to retain direct command over the Communist armies in the field. Communist-Kuomintang friction culminated in the New Fourth Army incident of January 1941, when Nationalist and Communist armies clashed. An uneasy alliance continued through May 1944, at which time discussions between representatives of the Kuomintang and the Chinese Communist Party began in Sian.

The United States tried on several occasions to temper Kuomintang-Communist tensions. During the spring of 1944, President Roosevelt appointed Vice President Henry A. Wallace to travel to China, and he carried out talks with Jiang in Chungking in late June. Major General Patrick J. Hurley later arrived in Chungking on September 6, 1944, and also tried to fortify China's anti-Japanese determination. The Nationalists, trained and led by U.S.

advisers, finally mounted an offensive in the spring and summer of 1945. Nonetheless, it could be asserted that throughout the war years neither the Chinese Nationalists nor the Communists could do much to hinder Japanese movements and operations in China. As Japanese power waned, the Kuomintang and the Communists gradually became embroiled in their civil struggle.

Following the Yalta Agreement, the Nationalists and the Soviet Union negotiated and signed their own agreement on August 14, 1945. Although this agreement guaranteed Chinese sovereignty in Manchuria, by early November 1945 it became clear that Soviet withdrawal would lead to the immediate occupation of Manchuria by the Chinese Communists. The Kuomintang therefore negotiated with the Soviets to extend their stay and to allow Kuomintang troops to enter the region. The Soviet evacuation was eventually delayed four more times, until early May 1946, by which time the Chinese Communists had consolidated their control through Manchuria (and the Soviets had stripped Manchuria of its industrial plant).

In December 1945, President Truman appointed General George Marshall (former chief of staff of the U.S. Army) as his special envoy to replace Hurley. The president instructed Marshall to work for a cease-fire between the Kuomintang and the Chinese Communists. He also urged the peaceful reunification of China by the holding of a national convention, as earlier agreed to by Chiang and Mao. Marshall's mission appeared to produce immediate results, and a cease-fire went into effect on January 10, 1946. On February 25, agreements were announced that specified the reorganization of the national government along constitutional lines, revision of the 1936 constitution, and the creation of one army under a unified command.

Although the garrisoning of Communist troops in Manchuria did not violate these agreements, as the Russian forces withdrew during mid-March, the Communists quickly took their place. Kuomintang troops in Mukden defeated the Chinese Communist forces within twenty-four hours, but the Kuomintang consolidated full control only on May 23.

With the cease-fire broken, Marshall withdrew as mediator but continued to act as the intermediary between the Kuomintang and the Chinese Communists. In this capacity, he supported further negotiations with the Chinese Communists, but Chiang declared that this would be the last time he would negotiate. The major stumbling block to a new agreement was the Communists' insistence on the continuation of all existing local governments in northern China after the Communists evacuated their troops. This was unacceptable to the Kuomintang. As a result of this failure, the Marshall mission was formally terminated on January 6, 1947.

After the United States halted its active support of the Kuomintang, the Chinese Communists gradually gained the upper hand. On April 23, 1949, Communist forces overran Nanjing and began the task of consolidating control over all of continental China, forcing the Kuomintang retreat to Taiwan. On October 1, 1949, Mao declared the formation of the People's Republic of China from the Gate of Heavenly Peace in Beijing.

FURTHER READINGS

Corr, Gerard H. *The Chinese Red Army: Campaigns and Politics since 1949* (1974).

Dreyer, Edward L. *China at War, 1901–1949* (1995).

Hsu, Immanuel C. *The Rise of Modern China* (1995).

Liu, F. F. *A Military History of Modern China*, 1924–1949 (1956).

Spence, Jonathan D. *The Search for Modern China* (1990).

Bruce A. Elleman

SEE ALSO Chennault, Claire Lee; Chiang Kai-shek; People's Liberation Army; Stilwell, Joseph Warren

Clark and Iba Airfields, Japanese Bombing of

For high-level U.S. war planners the defense of the Philippine Islands from Japanese attack would hinge on air power. The Japanese agreed that they needed to reduce General Douglas MacArthur's fledgling air force before they could invade the Philippines. To do that, they massed significant air power on Formosa for an attack the morning of December 8, 1941. Takeoff was scheduled for 0300 hours (Philippine time) for a flight that would last three and a half hours, one way. The plan was to reach Nichols and Clark Fields—the main U.S. fighter and bomber bases—at about 0630 hours, using the dark to avoid interception but arriving in time to use first light.

But Monday morning on Formosa began badly. Mists came in from the sea, closing Formosa's airfields and grounding the navy's Eleventh Air Fleet. The fog was so thick by the scheduled takeoff time that pilots could see barely a few yards. With all hope of surprise completely gone, Formosa's planners canceled the attack on Nichols Field, just south of Manila, where two squadrons of P-40Es were based. They switched twenty-seven of the fifty-four bombers slated to attack Nichols to the pursuit-squadron base at Iba Field on Luzon's west coast. They did not want Iba's one squadron of P-40Es hitting the bombers in the flank as they passed by on their way to Clark.

Eleventh Air Fleet's staff also worked up a diversion: The remaining twenty-seven bombers of the canceled Nichols force would fly south before the main force, to lure Iba's P-40s up and exhaust their fuel before the main Clark and Iba strike forces arrived. Those twenty-seven bombers would then join the main strike as it arrived over Iba—they hoped, just as the U.S. warplanes had to land for fuel.

The fog began to clear at 0800 hours. Takeoff would start at 0900 hours. Eleventh Air Fleet made one final change: It canceled the twenty-seven navy bombers that had just been scheduled to draw off Iba's fighters. If those planes started the battle with the diversion, it would add another two hours to the already badly delayed time schedule, and aircraft would be returning to Formosa after dark. Unwilling to accept any more delays, Japanese planners rolled those planes back into the strike force aimed at Iba.

Fifty-four navy Mitsubishi twin-engined, twin-tailed Type 96 bombers (Nells) from the Takao Group and fifty Zeros from the 3d Air Group moved into their takeoff routine. Their target was Iba Field. Fifty-four Mitsubishi G4M1 Type 1 twin-engined, single-tailed bombers (Bettys) from the Kanoya Group began taxiing for take-off. The Tainan Air Group's forty-four Zeros moved into position ready to follow. Their target was the major base at Clark.

The first bomber started down the strip at 0900 hours. By 0945 hours, the last Japanese aircraft were in the air. The Zeros split. One group stayed to escort the bombers, while the second group flew ahead to engage what should be wide-awake U.S. pilots in pursuit craft. The first Zeros approached Clark in central Luzon just before 1230 hours with the mission of clearing the skies of defending aircraft.

After all their concerns while fog-bound on Formosa, the Japanese were not prepared for what they saw: U.S. aircraft squatted on Clark like sitting ducks. Japanese pilots could not believe it. What they did not know was that the big four-engine B-17s had just returned from more then three hours in the air, and that the one squadron of pursuit aircraft based at Clark had set down to refuel after having been up for two and a half hours. Nor did they know of the paralyzing indecision over missions and targets that had plagued U.S. commanders. Equally astounding to the Japanese was their perception that no one on the ground could see them circling high above the field.

Various P-40s were flying into and out of Clark air space. Some rushed south to Manila and then north back to Clark. Eight came in from Iba at top speed burning up gas, looked for Japanese, saw none, and turned back to Iba to refuel. Four flew in from Nichols, saw nothing, and departed. A few P-40s pulled out of their formations and headed home because oil from brand-new engines had sprayed their windshields. Individual aircraft tried to link up with missing squadron mates or arrived at Clark after responding to radio instructions. Amazingly, not a single P-40 pilot saw or recognized the Zeros.

Down below, three B-17s selected for a Formosa reconnaissance sat with their engines running. For some reason, Clark's bombers had not received an earlier warning about the incoming Japanese or an order to scramble the Clark-based pursuit squadron. Everyone accepted that no news from the Air Warning Service was good news. Armorers were loading bombs into the two squadrons of B-17s. The two battalions of antiaircraft artillerymen protecting Clark sat at their 37-mm and 3-inch guns and their .50-caliber machine guns.

An irregular pulsing drone, a low moaning, passed over Clark at about 1230 hours, and the shocked Americans looked up. Above them at about 22,000 to 25,000 feet flew two groups, one behind the other—first twenty-seven, then twenty-six Japanese bombers. The seven-man bomber crews tensed behind their defensive machine guns. They expected fighters to pounce on them at any moment. Betty bombers had sacrificed all armor and survivability to achieve their long-range characteristics. Almost any sort of hit in their totally unprotected and immense wing tanks would knock them down. Their arrival at Clark was a total technological surprise, even though the Betty had made its combat debut over China. Like the Zero, the Betty had been unknown to the Americans.

Sixteen P-40Bs of the 20th Pursuit Squadron frantically taxied onto the runway. They had finally seen the Japanese, whose bombardiers now had in their sights the targets they had studied so long. What the Japanese did not have was U.S. fighters or antiaircraft bothering them as they approached, so their aim was superb. The Japanese fighters who had expected to initiate the attack by breaking up defending pursuit squadrons had nothing to do. All the P-40s that had flown in and out of Clark air space over the past ten minutes had disappeared. For the next fifteen minutes, the Japanese dropped long strings of 300-pound demolition and smaller incendiary bombs in the most phenomenally accurate strike that Japanese horizontal bombers made in all of World War II.

Most of the U.S. bombers were relatively well dispersed and protected by blast pens—as best they could be, considering that dispersal facilities had not yet been completed—and escaped damage from the high-level bombers. The Americans had hardly begun to recover before a large formation of thirty-four Zeros lined up and attacked the field from south to north. A terrible blow was the loss of Clark's single tower radio, which was needed for ground-to-fighter communications; Zeros strafed the tower and damaged the transmitting and receiving gear.

The surviving B-17s were now trapped, and the blast pens and dispersion that had saved them from the horizontal bombers were now of no help. Japanese Zeros shot the flying fortresses to pieces, despite return fire from crewmen manning the planes' .50-caliber machine guns. The 200th Antiaircraft Artillery Regiment had guns around Clark, but many of the most experienced men—draftees over 35 years old—had already sailed back to the United States. Skeleton crews had originally manned the guns, so the antiaircraft gunners could not engage even the first several flights.

More than an hour after they had started their low-level attacks, the last of the Japanese wheeled back to the northwest. Clark Field was a near-total wreck. Fifteen B-17s were destroyed, and another four were badly damaged and could not fly without repairs. One OA-9 observation aircraft and several old B-10s and B-18s were also destroyed. Sixteen of the 20th Pursuit's twenty-three modern P-40Bs were destroyed. Smoking aircraft littered the field, gasoline dumps were aflame, and it seemed as though every building was on fire.

The Clark Field disaster overshadowed another disaster taking place simultaneously at Iba Field. The 3d Pursuit Squadron had flown its P-40Es off the grass strip at about 1145 hours in a high-speed run to intercept Japanese reported heading for Manila. They failed to spot any Japanese, and the planes raced back when they heard the Iba Field radio warn of an enemy force coming in from the sea.

Interceptor Command headquarters failed to hear this message (two squadrons of P-40s were patrolling over Manila Bay awaiting orders), so no help was sent to Iba. The 3d Pursuit reached Iba low on fuel. The pilots were tired and frustrated by two successive failed interception attempts. The squadron entered the landing pattern at 1245 hours. As the first P-40 landed, fifty-four twin-engined Nell bombers and fifty Zeros struck. The Japanese were putting half their bombers and more than half their fighters against just 20 percent of the U.S. pursuit strength—more than a hundred planes against eighteen.

A nice bomb pattern started at the northwest corner of Iba Field. Barracks and service buildings were hit, and much of the equipment used to maintain the planes was destroyed. The critical radar that had been giving warnings of enemy formations, and which was still reporting even as the bombs fell, was blown apart, and every man on duty was killed. Loss of the Iba radar would prove fatal for subsequent attempts to defend Luzon's air space.

A few U.S. pilots rallied, opened their throttles, and desperately clawed for altitude. They turned into the enemy even as they kept one eye on their near-empty fuel gauges. Although the Americans could never make up for their initial disadvantage in altitude and speed, they attacked the Japanese Zeros despite being outnumbered more than 4 to 1. The Japanese shot down five P-40s, and swirling dogfights ran three more Americans out of gas.

Although the 3d Pursuit Squadron failed to shoot down a single Zero, its desperate attack prevented the Japanese from the unopposed strafing attacks that had so devastated Clark. Regardless, the 3d Pursuit had lost sixteen P-40s—nearly the entire squadron—as well as forty-five trained pilots, mechanics, and radar operators. Telephone, teletype, and radio links to the rest of Luzon were cut; the airfield could not communicate.

The sun was reaching for the horizon off Formosa when the returning bombers came into view. After the initial morning activity required to get the attack force airborne, life on the airfields had returned to normal. The only indication that war had started was Tokyo's filling the airwaves with urgent inquiries about the attack. The Japanese knew that they had started badly behind schedule and were worried about the outcome. The first comments from the returning bomber pilots showed their bewilderment: "Are we really at war?" They had met very little opposition, and the U.S. planes had been lined up on the ground as though it were still peacetime.

Japanese intelligence experts were hard-pressed to credit the claims of their pilots. No one had dared anticipate the crushing victory that they had just won. Everyone had expected a hard fight and a certain minimal success, but nothing like this. Loss estimates for the first month had ranged from 25 to 40 percent. So it was a miracle that only seven fighters failed to return and that every bomber came home. The Japanese believed that they had destroyed all fifteen of the U.S. fighters they had encountered in the air, and they estimated that they had destroyed forty to fifty bombers and fighters at Clark and twenty-five fighters at Iba.

Information of the twin disasters began to arrive at MacArthur's headquarters and stunned the officers there. The air battle on which the defense of the Philippines hinged had been fought and lost, despite U.S. forces being fully alerted. Half the heavy bomber force—the offensive arm that was to deny the waters around the islands to an invasion fleet—was gone. Two of MacArthur's four modern pursuit squadrons had been destroyed. Service and support operations for the remaining aircraft had been disrupted. Iba radar—the only radar in operation—was gone. The war was a mere eleven hours old, the Japanese had been over Luzon for one hour, and the decisive air battle had already been lost. The Clark and Iba raids were the greatest purely air disaster in U.S. military history.

FURTHER READINGS

Allicin, P. *Bataan: The Judgment Seat. The Saga of the Philippine Command of the United States Army Air Force, May 1941 to May 1942* (1944).

Bartsch, William H. *Doomed at the Start: American Pursuit Pilots in the Philippines, 1941–1942* (1992).

Brereton, Lewis H. *The Brereton Diaries: The War in the Air in the Pacific, Middle East and Europe, 3 October 1941–8 May 1945* (1946).

Craven, Wesley F., and James E. Cate, eds. *The Army Air Forces in World War II*, vol. I, *Plans and Early Operations, January 1939 to August 1942* (1948).

Edmonds, Walter D. *They Fought with What They Had* (1951).

Sarai, Saburo. *Samurai!* (1957).

Schemata, Cacao. "Air Operations in the Philippines." *The Japanese Navy in World War II: An Anthology of Articles by Former Officers of the Imperial Japanese Navy and Air Defense Force* (1969).

Shores, Christopher, and Brian Cull, with Yasuho Izawa. *Bloody Shambles. The Drift to War to the Fall of Singapore* (1992).

John W. Whitman

SEE ALSO Army Air Corps/Air Forces, U.S.; Philippines, Fall of

Coastwatchers

Concerned about the vulnerability to invasion of Australia's exposed northeastern coast, in 1919 the Royal Australian Navy established the Islands Coastwatching Service—the Coastwatchers—in the series of islands stretching across that area (including Papua New Guinea, the Solomons, and the New Hebrides). As Japanese ambitions became apparent, the navy appointed Commander Eric A. Feldt to make the coastwatching network as effective as possible, training and equipping existing Coastwatchers and adding new ones as needed to fill gaps in the line. The characteristics he looked for in Coastwatchers—self-reliance, inventiveness, quick thinking, and patience while being restive and rebellious about day-to-day routines of established civilization—cut across all national, military, civil, age, and skill categories. Feldt found willing recruits among the traders, settlers, colonial officials, and adventurers who lived on the remote, undeveloped islands.

The period of menace to the Coastwatchers lasted from the beginning of the war until September 1944. Moving south through the Dutch East Indies, the Japanese occupied the Solomons, including Guadalcanal, by June 1942. Although some Coastwatchers were captured, killed, or driven off, many survived in the bush as Allied forces began fighting their way back up the island chain that summer. The Coastwatchers reported the movement of Japanese air and naval forces in the "Slot," the portion of the Solomon Sea between two lines of islands that ran roughly parallel to each other from Bougainville in the north to Guadalcanal in the south; they rescued downed fliers and sailors and helped to evacuate noncombatants. Although Feldt intended that Coastwatchers not participate in combat (he even pointedly code-named their network "Ferdinand," after the peaceful bull of literary fame), they occasionally did get involved in the fighting.

The Coastwatchers were top secret during the war. Rescued personnel were cautioned not to mention them in public. Although books and films have since memorialized them, Coastwatchers have not received their due in proportion to the importance of their role. Perhaps the most famous rescues in which Coastwatchers assisted were those of Lieutenant (junior grade) John F. Kennedy and his crewmates on PT-109 and the crew of USS *Helena*.

The Coastwatchers established close ties to local people, who in turn often supported their mission with food or shelter. The Japanese were aware of the presence and value of the Coastwatchers and exerted great effort to apprehend them. But the densely jungled, relatively unmapped and unknown island interiors as well as Feldt's strategies and tactics—and, in some cases, heroic native resistance—prevented inordinate losses.

In the first two and a half years of the Pacific war, the Coastwatchers were invaluable to the Allied effort. When the island-hopping offensive ended their observation role, they fought as guerrillas against Japanese soldiers holding out in the bush on reconquered islands and in garrisons on passed-by islands. Yet it was during their period at the forefront that the Coastwatchers performed a crucial role, and many Allied personnel lived to fight another day because of them.

FURTHER READINGS

Coggins, Jack Coggins. *The Campaign for Guadalcanal* (1972).

Craven, Wesley F., and James Lea Cate, eds. *The Army Air Forces in World War II,* vol. 4, *The Pacific: Guadalcanal to Saipan, August 1942 to July 1944* (1950).

Donovan, Robert J. *PT 109: John F. Kennedy in World War II* (1961).

Feldt, Eric A., O.B.E. *The Coastwatchers* (1946, 1959).

Lord, Walter. *Lonely Vigil: Coastwatchers of the Solomons* (1977).

Spector, Ronald H. *Eagle against the Sun: The American War with Japan* (1985).

Steven Agoratus

SEE ALSO Australia; Guadalcanal, Battle for

Comfort Women

Japanese military prostitutes known as *Jugun Ianfu* ("military comfort women") worked in *iansho* ("comfort centers," or military brothels) for the Imperial Japanese Army and Navy. Systematic military sexual exploitation of women by the Japanese began in 1894–1895 when the Imperial Japanese Army recruited prostitutes during the Sino-Japanese War. In World War II the first comfort centers under direct Japanese military control were opened at Shanghai in 1932. Fearing international criticism following reports of more than two hundred rapes by Japanese troops, Lieutenant General Okamura Yasuji brought in comfort women. Reports of rape declined, providing a rationale for comfort women; the military also considered the medically supervised comfort stations a means of combating sexually transmitted diseases and improving morale.

Comfort stations did not become widespread, however, until after the "rape of Nanking" in 1937, when Japanese soldiers ran amok for weeks. As the war spread, comfort centers existed virtually wherever troops were stationed, although Japan's Diet did not legalize the practice until August 1944. Direct army control of comfort stations usually occurred only in forward areas. Private operators ran them in noncombat regions. These proprietors had to be Japanese (which included Koreans and Taiwanese) with business experience and had to file a business plan with the military. They held paramilitary status and rank, while the army retained overall supervision and provided transportation, health services, and other support. The military considered comfort women a high priority and even euphemistically listed them as "munitions" or "canteen supplies" to ensure their prompt arrival.

The number of women and girls involved in this practice is staggering: an estimated 100,000 to 200,000. Perhaps 80 percent of them were Korean, while others came from China, Taiwan, the Philippines, and other Asian countries. Of the Koreans, an estimated 80 percent were between 14 and 18 years old when first "recruited," but some were as young as 12. Although some contracted themselves as prostitutes, for most their recruitment involved deception, coercion, and force. Initially promised employment in restaurants, canteens, and factories, they discovered their fate only when arriving at their destination, and there was no turning back. Others recount that their own families forced them to give themselves up in order to save male family members from being drafted into the military or forced labor. Under National General Mobilization regulations the Japanese seized Korean girls in virtual slave raids. In conquered areas troops forcibly conscripted women from the local population or prison camps; the latter included European women.

Comfort women experienced a variety of horrors. Initiates underwent a period of "breaking in," as might befit a horse, during which they were repeatedly beaten, raped, and subjected to other degradations before being pressed into regular service, which involved having sexual intercourse with up to thirty or forty men daily. One Japanese fighter pilot said of them: "Their bodies must have been worn out. Soldiers usually had no women around them, so they must have acted like beasts at the comfort quarters." Women who became pregnant usually had abortions—often forced. Others carried babies to term, while continuing to service troops. Some report having operations performed on them to stop menstruation and to prevent pregnancy. Besides sexually transmitted diseases, they suffered from illnesses ranging from beriberi to malaria. Escape was nearly impossible, because the women were often overseas. Some attempted suicide; those who failed were forced back into service.

The comfort stations were used by both enlisted men and officers, who paid along a sliding scale based on rank. A typical fee for a private earning about 15 yen a month was 1.5 yen. Higher ranks paid more: 2 yen for NCOs, 2.5 yen for junior officers, and 3 yen for senior officers. These rates were for thirty to forty minutes, although there was considerably less time when large groups of enlisted men arrived—usually not more than ten minutes each. Rates occasionally varied according to the race of the woman. Japanese preferred Japanese and Okinawan women and would pay more for them than for "less desirable" Southeast Asians.

The women seldom saw any of this money. Soldiers usually gave them tickets or vouchers, which they handed over to the proprietor. Some saved money from tips. Others were paid half the value of the tickets they received, but with this money they had to pay for food to supplement their basic rations and for clothing and other supplies. Because most of the women were illiterate, they were often cheated out of their savings. Even so, some were able to send earnings home to their families. Others kept their savings in Japanese accounts, which they lost after the war.

Comfort stations operated under a number of rules. Most prohibited drinking in a room, required the use of condoms, and refused to give refunds. The condom rule was especially difficult to enforce; when shortages occurred, the women washed used condoms for reuse. Comfort women also had to douche or at least wipe themselves with disinfectant after each customer. Specific rules also ostensibly protected them against violence from soldiers, and they usually received two days off a month for menstruation. They had to undergo regular medical inspections, and those suffering from infection or disease were forbidden to work. Personal relationships were also forbidden, but they did sometimes occur. Proprietors were forbidden from undue profiteering or breaching military discipline. Each comfort station had to keep accounts of all transactions and would be closed for failing to do so. Many official rules were often observed more in the breach, as proprietors found it difficult not to exploit ignorant farm girls.

When the defeat of Japan became imminent, many comfort stations reported their greatest volume as troops sought some final pleasure. In addition, comfort women were recruited to other duties, such as nursing assistants. In the face of Allied advances, some comfort women were evacuated. Most stayed until the end, abandoned by the troops they served. On Tare, the Japanese massacred comfort women hiding in a bunker, and in the Philippines they beheaded them; the military considered the women an encumbrance and an embarrassment if discovered by U.S. troops. On Saipan, the women joined many of the island's civilian population in drowning themselves rather than falling into American hands. (This did happen to a small number of comfort women after the siege of Myt-kyina in northern Burma, and the Americans apparently treated them well.) A few comfort women were able to exact revenge when Japan fell. In a Malaysian comfort station the women killed the couple running the center when news came of Japan's surrender.

After the war, comfort women faced a tenuous future. Fewer than 30 percent survived the conflict, and up to 90 percent of these suffered lasting physical disabilities, including the inability to bear children. All bore psychological scars—particularly those from cultures like Korea's that place high value on chastity. Too ashamed to return home, some remained where they were. Most were re-

patriated (although some, on sight of their homeland, threw themselves overboard and drowned). A number of the women continued to work as prostitutes after the war, often serving occupation forces in Japan at the behest of officials hoping to reduce the chances that their own women would be raped.

Little was done to address the issue of comfort women after the war. The only cases tried as war crimes involved Dutch women in Indonesia. In one trial, before the court passed sentences, three of the principal Japanese officers committed suicide; eight lower-ranking officers received prison terms of two to seven years. In the second trial, one Japanese officer was sentenced to death, and the others were sent to prison for two to fifteen years. The Allies lost interest in pursuing such matters in the face of cold war tensions and particularly the Korean War. In 1956 the Japanese–South Korean Basic Treaty gave the South Korean government the right to handle all matters of compensation for wartime suffering; Japan provided $800 million in grants, credit, and loans to South Korea to be distributed in compensation for outstanding claims. The treaty never acknowledged the issue of comfort women, and it absolved Japan of any further claims.

With the relaxation of restrictions on free speech in Korea, a growing feminist movement was encouraged to address the issue of comfort women. Professor Yun Chung Ok of Ehwa Women's University formed a group within the Korean Church Women's Alliance, which became the center of demands for action. In 1990 a number of Korean women's groups petitioned the Japanese embassy for redress. But it was not until 1991 that Kim Hak Sun became the first comfort woman to publicly tell her story. Other disclosures followed as part of a class action suit against the Japanese government in Tokyo district court in December 1991. Although the Japanese government denied that the army was directly involved in the comfort women trade, in January 1992 the Japanese daily *Asahi* published documents that forced the government to admit the army's role, and in 1993 the government acknowledged the recruiting and stationing of comfort women against their will. In August 1994 Prime Minister Tomiichi Murayama in an apology to Korea announced a ten-year $1 billion program to undertake cultural and vocational projects. The program did not include direct compensation to surviving comfort women, but it called for a $10 million private donation fund to be managed by the Japanese Red Cross. Individuals would receive lump payments of $10,000. The plan was criticized as being too generous by Japanese conservatives and as being insufficient by a number of Japanese and international groups. Even now, many issues relating to comfort women remain unresolved.

FURTHER READINGS

"An Appeal for Donations for the Asian Women's Fund by the Proponents" (July 18, 1995). "Statement by Prime Minister Tomiichi Murayama" (July 1995). http://www.kantei.go.jp:80/foreign/women-fund.html

Chai, Alice Yun. "Asian-Pacific Feminist Coalition Politics: The Chongshidae/Jugunianfu ('Comfort Women') Movement." *Korean Studies* 17 (1993):67–91.

"The 'Comfort Woman' System: Enslaving Women in World War II." *The East* (September 1994).

Dolgopol, Ustina, and Snehal Parajape. "Comfort Women: An Unfinished Ordeal." Geneva: International Commission of Jurists (1994).

Go, Lisa. "An Unbroken History of Japan's Sex Slaves," ASA-News (April 1994); also available at: gopher://csf.Colorado.EDU:70/00/ipe/Geographic_Archive/asia/women/Japanese_Sex_Slaves

Hicks, George. *The Comfort Women* (1994).

Korean Council for the Women Drafted for Military Sexual Slavery by Japan. "The Reality of Survivors and Activities of the Korean Council for the Women Drafted for Military Sexual Slavery by Japan" and "Slavery by Japan." http://www.korea.com/general/reality.html

Ruff-O'Herne, Jan. *50 years of Silence* (1994).

Taiwan Women's Forum. "A Report on Tawianese Comfort Women." http://www.seed.net.tw:80/~newcongr/women/comfw.html

Tokchi, Kim. "I Have Much to Say to the Korean Government." *Index on Censorship* 3 (1995).

War Victimization and Japan. International Public Hearing Report. Tokyo: Executive Committee, International Public Hearing Concerning Post War Compensation by Japan (1993).

Daniel D. Liestman

SEE ALSO Army, Japanese

Communists

See Chinese Communists versus Nationalists.

Coral Sea, Battle of the

The Battle of the Coral Sea (May 1–7, 1942) marked the first time in history that two fleets fought each other using only airplanes, with the opponents never coming within sight of one another. Like the Battles of Midway, the Philippine Sea, and Leyte Gulf, this was a multiforce, several-day affair. And like the Battle of Midway, actual ship losses were small compared with the size of the forces involved; only a few crucial ships—the aircraft carriers—had to be sunk or damaged for the battle to be terminated.

The Japanese strategy for the first phase of the war had succeeded beyond all expectations. The Allied fleets had been severely weakened and pushed back. The Philippines, Guam, Malaya, and other Allied bases were quickly captured, and the Allies were retreating on the Asian continent. Now that the vital oil fields of the Southern Resources Area had been seized, there was a brief pause in operations. There was much high-level discussion over how to carry out phase 2, the consolidation of gains and the extension of the defensive perimeter of the Greater East Asian Co-Prosperity Sphere. It was decided to continue to push southward, to interrupt Allied supply lines and to isolate Australia. The major effort would be an amphibious invasion of Port Moresby (Operation MO) on the south coast of the island of New Guinea, relatively close to northern Australia. At the same time a base would be established in the southern Solomon Islands. Ships and planes operating from these new bases would control a major portion of the Coral Sea north of Australia, would hinder Allied attacks on the Japanese base of Rabaul on the island of New Britain, and could directly attack the Australian continent. U.S. naval forces would be lured south, away from Hawaii (even though Admiral Isoroku Yamamoto, commander in chief of the Combined Fleet, was hoping for a decisive battle at Midway with the remnants of the U.S. fleet).

The speed and ease of the Japanese conquests led to a condition that some Japanese themselves termed "victory disease." The overconfidence of the Japanese military led them to underestimate U.S. strength and possible actions—and not even to consider the possibility that the Americans might have broken their naval codes. Even though the pressure was on to prepare for the upcoming larger and more important Midway operation (Operation MI), the Japanese high command decided that they were strong enough to continue with the Port Moresby invasion. As it turned out, they lacked both luck and effective leadership.

The Allied strategy was defensive by necessity. Sea and aerial lines of communication from North America to Australia and New Zealand had to be protected. The Allied air and naval forces had taken a tremendous beating at Pearl Harbor and in the Netherlands East Indies. Large numbers of British Commonwealth troops had surrendered in Malaya, in an incredible debacle. The Allies had to adjust to the speed of the Japanese advance and to the importance of air power. The large Philippine garrison on the Bataan Peninsula had finally capitulated on April 9, 1942. Only the island fortress of Corregidor, at the mouth of Manila Bay, remained heroically defiant, although it was hopelessly isolated and could not last long. General Douglas MacArthur, the U.S. commander in the Philippines, made a hazardous journey to Australia in early March to assume command of Allied forces in the southwest Pacific. Here he was confronted by near panic and very weak defenses. It would take a long time to organize, train, and equip sufficient numbers of troops and to build the ships and planes before the Allied counteroffensive could begin to roll back the Japanese tidal wave. The United States was the only military power able to field significant forces in the Pacific (most of the Australian and New Zealand divisions were fighting in North Africa at the time), but these would have to be applied only at critical points so they would not be wasted. The Coral Sea was one of those critical points.

The Imperial Japanese Navy forces assigned to Operation MO consisted of the striking force under Vice Admiral Chuichi Hara, composed of the sister carriers *Shokaku* ("Flying Heron") and *Zuikaku* ("Joyous Heron") (Carrier Division 5), escorted by two heavy cruisers and six destroyers (commanded by Vice Admiral Takeo Takagi), which left Truk on April 20. Admiral Sadamachi Kajioka commanded the Port Moresby invasion force of nine transports and eight escorts, with Vice Admiral Nobuji Goto in charge of the covering force of one carrier, a destroyer, and four cruisers. This force first protected the Tulagi invasion element before moving north to cover the Port Moresby invasion force. Regional command was entrusted to Vice Admiral Marimi Inonue, commander of the Fourth Fleet in Rabaul, on the island of New Britain, north of the Solomon Islands. This Australian base had been occupied by the Japanese at the end of January 1942. Japanese planes had greater range and firepower than the planes of their opponents, and their pilots had more combat experience. Japanese flying boats on reconnaissance missions could cover more of the Coral Sea than could Allied search planes based in Australia or New Caledonia, thus leaving little room for the Allied navies to operate unobserved.

Admiral Chester W. Nimitz, commander in chief of the U.S. Pacific Fleet based at Pearl Harbor, Hawaii, had far fewer ships to commit to the South Pacific theater. Admiral William "Bull" Halsey, the main U.S. carrier commander at this time, and his Task Force 16 (TF16)—carriers *Enterprise* (CV-6) and *Hornet* (CV-8), along with

their escorts—were returning to Hawaii from the Doolittle raid on Tokyo (April 18). They would be sent south just as soon as possible after replenishment, but they would arrive too late to see any action. (A shortage of naval auxiliaries prevented replenishment at sea at this time, which would have enabled Halsey to get to the region at least a week sooner.) USS *Saratoga* (CV-3) was still on the West Coast, being repaired after a torpedo hit suffered on January 11. There were only two striking forces available to Nimitz. USS *Lexington* (CV-2, sister ship of *Saratoga*) along with five destroyers and tanker *Tippecanoe* (AO-21) formed Task Force 11 (TF11). It had just completed three weeks of rest and resupply at Pearl Harbor and had sailed south in early April. Rear Admiral Aubrey Fitch had replaced Admiral Wilson Brown as task force commander on April 3, because U.S. Chief of Naval Operations Admiral Ernest King felt that Brown was not aggressive enough. Rear Admiral Frank Jack Fletcher's Task Force 17 (TF17) was composed of carrier USS *Yorktown* (CV-5), three cruisers, six destroyers, and oil tanker *Neosho* (AO-23), which had survived the attack on Pearl Harbor. This task force had been quietly patrolling the South Pacific for the last two months. The personnel were worn out from constant patrol activity. General MacArthur contributed heavy and medium air force bombers and aerial reconnaissance from Australia, but they were not able to effectively participate in this battle. The few navy Consolidated PBY Catalinas operating from New Caledonia had a similar lack of success. (Greater success in sighting the Japanese might have been achieved if seaplane tender *Tangier* [AV-8] and its planes had been moved north to the Santa Cruz Islands, closer to the scene of action.) There were also communication problems between the army in Australia and the navy. In addition, the command structure was unnecessarily complicated. Even though the battle would be fought within MacArthur's southwest Pacific theater of operations, Nimitz was in charge of the task forces and their movements. There was no regional commander who could effectively coordinate the various aerial and naval forces.

Nimitz had two unquantifiable advantages. First and most important was his superior information on enemy activities and intentions, gathered through signals intelligence (SIGINT). This allowed him to position his forces both to counter the Japanese *before* they made their moves and to gauge their strength to a reasonable degree. The Japanese were unable to collect or utilize intelligence in a similar manner. They thought that only one U.S. carrier would be available and that it would be accompanied by battleships. U.S. intelligence proved to be a force multiplier throughout the war, but it was never more valuable than in this first year, when the Allies were at their weakest.

A second advantage (although it did not seem like one at the time) was that Nimitz had fewer forces to coordinate, and so he was forced to formulate a simple and flexible plan that concentrated his forces. In contrast, the Japanese had several squadrons scattered across the region—a strategy that required coordination and good communications, which were not always in evidence. This was a feature of Japanese operations throughout the war, and in the end it would prove to be more dangerous to themselves than to the Americans.

The U.S. Pacific Fleet commander learned on April 17 about the southward movements and concentrations of Japanese ships, and he guessed that their target was Port Moresby. Admiral Fletcher was the senior officer afloat and was designated commander of the two task forces available in the area. He was instructed to attack enemy ships and planes, inflicting as much damage as possible, and to prevent the Japanese from seizing Port Moresby.

Admiral Fitch and *Lexington* met up with Fletcher east of Espiritu Santo on May 1, and they began to refuel. (One feature of Fletcher's wartime operational career was his constant refueling, as he did not want to have to fight without full bunkers. Certainly this is understandable, but it tempered his movements and frustrated his colleagues, particularly during the abortive Wake Island relief effort of late December 1941.) Fitch was ordered to continue a slow refueling while TF17 moved north the next day. When Admiral Fletcher heard from Australia on May 3 that the Japanese under Rear Admiral Kiyohede Shima had occupied Tulagi Island in the Solomons and were busy establishing a seaplane base, he headed north without delay. Japanese planes operating from this base could have easily detected the task forces, reducing their freedom of action. Thus Fletcher moved quickly to strike at the enemy.

Fletcher was lucky. Admiral Hara and his two big carriers were refueling near Bougainville, at the north end of the Solomons, and were flying off planes assigned to Rabaul. Thus they were unable to provide air cover for the Tulagi invasion forces. Long-range flying boats were not yet operating from Tulagi, and Japanese air and submarine patrols did not sight the Americans. TF17 was able to run unobserved to Guadalcanal under the cover of a cold front. Admiral Fletcher maintained radio silence and did not call *Lexington* to come forward (nor did he even send a plane over to let Admiral Fitch know what was happening, which was perhaps a mistake). The Americans achieved total surprise.

On May 4, *Yorktown* launched three air strikes against Japan's Tulagi invasion force but inflicted only minor damage, despite the exaggerated claims of the naval aviators (boasting was common on both sides). Japanese losses included a destroyer, three minesweepers, four landing barges, and several aircraft. Admiral Nimitz later wrote that he was disappointed by the minimal results for the effort expended, but these were relatively green fliers who needed more experience. It can be argued that Fletcher made a mistake by not waiting until *Lexington* had joined up, which would have increased the strength of the strike and the probability of hits, but Fletcher probably felt pressure to do something before heavier Japanese support forces arrived and while the weather was favorable. The fact that U.S. Chief of Naval Operations Admiral Ernest King did not like him and was demanding action might also have influenced Fletcher's thinking. Moreover, by attacking at Tulagi, Fletcher had advertised that U.S. carriers were in the area, when it might have been better to remain farther south, waiting for the Japanese carrier forces to appear. Had those been closer to Tulagi, they could have caught TF17 when it was weak. But TF17 also could have been spotted at any time by air or submarine searches, and its chance to strike at the enemy with surprise might have been lost if not exercised on May 4. By striking when it did, TF17 was able to destroy several seaplanes that could have aided Japanese forces in the coming battle.

The two U.S. task forces rejoined on May 5 some 300 miles south of Guadalcanal, and Admiral Fletcher again ordered refueling. Fletcher reorganized his forces, with Admiral Fitch controlling the carriers (TF 17.5); British Rear Admiral John G. Crace leading a mixed U.S.-Australian surface support group of three cruisers and two destroyers (TF 17.3, better known as TF 44, which had recently arrived); and Rear Admiral Thomas C. Kinkaid (who would gain fame later as MacArthur's favorite admiral while leading the Seventh Fleet) commanded an attack group of five cruisers and five destroyers (TF 17.2). For some reason Fletcher did not tell Admiral Fitch that he would be commanding the air group until shortly before operations commenced the next day. On May 6 the force moved north to be within range of the Jomard Passage, off the southeast tip of New Guinea, where the Japanese troop transports were heading on their way to Port Moresby. Anticipation of the coming battle was high, but U.S. troops' spirits were dampened by the news that the Corregidor garrison had been forced to surrender to the Japanese.

In probably his most risky decision of the battle, Fletcher, early on the morning of May 7, directed Admiral

Crace's support group north toward the Louisiade Archipelago to intercept the Japanese convoy sailing through the Jomard Passage. This illustrated that the advantages of air power were not yet fully apparent to the U.S. commanders. By taking this action, Fletcher put Crace's ships in an exposed position, unprotected by friendly fighters, and at the same time reduced the antiaircraft protection for his invaluable carriers. The record of losses of Allied surface combatants to aerial attacks at Pearl Harbor, and off the Malaya coast, and in the Indian Ocean did not appear to be a significant factor here. Fletcher was perhaps counting too much on the power of big guns. Yet there is some indication that the presence of Crace's small force helped influence the Japanese to reverse their troop transports, and their land-based air attacks were directed against Crace's ships instead of the U.S. carriers. As it was, Crace's group played no other productive part in the battle; it was attacked by both U.S. and Japanese land-based planes on May 7, but it successfully evaded all bombs and then headed for Australia.

On the morning of May 7 both sides sent out search planes, but in opposite directions: U.S. planes went north toward the invasion force, and Japanese planes went south. At 0840 hours, a Japanese scout radioed a sighting of a carrier and escorts; these were actually detached oil tanker *Neosho* and escorting destroyer *Sims* (DD-409). Admiral Hara launched three waves—virtually all his attack planes—to hit this supposed U.S. carrier. *Sims* quickly sank with heavy casualties after bomb hits, but *Neosho* managed to stay afloat until the crew was rescued on May 11, after which the tanker was scuttled by USS *Henley* (DD-391). Admiral Fletcher was undoubtedly happy that he had refueled when he had the chance, inasmuch as empty *Tippecanoe* had already retired from the area.

The sacrifice of these two ships allowed TF17 to go undisturbed as it attacked the enemy to the north. Matching the error of the Japanese scout, U.S. fliers misidentified the ships of the Japanese invasion support group. Acting on this misinformation, Admiral Fitch launched ninety-three planes at 0930 hours, and they attacked Admiral Goto's covering force at around 1100. Light carrier *Shoho* quickly sank after twenty bomb and torpedo hits. But because no one was directing the U.S. attack at the scene, no coordinated strikes were made against other Japanese ships. Commander Robert Dixon may have proclaimed the famous sentence "Scratch one flattop!" when he radioed back a situation report; but both sides used so many planes for these targets that few aircraft were left behind to defend the task forces or to attack other enemy forces, had they been sighted. A sighting by one side or

the other should have occurred, because at one time the two forces were only 70 miles apart. Both sides suffered from faulty communications and inefficient aerial reconnaissance.

The evening of May 7 proved to be exciting as well. Admiral Hara, knowing that U.S. ships had to be somewhere close by, gambled on the element of surprise and the skill of his more experienced aircrews. He sent twenty-seven planes to attack in the dark. But the Japanese failed to find TF17 and ended up tangling with Grumman F4F Wildcat fighters. Some Japanese pilots did run across the U.S. carriers and, thinking that they were friendly, mistakenly tried to land on them. They quickly realized their error when they were greeted by antiaircraft fire. Only six Japanese planes returned safely to Carrier Division 5. The radar on board *Lexington* spotted them circling in a landing pattern above the Japanese carriers, giving the Americans some idea of just how close the two forces were.

Admiral Fletcher also briefly contemplated taking a chance that night. Evidence from radar plots and radio direction-finding equipment indicated that the Japanese forces had to be very near by. A night surface attack by destroyers was discussed but was eventually rejected. (Admiral King held the opinion that the attack should have been attempted.) Such an attack would have used too much of the destroyers' fuel when there was no tanker available. Also, Japanese forces were not definitely located (and were in fact moving away), the torpedoes did not work well, and U.S. surface radar and tactics needed refinement. Conversely, the Japanese were masters of night warfare and had the most efficient torpedoes. It is entirely possible that all the U.S. ships might have been sunk in such an engagement. It was more important to keep the destroyers at hand as carrier escorts.

During the hours of darkness the Japanese carrier task force moved north to cover the transports, while the U.S. ships sailed south to put some distance between themselves and the powerful enemy they had not yet located. A disturbed Admiral Inonue in Rabaul ordered the Port Moresby invasion force to reverse course until matters could be sorted out.

Both sides knew that May 8 would be the day of decision. Weather conditions favored the Japanese in this portion of the battle. They operated under cloud cover, and the southerly winds allowed them to sail toward the enemy while launching aircraft. In contrast, U.S. carriers operated under sunny skies and were forced to steam away from the enemy in order to fly off planes.

Although both sides sent off aerial scouts at about the same time the next morning, the Americans got the first break, discovering the enemy at around 0930. The navy's

Douglas SBD Dauntless dive-bombers arrived over the Japanese carriers at 1030 (as would happen a month later at the Battle of Midway), but they waited for the slower (and ineffective) Douglas TBD Devastator torpedo planes to arrive so that they could make a coordinated attack as planned. This delay allowed *Zuikaku* to hide under a rain squall, so *Shokaku* had to bear the brunt of the U.S. aerial onslaught. The obsolescent torpedo planes and their deficient torpedoes were avoided through radical maneuvering, but two bomb hits started a major fire. The damaged *Shokaku* transferred its planes to its sister carrier and limped off to the Japanese naval bastion of Truk in the Caroline Islands, almost foundering on the way.

Meanwhile, Japanese planes were attacking their targets. According to contemporary naval doctrine, the U.S. force had split into two groups, which actually weakened its antiaircraft defense. Fighter direction techniques were still being developed and did not function well during this battle. Older and larger "Lady Lex," built on a battlecruiser hull, could not maneuver as well as smaller and faster Yorktown, and it absorbed two bombs and five torpedo hits on the port side. But U.S. damage control was generally superior to Japanese, and the fires seemed to be under control; it appeared that the ship would be able to resume operations that afternoon. However, gasoline fumes from a damaged aviation fuel tank seeped into a room where a generator was operating; a spark ignited an explosion and an uncontrollable fire. Rocked by a massive explosion at 1347, *Lexington* could not be saved, and Captain Frederick C. Sherman ordered the ship abandoned. The carrier was sunk by torpedoes from USS *Phelps* (DD-360) at latitude 15°20′ south, longitude 155°30′ east.

In the afternoon Admiral Nimitz ordered TF17 to retire southward, fearing for the safety of *Yorktown* (which now made up one-third of available U.S. carrier strength in the Pacific). Admiral Inonue, believing the exaggerated reports of full victory, directed Vice Admiral Takagi back to Truk. However, Admiral Yamamoto in Tokyo wanted to make sure that all enemy carriers had been sunk, and he ordered Takagi to reverse course. By the time Takagi turned back, the U.S. ships were steaming toward New Caledonia and Tonga, eventually to return to Pearl Harbor on May 27. There would then occur another miracle, as 3,000 men working three days straight repaired *Yorktown* just enough so that it could fight at the Battle of Midway.

The Battle of the Coral Sea might be counted as a tactical victory for the Japanese, in that they lost only a small carrier, a destroyer, and a few small craft; the United States lost *Lexington*, a destroyer, and an oil tanker. Airplane losses were 43 out of 122 for the Japanese and 33 out of 121 for the Americans. But most historians view this battle as a U.S. strategic victory, in that (1) the Japanese never again undertook a seaborne invasion of Port Moresby and, perhaps more important, (2) they lost many planes and an experienced aircrew, and two big carriers were removed from the upcoming Midway operation—where they might have provided the margin needed to prevent U.S. victory. The Pacific Fleet gained invaluable experience in aerial combat, antiaircraft defense, the use of radar and fighter direction techniques, and in evaluating Allied and Japanese aircraft performance. They also gained confidence that the Imperial Japanese Navy could be defeated.

With hindsight one can see where different, and perhaps better, results might have been achieved had the Americans been bolder. Certainly a surprise surface attack on the night of May 7 might have achieved great things, but it might have been a disaster just as easily. Admiral King in Washington criticized Fletcher for not making a night attack, but Nimitz supported Fletcher's decisions. Armchair admirals must remember that Admiral Fletcher commanded half the navy's invaluable carrier force in the Pacific during this battle. This was a resource that had to be exposed with care, since the new, fast, *Essex*-class carriers and their planes would not be available until 1943. Had *Yorktown* also been sunk at the Coral Sea battle, there might have been no "Miracle at Midway" (to borrow Gordon Prange's title on the subject). Admirals William F. Halsey and Raymond A. Spruance—the two most famous U.S. carrier commanders of the war—might well have fought the battle quite differently, but they were not on the scene. A careful study of the literature is necessary to understand who knew what, when they knew it, and what resources they had to combat the enemy. Admiral Fletcher has been frequently criticized, but he did what he had to do: He stopped the Japanese advance and brought *Yorktown* home to fight one more time. The Battle of the Coral Sea was the first of four situations (followed by Midway, the Guadalcanal campaign, and the battle off Samar in October 1944) where skill and luck allowed the U.S. Navy to triumph against a numerically stronger opponent.

FURTHER READINGS

Belote, James H., and William M. *Titans of the Seas: The Development and Operations of Japanese and American Carrier Task Forces During World War II* (1975).

Johnston, Stanley. *Queen of the Flat-Tops* (1942).

Lundstrom, John B. *The First Team: Pacific Naval Air Combat from Pearl Harbor to Midway* (1984).

Millot, Bernard. *The Battle of the Coral Sea* (1974).

Morison, Samuel Eliot. *Coral Sea, Midway and Submarine Actions: History of United States Naval Operations in World War II,* vol. 4 (1949).

Regan, Stephen D. *In Bitter Tempest: The Biography of Admiral Frank Jack Fletcher* (1994).

U.S. Department of the Navy, Naval War College, Department of Analysis. *The Battle of the Coral Sea, May 1 to May 11 Inclusive, 1942.* Strategical and Tactical Analysis series (1947).

Willmott, H. P. *The Barrier and the Javelin: Japanese and Allied Pacific Strategies February to June 1942* (1983).

Daniel K. Blewett

SEE ALSO Aircraft Carriers: Japanese, U.S., and British; Navy, U.S.

Corregidor

On February 3, 1945, General Douglas MacArthur, Southwest Pacific Area commander, directed Lieutenant General Walter Krueger of the Sixth Army to seize Corregidor, a U.S. Army island coastal fortification complex seized by the Japanese in 1942. Enemy possession of "the Rock" threatened Allied ship movements in Manila Bay and offered a potential sanctuary for troops fleeing Luzon. MacArthur told Krueger to take Corregidor by parachute or amphibious assault or joint effort.

Sixth Army readied a scheme combining a primary attack by the 503d Parachute Regimental Combat Team (RCT) from Mindoro followed by a landing of a reinforced battalion of the 34th Infantry, 24th Division, from Mariveles on the Bataan Peninsula. The use of airborne troops would reduce casualties and effect surprise. Planners rejected Kindley Field, on the island's eastern tail, as a drop zone because of its distance from important topographical features and because its openness would expose descending troopers to a concentrated enemy fusillade. Instead, "Topside"—to the west, with a former golf course and parade ground—was chosen. Sixth Army intelligence was aware that an easterly breeze and jump height of 400 feet could drop parachutists outside their designated areas. The planners considered the amphibious operation necessary because resupply and evacuation by air were nearly impossible. Besides, the landing force could take Malinta Hill before the defenders overcame the paralysis caused by preliminary bombardment and airborne attack. To reduce the amphibious force's prospective losses, the shore-to-shore operation would take place two hours later than the parachute jump. General MacArthur endorsed the joint airborne-amphibious proposal

on February 5, initially scheduling D-day for February 12; however, the assault was put off until February 15.

Corregidor and smaller islets were garrisoned by the Manila Bay Entrance Force, commanded by Captain Akira Itagaki of the Imperial Japanese Navy, headquartered on the Rock and under Rear Admiral Sanji Iwabuchi in Manila. Itagaki expected an amphibious assault. His 5,000 men on the island actually numbered considerably more than the 850 enemy reckoned by Sixth Army.

Bombardment of Corregidor started with air raids on January 22, complemented by naval gunfire on February 13, while minesweeping commenced in preparation for the capture of Mariveles. The amphibious operation would remain under the direction of the navy until a beachhead was secured. The parachute drop would be subject to the authority of the Fifth Air Force until the troops hit the ground. Then operational control would transfer to the Sixth Army's 11th Corps, who would organize Rock Force under Colonel George M. Jones, the 503d RCT's commander.

On February 16 paratroopers landed on Corregidor against light resistance, mainly small-arms fire. Despite heavier than expected first-jump casualties resulting from the drop altitude, the troops established a position and then won Topside in quick order. Meanwhile, the 3d Battalion, 34th Infantry, departed Mariveles Harbor, and, protected by paratroopers' machine guns on the southeast side of Topside, disembarked on the island's south shore with only the fifth wave taking enemy fire. Once ashore, the amphibious force advanced and gained a firm grip atop Malinta Hill. Distracted by descending paratroopers from the amphibious threat, the Japanese were surprised. Captain Itagaki was killed by troopers falling about his post, and organized opposition collapsed.

With Rock Force on Corregidor, military operations degenerated into an extensive mop-up. The island's small dimensions and uneven surface together with the overall stationary and disrupted enemy defense forestalled tactical movement by outfits above platoon size, and the battle became a series of small-unit actions in a succession of unconnected engagements. Japanese resistance centered on a network of caverns and underground passageways. Infantry assaults combined direct howitzer and small-arms fire, aided by naval fire support and napalm-bearing aircraft and supplemented by white-phosphorus grenades and flamethrowers to flush out the enemy. When dug-in defenders refused to surrender, engineer demolition specialists shut off cave openings.

Unsuccessful Japanese counterattacks at the southern and southwestern edges of Topside on February 19 and a modest-size Banzai assault at Wheeler Point on February

23 exhausted the enemy's offensive capability. Once the section east of Malinta Hill was secured and roadways passing by way of Middleside were cleared, the campaign subsided into a series of small-scale counterattacks and subterranean explosions, culminating in the massive Japanese detonation of an underground supply dump at Monkey Point. More than 200 Japanese defenders died, while Rock Force suffered about 50 deaths and 150 injured. Except for some mopping up, the huge blast signaled the conclusion of concerted resistance on the island. By the time General MacArthur returned to Corregidor on March 2 for a flag-raising observance, Rock Force had sustained over 1,000 casualties and had inflicted 4,500 fatalities on the enemy while taking 20 captives.

Despite posing no danger to Allied ship movements in Manila Bay, the islets of Caballo, Fort Drum, and Carabao were seized and neutralized. Caballo, below Corregidor, was captured by April 13 after bombardment and reduction of the Japanese on heights close to the island's center. When surviving defenders retreated into pits and tunnels beneath a hill, they were eliminated by oil poured into their positions and set afire. Fort Drum—the "Army's Concrete Battleship," located about 5 miles south of the Rock—was a structure of 25 to 36 feet of poured, reinforced concrete, tapering to 20 feet at its cap,

and accessible only by a sloping walkway on its eastern rim. After the ritual demands for surrender and the equally ritual hail of bullets in reply, army engineers pumped in a lethal mixture of petroleum and napalm. A massive explosion killed the entire enemy garrison, in contrast to the Japanese bombardment in 1942, which had inflicted only one minor injury. Subsequent to a forty-eight-hour bombardment of Carabao, located a mile from Ternate, troops went ashore on April 16 and found the island unoccupied. Corregidor, which had held out so strongly against the Japanese in 1942 (at a time when all European Asian colonial forts were almost supinely surrendered to the enemy), had fought its last battle.

FURTHER READINGS

Belote, James H., and William M. Belote. *Corregidor: The Saga of a Fortress* (1967).
Devlin, Gerard M. *Back to Corregidor: America Retakes the Rock* (1992).
Morison, Samuel Eliot. *The Liberation of the Philippines: Luzon, Mindanao, the Visayas, 1944–1945* (1959).
Smith, Robert Ross. *Triumph in the Philippines* (1963).
Rodney J. Ross

SEE ALSO Krueger, Walter; Philippines, Fall of

D

Darwin, Japanese Bombing of

On February 19, 1942, the war-crowded northern Australian harbor of Port Darwin was struck by 198 Japanese bombers. This coordinated land- and naval-based air strike surprised the ill-prepared defenders and devastated the port and the shipping concentrated within its harbor. Arriving in two waves, the forty-five minute attack sank eight ships, ran four aground, and severely damaged another eleven. More than 240 people were killed, mostly aboard the ships. Two more ships were destroyed as the planes transited home. They also struck the nearby Royal Australian Air Force (RAAF) base, destroying *all* the aircraft on the ground and downing all but one of the Australian fighters in the air. A follow-up raid finished off the base and inflicted so much wanton destruction that its military personnel fled to the south in panic. Total Japanese losses were only two aircraft. Darwin and its surrounding area endured more than a dozen air raids over the next fifteen months, but none would be as devastating as this first raid nor even approach its psychological impact.

Darwin's defenses had been neglected during the prewar period, but the most glaring deficiency in the port's defenses was the almost total lack of cooperation among the agencies involved. The resident administrator, Charles Abbott, aloof and ineffectual, had antagonized the local population, including the civil defense and military leaders. Lacking the cooperation of the local population, he had failed to evacuate nonessential personnel, organize the civil defense organization, or establish communications with local military leaders. For their part, the local unions openly thwarted Abbott's authority, and the civil defense officials blatantly ignored him when he did attempt to organize matters. The local military leaders also made their preparations separately. The Royal Australian Navy (RAN) had established a potentially effective system for protecting shipping offshore and in the port but had not established communications with the RAAF's warning network. Thus, RAN forces could neither receive early warning of attack nor coordinate their activities with the air force. The RAAF's only radar set in the area was inoperable on February 19. Moreover, the air force had a policy of withholding air warning until incoming aircraft were indisputably identified as Japanese, which meant that the bombs were practically falling before air-raid alarms could be issued. None of the defense agencies had practiced together or conducted an air-raid drill since the early weeks of December. That left them ill-prepared and confused as the attack developed. Finally, a series of false alarms had worn down local morale, undermined alertness, and led to the RAAF's tightening its already stringent identification procedures.

Darwin had become a target because of its importance as an Allied forward base and logistics center. It was the only significant port in northern Australia and the only one from which the Allies could support their forces in Java and the southwest Pacific. The Imperial Japanese Navy staff had argued that Australia had to be seized, but the army had resisted, indicating that the continent required more troops to subdue and garrison than Japan had to expend. So Australia's northern ports had to be neutralized instead, and the islands above it had to be seized as a buffer to prevent Allied counterstrokes against Japan's intended "inner perimeter" of vital islands and resource centers. Destroying Darwin was the first step in that process and offered the additional advantage of diverting Allied resources to Australia's defense and away from the fighting in Southeast Asia.

The air strike was planned and led by the same team, Commanders Genda and Fuchida, that had struck Pearl Harbor in Hawaii some two months earlier, using roughly the same methods and enjoying roughly the same results for roughly the same reasons (but the garrison at Darwin did not have the excuse that defenders had no idea they were at war). As far as the Japanese were concerned, the Allies were slow learners, particularly in light of the quite similar near-obliteration of U.S. air power in the Philippines by the Japanese raid on Clark Air Field. But in the Darwin strike the sea-based air wing was supported by a land-based element operating out of the recently captured airfields in the Dutch East Indies. The carrier-based aircraft would strike first, taking out the port, its shipping, and its defenses. They were escorted by thirty-six Zeros—arguably the best fighter aircraft in the Pacific at that time. The land-based horizontal bombers would then launch the second-phase attack, taking out the airfields and supporting facilities. The Japanese hoped to catch the Allied fighters on the ground, being serviced after the first raid. The plan succeeded beyond their fondest hopes.

The carrier aircraft took off at 8:45 A.M. and formed up for their one-hour flight to Darwin. Interestingly, both the carrier- and land-based aircraft were detected and reported by Australian coastwatchers some thirty minutes before they arrived over Darwin (again like the Pearl Harbor raid). Also, the carrier aircraft had struck an Allied convoy north of Darwin the previous day, and its surviving elements had sought refuge in the port. Although the convoy commander expected the Japanese to finish them off in Darwin, he never passed this assessment on to local officials. Instead, he despatched two destroyers and an oiler to refuel east of Darwin, and he placed his crews on alert. Coastwatchers' reports were ignored pending further verification, and authorities ashore remained unaware of the convoy commander's assessment. As a result, the raiders arrived unexpectedly and uncontested.

The ferocity and effectiveness of the Japanese attack stunned Australian authorities, but in the long run the surprise may have served them better than it did the Japanese (again as at Pearl Harbor), for it energized the Australians into action. No longer were civil defense officials ignored. Air-raid drills began in earnest throughout the country. Nonessential personnel departed Darwin willingly—indeed, enthusiastically (the exodus was sometimes termed "the Darwin Races")—and a new, more effective administrator was appointed. A royal commission was formed to study what went wrong, and despite the obstruction and outright falsification of records by local authorities, the commission discovered the problems and made some specific recommendations to prevent similar disasters in the future. The local RAAF commander was replaced, the services were forced to establish a common air-defense reporting network, and warning procedures were liberalized to ensure earlier response. Now false

alarms were preferable to further surprises. Although the Japanese continued their sporadic attacks against Port Darwin over the next fifteen months, as time went by the raids inflicted significantly less damage and led to higher losses for the Japanese.

FURTHER READINGS
Connaughton, Richard. *Shrouded Secrets* (1994).
Hall, Timothy. *Darwin: Australia's Darkest Hour* (1980).
Piekalkiewicz, Janusz. *The Air War 1939–1945* (1985).

Carl O. Schuster

SEE ALSO Australia

Detachment 101
See Office of Strategic Services, Detachment 101

Dive-Bombers
The aviation revolution during the interwar years produced a number of different types of aircraft to deal with specific wartime situations. The United States, Germany, and Japan saw the dive-bomber as the perfect weapon to hit a relatively small and moving target like a ship. Coming in nearly straight down and low was essential for good aim. In the hands of pilots in both the European and the Pacific theaters the dive-bomber repeatedly proved its worth in naval combat.

The United States lead the field, both in doctrine and equipment. The U.S. Marine Corps first used dive-bombers in action in Nicaragua in July 1927. By 1931, the U.S. Navy's experiments with the Curtis Hawk caught the attention of the Japanese. They ordered two He50s from the German manufacturer Heinkel for their own tests. Within the next ten years both the U.S. and the Japanese navies had developed the Douglas SBD Dauntless (U.S. Army Air Forces designation: A-24) and the Aichi D3A Type 99 Val variants, respectively, that would serve each during much of the war. During the critical carrier battles of 1942 these two types of dive-bombers accounted for 70 percent of all ships sunk.

Most dive-bombers had similar specialized features. Steep dive angles were required both to ensure accuracy and to offer the minimal exposure to antiaircraft fire. In early models, however, the angle caused the bomb to damage or destroy the plane's propeller as it left the aircraft. Bomb-displacing gear (called a "fork" or "crutch")—first added by the United States in 1931—threw the bomb clear of the propeller. Stability was paramount for accurate dive-bombing, but the slipstream from the wings buffeted the tail; therefore, dive brakes (perforated flaps along the wings' trailing edge) were added.

Bomb sights also evolved throughout the war. The three-magnification telescope sight on the first four marks of Dauntlesses, for example, tended to fog up as the plane plunged through thousands of feet of altitude with differing air temperatures and humidity. To solve that problem, the SBD-5 Dauntless mounted a reflector gunsight similar to the sight mounted on fighters.

The Dauntless was the standard U.S. Navy dive-bomber in 1941. It had a top speed of 250 mph and a loaded range of 1,300 miles. Dauntless variants included the scout (with 100- and 500-pound bomb combinations) and the bomber (one 1,000-pound bomb). The Val carried one 550-pound bomb at 240 mph to a range of 1,250 miles (five hours' endurance), and it sank more Allied ships during World War II than any other Axis aircraft. It remained in production until the end of the war. Both the Dauntless and the Val had a crew of two and were difficult to shoot down when bombless, although neither had self-sealing fuel tanks. Midway through the war both navies fielded new but unsatisfactory dive-bombers, the Curtiss SB2C Helldiver and the Yokusaka D4Y Judy, respectively.

The Helldiver replaced the Dauntless, coming to the fleet in 1943. But its structural problems required major modifications, so it deployed in large numbers only in mid-1944. The Helldiver had an internal bomb bay and flew 20 mph faster than the Dauntless, but it carried the same bomb load; however, it was much harder to fly and maintain. Overall, it did not represent much of an improvement over the Dauntless. The Judy mounted the Japanese version of the engine which powered Messerschmidt fighters. Flying at 360 mph, it was by far the world's fastest dive-bomber. Like the Helldiver, however, it had reliability problems. It was underarmored and also lacked self-sealing fuel tanks. The Judy never completely replaced the Val, anymore than the Helldiver replaced the venerable Dauntless.

Doctrinally, dive-bombers of both navies usually worked in close coordination with torpedo bombers and in many cases with level bombers and even high-altitude bombers. Because the defensive measures that ships took against each type of attacking aircraft were different, this combined-arms approach was very effective.

Typical dive-bomber tactics are exemplified by the Dauntless. A squadron of eighteen aircraft generally cruised at about 18,000 feet. At that altitude pilots made visual contact with the target, 30 to 40 miles away. The commander would try to get the squadron into ideal position, down-sun and up-wind. Pushover altitude was about 15,000 feet. The pilot had thirty-five to forty seconds to acquire the target, line up the shot, steady the aircraft, judge cross-wind and drift, release the bomb, and pull out of the dive in a 5–6G maneuver. All the while enemy fighters and antiaircraft fire tried to shoot him down or cause him to miss. Bomb release was at approximately 1,500 to 2,000 feet, and fuse settings varied among the squadron's planes to cause above- and below-deck damage. The SB2Cs which sank *Yamato* dived at an angle of 65 to 80 degrees.

Dive-bombers working in concert with torpedo planes sank battleships USS *California, Tennessee,* and *West Virginia* at Pearl Harbor and USS *Lexington* at the Battle of Coral Sea. At the Battle of Midway, Japanese Vals sank carrier USS *Yorktown.* Dauntlesses sank all four Japanese aircraft carriers lost at Midway. Dive-bombers teamed with torpedo bombers to sink light carrier *Shoho* at Coral Sea, *Hiyo* at the Philippine Sea, and *Zuiho* at the Battle of Leyte Gulf. Combined U.S. naval aircraft types also sank battleships *Haruna, Hyuga,* and *Ise* and the super-battleships *Musashi* and *Yamato.* A far greater number of cruisers, destroyers, and merchantmen were also sunk by dive-bombers of both sides. Dive-bombers in all Pacific theaters were instrumental in turning naval warfare in World War II into an aviation-dominated conflict. Dive-bombing was found to be perfectly within the capabilities of fighter aircraft, while specially designed dive-bombers like the JU-87 Stuka found themselves outclassed by current fighter models.

Robert Kirchubel

SEE ALSO Aircraft: Japanese, U.S., and British

Doolittle (Tokyo) Raid

The Tokyo raid of April 18, 1942, led by U.S. Army Lieutenant Colonel James H. Doolittle, was the best known of a half dozen aircraft carrier raids conducted by the United States in the months following the attack on Pearl Harbor. This first U.S. bombing raid on the Japanese home islands was a fillip to morale rather than any meaningful strike at the Japanese. Nonetheless, it had an important influence on Japanese policy.

Beginning with Pearl Harbor, the United States sustained a series of costly defeats. Morale was low in early 1942, and President Franklin D. Roosevelt rarely failed to stress to his military chiefs the need to strike Japan. Captain Francis S. Low, an operations officer on the staff of Chief of Naval Operations Admiral Ernest J. King, suggested to his chief that army bombers utilize aircraft carriers for a raid; Captain Donald W. Duncan, King's air officer, implemented the plan. After King approved the concept, in mid-January 1942 he sent Low and Duncan to meet with the U.S. Army Air Forces (USAAF) commanding general, Lieutenant General Henry W. "Hap" Arnold, who embraced the project enthusiastically. Arnold picked Lieutenant Colonel Doolittle of his staff as the army coordinator.

Japanese picket ships were known to be stationed 500 miles off the home islands. For that reason attacking planes would have to be launched at 550 miles out. Despite Low's hope, army bombers could perhaps take off from carriers but would not be able to return to them. After striking Tokyo they would have to fly on to China and land there—a flight of 2,000 miles. The B-25 Mitchell was the one army bomber that could take off from a carrier and had that range. The plan called for the B-25s to bomb Japan at night, striking Kobe, Osaka, Nagoya, Tokyo, and Yokohama; they would land at Chinese airfields the next morning. The carrier selected for the bombers was *Hornet* (CV-8, commanded by Captain Marc A. Mitscher).

On February 2, two B-25s were successfully launched from *Hornet* in operations off Norfolk, Virginia. Later that month *Hornet* sailed through the Panama Canal and joined the Pacific Fleet. At the same time, B-25 crews were training at Eglin Field, Florida. They came from the 17th Bombardment Group and the 89th Reconnaissance Squadron—the units most experienced with the relatively new B-25. Doolittle also secured permission, despite his age (45), to lead the mission.

Each B-25B was modified. The Norden bombsights were removed to keep them from possibly falling into enemy hands, collapsible 60-gallon fuel tanks replaced lower turrets, heavy radios were removed, and fake .50-caliber guns fashioned from broomsticks and painted black were bolted on each plane's tail.

On April 1 at Alameda Naval Air Station, California, the fifteen B-25s called for in the plan were hoisted on board. Doolittle thought there was room for one more and suggested that a sixteenth be lifted on. Mitscher concurred, the idea being that this bomber would be flown off *Hornet* and return to land to show that it could be done; none of the pilots, including Doolittle, had actually flown a B-25 off a carrier. Once the carrier was at sea, however, the sixteenth plane was added to the strike force. The USAAF contingent numbered seventy officers and sixty-four enlisted men.

On April 2 *Hornet* sailed from San Francisco. That afternoon Mitscher announced their destination over loudspeaker to the carrier's crew and to escorting vessels by signal flag. Wild cheers greeted the news. On April 13

carrier *Enterprise* (CV-6, Captain George D. Murray, with task-force commander Vice Admiral William Halsey aboard) and its escorts rendezvoused with *Hornet*'s force. *Enterprise* was to provide air cover (with the B-25s occupying more than half of *Hornet*'s flight decks, its elevators would be unable to bring up fighter aircraft). Task Force 16 consisted of the two carriers, four cruisers, eight destroyers, and two oilers. Two U.S. Navy submarines also operated near the Japanese coast to report on enemy ship movements and weather conditions.

Task Force 16 followed the approximate route (in reverse) taken by the Japanese in the Pearl Harbor attack. The Japanese were already aware from radio traffic that something was in the offing, perhaps an attack on Japan itself. Combined Fleet Headquarters ordered naval aircraft concentrated in the Tokyo area and alerted picket boats operating offshore beyond the range of carrier aircraft. On April 15 the Americans heard "Tokyo Rose" broadcasting that no enemy bombers would ever get within 500 miles of the Japanese capital.

On April 17 stormy weather made seas rough enough for water to break over *Hornet*'s flight deck. The carriers and cruisers increased speed, while the destroyers and tankers dropped out to be picked up on the return.

At 0300 on the morning of April 18 about 650 miles off the Japanese coast, ship radar detected two picket vessels. At 0600 the pilot of an SBD Dauntless from *Enterprise* sighted a Japanese patrol boat and radioed that he thought he had been spotted. An hour later another Japanese patrol craft (Patrol Boat No. 23, *Nitto Maru*) was sighted from *Hornet*, which picked up its radio transmission reporting the presence of "three" enemy carriers. Halsey dispatched cruiser *Nashville* to sink *Nitto Maru*.

The original plan was to fly off the B-25s on the afternoon of April 19, but that schedule was now advanced. At 0800 on April 18 Halsey flashed this message to *Hornet*: "Launch planes. To Colonel Doolittle and his gallant command Good Luck and God bless you." Gas tanks were topped off, and each B-25 took aboard ten 5-gallon cans of fuel; placed in the tail, they were a substantial fire risk. Each plane carried only four bombs; most had three 500-pound high-explosive bombs and one 500-pound incendiary cluster. A unique call sounded over *Hornet*'s speaker system: "Army pilots, man your planes." With only 4 feet of clearance between the B-25's wing tip and the carrier's island structure, white lines painted on the deck served as guides for the left wheel and nose wheel of each plane as it took off. Any miscalculation might have brought disaster.

Doolittle's B-25 was the first launched, at 0820 hours. One by one the remaining planes took off, and all were away by 0920. Halsey immediately ordered Task Force 16 to turn about and steam at flank speed.

The B-25s achieved total surprise because the Japanese assumed an attack range of 200 miles and hence a later launch. Bad weather over Task Force 16 also hid it from search planes, although one Japanese pilot on morning patrol radioed that he had seen a twin-engined bomber about 600 miles from Tokyo—a report that was discounted. At 1230 Tokyo time Doolittle's plane dropped the first bombs.

No B-25s were downed over Japan, and only one was hit by antiaircraft fire. Air-raid sirens sounded only after the U.S. planes had struck. Subsequently, however, all the bombers were lost. The fields in China were not ready to receive the planes, and all crews had to bail out or crash-land. One plane landed at Vladivostok; the Russians promptly interned it and its crew. Eleven crews bailed out, and the four others attempted crash landings. Three crewmen died of injuries, and eight were captured by the Japanese, tortured, and interrogated. On August 28, 1942, at Shanghai, all those captured were "tried" by a military court on charges of bombing and strafing civilian targets. Three were executed. Of the remaining five, one died in prison; the other four survived the war.

The Japanese sent both planes and ships in pursuit of Task Force 16, but it escaped. Combat air patrols from *Hornet* and *Nashville* did attack a number of Japanese patrol boats, and they sank three. Three U.S. aircraft were lost to weather rather than enemy fire.

The raid inflicted little material damage to Tokyo. Doolittle later said that he had expected to be brought home and court-martialed for this failure. Instead, he found himself a hero; presented the Medal of Honor, he was also leaped ahead two ranks to brigadier general. President Roosevelt told Americans that the raid had been launched from "Shangri-la," the mythical Asian never-never land in the prewar James Hilton novel *Lost Horizon*. (It was a year before the details of the raid were made public; a later carrier was actually christened *Shangri-la*). The Doolittle raid served also as the inspiration for the popular film *Thirty Seconds over Tokyo*.

The Doolittle raid and the other U.S. carrier attacks had far-reaching effects. They were a great boost to American morale and an embarrassment to the Japanese, leading them to shift four precious fighter groups to the defense of Tokyo and other cities. The raid also provoked a punitive expedition by the Japanese army in China. Fifty-three battalions killed perhaps 250,000 Chinese in a massive campaign of retribution. (Chiang Kai-shek had opposed the raid for this very reason.)

Most important for the future of the war, the Doolittle raid increased support in Tokyo for pushing the outer defensive ring farther, as well as for Admiral Yamamoto's plan to draw out the U.S. fleet and destroy it. On May 5, imperial headquarters directed Yamamoto "to carry out the occupation of Midway Island and key points in the western Aleutians in co-operation with the Army." This led to the decisive Japanese defeat in the Battle of Midway.

FURTHER READINGS
Glines, Carrol. *Doolittle's Tokyo Raiders* (1981).
Jablonski, Edward J. *Airwar*, vol. II, *Tragic Victories* (1971).
Morrison, Samuel Eliot. *History of United States Naval Operations in World War II*, vol. 3 (1961).

Spencer C. Tucker

SEE ALSO Army Air Corps/Air Forces, U.S.

Downfall, Operation

Operation Downfall was the projected invasion of Japan, consisting of two major amphibious operations, each larger than the Normandy invasion. Operation Olympic, scheduled for November 1, 1945, envisioned a landing in southern Kyushu to seize ports and air bases for the invasion of Honshu. Operation Coronet, scheduled for March 1, 1946, anticipated an assault on the Kanto Plain of Honshu, followed by the seizure of Tokyo and, if necessary, Osaka and Nagoya.

The Japanese planned a desperate, last-ditch defense of the home islands, including the mass use of suicide units and, possibly, poison gas and Allied prisoners of war as hostages. The Americans also studied the use of chemical and battlefield atomic weapons. The battle for Japan would have been the most savage in the history of either nation, perhaps of modern times, and many thousands of American and Japanese lives were saved when Japan surrendered and these invasions became unnecessary.

At the Allied wartime conferences from 1943 to 1945, the political basis for the invasion of Japan was established, and important military decisions were taken relative to the invasion. At the Casablanca Conference in January 1943, President Franklin Roosevelt propounded the doctrine of "unconditional surrender," which meant that America's war aim was nothing less than the total elimination of German, Italian, and Japanese military power. This had no immediate military implications in the Pacific, because any assault on the Japanese home islands still lay far in the future. Moreover, at Casablanca the Americans and the British affirmed their intention to focus their forthcoming military efforts on defeating Germany first. However, the doctrine of unconditional surrender would have major political significance for the end of the Pacific war.

Anglo-American discord was evident at the Washington Conference in May 1943. The British argued for a strict defensive in the Pacific, in order to concentrate on Europe, but the Americans urged new Pacific offensives. The Americans particularly wanted the British to open the Burmese supply route to China, so that the Chinese could seize territory from which to launch a U.S. bombing campaign against Japan in advance of a combined Anglo-American-Chinese invasion.

Further planning led to sharp disagreement at the Quebec Conference in August 1943. American planners called for U.S. offensives in the central and southwest Pacific and for a British effort to liberate Burma, leading to an invasion of Japan in 1947. The British were correctly skeptical of Chinese military capabilities and saw no urgent need for an offensive in Burma. They preferred to emphasize the U.S. drive in the central Pacific, which they thought would be decisive. Furthermore, the U.S. Joint Chiefs objected to this projected timetable and instructed the planners to develop a design for the defeat of Japan no later than one year after the defeat of Germany.

At Teheran in December 1943, Roosevelt offered Stalin a postwar world order based on U.S.-Soviet cooperation, in which peace would be secured by the elimination of Russia's two traditional geopolitical rivals, Germany and Japan. The Teheran Conference thus made the invasion of Japan all but inevitable; no compromise Japanese-American peace could be possible now, because Japan had to be stripped of its empire and military power in order to secure postwar U.S.-Soviet cooperation. At the Cairo Conference in December 1943, Roosevelt made public the pledge to deprive Japan of its empire. He proclaimed that Japan would be expelled from all territories occupied since 1914, that China would regain all its lost territory, and that Korea would be granted independence, "in due course." Inasmuch as no self-respecting Japanese could countenance surrender on this basis, the invasion and utter defeat of Japan would most likely be necessary to enforce this edict. Furthermore, by this time it was clear that China was incapable of taking the offensive against Japan. Therefore, at Cairo the Combined Chiefs of Staff issued an "Overall Plan for the Defeat of Japan." According to this plan, the main effort against Japan would be made amphibiously in the Pacific, and Japan itself would be invaded if air and sea blockade failed to induce unconditional surrender. Plans for Chinese and British offensives were shelved after the Cairo Conference.

Before the war, the U.S. Navy's War Plan Orange assumed that Japan could be forced to surrender through naval blockade and aerial bombardment. The war plan thus envisioned the destruction of the Japanese fleet and the seizure of peripheral bases as prerequisites for effective bombing and blockade. Although prewar planners admitted that blockade and bombardment to defeat Japan might take a long time—two years or more—they did not believe an invasion would be feasible, except as an extreme measure.

The arguments for blockade and bombing as viable alternatives to invasion continued well into 1944. For example, in late 1944, Admiral King argued for an invasion of Formosa (Taiwan) instead of Luzon, because this would better support the blockade of Japan. Admiral Leahy also maintained that a siege of Japan would take more time but would incur fewer casualties than an invasion. In September 1944, the Combined Chiefs agreed that the war against Japan would require "invading and seizing objectives in the heart of Japan," and in November 1944 the U.S. Joint Chiefs approved a plan to invade Kyushu in September 1945. King and Leahy accepted these decisions but continued to argue for the seizure of bases in China and Korea to complete the blockade. In March 1945, King proposed seizing lodgments in China, Korea, and the Tsushima Islands to provide fighter cover over Kyushu. General Marshall countered that such operations would absorb large U.S. forces without leading to decisive results. He favored an all-out assault on Kyushu as soon as the forces were available.

Southern Kyushu was a particularly attractive target for U.S. planners. It was within range of land-based fighters on Okinawa, and bases in Kyushu would enable land-based air invasion of central Honshu. Capturing Kyushu would permit the navy to break into the Sea of Japan, thus cutting the Japanese off from the Asian mainland. Southern Kyushu also featured excellent bay ports—Kagoshima and Ariake—from which the invasion of Honshu could be staged. Despite these attractions, the terrain behind the possible invasion beaches in southern Kyushu was not so favorable. The beaches were backed by cliffs and terraces, into which Japanese defenders could burrow, and roads leading from the beaches passed through narrow defiles.

The fall of Okinawa in April 1945 raised the question of a commander for the invasion of Japan. The two drives across the Pacific commanded by General Douglas MacArthur and Admiral Chester Nimitz had now met, and the assault on Japan would require close army-navy cooperation. After considerable interservice squabbling, it was agreed that Nimitz would be responsible for the naval and amphibious phases of the operation and would correlate his plans with MacArthur, who would be responsible for the ground campaign.

MacArthur envisaged a nine-division assault on Kyushu. Lieutenant General Walter Krueger's Sixth Army, consisting of three corps of three divisions each, would land on three separate beaches and then move north to capture airfields and the port of Kagoshima. Two more divisions would be held in floating reserve. The attack carriers of Admiral William Halsey's Third Fleet would provide air cover, and Admiral Raymond Spruance's Fifth Fleet would provide amphibious transport and shore bombardment. Major General George Kenney's Far East Air Forces would provide additional air support from Okinawa. As planned, the invasion would involve more than 3,000 ships (including 22 battleships and 63 aircraft carriers), 1,850 land-based combat aircraft (in addition to almost 2,000 carrier planes), some 353,000 combat soldiers and marines, and 230,000 service troops (including more than 100,000 engineers to build new bases on Kyushu).

Planning for the invasion of Honshu began with the assumption that ports and airfields on Kyushu had been secured successfully. Two beaches south of Tokyo—Sagami and Kujukuri—were selected as invasion sites. Three infantry and three marine divisions of Hodge's First Army would land at Kujukuri, drive across the Boso Peninsula, and open Tokyo Bay and the port of Choshi. Four infantry divisions of General Robert Eichelberger's Eighth Army would land at Sagami and capture Yokosuka. Reinforced by two armored divisions and two more infantry divisions, Eighth Army would then move north to capture Yokohama and to assist First Army in taking Tokyo. Like Operation Olympic, Operation Coronet envisioned a massive engineering effort to repair ports and build new airfields. Should the Japanese refuse to surrender after the fall of Tokyo, additional operations would be launched against northern Kyushu, Nagoya, Osaka, and Hokkaido in the summer of 1946.

The projected invasion of Japan would require the redeployment of a million troops from Europe to the Pacific, and this created enormous emotional and logistical problems in the summer of 1945. Bases for these troops did not exist, and service troops in the Pacific would be hard-pressed to build new facilities. The lack of rail connections and ports on the U.S. West Coast meant that troops should ideally be shipped directly from Europe to the Pacific, but considerations of morale and public opinion demanded that the troops be redeployed through the United States. More taxing was the problem of demobilization. The U.S. policy of individual replacement resulted in units that consisted of both veteran and green troops, and entire units could not be demobilized without unfairly penalizing veterans in units not selected. Thus, the War Department devised a system of individual demobilization that favored combat veterans.

Unfortunately, individual demobilization was a recipe for chaos. Unit cohesion and efficiency were disrupted, and the process created divisions filled with green troops. These redeploying divisions were supposed to undergo eight weeks of retraining in the United States before leaving for the Pacific, but schedule changes and personnel turnover disrupted this plan. Many men resented being sent to the Pacific, and morale in these units was at rock bottom. The situation in the U.S. Air Corps was little better. Individual demobilization even affected units already in the Pacific, which were gutted of both veteran and noncommissioned officers. In short, the United States was preparing to invade Japan with a great many green troops who had little training and low morale. This inexorably would have resulted in thousands of unnecessary casualties, had the invasion actually taken place.

After the war, President Harry Truman and Secretary of War Henry L. Stimson claimed that dropping the atomic bombs on Hiroshima and Nagasaki saved the lives of a million U.S. troops who would have been killed in an invasion of Japan. The wartime record does not support such a large casualty estimate. In early 1945, MacArthur's staff predicted about 23,000 casualties in the first thirty days of the invasion of Kyushu—a loss rate comparable to Okinawa's. Nimitz's staff predicted 49,000 casualties in thirty days on Kyushu. It was generally agreed that casualty rates on Kyushu would not exceed those of Luzon, because Kyushu—like Luzon but unlike the smaller Pacific atolls—offered room to maneuver and avoid Japanese fixed defenses. On the other hand, Kyushu was one of the home islands, and the Japanese must have been expected to fight all the harder on their own "sacred soil," so U.S. casualties might well have exceeded these estimates.

The Americans developed chemical weapons during the war to be held in reserve should Germany or Japan initiate chemical warfare. In March 1945, the War Department investigated the question of using chemicals to destroy the rice crop on the Japanese home islands. The Joint Chiefs of Staff concluded that such spraying would be effective, but its impact would peak at the time Japan was expected to surrender, and occupation forces would then have to feed millions of starving people. The War Department investigated using gas to attack caves and bunkers, and tests in Utah proved that this would be effective even against masked defenders. (There was even a harebrained proposal to invade the caves with thousands of near-frozen, immobilized bats, attached to incendiary devices!) Although no final decision was reached about the use of gas, appropriate plans and preparations were made. Gas masks and protective clothing were shipped to the Pacific, and stocks of chemical munitions were moved forward to Luzon in the summer of 1945. The Joint Chiefs even contemplated using atomic bombs in a tactical role to support the invasion. In postwar interviews, General George C. Marshall claimed that nine atomic bombs would have been used against Japanese troop concentrations on Kyushu immediately before Operation Olympic.

The Japanese began considering the defense of the home islands after the fall of the Mariana Islands in the summer of 1944. Japanese strategy thereafter was to delay and wear down U.S. forces, so that a negotiated peace would be possible, and meanwhile to prepare a last-ditch homeland defense. Little progress had been made by the spring of 1945, when the loss of Iwo Jima and Okinawa brought homeland defense to the forefront. The Japanese correctly predicted that the Americans would first seize southern Kyushu with fifteen divisions and then invade Honshu with thirty divisions. Analysis of the terrain in Kyushu enabled the Japanese to predict correctly the U.S. objectives, and invasion beaches and defenses were prepared accordingly.

The Japanese decided to fight "at the water's edge," because experience showed that once U.S. troops got ashore in strength, they could not be stopped. Japanese strategy was to fortify the invasion beaches in order to contain the invaders until mobile reserves could be brought up to crush them. Two types of forces were mobilized to support this strategy: static coast-defense divisions and mobile, better-trained counterattack divisions. Between March and June 1945, Japan raised forty-two new divisions (twenty-seven static and fifteen mobile) for homeland defense, as well as a large number of independent tank and infantry brigades. In addition, four veteran divisions were transferred from Manchuria to Japan. The new forces, formidable as they seemed on paper, were poorly trained and equipped and lacked adequate means of supply and transport. Masses of boys and girls were also being trained in the use of bamboo spears against the invaders.

Since the Japanese navy and air force had been all but annihilated, the Japanese intended to rely on suicide units in their place for homeland defense. As soon as the enemy fleet appeared, mass attacks would be launched, concentrating on invasion transports. The Japanese expected to have 10,000 suicide planes available at the time of the invasion and planned to employ 5,000 for the defense of Kyushu. These would be used in conjunction with some 2,000 fast suicide boats, nearly 400 midget submarines, and several hundred manned torpedoes. The Japanese hoped that these kamikazes would destroy from 15 to 50 percent of the invasion force before it reached the shore.

In July 1945, the Japanese, expecting the next U.S. assault to fall on southern Kyushu, began reinforcing the island. In April the region had only three divisions for its defense, but in August there were thirteen divisions, five tank brigades, and three mixed brigades in southern Kyushu. These forces were deployed to cover what were correctly thought to be the likely invasion beaches, with a counterattack force in reserve.

The reinforcement of Kyushu came at the expense of central Honshu. In August, thirteen divisions, ten brigades, and three tank brigades were deployed for coastal defense, and six mobile and three tank divisions were held in reserve as a counterattack force. Prospects for a successful defense of Honshu after the loss of Kyushu would not have been good—nearly all the suicide units would have been spent, and the Honshu terrain was intrinsically less favorable to the defender. The Japanese had to cover three possible invasion beaches, and if the enemy broke through the coastal defense anywhere, there was little to prevent the fall of Tokyo.

After Japan's surrender, the U.S. Army studied the proposed invasion of Japan and concluded that, had Japan not surrendered, Kyushu would have been taken in no more than two months at a cost of 75,000 to 100,000 American casualties. Japanese casualties would have been huge—certainly in the many hundreds of thousands, and perhaps in the millions—given the combined effects of the invasion, continued B-29 raids, and the possible use of weapons of mass destruction. However, the invasion of Honshu would have been a less difficult operation than Operation Olympic, because the Japanese would have spent their last reserves defending Kyushu. No serious study of the proposed U.S. invasion of the Japanese home islands has projected anything less than a horrific death rate for both sides. Questions about the morality or even the military necessity of dropping the atomic bomb are best posed in the context of the casualty rates that would have been suffered in the invasion of the Japanese home islands.

FURTHER READINGS

Allen, Thomas B., and Norman Polmar. *Codename Downfall: The Secret Plan to Invade Japan* (1995).
Skates, John R. *The Invasion of Japan: Alternative to the Bomb* (1994).

U.S. Army Air Forces in the Pacific. *"Downfall": Strategic Plan for Operations in the Japanese Archipelago* (1945).

James Perry

SEE ALSO MacArthur, Douglas; Roosevelt, Franklin Delano

Driniumor River Operation

The Japanese initiated the Driniumor River operation in response to General Douglas MacArthur's successful attack, on April 22, 1944, on their base at Hollandia on New Guinea's north-central coast. The U.S. occupation of Hollandia isolated Lieutenant General Hatazo Adachi's 55,000-man strong Eighteenth Army in the Hansa Bay–Wewak area to the east. Adachi realized that his surrounded army possessed finite and dwindling resources, so he decided that he could best help his compatriots at the other end of New Guinea by diverting as many U.S. troops and as much equipment as possible from MacArthur's fast-moving offensive toward the China-Formosa-Luzon region. To do this, Adachi zeroed in on Aitape, a U.S. base between Hansa Bay–Wewak and Hollandia. The Japanese lacked trucks, so they had to carry most of their equipment and supplies through the trackless jungle. Even so, by May 1944 Adachi and some 20,000 Japanese troops from his 20th, 41st, and 51st Divisions gradually closed in on Aitape and began skirmishing with U.S. troops in and around the Driniumor River area east of Aitape.

MacArthur's ground-forces commander, Lieutenant General Walter Krueger, worried about Aitape's vulnerability to just such a Japanese assault. U.S. intelligence was aware of the Japanese buildup, but no one was sure when the enemy would attack. To be safe, Krueger deployed Major General William Gill's veteran 32d Infantry Division to Aitape soon after it fell to the Americans as part of the Hollandia operation. As evidence of the Japanese strength in the area mounted, Krueger reinforced Aitape with Brigadier General Julian Cunningham's dismounted 112th Cavalry Regimental Combat Team (RCT) on June 28 and with Colonel Edward Starr's 124th RCT from the 31st Infantry Division on July 3. Neither unit had much combat experience, but Krueger hoped that they could hold out with the 32d Division until Major General Leonard Wing's veteran 43d Infantry Division arrived from the Solomon Islands. In forcing Krueger to deploy all these units to Aitape, Adachi succeeded in partially fulfilling his mission even before he committed his men to battle.

To command the growing forces at Aitape, Krueger sent in Major General Charles Hall and his XI Corps headquarters. Krueger wanted to eliminate the Japanese threat quickly so that the Americans could continue their offensive westward to the China-Formosa-Luzon region unfettered, and so he ordered Hall to attack the Japanese as far eastward as possible. Some of Hall's subordinates, however, urged the XI Corps commander to let the Japanese batter themselves against Aitape's well-established fortifications, which, while more time-consuming than Krueger's strategy, promised to minimize U.S. casualties. In the end, Hall compromised. He wanted to use the 43d Division to launch an amphibious assault behind the advancing Japanese, but the unit was slow in arriving. In the meantime, he developed two defensive lines—one around Aitape and the other to the east along the Driniumor River—under Brigadier General Clarence Martin. He garrisoned the Driniumor River line with the 112th RCT and elements from the 32d Division.

As July wore on, Krueger became increasingly impatient for the Japanese to show themselves, and he ordered Hall to dispatch a reconnaissance in force across the Driniumor to look for them. Hall reluctantly complied, even though this meant depleting his Driniumor River line. Two large patrols crossed the river on July 10. The one to the south near Afua, around the Driniumor's headwaters, found no Japanese, but the northern force ran into innumerable enemy roadblocks as it pushed eastward down the coast. That night, Adachi's forces launched an all-out attack against U.S. forces along the Driniumor. Pre-positioned U.S. artillery, mortars, and machine guns inflicted heavy casualties on the charging Japanese and bloodied the river, but Adachi's men succeeded in establishing themselves on the Driniumor's west bank. Alarmed by the scope of the assault, Martin asked for and received permission from Hall to fall back after he recovered the men east of the Driniumor. By then, however, Hall had lost confidence in Martin and relieved him, replacing him with Gill. The Japanese, meanwhile, paused after crossing the river, giving Hall time to bring up reinforcements from the Aitape line. Three days after the Japanese attack, Hall used these reinforcements to counterattack and drive the Japanese back across the Driniumor in bitter fighting. Combat along the river remained intense for the rest of July, especially around Afua, where at one point the Japanese surrounded elements of Cunningham's 112th RCT and the 32d Division's 127th RCT.

While fighting raged along the Driniumor, Hall waited impatiently for the 43d Division so he could launch a full-fledged counteroffensive designed to destroy Adachi's forces. Unfortunately for Hall, the 43d arrived in driblets, with worn-out equipment. Because the 43d was in no shape for immediate commitment to battle, Hall decided to substitute the 124th and use it to sweep the Japanese from the Driniumor's east bank. Nicknamed "Ted Force" after its commander, Colonel Starr, the 124th RCT and a battalion from the 43d Division crossed the Driniumor on July 31 against little opposition. Swinging south, Ted Force met few Japanese until it approached the Afua area and slugged it out with the Japanese in the ridges and gullies there. Even before Ted Force began its eleven-day trek, however, Adachi had concluded that he could not beat the Americans along the Driniumor, so he ordered a retreat back to Hansa Bay–Wewak. Starr's men lost 61 killed and 180 wounded in their encounter with what turned out to be the Japanese rear guard.

The Driniumor River fighting cost the Americans 597 killed, 1,691 wounded, and 85 missing. The Japanese, for their part, suffered some 8,800 casualties. The Americans stripped Adachi's Eighteenth Army of its offensive potential and safeguarded Aitape and Hollandia, permitting MacArthur's offensive to continue unhindered. Adachi, for his part, could take comfort in the knowledge that he had diverted significant U.S. resources that would otherwise have been deployed elsewhere. His attack did not, however, buy enough time for the Japanese to build up enough strength to stop MacArthur's offensive through western New Guinea.

FURTHER READINGS

Krueger, W. *From Down Under to Nippon* (1953).

"Operational History of the Tabletennis (Noemfoor Island) Operation." Washington National Records Center, RG 407, Box 1508.

Taafe, S. *MacArthur's Jungle War: The 1944 New Guinea Campaign* (1998).

"Unit History, 158th Infantry Regiment." Washington National Records Center, RG 407, Box 21182.

Stephen R. Taaffe

SEE ALSO New Guinea

Drought, James M.

A Roman Catholic priest from the Catholic Mission Society at Maryknoll, New York, Drought conducted a series of unofficial negotiations with Japanese leaders in late 1940 and early 1941.

In autumn of 1940 Drought arrived in Tokyo bearing letters of introduction to several Japanese business leaders from Lewis L. Strauss (the postwar chairman of the Atomic Energy Commission) of the banking firm of Kuhn, Loeb and Company. At least one of these business leaders, Ikawa Tadao of the Cooperative Bank of Japan, was known to have connections to Prince Konoe Fumimaro, the Japanese prime minister. War between the United States and Japan, Drought argued, would be a disaster for everyone except Hitler, who stood to profit while American attention was directed away from Europe. In a letter to Ikawa dated November 29, the priest (now joined by his superior from Maryknoll, Bishop James Walsh, a prelate also with political connections) called for a Japanese "Monroe Doctrine" for Asia, in which Japan would be granted political predominance in China, Indochina, Thailand, Malaya, and the Dutch East Indies. These areas would thus be protected both from European imperialism and communism. These suggestions met with an enthusiastic response by the Japanese, and Ikawa was encouraged to pursue his association with Drought.

Walsh and Drought then returned to the United States, where they were granted a meeting with President Franklin Roosevelt through the good offices of Postmaster General Frank Walker, an ardent Catholic and longtime friend of Bishop Walsh. At that meeting, the pair presented a memo which hinted that Japan might alter its commitment to the Axis Alliance and that the Japanese sought U.S. cooperation in settling the war in China. Roosevelt and Secretary of State Cordell Hull were less than enthusiastic about Drought's suggested "Far Eastern Monroe Doctrine" but were encouraged to continue the negotiations.

The two priests proceeded to New York, where they resumed negotiations with Ikawa, and the three were joined soon thereafter by Colonel Iwakuro Hideo, the assistant director of the Central Bureau of Military Affairs. In April they produced a "Preliminary Draft of Agreement in Principle" (later more commonly known as the "Draft Understanding") which was promptly sent to Secretary of State Hull. The Draft Understanding provided for the withdrawal of all Japanese troops from China "in accordance with an agreement to be reached between Japan and China"; recognition of the Japanese satellite, Manchukuo; and the resumption of normal trade relations between Japan and the United States. Furthermore, it called for a meeting between Roosevelt and Prince Konoe, to be held at Honolulu.

Hull refused to comment directly on the Draft Understanding but hinted that he might be willing to use it as a starting point for further negotiations. He qualified this, however, by attaching four principles that were to form the basis for any U.S.-Japanese understanding. These included respect for the territorial integrity and sovereignty of all nations, noninterference in the internal affairs of other nations, the essential equality of nations, and the nondisturbance of the status quo in the Pacific. (All but the last principle would seem to rule out any U.S. "accommodation" to the Japanese seizure and control of Manchuria.) He then passed this on to the Japanese ambassador, Nomura Kichisaburo, who ignored the four principles but cabled the Draft Understanding to Tokyo.

In Japan the Draft Understanding was assumed to be the official position of the U.S. government (which it certainly was not), and it was greeted with immense relief by most Japanese leaders, who sought to avoid a costly war with the United States. Foreign Minister Matsuoka Yosuke, however, was outraged that negotiations had been taking place without his knowledge. He suspected, quite correctly, that the Draft Understanding did not represent the official policy of the United States, and he refused to take it seriously. Drought's initiative, finally, amounted to virtually nothing, except that it reflected a sincere desire among the leadership of both the United States and Japan to reach some sort of mutually acceptable arrangement in Asia and the Pacific.

FURTHER READINGS

Butow, Robert J. C. *The John Doe Associates: Backdoor Diplomacy for Peace* (1974).

Lu, David J. *From the Marco Polo Bridge to Pearl Harbor* (1961).

Ike, Nobutaka, ed. *Japan's Decision for War: Records of the 1941 Policy Conferences* (1967).

John E. Moser

Dutch East Indies

The Dutch East Indies, also called the Netherlands East Indies, are an archipelago of more than thirteen thousand islands off the Southeast Asean Mainland, including Java, Sumatra, Dutch Borneo, Celebes, and western New Guinea. The population in 1930 was 60.7 million, with nearly 70 percent living on Java and the nearby island of Madura. The Netherlands gradually conquered Java and the other islands during the fifteenth century to form a colony. After the German conquest of the Netherlands in May 1940, the Dutch government in exile, based in London, assumed responsibility for the colony.

After the outbreak of Pacific war, the ABDA (American-British-Dutch-Australian) Command was formed on January 15, 1942, to defend Malaya, Singapore, the Dutch East Indies, and the northwestern coasts of Australia. Sir General Archibald Wavell (1883–1950) commanded from headquarters in Lembang, on Java.

On December 20, 1941, units of Lieutenant General Imamura Hitoshi's Sixteenth Army—having departed from Mindanao in the Philippines—attacked Dutch Borneo, Celebes, and other islands. Other units of the Sixteenth Army took the city of Palembang in southern Sumatra on February 16, 1942, capturing intact a large oil refinery. Most other oil facilities on Sumatra and Borneo were captured either intact or with little damage. During these operations, 500 Japanese paratroops were used for the first time, to take an airfield south of Menado on Celebes. On February 25, the ABDA Command was dissolved.

Having conquered most of the rest of the Dutch East Indies, the Japanese embarked two invasion forces for Java under the command of Vice Admiral Ibo Takahashi. On February 27, 1942, the first of three naval battles was fought between the Japanese covering force and the cruisers and destroyers from the former ABDA command. The Japanese navy decisively won the Battle of Java Sea. On March 1 Japanese forces landed at two locations on Java, and on March 8 the Royal Netherlands East Indies Army of 93,000 men under General Hein ter Poorten surrendered, as did 5,000 Australian, British, and American personnel. Japan sent the native Indonesian soldiers home and interned 170,000 European prisoners of war and European civilians.

Only on Timor was there any effective opposition to the Japanese. Timor was divided between the Dutch and the neutral Portuguese. On December 17, 1941, Australian and Dutch forces occupied the Portuguese part of Timor. Although the Portuguese objected to this violation, they made no armed opposition. On February 19, 1942, 6,000 Japanese troops invaded Timor. Six hundred thirty paratroopers were also dropped, most of whom were killed by the Allied defenders. The Dutch and Allied forces were quickly defeated, but included as part of the Australian defenders was a commando unit, the 2d Independent Company of the 2d Imperial Force. This intrepid unit retreated into the mountainous interior of the island with a considerable amount of supplies, including 160,000 rounds of ammunition. Although trained to fight in the deserts of North Africa, these 300 Australians inflicted some 1,500 casualties while losing only 40 men. The island natives actively assisted the Australians. In September 1942 a second commando company was infiltrated onto the island. To handle these annoying guerrillas, the Japanese added another 15,000 soldiers to the island, impelling the Australian high command to extract its forces by destroyer and submarine during December 1942 and the following month.

As a key component of the Greater East Asia Co-Prosperity Sphere, the Japanese expected the Dutch East Indies to supply raw materials for the factories of Japan, Korea, Manchukeo, northern China, and Formosa; they especially wanted the all-important oil from Sumatra and Borneo. Sumatra was administered by Japan's Twenty-Fifth Army; Java, by the Sixteenth Army; and Borneo and the eastern islands, by the navy. This division of administrative responsibility created policy confusion and differences in the treatment of the natives. Japan recruited the native nationalist leadership to administer the country under the "guidance" of the Japanese army and navy. The leading prewar agitator for independence, Sukarno (1901–1970), cooperated enthusiastically.

In January 1943, Prime Minister Tojo announced that Burma and the Philippines would be given independence within a year. This was a method of co-opting their populations into the Japanese war effort. It was not until September 7, 1944, that Prime Minister Koiso proposed independence for the Dutch East Indies for an unspecified future date. As the tide of war turned, the Japanese made efforts to mobilize the population. This included anti-Dutch propaganda, military training for youth groups, and the creation of the 25,000-man Heiho, or auxiliary forces, which were part of the Japanese armed forces. Another volunteer army (called *Peta*), of 57,000 men, was organized as guerrillas and commanded by natives. Japan made plans to grant independence to the Dutch East Indies in September 1945.

The closing of the export market devastated the economy of the islands, while the loss of tankers and shipping to Allied submarine warfare limited the amounts of oil and other resources that the Japanese could bring to their home islands. Although most of the native population supported Japan, this support eroded from 1943 to 1945 because of the confiscation of rice for the Japanese occupation forces, the brutal behavior of some Japanese troops, and the forced recruitment of laborers (called *romusha*), many of whom were sent overseas and never returned. By 1945, the populations of Java and other islands were mired in poverty and facing famine.

In 1944, Australia's 7th and 9th Infantry Divisions were detailed to retake Borneo from the Japanese, supported by U.S. naval and air power. Small units of commandos were first parachuted into the interior of the island to organize the native population. From May 1 to July 1, 1945, the Australians made multiple landings around Borneo. During July and August, the remaining Japanese forces were mopped up. On September 10, 1945—more than a month after the United States dropped atomic bombs on Hiroshima and Nagasaki—the Japanese commander of Borneo, Lieutenant General Masao Baba, surrendered. Seven weeks later the last fugitive Japanese unit was captured. With the exception of Dutch New Guinea, no other parts of the Dutch East Indies were reconquered by the Allies before the end of the war.

By its extraordinary feats of arms at the beginning of the war, Japan had shown the native population that the Dutch could be defeated. On August 17, 1945, three days after Japan's unconditional surrender, Sukarno and the nationalists declared independence and announced the formation of the Republic of Indonesia. With the war over, British, Indian, and Dutch troops landed to accept the surrender of the Japanese forces remaining in Indonesia. They found a politicized populace who believed in independence and who had ready-made military forces in the various groups like *Peta*. Some Japanese army and navy units helped the Allies, while others turned their weapons over to the Indonesians. Former Dutch colonial army soldiers—feeling that the Dutch surrender in 1942 had released them from their oath of service—joined the rebels, as did up to four hundred Japanese soldiers. Fierce clashes between Allied troops and Indonesian rebels soon occurred. The heaviest battle occurred at the Javan city of Surabaya, where 6,000 British-Indian troops landed on October 25, 1945. A month later the city was in ruins from aerial and naval bombardment, with 6,000 Indonesians dead and many Allied casualties, including the British commander, Brigadier A. W. S. Mallaby. This convinced the British to remain neutral in the ensuing revolutionary war. After four years of trying unsuccessfully to suppress the republic, the Dutch admitted defeat. On December 27, 1949, the Netherlands formally ceded sovereignty of the Dutch East Indies to the new nation of Indonesia.

FURTHER READINGS

Lebra, Joyce. *Japanese-Trained Armies in Southeast Asia: Independence and Volunteer Forces in World War II* (1977).

Sato Shigeru. *War, Nationalism and Peasants: Java under the Japanese Occupation 1942–1945* (1994).

Eric Swedin

SEE ALSO Army, Japanese; Greater East Asia Co-Prosperity Sphere; Navy, Japanese

Eastern Solomons, Battle of

This naval battle was the third carrier-versus-carrier clash of the Pacific war. Designated by the Japanese as the "Second Battle of the Solomon Sea," this naval air engagement was fought in late August 1942, in a wide expanse to the north and northeast of the islands of Malaita and Guadalcanal and in the vicinity of the Stewart Islands.

The battle was the outcome of the first major effort by the Japanese to regain control of Guadalcanal following the Battle of Savo Island on the night of August 8–9. To accomplish this, the Japanese intended immediately to reinforce their Guadalcanal garrison with army and naval troops: the Ichiki Detachment and the Yokosuka 5th Special Naval Landing Force. They also hoped to crush U.S. naval and air power in the area by employing a formidable portion of the Japanese navy's Combined Fleet in this operation.

The first phase of the landing of troop reinforcements was completed on the night of August 18–19, when six destroyers of the Japanese navy's Eighth Fleet put ashore at Taivu Point the first echelon, about 900 men, of the Japanese army's Ichiki Detachment. The next landing, involving 1,500 men (the Yokosuka 5th Special Naval Landing Force and the second echelon of the Ichiki Detachment), was scheduled for the night of August 23.

For the second landing, the Japanese intended that their Eighth Fleet be supported by a powerful body of ships from the Combined Fleet. Designated the support force, this group of warships included the three aircraft carriers of the recently reorganized Carrier Division 1 (*Zuikaku, Shokaku,* and *Ryujo*); battleships *Hiei, Kirishima,* and *Mutsu;* seaplane carrier *Chitose;* and several dozen cruisers and destroyers. Vice Admiral Nobutake Kondo, commander in chief of the Second Fleet, was given tactical command of the support force. Vice Admiral Gunichi Mikawa's Eighth Fleet, which was rein-

forced with a destroyer squadron, would provide the escort ships for the troop convoy. The 25th Air Flotilla, a Rabaul-based unit of Vice Admiral Nishizo Tsukahara's Eleventh Air Fleet, would provide air support.

The U.S. Navy's Task Force 61, under the command of Vice Admiral Frank Jack Fletcher, was positioned southeast of Guadalcanal in anticipation of a Japanese counteroffensive. TF 61 contained three carrier task forces (designated TF 11, 16, and 18), each of which had one fleet carrier (*Saratoga, Enterprise,* and *Wasp*) as its nucleus. The carriers' air groups totaled about 250 aircraft. TF 61 also included the new battleship *North Carolina,* seven cruisers, and eighteen destroyers. Fletcher would be supported also by army and marine aircraft as well as long-range navy reconnaissance planes, based nearby.

The main body of the Japanese fleet, the support force, approached Guadalcanal from the direction of Truk. It consisted of a carrier strike force under the command of Vice Admiral Chuichi Nagumo; a vanguard body, proceeding slightly ahead of the carriers, under the command of Rear Admiral Hiroaki Abe, which consisted of two battleships, four cruisers, and a destroyer screen; and an advance force of six cruisers, *Chitose,* and a destroyer screen, under the direct command of Vice Admiral Kondo, which provided distant cover on the support force's eastern flank. A skirmish line of Japanese submarines scouted well ahead of the main body. The transport group (formally designated the Guadalcanal Reinforcement Force) took a separate and more direct route. It consisted of armed merchant cruiser *Kinryu Maru,* two army transports, and four patrol boats laden with troops and supplies, escorted by Destroyer Squadron 2, commanded by Rear Admiral Raizo Tanaka aboard the squadron's flagship, light cruiser *Jintsu.* To the southwest were four Eighth Fleet heavy cruisers, under the command of

Vice Admiral Mikawa, that provided close cover for the transport group.

In the event that they were not confronted by U.S. carriers, the Japanese planned for light carrier *Ryujo,* escorted by heavy cruiser *Tone* and two destroyers, to break away from the carrier strike force and proceed south toward Guadalcanal. The *Ryujo* group was to provide cover for the transport group, and its carrier aircraft were to attack the Guadalcanal airfield (Henderson Field), which had become operational on August 20. Nagumo's fleet carriers, *Shokaku* and *Zuikaku,* would proceed farther to the east, prepared to deal with any U.S. carriers that might be lurking in the area. Should Kondo's support force prove successful in establishing control of the air and sea in the vicinity of Guadalcanal, the landing of the reinforcement troops would then commence. The landing, however, was rescheduled for the evening of August 24.

On August 23 U.S. air searches detected the slow-moving Japanese transport group, prompting Fletcher to launch an air strike, consisting of thirty-one dive-bombers and six torpedo bombers from *Saratoga.* Twenty-three Guadalcanal-based marine aircraft joined in the attack. Neither air group, however, located the Japanese transports, which had been ordered to retire temporarily to the north on learning of the presence of U.S. carriers.

At that point, Fletcher believed that he had an opportunity to refuel some of his ships before engaging any Japanese carriers. Intelligence reports, which proved inaccurate, indicated that the enemy carriers were well to the north, either at the Japanese naval base at Truk or beyond. Fletcher thereupon detached TF 18—*Wasp* task force, under Rear Admiral Leigh Noyes's command—to the south to refuel, thereby reducing his air strength by one carrier and approximately eighty aircraft. On the eve of the battle Fletcher had 153 operational carrier aircraft, while Nagumo had 177.

On the following day, August 24, TF 61's morning air search, which extended out 200 miles, made no significant sightings. But long-range army and navy patrol planes operating in the area made a number of sightings, including that of the *Ryujo* group, which had broken away from Nagumo's carrier strike force at 0400 hours to deliver an air strike against Henderson Field.

By late morning, therefore, Fletcher knew that at least one Japanese carrier (*Ryujo*) was nearby, although it was outside the range of his carrier planes. But he had not yet received any sighting reports on Nagumo's two fleet carriers, which he suspected were participating in this operation. Fletcher elected at this point to launch another air search to confirm the earlier sightings and to determine if other Japanese carriers were in the area. At his direction,

Enterprise launched an armed air search of twenty-three planes, beginning at 1229 hours, while *Saratoga* prepared for the launching of an air strike. Rear Admiral Thomas C. Kinkaid, commander of *Enterprise* TF 16, was also directed to prepare a strike force to be held in reserve for use against a "possible" second carrier, should one be located. At around 1345 hours *Saratoga* launched thirty dive-bombers and eight torpedo bombers, led by Commander Harry Felt, to attack the *Ryujo* group.

Soon thereafter, Fletcher received further search reports from his long-range aircraft, and although they were tracking the movements of the *Ryujo* group, he was not certain whether the reports pertained to *Ryujo,* now apparently at a different and unexpected location, or to a second carrier. Fletcher attempted, therefore, to divert Felt's air strike to a location where a carrier had been more recently sighted. He was unable, however, to establish radio contact with Commander Felt.

Throughout this day, Fletcher was plagued by difficulties with communications, mainly because of radio transmission and reception problems. As a result, some search reports were not received; others were incomplete or inaccurate. (The Japanese experienced similar problems.) The first sighting report that Fletcher received of Nagumo's two fleet carriers was made by elements of the afternoon armed air search. Unfortunately for Fletcher, the report was incomplete; it did not contain information about the carriers' locations.

Dawn searches conducted by aircraft from Admiral Kondo's advance force and Admiral Nagumo's strike force had also proved unsuccessful. But a late-morning air search conducted by float planes from Admiral Abe's vanguard force succeeded in locating TF 61. Based on a sighting report made at about 1405 hours by a float plane from cruiser *Chikuma,* Nagumo's fleet carriers launched two dive-bomber air strikes. The first, launched at 1507, consisted of twenty-seven dive-bombers, escorted by fifteen fighter aircraft. The second, launched at 1600, consisted of twenty-seven dive-bombers and nine fighters.

Admiral Fletcher had concluded that his task force's location had been reported to the Japanese carriers. His air patrols and radar had detected a number of Japanese search planes throughout the day. At 1610, when it became apparent to him that his ships would be subjected to an air attack soon, Fletcher gave orders for *Enterprise* and *Saratoga* to launch air strikes directed at one of the more recent carrier sightings, which proved to be a sighting of *Ryujo.* Beginning around 1615, shortly before the first Japanese air strike began its attack on TF 61, *Saratoga* launched two dive-bombers and five torpedo bombers.

Soon thereafter, eighteen bombers were launched from *Enterprise.*

The first air group on either side to reach its intended target was *Ryujo*'s strike force of twenty-one planes, which had been launched beginning at 1300 hours. Linking up with a Japanese land-based air strike that had originated in Rabaul, *Ryujo* aircraft began their attack on Henderson Field around 1430. The airfield suffered minor damage, and the *Ryujo* air group lost six aircraft during the attack.

Only a short time after its air group had begun to attack Henderson Field, *Ryujo* was challenged by several aircraft from Fletcher's afternoon armed air search, but no hits were scored. The *Saratoga* air strike led by Commander Felt succeeded in locating *Ryujo* and began its attack on the light carrier at around 1550, scoring bomb and torpedo hits. *Ryujo* sank at around 2000 hours, with an estimated 121 fatalities.

Of the two air strikes launched from Nagumo's carriers, the first strike, led by Lieutenant Commander Mamaruo Seki, attacked *Enterprise* TF 16 at 1641 hours, scoring three direct hits on the carrier. Several of the dive-bombers unsuccessfully attacked *North Carolina.* But approximately seventy men were killed and another ninety-five were wounded aboard *Enterprise.* Although the ship's crew would soon be able to restore the carrier to operational status, the carrier suffered temporary loss of steering at about the time that the second Japanese air strike arrived in the vicinity. However, that air group failed to locate TF 61.

The air strikes launched by *Enterprise* and *Saratoga* on the eve of the Japanese air attack on *Enterprise* had mixed results. The eighteen bombers launched by *Enterprise* failed to find the enemy. The *Saratoga* air strike located Kondo's advance force and seriously damaged *Chitose.*

The air battles of August 24 had taken their toll on the air units, both land- and carrier-based, of both sides. But it was clear that the Japanese had suffered far greater losses, losing sixty-five aircraft, while the Americans lost twenty-five.

TF 61 withdrew to the south on the evening of August 24 in an effort to avoid a night surface engagement with the numerically superior forces of the Japanese. Admiral Kondo's forces continued to pursue the Americans until around midnight, when Kondo opted to withdraw to the north.

Neither the Japanese nor the American carrier forces were inclined to resume the battle on August 25. Nonetheless, the Japanese continued in their efforts to land the troop reinforcements on Guadalcanal. Admiral Tanaka ordered five of his destroyers to push ahead for the purpose of bombarding Henderson Field during the night of August 24–25. The shelling did not neutralize the airfield, however. Eight marine and navy dive-bombers, escorted by ten fighter aircraft, departed Henderson Field at dawn. The bombers succeeded in locating Tanaka's transport group, scoring one direct hit on light cruiser *Jintsu* and setting transport *Kinryu Maru* ablaze. *Jintsu,* seriously damaged, was forced to retire from the action, leaving the escort ships to undertake the rescue of those aboard the sinking *Kinryu Maru.* Later, U.S. Army B-17s attacked the transport group, sinking destroyer *Mutsuki* (one of the few times that high-level bombers ever hit, let alone sank, an enemy warship). Accordingly, the remainder of the transport group withdrew, and the effort to land the reinforcement troops was canceled at 0930. The Japanese had damaged a U.S. Navy carrier, while the Americans had sunk a light Japanese carrier. Nonetheless, the fact that their task force had to retire (retreat) in the face of the enemy, even if numerically superior, rankled throughout the fleet. But the Japanese reinforcement of Guadalcanal was stymied, and the Americans still held in growing strength on Guadalcanal.

FURTHER READINGS

Frank, Richard B. *Guadalcanal* (1990).

Hammel, Eric. *Guadalcanal: The Carrier Battles* (1987).

———. *Carrier Clash: The Invasion of Guadalcanal and the Battle of the Eastern Solomons, August 1942* (1997).

Lundstrom, John B. *The First Team and the Guadalcanal Campaign* (1994).

Morison, Samuel Eliot. *The Struggle for Guadalcanal* (1954).

George H. Curtis

SEE ALSO Guadalcanal, Battle for; Navy, U.S.

Eichelberger, Robert Lawrence (1886–1961)

Robert L. Eichelberger, a general officer in the Pacific Theater in World War II, was born in Urbana, Ohio, on March 9, 1886. In 1905 he was nominated as a cadet to the U.S. Military Academy, from which he graduated in the class of 1910. Between 1910 and 1915 Eichelberger's regiment, the 10th Infantry, spent considerable time in the Panama Canal Zone. From 1915 to 1916 he served on the U.S. border with Mexico during the futile expedition to capture the Mexican bandit leader Pancho Villa, whose forces had raided towns on the U.S. side of the border. Eichelberger next spent two years training troops for service in World War I, before assignment to the general staff in Washington under Major General William S. Graves, the executive assistant chief of staff.

In the summer of 1918 Eichelberger and Graves were ordered to Europe with the 8th Division, an assignment countermanded when President Woodrow Wilson appointed Graves commander of the American Expeditionary Force in Siberia. Eichelberger accompanied Graves to Vladivostok as assistant chief of staff and intelligence officer, a post in which he remained until the expedition ended in 1920. Eichelberger's Siberian experience marked the beginning of his lifelong interest in Asian affairs. The multinational Siberian intervention, supposedly to protect Allied supplies and the strategic Trans-Siberian Railroad from German appropriation, allowed Britain and France to attempt to overthrow the new Bolshevik government of Russia, and Japan to try to annex Russian territory. This assignment, which allowed Eichelberger to observe firsthand Japan's determination to gain territory in East Asia, in this case at Russian expense, instilled in him a lasting distaste for that country. He later recalled:

[The Japanese] had agreed solemnly to send in 12,000 troops and had sent in 120,000. They intended to stay. Out of my Siberian experiences came a conviction that pursued me for the next twenty years: I knew that Japanese militarism had as its firm purpose the conquest of all Asia. (Eichelberger, xiv)

In 1921 Eichelberger was posted to the Philippines as chief of military intelligence but spent much of his time in China, where he set up intelligence offices in various cities. As military aide to the Chinese delegation at the Washington Naval Disarmament Conference in 1921, Eichelberger suffered his "first doubts" over the conference's achievements when he noted the jubilation of Prince Tokugawa, leader of the Japanese delegation.

Between the wars, Eichelberger transferred from the infantry to the adjutant general's department, which he hoped would provide a faster route to promotion. He attended advanced staff courses, spending one year studying at Fort Leavenworth (1925–1926) and another year (1930–1931) at the Army War College in Washington, D.C. The intervening years he spent at Leavenworth, first as an instructor and later as adjutant general. From 1931 to 1935 he was adjutant general and secretary of the Academic Board at West Point. In 1935 Eichelberger was appointed secretary to the U.S. Army General Staff, serving first under Douglas MacArthur and then under Malin Craig. Believing that war was increasingly likely, in 1938 Eichelberger returned to the infantry and spent the next two years on the West Coast as colonel of the 30th In-

fantry Regiment and assistant commander of the 3d Division, to which his regiment belonged. In 1940 he was posted to West Point as superintendent of the military academy. There he emphasized the teaching of modern military methods, including training in motorized warfare and aviation. After the Japanese attack on the U.S. Navy facility at Pearl Harbor, Hawaii, in December 1941, Eichelberger requested a combat assignment. In March 1942 he took command of the 77th Division, and in June 1942, of 1st Corps, which was undergoing training in amphibious warfare.

At the request of his former superior, Douglas MacArthur, the Allied supreme commander in the Southwest Pacific theater, in August 1942 Eichelberger took his corps headquarters to Australia, where he quickly realized that the army general staff and politicians in Washington accorded the Pacific theater a far lower priority than the European. The result was that for some months his men were chronically undersupplied and underequipped. The demoralized Allied forces in the Pacific needed a victory, and in October 1942 MacArthur ordered Eichelberger to take command of the dispirited and flagging ground troops in Buna, New Guinea, which the Japanese had occupied in June 1942. He told his subordinate, with typical grandiloquence: "I want you to take Buna, or not come back alive" (Eichelberger, 21). Eichelberger promptly replaced several senior officers, including the 32d Division's commander. After a difficult campaign in adverse jungle conditions, with his troops often short of food and basic supplies and suffering from various debilitating tropical diseases, Eichelberger accomplished his assignment. This victory, in January 1943, was the first major defeat U.S. forces inflicted on Japanese ground troops. It facilitated the construction of air bases from which the Allies could attack the larger Japanese fortress at Rabaul, New Guinea. This greatly enhanced the U.S. ability to dominate the sea routes and supply its Australian-based troops in the Pacific.

As the Buna campaign ended, Eichelberger was named commander of the entire Advance New Guinea Force. Despite his pleas, for most of 1943 he was restricted to training rather than further combat assignments; MacArthur refused to allow him to transfer to the European theater, where Eichelberger's rank entitled him to command fighting troops. Eventually Eichelberger's 1st Corps was assigned to the Sixth Army under General Walter Krueger. It contributed heavily to implementation of the island-hopping strategy of approaching the Japanese-held islands by sea, as opposed to engaging Japanese forces on the Asian mainland. He won further victories in campaigns in New Guinea, Hollandia (Djajapura in present-day Indonesia), New Britain, the Admiralty Islands, Numfoor, and Morotai—and, perhaps most spectacularly, in May 1944 in cave warfare at Biak, one of the Schouten Islands, just off the coast of northern New Guinea. In the latter campaign Japanese forces had retreated to the island's network of volcanic caves, an action demanding the development of new tactics. These campaigns gave Eichelberger great respect for the determination and dogged fighting qualities of the Japanese troops, even as he condemned such atrocities as Japanese aircraft machine-gunning surviving fliers who parachuted from downed U.S. planes.

In September 1944 Eichelberger took command of the newly formed Eighth Army, which launched the invasion of the Philippine Islands in October, beginning with the island of Leyte, which was taken on Christmas Day. A few months earlier President Franklin D. Roosevelt had decided Allied troops should bypass the Philippines and strike closer to Japan, but in July 1944 MacArthur persuaded him to reinstate the Philippine campaign, citing both military reasons and the moral imperative that the United States keep faith with its suffering Philippine ally. The Eighth Army launched numerous scattered invasions of the islands, including Leyte, Luzon, Palawan, the Zamboanga Peninsula, Panay, Bohol, Negros, Mindanao, Mindoro, Marinduque, Cebu, Capul, Samar, and numerous smaller islands. According to Eichelberger, between the fall of Leyte and the Japanese surrender, the Eighth Army launched a total of fifty-two seaborne invasions.

Eichelberger, who insisted on wearing his three stars despite the risk of attracting sniper fire, was known as a general who stayed close to his men and shared the experience of combat with them. During the widely dispersed Philippine campaign he became known for his flying visits to the far-flung troops under his command, journeys he and his intrepid pilot sometimes undertook in decidedly hazardous conditions. His memoirs pay frequent tribute to the courage of the infantrymen he commanded and the often appalling conditions and shortages of basic supplies that they endured.

In August 1945 it was expected that, with the Philippine campaign largely complete, the Eighth Army would shortly take part in the invasion of the Japanese home islands. The dropping of atomic bombs on Hiroshima and Nagasaki short-circuited these plans. On August 30, 1945, Eichelberger took part in the beginning of the occupation of Japan. He headed a small detachment of the 11th Airborne Division that landed at Atsugi Airfield in Japan to greet MacArthur. In a decidedly tense atmosphere and under conditions of strict security, but

without encountering serious resistance, U.S. forces established themselves, first at Yokohama, then in Tokyo. For the next three years Eichelberger served under MacArthur, named supreme commander of the Allied forces in the Pacific (SCAP), as commander of the U.S. occupation forces in Japan. In this capacity he arrested several prominent Japanese figures, including ex-prime minister Tojo, and presided over the subsequent war crimes trials.

Although the Eighth Army had no responsibility for making policy, which was devised and announced by MacArthur's SCAP headquarters, it was responsible for enforcing MacArthur's directives. In the latter part of his stay Communist-inspired riots in Tokyo, Osaka, and Kobe alarmed the staunchly anticommunist Eichelberger, who used U.S. troops to suppress them. During his three years in Japan, Eichelberger traveled constantly throughout the nation, ensuring that U.S. directives were enforced. Although he felt that Japan had "brought disaster upon [itself] and that its people must work out their own salvation" (Eichelberger, 276), the general anticipated a future in which, for reasons of mutual self-interest, the United States and Japan would be allies against the Soviet Union and Communist China, if not friends.

On his retirement in 1948, Eichelberger was the most senior of the twenty-two lieutenant generals in the U.S. Army. In retirement he served as a consultant to the Department of Defense and wrote his memoirs, which were refreshingly free of the personal vituperation and backbiting that characterized similar works produced by other military men in the Pacific theater. Eichelberger felt, with some justification, that whereas generals in the European theater received appropriate public recognition for their achievements, in the Pacific every other military man's accomplishments were relentlessly overshadowed by MacArthur's remorseless appetite for public adulation. In 1954 Eichelberger was promoted to full general. He died at Asheville, North Carolina, on September 22, 1961.

FURTHER READINGS

Chwialkowski, Paul. *In Caesar's Shadow: The Life of General Robert Eichelberger* (1993).

Eichelberger, Robert L. *Our Jungle Road to Tokyo* (1950).

Luvaas, Jay, ed. *Dear Miss Em: General Eichelberger's War in the Pacific, 1942–1945* (1972).

Mayo, Lida. *Bloody Buna* (1974).

Shortal, John F. *Forged by Fire: General Robert L. Eichelberger and the Pacific War* (1987).

Priscilla Roberts

SEE ALSO Biak, Battle for; Buna, Operations at; Japan, Occupation of; MacArthur, Douglas

Engineers, Allied Services

General Douglas MacArthur described his military operations in the southwest Pacific as the "engineers' war." And, in truth, Allied success basically depended on engineers' seizing and improving air and ground bases for troops. Allied engineers in the South Pacific theater were vital to the war effort both in combat itself and in logistical support. They encountered conditions quite different from their counterparts in Europe, enduring temperature extremes from the humid tropics to the frigid tundra. In the end the Allied forces utilized their superior technology and management skills to defeat the Japanese.

War Plan Orange, the main prewar defense plan, accepted the probable loss of the Philippines to the Japanese but did provide for extensive tunnel systems in the Philippines that had enabled U.S. troops to hold out at the Corregidor fortifications for months longer than their British counterparts at Malaya and Singapore. Other engineering projects before the attack on Pearl Harbor were far more modest, and the Japanese offensive interrupted almost all of them.

In 1939, the U.S. Corps of Engineers consisted of twelve units—ten combat and two topographic. During the war this force was expanded to twenty-five units, of which eighteen were combat. Major General Hugh John "Pat" Casey served as MacArthur's chief engineer during World War II. He had arrived in the Philippines in 1937 to oversee hydropower development and flood control projects. His familiarity with Pacific topography proved useful to Allied engineers.

With the attack on Pearl Harbor, it became obvious that prewar preparations were insufficient. Engineers helped to clean up the harbor and strengthen defenses at Panama, Alaska, Hawaii, and Pacific outposts. Personnel and materiel shortages added to the urgency after the attack; the immense amounts of work to be accomplished—and the desperate need to develop an organizational protocol and to procure equipment—exacerbated conditions.

Despite the urgency, officials attempted to select only the best as military engineers. Rigorous examinations weeded out the mediocre, and the men chosen had excelled in their various engineering fields, especially civil and hydraulics engineering. Professors and students from engineering colleges and researchers from engineering firms across the United States joined engineers from Allied nations. U.S. military engineer candidates completed the Engineer Officer Candidate Course and were expected to understand basic engineering methods and materials in order to assess, comprehend, and solve problems quickly. The military provided them with technical manuals showing how to design and construct needed structures, although in the Pacific engineers discovered that ingenuity and innovation tailored to each site were often more practical than the "textbook solution." The men also underwent combat training, learning to work and fight as an unit.

Because the Pacific war was fought mainly on, over, and below water, the military recruited boat, harbor, and shore engineers; many amphibian engineers assigned to the Pacific had gained similar experience in the European theater. They prepared for ship-to-shore operations, transporting troops and supplies, scouting landing sites, and improving beachheads. This was a new field of warfare, and the amphibian engineers developed shore-to-shore techniques at Camp Edwards, Massachusetts. They also trained at Camp Gordon Johnston, Florida, developing beach reconnaissance techniques.

The U.S. Corps of Engineers sent six brigades and two battalions to the South Pacific. The U.S. Navy's Seabees added a vital naval construction battalion, and two African American labor battalions—the 43d and 46th General Service Regiments—assisted the engineers. Allied engineers joined their efforts to control the Pacific terrain and create usable structures. For example, the Australia 808th Engineer Aviation Battalion added its effort early in the war, reassembling small boats and installing engines in Australia to ease transportation of Allied equipment to the Pacific. U.S. and Allied military engineers could be found from the Panama Canal to India and from Alaska to Australia. The engineers' primary goals were construction and mobilization of forces in combat zones, building roads, bridges, and air bases for troops. They also built civil works and were engaged in research and development.

In addition to the traditional combat battalions, the engineers comprised general service regiments and specialized units. Engineers served in shop battalions and even in model-making detachments. They constructed ports, dredged channels, and built pipelines. There were never enough engineers in the Pacific, and officers recruited civilian labor as workmen and contractors.

Engineers captured international attention in this war. *Time* magazine commented, "The War in the Pacific is moving with the speed of the bulldozer." Troops advanced according to engineering achievements; landings were scheduled only after engineers built forward air bases and secured beaches, often in cooperation with Allied engineers. Topographical engineers mapped uncharted and vast areas, using aerial photographs. Amphibian engineer units led landings and performed vital shore-to-shore missions, while combat engineers with each division supported the combat troops. Engineers swept for mines, placed markers on the beaches to guide ships, and assembled metal roadways for the "alligators" (the amphibian tractorlike landing craft). Their services were crucial for troop landings.

Engineer construction units then transformed the jungles, swamps, and mountains into useful sites for ports and bases "without which our air operations and forward movement would have been impossible," as General Casey emphasized. The engineers built camps, air bases, posts, roads, facilities to store and distribute petroleum, hospitals, depots, and utilities in undeveloped areas. Effective under pressure, they evaluated the environment and resourcefully and efficiently created useful structures.

Engineers improvised because they rarely had adequate supplies, equipment, or spare parts. Using indigenous materials such as coral and palm leaves, they invented simple tools and attempted to avoid the extravagant, prewar construction standards demanded by some officers. Pacific engineers sought simpler and often more efficient designs, such as parallel runways rather than crossed lanes. "Casey Cookies"—a combination of bamboo, dynamite, nails, and mud—substituted for hand grenades, and "Casey Coffins" were antitank mines made from cigar boxes. Empty gasoline drums were used to make piers and bridges, with rope serving for temporary spans. Engineers built their own sawmills to prepare logs for bridges and structures.

The immense distances in the South Pacific theater posed many challenges in transporting troops, reinforcements, and supplies. Japanese airfields were poorly built, so Allied engineers prepared sites for hundreds of new air bases. Taking into consideration the soil, heat, and humidity, engineers quickly but soundly constructed landplane and seaplane facilities that were considered pioneering efforts because of the natural obstacles and abnormal conditions in which they were built. Temporary landing strips were prepared until permanent runways could be built. Engineers cut trees, filled bomb craters, and used perforated metal strips to build airstrips. Drainage was essential because of heavy rainfall, and engineers dug ditches, laid pipe, and sandbagged areas. They used coral from nearby reefs to avoid shipping thousands of tons of cement from the United States. After runways were built, engineers erected hangars and other vital buildings, using prefabricated materials.

Engineers were responsible for keeping troops mobile despite natural or man-made obstacles. Lieutenant General Eugene Reybold, then chief of engineers, asserted, "Keeping a mechanized Army on the move through a 7,000-island maze of water-broken, roadless country like

the Philippines has required some pretty unusual engineering." Engineers constructed thousands of bridges, capable of supporting troops and tanks, from a variety of materials, including pierced steel plank. Temporary bridges spanned culverts and ravines as footbridges, while ferries and pontoon boats also aided river crossing, as did improvised floats to evacuate the wounded.

Railroads and roads were necessary to transport supplies and troops and to evacuate casualties. In the China-Burma-India theater, engineers improved the Burma Road and constructed the Ledo Road, carving the route through the jungle and mountains. Throughout the South Pacific, engineers strung cables from mountain peaks for communications. Everywhere, they installed sewage and water systems, built power plants and wired buildings for electricity when possible, and waterproofed vehicles. Allied engineers produced and distributed millions of maps; they also made mine maps to outline where mines had been emplaced.

Engineers had many strenuous and demanding missions. On land, they rebuilt and overhauled captured Japanese equipment. Earlier, engineers also had had the duty, when Allied troops abandoned an area, to destroy bridges, roads, and equipment that might prove useful to the enemy. A February 1943 issue of *The Military Engineer* summarized the effort: "The Military Engineer in time of war is rough, tough, and fast. His whole mental make-up and characteristics must be adjusted to that tempo if he is to accomplish his job."

As the Pacific war intensified, the number of engineers in the theater increased. Major General Casey was chief engineer of General Headquarters of the Allied Force in the Southwest Pacific Area with an estimated force of 275,000 officers and men. The 2d Engineer Special Brigade was established in 1942, making its first combat landing in June 1943 at Nassau Bay. Conducting the greatest number of amphibious combat operations by any unit in the southwest Pacific (an estimated eighty-seven amphibious landings), these "unusual engineers" were regarded as "indispensable."

Military leaders considered the Engineer Special Brigade the most efficient landing group in amphibious warfare. The brigade's motto was "Put 'Em Across." Specifically organized for Pacific service, these engineers were carefully selected then trained in the United States and Australia. They were the first to use rocket barrages in the southwest Pacific, at New Guinea. At Biak they shot down enemy planes and directed rockets into caves where enemy troops had hidden. The engineers evacuated troops, created floating observation posts for artillery, and wiped out Japanese mortar positions with dynamite and grenades while also performing their engineering duties. The 2d Engineer Special Brigade earned seven Presidential Unit Citations for its service.

Allied engineers encountered a variety of conflicts and obstacles in the South Pacific. The terrain and climate, as noted, posed the most problems. The lack of indigenous industry slowed construction projects, as did the vastness of the Pacific theater. Allied engineers had few building materials to work with because shipping was restricted and long distance, and they often had to improvise with available resources. The lack of adequate distribution systems also created delays in shipping. Many commanders did not comprehend the engineers' missions. The absence of long-range planning hindered engineering work. Officers disagreed about how engineering units should be assigned, and an informal policy emerged in which engineers were sent where needed in an emergency, despite regulations.

Although U.S. Navy and Army construction engineers coordinated projects with Allied armies' engineers, an imbalance existed, with too many engineering units specializing in a specific service and too few in others. Engineers often performed work for which they were untrained and unfamiliar. Some engineer officers lacked an adequate engineering background to plan and undertake projects and also had no practical experience.

Engineering was a dangerous service in the South Pacific. Troops were killed or mutilated in accidents. Construction engineer Joseph F. McDonald Jr., a stringer for the United Press on Wake Island, was captured in late December 1941 and held in captivity until September 1945. At Finschhafen, New Guinea, Private Junior N. Van Noy, of the 532d Engineer Boat and Shore Regiment, "almost singlehandedly broke up a Japanese amphibious counterattack" on October 17, 1943. He was posthumously awarded the Medal of Honor—the first engineer soldier to earn that honor in World War II.

The "Army Poets" column in *Stars and Stripes* printed "Salute to the Engineers," remarking that "your mechanized cavalry's quite all right / And your Doughboy has few peers, / But where in hell would the lot of them be / If it weren't for the Engineers?" Engineers on the home-front supported their colleagues in the Pacific by research and sending information and materials. Secretly, selected engineers worked on the atomic bomb project.

By June 30, 1945, Allied engineers in the South Pacific had facilitated the successful landing of almost two million passengers and 1,530,056 tons of cargo, traveling 4,500,000 miles. Engineers built airfields and pipelines in China to support military occupation forces and helped to remove debris and repair and rebuild shelters, businesses, hospitals, and other crucial structures.

By the end of World War II, seven hundred engineering units—approximately 235,764 men—had served in the South Pacific. Many received awards for their service, and all benefited from their combat experience in postwar employment opportunities. The Corps of Engineers Historical Foundation was established, and the corps published the eight-volume *The Engineers of the Southwest Pacific, 1941–1945*. Other histories and memoirs of Pacific engineers were issued. General Casey remained Mac-Arthur's chief engineer and improved U.S. bases in the Pacific to reinforce the Allies' postwar military presence, and, impressed by their South Pacific performance, Mac-Arthur recommended that the Engineer Special Brigade be included in the postwar army.

FURTHER READINGS

Bowman, Waldo G., et al. *Bulldozers Come First: The Story of U.S. War Construction in Foreign Lands* (1944).

Casey, Hugh. *Engineer Memoirs: Major General Hugh J. Casey, U.S. Army* (1993).

Dodd, Karl C. *The Corps of Engineers: The War against Japan* (1966).

Fowle, Barry, ed. *Builders and Fighters: U.S. Army Engineers in World War II* (1992).

Giles, Janice Holt. *The Damned Engineers* (1985).

Heavey, William Francis. *Down Ramp! The Story of the Army Amphibian Engineers* (1947).

Woodbury, David O. *Builders for Battle: How the Pacific Naval Air Bases Were Constructed* (1946).

Elizabeth D. Schafer

SEE ALSO Army, U.S.; Pick, Lewis A.

Eniwetok

Eniwetok is an atoll consisting of some forty islets surrounding a large lagoon. It is located in the Ralik chain of the Marshall Islands in the Central Pacific. Eniwetok was mandated to Japan by the League of Nations in 1920. At the time war broke out in the Pacific, it lacked any substantial military infrastructure. Construction of a seaplane base had begun in August 1941, but it was still incomplete, and no combat forces were present. Eniwetok's defenses were so meager that in February 1942 it was actually removed as a target for Admiral William Halsey's Task Force 8; submarine reconnaissance reported that there was nothing there worth attacking.

Eniwetok became an important outpost only in 1944, when Japanese ground forces were dispatched to fortify the atoll's islands as a barrier against the U.S. advance. In mid-1943 the Japanese high command began Operation Z, a plan to move troops from Manchuria and use them to bolster the defenses of the Pacific perimeter. Allied control of sea lanes prevented this operation from being carried out. Nonetheless, the Japanese army's crack 1st Amphibious Brigade, under Major General Nishida Yoshima, did arrive a mere six weeks before the invasion occurred. Although General Nishida's efforts to create fortifications were greatly hampered by U.S. bombing, a series of defenses were quickly erected on Eniwetok's major islands.

The 1st Amphibious Brigade's troops were spread out among several of the atoll's largest islands, together with a variety of manpower which included Korean laborers and administrative personnel. Parry Island contained the largest concentration of troops (about thirteen hundred); Engebi held only slightly less (twelve hundred); and Eniwetok Island itself held only about eight hundred. Without the time to build elaborate defenses, General Nishida oversaw the construction of a series of tunnels connected at a central location. The troops hitting the beaches at Eniwetok dubbed these "spider holes." Other defenses included pillboxes made from concrete and coconut logs. Both Eniwetok and Engebi had small airfields but no aircraft.

The assault on Eniwetok—Operation Catchpole—began on February 17, 1944. It was linked in many ways with the just-completed Operation Flintlock, at Kwajalein. Once again, U.S. Army and Marine troops operated jointly. In this case 22d Marines formed the assault unit, with the army's 106th Regimental Combat Team acting as a floating reserve (this was the 3d regiment of the 7th Infantry Division previously in action at Kwajalein). The attack would closely follow the script established in earlier island landings.

First, carriers of Admiral Spruance's Fifth Fleet pounded Truk the first two days of the landing, destroying several hundred aircraft and twenty transport vessels in order to prevent any effort to assist Eniwetok's defenders. Then, amphibious forces using maps captured at Kwajalein entered the lagoon at Eniwetok and seized two small, undefended islands, Camelia and Canna, for use as fire-support bases. Soon afterward naval gunfire, aerial bombardment, and ground-based artillery were unleashed on Engebi. On the morning of the February 18 the marines landed. Japanese resistance was weak on the beaches; the majority of troops who survived the bombardment had taken refuge in the palm grove in the center of the island. Tanks were brought up, and their resistance was swiftly broken. Engebi was declared secure after six hours. U.S. casualties were 85 dead and 521 wounded, while Japanese losses were 1,276 killed and 16 surrendered.

Among the wreckage on Engebi were documents indicating the Japanese troops' dispositions on the various islands of Eniwetok Atoll. After interrogating the few prisoners, local intelligence officers were led to believe that 550 soldiers and from 200 to 300 service personnel were stationed on Eniwetok Island and that approximately 1,300 were on Parry. This came as a surprise to intelligence officers, who had failed to detect a large presence of troops on either island. Plans to hit both islands at once were changed, and Eniwetok became the next target.

The following day the 1st and 3d Battalions of the U.S. Army's 106th Infantry regiment came ashore supported by Marine Corps tanks. Almost immediately it was recognized that the navy's preinvasion bombardment had been insufficient. Little headway was made initially because a ridge prevented tanks and amphibious tractors from moving much beyond the beach. Troops on the beach came under heavy fire, and soon the Japanese mounted counterattacks. The weary 22d Marines was quickly ordered ashore. Even with this support, the fighting on Eniwetok went on for four days. At the end, U.S. losses were 37 killed and 94 wounded, while the Japanese loses were estimated at 800 killed. Despite the overall success, some recriminations took place afterward, with ground forces faulting the navy for limiting its initial bombardment. However, the army acknowledged that 3d Battalion 106th had shown an "extreme caution" that had delayed the advance.

The assault on Parry Island took place on February 22—a delay of several days because of the tough going on Eniwetok. Once again 22d Marines was given the assignment. Determined not to repeat past mistakes, the navy conducted a truly massive bombardment of Parry before the assault. The weight of the bombardment was nearly five times that used days earlier. As a result, the landing went smoothly. Several small Japanese tanks attempted to assault the beachhead but were quickly dispatched. The battle was carried on throughout the night under the glow of navy star shells—a first for amphibious operations. By the next morning Parry was secure. The marines had suffered 73 killed and 261 wounded, while 1,027 Japanese dead were counted.

Only four days after the fall of Eniwetok Atoll, aircraft began operating from the captured airfield. The base would soon grow to become one of the largest in the Pacific—a major refueling center and home to Admiral Marc Mitscher's famous Task Force 58. All the facilities were greatly expanded, and more than 11,000 men garrisoned the various islands. Besides operating as a major supply depot, Eniwetok's air bases were used to suppress the bypassed islands of the Marshalls and Carolines.

FURTHER READINGS
Morrison, Samuel Eliot. *History of United States Naval Operations in World War II: Aleutians, Gilberts and Marshalls, June 1942–1944,* vol. VII (1955).
                                                    Michael C. Walker

SEE ALSO Island-Hopping and Leapfrogging, U.S. Strategies; Marine Corps, U.S.

"Europe First" Decision

Although there had been somewhat close strategic military cooperation between the United States and Great Britain dating from 1939, the Japanese attack on Pearl Harbor, Hawaii, on December 7, 1941, brought the United States directly into the war and necessitated even closer collaboration between the two powers over matters of strategy and both military and industrial interaction. After a conference between President Franklin D. Roosevelt and British Prime Minister Winston Churchill, the two Allied powers determined to concentrate on winning the war in Europe before undertaking a major effort in the Pacific. This "Europe First" decision became the cornerstone of Allied strategy during World War II.

From December 24, 1941, to January 14, 1942, Roosevelt and Churchill along with their senior advisers and military planners held a series of meetings in Washington, D.C., that was originally code-named Arcadia but later became known as the First Washington Conference. Churchill asked for the meeting in order to ensure that the United States not become so absorbed with the Japanese offensives in the Pacific that it would neglect the Atlantic dimension of the war. The purpose of the conference was to formalize joint strategy between the two powers and lay the foundation for the wartime partnership. Churchill was a guest in the White House, and the president and the prime minister established a warm working relationship that would continue throughout the war.

Significantly, representatives from the Soviet Union were not invited to the conference. This omission contributed to Soviet leader Joseph Stalin's mistrust of the ultimate aims of the Anglo-American partnership. (Then again, the Soviet Union maintained a studied neutrality until the last few days of the Pacific war.) But representatives from other major Allied powers—such as Australia, Canada, China, and the Netherlands (which still retained numerous colonies and military assets in the Pacific)—were also not invited.

The first main issue to be dealt with during the conference was which theater, Europe or Asia, should be the central focus of the initial Allied effort. In Europe, Germany had conquered the continent, and German troops were only 20 miles outside Moscow. Meanwhile, in the Pacific, the Japanese had scored major victories at Pearl Harbor and in the sinking of British naval Task Force Z (made up principally of the capital ships *Prince of Wales* and *Repulse*) and were making rapid ground advances throughout the Pacific; a day after the conference began, the Japanese conquered Hong Kong.

Despite the success of the Japanese in the Pacific, Churchill adamantly believed that the main threat to the Allies came from Nazi Germany and that the major thrust of the Allied war effort should be to defeat the Germans first and then to concentrate on Japan. Churchill believed that Japan could easily be defeated after Germany was forced out of the war. The prime minister wanted to increase aid to the Soviet Union in addition to relieving pressure on both Moscow and Egypt by opening a second front in the Mediterranean. Churchill was worried that the impact of Pearl Harbor and other Allied losses in the Pacific might tempt the United States to adopt an "Asia First" policy in order to satisfy domestic concerns.

Roosevelt and senior U.S. military officers were inclined to agree with Churchill. Before the Japanese attack, Chief of Naval Operations Admiral Harold R. Stark and Army Chief of Staff General George C. Marshall had developed a strategy known as Rainbow 5, which called for the concentration of U.S. forces in the Atlantic while only the minimal forces needed to contain the Japanese would be stationed in the Pacific. Senior U.S. officials, including Roosevelt, were concerned that Great Britain would be unable to continue its pace of military spending. They surmised that the United States would have to shoulder the significant financial burden of the war and provide a notable portion of the military equipment and troops to defeat Germany.

Roosevelt was also disturbed by the possibility that the Germans were on their way to developing an atomic bomb. Reports from Great Britain and the president's own Advisory Committee on Uranium confirmed both the possibility of constructing an atomic weapon and the potential that Germany would do so first. This was especially true after the Germans were able to capture several leading nuclear physics laboratories and their personnel, including the renowned French scientist Pierre Joliot-Curie. Roosevelt was particularly interested in ensuring that Germany be defeated before it could develop any fission bomb.

On the other hand, several of the president's military advisers pointed to the raid on Pearl Harbor and other Japanese victories in the Pacific and argued that it would be necessary to devote significant resources to the Pacific theater in order to slow or stall the Japanese. This was especially true of some senior U.S. naval officers who feared that the Japanese would be able to establish maritime supremacy in the theater. In military staff meetings between the two nations the British had already admitted that they would probably not be able adequately to defend their Far East empire. In order to counter such sentiments, Churchill pledged that the main British post in Southeast Asia, Singapore, could be held for at least six months (a promise that the Americans, realistically, did not believe and that soon enough proved totally wrong). In addition, the new chief of the U.S. Navy, Admiral Ernest King, feared that Roosevelt was allowing Churchill to set the priorities of U.S. strategy without sufficient consultation between the president and senior military commanders. King feared that the British were going to be able to insert their own national goals and interests as the basis for Allied strategy. (King's persistent Anglophobia clouded his judgment somewhat throughout the war.)

In the end, the Allies made compromises that basically satisfied the British and the Americans. It was decided to devote the majority of Allied resources to defeating the Germans and to maintain only enough force in the Pacific theater to contain the Japanese from gaining any meaningful military advantage. The "Europe First" decision thus became the foundation for Allied strategy throughout the remainder of the war.

FURTHER READINGS

Beitzell, R. *The Uneasy Alliance: America, Britain and Russia, 1941–43* (1972).
Costello, John. *The Pacific War* (1981).
Feis, H. *Churchill, Roosevelt and Stalin* (1967).
Issraeljan, Victor. *The Anti-Hitler Coalition* (1971).

Tom Lansford

SEE ALSO King, Ernest J.; Roosevelt, Franklin Delano

Fertig, Wendell W.

Wendell W. Fertig was a civilian mining engineer, a prosperous consultant in Manila, and a prominent leader of Filipino-U.S. guerrilla forces during the Japanese occupation and the American retaking of the Philippines. He was commissioned into his reserve rank of lieutenant colonel during mobilization of the Philippines in the fall of 1941. He fought first on the main island, Luzon, and then on the Bataan Peninsula and Corregidor. A PBY flying boat flew him off Corregidor before the island fell, but it crash-landed on the Philippine island of Mindanao en route to Australia.

When Corregidor fell and Lieutenant General Jonathan M. Wainwright surrendered all U.S. Army forces in the Philippines, Fertig was still on Mindanao. Someone asked Fertig what he was going to do, and he answered, "Any damn thing but surrender." He refused to hide. He knew Filipinos well because he had worked with them in his mining days. And he knew Mindanao. He considered himself the sole U.S. Army officer still free, and he decided to turn guerilla. Tall, deep-chested, and athletic, he avoided capture via some daunting hikes through terrible terrain and linked up with a Philippine constabulary captain who was organizing guerrillas.

Fertig hoped to collect the numerous independent and often feuding guerrilla bands under one command and organize them into lawful U.S. troops. He decided to bring rival chieftains under control by claiming the rank of brigadier general and by representing himself as having come from General Douglas MacArthur's headquarters. Most Filipinos revered MacArthur, and the use of his name brought immediate results. Fertig wanted everyone to know who he was, that he represented the United States, and that he would resist the Japanese. He sported a neatly trimmed red goatee, wore a uniform, and went

about armed. Fertig believed that fate had chosen him to be the scourge of the Japanese.

Until this time, Fertig had had no contact with MacArthur in Australia. He signed his own orders assuming command of Mindanao on October 1, 1942, and declared a state of martial law. He established the Free Philippine Government, which operated on Mindanao but was loyal to the government in exile. Fertig proclaimed that resistance would continue and that aid would come. He actually had no army, no money, and no transportation, but the men he did have immediately liberated huge tracts of Mindanao from weak Japanese garrisons.

Through 1942 and into 1943, Fertig and his guerrillas operated as though the Japanese were not a factor. He used whatever techniques worked. He earned money for his guerrillas by setting up hairdressers for Filipino women. He rented out a dance band! He commissioned independent young Americans who had evaded the surrender and had sought him out. He delegated authority to Filipinos and trusted them to run their own affairs. Telephones and telegraphs sent messages over hundreds of miles.

Farmers doubled their crops to feed the guerrillas. Civilians crowded towns lit by electricity. Fertig's men stamped out banditry and rogue guerrillas who preyed on Filipinos. At night, sail-driven craft and launches powered by coconut oil crossed between islands to reestablish commerce. The Japanese were aghast that the Filipino cities and towns they had conquered were lit by electricity run by Americans, that trucks moved freely across the island, and that a U.S. general commanded Mindanao in open and ostentatious defiance of their rule.

Fertig's men had constructed a radio and had been calling Australia blind since December 1942. They were using an old code, one that the army had suspended after Wainwright's surrender. San Francisco heard these calls but, fearing Japanese trickery, ignored the messages. Fertig decided to send three U.S. officers by an open boat all the way to Australia. In an astounding display of navigation and good luck, these men arrived with a simple call-sign code so that Australia could talk to Mindanao.

Fertig received his first radio response from San Francisco in early 1943. MacArthur, not at all surprisingly, wanted to bring all Philippine guerrillas under his control. He sent a representative into Mindanao to evaluate the effectiveness and leadership abilities of the numerous guerrilla chieftains. The first U.S. guerrilla chief that Lieutenant Commander Charles Parsons recognized was Fertig on Mindanao.

After MacArthur's headquarters coordinated with Fertig, Mindanao became a supply base for guerrillas on other islands. Submarines landed weapons, radios, and medicine. Ammunition, propaganda, and other aid from Australia gave the guerrillas new hope and capabilities. Ultimately, six guerrilla divisions consisting of regiments, battalions, and companies would operate on Mindanao.

But not all was well. No army can allow guerrillas to operate unchallenged behind its lines, and Japan was no exception. In late May 1943, the Japanese poured troops into Mindanao, shattered guerrilla organizations, and ended a golden age of the guerrilla. Ruthless assaults cowed civilians and drove them into Japanese-occupied towns. Fertig wrote in his diary, "Unless a United States offensive starts very soon, we are lost, for we cannot meet the full force of the enemy." (Fertig had a lot to learn yet about guerrilla warfare. Guerrilla strategists never attempt to meet "the full force of the enemy; rather, they melt away and attack where the enemy is weak.) The Japanese used forced Filipino labor to harvest and transport crops, and they burned the remotest barrios they could find. Although they were unable to find and kill many guerrillas, they had no trouble finding and killing civilians. But the Japanese also had a lot to learn about guerrilla warfare, and they seemingly never learned much. Japanese terror brought more volunteers to Fertig than he ever could have recruited himself. When a peasant's house is burned down and his family killed, he has little choice but to join the guerrilla bands who can offer food and a chance for revenge.

Throughout it all—through the defeats, hunger, and false hopes—Fertig kept his loosely knit organization intact. Learning his guerrilla warfare lessons well, his troops now fell back before heavily armed enemy columns, then reassembled once the immediate threat had passed. Information flowed to MacArthur about Japanese installations, troop movements, and plans, thus building for Fertig some sort of "debt" on the part of MacArthur's

headquarters. The hard-core, full-time guerrillas sniped, slipped away, and sniped again. Their wounded by then could often be evacuated to Australia by submarine, and their next of kin were officially promised compensation. No longer would brave men be left to die by the side of some jungle trail and their widows be reduced to penury. Unable to find the lightfooted guerrillas, the Japanese broke their forces into smaller and smaller columns and drove deeper and deeper into unknown territory. Filipinos who had run from the large columns found themselves numerically superior to these smaller detachments. The guerrillas ambushed the most careless of the enemy patrols. The Japanese-created counterguerrilla Filipino puppet constabulary was worse than useless for the task. Many of its members were lackadaisical, hated the Japanese, and hoped for a U.S. victory. Certainly, there was no widespread purge of "collaborators" after the Japanese were driven out of the islands.

When U.S. aircraft returned to Philippine skies and U.S. armies landed on Leyte and Luzon, Japanese garrisons on Mindanao retreated into small lodgments. Fertig's guerrillas pursued them as they fled. When the Americans finally landed on Mindanao, organized guerrillas were available to provide information, confine Japanese to their garrisons, and offer nearly unlimited manpower. They also performed sterling work in calling off U.S. artillery and air strikes on towns and villages that had already been cleared of the enemy, thus saving thousands of lives and livelihoods. Fertig and his guerrillas were among the most successful of all American guerrilla units.

In the early 1950s, with the intensification of the cold war, Fertig was assigned to Fort Bragg, North Carolina, where he and another Philippine guerrilla veteran, Brigadier General Russell Volckmann, called on their vast guerrilla experience to draw up insurgency doctrine and manuals for the fledgling U.S. Army Special Forces.

FURTHER READINGS

Haggerty, Edward. *Guerrilla Padre in Mindanao* (1946).

Ingham, Travis. *Rendezvous by Submarine: The Story of Charles Parsons and the Guerrilla Soldiers in the Philippines* (1945).

Keats, John. *They Fought Alone* (1963).

Volckmann, Russell W. *We Remained: Three Years behind the Enemy Lines in the Philippines* (1954).

John W. Whitman

SEE ALSO Army, U.S.-Filipino; Philippines, Anti-Japanese Guerrillas in; Philippines, Fall of

Fiji

The 320 Fiji Islands are scattered through an archipelago that lies 3,160 kilometers northeast of Sydney, Australia. The largest island of the group, Viti Levu, was recognized after World War I as having a harbor of great strategic importance. Japanese conquests in the Pacific during 1941 suddenly increased the military value of Fiji as one of the last island groups between Australia and the United States.

In 1936 the British Overseas Defense Committee concluded a study of the Pacific area with a recommendation that the Royal Navy and the armed forces of New Zealand be responsible for the defense of Fiji. Two years later, the New Zealand chiefs of staff sanctioned an increase to brigade size of the Fiji Defense Force, the construction of airfields, and the siting of coastal artillery. Nevertheless, by September 1939, Fiji was still totally unprepared to defend itself against invasion, and plans were drawn up by members of the Royal Australian Artillery for the installation of coastal defense batteries. Hastily emplaced dummy and obsolete guns were soon replaced by the first operational battery, situated at the capital, Suva, on the eastern side of Viti Levu. The 6-inch guns fired their first proof shot on March 11, 1940.

Soon afterward, three additional 6-inch artillery batteries were operational under the command of the 1st Heavy Regiment, Fiji Artillery. A warning shot was fired at a Japanese cargo ship on December 6, 1941, for failing to stop when requested. The defense of Fiji at this time was the responsibility of the 2d New Zealand Expeditionary Force, and the number of coastal artillery batteries was increased to five to cover the eastern and western approaches to Viti Levu.

As the threat of a Japanese landing increased, the U.S. 37th Infantry Division arrived at Suva on June 10, 1942, to defend the island while preparing for later operations. The Fiji Defense Force was placed under the command of the U.S. Army and the coastal artillery taken over by the 251st Artillery Regiment.

Meanwhile, in Japan, enthusiastic and overconfident naval staff members were proposing such grandiose ventures as the invasion of Australia, Hawaii, and India. On May 18, 1942, Lieutenant General Haruyoshi Hyukatake, commander of the Seventeenth Army, was ordered to prepare for amphibious landings on New Caledonia, Samoa, and Fiji. From these newly acquired islands, sustained attacks could be mounted against Australia and New Zealand to disrupt the buildup of Allied forces and sever communications with the United States. These operations, however, were postponed and eventually were canceled following the defeat of the Imperial Navy in the Battle of Midway.

By the end of 1942, the threat of invasion had passed and the majority of U.S. forces had been transferred from Fiji. The closest that war came to the islands was the reconnaissance flights of aircraft launched from the Japanese submarines *I-10* and *I-25*, and a Japanese submarine's unsuccessful attempt to torpedo the armed merchant cruiser HMS *Manowai* on January 16, 1942. With the likelihood of Japanese attack eliminated, the manning of coastal artillery ceased on February 10, 1944. Members of the Fijian army participated in several Pacific Island battles, such as the Solomon Islands, where their prowess for guerrilla jungle fighting became legendary.

FURTHER READINGS

Muehrcke, Robert. *Orchids in the Mud* (132d Infantry Regiment Association, 1985).
"Fiji Patrol in Bouganville." *National Geographic* (January 1945).
Pacific Islands Yearbook, 16th ed. (1989).

David M. Green

Film Treatment of the Pacific War, U.S.

When war broke out in the Pacific, filmmakers in Hollywood were caught off guard about as much as were the U.S. military forces in Pearl Harbor. Although the growing menace of the Third Reich had already been dealt with by the major U.S. studios in films like *Confessions of a Nazi Spy* (1939), *The Mortal Storm* (1940), and *Escape* (1940), there were no comparable treatments of the dangers represented by the increasing militarism and expansion of the Japanese empire during the late 1930s.

However, within days after the U.S. declaration of war on December 8, 1941, the Hollywood studios—like the civilian plants that were quickly converting to war work—were now actively looking for ways in which they could help the Allies win the war. President Franklin D. Roosevelt, well aware that Hollywood was one of the most powerful persuaders on the planet, established the Office of War Information's Bureau of Motion Pictures on December 18, 1941, directing the U.S. government to "consult with and advise motion picture producers of ways and means in which they can usefully serve the National Defense Effort."

Like most other large manufacturers in search of maximum profits, the Hollywood studios by the mid-1930s had already succeeded in standardizing and stabilizing their productions. One of the primary ways they achieved this was through the gradual evolution of film *genres*, popular narrative forms that followed certain conventions delineating a film's setting, characters, and plot. In December 1941, Hollywood was very much in need of a formula for the World War II combat films it wanted to produce, but it was obviously reluctant to turn to the genre it had created for World War I, because many of those films—including such acclaimed productions as *The Big Parade* (1925) and *All Quiet on the Western Front* (1930)—were unsuitably pacifist, dealing largely with the horrors and futility of war and the international brotherhood of men in combat.

Perhaps not surprisingly, the Hollywood studios turned instead to one of the oldest and most reliable of film genres, the Western, which they adapted with just a few alterations to create the World War II combat film. Just as the Western was set on the sparsely settled untamed frontier, so too was the World War II combat film set in a fierce wilderness, epitomized by the remote barren islands and thick jungles of the Pacific theater. Similarly, the Western's focus on a conflict between the forces of civilization (often represented by an isolated community of cavalry troopers or settlers) and the forces of savagery (usually represented by warlike Native Americans) was ideally suited for portraying combat in the Pacific. Because of racial differences, an Asian enemy like the Japanese could more easily be transformed into barbaric savages than a European enemy like the Germans, who after all too closely resembled a sizable percentage of the U.S. population. Moreover, the surprise attack at Pearl Harbor on a quiet Sunday morning, while two Japanese diplomats were in Washington to discuss peace, had convinced many that the Japanese were innately deceitful and devoid of fair play. The Western's formulaic plot device of an isolated group that constitutes a small pocket of civilization remained essentially unchanged, albeit transformed from cavalry troopers or stagecoach passengers into a submarine or battleship crew, an air force squadron, or an infantry platoon on patrol.

In many cases, the Hollywood studios simply shifted personnel from Westerns to war films: stars like Errol Flynn, John Wayne, and Tyrone Power; directors like John Ford and Raoul Walsh; screenwriters like Dudley Nichols and Lamar Trotti. The one significant alteration that became necessary in shifting from the Western to World War II was the representation of the protagonist. Whereas the Western hero usually stood alone, free and independent (though usually allied with the group representing civilization), the World War II combat unit had to remain united. There could be no room for solitary cowboys maintaining self-reliance and free-spirited individualism.

Nevertheless, because American-style individualism could not be completely ignored, Hollywood's solution was to create World War II crews and platoons that were made up of distinct individuals, each representing a certain American type: dominant white Anglo-Saxon Protestants (officers), Irish Catholics, Jews (usually from New York), African Americans (even though integrated combat units for the most part did not exist before 1950), Mexican Americans, Polish Americans, Italian Americans, farmers, cabdrivers, steelworkers, Southerners, Midwesterners, and New Englanders. These types of diversity (religious, racial, ethnic, occupational, and geographical) symbolized the democracy and harmony within the United States that needed to be preserved and that presumably were the reason why the country was fighting in World War II.

The first half-year of the war in the Pacific was a series of disasters for the United States: devastation at Pearl Harbor in December 1941, the fall of Guam and Wake Island later in the month, the loss of the Philippines and the Bataan death march in April 1942, and defeat at Corregidor in May. Nevertheless, the Hollywood studios put the brightest face they could on a dark situation and released more than a dozen films in 1942 on the Pacific war, including *Little Tokyo, U.S.A.,* which portrayed treacherous Japanese espionage in Los Angeles; *A Yank on the Burma Road,* in which a former cabdriver from New York leads a force of Chinese guerrillas against the Japanese (the American would always lead, even in a foreign country); *Submarine Raider,* featuring a U.S. submarine against a Japanese aircraft carrier; *Flying Tigers,* featuring jaunty American heroes in the air; and *Wake Island,* recreating its heroic defense by 377 marines against overwhelming odds.

Released in early September 1942, *Wake Island* was not only the first Hollywood production to be based on an actual battle from World War II but was also one of the most representative and influential films of the war. The opening titles, which connect the events of Wake Island to Valley Forge and Custer's Last Stand, praise the "men who fought savagely to the death, because in dying they gave eternal life." The film quickly establishes the deceit of the Japanese before they attacked Pearl Harbor, then portrays the ways in which the Americans on Wake Island unite in defense of freedom and civilization.

In early 1943 came two more seminal films about the Pacific war: *Air Force,* in which the crew of a B-17 makes its way through enemy territory at Pearl Harbor, Wake Island, and Manila; and *Bataan,* in which thirteen volunteers (perhaps representing the thirteen original colonies, perhaps Jesus and the Twelve Apostles) stay behind on a suicidal mission to protect the Allied retreat down the Bataan Peninsula. Both films feature a diverse group of loyal U.S. servicemen working in harmony against a sinister band of Japanese, who do not fight fairly (attacking women and children, feigning surrender and then stabbing their captors in the back) and who slither along the jungle floor like treacherous snakes. When only one American is left on the Bataan to fight the Japanese hordes, the camera closes in on him laughing and shouting defiantly:

> Come on, suckers, come and get it. Come on, suckers, whatsa matter with you? What are you waiting for? Didn't think we were here, did you, you dirty rotten rats? We're still here, we'll always be here. Why don't you come and get it?

The film's written epilog (with "The Battle Hymn of the Republic" on the soundtrack) concludes:

> So fought the heroes of Bataan. Their sacrifice made possible our victories in the Coral and Bismarck Seas, at Midway, on New Guinea and Guadalcanal. Their spirit will lead us back to Bataan!

Indeed, *Back to Bataan* became the title of a later Hollywood film about World War II in the Pacific.

The pattern established by *Wake Island*, *Air Force*, and *Bataan* continued to guide Hollywood productions until the end of the war. Major films from 1943 include *Guadalcanal Diary*, *Bombardier*, *Corregidor*, *Behind the Rising Sun*, and *We've Never Been Licked*. Films from 1944 include *Destination Tokyo*, *Gung Ho! The Fighting Seabees*, *Marine Raiders*, *A Wing and a Prayer*, *Thirty Seconds over Tokyo*, *Purple Heart*, and *Dragon Seed* (the last is one of several wartime films that celebrated the fighting spirit of the Chinese Nationalists, much as *The Good Earth* had done as early as 1937). Examples from 1945 include *Objective Burma*, *Blood on the Sun*, *Betrayal from the East*, *God Is My Co-Pilot*, *Pride of the Marines*, *Back to Bataan*, and *The Story of G.I. Joe*. Almost invariably, these films corresponded closely to the paradigm of the "good war": that the fighting was started unfairly by the other side; that the conflict was unambiguous and unironic, with a clear resolution in the end; and that U.S. forces were innocent (indeed, often the underdog), fighting the enemy with old-fashioned know-how, commonsense ingenuity, and undaunted courage.

In contrast, the Japanese enemy was almost invariably portrayed as unscrupulous, brutal, and inhuman. "They're degenerate, immoral idiots. Stinking little sav-ages," declares a newspaper correspondent in *Objective Burma*. "Well, it's kill or be killed; besides they ain't people," maintains a sergeant in *Guadalcanal Diary*. The animal imagery may have varied, as the Japanese were likened to bugs that "glow in the night" (*Flying Tigers*), "monkeys who live in trees" (*Gung Ho!*), and "yellow-skinned, slanty-eyed devils" (*Bataan*); but the consistent message to Japan from the Hollywood films produced between 1942 and 1945 was (as one screen aviator in *The Purple Heart* put it):

> This is your war. You wanted it. You asked for it. And now you're going to get it. And it won't be finished until your dirty little empire is wiped off the face of the earth."

Even semiofficial films, like those in the Why We Fight series, were little better. The feature dealing with the war with Japan speaks of the "Jap's" "little brain."

Immediately following the conclusion of hostilities in 1945, the production of war films suddenly ceased, as though Hollywood had calculated that the U.S. public would no longer be interested in its partisan portrayals of World War II. A few years later, however, the Pacific war began to return to the screen, usually following the same generic conventions as the films made from 1942 to 1945, but with a gradual softening of tone in the depiction of the Japanese enemy. With the resolution of the war a matter of historical fact, the films from the postwar period acquired not only a more realistic mood, which might appeal to the 16 million veterans in the audience, but also a more nostalgic mood, as though seeking to mythologize the war in the memory of the public.

The seminal film of the postwar period was *Sands of Iwo Jima* (1949), dedicated to the U.S. Marine Corps, "whose exploits and valor have left a lasting impression on the world and in the hearts of their countrymen." Starring John Wayne—perhaps the one actor who best typified the tough and courageous U.S. serviceman—*Sands* recreated important historical moments: fighting on the islands of Tarawa and Iwo Jima and the legendary raising of the U.S. flag on Mount Suribachi. Although frequently criticized today as an overly sanitized example of "guts and glory," *Sands* was also startlingly realistic for audiences in 1949, particularly in its ending: After the battle is won, John Wayne's character is suddenly and fatally shot by a sneaky Japanese sniper. (Racist attitudes are not entirely eschewed in *Sands*. Although John Wayne straightforwardly letter tells his men that they will be up against "Japanese Marines, and they're tough," a later episode features a flamethrower tank moving up to a Japanese bunker: "All right, Mac, give 'em a hot foot!")

During the next twenty years, in the wake of *Sands of Iwo Jima,* roughly fifty films of the Pacific war were released. Most of them were more realistic than anything produced during the war years; but most also reinforced the generic conventions of their predecessors. Conspicuously absent, for instance, were films focusing on the war's final campaign, when U.S. atomic bombs vaporized the cities of Hiroshima and Nagasaki in August 1945, as though filmmakers sensed that the lines between savagery and civilization might be confused by too graphic a portrayal of the country's winning weapons at work. Accordingly, among the most notable films of the postwar years were *The Halls of Montezuma, Operation Pacific,* and *Flying Leathernecks* (all 1951); *The Wild Blue Yonder, Submarine Command,* and *Okinawa* (all 1952); *Thunderbirds, From Here to Eternity,* and *Above and Beyond* (all 1953, with the last film delicately portraying the events leading up to the bombing of Hiroshima); *Beachhead* (1954); *Battle Cry* (1955); *Away All Boats* and *Between Heaven and Hell* (both 1956); *The Bridge on the River Kwai* (1957); *Run Silent, Run Deep* and *The Naked and the Dead* and *In Love and War* (all 1958); *Up Periscope* and *Battle of the Coral Sea* (both 1959); *Never So Few* and *Hell to Eternity* (both 1960); *The Battle at Bloody Beach* and *Operation Bottleneck* (both 1961); *Merrill's Marauders* and *No Man Is an Island* (both 1962); *PT-109* and *Cry of Battle* (both 1963); *The Thin Red Line* (1964); *None but the Brave* and *Ambush Bay* (both 1965); *Beach Red* (1967); and *Hell in the Pacific* (1968).

By the end of the 1960s, partly in response to the scenes of the Vietnam War that were being televised daily, the two threads of greater realism and higher mythologizing had developed even further, resulting in a new hybrid: the large-scale epic film that tried to recreate the Pacific war in precise detail. Although *In Harm's Way* (1965)—a throwback that in many ways could have been filmed in 1945—may have been the earliest film in this category, the best known was certainly *Tora! Tora! Tora!* (1970), which tried to explain, from both the American and the Japanese points of view, the events leading up to the attack on Pearl Harbor. Similar epic recreations were seen in *Midway* (1976) and *MacArthur* (1976).

When films about Vietnam began to proliferate in the late 1970s, the portrayals of that larger and earlier war in the Pacific all but disappeared from the big screen. On the small screen, however, World War II could still be found often: in the form of television miniseries, cable-network documentaries, and even home video rentals of World War II combat classics. By the end of the 1990s,

the Pacific war on film had become a relatively rare phenomenon, seen primarily as the subject of big-budget films with artistic pretensions, such as Steven Spielberg's *Empire of the Sun* (1987) and Terrence Malick's *The Thin Red Line* (1998). These two films, which may herald a new direction for the Pacific war film in the twenty-first century, try to move the viewer away from the narrative action of the war and more toward the interior states of mind of the war's participants.

FURTHER READINGS

Basinger, Jeanine. *The World War II Combat Film: Anatomy of a Genre* (1986).

Dick, Bernard F. *The Star-Spangled Screen: The American World War II Film* (1985).

Doherty, Thomas. *Projections of War: Hollywood, American Culture, and World War II,* (2d ed. 1999).

Koppes, Clayton R., and Gregory D. Black. *Hollywood Goes to War: How Politics, Profits, and Propaganda Shaped World War II Movies* (1987).

James T. Deutsch

SEE ALSO Home Front, U.S.

Forrestal, James (1892–1949)

An investment banker, James Forrestal was recruited by President Franklin Roosevelt to serve in his administration in the summer of 1940. Born in 1892 in Beacon, New York, Forrestal was educated at Dartmouth College and Princeton University. Within weeks of graduation from Princeton in 1916 he joined the firm that became Dillon Read and Company, as a bond salesman. As the United States entered World War I, Forrestal trained at the then-hybrid specialty of naval aviator. After completing training, he was assigned to duty at the Navy Department in Washington, D.C., and did not serve in a combat role during the war.

After the close of hostilities, Forrestal returned to Dillon Read and quickly rose to top management. By 1938, at age 46, Forrestal became company president and was highly regarded on Wall Street. By this time he had developed a vast array of commercial and industrial contacts throughout the country. President Roosevelt and one of his key advisers, Harry Hopkins, were aware of the coming need to recruit high-level businessmen for the purposes of expanding the nation's industrial base and preparing it for the looming large-scale war. An added difficulty in this task was that many on Wall Street and in corporate management did not strongly support the liberal policies being pursued by the Roosevelt administration. Though staunchly capitalistic, Forrestal, unlike many of his peers in manufacturing and finance, supported the principal New Deal banking and financial reforms; and White House officials—Harry Hopkins, in particular—took notice.

Events developed quickly for Forrestal and the U.S. Navy during the summer of 1940. In June, Hopkins persuaded Forrestal to come to Washington and be one of four newly established special administrative assistants to President Roosevelt. Forrestal was assigned projects dealing with Latin America, but he felt that his duties were inconsequential for a nation on the verge of entry into a great military conflict. Within three weeks of his initial appointment, however, he was already being considered for assignment with the Navy Department.

Congress had authorized the new position of Undersecretary of the Navy, and with Roosevelt's support Forrestal was sworn into that position on August 22, 1940. In the previous month Roosevelt signed into law the "Two-Ocean Navy bill," which had been introduced by Carl Vinson, veteran chairman of the House Naval Affairs Committee. The bill authorized a 70 percent expansion of naval construction. The navy, throughout its history up to World War I, had essentially focused on the Atlantic Ocean; and because the United States had chosen to keep its standing peacetime forces at reduced levels, the navy was in no position to conduct large-scale operations on two oceans in 1940. Roosevelt, with the assistance of men like Forrestal, sought to vastly increase the navy's capability.

Roosevelt had spent eight years in the Wilson administration as assistant secretary of the navy, and he remained a staunch supporter of the U.S. Fleet throughout his political career. He also had, at times, expressed his frustration at attempting to make any lasting changes in the traditional manner in which the navy had conducted its business. "Attempting to promote change in the Navy," he reportedly commented, "is much like punching at a large feather bed mattress. You can exert yourself all you like, but the thing simply falls back to its original form."

Although Forrestal saw no combat during World War I, had been trained in naval aviation and understood the role that air warfare would play in naval strategy should war break out between the United States and the Axis powers. Even up to and briefly after Japan's air raid at Pearl Harbor on December 7, 1941, much of the conventional wisdom in the minds of U.S. naval commanders held that the battleship remained the premier capital ship and was the weapons system around which naval engagements would be won or lost. Roosevelt realized the necessity of having key personnel in the Navy Department

who had knowledge of naval air, had a forward-looking perspective, were not afraid to take risks, and possessed skills that he deemed essential to expanding the country's war might. He commented to Harry Hopkins in late 1939: "Find men with organizing ability to handle the problem of industrial production of war materials."

Forrestal turned out to be the right man for the job. Besides having superior analytic and management skills, he thoroughly understood business organization. His wide association with industrial leaders and his investment-banking financial acumen made him superbly qualified to prepare the navy for a massive industrial expansion. Forrestal was a master in the art of persuasion and was able to convince others to work toward the realization of his creative ideas. He was also highly successful at enlisting hard-to-get individuals to join the Roosevelt administration's efforts. His specialty was the recognition of organizational and managerial talent, and he was widely regarded for his ability to find the right person for a particular job.

Beginning in mid-1940, the increased high volume of naval production required innovative procedures to handle the increased amount of everything from paperwork to propellers. Forrestal found that no overall organization within the department was responsible for coordinating the procurement activities of the bureaus, which lacked trained people competent to deal with questions of research, design, purchasing, production, and transportation. Moreover, the navy lacked a general counsel's office with capable lawyers to ascertain the complex legal ramifications of the increased commercial traffic. By July 1941, Forrestal had installed the Procurement Legal Division to give its advice on contract negotiation, preparation, and performance.

Early in 1942, Forrestal established the Office of Procurement and Material (OPM) to deal with planning, statistics, and resources; this was widely considered one of the soundest and most productive measures initiated in logistical management at the time. Forrestal realized that if the navy were to compete for scarce materials and manpower with the army, the merchant marine, Lend Lease, and the civilian economy, it must have some way of making an accurate and documented statement of its needs (in ships and guns, trained personnel, supply depots, and other vital resources) in order to prosecute successful naval operations on a global scale.

In his 1944 analysis of the situation at Pearl Harbor when it was attacked, Forrestal wrote: "Number four: Submersion of Chief of Naval Operations (CNO) in details of material to the extent that he became insensitive to the significance of events." By having personnel capable of performing the "details of material" and of implementing a coherent industrial policy, the navy freed its commanders and strategists to concentrate on defeating the enemy.

In April 1944, Secretary of the Navy Frank Knox died suddenly, and Forrestal succeeded him. Knox had acted as a buffer between Forrestal and Admiral Ernest J. King, the high-powered chief of naval operations, in the early stages of their working together. Because of these efforts, King came to appreciate the value and talents that Forrestal brought to the navy's effort. By the time of Knox's death, the two had achieved a pragmatic working relationship. Forrestal's industrial and organizational skills allowed King to move beyond "matters of material" and to concentrate on a naval campaign that brought victory in the Pacific war.

The U.S. Navy at the beginning of World War II had little resemblance to the fleet that finished it. When Forrestal assumed control of material development, the navy consisted of 1099 vessels of various sizes. By June 1945, the fleets included in their inventories some 50,759 vessels, and personnel increased from 160,997 to 3,383,196. The navy added 92 aircraft carriers, 8 battleships, 35 cruisers, 148 destroyers, and 140 submarines. The U.S. Navy had emerged as the largest and most powerful in the world—a position it still easily holds. Admiral King ensured that the navy received the right combination of ships and weapons systems; and Forrestal ensured that the jobs of planning, production, control, and delivery were completed in an organized and efficient manner.

Forrestal remained secretary of the navy until 1947, when the Department of Defense was established by the National Security Act. He was one of the chief planners in unifying the three armed services under a single executive department of the federal government. He became the nation's first secretary of defense in 1947 but resigned in 1949 because of poor health. For several decades he had worked endless hours to advance his country's interests, and the effort finally caught up with him. James Forrestal, in failing physical and mental health, took his life at age 57. He was buried with full military honors at Arlington National Cemetery.

FURTHER READINGS

Dorwat, Jeffery M. *Eberstadt and Forrestal: A National Security Partnership, 1909–1949* (1991).

Hoopes, Townsend. *Driven Patriot: The Life and Times of James Forrestal* (1992).

Rogow, Arnold A. *James Forrestal: A Study of Personality, Politics, and Policy* (1963).

James McNabb

SEE ALSO Navy, U.S.

Franco-Thai War

Between November 1940 and January 1941, Vichy France and Thailand waged an undeclared and now nearly forgotten war. Thailand began it to regain the three rich rice-growing provinces of Battambang, Siemréap, and Sisophon, which then-Siam had annexed in 1862 from Cambodia (Kampuchea) but which the French had forced the Thais to restore in 1907. Thailand also claimed territory in Laos, which the French had also forced it to return in 1904. In early June 1940, Thailand concluded a nonaggression pact with France, but after the defeat of France by Germany the Thais lost interest in ratifying it. The pro-Japanese military government of Marshal Pibul Songgram (which had changed Siam's name to Thailand) sought to capitalize on France's weakness. In October Bangkok mobilized its military reservists.

With reservists, the Thai army in 1940 numbered nearly 50,000. The Thai air force had about 270 planes—150 of them combat types, mostly of U.S. manufacture. The navy also had two dozen obsolete land-based aircraft, but Japan delivered ninety-three planes in December 1940. The Thai navy had 10,000 men. Its vessels consisted of royal yachts, a British-built World War I destroyer, and two British-built small gunboats and eight torpedo boats. Italy supplied nine small torpedo boats, two minesweepers, and nine minelayers. Italy was also building two light cruisers for the Thais, but these were not available and in fact were sequestered by Italy in 1941. Japan delivered two modern armored coast-defense anti-aircraft vessels, four small submarines, two escort/training ships, and three small torpedo boats. In addition to fighting ships, the Thai navy also had a number of auxiliaries. Despite its relatively large number of vessels, the navy suffered from serious shortcomings. Older vessels were of limited fighting value, the modern Italian torpedo boats were too flimsy for service in rough seas, and the Japanese submarines could not dive. Also, the navy's sailors were poorly trained, and many of its officers were political appointees.

The French had 50,000 men in their Indochina army, but 38,000 of these were native troops of questionable loyalty. The heart of the French military was the 5,000-man 5th Foreign Legion Regiment. The French also had thirty World War I tanks. Much of their artillery was also outdated, and they were short of ammunition. The French air force had fewer than a hundred planes. French naval units in Indochinese waters consisted of an old light cruiser (*La Motte-Picquet*), two gunboats, two sloops, two auxiliary patrol craft, and several noncombatants. Most French warships were old and poorly armed and suffered from mechanical problems.

France appeared vulnerable. Not only had the Germans defeated metropolitan France, but the country was under pressure from Japan. In September 1940 Japanese troops invaded Tonkin, killed 800 French troops, and secured occupation concessions and airfields. In what it believed were highly favorable military and diplomatic conditions, Bangkok decided to reassert its claims.

From mid-November 1940 the Thais sent military units across the Mekong River into eastern Cambodia; these led to skirmishes with the French. The French military was temporarily sidetracked by the November 22 Indochina Communist Party uprising in Cochin China (South Vietnam) but crushed it the first week in December.

French High Commissioner Admiral Jean Decoux decided to answer the Thai attacks with a land and sea offensive. The land portion began on January 16, 1941, when a mixed French brigade attacked Thai positions at Yang Dom Koum but failed because of insufficient manpower and heavy weapons. The Thais, who had planned their own offensive for the same day, then counterattacked, supported by tanks, but were beaten back with grenades. Both sides then withdrew from the immediate area, although Bangkok claimed a major victory.

Simultaneously, fighting erupted at sea. The French navy planned bold attacks on the Thai naval detachment at Koh Chang and at the principal navy base at Sattahib. The initial strike was to be carried out by virtually the entire flotilla: the venerable *La Motte-Picquet,* two gunboats, and two sloops. On January 16 this force sailed for the Gulf of Siam and Koh Chang, which guarded the passage to Sattahib. The French warships, led by three seaplanes (which fixed the position of the Thai vessels but also revealed the presence of the French), attacked their enemy early on the morning of January 17. In the ensuing 90-minute action at Koh Chang the French sank three Thai torpedo boats, forced one of the two heavy coast-defense warships to run aground, and mortally damaged its sister ship. The French then retired with no direct hits or losses to themselves.

This action was significant (if now almost forgotten) in that it was the only naval engagement in either world war which the French fought alone without allies. It is remarkable also in its one-sided nature, despite the fact that the Thais—forewarned by the French seaplane reconnaissance—opened fire first. The elderly French cruiser mounted only eight 6-inch guns as opposed to the four 8-inch batteries of the thoroughly modern Thai coast-defense warships (miniature battleships, in reality). Obviously, naval skill and professionalism by the French had made the difference.

There was little air action during the war, although the Thais did use their vintage Curtiss Hawk III biplanes in a dive-bombing role. The French had a plan, not implemented, to fire-bomb Bangkok from the air.

The indecisive land and air actions and the one-sided naval battle did not end the conflict. Rather, the Japanese threatened to intervene on the Thai side. On January 31 a Japanese-dictated armistice was signed at Saigon aboard the Japanese cruiser *Natori.* In March, pressured also by Germany, the Vichy government accepted Japanese mediation. By Japanese edict, on May 9, 1941, France and Thailand signed a peace treaty in Tokyo whereby France transferred to Thailand three Cambodian and two Laotian provinces on the right bank of the Mekong River, ceding some 42,000 square miles in all. France—abjectly defeated in Europe, unable to defeat an inferior military power in Asia, dictated to by Japan, and pressured by Germany to give up five colonial provinces—had drunk of the cup of humiliation. But its crushing of the Communist rebellion and its daring Nelsonic victory at Koh Chang made the drink palatable.

In September 1945 the Thais were forced to return their recently acquired territory and accept the Mekong as the boundary between their country and Laos and Cambodia. That the issue probably had yet been settled was seen in lingering border skirmishes along the Mekong in 1946, in clashes from May 1987 to February 1988 between Thailand and Laos, and in continuing Thai support of the genocidal Khmer Rouge movement in Cambodia.

FURTHER READINGS

Decoux, Jean. *A La Barre de L'Indochine* (1949).
Meisler, Jurg. "Koh Chang: The Unknown Battle, Franco-Thai War of 1940–41." *World War II Investigator,* 2, 14 (1989): 26–34.
Mordal, Jacques. *Marine Indochine* (1953)
———, and Gabriel A. J. P. Auphan. *La Marine Française pendant la Deuxième Guerre Mondiale* (1958).

Spencer C. Tucker

SEE ALSO French Indochina; Thailand

Fraser, Bruce A. (1888–1981)

Admiral Sir Bruce Austin Fraser was appointed commander in chief of the British Pacific Fleet in 1944, a post which he held until the end of the war. Fraser had held the position of Third Sea Lord and Controller of the Royal Navy when World War II broke out. He was responsible for the expansion of the fleet and the integration of the reserve units into regular service. In 1941, he was knighted and promoted to Vice Admiral and appointed as second in command of the Home Fleet. In this post, he was responsible for the Allied Arctic convoys from Britain to northern Russia. He was promoted to commander in chief of the Home Fleet in 1943. He personally commanded the British squadron which engaged and sank the German battleship *Scharnhorst* on December 26, 1943. Fraser also oversaw the naval blockade of Norway.

In 1944, British Prime Minister Winston Churchill convinced U.S. President Franklin D. Roosevelt to allow the British to station a major fleet in the Pacific in order to reestablish a presence as former colonies were liberated and to share in the defeat of the Japanese. Fraser was appointed to command the Far East naval units in November 1944. Churchill picked Fraser because he was a proven sailor, had a natural talent for public relations, and was adept at handling the press; most important, he got along well with the Americans.

The main British fleet consisted of four aircraft carriers, two battleships, five cruisers, and fifteen destroyers. Because it was recognized that the British fleet would often operate with American units, Fraser decided to establish his command ashore at Sydney and appoint Vice Admiral Sir Bernard Rawlings to command the fleet at sea, since Fraser's seniority meant that he would outrank all the U.S. fleet commanders if he were to take personal command of the fleet.

Fraser was chosen by Churchill as much for his diplomatic abilities as for his military acumen. The British Pacific Fleet was only a fraction of the size of the U.S. naval presence in the Pacific, and it was recognized by both the Americans and the British that the British fleet would have to serve essentially as a junior partner to U.S. naval forces. In addition, the British lacked the logistical base to support fleet operations over an area as large as the Pacific theater and would, consequently, be dependent on American logistic capabilities. These factors were the source of the U.S. Joint Chiefs of Staff opposition to the British deployment, and it would be up to Fraser to overcome such opposition and to develop a niche for the British fleet without completely subordinating his units to the Americans. (The U.S. Navy's Chief of Naval Operations, the crusty Anglophobe Admiral Ernest King, was never reconciled to the presence of the Royal Navy in "his" Pacific.)

The British naval base at Colombo became the early center of the British Pacific Fleet as Fraser worked to build up the fleet and have necessary modifications made to the ships. The admiral wanted the British aircraft carriers modified so that they could carry seventy-two, instead of

their original fifty, aircraft; and he wanted the slower British aircraft, such as the Sea Hurricanes or the Barracuda torpedo bombers, replaced with proven U.S. aircraft, such as the Corsair fighters or the Avenger torpedo bombers. In addition, Fraser needed to assemble the supply and repair ships needed to support the fleet. By February 1945, he felt that the fleet was sufficiently prepared, and it sailed to its designated home port of Sydney, Australia.

In Sydney, Fraser's skills as a diplomat were tested when he found himself in the middle of a dispute over the deployment of the fleet. The U.S. naval commander, Admiral King, wanted to attach the British fleet to General Douglas MacArthur's Southwest Pacific Command, where it would be used to support the reconquest of Borneo. Fraser wanted the fleet used in the much more visible campaign centered on the assault of Okinawa. In addition, the admiral wanted to continue working with U.S. Admiral Chester Nimitz, with whom he had formed a warm working relationship, rather than be transferred to MacArthur's command.

Eventually, King was persuaded to allow the British Pacific Fleet to be designated Task Force 57 and attached to the U.S. Fifth Fleet attacking Okinawa. Although under the nominal control of fleet commander Admiral Raymond Spruance, Fraser made sure that the tactical command of the British fleet remained in the hands of Rawlings. Thus, although their operations were coordinated with the Americans, the British operated in a semi-independent manner.

Meanwhile, Fraser had to carry out a balancing act that meant negotiating between the Admiralty in London, the U.S. naval command at Pearl Harbor, and the Australian supply officials in Sydney. For instance, the Admiralty was keen to dispatch British submarines to the Pacific, but there were no facilities for the additional vessels in Fremantle, Australia. Fraser was able to arrange the construction of a base in the U.S.-occupied Philippines, and the submarines were transferred three months later.

The two most pressing problems for Fraser during his tenure were the exact nature of the relationship between British and U.S. forces and the need to supply the fleet. As Task Force 57, the British fleet had performed well, but with new operations came a need to redefine the command structure. Fraser allowed the British fleet to be redesignated Task Force 37 and placed under the immediate command of U.S. Admiral William Halsey. Although the British were still technically independent, for the remainder of the war they functioned as one of Halsey's task forces. Fraser's willingness to compromise ensured Allied unity of effort until the war's end. For all the British Pacific Fleet's problems with logistics, U.S. naval personnel

turned envious of their British allies during Japanese kamikaze attacks, particularly those off Okinawa. The Royal
Navy carriers' armored flight decks made it possible, as
British personnel put it, simply "to sweep away" the
wreckage of Japanese suicide aircraft and to get on with
operations. This was a pardonable exaggeration, because
the Japanese suicide attackers and more conventional ordnance could penetrate the timber and light-metal construction of U.S. Navy carriers' flight decks more or less
at will. (There is nearly always a "trade-off" in such matters: the British carriers' armor reduced their aircraft
capacity considerably below that of comparable U.S.
carriers.)

The inability of the British fleet to resupply itself at
sea as did the U.S. Navy was one factor which necessitated
close cooperation with the Americans. When the British
fleet was dispatched to the Pacific, it did not have an
adequate supply train, and Fraser battled the Admiralty
to increase the fleet's repair and supply vessels, but is was
not until late in 1945 that the British could be said to be
adequately supported.

At the end of the war, Admiral Fraser represented
Great Britain at the surrender ceremony in Tokyo Bay
and oversaw the repatriation of prisoners of wax and the
surrender of those territories which the Japanese still retained. After the war, Fraser was promoted the the position of First Sea Lord, a well-deserved appointment.

FURTHER READINGS

Costello, John. *The Pacific War* (1981).
Smith, Peter. *Task Force 57: The British Pacific Fleet,
1944–1945* (1969).
Winton, John. *The Forgotten Fleet: The British Navy in
the Pacific, 1944–1945* (1970).

Tom Lansford

SEE ALSO Navy, Royal; Okinawa, Battle for

French Indochina

On the eve of World War II, French Indochina consisted
of Vietnam (divided by France into Cochin China, An
Nam, and Tonkin), Cambodia, and Laos. Officially, only
Cochin China was an outright colony; the others were
protectorates, but France exercised full control. Administration was through a governor general who was responsible to the minister of colonies in Paris.

Nationalism reached Indochina following World War
I. President Woodrow Wilson's self-determination of peoples and the example of the Nationalist (Kuomintang)
government in China inspired Indochinese nationalists.

In the 1920s the French rejected demands of moderate
nationalists for reform through cooperation with France,
and in 1930 there was an uprising in Tonkin by the Viet
Nam Quoc Dan Dang (VNQDD, or Vietnamese Nationalist Party). It was the most effective indigenous non-
Communist political and military organization in Vietnam at the time. French troops, forewarned, suppressed
the uprising and destroyed the Vietnamese Nationalist
Party as an effective organization. This left the field to the
Communists. In 1930 Ho Chi Minh had achieved a fu-
sion of several Vietnamese Communist groups into the
Indochinese Communist Party (ICP). Combining nationalism and communism, on the outbreak of World
War II the ICP was the strongest anti-French underground organization.

World War II had a tremendous impact on the region.
Taking advantage of fighting in Europe, in September
1940 the Japanese attacked Lang Son and Hai Phong in
Tonkin. The French suffered 800 dead in the fighting
before the Vichy government agreed to grant Japan the
right to garrison 6,000 men and use certain airfields in
Indochina, as well as the right to transit 25,000 men.
Japan had been at war with China since 1937, and this
move was supposedly to close supply routes to Nationalist
forces in Chungking. With the German defeat of France
and the Dutch, and with Great Britain fighting for survival in Europe, Japan had its "golden opportunity" in
Asia. In July 1941, after the German invasion of the Soviet Union, Japan occupied southern Indochina. This
placed its aircraft within range of Siam (Thailand), Malaya, and the Dutch East Indies, and it prompted a joint
U.S.-U.K.-Netherlands economic embargo, which in
turn triggered the Japanese decision to plan for war with
the United States. Ironically, in view of what happened
two decades later, it was the U.S. "line-in-the-sand" approach to Japanese expansion in Vietnam that led to its
becoming a shooting participant in World War II.

The French (Vichy) government was unable to challenge Japanese actions in Indochina, but the Japanese
made no concessions to Indochinese nationalist leaders
and merely utilized the existing French administration.
Although Tokyo recognized French sovereignty in Indochina, it had de facto control. The Japanese had free transit across Indochina, and they controlled its local military
facilities and economic resources, particularly its valuable
rice and rubber.

With Japanese troops in Indochina, Nationalist Chinese leader Chiang Kai-shek and his generals shared a
common objective with Ho and the ICP of trying to expel
the invaders. The ICP now became the center of resistance against the Japanese occupation. On November 22,

1940, the ICP led an uprising in western Cochin China, which was crushed the first week in December by the French military.

From November 1940 to January 1941 Thailand and France fought an undeclared war. The Thais, supported by Japan, sought to take advantage of French weakness to secure the return of Cambodian and Laotian provinces they had been forced to cede some thirty years before. After a series of inconclusive land and sea battles in May 1941 Tokyo dictated a settlement entirely in favor of Thailand.

In May 1941 Ho and his lieutenants in southern China established the Viet Nam Doc Lap Dong Minh Hoi (Vietnamese Independence League), which came to be known as the Viet Minh. This was an effort to bring together all nationalist groups to fight for independence against the French and Japanese.

Nationalist Chinese support for Ho and the Viet Minh vacillated, but the Viet Minh was the chief indigenous force contesting the Japanese in Indochina. By the end of 1943 Viet Minh commandos led by Vo Nguyen Giap penetrated into Tonkin. In November 1944 a large unit entered Tonkin, and during the winter of 1944–1945 the Viet Minh came to control much of its northernmost provinces.

As the principal resistants to the Japanese, the Viet Minh received aid from the U.S. Office of Strategic Services (OSS). This assistance consisted of small arms, communications equipment, medical supplies, and instructors to train the Viet Minh in guerrilla warfare techniques against the Japanese. In return, the Viet Minh provided weather data, rescued downed U.S. pilots, and provided valuable intelligence information. OSS operatives in Vietnam did not conceal their admiration for the Viet Minh and assured them of U.S. support in their struggle for independence. This was very much in keeping with the 1940 British-U.S. Atlantic Charter, which placed emphasis on self-determination of all peoples, as well as with President Roosevelt's personal inclination that France not retain its colonies.

By early 1945 it was evident that Japan had lost the war. Gaullist influence spread among the French in Indochina who were determined that they would liberate the area themselves. The Japanese struck first, and on March 9, 1945, they arrested every French administrator and soldier they could find. Only about six thousand French troops and two small naval auxiliary vessels escaped. On March 10 the Japanese made some moves toward establishing a national Vietnamese government. To secure support they granted "independence" to Indochina and appointed Bao Dai (the French-controlled emperor of An Nam who had spent the war years at Huê) as head of state of Vietnam.

When Japan surrendered on August 15, there was a power vacuum in Vietnam, into which Ho and his supporters moved. On August 17–18 pro–Viet Minh elements in Hanoi staged an uprising, and on August 19 Viet Minh troops entered the city. Bao Dai abdicated a week later. At the same time the Viet Minh's southern arm (the Committee for the Liberation of Nam Bo) took control of Saigon. On August 29 in Hanoi, Ho announced the formation of a provisional government of the Democratic Republic of Vietnam (DRV) with its capital at Hanoi. On September 2 he officially proclaimed the independence of the DRV.

The Potsdam Conference (July 17–August 2, 1945) stipulated that British troops would take the surrender of Japanese forces and occupy the southern half of Vietnam up to the 16th parallel; Chinese troops would do the same north of that line. Nothing was said about the ultimate disposition of Indochina, although it seems probable that had Roosevelt lived, it would not have been returned to French control. The British commander in the south, Major General Douglas Gracey, however, released the French from their prison camps and allowed them to reestablish control over southern Vietnam. Soon they again controlled Cambodia and Laos. Tonkin was another matter, however. Finally in March 1946 a compromise was worked out with Ho Chi Minh (the Ho-Sainteny Agreement) providing for French recognition of the DRV as a free state within the French Union. France also agreed to a plebiscite in the rest of Vietnam to see if it wanted to be reunited with the north. By making concessions regarding rights in China, France also secured the withdrawal of Chinese Nationalist troops from the DRV.

French High Commissioner Admiral Thierry d'Argenlieu's decision (taken without approval from Paris) to violate the terms of the Ho-Sainteny Agreement and his belief that only military force would teach the leaders of the DRV who was really in command in Indochina led to the first Vietnam War.

FURTHER READINGS
Duiker, William J. *The Communist Road to Power in Vietnam* (1981).
———. *The Rise of Nationalism in Vietnam, 1900–1941* (1984).
Fall, Bernard. *The Two Vietnams* (1964).
Hammer, Ellen J. *The Struggle for Indochina* (1954).
Spencer C. Tucker

SEE ALSO Ho Chi Minh; Office of Strategic Services in the Pacific

Gandhi, Mohandas Karamchand (1869–1948)

Mohandas Karamchand Gandhi, one of the most inspiring figures of the twentieth century, led the movement for Indian independence throughout World War II and until the final relinquishment of British control in 1947. He was born on October 2, 1869, in Porbandar. His father served as revenue minister for the local ruler, though their caste was the third-ranking *modh bania; gandhi* means nothing more than "grocer" in Gujarati. At age 13, he entered an arranged marriage with Kasturbhai that eventually resulted in four sons. At 19, he left for London to study law, but he found little professional success on returning to India.

In 1893, Gandhi left India to practice law in South Africa, where he was much more successful. There he encountered colonial racism against fellow Indians who had initially been brought to Natal province as indentured laborers. Almost overnight, a pious, passive man became a moral force to be reckoned with. As part of his campaign against this discrimination, he developed the idea of *satyagraha* ("holding fast to the truth")—a nonviolent approach to civil disobedience and noncooperation with the colonial authorities. He turned from lawyering and became a *sadhu* ("sage"), living in poverty, fasting often, and avoiding marital relations. During the Boer War (1899–1902) and again during the Zulu Rebellion (1906), Gandhi organized an Indian ambulance corps and served with it.

After twenty years in South Africa, Gandhi left for India in July 1914. With the coming of World War I, he supported the British war effort in India by recruiting soldiers for the Indian army. After the war, in 1919—provoked by passage of the antisedition Rowlatt Bills—Gandhi inaugurated a satyagraha against the British in India. It turned violent, and British troops massacred nearly four hundred Indians at one meeting. This prompted Gandhi to wait awhile before again pushing the British with another mass campaign. When his followers resorted to violence, Gandhi again called off the campaign. He wanted independence for India, but not at the cost of violence.

Gandhi converted the Indian National Congress from an upper-middle-class organization into an effective mass movement. During the next two decades, the National Congress grew in power, and Gandhi was jailed several times. In 1930, he launched another satyagraha, this time against the salt tax. He also crusaded against the prejudices and discrimination that the lowest caste, the "untouchables," experienced.

The approach of World War II occasionally drew Gandhi's attention from India. Writing about the Jews under Hitler in 1938, he admitted, "If there ever could be a justifiable war in the name of and for humanity, a war against Germany, to prevent the wanton persecution of a whole race, would be completely justified"; he added, however, "I do not believe in any war." He advised nonviolent resistance as the best course of action, although he recognized that this might easily result in a "general massacre of the Jews." (The likelihood of mass death resulting specifically from the absence of war was a conundrum that Gandhi and most pacifists could not resolve.)

Gandhi hated fascism, but he hated war even more and disagreed with other leaders of the National Congress over how much India should support the British war effort. It was only after the failure of the Cripps mission in March 1942 to arrive at a blueprint for eventual independence that other National Congress leaders were persuaded toward Gandhi's position. Gandhi was particularly irritated by successful British efforts to recruit Muslim support for the war and drive a wedge between Muslims and Hindus.

On August 8, 1942, the Indian National Congress adopted a resolution calling on the British to "Quit India." This was Gandhi's last great satyagraha. He and other National Congress leaders were rapidly arrested, and the resulting protests turned into riots. By the end of September, the dissent had petered out, although some activity continued for another year. By the end of 1943, by British count, 208 police stations and 749 other government buildings in India had been either destroyed or badly damaged. More than twenty-five hundred civilians had been killed or injured, and some sixty-six thousand Indians had been detained during this crisis.

Gandhi spent the next two years under house arrest in the Aga Khan's palace outside Poona. He was released on May 6, 1944, when medical opinion determined that his health was so poor that he would be unable to participate in politics again. The doctor was wrong, and Gandhi was an active participant in the postwar negotiations which resulted in India's independence. At considerable risk to his own life, he traveled to areas where communal violence among Hindus, Muslims, and Sikhs was killing and displacing thousands—always calming the anger and urging peace. But his dream of a united India whose masses practiced the doctrine of nonviolence was not realized. An independent Pakistan was created for the Muslims at the same time that India became independent on August 14, 1947.

On January 30, 1948, a young Hindu fired three shots at Gandhi. The assassin was offended by Gandhi's efforts to achieve unity and peace; and so the apostle of nonviolence died a violent death. Although Gandhi became known for his politics, his main focus in life was spirituality. His father's household had been tolerant of other religions, and his mother was very religious. Later, he read the Koran, Tolstoy's writings on Christianity, and Hindu scriptures. He concluded that all religions were true but flawed because of the imperfections of people. He found his greatest source of inspiration in the Hindu *Bhagavad Gita*. Throughout his long life, Gandhi was a prolific author; his writings fill ninety published volumes. A man of vision, Gandhi inspired many social and political activists—including Martin Luther King Jr.—with his message of tolerance and nonviolence.

FURTHER READINGS
Judith M. Brown. *Gandhi: Prisoner of Hope* (1989).

Eric Swedin

SEE ALSO India; Indian National Army

Gilbert Islands

Located in the west central Pacific Ocean, approximately 2,800 miles northeast of Australia, the Gilbert Islands, (now Kiribati), a British crown colony since 1916, were among the first targets of Japanese expansion in the Pacific in 1941. Subsequently, in 1943, the Gilberts served as the starting point for an Allied offensive in the central Pacific that, by 1945, carried U.S. forces to the doorstep of the Japanese home islands.

On December 10, 1941, shortly after their attack on the U.S. naval facility at Pearl Harbor, Hawaii, and the onset of their campaign to conquer the Southern Resources Area, the Japanese occupied Makin, the northernmost of the sixteen coral atolls making up the Gilbert chain. Initially they maintained a force of fewer than one hundred men in the Gilberts. However, in the late summer of 1942, the Japanese perspective on the Gilberts and the entire central Pacific changed radically. A submarine-borne hit-and-run raid against Makin, carried out by U.S. Marines commanded by Lieutenant Colonel Evans F. Carlson on August 17, 1942, persuaded Japan's military leadership that the defensive perimeter established during the first six months of the war to protect the Southern Resources Area was vulnerable in the central Pacific. Beginning in late August 1942, the Japanese dispatched troops from the Marshall Islands, the Caroline Islands, and Japan itself to the Gilberts and other British mandates south of the Marshalls. These troops occupied the Gilberts in force and established garrisons on previously unoccupied Nauru and Ocean Island, both located west of the Gilberts.

In strengthening their position in the Gilberts, the Japanese built up their forces and defenses primarily on Tarawa, a triangular atoll located in the northern portion of the chain. Thus, although they reinforced Makin, site of the Carlson raid, the Japanese dispatched the bulk of the troops earmarked for the Gilberts to Tarawa, deemed the most likely target of an Allied invasion. In September 1942, Japan's leadership transported to Tarawa, the Yokosuka 6th Special Naval Landing Force (redesignated the 3d Base Force in February 1943). This force, the first sizable unit sent to the Gilberts, was joined in May 1943 by the Sasebo 7th Special Naval Landing Force.

The Japanese concentrated the vast majority of their forces committed to Tarawa on Betio, an island located at the southwest corner of the atoll. Two and a half miles long and 800 yards across at its widest point, Betio held an airfield that became operational in January 1943. By November of that year, the Japanese garrison defending Betio numbered 4,836 men, including more than three thousand trained combat soldiers, and the island had been transformed into a formidable bastion. Betio's defenses included more than one hundred pillboxes, machine gun posts, and reinforced concrete bunkers; a coconut log seawall, 3 to 5 feet high, surrounding the island; and more than two hundred guns, ranging from British 8-inch naval guns brought from Singapore to dug-in tanks. Additionally, the Japanese made the ocean approach virtually impassable with concrete tetrahedrons wired together, with mines among them. When the Japanese completed their defensive preparations on Betio, the only viable approach for an invader was from the northwest, via Tarawa's lagoon. However, a reef, located from 500 to 1,000 yards offshore, made this route treacherous. Confident that Betio was impregnable, Rear Admiral Keiji Shibasaki, commander of Japanese forces there, boasted that the island could not be taken if a million men tried for a hundred years.

While the Japanese prepared to defend the Gilberts, the Allies, who had seized the initiative with difficult victories on Guadalcanal (August 1942–February 1943) and New Guinea (September 1942–January 1943), mapped out their strategy for the Pacific war, for both the short and the long terms. In late May 1943, the U.S. joint chiefs of staff adopted the somewhat misnamed "Strategic Plan for the Defeat of Japan." This plan provided that Allied forces would mount offensive operations in the central, southwest, and southern Pacific in 1943 and 1944, with top priority assigned to a central Pacific drive westward from Pearl Harbor. Approved by the Anglo–American combined chiefs of staff at the Trident Conference (Washington, D.C., May 11–25, 1943), the "Strategic Plan" established the future course of Allied—U.S. in particular—operations in the Pacific war.

Having decided on a central Pacific offensive, American military planners selected the targets to be attacked. Although the chief advocate of the central Pacific drive, Admiral Ernest J. King, the head of the U.S. Navy, preferred the Marshall Islands, it quickly became apparent that this could not go forward in 1943 without severely curtailing General Douglas MacArthur's operations in the southwest Pacific and Admiral William F. Halsey's in the South Pacific. American strategists therefore selected the Gilbert Islands as the first objective of the central Pacific offensive, postponing the invasion of the Marshalls until early 1944. Admiral Chester W. Nimitz, whose forces were to mount the central Pacific drive, welcomed this decision, knowing that the Gilberts lay within range of land-based bombers and that they would provide an excellent staging ground for the Marshalls' operation.

On November 21, 1943, American forces invaded the Gilberts and initiated the central Pacific offensive. Code-named Operation Galvanic, the invasion involved simultaneous amphibious attacks against Betio, Tarawa, and Makin. Supported by the eight carriers, seven battleships, seven heavy cruisers, three light cruisers, and thirty-four destroyers of Vice Admiral Raymond A. Spruance's Fifth Fleet, the 2d Marine Division assaulted Betio while the 165th Regimental Combat Team of the U.S. Army's 27th Division struck Makin.

Prior to the landings on Betio, U.S. naval and air forces subjected the small island to the heaviest bombardment of the Pacific war to that point. Over the course of two and a half hours, U.S. ships and planes fired some 3,000 tons of shells. Although it wrecked Japanese communications and left the defenders temporarily dazed, the preinvasion bombardment did not last long enough to neutralize Betio's defenses. Furthermore, communications problems resulted in the bombardment's being lifted too early. Consequently, U.S. marines attempting to reach shore encountered a deadly barrage of fire.

To make matters worse for the invaders, the Americans had enough amphibious tractors (amtracs/LVTs) for only the first three waves of marines. Subsequent waves had to be transported in standard landing craft (LCVPs). Although the amtracs could get over the reef surrounding Betio, the LCVPs, because of an unusually low tide, could not, many running aground and becoming easy targets for Japanese guns. Marines not killed or wounded in the stranded LCVPs attempted to wade ashore through shoulder-deep water for hundreds of yards. Many were killed or wounded by Japanese fire. Despite the fierce resistance, some five thousand marines made it ashore by nightfall, establishing a beachhead only 300 yards deep. Some fifteen hundred marines had died or were wounded.

The bloodletting on Tarawa continued for the better part of three days. Utilizing flamethrowers and high explosives, marines gradually forced the Japanese defenders to give up their fortified positions. Simultaneously, a rising tide allowed the landing of tanks, artillery, and reinforcements while naval guns and carrier planes blasted away at enemy positions. Forced into the narrow eastern tail of Betio, Japanese forces, on the night of November 22, launched a series of suicidal counterattacks that resulted in their annihilation. On the afternoon of November 23, Major General Julian Smith, commander of the 2d Marine Division, announced the end of organized resistance. For the Americans, victory on Tarawa came at great cost: 991 dead and 2,311 wounded.

On Makin, the 6,500 U.S. assault troops encountered greater resistance than anticipated from the 798 Japanese defenders. Although the landings on Butaritari, the largest island of Makin atoll, met no real opposition; the Americans needed four days to clear the atoll. Compared with Tarawa, U.S. casualties were light: 218 total, 66 killed. Naval losses, in contrast, were more significant. As the fighting on Makin wound down, a Japanese submarine sank *Liscome Bay,* a U.S. escort carrier supporting the operation, killing 642 officers and enlisted men.

After capturing Tarawa and Makin, U.S. forces seized the remaining atolls of the northern Gilberts. Abaiang, Maiana, and Marakei atolls, lying respectively north, south, and northeast of Tarawa, fell quickly. So did Apamama (Abemama), located some seventy-six miles south of Tarawa. By December 1943, the northern Gilberts, stretching 180 miles from Makin to Apamama, had been seized by the Americans.

The heavy casualties incurred by U.S. forces in the Gilberts, especially the three thousand-plus suffered on Tarawa, shocked public opinion in the United States and raised the question of whether possession of a few hundred acres of coral justified the price. U.S. military planners and strategists certainly believed that the strategic gains and tactical lessons learned indeed outweighed the costs. The Gilberts provided air bases from which U.S. reconnaissance planes, bombers, and fighters offered invaluable support during the February 1944 invasion of the Marshall Islands. Equally significant, in the wake of the Tarawa experience, U.S. commanders made significant changes in equipment, tactics, the angle of naval fire, and the length and nature of preinvasion bombardments that greatly facilitated future amphibious assaults in the Pacific war.

FURTHER READINGS

Costell, John. *The Pacific War, 1941–1945* (1982).

Crowl, Philip, and Edmund G. Love. *Seizure of the Gilberts and Marshalls.* In the series U.S. Army in World War II. (Office of the Chief of Military History, Department of the Army, 1955).

Morison, Samuel Eliot. *History of United States Naval Operations in World War II.* Vol. 7, *Aleutians, Gilberts, and Marshalls, June 1942–April 1944* (1951).

Spector, Ronald. *Eagle Against the Sun: The American War with Japan* (1985).

Bruce J. DeHart

SEE ALSO Makin Atoll; Tarawa, Capture of

Goodenough Island

Part of New Guinea, Goodenough Island was the site of a Japanese amphibious landing in August 1942—one of very few such Japanese operations after the empire's initial

offensives between late 1941 and early 1942. The attack was part of the main campaign to drive Australian and U.S. troops out of New Guinea, and the immediate goal was the capture of Milne Bay and in particular the Gili Gili plantation, which had a pier as well as one completed and two partly completed Allied airfields. The former plantation could be used as a seaport and air base to support an ongoing offensive against Port Moresby.

The operation was flawed from the beginning. Japanese intelligence had reported that only three companies of infantry and thirty airplanes defended the area, which in fact housed some 8,500 Australian infantrymen and artillerymen and some 1,300 American engineers. Believing this mistaken report, Japanese commander Vice Admiral Gunichi Mikawa initially dispatched only 1,500 marines for the invasion; an army battalion that had originally been assigned to participate was shifted instead to Guadalcanal. Admiral Mikawa further weakened his force by splitting it into two sections. One section, composed of about 1,100 men, was to land on the Papua Peninsula at Rabi and march 3 miles up the coast to Gili Gili, while the remaining 353 men were to take Goodenough Island and march overland to support the attack on Gili Gili.

One of the ever-faithful Australian Coastwatchers spotted the convoy carrying the overland troops on August 24. The next day those troops landed on Goodenough Island—where the Allies launched air strikes which destroyed the seven landing barges of the Japanese and stranded the detachment on the island. When the Japanese destroyer *Yayoi* attempted to extract the troops, it was also destroyed by Allied airplanes. To complicate matters, the other Japanese force missed its intended landing spot and ended up 7 miles from Gili Gili. The Japanese advance quickly bogged down in heavy fighting as the superior numbers and artillery of the Allied troops inflicted substantial casualties. Even with some 800 reinforcements who landed on August 29, the Japanese were unable to capture their objective. Meanwhile, continued Allied air strikes destroyed most of the invaders' ammunition and supplies. By September 1, the Japanese were forced to begin evacuating both landing sites after approximately half their troops had been either killed or wounded. By September 6, they had completely withdrawn from Milne Bay.

On October 22, General Douglas MacArthur dispatched some 800 Australians to retake Goodenough Island. The Australians landed at either end of the island and attacked the Japanese from two directions. The Japanese retreated, again suffering heavy casualties. On October 26, under cover of darkness, a submarine managed to evacuate the remaining Japanese troops—an indication of the tiny number of survivors. For the remainder of the war Goodenough Island served as an Allied air base. The battle in Milne Bay marked the first significant Allied land victory over the Japanese during the war, predating the far more celebrated Allied victory at Guadalcanal.

FURTHER READINGS

Costello, John. *The Pacific War* (1981).

Gailey, Harry A. *The War in the Pacific: From Pearl Harbor to Tokyo Bay* (1995).

Morrison, Samuel Eliot. "Breaking the Bismarck Barrier." *History of United States Naval Operations in World War II,* vol. 6 (1950).

Tom Lansford

SEE ALSO New Guinea

Greater East Asia Co-Prosperity Sphere

Japan is rich in people but poor in natural resources. Not until the Meiji Revolution in 1868 did the country embark on a path of Westernization and industrialization, abandoning its previous penchant for isolation. The new factories required raw materials and export markets, and so Japan joined in the efforts, through treaty rights, to carve up China into spheres of national influence. As a consequence of the Sino-Japanese War of 1894–1895, Korea and Formosa (Taiwan) became Japanese colonies. A decade later, Japan's search for raw materials collided with Russian interests and led to the Russo-Japanese War of 1904–1905, which resulted in a Japanese victory and extensive treaty rights to southern Manchuria. As a reward for joining the Allies during World War I Japan acquired League of Nations mandates over former German possessions: the Marshall, Caroline, and Mariana island groups.

On September 18, 1931, the Japanese Kwantung Army created the "Manchurian incident" with China as a justification to occupy Manchuria. The army set up a puppet government under the former Chinese emperor, Pu Yi, to administer the new country of "Manchukuo." Factions within Japan's army again pulled the country into war with the "Marco Polo Bridge incident" on July 7, 1937, which resulted in general warfare with China and the occupation of much of the Chinese coast. These aggressions provoked the United States into increasingly harsher responses to Japan until the Pacific war erupted after the attack at Pearl Harbor on December 7, 1941.

In the decades since the Pacific war, Japanese scholars have paid little attention to the ideology of the Greater East Asia Co-Prosperity Sphere, whereas before and dur-

ing the war there was a plethora of writing on the ideological goals of Japan in Asia. Two forerunners to the sphere were the East Asia Co-Operative Body and the New Order in East Asia, both of which concentrated on Manchuria. What gradually emerged was a strategy whereby an inner core of industry that was concentrated in Japan, northern Korea, Manchukuo, northern China, and Formosa would be fed by an outer core of resource regions and export markets, including the Dutch East Indies, the Philippines, Malaya, Indochina, Thailand (Siam), and Burma.

The Greater East Asia Co-Prosperity Sphere was not a master plan but rather an amalgamation of previous ideas under the pressures of war. As the war began to turn against Japan after the Battle of Midway, the political aspects of the sphere gained greater importance. An Imperial Conference on May 31, 1943, decided gradually to grant independence to the outlying regions so that their populations might be motivated more effectively to participate in the war effort. Burma was granted "independence" on August 1, 1943, as were the Philippines on October 14, 1943. These new "nations" were given only nominal independence, in that Japan reserved for itself certain economic and military privileges in them. Korea and Formosa, on the other hand, were considered part of Japan. Thailand—the only nation which was a Japanese ally rather than a conquest—was granted certain border areas in return for economic privileges. The Dutch East Indies were to remain a colony, although this changed as prospects for victory grew worse; plans to grant "independence" in September 1945 were cut short by Japan's surrender to the Allies.

It was not until November 1, 1943, that the Greater East Asia Ministry was set up, separate from the Foreign Ministry, the army, and the navy. This ministry conducted foreign relations within the sphere, while the Foreign Ministry conducted diplomacy outside the sphere—yet another indication that the sovereignty of those countries within the sphere fell into a "special" category. Even with the establishment of this ministry most of Southeast Asia remained under the direct administration of either the army or the navy: The army administered the Philippines, Malaya, Java, Sumatra, and Burma, while the navy administered the Celebes, the Moluccas, New Guinea, and the Bismarck Archipelago.

In November 1943, Japan brought representatives of its puppet governments to Tokyo for the Greater East Asia Conference. The Nanking government, Manchukuo, and Thailand were also represented. Japan was not yet ready to give even nominal recognition to Indonesia, and so Indonesian nationalist leader Sukarno was not invited.

This conference presented a belated justification for the Pacific war. Part of the Joint Declaration of the Greater East Asia Conference read:

> The United States of America and the British Empire have in seeking their own prosperity oppressed other nations and peoples. Especially in East Asia, they indulged in insatiable aggression and exploitation, and sought to satisfy their inordinate ambition of enslaving the entire region, and finally they came to menace seriously the stability of East Asia. Herein lies the cause of the present war.

(For some reason the French imperialists were not included in this bill of indictment.) Angered by this exploitation, the Japanese had risen up and repelled the Caucasian exploiters, "liberating their region from the yoke of British-American domination, and ensuring their self-existence and self-defense." The slogan "Asia for the Asiatics" neatly summed up the role of Japan as supposed liberator.

Although the Japanese insisted that the sphere was not an empire, they did feel racially superior to their fellow Asians. Along with Thailand, Japan was the only Asian nation which had not been colonized or defeated by the Western powers. The Japanese language was taught in the schools of the newly conquered territories, and new textbooks were introduced. The arrogance of some Japanese soldiers also served to turn the natives away from their propaganda. And, always serving as a grim reminder, there was the example of Japan's atrocious treatment of the Chinese. Within the new territories the economies were administered by the Japanese in ways that contributed to the war effort but not necessarily to the well-being of inhabitants. Military purchases were paid for in military scrip, which led to inflation later in the war. At least the former colonialists had paid in dollars, pounds, or francs for what they took out of the area.

Neglect by the Imperial Japanese Navy of convoy duty resulted in heavy loses of Japanese freighters and tankers to U.S. submarines. Thus the maritime sinews that were to bind the sphere to Japan were almost severed. Rice exports to Japan from Indochina, Thailand, and Burma were reduced from 1.4 million metric tons in 1942 to 74,000 tons in 1944. Iron ore from the Philippines dropped to a mere 10 percent of prewar levels. Of the 50 million barrels of oil produced in 1943, only 10 million barrels of crude and 5 million barrels of refined actually reached Japan. In 1944, those figures had dropped to 1.6 million barrels of crude and 3.3 million barrels of refined. This shortage of raw materials and fuel meant that Japa-

nese factories were idle or only partly productive and that new military pilots could receive only the most rudimentary training.

In the end, the sphere did not serve the purpose either of uniting East Asia against the Allies or of harnessing the region's economy to the Japanese war effort. By the end of the war, the economy of East Asia was devastated not only from war damage and the dislocation of markets but also from the effects of Japanese oversight, which was focused solely on the war effort.

Despite the eventual defeat of Japan, the Japanese occupation did speed the dissolution of the great European colonial empires—although the British, French, and Dutch were hardly aware of this development. In Vietnam a resistance movement under Ho Chi Minh was organized and bloodied against the Japanese occupiers. In Burma and Indonesia, local forces were trained and nationalist leaders were encouraged, leading directly to later independence movements. Although India was never occupied by Japan, the Indian National Army and the Free India Provisional Government helped inspire the Indian population on their quest for independence. Korea was liberated from Japanese occupation, and Formosa (Taiwan) was returned to Chinese control.

Overall, the utter failure of the Greater East Asia Co-Prosperity Sphere did serve to discredit Japanese imperialism. Since the war, Japan has demonstrated its conviction that the path to a sphere of economic influence and prosperity in East Asia is through trade and economic expansion, not military conquest.

FURTHER READINGS
Beasley, W. G. *Japanese Imperialism, 1894–1945* (1987).
Jones, F. C. *Japan's New Order in East Asia: Its Rise and Fall 1937–1945* (1954).
Lebra, Joyce C. *Japan's Greater East Asia Co-Prosperity Sphere in World War II* (1975).

John E. Moser

Grenades and Land Mines, Japanese

Two forms of infantry weapons—grenades and land mines—complemented the small arms used by Japanese army and naval landing forces in World War II. These forces employed numerous types of hand grenades, which generally ranged in weight from about 10 to 20 ounces. The Model 91 (1931) fragmentation hand grenade was identified by its black, serrated, cast-iron body; brass safety cover; and perforated base-propellant container. Its fuse had an 8- to 9-second burning time.

The Model 91 was thrown by hand or launched by means of a rifle adapter via a special tail assembly. Although it could also be launched by either the Model 10 (1921) or the Model 89 (1929) 50-mm grenade discharger via the base-propellant charge, the heavier Model 89 discharger was used almost exclusively. The Model 97 (1937) fragmentation hand grenade was almost identical to the Model 91 except that it had no base-propellant charge, so that it could not be launched or discharged, and it had a 4- to 5-second delay. The Model 97 was issued to all frontline Japanese troops and could also be employed as a booby trap.

The Model 99 Kiska (1939) hand grenade had a smooth cylindrical body with a flange at either end. This grenade was armed by removing the safety pin and striking the head of the fuse assembly against a hard object; the grenade was then immediately thrown, and it exploded in four to five seconds. The Model 99 was also launched by means of a rifle-type or cup-type Model 100 rifle adapter; when launched, it had a range of about 100 yards. The Model 23 grenade (year of origin unknown) was both thrown and used as a booby trap. It looked somewhat like the Model 97 but had lugs and rings attached to its side so it could be anchored in place. It was filled with granular TNT; its fuse was ignited by a pull string and had a 5-second delay.

The Japanese also used a high-explosive stick hand grenade with a "potato-masher" shape that had been used by German forces in World War I. It had a wooden handle and a metal cap, and its 4- to 5-second fuse was armed by removing the metal cap so that the pull ring inside the handle could be reached. Two forms of incendiary grenades also existed. One was a white-phosphorus-filled ½-kg grenade which was thrown or projected from the Model 89 discharger. The other was an incendiary stick hand grenade; it had curved rather than flat ends, which differentiated it from the high-explosive stick hand grenade. This grenade was filled with forty scatterable rubber pellets impregnated with a solution of phosphorus carbon disulphide. One variant had a phosphorus smoke filling. This grenade was armed by removing the safety pin and then striking the percussion cap against a hard surface.

The Japanese also employed a "Molotov cocktail" incendiary grenade filled with a mixture of oil and gasoline. This glass-bottle grenade had an impact-driven fusing device and exploded on contact. There was also a frangible smoke grenade, composed of a flat-bottomed, 3-inch-diameter glass flask filled with either titanium tetrachloride or a mixture of titanium and silicon tetrachloride. Also evident were two different types of frangible hydrocyanic acid grenades and a special hollow-charge antitank

grenade, based on the German model, utilizing a cup-type rifle adapter.

The Japanese military employed three basic types of land mines and a standardized type of Bangalore torpedo (described below). The Model 93 (1933) mine was called the "tape-measure mine" because it looked like the case of a tape measure. This pressure-sensitive mine was painted yellow or olive drab and weighed about 3 pounds. It was used for both antipersonnel and antitank purposes. The Model 99 (1939) armor-piercing mine was referred to as the "magnetic antitank bomb" or the "magnetic armor-piercing grenade." Four magnets were attached to this flat, disc-shaped mine, which allowed it to be placed onto a tank or against the iron door of a pillbox. These mines were filled with TNT and weighed 2 pounds, 11 ounces. They were usually coupled together for a penetrative effect of up to 1¼ inches of armor plate.

The Model 96 (1936) mine was used both on land and under water. It looked like the top half of a standard spherical naval mine, weighed about 106 pounds, and had two projecting lead-alloy contact horns. Detonation occurred as a result of pressure applied to either horn; the pressure crushed a glass vial of electrolytic fluid contained within the horn, which triggered a chemical electric fuse.

The Bangalore torpedo was olive drab in color and consisted of a common piece of 2-inch pipe, about 40 to 46 inches long, which was packed with TNT and cyclonite. Threaded ends on these 10-pound pipe bombs allowed for an indefinite number of them to be linked together. The Bangalore was activated by pulling a lanyard, which fired a friction primer, and was commonly used to destroy barbed-wire entanglements. One variant was filled with 6 pounds of picric acid and was employed as an antitank mine.

FURTHER READINGS

U.S. War Department. *Japanese Infantry Weapons,* Special Series, No. 19 (1943).

U.S. War Department. *Handbook on Japanese Military Forces,* TM-E 30-480 (1944, 1991).

Robert J. Bunker

SEE ALSO Army, Japanese

Grenades and Land Mines, U.S.

For U.S. Marine Corps and Army units, the hand grenade was one of the most useful weapons in the Pacific war. After the pin was pulled to release a safety mechanism, the grenade was detonated by a timed fuse. U.S. troops typically threw their grenades at enemy positions and in close-quarter combat. Grenades proved to be deadly weapons in jungles or caves, which were often the setting in the Pacific theater. In addition, grenades laid smoke, penetrated armor, or destroyed fortified emplacements. Because rifle grenades had a limited range of only 30 to 40 yards, launchers were added to modified rifles to increase their range to 250 yards.

U.S. soldiers and marines typically used three types of hand grenades. First, the fragmentation grenade had a cast-iron body which held an explosive TNT charge. When the grenade was detonated, small pieces of shrapnel, or "fragments," saturated the surrounding area. The MkII, otherwise known as the M2, was the most recognizable and widely used grenade in World War II. It looked like a pineapple, weighed 1.31 pounds, and had a 4- to 4.8-second fuse. When detonated, the M2A1 threw approximately a thousand pieces of shrapnel in a killing radius up to ten yards; however, fragments could be dangerous up to fifty yards.

Second, the M15 WP, or white-phosphorous, grenade had a cylindrical body made of sheet metal which was filled with white phosphorous. When detonated, the white phosphorous burned fiercely and created smoke. This grenade produced a smoke screen, harassed the enemy, and caused some casualties; in addition, fragments of the burning chemical were also thrown through the air and could cause more serious injuries. In a confined space, the grenade's smoke and fumes could also seriously injure an enemy soldier's eyes and respiratory system. The M15 WP grenade was particularly effective in assaulting Japanese-held caves or pillboxes. It weighed almost 2 pounds, had a 4 to 4.8-second fuse, and burned for fifty to sixty seconds in a blast radius of less than 30 yards. Nicknamed "Willie Pete," the M15 WP saw limited use in World War II yet acquired a loyal following among U.S. troops.

Third, the MkIIIA1 (M3A1) concussion grenade had a cylindrical body made of pressed fiber and contained TNT. It was employed in house-to-house fighting and against bunkers and pillboxes. Although initial models of the MkIIIA1 were designed to detonate on impact, later models employed the safer timed-fuse detonation. The blast disoriented the defenders and perhaps damaged the structure they were in. This grenade weighed about 14 ounces and had a 4 to 5-second fuse. The MkIIIA1 grenade saw limited use in World War II. When the goal was to cause a concussion, the simple demolition bag containing an explosive charge was more powerful and therefore more popular and more widely used.

For greater ranges of up to 250 yards, rifles were used to launch grenades. U.S. troops liked this option because

they could easily operate slightly modified standard weapons such as the Garand, Springfield 1903, and M1 carbine. In fact, many preferred the rifle grenade launcher over the bazooka. Rifle grenades required special ammunition that did not have the normal slug or bullet; instead, the cartridge contained only powder. When ignited, the powder burned and produced the expanding gas that launched the grenade at the end of the rifle's barrel at a velocity of approximately 200 feet per second. The barrel was fitted with an adapter which helped propel and aim the grenade. Impact, rather than a timed fuse, detonated the charge. The U.S. Army developed special rifle grenades including the M9A1 antitank grenade, the M17 fragmentation grenade, and the M19 white-phosphorous grenade. Of these, the M9A1 grenade could penetrate 4 inches of armor—almost equal to a bazooka's penetration. In weight and blast radius, other rifle grenades had specifications similar to hand grenades.

In addition to grenades, U.S. forces also used land mines to defend a position quickly and cheaply. Land mines fell into two categories: antipersonnel and antivehicle. Antipersonnel land mines were buried under a few inches of soil and contained less than a pound of explosives that was detonated by light pressure or a trip wire. The antivehicle land mine contained from 3 to 22 pounds of explosives and was detonated by more than 300 pounds of pressure. After detonation, a land mine's explosive charge exploded upward—killing the soldier who had stepped on it or disabling the vehicle which had driven over it.

FURTHER READINGS

Canfield, Bruce N. *U.S. Infantry Weapons of World War II* (1994).

Forty, George. *U.S. Army Handbook, 1939–1945*, 2d ed. (1995).

Rottman, Gordon L. *U.S. Marine Corps World War II Divisions, Brigades, and Regiments* (1995).

Sledge, E. B. *With the Old Breed at Peleliu and Okinawa* (1981).

Thompson, Henry C., and Lida Mayo. *The Ordnance Department: Procurement and Supply* (1960).

David Ulbrich

SEE ALSO Army Ground Forces, U.S.; Marine Corps, U.S.

Guadalcanal, Battle for

The Imperial Japanese Navy took possession of Guadalcanal Island on June 8, 1942, during the advance to the south—part of their plan to expand their defense perimeter. They planned to build an airstrip on Guadalcanal to safeguard their major air base at Rabual and to provide a springboard for expansion farther south. A convoy of twelve ships arrived on July 6 and landed the navy's 11th and 13th Construction Units, which were strong in manpower but weak in vehicles and construction equipment. The units set to work to build a tamped coral airstrip. This advance imperiled Australia and the lines of communications back to the United States. If the Japanese continued past the Solomon Islands, their aircraft might drive U.S. shipping into an intolerable detour.

The Japanese did not consider Guadalcanal and the nearby island of Tulagi exceptionally important. Their eyes were fixed on the New Guinea campaign. Although they began to construct the airfield on Guadalcanal, and although the first aircraft were expected to arrive on August 16, no one knew where the aircraft to use the field would come from. Nor were many Japanese concerned that the United States would descend on the area. Common wisdom at imperial general headquarters was that the Americans could not launch an offensive until 1943. Common wisdom was wrong.

The United States, too, was looking at the Solomons. The public would not condone idleness in the Pacific, and Chief of Naval Operations Admiral Ernest J. King was determined to embark on operations in the southwest Pacific even if he had to do it without army troops. He wanted to preempt enemy moves into the Solomons. Airfields and the question of sufficient air power overshadowed all other planning considerations. King's uncompromising will drove the Guadalcanal plan into a reality despite logistical and air-support shortcomings. The Americans planned a step-by-step offensive. Land-based aircraft would cover each landing. But first the Americans needed an initial lodgement, and they would have to gain and maintain aerial superiority over any amphibious landing area.

King had his own landing force: Major General Alexander A. Vandegrift's 1st Marine Division, made up of high-caliber youngsters led by a small number of "the old breed." There were insufficient transports to carry the full division, so officers stripped out 75 percent of the division's heavy vehicles and everything else they thought could be left behind. All this gear was scheduled to follow. U.S. military planners disagreed on how long aircraft carriers would stay in harm's way to support the landing. As noted, air power was central to all plans. Rear Admiral Frank J. Fletcher, the Expeditionary Force commander, finally agreed to stay three days.

August 7 saw U.S. warships and transports standing off north-central Guadalcanal. The invasion convoy had achieved complete tactical surprise, in part because heavy clouds and rain obscured the ships during the run into the beaches. Even more important was the complete strategic surprise. The Japanese had not foreseen this landing, nor did they immediately realize its significance.

Five infantry battalions landed on Guadalcanal without opposition, for the Japanese navy's construction units had fled. Movement into the jungles went slowly. The men were cautious, the jungles intimidating. The marines experienced serious difficulties unloading cargo. The 300-man naval shore party was completely inadequate to hoist supplies out of small boats and move them ashore. Transports put their cargoes into boats faster than the shore party could unload them at the beach. So chaotic did the situation become that unloading was postponed early the next morning.

Japanese naval air forces reacted swiftly to the landing—too swiftly, as it turned out. The 11th Air Fleet's Rabaul-based 25th Air Flotilla launched an attack the day of the landing with twenty-seven twin-engined Bettys. Eighteen Zeros from the veteran Tainan Air Group escorted them. There were big problems with this attack. The range from Rabaul to Guadalcanal would stretch the endurance of the navy Zeros, even with belly tanks. Shorter-range army Zeros could not make the trip. The bombers could cover the distance, but they had been loaded with bombs for a mission against Milne Bay on New Guinea; rather than rearm with torpedoes to strike ships, they took off with bombs.

Nine fixed-landing-gear Val dive-bombers also took off, but they were too short-ranged to make a round trip. Nor did Japanese planners synchronize the Val attack with the high-flying Bettys. They told Val pilots to either ditch next to a destroyer or flying-boat ditching station or to reach the crude Buka airstrip on northern Bougainville Island. The haste with which the Japanese launched the aircraft typified all their subsequent actions.

The Bettys arrived at 1315 hours to find the U.S. transports (warned by Australian Coastwatchers) under way and the F4F carrier-borne Wildcats ready to intercept. Not a single Japanese bomb hit the twisting ships. The Japanese lost three Bettys shot down and two so badly damaged that they ditched or crash-landed. When the nine unescorted Vals arrived, they hit a destroyer with one bomb at the cost of five Vals shot down and the remaining four ditching on the return flight. Twelve U.S. aircraft were lost, and although no transports had been hit, the raids had disrupted unloading for three hours.

The Japanese attacked again on August 8 with twenty-three torpedo-laden Bettys escorted by fifteen Zeros. Their principal target had been the three U.S. carriers supporting the landing. But reconnaissance aircraft could not find the carriers, so the Japanese struck at the landing. They came in low, only to be met by tremendous anti-aircraft fire from U.S. warships and transports, which downed two Zeros and all but five of the twenty-three vulnerable Bettys. The only positive result for Japan of this grievous aerial loss was one U.S. destroyer damaged and one transport sunk. Such an aircraft loss rate is utterly insupportable for any armed force, and it was especially so for resource-poor Japan.

The Japanese navy, much like the army, sometimes lost sight of its objective. After sinking three U.S. and one Australian heavy cruiser the night of August 8–9, Vice Admiral Gunichi Mikawa could have sailed into the transport area and written finis to the entire U.S. operation. His ostensible mission had been to do just that, but he declined to do so, partly out of concern that U.S. carrier aircraft might catch him in the morning if he stayed to do the job (the carriers were actually out of range). Then, on August 9, the 25th Air Flotilla chose to expend its punch against a crippled U.S. "battleship" rather than against transports still unloading off Guadalcanal's beaches. So the Japanese wasted two chances to hit the transports.

The hurried departure of U.S. transports on August 9 with much of the 1st Marine Division's gear, supplies, and even many of its men left those ashore in a precarious position. The marines immediately exploited abandoned Japanese supplies. They also hauled the supplies that the U.S. transports had landed into the jungle and dispersed them. Marine fighting strength consisted of just five infantry battalions, three field artillery battalions (two of 75-mm pack howitzers and one of 105-mm howitzers), and the 3d Marine Defense Battalion.

On August 15, four U.S. destroyer-transports arrived with food, ammunition, and equipment for the air base. News also arrived that aircraft were expected to arrive on August 18 or 19. Also on August 15, Japanese aircraft dropped woven baskets of food to their men; a note inside read that help was on the way. On August 16, a Japanese destroyer arrived at Tassafaranga Point with 113 men of the 5th Yokosuka Special Naval Landing Force. The race to put reinforcements ashore had begun. August 20 was a great day for the U.S. Marines: Their first aircraft arrived on the field. Nineteen F4F Wildcats and twelve SBD-3 dive-bombers took up residence.

The Japanese Seventeenth Army at Rabaul had responsibility for army operations on Guadalcanal. Seventeenth Army examined the lack of U.S. aerial activity at the field (before August 20) and the absence of U.S. surface forces at sea and determined that the Americans had launched a reconnaissance in force or had, in fact, withdrawn. Japanese army commanders at Rabaul were dazzled by their own optimism, did not understand how quickly the jungle and disease could kill, misjudged the terrain, and underestimated their enemy, both in actual numbers and in military prowess. Everyone was anxious to attack. Staff work was sloppy, especially concerning logistics. Moving men on warships to Guadalcanal was quicker, easier, and safer than transporting bulky supplies and heavy equipment on vulnerable, slow transports, so only light combat troops were dispatched.

The first Japanese army troops to land were the Ichiki Detachment, the 28th Infantry led by Colonel Kiyono Ichiki. Ichiki's mission was to capture the airfield. If he could not do that, he was to await reinforcements. Ichiki disembarked from destroyers early on August 19 with 900 men—the lead elements of his regiment. More than half of his men were scheduled to follow. Ichiki believed, as did most Japanese army officers, that a night attack with cold steel could defeat an enemy. And he would try it with the men he had on hand. His soldiers carried but 250 rounds per man and seven days' rations.

Ichiki's men attacked the night of August 20–21 in what would be known as the Battle of the Tenaru River. They launched a night attack in hardly more than battalion strength and were crushed by U.S. Marine fire. The marines counterattacked at daylight in a handsome maneuver that annihilated the surviving Japanese; 767 Japanese died.

The quick demise of Ichiki's men should have warned the Japanese that taking Guadalcanal might be more difficult than they had figured. Yet Ichiki's attack and those that followed were consistent with Japanese doctrine and, in fact, illustrated the only way they could fight. The Japanese had to believe that their enemies were weak, unskilled, and lacking in determination. Shock action by light infantry can prevail when meeting such an enemy. But if it turned out that the Americans were strong, skilled, and determined, then their use of superior firepower and materiel meant that Japan would lose the war.

Japan's air operations were not going much better than its operations on the ground. Even at the major base of Rabaul, Japanese airmen found it exceedingly difficult to bring in the ground crews and equipment needed to support their aircraft. Regular attacks on Rabaul by General Douglas MacArthur's aircraft added to losses and damage. The long round trip from Rabaul to Guadalcanal tired fliers and wore out aircraft. It also meant that Japanese aircraft always arrived between 1130 hours and 1430 hours, giving their attacks a predictability that helped the Americans immensely. Japan needed better bases for its air war. Planners decided to construct a base at Buin, on the southeast tip of Bougainville. But the ground was soggy, the Japanese lacked adequate airfield construction capability, and work progressed slowly.

The next significant Japanese army ground effort was launched by Major General Kiyotake Kawaguchi's 35th Brigade. It left Truk Island in the Carolines on August 24. U.S. Marine aircraft from Henderson Field attacked four destroyers carrying a battalion of 600 men; they sank one destroyer, crippled one, and damaged one. A second echelon of three destroyers turned about and headed for safety. Yet the Japanese were persistent, and destroyers put 450 men of the 1st Battalion, 124th Infantry, and 300 men of Ichiki's Second Echelon ashore the night of August 29. Two nights later, General Kawaguchi arrived with 1,200 men on eight destroyers.

The Japanese would never solve their reinforcement and supply problems. Their aircraft could not provide adequate cover to slow transports or to daylight efforts. U.S. dive-bombers from Guadalcanal forced the Japanese to abandon large transports and use fast destroyers. A destroyer's speed allowed it to quickly land men and escape north, out of range, before daylight. But destroyers made bad transports. They had no materiel-handling equipment; they were not designed to carry equipment, vehicles, and artillery; and deck cargo encumbered their ability to fight.

Even so, the "Tokyo Express" sufficed for a while and at times prevailed. On the night of September 4–5, for instance, one light cruiser and eleven destroyers delivered 1,000 men of the 2d Battalion, 4th Infantry, and the rest of Ichiki's Second Echelon. As a bonus, the Japanese sank two U.S. destroyer-transports. Other means of reinforcement were more dangerous. U.S. SBD dive-bombers broke up an attempt to ferry men on sixty-one barges between September 3 and 5 and inflicted heavy casualties.

Major Kawaguchi was now on Guadalcanal and made his plans. He had the 2d Battalion, 124th Infantry, on the west side of the U.S. Marine perimeter. East of the perimeter, Kawaguchi's four other battalions (1/124, 3/124, 2/4, and Ichiki's Second Echelon) included a small number of artillery, engineers, antitank guns, etc., and totaled roughly 5,200 men. Kawaguchi believed that this force would be enough. Japanese intelligence told him that only 2,000 Americans were on the island, and he turned down another battalion offered by the Seventeenth Army. Few Japanese officers yet appreciated the deadliness of U.S. firepower.

Kawaguchi planned to hack through Guadalcanal's jungle and attack from the south. Hardly 2,500 yards south of Henderson Field lay a low ridgeline that gave easy access to the field. Here stood a composite battalion of marine raiders and paratroopers, about 840 men. Kawaguchi's men would carry only two days' rations, for they expected to eat captured American food. Kawaguchi had planned to attack the night of September 12–13, but the jungle so scattered, slowed, and exhausted his men that he had not gotten everyone into position. The Japanese attack during the night of September 12–13, which was supported by a light cruiser and destroyers firing into targets near the ridge, misfired and bogged down in swampy jungle.

The next night (September 13–14), three battalions of Japanese infantry prepared to try again. Supported by heavy mortar fire, two battalions swarmed up the ridge, but the third battalion was so poorly led that it failed to enter the fight. Marine artillery and infantry repulsed the determined Japanese and killed 500 during a hellishly long and brutal night. The terrain feature over which they fought became known as Bloody Ridge. A small supporting attack by the Japanese farther east came to naught, and an uncoordinated western attack the next night also failed.

Although the Japanese decided on September 16 to dispatch the 2d Division and part of the 38th Division to Guadalcanal, and although new air units massed at Rabaul, the Americans were winning the reinforcement race. On September 18, the 7th Marines arrived with all their equipment, weapons, ammunition, and supplies. The 1st Marine Division now had 19,251 men on Guadalcanal. General Vandegrift felt more secure with these men ashore, and he believed that an active defense was in order. He had ten battalions of infantry on Guadalcanal as well as a raider battalion, four battalions of field artillery, the marine defense battalion, and two light tank companies. In late September, Vandegrift sent three battalions against Japanese positions on the west flank of the perimeter. But the operation went poorly and cost the marines numerous casualties.

Vandegrift launched a second try, at the Matanikau River on October 7. This time he used six battalions with air and artillery support. Three battalions abreast on a narrow front rolled into the Japanese 4th Infantry—itself preparing to attack—hit them with small arms and artillery, and scattered them. The Japanese lost nearly seven hundred men. The marines were now convinced that they could strike out at and defeat the enemy on his own ground.

The Japanese set about organizing another attack. Ichiki's detachment had failed. Kawaguchi's brigade had failed. This time it would be Lieutenant General Masao Maruyama's 2d Division, brought in by transports and destroyers of the Tokyo Express. Lieutenant General Harukichi Hyakutake and the Seventeenth Army staff also arrived. American strength had grown to 23,000 men, and so the Japanese would be attacking with extremely low force ratios. The Japanese could mass at the point of their attack, but the U.S. Marines could maneuver reserves using interior lines to that same point. A supporting attack in the west along the Matanikau River the night of October 23 boiled up against marine lines. Once again, marine antitank, artillery, and small-arms fire smashed the attack. And for the Japanese, the supporting attack was a complete waste; the main attack itself had fallen behind schedule.

Early the morning of October 25, nine battalions of Japanese infantry assembled south of Bloody Ridge. The inadequate trail the Japanese had hacked through 30 miles of jungle had claimed almost all their artillery and mortars. There had been no farms or towns to pillage, and the men were exhausted, hungry, and even delusional. More than half the foot soldiers were lost and would not enter the battle.

Once again, it would be an unsupported, piecemeal attack—spirit against steel. Once again, screaming Japanese infantry running forward in a night attack proved no match to dug-in marines reinforced by U.S. Army infantry and supported by artillery. Japan's 29th Infantry lost nearly three hundred men on or within marine lines, while many more perished from U.S. artillery and mortars. Entirely unable to react to this disaster and plan something different, the Japanese resumed the battle in the same place the following night. Once again, half the attacking force missed the battle; they reacted to a phantom threat to their flank and went onto the defensive. U.S. Army and Marine troops vanquished the remainder of the 2d Division who did attack.

On November 1, General Vandegrift sent the 5th Marines and a composite group west across the Matanikau River, while naval vessels and army and navy aircraft struck at Japanese positions. The next day, the Tokyo Express landed another 1,500 men east of the perimeter. U.S. Army and Marine troops attacked and mauled the eastern landing. The Japanese had planned to land the rest of the 38th Division and its heavy equipment by large transports.

Elements of the 38th Division continued to arrive. November 7 saw 1,300 Japanese land, and another 600 came ashore on the night of November 11. The 51st Division and the 21st Independent Mixed Brigade were alerted for movement to Guadalcanal. But American reinforcements were overtaking anything the Japanese could bring in. On November 12, another U.S. Army regiment, U.S. Marine aviation engineers, and U.S. Marine air-wing personnel landed. Not a man or an ounce of supplies was lost.

The battleship-cruiser action ("The Battle of Friday the 13th") and the battleship action the night of November 14–15 stopped Japanese warships from bombarding Henderson Field. When the major Japanese transport effort carrying elements of the 38th Division (eleven transports, 7,000 men, supplies for 30,000 men for twenty days, 31,500 artillery shells) arrived within range of Henderson Field on November 14, repeated air attacks from the undamaged field and from USS *Enterprise* sank six transports and a heavy cruiser. The Japanese pressed on with the remaining transports and escorts. Four transports reached the island and beached. Although 2,000 Japanese got ashore, Henderson Field's army and marine fliers, army and marine artillery, and a U.S. destroyer pounded the ships as well as heavy equipment and supplies that had been landed. It was the death knell of Japanese hopes.

Here was the critical problem: The Japanese could not sustain a long, drawn-out campaign, so they had to succeed in their "first" attack. Because they "would succeed," they concluded that they did not need to deploy the logistics necessary for a long campaign. Soldiers launched frontal attacks because they did not have equipment and supplies for more sophisticated tactics or for lengthy fights. Troops manpacked their artillery. The trails they cut toward Henderson Field were too steep and narrow for heavy artillery, and even mountain guns had to be left behind. There were no medical units, no kitchens, and no transportation. Soldiers had little food, no change of clothes, and virtually no supplies.

Japan's Seventeenth Army needed 200 tons of provisions a day in late October to support its peak strength of 30,000 men—or at least five destroyer-transports a day simply to sustain the forces on hand. A buildup would require more. The Seventeenth Army staff calculated that Guadalcanal needed forty-two transports and a hundred destroyer loads in addition to the roughly six destroyers that were actually arriving every three days. Only 20 percent of supplies dispatched from Rabaul were actually reaching Guadalcanal.

By the end of November, the Japanese supply situation had become disastrous. They cut rations to one-sixth normal for frontline troops and to one-tenth for others. Japanese soldiers suffered so badly that men literally starved to death. Disease ran untreated through the ranks. Guadalcanal earned its Japanese nickname of "Starvation Island." Floating supplies from destroyers to shore proved too slow. So the Japanese used destroyers to drop large, sealed, roped-together metal drums filled with rice and barley, which boats and swimmers would tow to shore. At worst, perhaps the drums would float to shore.

Twenty-five thousand Japanese troops were depending on destroyer drops, and the drums were not enough, especially since U.S. aircraft and PT boats were becoming more effective in harassing and even blocking those efforts. As December opened, U.S. air strength had risen to 188 aircraft, Henderson Field was building more and more steel-matted runways, and shellings of the field by Japanese warships and long-range artillery had ceased.

December brought a major decision from the Japanese. Guadalcanal would be evacuated. The Japanese navy could no longer expend its ships to supply the garrison. Although army troops (50,000 at Rabaul alone) might continue the attacks against Henderson Field, the navy could not get them there or sustain them. The decision to evacuate the garrison was a shocking admission by Japan that it had lost the costly air, sea, and ground conflict in and around Guadalcanal. The great, heady conquests of 1941–1942 had ended.

The 1st Marine Division was leaving, to be replaced by the army's Americal Division. Army Major General Alexander M. Patch took command when General Vandegrift departed. Patch also had two marine regiments of the 2d Marine Division as well as another army regiment. By January 4, 1943, the entire 25th Division was ashore, as were the rest of the 2d Marine Division. Food, medicine, and ammunition were arriving in increasing quantities. An army corps headquarters, the XIV, arrived to control the three divisions. The first corps-level operation was about to begin.

U.S. attacks out of the perimeter in January met stubborn, deadly resistance. Yet marine and army troops killed hundreds of Japanese and pressed westward along Guadalcanal's northern coast. The Japanese used destroyers to evacuate the surviving 11,706 men. The last destroyer pickup occurred the night of February 7–8.

The battle for Guadalcanal offered ominous portents to the Japanese. The army found that it could not defeat the despised Americans and that its doctrine was fatally flawed. Spirit, advanced infantry tactics, and cultural superiority over steel had failed. Two-thirds (20,800) of the Japanese who set foot on Guadalcanal died. Japan's air forces found that they lacked air bases and base support, trained pilots, and sufficient numbers of aircraft. They had no strategic bombers like the B-17 and B-24 with which to interdict American logistics and suppress distant air bases.

Even worse, U.S. fighter aircraft had matched and exceeded the Zero's performance. Japanese naval air forces had been badly bled. Highly trained crews had died, and Japan's training base could not make good the losses. The Imperial Japanese Navy's string of night-surface victories had been broken as the U.S. Navy learned its trade. The Americans had wrested their first conquest from Japanese hands. Losing Guadalcanal was not just a local defeat; it carried the most serious implications, and the Japanese could not see how to reverse the situation. U.S. forces would only grow stronger. Japan would only weaken. No one could see how to counter the American approach to war—that of mass, firepower, and mechanization.

Both sides at Guadalcanal had been presented with numerous opportunities to win or lose the campaign. Each operational and tactical decision had resonated with significance. Before this campaign, the Imperial Japanese Army had been invincible. During and after it, the army lost every engagement it fought. Lessons learned—especially the absolute necessity of air, engineer, and logistical support—served the Americans through the rest of the war. The Japanese, with their totally inadequate industrial base, benefited little from what they learned.

Japan lost the war when it lost Guadalcanal. Unfortunately for all concerned, Japanese leaders refused to recognize that fact. The war would grind on for nearly three more years.

FURTHER READINGS

Coggins, Jack. *The Campaign for Guadalcanal* (1972).

Craven, Wesley F., and James L. Cate. *The Army Air Forces in World War II*, vol. 4, *The Pacific: Guadalcanal to Saipan August 1942 to July 1944* (1950).

Frank, Richard B. *Guadalcanal* (1990).

Miller, John. *United States Army in World War II. The War in the Pacific. Guadalcanal: The First Offensive* (1949).

Tregaskis, Richard. *Guadalcanal Diary* (1943).

John W. Whitman

SEE ALSO Army, Japanese; Navy, U.S.; Savo Island, Battle of

Gurkhas

Many professional soldiers have for years considered the Gurkhas the best infantrymen in the world. Even before World War II the tough but small mountain farmers from Nepal had earned a well-deserved reputation for discipline, intelligence, and loyalty. No other soldier in the history of the British army has been more respected by his officers and more feared by his enemies than "Johnny Gurkha."

The British and the Gurkhas first met, as enemies, in 1814. Over the course of two campaigns that ended in stalemate, the two sides developed a strong mutual respect, concluding that in the future it would be wiser to fight on the same side. In 1816 Lieutenant Frederick Young raised the first Gurkha regiment for the East India Company, and the Gurkhas have remained loyal to the British ever since—most significantly during the Indian Mutiny of 1857.

Although Nepal never was part of the British raj, the soldiers of the Gurkha Brigade fought for Great Britain in World War I in France and Flanders, Mesopotamia, Persia, Egypt, Gallipoli, Salonca, and Palestine. In 1915 the first Gurkha soldier earned the Victoria Cross. By the end of the war the Gurkhas—and especially their famous weapon, the *kukri*, a short, curved sword—had developed a notorious reputation among German and Turkish troops.

Even as early as the Munich Crisis in 1938, the maharajah of Nepal offered assistance to Great Britain in the form of more Gurkha units. But the appeasement-minded government of Prime Minister Neville Chamberlain politely declined the offer.

When the war actually started, the maharajah renewed his offer, and for some incomprehensible reason it again was refused. Finally, in 1940, the British government ordered its minister in Nepal to request permission to raise ten additional battalions and for Gurkhas to serve overseas. The maharajah, for his part, never could understand why the British had waited so long.

In 1939 there were ten Gurkha regiments of two battalions each serving in the Indian army. Initially, each regiment expanded to four battalions. By the end of the war, fifty-five Gurkha battalions were in service. This represented some 250,000 troops out of a total Nepalese population of only 8 million.

The 1st Gurkha Rifles served in Burma. The 2d Gurkhas served in Burma, Persia, Italy, Greece, Malaya, and North Africa. The 3d, 4th, 5th, and 6th Gurkhas had battalions in both Burma and Italy. The 1st Battalion, 7th Gurkhas, fought in Burma; the 2d Battalion fought in North Africa. As in World War I, the 2d Battalion, 7th Gurkhas, were captured and later reconstituted; the new 2/7th served in Syria, Lebanon, Palestine, and Italy. The 8th Gurkhas had battalions in Burma and Italy. The 10th Gurkhas had battalions in Syria, Iraq, Italy, Palestine, and Burma.

Two new regiments were raised during the war. In order to achieve efficiencies of scale in instruction, training battalions were formed to provide replacements for pairs of rifle regiments. Thus, the 14th Gurkha Rifles provided replacements for the 1st and 4th Gurkhas; the 29th Gurkha Rifles, for the 2d and 9th regiments; the 38th Gurkha Rifles, for the 3d and 8th; the 56th, for the 5th and 6th; and the 710th, for the 7th and 10th.

The Gurkha regiments had such a good reputation that regular British officers competed fiercely for assignment to these units. Before the war, all such officers were required first to achieve proficiency in Gurkhali. With the rapid expansion of the wartime British military, many emergency commissioned officers (ECOs) were assigned to Gurkha units. Language turned out to be a major handicap for these ECOs—most of whom had never been east of Suez.

Nonetheless, more than one British officer made advantageous use of his knowledge of Gurkhali. During the retreat from Burma, the commander of I Burma Corps, Major General (later Field Marshal) William Slim and both of his subordinate division commanders were former Gurkha officers. Although the Japanese routinely tapped the British field-phone lines, the three generals communicated in Gurkhali. Many Japanese understood English, but almost none could translate Gurkhali.

In the Gurkha units themselves, the critical connecting link between the British officers and the senior Gurkha noncommissioned officers (NCOs) were the Gurkha officers. As viceroy's commissioned officers (VCOs), they held their commissions from the viceroy of India rather than from the British king-emperor. Using Indian army rank titles, the highest of these VCOs was a *subadar* major, the equivalent of a major. A Gurkha *subadar* was a captain, and a *jemadar* was a lieutenant. In the enlisted ranks, a *havildar* major was a sergeant major; a *havildar*, a sergeant; a *naik*, a corporal; and a lance *naik*, a lance corporal.

Through no fault of their own, Gurkha units suffered some major losses in 1942. When Singapore surrendered to a Japanese force inferior only in numbers that February, the entire 2d Battalion of the 2d Gurkhas were among the almost 138,000 British prisoners taken. The unlucky 2d Battalions of the 5th and 7th Gurkhas also were captured with the fall of Tobruk, in North Africa, on June 21 of that same year.

But for the rest of the war, the Gurkhas made a significant contribution to the Allied effort in Italy. Battalions from eight Gurkha regiments fought there as part of the British Eighth Army, with three Gurkha soldiers earning the Victoria Cross. During the fighting for the Gustav Line the 1st Battalion, the Gurkha Rifles, particularly distinguished themselves by hanging on for sixteen days to a position appropriately known as Hangman's Hill. After the fight, only eight officers and 177 soldiers survived out of nearly a thousand.

More Gurkha battalions served in Burma than in all other theaters combined. During the retreat from Burma, four Gurkha battalions were savaged in February 1942 while trying to withdraw across the Sittang River. By the time they made it across the river, the combined survivors of the 1/7th, 3/7th, 1/3d, and 2/5th Gurkhas did not even equal one full-strength battalion.

The 3/2d and 3/6th Gurkhas took part in both of Major General Orde Wingate's first and second Chindit expeditions, while the 3/4th and 4/10th Gurkhas also participated in the second. All were wartime-raised units. Wingate specifically selected the newly raised battalions because he thought they could more easily be trained in accordance with his own peculiar form of operations. But Wingate had misread his Gurkha units and failed to use them to the best advantage. He did not keep the Gurkha battalions together as whole units. Apparently ignoring the fact that most Gurkhas spoke little English, Wingate had the battalions broken up into smaller subunits that were mixed with British units, under officers who spoke little or no Gurkhali. Many of the new and inexperienced recruits, some of whom were only 16 or 17 years of age, were assigned as mule skinners—under the assumption that all Nepalese knew how to handle mules. They did not.

The results were not good, and Wingate was the only British officer in more than 130 years to criticize the Gurkhas. He claimed they were mentally unsuited for the Chindit role of deep penetration and guerrilla warfare. This was totally false, because the Gurkha soldier had a natural skill as a tracker and an ability to move through the jungle with a silence and patience far beyond the capabilities of the Japanese. The Gurkha record in guerrilla and counterguerrilla operations since 1948 proves just how far off the mark the eccentric and opinionated Wingate was on this point.

As the war progressed, the Fourteenth Army under Slim eventually prevailed and pushed the Japanese out of Burma. Several Gurkha battalions were under the Fourteenth Army—which called itself, with perverse pride, "The Forgotten Army." Slim did not make Wingate's mistakes in employing his Gurkha units. The decisive battles of the Burma campaign were fought at Imphal and Kohima—where the 2/5th Gurkhas lost almost eight hundred of its own.

When the war ended, the wartime Gurkha units were disbanded as quickly as they had been raised. The tiny kingdom of Nepal paid a high price for supporting its British ally. A total of 7,544 Gurkha soldiers were killed in action or died of wounds or disease, while another 1,441 were listed as missing and presumed dead. An additional 23,655 Gurkhas were severely wounded—amounting to an overall casualty rate of a most heavy 13 percent. On the other hand, Gurkhas won some 2,734 decorations for gallantry, including ten Victoria Crosses (seven in Burma) out of the total of 178 awarded throughout World War II.

When India gained its independence from Great Britain in 1947, the New Indian Army and the British army divided the Gurkha regiments. Six regiments remained with the Indian army, and four transferred to the British army. In January 1948, these four—the 2d, 6th, 7th, and 10th Gurkhas Rifles—sailed for a new home in Malaya. In subsequent years, the Gurkhas provided the backbone for Great Britain's successful campaigns in Malaya and Borneo and patrolled the border between Hong Kong and China. More recently, a battalion of the 7th Duke of Endinburgh's Own Gurkha Rifles fought in the 1982 Falklands campaign.

The motto of the Gurkhas is "Better to die than live a coward." Sir William Slim once said of them, "The Almighty created in the Gurkha an ideal infantryman . . . brave, tough, patient, adaptable and skilled in fieldcraft." Unfortunately, with the return of Hong Kong to China in 1997, the future of the Gurkha regiments in the British forces remains in question.

FURTHER READINGS

Byron, Farwell. *The Gurkhas* (1984).
Masters, John. *Road Past Mandalay* (1965).
Smith, E. D. *Britain's Brigade of Gurkhas* (1973).
———. *Johnny Gurkha: Friends in the Hills* (1985).

David T. Zabecki

SEE ALSO India

H

Halsey, William Frederick, Jr. (1882–1959)

U.S. fleet admiral and Third Fleet commander in World War II. William "Bull" Halsey, the son of a naval captain, attended the U.S. Naval Academy on an at-large presidential appointment. After graduating in 1904 and being commissioned an ensign in February 1906, he participated in the global cruise of the "Great White Fleet" (1907–1909) and was promoted to lieutenant upon his return. In 1909, Halsey began a twenty-three-year tour in torpedo warfare and escort duties when he took command of torpedo boat *Dupont*. Between 1909 and 1916 he commanded several destroyers and participated in the U.S. punitive expedition into Mexico, following raids into the United States by Pancho Villa and his men (1916) before being posted to the executive department of the U.S. Naval Academy.

During World War I, Halsey, a lieutenant commander, participated in antisubmarine escort duty and commanded a series of destroyers (*Duncan, Benham,* and *Shaw*). He never sighted an enemy submarine, however.

Halsey held postwar commands aboard destroyers *Chauncy, John Francis Burnes, Wickes, Dale,* and *Osborne*. He also saw duty at the Office of Naval Intelligence (1921–1922) and as naval attaché in Germany (1922–1924) and, concurrently, Norway, Denmark, and Sweden (1923–1924). Promoted to captain in 1927, Halsey became enamored of naval aviation but failed to meet the vision standards required for flight training. He then commanded Destroyer Squadron 14 (1930–1932) and attended the Navy War College (1930–1932) and the Army War Colleges (1932–1933).

In 1935 Halsey's career path changed when he was certified as a naval aviator at the age of 52. He subsequently commanded aircraft carrier *Saratoga* (1935–1937) and Pensacola Naval Air Station. Promoted to rear admiral in March 1938, Halsey became commander of Carrier Division 2 on board carrier *Yorktown,* and from 1939 to 1940 he commanded Carrier Division 1 on board *Saratoga*. At the outbreak of World War II, Halsey, who had been promoted to vice admiral in June 1940, was senior carrier captain in the Pacific and served as commander Aircraft Battle Force and commander Carrier Division 2. During the Japanese attack on the U.S. naval base at Pearl Harbor, Hawaii, in December 1941, Halsey's carriers were at sea and thus escaped damage. In early 1942 Halsey, as commander of carriers, Pacific Fleet, and of Task Force 16, led attacks on the Marshall, Gilbert, Wake, and Marcus islands. James Doolittle's raid on Tokyo in April 1942 was launched from *Hornet,* then under Halsey's command. Halsey did not participate in the Battle of Midway in June 1942 because of illness but returned to lead the U.S. South Pacific Force to victories at Guadalcanal and Santa Cruz in October and November 1942. He was promoted to admiral in the latter month.

After the Japanese were driven from Guadalcanal in February 1943, Halsey led the offensive against the Solomon Islands throughout 1943 and 1944, including the capture of New Georgia, Vella Lavella, and Bougainville. Other Japanese-held islands were bypassed, including the stronghold at Rabaul on New Britain, which was effectively surrounded and neutralized with superior airpower.

In June 1944 Halsey was appointed commander of Third Fleet. Throughout the remainder of the major campaigns of the war in the Pacific, he collaborated with Admiral Raymond A. Spruance as head of the Pacific Fleet—one planning while the other fought. In August 1944 Halsey's Third Fleet provided cover for landings in the Palau Islands. In September he began air attacks on the Philippines in preparation for the upcoming invasion. Upon discovering that Japanese forces were weaker than had been surmised, Halsey successfully urged that the landings on Leyte be moved forward to October 20. Halsey's Third Fleet provided cover for the assault forces. Shortly after the landing the Japanese fleet sortied out to fight, using a plan which played upon Halsey's natural aggressiveness. At the Battle of Leyte Gulf, the Japanese used a large decoy force of planeless carriers to draw Halsey to the north while other Japanese surface ships slipped in to attack the landing forces. Halsey had to be ordered by Admiral Chester Nimitz to break off his attacks on the decoy Japanese carrier fleet and return to protect the beachheads. Valiant efforts by smaller U.S. forces saved the landing areas, but the Japanese short-term breakthrough revealed communication and command problems between U.S. naval forces.

Halsey drew increased criticism in December 1944 when he sailed his Third Fleet into a typhoon (December 17–18), losing three destroyers and at least eight hundred men. Although faulty weather information played a role in the disaster, historians have also blamed Halsey's judgment and management. He turned over command of Third Fleet to Spruance on January 26, 1945, but resumed control in May with the new battleship *Missouri* as his flagship. Halsey's fleet provided air cover for the assault on Okinawa that began on April 1, 1945. On June 4–5 he again steered his fleet into a typhoon. Throughout July and August, Halsey's unit attacked the Japanese home islands. The Japanese surrender took place aboard Halsey's flagship on September 2, 1945, in Tokyo Bay.

Halsey relinquished command in November 1945 and was promoted to fleet admiral in December. After making numerous public appearances throughout 1946, he requested and received an early retirement in March 1947.

In the early stages of the war, Halsey's aggressiveness and dynamism bolstered morale, but he has been criticized for his makeshift planning, careless techniques, and inefficient administration. Also, by late 1944 his health had been strained. Despite these shortcomings, Halsey was one of the best-known and most respected naval commanders, and had earned fierce loyalty from his men. He died at Fishers Island, New York, on August 16, 1959.

FURTHER READINGS

Frank, Benis M. *Halsey* (1974).
Halsey, William F., and J. Bryan III. *Admiral Halsey's Story* (1947).
Woodward, C. Vann. *The Battle for Leyte Gulf* (1947).
Laura Matysek Wood

SEE ALSO Leyte Gulf, Battle of; Navy, U.S.; Nimitz, Chester William; Spruance, Raymond Ames

Hart, Thomas C.

U.S. naval officer, commander of the U.S. Asiatic Fleet at the beginning of World War II in the Pacific. An 1897 graduate of the U.S. Naval Academy, Hart served in Cuban waters, commanded a submarine division in 1916, and led two submarine divisions to Europe during World War I. After graduation from the Army War College and Naval War College, Hart was captain of battleship *Mississippi* (1925–1927), and then commanded all submarines in both the Atlantic and the Pacific. He became superintendent of the U.S. Naval Academy in 1931. He went to sea again in 1934, commanding a division of heavy cruisers.

Hart was in Manila, Philippines, on December 8, 1941, when the United States declared war on Japan. He and his small fleet had operated out of Shanghai, China, until the autumn of 1940. As rumors and dangers of war increased, Hart sailed his flagship, cruiser U.S.S. *Houston*, to Manila Bay. His small fleet was spread from China to Hong Kong to Singapore. It was not, and was never meant to be, a fighting fleet; it was a political instrument, meant to show the flag. Nevertheless, Hart began recalling most of the ships and concentrating them in the Philippines.

Hart ordered PBY reconnaissance flights to Cam Ranh Bay, French Indochina (now Vietnam) and nearby harbors, as well as to the Spratly Islands, between the Philippines and Indochina. When these flights proved to be overtaxing Hart's resources, the Far East Air Force assumed responsibility for some of the flights.

Hart had twenty-two submarines at sea on December 22, 1941, the day of the main Japanese landing in Lingayen Gulf, but they were scattered across the Philippine and South China seas, a deployment that was useless. His positioning of his submarines was an inexplicable lapse that immeasurably increased the odds of success in Japan's favor. Only seven submarines attacked or tried to attack the invasion fleet. Nine others were within striking distance but were not ordered into action. The submarines were made ineffective by poor torpedoes, poor tactics, and some reticent skippers.

General Douglas MacArthur's defense of Luzon collapsed the moment the Japanese stepped ashore. On December 24, 1941, MacArthur advised his forces that he would soon declare Manila an open city. This surprised Hart. Since the war had begun, he had received no notice that such a move was contemplated. Because of that lack of intelligence, Hart had made Manila the logistical base from which he was conducting his submarine war.

Hart now had too little time in which to evacuate equipment. The sudden loss of Manila's infrastructure deprived him of his headquarters, his communications, and his base for supplies and services.

Hart decided to leave. At noon on Christmas Day, 1941, he turned over command of all Philippine naval personnel and facilities. The next morning he sailed in the submarine *Shark*. He arrived in Surabaja, Java (now Indonesia), on the afternoon of January 1, 1942. Realizing that the failures in the Philippines had compromised his effectiveness, he immediately cabled the Navy Department, recommending that another officer be assigned to command the naval forces of the nascent American/British/Dutch/Australian command (ABDA). But because he was on the scene, Hart got the job. Unfortunately, there was no unified strategy. ABDA's naval forces were meager and unbalanced, and no reinforcements were expected from the United States.

The Dutch resented U.S. and British domination of ABDA and had little faith in Hart. The British thought Hart had an exaggerated view of Japanese capabilities, and that he was pessimistic and used up from his Philippine experiences.

Hart knew Java would soon fall; he wanted to keep his lines of communications open; and he wanted to strike with cruisers and destroyers at advancing Japanese forces. The British wanted to use these same ships to protect convoys to Singapore. The Dutch naturally wanted the ships to defend Java. Confusion increased when the U.S. government tried to manage Hart's personnel and operations from a distance.

Although Hart initiated the successful destroyer action at Balikpapan, Borneo (now Indonesia), on January 24, 1942—the first U.S. Navy surface action since 1898—it was suggested that he step down because of poor health. A loyal officer, Hart relinquished command on February 14, 1942. He later served as Admiral Harold R. Stark's counsel during a U.S. Navy inquiry on the Japanese attack on the U.S. naval base at Pearl Harbor, Hawaii, on December 7, 1941. He accepted appointment as a U.S. senator from Connecticut on February 15, 1945.

FURTHER READINGS

Blair, Clay, Jr. *Silent Victory: The U.S. Submarine War Against Japan* (1975).

Hart, Thomas C. "Narrative of Events, Asiatic Fleet, Leading up to War and from 8 December 1941 to 15 February 1942." U.S. Army Military History Institute, Carlisle Barracks, Pa.

Leutze, James R. *A Different Kind of Victory: A Biography of Admiral Thomas C. Hart* (1981).

Morison, Samuel Eliot. *History of United States Naval Operations in World War II.* Vol. 3, *The Rising Sun in the Pacific, 1931–April 1942* (1948).

"The Reminiscences of Thomas C. Hart." Interviews conducted by John T. Mason, Jr., December 5, 1961, and January 24, 1962. Oral History Research Office, Columbia University.

John W. Whitman

SEE ALSO ABDA Command; Navy, U.S.; Philippines, Fall of

Hata Shunroku (1876–1962)

Japanese army field marshal best known for championing Japanese domination of East and Southeast Asia. As a member of the Supreme War Council in 1937, he helped to plan the invasion of China, and he commanded the China Expeditionary Force in 1938. He directed the assault on the city of Hankow and was in overall command when numerous atrocities were committed against Chinese civilians. He either did nothing to prevent the atrocities, or did not take the necessary steps to ensure that orders for the humane treatment of civilians and prisoners were obeyed. Subsequently, however, when Hata's forces captured the city of Wuhan during the same campaign, he disciplined his troops strictly, thereby avoiding widespread atrocities.

Hata returned to Tokyo as war minister from 1939 to 1940. He favored Japan's alliance with Germany and Italy; his resignation in July 1940 brought down the cabinet of Admiral Yonai Mitsumasa, a bitter opponent of the alliance with the Nazis. As a result, Konoe Fumimaro formed his third cabinet with Tojo Hideki as war minister. One of the first actions of the new government was to accept the alliance with Germany and then with Benito Mussolini's Italy.

From 1941 to 1944, Hata again commanded the China Expeditionary Force. For much of this period he focused more on controlling areas under occupation than on conquering new territory. He hoped to pacify regions of China by using "model peace zones," where tight military, economic, and political security could be maintained. The program was not particularly successful; the Chinese Nationalists and the Communists were able to maintain a presence even in the most secure model peace zones. Hata also helped to plan and implement Japan's Ichigo offensive in 1944. The objective of this operation was to seize the air bases in southern China that U.S. Air Force General Claire Chennault was using to attack Japanese positions. Chinese resistance was ineffective, and by the end of the year the air bases had been destroyed and almost half a million Chinese soldiers had been killed or wounded. Hata's final assignment was to prepare for the presumed decisive battle on the home islands of Japan as commander of the Second General Headquarters in Hiroshima.

Hata was one of the twenty-eight class A war criminal suspects brought to trial by the International Military Tribunal for the Far East in Tokyo. He was found guilty of six counts: as one of the "leaders, organizers, instigators or accomplices in the formulation of a common plan or conspiracy . . . to wage wars of aggression, and war or wars in violation of international law"; for waging an unprovoked war against China and aggressive wars against the United States, the British Commonwealth, and the Netherlands; and for deliberately and recklessly disregarding his duty to prevent atrocities. He was found not guilty of waging an aggressive war against the Soviet Union and of ordering or permitting the inhumane treatment of prisoners of war. He received a sentence of life imprisonment but was paroled in 1954.

FURTHER READINGS

Brackman, Arnold. *The Other Nuremberg* (1987).
Dreyer, Edward. *China at War 1901–1949* (1995).

Stephen J. Valone

SEE ALSO Army, Japanese

Hirohito (1901–1989)

Emperor of Japan from 1926 until his death in 1989. The extent of Hirohito's influence on, and involvement in, the decisions that led to Japan going to war against the United States are the subject of intense debate among historians. Some have argued that the emperor was a mere figurehead who had little, if anything, to do with the specific policies and plans that led to the outbreak of hostilities with the United States in 1941. These historians paint the picture of a respected but powerless figure unable, despite grave misgivings, to halt the militarists who dominated the armed forces and the government.

Other historians have maintained that Hirohito was deeply involved in all aspects of prewar Japanese policies, including the decision to attack China in the 1930s and the decision to mount a surprise attack on the American naval base at Pearl Harbor, Hawaii, in December 1941—an attack that resulted in an American declaration of war against Japan.

Hirohito was born in 1901 in Tokyo. As a young man he developed an interest in marine biology, which remained his passion throughout his life. Although he was brought up amidst the confining rituals and traditions of the imperial palace, Hirohito was the first Japanese crown prince to travel to Europe (1921) and to be exposed to Western influences. In 1924 he married the princess Nagako Kuni.

Hirohito ascended the throne at the age of 25 on the death of his father. He had been prince regent since 1921 because of his father's worsening mental illness. As was the custom in Japan, his reign was given a name: "Showa," meaning "enlightened peace," an ironic appellation given the events of the next twenty years.

Constitutionally, Hirohito had supreme authority, but in practice, the emperor was supposed to only ratify the policies of his ministers. Within the framework of the debate concerning the degree and nature of Hirohito's involvement in the policies that led to war, there is little disagreement that the emperor used his influence to persuade a bitterly divided military and government to chose peace in August 1945. The country was exhausted militarily and psychologically. Its navy and air force had been obliterated, and two of its main cities—Hiroshima and Nagasaki—had been reduced to rubble by atomic bombs. On August 9 came the devastating news of the Soviet declaration of war against Japan.

Yet, many within the Japanese government and the military argued that the nation should fight to the last man, woman, and child. The Japanese revered the figure of the emperor, so it was only he who could ask the people to "bear the unbearable"—unconditional surrender. On August 15, 1945, Hirohito's voice was heard for the first time over the radio as he addressed his subjects and informed them that the war had "not exactly gone to Japan's advantage."

In 1946, at the insistence of the United States, Hirohito publicly repudiated his traditional quasi-divine status. Under the new Japanese constitution, drafted by the Americans, he became a constitutional monarch. He appeared now in public wearing an ordinary business suit and a hat. The imposing figure seen on a white horse wearing a military uniform in the years before the war now seemed like an ordinary middle-aged Japanese businessman. He had survived the war because the Americans believed his person and role were necessary to hold the defeated nation together. Although some had argued that Hirohito should be tried as a war criminal, he was, in fact, allowed to remain in his palace. But he was now a man and no longer a god. Hirohito adapted well to the new role imposed on him by the defeat of his country in the Pacific war.

At the time of Japan's surrender, Hirohito had forty-four more years of life left to him. When he died in 1989, he had become a revered figure once again, but in his second incarnation, he represented not only the new

Japan but its connection to the troubled past. Hirohito was succeeded by his son, Akihito.

FURTHER READINGS
Irokawa, Daikichi, ed. *The Age of Hirohito: In Search of Modern Japan* (1995).
Wetzler, Peter. *Hirohito and War: Imperial Tradition and Military Decision Making in Prewar Japan* (1998).
Richard Steins

Hiroshima

See Atomic Bomb, Decision to Use against Japan

Historiography of the Pacific War

Before World War II, the writing of military history was focused on weapons, battle narratives, biographies of great leaders, and the analysis of strategy and tactics. Academia ignored the field in general, leaving the practice of military history to popular writers, military officers, and antiquarians. After World War II, the U.S. government funded exhaustive efforts to write the history of the war. Because of the cold war, there was also more funding for military history in general. Beginning in the 1960s, there emerged among historians a movement to create a "new military history," a not very original term, which shifted beyond the battlefield to examine the social context of military institutions, as well as technology, class, race, art, psychology, mass culture, even antiwar sentiment. The techniques of the social sciences were harnessed to delve into the actual experiences of soldiers under fire and of societies at war. One historian characterized this change as the movement from "drums and trumpets" to "the military in society."

In general, military history is written to satisfy one of four audiences: the popular reader, military historians, other academic historians, and military officers. It is rare for a book to satisfy them all. At the risk of caricature, it can be said that these audiences have different expectations of their military history. The popular reader wants battle narratives with a human dimension, portraying the glory and brutality of war. Military historians want interpretations and documented details that contribute to a more accurate interpretation of the past. Other academic historians want to know how wars and military institutions affected mainstream society and transformed cultures. Military officers desire combat lessons from their history: how to win battles in the next war.

As the ardor of patriotic commitment to the war against Japan cooled, historians started to question Amer-

ican decisions: use of the atomic bomb, interment camps for West Coast residents of Japanese descent, the efficacy and morality of the strategic bombing campaign, and the treatment of Japanese war criminals. These questions cut to the heart of the metastory that Americans accept about World War II. As time passes, the metastory will, it is hoped, become more accurate. As part of the evolving story, the next wave of the new military history is now occurring: race, gender, and other topics that intrigue contemporary academia are being researched and explained.

In one important way the historiography of World War II is unique. In previous wars historians could rightfully argue relative questions of war guilt and atrocities; with the passage of time the conviction of the absolute rightness of one's own side would weaken as the heat of wartime passion usually subsided. But even the passage of half a century has not weakened the conviction of the absolute evil of Nazism or the aggressive and brutal nature of the Japanese militarists. If anything, new documentation about the Nazi holocaust or Japanese bacteriological warfare experiments on human guinea pigs or the "Rape of Nanking" renews the repugnance felt by the enemies of the Third Reich or imperial Japan. Even such morally dubious Allied actions such as the bombing of Dresden have not, for the most part, induced many "moral equivalence" arguments among academic historians. In addition, significant work is still being done in the older topics of interest. Historians can still, for example, argue the merits of one fighter aircraft over another.

Historical Sources

World War II was different from previous wars in that historians accompanied U.S. forces into combat, documenting their observations and preserving records. Besides paper records, wartime films, and audio recordings are available. As a result, historians have a wealth of source material to draw upon when examining the Pacific war. "Raw" military records in the United States are located at the Modern Military Records Branch of the National Archives and the U.S. Naval Historical Center, both in Washington, D.C.; the Air Force Historical Center at Maxwell Air Force Base in Alabama; and the Marine Corps Historical Center at Quantico, Virginia. All have professional staffs and contain voluminous primary archival material not found in the National Archives. For example, the log of a particular aircraft carrier would be found at the National Archives, but a navy study of, say, carriers in combat, or of their design or construction, would most likely be at the Naval Historical Center.

There is also published primary material. For example, Donald Detwiler and Charles Burdick edited a 15-volume work, *War in Asia and the Pacific, 1937–1949: Japanese and Chinese Studies and Documents* (1980). There are numerous personal accounts and oral histories, such as John R. Mason, *The Pacific War Remembered: An Oral History Collection* (1986). Oral history has a tendency to deliver the emotion and flavor of a time and place strongly, at the same time often mixing up the precise details; it declines in value as the participants are distanced from the event.

Selected Bibliography

Important bibliographies include Robin Higham, *A Guide to the Sources of United States Military History* (1975), and the supplements edited by Higham and Donald J. Mrozek, *A Guide to the Sources of United States Military History: Supplement I* (1981), *Supplement II* (1986), and *Supplement III* (1993). John J. Sbrega's *The War Against Japan, 1941–1945: An Annotated Bibliography* (1989) contains 5,200 entries.

For general ruminations about the practice of military history, see R. J. B. Bosworth, *Explaining Auschwitz and Hiroshima* (1993); and the volume edited by David A. Charters, Marc Milner, and J. Brent Wilson, *Military History and the Military Profession* (1992).

Though early U.S. wars have official histories, none of them come close to achieving the comprehensive U.S. Army's Office of the Chief of Military History/Center of Military History's ongoing, 75-volume "Green Books" on World War II. Samuel Eliot Morison devoted most of his 15-volume *History of United States Naval Operations in World War II* (1947–1962) to the Pacific war. The marine corps has published multiple monographs, including the 5-volume *History of U.S. Marine Corps Operations in World War II* (1958–1968). The air force issued a 7-volume history, *The Army Air Forces in World War II* (1948–1958). The army's ongoing contribution is detailed in Richard D. Adamczyk and Morris J. MacGregor, *United States Army in World War II: Reader's Guide* (1992). Two examples typify the breadth of this impressive research effort: Karl C. Dod, *The Corps of Engineers: The War Against Japan* (1966); and Robert Ross Smith, *The War in the Pacific: Triumph in the Philippines* (1963). There is always some concern about bias within government-funded research, but overall, the "Green Books" are solid works. For many phases of the war and many smaller battles, they are the only secondary works available. Some eighty volumes of the British *Official History of the Second World War* have been published. The

Australians have published the 21-volume *Australia in the War of 1939–1945* (1952–1968).

The causes of the Pacific war was a controversial topic during and immediately after the war, and still continues to attract attention. This topic is divided into two categories. The first focuses on the Pacific war before the Japanese attack on the U.S. naval base at Pearl Harbor, Hawaii, in 1941; examples are Takehiko Yoshihashi, *Conspiracy at Mukden: The Rise of the Japanese Military* (1963); Alvin D. Coox, *Nomonhan: Japan Against Russia, 1939* (1985); and Ben-Ami Shillony, *Revolt in Japan: The Young Officers and the February 26, 1936 Incident* (1973). In 1962–1963, Japan's largest newspaper published the 7-volume *Taiheiyō sensō e no michi: Kaisen gaikō shi* (Road to the Pacific War: A Diplomatic History of the Origins of the War), from which James William Morley has made selections and edited a useful series: *Japan Erupts: The London Naval Conference and the Manchurian Incident, 1928–1932* (1984); *The China Quagmire: Japan's Expansion on the Asian Continent, 1933–1941* (1983); *Deterrent Diplomacy: Japan, Germany, and the USSR, 1935–1941* (1976); *The Fateful Choice: Japan's Advance into Southeast Asia, 1939–1941* (1980); and *The Final Confrontation: Japan's Negotiations with the United States, 1941* (1994). Some historians advance the argument that Japan's failure to win the earlier wars in China and Mongolia forced it into war with the United States. The second category focuses on U.S. entry into the war. Examples include James R. Leutze, *Bargaining for Supremacy* (1977); Roland H. Worth, Jr., *No Choice but War: The United States Embargo Against Japan and the Eruption of War in the Pacific* (1995); and Stephen E. Pelz, *Race to Pearl Harbor: The Failure of the Second London Naval Conference and the Onset of World War II* (1974).

The attack on Pearl Harbor continues to hold the attention of historians and those prone to entertain conspiracies. The definitive, exhaustive work is the trilogy by Gordon W. Prange, *At Dawn We Slept: The Untold Story of Pearl Harbor* (1981); *Pearl Harbor: The Verdict of History* (1986); and *December 7, 1941: The Day the Japanese Attacked Pearl Harbor* (1988). John Toland unconvincingly argues that Franklin D. Roosevelt (FDR) knew in advance about the President surprise attack in *Infamy: Pearl Harbor and Its Aftermath* (1982). (Those who believe that FDR knew about the Pearl Harbor attack seem to *want* to believe that he knew about it.)

Useful biographies include Barbara W. Tuchman, *Stilwell and the American Experience in China, 1911–1945* (1971); Thomas B. Buell, *Master of Sea Power: A Biography of Fleet Admiral Ernest J. King* (1980); William Manchester, *American Caesar: Douglas MacArthur 1880–*

1964 (1978); and Hiroyuki Agawa, *The Reluctant Admiral: Yamamoto and the Imperial Navy* (1979). Most major U.S. leaders either wrote autobiographies or memoirs or authorized biographies. An interesting variation is the autobiographical novel, such as Leon Uris's *Battle Cry* (1953).

In the mid-1970s, declassification of documents which revealed the existence and scope of the Ultra code-breaking efforts are redefining our understanding of U.S. strategy and campaigns in the Pacific. The full impact of this information has not been completely integrated in any comprehensive work. Edward J. Drea's *MacArthur's ULTRA: Codebreaking and the War Against Japan, 1942–1945* (1992) is an example of what is yet to be accomplished with this new information. Even though the war ended more than fifty years ago, there are still some classified documents, especially in Great Britain, which, when released, may radically change interpretations of selected aspects of the war.

Home-front propaganda on all sides demonized the enemy, freely drawing on racist themes. Studies of propaganda demonstrate that the Pacific conflict was in many ways as vicious as the Nazi-Soviet conflict and as laden with ethnic and racial themes. See John W. Dower, *War Without Mercy: Race and Power in the Pacific War* (1986); and Craig M. Cameron, *American Samurai: Myth, Imagination, and the Conduct of Battle in the First Marine Division, 1941–1951* (1994).

The decision to use atomic weapons continues to reverberate within the American and Japanese psyches. Representative works on this subject include John Hersey's classic *Hiroshima* (1946); Richard Rhodes, *The Making of the Atomic Bomb* (1986); Robert Jay Lifton, *Death in Life: Survivors of Hiroshima* (1967); Richard H. Minear, *Hiroshima: Three Witnesses* (1990); and the exhaustive work by Gar Alperovitz, *The Decision to Use the Atomic Bomb and the Architecture of an American Myth* (1995). A Japanese group, the Pacific War Research Society, published *The Day Man Lost: Hiroshima, 6 August 1945* (1972). Part of the argument over Hiroshima and Nagasaki is whether the proposed invasion of Japan's home islands was necessary; this is examined in John Ray Skates, *The Invasion of Japan: Alternative to the Bomb* (1994).

World War II had a profound impact on American culture. See John M. Blum, *V Was for Victory: Politics and American Culture During World War II* (1976); and Doris Weatherford, *American Women and World War II* (1990). Part of the cultural impact was on films, both during and after the war, as described in Bernard F. Dick, *The Star-Spangled Screen: The American World War II Film* (1985); and Colin Shindler, *Hollywood Goes to War: Films and*

American Society, 1939–1952 (1979). Oral history provides a vivid window into the experiences of a nation at war in Studs Terkel, *"The Good War": An Oral History of World War Two* (1984). The myth of the "Good War" has lent a rosy tint to the complexity of World War II, obscuring unpleasant truths. For a gentle debunking, see Michael C. C. Adams, *The Best War Ever: America and World War II* (1994); less gentle is Paul Fussell, *Wartime: Understanding and Behavior in the Second World War* (1989). On the Japanese home front, see Haruko Taya Cook and Theodore F. Cook, *Japan at War: An Oral History* (1992); and Thomas R. H. Havens, *Valley of Darkness: The Japanese People and World War Two* (1978).

There is a dearth of work on the war from the Japanese perspective, though recent efforts are yielding fruit. From American historians, see John Toland, *The Rising Sun: The Decline and Fall of the Japanese Empire* (1970); and David C. Evans, *The Japanese Navy in World War II: In the Words of Former Japanese Naval Officers* (1986). From Japanese historians, see Iwaichi Fujiwara, *F. Kikan: Japanese Army Intelligence Operations in Southeast Asia During World War II* (1983); Saburo Hayashi, *Kogun: The Japanese Army in the Pacific War* (1978); and Saburo Ienaga, *The Pacific War: World War II and the Japanese, 1931–1945* (1978), an antiwar polemic.

In evaluating the long-term consequences of the war on Japan, much has been made of the postwar American occupation, where MacArthur is often portrayed as a latter-day shogun. See John W. Dower, *Japan in War and Peace: Selected Essays* (1993) and Theodore Cohen, *Remaking Japan: The American Occupation as New Deal* (1987). For Japan's effect on the postwar break-up of colonial empires, see Willard H. Elsbree, *Japan's Role in Southeast Asian Nationalist Movements, 1940 to 1945* (1953) and Joyce C. Lebra, *Japanese-Trained Armies in Southeast Asia: Independence and Volunteer Forces in World War I* (1977). Another long-term consequence of the war all the debate and repercussions from Japanese atrocities, a story that is still unfolding. Some contemporary Japanese historians and politicians are wrestling with the moral fallout from issues like the sack and rape of Nanking, Unit 731, comfort girls, and the ill-feelings of nations who were part of the Greater East Asia Co-Prosperity Sphere.

Recent high-quality general works include Ronald H. Spector, *Eagle Against the Sun: The American War With Japan* (1985) and Meirion and Susie Herris, *Soldiers of the Sun: The Rise and Fall of the Imperial Japanese Army* (1991). The Time-Life series on World War II (1977–1983) is informative, with a broad reach of topics and, of course, is well illustrated.

There are occasional efforts to put forward radically revisionist versions of the Pacific war. These include the straw-man argument of Bruce M. Russett, *No Clear and Present Danger: A Skeptical View of U.S. Entry into World War II* (1972); the important work by Akira Iriye, *Power and Culture: The Japanese American War, 1941–1945* (1982); and John Toland's *Infamy*. One of the most important works is John Ellis, *Brute Force: Allied Strategy and Tactics in the Second World War* (1990), which demonstrates the overwhelming materiel and manpower superiority of the Allies in all theaters of the war. From a purely resource-based perspective, what is amazing is not that the Allies won, but that the Japanese did as well as they did. Also very informative is John Ellis, *World War II: A Statistical Survey. The Essential Facts and Figures for All the Combatants* (1993).

The Soviet Union's opportunistic 4-day campaign against Japan at the end of the war is little documented, except for the expected chest-thumping official, heroic Soviet chronicles.

World War II was humanity's greatest enterprise, and the torrent of publications—academic, general, or sensational—on that catastrophe shows no sign of abating, let alone ending.

Eric Swedin

SEE ALSO History Program: Japanese Air Force; History Program: Japanese Military; History Program: U.S. Army Military

History Program, Japanese Air Force

In 1955, the Japanese government established the Office of Military History (OMH) within the Japanese Ministry of Defense, and systematically collected all official documents relating to the Asia-Pacific war. It now possesses more than 83,000 documents relating to the army and 33,000 documents relating to the navy. By the early 1970s, the OMH had published 102 volumes of *Senshi sosho* (The Official Military History), of which fourteen volumes were devoted to air force strategies and operations: volume 7, *Military Air Force Operations in Eastern New Guinea;* volume 19, *Japanese Mainland Antiaircraft Operations;* volume 22, *Military Air Force Operations in Western New Guinea;* volume 34, *Military Air Force Operations in Southern Strategy;* volume 36, *Military Air Force Operations in Okinawa, Taiwan, and Iwo Jima;* volume 48, *Military Air Force Operations in the Philippines;* volume 52, *Armament and Management in the Military Air Force* (part 1); volume 53, *Military Air Force Operations in Manchuria;* volume 61, *The Third Air Force Fleet Operations in Burma*

and Dutch Indonesia; volume 78, *Armament and Management in the Military Air Force* (part 2); volume 87, *Development, Production, & Supply of Military Air Force Weaponry;* volume 94, *Armament and Management in the Military Air Force* (part 4); volume 95, *General History of Navy Air Force;* and volume 97, *Construction & Basic Resource Management of the Military Air Force.*

The volumes of *Senshi sosho* demonstrate that the weakness of Japan's air force was one of the decisive factors in the nation's defeat. According to *Senshi sosho*, the Japanese air force had several critical defects. First, the military established its air force on the assumption that it would be used to fight against the Soviet Union in Manchuria. Because the Russian air force would always be larger than the Japanese air force, the latter primarily prepared itself for air-to-air battles. In October 1941, however, general headquarters decided to use the military air force in Southeast Asia. The military air force did not have enough time to adjust itself to the rapid strategic changes. The primary aim of the new southern strategy was to assault the Philippines and Malaya (now Malaysia) simultaneously; to destroy the main bases of the United States, Great Britain, and the Netherlands; and to occupy strategically important areas. Under such an ambitious plan, the air force had to cover a large area, which necessitated an extremely long supply line.

Second, Japan's relatively lower productivity, outdated technology, shortage of natural resources, and lack of manpower were responsible for the weakness of the Japanese air force. The Allied powers, using more efficient construction machinery, for example, were able to build an air base in a week or so, whereas Japan, depending primarily on manpower, needed several months to do the same job. Japanese air force radar, communication systems, and weaponry were quite inferior to those of the Allies. The use of kamikaze suicide squads was a result of Japan's desperate need to conserve fuel and weapons. Neither the military nor the navy provided air force personnel with appropriate training based on any kind of long-term, systematic program.

Third, even though both the military and the navy recognized the importance of the air force, they paid only secondary attention to the need to strengthen it. The military considered its ground force strategy to be the main thrust of its operations, and the navy believed that a frontal assault using battleships was its primary focus. Since the 1920s, there had been some in the military who had called for Japan to have an independent air force. In December 1938, the military established the Military Air Force Bureau and appointed Lieutenant General Tojo Hideki, War Department vice minister, as its head. Top members of the military, such as Lieutenant General Yamashita Tomoyuki and General Kawabe Shozo, later became heads of the Military Air Force Bureau, but the idea of establishing an independent air force and giving it top priority made no headway at general headquarters, where the prevailing thought was still firmly rooted in traditional strategy.

Fourth, general headquarters could not coordinate the operations of the military and the navy air forces. Since one of the key factors in securing victory in the Asia-Pacific war was a successful military-navy-air force joint operation to acquire air bases in the Pacific region, this lack of coordination eventually proved fatal for Japan.

The volumes of *Senshi shosho* repeatedly insist that general headquarters failed to understand the critical importance of the air force in the Asia-Pacific war. They suggest that successful air force operations would have required greater productive power; better coordination among the military, the navy, and the air force; a smoother flow of natural resources; more advanced technology; and a more appropriate level of manpower. As it was, the great success of the Japanese air force in the opening weeks of the Pacific war blinded that service to the imperative need for modernization and doomed it to defeat. Individual weapons, such as the Zero fighter, were fully the equal, and more, of anything in the Allied air arsenal, but by 1943 even this splendid warplane was outclassed by U.S. fighters. The interservice rivalries that afflicted the Japanese army and navy also crippled the Japanese air force.

Yone Sugita

History Program, Japanese Military

The Japanese imperial government compiled no official, written military history during the Asia-Pacific war. The military destroyed a great number of official documents at war's end, but many individual officers secretly preserved the most critical documents.

During the U.S. occupation (1945–1952), because the Japanese official documents were not available and the general headquarters for the Allied powers (GHQ) reviewed all books before publication, only a few military history books were published. In fact, GHQ encouraged exposés of the Japanese military. Nishiura Susumu, military adjutant general and the first director of the Office of Military History (OMH) of the Defense Vestibule School, wrote his memoir immediately after the war. Using inside information, he meticulously wrote about the Japanese Army Department, including his opinion that many generals were incapable of strategic and tactical studies. This memoir was finally published in 1980 as

Showa sensoshi no shogen (Records of Showa War History). *Gun sanbocho no shuki* (Notes of a Chief of Staff), by Major General Tomochika Yoshiharu, former chief of staff of the 35th Army in the Philippines, was published in 1946. This was the first military history book written by a Japanese military officer to be available to the public in the postwar era. It demonstrated the cruelty of the war, the incompetence of the military leaders, and even the decadence of the rank and file.

In May 1948, GHQ allowed the Japanese to translate and publish books in Japan. That same year, Nakano Goro wrote *Kakute gyokusai seri* (This Is How We Died in the War). This first comprehensive military history book written by a Japanese in the postwar era was virtually a translation of selected narratives on the Asia-Pacific war from various military histories published in the United States during and after the war.

The Japanese navy published its war history books before the army did. In 1949, Rear Admiral Takagi Sokichi wrote *Taiheiyo kaisenshi* (The Pacific Naval War History). This book contains accounts not only of naval operations and combat but also of the general policy, diagnosis, and strategic scheme of each naval battle. In 1950, Admiral Toyota Soemu, former commander in chief of the Japanese Combined Squadron, published his oral history, *Saigo no teikoku kaigun* (The Last Imperial Navy). This work consisted of the admiral's reminiscences, conjectures, and hearsay accounts, all indicating that there was severe antagonism between the navy and the army. Toyota insists that the navy had competent leaders, whereas the army was rife with inept officers. He concludes that General Tojo was primarily responsible for the loss of the war. In 1951, Vice Admiral Fukutome Shigeru, chief of staff of the Japanese Combined Squadron, published his memoir, *Kaigun no hansei* (Reflection of the Navy). From the perspective of the Navy General Staff Office, he analyzes naval operations and probable causes of the defeat. Fukutome concludes that the low level of technology and science deployed at the time, especially with respect to the relative inferiority of the air force and the crypto system, was a major cause of defeat.

After the end of the postwar U.S. occupation, the Office of Military History of the Japanese Ministry of Defense collected many of privately held wartime documents. The resulting official works include *Kimitsu senso nisshi* (The Secret Wartime Journals), *Daihonei seifu renraku kaigi shingiroku* (The Minute Book of the General Headquarters-Government Liaison Meetings), *Daihonei seifu renraku kaigi kettei tsuzuri* (The Decisions of the General Headquarters-Government Liaison Meetings), *Dai riku mei* (Great Army Orders), *Dai kai mei* (Great

Navy Orders), *Dai riku shi* (Great Army Directives), *Dai kai shi* (Great Navy Directives), *Joso shorui* (The Addresses to the Emperor), and *Kimitsu sakusen nisshi* (The Secret Journals of Tactics). In addition to those official documents, a large number of high-ranking military officials and rank and filers left behind their diaries, memos, and notes written during the war.

Two years later, a high-ranking army officer wrote a military history of the army. Hayashi Saburo, who had held a series of important positions, such as chief of the Russian Bureau, chief of the Regimentation and Mobilization Bureau, and secretary to the war minister, published *Taiheiyo senso rikusen gaishi* (A General History of the Army Battles in the Pacific War, translated by Hayashi Saburo, Marine Corps Association, 1959). This first book to be written about army operations during the Asia-Pacific war focused on the direction of the war by army headquarters. Hayashi Saburo argues that Japan did not have a united war effort that fully integrated military, economic, and diplomatic policies; rather, the army and the navy had separate, often contradictory, strategies. In addition, he argues that a lack of technology and weapons, compounded by the rigidity of the decision-making process, constituted a major cause of Japan's defeat.

After the peace treaty with Japan was signed at San Francisco in 1951, many official and quasi-official documents began to appear in public. In 1952, Tanemura Sakou, formerly chief of the War Conduct Section of the General Staff Office, published *Daihonei kimitsu nisshi* (Secret Journals of the Imperial General Headquarters). Tanemura had worked in the General Staff Office for more than five years (December 1939–August 1945) and had dealt with most of the strategic policies throughout the war. This book was based on the official *Kimitsu senso nisshi* (The Secret Wartime Journals), noted above, to which he added his memories and experiences. Tanemura made the common criticism of the lack of consistency in war directives, the open conflicts between the army and the navy, the navy's indecisive and uncompromising attitudes, and the Imperial General Headquarters' myopic view of the war in general. He believed that the major Allied powers had supreme national leaders who could make comprehensive decisions covering political, military, and economic matters, whereas Japan sorely lacked such a powerful, central figure. He concluded that this absence of strong, centralized leadership in Japan was a primary cause of confusion and lack of effectiveness in the general headquarters.

At about this time, former officers who had became frustrated with the muckrakers began to strike back. Vice Admiral Kusaka Ryunosuke, chief of staff of the Japanese

Combined Squadron, published *Rengo kantai* (The Japanese Combined Squadron) in 1952; in it he insists, improbably, that only slightly more effort would have brought victory to Japan.

In 1953, using the newly available official documents, Colonel Hattori Takushiro, chief of the Operations Bureau of the General Staff Office, published the first full-scale, quasi-official military history work, the four-volumes *Dai toa senso zenshi* (The Complete History of the Great East Asia War, English translation available). Hattori worked for the General Staff Office from July 1941 until March 1945, when the army dispatched him to China. At war's end, he joined the Military History Section of the Veterans Administration, then the Archival Section of the Veterans Bureau. He also was a member GHQ's project to write MacArthur's military history. His book covers not only top decision-making processes but also the events of important operations and battles, in order to present a complete picture of the war. It explains Japan's military and political strategies, demonstrating that there was no single institution to integrate military and political strategies in the Japanese government. The work also attests that because of the severe hostility between the army and the navy, there was no comprehensive military strategy in Japanese headquarters. Even though he tries to present an unbiased historical account, Hattori exaggerates somewhat the heroism of the Japanese soldier, and makes this book into something of a requiem for the war dead and a means to save face for the veterans who survived. The book focuses on the war between the United States and Japan, with little mention of the Sino-Japanese war. Because this book does not go into as much detail regarding the operations of the navy as it does those of the army, navy veterans were understandably dissatisfied. Despite these shortcomings, this book acquired enduring fame and became one of the most important military history books on the Asia-Pacific war.

Itoh Masanori, a navy war correspondent, published a five-volume history of the army, *Teikoku rikugun no saigo* (The End of the Imperial Army; 1959–1961). Masanori believes that a strong national leader with a far-reaching perspective should have ruled wartime Japan. He blames the failure to devise and implement effective military strategies on the fact that the generals governed politics in Japan. According to Masanori, even though Japan had a strong, well-trained army and the Japanese people devoted themselves to the war effort, only a handful of these "political generals" made and implemented the strategic mistakes that lost the war. When the Japanese began to enjoy the fruit of economic growth, there was an understandable backlash against what they perceived as the reckless militarism of the war.

In 1960, the 7-volume *Jitsuroku taiheiyo senso* (Documentary History of the Pacific War) was published. Volumes 1 through 5 deal with operational processes, and volumes 6 and 7 relate to the situation on the home front and secret stories of the war's beginning and ending. These volumes compile the experiences of line and/or staff officers of important operations, as well as those of officers and rank and filers who actually participated in the battles. They are important documents for understanding the actual processes in various battles.

In 1966, Satoh Kenryo, former adjutant general of the army, published *Dai toa senso kaikoroku* (Memoirs of the Great East Asia War). The author argues that while Japan and the United States fought against each other on the battlefield, on the home front the army and the navy were doing much the same. He describes his confrontation with navy officers over the production of weapons and their allocation. This book exposes a fundamental strategic difference between the army and the navy: the former considered defensive as well as offensive strategies, whereas the latter concentrated on the offensive.

The Shidehara cabinet established a commission of inquiry to edit the official military history in 1945, but antimilitary feelings among the Japanese people and a lack of funding cut short this project. Former military officers led by Hattori Takushiro insisted that editing the official military history be a national project, but it was some time before this came to fruition. Finally, in 1955, as noted, the Japanese government established the Office of Military History (OMH) in the Ministry of Defense, and began systematically to collect the official documents. The OMH now possesses more than eighty-three thousand documents relating to the army and more than thirty-three thousand documents relating to the navy.

After eleven years of preparation, the OMH began to publish *Senshi sosho* (The Official Military History) in 1966. Over the next fourteen years it published 102 volumes. The serious conflicts between the army and the navy that marked the war years continued even after the war and influenced the editorial policies of the *Senshi sosho*. The army and navy officers could not agree on the exact causes of the war and or of the defeat. In the end, the OMH had to publish two separate series of volumes: sixty-eight volumes on the army, thirty-three volumes on the navy, and one chronological volume.

Because this was an official project, the editors focused solely on the documentation of the available records and accepted them as faithful representations of historical evidence, without examining or interpreting them. The OMH spent a substantial amount of time and funding on interviewing more than a thousand former military officers a year and verified their statements through existing documents. Despite these efforts, the work was clearly deficient. Because the research had begun ten years after the end of the war, many documents had been destroyed or scattered, numerous important officers had died, and the memories of survivors could not be considered reliable. In addition, because the editorial board consisted primarily of former military officers rather than professional historians, the editors could not fully integrate the substantial amount of information, but only enumerated documentary facts.

Notwithstanding those shortcomings, *Senshi sosho* disclosed many important but lesser known facts, especially regarding the navy. The navy assumed that Germany would win the war in Europe and Japan would hold out long enough for the United States to lose its will to fight in the Pacific. The navy believed that once Japan occupied the southern region and secured the necessary raw materials, it could endure an extended war. Consequently, it focused on preparing for the early phase of the war but did not make elaborate long-term plans. Moreover, the navy did not coordinate its strategies with the army either before or even after the outbreak of the war. Admiral Yamamoto Isoruku, commander in chief of the Japanese Combined Squadron, seemed to recognize that the navy's general policy would not be feasible, and only in the unlikely event of a short-term war might Japan's aggression lead to victory. His emphasis on a strong offensive greatly influenced the navy during the war.

In 1975, Vice Admiral Hoshina Zenshiro, former chief of the Military Supplies Bureau of the navy and later its adjutant general, published *Dai toa senso hishi* (A Secret History of the Great East Asia War). The work consists of Hoshina's wartime memoirs, which cast light on important developments within the core of the navy during the war. According to Hoshina, he opposed war with the United States, and once the conflict broke out, he sought the timing and methods to end it as soon as possible under favorable terms and conditions.

In 1979, Imoto Kumao, who had worked in the Operation Section of the General Staff Office during the war, published *Sakusen nisshi de tsuzuru dai toa senso* (The Great East Asia War Through the Operation Journals). This work praises the bravery of the Japanese soldier on the battlefront and criticizes the policies of the General Staff Office. Imoto uses the term *konpon gonin* (fundamental fault) to explain the causes of Japan's defeat. He argues that the general headquarters made many fundamental mistakes in waging the war. These underlying faults had been shaped in a long-term and complicated process, and they became firmly established before the outbreak of the Asia-Pacific war. One of the most important *konpon gonin,* once again, was the existence of considerable enmity and lack of communication between the army and the navy. At the outbreak of the war, the army wrongly assumed that the navy would be able to repel the U.S. Pacific Fleet. The army did not recognize that this assumption was overly optimistic, and its own efforts were dragged down by the weakness of the navy. In other words, Imoto contends that it was the army's overestimation of the relatively weak navy that ultimately brought about Japan's defeat.

The most important Japanese military history works dealing with World War II in the Pacific arrive at a number of common conclusions:

1. The Japanese general headquarters was basically incapable of arriving at effective political and military strategies for prosecuting the war; however, the soldiers fought bravely on the battlefront and the Japanese people worked hard on the home front. In other words, it was the top decision makers who were at fault.
2. Japan did not have a supreme national power center that could integrate political, economic, and military strategies. Moreover, there was an uncompromising divisiveness between the army and the navy, which prevented the general headquarters from making and implementing effective military strategies.
3. The United States defeated Japan because of its overwhelming productive power and advanced technology, not its greater bravery or sacrifice.

Nonetheless, reading these accounts of the Pacific war, with their remarkably similar conclusions as to festering animosity between the army and the navy, the lack of effective political leadership, and Japan's technological backwardness and inferior industrial base, it is difficult to avoid the conclusion that, aside from the incredible bravery of the individual Japanese soldier, Nippon's initial victories in the Pacific war were due as much to luck and to Allied incompetence as to any innate Japanese ability to wage long-term, large-scale war.

Yone Sugita

SEE ALSO Historiography of the Pacific War; History Program, Japanese Air Force

History Program, U.S. Army Military

The U.S. Army's military history detachments of World War II had their origins in the 1918 creation of the Historical Branch of the War Plans Division within the army's general staff. Secretary of War Newton Baker directed that this permanent historical unit collect, index, and preserve the records generated during World War I, and prepare a limited number of historical monographs.

The army, however, did not follow through on this promising beginning. Savage postwar budget cuts saw the army hard pressed to carry out even the most basic training or replacement of equipment, and there was practically nothing remaining for something so esoteric to most officers as military history. Basically, between the wars, the U.S. Army had only the most attenuated of historical sections, and its duties were primarily archival. In fact, the army's official history of World War I was not published until 1948, three years after the end of World War II. By that time there was a sense of déjà vu about the whole project, which was especially evident in its title, *History of the U.S. Army in the World War,* as though the army was not yet aware that there had been a subsequent world war.

General John J. Pershing's staff did arrange for staff rides over the battle sites of World War I, the Army War College (which did have a small historical section) supervised some student historical projects, the Army Command College and General Staff College conducted staff rides over Civil War battlefields, and the surgeon general published a history of the army's medical experience in World War I. All of this was a very small effort, of course, in comparison with the historical work carried out by the other major powers in the wake of World War I and in the interwar years.

But with the entry of the United States into World War II this rather dismal on March 4, 1942, military situation ended. Starting at the top, President Franklin D. Roosevelt directed that all executive departments and agencies to arrange for the preservation of their wartime records and for the compiling of histories of their experiences during the conflict. Both the chief of staff of the army, General George C. Marshall, and the assistant secretary of war, John J. McCloy, had already determined that the army would have a permanent history program and that it would publish studies of the current conflict in a timely manner.

Thus, in August 1943, the army established the Historical Branch within its Intelligence Division (G-2), where its personnel would have close contact with linguists, area specialists, professional investigators, geographers, travelers, writers, and others, thereby giving the new organization a solid cross-cultural and cross-disciplinary foundation. Several distinguished academic historians were brought in who insisted that the series for World War II be basically narrative, as opposed to the binding together of official dispatches and after-action reports that was the format of the *Official Records* of both the Civil War and World War I. McCloy needed little urging to adopt the new format and, in fact, the project was later raised to the level of a division of the War Department Special Staff. An advisory committee proposed that the army's historical section provide first for professional recordkeeping, then a series of up-to-date monographs for the immediate postwar use of the service schools, then for a good popular history, and finally for the authoritative official histories.

In order to supplement the historical work carried out below the theater level, in April 1944 the War Department established information and historical teams (two officers and two enlisted men) and dispatched them to subordinate units in the field, where each did most of its work equipped primarily with a typewriter and the army's ubiquitous quarter-ton personnel carriers (jeeps). Most of these personnel were reservists or had been involved in the historical profession in civil life.

The army then organized historical teams, which produced fourteen studies in the Armed Forces in Action series. In addition, a large number of unpublished history manuscripts relating to World War II topics were deposited in the Historical Branch when postwar budget cutbacks forestalled their publication.

These teams used the interviewing techniques of the former journalist Samuel L. A. ("SLAM") Marshall, who was able to weave human interest accounts into the "big picture" of operations and campaigns. Marshall's oral interviewing techniques have remained a standard for army historians ever since. In fact, it could be argued that Marshall (who later rose to the rank of brigadier general) practically founded the oral history concept that is so much a part of post–World War II historiography, civilian as well as military.

For all of the good work of "SLAM" Marshall and his fellows, many action-oriented army commanders did not realize the importance of accurate historical accounts of their units in battle, and often used the historical teams to guide visiting VIPs or in public relations assignments. Records were often lost or thrown out in battle or its aftermath, and officious intelligence officers were likely to be loath to allow mere historians access to their prized secret documents. In fact, the most common question asked of army historians, either in the field or at headquarters, was "Just what do you guys do?" Army historians

also had to compete with unit histories written under command imprimatur and paid for by unit members' subscriptions—and completely positive in tone: "Under the inspired leadership of General Jones, the _th seized all of its assigned objectives, driving the enemy before it." These official unit histories still bedevil anyone attempting to write objective military history. In all, considering the low priority, the official ignorance, and the indifference of so much of the army leadership to military history, it is indeed a tribute to these field and headquarters historians that so much lasting history was written.

Each theater of operations was assigned one supervising historian. In the Pacific, one each was assigned to the central, south and southwest Pacific theaters. The actual historical research and writing were done by a team consisting of a lieutenant colonel who served as the senior historian, one officer and two enlisted historians who composed a monograph unit, a clerk-typist, and a varying number of contact teams consisting of two enlisted and two commissioned historians. Some three-hundred enlisted and commissioned personnel comprised the nine Information and Historical Service units. These units were supplemented by thirty-six teams, twenty of which supported the U.S. Army Air Forces.

However, their efforts were hampered by the late fielding of the army historical program. Personnel turnover, particularly in the first postwar months of demobilization, and administration, transportation, and supply difficulties also hindered the work, as did security considerations and faulty filing, not to mention the deaths, wounding, and transfers of key personnel. All of these problems basically originated in certain senior commanders' lack of knowledge about or interest in the army historical program. Many, perhaps a majority, felt that there was a war to be won, the troops would be sent home at the end of hostilities, and that should be an end to the matter. More thoughtful commanders also felt that war was changing so rapidly that the "lessons learned" from World War II would be obsolete before they were even written up.

Nonetheless, most of the historical teams assembled by the U.S. Army in the Pacific war did good work in an environment hardly conducive to deep historical research and deliberate writing. It is particularly impressive that the army histories of World War II went beyond the battles and campaigns, with volumes on global logistics, strategy, procurement, the employment of black troops, and other topics.

The U.S. Army historical program of World War II laid the scholarly foundations for the impressive postwar "Green Books" histories, which set standards of military history research and writing and have become basic documents of the American participation in World War II.

The U.S. Navy and U.S. Air Force chose an entirely different means of documenting their activities in World War II. Both retained established academic historians to write their histories in the postwar years. The navy selected the eminent Harvard historian Samuel Eliot Morison, whose his magisterial fifteen-volume *History of United States Navy Operations in World War II* was published between 1947 and 1962. Hardly less impressive were the official volumes of the U.S. Army Air Corps/ Forces, by James Lea Cate and Wesley Craven. Professor Morison, a keen yachtsman in civilian life, was commissioned a lieutenant commander in the U.S. Naval Reserve and witnessed many of the battles and campaigns that he later chronicled. (He retired as a rear admiral in 1951.)

These authors can be honest in their critiques of early shortcomings in their respective services, none more so than Morison. But all also wrote from basically a positive viewpoint, a not unreasonable position, considering the nature of the opposition: in their narratives, mistakes are corrected and shortcomings are eliminated on the road to victory. Later histories of the war by academic historians are considerably more critical, emphasizing, for example, the pervasive racism of the services at the time, or the fact that U.S. forces usually far outnumbered their opponents. There is no naval or air equivalent to the army's bold "Green Book" volume *The Employment of Negro Troops* (1965), which could in all fairness have been entitled *The Mis-Employment of Negro Troops*.

Overall, the official U.S. military histories, whether written in-house, like those of the army, or by outside contractors, have withstood the initial fastidious skepticism of academics, and remain basic sources for the history of the United States war effort, used alike by academic historians and the more literate public.

FURTHER READINGS

Conn, Stetson. *Historical Work in the U.S. Army, 1862– 1954* (U.S. Army Center of Military History, 1930).

Hunt, Richard A. "The Military History Detachment in the Field." In John E. Jessup, Jr., and Richard W. Coakley, eds., *A Guide to the Study and Use of Military History* (1979).

Naisawald, Louis. "The New Look in Military History: A Comparison of the United States Army's Historical Treatment of the American Civil War and World War II." *Military Review* (September 1954).

Spector, Ronald. "An Improbable Success Story: Official Military Histories Twentieth Century." *The Public Historian* (Winter 1990).

Wright, Robert K., Jr. "Clio in Combat: The Evolution of the Military History Detachment." *The Army Historian* (Winter 1985).

John Schliffer

SEE ALSO Historiography of the Pacific War; History Program, Japanese Air Force

Ho Chi Minh (1890–1969)

Primary organizer and leader of an anti–Japanese and anti–French Communist and nationalist guerrilla movement in Indochina during World War II. He later conducted a successful war of national unification, defeating the French and the Republic of Vietnam, and compelling the United States to withdraw from Vietnam.

Born Nguyen Tat Thanh on May 19, 1890, in Kim Lein, a small village in Nghe An province, central Vietnam, Ho was the son of a minor mandarin official who was dismissed from government service because of his nationalist activities. As a youth, Ho attended Quoc Hoc lycée in Hue, to prepare for a career in government, but left school in 1911 without graduating. He boarded a French steamer to see the world, traveling widely and earning a living as a laborer, galley hand, gardener, photographer's assistant, and laundry worker. During these years he visited Boston, New York, and London, among other places, before ending up in France during World War I.

In Paris, Ho Chi Minh became involved in Vietnamese nationalist activities, and in 1919 he presented a petition to the Big Four at Versailles demanding that the principle of self-determination embodied in President Woodrow Wilson's Fourteen Points be applied to French Indochina. Although his petition was ignored, Ho stayed in France and joined the French Socialist Party in 1919. The next year he broke away from this group to help found the French Communist Party. Strongly drawn to Lenin's ideology, especially his *Thesis on the National and Colonial Questions,* Ho attended the Communist International in Moscow in 1922. In 1923, he left France to live and study in Moscow, where he soon became an expert on colonial issues as well as a professional political organizer.

In 1925 Ho was sent to China as an assistant to the Communist International's adviser to the Chinese Nationalist Kuomintang. While in Canton he organized Vietnamese political exiles into the Vietnamese Revolutionary Youth Movement, edited the political journal *Thanh Nien,* and wrote his only book, *The Road of Revolution.* After the 1927 Communist-Kuomintang, Sino-Soviet split, Ho returned to Moscow before traveling to

Thailand, Canton, and Hong Kong, where he founded the Indochinese Communist Party in 1930. Ho remained in China throughout the 1930s, building the party and keeping in contact with nationalist and Communist groups in Indochina.

After France was defeated by Nazi Germany in June 1940, Japan quickly moved into Indochina in August, the country then being loosely controlled by the pro–Axis Vichy French regime. By the end of 1941, the Japanese dominated Indochina, stationing troops and air and naval forces there. The displacement of the French by the Japanese provided a unique opportunity for Vietnamese nationalists to gain a greater role in political affairs and to agitate for independence under Japanese hegemony, although the Japanese had no intention of granting any sort of real freedom to Vietnam.

From his place of exile in southern China, Ho Chi Minh and other Vietnamese nationalists recognized the implications of the French defeat and of the Japanese occupation. Realizing that the growing nationalist movement would need leadership which he could provide, on May 19, 1941, in a cave near the village of Pac Bo in Cao Bang province, Ho met with Vietnamese Communist leaders to plan strategy. At the conference it was agreed that all Vietnamese, of whatever class or occupation, must be mobilized to achieve independence. To reach this end, an all-encompassing national front organization, the League for the Independence of Vietnam (Viet Nam Doc Lap Dong Minh, or Viet Minh), was formed. Cao Bang would be the movement's main base with recruiting and guerrilla training bases nearby.

Although the Viet Minh was a union of all anti–French and anti–Japanese groups, and although Ho realized that only a broad-front democratic coalition could win international support for Vietnamese independence, he himself was closely associated with the Chinese Communist movement and its leader Mao Tse-tung (Mao Zedong). Ho was therefore jailed by Nationalist Chinese leader Chiang Kai-shek between August 1942 and September 1943. Ho was freed only after members of the U.S. Office of Strategic Services (OSS) based in Kun-ming, China, insisted that he be released and returned to Indochina, where he could fight the Japanese with American-supplied arms, money, and training.

When Chinese Nationalist general and warlord Chang Fa-kwei decided to support and fund the Viet Minh as the primary anti–Japanese guerrilla and intelligence group in Vietnam, he urged Ho to change his name and downplay his Communist background and leanings. Ho did so, selecting the name Ho Chi Minh (Ho, Shedder of Light) in 1943. With this all-important Chinese stamp of official approval, the Viet Minh automatically qualified for more funding from the U.S. mission in China. Ho and the Viet Minh never received substantial aid from the Nationalist Chinese during World War II or from either Chinese or Russian Communists. Ho's real support came from Americans in the OSS who viewed the Viet Minh as the only anti–Japanese force of any use or consequence then active in Vietnam.

In December 1944, Ho ordered the creation of a Viet Minh military division to be called the Vietnamese Liberation Army, under his colleague Vo Nguyen Giap. During the winter of 1944–1945, Viet Minh guerrillas gained control of three northern provinces in Tonkin and sporadically fought both the French and the Japanese. The Viet Minh were also instrumental in rescuing U.S. fliers belonging to the U.S. 14th Army Air Force who were downed over Indochina.

With defeat imminent in 1945, and aware that the French were plotting their overthrow, Japanese forces in Indochina launched a preemptive coup d'état against the French colonial government in March, establishing direct Japanese control of the entire country. Realizing that whatever French aid and support had existed in Indochina was now gone, the OSS turned to the Viet Minh to fill the vacuum. In the spring of 1945, the Viet Minh began to receive significant amounts of military, medical, and material aid from the OSS in Kunming. The Viet Minh in turn accompanied OSS agents on sabotage missions and provided them with general intelligence concerning Japanese movements and dispositions in Indochina. OSS officers served with, and helped train, the Viet Minh at Pac Bo, Cao Bang, and Lang Son.

Seizing the opportunity to supplant both the French and the ever weaker Japanese, Ho Chi Minh and Vo Nguyen Giap moved quickly to take control of the countryside in the spring of 1945. Already controlling much of rural Tonkin, the Viet Minh quickly spread their influence to other parts of the countryside and the major urban areas of the north. In August 1945, when word of the Japanese intention to surrender reached Ho Chi Minh, the Viet Minh quickly took real control of the country. On August 13, Ho formed a provisional government, the National Liberation Committee of Vietnam, and seized Hanoi on August 19 and Hue on August 23. Between August 18 and 28, other units of the Viet Minh, now the largest and strongest political force in Indochina, took control of some sixty district and provincial capitals. On August 29 the Viet Minh formed a national government, the Provisional Government of the Democratic Republic of Vietnam, with its capital in Hanoi. On August 30, Emperor Bao Dai, the French- and Japanese-recognized ruler of Vietnam, presented the imperial seal and sword, the twin symbols of Vietnamese sovereignty, to the Viet Minh and abdicated, leaving Ho Chi Minh and the Viet Minh with the only real power in Vietnam.

With the aid of an OSS agent, Archimedes Patti, Ho Chi Minh wrote a declaration of independence for Vietnam modeled after the American document and proclaimed the creation of the Democratic Republic of Vietnam on September 2, 1945, before a Hanoi crowd of half a million people. OSS personnel joined in the festivities, and several U.S. Army officers stood on the platform with Ho and Giap while a flight of U.S. warplanes flew over the city and "The Star-Spangled Banner" was played.

In April 1946, Ho became president of an autonomous Vietnam within French Indochina, but fighting had already erupted between Viet Minh forces and the French, who sought to reestablish their prewar colonial rule. Ho began a full-scale guerrilla war against the French that same year. Viet Minh military forces under Vo Nguyen Giap, with Ho's political organization and direction, defeated the French in 1954 and Ho became the president of the People's Democratic Republic of North Vietnam, a Communist regime. He established a new guerrilla movement against the anticommunist Republic of South Vietnam in 1959 and fought against both that government and the United States after 1965. Ho died on September 3, 1969. He did not live to see Vietnam officially unified under Communist rule, an event that occurred in 1976, at enormous cost. At no time during his life did Ho Chi Minh keep a diary, write his memoirs, or dictate his biography, so in many ways he remains an enigmatic figure.

FURTHER READINGS

Lacouture, Jean. *Ho Chi Minh: A Political Biography* (1968)

Maclear, Michael. *The Ten Thousand Day War: Vietnam, 1945–1975.* (1981).

Spector, Ronald A. *Advice and Support: The Early Years, U.S. Army in Vietnam* (U.S. Army Center of Military History, 1983).

Clayton D. Laurie

SEE ALSO Office of Strategic Services in the Pacific

Holcomb, Thomas (1879–1965)

Seventeenth commandant of the U.S. Marine Corps (1936–1943). Born on August 5, 1879, in New Castle, Delaware, Holcomb began his military career as a marine second lieutenant in April 1900. Holcomb had a variety of assignments from China to the Philippines and impressed his superiors with his abilities. He also launched the marine corps rifle team and competed on the team at the national matches, winning the national championship in 1911. During World War I, Holcomb distinguished himself as commanding officer of the 2d Battalion, 6th Marines, in the American Expeditionary Force. His leadership at the Battles of Belleau Wood, Blanc Mont, and Soissons won him decorations that included the Navy Cross, the Silver Star with three oak-leaf clusters, and France's Croix de Guerre with palm. Eventually, Holcomb joined the staff of the U.S. Army's 2d Division. His service in France gave him invaluable experience in administration and leadership.

During the 1920s, Holcomb graduated with distinction from the U.S. Army's Command and Staff College, served at Marine Corps Headquarters in the Division of Operations and Training, and commanded the American legation in Peking, China. In the early 1930s Holcomb, now a colonel, attended both the Navy War College, and the Army War College, and served in the Office of Naval Operations in Washington, D.C. In 1935, Holcomb was promoted to brigadier general and was appointed superintendent of the Marine Corps Schools at Quantico, Virginia.

The interwar years were lean for the marine corps. It faced numerous problems: severe overextension; promotion bottlenecks leading to overage, conservative higher officers; low morale; interservice rivalries; and budgetary restraints. At a low point during the Great Depression, Holcomb assumed the rank of major general commandant of the marine corps in December 1936. His experience and education helped prepare him for the two greatest challenges of his career: expanding the corps and fighting World War II. He guided the corp's massive expansion from approximately 17,000 marines in 1936 to nearly 65,000 in late November 1941, and more than 300,000 when he retired at the end of 1943. The corps's expenditures grew as quickly: from $21 million in 1936 to $67 million in 1941 to $493 million in 1943. Holcomb played two pivotal roles in this growth: as salesman cajoling the civilian government into supporting the corps and as administrator supervising its expansion. His performance and the need for talented leadership led President Franklin D. Roosevelt to appoint Holcomb to a second term as commandant in 1940.

Gaining popular support from the American people provided the best avenue to gaining financial support from Congress. In an ambitious public relations campaign in all available media, Holcomb stressed the corps's unique capability as a base defense force. Less conspicuously, he publicized the offensive role of amphibious assault. Holcomb consistently portrayed the corps as an integral part of the navy and of America's defense. Beyond courting public support, he initiated better relations with Congress. He devoted significant energy to encouraging passage of bills that benefited the corps. Holcomb took several steps to minimize the problems of appropriations. First, he demanded that his subordinates document every cent of their projected expenses. When testifying before Congress, he never bluffed or overestimated the importance of a given request. Instead, Holcomb admitted any lack of justification within his projections when questioned by legislators. He then sought a satisfactory answer for the legislators as soon as possible. Holcomb's fiscal thoroughness and honesty won him respect from Congress. Thus, when important votes occurred, Congress was inclined to be sympathetic to the corps's plight.

In the 1930s, Marines still used World War I vintage weapons and equipment. The Springfield 1903 rifle remained in most marines' hands well into 1943; the M-1 Garand slowly replaced it. To make matters worse, Holcomb and the corps struggled with the task of robbing Peter to pay Paul. Sufficient equipment and manpower did not exist to fulfill the corps's amphibious assault, base defense, aviation, and ship and shore missions. Nevertheless, Holcomb had to juggle all these priorities. The outbreak of war in Europe in September 1939 was a major turning point for the corps. Guaranteeing the existence the marine corps or finding a mission for it ceased to be an issue. Expansion surfaced as the major issue—not if, but how much and how fast. Holcomb found it much easier to enlarge training facilities, increase recruitment, and develop equipment such as landing craft. Still, the reality of unpreparedness persisted because appropriations and procurement progressed very slowly. The corps remained perpetually six months behind schedule to meet its ever widening responsibilities.

To increase the corps's administrative efficiency, Holcomb split Marine Corps Headquarters into several divisions and departments: Plans and Policies, Aviation, Public Information, Reserve, Recruiting, Inspection, Personnel, and Supply. Each performed specific tasks in Holcomb's decentralized style of management. This corresponded with the commandant's established function as administrator rather than field commander. Delegation of authority allowed Holcomb to concentrate on matters external to the corps, such as interservice and civil-military relations.

After the Japanese attack on the U.S. naval facility at Pearl Harbor, Hawaii, in 1941, Holcomb helped coordinate the initial U.S. counteroffensive across the Pacific

from Washington, D.C. He delicately balanced the corps's missions and activities among the joint chiefs of staff, Admiral Chester Nimitz, and General Douglas MacArthur. Holcomb had to contend with being subordinate to the joint chiefs of staff in Washington. Moreover, the corps was clearly subordinate to the army and navy in the Pacific and southwest Pacific theaters, commanded by Nimitz and MacArthur, respectively. Meanwhile, Holcomb rose to the rank of lieutenant general in January 1942, making him the highest-ranking marine to that point in the corps's history.

Establishing a chain of command became one of Holcomb's most immediate problems. As part of the Department of the Navy, the marine corps occupied a subordinate position in the strategic decision-making process. However, at the tactical level, unifying command under a navy flag officer could prove to be problematic because the navy's commanders often had little experience with or understanding of amphibious assault tactics.

The command structure during the Guadalcanal campaign was an example of unity of command problems. The overzealous Rear Admiral Richmond K. Turner failed to give marine Major General Alexander A. Vandegrift enough latitude to exercise tactical leadership after the initial landing. Vandegrift commanded the reinforced 1st Marine Division, which was to take and hold an airfield on Guadalcanal. Instead, Turner attempted to micromanage all aspects of the Guadalcanal operation.

Planning and executing successful amphibious operations necessitated giving marine commanders equity and autonomy in the command structure. Holcomb solved this problem by proposing that marine commanders have parity with navy commanders during the planning and the subsequent tactical operation on land. Navy commanders would exercise undisputed control only during actual landing operations. In theory, unity of command existed with the theater commander. However, even this arrangement was no long-term solution because the Pacific was divided between MacArthur and Nimitz.

Holcomb had to be strongly persuaded to include women and African Americans in the corps; many marines of all ranks shared his attitude. In 1943, the women marines were established and eventually grew to a strength of 23,000. African American units came on line in 1942, but they were relegated to labor and other segregated units.

Looking back on the first two years of World War II, it can be seen that Holcomb played a central part in the history of the marine corps and in its successful prosecution of the Pacific war. He increased the esprit de corps among marines by establishing the corps as an indispensable piece of U.S. Pacific strategy. Much of the corps's success and glory can be credited to Holcomb's efforts and foresight. He was placed on the retired list on January 1, 1944, advanced to general, and then recalled to active duty until April 1944. In the interim, Holcomb actively helped to ensure the corps's continued growth and success. Finally, he was removed from its active rolls after more than forty years of service. Alexander A. Vandegrift, Holcomb's successor as commandant of the marine corps, continued his ambitious expansion plan, which saw the corps increase to more than 450,000 marines by mid-1944. From 1944 until 1948, Holcomb served as minister to South Africa. He then retired to a farm in Maryland. He died on May 24, 1965.

Perhaps military historian John W. Gordon pays the best tribute to Holcomb, comparing him in "personality, style, and even intellectual equipment" to General George C. Marshall, chief of staff of the U.S. Army during World War II. In fact, Gordon believes that "Holcomb was a sort of "mini-Marshall" in his juggling far tinier resources but coping with the vaster geographic sweep of the Pacific. Gordon's sentiment exemplifies an almost universal admiration for Holcomb among enlisted marines, officers, and historians.

FURTHER READINGS

Gordon, John W. "General Thomas Holcomb and 'The Golden Age of Amphibious Warfare.' " *Delaware History* (September 1985).

Millet, Allan R. *Semper Fidelis: The History of the United States Marine Corps*, rev. ed. (1991).

Ulbrich, David J. "Thomas Holcomb and the Advent of the Marine Corps Defense Battalion, 1936–1941." M.A. thesis, Ball State University (1996).

U.S. Marine Corps. *History of U.S. Marine Corps Operations in World War II*, 5 vols. (1958–1968).

Vandegrift, Alexander A., and Robert B. Asprey. *Once a Marine: The Memoirs of General A. A. Vandegrift, USMC* (1964).

David Ulbrich

SEE ALSO Marine Corps, U.S.; Vandegrift, Alexander A.

Hollandia

By early 1944 Allied forces in the Southwest Pacific Area (SWPA), commanded by General Douglas MacArthur, had advanced as far west along the coast of northeast New Guinea as Saidor. Originally MacArthur had next planned to attack Hansa Bay, 200 miles northwest of Saidor, on April 26. But with the capture of the Admiralty Islands in early March, MacArthur decided to leap 580 miles northwest to Hollandia (now Djajapura), in Dutch New Guinea (now Irian Barat).

Hollandia was a major Japanese air and supply base. The port and the surrounding area, stretching 25 miles along the coast from Humboldt (now Kayo) Bay to Tanahmerah Bay, was dominated by the 6,000-foot-high Cyclops Mountains, which run parallel to the coast with steep cliffs dropping down to the sea, and Lake Sentani to the south. The Dajaoe Plain, located between the mountains and the lake, was suitable for air bases, and by 1944 the Japanese had constructed three compacted-earth airstrips there: Hollandia, Sentani, and Cyclops dromes. A fourth airstrip, Tami Drome, had been built about 20 miles east of Lake Sentani, near the mouth of the Tami River.

The leap to Hollandia had several major advantages for MacArthur. First, it would enable him to avoid potentially bloody battles at Hansa Bay and Wewak, where there were strong concentrations of Japanese troops, and to isolate the Japanese Eighteenth Army in eastern New Guinea. Second, it would accelerate the pace of the New Guinea campaign, because the current schedule did not call for the seizure of Hollandia until the fall of 1944. And third, it would provide him with an ideal springboard for his ultimate move to the Philippines. The port of Hollandia was the best sheltered anchorage on a lengthy stretch of the northern coast of New Guinea, and for some time MacArthur's staff had been preparing plans to turn the area into a major base area for future operations in western New Guinea and the Philippines. According to their plans, Hollandia would serve as a staging area for 100,000 troops and be able to handle supplies to support twice that number. In addition, there would be two airstrips for heavy bombers, an airship for fighters, and an emergency field.

The catalyst for MacArthur's decision to leap to Hollandia was the work of his Central Bureau, or cryptoanalyst section. Monitoring Japanese radio traffic in February, it determined that Hollandia was weakly held, apparently because the Japanese expected that MacArthur would be bogged down in the jungles of eastern New Guinea and would not be near Hollandia for some months. To the east, in northeast New Guinea, Lieutenant General Adachi Hatazo commanded three divisions that were retreating from the Saidor and Madang areas to the Hansa Bay–Wewak region, where the Japanese expected MacArthur to attack in May. To the west, in Dutch New Guinea, the Japanese Second Army had 50,000 troops in three divisions, with the easternmost stationed in the Wadke–Sarmi vicinity, about 300 miles west of Wewak. Hollandia, between Wewak and Wadke–Sarmi, was the soft center of the Japanese defensive position and was garrisoned by about 11,000 troops. Most were service personnel and pilots and crews from the Japanese 6th Air Division. Only about one-fifth were combat troops.

Even with the relatively small number of Japanese defenders, the 580-mile leap to Hollandia was risky because it exceeded the range of MacArthur's land-based fighter planes. But after agreeing to the Hollandia operation on March 12, the joint chiefs of staff instructed Admiral Chester W. Nimitz, commander of the U.S. Pacific Fleet and the Pacific Ocean areas, to lend his powerful Fifth Fleet aircraft carriers to MacArthur. At the same time, Lieutenant General George Kenney, commander of MacArthur's overall air forces and of the U.S. Fifth Air Force, sped up efforts to extend the range of the P-38 fighter through the modification of the wing tanks to increase its range from 350 miles to 650 miles. With the newly converted long-range P-38s, Kenney could now provide fighter protection for his B-17 and B-24 heavy bombers in their raids against Hollandia from their nearest base, Nadzab, in the lower Markham River valley, 448 miles from Hollandia.

In early 1944 the Japanese had begun to build up their air units to challenge the Allies for air supremacy over New Guinea. During March, however, Kenney's bombers struck heavy blows against the Japanese air bases at Wewak, Hansa Bay, Aitape, and Hollandia. The attacks were so effective that Lieutenant General Teramoto Kunachi, commander of the Japanese Fourth Air Army, decided to move his forward units at Wewak back to Hollandia. Most of the ground crew specialists had to withdraw by land, and the jungle claimed several hundred of them. On March 30, March 31, and April 3, Kenney's bombers hit Hollandia in devastating raids that damaged or destroyed nearly four hundred of the 6th Air Division's planes and ruined installations, antiaircraft gun emplacements, and fuel and ammunition dumps. Although additional raids continued to the day of the Hollandia landings, Kenney's first series of strikes virtually annihilated Japanese air strength in New Guinea and paved the way for MacArthur's ground troops.

Increasingly concerned about the weakness of his forces at Hollandia, General Anami Korechika, commander of the 2nd Area Army, ordered Adachi to move the 51st Division to Hollandia. But Adachi, convinced that MacArthur's next landing would be at Wewak or Hansa Bay, was slow to comply with Anami's instructions, telling him that it would be July before the division would arrive at Hollandia. Distressed by Adachi's reply, Anami sent his chief of staff to Wewak on April 12 to accelerate the transfer of the 51st Division.

Reluctantly, Adachi agreed to have two of the division's regiments start their march to Hollandia immediately. They were expected to arrive in early May. Anami also wanted to move the 36th Division from Wadke–Sarmi to Hollandia. However, General Count Terauchi Hisaichi commander of the Southern Army, ordered it to remain in its defensive positions.

During March and early April, MacArthur's staff prepared plans for the Hollandia operation, which was to be carried out by Lieutenant General Robert L. Eichelberger's 1st Corps. Dubbed Operation Reckless, it would be the biggest operation in SWPA to date. Two regiments from the 24th Division, commanded by Major General Frederick A. Irving, were to land on two beaches at Tanahmerah Bay and, using native trails, work their way around the Cyclops Mountains and move toward the three airfields located on the plain to the south. Simultaneously, two regiments from the 41st Division, commanded by Major General Horace H. Fuller, were to land 25 miles to the east at Humboldt Bay, and move toward the airfields from the west. Finally, the 163d Infantry Regiment from the 41st Division and the 127th Infantry Regiment from the 32d Division were to land at Aitape, 125 miles to the southeast, to secure the nearby fighter strips. Altogether, the operation would consist of 80,000 men and require 217 ships, organized into the 7th Amphibious Force, commanded by Rear Admiral Daniel E. Barbey and sailing from three staging areas, including Goodenough Island, more than a thousand miles to the south. To keep the Japanese off guard, MacArthur's command carried on an extensive deception effort to convince them that his next blow would come, as they expected, at Hansa Bay or Wewak.

On April 20 the three convoys of the 7th Amphibious Force rendezvoused north of the Admiralty Islands as part of a ruse to persuade the Japanese that a move toward the Caroline Islands or possibly Rabaul, on New Britain Island, was forthcoming. Then, after dark, they turned toward the New Guinea coast. Following heavy naval and air bombardment, the assault troops began to land on the morning of April 22. The Japanese garrison at Hollandia, commanded by Major General Inada Masazumi, commander of the 6th Air Division, was caught completely by surprise and put up only sporadic opposition. Many Japanese defenders—demoralized, greatly outnumbered, and ill equipped for battle (only one in ten had a rifle)—quickly fled into the interior. Overhead, naval aircraft flew protective missions, but they were not really needed, because Japanese aircraft did not seriously challenge the landings on April 22. On the night of April 23, however, two Japanese type 99 bombers did hit a supply dump for the 41st Division, setting off a chain reaction of explosions that killed 24, wounded 100, and destroyed 60 percent of the rations and ammunition landed since the morning of April 22.

Even after MacArthur's troops were ashore, the Japanese mounted no meaningful organized resistance. For the 24th Division, the terrain proved to be the biggest obstacle. The landing beaches at Tanahmerah Bay were hemmed in by nearly impassable swamps, and after the 21st Infantry Regiment had already landed, Eichelberger decided to shift the division's 19th Infantry Regiment to Humboldt Bay. The troops already landed had to have their supplies augmented by airdrops. Despite heavy rains and their being strung out over a long, narrow, muddy trail, they steadily moved forward, encountering no opposition except for the occasional sniper, even though a small number of determined defenders could easily have delayed them by using the many hairpin turns and defiles as ambush points. On April 26 they seized Hollandia Drome, pushing aside a few enemy troops in an unsupported defensive position.

To the east, the two regiments from the 41st Division also encountered light resistance. The town of Hollandia was captured on April 23 by the 162d Infantry Regiment without opposition. Small-scale Japanese counterattacks slightly delayed the advance of the 186th Infantry Regiment toward Lake Sentani; however, by the evening of April 26, it had overrun the other airfields and linked up with the 21st Infantry, connecting the two beachheads. Mop-up operations that produced several fierce firefights continued over the next weeks. Total American casualties were 159 killed and 1,100 wounded. The Japanese lost 3,300 dead and 600 prisoners, the latter an unusually large bag. At Aitape, meanwhile, the objectives were secured by the evening of April 25 at a cost of three dead. About 600 Japanese were killed and twenty-seven were taken prisoner.

As MacArthur's troops were completing their pincer movement in the Tanahmerah-Humboldt Bay area, Inada began to collect approximately 7,000 troops at the west of Lake Sentani. In early May they started to march through the jungle to Wadke-Sarmi, 140 miles to the west. Lacking adequate food and medical supplies, and harassed by patrols from the 24th Division, they suffered terribly. Thousands died from starvation, disease, or wounds. Only about a thousand survived the trek, all that remained of the nearly 11,000 defending the Hollandia area in March.

Operation Reckless was a major triumph for MacArthur. Skillfully applying intelligence from code breaking to operational planning, he dramatically split the Japanese forces defending New Guinea in half, leaving Adachi's Eighteenth Army isolated in eastern New Guinea, and provided himself with a superb base area from which he could increase the tempo of future operations in the SWPA. Quickly, American engineers began to develop a vast complex of military, naval, and air facilities at Hollandia, although, to the dismay of MacArthur, it was soon learned that the soil around Lake Sentani was too soft to support the planned heavy-bomber strips until extensive engineering was completed. Roads were constructed, pipelines were laid, and docks were occupied by 140,000 men. Following the destruction of Adachi's remaining offensive power in late August, the advance headquarters of all of MacArthur's organizations were moved to Hollandia. Their compounds were on a hillside overlooking Lake Sentani, with MacArthur's house at the top. Stories circulated that it was the "White House of the Southwest Pacific," but because of the demands of planning new operations, MacArthur spent a total of only four nights there before moving his headquarters to Leyte Island in the Philippines in October 1944.

FURTHER READINGS

Craven, Wesley Frank, and James Lea Cate, eds. *The Army Air Forces in World War II*. Vol. 4, *The Pacific: Guadalcanal to Saipan, August 1942–July 1944* (1950).

Drea, Edward J. *MacArthur's Ultra: Codebreaking and the War Against Japan, 1942–1945* (1992).

James, D. Clayton. *The Years of MacArthur*, vol. 2 (1975).

Morison, Samuel Eliot. *History of United States Naval Operations in World War II*. Vol. 8, *New Guinea and the Marianas, March 1944–August 1944* (1953).

Prefer, Nathan. *MacArthur's New Guinea Campaign* (1995).

Smith, Ross. *The Approach to the Philippines* (1953).

Taafe, Stephen. *MacArthur's Jungle War: The 1944 New Guinea Campaign* (1998).

John Kennedy Ohl

SEE ALSO Kenney, George C.; MacArthur, Douglas; New Guinea

Home Front, Japanese

When considering the situation in Japan during the Pacific war, it is important to remember that by the time of the Japanese attack on the U.S. naval base at Pearl Harbor,

Hawaii, in December 1941, the nation had already been at war with China for more than four years, and Japanese society had already grown accustomed to providing for the demands of the military. The economy, for example, had been fully geared to wartime production since the passage of the National Mobilization Act of 1938, which gave the armed forces first claim on all resources and manpower. The government saw to it that nearly all available raw materials were so assigned; thus consumer goods had become practically nonexistent. By 1940 the government was rationing matches and sugar, and rationing of rice and charcoal followed in 1941. By the end of the war, nearly every daily necessity had been added to the list. As a result, Japanese civilians used whatever substitutes were available. Synthetic fibers replaced cotton in clothing. Metal eating utensils vanished in favor of ones made of bamboo, and relatively clean-burning gasoline-powered buses were replaced by charcoal-burning vehicles that filled the air with soot.

Nor did the conquest of the "Southern Resource Area"—Indochina, Malaya, and the Dutch East Indies—help much. Although these areas were indeed rich in resources, the military laid first claim to their bounty. Moreover, there were increasing difficulties in getting these resources to the home islands as the war went on, not to mention the heavy costs of defending them—in vain, as it turned out. By 1944, Allied control of the shipping lanes, as well as the almost complete decimation of the Japanese merchant marine, meant that very few raw materials were reaching Japan.

Both socially and culturally, life in wartime Japan took on an increasingly somber tone. Western-style art and music could not be displayed or performed, and many other forms of art were discouraged as "frivolous." Romance novels, for example, were branded "useless literature of leisure," unfit for Japanese attention during the time of national crisis. Dance halls were closed, and by 1942 marches and patriotic anthems were the only musical pieces heard on the radio. Clothing fashions changed as well, with Western-style or colorful articles disappearing in favor of the simple khaki "people's uniform" for men and pantaloons for women.

Given that Japanese governments in the 1930s had so often complained of the country's overpopulation, it is ironic that the war brought a severe scarcity of manpower. By 1945 more than 7 million Japanese men were in uniform, so in order to keep the factories operating at home, it became necessary to recruit students and women, and to draft Korean and Chinese laborers from the Asian mainland. These substitute workers, however, were ill-fed and (especially the Koreans and Chinese) mistreated, and

therefore not very productive. Per capita production actually dropped between 1941 and 1944, whereas production in other belligerent nations increased dramatically.

Of course, all of the problems experienced by the Japanese at home were magnified after November 1944, when large-scale bombing of the home islands by U.S. aircraft began. Over the next eight months, sixty-six Japanese cities were targeted for destruction, and about 40 percent of each of them was left in ruins. By war's end approximately 20 percent of all the homes in Japan had been leveled by bombs. Nor was the destruction of homes the only negative effect for Japanese civilians; the resultant disruption of agriculture, shipping, and the fishing industry led to severe malnutrition. It is estimated that the daily caloric intake among the Japanese in 1945 averaged less than 1,800 calories, well below the 2,200-calorie minimum recommended by most nutritionists.

Naturally, maintaining public morale in the face of wartime deprivation was a major concern for Japan's political and military leaders. They were helped by the fact that in 1941, Japan had one of the world's most sophisticated mass media networks. Nearly 850 daily newspapers reached about 7 million households every day. Radio broadcasting brought news and entertainment to about half the population. Over twenty-seven hundred magazines were published, with a combined circulation of 6.5 million.

All of these media outlets were harnessed to the war effort. Outright criticism of the war, of course, was forbidden by law, but formal disciplinary measures were not usually necessary. Informal means, such as denying newsprint to publishers who refused to cooperate with censors, or blacklisting journalists who tended to report on negative aspects of the war, were far more common. In 1940, in order to control the press more easily, the government began encouraging newspapers to merge; as a result, only fifty-four remained in existence by 1943. Japanese home front propaganda was greatly assisted, of course, by the nation's relatively homogeneous population.

In spite of these measures, however, it remained possible to criticize certain government activities. Inefficiency and mismanagement in food distribution, local administration, and civil defense were frequent targets of editorial criticism. Even military strategy was not off-limits; in February 1944 the national newspaper *Mainichi shimbun* published an article titled "Bamboo Spears Are Not Enough," which chided the army for having given insufficient attention to the threat of Allied invasion. Although the author was soon conscripted into the army, no effort was made to punish the newspaper.

Nor were newspapers the only element of the propaganda campaign; artists, writers, musicians, and filmmakers were enlisted as well. Organizations such as the Great Japan Patriotic Writers Association, the Literary Patriotic Association, and the Roving Musical Patriotic Volunteer Corps organized creative people for the war effort and promoted a nationalistic spirit. Filmmakers did their part by producing a stream of propaganda films such as *The Story of Tank Commander Nishizumi* (1940), *The Battles of Hawaii and Malaya* (1942), and *Momotaro—Divine Troops of the Ocean* (1944), as well as dramatic newsreels that brought images of the new southern empire back to the home islands. Above all, however, writers offered patriotic slogans, such as "Luxury is the enemy," "Saving is the road to victory," and "Deny oneself and serve the nation."

The campaign to mobilize Japan for war extended to the neighborhood level. Every five to ten households were organized into *tonarigumi,* neighborhood associations under the control of the Home Ministry. Members of these groups were expected to keep an eye on their neighbors and encourage them to support the war effort in any way possible. They were also responsible for distributing rationed items and organizing parties to celebrate the departure of local soldiers and sailors as they went off to join the fighting.

The converse of the government's propaganda campaign was the suppression of ideas that might undermine the country's support for the war. Indeed, this predated even the fighting in China. The Peace Preservation Act of 1928 made it a crime to advocate the abolition of private property or the overthrow of the emperor. The Communist party was outlawed soon thereafter, and mass arrests of Marxists and socialists began as early as 1936. After the outbreak of the "China Incident" (as Japan's invasion of China was termed), liberals and pacifists were increasingly subjected to police harassment. In addition, organizations suspected of left-wing leanings, including most labor unions, were forced to dissolve.

At the same time, however, political repression never reached the extent that it did in Nazi Germany or the Soviet Union, even with Japan's infamous "thought police." It was generally possible to avoid police harassment simply by keeping quiet and obeying the law. And although prison conditions were abysmal, and the police were often brutal in their tactics, there were no concentration camps or mass executions in wartime Japan. Indeed, during the entire war only one Japanese civilian—Ozaki Hotsumi, accomplice of the Soviet spy Richard Sorge—was executed by the government. Moreover, while 74,000 people were arrested for violating the Peace Preservation Act, only about 5,000 were actually prosecuted. By the end of the war, fewer than 2,500 political

prisoners remained behind bars. The preferred method was to "rehabilitate" dissidents and force them to recant their views.

Another way in which wartime Japan differed both from its Axis partners and even from such Allied powers as Chiang Kai-shek's China and Stalin's Soviet Union, was in its political organization. Though Japan's form of government could hardly be called democratic, neither was it a dictatorship. The emperor, although in theory having absolute political power, remained a distant and detached figure who participated actively only when there was deadlock between the cabinet and the high command; he intervened, for example, to decide in favor of surrender to the Allies in August 1945. And although the emperor's portrait could be seen throughout Japan—in shop windows, school classrooms, military bases, and private homes—the emperor himself made very few public appearances, and never addressed his people. Indeed, his August 15 radio broadcast announcing the surrender was the first time that the overwhelming majority of Japanese had ever heard their ruler's voice.

Japan's political parties, which had been losing influence since the late 1920s, voluntarily dissolved themselves in 1940 to become part of the Imperial Rule Assistance Association (IRAA; *Taiseiyokusankai*), a single party designed to promote national unity. Nevertheless, the popularly elected Japanese Diet continued to function and pass legislation throughout the war. Indeed, aside from the United States, Japan was the only major belligerent to hold relatively free national elections during the war. The IRAA's candidates won nearly two-thirds of the vote in the 1942 elections, without overt government interference in the campaign. Though the Diet had little real power, the results were a reflection of the effectiveness of the government's propaganda efforts. Indeed, the most serious opposition came not from opponents of the war—who had been silenced by this time—but from extreme rightists who hoped to build a regime modeled after that of Nazi Germany.

During the war considerable political power accrued in the hands of the prime minister, Tojo Hideki, who gradually took on the added responsibilities of army minister, home minister, and munitions minister. However, Tojo was far from a dictator in the mold of Hitler, Stalin, or Mussolini, and he probably enjoyed less freedom of action than British Prime Minister Winston Churchill or President Franklin D. Roosevelt. The supreme command of the armed forces remained answerable only to the emperor, not to the prime minister, so that Tojo had no say in operational decisions. Nor did he ever command broad support among any segment of the population. The emperor remained the focus of popular loyalty, and several outspoken critics of Tojo in the armed forces (especially the navy) openly attacked his policies. Ultimately criticisms of Tojo's performance reached all the way to the imperial court, and the emperor expressed his desire that Tojo resign after the fall of Saipan to the Americans in July 1944, which Tojo did. At no time, then, could wartime Japan have been considered a true dictatorship.

In contrast to Japan's crushing military defeat in Asia and the Pacific, the home front war was one that Tokyo undoubtedly won. The campaigns to rally the Japanese people behind the war, and to suppress opposition to it, were by far the most effective elements of the government's war effort. Despite the series of costly defeats suffered by the armed forces between 1942 and 1945, despite sustained terror bombings of the civilian population by U.S. aircraft in late 1944 and 1945, despite the almost complete collapse of Japan's infrastructure and economy, most Japanese civilians remained loyal to their emperor and their political system until the actual moment of the emperor's surrender broadcast. While there were some indications of discontent—a semiactive black market in rationed goods, grumbling, and occasional appearances of subversive (mainly Communist-inspired) graffiti—there were no popular demonstrations, let alone uprisings, against the government. Its edicts were more or less willingly obeyed to the very end, when the Japanese people were informed by His Imperial Majesty's broadcast in nearly unintelligible court language that the war "has not gone entirely to Japan's advantage."

FURTHER READINGS

Cook, Haruko Taya. *Japan at War: An Oral History* (1992).

Dower, John W. "Japanese Cinema Goes to War." In his *Japan in War & Peace: Selected Essays* (1993).

———. "Sensational Rumors, Seditious Graffiti, and the Nightmares of the Thought Police." In his *Japan in War & Peace: Selected Essays* (1993).

Hane, Mikiso. *Modern Japan: A Historical Survey,* 2d ed. (1992).

Ienaga, Saburo. *The Pacific War, 1931–1945* (1978).

Shillony, Ben-Ami. *Politics and Culture in Wartime Japan* (1981).

John E. Moser

SEE ALSO Home Front, U.S.

Home Front, U.S.

Though the loss of 300,000 Americans in World War II can never be minimized, nor can the anguish of their survivors, still, for most Americans their home front experience was almost a positive one, because it finally brought to an end the seemingly endless Great Depression. Factory employment lines replaced bread lines. Help Wanted signs replaced No Help Wanted—This Means You notices. The U.S. home front was unique in its prosperity and in its unity, and in its comparatively light burden of war in terms of relative casualties and in the proportion of the young men actually mobilized. The Canadian home front, prosperous enough, was riven with the strife between Anglophones and Francophones to the extent that the dominion could not enact conscription until 1944 and no conscripts actually went overseas. The British Isles, of course, were under heavy aerial bombardment and strict rationing. Australia and New Zealand lost most of their young men for the duration, and the Soviets endured greater loss of life, destruction, and privations than were suffered by any and all of the rest of the Allies, save China, combined. In the words of one scholar, "War is hell. But for millions of Americans on the booming home front, World War II was also a hell of a war" (M. H. Leff, "The Politics of Sacrifice on the Home Front in World War II," *Journal of American History* 77 [1991]).

Yet on the eve of their entrance into World War II, the American people had been so divided over the wisdom of even preparing for the obviously coming conflict that the bill to extend the service of draftees beyond October 1941 was passed by a one-vote margin in the House of Representatives.

But the Japanese attack on the U.S. naval base at Pearl Harbor, Hawaii, in December 1941 so rallied the American people, so united them in a determination to win the war, that ever since then some critics have suspected that President Franklin D. Roosevelt somehow must have had a hand in it. The bitter arguments between America Firsters (so-called isolationists, whose isolation usually did not extend beyond Europe) and interventionists as America fought an undeclared naval war against Nazi Germany were swept away in a hot sense of anger at the "sneak attack" on Pearl Harbor and replaced by a dogged, united, and patriotic determination to gain revenge for the "sneak attack" and to win the war. Four days after Pearl Harbor, Hitler, in an act of folly equaled only by his attack on the Soviet Union, gratuitously declared war on the United States. (The Nazis for once respected the diplomatic amenities enough to issue a declaration of war.)

American wartime determination was not usually articulated in patriotic statements; when young men were asked why they had interrupted their careers to join the armed forces, the common reply was "There's a job to do." (Soon the question became academic; recruiting offices were closed and Selective Service took the able-bodied and eligible.) Indeed, the U.S. home front (much like the British and the Soviet) was a dynamic element of the history of World War II and one of the main reasons for the success of the Allies in fighting a global war.

The home front had many dimensions—economic, social, and political—as might be expected, but the overriding theme was the sense of unity and commitment to hard work. For those who remained at home, the war meant sacrifices—and jobs. Employment had of course been scarce during the Great Depression, which had lasted for more than a decade, and the opportunity to work, with about as much overtime as a worker could bear, benefited many Americans who had long been without steady income. To be sure, the war was not a pleasant way to furnish employment, but for millions of workers it meant a regular paycheck, a welcomed end to the Depression. It was this combination of a united spirit and a willingness to work to defeat enemies who represented pure evil, plus a physical plant that had not run at anything like full production since 1930, that led to the record surge of material output during the years 1942–1945: 80,000 landing craft, 100,000 armored vehicles, 2.4 million military trucks, 2.6 million machine guns.

This production "miracle" made the American soldier the best equipped in the world, always in quantity, usually in quality. (The British, for example, marveled at the gabardine in the uniform of the lowliest U.S. Army private; such cloth was reserved for officers in the British army.) Every U.S. soldier could have ridden to battle in U.S.-produced military vehicles without much crowding. This military cornucopia was also directed toward America's allies. Chinese Nationalist soldiers were equipped with U.S. weapons, British civilians ate Spam, and the Free French armor was entirely U.S.-made. As for the Soviets, their aircraft were built with U.S.-supplied aluminum, their supplies was sent to the front in trains often pulled by U.S.-built steam locomotives, and many of the air force's ground-attack aircraft were P-39s and P-63s turned out by Bell Aircraft of Buffalo, New York. And so many 2.5-ton all-axle-drive military trucks were sent to the Soviet Union that to this day, without knowing why anymore, Russians speak of all-axle-drive trucks as *Studeborkii*.

Mobilization began as early as August 1939, when President Franklin D. Roosevelt created the War Resources Board. Headed by Edward R. Stettinius, it made plans for organizing materials for the war effort. Roosevelt created the Office of Emergency Management in May 1940, and the Office of Production Management, led by William S. Knudsen, in January 1941. These first efforts

had limited impact. Roosevelt was careful not to move too far too fast, for fear of offending the majority of the general public, which, although sympathetic to the French until their defeat by Germany, to the Soviet Union after Hitler tore up his nonaggression pact with Stalin, and to the steadfast British, still intended to stay out of the war.

The Japanese attack on Pearl Harbor ended all questions about U.S. entry into the war, of course, and Roosevelt, realizing that the United States had to furnish materials for itself and, to a great extent, for its allies, created the War Production Board in January 1942. He selected Donald Nelson of Sears, Roebuck, and Company as its head, intending for Nelson to make it the principal agency for mobilizing the economy. Nelson could not reach that goal, however, due primarily to squabbling between branches of the armed forces and conflict between the military and civilian sectors. In May 1943 Roosevelt created the Office of War Mobilization and named James F. Byrnes as head. Byrnes was an excellent choice because of his stature in the Democratic Party and government circles. Previously a justice of the U.S. Supreme Court, he had prestige and influence, and he was known for his persuasive powers. Byrnes, who came to be regarded as the "economic czar," put the economy on a full wartime footing. By this time Roosevelt had established the Office of Price Administration (OPA) to set "fair" prices. He was roundly cursed for it by businessmen, but the OPA probably saved the nation from serious inflation of the type that had ravaged workers during World War I.

Other agencies had to be created, such as the War Labor Board, which tried to hold down strikes and wage increases. Although strikes were frequent—as many as 14,471 during the war, according to one authority—they did not really endanger the war effort. John L. Lewis, now head of the United Mine Workers' Union, and not one to let a world war interfere with improvement of his workers' conditions, became a target of particular hatred—"God damn your coal-black soul," one soldier wrote home—as he led the mine workers on several strikes. The federal government had to take over the mines for a short time. For the majority of Americans, John L. Lewis ranked slightly above a draft dodger. The heads of the Congress of Industrial Organizations (CIO) and the American Federation of Labor (AFL), by way of contrast, cooperated as fully as they felt possible with the president and the war effort.

Another strike, much less far-ranging than those of the miners, but even more bitter and revealing of underlying American racial attitudes, shut down the Philadelphia Transportation Company (PTC). The PTC, desperate for motormen to operate its streetcars, had made the radical step of beginning to train blacks for this work. White unionists protested and walked out of the carbarns. Roosevelt, realizing the key role that Philadelphia—with its Frankford Arsenal, shipyards, and a host of smaller industries—was playing in the war effort, diverted troops from training for overseas battlefronts to stand guard on streetcar platforms in order to keep the vehicles running. But the strike continued, tying up war industries, whose workers, in those years of strict tire and gasoline rationing, had few alternative means of getting to the job. Only the threat of being drafted into the army sent the union stalwarts back to their vital tasks. Nonetheless, after Pearl Harbor there was, in the vast majority of industries and businesses, a willingness to put aside union rules and the right to strike, and to get on with the job.

The early war years also saw a surge of industrial accidents as plants were run flat out and as new, unskilled workers and those whose skills had deteriorated during the long Depression years entered the workplace. In fact, in the first two years of the war more Americans were killed at their work stations than at the hands of the enemy.

One of the immediate changes on the home front was the migration of people. A large, and what came to be a permanent, relocation of Americans occurred as they moved to take advantage of new jobs, particularly to the industrial areas of the United States where the conversion to defense production was greatest. The Census Bureau reported that no fewer than 15 million Americans relocated during the war; the largest concentrations, as might be expected, occurred on the East Coast and the West Coast and in the industrial Midwest. Approximately 3 million people left the South, an area short of industry but abundant with manpower. Throughout the United States rural inhabitants moved into cities and urban residents moved to other cities. The result was a great strain on municipal services, schools, housing, and other parts of the civilian sector, as well as social strains evident in higher divorce, alcoholism, juvenile delinquency, and venereal disease rates. Some industrial cities experienced a boom in population growth: southern California gained more than 400,000 inhabitants and Michigan gained nearly 300,000. Some cities in the South also grew: Mobile, Alabama, gained more than 150,000 residents. These staggering numbers were a pattern repeated in many cities throughout the United States.

For the first time since about 1929, businessmen could feel that they were once again regarded as something more than exploiters of helpless workers. New industrial heroes emerged, such as shipbuilder Henry J. Kaiser and boat-builder Andrew Jackson Higgins, not to mention such veteran industrialists as Kaufman T. Keller of Chrysler, which was now busily setting world records in tank production.

But there was a dark side to this booming economy. Crowded living conditions were common. New arrivals jammed into housing districts, often living side by side with people of different races and backgrounds. Examples abounded of rent gouging for shacks and "hot-bed" boarding houses. In some areas shantytowns appeared or trailer camps were started where families crowded into flimsy, unsafe temporary shelters that might lack water and sewage facilities. Substandard living conditions were more or less tolerated in the name of patriotism, however; and when individuals complained, they were often rebuked by their fellow workers for not being committed to the war effort. Schools were overcrowded, some running on shifts, and many children, with parents either in the military or working long hours, were left unsupervised. The rate of juvenile delinquency accelerated along with the divorce rate. "V-Girls" haunted military encampments, ready for sex, paid or not, with servicemen.

Those migratory Americans traveled mostly by train; the airlines were hardly removed from their pioneer stage, and the interstate highway system was still far in the future. Long freight trains transported armored vehicles to the ports, and lengthy hospital trains carried the battle casualties from those same ports. Civilian passengers secured what accommodation they could, in the face of government priorities that put them at the bottom of the list. Often they found themselves trying to sleep on a hard bench in the small hours of the morning in some rural depot, waiting for an interminably delayed "milk run." Those with the right priority, of course, could find themselves on one of the crack streamliners that still ran, complete with club cars, diners, and luxury sleeping accommodations. Almost everyone on government business traveled by train; even German prisoners of war (POWs) found themselves in quite adequate day coaches, eating in dining cars, and the enemy wounded and officers took their ease in two-man compartments. (There was some publicity concerning those POWs eating in the dining cars while black U.S. soldiers ate behind screens "like contaminated animals," but the practice continued. The Geneva convention, of course, protected the enemy, not Americans.)

Like the factories, the American railroads in World War II ran flat out, and paid a price; railway mishaps proliferated, often with heavy loss of life. In one of the most serious, in 1944, the crack Congressional Limited derailed in North Philadelphia, killing more than seventy military and civilian passengers.

Despite the hardships, Americans were pleased with the new jobs and the extra money; real industrial wages increased by 50 percent, and farm income by no less than 200 percent. For many families the war enabled them to afford a car, although only used models were available, or to buy a refrigerator (again used) or a few pieces of furniture, all at high prices that would have seemed out of the question before the war. Diets improved for those who had lived on the edge of destitution during the Depression, and many enjoyed regular medical care for the first time in their lives. In the midst of war, openings of new supermarkets increased 400 percent over the immediate prewar years.

The war was an economic and social boon for the United States: it ended the Depression and set the economy on a course of improvement that lasted well past the immediate postwar period. But it should also be remembered that Americans did not at the time know how long this good fortune on the home front would last. The invasion of Europe could have caused many more grief-stricken next of kin stateside; a turn in the fortunes of war, a severe tightening of the economic screws. The war ended in 1945 without any of these dismal possibilities actually occurring.

The Pacific war was responsible for one of the most important and controversial relocations of people in the history of the United States—the internment of Japanese Americans living on the West Coast. Approximately 110,000 Japanese, consisting of issei, nisei, and sansei (immigrants, children of immigrants, grandchildren of immigrants, respectively), were distrusted by the American people, who feared they still were loyal to the Japanese emperor and might engage in espionage, particularly because a large portion of U.S. aircraft plants were located in California. Although some in the Roosevelt administration questioned the constitutionality of removing the Japanese from their homes and putting them into camps, the government went through with a plan to place the 110,000 in ten relocation centers in the western states. During the course of the war, most of them returned to their homes, but they found that their property and personal belongings were gone. This relocation proved to be an outright violation of civil rights, but it was justified at the time on the basis of the wartime crisis. The fears proved to be unfounded, although about 8,000 men actually preferred to be returned to the ruins of postwar Japan rather than renounce their loyalty to their emperor. Not until long after the war, during the 1990s, did the federal government agree to compensate the Japanese Americans for their losses.

With the population movements and wartime social stresses, it was not surprising that racial incidents scarred the home front, reaching a crescendo of violence in the summer of 1943. The Detroit race riot was the most bloody since the Civil War. In June rioting broke out along the city's lakefront and spread through the black ghetto, with members of both races engaging in rock throwing, beatings, shootings, and destruction of property. After two days the Michigan governor asked for federal assistance, and troops were sent to Detroit, to patrol city streets until order was restored. Twenty-five blacks and nine whites were killed and approximately seven hundred people were injured.

Racial violence also broke out in Philadelphia, the Harlem district of New York City, Houston, Washington, D.C., Pittsburgh, and Charleston, West Virginia. A rather bizarre outbreak was the "zoot suit" riot in Los Angeles, involving Hispanic youths and navy servicemen, with the latter objecting violently to the attire of the former.

The United States was still a society racially segregated by law in the southern and some western states, and by custom almost everywhere else. Even the Red Cross segregated its blood supply to accommodate those who had no objection to being injected with toxins from horses or swine, but would have balked at receiving blood from human beings of color. Schools, transportation, and medical, eating, and sanitary facilities were segregated by law in the South, and neighborhood segregation accomplished something like the same result in the rest of the nation. Lynchings of blacks continued, although at a steadily declining pace. Though national magazines made a conscientious effort to call for equal treatment, individual blacks seemed to "make the news" only if they were entertainers, rioters, or criminals. The stereotypical Hollywood image of the African American remained: a tap-dancing, amiable, dull-witted, razor-toting vagrant whose "feets hurt."

U.S. enemies were quick to point out the contradiction between the nation's publicly proclaimed aim of a world free from oppression and the realities of life in the wartime United States. Japan's "Asia for the Asiatics" campaign was given some veracity by the infamous relocation of the Japanese Americans, and Germany's propaganda minister, Dr. Josef Goebbels (a man who could give lying a bad name), piously commiserated with the fate of black Americans, brutalized by the "Judeo-Plutocratic Rosenfelt" administration.

African American troops, as rigidly segregated throughout the war as their civilian counterparts, erupted

create

into home front violence on numerous occasions, shooting down military police or white troopers and defying orders to disperse, or attempting to integrate "Jim Crow" base facilities. The usual response of white America was to demand a moratorium for the duration of the war on such "agitation" and to iterate the great progress made by blacks, who had been held in chattel slavery within living memory. President Roosevelt made encouraging noises on the subject; his wife, Eleanor, was rightly known for her commitment to improving the situation of blacks. But in truth, concern with the conditions of African Americans (as far as whites were concerned) was far more a postwar phenomenon. The overwhelming majority of white Americans could not see how alleviating racial inequality would do much to win the war.

One of the most remembered aspects of life on the home front was rationing, the process by which the federal government controlled the sale of a variety of commodities in order to ensure enough food and other items for its fighting forces and the general population. The major items to be rationed were tires, gasoline, leather (shoes), sugar, coffee, meat, and dairy products. In order to purchase these items, Americans had to have coupons. With the coupons, which shoppers were allowed to obtain at government distribution centers once a month, they could buy a limited amount of the particular items. Shortages were never serious, and only bubble gum and bananas were denied to the American public during the war.

Another form of rationing was the lowering of quality of many consumer goods. Metal toys vanished and were replaced by plastic or wooden makeshifts, wire clothing hangers were replaced by cardboard devices, and cuffs and vests were removed from men's suits. Many Americans remarked on the paradox of having "real money" for the first time, but so little of lasting quality to spend it on. Consumer goods that were not cheapened or rationed were still often in short supply. At times, liquor and cigarettes could be obtained only by someone "in the know" or by under-the-counter payments. Those who complained about absent or shoddy goods had to face the inevitable response. "Don't you know there's a war on?" But once the tide of battle turned in favor of the Allies, the patriotic appeal of rationing weakened, and even Americans who prided themselves on their patriotism found themselves patronizing the black market.

Motion picture theaters, of course, remained open, and the 1940s could be considered Hollywood's best decade. In addition to the expected war films, like *Lifeboat, Back to Bataan,* and *Thirty Seconds over Tokyo,* the film industry turned out features that made little or no reference to the war, such as *Shadow of a Doubt, Laura, Meet Me in St. Louis,* and *State Fair,* to name some of the best. Moviegoers had money in their pockets and little else to spend it on. Radio audiences, fascinated by broadcasts "live from London" or even from a B-17 bomber over Berlin, increased dramatically. (Television broadcasting, whose closing down for the war was hardly noticed by Americans, remained something for "the World of Tomorrow," along with the "autogyro in every garage" of the Sunday supplements.) Panicky bureaucrats shut down racetracks immediately after Pearl Harbor, but they were soon reopened in the interests of "morale," as were nightclubs.

Popular music for the most part ignored the war (one big exception being Spike Jones's hilarious spoof, "Right in der Fuehrer's Face!"), emphasizing instead the smooth big band sounds of the likes of Glenn Miller, boogie-woogie and nonsense songs ("Mairzy Doats"), and love ballads. Perhaps the most evocative of the last was "I'll be Seeing You," which expressed the deep longings for absent loved ones.

Big-league sports, decimated by the armed forces, had to rely on what might uncharitably be termed the "lame, the blind, and the halt," but major athletic contests were never canceled.

Social changes were probably the most far-reaching and permanent effects of the war, next to the complete overthrow of America's enemies. Due to the shortage of manpower, about 4 million women took jobs in the defense industries and other areas of the economy, temporarily raising the percentage of women in the workforce to approximately one-third. For the first time in American history the workforce had a large proportion of women, a condition that would not be repeated until the 1970s. This development had significant ramifications for family life: it left large numbers of children at home without supervision, and social observers, seeing a rise in juvenile delinquency, assumed that the absence of working mothers was responsible. A slight increase in the divorce rate occurred during the war and mushroomed after it, suggesting that the pressures of separation and loneliness and the stress associated with the new responsibilities of women were a direct consequence of World War II. Though some women benefited from the income earned in a new or better job, many suffered considerable hardship, particularly those who had children and whose husbands were in the military. These women had to raise their children without the economic and emotional support of a husband, and some lived in destitution. Prevailing attitudes, however, saw the women in the workforce as a temporary necessity, and in fact, at the end of the war, most women did return to full-time jobs—as homemakers. Basically, "Rosie the Riveter" had signed up only for the duration.

Even when women joined the armed services in completely gender-segregated voluntary organizations—the Women's Army Corps (WAC; originally and significantly called Women's Auxiliary Army Corps), Women's Air Force (WAF) the navy's WAVES (Women Accepted for Voluntary Emergency Service), the women marines, and the coast guard's SPARs (from its motto, "Semper Paratus; Always Ready")—these, too, were considered temporary arrangements. And, at least in the beginning, many Americans, male and female, presumed their members were little better than camp followers. In the final analysis, however, except for those who lost loved ones in the conflict, the war had a positive, if temporary, effect on women and their role in society despite the hardships endured by some.

World War II enhanced the presence of the federal government in the lives of all Americans, continuing the trend set during the New Deal in the 1930s. About 15 million men and women were in uniform, and several million civilians served in civil defense and support groups such as the United Service Organizations (USO) clubs. Even Americans not connected with the military were affected by the government's mobilization, through their jobs, their relocations, rationing, and so on. The government established a close link with higher education, upon which it depended for research in developing military and scientific projects. The Manhattan Project was the best known, although only after the dropping of the first atomic bomb. This link continued and accelerated after the war.

Toward the end of the conflict, some of the more popular New Deal programs that had been interrupted resumed operation. The overwhelming activities organized and managed by the federal government led Americans, who had come to look to government during the Great Depression, to become even more accepting and tolerant of active government intrusion, despite the strength displayed by the Republican Party in the 1942 elections. For example, there was little opposition to federal government financing of veterans' education, and the resultant, enormously popular, and successful "GI Bill of Rights" was extremely generous. It is still a matter of debate, however, as to what extent the GI Bill was a reflection of a more relaxed view of government assistance and how much was a shrewd realization by Congress of the enormous voting power of the returning servicemen and their adult family members, as well as sheer gratitude for the servicemen's sacrifices.

The war eradicated much of the pessimism of the Depression, replacing it with a restored faith in capitalism, albeit capitalism controlled by government. In the first wartime national elections, those of 1942, the Republicans scored impressive gains. For many pundits, it seemed that the basic Democratic alliance of Southern Bourbons and big-city ethnic machines was starting to unravel. The 78th Congress began an assault upon New Deal agencies, led by the Republicans and Southern conservatives. Many Republicans now entertained hopes that the American public would finally stop blaming them for the Great Depression, and that the public was growing tired of intrusive government in their lives and of high taxation, now that they had some income to tax.

And income was being taxed as never before; World War II brought the income tax (originally billed as "a rich man's tax") down to working-class Americans, along with the pay-as-you-earn system of collection.

But an indication that the pessimism of the Depression had not completely ended was the widespread belief, buttressed by various "experts," that the postwar years would see a depression similar to that of the 1930s, as millions of veterans reentered a job market shrunk by cancellation of war production. With this renewed but wary faith in the economy and with the end of the war coming into sight, a perception apparent by mid-1944, Americans were less willing to accept sacrifices, and a sense of discontent or loss of patience with the war became evident. (The popular comedian Jimmy Durante, protesting the red tape and bureaucratic control of lives, articulated his popular philosophy for the times: "Leave people the hell alone!") The black market became more active, and complaints about shortages and government regulations mounted. "Don't you know there's a war on?" could no longer be counted on to silence criticism.

Roosevelt did win a fourth term in the 1944 election, but by the smallest majority in his four campaigns. Looking back, it now seems incredible that his obviously failing health was not an election issue. But this was an era and a society in which press photographers scrupulously refrained from taking any photos of the president in his infirmity; today the Roosevelt library at Hyde Park, New York, has only two photos of Roosevelt in his wheelchair.

There was some hope that the fighting might end by Christmas 1944, much to the concern of military leaders, who lectured Congress and the public on the evils of "complacency." (Those same commanders were caught flat-footed in December 1944 by the Germans' counteroffensive in the "quiet" Ardennes sector of the western front.)

When the war did end and the country celebrated first VE Day and then VJ Day, Americans, military and civilian, sobered by the war's irretrievable human losses and by fears of a postwar depression, nonetheless looked forward to the opportunity to start new careers, to obtain more education, to have a more active and satisfying life "in a nice little place of our own just outside of town." And in large measure, for white Americans, in the postwar decades those hopes were fulfilled.

FURTHER READINGS

Costello, John. *Virtue Under Fire: How World War II Changed Our Social and Sexual Mores* (1985).

Erenberg, L. A., and S. E. Hirsch, eds. *The War in American Culture: Society and Consciousness During World War II* (1996).

Harris, Mark Jonathan, and Franklin D. Mitchell. *The Homefront: America During World War II* (1984).

Polenberg, Richard. *War and Society: The United States, 1941–1945* (1972).

Winkler, Allan M. *Home Front U.S.A.: America During World War II* (1986).

D. Clayton Brown

SEE ALSO Home Front, Japanese; Roosevelt, Franklin Delano

Homma Masaharu (1887–1946)

Officer in command of the Japanese army that conquered the Philippines. Homma was born at Sado Island on November 27, 1889, into a family of privileged landowners. He graduated with high marks from the Japanese military academy and from the staff college. During World War I he was sent to France as an observer on assignment to the British command along the western front. In the 1920s he served as Japan's resident army officer in India and later as military attaché in Great Britain. As head of the Japanese War Ministry's press section, Homma defended the Japanese occupation of Manchuria in 1931 and eventually commanded troops in northern China. After the capture of Nanking (Nanjing) in 1937, he openly urged the need for a prompt peace in order to avert a calamity. He also doubted the ability of Tojo Hideki as a prospective war minister. Homma was commandant of the Formosa (now Taiwan) Army before his return to Japan in preparation for the outbreak of war.

Homma, whose avocations extended to the composition of plays and poetry, expressed an independent mind almost unheard of within the inflexible Japanese command structure. For example, in a fiery manner he questioned the particulars of his new assignment and had been audacious enough to declare publicly that hostilities with England and the United States would be an act of insanity. By December 1941 Homma, with the rank of lieutenant general, was the supreme commander of all Japanese army units scheduled to invade the Philippines. The Fourteenth Army, headquartered in Formosa, contained only two divisions, the 16th and the 48th, supported by service and logistical elements. Furthermore, the government's timetable permitted use of the 48th Division for only fifty days, the period allotted for the Philippine campaign, because the unit was destined for employment in the Dutch East Indies (now Indonesia). Japanese strategy directed Homma to seize Manila, the capital; no preparation was made for a U.S. withdrawal into the Bataan Peninsula. On December 22, Homma put ashore the 48th Division at Lingayen Gulf and landed the 16th Division at Lamon Bay as wings meant to envelop Manila. Brushing aside resistance, his army raced for Manila but was delayed, despite its control of the air, at the Calumpit bridges while General Douglas MacArthur's forces hastened to Bataan. Homma's units eventually entered the city on January 2, 1942. However, to his disappointment, its capture failed to effect the archipelago's surrender.

Behind schedule and deprived of the seasoned 48th Division, Homma engaged the Fil-American army in Bataan with the green 65th Division, newly arrived from Formosa. He felt a repeated sense of urgency to step up his attack, notwithstanding inferior numbers and stubborn resistance, because of General Yamashita Tomoyuki's successful offensive in Malaya (now Malaysia). With the Fourteenth Army exhausted and the campaign stalled, Homma halted the offensive in early February and requested reinforcements. His soldiers were tired, diseased, and debilitated by wounds. By April his reinforced army, backed by airpower and artillery, renewed the attack and quickly forced the U.S. capitulation on Bataan. But headquarters had underestimated the number of prisoners to be handled and to be encamped at sites on Luzon; consequently, Japanese logistics collapsed and the Bataan death march resulted. Homma, already off schedule, moved next against Corregidor. Becoming more jumpy and agitated because of demands from general headquarters, he waited anxiously for the assault on the island fortress. He visited the debarkation point of Lamao to see off the attackers, knowing that an operational failure would lead to his dishonor. His anger boiled on May 5 when General Jonathan Wainwright, commander of Fil-American forces, declined to surrender all units in the islands—striking his clenched hands on a table, he threatened to keep fighting on Corregidor. Although Wainwright reconsidered and decided to surrender, Homma, greatly offended, told him to go back to Corregidor in order to capitulate to the Japanese officer at the scene.

Despite his victory, Homma was out of favor with the army general staff. His Philippines campaign had been too lengthy and expensive. Besides, there was displeasure with his forbearance toward the Filipino populace and his refusal to circulate anti–American propaganda. In late August he was ordered to Japan and placed on reserve. Following Tojo's downfall in December 1943, Homma was selected as minister of information by the incoming prime minister, Kiso Kuniaki. In September 1945, to his astonishment as well as that of the Japanese public, he was arrested and indicted for war crimes by the Allies, charged with accountability for the Bataan death march in particular. He was found guilty on February 11, 1946, and sentenced to die by firing squad. Despite an eleventh-hour plea by his wife to General MacArthur, he was executed on April 3, 1946, in Manila.

For a World War II Japanese general, Homma was an attractive personality, and his execution disturbed a number of Americans in the occupation forces. Many informed observers, at the time and since, have felt that he was executed primarily because he had defeated General MacArthur.

FURTHER READINGS

Morton, Louis. *The Fall of the Philippines* (1953).
Taylor, Lawrence. *A Trial of Generals: Homma, Yamashita, MacArthur* (1981).
Toland, John. *But Not in Shame: The Six Months After Pearl Harbor* (1961).
Whitman, John W. *Bataan: Our Last Ditch* (1990).

Rodney J. Ross

SEE ALSO Army, Japanese; Bataan Death March; MacArthur, Douglas; Philippines, Fall of

Hong Kong

Hong Kong was a British Crown colony of some four hundred square miles situated on the coast of southern China, near the city of Canton. The colony, which came under British rule in 1842 as a result of the Opium War, had a 1941 population of 1.6 million people, all of whom were Chinese except for 22,000 European civilians and military personnel. Prior to the war Hong Kong was the headquarters of the Royal Navy's China Squadron.

The issue of how to best defend Hong Kong, a small territory remote from Britain, or whether to defend it at all, in the event of a Pacific war, was the frequent topic of debate within the British government. In March 1935 General Sir John Dill, director of military operations, had concluded that the colony could not be defended. He had stated that it would be far better to risk losing Hong Kong than to man it too lightly, or to reinforce it to the point where it would become a Verdun-type symbol whose inevitable loss would destroy British prestige at home and abroad. Dill also concluded that the colony, little more than 400 miles from Japanese air bases on Formosa (now Taiwan), was much less strategically important than Singapore, the "Gibraltar of the East," 1,600 miles to the southwest.

As late as 1937 the British joint chiefs of staff continued to believe that Hong Kong could not be defended, even if reinforced, and that a garrison besieged there could not expect relief for at least ninety days under the very best of circumstances. Even if by some chance the colony could be held, its port would probably be destroyed or at least neutralized as a usable British base by Japanese airpower. Even as the possibilities of successfully defending Hong Kong were becoming weaker, an evacuation of the colony's civilian population was repeatedly delayed. Such a move, British leaders reasoned, would be interpreted as an abandonment of the Far East, with a resulting loss of face in a time of increasing crisis. It was also seen as damaging to the already low morale plaguing the Nationalist Chinese government. The British thus concluded that Hong Kong was an important, but not vital, outpost that was to be defended for as long as possible in the case of attack by Japan.

A final strategic review in 1939 put British interests in Europe far ahead of their interests in Hong Kong, especially considering that Japanese inroads in China were such that the colony was increasingly isolated. Indeed, by June 1940, sizable Japanese forces were entrenched on the Chinese mainland north of the colony, and other units manned positions athwart the Kowloon Peninsula, cutting Hong Kong off from the mainland. Although a withdrawal of the garrison was recommended in August 1940 by Dill, now chief of the imperial general staff, a recommendation accepted by Prime Minister Winston S. Churchill and his war cabinet, nothing was done to implement the decision. Yet as Anglo-Japanese relations became strained, the British did evacuate some European women and children to Manila in the Philippines in June 1941.

It was common knowledge that Japanese spies had been at work in Hong Kong for years before the war and that they had obtained accurate intelligence on British defenses and troop dispositions. The garrison, commanded by Major General Christopher M. Maltby, normally consisted of only four battalions, two British and two Indian, with additional small support units. In a surprising reversal of policy, however, the British accepted a near-inexplicable offer by the Canadian government to send two additional battalions to Hong Kong, thinking it would lend more credibility to the defense, however doomed it might be in the long run. Thus Canadian troops, the first to see action in World War II, sailed for Hong Kong on October 27, 1941. As weak as the British were on the ground, their air and sea arms were even more inadequate, consisting of seven aircraft, eight motor torpedo boats, and four other smaller gunboats. The twelve thousand regular troops were augmented by the Hong Kong and Singapore Royal Artillery and citizen soldiers of the Hong Kong Volunteer Defense Force.

General Maltby was faced with a difficult tactical situation, having to defend a great deal of territory with few resources. The principal defensive line for the colony was placed just three miles north of Kowloon in the Leased Territories rather than farther inland. Manned by three battalions of Indian and Scottish troops, it was far too long for the available forces. Another three battalions were deployed on Hong Kong Island itself, including the recently arrived Canadian units. Even though a Japanese assault had long been expected from the landward side of the colony, little else could be done considering the general British strategic situation in Asia at the time.

Early on December 8, 1941, Japanese bombers from Formosa destroyed all seven British aircraft in a surprise raid on Hong Kong's Kai Tak airfield, while twelve battalions of the Twenty-third Army's 38th Division, commanded by Lieutenant General Sano Tadayoshi, crossed the Sham Chun River into the Leased (New) Territories. In Britain, on hearing of the start of the attack, Prime Minister Churchill declared that the eyes of the world were on Hong Kong and that the garrison should resist to the end. Yet within twenty-four hours, by the evening of December 9, Japanese forces had breached the main British defenses, known for some obscure reason as the Gindrinker's Line, and had taken a crucial redoubt. This success made the already overextended British positions untenable and forced Maltby to order a retreat. British forces quickly fell back, and Kowloon was in Japanese hands by December 12.

After Maltby's withdrawal to Hong Kong Island, a move later described as too hasty, Sano began to bombard Victoria with artillery on December 13, soon followed by heavy air attacks. These bombardments badly damaged the British naval force and caused fires in the central business district. Following the delivery of a surrender ultimatum on December 14, an ultimatum which Maltby rejected, Japanese troops attempted to cross to Hong Kong Island the next day, but were repulsed. Three nights later, on December 18, the Japanese tried again, and landed in strength between North Point and Aldrich Bay. Their troops quickly penetrated the island's defenses and drove to Deep Water Bay in the south, splitting the British forces in two. Motor-torpedo boats tried to stem this tide by attacking vessels carrying Japanese reinforcements, but Japanese air superiority was complete and British naval losses were heavy. However, British resistance was so stiff that on December 20, General Sano was forced to halt all attacks in order to reorganize his forces.

Time, manpower, and resources, however, clearly favored the Japanese. By December 24 the surviving British defenders were exhausted, and water and ammunition supplies were nearly exhausted. The Japanese bombing and the resulting fires had destroyed water mains, and Japanese forces controlled the reservoirs serving the colony. On the afternoon of Christmas Day, 1941, a cease-fire was arranged, and that evening the British governor surrendered the colony unconditionally to Lieutenant General Sakai Takashi.

Hong Kong's garrison had held for eighteen days, far short of the ninety days predicted, but had put up a much stouter resistance than that offered at Singapore. Japanese casualties numbered approximately 2,700, and the British suffered 4,400 casualties. Only a few people managed to escape into China, and most Europeans become prisoners of war. In the aftermath of the surrender, as elsewhere in Asia and the Pacific, the Japanese committed numerous atrocities against Chinese and Europeans.

Hong Kong was in Japanese hands for the remainder of World War II, and was returned to Great Britain after a brief surrender ceremony at Government House on September 16, 1945.

FURTHER READINGS

Birch, Alan, and Martin Cole. *Captive Christmas: The Battle of Hong Kong, December 1941* (1979).

Lindsay, Oliver. *The Lasting Honour: The Fall of Hong Kong, 1941* (1978).

Clayton D. Laurie

Hurley, Patrick J. (1883–1963)

Military diplomat instrumental in effecting U.S. policy in China, 1944–1945. A prominent Republican who served in the administration of Herbert Hoover as assistant secretary of war, Hurley was President Franklin D. Roosevelt's personal representative on several missions during World War II.

Born in 1883 near Lehigh in Oklahoma Territory, Hurley was a coal miner and cowboy as a youth. After becoming a successful lawyer, he served as attorney for the Choctaw Indian nation (1911–1917). During World War I, Colonel Hurley saw action at St. Mihiel and near Louppy. From December 1929 to March 1933 he was assistant secretary of war; he encouraged military preparedness, increasing mechanization, and greater attention to aircraft. After returning to private law practice, Hurley gained wealth, in spite of the Great Depression, through oil and banking investments. From 1938 to 1941 he helped negotiate agreements with the Mexican government regarding American oil interests.

Hurley's pleas for an active command once the United States entered World War II were denied because of his age, but President Roosevelt chose him to coordinate Colonel John A. Robenson's special mission to get supply ships through the Japanese blockade to General Douglas MacArthur's beleaguered forces on Bataan. For this assignment Hurley was given the rank of brigadier general and was concurrently appointed U.S. minister to New Zealand as a cover for the blockade-running operation.

Hurley's job was to requisition guns, ammunition, and medical supplies, and the ships to carry them. He also worked out support for the mission from ABDA (American-British-Dutch-Australian) Command in the Dutch East Indies (now Indonesia). He experienced frustration and delays in securing ABDA Command assistance and finding crews willing to undertake the great hazards of penetrating the Japanese blockade of the Philippines. Hurley braved Japanese air attacks on flights between Java and Australia, and suffered a minor head wound in a Japanese air attack on Australia. Of the six ships he assembled at Darwin and the twelve dispatched by ABDA Command from Java, only three reached the Philippines.

A longtime friend of MacArthur, Hurley pressed for more aggressive U.S. action in the Pacific. He believed the Democratic administration in Washington was relegating Republicans to backwaters of the war effort. To impress on the outspoken Hurley the vital concerns of other war theaters and to draw on his experience in oil negotiations, Roosevelt sent him as his personal representative to Moscow.

On August 18, 1944, Hurley was commissioned Roosevelt's personal emissary to resolve the crisis that had developed in China, where feuds embroiled both British commanders and Chinese Nationalist leader Chiang Kai-shek with American General Joseph W. Stilwell. Hurley refused to go to China under auspices of the State Department because he disagreed with its Middle East policies; he went instead as a major general in the U.S. Army. Although he lacked an understanding of China and Chinese political matters, Hurley soon agreed with Chiang Kai-shek that Stilwell must be dismissed.

In November 1944 Hurley was named U.S. ambassador to China and charged with unifying and strengthening the Chinese war effort. His pro–Chiang bias further hindered the already impossible task of reconciling the Nationalist government and the Communists. He became convinced that foreign service officers working for Stilwell, as well as many U.S. journalists in China, had Communist leanings. Once Japan had surrendered and civil war had broken out in China between Chiang's and Mao Tse-tung's forces, Hurley resigned his post in November 1945.

After retiring from government service, Hurley resumed his business interests and practice of law. He joined Republican conservatives after World War II in alleging that Communist infiltration of the State Department lay behind the Yalta agreement and the fall of China to communism, and in urging continued U.S. support for Nationalist China. He died at Santa Fe, New Mexico, on July 30, 1963.

FURTHER READINGS

Buhite, Russell D. *Patrick J. Hurley and American Foreign Policy* (1973).

Lohbeck, Don. *Patrick J. Hurley* (1956).

"Hurley, Patrick J(ay)." In Eleanora W. Schoenebaum, ed., *Political Profiles: The Truman Years* (1978).

Camille Dean

SEE ALSO Chiang Kai-shek; Stilwell, Joseph Warren

Iba Airfield

See Clark and Iba Airfields, Japanese Bombing of

Ichigo, Operation

After the attack on the U.S. naval facility at Pearl Harbor, Hawaii, in December 1941, the Japanese were content to confine their military effort in China to the occupation of the major ports, the northeastern part of the country, and the industrial areas along the Yangtze River as far west as I-chang. In the fall of 1943, however, they began to plan for a major offensive to seize the airfields in eastern China that were currently being used by the U.S. Fourteenth Air Force, commanded by Major General Claire Chennault, as bases from which to attack Japanese shipping along the Yangtze River and the coast, and were also potential bases for U.S. long-range B-29 bombers to conduct raids against Japan itself. By early January 1944, Japan's plans had taken their final shape, and on January 17 general headquarters ordered the China Expeditionary Army, commanded by Lieutenant General Hata Shunroku, to seize the eastern China airfields and the Hunan–Kwangsi, Canton–Hankow, and Peking–Hankow railroad lines to ensure a secure line of land transportation from their stronghold in northern China to their forces in Southeast Asia. The Japanese also hoped to destroy several large formations of Chinese troops and to further the deterioration of Generalissimo Chiang Kai-shek's flagging political regime, perhaps to the point of surrender.

The Japanese offensive, code-named Ichigo (Operation Number One), was divided into two parts. In the first part, Kogo, forces from the North China Area Army would drive south in April across the Yellow River toward Hankow, supported by a feint toward the west. After Kogo, which was expected to last six weeks, Togo would begin, and within five months would include the capture of Heng-yang, Kweilin (Kuei-lin), Liuchow, and Nanning to secure the railroad lines and the capture of the U.S. airfields by forces moving south from Hankow and north and west from Canton. Ultimately, the Japanese would commit fifteen divisions, four independent mixed brigades, and one independent infantry brigade to Ichigo.

The Chinese were ill prepared to meet Ichigo. His war effort already feeble, Chiang Kai-shek had no meaningful plans to stem the Japanese assault. For some time he had relied for defense on Chennault's planes and Chennault's assurances that, if adequately supplied by the United States, his Fourteenth Air Force could contain any Japanese attack and possibly defeat it. Chiang, whose goal in 1944 was to preserve his regime, not fight the Japanese, favored this approach because it enabled him to hoard his limited military resources for use in the future against the Chinese Communists and provided a surrogate to fight the Japanese. Chiang's best troops (such as they were) were deployed against the Communists, and those in the path of the Japanese were provincial forces commanded by longtime antagonists who opposed his leadership and who had received only meager allotments from the arms shipments the United States had sent to China.

In March and early April, Chiang and Chennault sent warnings about the impending Japanese offensive to President Franklin D. Roosevelt and to Lieutenant General Joseph W. Stilwell, commander of the China-Burma-India theater (CBI), Chiang's chief of staff, and American lend-lease administrator for China. Chennault, in a letter to Stilwell, pointed out the need to protect his eastern bases and cautioned that the Fourteenth Air Force could not provide adequate support for the Chinese ground forces defending those bases unless it received priority in the assignment of supplies and concentrated its efforts against Ichigo.

Stilwell was not receptive to Chennault's warning. The two had been at odds since 1942 over strategy in the CBI, the allocation of the limited quantities of supplies earmarked for the theater, and the limited airlift available for transporting supplies from India to China by way of the "Hump" route over the Himalayas, the only supply route open to China. Chennault, with the support of Chiang, wanted top priority given to his Fourteenth Air Force, whereas Stilwell preferred to emphasize ground warfare, arguing that an air force was no better than the ground troops who defended its airfields. His plan was to train and equip Chinese troops, then use them in operations against the Japanese in Burma (now Myanmar) to open a land route to China and to defend the bases in eastern China. The War Department effectively killed Stilwell's plan by refusing to provide more than a minimum of equipment. But Stilwell plunged ahead, and in the spring of 1944 he was determined to use the Chinese troops he had already trained and equipped for offensives in Burma.

The Allied high command also had other concerns than Ichigo. The Japanese launched an offensive into India from Burma in the spring of 1944 that greatly strained the British forces defending India, and the U.S. joint chiefs of staff (JCS) had assigned highest priority in the CBI to Operation Matterhorn, a strategic bombing campaign against Japan using B-29s staged from bases near Cheng-tu in central China. To the JCS, Chennault's primary responsibility should be the protection of the Cheng-tu bases, even at the expense of strikes against Japanese shipping and the support of Chinese ground troops defending the eastern bases. Faced with too many demands and not enough supplies and airlift, Stilwell said that until the India situation improved, he saw no possibility of increasing supplies to Chennault, and diverted resources to his Burma campaign and Operation Matterhorn. These resources included 350 of Chennault's planes, leaving only 150 for operations in eastern China.

Ichigo was launched on April 17 when the Japanese Twelfth Army, under Lieutenant General Uchiyama Eitaro, crossed the Yellow River and began moving south along the Peking–Hankow railroad while elements of the First Army feinted to the west. Spearheaded by 500 tanks and armored cars and supported by squadrons of airplanes, the 100,000 Japanese troops participating in the Kogo phase of Ichigo encountered little opposition from the thirty-four divisions commanded by General T'ang En-po that were supposedly defending Honan province. Within two months the Japanese secured the railroad from Peking to Hankow and dispersed a Chinese force of 300,000 at a cost of 1,000 of their own dead. Having experienced famine, taxation, conscription, and misman-

agement by Chiang's regime, many peasants aided the Japanese and, armed with farm implements and crude weapons, attacked groups of retreating Chinese soldiers, dispersing 50,000 of them. Chennault's flyers mounted the only effective defense against the Japanese. By early May, they gained local air superiority and were regularly strafing Japanese columns and trains, and bombing the Yellow River bridges. But they were unable to close down the river crossings or significantly slow the Japanese advance.

The second phase of Ichigo opened at the end of May when Hata, who was promoted to field marshal on June 2, sent his 250,000 troops south across the Yangtze River into Hunan province, aiming at the railroad centers of Chang-sha, on the Hsiang River, and Heng-yang. Opposing Hata were 150,000 Chinese troops of the Ninth War Area, commanded by General Hsueh Yueh. He was not one of Chiang's favorite generals, and Chiang had deliberately withheld equipment from him. The Chinese were unable to mount an effective resistance because the Japanese avoided the strong Chinese positions and dispersed themselves to minimize the effect of Chennault's fighters and bombers. Chang-sha, which had withstood two previous attempts to capture it and had been a model of resistance, fell on June 21 after the Chinese Fourth Army abandoned the city without much of a fight and marched to the southwest.

As Ichigo progressed, relations between Stilwell and Chennault worsened. Chennault called for more aircraft, supplies, and fuel to be assigned to the Fourteenth Air Force, more arms for the Chinese troops defending eastern China, and a B-29 strike against Hankow, the main Japanese supply base. Stilwell, who despised Chennault and even tried to have him relieved as commander of the Fourteenth Air Force in early June because of their longstanding differences, was convinced that Chennault and Chiang were trying to make him the scapegoat for their misjudgment in emphasizing an air strategy. He further believed that the Japanese would eventually come to a natural stop as they outran their supplies. Rather than take away troops, supplies, and air support from his operations in Burma to defend eastern China, and divert Hump tonnage from Operation Matterhorn to Chennault, his plan was to reopen the land route to China and then, with a combined U.S.-Chinese army, clear a path to the China coast and seize a port. Nevertheless, when pressured by Chiang, he agreed to increase Chennault's allotment from Hump tonnage and asked the War Department's permission for a B-29 strike against Hankow. The War Department refused the B-29 strike and advised Stilwell that he should not make any Hump allocations that would interfere with Operation Matterhorn. Chennault never appreciated the high priority the War Department placed on Operation Matterhorn and directed his anger at Stilwell.

From Chang-sha, Japanese forces pushed south to the walled city of Heng-yang, seizing its airfield on June 26. Aided by a special shipment of arms and munitions authorized by Stilwell, the Tenth Chinese Army, commanded by Major General Fong Hsien-chueh, stood its ground and turned back several Japanese attempts to overrun the city. The Chinese, at least for a time, were ably supported by the Fourteenth Air Force. Long stretches of the railroad south from Hankow were torn up by bombs from Chennault's planes, and their attacks limited traffic to nighttime on the parallel Hsiang River. The combined efforts of the Chinese troops at Heng-yang and Chennault's pilots effectively stalled the Japanese advance. Chiang, however, would not approve any further shipments of arms and munitions to Hunan out of concern that they would strengthen his potential and real political rivals, and Chinese counterattacks failed to cut the Japanese supply line or relieve the siege of Heng-yang. Finally, on August 8, Heng-yang fell after a 47-day siege in which more than 15,000 of the 16,275 Chinese defenders perished. The Japanese suffered 20,000 casualties.

After the fall of Heng-yang, there was a lull in the fighting because the Japanese, who were being hurt by Chennault's air attacks, had to accumulate additional supplies for a further advance. The Japanese also used the lull to reorganize their forces, and to conclude Ichigo they created a new headquarters, the Sixth Area Army, commanded by General Yasuji Okamura. He resumed the Japanese advance at the end of August, with the Eleventh Army driving south along the railroad from Heng-yang and the Twenty-third Army driving north from Canton. Their objectives were Kweilin and Liuchow in Kwangsi province, the location of Chennault's major airbases in eastern China. Chinese resistance was light, but the Fourteenth Air Force did slow the Japanese advance again, despite meeting strong opposition from recently strengthened Japanese fighter squadrons. By November the Japanese were approaching the two cities, and on November 10 the Chinese evacuated both garrisons. Flushed with victory, the Eleventh Army pushed to the west toward Kweiyang (Kuei-yang), from which it could turn against the Chinese capital at Chungking or against Kun-ming, the major Chinese terminal for the Hump route. Other Japanese troops moved north from Indochina to link up with troops moving south from Liuchow, completing the continental corridor from northern China into Southeast Asia.

The weakness of the Chinese resistance angered the Americans and heightened the tension between Chennault and Stilwell. Chennault believed the Fourteenth Air Force's efforts proved that his theories of air strategy in China would have worked if he and the Chinese troops on the ground had been adequately supplied, and he criticized Stilwell for depriving them of their expected share of Hump tonnage. Stilwell argued that the Chinese defeats were the result of Chennault's and Chiang's faulty reliance on airpower for defending eastern China, and of internal Chinese politics, which had led Chiang to embargo the shipment of supplies to General Hsueh Yueh.

More important, Washington, long disappointed by the Chinese war effort, pressured Chiang to place Stilwell in charge of all Chinese combat troops as part of a larger attempt, initiated in the spring of 1944, to reinvigorate the Chinese effort. Chiang had agreed in principle to Washington's request, but he had no intention of placing his troops under Stilwell's command. In October, at his demand, Stilwell was relieved of his CBI commands, and Lieutenant General Albert C. Wedemeyer was placed in command of the newly created China theater.

When Wedemeyer replaced Stilwell, Chungking was in a state of near panic and Chiang's Nationalist China was on the verge of military and economic collapse. Wedemeyer promptly began an airlift of Chinese troops from Burma to help defend Chungking against an expected Japanese advance. But the Japanese had no plans to advance that far into China. Their supply line was now long and precarious, and they were worried about a possible U.S. threat to the China coast. In addition, they had achieved their principal objectives of eliminating the U.S. air bases in eastern China and securing the railroad corridor. It also is possible that the Japanese feared that seizing Chungking and eliminating Chiang's regime would free Chinese Communist troops to attack them, or that Chiang and the Japanese had reached an understanding that the Japanese would not attack Chungking and Kunming if Chiang would not supply or reinforce the Chinese troops guarding the U.S. air bases in eastern China. Whatever the reasons, Okamura pulled back the Eleventh Army when it was still 300 miles from Chungking, to consolidate control of the railroad.

In March 1945 the Japanese resumed their offensive against the Chinese and drove toward the air bases near Chekiang, less than 200 miles from Chungking. But Chinese troops and the Fourteenth Air Force held them in check. Two months later the Chinese recaptured Nanning, on the railroad south of Liuchow, and after that, Liuchow. When the Japanese surrendered in August, the Chinese were closing in on Kweilin.

Ichigo was a major blow to the Allied war effort in China. The Japanese occupied an area containing 100 million people, Nationalist China's granary, and a considerable part of the Nationalists' industrial base, thereby bringing the Chinese economy close to collapse. In addition, the Japanese completely cut off Chungking from any access to the coast, gained a rail route connecting northern China and Indochina, and inflicted 700,000 casualties on Chiang's armies. Finally, the Japanese forced the abandonment of seventeen airfields in eastern China from which Chennault's Fourteenth Air Force had been striking at their river and coastal shipping, and ended the possibility that China-based U.S. aircraft could provide close support for U.S. operations in the Pacific Ocean area.

Equally important, Ichigo had significant consequences for the future of China. It exposed as never before the inability of Chiang's regime to wage war and its willingness to throw provincial armies into decimating combat while conserving its U.S.-equipped divisions, costing it desperately needed popular support in its struggle for power with the Communists. At the same time, it presented the Communists with an opportunity to strengthen their position. Taking advantage of Chiang's defeats at the hands of the Japanese in Ichigo, they occupied more territory in China and expanded their army by 100,000 men, helping to pave the way for their ultimate triumph over Chiang in 1949.

FURTHER READINGS

Bagby, Wesley M. *The Eagle-Dragon Alliance: America's Relations with China in World War II* (1992).

Byrd, Martha. *Chennault: Giving Wings to the Tiger* (1987).

Eastman, Lloyd D. *Seeds of Destruction: Nationalist China in War and Revolution, 1937–1949* (1984).

Romanus, Charles F., and Sunderland, Riley. *Stilwell's Command Problems,* United States Army in World War II (1956).

———. *Time Runs Out in the CBI* (1959).

Samson, Jack. *Chennault* (1987).

Tuchman, Barbara W. *Stilwell and the American Experience in China, 1911–1945* (1970).

Wilson, Dick. *When Tigers Fight: The Story of the Sino-Japanese War, 1937–1945* (1982).

John Kennedy Ohl

SEE ALSO Chennault, Claire Lee; Chiang Kai-shek; Stilwell, Joseph Warren

Imperial Japanese Army
See Army, Japanese

Imphal and Kohima, Battles of

After taking Burma (now Myanmar) in 1942, the Japanese army contemplated a plan called Operation 21 to invade northeast India. However, the mountainous border region was deemed too difficult to supply and there were higher priorities, so the operation was shelved. It was also thought that an invasion "was likely to arouse ill-feeling amongst the Indian masses."

Facing the Japanese was the British Fourteenth Army, commanded by Lieutenant General William Slim. Slim had suffered through the retreat from Burma in 1942, and his corps was upgraded to an army in October 1943. Ever since their retreat, the British had been improving the roads around the mountain town of Imphal, laying in vast stores of supplies to support the eventual reconquest of Burma. While biding their time, the British high command allowed Orde Wingate's Chindits (guerrillas also known as Wingate's Raiders) to make a large-scale raid in February and April 1943.

Lieutenant General Renya Mutaguchi led the effort to mop up after the Chindits and was inspired with the idea of long-range operations into enemy territory without a secure line of communications. After assuming command of the Japanese Fifteenth Army, he advocated an invasion of northeast India. By 1944, the war was going poorly for Japan on all fronts, and Mutaguchi argued that a dramatic thrust against Imphal and Kohima would achieve several goals: (1) the taking of these supply bases would leave the British unable to attack Burma; (2) a victory was sorely needed by the Japanese nation; (3) perhaps the Indian National Army could provoke a revolt within India.

Surrounded by mountains and jungles, Imphal is on a plain some 3,000 feet high. During the dry season, the temperature soars well above 100°(F), leaving the ground parched and cracked. Sixty-five miles north along the only road into Imphal is the small mountain town of Kohima, at an elevation of 5,000 feet. The Japanese needed to take the two towns before the annual monsoon began in May. Troops, who were to carry only a month's supply of rice, were expected to capture enemy supplies and munitions for their use. Mutaguchi assumed that the Japanese would repeat their whirlwind success of 1942.

Beginning in October 1943, the Japanese 56th and 18th Divisions conducted operations in northern Burma to disrupt the Chinese forces facing them. On February 3, 1944, the Japanese 55th Division launched a diversionary attack from southern Burma against the 15th

Corps (5th and 7th Indian Divisions and 81st African Division) in Arakan, a state of Burma on the Bay of Bengal, near India. Retreating before the Japanese, elements of the two Indian divisions formed an "administrative box," an all-round defense tactic that relied on being supplied by air. The few Japanese aircraft were unable to stop their resupply. On February 24, out of ammunition and starving, the Japanese withdrew. Slim had committed two of his reserve divisions to this battle, thus achieving Mutaguchi's objective of drawing away forces from Imphal.

In early March, Japanese soldiers began to cross the Chindwin River, launching Operation U. The 33d Division, under Lieutenant General Yanagida, advanced from the south toward Imphal, while the 15th Division, under General Yamauchi, moved toward the town from the east. Seven thousand men of the Indian National Army's 1st Division accompanied Yamauchi. To the north, the 31st Division, under General Sato was to capture Kohima and drive beyond to the strategic rail center of Dimapur.

Slim had hoped that the Japanese would attack, and had planned a defensive battle to bleed the Japanese forces before launching an offensive of his own into Burma. British intelligence expected an imminent attack, but their troops were caught off guard nevertheless. The 33d Division conducted a series of pincer movements against the 17th Indian Light Division and 20th Indian Division, forcing them back toward Imphal. In response, the 5th Indian Division was flown into Imphal to reinforce the defenders, an operation completed by March 24.

The Japanese 15th Division and a regiment of the 31st Division tried to push through the 50th Indian Parachute Brigade at Sangshak and faced bitter opposition. Though the brigade was essentially destroyed, the Indian and British troops exacted heavy casualties and delayed the Japanese forces until March 24. On March 29, units of the 31st Division cut the Imphal–Kohima road, beginning the siege of Imphal. They trapped 150,000 British and Indian troops in Imphal and its airfields, requiring supply by air. Defensive boxes were set up around the city and supplied by airdrops. During the course of the siege, 12,000 reinforcements were flown in, along with 800,000 gallons of fuel, 423 tons of sugar, 919 tons of grains, and other supplies. Ten thousand wounded and ill were evacuated by air.

From April 1 to the end of May, the Japanese 33d and 15th Divisions fought to take Imphal. In the town were the equivalent of five divisions, including the 254th Tank Brigade, the only armored unit on either side. Because the Japanese had only a few antitank weapons, the 254th

was a major factor in the continuing battles around the perimeter of the siege. In May, the monsoon came early and dropped 400 inches of rain.

Having been delayed at Sangshak, the Japanese 31st Division surrounded Kohima and made its first major attack on April 6. The town was garrisoned by the 161st Indian Brigade. Typical of the Indian army, this brigade contained one British and two Indian battalions. Just 46 miles beyond Kohima was the important railway town of Dimapur. The railroad to Ledo ran through there, and it was from Ledo that the airlift to China was conducted. Lieutenant General Kawabe Masakazu of the Burma Area Army refused Mutaguchi's April 8 request to divert the 31st Division toward Dimapur. At the beginning of the campaign, Dimapur was virtually undefended, a situation the British were forced to remedy by flying in the British 2d Division. This airlift was completed by April 1, and two brigades of the division began to push down the road to Kohima to relieve the beleaguered 161st Brigade. They met units of the Japanese 31st Division entrenched in pillboxes and took until April 18 to reach Kohima; by then the defenders of Kohima were down to a circular defensive perimeter only a few hundred yards in diameter.

Though the siege was broken, the Battle of Kohima was not over. The Japanese dug in, and the British and Indian forces, supported by tanks, repeatedly attacked from May 3 to June 2. The Japanese held on during bitter and inconclusive fighting. General Sato finally took it on his own authority to order a retreat. Mutaguchi tried to countermand the order, and Sato cut communications. Kohima had cost 4,000 killed and wounded among the Indians, Gurkhas, and British, and over 7,000 casualties among the Japanese.

During June, the British gained the initiative around Imphal, but found the two Japanese divisions as tenacious and skilled as the 31st before Kohima. On June 22, the road to Kohima was reopened, lifting the siege. The British and Indian forces suffered some 13,000 casualties at the Battle of Imphal.

From the beginning, Mutaguchi found his ambitious operation frustrated. During May he relieved Yanagida of command of the 33d Division and Yamauchi of the 15th Division; on July 5, Sato was relieved of command of the 31st Division. On June 26, Mutaguchi finally advised an end to the campaign and withdrawal back to the Chindwin River. The Japanese troops continued to suffer until July 8, when Prime Minister Tojo eventually concurred and the retreat began. Of the 220,000 Japanese troops who started the campaign, only 130,000 survived. Their Indian National Army allies lost almost 2,000 dead, and another 1,500 either surrendered or deserted. Having been responsible for one of the greatest land defeats in Japan's history, Mutaguchi and his superior, Kawabe, were soon relieved of their commands, as were numerous staff officers.

FURTHER READINGS

Evans, Geoffrey, and Anthony Brett-James. *Imphal* (1961).

Rooney, David. *Burma Victory: Imphal, Kohima and the Chindit Issue, March 1944 to May 1945* (1992).

Eric Swedin

SEE ALSO India; Indian National Army; Slim, William Joseph; Wingate, Orde C.

India

With a population of 318 million, India was (in the hackneyed phrase of the time) still the "jewel in the crown of the British Empire" at the beginning of World War II. In a dominion deeply divided along religious lines, Muslims constituted the largest minority. Indian soldiers had served faithfully during World War I, and in August 1917, the British secretary of state for India, Edwin Samuel Montagu, announced that the British government intended to develop "self-governing institutions" within India. For the next two decades, the British government and the Indian National Congress, an independence movement founded in 1885, negotiated over the nature of these constitutional reforms.

When Great Britain declared war on Germany, the viceroy of India proclaimed India at war, without consulting any of the Indian leaders. Although many members of the Indian National Congress supported the cause against fascism, its officials serving as provincial officials resigned en masse to protest the callous way in which India was dragged into the war. The other great force among Indian nationalists was the Muslim League, under the leadership of Muhammad Ali Jinnah, who would settle for nothing less than an independent Muslim state of "Pakistan." Perceiving a way to weaken the power of the Indian National Congress, he threw Muslim support behind the British war effort.

The leaders of the Indian National Congress were Jawaharlal Nehru and Mohandas Karamchand Gandhi. Gandhi preached satyagraha (holding fast to the truth), a nonviolent approach to civil disobedience and noncooperation with the colonial authorities. On October 17, 1940, he launched a satyagraha against Indian participation in the war. Within six months, 14,000 Indian Na-

tional Congress members were in jail. Sensing the onset of the Pacific war, the British released them on December 3, 1941.

Within months, Malaya (now Malaysia), Singapore, and Burma (now Myanmar), British possessions all, fell, bringing a Japanese army almost to the Indian border. On April 5, 1942, a Japanese carrier task force under Vice Admiral Chuichi Nagumo attacked Ceylon (now Sri Lanka) in an attempt to destroy the British Eastern Fleet. The British were forewarned by a decoded message and had set sail in an attempt to intercept the Japanese fleet, but when they ran low on fuel, they retired to the Maldive Islands. The British did lose seven vessels, including cruisers *Dorsetshire* and *Cornwall,* but the Japanese raid failed in its goal of driving British naval power from the Indian Ocean.

In early 1942, the land-based defenses of India were quite poor, with only the 23d Indian Division guarding the frontier with Japanese-occupied Burma, but the Japanese made no effort to take advantage of this situation. The Indian army grew from a prewar strength of 350,000 to 2.5 million by the end of the war. As well as defending India, Indian army units served in North Africa, East Africa, Italy, Greece, Syria, Iraq, Persia, Burma, Hong Kong, Malaya, and Singapore. Casualties included 24,000 killed, 64,000 wounded, 12,000 missing, and 80,000 taken prisoner (most of the latter in the catastrophe at Singapore).

Although the majority of Indian National Congress members supported the Allied war effort, they did not want to continue to participate in the war if that meant continued British dominance. If the British left, what reason did Japan have to invade? This attitude was not entirely naive, in that Japan did not intend to incorporate India into its Greater East Asia Co-Prosperity Sphere. In May 1942, Sir Stafford Cripps, leader of the House of Commons in the Churchill coalition government, arrived with an offer of postwar independence. Negotiators failed to agree on the details of the offer and the offer was rejected as insufficient.

In August 1942 the Indian National Congress voted on a policy of "Quit India," Gandhi's last great satyagraha. More than fifty battalions of troops were deployed to suppress the effort, and by the end of 1942, 66,000 Congress supporters were interned or jailed, including Nehru and Gandhi. Deprived of leadership, the movement grew out of control and soon went beyond nonviolence. More than a thousand deaths occurred in ensuing riots. Sir Archibald Wavell, commander in chief in India, considered this "India's most dangerous hour." For the rest of the war, the British and Indian armed forces suffered numerous instances of sabotage and harassment by Indians opposed to the British presence. Matters were not helped by President Franklin D. Roosevelt's frequent prodding and needling of Prime Minister Winston Churchill over the question of Indian independence; the Americans had set themselves up in this war as the champions of colonial freedom.

Some Indians actively assisted the Japanese. The Indian National Army (INA) was formed from prisoners of war captured during the fall of Malaya, Singapore, and Burma. An important prewar independence leader, Subhas Chandra Bose, escaped from British custody to Germany, where he formed the Indian Legion from prisoners of war captured in Egypt, in the Western desert. Later he went to Japan, took command of the INA, and formed the Free India Provisional Government. Six thousand men in the INA 1st Division accompanied Japan's 15th Division during the Battle of Imphal in 1944 and suffered heavy casualties before retreating with the Japanese.

The war brought inflation and food shortages, devastating the Indian economy. The price of rice and other staples doubled by 1944. In 1943 a terrible famine in Bengal, caused by harvest failure and inadequate coordination of transport, led to the deaths by starvation of an estimated 3.5 million of the 60 million citizens of Bengal. Despite these hardships, by the end of the war India had become a financial creditor, rather than a debtor, to Britain.

India was an important source of manpower and raw materials for the Allies, and it also served a base for military operations. After the Burma Road was closed by the Japanese occupation of Burma, a long-term airlift was inaugurated from Ledo in north-eastern India. Five hundred air miles away, over "the Hump" of the Himalayas, was the Chinese Nationalist capital of Chungking. From July 1942 until the Burma Road was reopened on January 27, 1945, 650,000 tons of supplies were flown in over some of the most rugged terrain in the world.

In March 1944, the Japanese 15th Division invaded India in an attempt to secure better positions from which to defend Burma. After hard-fought sieges at the mountain towns of Imphal and Kohima, the Japanese were repelled.

At the end of the war, the changes that had came to India made it obvious that India would not suffer British imperial rule much longer. At midnight on August 14, 1947, after two years of ethnic disturbances which took at least a million lives, British rule ended with the independence of Pakistan (including what is now Bangladesh) and India.

FURTHER READINGS
Fay, Peter Ward. *The Forgotten Army: India's Armed Struggle for Independence, 1942–1945* (1993).
Voigt, Johannes H. *India in the Second World War* (1987).
                                                      Eric Swedin

SEE ALSO Bose, Subhas Chandra; Gandhi, Mohandas Karamchand; Imphal and Kohima, Battles of; Indian National Army

Indian National Army

In October 1941, Major Iwaichi Fujiwara arrived in Thailand to exploit Indian opposition to the British through propaganda and intelligence operations. His small group of officers was called Fujiwara Kikan, or F Kikan. In Bangkok he cultivated a relationship with Pritam Singh, a Sikh leader of the local Indian independence movement. When the war in the Pacific started, Fujiwara and Singh followed the Japanese attack into Malaya (now Malaysia). There they met the newly captured Captain Mohan Singh, a Sikh who was second in command of a battalion in the Punjab Regiment of the Indian army. After his battalion was shattered and surrendered on December 13, 1941, Captain Singh responded positively to Fujiwara's suggestion that they form the Indian prisoners into a revolutionary army. Some twenty-five hundred Indian prisoners of war soon joined the fledgling Indian National Army (INA). Two companies of the INA joined the Japanese in their assault on Singapore on February 7, 1942.

When Singapore surrendered on February 15, 50,000 Indian troops became prisoners of war. The official surrender of the Indian troops was on February 17, two days after the official British ceremony. This was yet another reminder of the discrimination they faced within the ranks of a colonial army. Fujiwara, Pritam Singh, and Mohan Singh spoke to the troops at their surrender and persuaded half of them to join the INA. The rest were treated as prisoners of war.

Japanese intentions toward India were always vague. India was not considered part of the Greater East Asia Co-Prosperity Sphere, but Japan had no intention of seeing it remain a British colony. Prime Minister Tojo explained to the Japanese Diet in early 1942 that "Without the liberation of India, there can be no real mutual prosperity in Greater East Asia."

In March 1942, Japan invited Indian nationalists who lived in areas that Japan controlled to a conference in Tokyo on Indian independence. Rash Behari Bose, an Indian exile who had lived in Japan since 1915, was selected by Tojo as president of the conference and was then elected president of the Indian Independence League, of which the INA was the military arm. After this conference, Fujiwara was replaced by Colonel Hideo Iwakuro and his Iwakuro Kikan. Whereas Fujiwara was an idealist, truly supportive of Indian nationalism, Iwakuro was more interested in exploiting the INA as a propaganda tool. A branch of Iwakuro Kikan based on Penang Island trained INA soldiers as spies and guerrillas—who, when sent into India, usually surrendered quickly. The Japanese army did not have the resources to train or arm a large army and did not desire the problems that such an ally might create.

Mohan Singh grew increasingly unhappy with the Japanese failure to create a true army. On December 29, 1942, he was arrested by Iwakuro. As a result, the senior officers of the INA asked to revert back to the status of prisoners of war. The INA fell from 45,000 men to only 8,000, and remained at this low point until the dynamic Subhas Bose arrived.

Subhas Chandra Bose was born to an upper-class Bengali family on January 23, 1897. In 1920, he resigned his recent appointment to the Indian civil service and devoted his life to achieving Indian independence. In 1938 and 1939 he was elected president of the Indian National Congress. He opposed the nonviolent disobedience of Mohandas Gandhi and Jawaharlal Nehru, advocating a more militant approach. He also argued that independent India should initially have an authoritarian government combining elements of fascism and communism; only after economic prosperity had been achieved should a democratic system be introduced. On July 2, 1940, the British arrested Bose on charges of sedition. On November 29, 1940, he announced that he would fast, Gandhi-like, until freed. Six days later he was released to go home while awaiting trial. He took the opportunity to escape to Kabul, Afghanistan, then continued through the Soviet Union to Berlin.

Cooperating with the Germans, Bose formed the Indian Legion in 1941 from Indian prisoners of war captured in North Africa. Three thousand to four thousand Indians served in three battalions under German officers who spoke only German. After the collapse of the INA in North Africa, Bose was smuggled out by U-boat to a rendezvous with a Japanese submarine southwest of Madagascar. He arrived in Tokyo on March 16, 1943.

Only Gandhi and Nehru were more popular than Bose as Indian independence leaders. Bose convinced the Japanese government to support his cause more fully and rallied the support of the expatriate Indian population in Southeast Asia. He renamed the INA the Azad Hind Fauj (Free India Army), and formed the Rani of Jhansi Regiment, composed of women and named for a heroine of the 1857 Indian Mutiny. The INA was a truly national organization, with Hindus, Muslims, and Sikhs serving together. Bose declined to accept a military rank, but soon became known as *Netaji* (Leader), a word with obvious fascist overtones.

Bose created the Free India Provisional Government (FIPG) On October 21, 1943, as the government for the INA to serve. In November 1943 Japan officially transferred the Andaman and Nicobar Islands in the Bay of Bengal to the FIPG. These islands were the only parts of India which Japan had conquered. The defense and administration of these islands, however, remained with the Japanese navy, not the INA. Also in November, Bose attended the Greater East Asia Conference in Tokyo. He was an observer, not a delegate, because Japan did not intend to incorporate India into the Greater East Asia Co-Prosperity Sphere.

In 1944, responsibility for the INA was transferred from the Japanese Twenty-fifth Army to the Fifteenth Army, and the INA relocated from Singapore to Rangoon, Burma (now Myanmar). In order to establish better positions to defend Burma, the Burma Area Army decided that the key mountain towns of Imphal and Kohima should be taken as a buffer zone. The Japanese army hoped to disrupt communications between India and China, and to use propaganda and the INA to incite revolution in India. This amounted to a limited invasion of India, and Bose insisted that the INA be involved as an allied army. He repeatedly declared, "The first drop of blood shed on Indian soil must be that of a soldier of the INA." He planned for the INA to continue to march beyond the initial Japanese objectives and provoke widespread revolution within India.

Six thousand troops in the three guerrilla regiments of the INA 1st Division accompanied the Fifteenth Army in its attack on Imphal. Ironically, considering Bose's disagreements with the men, two of these regiments were called the Gandhi and Nehru regiments. A second INA division was being trained in Rangoon. Imphal and Kohima were besieged, at the cost of heavy casualties. Finally starvation, disease, and lack of munitions forced Tojo to order the Japanese army to retreat on July 8, 1944. Of the 6,000 soldiers in the INA 1st Division, only 2,600 returned to Burma; 800 had surrendered and 715 had deserted. Four hundred had died in action, and 1,500 had died of disease or starvation. When British, Indian, and Chinese forces reconquered Burma in 1945, the INA collapsed. The entire INA 1st

Division surrendered, as did a 5,000-man INA garrison in Rangoon.

On August 17, 1945, a Japanese bomber carrying Bose crashed in Formosa (now Taiwan). Bose died hours later, of burns. Now that Japan had surrendered, he had been flying to Manchuria, hoping to meet with Russian officials and, in a scheme that even the devious Joseph Stalin would undoubtedly have rejected, recruit them to support the INA in its quest for an independent India.

With the war over, the INA troops came home to India. The British government considered them to be traitors and sent some of the soldiers to rehabilitation centers before allowing them to rejoin the Indian army. It was decided to court-martial some of the officers as an example. The trials were held in the Red Fort near New Delhi. The All-India Congress Committee funded the defense of these officers. The trial of the first three defendants started on November 5, 1945. The defense argued that the INA had not been part of the Japanese army, but an independent army serving an independent government.

The Indian populace considered the defendants to be heroes. Demonstrators surrounded the Red Fort, and riots erupted in Madras and Calcutta in support of the defendants. In February 1946 the Indian navy in Bombay mutinied, including among their demands a halt to the trials. The INA defendants were convicted and sentenced to life imprisonment. The sentences were immediately commuted to dismissal from the Indian army. Other defendants were tried in early 1946. On April 24, 1946, Nehru warned the British government of his opposition to any further trials. By now it was obvious that India would be independent before long, and the British ceased the trials. Contemporary British scholarship is in general contemptuous of the INA, dismissing its members as traitors who had no military impact. Indian scholarship portrays them as true patriots who contributed to the country's independence.

FURTHER READINGS

Bose, Sisir K. *The Flaming Sword Forever Unsheathed: A Concise Biography of Netaji Subhas Chandra Bose* (1986).

Corr, Gerald H. *The War of the Springing Tigers* (1975).

Fay, Peter Ward. *The Forgotten Army: India's Armed Struggle for Independence, 1942–1945* (1993).

Gordon, Leonard. *Brothers Against the Raj: A Biography of Indian Nationalists Sarat and Subhas Chandra Bose* (1990).

Lebra, Joyce C. *Jungle Alliance: Japan and the Indian National Army* (1972).

Pandit, H. N. *Netaji Subhas Chandra Bose: From Kabul to Imphal* (1988).

Sareen, T. R. *Japan and the Indian National Army* (1986).
Eric Swedin

SEE ALSO Bose, Subhas Chandra; Imphal and Kohima, Battles of; India

Indianapolis

Commissioned in 1932, cruiser USS *Indianapolis* was the first major U.S. Navy vessel built after the London Naval Conference of 1930. During World War II, *Indianapolis* fought with distinction at New Britain, New Guinea, the Aleutians, the Gilberts, the Western Carolines, the Marianas, the Marshalls, and Okinawa. Built with spacious living quarters and a distinctive swayback profile, the ship was very fast, and Admiral Raymond Spruance used it as his flagship for the Fifth Fleet. *Indianapolis* was fitted with such modern equipment as radar, radio, and fire control systems, but lacked sonar and suffered from an easily floodable design. In 1945 it was commanded by Captain Charles B. McVay III.

After having been badly damaged by kamikaze attacks off Okinawa in April 1945, *Indianapolis* sailed to San Francisco for repairs. On July 16 *Indianapolis* left San Francisco carrying a very precious cargo—the atomic bomb that would be dropped on Hiroshima. That same day, the Japanese submarine I-58 left Kure Harbor in Japan for a final mission. After a brief stop at Hawaii, *Indianapolis* reached its destination, the island of Tinian, on July 26.

After unloading the bomb, *Indianapolis* sailed to Guam under orders of the commander in chief, Pacific (CINCPAC). The ship arrived on July 27 and was then due to sail on to Leyte in the Philippines for posting to Vice Admiral Jesse Oldendorf's Task Force 95. Captain McVay conferred with Commodore J. B. Carter, Admiral Chester Nimitz's assistant chief of staff for operations, about his impending voyage to Leyte. Carter did not give McVay vital information about the activity of Japanese submarines along the route; four submarines were known to be operating in the area through which *Indianapolis* would pass, and another ship had recently been sunk in the area. Nor did the surface operations officer of the Marianas command, Captain Oliver F. Naquin, or the port director's routing officer, Lieutenant Joseph Waldron, give McVay this information.

Indianapolis left Guam on the morning of July 28, steaming at 15.7 knots with no escorts, and was due to arrive in Leyte on Tuesday, August 1, about dawn. That same day another ship about 170 miles ahead of *Indianapolis* on the same route reported spotting a submarine; the Marianas command sent a hunter-killer group to search for the submarine. *Indianapolis* was not diverted, nor did it receive direct information about these incidents.

Orders concerning zigzagging were convoluted. Fleet rules required all warships sailing in "dangerous" waters to zigzag in fair weather; at Guam, Captain McVay was given instructions to use his discretion on zigzagging. On the night of July 28 the weather was overcast, so he ordered no zigzagging; the ship was sailing at the rather fast speed of 17 knots.

Between 2345 hours and 2400 hours the Japanese submarine I-58 fired a spread of six torpedoes at a large, unknown target. Two, possibly three, of these torpedoes slammed into the starboard side, below the waterline, of *Indianapolis,* blowing off the bow. Without sonar, *Indianapolis* had no idea the submarine was nearby. The explosions severed all communication and electrical lines throughout the ship; in the confusion and chaos aboard, the engines were kept running, thus driving the ship under the waves. Many men were trapped below, and apparently the radios were not able to send a signal, so no one heard the SOS. Of the 1,199 men aboard *Indianapolis,* approximately 850 made it into the water to await rescue.

On July 30 Captain E. T. Layton at CINCPAC Combat Intelligence Office in Guam intercepted an encoded message from a Japanese submarine, claiming that it had sunk a large U.S. ship. Because U.S. high naval commanders felt that the Japanese navy was no longer a threat, this message was not believed. Commodore Carter also dismissed the message. Although *Indianapolis* was due in port on August 1, the port operations officer in Leyte Gulf, Lieutenant Stuart Gibson, made no report because he was required to file one only when a ship arrived. Captain Alfred Granum, operations officer for the Frontier Command, also at Leyte, was not told if *Indianapolis* had arrived and did not ask; all concerned just assumed that it had arrived or that, because it was the admiral's flagship, it had been rerouted without their knowing of the change. On July 31, army pilot Captain Richard G. LeFrancis claimed to have seen explosions while flying at night near the area where *Indianapolis* was torpedoed; he actually saw the flares shot into the air by the crew who were in the water.

On August 2, Lieutenant Wilbur C. Gwinn of the Marianas Command was flying his Ventura airplane, looking for Japanese ships and submarines that might still be supplying isolated outposts. Instead, he spotted *Indianapolis* survivors. At first, his messages stating that he had found naval survivors surprised his superiors, who could not imagine from which ship they might have come. Lieutenant Robert A. Marks and his PBY Catalina were dispatched to pick up the survivors; upon arrival he realized there were more survivors than he could recover. It slowly dawned on the rescuers, as they questioned the survivors, that they were from overdue *Indianapolis.* Of the 850 who had made it into the water on the night of July 28, only 316 survived, many of them having succumbed to delirium, sharks, and lack of water.

The survivors were rescued the day before the United States dropped the atomic bomb on Hiroshima; the timing could not have been worse. In looking to place blame, Captain McVay was issued a letter of reprimand and court-martialed—the first captain ever tried by the U.S. Navy for losing his ship in battle. Admiral Chester Nimitz, CINCPAC commander, recommended against court-martial, but Admiral Ernest King, head of the navy, felt someone was responsible for this tragedy and should be punished; he supported the court-martial. The captain of the Japanese submarine I-58, Mochitsura Hashimoto, acted as a witness for the navy, stating that he did not see *Indianapolis* zigzagging, although he felt it would have made little difference even if it had been. At the end of the court-martial, McVay was cleared of the charge of not ordering his men to abandon ship in time, but not cleared of the charge of not zigzagging, although whether he had actually violated the standing orders was not made clear. The navy also, more justifiably, issued letters of reprimand to four officers of the Philippine Sea Frontier Command who had failed to act upon *Indianapolis*'s nonarrival or warned it of impending danger; no one else was court-martialed. The letters of reprimand were later withdrawn from the four officers' files.

USS *Indianapolis* was the last U.S. warship sunk, the last submarine kill, and the last victim of the Imperial Japanese Navy in World War II. It was also the worst single-ship sea disaster in U.S. naval history. In fact, no U.S. warship has been sunk since the loss of *Indianapolis.* The timing of the disaster proved an embarrassment to the navy leadership, because it was difficult to acknowledge that such a disaster could happen, and that the survivors could be left for five days in the water, at the same time that the United States had won the war in the Pacific. Whatever the courts-martial verdicts, complacency was the true culprit.

FURTHER READINGS
Kurzman, Dan. *Fatal Voyage* (1990).
Morison, Samuel Eliot. *History of United States Naval Operations in World War II,* vol. 14, *Victory in the Pacific, 1945* (1960).

Laura Matysek Wood

SEE ALSO Navy, U.S.

Intelligence in the Pacific Theater

World War II in the Pacific was huge in scale, a situation which gave military intelligence more importance than ever before. The war covered a vast theater of operations involving enormous numbers of land, sea, and air combatants. Arguably, the fact that the war was between dramatically contrasting—and clashing—cultures and races resulted in unusually brutal combat. The determination of Japan to conquer and maintain control over large parts of China, Southeast Asia, and the Pacific region was symbolized by the military commitment to death before surrender. The declared U.S. goal of nothing less than the unconditional surrender of Japan reflected that nation's absolute commitment to total victory in the wake of the Japanese attack on the U.S. naval facility at Pearl Harbor, Hawaii, in December 1941.

Geography and the instruments of the modern battle reinforced the psychological commitment to total war. Although the Pacific theater was vast, modern ships and aircraft provided an extraordinary capacity to deliver both men and munitions over very long distances. For the first time in history, a single nation succeeded in holding dominance over the entire Pacific.

In this context, intelligence activities were severely challenged. The possibility of surprise attack, a technique which Japan had demonstrated with devastating effect in the Russo–Japanese War of 1904–1905, placed a premium on accurate intelligence. The extraordinary growth in radio and other forms of electronic communications since late in the nineteenth century put entirely new types and amounts of information at the disposal of both sides. The duel between opposing intelligence services became increasingly technological. Even before World War I, armed services had begun to use wireless radio to transmit information to units in the field and from the field to headquarters. As a result, interception of such traffic became crucial to the process of assembling the pieces of the puzzles of enemy intentions and movements.

Traditional human intelligence retained its central importance. As usual, espionage and sabotage agents were involved on both sides. In the anger—and hysteria—which resulted from the surprise attack on Pearl Harbor by Japan, many in the United States exaggerated the domestic threat from Japanese Americans, who proved to be remarkably patriotic, notably in combat in Europe but also in assisting Washington with information of various kinds that was useful to understanding the nation the United States was fighting. The advantage of the government of Japan at home in maintaining control over a homogeneous population, with a totalitarian system in place, was only partial compensation for the intractable problems of trying to control vast areas of the Pacific region.

One distinctive feature of the Allied intelligence effort was the use of carefully selected individuals to monitor movements of aircraft and ships. The Royal Australian Navy created the coast watcher service after World War I. Begun to protect the very extensive Australian coastline, the operation was gradually expanded during the 1930s to include the Solomon Islands, New Guinea, and the Bismarck Archipelago. Those involved were mainly farmers, missionaries, and government officers with good reason to be in strategically and tactically important isolated areas. Special teleradios were developed. Battery-operated, they had the capacity to function in the extreme temperatures and wetness of the tropics. They could send voice transmissions up to 400 miles, and telegraphic key transmissions up to 600 miles. The main drawback was their weight; carrying each radio to the selected location required up to sixteen porters. Human intelligence also was heavily used by the Japanese. Author William Manchester, a combat veteran of the Pacific war, has strong views as well as graphic descriptive powers in relating the events that took place. In the 1930s Japanese officers, disguised as bicycle salesmen, sidewalk photographers, and assorted tradesmen, appeared in the archipelago to survey Philippine defenses. Generally, however, the extent of behind-the-lines Japanese human intelligence was exaggerated, particularly to explain Pearl Harbor.

Electronic intelligence was much more significant than in any previous war. A great Allied advantage, ultimately of decisive importance, was that the United States had broken Japan's military codes before Pearl Harbor. Over time, Japanese military discipline could only partially compensate for this great disadvantage. The Japanese armada that advanced on Pearl Harbor at the beginning of December 1941 maintained strict radio silence that permitted it to move in almost total secrecy. There was a general sense at the U.S. base that an attack was coming, but no clear indication of where. The Hawaiian Islands and the Philippines were two very distinct possibilities, but there were others. Unfortunately for U.S. leaders and the U.S. military in the field—and of enormous importance to the Japanese—there was no effective sighting of the Japanese armada before the attack. It would have been very difficult, given the many attack options and the sheer size of the Pacific region.

Understandably, given the devastating nature of the attack on Pearl Harbor, there was intense acrimony in Washington afterward, with extensive hearings and investigations. Senior commanders were cashiered, and there was continuing debate over the degree to which they were individually guilty or were scapegoats. Political opponents and conspiracy theorists accused President Franklin D. Roosevelt (FDR) of directly undercutting fleet preparedness, even of foreknowledge of some type of Japanese attack, though evidence is lacking and any rational motive is impossible to define. (FDR was trying to prepare the United States for a war against Germany. Why would he wish to get into a war with Japan at roughly the same time?) In fact, the best explanation for the failure is a combination of complacency and conservatism. Complacency led the U.S. high command to feel more secure than reality justified; conservatism led them to fail to anticipate the reach and daring of the Japanese attack. Pearl Harbor was therefore not primarily a failure of intelligence; the experience, however, does demonstrate clearly the limitations of that dimension of war planning.

The attack on Pearl Harbor was accompanied by a coordinated attack on other centers of U.S. strength in the Pacific, including the substantial air, sea, and land facilities in the Philippines. Months of heavy fighting took place before the islands were finally conquered by the Japanese. Again, there was undeniable intelligence failure and complacency, reflected in the success of the initial assault on the Philippines. In both attacks the Japanese proved the importance of superior tactics, greater preparedness, strong discipline, and a willingness to take extreme risks. Even in the losing battle for the Philippines, however, U.S. electronic intelligence permitted an occasional surprise of the Japanese, especially in the air. If intelligence failures were important in the disaster at Pearl Harbor and related defeats in the Philippines, they were also vital to ultimate U.S. success in the war.

Perhaps the most dramatic example of intelligence playing a central role in the defeat of Japan was in the pivotal Battle of Midway in 1942. The seesaw battle, generally regarded as the turning point of the war in the central Pacific, ended in decisive victory for the United States. In advance of the battle, U.S. intelligence profes-

sionals were able to piece together the entire Japanese strategic plan, determining in advance virtually the entire order of battle, disposition of forces, intentions, and capabilities of the Japanese fleet. Even dates of movements and attack were pinpointed. A feint toward the Aleutian Islands was correctly evaluated. Gordon Prange, the distinguished analyst of the Pearl Harbor attack and of the Pacific war in general, has written that the Japanese defeat at Midway ultimately was not a command failure; it was an intelligence failure. Yet U.S. success at Midway did not mean such intelligence coups would become routine; this remarkable victory remains an exception, the combining of technical expertise with good luck. According to military historian Ronald H. Spector, Midway was the greatest single success produced by intelligence in the war with Japan, but it was far from typical.

The overall structure of intelligence activities in the Pacific reflected the complexities of military organizations—and senior personalities—involved. The inherent division between the navy's dominance of the central Pacific and General Douglas MacArthur's oversight of the southern and southwestern Pacific was no help to overall intelligence efficiency. Interservice rivalry, and at times hostility between different intelligence agencies, further complicated integrated efforts. In the Pacific Ocean Area, headed by Admiral Chester Nimitz, a joint staff organizational structure was reflected in the Joint Intelligence Center, Pacific Ocean Area, commanded by Brigadier General Joseph J. Twitty. The Joint Intelligence Center handled analysis of aerial photographs and captured documents, as well as interrogation of prisoners. The comprehensive effort included providing maps, charts, and terrain models, and production of the classified *Weekly Intelligence Bulletin*.

The Joint Intelligence Center was by no means inclusive, however. Code breaking remained a separate activity, commanded by the communications officer of the Pacific Fleet. The Special Estimates Section provided coordination between the two operations. MacArthur, predictably, ran a separate show. All intelligence operations in his southwest Pacific theater were part of his G-2 section. The section had overall authority, which provided the general with the means to direct intelligence priorities and analysis personally whenever he chose to do so.

As the war progressed, the workload of this intelligence organization became very substantial. A total of 50 tons of documents were captured in the campaign for Saipan. By 1944, over two hundred translators were employed. As the U.S. and related Allied war capabilities steadily grew, intelligence operations became more and more extensive. Intelligence was defensive as well as offensive, with efforts to conceal Allied operations as well as to discover enemy forces and plans. The home front remained just that; the high stakes involved are symbolized by the 1944 surprise visit of intelligence officers to offices of the popular U.S. science fiction magazine *Astounding,* which had just published a detailed short story by Cleve Cartmill featuring the development of an atomic bomb—a purely coincidental and purely imaginary discussion of a U.S. atomic bomb project. Intelligence activities remained crucial throughout the war and afterward. Beyond the search for vital information on fleet and troop movements, technical capabilities were instrumental in other aspects of the conflict. Accurate weather reports and photoreconnaissance played a role in the decisions concerning when and where to use the atomic bombs against Japan.

Information gathered during the war concerning the domestic economy and society of Japan was important for the military occupation following the surrender and for the rebuilding of that nation.

FURTHER READINGS

Manchester, William. *Goodbye Darkness—A Memoir of the Pacific War* (1981).

Prange, Gordon W. W., with Donald M. Goldstein and Katherine V. Dillon. *Miracle at Midway* (1982).

Spector, Ronald H. *Eagle Against the Sun—The American War with Japan* (1985).

Arthur I. Cyr

SEE ALSO Navy, Japanese; Pearl Harbor, Japanese Attack on

Intelligence Operations, Japanese

Intelligence Operations were one of the few areas where Japan's military services displayed any level of coordination, albeit more at the tactical and operational levels than at the strategic. It was also a rare arena in which Japan cooperated with other countries, primarily Germany but also Finland. Despite this achievement, Japanese intelligence had an uneven record. Both the military and foreign service signals intelligence agencies did outstanding work, although there is no evidence that they ever broke any high level Allied ciphers other than those of China. At the same time, however, photographic intelligence received very little emphasis until late in the war. In fact, the military services placed too much value on espionage networks and never established a screening process to evaluate reports against other sources. No effort was made to integrate reporting from the various sources available. As a result, Japanese intelligence was repeatedly victimized

by Allied deception efforts after late 1942, to Japan's cost as the Allies shifted over to the offensive.

At war's start, Japanese intelligence consisted of three main components: army, navy and foreign ministry Intelligence. Each concentrated on intelligence suitable to their service. A fourth component was added in 1942—the intelligence service of the Far East Asia ministry. It focused on internal security issues and information related to the collaborationist governments that administered Japan's newly conquered territories. Its agents and offices cooperated very closely with those of the foreign ministry and the occupying military intelligence and counterintelligence services. Unlike the other intelligence services, however, the Far East Asia ministry had no signals intelligence organization. It was totally dependent on its agents and contacts within the occupied countries.

The army's intelligence service was Japan's largest. Reporting to the minister of war, its agents ranged far and wide across the globe, but most operated in the Asian mainland. The *Kempeitai* controlled both the army's attachés in diplomat posts and its undercover operatives. Many of its agents were recruited from various patriotic societies, which often collected intelligence information and organized subversion on their own without prior coordination or approval from Imperial Army headquarters. Despite the occasional embarrassment this caused the government, the army's dominant political position precluded any effective action to curb its actions.

Army intelligence also had a very large and effective signals intelligence department. As with its espionage service, the army's signals service was directed primarily against China and Russia. The United States did not become a major target until 1940. Army signals service enjoyed mixed success in attacking enemy cipher systems but was very good at traffic analysis. It broke the ciphers Chinese Nationalist government regularly, but it did not do so well against the Communist Chinese or the Soviet cipher systems. Some low level U.S. Air Force ciphers were also broken, but the penetration was limited and inconsistent. No high-level Soviet, American, or British cipher systems were ever penetrated.

The navy's intelligence service was not as large as the army's, and it had a different geographic focus. The United States had been its primary target since the 1890s, and its interest in America's Hawaiian bases dated back to 1901. Britain was added in the late 1920s. Detailed information and files were developed on virtually every American and British naval base in the Pacific Ocean. Although the Imperial Navy also employed patriotic societies and their members for espionage, it relied much more on its own agents and used the society members for support. Its most successful intelligence operation involved the use of leased fishing craft staging out of Mexico with mixed Japanese-national and local ethnic Japanese crews. Much like the Soviet Union's seaborne spy ships, these "fishing craft" were equipped with radio monitoring equipment and stationed off San Diego and Los Angeles, the U.S. Pacific fleet's primary prewar operating bases. Some even ranged as far as San Francisco Bay. Espionage agents worked as waiters at local night spots frequented by the ships' officers and crews. In Hawaii, at least one agent actually worked as a waiter in the Pearl Harbor Officer's Club. Merchant ship crews were also employed to chart harbors and photograph ports and facilities. They even reported on warships they encountered at sea.

The navy also had a signals intelligence section, called the *Tokumu Han* or special services section. Its primary stations were located near naval stations such as Yokosuka and Sasebo, but it also had stations in China, Rabaul, and Formosa. New stations were built in Singapore and the Philippines during the war in an effort to improve the system's direction-finding accuracy. As with the army, the *Tokumu Han* had little success against high-grade ciphers, but it did successfully attack some U.S. Navy airwing and air reporting cipher systems. More significantly, it made some significant contributions to Japan's early success by locating Allied naval units. It also penetrated some low-level Soviet naval ciphers with the assistance of the Finnish intelligence services; however, it was not reliable enough to provide strategic warning of the Soviet attack against Japanese forces in Manchuria in August 1945.

Neither the army nor the navy employed special-purpose photo-reconnaissance aircraft to any extent. Most photography was taken by air crews using hand-held cameras. The army air force had one strategic reconnaissance squadron, the 1st Air Photographic Unit, and employed another, the 70th Independent Flying Squadron, based in New Guinea, for aerial reconnaissance. The navy did not establish a specialized aerial reconnaissance squadron until 1944. Allied fleet movements, bases, and ports were a high priority for both services. Air bases were added after mid-1942 and gained in importance as the war progressed.

As with the military intelligence services, the foreign ministry employed a vast array of human agents, including cultural and political attachés as well as espionage agents, to gather diplomatic intelligence about countries of concern. The American, British, and French consulates in Shanghai were penetrated, and the foreign ministry had the best Axis network operating in the United States and Soviet Union in 1942. For its American network, it used a Spanish intelligence agent. Penetrating America via

Mexico, the network used Spanish embassies and consulates to support its agents operating in Chicago, New York, and San Francisco. The network discovered the American nuclear weapons program and gained some limited insights into Allied radar and other technological developments. Fortunately for the Allies, decryption of Spain's diplomatic codes enabled the FBI to cripple the network by late 1943.

The foreign ministry's signals intelligence service attacked enemy and neutral diplomatic codes. Its successes include penetrating the French, American, Chinese, and Swedish diplomatic codes. The American naval attaché cipher and occasionally the Soviet diplomatic ciphers were also broken, albeit inconsistently. The foreign ministry received the assistance and cooperation of Germany's SS signals intelligence service beginning in 1944, although the extent to which that assistance benefitted the Japanese war effort remains unclear to this day.

All of Japan's intelligence services subverted Allied colonial authorities. Rash Behari Bose, leader of the Pan Asiatic League, and Subhas Chandra Bose of the Indian Independent League, represented a clumsy—but initially partially successful—effort to undermine British rule in India. The Japanese supported Ho Chi Minh's Vietnamese nationalist movement in Indochina, Muslim separatists in China and the Soviet Union, and the Indonesian nationalist movement in the Dutch East Indies. In many cases, they hired local nationalist movements to run the police and security services of the conquered territories. For example, Japanese occupation authorities in Indochina used Viet Minh troops to guard prisoner-of-war camps in that region.

Japan's massive human intelligence effort greatly facilitated its successes early in the war. Japanese maps of Malaya and Burma were often better than those of their British opponents. Moreover, Japanese intelligence knew a critical fact about Singapore that British prime minister Winston Churchill did not: that the city's landward defenses were inadequate and that its water came from the Malaysian mainland. Once the war began in earnest, however, Japan's espionage networks became unreliable as networks were rolled up by Allied counterintelligence services supported by the Allies' superior decryption services. Japanese leaders became increasingly blind to Allied plans and intentions after late 1942 and were therefore victimized by Allied deception efforts. By late 1944, virtually every Allied invasion or air attack achieved strategic surprise, forcing Japan to use inefficiently large garrisons as it attempted to defend everything. In the end, only the absence of alternate targets enabled the Imperial general staff to realize that the final invasion of Japan's home islands would follow the Okinawan invasion. The atomic bombing of Hiroshima and Nagasaki (1945) was itself a surprise, even though the Japanese had been aware of the American effort to develop a bomb almost from its inception. The empire's intelligence services's defeat was as complete as that of the empire itself.

FURTHER READINGS

Bennett, J.W., et al., Intelligence and Cryptanalytic Activities of the Japanese During World War II (1996).

Deacon, Richard. *A History of Japanese Secret Service,* (1983).

Wilcox, Robert K. *Japan's Secret War,* (1985).

Carl O. Schuster

SEE ALSO Army, Japanese; Navy, Japanese

Internment and Relocation of Italian Americans

When Italy declared war on the United States on December 11, 1941, there were 695,363 nonnaturalized Italian citizens in the United States. They were classified as "enemy aliens" and subjected to curfew and travel restrictions. Moreover, they were barred from employment in defense industries and were not allowed to possess firearms, ammunition, cameras, flashlights, and short-wave radios. In the aftermath of the Japanese attack on the U.S. naval base at Pearl Harbor, Hawaii, in December 1941, 264 suspected Italian Fascist agents were arrested nationwide.

The conflict between Italy and the United States affected primarily and more deeply the population of Italian extraction on the West Coast. The Western Defense Command estimated that there were 108,089 "enemy aliens" in that area, and Italians made up about 43 percent of these people. Most lived in California, especially in San Francisco.

On February 19, 1942, President Franklin D. Roosevelt signed Executive Order 9066, which authorized the secretary of war to "designate military areas from which any or all persons may be excluded." This wording was applicable not only to nonnaturalized persons but also to U.S. citizens. The measure was enacted primarily to allow the evacuation of Japanese Americans from the West Coast, but Lieutenant General John L. DeWitt, who was in charge of the Western Defense Command, opposed any racial preferential treatment and recommended the mass deportation and internment of German Americans and Italian Americans as well.

Roosevelt disagreed. In his opinion, Italian Americans were not a threat to U.S. security: "They are a lot of opera singers," he explained to Attorney General Francis Biddle. Similarly, Secretary of War Henry L. Stimson advised DeWitt not to disturb "Italian aliens and persons of Italian lineage except where they . . . constitute a definite danger."

Furthermore, Italian Americans were the single largest nationality group in the United States. Their relocation and internment en masse would have alienated the almost 5 million U.S. citizens of Italian descent, many of whom were employed in war industries, were fighting in the U.S. armed forces, and were a key component of the political coalition that had elected Roosevelt to the presidency.

Instead of the blanket policy adopted for Japanese Americans, a selective individual exclusion program was enforced against Italian Americans on the West Coast. Under its provisions, only specified "potentially dangerous" foreign-born naturalized Italian Americans could be considered for relocation on the basis of intelligence and other information. Boards of the Civil Affairs Division of the army's Wartime Civil Control Administration made the final decision on individual cases after hearings at which the accused could only answer questions; they were not allowed to testify on their own behalf.

Data in government records are unclear. Nevertheless, scholars have estimated that although hundreds of Italian aliens had to move out of areas located within 20 miles of the West Coast, only about a hundred U.S. citizens of Italian birth in the Pacific states were interned, primarily at Fort Missoula, Montana, and twenty-four more were served relocation orders. None was deprived of U.S. citizenship, although proceedings to revoke their naturalization were initiated for a number of them.

Those who were relocated included well-known prewar Fascist sympathizers like Ettore Patrizi and Renzo Turco. Patrizi was the editor-publisher of the San Francisco-based daily *L'Italia,* the most influential Italian-language newspaper on the West Coast; it received subsidies from the Italian government to spread Fascist propaganda. Turco had been a member of the Fascist League of North America in the late 1920s. According to the California Senate's Tenney "Committee on Un-American Activities," Patrizi and Turco directed the Fascist movement in California.

Many other relocated individuals, however, were simply "fellow travelers" of Italian dictator Benito Mussolini. Their ties to the Fascist regime originated less from ideological commitment than from ethnic defensiveness. Italian immigrants and their American-born offspring basked in the glory of Mussolini until their ancestral country entered World War II. Many felt that the alleged achievements of fascism were a partial redress for decades of anti–Italian intolerance and discrimination. Such pro–Fascist feelings made Americans of Italian ancestry a particularly vulnerable ethnic group because of concerns about sabotage and espionage by fifth columnists.

Relocation and internment took a heavy toll. Many Italian immigrants lost their jobs—especially in San Francisco, where a significant number worked as fishermen but were excluded from the waterfront for security reasons. Some had to find new employment as far east as Chicago and Detroit. Students were forced to leave school to follow their parents. At least four Italians committed suicide before the board hearings.

As early as June 27, 1942, restricted zones in the Western Defense Command were abolished with the exception of certain sensitive areas, and most of those who had been relocated could return to their homes. On Columbus Day, October 12, 1942, Attorney General Biddle announced that nonnaturalized Italians would no longer be classified as "enemy aliens." Remaining relocation orders were thereafter rescinded with few exceptions. Patrizi, for instance, remained confined in Reno, Nevada, until Italy signed an armistice with the United States in September 1943.

Only an infinitesimal minority of Italian Americans were disloyal to their adopted country after the outbreak of the war. Yet Italians' demonstrated loyalty to the United States played a marginal role in the decision of the Roosevelt administration. On the one hand, the United States was at war with Italy, a war declared by Italy on the United States. On the other hand, Roosevelt wished to appease Italian American voters so that the Democratic Party could regain their support in the forthcoming midterm elections. A significant percentage of the electorate of Italian extraction had gone over to the Republican Party two years earlier, following President Roosevelt's denunciation of Italy's 1940 attack on France. As Biddle later acknowledged, the reclassification of Italians was "good politics."

There was a general feeling in the United States at the time that the anti-ethnic excesses of World War I should not be repeated. Thus the rapid repeal of anti–Italian orders. Yet there was some lingering anti–Italian feeling. For example, the only known case of the lynching of a white man by blacks at this time occurred in 1944, in the Seattle area, when black troops hanged an member of the Italian Service Corps, which was composed of former Italian prisoners of war.

Compared with the 110,000–120,000 Japanese Americans who were interned, relatively few Italian Americans

on the West Coast were subject to relocation and internment. However, they, too, were victims of wartime anti-alien emotion in the United States.

FURTHER READINGS
Biddle, Francis. *In Brief Authority* (1962).
Blum, John Morton. *V Was for Victory: Politics and American Culture During World War II* (1976).
California Senate, Fifty-fifth Session. *Report of the Joint Fact-Finding Committee on Un-American Activities in California* (1943).
Facondo, Gabriella. *Socialismo italiano esule negli USA, 1930–1942* (1993).
Fox, Stephen. *The Unknown Internment: An Oral History of the Relocation of Italian Americans During World War II* (1990).
Scherini, Rose D. "Executive Order 9066 and Italian Americans: The San Francisco Story." *California History* (Winter 1991–1992).
Van Valkenburg, Carol Bulger. *An Alien Place: The Fort Missoula, Montana, Detention Camp, 1941–1944* (1995).

Stefano Luconi

SEE ALSO Home Front, U.S.; Internment of U.S. Citizens of Japanese Ancestry

Internment of U.S. Citizens of Japanese Ancestry

During World, War II the U.S. government removed and detained somewhere between 110,000 and 120,000 people of Japanese descent. Two-thirds of these were second-generation nisei and American citizens; and the rest were immigrant issei, barred from naturalization by federal law.

The removal of the Japanese Americans from the West Coast was the climax of a long history of discrimination and suspicion, now exacerbated by war. As early as 1932, federal agencies began surveillance of the Japanese American community. Buddhist temples, Japanese language schools, business associations, farmers, and fishermen drew particular scrutiny. By 1941 the government began categorizing the more than two thousand Japanese under surveillance. Group A were "known dangerous" and considered likely to engage in fifth column activities. Group B were considered potentially dangerous, but needed to have more intelligence gathered on them. Group C were considered to have pro–Japan inclinations and were suspected either of having contacts with spies or of engaging in propaganda activities. (Apparently there was no group presumed clear of any pro–Japanese taint.) Still, by October 1941, both the FBI and Office of Naval Intelligence (ONI) concluded there was no specific evidence of Japanese American involvement in any fifth column activities. In November, State Department representative Curtis B. Munson concluded that Japanese Americans generally posed little threat to national security and that those deemed dangerous were already under surveillance. Indeed, the subsequent declassification of Operation Magic messages shows that prewar imperial efforts to recruit Japanese Americans in espionage activities had singularly failed.

The Japanese American Citizens League (JACL) sought to affirm loyalty to the United States. In 1940 it began promoting its "Japanese-American Creed." The JACL, at the government's request, even informed on Japanese American community members; to refuse, its leaders reasoned, might be construed as disloyal.

Within forty-eight hours of the Japanese attack on the U.S. naval base at Pearl Harbor, Hawaii, on December 7, 1941, the FBI held 1,291 Japanese from groups A, B, and C. Authorities questioned and released some but held others indefinitely. The removal of community leaders disrupted the Japanese American social structure and led to the de facto transfer of power to the younger nisei, a particularly difficult situation for a culture which traditionally valued age and respected elders.

In the face of political and military pressure, President Franklin D. Roosevelt signed Executive Order 9066 on February 19, 1942, in spite of misgivings by Attorney General Francis Biddle and Army Chief of Staff George C. Marshall. The order allowed the War Department to designate military areas from which any person could be excluded. In March, while a congressional committee investigated the possibility of forcibly moving Japanese Americans, Lieutenant General John L. DeWitt, head of the Western Defense Command, declared California, western Oregon, and Washington, as well as southwestern Arizona, to be strategic areas from which all residents of Japanese descent would be prohibited. He sought wholesale evacuation rather than continued detention of those in the A, B, and C groups, or even creation of Japanese-free zones near strategic sites. He justified his demands by repeating the common racist mantra "A Jap's a Jap," meaning that U.S. citizenship or long residence in the United States meant nothing when it came to ultimate loyalty.

Nevertheless, Assistant Secretary of War John J. McCloy saw to it that DeWitt's final report stated that the government's action was based on "military necessity" rather than the general's racial arguments. DeWitt, with Army provost marshal Allen W. Gullion, and Karl Ben-

detsen, of the provost marshal's Office, were the three officials most directly responsible for designing the removal of Japanese Americans.

Implementation fell to the civilian-controlled War Relocation Authority (WRA), activated on March 18, 1942, under Milton Eisenhower (brother of General Dwight D. Eisenhower). Eisenhower did consider relocating Japanese in western states to work on farms, but western governors strongly objected. Eisenhower soon resigned because of stress, and Dillon Myer succeeded him on June 17, 1942.

Initially, the government hoped Japanese Americans would voluntarily migrate out of the prohibited military zones. However, only about five thousand did so; the largest voluntary resettlement community was Keetley Farms, Utah. Overall, most Japanese Americans did not relocate; they had nowhere to go and feared local opposition. By March 1942 the government realized widespread voluntary resettlement would not occur, and opted for forced removal.

With the announcement of mandatory relocation, many Japanese Americans found themselves forced to settle business and personal affairs quickly, sometimes within forty-eight hours. During the spring and summer of 1942, they gathered at assembly centers operated by the (ominously titled) Wartime Civil Control Administration. These centers—at Puyallup, Washington; Portland, Oregon; Mayer, Arizona; and Marysville, Sacramento, Tanforan, Stockton, Turlock, Salinas, Merced, Pinedale, Fresno, Tulare, Santa Anita, Pomona, and Manzanar, California—were often fairgrounds or horse tracks where evacuees lived in stables. By October all the centers closed because the evacuees left for relocation camps.

These ten camps technically were concentration camps, in that a segment of the population was concentrated there, but certainly were not death camps of Nazi infamy. Still, they had their own hardships. The camps—located in Manzanar and Tule Lake in California, Poston and Gila River in Arizona, Granada (Amache), in Colorado, Topaz in Utah, Jerome and Rowher in Arkansas, Minidoka in Idaho, and Heart Mountain in Wyoming—were in isolated areas and guarded by armed sentries who watched over the residents of the tar-paper-covered barracks. At Gila River, evacuees arrived in 100-degree heat to find the shelters not completed. So many residents of Heart Mountain fell ill during the harsh winters that they overwhelmed the camp hospital. Jerome was surrounded by swamps containing four species of poisonous snakes. Although most of the camps had gardens, it was not until 1943 that meals at some of the camps reached minimum army standards.

The camps presented a number of serious problems. On several different occasions guards shot unarmed inmates, occasionally fatally, and sometimes under suspicious circumstances. Tension among the evacuees led to other difficulties. At Poston, following the arrest of two issei for the beating of a suspected *inu* (informant; literally, dog), a protest broke out once it became known the pair faced trial in an Arizona court. In the face of a strike, camp administrators released one and agreed to try the other in the camp. The issei also agreed to stop the beatings and to seek better relations. In December 1942, violence erupted at Manzanar. The incident centered on the arrest of JACL critic Harry Ueno for the beating of Fred Tayama, a JACL leader and suspected *inu*. Supporters gathered to demand Ueno's release and threatened to punish other suspected informants. When the crowd did not disperse, military police (MPs) used tear gas. Protesters started an empty car and aimed it at the troops, whom it missed. The MPs then fired into the unarmed crowd, killing two and wounding at least ten others. The Poston and Manzanar incidents revealed underlying tensions and prompted an effort to separate the "loyal" from the "disloyal" evacuees.

There were other reasons for determining the loyalty of individual camp residents. By 1943 Myer was eager to resettle as many loyal evacuees as possible. Moreover, the War Department planned to create an all-nisei combat unit and sought loyal volunteers. Finally, the WRA realized many of the Japanese desired an opportunity to prove their loyalty. With the support of the JACL, the WRA and the War Department sought to determine loyalty with questionnaires. Questions #27 and #28 on each agency's form served as a litmus; the first asked if the respondent was willing to serve in the armed forces, and the other asked if the respondent was willing to forswear any allegiance to the emperor of Japan or other foreign power. Those responding "yes" to both were available for military service or resettlement. A number of nisei answered "no" to #27 to protest being asked to serve in the military while incarcerated or in deference to parental pressure. Question #28 question troubled others. For nisei it implied that they, native-born American citizens, held loyalty to the emperor. For issei, answering "yes" meant renouncing the only citizenship they possessed. Still, 84 percent answered #28 affirmatively. However, many Americans outside the camps interpreted the "nos" as disloyal. Most of those answering "no" were subsequently moved to Tule Lake.

Because Tule Lake had already experienced more strikes than any other camp and held the most residents refusing to answer the loyalty questions in the affirmative, the WRA designated it as a segregation center for "disloyals." Many original residents who were loyal or at least "fence sitters" soon found themselves living in an increasingly "disloyal" social milieu. A sense of mutual mistrust developed between the residents and the administration. Camp officials misinterpreted a series of altercations surrounding the visit of Dillon Myer in October 1943 as a riot, and declared martial law for three months. In addition, Tule Lake's stockade held approximately four hundred fifty inmates without hearing or trial under harsh conditions that reportedly included beatings. The stockade closed in August 1944 after the American Civil Liberties Union threatened a habeas corpus suit. In addition, Tule Lake held virtually all of the 5,589 Japanese Americans who renounced their citizenship. Radical pro–Japanese internees pressured many into such action through fear, intimidation, and, in one case, murder. In addition, many, fearful of retribution if they left the camp, saw renunciation as the only alternative. Most (5,409 in all) had second thoughts and sought restoration of their citizenship. A series of lawsuits stressing that the renunciations were made under duress prevented their removal until the matter was resolved. In spite of initial Justice Department opposition, 4,978 annulment requests were ultimately granted.

Very few of the nisei chose military service, even though the JACL petitioned President Roosevelt to restore the draft for Japanese Americans in November 1942 and the War Department created the 442d Regimental Combat Team. The army actively recruited nisei from the mainland and Hawaii to serve in the 442d and the Hawaii-based 100th Infantry Battalion. Most of the troops in both units came from Hawaii.

Of 23,000 eligible young men on the mainland, only 1,200 volunteered, and of these, the army inducted only 800. The Fair Play Committee (FPC) at Heart Mountain was the only organized draft resistance movement in the camps. Members said they would not report to the draft until their rights were restored. When draft notices were issued, sixty-three resisted and were sentenced to three years in prison. (They and twenty-two other resisters received presidential pardons in 1947.) The seven FPC leaders were convicted of sedition and sent to Fort Leavenworth, Kansas, but after the war their convictions were overturned. In spite of resistance in the camps, the magnificent battle, intelligence, and interpreter record of Japanese American troops did much to ease national hostility and led to increased opportunity for resettlement.

Myer considered resettlement a means to achieve his goals of breaking up traditional Japanese enclaves and Americanizing the Japanese Americans. Moreover, he saw it as a means of easing wartime labor shortages. As early as 1942 college students were released to attend inland institutions. Later that year, others left to do agricultural labor. Many families resettled in Denver and Salt Lake City. Later, Chicago and other Midwestern cities became popular destinations. Many issei camp residents were unwilling to leave, however. In the face of what they perceived as rampant anti–Japanese prejudice, they regarded the camps as secure places. As the camps closed, some issei resisted leaving, even committing suicide.

Several legal actions challenged relocation and internment. Fred Korematsu, Minoru Yasui, and Gordon Hirabayashi launched separate legal challenges to the curfew and exclusion orders. All three lost their cases before the Supreme Court, even though the court chose to sidestep the exclusion issues and addressed only the curfew violations. In 1944, *Endo* v. *United States,* it found that the detention of persons whose loyalty was not questioned was unconstitutional. On December 17, 1944—ironically, the day before the Supreme Court decided the *Endo* case—the War Department announced that release of the internees would begin on January 2, 1945. In the early 1980s evidence surfaced that the government had lied and withheld evidence in the three earlier cases. The trio (still living) filed to have their cases reheard, and their convictions were overturned.

The government ran other camps in addition to the relocation centers. The WRA operated a separate prison camp for selected "troublemakers." First established near Moab, Utah, it was later moved to Leupp, on the Navajo reservation in Arizona. Prisoners at the camps were often denied due process, seldom had hearings, and received sentences of indefinite length. Francis S. Frederick, chief of security at both Moab and Leupp, documented cases of mistreatment by military personnel and of capricious sentencing by other project directors or camp administrators. He passed this documentation on to director Paul G. Robertson, who, in turn, reported the information to his WRA superiors. The WRA closed Leupp in December 1943, fearing adverse publicity. The Immigration and Naturalization Service also ran seven camps which held some seven thousand issei and kibei (nisei educated in Japan) deemed most dangerous to the nation and the war effort—often they were simply leaders in the Japanese American community. The largest such camp, at Crystal City, Texas, also held German and Italian nationals. Other camps were located at Santa Fe and Fort Stanton, New Mexico; Seagoville and Kennedy, Texas; Fort Missoula, Montana; Fort Lincoln, North Dakota; and Kooskia, Indiana. These camps did not have the tensions of the WRA camps. Nevertheless, inmates reported

beatings and other mistreatment, including the shooting of three internees.

In November 1944, in the first cabinet meeting following the national elections of that year, President Roosevelt agreed to lift the exclusion because military necessity was no longer a justification. By early 1945 the government allowed Japanese Americans to return to their West Coast homes. The WRA provided those who left the camps voluntarily with a resettlement allowance of $25 for individuals and $50 for families, as well as train fare back to the place from which they had been evacuated. Tule Lake was the last camp to close, shutting down on March 28, 1946.

There were two major efforts to compensate Japanese Americans after the war. The Japanese Evacuation Claims Act of 1948 was intended to provide compensation for loss of property. The government paid out $38 million between 1950 and 1956. However, total repayment represented about 10 percent of the fair market value of the property at the time of incarceration. And in the meantime, what had been bean fields in 1942 had often become shopping malls and high-rise apartment blocks. The redress movement, which began among some JACL activists in the camps, sparked much debate and discussion. In 1980 Congress created the Commission on Wartime Relocation and Internment of Civilians. In 1983 the commission forthrightly determined that the promulgation of Executive Order 9066 was not justified by military necessity, and attributed the relocation order to racism and wartime hysteria. The commission recommended individual compensation of $20,000 to all surviving veterans of the camps. President Ronald Reagan signed the bill implementing these recommendations in 1988.

The relocation of the Japanese was basically the result of misplaced patriotic zeal, acting upon incipient anti–Asian racial feeling. No issei or nisei on the mainland committed a single documented act of espionage, sabotage, or fifth column activity. Ironically, in Hawaii, which would have faced invasion before the mainland and was home to some 150,000 people of Japanese descent, there was little movement to relocate a group that accounted for more than one-third of the population. Only 1 percent of Hawaii's Japanese residents were interned.

Some Americans not of Japanese ancestry have termed the subsequent sense of national shame about Japanese relocation as exercises in 20/20 hindsight; for them, no one who had not lived through the weeks of near panic after the Japanese attack on Pearl Harbor could honestly criticize what was perhaps a hasty and ill-conceived program, but one carried out in face of a mortal threat to the United States with far more consideration than the Japanese ever showed to any group who had the misfortune to fall under their control, such as the Filipinos. Nonetheless, even taking into consideration the arguments of perfect hindsight, the considered opinion of an overwhelming number of legal authorities and historians is that the removal of Japanese Americans remains one of the greatest blemishes on America's World War II record and a betrayal of American ideals. Aside from the belated compensations to the Japanese Americans, the only positive interpretation that can be made of the whole episode was that it was Americans themselves, whether of Japanese ancestry or not, who subsequently brought the whole sorry tale before the American public and succeeded in securing some measure of repentance and redress. (The relocation of Japanese Canadians was far less publicized, and in most cases they could not own land or vote until well after the war.) The enormous body of historical literature on the subject testifies to the fact that this is one episode that Americans are determined not to forget.

FURTHER READINGS

Bosworth, Allan. *America's Concentration Camps* (1967).

Commission on Wartime Relocation and Internment of Civilians. *Personal Justice Denied* (U.S. Government Printing Office, 1982).

Daniels, Roger. *Concentration Camps USA: Japanese Americans and World War II* (1971).

———. *The Decision to Relocate the Japanese Americans* (1975).

———. *Asian America: Chinese and Japanese in the United States Since 1850* (1988).

Daniels, Roger, Sandra C. Taylor, and Harry H. L. Kitano, eds. *Japanese Americans: From Relocation to Redress* (1986).

Drinnon, Richard. *Keeper of the Concentration Camps: Dillon S. Myer and American Racism* (1987).

Girdner, Audrie, and Anne Loftis. *The Great Betrayal: The Evacuation of Japanese-Americans During World War II* (1969).

Grodzins, Morton. *Americans Betrayed: Politics and the Japanese Evacuation* (1949).

Irons, Peter. *Justice at War* (1983).

Kumamoto, Bob. "The Search for Spies: American Counterintelligence and the Japanese American Community, 1931–1942." *Amerasia Journal* (Fall 1979).

Tateishi, John. *And Justice for All: An Oral History of the Japanese American Detention Camps* (1984).

TenBroek, Jacobus, Edward N. Barnhart, and Floyd W. Matson. *Prejudice, War and the Constitution* (1954).

Uchida, Yoshiko. *Desert Exile: The Uprooting of a Japanese American Family* (1982).

United States War Department. *Final Report: Japanese Evacuation from the West Coast* (U.S. Government Printing Office, 1943).

Weglyn, Michi. *Years of Infamy: The Untold Story of America's Concentration Camps* (1976).

Yatsushiro, Toshio. *Politics and Cultural Values: The World War II Japanese Relocation Centers and the United States Government* (1978).

Daniel D. Liestman

SEE ALSO Home Front, U.S.

Island-Hopping and Leapfrogging, U.S. Strategies

After the Japanese attack on the U.S. naval facility at Pearl Harbor, Hawaii, in December 1941, the United States and its allies found themselves in a desperate strategic situation in the Pacific. In May 1942, elements of the U.S. Pacific Fleet turned back the Japanese threat to Australia in a strategic victory at the Battle of the Coral Sea. Even with another decisive victory at the Battle of Midway in June 1942, however, going on the offensive in the Pacific placed almost impossible demands on the limited resources of the United States and its allies, especially when Allied grand strategy emphasized the European theater of operations.

The U.S. leaders, General Douglas MacArthur and Admiral Chester Nimitz, dominated the Allies' planning and operations in the Pacific war. Together with the joint chiefs of staff (JCS) in Washington, they adopted a two-pronged strategy divided between their respective areas of authority. MacArthur commanded the southwest Pacific theater and directed the southern prong of the Allied states, Australia and New Zealand. As the Pacific war progressed, MacArthur used Australia as a base of operations to drive through New Guinea and the Bismarck Islands in preparation for retaking the Philippines and eventually seizing Okinawa. From late 1942 through 1943, the Allied forces went on a slow, bloody offensive through the Solomon Islands and on New Guinea. Admiral Nimitz commanded the Pacific theater, which included the central, south, and north Pacific subdivisions. The northern prong of the Allied counteroffensive came under his control and struck westward across the central Pacific from the U.S. naval base at Pearl Harbor toward the Japanese home islands. Nimitz's forces were made up almost exclusively of Americans. Little offensive activity occurred in his command until late 1943, when the U.S. Navy mustered a sufficient number of aircraft carriers to ensure U.S. air superiority.

Advancing in either the southwest Pacific or the central Pacific after the Battle of Midway in June 1942 required the Allies to attain several objectives. First, the U.S. Pacific Fleet needed to keep the Japanese Combined Fleet in check, if not totally destroy it. Second, Allied air superiority had to be established and maintained with both land- and carrier-based aircraft. Third, Allied forces needed to carry out repeated large-scale amphibious assaults. Finally, rolling back the Japanese forces meant attacking a strategic defense-in-depth in the Pacific, where island chains potentially served as mutually supporting bases of operations. To reach all these overlapping objectives, the Allies employed "island-hopping" and "leapfrogging" strategies to maximize limited resources, shorten time, and reduce casualties.

In theory, island-hopping made sense as a solution to cracking an island-based defense-in-depth. This strategy can be understood in the following example.

U.S. amphibious and naval forces successfully subdue a Japanese island base, X. In the following month or two, fresh troops replace the exhausted assault forces and crush any stubborn Japanese resistance. Then this island is used as a staging point for assaulting the next enemy-held island, Y. Seabees and army engineers speedily repair or construct airfields and dredge harbors as Allied forces mass for the next leg of the campaign.

Island X serves as air base, safe anchorage, and supply depot for the men and materiel being ferried from Australia or Hawaii. Fresh marine and army divisions receive their last-minute training before their amphibious assault on island Y with support from naval forces and aircraft based on island X. This strategy was employed during the Solomons campaign and later at Iwo Jima and Okinawa.

Island-hopping proved to be a strategic necessity early in the Pacific war. As 1942 drew to a close and 1943 began, the Allies could muster only limited carrier strength because of losses around Guadalcanal. At one point in October 1942, USS *Enterprise* was the only operational aircraft carrier in the theater, and it desperately needed an overhaul. Until the new *Essex*-class carriers became operational, amphibious attacks could not be supported beyond the range of land-based aircraft. Consequently, hopping from island to island under cover of aircraft from nearby bases was the only practical option.

As more carriers became available, U.S. leaders also used a leapfrogging strategy which entailed isolating, bypassing, or circumventing Japanese bases. In theory, leapfrogging was most practical when U.S. forces had achieved air and naval superiority. Without air or naval offensive capabilities, the leapfrogged Japanese forces became impotent because they could not attack U.S. forces or receive supplies or reinforcements.

An example helps show how leapfrogging worked.

Three Japanese-held islands, A, B, and C, are situated roughly in a row; all have formidable defenses and some naval and airborne offensive capabilities. Allied air and amphibious forces begin by successfully subduing island A. Then this island becomes a staging point for supplies, men, and materiel for the next leg of the Allies' campaign. Seabees and army engineers prepare an airfield and harbor for the forces massing on island A. Meanwhile, Allied land- and carrier-based aircraft attack and destroy the Japanese air and naval forces on island B, thus isolating the base and depriving its garrison of any offensive capability. Finally, when sufficient forces are available on island A, Allied forces leapfrog island B and strike at island C.

For Pacific commanders, leapfrogging was best explained with a baseball analogy: it was like "hitting 'em where they ain't." The leapfrogged Japanese base was isolated in the rear area and left to "wither on the vine." This strategy had two strategic benefits: U.S. forces could advance more quickly, and U.S. commanders could conserve their men and materiel. The leapfrogging strategy was employed at Rabaul, Truk, Mindanao, and the Caroline Islands.

Allied campaigns in the southwest and central Pacific alternated between hopping from island to island and leapfrogging an island. After the naval victories in the Battles of the Coral Sea and Midway earlier in 1942, the island-hopping strategy was used in New Guinea and the Solomon Islands from late 1942 into 1943. These islands were close to one another and thus easily lent themselves to island-hopping as well as base-hopping. Located near the southeastern tip of the Solomons, Guadalcanal was targeted as a primary strategic objective in Operation Watchtower, the Allies' first offensive in the Pacific. For six months, the fighting on Guadalcanal raged as both the U.S. and Japan reinforced their land forces in a battle of attrition. On the island, the 1st Marine Division stubbornly held a defensive position around Henderson Field, the all-important air base for success in island-hopping.

Meanwhile, ongoing battles occurred in the air above and in the seas around Guadalcanal. Allied air-power and sea power gradually cut the Japanese supply lines and denied support to the enemy forces remaining on this island. Guadalcanal was under Allied control by the end of 1942. Allied forces then progressed to the northwest through the Solomon chain in a campaign to take the Japanese stronghold at Rabaul on the island of New Britain. To the southwest, MacArthur's troops simultaneously moved over the Papuan peninsula of New Guinea. Together, operations on Guadalcanal and New Guinea served as preludes to a planned attack on Rabaul.

Located on New Britain in the Bismarck Archipelago, off the northern coast of New Guinea, Rabaul possessed powerful naval, air, and land forces which included more than 100,000 Japanese combatants. This base also controlled surrounding area and consequently blocked the Allied advance through the Solomons.

Initially, Rabaul was to be captured under Operation Cartwheel. However, at the Quebec Conference in August 1943, it became apparent that such an action would be much too costly in time, manpower, and materiel. The obvious solution was a modified Operation Cartwheel which called for leapfrogging or isolating Rabaul. In the battles that followed, Allied forces successfully encircled Rabaul by taking Bougainville, the Admiralty Islands, and other islands in the Bismarcks. Allied bombers and their fighter escorts traveled only 170 miles from Bougainville and pulverized the Japanese forces at Rabaul. After losing air and naval superiority, this base's offensive capabilities and its threat to the continued Allied advance were negligible. In addition, Allied prizes such as the Admiralties served as important staging points for future operations. Although ultimately a strategic success, leapfrogging Rabaul took more than seven months of hard fighting.

As 1943 drew to a close, deployment of *Essex*-class aircraft carriers irreversibly tipped the scales of air power in favor of the United States and enabled Admiral Nimitz's central Pacific offensive, code-named Granite, to progress in earnest. Carrier-based air superiority conveyed two fringe benefits: strategic mobility and relative naval supremacy. With carrier-based aircraft, Nimitz therefore had much greater strategic mobility. Conversely, without adequate air cover, the Imperial Japanese Navy's effectiveness was greatly decreased because its transportation and communications were severely limited.

Nimitz utilized the basic form of the War Plan Orange from the interwar years. Having appeared in various versions, this plan essentially called for the U.S. Pacific Fleet to fight its way across the central Pacific to relieve or recapture the Philippines. En route, the plan anticipated that the Orange (the color designation for Japan) fleet would be defeated in a decisive sea battle. Simultaneously, War Plan Orange anticipated that marine units would seize and defend "advanced bases" in Micronesia, more than a thousand islands stretching across the western Pacific approximately two thousand miles southwest of Hawaii.

Micronesia included the Gilbert, Marshall, Caroline, and the Mariana chains of islands and atolls. They rose out of coral or volcanic reefs and often amounted to no more than a few square miles. After being taken by U.S. forces, advanced bases in Micronesia were used to support subsequent operations. Consequently, the central Pacific strategy included not only island-hopping in a given island chain but also hopping from chain to chain.

Beginning in November 1943, U.S. carrier-based aircraft reduced Japanese air power in the Gilberts and screened the amphibious assault forces in case the Japanese navy contested U.S. landings. Anticipated counterattacks from Japanese bombers based in the Marshalls did not occur. More than 108,000 men in the U.S. Fifth Fleet and 5th Amphibious Corps focused on strong points in the Gilberts, such as Makin and Tarawa. Makin was relatively easy to subdue. Tarawa, however, proved to be more difficult; marines met its fanatical Japanese defenders on the beach. Taking this island was necessary because it provided needed practice in the complex combined arms operations of amphibious warfare: air and sea bombardments had to coordinate with amphibious landings. Tarawa's airfield was also needed to a lesser extent for bombing operations against the Marshalls, a larger island chain 600 miles to the northwest.

The Marshalls stood next in line, and capturing them had several strategic benefits. The most important islands were Kwajalein and Eniwetok, both of which had airfields and naval anchorages. Japanese forces used Kwajalein as a logistics and communications hub for the rest of the Marshalls as well as the Gilberts. Eniwetok was an atoll which formed a natural harbor and could provide protection for major surface vessels.

Neither island was defended by significant numbers of Japanese troops. Although the fighting was bloody, the Marshalls were quickly subdued by February 1944, within three months of the start of the central Pacific drive. After the Marshalls were taken, they formed the base of operations for the planned conquest of the Carolines. The navy refurbished and expanded the base at Eniwetok, which functioned as an advanced fleet anchorage for U.S. major combat vessels. Having such a base more than two thousand miles from Pearl Harbor proved invaluable to the next step in the central Pacific campaign. Aircraft from Eniwetok flew sorties against Wake Island and Truk in the Carolines.

Rather than continuing to hop from Marshalls to the Carolines to the Marianas, Nimitz decided on a two-stage maneuver in Operation Forager: first, leapfrog the Carolines, then seize the Marianas. The Micronesian island chains are not in a straight line, and the Carolines represented a formidable obstacle flanking the Marianas to the northwest and New Guinea to the south. Japanese naval and air forces at Truk in the Carolines presented the most significant threat to the Allied campaign; this base potentially blocked advances in both the central Pacific and the southwest Pacific. Dubbed the "Gibraltar of the Pacific," Truk's main island served as a major headquarters and base for the Japanese Combined Fleet where vessels like the super battleship *Musashi* were stationed. The U.S. Pacific Fleet leapfrogged the Carolines when U.S. air attacks from carriers and Eniwetok devastated the Japanese forces at Truk. The Japanese Combined Fleet fled, and U.S. aircraft destroyed most of Truk's aircraft on the ground.

With Truk's threat effectively neutralized, the second stage of Operation Forager went forward. It rivaled Allied operations in Europe and the Mediterranean Sea in vastness and complexity. The U.S. Fifth Fleet included 535 combat and auxiliary vessels which carried more than 127,500 troops, two-thirds of whom were marines. This armada was a self-sufficient expeditionary force. The logistical challenges of Operation Forager appeared almost insurmountable; the Fifth Fleet sailed more than a thousand miles from Eniwetok to the Marianas, where it conducted an amphibious assault against several Japanese-held islands. If that was not enough, U.S. planners fully expected that attacking the Marianas would draw a counterattack by the Imperial Japanese Navy. Nevertheless, Operation Forager was a success in part because of good planning and effective leadership.

In the Mariana Islands, amphibious assaults on Saipan, Tinian, and Guam occurred during the summer of 1944. Desperate Japanese defenders did not yield the Marianas without inflicting heavy casualties on U.S. forces. However, despite the cost in lives at the tactical level, leapfrogging the Carolines and securing the Marianas paid off handsomely at the strategic level. First, much time and many lives were saved overall. In addition, Allied occupation of these islands cracked Japan's inner defensive perimeter and thus opened a way for Nimitz's forces to converge on the Philippines and link up with MacArthur. Likewise, the strongly defended island of Iwo Jima was a short hop from the Marianas.

In 1944, another benefit became clear as the B-29 Superfortresses were deployed in the Pacific. With this aircraft's exceptionally long range and with less then 1,300 miles between the Marianas and the Japan home islands, B-29s could bombard the heart of the shrinking Empire of the Rising Sun. Last, the Japanese regarded Saipan as part of their home territory, and thus losing the island was not only a strategic but also a morale blow.

As the central Pacific drive moved through Micronesia and secured the Marianas, MacArthur's forces had been moving quickly along the northern coast of New Guinea during mid-1944. The Japanese base at Wewak was leapfrogged, and Hollandia was subsequently attacked. The once formidable Hollandia fell quickly after a heavy air bombardment, and its airfields in turn supported base-hopping operations against Wakde, Biak, Noemfoor, and Sansapor. By July 1944, three months after the initial isolation of Wewak, MacArthur and his forces controlled New Guinea and began preparing for an invasion of Mindanao and other islands of the Philippines.

In mid-1945, a debate raged among MacArthur, Nimitz, and the JCS. The Allies had to choose between two strategic options: leapfrog the Philippines as a whole and capture Formosa (now Taiwan), off the coast of China, or invade and subdue the Philippines. Chief of Naval Operations Ernest J. King and the JCS favored the first option. To them, it offered grand strategic benefits because the Philippines could be bypassed, and because Formosa could be used as the final stepping-stone for an invasion of Okinawa and the Japanese home islands. Conversely, the second option entailed a potentially lengthy operation to subdue the 7,000-island archipelago. MacArthur insisted on making good on his promise to return to the Philippines, and in the end he would not be denied. Nimitz also argued for an invasion of the Philippines to establish bases for operations against Japan itself. President Franklin D. Roosevelt intervened and ended the debate by mandating an invasion of the Philippines.

It should be noted that logistics and timetables played critical roles in the decision to capture the Philippines instead of Formosa. Planners expected that the assault on Formosa would require nine divisions. Such an operation was possible only in early 1945, when sufficient manpower became available. So, in the case of the Philippines, the leapfrogging strategy was rejected for the same reasons usually cited as benefits.

Once the invasion of the Philippines commenced in October 1944, both island-hopping and leapfrogging were employed in the campaign. Airfields were constructed after advances had been consolidated, and they supported the next phases of the operations. U.S. naval forces fought a series of battles with the remains of the Japanese Combined Fleet to retain air and naval superiority, despite some potentially disastrous mishaps and repeated kamikaze raids. The best example of leapfrogging in the Philippines was bypassing of the large island of Mindanao in the south part of the archipelago; instead, MacArthur's forces attacked Leyte. After securing Mindoro as a base for aircraft, MacArthur then used an island-hopping strategy by invading Luzon, which was brought under practical Allied control early in 1945.

With the most important Philippines islands as staging areas, the largest Allied armada in World War II made the hop from the Philippines to Okinawa in April 1945. After two months of some of the war's bloodiest fighting, Okinawa fell. Not even a suicide mission by *Yamato,* Japan's remaining superbattleship, could change the outcome. By the late summer of 1945, the invasion of southern Japanese home islands was expected to be launched from Okinawa—the last and most dreaded island-hopping operation.

Because of the "Europe-First" grand strategy in World War II, limited resources were available to the Allies in the Pacific. Only enough men and materiel were available for relatively small operations. Island-hopping and leap-frogging constituted a means to build several small steps into a large advance. This can be seen in the New Guinea, Philippines, and central Pacific campaigns. Moreover, using both island-hopping and leapfrogging in the two-pronged (southwest and central Pacific campaigns) strategy consistently kept the Japanese off balance. Also, hundreds of thousands of Japanese troops were tied down in the China-Burma-India theater. As a result, the Japanese were never able to take full advantage of their interior lines of communication and transportation because they had lost air, and consequently naval, superiority. They never concentrated their forces sufficiently to deal a deadly blow to either Allied advance, thus making their defeat all but inevitable.

FURTHER READINGS

Isely, Jeter A., and Philip A. Crowl. *The U.S. Marines and Amphibious Warfare: Its Theory and Practice in the Pacific* (1951).

MacArthur, Douglas. *Reminiscences* (1964).

Miller, Edward S. *War Plan Orange: The U.S. Strategy to Defeat Japan, 1897–1945* (1991).

Morison, Samuel Eliot. *The Two-Ocean War: A Short History of the United States Navy in the Second World War* (1963).

Nimitz, Chester, and E. B. Potter. *The Great Sea War* (1960).

Spector, Ronald H. *Eagle Against the Sun: The American War with Japan* (1985).

U.S. Army. *The War in the Pacific,* 11 vols. In the series The United States Army in World War II (1948–1962).

U.S. Marine Corps. *History of U.S. Marine Corps Operations in World War II,* 5 vols. (1958–1968).

Weinberg, Gerhard L. "Grand Strategy in the Pacific War." *Air Power History* (Spring 1996).

David Ulbrich

SEE ALSO Bougainville, U.S. Operations Against; Eniwetok; Guadalcanal, Battle for; Hollandia; New Britain; New Guinea; Okinawa, Battle for; Tarawa, Capture of; Truk

Italian Americans
See Internment and Relocation of Italian Americans

Iwabuchi Sanji (d. 1945)

Japanese naval officer in charge of the defenses of Manila, the Philippines, in 1945. Iwabuchi graduated from the Japanese Naval Academy in 1915. In April 1942, he named captain of battleship *Kirishima,* which saw action at the Battle of Midway as well as in the Solomon Islands before it went down near Savo Island late that year. By the spring of 1943, Iwabuchi had advanced to rear admiral, and in November 1944 he was named commandant of the 31st Naval Special Base Force in Manila.

The U.S. landing on Mindoro in December 1944 caused Vice Admiral Okochi Denshichi, commander of the Southwestern Area Fleet and senior Japanese naval officer in the Philippines, to strengthen the navy's fortifications in the capital. He assigned about 4,000 combat-ready men to a fresh unit he called the Manila Naval Defense Force. To command the newly formed organization, Okochi turned to Iwabuchi, whose Thirty-first Naval Special Base Force was stationed in and about the city. Iwabuchi's 16,000 men were to defend Nichols Field and Cavite Naval Base, seed Manila Bay with mines, conduct suicide boat missions in the bay, prepare for the removal of vessels belonging to the 31st Naval Special Base Force, and, in the end, ensure the demolition of every Japanese naval installation and logistical cache in the Manila area.

Iwabuchi's independent attitude undermined the Japanese command structure around Manila. When Okochi withdrew from the capital with General Tomoyuki Yamashita, he assigned the 31st Naval Special Base Force to the Shimbu Army Group outside of the city, wishing to establish a unified command. However, Iwabuchi maintained that Yokohama lacked authority over him until completion of the missions given him by Okochi. Notwithstanding Yamashita's plans to evacuate and declare Manila an open city, Iwabuchi and the naval staff agreed that the capital should be defended to the last man, likening the city to an innate bastion held at considerable expense to the attacker. Much to Yamashita's chagrin, Yokohama consented to Iwabuchi's defensive scheme by instituting a consolidated command inside Manila and handing over residual army forces to Iwabuchi as superior authority on the scene.

Iwabuchi commanded close to 17,000 men in the Manila area. He organized his force into three combat units, a majority inside the city's confines with Intramuros, the venerable Spanish rampart, serving as his stronghold's center. He concocted a self-destructive battle to the finish, together with widespread demolitions. By February 12, 1945, the Americans were within the city and a constant fight of attrition developed, with avenue-to-avenue, structure-to-structure, and apartment-to-apartment combat. Despite Yokohama's repeated orders to disengage, Iwabuchi remained adamant, and on February 23, contacts between Iwabuchi and the Shimbu Army Group ended. As his line of command broke down, Iwabuchi's encircled troops perpetrated atrocities that contributed to no fewer than 100,000 Filipino deaths during the month-long battle. Iwabuchi, who died amid the mindless carnage that he had created, received a posthumous promotion to vice admiral. Yamashita survived to be hanged by the Americans, particularly for supposed war crimes against the civilians of Manila.

FURTHER READINGS

Connaughton, Richard, et al. *The Battle for Manila: The Most Devastating Untold Story of World War II* (1995).

Morrison, Samuel Ailed. *The Liberation of the Philippines: Luzon, Mindanao, the Vases 1944–1945* (1959).

Smith, Robert Robs. *Triumph in the Philippines* (1963).

Rodney J. Ross

SEE ALSO Yamashita Tomoyuki

Iwakuro Hideo

Iwakuro was a Japanese army officer expert in military intelligence. He served as military attaché to Washington in 1941 and was an outspoken opponent of war with the United States.

Early in his career Iwakuro had established the prestigious Nakano School, which trained many of Japan's finest secret agents. In the late 1930s he devised a scheme to destroy the Chinese economy by flooding that country with over a billion dollars' worth of counterfeit yen. By contrast, he was sympathetic to the plight of European Jews, and secured refuge in Manchuria for five thousand of them after they fled Nazi oppression. He managed to convince the leaders of the Kwantung Army in Manchuria that it was a simple matter of repayment of debt; after all, Iwakuro argued, a Jewish-owned firm—Kuhn, Loeb and Company—had provided financing to Japan during the Russo-Japanese War.

In December 1940, Ikawa Tadao, a trustee of the Co-operative Bank of Japan, asked Prime Minister Fumimaro Konoe to recommend someone in the army who might help expedite his ongoing negotiations with the U.S. priests James M. Drought and James Anthony Walsh. Konoe suggested Iwakuro, and the colonel did not disappoint. By this time he was serving as assistant to the director of the Central Bureau of Military Affairs. He helped Ikawa to secure funding for a trip to the United States to continue his negotiations, and participated in them in late March 1941. He stayed on as military attaché in Washington after the negotiations were completed in April.

In late July, when Iwakuro returned to Japan, he was struck by the level of animosity which had developed toward the United States since his departure only a few months earlier. He then embarked on a speaking tour, warning high-level military, political, and industrial groups that war with the United States would bring disaster for Japan. By this time, however, Iwakuro's superiors in the army had all but decided that war was inevitable, and they feared that his speaking tour would only encourage defeatism. On August 28, therefore, he was reassigned to the command of a regiment in French Indochina, and his efforts to avert war with the United States went for naught.

FURTHER READINGS

Butow, Robert J. C. *The John Doe Associates: Backdoor Diplomacy for Peace* (1974).

Ike, Nobutaka, ed. *Japan's Decision for War: Records of the 1941 Policy Conferences* (1967).

Lu, David J. *From the Marco Polo Bridge to Pearl Harbor* (1961).

Oka, Yoshitake. *Konoe Fumimaro: A Political Biography* (1983).

Toland, John R. *The Rising Sun: The Decline and Fall of the Japanese Empire, 1936–1941,* 2 vols. (1970).

John E. Moser

Iwo Jima, Battle of

The fighting on the island of Iwo Jima in February and March 1945 was some of the most bitter of World War II. The capture of the island is considered a classic example of an assault operation and the ultimate test for the U.S. Marine Corps's twenty years of amphibious training and three years of war.

The capture of Iwo Jima was an essential step in the U.S. plan to secure island bases for the invasion of Japan. Okinawa and Iwo Jima were the islands desired, and Iwo Jima was selected to be taken first because it was thought to be the easier of the two to capture and because, unlike Okinawa, it was outside the range of kamikazes. Iwo Jima is halfway between the Marianas and Japan, only 700 miles from Tokyo. In Japanese hands it menaced B-29 bombers flying raids against Japan; in U.S. hands this threat would be ended, and the island could serve as an emergency stopping point for B-29s and as an air base for long-range U.S. fighters.

Iwo Jima is the central island of the Volcano group in the western Pacific. Quite small and shaped like a pork chop, it is about 5.5 miles long and 2.5 miles across at its widest point. Its most distinctive feature is Mount Suribachi, a 548-foot-high extinct volcano at the southern end. Also at the southern end, just north of Suribachi and extending from its base for more than two miles to the north and east, are beaches of what appears to be black sand but is actually a thick bed of light volcanic ash and cinders. The Japanese correctly assumed the beaches would be the invasion site. The northern part of the island is a plateau 350 feet high with inaccessible rocky sides.

Washington originally planned an invasion of Iwo Jima for October 1944, but delay in taking the Philippines caused slippage in the date. This resulted in far heavier casualties for the attacking marines, because the Japanese had time to turn the island into a formidable defensive bastion.

The Americans assumed the Japanese would fight hard for Iwo Jima, and this led to some discussion in Washington of employing poison gas before the attack. The United States was not legally bound to the treaty outlawing poison gas, but President Franklin D. Roosevelt was adamantly opposed to its use, and his decision left a heavy conventional bombardment as the only option.

Beginning in August 1944 and accelerating over the next several months, Iwo Jima was subjected to regular air attack by B-24 bombers of the Seventh Army Air Force, flying out of the Marianas. In early November, B-29s, also from the Marianas, made two strikes. Starting on December 8, 1944, Iwo came under daily attack. Three heavy cruisers bombarded the island three times in December and twice in January 1945. For two weeks beginning at the end of January, the Seventh Army Air Force bombed Iwo Jima day and night, and B-29s struck it twice. In all, 6,800 tons of bombs and 22,000 rounds of shells ranging from 5-inch to 16-inch were hurled at Iwo

Jima before the invasion, the heaviest such bombardment of the Pacific war. Even so, the bombardment was less than that called for by Lieutenant General Holland "Howlin' Mad" Smith. Some battleships were still in Philippine waters, and in the days just before the invasion, U.S. Navy carrier aircraft struck aviation targets in and around Tokyo. These raids, intended in part to remove the possibility of retaliatory Japanese attacks against the Americans at Iwo Jima, did nothing to reduce Iwo Jima's defenses.

The Japanese had long been aware of the probability of a U.S. invasion of Iwo Jima. They evacuated the small civilian population from the island and assigned to its defense some 14,000 army and 7,000 navy personnel. With six months to prepare, Iwo Jima's commander, Lieutenant General Tadamichi Kuribayashi, oversaw construction of an elaborate system of subterranean fortifications and worked to turn this obscure bit of volcanic rock into what one writer has called "probably the most ingenious fortress the world had ever seen."

The Japanese dug caves with angled entrances and constructed command posts and concrete pillboxes, some with 6-foot-thick walls. Much of this defense system was interconnected by tunnels. The defenders also buried tanks up to the turrets as instant pillboxes, and converted bombs into rockets to be launched electronically along 45-degree slanted wooden ramps. Mount Suribachi became a fortress. The Japanese were prepared to defend Iwo Jima to the last.

Although Kuribayashi assumed that the Americans would get ashore, he prohibited the earlier practice of futile banzai charges that satisfied honor but wasted manpower. He ordered his men to stay in their defensive positions and inflict maximum casualties on the attackers. General Smith later referred to Kuribayashi as the "most redoubtable" of all his Pacific war adversaries.

The battle for Iwo Jima saw a Japanese attempt to use human-guided torpedoes, known as *kaiten,* launched from I-boats (large submarines). The *kaiten* were directed by individual swimmers who "rode" the torpedoes. Although U.S. Navy hunter-killer antisubmarine units intercepted all *kaiten* successfully, these weapons signaled the extent to which the Japanese were prepared to resist the U.S. advance toward Tokyo.

Admiral Raymond A. Spruance commanded Fifth Fleet, and Vice Admiral Richmond Kelly Turner had overall charge of the invasion. Rear Admiral William H. P. Bundy had charge of the prelanding bombardment. Major General Harry Schmidt commanded the Marine 5th Amphibious Corps; his direct superior was General Smith.

For three days prior to the U.S. invasion, Bundy's ships rained shells on Iwo Jima. For the task he had eight battleships, five heavy cruisers, and a number of destroyers. Subsequently some criticized Admiral Turner for failing to extend the bombardment by another day, especially after poor weather had obscured many targets and all ammunition had not been expended. General Smith did not oppose Turner's decision, however; he had wanted the bombardment to begin earlier, not end later. A longer naval bombardment would, however, have lengthened the time the U.S. fleet was exposed to suicide attack. In any case, the bombing and shelling had only mixed results on the subterranean defenses. Although most Japanese held fire, a premature reaction on February 17 by some gunners to seven U.S. Navy LCI gunboats covering pre-invasion underwater-demolition teams revealed the locations of previously unknown Japanese emplacements, which were promptly shelled. All the LCIs were hit and one was destroyed; the underwater-demolition teams were recovered.

At 0645 hours on February 19, Turner gave the order "Land the landing force." The initial assault was by the 4th and 5th Marine Divisions; the 3d Marine Division was kept in floating reserve. At 0830 hours the first assault wave of sixty-eight LVT amtrac tanks left the line of departure. They hit the beaches at 0900 hours, almost precisely on time. The remaining assault waves landed in the next half hour, followed by twelve LSMs carrying medium tanks. The 5th Marine Division went ashore just north of Mount Suribachi; 4th Marine Division was on their right flank.

The landing, accompanied by a rolling barrage from the ships offshore, was easy. Optimists predicted Iwo Jima would be secured in a few days. But most Japanese defenders, deep in their caves, had survived the bombs and shells. When the marines landed and crowded onto the beaches, the Japanese opened a withering fire which pinned the Americans down. The loose volcanic ash on the beaches made movement by the assaulting troops difficult, and the men were easily visible from observation posts on Mount Suribachi.

Close naval gunfire support, especially from cruiser *Santa Fe,* allowed the marines to dig in and establish a beachhead. *Santa Fe's* 5- and 6-inch guns pounded the base of Suribachi. Battleship *Nevada* was another stalwart gunfire support platform. Aircraft from escort carriers provided air support. By nightfall the 5th Marine Division had pushed across the island's most narrow point, north of Suribachi. They also had reached the more southern of two Japanese airstrips. The day had been

costly. Of 30,000 marines sent ashore the first day, 600 lay dead and another 1,600 were wounded.

For the combatants Iwo Jima was truly an experience in hell. Fighting was bloody and foot by foot—there was little room for maneuver, and the Japanese fought from concealment. There were countless instances of individual heroism (after the capture of Iwo Jima, an incredible twenty-seven Congressional Medals of Honor were awarded).

On the morning of February 23, the marines successfully scaled Mount Suribachi and planted a U.S. flag on its summit. The picture taken by AP photographer Joe Rosenthal—for Americans the most famous of the war and the inspiration for the marine corps Memorial in Arlington, Virginia—was taken under combat conditions (but it was the second raising of a U.S. flag on Suribachi).

Meanwhile, the battle for the island, expected to take only ten days, dragged on for another month. By the beginning of March the Japanese had retreated to the northern part of the island. There is controversy concerning the failure of Admiral Turner and General Smith, with the island two-thirds taken, to land the 3d Regiment of the 3d Marine Division. General Schmidt very much wanted this last regiment of the floating reserve, but Smith told him that Turner believed it would only add to congestion on the island. The regiment was sent back to Guam. Some believe that had it been committed, the battle would have been shortened and there would have been fewer U.S. casualties.

On March 4 the first B-29, low on fuel after a raid on Japan, landed on an airfield hastily reactivated by U.S. Seabees. On March 15 General Schmidt pronounced Iwo Jima secured, but Japanese resistance continued for another ten days, and occasional snipers harassed U.S. forces after that date.

Through March 26 the marines and navy sustained losses of 6,812 killed and 19,189 wounded. Battle casualties totaled 30 percent of the entire landing force, and 75 percent in the infantry regiments of the 4th and 5th Marine Divisions. Most of the Japanese fought to the end. Kuribayashi was one of the last to die, on March 24. Of the Japanese garrison, only 216 men were taken alive. Marines counted 20,703 Japanese dead. Through May the 147th U.S. Army Infantry Regiment, which took over from the marines, accounted for an additional 1,602 Japanese dead and 867 prisoners.

There was also a cost at sea. Some kamikaze aircraft succeeded in penetrating the U.S. defensive fighter screen and struck carrier *Saratoga,* which resulted in the loss of forty-two aircraft, and the killing of 123 crewmen and the wounding of 192. Escort carrier *Bismarck Sea,* also hit by a kamikazes, exploded and sank with the loss of 218 men. Another escort carrier, a cargo ship, and an LST were damaged by kamikazes.

Iwo Jima was the first land under direct Tokyo administration captured by the U.S. in the war. Was the battle worth it? U.S. airmen certainly thought so. From March to August 1945, 2,251 B-29s force landed on the island. Many of these would otherwise have been lost. Iwo Jima also served as an important part of elaborate air-sea rescue operations to retrieve B-29 crews forced to ditch at sea. The 7th Fighter Command moved to the island, and soon long-range P-47 Thunderbolts and P-51 Mustangs were flying from Iwo Jima to accompany the B-29s on raids against Japan. Their presence enabled the big bombers to carry out midlevel daytime raids in addition to the low-level night attacks.

In 1968 Iwo Jima was returned to Japanese sovereignty, and ten years later Japan announced its intention to re-militarize the island "as a key strategic base for Japan's national defense." One former marine remarked at the time, "By hell, I'll run off to Canada before I help take it again."

FURTHER READINGS

Bartley, Whitman S. *Iwo Jima: Amphibious Epic* (Historical Division, U.S. Marine Corps, 1954).

Garand, George W., and Truman R. Strobridge. *Western Pacific Operations, vol. 4 of History of U.S. Marine Corps Operations in World War II* (Historical Division, U.S. Marine Corps, 1971).

Morison, Samuel Eliot. *The Two-Ocean War: A Short History of the United States Navy in the Second World War* (1963).

Ross, Bill D. *Iwo Jima: Legacy of Valor* (1985).

Smith, S. E., ed. *The United States Marine Corps in World War II* (1969).

Wheeler, Richard. *Iwo* (1980).

Spencer C. Tucker

Japan, Occupation of

With the sudden capitulation of Japan, a major nation surrendered, for the first time in modern history, without its territory having been invaded. (Germany passed from armistice to peace treaty after World War I, never having actually surrendered.) Consequently, U.S. armed forces assumed control of a government that was in place and functioning, from the capital down to the local towns and villages. However battered Japan had been by aerial bombardment in the last year of the conflict and whatever the enormous losses throughout the Pacific war, the government had retained absolute control of the nation. When that government, in the person of the divine Emperor Hirohito, ordered its people to cease resistance and to cooperate with the American occupiers, the nation immediately and completely did so. This was much to the bemusement of the Americans, who had had all too much of Japanese soldiers fighting to the last man and then committing seppuku. It could even be argued that "military government" might not be a strictly accurate description of the U.S. occupation of Japan, in that in August 1945 the U.S. military simply assumed the overall control of the functioning Japanese government from the emperor on down. More specifically, the Japanese government mandated, in the form of an imperial ordinance, that all acts prejudicial to the objectives of the occupation and all violations of that occupation's directives were now crimes under Japanese law, and could be tried in either military government or Japanese courts.

The seven-year occupation of Japan by the United States was arguably the most thoroughgoing—and successful—effort in modern history by one nation to change another's very way of life. Basically, Japan was to be reconstructed into something like an Oriental version of the United States. Yet its history, culture, and government were almost totally terra incognita, even to American university graduates. This ignorance of Japan extended to the State Department, conspicuously laggard in its planning for the Japanese occupation. Japan was to be re-created as a demilitarized and democratized nation with an economic free market, and also with a land-owning peasantry. The United States would not impose upon Japan any form of government not supported by the freely expressed will of its people, but would nurture the democratic process. Still, the U.S. military government (MG) would have the final word in the event of any difference of opinion with the Japanese authorities.

Because of the unexpectedly swift Japanese capitulation, and also probably because of America's "Europe First" strategy, there had been very little presurrender planning for Japan. Although such planning called for an Allied occupation through the Allied Council for Japan, General Douglas MacArthur ignored Soviet attempts to secure a significant share in the occupation. The British, Chinese, and French, lacking resources, were forced to accept what portions of his empire MacArthur chose to dole out. As an example of the non–Allied nature of this occupation, in the spring of 1949 MacArthur unilaterally abrogated any further Japanese reparations, to the fury of the Allied Council. His logic was impeccable: it made no sense to strip impoverished Japan, into which the United States was reluctantly pouring millions of dollars, if the main source of that nation's economic recovery were to be shipped away. Furthermore, to the inestimable benefit of the Japanese, the unilateral U.S. occupation meant that Japan was never territorially divided into zones of Allied occupation. Commerce, government, and the movement of people remained unhindered by artificial political barriers. The surrender was hard enough for this people; dismemberment of their land might have proved insupportable.

Few Americans could ever name the heads of MG in Germany, but the Japanese occupation was dominated throughout almost its entire term by one officer, General Douglas MacArthur, designated supreme commander for the Allied powers (SCAP). Even Emperor Hirohito, retained on his throne as a revered figurehead monarch, proved no competition. MacArthur seemed to have no difficulty in assuming the role of an aloof, benign overlord of the Japanese in place of the emperor. He also retained his post as commander in chief of U.S. forces in the Far East (USFFE). Surprisingly for those who view MacArthur as an uncompromising conservative, the prevailing tenor of the early years of the occupation of Japan had a New Deal, even "liberal," cast.

The structure of the MG was extremely complex, with three administrative layers between SCAP and MG teams at the prefectural level, and none had a Japanese counterpart. Just below SCAP was the U.S. Eighth Army, with a Military Government Section appended to its headquarters. Below the Eighth Army were two corps, I and IX, both of which had an MG staff section. Between the corps and prefectural teams were eight MG regional headquarters, each of which supervised a group of prefectural teams. At the prefectural level, the MG was exercised by a total of six groups, twenty-four companies, and twenty-eight detachments. ("Team" replaced "detachment" soon after.) The trained MG officers had left Japan by the summer of 1946. They were replaced by regular army officers transferred from troop duty, their only training a hastily organized course at Carlisle Barracks, Pennsylvania. Other officers, transferred directly from Japanese troop duty, did not have even that scanty training. Overall, MG forces at full strength numbered some five hundred officers (from all arms and services), an equal number of civilians from the civil service and Department of the Army, and 2,300 enlisted men, plus a variable number of Japanese civilians. An average MG team consisted of 10 officers, 10 civilians, 45 enlisted men, and 120 to 200 Japanese civilians (the latter serving as interpreters, janitors, drivers, mechanics, clerks, kitchen personnel, etc.).

In the absence of any Japanese resistance (as distinguished from labor unrest and riots), and with the prompt compliance to SCAP's initial directives, the Military Government Section of General Headquarters, Armed Forces Pacific, was dissolved. It was soon obvious that the main concern of the occupation would be with the nonmilitary aspects of Japanese life. The Eighth Army carried three principal agencies concerned with the MG: the Military Government Section; a field organization based on two corps headquarters and special MG units; and fifty-three MG teams, one team for each of the forty-six prefectures

and one for each of the seven administrative regions. With the exception of the three largest metropolitan teams, which reported to the Eighth Army commander, the regional and prefectural teams within each corps area were attached to the corps and operated under the direct supervision of the corps commander.

The Eighth Army Military Government (Special) Staff Section comprised seven divisions: Legal and Public Safety, Welfare, Economics, Finance, Medical, Supply and Procurement, and Repatriation. Soon the units were redesignated "teams" and were identified with the prefecture to which they were assigned. These prefecture teams included experts in commerce and industry, legal and government matters, information and education, civil property, public health, and public welfare. They were to work in daily contact with the agencies of the central Japanese government, of the prefectural governments, and of local governing and voluntary bodies, providing "on the spot" supervision and oversight of the execution of SCAP directives and ferreting out violations and noncompliance. However, punitive or disciplinary action was not delegated to the MG units. Rather, it was the duty of the MG to report violations of or failure to comply with SCAP directives to Tokyo for action. There would be no "military governors" as such in Japan; rather, there would be MG officers (who after 1949 were called civil affairs officers). In theory, at least, the occupation forces were in Japan simply to observe, investigate, and report Japanese compliance with the instructions of the supreme commander to the Japanese government. In fact, one MG officer was actually transferred out of Japan immediately after his wife, writing a society column in an American newspaper, committed the gaffe of referring to her spouse as a "military governor."

The teams varied in size from 6 officers and 25 enlisted men for minor prefectural teams, to 67 officers and 150 enlisted men assigned to the Tokyo-Kanagawa MG District Team. Nationwide, the number of MG personnel continued to decline, reaching 1,772 in August 1948. With so few troops, the Eighth Army had to recruit civil service personnel for positions in a wide variety of fields, such as economics, sociology, and government. Yet personnel shortages persisted despite good salaries and perquisites. From the start of the occupation, the MG was split between policy makers and administrators whose major priority was to build Japan anew along democratic lines, and those who were more concerned with Japan's role as a bastion against communism, either the domestic variety or the threat posed by the Soviet Union.

The first postsurrender duty given by SCAP to the Japanese was the repatriation of all Japanese troops from their overseas territories, particularly Korea and Formosa, as well of all Koreans and Formosans in Japan who wished repatriation to their homelands. Some 1,250,000 persons were thus repatriated, with remarkable efficiency.

The demilitarization of the nation came simultaneously with repatriation and was fully as successful. The one significant blot on the occupation's demilitarization record, and on that of MacArthur personally, was the executions of Japanese generals Yamashita Tomoyuki and Homma Masaharu, who probably would not have been convicted of war crimes in any impartial court of law, but who had been unlucky enough to have badly defeated MacArthur and other Allied commanders in the early months of the war. This was no example of an independent judiciary that the Japanese would wish to emulate, but most Japanese seemed to blame their own discredited warlords rather than the Americans for their current misery.

That misery was as much spiritual as physical. There had been very little opposition to the war policies of the Japanese leadership; the Japanese people entered the war as the most united and enthusiastic of all of the belligerents, and now they had been ordered to surrender to and cooperate with the "barbarians." Understandably, in light of the MG's grand vision of purging Japan of centuries of militarism and feudalism, censorship played a large part in the occupation of Japan. Initially, everything from radio, press, news agencies, concert halls, and libraries to geisha houses and picnic grounds was to be controlled, although freedom of speech, press, religion, "and (eventually) freedom of assembly" were to be permitted "as soon as practicable," subject to the exigencies of security and law and order. Taboo were ultramilitaristic, ultranationalistic, and feudalistic themes. Thus even Kabuki and No theatrical productions were in trouble in the early days of the occupation. Films, too, were carefully scrutinized for offending material. Out went *Symphony of Revenge, Swords Flash in Cherry Blossom Time,* and *Human Bullet Volunteer Corps.* The official history of SCAP blandly asserted that the "Press Code for Japan and Radio Code for Japan" were based "on ethical practices in the United States," which would surely have been news to American media executives. Further, this censorship was admittedly used equally to keep abreast of "violence, strikes, communist activities or any other developments which were of a subversive or possibly subversive nature."

The MG's Information Dissemination Section (IDS) conducted propaganda and information programs that gradually became considerably more sophisticated and popular. (The MG censorship office followed the mold of totalitarian regimes by prohibiting any public reference to its own activities.)

It was all part of the dilemma of how one could encourage freedom while restricting freedom of expression, something that, admittedly, bothered MG censors. However, during the immediate postwar years, the censorship gradually eased, with a trend from pre- to post-censorship.

The MG had its own, excellent source of information about Japanese attitudes with its Allied Translation and Information Service (ATIS), an intelligence organization dating back to World War II in the Pacific. Although MacArthur was personally aloof from the Japanese people, through ATIS he was quite well informed on their activities and opinions.

In 1947, the MG-drafted new Japanese constitution grandly proclaimed that "The feudal system of Japan will cease." This reorientation mandated the disestablishment of the Shinto religion; the emperor's renunciation of "the false conception that the Emperor is divine and that the Japanese people are superior to other races and fated to rule the world"; the removal of restrictions on political, civil, and religious liberties; dissolution of holding companies; rural land reform; and reform of the civil service and education. The total control by the police over the everyday life of the Japanese people was weakened by an ambitious decentralization program, and the infamous "Thought Police" were disbanded.

The "purge program" was based on a joint chiefs of staff directive dated November 3, 1945, which stated that "you will assume that any persons who have held key positions of high responsibility since 1937 in industry, finance, commerce or agriculture have been active exponents of militant nationalism and aggression," a blatant violation of Anglo–U.S. legal principles. At lower levels, the purge was to be handled by local Japanese boards. It fell most heavily on the "militarists," who were removed from any positions of power. Neither they nor any spiritual descendants have disturbed the peace over the last half-century.

The civilian ultranationalists, in some ways fully as bloodthirsty as their military counterparts, also were purged from positions of authority. Nonetheless, though no longer assassinating politicians who stood in their way, they maintained a shadowy existence as an ultrarightist force, gained new strength during the Korean war, and reestablished former ties with organized crime. The bureaucrats and the financial and industrial elite survived for the most part, and were not reduced to manual labor or penury.

Some of these purges seemed to go "by the numbers." When one local board was excoriated by higher MG authorities for "incompetence" and "inefficiency," it immediately raised the percentages of "purgees" from 0.4 to 1.3 percent. Even when nonmilitary elites were purged, they were usually replaced by men with similar training and attitudes.

More lasting good came from the MG-inspired "Daily Life Security Law," Japan's first comprehensive welfare legislation. Because the law placed the burden of responsibility for public welfare on local government, MG teams were required to see that the prefectural and municipal officials understood the law and complied with its numerous provisions. All too often these officials proved lethargic and their work was handicapped by the lack of trained social workers. In time, however, the law basically brought Japan up to the social security standards of industrialized Western nations.

Judicial reform encompassed a new structure of basic law, new civil and criminal codes, and a new system of court procedures; the Supreme Court was given the American power to declare laws unconstitutional. However, the Japanese did not adopt the American habit of litigiousness.

The MG saw to it that nationwide elections were held in 1946. A succession of ministries resulted, which would indicate a certain political freedom, until the election of the long-lasting Yoshida regime, which set Japan on its path of global economic power.

The most publicized achievement of the MG was the inauguration of a new constitution. The official myth is that Japanese officials and politicians, aware of the Allies' dissatisfaction with the existing constitution, themselves drew up this new instrument of state, in close consultation with MG officials. In reality, General MacArthur's headquarters rejected a first draft that was indeed drawn up by the Japanese cabinet. Then, in the closest secrecy, MacArthur's government section chief, Brigadier General Courtney Whitney, drew up a revised draft (presumably in English), presented it to a distraught Japanese cabinet, and forced it through a reluctant Japanese Diet, allowing only the most minimal of changes. (A Japanese news magazine impertinently published the story of a citizen who, when asked what he thought of Japan's new constitution, replied, "Oh, has it been translated into Japanese already?") The document was full of American idioms and political theories that at first were almost unintelligible to Japanese readers. MacArthur blandly praised the Japanese people for having produced so exemplary a document, and the new "Japanese" constitution, whatever its provenance, went into effect on May 3, 1947. It has endured to this day.

Economic recovery was another urgent SCAP priority. Japanese industrial production was then at about one-tenth of prewar levels, and even this meager effort was mainly in the line of such makeshifts as turning army helmets into pots and pans or wood pulp into an ersatz cloth that soon reverted to its previous state in the rain. The ubiquitous black market could be seen as another, and extremely significant, "industry." On the other hand, despite heavy U.S. bombing in the closing months of the war, Japanese industry was damaged, not destroyed, notwithstanding the claims of the advocates of "victory through airpower."

The main problems of the Japanese postwar economy lay in a lack of raw materials and transportation, and the departure of the Chinese and Korean slave laborers. The U.S. occupation had initially, and naively, believed that it could leave the economic situation and its reform to the Japanese themselves. The problems were too great, however, the industrial plant too damaged, transport too chaotic, and the Japanese people too close to starvation.

Coal seemed to be at the root of most economic and industrial problems. Coal production was slowed by lack of equipment and food; increased food production depended upon fertilizer; and the production of fertilizer depended upon the production of more coal. Initial emergency aid was soon replaced by longer-range economic reform, although the fruits of the U.S. economic policies were not particularly evident until the boom induced by the Korean war in 1950. The MG realized that production could not begin to increase until the Japanese worker could be fed better. Official rations had dropped to 1,050 calories per person per day—about one-fifth the amount consumed by an average U.S. occupation soldier. Even so, the rations were often late and, when they arrived, were filled out with such unpalatable substances as acorn meal and the residue from the production of soybean meal. Guided by identification charts printed in newspapers, housewives foraged through the countryside for edible weeds. In reality, no one was expected to live on the official rations. There may have been few, if any, deaths from starvation, but civilians weakened by malnutrition were easy prey to disease and certainly could not work at their highest level.

Furthermore, the day-to-day struggle for food consumed time that could have been spent at the factory, office, or mine. The only answer was the importation of food, a course of action resisted by those mindful of the destruction and starvation inflicted on millions of innocents by the vanquished aggressor nations. General MacArthur, acting on the premise that "you cannot teach democracy to a hungry people," directed the emergency importation of foodstuffs and medicines into Japan, on the grounds that the health and security of the U.S. occupation forces there would be in danger if the situation were to continue. He grandiloquently wired a hesitating State Department, "Give me bread or give me bullets."

Food imports were not always handled wisely. For example, occupation officials imported large quantities of cornmeal, explaining to the citizenry that corn bread and corn muffins were considered delicacies in the United States. All it took was the addition of some shortening, wheat flour, eggs, milk, butter, and salt. . . .

Sanitary conditions initially threatened a large-scale outbreak of disease. The Japanese personally were extremely clean, but retained a paradoxically casual attitude toward public health, a situation made much worse by the war. MG sanitation personnel had their educational work cut out for them, but usually prevailed by emphasizing to this disciplined and conforming people that it was "for the good of everybody," particularly the children.

The MG Medical Section initiated mass inoculations in 1946 against a serious smallpox threat and the localization of cholera brought to the home islands by repatriates. Less pressing but hardly less important were the MG health campaigns against venereal and gastrointestinal diseases and tuberculosis.

To hold down inflation, the occupation embarked upon a price-control program, which had little effect and only fueled the black market all the more. The Japanese economy did little more than mark time until about 1950–1951.

One of the more successful economic programs of the MG, on the other hand, was the breaking up of the giant *zaibatsu* financier families, or "money clique." The Japanese Holding Company Liquidation Commission, closely supervised by the MG, saw to it that the stocks of the *zaibatsu* eventually were sold off. In the meantime, the money trusts were deprived of control over those stocks. Attempts to break up other Japanese monopolies had considerably less success. The policy was incomprehensible to the Japanese. They felt that economic consolidation was the way the world was obviously going, and that only a nation as wealthy as America could afford to be so wasteful as to ignore the economies of scale, and mobilization of capital and enterprise, that monopolies supposedly afforded. MacArthur asserted that he was not opposed to encouraging a capitalist economy in Japan, but if the purge of tainted top managers would delay or disrupt Japanese recovery, so be it.

The occupation can also be credited with "setting the workers free" with its labor union policies. The Socialists firmly believed that MacArthur did not go nearly far enough. Even so, by early 1948 Japanese workers enjoyed a system of workers' compensation, insurance legislation, regulated workplace standards, hours of work, and vacations with pay that was enforced on a uniform basis by labor standards administrative offices in each prefecture. This reform, although certainly at the behest of MacArthur, was carried out by the Japanese government.

Perhaps as a result, Japan was racked with strikes and labor disorders in the first few years of the U.S. occupation. In March 1948 leftist-controlled unions of government workers brought the nation to the verge of a crippling strike that MacArthur had to prohibit. He responded with a purge of Communist leaders in June 1948. In the spring of 1949 a Korean mob occupied the Kobe prefectural office and had to be removed by Eighth Army troops. In June of that year, Communists seized a police station in the town of Taira (Iwaki) and held it for the better part of the day. In 1949 government and private employers, with MacArthur's active encouragement, struck back, firing some twenty thousand workers considered Communists or fellow travelers. (In December 1948, public sector workers had had their right to strike taken from them.)

Throughout the reform program MacArthur seems to have been sensitive to Japanese cultural norms and to have avoided overt "pushing" of the Japanese into reforms and transformations that the Americans favored. One of the best, and most successful, examples of his deference to Japanese mores did nothing less than transform rural Japan from a collection of landless peasants to one of landowning proprietors. As early as 1947 the Japanese government purchased more than 2 million acres of land for redistribution. In October 1948, the Diet, acting at the behest of MacArthur, passed the Farm Land Reform Law, which prohibited absentee landownership. Some thirteen thousand locally elected land commissions, each consisting of five tenant farmers, two owner-cultivators, and three landlords, were established. They in turn chose prefectural land commissions that were supervised on the national level by the Central Land Commission (and, of course, indirectly by MacArthur). With commendable speed and efficiency some 75 percent of tenant farmers became small landowners. MG officers made routine visits to the most remote villages to symbolize MacArthur's commitment and to see that the job was getting done. This was unprecedented land reform (except in the Philippines in the 1950s and in South Vietnam in the 1970s, also under U.S. prodding). The Soviet representative on the Allied Council was unimpressed, and unsuccessfully demanded the immediate uncompensated confiscation of all land and its redistribution to the peasants. Japanese land reform was successful primarily because MacArthur could call upon a broad range of knowledge of Japan in the U.S. government and academe. (This bank of knowledge of Japan had not been called upon in the first months of the occupation.) It also helped considerably that Japan was by far the most Western of any Asian nation at the time.

In education, the MG concerned itself with the removal of "objectionable" courses, practices, and textbooks, and ordered the Japanese government to reform its centralized school system forthwith. The first MG-directed education reforms were negative and unarguable: the prohibition of any teaching of ultranationalism and militarism, racial superiority, the subordination of the individual to the state, even of rote learning, as well as of texts and teachers who propagated these ideas. By April 1947, some 22 percent of the nation's school officials had resigned or had been removed by Japanese screening committees. In all, approximately 700,000 individuals were investigated, of whom only 3,000 were judged unfit to continue in the field of education. MG education enthusiasts even attempted to import American-style parent–teacher associations, without much success, because teachers remained authority figures in postwar Japan.

The Japanese could be forgiven their doubts about the reforming of schooling along U.S. lines. Early in the occupation a U.S. education commission was brought to Japan to, in the words of one of its members, "supplant nationalism, militarism, and mental slavery by democracy and freedom of thought"—which the educators admitted was something of "a large order." These evils were to be replaced by emphasis on "the dignity and worth of the individual, on independent thought and initiative and on developing a spirit of inquiry." More dubiously, the Americans had dreams of something like two hundred universities to replace the six prewar imperial institutions of higher education, another "reform" quietly throttled by the Japanese.

Bothered by Japanese education control from the top, the MG civil information and education section saw to it that popularly elected school boards were eventually constituted in each prefecture and in most municipalities. Most of these officers were school administrators and professional educators; local MG education officers had limited academic backgrounds. In the only gesture ever made toward the reinstatement of those who had lost positions because of their opposition to the old regime, such teachers were given preference in hiring.

The new social studies textbook was completed by the fall of 1946. Prepared by Japanese scholars, the text was indeed purged of the traditional glorification of militarism, ultranationalism, and Shintoism. Nonetheless, the "evidence shows . . . [its] values sprang not from American but Japanese sources."

Education reform was not singular in this regard. One authority on the occupation of Japan perceptively concluded, "For almost every proposed reform there was found a Japanese who long before the occupation had developed a commitment to the concept involved."

Furthermore, "Japanese educators and particularly the university professors were conscious only of their own wider experience or greater erudition and tended to be supercilious toward these American educational officers and their ideas." By the end of 1948, the MG's Election Management Commission recognized four major political parties, plus some 1,250 other registered political groups, all officially working for democracy. The former head of the Government Section noted: "The 1,250 parties seem bewilderingly numerous, yet no one but the American is in the least confused. . . . An Oriental will form a group, dignified by a high title, at the drop of a hat."

Almost as significant as these numerous political "groups" were the *oyabun-kobun* (literally "fatherlike–childlike"), a network of near-feudalistic patron–protégé organizations, which permeated Japan and, in the words of the assistant chief of the Government Section, extended "from the smallest rural village to the highest echelons of the national government." This officer logically argued that "this clannish and clandestine combination of bosses, hoodlums, and racketeers is the greatest threat to American democratic aims in Japan." These groups did bring up frightening parallels with the secret societies that had assassinated democratic-leaning politicians and military officers and that did as much as anything else to place Japan on its path of conquest in the 1930s. It cannot be denied that the *oyabun* flourished all the more in the difficult years of occupation immediately following the surrender.

Far more significant than any postwar secret groupings was the new Japanese political elite and bureaucracy. The prewar political elite had been almost entirely removed. A new political elite found its home for the most part in the Liberal-Democratic Party, which governed and dominated Japan without interruption for more than three decades after its organization in 1955.

The year 1948 saw the transition from something of a punitive occupation to one more concerned with economic rehabilitation. Japan was now looked upon as a potential bulwark against Communist expansion in the Pacific, its well-being a matter of American national interest. The indirect Japanese occupation was to become even more indirect. Surprisingly, many Japanese authorities were alarmed by the rather unexpected turning over to them of so much more responsibility. They feared shame and loss of face if they failed in their new responsibilities, and in many cases pleaded for the retention of uniformed U.S. Army troops for moral support. In January 1948, Secretary of the Army Kenneth C. Royall called for a reassessment of U.S. policies in Japan, in particular the December 1946 "Law Relating to the Prohibition of Excessive Concentrations of Economic Power" and the Antimonopoly Law of April 1947. Royal noted "an area of conflict between the original concept of broad demilitarization and the new purpose of building a self-supporting nation," and concluded that the *zaibatsu* were "the ablest and most successful leaders of that country, and their services would in many instances contribute to the economic recovery of Japan."

By then the *zaibatsu* had mostly been removed, but younger executives were already taking their places. Even then, purgees were not prohibited from moving into new lines of work. The chairman of the Mitsui Bank, for example, simply moved over to the chairmanship of Sony, "where his distinguished talents were put to splendid use," in the words of the MG official who helped to plan the *zaibatsu* purge. A contemporary American author noted "the peculiar cross-industry structure of industrial control under which certain Japanese firms have manufactured everything from parasols to locomotives," well before U.S. businessmen made their supposedly unique discovery of the benefits of the conglomerate.

As early as the beginning of 1948, prefectural MG officials were doing no more than referring cases of noncompliance to the prefectural governments and suggesting remedies. Increasingly, MacArthur was governing Japan by "remote control" through Japanese authorities.

Although Japan lacked a land border with any other nation and was spared a Soviet zone of occupation, MacArthur worried about Communist unrest and Soviet pressure. The Korean war of course intensified these fears; but by then Japan was well on the road to self-government, and the treaty of peace and the end of the occupation were only a year and two years away, respectively.

The year 1948 also saw the first lasting economic improvement since the end of the war. In March the Draper mission, headed by the undersecretary of the army and composed of prominent American businessmen, concluded that Japan was to become the workshop of Asia. Rather than reparations out of Japan, investment would now flow into Japan from America. In 1949, Joseph Dodge, who had presided over the successful reform of the German currency, became MacArthur's financial adviser. Also in that year the Diet submitted its first balanced budget.

In 1950 the Korean war solidified and accelerated Japan's economic recovery and left the nation poised for global economic eminence. In sum, and looking back, it can be confirmed that under U.S. occupation and military government, Japan "followed the great tradition of adaptation, importation, and consolidation, which the Japanese have followed on other occasions in their history."

In 1952 the World War II Allies, with the conspicuous exception of the Soviet Union, signed a peace treaty with Japan that officially stripped it of its imperial possessions, but otherwise was a nonpunitive instrument that afforded Japan an honorable place among the nations of the world.

FURTHER READINGS

Cohen, Theodore. *Remaking Japan: The American Occupation as New Deal* (1987).

Harries, Merion, and Susie Harries. *Sheathing the Sword: The Demilitarization of Postwar Japan* (1987).

Kawai Kazo. *Japan's American Interlude* (1960).

Martin, Edwin. *The Allied Occupation of Japan*, 2d ed. (1972).

Nimmo, William F., ed. *The Occupation of Japan: The Impact of the Korean War*. Proceedings of a symposium sponsored by the General Douglas MacArthur Memorial, October 16–17, 1986 (1990).

———. *History of the Navy—Military Activities of the Occupation of Japan* (GHQ Statistics and Reports Section, 1952).

———. *Reports of General MacArthur. MacArthur in Japan: The Occupation: Military Phase* (SCAP General Staff, 1950, 1966, 1994).

Supreme Commander for the Allied Powers. *History of the Non-Military Activities of the Occupation of Japan*. NARA MP 65-4, rolls 1–13.

Ward, Robert, and Frank J. Shulman. *The Allied Occupation of Japan, 1945–52: An Annotated Bibliography on Western Language Materials* (1974).

Wolfe, Robert, ed. *Americans as Proconsuls: United States Military Government in Germany and Japan, 1944–1952*. Proceedings of Symposium "Americans as Proconsuls," National Museum of History and Technology, Smithsonian Institution, May 1977 (1984).

Stanley Sandler

SEE ALSO MacArthur, Douglas

Jet and Rocket Aircraft, Japanese

One of the few areas of German-Japanese cooperation during World War II was in aviation. The Japanese had purchased German fighters (Heinkel 112Bs) and long-range transports (Fw 200s) before the war, and received technical data, tools, and blueprints in exchange for critical war materials such as tungsten and quinine. Therefore, in the fall of 1944 Hitler authorized the provision of key tools, blueprints, and data about the Messerschmitt 163 and 262 rocket and jet fighters, respectively, to Japan. In fact, the Japanese bought the production rights for both aircraft. Despite the July 1944 sinking of the U-boat carrying the manufacturing specifications, work progressed fairly steadily on the rocket fighter. The Japanese jet projects enjoyed greater fortune, receiving the key materials just a few months later. Both prototypes were completed in early March 1945 and made their maiden flights in July, but neither ever went beyond prototype testing and would not have been ready for production until mid-1946 at the earliest.

Had they achieved operational status in any significant numbers, the Nakajima Kikka and Ki-201 jet fighters would have been formidable opponents for the B-29s over Japan, as would the Mitsubishi J8MI rocket fighter. These projects indicated the high priority Japan had given to air defense by 1944, but they came too late to make a difference. Both aircraft closely resembled their German models but were not exact copies, and their performance was somewhat lower.

FURTHER READINGS

Green, William. *War Planes of the Second World War, Fighters,* vol. 3 (1961).

Gurney, Gene. *The War in the Air* (1962).

Smith, Richard, and Eddie Creek. *Jet Planes of the Third Reich* (1982).

Carl O. Schuster

SEE ALSO Aircraft: Japanese, U.S., and British; Army Air Force, Japanese

Journalistic Coverage of the Pacific War, U.S.

American war correspondents in the South Pacific theater experienced considerably more hazardous and difficult conditions than did their counterparts in Europe. Hindered by stringent censorship rules and geographical obstacles, they were in many cases unable to report fully until after the war. Although reporters assigned to the Pacific theater were not considered as important as journalists in Europe, and were paid less, they provided valuable information to the military and the public. Overall, the United States sent the most journalists to World War II fronts, with the possible exception of the Soviet Union: an estimated 1,646 accredited reporters.

Because of Japanese aggression in China, American correspondents were already stationed throughout the Pacific—at Hong Kong, Shanghai, Manila, and Tokyo—when the United States entered World War II. But Bill Dunn of CBS was the only broadcast war correspondent who covered the Pacific from the Japanese attack against the U.S. naval facility at Pearl Harbor, Hawaii, in December 1941 to V-J Day in August 1945.

Honolulu became the center for U.S. Pacific press war news. Immediately after war was declared, American reporters flocked to San Francisco. By early January, the War Department had accredited 115 correspondents in the Pacific. Each reporter was required to wear an officer's uniform without rank insignia; a green brassard on the left sleeve (and later a shoulder patch) designated correspondent status. The correspondents were attached to a field force commander's headquarters and received the same privileges as officers regarding transportation and accommodations. They were allowed to use government communication facilities. If captured, they were expected to be treated the same as captains. Visiting correspondents did not wear uniforms but were expected to display the brassard and were usually accompanied by an officer who set their itinerary.

Marine correspondents served the dual roles of enlisted marines assigned to line regiments and of journalists. These combat correspondents carried rifles and typewriters in their battle gear and focused on soldiers, not the overall war. Marine Dan Levin recalled that marine correspondents wrote "Joe Blow" stories about individual marines, often heroic, to be published in hometown papers.

The U.S. government had mandated that all combat photographs, whether taken by commercial or by military photographers, had to be made available to all press outlets. The Still Photographic War Pool deployed photographers from its participating organizations to most combat areas. Their products were then pooled and forwarded to publications in the continental United States. All photographs, of course, were censored in the field and then at the War or Navy Department.

Although war photographers shared the same frustrations as U.S. military commanders that their field of operations was "second string" to Europe, their photographs were the ones that remained fixed in the minds of Americans more often than those taken in Europe, starting with the stunning photo of the blowing up of destroyer *Shaw* at Pearl Harbor, which has remained *the* representation of the opening disaster of the Pacific war.

One has only to think of the raising of the flag on Iwo Jima, an absolute icon of U.S. participation in the Pacific war, which was perpetuated in bronze in the Marine Corps Memorial outside Washington, D.C. That single photo, in the words of the Secretary of the Navy James Forrestal (who was at Iwo Jima), "guaranteed that there would be a Marine Corps for the next hundred years." Then there was the first photograph of U.S. dead released to the American public, an evocative photo of several fallen soldiers on the beach at Buna, New Guinea.

Editors in the United States were more interested in spectacular European campaigns than in events in the South Pacific. Nonetheless, many Pacific reporters gained international reputations for their coverage whereas, paradoxically, fewer reporters in Europe were as well known. In the Philippines, Clark Lee and Melville Jacoby were among the best-known correspondents, as were Daniel De Luce and Jack Belden in Burma, Richard Tregaskis on Guadalcanal, Cecil Brown at Singapore, and Ira Wolfert in the Solomons.

Conditions in the South Pacific theater proved more difficult than those in Europe for correspondents to cover. American journalists in the South Pacific endured Japanese snipers and suicide attacks. The distances between Pacific islands where fighting occurred resulted in poor communications and lack of access to action. The war at sea made it physically impossible for correspondents to follow troops as they would on land. But some more adventurous reporters overcame these difficulties through various stratagems to secure "scoops." They also endured heat, humidity, monotony, and at least the possibility of acquiring exotic diseases along with their stories.

Without advanced technology, reporters had to rely on erratic telephone and telegraph lines in the jungle. Radio broadcasts were crucial after the Japanese cut the Pacific cable. Later, mobile press centers with radio transmitters followed troops when possible; often they erected their antennas on the beaches immediately after the landings. Reporters worked in blacked-out tents, secured their copy in waterproof canisters, and transported it by jeep to beachhead rendezvous. Rough seas delayed press boats and mortar fire often confined reporters to foxholes.

Even so, censorship was perhaps the greatest problem that American correspondents in the South Pacific encountered. The Pacific theater was the strictest in controlling information. The U.S. Pacific Fleet Service Force established a public relations unit which released official reports, and there was a feeling among the "brass" that this was all that was needed to keep the American public informed. Yet, in March 1942 General Douglas MacArthur told reporters they were "one of the most valuable components" in the Pacific war because "in democracies it is essential that the public know the truth." Optimism dimmed, however, as MacArthur's press officers stressed that only stories promoting MacArthur's bravery would pass censors. Stories listing high casualties or praising other officers would be suppressed.

MacArthur sought publicity that would promote him as a military genius. He insisted on taking credit for actions in which his role was merely peripheral. He ordered photographs to give the illusion that he was "on the line" when actually he rarely visited the front, and was known by the embittered troops on Bataan as "dugout Doug." When he was evacuated from the Philippines to Australia, he insisted that headlines boast about his power and leadership. In all, MacArthur considered journalism another myth-making machine, along with his staff. Demoralized journalists assigned to MacArthur's command wrote a verse:

Put on your spurs and pick up your whip;
Know ye the pleasures of censorship!
Take a deep drag on the juice of the poppy
And then cut the hell out of everyone's copy!

The permanently irascible Admiral Ernest King, chief of naval operations, also distrusted the press. He insisted on reviewing releases, worrying that the navy's credibility might be damaged and the public made cynical.

All news in the southeast Pacific was required to go through General MacArthur's headquarters, and news in the central Pacific needed navy approval. Government censors controlled war news and promoted secrecy, using generic datelines like "Somewhere in New Guinea." News releases often did not report what was really happening; others were overly optimistic and misleading. One military censor dryly noted, "I wouldn't tell the people anything until the war is over, and then I'd tell them who won."

Censors often rewrote articles until they resembled slick public relations pieces depicting the troops as perfect Americans; indications of drinking, immorality, looting, or black market activity were carefully excised, as were references to morale problems, disciplinary actions, and race violence. It is indicative of the situation that the numbers of U.S. servicemen judicially executed in the European theater became available soon after the war; they still are elusive for the Pacific theater. In fact, a great percentage of news about the South Pacific front was actually written by personnel in Honolulu or Washington, D.C. Unfamiliar with the territory and local situations, they often cut out crucial facts and details or made ludicrous mistakes.

American correspondents were not allowed in the Pacific theater unless they were accredited and signed a waiver. Each armed forces-accredited correspondent took an oath to submit his copy to a censor; they were briefed before each mission and taken to the embarkation point with the troops. The major news services had agreed to establish a reporter pool, and correspondents on the scene drew lots to see who would photograph and write each story. Although most American reporters obviously believed the public was entitled to know the facts of the war, they also believed in a modicum of censorship to protect security. Nonetheless, faced with the strict censorship in the Pacific, many soon requested reassignment.

The 1942 Battle of Midway was the worst-reported naval battle in the war and the only time the World War I Espionage Act was invoked, unsuccessfully, to punish censorship violations in World War II. Reporter Stanley Johnston published a story with the headline "Navy Had Word of Jap Plan to Strike at Sea." Johnston was actually in Chicago when the article appeared, but he had used a dispatch from Admiral Chester Nimitz about movements of Japanese ships for his source and had deduced his conclusion. His story was so accurate and detailed that it threatened military security, mainly because he implied that the Americans had broken the Japanese secret code (which they had) and military officials feared the Japanese would change it.

Sometimes reporters outsmarted the military censors. During the summer of 1942, American reporters were forbidden to inform their editors about the impending landings at Guadalcanal in the Solomons. But censors did not catch John Hersey's reference to "wise men," alluding to King Solomon, and his astute editors printed the story when the invasion began.

In 1943, Admiral William F. Halsey, commander in chief of the South Pacific, and MacArthur restricted air transportation for civilian correspondents. Considering flying essential for their work, Vern Haugland, Harold Guard, and Lee Van Atta nonetheless flew to New Guinea and were then expelled from the theater. They appealed to Admiral Nimitz, who withdrew Halsey's and MacArthur's orders and even assigned an officer of air transportation for correspondents.

Admiral Nimitz also agreed to reform censorship in an attempt to coordinate and make submission procedures more efficient, but reporters considered the changes even more time-consuming. Also in 1943, Office of War Information chief Elmer Davis asked President Franklin D. Roosevelt to lift the ban on combat photographs so Americans could be aware of the realities of war. Soon after, *Life* published George Strock's photograph of three dead American soldiers on a southwest Pacific beach, sending a shock wave through the land. However, W. Eugene Smith's photograph of a dead Marine at Saipan was censored as too grotesque. Also excised for the most part were photos of Japanese skulls being used as candleholders, ashtrays, and other items.

As troops prepared to seize Pacific islands during the fall of 1943, the U.S. Pacific Fleet public relations unit offered to arrange interviews, promising a "story gold mine." Reporters were cheerfully informed that the military would now "do anything for you that will help to get your yarn." Changes, however, were minimal, correspondents still were assigned to a pool, sharing stories.

More positively, by Christmas 1943 the Signal Corps had developed transmitters to broadcast from Sydney, Australia, to the U.S. West Coast, alleviating delays for many reporters. In February 1944 the largest group of Pacific correspondents, approximately forty reporters, covered the attack on the Marshall Islands. And General MacArthur saw to it that no fewer than fifty correspondents accompanied him on his return to the Philippines, which was the most covered event in the Pacific. The event was restaged several times for military photographers to get just the right angles. MacArthur's "I have returned" speech was widely broadcast throughout the Philippines.

In 1944, the Pacific War Correspondents Association was established in Honolulu and worked with Admiral Nimitz's headquarters to ease censorship. Reporting conditions did improve: correspondents could attend briefings; blue seals were now placed on copy, which was sent on courier plane to hasten delivery; and correspondents were allowed on aircraft carriers and could request to be flown to battle sites. Censorship, however, remained firm. *Newsweek* irreverently declared, "The two most important American war correspondents are the two men who sit in Washington and prepare the Army and Navy communiqués." American correspondents were forbidden to disagree with the official version of a story, and often the military writers were missing key facts to pass on to correspondents. For example, at the Battle of Leyte Gulf in October 1944, the navy remained unaware of the extent of damage and losses on both sides. In other instances the navy hid damage inflicted by kamikaze pilots, but correspondents who located damaged vessels in shipyards soon realized the true extent of the destruction. The military also suppressed stories about tensions and clashes between Americans and Australians, such as the "Battle of Brisbane," where an American MP killed an Australian soldier and hurt eight more in a brawl at a railway station.

Opinions differ concerning the quality of American correspondents' reporting in the South Pacific. Historian Fletcher Pratt called it "nearly the worst reported" war in history, blaming the dependence on the military for the production of propaganda and "fluff pieces" to satisfy officers and politicians. A former war correspondent, Pratt published "How the Censors Rigged the News" in the February 1946 *Harper's* magazine (i.e., after the end of hostilities):

> The war was reported in terms of a social function by the Fifth Street Ladies Club—the name and addresses were correct and all the necessary ones got in. . . . There was almost never any sense of the hurry, passion, and continual surprise that are the essence of real fighting . . . or the ineffable boredom and desperate devices for self-entertainment that are the focus of preparation for battle.

To be fair, such strictures could hardly apply to reporters of the caliber of Ernie Pyle, for example, after he had transferred his reporting to the Pacific.

> On the other hand, Secretary of War Robert P. Patterson claimed that the war correspondents and photographers were "honest, competent, and patriotic," with very few exceptions.

But Patterson was hardly a disinterested observer. The immediate postwar U.S. literary scene saw a flood of factual accounts of the Pacific war, now that reporters could write as they pleased.

Artists composed a significant segment of war correspondents. Tom Lea painted portraits for *Life*, portraying the invasion of Peleliu. David Fredenthal, who joined the Army Art Unit in 1943, realistically painted watercolors of the island invasions at Arawe, New Britain. Milton Caniff's "Terry and the Pirates" comic strip helped Americans understand the war in the Pacific and promoted patriotism.

American correspondents included minorities like Vincent Tubbs of the *Baltimore Afro-American* and Annalee Jacoby from *Liberty* magazine, who was also the only woman correspondent accredited in the Southwest Pacific Area command. Sonia Tomara covered the China-Burma-India theater for the *New York Herald Tribune*, flying on combat missions. Bonnie Wiley of the Associated Press was the first woman correspondent to accompany an island invasion force, observing from a hospital ship. Shel-ley Smith Mydans, trapped in the Philippines, wrote a novel, *The Open City*, about her internment in the Philippines.

Troops published their own newspapers until restricted by MacArthur; the 854th Engineer Battalion on Okinawa, for example, printed *The Latrine Rumor*, whose very title must have infuriated MacArthur. There were Pacific editions of *Yank* and *Stars and Stripes*; the *Navy News* printed a Guam edition; and the *Daily Pacifican* represented armed forces in the Philippines. In addition to the harsh conditions already noted, American correspondents often found themselves in harm's way. United Press reporter Joe James Custer lost an eye at Guadalcanal. He commented that many correspondents were in poor shape and should have gone through basic training. "It's a hard, physical grind, working 24 hours a day, with a nap only now and then," he noted, adding that reporters should "learn hand-to-hand combat and the tricks of war." They seemed to do just that on the job. At Tarawa, correspondents dug foxholes next to the military on the beachhead, they bailed out of disabled aircraft, and they survived on jungle plants until they were rescued. Others died from their privations and hazards or were killed by the enemy. Several received the Purple Heart. The military reported that 112 American correspondents were wounded and 37 died in the war, an astonishing casualty rate four times, in proportion, to that of the troops. Ernie Pyle was undoubtedly the most famous reporter killed in the Pacific. And the *New York Times* reporter Byron "Barney" Darnton, considered by many to be the best overall correspondent in the Pacific, died when hit by a bomb fragment as he covered advance troops in northern New Guinea. Several American correspondents killed in the Pacific were memorialized with a Liberty ship named in their honor.

No fewer than fifty reporters were imprisoned by the Japanese. Joseph F. McDonald, Jr., a stringer for the United Press on Wake Island, was mistakenly identified as the first American correspondent killed in the Pacific; in fact, he was captured in late December 1941 and remained in captivity until September 1945. Otto D. Tolischus of the *New York Times* told how the Japanese tortured his fellow reporter, attempting to obtain his confession that he was a spy.

When the European war ended in May 1945, correspondents from that front transferred to the Pacific. A pool of 200 reporters covered the Japanese surrender ceremony and transmitted photographs from USS *Missouri* in Tokyo Bay. Correspondents also landed with the occupation forces and took advantage of opportunities during the early occupation to secure stories from such notables as Tokyo Rose, the pseudonym American soldiers gave to the female Japanese propaganda broadcasters in the Pacific war. By October, the Tokyo Correspondents' Club was established to focus on censorship issues, transportation needs, and other crucial concerns. At the end of that month, General MacArthur disaccredited all correspondents attached to the armed forces. As instant civilians they now had to pay their way home on military transports.

American correspondents also reported on the atomic bomb. William Laurence, a science reporter for the *New York Times* dubbed "Atomic Bill," explained technical aspects of the bomb to the public and suggested peacetime uses for its energy. As early as the summer of 1940, he had commented that atomic fission was possible, warned about the possible advances of German physicists, and noted that American scientists were disappearing. He was told about the Manhattan Project and became its official chronicler, preparing false releases to cover up test detonations. Laurence had observed the plane take off with the bomb and was on board an accompanying B-29 bomber to see it used on Nagasaki. He won a Pulitzer Prize for his series on the atomic bomb.

General MacArthur declared southern Japan off-limits to the press and increased censorship, stressing that no stories about the bomb's effects would be written and encouraging U.S. prisoner of war liberation stories to be prepared instead. The air force flew in American reporters Homer Bigart and Laurence to join the left-wing London reporter Wilfred Burchett, who described radiation sickness. Hiroshima was then closed to the press. In 1946 the *New Yorker* sent John Hersey to chronicle the atomic bomb's effects; his account was later expanded into his book *Hiroshima*. Hersey had previously written *Into the Valley: A Skirmish of the Marines,* about a failed marine sortie on the Mataniko River in Guadalcanal during the fall of 1942. Understandably, Hersey was not MacArthur's or Halsey's favorite war correspondent.

Several American correspondents published their wartime memoirs. Clark Lee's *They Call It Pacific* is considered one of the best. Other significant autobiographical works include Richard Tregaskis's *Guadalcanal Diary* and William Dunn's *Pacific Microphone.* Excerpts of correspondents' wartime articles, including Ernie Pyle's, have been anthologized. Numerous American journalists received Pulitzer Prizes for their work in the South Pacific theater, including Joe Rosenthal for his immortal photograph of U.S. Marines raising the American flag on Iwo Jima. After World War II, most American reporters who covered the South Pacific resumed their journalism careers at home or secured contracts as foreign correspondents in other regions and wars.

FURTHER READINGS

Collier, Richard. *The Warcos: The War Correspondents of World War Two* (1989).

Cornebise, Alfred. *Ranks and Columns: Armed Forces Newspapers in American Wars* (1993).

Desmond, Robert W. *Tides of War: World News Reporting 1940–1945* (1984).

Levin, Dan. *From the Battlefield: Dispatches of a World War II Marine* (1995).

Voss, Frederick S. *Reporting the War: The Journalistic Coverage of World War II* (1994).

Elizabeth D. Schafer

SEE ALSO Home Front, U.S.

Kamikazes

Born of desperation, the Kamikaze Special Attack Corps was organized during the final stages of World War II to fly suicide missions against Allied naval forces. Named for the "divine wind," a thirteenth-century typhoon that supposedly had saved Japan from invasion by Kublai Khan's fleet, naval kamikaze units were first proposed by Vice Admiral Takijiro Onishi.

On October 25, 1944, during the Battle of Leyte Gulf, the kamikazes made their debut when Lieutenant Yukio Seki, flying a Mitsubishi Zero armed with a 550-pound bomb, struck light aircraft carrier USS *Santee*. Two other kamikazes narrowly missed light carriers *Sangamon* and *Petrof Bay*. By noon, kamikazes had seriously damaged aircraft carriers *Suwannee, Kitkun Bay*, and *St. Lo*. The latter broke in two and sank, victim of a single kamikaze.

Impressed by these early results, the Japanese expanded kamikaze operations. The army began preparations for the kamikaze units and adapted more types of aircraft for suicide missions. The original Zeros were soon joined by Val and Judy dive-bombers as well as Frances twin-engined bombers. On November 25, 1944, six Zeros and two Judys, led by Lieutenant Kimiyoshi Takatake, slightly damaged heavy aircraft carrier *Essex*. Two sister carriers as well as light carrier *Independence* were extensively damaged.

On January 25, 1945, in an all-out effort, the last kamikaze attacks in the Philippines failed to stop U.S. landings at Luzon. Later that month the Japanese First Air Fleet transferred its aircraft to Formosa (now Taiwan), where it continued operations. On January 21, 1945, Formosa-based kamikazes seriously damaged aircraft carrier *Ticonderoga*.

Early kamikaze aircraft were slightly modified production aircraft, but in August 1944 the Naval Air Research and Development Center began experiments with a spe-cialized, piloted glide-bomb. Suggested by Ensign Mitsuo Ota, this Marudai Project was commanded by Captain Motoharu Okamura. Its single-seat glider, christened Oka (Cherry Blossom) II, armed with a 2,640-pound warhead, was designed to be carried to its target by a twin-engined Betty bomber. Linguistically alert Americans soon dubbed the novel weapon Baka (Fool).

A new volunteer unit, the Jinrai Butai (Corps of Divine Thunder), was organized to pilot the new Oka IIs. First intended to operate from bases in the Philippines, Formosa, and Okinawa, the Jinrai Butai was temporarily crippled by the loss of fifty Okas. They were being transported by aircraft carrier *Shinano* when it was sunk on November 29, 1944, by U.S. submarine *Archerfish*.

On March 21, 1945, Lieutenant Commander Goro Ionaka led the first major Oka assault against U.S. forces. His flight of sixteen Type 1 Betty bombers, each carrying a single Oka, as well as two conventionally armed Bettys, was jumped by U.S. F6F Hellcats 300 miles southeast of Kyushu. The F6Fs downed all of the Japanese bombers as well as fifteen of their thirty Zero escorts. A second and final raid against U.S. warships at Okinawa incorporated seventy-four Okas. Although a few of the manned bombs found targets, most were shot down while still attached to their mother planes.

Although never operational, several advanced piloted-bomb prototypes were in various stages of development at war's end. These included the jet engine-powered Oka Model 22, the turbojet Kikka (Mandarin Orange Blossom), the pulse-jet *Baika* (Plum Blossom), and the Shinryu (Divine Dragon) glider launched by solid-fuel rockets. The army produced the Tsurugi (Sword), a version of the navy's reciprocating engine-powered Toka (Wisteria Blossom).

As Allied forces closed in on the Japanese home islands, more than half of the available Japanese pilots operated as kamikazes in Operation Kikusui (Ten Go). In desperate attacks, kamikazes from the First, Fifth, and Tenth Air Fleets based at Kyushu and the First Air Fleet from Formosa concentrated on Allied carriers. In the war's final days, kamikaze pilots flying every type of available aircraft damaged aircraft carriers *Wasp, Franklin, Hancock, Intrepid, Bunker Hill,* and *Enterprise,* as well as numerous other vessels. In all, approximately five thousand kamikaze crewmen in both army and navy units died during the war. Of 2,363 navy planes that participated in kamikaze missions, 1,189 completed their attacks.

Kamikazes proved to be one of the most effective weapons of the war. Although the numbers of available pilots and aircraft dwindled toward war's end, kamikazes inflicted horrendous losses on Allied ships and crews. In the battle for Okinawa the U.S. Navy lost 36 ships sunk, 368 damaged, 4,907 seamen killed or missing and 4,874 wounded, its highest losses for any Pacific campaign. The desperate kamikaze attacks were also instrumental in convincing the Americans to use the atomic bomb.

On August 15, 1945, the day after Japan's surrender, Vice Admiral Matome Ugaki, the Kyushu kamikaze commander, died leading an attack off Okinawa. Vice Admiral Takijiro Onishi, vice chief of the Naval General Staff and father of the kamikazes, committed suicide.

FURTHER READINGS

Griess, Thomas, ed. *The Second World War: Asia and the Pacific* (1984).

Liddell Hart, B. H. *History of the Second World War* (1970).

Okumiya, Masatake, Jiro Horikoshi, and Martin Caidin. *Zero!* (1956).

Parrish, Thomas, ed. *The Simon and Schuster Encyclopedia of World War II* (1978).

Jeff Kinard

SEE ALSO Army Air Force, Japanese; Navy, Japanese

Kelly, Colin (1915–1941)

Captain Colin P. Kelly, Jr., American hero of the early Pacific war, graduated from West Point in 1937 and joined the Army Air Corps. As a B-17 Flying Fortress commander and squadron operations officer for the 14th Bombardment Squadron, he flew his bomber to the Philippines in September 1941 as part of the War Department's efforts to reinforce General Douglas MacArthur's Philippine Army.

The 26-year-old Kelly and his eight-man crew were in their B-17 scouting for a Japanese aircraft carrier on De-

cember 10. No one saw a carrier, but they did spot heavy cruiser *Ashigara.* Kelly had only three 600-pound bombs on board, having been forced off the main bomber base of Clark Field to avoid an enemy raid. He flew a practice run on *Ashigara,* then returned and released all three bombs from 22,000 feet. Kelly's crew thought that one bomb had hit amidships. Smoke billowed from the cruiser, and an oil slick gleamed in the water. All was an illusion, however, for the bombs were near misses.

Kelly's attack drew the attention of no fewer than twenty-seven Japanese Zero fighters. The Zero pilots were covering an amphibious landing along Luzon's west coast at Vigan, and were surprised when they saw three water impact marks from Kelly's bombs near the *Ashigara.* They were even more surprised when they spotted just one unescorted B-17.

The Zeros had to use full throttle to catch the speeding bomber. Fifty miles north of Clark Field, the Japanese were almost in range. Suddenly, three Zeros from another force attacked Kelly. Their fire seemed to make no impression on Kelly's B-17. Seven of the Viga Zeros joined the newcomers and swung into a long file. Each plane made a solo attack and then gave way to the next.

After all the planes had made a pass, the Japanese pilots were flabbergasted. It did not seem that a single bullet or cannon shell had hit Kelly's plane. Both the Americans and the Japanese had a lot to learn about aerial combat in these first days of the Pacific war. The Zeros were inexperienced at attacking B-17s, and the large size of the bomber caused them to open fire at too great a range. The high speed of the B-17 also affected their aim. Kelly's gunners were busy during the attacks, although their fire was no more effective than that of the Zeros. Then one Zero pilot dived in close, directly for the tail, and two other Zeros closed up on him.

Kelly fishtailed the plane left and right to allow his waist gunners clear shots toward the rear (there were no tail guns in this early model B-17). Zero pilot Petty Officer Sakai Saburo opened fire. He sawed pieces off the bomber's right wing, killed one crewman, and created a fuel leak. In return, Kelly's gunners riddled the wings of two Zeros. Sakai continued to fire until the fuel leak geysered and he ran out of ammunition. Another Zero closed in. Kelly's bomber was now doomed. Three men bailed out of the burning aircraft at 7,000 feet. Then the bomber entered overcast, and the Japanese lost sight of their target. Kelly was trying to reach Clark Field, but he was not going to make it. He held the aircraft level enough for three more men to jump. When Kelly tried to follow them, the plane exploded, and he became tangled in the falling wreckage.

The Americans checked *Jane's Fighting Ships* to determine what Japanese warship Kelly had bombed, and they settled on battleship *Haruna* or a sister ship. The Japanese pilot credited with shooting Kelly down, Petty Officer Sakai, had once served aboard the *Haruna,* the very battleship the Americans claimed Kelly had sunk. Kelly was the first West Point aviator to die in World War II. A grateful nation, desperate for some good news, awarded him the Distinguished Service Cross for "sinking" the *Haruna.*

FURTHER READINGS

Brereton, Lewis H. *The Brereton Diaries: The War in the Air in the Pacific, Middle East and Europe 3 October 1941–8 May 1945* (1946).

McClendon, Dennis E., and Wallace F. Richards. *The Legend of Colin Kelly* (1994).

Sakai Saburo. *Samurai!* (1957).

John W. Whitman

Kempeitai

First established by order of the Meiji Council of State in 1881, the Kempeitai (individual officers were called kempei) was Japan's military police force, although it had responsibilities far beyond those of similar organizations in other nations.

Although originally organized to enforce conscription laws, the scope of Kempeitai responsibility expanded quickly. There were two distinct branches: the General Affairs section, which was responsible for maintaining discipline and "thought control" in the armed forces, and the Services Section, which engaged in police unit training, security, and counter-espionage. The Kempeitai's varied functions meant that the organization was responsible to three different cabinet ministries—the War Ministry for its normal military activities, the Home Affairs Ministry when it served as an auxiliary to the civil police, and the Justice Ministry in its law enforcement capacity. There were also Field Kempei Units (*yasen Kempeitai,* stationed outside Japan in the occupied territories, which were responsible to the commanders-in-chief of the various area armies to which they were assigned).

Until the late 1930s, the Kempeitai remained relatively small; in 1937, for instance, the organization had only about three hundred officers and six thousand lower ranks. The rise of General Hideki Tojo, however, gave the organization a powerful ally in the cabinet. Tojo had served as commander of the kempei unit attached to the Kwantung Army in Manchuria, and as war minister and, after October 1941, prime minister, he steadily worked to expand the organization's size and scope. By the time of Japan's surrender in August 1945 there were more than thirty-six thousand kempei stationed throughout Japan and its occupied areas.

Officers of the Kempeitai generally represented the elite of the Japanese armed forces. They tended to be more educated and in better physical condition than the ordinary soldier, and each was required to spend six years in specialized training, including espionage, explosives, fifth-column organization, code breaking, burglary, disguise, and horsemanship. There were special Kempeitai training centers in Tokyo and Seoul, Korea, and a third was established in newly conquered Singapore in 1942.

In performing their duties, the kempei had broad powers of arrest, not only among the military (where a kempei could arrest an officer up to three ranks higher than himself), but among the civilian population as well. Kempei normally wore army uniforms, but were recognizable by their white and black (or sometimes red and khaki) arm bands emblazoned with the characters *ken* (law) and *hei* (soldier). They were responsible for keeping order in civilian internment centers and prisoner-of-war camps, where they enforced the rules, interrogated prisoners, and forced them into slave labor for Japan's war effort. But it was in the occupied territories that they wielded the most authority. As the branch of the military responsible for relations with native communities, they were empowered to requisition food and supplies, conscript forced labor, combat Allied propaganda and espionage, and generally to use any means necessary—including beatings, rape, torture, and execution—to maintain order.

It is little wonder, then, that they soon came to be feared throughout Asia, developing a reputation comparable to that of the gestapo in Europe. Some of the better-known atrocities in which they were involved include the experiments in bacteriological warfare carried out in the infamous Japanese bacteriological warfare center in Manchukuo/Manchuria, the trial and execution of captured American airmen throughout the war, and the forced recruitment of women in the occupied areas to serve as prostitutes ("comfort women") to Japanese troops.

When the Japanese government made its decision to surrender in August 1945, the leadership recognized that the kempei were likely to be targeted for retribution by enemy soldiers and native populations. Indeed, in the final days some kempei, stationed in POW camps, and acting perfectly in character, ordered the massacre of all prisoners to prevent them from identifying Kempeitai personnel. The Imperial General Headquarters, therefore, instructed all officers to disperse and vanish into the population, so that only about fifteen hundred kempei fell into Allied hands. On October 30, 1945, General Douglas MacArthur, Supreme Commander for the Allied Powers, formally ordered the dissolution of the organization. In the Far East War Crimes Trials, former kempei were prosecuted for 619 incidents—roughly a quarter of all war crimes committed by the Japanese armed forces. The court sentenced no less than 447 to death for their role in these atrocities and 312 were actually executed. One hundred twenty-five more were sentenced to life imprisonment. To the relief of literally millions, this most sinister and brutal of the institutions of imperial Japan had finally been ended.

FURTHER READINGS

Deacon, Richard. *Kempeitai: The Japanese Secret Service Then and Now* (1990).

Lamont-Brown, Raymond. *Kempeitai: Japan's Dreaded Military Police* (1998).

John E. Moser

SEE ALSO Army, Japanese

Kenney, George C. (1889–1977)

In the Southwest Pacific theater overall direction of the war fell to the theater commander General Douglas MacArthur, but the geographic realities of that area made airpower vitally important. These conditions gave his air commander General George C. Kenney a critically important role in the planning and conduct of the Southwest Pacific campaigns.

George Churchill Kenney was born in Nova Scotia on August 6, 1889, but grew up in Boston, attending Massachusetts Institute of Technology for three years before leaving school to work as a civil engineer. He joined the Army as an aviation cadet in April 1917. As an observation pilot in France during World War I he shot down two enemy aircraft, earning several decorations for bravery. Kenney remained in the Army after the war, acquiring a broad background in air operations as a test pilot, instructor at the Air Corps Tactical School, commander, and staff officer.

Kenney landed in Australia in late July 1942 at a low point in the Allied fortunes. The surprise attacks by the Japanese at Pearl Harbor (1941) and in the Philippines had effectively wiped out the American air units in the Pacific. When Kenney arrived it appeared that the Imperial forces might invade Australia. His predecessor Major General George Brett had wrestled with a multitude of problems, including a lack of spare parts, too few aircraft, inappropriate tactics, and poor training. By June 1942, MacArthur had lost confidence in Brett's ability to win the air war.

Gaining the trust and confidence of Douglas MacArthur became one of Kenney's first priorities. Kenney outmaneuvered MacArthur's imperious chief of staff Major General Richard Sutherland to gain unrestricted access to the theater commander, while reorganizing the air command and replacing incompetent air officers.

Kenney believed gaining air superiority was an essential prerequisite to attempting any other kind of air, ground, or sea operation. In pursuit of this goal he bombed Japanese aircraft on the ground and attacked them in the air, the latter effort aided by the Allies' ability to intercept Japanese radio transmissions, providing early warning of enemy bombing raids. During the ongoing battle for control of the air he also used aircraft to isolate Japanese garrisons by bombing the ships bringing supplies to the island or attacking enemy supply lines on the land. He argued forcefully for using aircraft in this interdiction role, rather than bombing enemy positions at the front lines. Nevertheless Kenney had to dispatch aircraft on front-line missions during the fighting on New Guinea in the last half of 1942. His pilots had difficulty locating and attacking targets on the ground through the thick jungle canopy and at times could not identify friendly forces, resulting in several attacks on American troops.

After MacArthur eliminated the Japanese in eastern New Guinea in January 1943, the Joint Chiefs of Staff ordered him to advance up the coast of New Guinea before capturing the Japanese stronghold at Rabaul in New Britain. Capturing this base would eliminate the ability of the Japanese to control the South Pacific and allow MacArthur to reconquer the Philippines and move on to Japan.

Although most maps of the Southwest Pacific in early 1943 show the Japanese controlling a wide swath of territory, in reality their defensive perimeter depended on holding a few key areas along the coast of New Guinea and on island outposts. MacArthur's highly successful leap-frog strategy avoided the strongly held, but widely separated, Japanese garrisons. In carrying out these plans he depended on air power to gain air superiority, interdict men and supplies, harass enemy communications, transport Allied soldiers and material to battle, provide protection for shipping and amphibious assaults, and, if required, to fly in direct support of the ground fighting. In short, MacArthur's campaigns turned on the strategies Kenney had developed during the first offensive in New Guinea.

Kenney demonstrated great flexibility in carrying out the many missions he was assigned. Far earlier than his European counterparts, he realized that airmen had been overly optimistic about the ability of bombers to reach their targets without the protection of fighter aircraft. Kenney installed droppable external fuel tanks to increase the range of fighter aircraft, allowing them to accompany the bombers to their targets. He also shifted from the prewar doctrine of high-altitude bombing to low-altitude attacks on Japanese shipping. The most dramatic and public success of this change occurred during the Battle of the Bismarck Sea in early March 1943, when Kenney's airmen devastated a 16-ship convoy off the coast of New Guinea. The attack not only wiped out the reinforcements and their supplies, but also shocked the Japanese high command, and they abandoned further attempts at reinforcing eastern New Guinea.

In June 1943, MacArthur began a series of amphibious assaults along the northern coast of New Guinea aimed at controlling the Huon Peninsula. Through the rest of the year MacArthur's forces moved westward to outflank the Japanese position at Rabaul in a series of well-integrated air, land, and sea operations. Although MacArthur originally planned on invading Rabaul after gaining control of the Huon Peninsula, his advance through New Guinea, coupled with Admiral William "Bull" Halsey's control over the Solomons and Admiral Chester Nimitz's efforts in the Central Pacific, made it possible to bypass Rabaul. In April 1944, MacArthur proposed an invasion at Hollandia, a move which would put him 500 miles closer to the Philippines and avoid the strongest Japanese positions in New Guinea. This operation was too far for Kenney to provide air cover, and MacArthur was forced to rely on aircraft carriers for air support. Kenney argued forcefully against the plan, citing the limited range and small bombloads of the carriers planes, as well as the need for aircraft carriers to routinely stop flying operations to take on fuel, food, and ammunition. Despite Kenney's objections, the attack on Hollandia went on as planned and encountered no major problems.

With New Guinea secure, MacArthur began planning his return to the Philippines. Although the initial plan was to land in the southernmost island of Mindanao, Halsey, after meeting little resistance during bombing raids in the Philippines, suggested a landing on Leyte. Bypassing Mindanao meant no land-based air support, forcing MacArthur to once again rely on aircraft carriers for air support. This time Kenney wisely refrained from voicing any criticism.

Although the ground troops landing on Leyte on October 20, 1944, encountered little resistance, the campaign took much longer and was far costlier than anticipated, in part because the decision to rely solely on aircraft carriers forced American ground forces to fight without air superiority. Aircraft carriers ably covered the initial landing but, battered by Japanese surface and air attacks and in need of refurbishment, they departed soon after the invasion. At the same time, airfield construction on the island was slowed by heavy rains and took much longer than originally planned, further eroding the Allied air advantage.

Kenney and the other air commanders erred badly in their planning for Leyte. They discounted engineers' concerns about building the airfields and failed to recognize the differences between earlier campaigns and the battle for air superiority in the Philippines. In previous operations in the Central and Southwest Pacific the limited number of airfields had made it possible to destroy every aircraft on the ground and cut off the flow of replacement planes. Neither was possible in the Philippines. The number of airfields scattered throughout the islands allowed the Japanese to disperse their aircraft, making it exceedingly difficult to find and destroy all of them, while the relatively short distance between Japanese-held Formosa and Luzon allowed the Japanese to pour large numbers of reinforcements into the fighting. Changes in Japanese tactics exacerbated these miscalculations. In contrast to previous operations in which the Japanese sent out small numbers of aircraft, the steady flow of reinforcements allowed them to use large formations, and the deadly kamikaze attacks proved almost impossible to stop. Only after the Japanese withdrew their aircraft from the Philippines in early January 1945 did the air attacks stop.

Although the Japanese air effort slowed the ground fighting, they could not win the war, and American soldiers finally captured Manila in March 1945. Kenney turned his attention northward—first, in support of the landings at Okinawa with attacks on the airfields on Formosa, and, later, preparing for an American invasion of the Japanese home islands. In both cases, Kenney made few changes to the strategy he had developed during the course of the war: first gain air superiority, then cut off the battle area, and, finally, on the day of the assault, put every available aircraft over the landing area. In the end, the dropping of the atomic bombs and the entry of the Soviet Union into the war in 1945 made the planned invasion unnecessary.

Kenney's efforts as the air commander were boosted by several advantages. He served with a theater commander who learned to appreciate the benefits offered by air power. In addition, the ability to intercept and decode Japanese radio transmissions, even those of a routine nature, gave Kenney an extremely accurate picture of Japanese air strength and enabled him to choose lucrative targets for large, concentrated raids, such as bombing an airfield soon after the Japanese had sent in large numbers of reinforcements. Signals intelligence also provided early warning of an impending air raid and gave Allied fighters enough time to gain altitude and attack the Japanese formations before they reached their targets. Kenney also used signal intelligence to great advantage in sealing off the Japanese garrisons. Searching for and finding ships in the vast expanses of the ocean was not an easy task. Without advance knowledge of the Japanese sailing schedules, more aircraft would have been needed to discover enemy ship movements, leaving fewer available to attack other targets.

Knowledge about the enemy's capabilities and intentions explain only part of Kenney's success; equally important was having enough aircraft available to carry out the missions. He moved supply depots closer to the combat air bases and focused those working in the rear echelon on increasing the number of combat-ready aircraft. While pilots and other aviators received most of the publicity, Kenney realized the importance of the hard-working mechanics and armorers to winning the war, and searched for ways to raise their morale by awarding military decorations and improving living conditions. Although the number of aircraft in his command increased slowly, the total number of sorties flown grew rapidly, an indication of the strenuous efforts expended on flying the same few aircraft more often.

War is not a one-sided enterprise, and Kenney's strengths and methods exacerbated the weaknesses of the Japanese. They never seriously considered the possibility that their radio codes had been broken, nor were they able to break the codes used by the Allies—a sizable advantage in planning air operations. Likewise, Japanese aircraft production never kept pace with the American effort, while the supply and maintenance organizations of the Japanese air arms were woefully incompetent. Kenney's tactics also met with great success against the Japanese. The low-level attacks against merchant shipping were extremely effective and resulted in few losses, largely because the Japanese ships were only lightly armed and ill-equipped to defend themselves against air attacks. Similarly, the relatively few anti-aircraft guns and weaknesses in the air raid warning networks made low-altitude attacks against Japanese air bases effective.

Kenney's prewar experience prepared him well for his role while at the same time he proved capable of meeting a wide range of problems with innovative solutions, a formidable combination in any commander. He built and

maintained a strong and effective working relationship with MacArthur and focused on using air power to avoid large concentrations of enemy forces and outflank the enemy through the air. After gaining control of the skies by defeating the opposing air force, Kenney's airmen isolated enemy positions, supported the amphibious invasions, and transported troops and equipment to the battle area. Although the basic strategy of outflanking the enemy is as old as war itself, MacArthur's campaigns in the Southwest Pacific would not have been possible without intelligently applied air power. In this regard, General George C. Kenney, MacArthur's airman, proved instrumental to the Allied victory.

FURTHER READINGS

Griffith, Thomas E., Jr. *MacArthur's Airman: General George C. Kenney and the Air War in the Southwest Pacific* (1998).

Kenney, George C. *General Kenney Reports* (1949; reprinted, Office of Air Force History, 1987).

Wolk, Herman S. "George C. Kenney: MacArthur's Premier Airman," in *We Shall Return,* ed. William M. Leary, (1988).

———. "George C. Kenney: The Great Innovator," in *Makers of the United States Air Force,* ed. John L. Frisbee (Office of Air Force History, 1987).

Thomas E. Griffith, Jr.

SEE ALSO Army Air Corps/Air Forces, U.S.; Army Air Force, Japanese; MacArthur, Douglas

Kimmel, Husband Edward (1882–1968)

U.S. Naval officer. Husband Edward Kimmel was born in Henderson, Kentucky, on February 26, 1882, the son of Manning Marius and Sibbie (Lambert) Kimmel. His father, a West Point graduate, had served in the Confederate Army during the Civil War and later worked as a civil engineer and businessman. Kimmel attended Central University in Kentucky for a year before gaining an appointment to the U.S. Naval Academy in 1900. He graduated in 1904 and was commissioned an ensign in 1906 after sea duty and postgraduate study in gunnery at the Naval War College.

During the next ten years, Kimmel held a variety of assignments in which he earned a reputation as an expert in gunnery and ordnance. Following instruction in ordnance engineering at the Bureau of Ordnance in Washington, D.C., he served on the battleships *Georgia, Wisconsin,* and *Louisiana,* twice as assistant to the director of target practice at the Navy Department, as ordnance officer on the armored cruiser *California,* and as gunnery officer for the Pacific Fleet. He also participated in the Veracruz, Mexico, intervention of 1914 and served briefly as an aide to Assistant Secretary of the Navy Franklin D. Roosevelt in 1915.

After the United States entered World War I in 1917, Kimmel went to Great Britain to advise the Royal Navy on new techniques for gun spotting. He then became staff gunnery officer for the American battleship squadron attached to the Royal Navy's Grand Fleet. Following World War I, Kimmel held successively more important positions while rising to the rank of rear admiral in 1937; he was noted within the Navy for his professionalism and drive. Kimmel's assignments included service at the Naval Gun Factory in Washington, command of destroyer squadrons, student at the Naval War College, liaison officer between the Navy Department and the State Department, director of ship movements in the Office of the Chief of Naval Operations, commander of the battleship *New York,* chief of staff of the fleet's battleship command, and budget officer of the Navy.

From 1939 to 1941, Kimmel commanded a cruiser division and then all cruisers operating in the Battle Force of the Pacific Fleet. Kimmel's outstanding performance in the latter post led Secretary of the Navy Frank Knox in February 1941 to advance him to the temporary rank of full admiral and name him commander of the Pacific Fleet and commander of the United States Fleet. During the next months, Kimmel put the Pacific Fleet, stationed at Pearl Harbor, Hawaii, through a vigorous training program in preparation for a possible war with Japan, and also refined plans for offensive operations into the Marshall Islands beginning on the first day of war.

On December 7, 1941, carrier-based Japanese aircraft caught American forces in Hawaii off guard and at least temporarily put out of commission all of the battleships of the Pacific Fleet. Despite this devastating blow, Kimmel planned to use his three aircraft carriers, which had survived the attack because they were at sea, to relieve Wake Island. Before this operation could be concluded, however, Kimmel was relieved of his command on December 17. In early 1942, a special commission investigating the Pearl Harbor disaster, headed by U.S. Supreme Court associate justice Owen J. Roberts, judged that Kimmel was guilty of "dereliction of duty" in his command. The commission's finding led Kimmel to retire in disgrace on March 1, 1942, with the permanent rank of rear admiral. Shortly afterward, Kimmel was employed by an engineering consulting firm in New York, a position he held until retiring in 1947. At the same time, he faced a number of inquiries that lasted until 1946 into the Pearl Har-

bor disaster. A Navy court of inquiry in 1944 concluded that Kimmel was not guilty of any offense or responsible for the defeat. But Admiral Ernest J. King, Chief of Naval Operations, reversed the court's verdict and ruled that Kimmel had committed errors of omission in failing to institute air patrols to the north and northwest of Pearl Harbor, the direction from which the Japanese aircraft came, and that he had demonstrated that he "lacked superior judgment necessary for his post." A Joint Committee of Congress reinforced King's findings in 1946, charging that Kimmel was guilty of "errors of judgment."

In his defense, Kimmel and his supporters argued that authorities in Washington had denied him the intelligence and numbers of long-range aircraft that were necessary for him to discharge his duties properly and that he was made a scapegoat to cover up the failings of his superiors. Some even suggested that President Franklin D. Roosevelt knew of the Japanese attack ahead of time (and also knew ahead of time that Hitler would declare war on the United States) and had deliberately withheld vital intelligence from Kimmel in order to have Japan strike the "first blow," all as part of a plot to get the United States into war against Germany through the "back door." Kimmel's critics argued that he had been adequately informed to appreciate that Japanese-American relations were at the breaking point in early December 1941 but was not sufficiently alert. Like the authorities in Washington, Kimmel was aware that war was imminent, and like them, he shared the general belief that it would commence in the Far East and that an attack against Pearl Harbor, while a possibility, was not likely. Rather than focus on Japan's capabilities and all of its possible courses of action, he directed much of his attention to the operations he would undertake once the war was underway. In the final analysis, Kimmel, as the man on the spot, must bear a significant share of the responsibility for the Pearl Harbor defeat. While he was not always well served by the authorities in Washington, he was not prepared for war when it came. Kimmel died in Groton, Connecticut, on May 14, 1968.

FURTHER READINGS

Beach, Edward L. *Scapegoats: A Defense of Kimmel and Short at Pearl Harbor* (1995).

Costello, Joseph. *Days of Infamy* (1994).

Gailey, Harry A. *The War in the Pacific: From Pearl Harbor to Tokyo Bay* (1995).

Harris, James Russell. "Admiral Kimmel and Pearl Harbor: Heritage, Perception, and the Perils of Calculation," *The Filson Club History Quarterly* 68 (1994).

Kimmel, Husband E. *Admiral Kimmel's Story* (1956).

Morison, Samuel Eliot. *History of U.S. Naval Operations in World War II*, vol. 3, *The Rising Sun in the Pacific* (1948).

Prange, Gordon. *At Dawn We Slept: The Untold Story of Pearl Harbor* (1981).

Richardson, J. O. *On the Treadmill to Pearl Harbor* (1973).

Spector, Ronald H. *Eagle Against the Sun* (1985).

John Kennedy Ohl

SEE ALSO Pearl Harbor, Japanese Attack on; Short, Walter Campbell

King, Edward P. (1884–1958)

Commander of US-Filipino forces on Luzon at the time of the surrender to the Japanese, Edward P. King was born in Atlanta in 1884. He graduated from the University of Georgia in 1903 and then went on to the University of Georgia School of Law. King entered the U.S. Army through the Georgia National Guard in 1908.

King completed the U.S. Army Artillery School program and was posted to the Philippines in 1912, where he served as commander of Fort Stotsenburg. When he returned to the United States he served three times in the office of Chief of Field Artillery and attended the Command and General Staff School. King's talents were recognized and he served as an instructor at the Army War College and attended the Naval War College. While at the War College he served as Director of the War Plans Section. Upon his second posting to the Philippines, King was promoted to brigadier general.

In September 1940, King was assigned to the U.S. Army Forces Far East (USAFFE) as the artillery officer, and later served under General Douglas MacArthur. King was an artillery officer with a reputation for modesty and politeness, which made him popular with enlisted men and officers, both Filipinos and American. He also was an energetic staff officer who significantly improved the quality of the Philippine army artillery units. Despite the lack of modern equipment and incomplete equipment for the old pieces that were delivered, King managed to build a force that was the major problem for the Japanese once they landed. For a brief time King commanded North Luzon Force in December 1941. After MacArthur departed the Philippines in early 1942 following the Japanese invasion, and General Jonathan Wainwright assumed command of USAFFE, Wainwright appointed King to command Luzon Force on Bataan. King commanded a combined American-Filipino force of 80,000 divided into two corps, I and II, and a reserve, the Philippine Division.

The vast bulk of the command was made up of Philippine army units with limited equipment.

The whole of the force suffered from disease, malnutrition, and the fatigue of almost four months of constant fighting. It would fall to King to lead these troops in their last hopeless battle. King made minor adjustments to the formations before the Japanese attacked. His major energies were focused on matters of logistics.

On April 5, 1942, the Japanese opened their final offensive on Bataan. The exhausted and sick defenders put up stiff resistance. The I Corps forces were forced back and the ordered counterattacks stalled. On the morning of April 9, 1942, King, concerned for the survival of his troops, surrendered. Despite orders from MacArthur and protests from some of his subordinates, King made the most difficult decision of his life and capitulated.

King had expected better treatment of his troops by the Japanese. But the Bataan death march killed more of King's men than did the fighting. The commander marched into captivity with his men and was repatriated after the war in August 1945. On several occasions King suffered at the hands of his captors and endured numerous near-fatal illnesses. He died in North Carolina in 1958.

FURTHER READINGS

Morton, Louis. *United States Army in World War II: The War in the Pacific—The Fall of the Philippines.* U.S. Army Office of the Chief of Military History (1953).

Rutherford, Ward. *Fall of the Philippines* (1971).

Toland, John. *But Not in Shame* (1961).

Jim Birdseye

SEE ALSO Army, U.S.-Filipino; Bataan Death March

King, Ernest J. (1878–1956)

U.S. Chief of Naval Operations through most of the Pacific war, Ernest King was born in Cleveland on November 23, 1878, and rose to command the largest navy in history, totaling more than eight thousand ships, twenty-four thousand aircraft, and about three million people. Noted throughout his career for his candor and bluntness, Admiral King guided the U.S. Navy in its most difficult days, often shaping Allied strategy in the Navy's favor by sheer force of will. An anglophobe who deeply distrusted the British, Admiral King fought any proposal that detracted from the Pacific campaign, which he saw as America's primary theater of war. His obstinance often interfered with overall Allied strategy, but that same stubbornness enabled him to overcome obstacles inhibiting the construction of the ships, submarines and aircraft needed to support a worldwide war effort. As such, he stands out as one of the war's major figures.

Accepted into the U.S. Naval Academy in 1897, Admiral King first saw action by finagling his way aboard cruiser *Indianapolis* during the Spanish American War. Graduating in 1901, he first served as navigator aboard survey ship *Eagle* before moving on to the new battleship *Illinois* for its European "show-the-flag" cruise of 1902. It was aboard this ship that he passed his exam for ensign and was commissioned in 1903. An aggressive and forthright officer, he seemed destined for greatness except for two weaknesses which his superiors noted in his official record: drinking and an arrogance that almost bordered on insubordination. The former he corrected, at least publicly. The latter stayed with him to his grave.

King served in a variety of sea tours in weapons, administration, and engineering between 1903 and 1909, including a brief tour as an instructor at the Naval Academy. He went from there to duty as flag secretary to the commander of the Atlantic fleet. He returned to the Naval Academy three years later as commander of the Experimental Station. That duty was followed by successive tours as commander of two destroyers and a four-ship destroyer squadron. He was then selected to be the engineering officer on the staff of Admiral Henry Mayo, commander of the Battleship Force, Atlantic Fleet, in 1915. He followed Admiral Mayo when the admiral became Commander of the Atlantic Fleet later that year. Two years later, Admiral Mayo and his staff took the Atlantic Fleet to Europe as the United States entered World War I. It was a profound experience, attending planning conferences and dealing with the Washington and Royal Navy bureaucracies. King came away from it with a strong appreciation for the difficulties of commanding a fleet at war and a deeply ingrained contempt for bureaucracies.

But his personality won him few friends, and he found himself commanding a supply ship after the war. He was then given command of the submarine station in New London, Connecticut. It was there that he first came to national prominence by raising the sunken submarine, *S-51*. Still unable to get a surface command, Captain King leaped at the opportunity to command seaplane tender *Wright,* in an aviation unit. That was followed by a brief tour as assistant head of the Aeronautics Bureau and then finally, command of the great aircraft carrier *Lexington* in June 1930. Two years later, he transferred to the Naval War College.

Selected to flag rank in August 1932, Rear Admiral King took charge of the Aeronautics Board just as the worst of the Great Depression struck. It was a difficult time in that the economy was forcing cuts in all aspects of government spending. Admiral King quickly learned how to deal with Congress, cajoling and lobbying aggressively to retain funding of aviation programs. Many of the aircraft he fostered provided great service in the war (for example, the PBY Catalina seaplane). In 1935, he was given command of the Pacific Scouting Force out of San Diego. He made Vice Admiral in 1938 and took command of Aviation Forces and Bases, a position that gave him control over five aircraft carriers and all Pacific Fleet shore-based aircraft. In that capacity, he became the first senior officer to advocate the detachment of the faster aircraft carriers from the battleships to conduct independent strikes, escorted only by destroyers and fast cruisers. Unfortunately, it was an idea beyond the vision of the Navy's leadership at the time.

Admiral King was moved to the Navy's General (advisory) Board as a Rear Admiral in 1939, a significant demotion that signaled he was headed for retirement. The reason for this assignment has never been clarified, but many felt that it was due to King's drinking and crude, acerbic personality. It is more likely that he had no friends in high places to sponsor his further advancement.

King was saved in 1940 by a chance selection to accompany the secretary of the navy on a fact-finding mission. Impressed by King's vision and drive, Secretary Charles Edison urged President Franklin D. Roosevelt to appoint King as commander of what would become the Atlantic Fleet, a position King attained as a four-star admiral in February 1941. He was appointed commander of the U.S. Fleet on December 17, 1941. In that position, he had authority over all Navy bureaus and departments and was answerable directly to the president. He also became one of the primary members of the Combined Allied Staff for the prosecution of the war. He went on to become Chief of Naval Operations in March 1942.

A strong advocate of the Pacific campaign, Admiral King alternately supported and opposed General George C. Marshall's "second front" plans in order to gain the most resources he could to fight Japan. He contested General Douglas MacArthur's views on Pacific strategy, opposing the assault on the Philippines. He was just as forceful with the civilian bureaus and companies that built his ships and supplied his fleet. He wanted the best ships and aircraft money could buy, but at prices the nation could afford. As before the war, his domineering personality made him few friends. Several well-authenticated anecdotes illustrate the man: His daughter said that her father was "even tempered, he's just mad all the time," and President Roosevelt joked that his Chief of Naval Operations "shaved with a blow torch." Admiral King retired in December 1945 and began work on his memoirs. He died following a series of strokes on June 25, 1956.

Tough, competitive and parochial, he was the strongest leader the U.S. Navy has ever known. He was a visionary in the fullest sense of the word. In addition to his views on carrier airpower, he forced the Navy to develop the fleet train concept that was so critical to the Pacific campaign (enabling ships to be supplied and repaired without returning to home bases). No other officer has had such complete authority over so large a navy institutions and few could have wielded it so well.

FURTHER READINGS
Keegan, John, ed. *Who Was Who in World War II* (1984).
King, Ernest J., and W. M. Whitehall. *Fleet Admiral King* (1952).
Pfannes, Charles E., and Victor Salamone. *The Great Admirals of World War II,* volume I (1983).

Carl O. Schuster

SEE ALSO Navy, U.S.

Knox, Frank (1874–1944)

U.S. secretary of the navy from 1940 until his death in 1944. Frank Knox presided over the dramatic expansion of U.S. naval forces after the United States entered World War II (1941) and fought a two-front naval war in the Atlantic and Pacific. A prominent Republican politician, Knox was appointed navy secretary by President Franklin D. Roosevelt, a Democrat, as part of FDR's attempt to expand bipartisan support for his foreign policy.

William Franklin Knox was born in Boston. A graduate of Harvard, he served with Theodore Roosevelt's Rough Riders in the Spanish-American War (1898). In 1901, Knox became the publisher of a newspaper in Sault Ste. Marie, Michigan. During World War I, which the United States entered in 1917, Knox served as an officer in the U.S. Army. He returned to the newspaper business after the war, and in 1927 moved to Boston, where he took charge of the *Boston American and Advertiser.* In 1928 he was appointed general manager of all the Hearst newspapers. In 1931, Knox bought controlling interest in the *Chicago Daily News,* and he remained its publisher until 1940.

Strongly committed to the Republican Party, Knox was nominated for the vice presidency as Alfred M. Landon's running mate in 1936. The Landon-Knox ticket was crushed in the general election, winning a mere 8 electoral votes to Roosevelt's 531.

Knox was a consistent opponent of FDR's domestic New Deal, but in foreign policy, he, like Roosevelt, was an internationalist who believed that the United States could not retreat into isolationism and was destined to play a role in an increasingly unstable world. Roosevelt believed that America's involvement in the war in Europe, which had broken out with Germany's invasion of Poland in 1939, was unavoidable. In an effort to gain support in the Republican Party for his foreign policy, he appointed two prominent Republicans to his cabinet in 1940. Henry L. Stimson, former secretary of war under President William Howard Taft and secretary of state (1929–1933) under President Herbert Hoover, was appointed secretary of war, and Frank Knox was appointed secretary of the navy.

At the time of Knox's appointment, the navy had some one thousand vessels in its inventory. By the end of the war, that number had increased to more than fifty thousand. A navy of some one hundred sixty thousand personnel in 1941 had also increased to more than 3.4 million. Knox died in office in 1944 and was succeeded by James V. Forrestal.

FURTHER READINGS
Marolda, Edward S. *FDR and the U.S. Navy* (Franklin and Eleanor Roosevelt Institute Series on Diplomatic and Economic History, 1998).

Richard Steins

SEE ALSO Navy, U.S.

Kobayashi Ichizo

A former president of the Tokyo Electricity Board, Kobayashi was named minister of commerce and industry in the second cabinet of Prince Fumimaro Konoe.

In September 1940, Konoe appointed Kobayashi to head an economic mission to the Dutch East Indies. The United States had only recently reduced its oil exports to Japan, to protest the occupation of northern Indochina. The Kobayashi delegation was to try to obtain Japanese access to the oil, rubber, and tin resources of the Dutch East Indies, or, failing that, to negotiate the simple purchase of oil. The mission, however, ran into trouble from the start. The Dutch became particularly apprehensive about dealing with the Japanese after it was announced that Japan had on September 27 concluded the Tripartite Pact with Germany and Italy. (It should be remembered that the Japanese were dealing with a Dutch government-in-exile; Germany had overrun the Netherlands in May 1940.) The Indies government feared that any oil shipped to Japan might be used, directly or indirectly, to assist the

German war effort, and thus they began to employ various delaying tactics. Because Kobayashi lacked specific instructions, the negotiations produced nothing more than an agreement by the Dutch to sell Japan less than 1.5 million tons of crude, far below what Tokyo had initially anticipated. Kobayashi returned to Japan in late October, believing that the last chance for a peaceful settlement of Japan's increasingly desperate oil situation had been lost. The cabinet decided soon after that the Dutch East Indies would have to be forced to sever its ties with the United States and Britain and become part of the Greater East Asia Co-Prosperity Sphere.

In July 1941, Kobayashi further distinguished himself as the only member of the cabinet to warn that Japan lacked the resources to support a land war in Asia and a naval war with the United States simultaneously. As a civilian, however, his views were discounted.

FURTHER READINGS

Ike, Nobutaka, ed. *Japan's Decision for War: Records of the 1941 Policy Conferences* (1967).

Barnhart, Michael A. *Japan Prepares for Total War: The Search for Economic Security* (1987).

Lu, David J. *From the Marco Polo Bridge to Pearl Harbor* (1961).

John E. Moser

Konoe Fumimaro (1891–1945)

Konoe served as prime minister of Japan on three occasions between 1937 and 1941. A member of a distinguished family and a personal confidante of the emperor, he was undeniably the most prestigious civilian politician of pre–Pearl Harbor Japan.

Konoe was born into the ancient Fujiwara clan, a politically powerful family that was distantly related to the emperor himself. He studied philosophy and law at Kyoto Imperial University, where he became attracted to European radical thought. In 1916, at the age of 25, Konoe assumed his family's hereditary seat in the House of Peers. In his early years in politics he became the protege of Prince Kimmochi Saionji, former prime minister and eminent liberal. Indeed, one of the prince's earliest legislative efforts was his push for universal manhood suffrage, a campaign that gave a tremendous boost to his popularity among the masses. Yet differences between Konoe and Saionji soon developed in the field of foreign policy when the pair served in the Japanese delegation to the Paris Peace Conference in 1919 that ended World War I. Konoe, to his mentor's dismay, was outspokenly critical of the treaties drafted at Paris, which he claimed were

nothing more than a cover for Anglo-American global hegemony. Moreover, he argued, "have-not" nations such as Japan had a right to resort to force in order to overturn an unjust international system. Eleven years later, when Japanese troops occupied Manchuria, Konoe's was among the loudest voices defending the move, which was denounced in the rest of the world.

Such views, as one might imagine, made the young prince quite popular among powerful circles in the military and various ultra-nationalist organizations, who in turn assisted his rise to political prominence. In 1921 he was elected president of the Imperial Diet and was elected vice president of the House of Peers ten years later.

As the military gained in political strength in the 1930s, Konoe increasingly appeared to be the only politician both acceptable to the military and capable of restraining it. Therefore Saionji, despite his concerns about his protege's ideas on foreign policy, began to press the prince to accept the position of prime minister.

In June 1937, when Konoe was only 46 years of age, he assumed the prime ministership for the first time. His immediate priority was to draft a law granting amnesty to all members of militaristic, ultra-nationalist organizations who had plotted to overthrow the government in the early- to mid-1930s. That project was soon overshadowed, however, by events in China. In July, Japanese troops exchanged fire with Chinese Nationalist forces at the Marco Polo Bridge, just outside Peking. Konoe sought a quick settlement of the affair but feared that there was nothing that the government could do to restrain an army bent on conquest in China. Thus, when hostilities spread to the port of Shanghai, Konoe and his cabinet quickly approved the dispatch of several divisions from the Japanese home islands to China. The so-called "China Incident," therefore, rapidly escalated from a local skirmish to a full-scale war.

In November 1938, Konoe announced Japan's terms for ending the war in China. These demands, which came to be known as the "Konoe Principles," included recognition of Japan's satellite regime in Manchukuo (Manchuria), joint cooperation between Japan and China against communism, and economic cooperation in the development of certain parts of North China. Japan, he claimed, sought nothing less than the establishment of a "New Order" in Asia, in which China, Japan, and Manchukuo would work together to protect Asia from communism and western imperialism alike. While seemingly mild, however, the specifics concerning the implementation of the Konoe Principles were far harsher and included the indefinite stationing of Japanese troops in

North China. These terms were resoundingly rejected by the Nationalist leader, Chiang Kai-shek.

As the China war ground on with no hope of a quick conclusion, Konoe made repeated attempts to resign his position. He was dissuaded from this on several occasions in 1938, but was finally allowed to resign in January 1939. He immediately moved into the largely ceremonial post of President of the Privy Council. In June 1940 he resigned from that position as well, ostensibly to dedicate himself full-time to the establishment of a new political order for Japan. This new order, as he envisioned it, would arise spontaneously from among the people, overthrowing the current Western-style party system, which he claimed was corrupt and incapable of governing Japan in a changing world. The new order would replace political and economic liberalism—denounced as "un-Japanese"—with a renewed notion of service to the emperor and the state.

Konoe's message resonated with a Japanese public still in the thrall of economic depression. Yet he remained vague about how the new order would actually function and how it would be constituted. As a result, a wide variety of groups, both military and civilian, rallied to Konoe's banner, hoping to use the former prime minister's immense prestige and popularity to advance their own agendas. The result was the formation of the *Kokuhonsha*, the New Order Movement.

Yet Konoe could not remain out of the government for long. In July 1940 the army engineered the fall of the cabinet of Mitsumasa Yonai, who was viewed as too pro-Western, and persuaded Konoe to assume the prime minister's post once more. The second Konoe cabinet included the ardent militarist Hideki Tojo as war minister and the nationalist firebrand Yosuke Matsuoka as foreign minister. Over Tojo's appointment Konoe had no control, for by the late 1930s the choice for that position lay entirely with the army. Responsibility for naming Matsuoka as foreign minister, however, lay squarely with the prime minister. Japanese moderates had serious misgivings about his strong anti-Western rhetoric, and even the emperor suggested that Konoe might reconsider his decision. But the prince was attracted to those with strong and unconventional personalities, and he viewed Matsuoka as an ideal choice to direct Japan's new course in foreign affairs.

Domestically, Konoe's first order of business was the overhaul of the political system in an attempt to create a strong national defense state capable of carrying the China war to a successful conclusion. The major political parties, eager to prove their patriotism, obligingly dissolved themselves, their leaders accepting positions of power within the New Order. In their place the *Taisei-youkusankai*—loosely translated as the Imperial Rule Assistance Association—took control of the government on October 12. Japan had become a totalitarian state, though unlike the regimes of Germany, Italy, or the Soviet Union, the Imperial Rule Assistance Association did not require a charismatic leader to serve as the center of a cult of personality. In keeping with Japanese culture and tradition, decisions would be made by way of consensus carefully formed among the leadership, not by the edict of a single dictator.

The creation of a new order at home was accompanied by vigorous efforts to realize Konoe's dream of a novel order for Asia. In September 1940, Japanese troops occupied the northern half of the French colony of Indochina, thus opening a new southern front against the Chinese Nationalists. Five days later Japan signed the Tripartite Pact, an alliance binding Japan's fate to that of Germany and Italy. Konoe had no particular love for Nazi Germany but viewed the pact as a means of avoiding diplomatic isolation. Furthermore, he saw it as a means of improving relations with the Soviet Union, bringing the China war to an end, and most important, dissuading the United States from further involvement in Asia. The Tripartite Pact failed to achieve the first two goals and accomplished the exact opposite of the third; far from turning the United States away from Asia, it led to an American embargo of scrap metal and several other materials vital to the Japanese war effort.

This strong reaction by the United States to Japan's new course gave Konoe pause. He had counted on American preoccupation with Europe in order for Japan to achieve its goals in Asia, and he was terrified by the thought of war with the United States. The prime minister instructed Matsuoka to give priority to negotiations with the Washington, and when the foreign minister balked at this, Konoe authorized continued talks through less official channels. When Matsuoka began to demand that negotiations with the United States be broken off altogether, the prince went to the extreme of resigning on July 17, 1941, only to reconstitute his government three days later with a new foreign minister, the far more moderate Admiral Teijiro Toyoda.

While negotiations continued with the United States, the need remained for sources of raw materials to replace those being embargoed by Washington. On July 28, 1941, Japanese forces entered the southern half of Indochina—another step on the road to Konoe's new order in Asia. Washington responded by freezing Japanese assets in the United States and by banning all oil exports to Japan. The situation was becoming desperate indeed, for Japan was almost completely dependent on U.S. oil.

As the military began to clamor for war, Konoe became convinced that only a personal meeting between himself and President Franklin D. Roosevelt could settle matters once and for all. Tojo and the military were skeptical, for they had by this time reached the conclusion that the United States would accept nothing less than full withdrawal from China. They agreed to go along, however, but insisted on a deadline for negotiations. If no breakthrough were reached by October 15, plans would go ahead for war with the United States.

Roosevelt, for his part, was initially receptive to the idea of a meeting, even going so far as to suggest Juneau, Alaska, as a possible location, but he was dissuaded by his secretary of state, Cordell Hull. Before any meeting could be held between the two leaders, Hull insisted that some understanding be reached regarding key issues such as China, Indochina, and the Tripartite Pact. Otherwise, he warned, any meeting might imply American endorsement of the Japanese position; the result would be, in Hull's words, an "Asian Munich." Konoe, however, was prevented by Tojo from making any promises in advance, and his long sought after diplomatic breakthrough failed to materialize. When the October 15 deadline arrived, Konoe, unwilling to accept the prospect of war with the United States, resigned as prime minister for the final time. When no civilian politician stepped forward to succeed him, Tojo himself set up a new cabinet.

Konoe was never optimistic about Japan's chances in a war against the United States, even during the heady days of victory in early 1942. In 1944 he became one of the first prominent Japanese leaders to call for an early end to the fighting (at a time when any common civilian would have been tortured and shot by the infamous "thought police" for such opinions). He began to advance the theory that the war had actually been engineered by "communistic" forces within the military, who hoped that a war would trigger revolution. In February 1945 he spoke to the emperor, telling him that the war was already lost and that only a quick peace could avert communist revolution. To that end he offered to go to the Soviet Union to seek Stalin's help in ending the war. The U.S.S.R., however, declared war on Japan before any such visit could take place (August 1945).

With the arrival of the American occupiers after the end of hostilities, Konoe hoped to have some role in the postwar reconstruction of Japan. He met with the Allied commander, General Douglas MacArthur, who encouraged his continued participation. But when the former prime minister formed a committee to draft a new constitution for the new government of Japan, the occupiers quickly began to distance themselves from his efforts. On December 6, MacArthur's headquarters announced that Konoe's name had been added to the list of those to be arrested for alleged war crimes. Devastated, Konoe committed suicide rather than suffer the indignity of a trial. He was condemned posthumously for his role in bringing totalitarianism to Japan.

Contemporary accounts before Pearl Harbor tended to portray Konoe as a moderate, if not a liberal, who fought to control the military; indeed, the prince himself did a great deal to encourage this characterization in his attempts to negotiate with the United States. After Pearl Harbor this changed, and he came to be viewed as a mere tool of Tojo and the army. More recent scholarship, however, has shown both of these interpretations to be oversimplifications. Konoe saw himself first and foremost as an aristocrat, not a politician. He disliked the increasing political power of the military in the 1930s, but saw an aggressive foreign policy as a means of providing an outlet for their nationalist aspirations. Nevertheless, in times of trouble he was prone to attacks of what one of his contemporaries called "weak nerves." Crises both foreign and domestic tended to paralyze him, often triggering real or imagined illnesses; indeed, *Time* magazine called him the "divine hypochondriac" and claimed that he had "spent one-half of the days since he was 25 in bed."

In the end, it can be said that Konoe failed to appreciate the relationship of means to ends. He had grandiose visions of a new order for Asia but was unwilling to face the risk of war that was implicit in creating such an order. Likewise, he strove to create a totalitarian state in Japan but shrank from the sorts of methods employed by other one-party regimes (Germany, Italy, or the Soviet Union) to crack down on dissent. As historian F. C. Jones wrote of him, "he was a man of weak and irresolute character, prone to take the line of least resistance, to procrastinate as much as possible, and to lay down the burden of office when evasion would no longer serve him." Perhaps during a less turbulent period Konoe would have made an admirable leader, but in the climate of pre–Pearl Harbor Japan, he proved utterly unfit for office.

FURTHER READINGS

Berger, Gordon M. *Parties Out of Power in Japan, 1931–1941* (1977).

Boyle, John H. *China and Japan at War 1937–1945: The Politics of Collaboration* (1972).

Butow, Robert J. C. *Tojo and the Coming of War* (1961).

Ike, Nobutaka (ed.). *Japan's Decision for War: Records of the 1941 Policy*.

Jones, F. C. *Japan's New Order in East Asia* (1954).

Lu, David J. *From the Marco Polo Bridge to Pearl Harbor* (1961).

Oka, Yoshitake. *Konoe Fumimaro: A Political Biography* (1983).

John E. Moser

Korea and Koreans

The surrender of Japan on August 14, 1945, brought Japanese rule to an end on the Korean peninsula. It also brought to an end Korea's participation in the war in the Pacific. Korea's involvement in the war was part and parcel of the Japanese occupation and administration of the Korean peninsula under the auspices of Japan's Greater East Asia Co-Prosperity Sphere. Japan, eager to exploit the natural resources as well as the manpower available on the Korean peninsula, developed the Korean economy through the construction of heavy industry and modernization of agriculture. Koreans were conscripted as laborers. Korean men fought in the Japanese army or, at the behest of Japanese colonial authorities, were utilized as slave labor on the Japanese mainland and around the Pacific basin. Thousands of young Korean women and girls were forced into prostitution as so-called comfort women who were shipped to front-line Japanese army units during the war in the Pacific.

For Japan, Korea was to be an inexpensive export granary as well as a market for Japanese finished goods. Thus, the modernization of the infrastructure included the construction of roads and railways, such as the high-speed rail line connecting of the port city of Pusan with Seoul, designed to expedite trade with Japan. Industrialization was concentrated in only Hamgyong and Kyonggi provinces and was limited to heavy industry to meet the needs of the growing Japanese economy. This increased level of economic industrialization further bound the Japanese and Korean economies.

Japan also sought to mobilize the Koreans themselves and to inculcate Japanese values in the Korean populace. As part of their mobilization scheme, the Japanese closed Korean-language schools and forced Korean children into Japanese-language schools. The speaking and reading of Korean were forbidden, even outside schools. Korean language newspapers were closed. Propaganda emphasized Japanese cultural and social values, and any form of dissent was quickly silenced. Koreans were required to recite "loyalty" oaths such as the "Pledge for Imperial Subjects" and were also required to visit Shinto shrines to demonstrate their loyalty. Japan's assimilation policy reached its zenith at the onset of the war in the Pacific when the Japanese invited the Korean people to adopt Japanese names in place of their personal Korean names. The concept of Confucian filial piety was extremely important and respected in Korean society, but the Japanese sought to sever Koreans' ties to their past and their ancestors. Japan justified its policies by claiming that it was bringing morality and economic development to Korea, and that the privileged position of the Japanese was based on their moral superiority.

The impact of the second Sino-Japanese War, which began in July 1937, was immediately felt on the Korean peninsula. Korean commerce and industry displaced the disrupted Chinese labor markets and exports to Manchukuo and northern China. Korean entrepreneurs followed the Japanese military into Manchukuo, supplying the increasing needs of the Japanese army as well as the Japanese-installed colonial administration of Manchukuo. War-related industries such as petrochemicals and textiles were quickly expanded while the development of heavy machinery and machine tools was rapidly increased. Yet, while Korean industry expanded, conditions at home deteriorated rapidly. Many Koreans died from disease, from shortages of medicine, and in workplace accidents.

The beginning of mass participation by Korean civilians in the Japanese war effort began in 1938, when a special government edict allowed young Korean boys and men to volunteer in the Japanese Imperial Army as "special army volunteers." The Japanese army utilized these Korean volunteers as cheap labor to develop and exploit the rich natural resources in Manchuria. It was at this time that the Japanese formed the so-called "Comfort Corp" a euphemism for organized houses of prostitution that included thousands of Korean comfort women who served the sexual needs of front-line Japanese troops. Young girls, often from rural hamlets, were tricked into the Comfort Corp with promises of well-paying jobs. Instead, these young girls, far from home, were forced to serve as prostitutes for the Japanese army.

But increased manpower needs throughout the Japanese empire eventually deprived the nascent Korean industry of Japanese managers, while Korea's resources were allocated to support Japan's increased war effort. Korean oil refineries, cement plants, and machine-tool factories provided much-needed supplies for Japan's war effort. Since most avenues for advancement required acquiescence to Japanese dominion, many Koreans chose to collaborate with the Japanese. A few hard-working and industrious Koreans managed to become engineers, technicians and businessmen who later constituted the core of the Korean economic miracle.

The onset of American involvement in the war in the Pacific increased the manpower needs of an already overstretched Japan. The war with the United States meant increased hardship as Japan now fought on a broad range front, from New Guinea in the South Pacific to Burma in Southeast Asia. After 1941, increasing numbers of Koreans were conscripted as labor to work in Japan and others parts of Japan's Greater East Asia Co-Prosperity Sphere. Koreans workers labored in the mines and factories of northern Korea, Manchuria, and Japan. Koreans also served as prison camp guards in Manchuria as well as in building military facilities in northern Korea and China. School days were shortened, and students were required to labor on construction projects and in the fields in an effort to mobilize every available worker.

By 1943, the Japanese were using forced conscription of Korean males to supply the need for soldiers and slave laborers. The Japanese began forcibly removing Koreans to northern Korea, Manchuria, and the Japanese mainland in order to meet the increasing labor needs of wartime Japan. Koreans were later drafted to serve in support roles for the Japanese army in the war around the Pacific basin. By the end of 1944, no fewer than 4 million Koreans lived outside Korea.

Japan's surrender on August 14, 1945, brought an end to Japan's domination and exploitation of Korea. Japan's occupation of Korea had seen both the economy and Korean society change. During the war in the Pacific, Korea had become linked to Japan both economically and socially. Rapid industrialization had led many Koreans from small towns and hamlets to work in the factories that fueled Japan's war effort. Korean industry had become inexorably linked with that of Japan, tying cheap agricultural imports with the export of finished goods. Significant numbers of Koreans resided outside Korea by 1945. But the Korean infrastructure had been run down during the war years, and the Japanese legacy to Korea, aside from a skeletal infrastructure, was the bitter and long-lasting resentment by Koreans of all things Japanese.

FURTHER READINGS

Chang Yunshik. *Colonization as Planned Change: The Korean Case* (1971).

Dong Wongho. "Assimilation and Social Mobilization in Korea" in Nahm, Andrew (ed.) *Korea Under Japanese Colonial Rule* (1973).

Eckert, Carter J., Ki-baik Lee, Young Ick Lew, Michael Robinson, and Edward Wagner. *Korea Old and New: A History* (1990).

Hicks, George. *The Comfort Women; Sex Slaves for the Japanese Imperial Forces* (1995).

Howard, Keith. *True Stories of the Korean Comfort Women* (1996).

Lone, Stewart, and Gavan McCormack. *Korea Since 1850* (1993).

Myers, Ramon H., and Mark R. Peattie, eds. *The Japanese Colonial Empire, 1895–1945* (1984).

Tennant, Roger. *A History of Korea* (1996).

Keith A. Leitich

SEE ALSO Army, Japanese; Comfort Women; Greater East Asia Co-Prosperity Sphere; Manchuria

Krueger, Walter (1881–1967)

General Walter Krueger served as General Douglas MacArthur's senior ground forces commander in the Southwest Pacific from 1943 to 1945. Born in Flatow, West Prussia (now Zlotow, Poland), the son of a Prussian army officer, Krueger's family emigrated to the United States when he was 8 years old. Caught up in the patriotic fervor of the day, he left high school at the outbreak of the Spanish-American War (1898), enlisted in the army, and went on to serve in Cuba and the Philippines, rising from the rank of private to that of lieutenant.

Deciding on a military career, Krueger experienced a variety of command, staff, and academic assignments. He gained considerable attention among his peers by translating Colonel William Balck's *Tactics,* a highly regarded study by a German authority on tactical principles that was adopted by U.S. Army service schools. Following duty in France during World War I, Krueger attended senior staff colleges, then held a series of ever-higher commands that culminated in his promotion to lieutenant general in 1941 and to leadership of Third U.S. Army.

Krueger hoped for a combat assignment following U.S. entry into World War II but instead was given training duties. He performed this task with characteristic energy and skill as he helped transform a flood of volunteers and draftees into an effective fighting force. In January 1943, to Krueger's great delight, MacArthur selected the 62-year-old soldier to command the new Sixth Army in the Southwest Pacific. The appointment was based both on MacArthur's respect for Krueger's abilities and his desire to place a senior U.S. officer in charge of ground forces in the chain of command under the Australian General Thomas Blamey.

Krueger arrived in Australia to find the men of his new command scattered over two thousand miles, poorly supplied, ravaged by disease, and generally dispirited. He immediately took action to restore the fighting efficiency of his troops. Thanks to his tireless and effective efforts, by May 1943, Sixth Army (which first went into action under the designation of Alamo Force) was ready to embark on MacArthur's ambitious strategic plan for isolating the major Japanese base of Rabaul.

Krueger's soldiers first seized the islands of Kiriwina and Woodlark, north of the southwestern tip of New Guinea; these became the site for air bases to support MacArthur's drive along the northern coast of New Guinea. In a series of amphibious operations over a 6-month period, Sixth Army/Alamo Force advanced from Lae to Mandang, then landed at Arawe and Cape Gloucester and seized western New Britain.

The pace of operations accelerated in 1944. In February, Krueger's forces assaulted the Admiralty Islands, completing the encirclement of Rabaul. Sixth Army then continued its drive along the northern coast of New Guinea, with hard-fought battles from Hollandia-Atape to Sanspor. By the end of the summer, the Japanese forces on New Guinea had been defeated.

Obviously pleased with the performance of Sixth Army's commander, MacArthur selected Krueger to lead the assault on Leyte in the Philippines. Americans returned to the Philippines in October 1944, but it took until December to defeat a tenacious Japanese foe. During the campaign, 56,263 Japanese soldiers died; Sixth Army lost 2,888 killed and 9,850 wounded.

The Leyte campaign proved only a preliminary to the battle for the main Philippine island of Luzon, which began in January 1945. During the drive on Manila, an impatient MacArthur clashed with his senior field commander. Anxious to occupy Manila by his birthday, MacArthur pressed Krueger for more aggressive action. Krueger, however, refused to commit his forces before receiving reinforcements. MacArthur, Krueger noted, could have ordered an assault, "but he refrained from directing me . . . to take a risk I considered unjustifiable with the forces available to me at the time."

Following the capture of Manila in early March, Sixth Army was assigned the arduous task of engaging the main Japanese forces on Luzon, which were strongly entrenched in the mountainous terrain east and north of the capital. It took Krueger until June to defeat the largest Japanese army encountered by American troops in the Pacific war. The cost proved high. Nearly a quarter-million Japanese died in the fighting, along with 8,140 Sixth Army dead and some 30,000 wounded.

MacArthur may have had his problems with Krueger's cautious use of his forces during the drive on Manila, but he never lost confidence in his subordinate. Aware of his own tendency toward impetuosity, he prized Krueger's prudence. Faced with the certainty of hard fighting on the Japanese home islands, MacArthur selected Krueger to lead the planned invasion of Kyushu in November 1945. The end of the war, however, prevented the bloodbath of a final ground campaign.

Krueger received little publicity during the war, as MacArthur dominated the press releases from the theater. Indeed, in June 1945 the *Christian Science Weekly Magazine* published an article on Krueger, who now held four-star rank, under the title, "Mystery Man of the Pacific." Uninterested in public acclaim and without political ambition, Krueger was content to do his job to the best of his ability. MacArthur no doubt prized Krueger's modesty as well as his leadership talents.

A strict disciplinarian who cared deeply about the welfare of the enlisted men under his command, Krueger lacked the charisma of a Patton or Halsey. He planned his campaigns with meticulous care, then conducted them with prudence and skill. Consistent rather than bold in his leadership, Krueger successfully led Sixth Army to victory in twenty-one major engagements against a determined enemy. Known as "a soldier's soldier," Krueger died in Valley Forge, Pennsylvania, on August 20, 1967, and was buried in Arlington National Cemetery.

FURTHER READINGS

Krueger, W. *From Down Under to Nippon* (1953).
Leary, William M., ed. *We Shall Return! MacArthur's Commanders and the Defeat of Japan, 1942–1945* (1988).
Taafe, Stephen R. *MacArthur's Jungle War: The 1944 New Guinea Campaign* (1998).

William M. Leary

SEE ALSO Army Ground Forces, U.S.; MacArthur, Douglas

Kurile Islands

The Kurile Islands lie at the mouth of the Sea of Okhotsk in the Russian Far East, stretching for 700 miles between the Japanese home island of Hokkaido to the south and the Kamchatka peninsula to the north. They fell under Japanese control through two treaties with Imperial Russia in the nineteenth century. The first agreement in 1855 secured the southern portion of the islands while the second in 1875 enabled control of the northern part.

The Japanese used their naval and air bases in the archipelago for various operations during the Pacific war. Hittokappu Bay in the southern island of Etorofu was the anchorage from which the Pearl Harbor strike force sailed on November 26, 1941. The Kuriles were also used in the amphibious assault on the American bases on Attu and Kiska in the Aleutians, which both fell in June 1942 to the Japanese as part of their Midway campaign. This operation represented the last time that the Japanese could conduct offensive operations unmolested from these islands. American forces recaptured Attu and Kiska in the summer of 1943 and launched naval and air attacks from them against the Kuriles for the rest of the war. The islands also suffered from lack of sufficient war material from 1944 onward due to attacks by U.S. submarines on Japan's supply convoys.

The fate of these islands in the postwar world was the product of their geographic importance. Ever since the outbreak of the Pacific war the Allies had hoped that the Soviet Union would commence hostilities against Japan. Soviet premier Joseph Stalin stated at the end of the 1943 Moscow Conference that the U.S.S.R. would fight Japan following the defeat of Germany. There was, however, a price for such intervention. Stalin did not speak openly of his conditions for Russian entry into the Pacific War, but at the Tehran Conference in November 1943, he revealed them to Roosevelt in three private meetings. The Soviet leader desired the Kurile Islands in order to control the straits leading into the Sea of Okhotsk to Siberia. The Allies approved this demand at the Yalta Conference in February 1945 as one of the territorial conditions for Soviet entry into the Pacific War.

This agreement did not make Soviet possession of the Kuriles a reality. The Soviets prepared an assault force to this end and on August 18, 1945, the archipelago became the site of the last battle of the Pacific war. Japanese forces resisted, but by August 21 the two sides had negotiated a cease-fire. On September 4, 1945, the Russians completed their occupation of the Kurile Islands, despite Japanese protests that they should be allowed to keep the southern half of the chain. The ownership of the Kuriles remained an enduring dispute between the two countries in the postwar world.

FURTHER READINGS

Craig, William. *The Fall of Japan* (1967).
Rees, David. *The Defeat of Japan* (1997).
Wells, Anne Sharp. *Historical Dictionary of World War II: The War Against Japan* (1999).

Eric W. Osborne

SEE ALSO Aleutian Islands Campaign; Yalta Conference

Kurusu Saburo

Kurusu was a career diplomat who served as Japanese ambassador to Germany in 1939–1940 and as special envoy to the United States in November 1941.

As ambassador to Germany, Kurusu presided over a period of chilly relations between Berlin and Tokyo. The Japanese leadership deeply resented the August 1939 conclusion of the nonaggression pact between Hitler and Stalin, which they viewed as a clear violation of the Anti-Comintern Pact of 1936. The German government, moreover, refused to recognize Japan's Greater East Asia Co-Prosperity Sphere or to lend any assistance in bringing the war in China to a successful conclusion; the Germans had, in fact, been giving military assistance to the Chinese Nationalist government. This situation changed considerably when the pro-German Yosuke Matsuoka became foreign minister in July 1940; by the end of September, Kurusu signed the Tripartite Pact with Germany and Italy on Japan's behalf.

In November 1941, Kurusu was sent by Prime Minister Hideki Tojo to Washington to assist the ambassador, Kichisaburo Nomura. Though Nomura enjoyed friendly relations with President Franklin D. Roosevelt and Secretary of State Cordell Hull, the ambassador had trouble with the English language, leading to at least one serious diplomatic misunderstanding. Kurusu, by contrast, was thoroughly fluent in English; indeed, he was married to an American woman, a fact which Tojo believed might help convince Washington of Japan's peaceful intentions.

Kurusu, however, failed to make any positive impact on the course of U.S.-Japanese relations. Hull in particular remembered him as the man who signed the Tripartite Pact for Japan, and believed (rather unfairly) that he was part of the ultra-nationalist clique which was pushing for war. Kurusu's position was not helped by the fact that he brought with him no new offers from Tokyo, only a vague promise that Japan would not allow Germany to determine its foreign policy.

After several days in Washington, Kurusu concluded that there was no point in trying to reach a general settlement of all outstanding issues between Japan and the United States as long as Hull maintained his insistence on the total evacuation of all Japanese troops from China. He and Nomura, therefore, instead drafted a modus vivendi designed to avert a war in the immediate future. Under the modus vivendi, Japan would evacuate southern Indochina and pledge not to invoke the Tripartite Pact in the event of a war between the United States and Germany. In return the United States would agree to resume oil shipments to Japan.

Hull showed little interest in the modus vivendi, fearing that any agreement made with Japan, no matter how short term, might imply that the United States condoned Japanese action in China. But Hull's refusal to deal proved irrelevant, given that the Tojo cabinet never had any intention of withdrawing from southern Indochina. By November, Tokyo had decided irrevocably on war with the United States, and the Kurusu mission proved to be nothing more than an elaborate bit of window-dressing to discourage the United States from preparing for a Japanese attack, though Kurusu himself appears to have been unaware of this fact.

The war that Kurusu had honestly tried to avoid came home to the diplomat in a tragic and almost unbelievable denouement. The diplomat's son, an army pilot was forced due to a malfunction to make an emergency landing in the Japanese countryside. There he was beaten to death by peasants who believed that he was an American.

FURTHER READINGS

Morley, James W. (ed.). *The Fateful Choice: Japan's Advance into Southeast Asia, 1939–1941* (1980).

Schroeder, Paul W. *The Axis Alliance and Japanese-American Relations* (1958).

Butow, Robert J. C. *The John Doe Associates: Backdoor Diplomacy for Peace, 1941* (1974).

Lu, David J. *From the Marco Polo Bridge to Pearl Harbor* (1961).

John E. Moser

SEE ALSO Pearl Harbor, Japanese Attack on

Kwantung Army

The Kwantung Army (named after the peninsula on which Port Arthur is sited) was a Japanese force that could claim to have fired the first shots of World War II and also fought in its last campaign.

The Kwantung Army arrived in 1905 after the Russo-Japanese War to occupy newly acquired Liaotung Peninsula and Port Arthur. Its mission expanded in the 1920s to guard Japanese commercial interests, chiefly the railroads in Manchuria. Manchuria was then a wild frontier territory ruled by Chinese war lords. The Kwantung Army became a hotbed of *gekokujo* (insubordination), which was institutionalized and legitimized by tradition in the Japanese military during the early interwar period. The field-grade officers who were the de facto leaders of the *gekokujo* movement wanted Manchuria for a Japanese version of *lebensraum* (room to live), raw materials for Japan, and a market for Japanese goods.

By the early 1930s, the Kwantung Army's penchant for unauthorized action and immunity from General Headquarters and cabinet control plus involvement in domestic Chinese politics combined to lead Japan toward general war in Asia. Already on April 4, 1928, its soldiers assassinated the chief war lord in Manchuria, Marshal Chang Tso-lin.

The Kwantung Army sought a major provocation for an excuse to occupy all of Manchuria. On September 18, 1931, it caused just such an incident at Mukden. Several of its soldiers were injured by gunshots during night maneuvers there, and the Japanese blamed the Chinese and accordingly attacked the city the next day.

Against Tokyo's orders the Kwantung Army swept across Manchuria, easily taking cities linked by rail. It took the south Manchuria line between Port Arthur and Changchun by the end of September. The Kirin-Mukden route was cleared the next month. The only real resistance to the Japanese came along the Siping-Tsitshar railroad, which they secured in November. They then pushed all the way Great Wall. The campaign ended with the occupation on Harbin on February 5, 1932. Two weeks later the Kwantung Army—approximately corps-sized by then—established the puppet "Manchukuo" regime. On March 1, 1933 it proclaimed the "Manchukou Empire." Not surprisingly, Nazi Germany was one of the first governments to recognize this bogus empire.

The League of Nations, occupied elsewhere, proved powerless. Britain and France were unable to maintain the post–World War I system, while Germany and Italy watched these developments with great interest. Another contrived incident at the Marco Polo Bridge southwest of Peking in July 1937 began a second wave of aggression. The Kwantung Army, along with the North China Area Army and elements of the Japanese military in Korea, invaded northern China. This aggressive force moved west from Manchuria to the Chahar province, occupying Kalgan. On August 27, it penetrated Shansi province, taking Taung on September 13. In concert with Mongolian satellite forces, the Kwantung Army then headed into Suiyuan province, capturing Kueisui on October 14 and Paotow on October 17. It established another puppet state, the "Mongolian Federated Autonomous Government," a week later.

By late 1938, a stalemate had settled over China. Garrison duty along the Soviet border did not suit the Kwantung Army, so it went looking for new intrigues. In May 1939 it entered Soviet eastern Mongolia and occupied the city of Nomonhan, 10 miles inside the border. Here it faced a modern European force instead of the poorly led, equipped, and trained Chinese. The Soviet Twentieth Army under rising star General Georgii Zhukov (who had somehow excaped Stalin's bloody purges of the military), severely mauled the Japanese between August 20–31, 1939. The Japanese army had prepared for decades to defeat the Russian army, just as the navy prepared to destroy the U.S. Navy. But after Nomonhan, the Kwantung Army never rose to challenge the Soviets—not even during the Axis's hour of need during 1941–1942 in Russia.

By 1944, the Japanese high command had stripped much of the idle Kwantung Army in order to reinforce Pacific islands (and warfare for which it was much better suited). Just as it had dismissed Germany's blitzkrieg (lightning war) methods, organization, and material before Nomonhan, the Kwantung Army had learned nothing from the German Wehrmacht's experiences against the Soviets. With outmoded thinking and no modern tanks or antitank weapons, it would be completely outclassed when the Red Army turned its full attention eastward in 1945.

The Kwantung Army still fielded a powerful force, however. In August 1945 it numbered twenty-four divisions and eleven brigades in Manchuria alone, and counting contributions of Manchukuan and Inner Mongolian forces, this equaled 787,000 troops. It possessed 1,215 armored fighting vehicles and 6,700 guns, though most were obsolete. Of its 1,800 aircraft, only 300 were of front-line quality. The army was unprepared for the realities of combat against the post–V-E Day Red Army.

Under Marshal A.M. Vasilevsky, 1.6 million Soviet troops attacked on August 9. Though outmatched, the Japanese put up a typically ferocious defense. Although they suffered more than 40,000 casualties (while inflicting only 8,219) they offered little meaningful resistance. Partly out of ignorance and partly out of willfulness, the Kwantung Army fought past the August 15 armistice. On August 16 it ignored Tokyo's instructions to cease fire. Only on the next day, under personal orders of the emperor, did it formally surrender.

The Kwantung Army represented the worst traits of the Japanese military: ruthless militarism that placed itself above any superior authority, rigid thinking that ignored six years' martial evolution, and inability to adapt. It succeeded only when facing an inferior foe; when opposed by an enemy of equal or better quality it simply could not compete.

Nonetheless, even this army did not deserve the fate the victorious Soviets meted out to it: long years of imprisonment in labor camps and heavy indoctrination programs, in total violation of international law and the accepted rules of warfare. For years after the formal end of hostilities, veterans of the Kwantung Army were returning to Japan. But many never made the trip home.

FURTHER READINGS

Gilbert, Martin. *The Second World War* (1989).
Hoyt, Edwin, *Japan's War* (1986).
Wilmot, Chester. *Empires in the Balance* (1982).

Robert Kirchubel

SEE ALSO Army, Japanese

L

Laurel, José Paciano (1891–1959)

A Filipino politician, José Paciano Laurel was president of the Japanese-sponsored Philippine republic. Born at Tanauan, Batangas Province, on March 9, 1891, Laurel obtained law degrees from the University of the Philippines in 1915, Yale University in 1920, and the Tokyo Imperial University in 1938. In the Philippines, he served as interior secretary in 1923, senator and floor leader in the assembly between 1925 and 1931, and associate justice of the supreme court from 1936 until the outbreak of war, when he quit to become justice secretary.

Known for his intelligence and executive skill, Laurel also won recognition for killing a rival over a female in 1909. He represented himself and gained a verdict of lawful self-defense in 1912, despite his conviction in a lower court. In the subsequent decade, he strove to attain an impressive record and by 1923 had become an established figure in the Philippine oligarchy. However, his quick ascent was unexpectedly checked when he and fellow cabinet members resigned after involvement in a conflict with Governor-General Leonard Wood over a U.S. policeman.

Laurel, a fervent nationalist, detested colonialism and believed racial self-respect was important in the molding of a nation-state. He condemned the Filipino mania for Occidental norms and favored a school program encouraging indigenous beliefs and national solidarity. In 1936, he sent a son to study at Tokyo's Imperial Military Academy. Although his legal views and political philosophy were Western, particularly Spanish, Laurel wanted a Philippine state created on an Oriental foundation. An admirer of Japanese society, he served as a prewar lobbyist for Tokyo businessmen.

After Pearl Harbor and before he fled the Philippines, President Manual Quezon assigned Laurel to remain in Manila and to help coordinate the political changeover to Japan's occupation. Laurel's legal and personal ties with the Japanese, Quezon surmised, might alleviate the severity of their newly imposed authority. Laurel objected to the appointment, yet the president insisted. When Laurel asked how he should deal with the invader, General Douglas MacArthur said he and other Filipino officials could do what they considered imperative barring a loyalty pledge to the Japanese empire. If such an action was taken, the general added, execution would be the consequence when the Allies returned.

Laurel became a member of the transitional Executive Commission. Chairman Jorge Vargas placed him on the committee to frame the Articles of Organization of the Philippine Council of State, a document giving formal status to the provisional council as the most elevated advisory agency in the archipelago. Once published on January 29, 1942, it concluded the formation of a Japanese-backed regime. Vargas then chose Laurel as justice commissioner.

In 1943, Laurel departed justice and, as commissioner of the interior, issued a letter exhorting the Filipino clergy to encourage their faithful to be loyal and favorable to the puppet government. Under Japanese auspices, the commission organized the Central Pacification Committee, directed by Laurel, which partitioned the Philippines into seven regions with an important prewar functionary charged with keeping the peace in each. Laurel himself was answerable for Mindanao and Sulu. As a commissioner, he also commanded the District and Neighborhood Associations throughout the country and oversaw local governors and provincial officials.

That same year the Japanese formed the Preparatory Commission for Philippine Independence, selecting Laurel as its president. Of the six standing committees established to prepare the new frame of government, actual authority resided in the Committee on Drafting, chaired by Laurel. Hoping to concentrate power in the chief executive, Laurel consented to the debilitation of the legislature, and once Vargas proposed him as president, the lawmakers chose him unanimously.

As president, Laurel planned to utilize the Japanese presence to renew Philippine culture and values. Applauding the Japanese Military Administration as pursuing the genuine well-being of Filipino people and their rapid advance toward self-government, he pushed moral awareness and the creation of a citizenry committed to the general interest. He also advocated a Filipinization agenda, establishing the National Education Board to consider changes and the Bureau of Oriental Culture to promote Tagalog and native ways of life. Although he initially pleaded for diplomatic recognition by the world community, he signed a military accord with Tokyo shortly after his inauguration. Addressing domestic economic and security matters, he decreed capital punishment the penalty for bribery, black-marketing in foods, and racketeering. When rice production dropped below civilian requirements, he replaced the Japanese-operated National Rice and Corn Corporation with the Bigasang Bayan. At first, Laurel tried to win the support of the resistance, and his pardon bill passed through the legislature without dissent. At Japanese urging, he enlarged the constabulary force, creating new regional training facilities and establishing the Order of Tirad Pass for effectives who demonstrated bravery. The constabulary was apparently thoroughly infiltrated by the resistance, and constabulary members sensed that the Americans would soon return and that they would have to give an account of themselves. Yet Laurel rejected the conscription of Filipinos and opposed the formation of a pro-Japanese force of volunteers. In 1944, he ordered military governors to provide laborers to the Nipponese army, demanding the cooperation of every male between the ages of 18 and 50. Laurel presided over the Kalibapi, or Association for Service in the New Philippines, a Japanese-sponsored supra-party.

As U.S. invaders approached the Philippines, Laurel pressed the legislature to declare a state of emergency, an action that authorized enhanced presidential power. On September 22, he issued a proclamation recklessly declaring war on the United States. Fleeing to Baguio in 1945, he was brought to Japan to set up a government in exile. Once Tokyo surrendered, Laurel announced the termination of the Republic of the Philippines. Returned to his homeland and jailed, he gained release on bail and managed to postpone his trial. In 1947, he was proposed for the senate and the presidency prior to an appearance before the People's Court. Eventually his case was thrown out via pardon. Laurel died on November 6, 1959. Many observers of the postwar Philippine scene have speculated that the mildness with which the postwar Philippine government treated Laurel indicated either that he was acting more or less as instructed by the Americans or that the Filipino legal elite admired his anti-American stance, or both.

FURTHER READINGS

Agpalo, Remigio E. *Jose P. Laurel: National Leader and Political Philosopher* (1992).

Friend, Theodore. *The Blue-Eyed Enemy: Japan against the West in Java and Luzon, 1942–1945* (1988).

Lansang, Jose, ed. *War Memoirs of Dr. Jose P. Laurel* (1962).

Steinberg, David Joel. *Philippine Collaboration in World War II* (1967).

Rodney J. Ross

SEE ALSO   Roxas, Manuel; Osmena, Sergio; Quezon, Manuel; Philippines, Fall of

Leahy, William D. (1875–1959)

U.S. naval commander. Although William D. Leahy retired as chief of naval operations (CNO), the highest professional post in the U.S. Navy, in 1939, he went on to serve through most of World War II in appointments near or at the highest levels of government—none of them in the navy itself, let alone at sea. Leahy was born in Iowa in 1875. He graduated fifteenth in his class from the U.S. Naval Academy in 1897, and for the next two decades saw as much active service as an American sailor could at that time. Leahy served in the Spanish-American War, the Philippines uprising, and the Boxer Rebellion; was chief of staff for the occupation of Nicaragua in 1912; served in the Haiti campaign of 1916; and commanded USS *Dolphin* in the punitive expedition into Mexico against Pancho Villa of 1916. This last appointment proved fateful. *Dolphin* was then the secretary of the navy's dispatch boat. While in command, Leahy befriended the young assistant secretary of the navy, who made several cruises on her—Franklin Delano Roosevelt.

Leahy became close enough to Roosevelt to make several visits to the latter's homes at Hyde Park, New York, and Campobello, New Brunswick, fostering, according to Leahy, "a deep personal affection that endured unchanged until [Roosevelt's] death." For the next twenty years Leahy rose steadily up the navy chain of command, not seeing much of his old friend. But the bond paid off handsomely in January 1937 when President Roosevelt appointed Leahy CNO. Together, the two friends oversaw a great expansion of the navy and steady, if slow, progress in preparing it for war. From late 1937 Leahy was sure the United States must sooner or later resort to war to crush Japanese aspirations to dominate Asia and the Pacific, and pushed hard for a firm stand against Japanese expansion. On his watch, much progress was made in formulating strategic plans for coalition warfare that later formed the basis of U.S. grand strategy. Leahy played a major role in secret prewar talks that paved the way for wartime cooperation with the British, and in making the navy plan to take offensive action against Japan as soon as possible. When he was relieved on reaching retirement age in August 1939, the president saw to it that he was not put out to pasture, naming him governor of Puerto Rico. This post kept Leahy active until 1940, when events prompted Roosevelt to bring him back toward the center of national affairs.

In December 1940, Roosevelt sent Leahy to Vichy France, naming him ambassador to the government left in control of "unoccupied France" by the armistice agreement reached after the German victory over France earlier that year. He made little impact on the French but impressed Roosevelt so much, with his devotion to carrying out the president's policy, that the president brought him into the inner circle. Leahy was recalled in April 1942—to a nation now waging global war. This unprecedented challenge posed new and vast problems in organizing and directing total war on the grand scale. Leahy's return enabled the organization to be addressed.

The chain of command for the central direction of the war brought President Roosevelt, as commander in chief of the armed forces, together with the newly established joint chiefs of staff (JCS), a combination of the professional heads of the services into a committee whose job was to advise the president on military strategy and to implement all decisions. There was as yet no channel of liaison between the two. General George C. Marshall, chief of staff of the U.S. Army, suggested that Leahy be placed in a new post. Senior in service to the chiefs of staff, liked by them, and above all trusted by the president, Leahy was the ideal choice to be the channel by which the president's views and the advice of the JCS could be passed between the two. In that capacity Leahy could also act as chairman of the JCS, which would restore a balance of two admirals and two generals. The logic of this proposal convinced all concerned, so on July 20, 1942, Leahy was recalled to active service as the first chief of staff to the commander in chief.

Leahy served in this capacity for the rest of the war. This position put him at the very heart of making "war from the top." Leahy's influence always rested on his relationship with the president, which by the last year of

Roosevelt's life was very close indeed. Leahy saw the president daily, attended nearly all the major conferences during the war, and exerted much indirect influence on Roosevelt by shaping the military information and issues that reached him. This access also brought a miscellaneous group of people to Leahy's office, seeking help and support from the White House. Leahy chaired both the JCS and, frequently, the combined chiefs of staff, the body that brought together the American and British staffs to direct the coalition war. On these bodies Leahy was often active, sometimes assertive, but rarely a prime mover. In their deliberations the admiral never opposed any decision of the president, and rarely disagreed on strategic issues with the acerbic Admiral Ernest King, now CNO. Over time, General Marshall came to feel that Leahy acted more as the voice of the president than of the JCS, but the chairman nevertheless retained the respect and confidence of his peers.

Leahy supported the Allied policy to concentrate on defeating Germany first, but shared the general desire of his service to put greater force into the war against Japan. Regarding strategy for the defeat of Japan, Leahy was fairly open-minded, in 1944 supporting General Douglas MacArthur's desire to liberate the Philippines and in 1945 opposing plans to invade Japan—arguing it would be expensive and unnecessary, because Japan could be defeated by bombing and blockade. Leahy regarded the Japanese with contempt, openly describing them as "savages" and "barbarians" whose power must be "utterly destroyed." Yet he was the only member of the high command to argue against dropping the atomic bomb. At first he wrongly predicted the bomb would be an expensive failure ("and I speak as an expert in explosives"), then he criticized its use on moral grounds, claiming it marked a reversion to uncivilized ways of warfare. Leahy also argued that the emperor of Japan should be allowed to remain on the throne, to make it easier for Japan to surrender and for American forces to occupy and reorganize the country.

Leahy's efforts inspired President Roosevelt to persuade Congress to authorize a new rank that he was the first to hold, being promoted five-star fleet admiral in December 1944. His experience, stature, and direct manner gained him the confidence of the next president, Harry Truman, who retained him as chief of staff until March 1949. Leahy shared Truman's growing suspicion of the Soviet Union and joined in the hardening of U.S. policy as the cold war developed. But he was never as close to this president, and retired in some frustration after fighting and losing a last battle to prevent the creation of a unified Department of Defense. Leahy did perform one last service at Truman's request, in 1950 publishing a volume of wartime memoirs based on his notes, titled *I Was There*, to defend the Democratic administration against growing controversy over cold war–driven issues. Leahy died in 1959.

FURTHER READINGS

Burns, J. M. *Roosevelt: The Soldier of Freedom* (1970).

Greenfield, K. R. *Command Decisions* (1960).

Hayes, G. P. *The History of the Joint Chiefs of Staff in World War II: The War Against Japan* (1982).

Kimball, W. F. *Forged in War: Churchill, Roosevelt and the Second World War* (1998).

King, E. J. *A Naval Record* (1952).

Leahy, W. D. *I Was There* (1950).

Major, J. "William Daniel Leahy," in R. W. Love Jr., ed., *The Chiefs of Naval Operations* (1980).

Miller, E. S. *War Plan Orange* (1991).

Pogue, F. C. *The Supreme Command* (1954).

Brian P. Farrell

LeMay, Curtis (1906–1990)

U.S. Army Air Forces and Air Force officer, widely acknowledged as the architect of U.S. strategic air power during the early period of the cold war, Curtis LeMay was born in Columbus, Ohio, on November 15, 1906. He attended Ohio State University and enrolled in the Reserve Officers' Training Corps after unsuccessfully trying to enter West Point. He left college before he finished his degree in order to enlist in the National Guard as a flight cadet. LeMay received his pilot's wings in October 1929 and joined the 27th Pursuit Squadron at Selfridge Field, Michigan.

LeMay completed the requirements for his civil engineering degree in 1932. In late 1936, he requested a transfer to a bomber unit after concluding that bombers would have more decisive an impact than fighters in any future war. He was assigned to the 2d Bombardment Group at Langley Field, Virginia.

LeMay quickly developed a reputation as the best navigator in the air force. In 1937 and 1938, he was the lead navigator on two mass flights of B-17 bombers to South America. They were the first mass flights of land planes in history, and the group received the Mackay Trophy. He also was the lead navigator on a number of exercises to test the capability of bombers to intercept ships at sea—locating USS *Utah* in 1937 and then Italian liner *Rex* in 1938.

In 1939, LeMay attended the Air Corps Tactical School at Maxwell Field, Alabama. In late 1940, Captain LeMay took command of a bomber squadron stationed at Westover Air Force Base, Massachusetts. He participated with the Royal Canadian Air Force in a number of ferrying operations across the Atlantic to Great Britain. He advanced to major in March 1941, to lieutenant colonel in January 1942, and to colonel in March 1942.

In May 1942, LeMay assumed command of the 305th Bombardment Group in Muroc, California. He was given the mission of training the unit to be one of the first to enter the European war. LeMay was a hard-driving and demanding trainer, and during that period he earned the nickname that followed him for the rest of his life—"Iron Ass."

The 305th arrived in Britain in the fall of 1942, and LeMay quickly won a reputation as an innovative tactician. Almost immediately he challenged the then-current practice of bombers flying evasive patterns while trying to bomb their targets. The belief was that any bomber that flew in a straight line for more than ten seconds in a combat zone would be shot down. LeMay produced a mathematical analysis demonstrating otherwise.

To prove the point, he personally led the 305th in an attack on the German-held port of Saint-Nazaire. None of his bombers was shot down, although they held a straight course on the final bomb run for seven minutes. The bombing scores also improved dramatically, and LeMay's technique shortly became standard practice. LeMay also pioneered a tactical formation using all eighteen bombers of a group arranged so that the formation's firepower could defend the group against fighter attack from any angle.

On August 17, 1943, LeMay led the famous "shuttle mission" against Regensburg, taking off from Britain and landing in North Africa. In June 1943, he assumed command of the Eighth Air Force's 3d Bombardment Division. He was promoted to brigadier general in September 1943 and to major general on March 2, 1944. At the age of 37, LeMay became one of the youngest officers in U.S. military history to hold that rank.

LeMay was transferred to the China-Burma-India theater in August 1944 to head the XX Bomber Command. His B-29s made attacks on Anshan and other Japanese-controlled Manchurian industrial centers in July and September. In January 1945, he moved to the Pacific to command the XXI Bomber Command based on Guam.

LeMay then made what has been described as one of the most momentous decisions in modern warfare. Although the B-29 bomber had been designed for high-altitude missions, LeMay ordered the warplanes stripped of defensive armament so they could carry more bombs and be used in low-level night attacks against Japan. He also ordered his crews to attack singly, not in formation. His pilots were disbelieving at first, but the new tactics proved highly effective without an increase in aircraft losses.

Using this technique, the XXI Bomber Command attacked Tokyo with 335 B-29s on the night of March 9, 1945. Its B-29s destroyed a large portion of Tokyo and its industrial area in one of the greatest single disasters in military history.

LeMay was still in command of the XXI Bomber Command when it became the Twentieth Air Force, the United States' first strategic strike force, operating directly under the control of the Joint Chiefs of Staff. Shortly after, LeMay became the chief of staff of General Carl Spaatz's U.S. Strategic Air Forces. In that position, he played a major role in planning the nuclear strikes on Hiroshima and Nagasaki.

After the war, LeMay served briefly as the head of air force research and development. He was promoted to lieutenant general and assumed command of the U.S. Air Forces in Europe in October 1947. He commanded the air operations of the Berlin airlift in 1948–1949. In October 1948, LeMay became the commander of Strategic Air Command (SAC). He held that position for nine years and turned SAC into the ultimate nuclear striking force of the cold war. During his tenure, SAC introduced the global-reaching and nuclear-capable piston-and-jet-engine B-36, then the all-jet B-47, then the B-52, and, finally, nuclear-tipped intercontinental ballistic missiles. In 1951, LeMay became America's youngest four-star general since Ulysses S. Grant.

LeMay served as the chief of staff of the U.S. Air Force from 1961 to 1965. He advocated the use of nuclear weapons in the Cuban missile crisis of 1962. During the Vietnam War, he was again a strong advocate of using whatever means necessary—including nuclear weapons—to win. "Bomb 'em back to the stone-age" was one notorious quote attributed to him.

After his retirement, LeMay became an executive for an electronics firm. He briefly entered politics as the vice presidential running mate of third-party candidate George Wallace in the 1968 elections. LeMay also was a longtime member of the National Geographic Society's board of trustees.

LeMay was the image of the tough, no-nonsense, cigar-chomping air commander. During the Vietnam War period and the later cold war, he became almost a caricature of the ultimate cold warrior. He also became a special target of hatred among radical antinuclear groups because of his roles in the Hiroshima and Nagasaki attacks and the buildup of SAC. Despite the "revisionist" perspective,

LeMay, for better or worse, was one of America's most important and influential military commanders. General Spaatz once referred to him as the greatest air combat commander of World War II. He died at March Air Force Base, California, on October 1, 1990.

FURTHER READINGS
Coffey, Thomas M. *Iron Eagle: The Turbulent Life of General, Curtis LeMay* (1986).
Larrabee, Eric. *Commander in Chief: Franklin Delano Roosevelt, His Lieutenants, and Their War* (1987).
LeMay, Curtis E., with MacKinlay Kantor. *Mission with LeMay* (1965).

David T. Zabecki

Lexington

U.S.S. *Lexington* was the largest warship of the U.S. Navy ever to be sunk at sea. It was the second U.S. aircraft carrier, and the fourth U.S. warship, of that name. Construction began in 1920 on what was to be a new battle cruiser, but was halted during the Washington Conference of 1921. Completed in 1927, *Lexington,* and its sister ship *Saratoga*, were the largest warships afloat at the time. Each ship was 888 feet long, with a 106-foot beam, and drew twenty-four feet of water. Long, heavily armored, and fast, *Lexington* represented the cutting edge of carrier technology at the time and was soon unofficially called *Lady Lex*.

For most of the 1930s, the *Lexington* was one of only three U.S. carriers (the other two being the pioneer (but now obsolete) small and slow *Langley* and *Saratoga*). Based in San Pedro, California, this ship was instrumental in the training of naval fleet pilots and their aircraft in carrier operations, except for those attached to Pearl Harbor or the Canal Zone. In July 1937, *Lexington* aided in the search for aviator Amelia Earhart, who was thought to have crash-landed in the Pacific during her attempt to fly around the world. By the end of the decade, *Yorktown* and *Enterprise* had joined the fleet, and *Wasp* was under construction. The outbreak of war in Europe, and growing U.S. concerns as to the intentions of Japan, led to the acceleration of aviator training. In addition, U.S. carriers were deployed more broadly across the Pacific, in an attempt to resupply and strengthen U.S. holdings (such as Wake and Midway islands) in the event of war.

These fears proved to be well founded. With the Japanese surprise air attack on the U.S. naval base at Pearl Harbor, Hawaii, on December 7, 1941, U.S. forces in the Pacific, including a number of submarines, began to engage the enemy. The U.S. carrier fleet, however, saw little coordinated action except for raids until mid-1942. In April, U.S. Navy Intelligence, having broken the Japanese code, ascertained that the next Japanese move in the South Pacific would be in the area of the Coral Sea. Admiral Chester Nimitz created Task Force 17, a 2-carrier group consisting of *Lexington* and *Yorktown,* under the command of Rear Admiral Frank Jack Fletcher. This task force was ordered to proceed to the Coral Sea, and to intercept and destroy any Japanese forces they encountered along the way.

The Japanese plan was to secure the island of Tulagi and Port Moresby, New Guinea by invasion and to destroy any U.S. naval forces they could. The stakes were high for both sides. The Japanese hoped to expand their newly won defensive perimeter outward, so as to protect their important base at Rabaul, New Britain. This base had come under U.S. attack, including one recent raid in which *Lexington* had participated. Furthermore, Japanese strategists regarded U.S. carrier-based aircraft as the biggest remaining obstacle to Japan's ambitions in the Pacific, and logically concluded that the carriers must be destroyed. For the Americans, failure to stop the Japanese advance would leave Australia open to possible invasion while weakening a Pacific force that already had too many responsibilities and too few resources.

The Battle of the Coral Sea (May 3–May 8, 1942) was the first major carrier battle of the war, and one in which the opposing carrier groups never came within sight of one another. Instead, the battle was fought by carrier-launched aircraft. The Japanese made an unopposed landing at Tulagi on May 3, and were attacked by planes from the *Yorktown* the following morning. Poor weather hampered U.S. and Japanese forces for the next two days as each group sought out the other without success. On May 7, Japanese planes located and attacked two U.S. ships, oiler *Neosho* and destroyer *Simms;* U.S. aircraft stumbled across Japanese carrier *Shoho,* which they promptly sank. The decisive day for the opposing carrier forces was May 8. By midmorning, Japanese carrier *Shokaku* was damaged to the extent that it could not launch planes and was ordered back to Truk. Meanwhile, an attack group of sixty-nine Japanese planes located and attacked *Lexington* and *Yorktown.* The larger and less maneuverable *Lexington,* which was more heavily armored, bore the brunt of the damage, sustaining three torpedo hits. Both elevators were jammed, the aviation fuel system on the port side was disrupted, two severely damaged aircraft were pushed overboard (with the possibility that more might have to follow), and no aircraft could be lowered to the hangars. Despite the damage, there did not seem to be any immediate threat to the ship once the attack ceased. The carrier gradually increased speed until it had resumed 24 knots and prepared to recover the aircraft. The optimistic assessment of the repair crews did not hold for long, however. About an hour after the attack had ceased, a massive explosion rocked the ship, setting off a chain reaction of smaller explosions throughout the vessel.

In fact, the assessment of the damage control parties was not as far off as might be assumed, in that the initial damage from the three torpedo hits alone was not enough to sink the ship. It was a series of unfortunate, and to some extent preventable, circumstances that led to the massive explosion. The aviation fuel compartments, whose purpose was to hold vapors normally collected by the ventilation system, had been ruptured during the attack. This damage was neither discovered nor addressed by the damage parties. Vapor from these compartments seeped through the ship and became concentrated in a section where ventilation had failed. Since this area had been evacuated, the buildup of vapors went unnoticed for some time. Although dispersal through natural ventilation was the main precaution against dangers posed by the vapors, other safety measures, such as heavy insulation around electric circuits, had been employed during construction of *Lexington.* Unfortunately, the motor generators had been left running in the evacuated section of the ship, although they were known to be overheating owing to misalignment. The carrier's executive officer blamed a spark from one of these generators for setting off the massive explosion that doomed *Lexington.*

Even this damage was not at first considered fatal, but despite an enormous effort by the damage control teams, Captain Frederick C. Sherman gave the order to abandon ship at 1707 hours. Sherman's report to the Navy Department stated that he had lost 26 officers and 190 men, out of a complement of 2,951. He concluded that in addition to this remarkable fact, "the ship and crew had performed gloriously," and it seemed too bad that she had to perish in her hour of victory. *Lady Lex* lingered, without its crew and in its extremely damaged state, until the order was given by Admiral Kinkaid to finish the job. Destroyer *Phelps* put five torpedoes into the doomed ship before it sank at 1952 hours.

The loss of *Lexington,* though significant, must be considered in light of other factors. The Battle of the Coral Sea was a tactical defeat but a strategic victory for U.S. forces. Despite the loss of men and materiel, U.S. forces had prevented the Japanese from capturing Port Moresby and Tulagi and extending their defensive perimeter. Furthermore, the loss of *Shoho* and heavy damage to *Shokaku,* as well as the loss of the almost irreplaceable Japanese pilots, would have an impact on the Japanese performance during the Battle of Midway, which was both a strategic and a tactical victory for the United States and crippled the air arm of the Japanese Imperial Fleet. The name *Lexington* lived on in a new American carrier that served with distinction for the rest of the war.

FURTHER READINGS

Bennett, Geoffrey. *Naval Battles of World War II* (1975).

Brown, David. *Carrier Operations in World War II* (1974).

Hoehling, A. A. *The Lexington Goes Down* (1971).

Hoyt, Edwin P. *Blue Skies and Blood: The Battle of Coral Sea* (1975).

Mason, John T. *The Pacific War Remembered: An Oral History Collection* (1986).

Miller, Nathan. *War at Sea: A Naval History of World War II* (1995).

Morison, Samuel Eliot. *The Two-Ocean War: A Short History of the United States Navy in the Second World War* (1963).

Willmott, H. P. *The Barrier and the Javelin: Japanese and Allied Pacific Strategies, February to June 1942* (1983).

Melissa R. Jordine and Kenneth A. Millard

SEE ALSO Coral Sea, Battle of the

Leyte Gulf, Battle of

Whether in terms of ships or men involved or extent in area, the October 23–26, 1944, Battle of Leyte Gulf was the largest naval engagement of modern times, perhaps in all naval history. Its 282 vessels (216 U.S., 2 Australian, and 64 Japanese) outnumbered the 250 ships of the 1916 Battle of Jutland. The battle involved nearly two hundred thousand men and encompassed an area of more than one hundred thousand square miles. It saw all aspects of naval warfare—air, surface, submarine, and amphibious—as well as the use of the largest guns ever at sea, the last clash of the dreadnoughts, and the introduction of kamikazes. The Battle of Leyte Gulf saw fine planning and leadership, brilliant deception, failed intelligence, and great controversy. Americans have often ignored it and instead chosen to remember the battle of Midway (1942) or the Normandy invasion in Europe (1944), perhaps because Leyte Gulf came late in the war, when the tide had already turned and a U.S. victory seemed a mere matter of time.

The Battle of Leyte Gulf resulted from President Franklin Delano Roosevelt's decision to follow the conquest of the Mariana Islands with recapture of the Philippines. This was Commander of Southwest Pacific Forces General Douglas MacArthur's idea; Chief of Naval Operations Ernest J. King wanted to land on Japan's colony of Formosa. The latter made sound military sense; the former, political sense.

On October 20, the U.S. Sixth Army began an invasion of Leyte. More than one hundred thirty-two thousand men went ashore the first day. Warned by the preliminary bombardment, the Japanese put into effect a last-ditch and overly complicated contingency plan.

As early as July 21, 1944, the naval general staff in Tokyo had issued a directive for subsequent "urgent operations." The Combined Fleet was to maintain the strategic status quo and take advantage of tactical situations to seize the initiative "to crush the enemy fleet and attacking forces." On July 26, the naval general staff informed Combined Fleet Commander Admiral Soemu Toyoda that the "urgent operations" would be known by the *Shō* (Victory) code name. The Japanese had four of these to combat the next U.S. offensive; *Shō Ichi Go* (Operation Victory One) covered defense of the Philippine archipelago, to which the Japanese decided to commit the entire Combined Fleet. Toyoda knew it would be a gamble. He said after the war, "If things went well, we might obtain unexpectedly good results; but if the worst should happen, there was a chance that we would lose the entire fleet. But I felt that chance had to be taken." Toyoda knew all too well that should the Americans retake the Philippines, "the shipping lane to the south would be completely cut off, so that the fleet, if it should come back to Japanese waters, could not obtain its fuel supply. If it should remain in southern waters, it could not receive supplies of ammunition and arms. There would be no sense in saving the fleet at the expense of the Philippines."

Japanese naval air strength had been severely reduced in the June 1944 Battle of the Philippine Sea ("The Great Marianas Turkey Shoot"), and during October 12–14 U.S. carrier planes and army B-29s hit Japanese airfields on Formosa, Okinawa, and the Philippines. These strikes had the effect of denying the Japanese navy badly needed land-based air support; this fact alone probably doomed the Japanese plan. The Japanese did add extra antiaircraft guns to their ships in an attempt to offset the lack of air power, but offensively they had to rely on naval gunnery and some three hundred thirty-five land-based planes in the Luzon area.

The Japanese hoped to destroy enough U.S. shipping to break up the amphibious landing. There were four prongs in the Japanese attack. A decoy force was to draw the U.S. fleet north while two elements struck from the west on either side of Leyte to converge simultaneously on the landing area in the Leyte Gulf and destroy Allied shipping there. At the same time, shore-based aircraft were to inflict maximum damage on U.S. forces assisting the landings. At best, the complex plan was a long shot.

On October 17, on receiving information that U.S. warships were off Suhuan Island, Admiral Toyoda alerted his forces. The next day the Japanese intercepted U.S. messages regarding the approaching Leyte landings, and Toyoda initiated *Shō Ichi Go.* The original target date for the fleet engagement was October 22, but logistical difficulties delayed it to October 25.

Vice Admiral Jisabuto Ozawa's decoy Northern Force (or Third Fleet) consisted of heavy carrier *Zuikaku,* three light carriers, two hybrid battleship-carriers, three cruisers, and eight destroyers. Ozawa had only 116 planes, flown by half-trained pilots. His force sortied from Japan on October 20 and on the evening of October 22 turned south toward Luzon. The Japanese had high hopes for this decoy force.

Japanese submarines off Formosa were ordered south toward the eastern approaches to the Philippine archipelago, and shortly before October 23 what remained of the Japanese 2d Air Fleet began to arrive on Luzon.

The strongest element of the Japanese attack was the 1st Division Attack Force. It reached Brunei Bay in northwest Borneo on October 20, refueled, split into two parts, and resumed its movement two days later. The Center Force under Admiral Takeo Kurita had the bulk of Japanese attack strength, including the two super battleships *Musashi* and *Yamato.* With their 18.1-inch guns, these 862-foot-long, 70,000-ton behemoths were at the time the largest warships ever built. Kurita also had three older battleships, twelve cruisers, and fifteen destroyers. Center Force sailed northeasterly up the west coast of Palawan Island and then turned eastward through the waters of the Central Philippines to San Bernardino Strait. Meanwhile, the Southern Force (C Force) of two battleships, one heavy cruiser, and four destroyers, commanded by Vice Admiral Shoji Nishimura, struck eastward through the Sulu Sea in an effort to force its way through Surigao Strait between the islands of Mindanao and Leyte. It was trailed by the 2d Diversion Attack Force commanded by Vice Admiral Kiyohide Shima. He had two heavy cruisers, one light cruiser, and four destroyers. Shima's warships left the Pescadores on October 21, steamed south past western Luzon, and refueled in the Calamian Islands. Shima's force was late joining that of Nishimura and followed it into Surigao Strait.

Opposing the Japanese were two U.S. Navy fleets: the Seventh, commanded by Admiral Thomas C. Kinkaid and operating under General MacArthur's Southwest Pacific Command; and the Third, commanded by Admiral William F. Halsey and under Admiral Chester Nimitz at Pearl Harbor. Leyte was the first landing to involve two entire U.S. fleets and the first without unified command. This divided command had unfortunate consequences.

Seventh Fleet was divided into three task groups—the first consisted of Admiral Jesse D. Oldendorf's six old battleships, sixteen escort carriers, four heavy cruisers, four light cruisers, thirty destroyers, and ten destroyer escorts. The other two elements were amphibious task groups carrying out the actual invasion. Seventh Fleet had escorted the invasion force to Leyte and now provided broad protection for the entire landing area. Because most of Halsey's amphibious assets had been loaned to Kinkaid, Third Fleet consisted almost entirely of Admiral Marc Mitscher's Task Force 38: fourteen fast carriers (more than a thousand aircraft) organized into four task groups containing six battleships, eight heavy cruisers, thirteen light cruisers, and fifty-seven destroyers. Third Fleet's orders called for it to secure air superiority over the Philippines, protect the landings, and maintain pressure on the Japanese. In addition, the fleet was to take advantage of, or create, any opportunity to destroy a major part of the Japanese fleet.

Both western Japanese attacks were detected early. The Battle of Leyte Gulf was actually a series of battles, the first of which was the October 23–24 Battle of the Sibuyan Sea. Early on the twenty-third U.S. submarines *Darter* and *Dace* discovered Kurita's Center Force entering Palawan Passage from the South China Sea and alerted Admiral Halsey, whose Third Fleet guarded San Bernardino Strait. The submarines sank two Japanese heavy cruisers, *Atago* (Kurita's flagship) and *Maya,* and damaged a third. Kurita transferred his flag to *Yamato,* and his force continued east into the Sibuyan Sea, where, beginning on the morning of the twenty-fourth, TF 38 launched five air strikes against it. The first wave of carrier planes arrived at 1025 hours and concentrated on *Musashi,* which took nineteen torpedoes and nearly as many bombs before it went to the bottom with half of its nearly 2,200-man crew. These all-day air attacks also damaged several other Japanese vessels. At 1440 hours on October 25, U.S. pilots reported Kurita had reversed course and was heading west; Halsey incorrectly assumed that his part of the battle was over. He did issue a preliminary order detailing a line of battleships known as Task Force 34 to be commanded by Vice Admiral Willis A. Lee. Admiral Kinkaid was aware of that signal and assumed that TF 34 had been established.

Meanwhile, Japanese land-based planes from 2d Air Fleet harassed a portion of TF 38. Most were shot down, but they did sink light carrier *Princeton* and badly damaged cruiser *Birmingham.* Moreover, unknown to Halsey, after nightfall Kurita's force changed course and resumed heading for San Bernardino Strait.

Warned of the approach of the Japanese Combined Fleet, Admiral Kinkaid placed Rear Admiral Oldendorf's six Seventh Fleet old fire-support battleships (all but one veterans of Pearl Harbor), flanked by eight cruisers, across the south of Surigao Strait in an intercepting position. Oldendorf also lined the strait with thirty-nine patrol torpedo (PT) boats and twenty-eight destroyers.

The October 24–25 Battle of Surigao Strait was a classic example of the "crossing of the T." Admiral Oldendorf's PT boats discovered the Japanese moving in line-ahead formation, but Nishimura's force easily beat them back. Although the U.S. battleships usually get the credit for the Surigao Strait victory, the U.S. destroyers inflicted most of the damage. Two converging torpedo attacks sank battleships *Fuso* and three destroyers. Then the Japanese line was "capped" by Oldendorf's battlewagons. All Japanese warships save destroyer *Shigura* were sunk. Nishimura, obedient to the code of the Bushido warrior, went down with his flagship, battleship *Yamashiro*.

Rear Admiral Oldendorf had accomplished what every war-ambitious battle-gaming student at the Naval War College had dreamed of in pre–Pearl Harbor days: the crossing of the enemy fleet's "T." And earlier he would have indeed gained the immortality awarded to Admiral Togo Heihachiro at Tsushima. But in these times, there was something almost anachronistic about the feat, even though Nishimura's fleet was annihilated. Battleship-to-battleship combat, perhaps unfairly, now resembled jousts by knights in armor.

Shima's force, bringing up the rear, was attacked thirty minutes later by PT boats, which crippled a light cruiser. His force then attempted an attack, but his flagship collided with one of Nishimura's sinking vessels. Oldendorf's ships pursued the retreating Japanese. Another Japanese cruiser succumbed to attacks by land-based planes and planes of Admiral Thomas L. Sprague's escort carriers. The rest of Shima's force escaped when Oldendorf, knowing his ships might be needed later, turned back. By 0430 hours on October 25, the southern Japanese pincer was no more.

Meanwhile, during the night of October 24–25, Kurita's force, hoping to join Nishimura in Leyte Gulf, moved through San Bernardino Strait, issued unopposed from it, and turned south. In the most controversial aspect of the battle, near midnight Halsey left San Bernardino Strait unprotected to rush with all available units of Third Fleet after Admiral Ozawa's decoy fleet, which had been sighted far to the north. Halsey's decision was in part the result of criticism earlier leveled at Admiral Ray-

mond A. Spruance for not leaving landing forces at Saipan to pursue an attacking Japanese force. Several of Halsey's subordinates registered reservations about his decision, but the admiral would not be deterred. Compounding the error, Halsey failed to inform Admiral Kinkaid, who in any case assumed TF 34 was protecting the strait. Halsey's decision left the landing beaches guarded only by Seventh Fleet's Taffy 3 escort carrier group commanded by Rear Admiral Clifton A. F. Sprague. It was one of three such support groups operating off Samar. Sprague had six light escort carriers (CVEs: "Combustible, Vulnerable, Expendable," as their crews well knew), three destroyers, and four destroyer escorts.

Fighting off Samar erupted about 0630 hours on October 24 when Taffy 3 found itself opposing Kurita's four battleships, including *Yamato* with its 18.1-inch guns, six heavy cruisers, and ten destroyers. The aircraft from all three Taffys now attacked the Japanese. Unfortunately, the planes carried the wrong ordnance—relatively harmless fragmentation bombs for use against land targets—but they put up a strong fight, dropping bombs, strafing, and generally harassing the powerful Japanese warships. Sprague's destroyers and destroyer escorts also joined the fight. Their crews skillfully and courageously attacked the far more powerful Japanese warships, launching torpedoes and laying down a smoke screen to try to obscure the escort carriers. These combined attacks forced several Japanese cruisers to drop out of the battle.

Nonetheless, by 0910 hours, Kurita's warships had sunk *Gambier Bay*, the only U.S. carrier ever lost to gunfire, destroyers *Hoel* and *Johnston*, and destroyer escort *Samuel B. Roberts*. Kurita now lost his nerve. Believing he was being attacked by aircraft from TF 38, and just when he might have had a crushing victory, at 0911 hours he ordered his forces to break off the attack, his decision strengthened by the fact that the southern attacking force had been destroyed. After the war, Kurita said, "The conclusion from our gunfire and anti-aircraft fire during the day had led me to believe in my uselessness, my ineffectual position, if I proceeded into Leyte Gulf where I would come under even heavier air attack." Several days of near-incessant attacks may also have frayed Kurita's nerves. Kurita hoped to join Ozawa's force to the north but changed his mind and exited through San Bernardino Strait. Sprague later noted that the failure of Kurita's force "to completely wipe out all vessels of this Task Unit can be attributed to our successful smoke screen, our torpedo counterattack, continuous harassment of the enemy by bomb, torpedo, and strafing air attacks, timely maneuvers, and the definite partiality of Almighty God." The four ships lost by *Taffy 3* were the only U.S. warships sunk by Japanese surface ships in the Battle of Leyte Gulf.

At 2140 hours, Kurita's ships reentered San Bernardino Strait. As the Japanese withdrew, they were attacked by aircraft from Rear Admiral John S. McCain's task force of Halsey's fleet, which sank only one destroyer. Meanwhile, Admiral Sprague's escort carriers and Oldendorf's force returning from the Battle of Surigao Strait came under attack from land-based kamikaze aircraft, the first such attacks of the war. These sank escort carrier *St. Lô* and damaged several other ships.

Earlier, at about 0220 hours on October 25, Mitscher's search planes of Halsey's force located Ozawa's northern decoy force. At dawn, the first of three strikes was launched in what became known as the Battle of Cape Engaño. Ozawa had sent most of his planes ashore to operate from bases there and thus had only antiaircraft fire with which to oppose the attack. While engaged against Ozawa, Halsey learned of the action off Samar when a signal came in from Kinkaid at 0822 hours, followed by an urgent request eight minutes later for fast battleships. Finally, at 0848 hours, Halsey ordered Vice Admiral McCain's Task Group 38.1 to make "best possible speed" to engage Kurita's Center Force. It was en route from the Ulithi to rejoin the other elements of TF 38 with more carriers and planes than any of the three other task groups in Halsey's force, so it made good sense to detach it. Several minutes later, Halsey was enraged by a query from Nimitz at Pearl Harbor: "WHERE IS RPT WHERE IS TASK FORCE THIRTY-FOUR RR THE WORLD WONDERS." ("THE WORLD WONDERS" was apparently meaningless "padding" attached to messages to confuse enemy intercepts. But in this case, the padding made sense, to the mercurial Halsey's fury.) At 1055 hours, Halsey ordered all six fast battleships and Task Group 38.2 to turn south and steam at flank speed, but they missed the battle. After the war, Kurita admitted his error in judgment; Halsey never did. In fact, Halsey said his decision to send the battleships south to Samar was "the greatest error I committed during the Battle of Leyte Gulf." Historian Thomas Cutler believes that if Halsey had left part of his force behind instead of taking the entire Third Fleet, "all other errors would have been canceled out."

By nightfall, U.S. aircraft, a submarine, and surface ships had sunk all four Japanese carriers of Ozawa's force as well as five other ships. In effect, this blow ended Japanese carrier aviation. But the battle of annihilation that would have been possible with the fast battleships had slipped from Halsey's grasp. Still, of Ozawa's force only two battleships, two light cruisers, and a destroyer escaped. Including retiring vessels sunk on October 26 and 27, Japanese losses in the battle were twenty-nine warships (four carriers, three battleships, six heavy and four light cruisers, eleven destroyers, and a submarine) and more than five hundred aircraft. Japanese personnel losses amounted to some ten thousand five hundred seamen and aviators dead. The U.S. Navy lost only six ships (one light carrier, two escort carriers, two destroyers, and a destroyer escort) and more than two hundred aircraft. About twenty-eight hundred Americans were killed and another thousand wounded. The Battle of Leyte Gulf ended the Japanese fleet as an organized fighting force.

FURTHER READINGS

Cannon, M. Hamlin. *Leyte: The Return to the Philippines.* United States Army in World War II: The War in the Pacific. U.S. Army Center of Military History (1993).

Cutler, Thomas J. *The Battle of Leyte Gulf, 23–26 October 1944* (1994).

Field, James A., Jr. *The Japanese at Leyte Gulf: The Shō Operation* (1947).

Morison, Samuel Eliot. *History of United States Naval Operations in World War II,* vol 12, *Leyte* (1975).

Potter, E. B. *Bull Halsey* (1985).

"United States Strategic Bombing Survey, Employment of Forces under the Southwest Pacific Command" (February 1947).

Woodward, C. Vann. *The Battle for Leyte Gulf* (1947).

Spencer C. Tucker

SEE ALSO Aircraft Carriers: Japanese, U.S., and British; Halsey, William Frederick, Jr.; Navy, Japanese; Navy, U.S.

Lim, Vicente (1888–1944/45)

Filipino military officer and strategist Vicente Lim was born to the south of Manila at Calamba, Laguna Province, on February 24, 1888, to a Chinese father and Chinese mestiza mother. Despite his parentage, he identified more with Philippine society, although he believed his Chinese legacy worthy of note. For instance, on his U.S. Military Academy application, he mentioned his father as a Philippine citizen yet of Chinese kinship. Lim attended the Liceo de Manila and finished the teacher-training curriculum at the Philippine Normal School. He taught in public school, then returned to the normal school. In 1908, he failed the qualifying test for West Point proctored by the Philippine Bureau of Civil Service. Nonetheless, Governor-General James F. Smith named him an alternate candidate. Lim then retook and passed the examination, reaching the academy in March 1910.

Lim's military career probably had begun before his arrival at West Point. As a child, he organized other youngsters to run as messengers for insurgent General Miguel Malvar's army, active in his home province during the Philippine insurrection (a youthful indiscretion he undoubtedly omitted from his academy application). At the academy, he performed adequately in mathematics as well as chemistry and surpassed others in Spanish. Cadet Lim placed on or close to the foot of his class in the wholly military courses, training exercises, and practical military engineering. He was commissioned a second lieutenant on June 12, 1914, ranking seventy-seventh in a class of 100 graduates.

Lim returned to the Philippines near the end of 1914. Assigned to Scout service and sensing that postings in remote provinces would be confining, he asked President Manuel Quezon to transfer him to Europe as a military observer. His first year home he grumbled to Quezon of the affronts and spiteful abuse he endured because of his dark skin. In 1922, while on duty with the 45th Infantry Regiment at Fort McKinley, the quick-tempered Lim turned down an assignment to Corregidor Island when he realized the transfer was to create room for arriving U.S. officers. Back in the United States, he became the only Filipino officer to study at the Command and General Staff School before the establishment of the Philippine army and the sole Filipino graduate from the Army War College. Home by 1929, he was named commandant of cadets at Manila's San Juan de Letran College. Lim assumed he would be appointed chief of constabulary in 1931 in the eventuality of Philippine independence. But after leaving the U.S. military as a lieutenant colonel because of a weak heart, he joined the Philippine army as a brigadier general. By 1938, he had advanced to assistant chief of staff, chief of the War Plans Divisions, and deputy chief of staff. He studied at the Baguio Command and Staff School before his posting as the Philippine army's 41st Division commander.

For defense of the Philippines, Lim believed the Philippine army should originate anew, without an institution like the existing constabulary as its core. Preferring to begin with a strong officer establishment, he expressed disappointment in 1940 with the quality of officers being produced by the Reserve Officer Service School. He took the Japanese threat seriously and journeyed to Mindanao to emphasize the potential ties between Davao's Nipponese population and Tokyo's military forces. Yet on March 27, 1939, Lim told President Quezon that he was considering leaving the army because of its many problems.

The president disallowed his resignation and asked him for his thoughts. Lim then complained of the army's low morality, citing instances of forgery, stealing, dishonesty, and such. He likewise questioned the purchase from the United States and Great Britain of discarded weapons, such as the World War I–vintage Enfield rifle, which was inexpensive but of limited range. Criticizing General Douglas MacArthur's plan for the creation of a large army of draftees, Lim proposed cutting the recruits by 50 percent and investing the saved moneys in upgrading officer performance and hardware acquisition. He perceived the role of MacArthur and his military mission as advisory instead of command. When MacArthur stated the Philippine army was to be responsible for citizenship education in the secondary schools, Lim accused him of acting outside the lines of his authority and infringing on the general staff. Nevertheless, Lim realized the need to rely on U.S. naval power to offset the Japanese while the Philippines supplied ground forces. Once war started in Europe, he continued to have qualms about MacArthur's scheme and suggested the field marshal be dismissed unless he altered his way of thinking.

In 1939, Lim foresaw Japan's impending invasion of Southeast Asia. Two years later he sent his wife and younger children to join his sons in the States. When the Japanese attacked the Philippines, he and his fellow officers remained faithful to their benefactor. Already promised independence by 1946 and receiving military protection, economic preferences, and health and educational advantages, Filipinos in 1941 were loyal to the United States, as even the Japanese could see. While leading the 41st Division on the Bataan, General Lim gained distinction defending a section of the Abucay position. Despite their commander's suffering from a bad heart and aching tooth that confined him to his command post and prevented his visiting the front, Lim's unit's stubborn resistance secured the middle of the II Corps line in the face of repeated Japanese onslaughts. Later the 41st sat astride Japanese General Akira Nara's path west of Mount Samat, which cut 5 miles through II Corps territory and connected various trails running east and west. (Ironically, Lim and Nara had attended Fort Benning Infantry School together in 1928, and Nara favorably recalled his former classmate.) Lim became very ill during the campaign, enduring fever outbreaks every afternoon brought about by malaria along with the annoying infection in his tooth, which he refused to leave his post to have extracted because he feared his men would suspect him of abandoning them. Captured during the fall of Bataan, he wearily trudged northward with his troops in the infamous death march.

Once released by his Japanese captors, who wished to alienate the Filipinos from the Americans, Lim became active in the underground resistance. He vanished in Mindoro after departing Manila for Negros in an attempted getaway to Australia by submarine. Recaptured by the Japanese, he was returned to Manila, tortured at Fort Santiago, and executed sometime between November 1944 and January 1945.

Whatever the shortcomings of the Americans in their dealings with the nascent Philippine army, there was such an army, and it had Filipino general officers, such as Lim, something the British, French, and Dutch in their Pacific colonies had hardly even contemplated. Thus the Filipinos were the only Pacific peoples under foreign domination to fight in any numbers against the Japanese.

FURTHER READINGS

Friend, Theodore. *Between Two Empires: The Ordeal of the Philippines, 1929–1946* (1965).

Jose, Ricardo Trota. *The Philippine Army, 1935–1942* (1992).

Lim, Vicente. *To Inspire and to Lead: The Letters of Vicente Lim, 1938–1942* (1980).

Whitman, John W. *Bataan, Our Last Ditch: The Bataan Campaign, 1942* (1990).

Rodney J. Ross

SEE ALSO Philippines, Fall of the

Logistics, Japanese

Japan could not envision war on the scale understood by the West. The Japanese had not fought World War I–sized battles and had not experienced the logistical challenges faced by Western armies. Poor logistics planning, lack of foresight, and an inability to appreciate logistics requirements characterized their Japanese supply efforts throughout World War II.

Although the Japanese talked about total war, they did not understand it. Although they "battled," they did not "war." They searched for the decisive battle, only dimly aware that a decisive logistics battle was underway, that victory would be decided in factories, and that they were losing. Few wars have been started by countries less able to sustain the effort than Japan. Although the Japanese began the war over access to oil and southeast Asian resources, they did not clearly see war in logistical or economic terms, either for themselves or for their enemies.

The Japanese were especially vulnerable logistically. Japan was not rich. Planners were chronically hampered by "have-not" realities in money, resources, and manufactur-

ing. They thought small, expected to fight outnumbered, and assumed that their "spirit" (*bushido*) would overcome enemy materiel. They did not adequately allow for wastage, made no provision for pipeline supplies (items en route but not yet available to front-line units), and did not adequately estimate what supplies would inevitably be lost in transit.

As crippling as materiel shortcomings was the psychological outlook of the Japanese. Tactics, not strategy or logistics, was the Japanese strength. Their admirals and generals considered themselves warriors, not supply men (also not ordnance men, maintenance men, intelligence men, medical men, or communications men). From the Combined Fleet to the Imperial Army to airmen of both services, the focus was on battle. The Japanese officer was a participant in the conflict rather than a Western-style manager of violence. Feeding the men, ensuring that equipment existed, and ensuring soldier health was not what a warrior did. Raising doubts, or warning about logistical unsupportability, could ruin an officer's reputation.

The army was confident that it could campaign with lightly equipped and lightly supported infantry forces, so they deliberately skimped on support troops. Although Japan mobilized an impressive 175 divisions for World War I, it failed to equip them in the Western sense. Supply depots in Japan were poorly planned, badly equipped, and inadequate to handle large-scale, wholesale distribution of supplies. Warehouses were inaccessible to freight cars and lacked handling equipment.

The Japanese based their resupply planning on expenditure rates from the Russo-Japanese War of 1905 and from experiences in China. Ammunition was issued at a rate that supplied the number of rounds necessary for each weapon in a division for four months. Planners assumed only twenty days of firing during those four months. Experience quickly showed that triple this amount was needed in modern warfare, and even that experience was based on ammunition that had been available, not what could or should have been expended. Factories, however, could not meet modern needs.

There were no fleets of trucks to provide support, no sprawling quartermaster or maintenance facilities, no vast depots to refurbish worn and damaged equipment. No great training bases turned out a steady flow of radio operators, cooks, clerks, navigators, truck drivers, POL managers, ordnance men, aerial gunners, medics, or mechanics. Commanders showed little interest in sending their men to the ordnance school in Japan, nor did they establish schools or training programs at tactical units or in geographic army areas. Commanders and planners completely lacked appreciation for the vast numbers of technicians required to support a modern army.

Service schools paid little attention to logistics and engineering support of combat forces. Logistics, science, and technology were not important subjects. It was difficult to get military academy students to study logistics. The best men did not become logisticians. One Japanese described supply officers as old, narrow thinking, and incompetent. "In our army," wrote an army-level chief of staff, "the officers do not like to study logistics—it does not interest them—they want to study only how to fight." Another Japanese recalled that staff officers found logistics work dull and thoroughly distasteful, so they skipped it.

Navy officers might have been more attuned to logistics than army officers, for they could not live off the land as the army did to some degree, especially in food. If there were no fuel or spare parts, ships did not sail and aircraft did not fly. The navy, however, was schooled in carrying everything they needed aboard ship and did not understand the army's need to transport bulk items and the army's long-term, sustained requirements when in austere theaters.

In the heady days of early 1942, the navy pressed the army to go well beyond Japan's original strategic goals. The startling successes of the initial campaigns encouraged tacticians to improvise (and caused logisticians to despair). Five divisions, the navy advocated, should invade Australia. But the navy had not analyzed tactical or logistical requirements. Nor had they considered the impossible strain the invasion of a vast, empty continent would impose on shipping.

The barrens of northern Australia could not feed an invasion force. The army in the Malay operation had used 710,000 tons of shipping for three divisions, and the Philippine landing had needed 650,000 tons for two divisions. The army countered that Australia would need twelve divisions and 1,500,000 tons of shipping specifically for the army, not counting the fleet train necessary to support the main body of the Combined Fleet. "The tea in this cup represents our total strength," the army planner told his Navy counterpart as he poured the tea on the floor. "You see it goes just so far."

The Japanese gambled on a quick negotiated peace. They did not have the technology or raw materials for a sustained war against an industrial power the size of the United States. They underestimated their own rates of consumption, badly underestimated U.S. ability to produce war materiel, and underestimated how quickly the Americans could launch a counteroffensive. Strategy did not drive logistics planning or industrial production. Plans were based on what could be produced, not on what

was needed. Strategic planners did not often restrain themselves based on logistical unsupportability. As a result, logistics planning consisted of little more than allocating scarcities.

The Japanese had planned their tactics, logistics, and personnel around one decisive naval battle that would win the war, but then, so had Western navies. They did not organize their industrial, manpower, or training base for the long haul, and they repeatedly ignored logistics until disaster had overwhelmed them. Japanese officers were not stupid. Some knew that sustainment of the fighting line was important. But their tactical efforts always overreached their logistics.

The Japanese accomplished their early war aims by conquering lands with raw materials, but local commanders proved unable to develop those resources. Even worse was the drain on shipping that carried and sustained the advance into the Solomons. What Japanese proconsuls did extract from Borneo, Java, Malaya, and Sumatra ran into shipping bottlenecks, for there was insufficient shipping. Although the Japanese had nearly a year to integrate captured countries into their economy before the American counteroffensive began, they were inefficient in doing so.

Manchuria

The Army's logistics system in 1941 was focused on the Soviet threat—severe cold, light weapons, a sizable industrial base in Manchuria with a large rail distribution system, and supply over poor roads supported by immense numbers of horses—65,000 horses in Manchuria alone. Korea, China, Manchuria, and Formosa were all self-supporting in food, and fair quantities of supplies existed there. Japan did not feed those armies. They fed themselves. Those conditions, with which army officers were familiar and comfortable, did not translate well into the Pacific.

Indochina

As the Japanese advanced into the Pacific, their aircraft operated from miserable, unimproved airstrips. Before the war, when the army asked Tokyo for money to upgrade French airfields seized in Indochina, Tokyo restricted what could be spent. Airfield work was totally dependent on coolie labor, thousands of men wielding shovels. Not a single motor-powered piece of construction equipment was available.

Philippines

Even in their early operations, the invading Japanese could not adequately supply their forces. The logistics system had been successful in the past, for it had worked against Russia in 1905 and in China since 1937. But sea lines of communications (LOCs) had been short, uninterrupted by submarine or air attack. The Japanese had not begun serious logistics planning for the Pacific operation until just two to three months before war began, and that planning was inadequate, optimistic, and lacked contingencies.

Japanese soldiers sent overseas received one month's supply of food. It was then their responsibility to forage off the locals. Japanese soldiers picked clean populated areas. In a 2-kilometer stretch of road on Luzon in December 1941, they collected carabao, tied them head to tail, then slaughtered and ate them. Chickens also met untimely fates. The Japanese looked at nearly everything made of wood as fuel for a cooking fire. Chairs, tables, and beds went into the flames.

Once off-loaded from ships, supplies moved to the troops on rail, trucks, horses, and native porters. Fifty-eight hundred horses landed with the army invading Luzon. Practically all supplies were securely wrapped in heavy, tightly woven straw bags and matting, easily carried by men, cart, and pack animals. Gasoline and diesel fuel were packaged in 18-liter cans (4.76 gallons) for ease of handling.

The supply system on Bataan broke down in early 1942. The normal ration of sixty-two ounces fell to twenty-three. Quinine exports from Java to Japan had been embargoed for about a year before war started, and fourteenth Army had invaded the Philippines with only one month's supply of quinine. Field hospitals were shacks with grass floors, overcrowded, and poorly equipped. Japanese doctrine allocated medical supplies to its soldiers at roughly one-quarter that of U.S. rates. But because it was a low priority item, less than half of the authorized quantities were ever shipped. If lucky, 70 percent of that half reached the troops.

Malaya/Singapore

The 3-division march on Singapore was executed with the strongest tank, engineer, communications, medical, and railroad augmentation ever given a Japanese army. Planners had stripped other theaters nearly bare of specialized troops. Much of the fuel and food came from captured British stocks as did 3,600 trucks and cars to move it. When the Japanese made artillery ammunition their top supply priority—in fact, the only item to be moved—logisticians could move it because they did not have to transport food or gasoline.

General Tomoyuki Yamashita knew that the British seriously outnumbered him, and if he had to fight for long in the city, he would fail. (But this the deluded British commander did not know and it is unlikely he would have done much about it if he had.) The premier ground force, the best-manned, best-led, and best-equipped force the Japanese possessed had, in reality, run out of ammunition. Even so, Japanese tactics and aggressiveness had so demoralized the British that Yamashita did not need any more ammunition. The British surrendered in good time.

Burma

The Japanese drove the British out of Burma through superior light infantry tactics. So horses, mules, and oxen moved their supplies. The Japanese left their heavy artillery behind. When soldiers asked for maps, they were told, "go and see." They saw and conquered. After they captured Rangoon, the Japanese found that the railroad running north out of that port city was indispensable for their logistics even though it was much too limited completely to support combat operations. Only when the Japanese launched their traditional lightning attacks of encirclement into India in March–April 1944 did they fail.

India

Staff studies for the India invasion did not address the chance of success. Instead, the arbitrary assumption that the invasion would occur drove the studies. One hundred miles of trackless jungle and mountains barred the way. There was only a small civilian economy and food source to exploit. When Fifteenth Army's chief of staff, a soldier well-versed in logistics, requested that the operation be reconsidered due to logistics unsupportability, the army commander fired him.

The Japanese planned a short, 3-week campaign into India for early 1944. Each division would carry ammunition for twenty days. Soldiers man-packed as much food as they could carry, elephants and oxen carried supplies (the 31st Division alone collected 3,000 horses and 5,000 oxen, but only three days of forage), and the men were told to be prepared to eat grass when food ran out. They drove meat on the hoof (until the cattle died), ate the oxen when the oxen died, and expected to subsist on captured British rations and arms. Sixty percent of the pack horses died. Unable to capture supplies, lacking communications and heavy weapons, and short of ammunition at the end of intolerably long supply lines, the bloodied Japanese staggered away from British materiel superiority. The Japanese "bamboo spear" philosophy—to wit, invincible spirit and bravery overcoming materiel strength—failed.

Southwest Pacific

In 1942, the major Japanese fighter base at Lae on New Guinea had no maintenance shops, no hangers, and no tower. The field was so small that pilots compared it to landing on a carrier. Three decrepit trucks supported the field. Men with shovels and wheelbarrows repaired cratered runways. From April 1942 until the Japanese lost the field in September 1943, they made no attempt to improve it, nor did they build any port facilities to expedite unloading of seaborne supplies.

The navy general staff was poor at logistics and construction planning and had not planned for mutually supporting airbases. In the first ten months of war, the Japanese navy would build only one new airbase, at Buin on Bougainville, and it had but one runway. The field at Guadalcanal bore bitter fruit when the Americans seized it. The expansion of the existing Buna field was so disrupted by American air attack that the Japanese gave up using it in late September.

The Buin runway on Bougainville was soft and slippery during rains. When ground crews reported that the field was unfit for operations, the chief of staff of the Combined Fleet—rather than arrange for construction assets to properly complete the field—groused in his diary, "How weak-minded they are! This is the time when every difficulty should be overcome. Don't grumble, but try to use it by all means!" Fliers used it and damaged about ten aircraft a day when the runway was wet.

Guadalcanal

The Japanese navy work force that landed on Guadalcanal was heavy on manpower and short on vehicles. They used nine road rollers, six trucks, mixers, and sundry equipment to build a tamped coral strip. After they lost the field, each piecemeal attempt to retake it failed. No serious logistics effort supported these attacks. Too few men were landed, they gambled on surprise when none existed, and a supply train in the Western sense did not exist.

Guadalcanal was the highwater mark of Japanese expansion in the south, and it was also the exemplar of Japanese logistics. Japanese doctrine had painted itself into a corner. Without the resources to build 4-engine bombers, they could not inhibit the American logistical and air base build up at Espiritu Santo and Noumea. Unprepared quickly to build multiple airfields, they could not bring in the aircraft they had. Unable to control the skies over their own LOCs, they could not deploy available ground assets into the fight. The nation could not afford adequate logistics and engineering, and they therefore could not plan for it.

The navy had to fuel its ship from tankers at Truk in 1942 because, although Truk was supposed to be an advanced naval base, the piers, dry docks, power plants, cranes, repair shops, and depots required to service a large fleet did not exist. Labor parties hand loaded goods and supplies into barges and sampans which shuttled them from ship to shore. A lack of cargo handling equipment, lifting equipment, and skilled labor slowed cargo ship turn around.

Food and ammunition constraints on Guadalcanal drove tactics. Because they could not sustain a long campaign, the Japanese had to succeed quickly. Because they "would succeed," no matter what, they concluded that they did not need the logistics necessary for a long campaign. They could not afford to fail, so they had no backup plan in case of failure. Soldiers launched frontal attacks because they did not have equipment and supplies for more sophisticated tactics or ammunition and food for lengthy fights.

No one had thought through the logistical requirements. Commanders were anxious to attack. Moving men on warships was quicker, easier, and safer than transporting bulky supplies and heavy equipment, so only light combat troops were dispatched. Soldiers carried their own food (which ran out) and manpacked their own artillery (which wore them out). Trails cut by hand from the landing beaches toward Henderson Field were too steep and narrow for heavy artillery. Even mountain guns were left behind. There were no medical units, no kitchens, and no transportation, few mosquito nets, and no plan for malaria control. Soldiers had little food, no change of clothes, and virtually no supplies. It was war on the cheap, little more than foot soldiers throwing themselves at a fully equipped combined arms team that was dug in, linked by communications, and well-supplied. The Japanese battled. The Americans waged war.

There was no civilized infrastructure on Guadalcanal to provide food, so Japanese soldiers lived on what the navy supplied. American air attacks hit so many transports and freighters that the navy canceled normal resupply efforts. Instead, destroyers dashed to the island and used on-board launches and collapsible boats to ferry supplies ashore. Navy twin-engine Bettys air dropped token quantities of supplies. Submarines brought in some food, but not nearly enough.

The Japanese cut rations to one-sixth normal for front line troops and to one-tenth for others. When boating supplies from destroyers to shore proved too slow, the Japanese used destroyers to drop large, sealed, metal drums filled with rice and barley, hoping that boats and swimmers could tow them to shore or, at worst, that they would float to shore. Only one-quarter of the 20,000 drums were ever recovered. Even those supplies faltered under American interdiction and proved utterly inadequate.

Air Warfare

The Pacific war was a fight to seize airfields. Yet the Japanese had not developed the airfield construction techniques and equipment necessary for an air war. Nor had they created units equipped for air base construction, maintenance, and supply. They had no concept of the maintenance, supply, and dispersal facilities needed for modern air warfare. Maintenance units lagged behind during the early advances and were too few in number. Depots where engines could be changed and major repairs made were few and scattered.

Japanese pilots took off from small, wretched, unpaved airstrips. Half the aircraft lost to 23rd Air Flotilla in the first three months were from crackups on bad runways. Without mechanized equipment to cut dispersal areas, aircraft were vulnerable to attack on the ground. Food was bad. Barracks were jungle slums. Disease felled pilots and left serviceable aircraft grounded. Ground crews pushed aircraft around fields, for there were no tractors to pull them. Getting heavy field and shop equipment to forward bases was difficult, so engine changes and body work were hampered.

A lack of standardization in weapons and equipment plagued logisticians. American army and navy aircraft carried three types of machine guns (.30-caliber, .50-caliber, and 20mm). Japanese aircraft carried fifteen. Navy aircraft could not resupply with ammunition at army depots, and vice versa, because of different gun-barrel chamber dimensions. Major differences in radio equipment resulted in poor intercommunication between army and navy aircraft.

Japan lost 182 of the initially available 240 G3M2 and G4M1 twin-engine bombers in the first ninety days of war, and Japanese industry was hard put to replace them. As early as April 1942, before the battle of Midway, the navy was bemoaning the nation's insufficient aircraft production facilities. More important than the aircraft were the pilots. Lost at Midway were well-trained veterans of China, and their replacements would never have the experience and talent of the prewar pilots, probably the best naval aviators in the world at the time.

The Japanese had failed to construct ferry sites and auxiliary airfields between Rabaul and Guadalcanal, 675 miles away. Japanese aircraft at Rabaul had to fly to their extreme limits simply to reach the island. Eighteen Type 99 dive bombers ditched into the sea in the first two days

of the Guadalcanal campaign when they ran out of gas. Excessive tactical optimism and a shortage of construction units repeatedly postponed intermediate airbase construction.

Attrition on ferry routes averaged 2 to 5 percent from 1942 to 1944 and rose to 10 percent in 1944. Japan lost 4,000 aircraft in ferry accidents versus 909 American aircraft lost in ferry accidents in all theaters. In later campaigns, the Japanese would lose up to 30 percent of their aircraft ferrying them to the front. Poor airstrips, poor maintenance, inexperienced ferry pilots, and a lack of repair parts increased noncombat losses. The decline in the quality of spare parts was so marked that accident rates soared. Repair-parts shortages were so serious that it became policy to ship complete end items to mechanics who then cannibalized them for parts.

Ground Warfare

The attack on Port Moresby in 1942 collapsed when the Japanese could not maintain their supply lines over the Owen Stanley Range in New Guinea. They had landed two naval construction units (3,000 men), a large army bridge and road construction unit (1,000 men), and more than three hundred pack horses, but that would not be enough. Logisticians had not stocked reserves of food before the crossing began. The Japanese dragooned, mistreated, and then murdered New Guinea laborers and porters, thereby foreclosing that source of manpower.

The fighting troops were unable to capture rations. Then Allied air attacks hit bridges, ships, barges, and supply dumps and forced Japanese supply columns off the one trail. On September 17, when almost within sight of Port Moresby, not a single grain of rice remained. The subsequent retreat was more grueling than the advance. The Japanese had already plundered the few native gardens during the advance, so they now ate roots, grass, and the occasional dead Australian.

The Japanese tried to build roads in February 1943 to support their New Guinea campaign, but they never had enough machinery, they did not understand road-building techniques, and their trucks were not powerful enough to climb steep slopes. Only 20 percent of all authorized trucks arrived at the front, and here conditions were severe and repair facilities least developed. The Japanese never developed anything approaching the quality of the U.S. Army's indestructible 2½-ton, six-wheeled, all-powered axle truck. Troops overloaded inferior-quality trucks by as much as 100 percent. Tire shortages, poor springs, and bad roads shook trucks to pieces and created an impossible maintenance backlog. The Japanese did not use the echelon system of maintenance, so attempts by unqualified personnel to make major repairs often ruined equipment.

The Japanese had not developed heavy engineer equipment in the prewar years. They did have some medium weight prime movers and earth-moving equipment, yet they did not take that medium equipment into forward areas in any quantity. Even had they desired, they could not have matched American experience in producing and using heavy engineer equipment.

Cargo ships tried to unload outside the range of U.S. land-based aircraft. Then army shipping engineer regiments (normally 1,000 or more men with 135 barges or boats) and sea transport battalions (50 to 150 sailing vessels) staged the cargo forward on barges, moving 40 to 80 miles each night. A typical Rabaul to New Guinea trip stretched 391 miles and took eleven nights.

Although dispersal of supplies into small packets on land and sea reduced the effectiveness of American air attacks, it made for an inefficient logistics system. Economies inherent in scale were lost, and their system of records and accounts was swamped. Supplymen across the Pacific lost track of where the dispersed supplies were stored. Spoilage and American attacks destroyed between 30 and 50 percent of all food shipped to the front. Logisticians were so stressed simply maintaining the front lines on a hand-to-mouth basis that they could never expand rear bases or stock reserve supplies.

As repair parts became scarce, as fuel dried up, and as mechanic support was overwhelmed, aircraft availability dropped 75 percent. High quality lubrication oil for aircraft and vehicles became scarce. The Japanese made do with lesser brands and reduced the life of their engines. American naval activity, mines, and air attacks cost the Japanese so many destroyers while they were operating as transports that barges replaced them. Japanese submarines had virtually ignored U.S. LOCs in favor of tactical support of the fleet. Many boats left traditional war patrols and slipped supplies into isolated garrisons. Big boats specially configured carried 50 tons internally and 40 externally. But submarine resupply was so small when matched against requirements that it was trivial.

Shipping

The Americans waged a gnawing war of attrition against Japanese shipping. Submarines and aircraft so interrupted normal surface transportation that the Japanese turned to small convoys of luggers, powered barges, and light craft. Necessity drove the Japanese to develop small craft into the principal tool of forward area resupply delivery. Thousands of barges, junks, and native craft crept from island to island, up rivers, and across dangerous waters.

It was, however, little more than a garden hose of supply on a wild fire of demand. Japan needed a strong, big-ship merchant marine. Uninterrupted movement of ships was vital to the war economy. The merchant marine brought in oil, iron ore, coal, bauxite, rubber, and food. From Japan flowed weapons, ammunition, and aircraft to defend the empire. There were three principal sea LOCs: Japan to Singapore, Japan to Palau, and Japan to Truk. Feeder lines snaked out from those three ports to front line units. Every Japanese LOC was a sea LOC.

Japan lost 180 ships to American submarines in 1942, not a serious toll. Yet less than a year after war began, demands for military shipping, inefficiencies inherent to military operations, and losses from air attacks left military and industry crying for more ships. In 1943, 335 ships went under from submarine attack alone. The Japanese merchant marine lost 20 percent of its capacity. The decline in ships meant that concrete, lumber, steel, barbed wire, and coast defense cannon could not get to the islands Japan hoped to defend.

The Japanese were reluctant to begin convoys or to assign adequate antisubmarine warfare vessels to protect convoys. The navy considered antisubmarine operations dull, defensive, and unglamorous. They had not established the staff, devoted the time, nor developed the doctrine to study and organize defensive tactics for merchant shipping. The decisive battle/short war assumption had excluded any need for long-term escorting. Japan had launched the war to seize resources but had not considered how to protect the sea LOCs over which the resources were to be shipped.

American submarines inflicted grievous losses on shipping and reduced supplies to deployed forces. Torpedoes sank 603 ships in 1944, and the Japanese lost more than half of their cargo carrying capacity. Even had the Japanese decided to give top priority to convoying and antisubmarine warfare, they did not have the assets or the technology to turn the tide.

Saipan

The transfer of men to Saipan and Luzon in 1944 occurred at a time of growing submarine, land-based, and carrier air threats. A convoy carrying the second echelon of 43d Division to Saipan lost five of its seven ships. The delays inherent in submarine threats doubled the normal sailing time between Japan and Saipan. Saipan's commander warned the navy that unless cement, steel reinforcing rods, barbed wire, and lumber were shipped in, his soldiers could do nothing but sit around with their arms folded.

Philippines, 1944–1945

Submarines and aircraft cut Luzon off from Japan. Japan could dispatch only 60 percent of planned supplies to Luzon, and of that, most failed to arrive. Yet because Manila had served as a main supply point for shipment of army and navy supplies farther south, and because interrupted sea LOCs prevented subsequent shipment out of the Philippines, the Japanese on Luzon found themselves with the best supply situation any garrison had yet seen. "Best," however, is relative.

Even with the best supply situation experienced by a Japanese army since 1942, they had too little, and they could not move what they had. There was no central logistics authority in Manila where 70,000 metric tons of supplies were piled helter-skelter. It would take six months to move it all, and that time did not exist. Trucks lacked fuel. The Japanese had failed to maintain Luzon's roads and railroads and were therefore unable to use them efficiently to move supplies to their redoubts.

They could move only 4,000 metric tons out of Manila against a requirement for 13,000 metric tons of the most vital supplies. The one tank division on Luzon had fuel for just seven hours of movement. The food shortage grew so bad that rations had to be cut from 3 pounds per man per day to 9/10 of a pound.

Okinawa

Okinawa was only a few hundred miles from Japan, and Japan was desperate to defend that island, so troops there were well-supplied. Native islanders augmented manpower for construction and logistical support. The Okinawa defenders armed themselves with large numbers of artillery pieces, mortars, antiaircraft guns, antitank, and automatic weapons from supplies intended for shipment to the south. And they had plenty of ammunition. The result was a spirited, but in the end doomed and bloody, defense.

Home Islands

The Japanese in Japan proper were in a most unusual position. On the debit side, two-thirds of the army's weapons and ammunition were outside the home islands and unable to return. On the credit side, there were no sea LOCs anymore. Each island would become a battlefield. Although most military industry had been bombed to rubble, manpower existed, aircraft had been hidden away, some food was available, and simple weapons necessary for a ground fight existed.

From February through June 1945, the Japanese mobilized twenty-nine brand-new coastal defense division, sixteen maneuver-attack divisions, and thirty independent mixed brigades and regiments, all to be equipped from current production. Some divisions reported to their defense sites without equipment. By August, there were fifty-seven divisions in the home islands, weapons for forty, and ammunition for thirty.

Japan's rail system was falling apart from deferred maintenance, overuse, and inexperienced workers. Only 12,000 motor vehicles (actually autos) were scheduled for the 400,000 newly mobilized men. Cargo mobility would come from 470,000 horses and 70,000 carts—horse-drawn, bicycle-drawn, and hand-drawn. Weapons were scarce. Some of the new coastal defense divisions did not have artillery regiments. Food became short as the demand rose to feed men arriving from Manchuria as well as the new units. This last, all-out logistic effort would not be tested, for the war ended before the Americans landed.

Conclusion

Unable to afford strategic bombers and misusing their submarines, the Japanese could not seriously inhibit the build-up of American strength. Uninterested in logistics, their warrior-centered philosophy shattered on Western matériel superiority. Unable to devote more resources to antiaircraft weapons, build dispersal and ferry sites, or match American fighter strength, they lost control of the air. Unable to field and transport masses of artillery and ammunition, their infantry was always outgunned. Unable to protect merchantmen or replace shipping losses, the entire logistics structure dwindled and died.

The Allies tried numerous Japanese for war crimes at the end of the war. Some should also have been tried for criminal neglect of logistics, or more accurately, for starting a war they could not support.

FURTHER READINGS

Craven, Wesley F., and James E. Cate. *The Army Air Forces in World War II*, vol 4. *The Pacific: Guadalcanal to Saipan, August 1942 to July 1944* (1950).

———. *The Army Air Forces in World War II*, vol 5. *The Pacific: Matterhorn to Nagasaki, June 1944 to August 1945* (1953).

Hayashi, Saburo. *Kogun: The Japanese Army in the Pacific War* (1959).

Parillo, Mark P. *The Japanese Merchant Marine in World War II* (1993).

Sakai Saburo. *Samurai!* (1957).

United States Strategic Bombing Survey. *The Effect of Air Action on Japanese Ground Army Logistics*, No. 64 (1947).

John W. Whitman

SEE ALSO Army, Japanese; Army Air Force, Japanese; Navy, Japanese

Logistics, U.S.

The war in the Pacific and the Far East was a war of magnificent distances. As such it required logistics efforts of unimagined magnitude and complexity to sustain it. Fortunately for the United States, the thousands of miles separating one base or strategic area from another were mostly nautical miles. This meant that the economic distances, that is, the distances in terms of cost of transportation, were but a fraction of what they would have been over land. If the sea lanes could be kept open for the United States and its allies, and closed to the enemy, the logistic advantage was likely to be decisive. But the Japanese in the early months of the conflict advanced so rapidly that they neglected to go to all-out mobilization until reversals of fortune demanded it. In the end it was they who had too little too late.

And there was water. Water everywhere. The rolling waves of the immense ocean, the still lagoons of the coral atolls, the rushing rivers and stagnant pools of the jungles, the rains of tropical storms and monsoons, and with little exception it was always hot. The moist, steaming heat of warm seas and hot bush. The main exceptions were the moist, foggy cold of winters in the Aleutians and the dry cold of the thin air of the Burmese and Chinese mountains. As the war spread across the vast reaches of the western Pacific and the South Seas, throughout East Asia and back again, the sheer exertion required to exist often overshadowed the special skills of artillery adjustment or rifle marksmanship. An environment of tropical seas and islands cast logistics in a wholly different light from that found in the more familiar surroundings of Europe. Railway networks and finished highways were foreign to most of the combat areas. Logistics organization, allowances of equipment, days of supply, and standard operating procedures developed for continental warfare were largely inappropriate. Dispersal of forces and supplies over great distances and reliance on water transportation to bring them together were the common order. Rapid deterioration of supplies in the hot, wet climate complicated supply storage and distribution. Widespread malaria multiplied the problems of medical care and troop effectiveness. Lack of ports and other facilities, lack of maps and terrain data made true mountains out of molehills for all kinds of operations. The jungle guaranteed that no move inland nor any construction of airfields and base facilities would be simple or easy.

Considered by many military observers to be incapable of striking effectively in more than one place at a time, the Japanese on December 7, 1941, attacked not only Pearl Harbor, but also Kota Bharu in British Malaya; Singora and Pattani in Thailand; Singapore, Guam, Hong Kong, Wake, and the Philippine Islands. Thereafter Japanese forces spread swiftly throughout the Western Pacific, the East Indies, and points southward.

They were supported by a war economy that had begun orientation toward war production as early as 1928 and since that time had expanded by more than 500 percent with an increase of total output of 85 percent. Aircraft, aluminum, machine tool, automotive, and tank industries had sprung up from almost nothing. Acquisitions in Manchuria and China had helped relieve Japan of shortages of coking coal, iron ore, salt, and food; expansion through Malaya and the East Indies would augment sources of critical raw materials, most importantly oil and food.

Still, Japan was in no position to wage a long war; Japanese industry was at the mercy of its sea communications. No major Axis power could have been less self-sufficient. The industrial potential of Japan was no more than 10 percent of that of the United States, but the Japanese had expanded their industrial capacity so rapidly in the last few years, already geared to war production, that many authorities tended to underrate the current strength of Japan.

The tenuous naval superiority that Japan gained in the Western Pacific by the devastation of the U.S. fleet at Pearl Harbor in December 1941, and its 2-to-1 numerical superiority in aircraft in the area, eventually could be overcome by the capacity of the enraged United States to restore and greatly increase its naval strength while building up ground and air forces. Its enormous advantage in total industrial potential gave to the United States a critical logistic advantage in a long war.

Aside from the replenishment of Hawaii, the first wartime logistic activity of the United States in the Pacific was a forlorn attempt to get sustenance and ammunition to the beleaguered forces in the Philippine Islands—mostly on the Bataan Peninsula of Luzon and the island fortifications of Corregidor at the entrance of Manila Bay.

The Orange and Rainbow war plans had included, almost to the last months before war, an assumption that the Philippines could not be held long against a full-scale attack. Consequently, there had been no buildup of supplies to support a prolonged defense, though the expectation had been that Bataan could be held for at least six months.

Doubtless the decision of General Douglas MacArthur to try to resist on the beaches instead of adhering to the plan for an immediate and orderly withdrawal into the peninsula hastened the loss of Bataan, for quantities of supplies sent forward for the beach defense had to be abandoned during the hasty withdrawal that followed.

Large food dumps were also abandoned in Manila, a particularly cruel loss, as the Bataan garrison suffered more from hunger than any other ill during the siege. Then, when the few efforts to run the tightening Japanese blockade were unavailing, supplies, already short, began to dwindle alarmingly. It turned out that food was the most critical item of supply on Bataan. Within a few weeks the daily ration had to be cut in half. Soon soldiers were driven to forage for whatever they could find, including pack mules, dogs, iguanas, and snakes. The end came on April 8, 1942.

Corregidor held out for another four weeks. There the most critical item was ammunition. President Roosevelt tried to hold out some rays of hope when there was no hope. He directed that six converted World War I destroyers be pressed into service for a shipment of 10,000 tons of ammunition to the Philippines. Unfortunately, delays in assembling crews and then finding safe routes were such that the ships had to offload at Cebu in the central Philippines. One thousand tons finally got to Corregidor. Submarines carried in 1 million rounds of small arms ammunition and 3,500 rounds of 3-inch antiaircraft ammunition. But as so often had been the case in the early years of this war, it was far too little, too late.

After the fall of the Philippines, the big effort was for a massive buildup of troops and supplies in Australia to turn that continent into a grand base for the long voyage to Tokyo. In spite of the strategic decision of "Germany first," several times as many troops and supplies now were going to the Pacific as to Europe. The naval battle of the Coral Sea in May 1942 blunted the Japanese threat to Australia and the decisive naval battle of Midway in early June opened the sea lanes to more traffic. After eight months and the expenditure of thousands of man hours in labor and the diversion of hundreds of ships to the task, 1,117,000 measurement tons of supplies and equipment had been delivered to the areas of Sydney and Melbourne—still about as far from Tokyo as when they had left San Francisco. At the same time over 312,000 tons were going to the South Pacific, mostly to New Zealand and New Caledonia; over 1 million tons were destined for the Central Pacific, mostly to Hawaii; over 800,000 tons to Alaska, and about 128,000 tons to the China-Burma-India theater.

But not all the Japanese were in the home islands, and the question arose, should those on the periphery be attacked first?

The first offensive was indeed against peripheral forces in the Solomon Islands, specifically the island of Guadalcanal and the adjacent small islands of Tulagi and others of the Florida group, where a Marine amphibious force landed on August 7 and 8, 1942, and Army reinforcements went in two months later. The forces on Guadalcanal had to be supported from Auckland, New Zealand, 1,500 miles away, and later from a forward base at Nouméa, New Caledonia, 900 miles from Guadalcanal, where there was an excellent harbor but very limited docking facilities.

Meanwhile, MacArthur was on the move in Australia. On July 20, 1942, he transferred his headquarters from Melbourne northward to Brisbane. That still was a long way from the Japanese threat, and in ensuing months the Southwest Pacific headquarters developed a forward base at Townsville, another 900 miles up the coast. Now MacArthur and the Australians worried about Japanese reinforcements on New Guinea and an attempt to overrun the Australian territory of Papua, the southeastern quarter of that big island. It appeared that the Japanese still were aiming at Australia itself.

MacArthur determined to meet the threat head-on in Papua. The question was, how to get men and supplies and equipment through the Japanese-infested waters. Lieutenant General George C. Kenney, commander of the Fifth U.S. Air Force and of Allied Air Forces in the area, proposed to move the forces into New Guinea by air shuttle. This unprecedented operation began in September 1942 with the movement of an infantry battalion of the 32d Division by air from Brisbane to Port Moresby on the southeast coast of Papua. Other troops followed from Townsville. To accomplish the mission, General Kenney pressed into service Australian civilian transport planes, newly arrived B-17 bombers—some with civilian crews—and some old German-built Dutch planes, as well as the few C-47 (the civilian Douglas DC-3) transport planes at his disposal. The bombers were even able to carry a 4-gun battery of 105-mm howitzers.

The next step was an air shuttle over the rugged, jungle-choked Owen Stanley Mountains for support of the campaign against Buna and Gona on the north coast of Papua. In October and November close to fifteen thousand American and Australian troops crossed those mountains by air. Then the air units were called upon to carry supplies to the forward positions. They even included the delivery of some 2½-ton trucks by the expedient of cutting the frames in two with acetylene torches so that the trucks could be stowed on aircraft. About twenty C-47s, with bombers reinforcing them from time to time, carried a weekly average of two hundred thousand tons of supplies to various points in Papua.

Ground troops, under the supervision of air officers, packaged the supplies, wrapped them in excelsior, and sewed burlap sacks around them so that they could be tossed from doors or dropped from bomb bays for free falls at a time when parachutes were scarce. Other supplies were delivered by air landing at forward air strips. On November 6, 1942, MacArthur moved his advance base to Port Moresby. Thereafter he commuted frequently between Brisbane and New Guinea.

The Guadalcanal and New Guinea operations were major steps in securing the supply lines to Australia. By the end of December the strength of army forces arrayed against Japan had reached 464,000 men. This was some 200,000 more than had been anticipated in plans approved the previous spring. Those deployed against Germany and Italy amounted to about 378,000, some 50,000 fewer than had been planned.

Reliance on oversea lines of communication, not only from the United States but within the theaters, together with the long series of amphibious operations, threw army, navy, and marine forces into close and continuous contact throughout the war in the Pacific. The situation cried out for the integration of logistics for the support of joint operations, but this was more evident to commanders on the scene than to planners in Washington. Admiral Chester Nimitz and Lieutenant General Delos C. Emmons, commander of army forces in Hawaii, independently made recommendations to Washington for a system of joint supply. Their pleas fell on deaf ears, largely because the commanding general of Army Service Forces, Major General Brehon B. Somervell, mistrusted the navy's logistic organization and feared that army interests would suffer.

Nevertheless, the commanders in the theaters took steps toward effective logistic cooperation. As early as May 1942, Ghormley had established a joint purchasing board to coordinate local procurement in New Zealand and on smaller islands in the area. Subsequently, the army assumed responsibility for obtaining provisions as necessary from the continental United States for all shore-based forces except those in Samoa, while the navy supplied gasoline and oil for all forces.

The machinery of logistic support varied greatly between army and navy. The army, geared mainly for massive land campaigns, had developed a system of centralized control and orderly distribution. The navy, concerned mostly with supporting forces at sea, encouraged decentralization, concentrating its depots at the ports, relying on the supply bureaus to meet their responsibilities without close overall command, and granting autonomy and flexibility in supply distribution to units in forward areas. By early 1942 the navy had developed auxiliary units that amounted to floating bases, one of the great logistic innovations of the war. With fuel, ammunition, provisions, and other supplies, as well as repair facilities, now afloat, the fleets had the long legs needed to move and fight almost indefinitely without the need to return to any fixed base. It was a system that might have served the army better than the system of island bases in many areas.

Wasteful duplication of effort and the need to make the most economical use of available shipping kept up the pressure for logistic coordination. At last the army chief of staff, General George C. Marshall, and the chief of naval operations, Admiral Ernest J. King, arrived at an agreement. In March 1943 they issued the "Basic Logistical Plan for Command Areas Involving Joint Army and Navy Operations." The crux was to put the responsibility for coordination on the shoulders of theater commanders—where the most significant steps in that direction already were being taken. In May, Nimitz directed Admiral William F. Halsey, Jr., who had succeeded Ghormley as commander of the South Pacific, to set up a more formal structure for logistic coordination in the area. Thereupon Halsey established a Joint Logistics Board on which army, navy, and marine service support commanders did formally what they already had been doing informally.

The command and administrative structure developed directly under Nimitz had special complications growing from the fact that at the same time he was commander in chief of the Pacific Ocean Areas, commander of the Central Pacific and the North Pacific Areas and commander in chief of the Pacific Fleet. Nevertheless it was in Nimitz's commands that joint logistics reached its highest development. In September 1943, Nimitz organized a joint staff for his headquarters at Pearl Harbor. It was the only truly functioning theater joint staff of the war, but it became the prototype for later unified command staffs. It comprised four staff sections, each including army, navy, and marine corps officers. These sections were: J-1, Plans, under a naval officer; J-2, Intelligence, under an army officer (there were also some British and Australian officers in this section); J-3, Operations, under a naval officer; and J-4, Logistics, under an army officer. Later a fifth section, J-5, General Administration, was added under a naval officer.

The J-4 section had branches for transportation, fuel, supply, and advanced bases. Although there was friction at times between commanders of the different services, the arrangement on the whole worked smoothly.

Control of shipping was the key to logistic coordination. As reflected in the relative lack of congestion and rapid turnaround of cargo ships, shipping control in the Central Pacific was superior to that in any other theater.

Under a system of joint theater planning and joint base commands, ships were echeloned according to detailed plans to assure that supplies would arrive as needed and in the proper order. Army engineers and navy construction battalions (Seabees) accomplished wonders in building air bases and support bases for amphibious operations in the offensive westward across the Pacific.

MacArthur's General Headquarters (GHQ), Southwest Pacific Area, remained essentially a U.S. Army staff, even though it was an allied as well as a joint command. MacArthur did add American and Australian naval officers and Australian army officers as technical assistants at various levels. Having no unified organization either for planning or operations with respect to supply, transportation, communication, construction, or logistic services at lower levels, and only limited measures for joint procurement or cross servicing, GHQ coordinated theater logistics mainly through a system of priorities control over shipments of cargo into the area.

For support of particular campaigns there was a consolidation of American and Australian forward supply services. For support of the offensive in New Guinea, GHQ in October 1942 organized in Papua the Combined Operational Service Command to control all activities of the Allied lines of communication. The deputy commander of the U.S. Army Services of Supply served was its commander, with an officer of the Australian Staff Corps as his deputy.

The Services of Supply (SOS) in the Southwest Pacific had to bend conventional organization to adapt to conditions, and it suffered from a lack of precise definition of responsibilities, for its staff had to operate in the shadow of GHQ. As the combat situation developed, SOS organized six base sections in Australia and an advance section in New Guinea, but it did not operate in close support of the combat units. Ordinarily, each task force commander improvised a service command to organize and operate his rear area until combat operations had been completed in the vicinity; then facilities would be turned over to SOS as combat operations moved on. However imperfect his organization, MacArthur fully appreciated the logistic factor, and he was especially concerned about the shortage of service troops. "The great problem of warfare in the Pacific is to move forces into contact and maintain them," he asserted. "Victory is dependent upon the solution of the logistic problem."

Warfare on the Asian mainland was in a world of its own. It too was hot, it had dense jungle growth. It also had high mountains. But there were no ocean seas close at hand to carry troops and supplies and equipment close to the sites of action. The command structure was a com-plicated one. The China-Burma-India (CBI) theater was a U.S. Army theater that had grown up without any official designation as such, but where Lieutenant General Joseph W. Stilwell was recognized as theater commander and commander of Chinese as well as U.S. troops in Burma and India. It extended over the area of the China theater, which was an Allied theater under the command of Chinese Nationalist Generalissimo Chiang Kai-shek, with Stilwell as chief of staff, independent of the Combined Chiefs of Staff; over Burma which lay within the area of another Allied command, the Southeast Asia Command (from August 1943), under Lord Louis Mountbatten of Great Britain, with Stilwell as deputy commander, and over India, which comprised a separate British command responsible to the government of India.

For supplying the oversea theaters from the continental United States, the ports of embarkation served in effect as supply-regulating points. Port commanders were responsible for the flow of supplies into and out of their ports in accordance with the needs of the theaters. Each port was responsible for shipping supplies to a certain area: San Francisco for the Pacific, Los Angeles for China-Burma-India, Seattle for Alaska. Other ports might be used as outports of the major terminals, but always under the direction of the port commander having jurisdiction for the area.

The ports regulated the shipment of troops as well as of supplies. Camp Stoneman, with facilities for 30,600 men, served as the principal staging area for San Francisco. Units were supposed to arrive in the staging area at full strength and with full personal and organizational equipment. However, most units had to be supplied some equipment, either due to deficiencies or because new items had become available.

Supply generally was automatic from the United States to a new theater. Then after a few months a system of reports and requisitions would come into play for most items. Requisitions would go to the designated port of embarkation where the Overseas Supply Division, a staff agency of Army Service Forces, would edit the requisitions and send extracts to the supply depots furnishing the types of goods called for. Requisitions for controlled or special items (such as ammunition or items in short supply) went to the headquarters of the technical service concerned or to Army Service Forces headquarters.

One of the greatest problems in oversea supply was in the coordination of shipping. There was no real unification of supply lines to the Pacific theaters. A measure of coordination did emerge from the formation of the Joint Army-Navy War Shipping Administration Ship Operations Committee set up informally in San Francisco early in 1943. Serious shipping shortages that year made joint action imperative. For a time in August and September troop shipments against agreed priorities were forty-five days behind schedule. Within another year the system was working smoothly.

Still, a comparable joint priority list for shipping cargo never was achieved. The very length of the supply lines made planning most difficult. It took almost as much shipping to move and maintain 40,000 American troops in Australia as for a force of 100,000 men in the British Isles. It was impractical also to establish central reserve stocks and a systematic flow of supplies through a series of depots. Neither was it practical simply to make whole-sale deliveries of supplies to the theaters and expect the theaters to make "local" deliveries to points extending over two or three thousand miles. Standard procedure came to be for the theaters to determine requirements and forward requisitions, then for deliveries from the United States to be made to many individual bases. In 1944, Army shipments from the United States were going to some seventy different destinations in the Pacific.

Plagued by inadequate facilities for ship discharge at the receiving end and with too few service troops, harried port officers pressed into service combat troops, navy and marine units, and native labor to try to overcome the congestion of shipping that followed from one base to the next as the fighting moved forward in the Pacific theaters—probably the greatest continuing logistic problem in those areas. Congestion reached critical proportions at Nouméa, New Caledonia, in the autumn of 1942; the shipping tie-up there scarcely had been over-come when it reappeared at Guadalcanal as preparations mounted for further offensives in the northern Solomons and then in the Marianas. In the Southwest Pacific such critical congestion appeared later, for as long as supplies continued to go into the Australian base, the well-developed ports of Brisbane and Sidney were adequate, even if their longshoremen stubbornly worked to a lack-adaisical peacetime routine, which featured numerous tea breaks. Further, the Southwest Pacific was able to rely to a greater extent on local procurement; indeed Mac-Arthur's staff reported that in the last half of 1942 the Southwest Pacific received a smaller tonnage of supplies from the United States than the theater itself shipped out to the neighboring South Pacific. Then, as Southwest Pacific offensives moved forward, serious congestion appeared successively at Milne Bay and Hollandia (New Guinea).

A related problem was in the displacement forward of rear bases. Efforts for efficient roll-up were only partially successful, and huge quantities of supplies went to waste, left on islands hundreds or thousands of miles to the rear of the action. It was easier to rely on further shipments from the United States than to find shipping and labor to reload supplies on distant island bases. Still, this argument made little sense to service troops who had so laboriously unloaded the cargo in the first place.

Frequent and sudden changes in objectives and advances in timing, resulting from and leading to further unanticipated success, created special problems for supply officers. But the ocean environment permitted a degree of flexibility otherwise impossible. Ships bound for one island could be diverted to another without serious loss. If at times the supply lines bent under the strain, they never broke. The momentum of the stepped-up offensives, once gained, never diminished.

To make direct shipments of supplies from the United States to the bases most effective, a way had to be found around the "normal" procedures of sorting, storage, and distribution. To this end the Central Pacific in 1943 introduced a system of block loading. At first defined as all supplies needed for 1,000 men for twenty days, later extended to thirty days, blocks were made up in two ways. For the initial phase of an operation, a block included all types of supplies needed by the number of men for the number of days. For resupply, one ship would carry only one class of supply; a group of ships then would be dispatched in a convoy or within a specified sailing period so that together they would provide all classes of supply. The theater would simply order so many standard blocks to be delivered to a designated advance bases.

Beyond routine supply that could be calculated in advance, requirements had to be met in other ways. Although procedures continued to be more regularized as the war wore on, improvisation of supply and transportation continued to the end. Conditions never could be precisely anticipated, though the War Department never ceased trying. The Operations Division set up a "project system" keyed to specific construction projects months in advance, when the exact nature of the project could only be guessed. Other kinds of special supplies had to be ordered to meet special needs as they arose: canvas buckets, water cans, and extra canteens for an island where fresh water was short; machetes for hacking through thick jungle growth; special tropical clothing; insect repellents and first aid for bites. On some of the islands quartermaster units were able to step up their operations by the use of palletized loads. Front-line supplies at various times were brought up in jeeps and trailers over freshly cut roads and trails were hand carried or were dropped by aircraft.

In the China-Burma-India theater the central objective as well as the central problem was logistical. The major purpose of the campaign in Burma was to establish effective communications with China. The greatest obstacle to the successful completion of that campaign was the moving up of supplies to support the forces engaged. Pack animals and natives carried supplies to the front when possible. Long-range penetration columns, such as Wingate's Chindits (British) and Merrill's Marauders, operating in the Japanese rear, depended for months on air drops.

But major operations and getting effective support to the Chinese depended on expansion of the line of communication across Assam, the northeast province of India. Tremendous efforts went into improving the port of Calcutta, into stepping up traffic on the Bengal and Assam Railway, into getting all possible use of the Brahmaputra barge line, operated by several British companies, into the construction of airfields in Assam, and into laying pipelines from Calcutta and Chittagong to Upper Assam. All this was necessary for the completion of the Ledo Road. This road was the vital link from the old Burma Road across the rugged mountains and swampy valleys to bring up supplies for air delivery over "the Hump"—the 500-mile route over the mountains—to China as well as for the support of current combat operations in the north Burma area. In May 1943, scarcely 5,000 tons of supplies were delivered over the Assam line of communication; within the next eighteen months that figure rose to 125,000 tons. The Ledo Road, renamed the Stilwell Road, was not completed until January 1945, and not until just a few weeks before the end of the war did fuel begin flowing through the pipeline to Kunming.

The most significant innovation of the scores of amphibious operations in the Pacific was the use of special vessels designed for the purpose: combat loaders and various types of landing craft. Combat loaders were transport ships specially rigged for carrying assault forces and cargo to the vicinity of hostile shores for landing by boats and lighters carried on board. These vessels were mainly of three types—the attack personnel transport (APA), the converted destroyer transport (APD) for carrying personnel and equipment, and the attack cargo transport (AKA), mainly for cargo.

As for special landing craft, the Japanese had used some vessels of this kind in their invasions of the Philippines and Malaya, and the British had made some use of similar craft in North Africa. But it was for the United States to develop new designs and undertake production on a big scale. Soon these came to be regarded as critical items of equipment, and strategic decisions and the timing of operations frequently hinged on their availability.

The common characteristics of these vessels were a bow that could be opened to permit lowering a ramp or a bow which itself could be lowered as a ramp, so that troops, trucks, and tanks could move out directly onto the beaches under their own power. They were of shallow draft, with controlled water ballast so that a vessel could be beached at low tide and floated off at high tide. These vessels were of two general categories, landing ships and landing craft.

The landing ships were ocean-going ships especially useful for shore-to-shore operations. Of the dozen or so types, the most important were the LST (landing ship, tank) which might carry, for instance, twenty medium tanks on its tank deck and eleven 2½-ton trucks on its main deck; the LSM (landing ship, medium), and the LSD (landing ship, dock), a floating drydock that carried landing craft and amphibious vehicles and launched them by flooding the hold.

The most common of the landing craft were the LCI (landing craft, infantry), the large version of which could carry 200 men or 75 long tons of cargo; various models of the LCT (landing craft, tank); the LCM (landing craft, mechanized), and the LCVP (landing craft, vehicle, personnel) that could carry 36 men and one 2½-ton truck or 4 tons of cargo.

In addition to these ships there were amphibious vehicles that could be launched from ships and proceed across water up onto the beaches under their own power. These included the "alligator," (later "Amtrak") an amphibious tractor used to carry troops and equipment ashore; the amphibious 2½-ton truck (DUKW), and the amphibious tank, for combat support.

The shipping required for an amphibious assault force varied according to the length of the voyage, the mission, special equipment, and the proportion of landing craft and amphibious vehicles carried. For a relatively small operation and short voyage, a force equivalent to a reinforced infantry division of some 22,000 men, with 3,600 vehicles, in a fairly typical case might take nine APAs, six AKAs, thirty-six LSTs, twelve LSMs, and three LSDs.

Southwest Pacific forces got their first test in the ways of amphibious warfare in operations along the north coast of New Guinea, perfected them in campaigns against islands from Biak and Noemfoor to Morotai, and reached their highest achievement in the return to the Philippines.

For operations over any extended distance in the Southwest Pacific, troops generally were transported in APDs and landed by landing craft carried on board. When coral reefs blocked the way to the beaches, assaulting forces used Alligator/Amtrak amphibious tractors and

DUKWs to get ashore. As soon as a way had been cleared, LCTs carrying tanks and shore party engineering equipment were launched from the flooded wells of LSDs. Then successive waves of infantry would go in on LCIs. About an hour after the initial assault, LSTs began arriving with vehicles, supplies, and additional troops, all to be unloaded before nightfall. All types of landing vessels might by used for follow-up landings on succeeding days. Echelons would continue at 3- to 5-day intervals until Army Services of Supply could take over responsibility for reinforcement and resupply with its own merchant shipping.

For shore-to-shore operations, MacArthur relied on Army engineer special brigades to man fleets of landing craft, to organize shore party teams for unloading the assault vessels and setting up supply dumps, and to provide lighterage and local transportation for supply build up. Only in the Southwest Pacific Area did the navy not man all the vessels in such operations. After training at the Engineer Amphibian Command on Cape Cod, Massachusetts, the 2d Engineer Amphibian Brigade (later redesignated the 2d Engineer Special Brigade) went to the Southwest Pacific in November 1942; a second brigade arrived in October 1943, and a third in May 1944.

Beach parties, as distinct from shore parties, were navy units charged with coordinating the arrival of boats and ships on the beaches, seeing to the evacuation of casualties into the waiting vessels, and getting the vessels off the beaches once they had been unloaded. In these duties the beach parties had to work closely with the shore parties. Ultimately the VII Amphibious Force, controlling the navy beaching vessels of MacArthur's command, organized and trained eight beach parties, each made up of three naval officers and eighteen seamen.

While MacArthur's forces moved northwestward and those of Admiral Nimitz moved westward across the Central Pacific, controversy developed between army and navy leaders over the major objectives in the western Pacific. Mainly the debate was on whether Luzon or Formosa should be the main target and whether one or the other might be bypassed. Differences broke along service lines, partly because an attack on the Philippines under MacArthur would be mainly an army show, while an attack on Formosa would be by Nimitz's forces and would be mainly a naval operation. MacArthur insisted that liberation of the Philippines was a political and moral responsibility. After all, the Philippines were an American possession, and he had promised, "I shall return." Admiral King, pressed his colleagues on the Joint Chiefs of Staff for a direct attack on Formosa. This would cut off the Japanese in the Philippines from homeland support, and

liberation of the Philippines then would come about anyway.

Whatever ulterior motives may have been at work, the argument hinged mainly on logistics. An officer of the Army Services Forces planning staff expressed concern about the great distances over open seas that supplies would have to be transported in the Central Pacific approach. This would be slow, the supply lines would be more vulnerable, and there would be complications of transhipment. Moreover, army planners had serious misgivings about whether the Marianas and Palaus could provide the bases necessary for mounting the massive assaults needed against the Japanese inner defenses. MacArthur insisted that the Philippines were essential for mounting further operations toward the Japanese home islands.

Navy logistics officers, however, saw the situation quite differently. While the army held to its belief in large land bases, and while operations in the Southwest Pacific had been over relatively short water distances (frequently shore-to-shore and involving only the smaller landing craft), in the Central Pacific long approaches over wide expanses of open ocean had become the rule. The navy was developing elaborate techniques for floating bases using combat loaders and fleet auxiliaries, and relying upon aircraft carriers for air support. Admiral King was not thinking of relying on bases in the Marianas for more than a small fraction of the build-up for a major offensive against Formosa. On the contrary, such an operation would be mounted from many widely separated sites in the Pacific and would rely on direct shipments from the United States, by way of the Marianas, for follow-up support.

Always reluctant to choose between MacArthur and Nimitz, the Joint Chiefs finally were persuaded that logistic resources would be available for the attack on Luzon, but not for Formosa until cargo shipping and service troops could be spared from the war in Europe. MacArthur developed a new schedule that called for a landing on Morotai on September 15, on the Talauds on October 15, on Saregani and Mindanao in the southern Philippines on November 15, and on Leyte in the central Philippines on December 20. On this basis MacArthur hoped to be able to land on Luzon in the Lingayen Gulf region by February 20, 1945.

Then in September 1944, Admiral Halsey, after raids by his carrier planes on the central Philippines, sent a recommendation to Nimitz that the proposed operations against the Talauds and Mindanao, as well as plans for Central Pacific forces to take Yap, be canceled in favor of a direct thrust to Leyte. Nimitz approvingly forwarded the recommendation to the Joint Chiefs of Staff, then in session at the second Quebec conference, and he added an offer to put forces scheduled for Yap at the disposal of MacArthur for an invasion of the Philippines. A query to MacArthur by the chiefs brought a quick reply that he could be prepared to land on Leyte on October 20. That was approved.

Now with this turn in favor of MacArthur, the Joint Chiefs did not forget Nimitz. Agreeing that it would be wise to bypass Formosa, they issued a directive to Nimitz to make a landing on Iwo Jima in the Bonins on January 20 and in the Ryukyus, approaching the southern islands of Japan, by March 1.

Was it feasible to marshall the vast forces and supplies needed to make a decisive attack on the Philippines in the time indicated? The answer was yes.

On September 13, the XXIV Corps, with two divisions presumably headed for the invasion of Yap, embarked at Honolulu and proceeded to Manus Island for completion of staging for the new objective. There the assault troops transferred from AKAs to LSTs. A month later Sixth Army headquarters, with the Sixth Army Service Command, X Corps headquarters, and the 24th Infantry division sailed from Hollandia, New Guinea. Two days later the 1st Cavalry Division, coming from Manus, joined them. The whole force, arriving off Leyte as scheduled, amounted to 150,000 men, with 518 ocean-going troop and cargo ships supported by about 180 warships. (The Allied D-day landing force in Normandy on June 6 totalled 132,700 men.)

Retaining supplies and equipment provided in anticipation of the Yap operation, the XXIV Corps brought a 30-day supply of rations and medical supplies, twenty days of clothing, weapons, vehicles, fuels, and construction materials, seven units of fire for artillery weapons, and five units for other weapons. The X Corps was to take ashore thirty days of engineer supplies, two units of fire for all weapons, and ten days of all other supplies. Resupply stocks were being shipped from the United States and Australia to New Guinea, where they would remain on call. In addition, ten Liberty ships, eight at Hollandia and two in the Palau Islands, were to be held loaded in floating reserve.

Within an hour after the landings, supplies began to pour onto the beaches. Unfortunately, many of the ships had not been properly combat-loaded and thus could not be unloaded in the order needed. Ships crews and soldiers detailed to stay on board for unloading did their best to get vehicles and supplies from the APAs, AKAs, and LSTs onto LSMs that served well as lighters. Shore parties from two regiments of the 2d Engineer Special Brigade controlled the unloading on the beaches in the X Corps zone.

Since the XXIV Corps came from the Central Pacific area, it had no engineer special brigade, but it formed provisional shore parties from two combat engineer groups to work the beaches in its area.

Congestion soon ruled the beaches. Some of the shore parties did not land soon enough to develop proper organization before supplies began to arrive. Some of the approaches in the north were too shallow for the LSTs, and they had to withdraw under fire. Other LSTs were diverted from one beach to another to meet changing needs. Many of the boats, carelessly loaded, were difficult to unload. Beach parties brought in supplies faster than shore parties could handle them.

One bright spot in the scene of chaos was the shore party that served the 7th Division near Dulag. It resorted to what it called the "drugstore system" of delivering supplies by DUKW amphibious trucks directly from LSTs to front-line units without going through the busy supply dumps in the midst of their build-up. In this way requisitions could be filled within an hour. After about six hours, regimental dumps about five hundred yards inland could be used for all requisitions in that area.

On the first day, a total of 107,450 tons of equipment and supplies were landed. The early congestion on the beaches was quickly relieved, but soon greater congestion set in. Swamps and rice paddies made it difficult to find suitable areas for supply bases and hospitals or to make much headway on the construction of airfields. Roads laboriously cut through by engineers quickly disintegrated.

The American victory in the great naval battle of Leyte Gulf in late October 1944, assured the security of the surrounding seas.

During November the Sixth Army Service Command established its major base at Tacloban. There, two deep-water berths were found intact, and engineers built additional docking facilities and several lighterage wharves. In addition, the service command established a sub-base at Dulag and a supply point at Carigara. Unfortunately, successive resupply convoys kept arriving before the preceding ones could be unloaded, and Japanese bombers kept attacking the ships.

Getting supplies ashore was only one problem. The other was getting them up to the advancing combat units. As roads became unusable, Navy vessels and amphibious vehicles carried supplies around the coastline to points as near the troops as they could get. When vehicles could not be used, service units organized carrying parties of soldiers and Filipino civilians to carry supplies forward. Often air drops were used to supply units otherwise isolated.

When the Japanese brought in additional troops to try to hold Leyte, MacArthur, too, sent in reinforcements from his reserve units, including the 112th Cavalry Regimental Combat Team, the 11th Airborne Division, elements of the 38th Infantry Division, and the 32d and 77th Infantry Divisions. All these brought with them further logistic complications, but the dispatch of additional amphibious vessels kept up the tenuous supply lines.

It took nearly two and one-half months for the Leyte operation to be completed. At that time a general level of five to ten days' supply had been built up and maintained for several weeks.

Still it was possible to adhere fairly closely to the stepped-up schedule for the invasion of the main island of Luzon. After a series of landings on Mindoro from December 15, two corps (four divisions) landed in early January in the Lingayen Gulf area of Luzon, and other landings farther south were made on January 31 and February 15. Over-the-beach supply operations now showed improvement, not only due to more favorable terrain and weaker resistance but also because of better organization. But, as nearly always, there was a shortage of labor for unloading supply ships, now aggravated by a disposition on the part of many of the troops to disappear from their tasks in favor of fraternizing with local Filipinos.

Meanwhile, large-scale movements were underway across the Central Pacific. Four months before the Leyte operation, the Central Pacific Force already had launched an amphibious operation of comparable magnitude. With only three months of planning, the operation was carried out 3,600 miles away from the main base in Hawaii. The force of 127,500 men—two-thirds Marine and one-third Army—with 535 transports and warships, arrived on June 15 in the Marianas after a 1,000-mile voyage from Eniwetok and launched successive attacks against Saipan, Tinian, and Guam.

Joint procedures for logistic support of amphibious operations had reached a high pitch of efficiency in the Central Pacific. Directives from Admiral Nimitz's headquarters ordinarily spelled out three phases for an operation. Control over logistics was in the hands of the commander in each phase. The first, the assault phase, came under the task force commander, usually Vice Admiral Richmond Kelly Turner. The second, the land operations phase, came under the ground forces commander, usually Lieutenant General Holland McTyeire Smith, Marine Corps. The third phase, the garrison or base phase, came under a commander of the service having major responsibility. Most of these were navy, but as the campaigns moved westward, the army was assigned major responsibility for base development on Makin in the Gilberts,

Kwajalein in the Marshalls, Saipan in the Marianas, and Anguar in the Palaus. In planning for base materials, the navy eschewed the army's keyed project system. Instead it made up standard units that could be called for in the numbers needed for the development of any particular base. The system in effect extended block-loading, and, to a degree automatic supply, to nearly all categories.

By far the greatest battle, in terms of numbers, against the Japanese was the last. For the invasion of Okinawa, a large island in the Ryukyus about three hundred forty miles south of the Japanese home island of Kyushu, an assault force 183,000 soldiers and marines, with 747,100 measurement tons of cargo, went aboard 430 assault transports and landing ships at ports on the U.S. West Coast, Hawaii, Espíritu Santo in New Caledonia, Guadalcanal, the Russell Islands, Saipan, and Leyte. They rendezvoused at Eniwetok, Ulithi, Saipan, and Leyte. Additional ships brought follow-up units to bring the total force to more than half a million men and 1,213 warships. On April 1, 1945, two marine divisions and two Army infantry divisions of Lieutenant General Simon Bolivar Buckner's newly formed Tenth Army went ashore on the southwest coast of Okinawa.

The navy commander of the task force, Admiral Turner, was responsible for delivering the troops and supplies to the beaches. General Buckner was responsible for landing the supplies and moving them to dumps. Island Command Okinawa was organized as an army service command of the Tenth Army to provide immediate logistic support and base development. The assault units carried a thirty-day supply of rations, clothing, fuel, and other essential units, and five units of fire of ammunition. Automatic resupply was in twenty-one shipments scheduled to leave the United States at 10-day intervals (beginning February 20) for regulating stations at Ulithi and Eniwetok, where they would wait for calls from General Buckner.

Careful planning and a surprising lack of enemy resistance made possible fast and effective organization of the beaches after the landings. For four or five hours during flood tide, landing craft could cross the reef and discharge cargo directly onto the beach. Larger ships had to be unloaded at the reef. General unloading began on April 3, and in the absence of enemy interference, continued through the nights under floodlights. Navy beachmasters directed the movements of incoming ships. Control of the beaches passed successively up the chain of command until the 1st Engineer Special Brigade and the Island Command, under Tenth Army headquarters, assumed control on April 9.

Storms interrupted unloading, and cargo kept coming in faster than it could be handled. At the end of May the Joint Freight Handling Facilities, under navy command, relieved the 1st Engineer Special Brigade of shore-party operations, and its quartermaster service and truck companies were transferred to the 53d Medium Port under that joint headquarters.

The initial Japanese reaction was deceptive. After five days Japanese troops began putting up strong defense from well-prepared positions, with support from hundreds of attacks by kamikaze (suicide) planes. The result was the heaviest casualties of the Pacific war. The air attacks also played havoc with supply activities. Failure to capture the port of Naha as had been planned put strains on over-the-beach supply operations. An inclination to unload vessels selectively only added to problems of congestion. The building of floating causeways and makeshift piers helped somewhat, but at the end of the campaign in June unloading of supplies was 200,000 measured tons behind schedule.

The end of hostilities on Okinawa brought no decline in logistic effort, for this was considered to be the staging area for the coming invasion of Japan. With the improvement of port facilities, discharge of cargo went up from a rate of 20,000 measurement tons a day in June to over 37,700 tons a day in July.

When Japan surrendered, MacArthur, to whose command the forces in the Ryukyus had been transferred on July 31, was preparing for the invasion of the home islands. On Luzon the Sixth Army was regrouping for its assigned invasion of Kyushu, and an advance detachment of the First Army had arrived from Europe to begin preparations for its part in the later invasion of Honshu.

Plans for redeployment of forces from Europe would have involved the most ambitious logistic operations of this or any war. They called for the movement of 1.2 million men from Europe to the Pacific (800,000 by way of the United States and 400,000 directly), the transfer of 5 million tons of supplies and equipment from Europe to the Pacific, and the return of another 5 million tons from Europe to the United States. After V-E Day (May 8, 1945) the Eighth Air Force quickly redeployed from Europe to the Far East, and the rapid redeployment of ground troops began. By this time more than 18,350,000 measurement tons of army cargo had been shipped to the Southwest Pacific area, more than 14,000,000 tons to the Central Pacific, and 3,540,000 tons to the South Pacific, while another 6,400,000 tons were going to the CBI and 6,900,000 tons to the Alaska area.

Although from the beginning many had urged a single theater command structure for the entire Pacific, the Joint Chiefs of Staff never had been able to bring themselves to a firm choice between MacArthur and Nimitz, and they did not do so now. MacArthur was given command over the planned invasion of Japan, but Nimitz was to be a co-ordinate, not a subordinate commander. Logistic machinery being developed for support of the operation was something of a throwback to the prewar concept, that is, separate army and navy commands with cooperation depending on agreement between the commanders concerned. An army-navy conference on shipping and supply in May and a conference at Guam in June between representatives of MacArthur and Nimitz developed joint arrangements for support of the Kyushu operation.

Already Army Service Forces in Washington and the theater army staff had prepared logistic plans for this invasion. The initial assault would be mounted and supplied from Pacific bases; resupply would be directly from the United States. The army would maintain major distribution points in the Philippines, with air depots on Guam, at Manila, and on Okinawa. In the absence of any further general agreement, the army and navy each would control the shipping for support of forces under its control. The army would have major control over shipping to common ports in the operational area. Regulating stations would be set up at Ulithi and Okinawa. There would be 482 special-loaded ships for Kyushu and 700 for Honshu.

The first operation was scheduled tentatively for November 1, 1945. It would be a three-pronged attack by the Sixth Army on Kyushu. The second operation, scheduled for March 1, 1946, was to be aimed initially at the Kanto plain east of Tokyo. This would involve a force of nine infantry divisions, two armored divisions, and three Marine divisions, under Eighth Army and Tenth Army, to be followed by First Army with one airborne and ten infantry divisions to be redeployed from Europe.

Then came the rapid turn of events in August leading to V-J Day. After the Japanese surrender it was necessary to put into effect only the recently drawn plans for unopposed occupation.

On August 28 advance parties arrived at the Atsugi airdrome, Tokyo. Main elements of the 11th Airborne Division began arriving early the next morning. By September 13, 21,721 men of the two divisions and higher headquarters had been flown to the Tokyo area.

An army service command was assigned to each occupation army. The XXIV Corps, with a newly assigned army service command assigned to it, went to Korea for occupation south of the 38th parallel.

At the same time, Headquarters, U.S. Forces China theater, organized advisory groups to supervise the turning over of military supplies to the Chinese and to assist in the movement of Chinese forces northward. China received special treatment in the continuation of lend-lease to enable Chinese forces to accept the surrender of Japanese troops in China and to complete a program begun during the war of providing equipment for a 39-division Chinese Nationalist army.

The end of the war in the Pacific was also the end of the greatest logistic operations in military history.

FURTHER READINGS

Ballantine, Duncan. *U.S. Naval Logistics in the Second World War* (1949).

Leighton, Richard M., and Robert W. Coakley. *Global Logistics and Strategy, 1940–1943* (1960).

Lutes, Le Roy. *Logistics in World War II: Final Report of Army Service Forces* (1948).

Morison, Samuel E. *The Two-Ocean War: A Short History of the United States Navy in the Second World War* (1963).

Army Forces Pacific. *Engineers of the Southwest Pacific,* 8 vols. (n.d.).

Stauffer, Alvin P. *The Quartermaster Corps: Operations in the War Against Japan* (1956).

Vagts, Alfred. *Landing Operations* (1946).

———. *Loading Operations* (1946).

James A. Huston

SEE ALSO Army Ground Forces, U.S.; Navy, U.S.

Los Baños Raid

As U.S. forces returned to the Philippines, General Douglas MacArthur became increasingly concerned that the Japanese would slaughter the more than two thousand prisoners held at Los Baños internment camp 20 miles below Manila. Thus in February 1945, he told General Joe Swing, commander of the 11th Airborne Division, that he wanted these prisoners rescued as soon as possible. The details of the operation were relegated to Swing.

Swing assigned the mission to Major Henry Burgess and the 1st Battalion of the 511th Parachute Infantry Regiment, based on the fact that Burgess's battalion, with 412 men, was the strongest in the division. As late as February 18, Burgess and his men were still involved in heavy fighting and did not know Los Baños existed. Within five days, however, they would be in and out of the objective after having executed one of the most successful raids of the war in the Pacific.

When Burgess received his orders, his summary of the available intelligence was simply that "there wasn't much." Lieutenant George Skau and the division reconnaissance platoon had been operating behind Japanese lines for four days and had gathered some information but not enough. On February 19, however, the raid's planners received an unexpected windfall when Pete Miles, a civilian engineer who had previously done demolition work for the army, reported to division headquarters after having escaped from Los Baños the day before. Miles had a wealth of information about the daily routine inside the camp, including the revelation that only those Japanese on guard duty were armed. Miles explained that the Japanese not on duty arose just before dawn and did calisthenics in an open area near their barracks, with their weapons locked in a rack in a short connecting room between the two long barracks where they slept.

With this key bit of information, the rescue plan had been finalized by February 21. The mission would begin at 0700 hours on February 23 with Lieutenant Skau's platoon and a group of Filipino guerrillas sneaking up to and killing the on-duty guards. At the same time, Lieutenant John Ringler's B Company and Lieutenant Bill Hettinger's machine-gun platoon would jump from nine C-47s to a small drop zone (DZ) next to the compound. The drop zone was ringed by barbed wire, a railroad track, and a high-voltage transmission line. As Ringler observed, "It'll be a tight fit, but we can do it." Once on the ground, the paratroopers would race across the camp to the weapons rack, hoping to arrive before the off-duty guards could react.

Even earlier, at 0400 hours, the rest of the battalion under the control of Major Burgess would load on fifty-four amphibious tractors, or "amtracs," slip into Laguna de Bay, and head for Mayondon Point, 2 miles north of the prison camp. The force would reach the landing point at 0700 hours, secure a beachhead, and continue to the prison in the amtracs.

On top of all this, Colonel Shorty Soule would lead a diversionary attack consisting of B Company of the 637th Tank Destroyer Battalion and elements of the 472d and 675th Field Artillery Battalions. This force would rush down the road from Manila toward Mamatid in order to fix the Japanese 8th Division positions near there.

On the morning of February 23, the raid got off to a good start. Skau's platoon had marked the DZ with colored smoke, and the jump was nearly perfect. Only one man was injured on the tight DZ. As the paratroopers descended, Skau's men destroyed the perimeter guards. Caught completely by surprise, the off-duty guards milled around in confusion. When they realized what was happening, it was too late. Ringler's men had already beaten them to the weapons rack.

Burgess's amtrac force was also having success. On reaching the compound, the lead vehicle smashed through the gate, creating a breach for the others to follow. Lieutenant Tom Mesereau positioned his C Company so as to block any reinforcements from the Japanese 8th Division. All was going according to plan.

The only snag in the operation was convincing the internees that their rescue was real. Ringler reported to Burgess that it was difficult to get the prisoners out of their shacks and barracks. Burgess, however, had the answer. The fire that had been started in the initial firefight was spreading toward the six amtracs parked near the guards' barracks and camp headquarters, and internees were rushing to the amtracs ahead of the flames. Burgess told Ringler to go to the south side of the camp, upwind, and torch the other barracks, in hopes of having a similar effect. The results were spectacular, as internees poured out and into the loading area. Troops started clearing the barracks in advance of the fire and carried out to the loading area more than 130 people who were too weak or too sick to walk. At 1130 hours, most of the camp was in flames, but the evacuation was complete.

However, time was still critical. Mesereau and his company had made contact with an enemy company, and there were indications that a much larger Japanese force was close behind. The first shuttle of about fifteen hundred internees and accompanying guards had left the beach at about 1000 hours. Burgess had the rest of his battalion and the reconnaissance platoon in a good defensive perimeter on the beachhead and about seven hundred twenty internees still waiting for evacuation. After completing their first round-trip, the amtracs returned to the beachhead, and at about 1500 hours all personnel were on board and under way. By this time, the Japanese had closed in and were beginning to find their range, but the amtracs had the head start they needed and escaped with little time to spare.

The raid had been an enormous success. To reach their objective the 11th Airborne had moved some twenty-five miles behind enemy lines by air, water, and land. In the process, they had rescued 2,122 prisoners, destroyed a Japanese camp, and killed at least 70 Japanese. Only three 11th Airborne soldiers and two guerrillas were killed. The only casualty among the internees was one woman, who was grazed by a bullet.

FURTHER READINGS
Breuer, William. *Retaking the Philippines* (1986).
Flanagan, E. M. *The Los Baños Raid* (1990).
Hogan, David W., Jr. *U.S. Army Special Operations in World War II.* U.S. Army Center of Military History (1992).

Kevin Dougherty

SEE ALSO Alamo Scouts; Office of Strategic Services in the Pacific

MacArthur, Douglas (1880–1964)

Douglas MacArthur comes the closest to being a mythic figure in the history of the United States and its army. Though well known, he is a difficult and complex personality to understand. MacArthur's aloofness, coupled with his ability to lead, gave rise to many different characterizations of the general, ranging from adulators claiming military genius to detractors asserting incompetence and outright insubordination. There is truth in both portrayals. He served as a general officer over a period of thirty-three years that included three major wars (World War I, World War II, and the Korean war), during which MacArthur exhibited bravery and physical courage. As a brigadier general in World War I, he could always be found near or in no-man's land, leading assaults or reconnoitering. During World War II and the Korean war, when he landed on the assault beaches just hours after the first troops, he often exposed himself to enemy gunfire. On the other hand, in 1942 he went to the fighting lines on Bataan only once.

MacArthur was able to adapt to changing conditions of warfare, learn from his mistakes or the mistakes of others, and incorporate new doctrines or theories into his method of warfare. He came to appreciate and rely heavily upon airpower, making sure his operations were always within the range of land-based or carrier aircraft. This willingness to adopt new theories is even more significant if one takes into account that he was nearing the end of his career when World War II began. MacArthur remained in command, and even those who did not personally like him thought he fought well against the Japanese, even though he made a number of serious mistakes, particularly in the retreat to Bataan.

MacArthur is also known for mastering amphibious operations, and incorporating the strategy of leapfrogging enemy strongholds, into his military repertoire. By no means did he invent this strategy; he claimed it was "as old as war itself." He did, however, bring amphibious operations closer to perfection, relying heavily on "hitting the enemy where they ain't." By employing amphibious landings that bypassed strongly held enemy positions in favor of attacking more lightly defended ones, while operating under the aegis of airpower, MacArthur became very adept and successful at amphibious warfare.

Outside of war MacArthur made significant contributions both to the U.S. Army and to peace. As superintendent of the U.S. Military Academy at West Point, New York, from 1919 to 1923, he began the long-needed modernization of the curriculum, despite opposition from traditionalists. As U.S. Army chief of staff, he fought to keep major budget cuts, necessitated by the Great Depression, from decimating the strength and fighting ability of the army. In the realm of peace, after World War II, MacArthur, as supreme commander of the Allied Powers (SCAP) in Japan, ran one of the most efficient and fair military occupations in history.

MacArthur's tremendous ego and confidence in his skills and talents made for difficult relationships and personality conflicts, especially with his superiors. He was not one to be satisfied with a subordinate role. Evidence of MacArthur's displeasure at not having full authority in his theater can be seen during World War II in his relations with Admiral Chester Nimitz and other naval officers and in his correspondence with his superiors in Washington, D.C. During the military occupation of Japan (1945–1951), MacArthur claimed that he was too busy to meet with President Harry Truman. The conflict of personalities between MacArthur and this president, present immediately after the conclusion of World War II, continued during the Korean war. MacArthur was warned about his public criticism of U.S. policy in Korea. Nevertheless, he continued his vociferous objection to U.S. policy, which ultimately became outright insubordination.

At the root of MacArthur's problem with superiors was the belief that although it was legitimate that the joint chiefs of staff (JCS) decided strategy, leeway should be given to the commander of the theater in which the operations took place. MacArthur believed that the theater commander had a better understanding of the geography, the objectives, the soldiers' capabilities and liabilities, and the enemy's strengths and weaknesses. He reasoned that he was willing to grant his subordinates significant latitude in carrying out assignments, so his superiors should allow him the freedom that he wanted to implement their policies.

Douglas MacArthur was born in Little Rock, Arkansas, into a military family. His father, a Union officer during the Civil War, performed numerous acts of bravery throughout the conflict, earning him the respect of his regiment. Martial life agreed with Arthur MacArthur, and he succeeded in acquiring a position in the regular army after the war was over, eventually reaching the rank of lieutenant general. One of his tours of duty included service as military governor of the Philippines, after having fought there during the Spanish-American War.

Douglas enjoyed life in a military family and felt at home surrounded by soldiers, horses, and the other equipment of military life. Not surprisingly, he aspired to a life in the military, hoping to equal, if not exceed, the exploits of his father. He obtained an appointment to West Point, becoming member of the class of 1903. MacArthur graduated at the top of his class, attaining some of the highest marks ever achieved at the U.S. Military Academy. Upon graduation he was commissioned a second lieutenant in the Army Corps of Engineers and sent to the Philippines, the first of many tours in that archipelago.

During the period between 1905 and World War I, MacArthur held a variety of staff and instructor positions, and also took part in the Vera Cruz expedition against President Victoriano Huerta of Mexico in 1914. In mid-1916, he was named military assistant to the secretary of war. In this post Major MacArthur dealt with problems of manpower in case the United States entered World War I, which by then seemed inevitable. He worked on plans that would send National Guard units to Europe to fight alongside the regular army. The United States did enter the war in April 1917, and to avoid the politically charged question of which National Guard division would have the honor of being first to Europe, MacArthur suggested the creation of a multistate National Guard infantry division, the 42nd "Rainbow" Division. In August 1917, MacArthur was promoted to colonel of infantry and given the assignment of chief of staff in the 42nd Division before it left for France.

MacArthur's performance during World War I was nothing short of remarkable. He took part in the Aisne-Marne operation (July 25–August 2, 1918) and commanded the 84th Brigade as a brevet brigadier general during the Battle of St. Mihiel (September 12–17). During the final campaign of World War I, the Meuse-Argonne (October 4–November 11), he led the "Rainbow" as the U.S. Army's youngest division commander. MacArthur was often seen by his soldiers on the front lines and personally led his soldiers into battle. He received a total of ten medals for valor and two Purple Hearts.

The next significant assignment for MacArthur was that of superintendent of West Point. This position allowed him to retain his first star and not be reduced to his permanent rank, as was the case with so many of the officers who received brevet ranks during the war. Army Chief of Staff Peyton March specifically had MacArthur in mind for this position because of his youth (39 years old) and his lack of vested interest in preserving the traditions and old habits of West Point. Although many army traditionalists, along with faculty and board members of West Point, were hostile to MacArthur's tampering with the curriculum, he succeeded in planting the seeds of reform during his tenure there. Changes included the codification of the honor code, the revitalization of the curriculum, the placing of more emphasis on the humanities and social sciences while still putting a premium on the sciences, and an attempt to eliminate hazing. MacArthur upset many influential military personnel, and consequently he did not serve out his last year at West Point. Instead, he returned to the Philippines.

While in the Philippines (1922–1925), MacArthur commanded a brigade in the Philippine Division. Even at this relatively early date, the U.S. plans for defending the islands did not please him. In fact, there was little to the "defense" of the Philippines, because at the first sign of a Japanese attack the U.S. Navy was to pull back to Hawaii and the small size of the U.S. Army did not allow for the appropriate number of troops to be stationed in the Philippines to prevent an invasion. MacArthur would later implement General Leonard Wood's plan to adopt a reserve system, based on the Swiss model. It was also firmly ingrained in MacArthur's mind that the key asset of the Philippines was the large harbor of Manila Bay, already heavily fortified by the Corregidor forts. Having secure possession of that anchorage meant having possession of the Bataan Peninsula and of Corregidor, small, rocky island off the peninsula's southern tip. These would be the areas to defend in the event of a Japanese attack. In January 1925, MacArthur received his second star, making him the youngest major general in the army.

For the next three years Major General MacArthur was back in the United States, first commanding the 4th Corps Area (Atlanta) and then assuming command of the 3d Corps Area (Baltimore). While serving in these capacities, he had to deal with shrinking army budgets, low enlistment rates, lack and obsolescence of equipment, and decrepit facilities. These conditions were the result of the fiscal conservatism of the presidential administrations and Congresses of the 1920s and to the growing antimilitarism sweeping the country. The highlight of MacArthur's term as 3d Corps Area commander was serving on the court-martial of the vocal airpower advocate, Colonel William "Billy" Mitchell.

In October 1928 MacArthur was sent again to the Philippines, this time as commander of the Department of the Philippines. Again he was outspoken in regard to the War Department's existing War Plan Orange to defend the Philippines in the event of war with Japan, calling the strategy "simply rotten." The navy's unwillingness to remain in the vicinity of the Philippines to obstruct an enemy invasion, or to maintain open supply lines, made a successful defense of the Philippines all but impossible. MacArthur was convinced that if the Philippines were to be defended, Filipinos would have to take an active part in their defense. His theory was that if the Japanese were confronted with hundreds of thousands of armed and trained Filipinos, coupled with the presence of U.S. forces, they would find an invasion too costly, both in lives and in money, and would decide against invading. The foundation for training and equipping the Filipinos was built during MacArthur's third tour in the Philippines (1935–1937).

In November 1930, MacArthur was sworn in as chief of staff of the army, a post carrying with it a temporary rank of full general (four stars). This was the highest and most prestigious position in the army. As chief of staff, his major task was to keep up the numerical strength and fighting capability of the army, at a time of continuing antimilitarism and during the Great Depression. MacArthur resisted any reductions in the size of the army by Congress or the closing of any of its installations. Under his tutelage the army developed mobilization plans for its expansion, civilian price control measures, and the retooling of industry in the event of war. He also supervised a limited program of modernization, including modest improvements in tactics, equipment (especially aircraft), training, and organization.

In 1932, during his time as chief of staff, MacArthur confronted the Bonus Army, a large group of World War I veterans who advocated receiving their "war bonuses" early because of the devastating effects of the Great Depression. This was one of the most controversial actions of his career, although he was not wholly to blame. Traditional accounts state that MacArthur ignored President Herbert Hoover's direct order not to disperse the Bonus Marchers. Recent scholarship raises the question of whether MacArthur ever received orders to halt before reaching the veterans' temporary housing. Although he overestimated the threat posed to the government by the Bonus Army, he was willing to oversee their removal. The Washington, D.C., police were actually in charge of the operation; army troops augmented the police force's numbers. If there were to be unfavorable repercussions or negative criticism of the way the eviction occurred, MacArthur was willing to take the blame. Pacifism and antimilitarism were so strong during this period that military officers, including MacArthur and Dwight D. Eisenhower, had to go to and from work in mufti. It did not help matters that MacArthur was wearing his best uniform while supervising the removal. The use of tear gas and the threat of bayonets only increased public outcry against an administration and military that were seemingly hostile to American citizens.

In October 1935 MacArthur reverted to his permanent rank of major general and returned to the Philippines. His primary mission was to organize Filipino military defenses in preparation for the islands' projected independence. The Philippine government headed by Manuel Quezon gave MacArthur the rank of field marshal in the Philippine army in August 1936. MacArthur thus held positions in the Filipino army and the U.S. Army, drawing salaries from both countries. Afraid that he would be reassigned and forced to leave the Philippines before his mission was completed, MacArthur retired from the U.S. Army at the end of 1937 and became President Quezon's military adviser. In this capacity he continued preparing the Filipino army for independence.

The War Department and the U.S. Navy still followed the strategy formulated under the War Plan Orange, with which MacArthur vehemently disagreed. Nonetheless, estimates from 1939 have shown the Filipino army would not have been a viable fighting force until after 1946. There were many problems that had to be surmounted, including a dearth of trained officers and an equal scarcity of modern weapons and equipment.

Considering the major obstacles that could not be overcome in the creation of a conventional army, it has been surmised that MacArthur prepared the Filipino army for a war it could not win. Instead, the argument goes, MacArthur should have trained the army in guerrilla tactics, because this style of warfare was the only legitimate option for this undertrained, understrength army. As the threat of war between Japan and the United States grew more imminent throughout the first half of 1941, MacArthur was recalled to active duty in July. He became commander of the newly created U.S. Army Forces in the Far East (USAFFE), and was promoted to lieutenant general. His military forces included the U.S. Army forces that were part of the Philippine Department and the forces of the Philippine Commonwealth, because President Franklin Roosevelt had federalized the Philippine military forces.

Lieutenant General MacArthur now had to integrate the diverse forces under his newly unified command. The quality of the forces ranged from raw Filipino recruits to highly trained American soldiers. The Filipinos lacked even the most basic equipment, and the U.S. forces were in need of significant numbers of artillery, tanks, and support vehicles. As for airpower, the United States and MacArthur overestimated the role that the bomber could play in defending the Philippines, at the same time refusing to send in sufficient numbers of fighter aircraft. During this period U.S. fighter planes did not equal the performance of their Japanese counterparts. U.S. defense planners during the prewar years emphasized the development of bombers and spent less money to improve and modernize fighters.

MacArthur knew the defense situation of the Philippines was far from ideal. He reported to Army Chief of Staff George Marshall that he was displeased with the fighting capability of Major General Jonathan Wainwright's Philippine Division. This force formed the core of the U.S. regular army troops in the Philippines. The USAFFE commander noted that these forces, although relatively well trained, lacked sufficient equipment and numbers. The Philippine Division was only two-thirds its authorized strength. The Filipino army was in even worse shape. It lacked basic firearms, clothing, equipment, and experienced and able officers and NCOs, and its soldiers spoke a multitude of languages. Although realistically aware of the numbers and capabilities of the forces under his command, MacArthur publicly pronounced that he was satisfied and encouraged with the defense forces of the Philippines. Perhaps this was to encourage the U.S. government not to write off the commonwealth and to include the Philippines in its defensive strategy for the Pacific, or at least to discourage the Japanese from attacking.

In part because of MacArthur's pleas to change U.S. Pacific strategy, but due largely to an effort to make a stand against further Japanese aggression, the joint chiefs of staff agreed to defend the Philippines by fighting on land and allowing MacArthur partly to scrap War Plan Orange-3. With this green light from the joint chiefs, the commander of the USAFFE began implementing his strategy of beach defense. The original plan had allowed for the major ships of the U.S. Navy in the Philippines to retreat to Hawaii and permitted the Japanese to land unopposed on the beaches of Luzon. The major fighting would then occur in the interior, giving the U.S. forces the advantage of shorter/interior supply lines while retreating onto the Bataan Peninsula and Corregidor. From these positions the defenders would deny the enemy the use of Manila as a harbor while waiting for reinforcements and resupply that would bring the besieged defenders relief before beginning their reconquest of the Philippines. The success of this defense strategy would rely on the quickness with which the U.S. Navy could provide reinforcements, a problem that became evident in the beginning of 1942.

MacArthur chose to use the strategy of defending the beaches in the event of a Japanese invasion: a gross lapse in strategic judgment, given the overall quality of his military force. Supplies that would have been stockpiled on Bataan and Corregidor were now dispersed throughout Luzon. By the end of November 1941, MacArthur had 85,000 men preparing to carry out his plan in case of a Japanese amphibious assault.

The Japanese attacked Pearl Harbor, the headquarters and anchorage of the United States Pacific Fleet, in Honolulu, Hawaii, on December 7, 1941. (The Philippines is on the other side of the International Date Line, so the date there was December 8.) The USAFFE commander was informed of the Pearl Harbor attack at 4 A.M. The Japanese designation of Pearl Harbor and not the Philippines as the initial target puzzled MacArthur. Over the next hours he ordered his forces on alert and sent up air patrols to warn of incoming aircraft. What followed were mistakes compounded by bad luck. The B-17s, which were key in the defense of the Philippines, should have been flown to Del Monte, an air base on the southern Philippine island of Mindanao. Here they would be out of range of Japanese land-based aircraft. Instead, MacArthur's orders were ignored and the commander of the Far Eastern Air Force (FEAF) sent only sixteen of his thirty-five bombers south.

Bad weather in western Formosa (now Taiwan) delayed the Japanese bomber attack on the Philippines. By late morning, the weather broke and the warplanes were soon on their way to Luzon, toward the key American air bases of Clark and Iba. The planes that had been searching for incoming Japanese aircraft were running low on fuel and would soon have to land to refuel. For some inexplicable reason, the air staff of FEAF allowed sixteen of the nineteen B-17s to be on the ground simultaneously. Of the three fighter squadrons, two were over Manila Bay, and the other was on the ground, when the Japanese bombers arrived. The devastating attacks took out the radar station and fighter planes on the ground at Iba, and at Clark the sixteen B-17s caught on the ground were damaged or destroyed. It was an "aerial Pearl Harbor" that was all the more inexplicable because the U.S. military authorities were well aware of the earlier Japanese surprise attack.

The initial Japanese landings on the Philippines began on December 10. Even after the reports that his Filipino troops were performing less well than expected reached MacArthur, he continued his beach defense, trying to meet the Japanese at all points. Why he chose to maintain this strategy, despite the inability of his forces to prevent the Japanese from advancing inland, coupled with a thoroughly weakened air force, remains a mystery. Even more bewildering, the day after the main Japanese amphibious assault (December 22) in Lingayen Gulf, north of Manila on the western coast of Luzon, MacArthur reverted to the War Plan Orange defense strategy that he had fought against throughout his career in the Philippines. However, he waited too long to change his strategy. By not preparing for the defense of Bataan, many of hardships the defenders had to endure were exacerbated. With the December 22 assault, the major forces of USAFFE on Luzon were in danger of being split in two. To prevent this, MacArthur needed the North Luzon Force to perform a fighting withdrawal, allowing time for the South Luzon Force to enter the Bataan Peninsula behind its lines. Wainwright and his North Luzon Force performed this maneuver superbly. However, the supplies that should have been on Bataan and Corregidor were spread throughout Luzon. The lack of planning and transportation, the captured depots, and the destroyed stores prevented adequate supplies from reaching Bataan. The original defense plans had anticipated 40,000 defenders and food and medical caches that would last six months. Instead, 105,000 ended up evacuating to Bataan, including soldiers from the U.S. and Philippine armies and civilian refugees. The supplies were less than enough for the planned 40,000. Immediately, MacArthur ordered the daily ration reduced by 50 percent, with further reductions imposed during the siege. By the time the Bataan forces capitulated, hunger and disease had made life nearly unbearable for the surviving defenders.

MacArthur, who was promoted to full general on December 22, declared Manila an open city upon his evacuation to Corregidor. The United States, by not disputing the control of the sea-lanes around Luzon and Japanese air superiority, condemned its forces that were left in the Philippines to death or capture by the Japanese. Although their situation was all but hopeless, the Bataan defenders managed to thwart the immediate use of Manila Bay by the Japanese, delaying their timetable by four months. In contrast to forces in Burma, Malaya, Singapore, and the Dutch East Indies, the U.S. forces in the Philippines offered stiff resistance. Because of their effort, MacArthur was given hero status in the United States. Unfortunately, his soldiers on Bataan did not have the same opinion. During these months of increasing privation on Bataan, MacArthur gained the nickname "Dugout Doug." Although it is true that MacArthur made only one visit to the peninsula, he did not deserve this criticism, for he coolly exposed himself on numerous occasions to enemy shell and aerial fire. Inexplicably, he chose to avoid being seen by his troops when he did so.

The joint chiefs of staff and President Franklin Roosevelt worried that MacArthur might be captured. Throughout the first months of 1942, Australians were growing increasingly worried about Japanese invasion. Having a general of MacArthur's stature reassigned to Australia would boost Australian morale and would show the U.S. commitment to defend the continent. With these factors in mind, President Roosevelt ordered MacArthur to leave the Philippines and to resume the fight against the Japanese from Australia. The joint chiefs agreed that the U.S. Army would use Australia as a supply base for launching future attacks against the Japanese. On the night of March 11, 1942, MacArthur, his family, and key members of his staff left the fortress island of Corregidor on PT boats, heading toward Mindanao. From there they would fly to Australia, where MacArthur would vow "I shall return" to the Philippines.

On April 9 the Bataan forces surrendered, and one month later those on Corregidor followed suit. MacArthur had intended to retain his position as commander of USAFFE and the overall command of operations in the Philippines. His plan was to divide the USAFFE into four commands, putting Wainwright in charge of only the forces on Bataan and Corregidor. The reason for this organizational arrangement was that with the inevitable collapse of Corregidor, Wainwright would have the authority to surrender only his forces, not the other USAFFE throughout the islands. Even with the surrender of U.S. forces on Bataan and Corregidor, other elements of USAFFE would be able prolong the resistance by carrying out guerrilla warfare. The War Department felt that this plan would be too difficult to command effectively from Australia. Wainwright soon began receiving messages addressing him as "Commanding General, USAFFE," allowing him a large degree of independence in conducting the war. The War Department disbanded the USAFFE and created a new department for Wainwright, the U.S. Forces in the Philippines.

When MacArthur reached Australia, he was received with adulation by an isolated land only too aware of how many of its young men had been thrown away in Malaya and Singapore by unaggressive British generals, and that now looked upon the United States, rather than Great Britain, as its main hope for victory. Also in March, MacArthur also received the Congressional Medal of Honor.

In Australia, MacArthur found only 25,000 American fighting men, the majority engineers and airmen. But what he needed were combat companies, tanks, artillery, and modern, serviceable aircraft. His dismay increased as he realized that the United States would not be returning to the Philippines in the near future.

But March 1942 did see the establishment of the Anglo-American combined chiefs of staff to devise Allied grand strategy. The United States became the major Allied power in the Pacific. The U.S. JCS, with divided army and navy factions, could not agree on one strategy or a single, unified command. The army was not willing to submit its forces to the navy, which it saw as relegating the army to a subordinate role. Army planners believed that the significant battles would be on land, culminating with an invasion of Japan. The navy would be needed to keep supply lanes and lines of communications open. The navy leaders, on the other hand, envisioned a war that would be comprised mainly of naval and amphibious operations, and wanted an admiral in command. The joint chiefs then agreed on dividing the Pacific into two major commands: the Pacific Ocean Areas, divided into three zones, under the domain of the U.S. Navy, and the Southwest Pacific Area (SWPA), under the command of the U.S. Army. The SWPA originally included Australia, New Guinea, the Bismarck archipelago, the Solomon Islands, and the Dutch East Indies. In April, MacArthur accepted the position of supreme commander of all Allied forces in the SWPA.

The lack of a single commander displeased MacArthur, but he was even more dissatisfied by the "Europe first" strategy agreed on by the combined chiefs of staff. He believed that the primary U.S. theater should be the Pacific, with the original mission of carrying out a strategic defense. The SWPA commander wanted more responsibilities and materiel for his theater.

Despite the "Europe first" strategy, by May 1942, 100,000 American troops (actually twice the number of U.S. troops deployed to the European theater) were stationed in or heading toward the SWPA to secure Australia from the threat of invasion. The neutralization or loss of Australia and New Zealand would dramatically affect U.S. strategy in the Pacific war, forcing the defensive line to be pulled back to Hawaii, if not farther.

MacArthur maintained an exhausting schedule in Australia, working long hours seven days a week. Scholars agree that MacArthur's staff, the "Bataan Gang," was second-rate (probably with the exception of his chief of staff, Richard Sutherland). Thus he was forced to spend much time overseeing even the smallest details during planning.

A perpetual limit on operations was the shortage of shipping, both supply vessels and amphibious landing craft. Often these ships had to be shared, and operations coordinated, between theaters when major operations were undertaken.

MacArthur's first mission was to secure Australia by removing the threat of Japanese invasion. He knew that a key factor in the defense of Australia was Port Moresby, on the southern coast of Papua, on the large island of New Guinea. From here the Japanese could use land-based planes to interdict naval traffic in the Coral Sea and threaten Australian cities. More significantly, Port Moresby would be the major staging area if the Japanese decided to invade Australia.

With approval from the JCS, MacArthur was ready to begin his counteroffensive five months after arriving in Australia. The battles of the Coral Sea and Midway in May and June 1942, the presence of Australian units with experience fighting the Italians and Germans in North Africa, the industrial output of Australia, the cooperative Australian prime minister, John Curtin, and his new air commander, General George C. Kenney, allowed MacArthur to take the initiative earlier than anticipated.

Near the end of August, Australian forces under MacArthur's command ejected the Japanese from their established beachhead at Milne Bay, on the southeasternmost tip of New Guinea. Milne Bay's air bases were later used to interdict Japanese forces in the Bismarck and Solomon Seas, and provided protection for U.S. operations in those island groups. MacArthur began his counteroffensive in August 1942, following the retreating Japanese north along the Kokoda Trail toward their strongholds of Buna and Gona, which MacArthur's forces attacked in the middle of November 1942. Problems arose from the beginning. If MacArthur had had the go-ahead to begin offensive operations at an earlier date, Gona and Buna might have been occupied by Allied forces before the Japanese had a chance to reinforce these positions. Faulty intelligence caused SWPA forces to be surprised at the large numbers of Japanese defenders.

Throughout this campaign MacArthur relied on the generals at the front and his staff to give him information on battlefield conditions and the progress of the attacks. Without an appreciation of the problems being encountered by his attacking forces, he was unable to understand and correct the mistakes of these battles. Some of the larger errors included sending U.S. troops into combat without the proper weapons. Infantry divisions did not have the weapons to conduct jungle warfare and reduce the fortified positions and bunkers: tanks, flamethrowers, mortars, and, especially, artillery. The typical infantry division was lightly armed (rifle companies with few machine guns), substituting mobility for heavy firepower. The division's heavy firepower was its artillery brigade of 105-mm and 155-mm howitzers, which were not present during the initial attacks because Sutherland believed it would be impossible to supply the needed ammunition. MacArthur's forces were also plagued by supply shortages, disease, and faulty close-air support. Consequently, the troops experienced nearly 50 percent casualties, including those killed, wounded, and struck by illness. The rifle companies of the 32nd Division were racked to the extent that it would take more than a year for the division to be rebuilt. The Australians captured Gona on December 9. Buna did not capitulate to the Americans until January 2, 1943, after the Americans brought in more ground forces and finally deployed tanks and artillery. During this campaign Allied forces suffered almost twice as many casualties as the Japanese.

MacArthur set about correcting these major deficiencies before the commencement of future operations. He made sure his troops had equipment and weapons suited for jungle war. Coordination and communication between ground forces and close-air support improved, as did artillery and infantry interaction. MacArthur realized that he lacked the naval forces needed to carry out amphibious landings. In response to this lack, the 7th Amphibious Force was created under Rear Admiral Daniel Barbey. MacArthur would come to rely heavily on this force to get his armies where they were needed.

General Kenney convinced MacArthur of the importance of airpower, converting a skeptical into one of the strongest advocates for airpower. In fact, MacArthur would not think about carrying out an amphibious landing unless it had air cover from either land-based or carrier-based aircraft. He adopted the leapfrogging strategy. The Japanese had employed this approach when they surrounded and isolated MacArthur's forces in the Philippines in 1941–1942. U.S. forces first used this method in the Aleutians in May 1943, when the strongly defended island of Kiska was bypassed in favor of the more weakly held island of Attu. MacArthur saw leapfrogging as the answer to the limitations placed on him as commander of the SWPA. It would allow him to conserve manpower, supplies, equipment, and shipping. These maneuvers would encircle enemy strongholds or sever their supply lines, rendering the stranded enemy forces impotent. If islands had to be attacked, MacArthur secured only enough territory to build and defend air bases, further reducing U.S. casualties.

At this point in the war MacArthur began to accompany the invasion fleets. Only hours after the initial assault waves, MacArthur would go ashore, often being exposed to enemy fire. He showed almost no concern for his personal safety as he reconnoitered the area. U.S. casualty rates during the dozens of amphibious operations were remarkably low because of the leapfrogging strategy, coupled with well-developed tactics and interservice coordination. Increasing American firepower (close air support, artillery, tanks, and naval gunfire) caused much heavier Japanese casualties, as did the Japanese method of fighting to the last man.

During March 1943 the Japanese attempted to reinforce Lae on the northern coast of New Guinea, and then to move inland and take Wau. Better intelligence and increased Allied air power warned of an approaching Japanese convoy from Rabaul, New Britain. General Kenney's Fifth Air Force sank and/or damaged many of the troop transports and escort vessels, preventing the armada from reaching Lae and forcing what was left of the convoy to return to Rabaul. The Battle of the Bismarck Sea on March 4, 1943, changed the military balance in New Guinea, giving the advantage to MacArthur's forces.

Throughout 1943 MacArthur was growing increasingly obsessed with returning to the Philippines, and attempted to get a higher priority for his SWPA command. The JCS formulated a two-pronged attack in the Pacific: Nimitz would spearhead a drive through the central Pacific while MacArthur would advance northwestward along the northern coast of New Guinea, toward the Philippines. His ultimate goal was the Vogelkop (now Doberai) Peninsula, on the extreme northwest part of New Guinea (now Irian Barat, Indonesia).

Before these drives could get under way, the Japanese stronghold of Rabaul would have to be neutralized. The JCS approved the Cartwheel operations, a series of thirteen amphibious operations by both Halsey and MacArthur, for the purpose of neutralizing Rabaul. One hundred thousand soldiers and a powerful air force garrisoned Rabaul, and the size of its harbor was such that the entire Imperial Japanese Navy could lie there at anchor. Army and navy planners could not ignore Rabaul. Originally it was to be captured, but the plan was later modified to permit the stronghold to be encircled and bypassed. MacArthur's operations in New Guinea at Lae and Finschhafen in September 1943, followed by an amphibious operation at Saidor in January 1944, succeeded in isolating Rabaul from the west. In December 1943 MacArthur conducted amphibious landings on southern and western New Britain, securing enough territory to set up air bases from which to attack Rabaul. At the end of February 1944, SWPA forces carried out successful amphibious landing in the Admiralty Islands, helping to cut off Rabaul from the north. The capture of Manus (Great Admiralty Island) and Los Negros provided MacArthur with an advanced naval base from which to continue the drive along the New Guinea coast. Nimitz's operations in the central Pacific drew off the remaining Japanese naval vessels and most of Japan's airpower, leaving only the powerful ground forces in Rabaul. Without naval or air units, Rabaul no longer posed a serious threat. By May 1944, Rabaul was effectively neutralized; the remaining forces there were allowed to "wither on the vine."

The next step for MacArthur was to continue his advance along the northern New Guinea Coast. The improved intelligence provided by ULTRA warned of a strong Japanese force at Hansa Bay and furnished information that the Japanese were vulnerable, 580 farther miles along the coast of New Guinea, at Hollandia (Djajapura, Irian Barat). The distance was too great for land-based planes to provide protection for the amphibious assault, so MacArthur obtained the use of the aircraft carriers from Nimitz's fleet to cover defend the invaders. MacArthur chose to bypass both Hansa Bay and Wewack in favor of the more daring invasion of Hollandia and Aitape on April 22, 1944. The airfields secured at these points provided air cover for the later invasion of Wakde Island (May 17). After SWPA forces secured Wakde, land-based warplanes there supported the amphibious assault on Biak Island (May 27). This process continued with the July 2 assault on Noemfoor (Numfoor) Island, culminating with the invasion of Sansapor on the Volgelkop Peninsula on July 30. MacArthur's forces advanced more than eleven hundred miles in a little over three months, leaving the Australians to carry out mopping-up operations throughout New Guinea; these forces often encountered tough resistance from encircled Japanese.

The next plan continued the movement toward the Philippines, employing the bypassing strategy, until by November 5 and December 20, MacArthur was able to return to the Philippine islands of Mindanao and Leyte, respectively. These plans were scrapped when Halsey received word that Leyte was only lightly held. MacArthur and Nimitz agreed that the timetable for the invasion of the Philippines should be moved up. On October 20, 1944, MacArthur, with the use of his Seventh Fleet and ships from Nimitz's fleet (a total of 700 ships and 1,000 planes) to provide protection and air cover, finally fulfilled his promise of returning to the Philippines. Resistance on Leyte was stronger than expected, but the landing force had a secure and well-supplied beachhead after the favorable outcome of the Battle of Leyte Gulf.

There were two schools of thought circulating in the JCS and the military departments on the best route for the invasion of Japan itself. The majority favored using Formosa (now Taiwan) to carry the invasion of the Japanese homeland, whereas MacArthur and others favored using the Philippines as the major assault base. The supply and shipping shortage would delay an invasion of Formosa until February 1945—and then only if that invasion was given priority over everything else, including the defeat of Germany. The invasion of Luzon could commence near the beginning of 1945 without needlessly hindering U.S. worldwide operations. The JCS agreed to reject the Formosa strategy in favor of the Philippines. Besides this being logistically sound, MacArthur believed that the United States owed the Filipinos as early a liberation as possible. On December 18, MacArthur was promoted to the newly created five-star rank of general of the army.

The Luzon landing occurred in Lingayen Gulf on January 9, 1945. The fighting on Luzon was some of the most difficult that SWPA forces encountered throughout the war. The some two hundred seventy-five thousand Japanese on Luzon were desperately short of munitions, supplies, and vehicles, and lacked the mobility and firepower of the U.S. troops. Pockets of resistance ended only with the surrender of Japan in mid-August. The U.S. Sixth Army was responsible for the operations on Luzon; instead of using his Eighth Army to help with the conquest of Luzon, MacArthur sent it southward to liberate other islands of the Philippines. The JCS did not intend MacArthur to liberate other islands of the Philippines, but he took it upon himself to decide how operations were to be carried out in his theater, not his last ignoring of JCS intentions.

MacArthur oversaw the last amphibious operations conducted in the war, by the Australians in the Borneo campaign at Brunei (June 10) and Balikpapan (July 1). Again he landed on the beaches only hours after the initial assault waves. MacArthur spent the rest of the war bringing his supply bases forward, consolidating his forces in the Philippines, and preparing plans for the invasion of Japan. The use of two atomic bombs on Hiroshima and Nagasaki, on August 6 and 9, respectively, made an invasion of Japan unnecessary. On August 14, 1945, MacArthur was named supreme commander of the Allied powers (SCAP), making him the officer who would take the Japanese surrender on Nimitz's flagship, battleship *Missouri,* in Tokyo Bay on September 2, 1945.

As SCAP, MacArthur was responsible for overseeing the demilitarization and demobilization, as well as the economic rebuilding, of Japan over the next six years. Some scholars point to MacArthur's military occupation as the highlight of his prestigious career—as MacArthur himself did in his later years. Several of his important reforms included giving women the right to vote and other rights; modernizing the health, welfare, and educational systems; imposing land reform; and instituting a free press. Before 1945, there was no guarantee of human rights or civil liberties in Japan. MacArthur set about creating a liberal constitution for Japan. These programs and institutions, begun under MacArthur, helped to eliminate Japanese ultranationalism, militarism, and feudalistic notions, replacing these beliefs with more modern and liberal, democratic concepts. He also prevented attempts by the Soviet Union to become a major partner in the occupation of Japan. As SCAP, he improved relations between the United States and Japan; all the more important in that Japan became the key country in the emerging Cold War against communism in the Far East.

After the North Korean invasion of South Korea on June 25, 1950, MacArthur was named supreme commander of United Nation forces in Korea (July 8). His brilliant (but not as dangerous as most accounts make out) landing at Inchon with the 10th Corps on September 15, 1950, permitted U.S. forces to cut North Korea's supply lines and eventually force its troops to return across the 38th parallel. MacArthur made two costly errors, one tactical and the other strategic. The tactical mistake was his allowing a large gap between the advancing Eighth Army and the 10th Corps as U.S. forces were approaching the border between North Korea and China. The more costly strategic error was the ignoring of Chinese Communist threats that they would enter the war if MacArthur's forces advanced too close to the Yalu River. On November 25, 1950, the Chinese launched a massive attack that took advantage of the gap and eventually pushed United Nations forces south of the 38th parallel. MacArthur's public criticisms of U.S. policy and the Truman administration regarding Korea continued after he had been warned to keep quiet. MacArthur's solution—an es-

calation of the war—was unacceptable to the Truman administration. Finally, in April 1951, Truman removed MacArthur from command, replacing him with General Matthew Ridgway.

MacArthur returned to the United States (which he had not seen for more than a decade) to near hysterical adulation. His speech before a joint session of Congress was an emotional masterpiece, ending with words that he made immortal: that he, like an old soldier, would "just fade away." Elements of the Republican Party were determined that this would not be the old soldier's fate, and touted him as a presidential candidate. A mistimed, hall-emptying speech at the 1952 Republican national convention spelled the end of such hopes. MacArthur accepted a somewhat honorific position with Remington Rand, an armament corporation. He did "fade away," except for a remarkable speech he gave months before his death to the assembled cadets at West Point. There, more eloquently than anyone else before or since, he emphasized the values of the U.S. Military Academy: "Duty, Honor, Country." This address aptly served as his eulogy. He died at Walter Reed Army Hospital in Washington, D.C., on April 5, 1964.

FURTHER READINGS
Drea, Edward J. *MacArthur's ULTRA* (1992).
James, D. C. *The Years of MacArthur,* 3 vols. (1970–1985).
MacArthur, Douglas. *Reminiscences* (1964).
Manchester, William. *American Caesar: Douglas MacArthur, 1880–1964* (1978).
Perret, Geoffrey. *Old Soldiers Never Die: The Life of Douglas MacArthur* (1996).
Petillo, Carol M. *Douglas MacArthur: The Philippine Years* (1981).
Taafe, Stephen R. *MacArthur's Jungle War* (1998).
James L. Isemann

SEE ALSO Amphibious Operations; Biak, Battle for; Corregidor; Hollandia; Island-Hopping and Leapfrogging, U.S. Strategies; Japan, Occupation of; Kenney, George C.; Leyte Gulf, Battle of; New Britain; Noemfoor Island; Philippines, Fall of the; Sutherland, Richard K.

Madagascar, Allied Invasion of

Following their surprise attack on the U.S. Navy facility at Pearl Harbor, Hawaii, on December 7, 1941, the Japanese military mounted a series of offensives to expand their strategic perimeter in the Pacific Ocean and in Asia.

These operations were extremely successful. Japanese forces not only inflicted humiliating battlefield defeats upon the Allied units mustered to oppose them, but also overran a considerable amount of territory in areas where the Allied powers had formerly been dominant. Such relentless progress by the Japanese armies and naval task forces was more than a political embarrassment for the Allies; it also created a major strategic problem. Owing to the unprecedented extent of their advance, the Japanese had gained control of military facilities and bases that placed their strike forces within easy reach of targets that the Allied high commands had previously considered invulnerable to Japanese attack.

Among the areas now open to such offensive operations was the Indian Ocean. This development created considerable alarm in London. Since the fall of France and the entry of Italy into the war, the Mediterranean had effectively been closed to Allied shipping; as a result, the passage of supplies through the Suez Canal had been halted. Consequently, the importance of the Indian Ocean as a logistical avenue had increased significantly. In addition to being the principal artery for the transportation of Middle Eastern oil to Britain and an important channel for the flow of equipment to the Soviet Union, it had become the major supply route for the British forces in North Africa. Were it to be severed, the British position in Egypt would quickly become untenable, a situation that would bring a complete Allied defeat in that theater. With the Japanese advance into the waters of the Indian Ocean, the cutting of this vital supply route seemed imminent. To forestall this possibility, the Allies decided to undertake the invasion of the strategically significant island of Madagascar.

Located off the southeastern coast of Africa, directly adjacent to the main shipping lane from the Cape of Good Hope, Madagascar (now Malagasy Republic) was in a geographic position with enormous military potential: it completely dominated the western approaches to the Indian Ocean. Consequently, were the Japanese to install themselves on the island and gain control of its ports and airfields, their forces would be in a position to pose a major threat to the Allied sea lines of communication to both India and the Middle East. That they might attempt to do this was no mere fantasy, but a distinct possibility that reflected the doubtful neutrality of the island's political authorities. Unfortunately for the Allies, Madagascar was a French colonial possession whose administration had declared its allegiance to the pro–Axis government at Vichy. From the Allied perspective this did nothing to inspire confidence in Madagascar's future. In 1940 the Vichy regime had allowed the Japanese military

to occupy Indochina, another of its outposts, and use it as a base from which to launch attacks against Allied forces that included the sinking of the British warships *Repulse* and *Prince of Wales*.

That such a government might be willing to afford the Japanese similar facilities in Madagascar seemed more than likely to the British, who knew that all that would be required to obtain compliance from the Germanophiles in the Vichy regime was a Japanese request backed by German pressure. Information provided by Allied intelligence reports suggested that this might soon be forthcoming, because, as decryptions of Japanese diplomatic telegrams made clear, the Germans were especially eager to impress upon their Asian allies the advantages of a landing in Madagascar. Given the devastating consequences were this to occur, the Allies decided not to wait for definite signs of an attack, but determined instead that they would preempt the Japanese. Thus Operation Ironclad was born.

As initially conceived, the purpose of the operation was not to capture the whole of the huge island of Madagascar, but rather to deny to the Japanese its main strategic area, the outstanding natural harbor at Diégo-Suarez (now Antsiranana) and the military facilities in its vicinity. To this end, despite pleas from South African Premier Jan Christiaan Smuts, who wanted the Allies to clear Madagascar of Vichy forces, the object of the assault was the northern tip of the island only. To undertake this mission, a substantial assault force was assembled. On the naval side, this consisted of the old battleship *Ramillies,* the new aircraft carriers *Indomitable* and *Illustrious,* and cruisers *Devonshire* and *Hermione,* accompanied by eleven destroyers, six corvettes, six minesweepers, five infantry assault ships, three troop ships, and six mechanical transports. Command of these maritime units, as well as overall command of the operation, was vested in Rear Admiral Neville Syfret. His land force commander, whose assault troops consisted of three infantry brigade groups and one commando group, was Major General R. G. Sturges of the Royal Marines.

Collecting so sizable a force at so perilous a moment during the war was no easy matter. The majority of the assault formations were infantry units headed for service in India. For them, the attack on Madagascar would be a temporary diversion. As for the naval armada, assembly of this force was made possible only by the intervention of the United States. Although U.S. units could not take part in the operation directly because Washington still maintained diplomatic relations with the Vichy government, they were nevertheless in a position to make a substantial indirect contribution. By relieving British forces of commitments elsewhere—in this instance, through the sending of U.S. naval reinforcements to the Atlantic—they allowed the Royal Navy to release ships for service in the Indian Ocean that had been tied up in other parts of the world.

Gathering the appropriate forces was not the only difficulty associated with this expedition. Equally problematic was military intelligence. Information on the disposition of Vichy forces on the island, as well as details of the layout of the harbor installations, was essential to the success of the initial assault. Although this information could be obtained with relative ease by aerial photography, it could not be done without the danger of arousing the suspicions of the Japanese, who might readily have been alerted to the approaching danger by the sudden and unexpected presence of Allied reconnaissance planes. Were it to be then also discovered that strong Allied naval forces were approaching the region, the purpose of the expedition might well have been deduced and the element of surprise, so essential to any seaborne assault, lost.

Consequently, as the convoys left Britain in the middle of March 1942 for Madagascar, the problem arose of gathering the necessary information for the assault force while keeping its final destination a secret. To achieve this, the first undertaking was a campaign of strategic deception. To hide the convoy's true purpose, an intricate cover plan was devised to mislead the Axis into believing that its objective was the Italian-occupied Dodecanese islands in the Aegean Sea. To this end, when the convoy reached Durban, South Africa, on April 22, 1942, briefings were held and maps distributed with this misinformation in mind. Possibly as a result of this counterintelligence campaign, when the convoy left Durban for Madagascar, its purpose had not been discovered by the enemy. Consequently, when it reached the seas around Diégo-Suarez on the evening of May 4, it was in a position to achieve total surprise.

Making full use of the cover of darkness, the assault was not launched until the early hours of the next day. The plan avoided a direct attack upon Diégo-Suarez itself, which was the focal point of the island's defenses, and called instead for troops to be landed at two inlets—Courrier Bay and Ambararata Bay—on the narrow isthmus just behind the major Vichy positions. To cover these landings, the Allies deployed artillery fire support from the warships and aircraft from the two carriers, which attacked the main harbor and airfield, destroying enemy naval and air forces before they could be mobilized. At the same time a diversionary attack, involving a false airborne landing by parachutes with dummies and a pyrotechnic naval barrage of star shells and rockets from

cruiser *Hermione* took place well to the southeast of the real target beaches.

This combination of a feint landing, close air support, and complete surprise proved highly effective. By 6:20 A.M., approximately two hours after the landings began, 2,000 troops had been put ashore and opposition on the beaches had been neutralized. The advance on the main objectives then began. At this point serious resistance was first encountered. The Vichy garrison, fighting for their colony against the British with a determination that they never exhibited when opposing the Japanese and rarely against the Germans invading their own country, attempted to stem the advance at a fortified defensive position blocking the route to the harbor and airfield. It took an additional landing by the Royal Marine detachment from *Ramillies,* as well as a barrage from the battleship's heavy guns, to break the garrison's resistance. At 10:50 A.M. on May 7, sixty hours after the attack began, the garrison surrendered.

The capture of Diégo-Suarez was not the end of operations on Madagascar. In September a campaign was launched to subdue the remainder of the island. Once again the Vichy forces put up a determined resistance, which was not overcome until November 5. More significant, however, than the rounding up of the remaining Vichy forces was the arrival of Japanese naval units in Madagascan waters. On the evening of May 30, two midget submarines launched from the parent submarines I.16 and I.20 penetrated the harbor defenses, torpedoing and seriously damaging *Ramillies*. This skillful attack demonstrated clearly that Madagascar was within range of Japanese offensive operations and clearly hinted at the carnage that could have been caused had Japanese forces been based on Madagascar. In forestalling this possibility, Operation Ironclad was patently worthwhile. Also, Madagascar was the first major amphibious assault undertaken by the British since the failed Dardanelles campaign in World War I. As such, it provided information about such assaults that would be of considerable use in later operations. More significant, however, was the fact that it was a success. Early 1942 was a difficult period for the Allies, one marked by continual advances by the Axis powers. The attack on Madagascar proved that the Allies could reach a theater of operations before their opponents and could mount a successful offensive. As a result, Allied morale was raised, and Allied domination of the approaches to the Indian Ocean was secured for the rest of the war.

FURTHER READINGS

Butler, J. R. M. *Grand Strategy,* vol. 2, part 2 (1964).
Hinsley, F. H. *British Intelligence in the Second World War,* vol. 2 (1981).

Ministry of Defence (Navy). *War with Japan,* vol. 3 (1995).

Roskill, S. W. *The War at Sea,* vol. 2 (1956).

Woodburn, Kirby S. *The War Against Japan,* vol. 2 (1958).

Matthew Seligman

SEE ALSO Navy, Royal

Magic, Operation

One of the key elements in the Allied victory in the Pacific was the ability of the Allies to decipher Japanese coded transmissions. This capability came about as a result of an intense effort by U.S. Army Intelligence to decipher the Japanese codes on the eve of the war. The attempts to break the Japanese codes came to be known as Operation Magic.

Although in 1929 Secretary of State Henry Stimson (supposedly saying, "Gentlemen do not read other gentlemen's mail") had closed down the State Department's "Black Chamber," that department's main cipher intelligence unit, there were six federal agencies involved in the effort to monitor Japanese coded transmissions: the Federal Bureau of Investigation, the Coast Guard, the Federal Communications Commission, the State Department, the U.S. Army, and the U.S. Navy. Through the 1930s, the army and navy intelligence sections devoted to breaking and reading Japanese codes took the lead in cryptanalytic services. Nonetheless, the relationship between the cryptanalytic sections of the two military branches was marked by animosity, mistrust, and duplication of effort.

The larger and far more organized section, which belonged to the U.S. Navy, was designated OP20G. This unit consisted of approximately forty men. In 1935, after a well orchestrated burglary of the office of the Japanese naval attaché in Washington, D.C., the navy was able to break the codes generated by the German-designed cipher machine Enigma, which was designated "Type A" by the Japanese. OP20G was able to build its own version of Enigma, which operated essentially as an electro-mechanical typewriter that transposed letters through three revolving rotors, and a stationary wheel. An electronic current went through each rotor and was reflected by the stationary wheel. Thus each current went through the three rotors twice. In addition, each rotor could be shuffled so that the possible variations of each letter sent through the machine was 105,456.

In 1935 the U.S. Army reorganized its code-breaking section of the SIS, and placed it under the command of an extremely gifted cryptanalyst, Colonel William F.

Friedman. Despite a minuscule staff, which numbered only eight in the mid-1930s, Friedman's section attempted to break Japan's diplomatic codes, unaware that OP20G had already done so. After the SIS team found that the encrypting machine used two sequences to encode, one substituting vowels for vowels and one substituting consonants for consonants, they were able to arrive at the overall pattern of the code. The SIS was then able to reconstruct the Enigma and read Japan's diplomatic messages. These messages were intercepted by six SIS radio stations, located in California, Hawaii, New Jersey, Panama, the Philippines, and Texas. A 1939 informal agreement between the army and navy gave OP20G the responsibility for handling Japanese military traffic; the SIS concentrated on diplomatic traffic.

For several years Friedman's team was able to read Japanese diplomatic messages encoded by Enigma and sent through what was known as the "Red Code." In 1939, however, the Japanese introduced a far more complicated version of Enigma, dubbed "Alphabetical Typewriter 97" or "Type B." Messages sent through this machine were known as "Purple Code" and initially could not be read by the SIS. The Japanese had replaced the rotors with electrical switches similar to those found in a telephone switchboard. Leo Rosen, an electrical engineer in the SIS, recognized what the Japanese had done, and Friedman's team set about attempting to design and construct a device that would allow them to decipher this new code.

With the threat of war drawing nearer and the difficulties raised by the implementation of the new Japanese code, both cryptanalytic branches were enlarged. OP20G was increased to some sixty men, and the SIS was more than doubled in strength to eighteen. Both sections worked, often with significant replication of effort, to break the new code. Despite the facts that the SIS had only one individual who could read Japanese and that the SIS had no analytic cipher equipment, in October 1940 they succeeded in building a copy of the Type B "Purple" machine, and thus broke the Japanese diplomatic code. The success of the operation led the American general overseeing the SIS, J. O. Mauborgne, to label those involved as "magicians" and the operation itself as "Magic." This soon became the official designation of intelligence material gathered through the SIS. Because of the small SIS staff and budget, Friedman's team turned to OP20G to aid it in producing more of the Magic machines. OP20G produced six more, of which the navy retained two for its own use.

Soon after breaking of the code, intelligence began to flow from intercepted Japanese diplomatic messages. By 1941, the SIS and OP20G were decoding all but about

2 percent of Japan's diplomatic traffic. The most significant information was sent by courier initially to the president, the secretaries of the navy, war and state, the directors of military and naval intelligence and the chief of war plans. Because these intercepts were edited and selected for content, those receiving the messages were not always able to get a complete overview of the rapidly deteriorating situation in the Pacific.

To further complicate matters, security lapses were discovered in the handling of the Magic information. In the spring of 1941, the Japanese embassy in Berlin received reliable information that the codes had been broken. Although the Japanese chose to disregard this information, when word of the leak reached Washington, it was decided to concentrate the information flowing from the Magic machines in the hands of the most senior officers. Henceforth, after July 1941, all Magic information sent to the Pacific went only through the expressed orders of the chief of naval operations. In addition, Hawaii had been designated to receive a Magic machine so that the Pacific Fleet would have its own intelligence capabilities. But a secret arrangement with the British sent that Magic machine and a spare to Great Britain in exchange for a British version of the most recent German Enigma machine, so that the United States would be able to read German codes. In addition, the United States and Great Britain agreed to share intelligence information about the Japanese. The United States would eventually use the combination of intelligence data gleaned from German transmissions and Japanese diplomatic messages between its embassy in Berlin and Tokyo to amass enough information about the planned German invasion of the Soviet Union to attempt to Stalin of the coming attack. Stalin of course ignored the warning.

As the dissemination of information was tightened and resources were diverted elsewhere, the Japanese navy revised its operational code. As the OP20G worked to break these new codes, there was little interaction between the navy group and the SIS. The combination of all of these factors meant that the commander of the U.S. naval forces in the Pacific, Admiral Husband Kimmel, did not tighten security or prepare for an attack even though Magic data pointed to the possibility of such an action, and on December 7, the Japanese were able to achieve about as complete a surprise in their attack on the U.S. naval facility at Pearl Harbor, Hawaii, as the Germans had in their invasion of the Soviet Union.

However, after Pearl Harbor, the American military would not want for intelligence information. As the war progressed, the Allies became increasingly adept at analyzing the deciphered codes. For instance, Magic data re-

vealed that Japan had no intention of attacking the Soviet Union, thereby allowing the Soviets to concentrate their forces against the Germans. In another instance, Magic data revealed significant information about the German defenses along the western coast of France after a Japanese military attaché sent a detailed report of the region's defenses from his office in Berlin to Tokyo. Magic transmissions also aided the Allies by detailing the damage inflicted by the Allied bombing campaign against Germany. Thus, by tapping into the diplomatic communications between the Japanese embassy in Berlin and Tokyo, Magic provided information on both the Pacific and European theaters of the war. The Magic information was compiled and distributed daily in what became known as the Magic Summary.

One of the most successful direct applications of Magic intelligence occurred at the Battle of Midway in June 1942. Magic data provided the Americans with both the approximate date and the direction of a Japanese attack against the Midway Islands. Magic also alerted the Americans that an attack on the Aleutian Islands would be a diversion. This knowledge kept the Americans from dispersing their already numerically inferior forces. In the end, the Americans won a resounding victory which marked the turning point in the war in the Pacific.

Throughout the rest of the war, Magic continued to provide the Allies with invaluable intelligence about both Germany and Japan. The ability to read the top-secret messages of the Japanese greatly aided Allied planners as they devised strategy. Operation Magic proved to be a major factor in the Allied effort against Japan and Germany.

FURTHER READINGS

Boyd, Carl. *Hitler's Japanese Confidant* (1993).
Drea, Edward J. *MacArthur's Ultra* (1992).
Parrish, Thomas. *The Ultra Americans* (1986).
Smith, Bradley F. *The Ultra-Magic Deals* (1993).

Tom Lansford

Makin Atoll

Part of the Gilbert Islands in the central Pacific, Makin atoll was the site of two battles in World War II. Both clashes occurred on the largest island of the coral atoll, Butaritari. The first, a hit-and-run raid on August 16–17, 1942, was conducted by the 2d Marine Raider Battalion (Carlson's Raiders). The second was the invasion and capture of the atoll on November 20–23, 1943, by elements of the U.S. Army's 27th Infantry Division. The marine raid, in which President Franklin Roosevelt's son James was a participant, was significant only in that it helped to bolster American morale early in the war—but it also warned the Japanese that their possessions in the Gilberts were inadequately defended. By the time Makin and its neighboring atoll, Tarawa, were attacked again in November 1943, the islands had been heavily reinforced and fortified. As a result, casualties—especially at Tarawa—were very high, causing critics to question the strategic wisdom of seizing the Gilbert Islands. Makin's strategic value was mainly as a seaplane base with a garrison consisting of about eight hundred, more than half of whom were Japanese and Korean laborers with no combat training.

The invasion of Makin (with the odd codename Operation Kourbash) was conducted primarily by the troops of the 27th Division's 165th Regimental Combat Team (RCT), a National Guard outfit perhaps better known by its previous designation as New York City's "Fighting [Irish] 69th" Infantry. The operation was planned by the 27th Division staff and was overseen by the staff of the newly formed V Amphibious Corps, commanded by Marine Major General Holland "Howlin' Mad" Smith. Smith, in turn, was responsible to the overall commander of the Gilbert Islands invasion force, Rear Admiral Richmond K. "Terrible" Turner.

From the air, Butaritari resembles a crutch lying on its side—it stretches about 11 miles from east to west and averages ¼ mile in width except at the westernmost end, the "armrest," where the first landings were made. The assault landings on Butaritari were preceded by extensive naval and air bombardment, but—as at Tarawa—this did little damage. The Japanese defenses on the island were concentrated in a 3000-yard-long "citadel" in the middle of the island, which was guarded to the east and west by antitank barriers and studded throughout with palm-log bunkers, trenches, machine-gun nests, and a few small gun emplacements. On the rest of the island the Japanese scattered a few snipers.

The 1st and 3d battalions of the 165th RCT landed on the western "armrest" of Butaritari at 8:30 A.M. on November 20, meeting negligible Japanese resistance. The coral restricted landing along all but a small stretch of the beach. Immediately, troops and supplies began to back up offshore. Were it not for the tracked mobility of a few amphibious tractors (LVTs), virtually no supplies would have made it ashore.

As the two battalions advanced eastward toward the citadel area, the width of the island rapidly diminished. By 10:30, the front line was so narrow—perhaps half a mile across—that the 3d battalion went into reserve, in anticipation of a landing on the far eastern tip of the

island the following day. At the same time that 1st battalion was taking over the front line, 2d battalion came ashore on the lagoon shore of Butaritari, in the heart of the Japanese defenses. Resistance was moderate. Only the tanks and LVTs in the first few waves could get over the coral reef to the shore—troops in all other landing craft had to debark and wade the last 250 to 300 feet.

The 1st and 2d battalions of the 165th RCT captured the western tank barrier by the end of the first day. The following day, 2d battalion moved east, clearing the central citadel up to the eastern tank barrier while 1st battalion mopped up Japanese left behind the front line. The original plan for the second day called for 3d battalion to land on the eastern tip of Butaritari and sweep west, but this was canceled because the desperate situation on nearby Tarawa required that these men be held out of combat in case they were needed there.

On the third day, 3d battalion was released from reserve and placed in the attack, covering 3½ miles of ground and killing or capturing another 200 Japanese. At nightfall, the dead-tired men dropped to the ground without digging in. They were convinced that only a few demoralized Japanese were left on the island. Thus, they were unprepared for the desperate, alcohol-fortified Japanese counterattack. A wild night of combat followed—dubbed "Saki Night" by the Americans—and in the morning the soldiers found more than fifty Japanese bodies in and around their perimeter, at the cost of three Americans killed. The weary troops quickly covered the last 2 miles to the eastern tip of Butaritari and reported "Makin Taken" at 10:30 on the morning of November 23. The cost to the Army was 66 killed in action or dead of wounds, 150 wounded in action, and 35 noncombat injuries.

Of special interest to military historians was the presence of Lieutenant Colonel S. L. A. Marshall, who had accompanied the invasion force in order to make a historical record. His interviews with a key unit on the morning after Saki Night led to the development of the unique system of postcombat interviewing that he used in three wars and taught to many other combat historians. Marshall later wrote, "The main part of my life's work came of the events of that day."

The navy had particularly bad luck during the Makin operation. Forty men were killed in a turret fire aboard battleship *Mississippi* during the preinvasion bombardment. Far worse was the loss of escort carrier *Liscome Bay* to a Japanese submarine in the early morning hours of November 24. The small carrier, struck in the magazine, exploded and sank with the loss of more than six hundred forty men.

The standard assessment of the army's performance on Makin was shaped by the immediate postwar publication of Holland Smith's memoirs, *Coral and Brass,* in which the general bitterly complained that the seizure of Makin had been "infuriatingly slow. Butaritari . . . should have been secured by dusk at D-Day. Any Marine Regiment would have done it in that time." Smith was also damning in his criticism of the rest of the army, the navy, the high command—pretty much anyone who wasn't a marine. But his criticism of the 27th at Makin stuck, and was echoed by later historians, including Samuel Eliot Morison in his *History of United States Naval Operations in World War II,* and even Philip Crowl and Edmund Love in the army's official history of the campaign, *The Seizure of the Gilberts and Marshalls.* Both histories blame the loss of the *Liscome Bay* on the army's failure to take the island in less then three days.

Recent scholarship, however, has tended to vindicate the 27th Division. Makin was captured according to the timetable laid out prior to the operation, despite the temporary withholding of troops from the operation by Smith in case they were needed on Tarawa. Furthermore, ships which were to be used to carry the assault troops back to Hawaii had not finished unloading until hours after the island was secured, due to the unanticipated difficulty in getting supplies across the reef. *Liscomb Bay,* which had to remain at Makin to protect those ships, would have been sunk even if the island had been taken on the first day.

Following the capture of Makin, an airstrip was built on the island from which raids were made against the Marshall Islands prior to their invasion and capture in early 1944.

FURTHER READINGS

Crowl, Philip, and Edmund Love. *Seizure of the Gilberts and Marshalls* (1955).

Gailey, Harry. *Howlin' Mad vs. the Army* (1986).

Marshall, S. L. A. *Makin* (1990). Reprint of *The Capture of Makin* (War Department Historical Division, 1946).

Morison, Samuel Eliot. *History of United States Naval Operations in World War II.* vol. 7, *Aleutians, Gilberts and Marshalls, June 1942–April 1944* (1951).

Les' Melnyk

SEE ALSO Amphibious Operations; Gilbert Islands; Smith, Holland McTyeire; Tarawa, Capture of

Malaria

"Doctor, this will be a long war if for every division facing the enemy, I must count on a second division in hospital with malaria and a third division convalescing from this debilitating disease." So spoke General Douglas MacArthur in despair at the inroads malaria was making on his troops.

Malaria was the "other enemy" in the war in the Pacific. It caused more deaths and hospitalized more soldiers than combat wounds. Military commanders who didn't see malaria as posing as serious a threat as the Japanese paid a high price. Although not the obvious enemy, it affected the outcomes of the fall of the Philippines, where it ravaged American troops; the battles of New Guinea and Guadalcanal, where it affected the Japanese more seriously that the Americans; and Burma, where weakened Japanese troops were unable to repulse a British invasion. It ultimately contributed to the defeat of the Japanese in the Pacific islands and South Asia.

Malaria is a bloodborne disease spread by the female *Anopheles* mosquito. The two most significant strains of malaria were *falciparum* and *vivax*. If not treated, *falciparum* malaria had a high mortality rate. Infected patients complained of a chilly sensation that lasted twenty to thirty-six hours, prostration, and headache. Complications included cerebral malaria, resulting in severe headache and delirium; and blackwater fever, so named because the patient's urine was darkened with dead blood cells. Both complications were usually fatal. Although *vivax* malaria had a lower mortality rate, it was both more common and more persistent. The patient initially complained of chills, followed by fever and sweats. The fever lasted from one to eight hours, and then the patient usually felt well until the next attack, approximately forty-eight hours later. If untreated, the symptoms subsided spontaneously in ten to thirty days, but could recur at varying intervals.

There were three aspects in the campaign against malaria. Environmental control involved the destruction of the mosquito habitat; swamps were drained and oil was poured in standing water to kill mosquito larvae. Behavior modification included efforts to teach soldiers how to protect themselves from infection, either by taking suppressive medication or by preventing mosquito bites through covering exposed skin or applying insect repellents. Medical treatment was provided to those infected with malaria so that they could return to service.

At the beginning of the war, quinine was considered the best treatment for malaria. It had been isolated in 1820 and its dosages were well understood. But the capture of the cinchona plantations in the Netherlands East Indies by the Japanese cut off quinine supplies to the Allies, forcing them to look at other antimalarial drugs.

Plasmochin, introduced in 1924, was the first synthetic antimalarial. Although it was highly effective in preventing relapses, Americans abandoned the drug early in the war because it was toxic and difficult to administer. Patients frequently reported stomach complaints, weakness, muscle aches, and dizziness. One of the more serious side effects was the destruction of red blood cells, particularly in persons of African ancestry.

Although Atabrine (quinacrine hydrochloride) had been introduced in 1931 as an antimalarial drug, there was no basis for determining dosages and it was thought to be both more toxic and less effective than the proven quinine. In 1943, clinical trials established appropriate dosage and proved that Atabrine could cure *falciparum* malaria and, if taken over a long period of time, *vivax* malaria.

China

Because the Chinese army didn't consider medical officers important or emphasize preventive medicine, malaria was common among its soldiers. A survey of a Chinese division in India found 90 percent malnourished, half with dysentery, and a quarter with malaria. The incidence of *falciparum* malaria was much higher compared with nearby Americans, and deaths were more frequent. The Chinese used Fraxine, a traditional pharmaceutical, to treat malaria; U.S. clinical trials concluded it was ineffective.

Australia

Although the Australian army had the medical means to combat malaria earlier than U.S. forces did, its troops suffered more from malaria because of their casual attitude toward prevention and their operations in highly malarial areas. In December 1943, the malaria rate was 890 per 1,000 per year, compared with the U.S. rate of 198 per 1,000 per year. Australia's war against malaria was the more urgent due to fears of the disease spreading to the mainland, a fear realized when a 1942 epidemic affected 7 percent of the population of Cairns, Queensland. As a result, troops in the region were required to take Atabrine, and soldiers who had contracted malaria in New Guinea were prevented from returning home. In another attempt to prevent the spread of malaria, aborigines were rounded up and placed in compounds free of mosquito breeding areas. N. Hamilton Fairley, director of the Australian Army Medical Corps, was placed in charge of the Combined Advisory Committee on Tropical Medicine, which pooled Allied medical efforts in the war against malaria.

Based on experience in Syria in 1941, the army established malaria control units to follow advancing troops and promptly implement malaria control measures. Mobile entomological sections were created in 1942 to study disease-bearing insects. In addition to assisting malaria control units by identifying mosquitoes, these units investigated repellents, established standards for insecticides, and evaluated aerial spraying. By 1944, Royal Australian Air Force Beaufort fighter-bombers were being used to spray DDT.

Malaria continued to ravage Australian troops due to lax malaria discipline until 1944. Several commanders neglected malaria control orders, fearing that they would lower morale. During the Huon campaign in New Guinea in 1943, the Australian 7th Division commanders didn't enforce malaria discipline and troops failed to take their Atabrine, in many cases because of rumors that Atabrine would permanently turn skin yellow and lead to impotence. In addition, soldiers discarded mosquito nets to lighten their burden and continued to wear shorts. Malaria accounted for more than 90 percent of the division's total hospital admissions for disease. By December 1943, the 7th Division's weekly preventive dosage was doubled and malaria discipline was enforced. The malaria rate dropped from 4,840 per 1,000 per year to 740 per 1,000 per year by January 1944.

The Australian army treatment used a combination of quinine, Atabrine, and Plasmochin, followed by a 6-week course of Atabrine.

India

Malaria was common in India long before World War II. The primary achievement of the Indian Medical Corps was the development of improved sanitation and mosquito eradication. Considerable research was conducted on mosquito ecology and an additional mosquito carrier of malaria was identified. By 1945, the daily malaria rate was 20 per 1,000 per day, down from the March 1943 rate of 95 per 1,000 per day. These efforts became the foundation for malaria eradication campaigns in postwar India.

In March 1941, the Anti-Malarial Unit (AMU) was formed, consisting of a malariologist, a surgeon with a small staff of ward servants, and laboratory assistants. These units worked with division field hygiene sections to supervise civilian labor used in mosquito eradication. However, when field hygiene sections moved to support advancing units, there was a time lag before the upper echelon could assume responsibility for mosquito eradication, resulting in a number of malaria outbreaks. The AMU was enlarged to a headquarters and four sections.

Each section was provided with its own transportation and civilian laborers. Whereas the number of AMUs varied according to the needs of the advancing armies, six AMUs were normally assigned to a corps, three of which were assigned to each division. Early efforts emphasized swamp drainage; a base in Manipur had over six hundred miles of drainage ditches constructed in 1944. DDT spraying supplanted these efforts, and over 454 million pounds of DDT was sprayed in 1944–1945.

The incidence of malaria varied with each unit, depending on how successful the medical officer was in persuading his commander of the importance of malaria prevention and the commander's willingness to enforce malaria discipline. Suppressive doses of Atabrine were not uniformly enforced throughout the Indian army. Personal protective measures in 1943 were mosquito netting and protective clothing. Although these measures were generally successful in base camps, protective clothing proved inadequate in the field. The decreasing incidence of malaria throughout the Indian army is generally attributed to improved sanitation.

In 1942 the Indian army treated malaria with a combination of quinine, Plasmochin, and Atabrine, later standardizing on an Atabrine-based therapy. Malaria forward treatment units, lightly equipped hospitals of two hundred to four hundred beds, treated patients close to the front.

New Zealand
Because New Zealand troops were stationed at New Caledonia, which had little malaria, few soldiers were exposed to the disease at the beginning of the war. By the time troops were deployed to the Solomons, where malaria was common, the lessons of malaria prevention and treatment had been learned and implemented by the New Zealand army. Soldiers benefited from fighting during the malaria "off season," when mosquitoes were less common, and from the mosquito control efforts of Allied forces. As a result, only 0.8 percent of the soldiers became sick with malaria during the war.

By January 1943, the army's Malaria Control Unit, with a total strength of thirty-six men, assisted in draining swamps and in identifying and classifying mosquitoes. The headquarters section included the commander and an entomologist with ten enlisted men, one trained in laboratory diagnosis of malaria. There were three sections, two headed by an entomologist and one by a combat engineer, each with seven enlisted men.

All combat officers were trained in antimalaria measures and were required to lecture their troops on malaria prevention. Although not permitted to bring short trou-

sers into malarious areas, many soldiers circumvented this rule by wearing their undershorts. Soldiers were issued insect repellent and given weekly suppressive dosages of Atabrine.

Medical officers received extensive training in the clinical diagnosis and treatment of malaria. In forward areas, all patients had blood drawn to test for infection, resulting in the diagnosis of many malaria cases. Battle casualties were routinely given a 3-day course of Atabrine. Each soldier kept a malaria record with him in his paybook.

United Kingdom
The malaria campaign of the Fourteenth Army, composed of African, British, and Indian troops, was so successful that it prompted rumors that Field Marshall William Slim deliberately chose to fight the Japanese in the most malarious regions of Burma in 1945, confident that his troops would withstand the disease better than the Japanese. He appointed an officer to each division to enforce malaria discipline. As a result, soldiers admitted to hospital with malaria decreased from a high of 60 percent of total strength in 1943 to around 10 percent in 1945.

The British army developed several antimalaria units during the war. The Malaria Control Company was responsible for coordinating civilian laborers eradicating mosquitoes by oiling breeding pools and draining swamps. By 1944, shortages of the insecticide pyrethrum resulted in the testing of DDT, which proved so effective that specially equipped Hurricane fighters sprayed large areas prior to the advance of the Fourteenth Army into Burma. The Base Malaria Field Laboratory performed malaria research, conducted surveys, prepared maps, and advised commanders on malaria prevention. The Mobile Malaria Field Laboratory, staffed with two malariologists, an entomologist, and seventeen enlisted laboratory technicians, investigated and controlled malaria problems in the field.

Slim made malaria prevention a command responsibility. Soldiers were issued uniforms impregnated with mosquito repellent. When soldiers were reluctant to take their Atabrine, because it was rumored to cause sterility, Slim began conducting surprise inspections with blood tests for Atabrine. If the result was less than 95 percent positive, the commander was removed. Only three officers were removed before the rest of the commanders began enforcing Atabrine discipline. Confidence in Atabrine improved, and by June 1943, infantrymen went to the regimental aid station if they missed their daily dosage.

At the beginning of the war, the British army treated malaria with a combination of quinine, Plasmochin, and

Atabrine, but later standardized on an Atabrine-based therapy

Japan

Although the Japanese had the apparent advantage in the war against malaria because they were more at home in the area and had access to quinine, the disease devastated their soldiers. During the Battle of Guadalcanal, nearly every soldier was infected and quarter of the troops died of a malaria. In New Georgia, between December 1942 and February 1943, the average hospital admission rate was at least 1,440 per 1,000 per year, double the U.S. rate in the region. On any given day, 40 out of 1,000 men were incapacitated due to malaria.

Attached to each division was a 50–150 man water purification unit responsible for controlling infection and ensuring a safe water supply. Their duties included malaria control by draining swamps and spraying breeding places with a liquid preparation called "earth." These units tended to function better around established bases than under combat conditions.

The Japanese used suppressive dosages of a combination of quinine and Atabrine. However, the dosages they used were insufficient or, worse, possibly suppressed only the less fatal *vivax* strain. The Japanese apparently had the same problems with compliance as their American counterparts; by the end of the Bataan campaign in 1942, section leaders had to line up their men daily to place the pills in their mouths. At the beginning of the war, insect repellents and mosquito nets were issued to soldiers upon arrival in the combat zone.

Most cases of malaria were treated with a combination of quinine, Atabrine, and/or Plasmochin, although anecdotal evidence suggests Atabrine was the drug of choice by 1944. Injectable treatments were used only long enough for the patient to recover sufficiently to take oral medications. The Japanese were aggressive in treating symptoms of malaria, and their patients routinely had to endure enemas, heart stimulants, and antacids as part of their treatment. Many of these efforts tended to exacerbate the disease rather than help the patient. Some units established 300-bed recuperation centers for malaria patients. Special emphasis was laid on exercises with diet to restore strength, and most men were returned to their units within forty-five days.

United States

Although the U.S. Army had had considerable experience in dealing with malaria in the Caribbean and Central America, very few American doctors had seen a malaria patient before the war. In 1941 and 1942, U.S. troops were ravaged by malaria. Convinced that malaria was the main cause of the U.S. defeat in the Philippines, General Douglas MacArthur began emphasizing malaria prevention. Military officers were judged on the malaria rates in their command. The turning point came in 1943, at the Battle of Guadalcanal, which saw the introduction of suppressive dosages of Atabrine. American efforts at malaria suppression were successful, and the malaria rate in New Guinea, that was 3,300 per 1,000 per year in January 1943, was reduced to 31 per 1,000 per year in January 1944.

The Army–Navy Malaria and Insect Control Organization was established in November 1942. The unit was headed by a malariologist and included a survey unit of eleven enlisted technicians headed by an entomologist, a control unit of eleven technicians headed by a sanitary engineer, and local area antimalaria squads that could be detached to conduct mosquito control operations in combat zones. Locally recruited labor gangs were hired to drain, oil, and clear swamps. The insecticide DDT, introduced in the Pacific by 1944, was sprayed by individuals from vehicles and from aircraft, such as modified L-4s, C-47s, A-20s, and B-25s. Although effective in mosquito control, DDT arrived too late to affect malaria rates. Between 1942 and 1944, U.S. Public Health Service officers ran the malaria-control efforts in China.

At the beginning of the war, soldiers were issued suppressive dosages of quinine until shortages forced the military to consider Atabrine. At first it was difficult to obtain soldier compliance, because the drug initially caused nausea, vomiting, and diarrhea; gave the skin a sickly yellowish hue—and was rumored to cause sterility. As proper dosages were established and effectiveness was proved, compliance improved. Soldiers received mosquito netting and DEET insect repellent. Education campaigns in the form of short films, pinup calendars and "Malaria Moe" cartoons encouraged soldiers to consider malaria as much the enemy as the Japanese, and to follow proper preventive techniques.

The Americans began the war using the quinine-Atabrine-Plasmochin treatment. However, shortages of quinine and disillusionment with Plasmochin left Atabrine as the antimalarial of choice. Malaria patients who could not retain or respond to oral medications were treated with injectable Atabrine or quinine. The general treatment of patients emphasized nutrition and fluid intake. Patients were given adequate rest and sleep, with the judicious use of sedatives. Recovery ordinarily took between ten and fourteen days.

All belligerent armies in the Pacific war had to resort to near-heroic measures to fight the age-old scourge of malaria. Whereas all of the Allied armies enjoyed considerable success in their antimalaria campaigns and eventually mastered the disease, the Japanese lost tens of thousands of fighting troops to this "other enemy."

FURTHER READINGS

Coates, John Boyd, ed. *Internal Medicine in World War II*, vol. 1, *Activities of Medical Consultants* (Office of the Surgeon General, Department of the Army, 1961).

———. *Internal Medicine in World War II*, vol. 2, *Infectious Diseases* (Office of the Surgeon General, Department of the Army, 1963).

———. *Preventative Medicine in World War II*, vol. 6, *Communicable Diseases, Malaria* (Office of the Surgeon General, Department of the Army, 1963).

Condon-Rall, Mary. "Allied Cooperation in Malaria Prevention and Control: The World War II Southeast Pacific Experience," *Journal of the History of Medicine and Allied Sciences* (October 1991).

Condon-Rall, Mary, and Cowdrey, Albert. *The Technical Services. The Medical Department: Medical Service in the War Against Japan* (U.S. Army Center of Military History, 1998).

Cowdrey, Albert E. *Fighting for Life: American Military Medicine in World War II* (1994).

Harrison, Mark. "Medicine and the Culture of Command: The Case of Malaria Control in the British Army During the Two World Wars," *Medical History*, 40 (1996).

Joy, Robert. "Malaria in American Troops in the South and Southwest Pacific in World War II," *Medical History*, 43 (1999).

MacNalty, Arthur, and Mellor, W. Franklin. *Medical Services in War: The Principal Medical Lessons of the Second World War* (1986).

Maisel, Albert Q. *Miracles of Military Medicine* (1943).

National Archives and Records Administration. *Allied Translator and Interpreter Section Reports, 1942–1946, South West Pacific Area* (microfiche).

Records of the Office of the Surgeon General, U.S. Army, Medical Intelligence Division. National Archives and Records Administration.

U.S. Army. *Jap Medical Problems in the South and Southwest Pacific*, Know Your Enemy, no. 17 (1944).

U.S. War Department. *Treatment of Clinical Malaria and Malarial Parasitemia*, Technical Bulletin MED 72 (1947).

Weina, Peter A. "From Atabrine in World War II to Mefloquine in Somalia: The Role of Education in Preventative Medicine," *Military Medicine* (September 1998).

Alan Hawk

Malaya, Japanese Conquest of

The Japanese conquest of Malaya and Singapore was one of the most one-sided campaigns in military history, a result as much of British blundering and lack of initiative as of Japanese valor and control of the air. The British had long controlled certain portions of Malaya, including the island of Singapore, as a crown colony. They had also worked out a number of defense arrangements with the federated and nonfederated Malay states. Malaya was one of the richest targets in what the Japanese called the Southern Resources Area, with large deposits of nickel, gold, and oil; nearly half of the world's rubber; and almost one-third of its tin. In addition to its abundance of raw materials, Malaya was important for another strategic reason. As long as the British retained Malaya, and more specifically Singapore, they could interfere with Japanese military activities in Southeast Asia, or in Indonesian or Philippine islands. In Japanese hands, Singapore could protect Japanese operations in the islands and would provide a springboard for further aggression.

Malaya figured prominently in the plans of the Japanese general staff. Japanese planners hoped to seize the Southern Resources Area and additional strategic islands by three principal offensive drives. The first was to be against Malaya and Singapore. The second was to start soon afterward, with a seaborne invasion of the Philippines. These two drives would then converge against Java, the heart of the Netherlands East Indies and a treasure-house of strategic minerals. Meanwhile, the Japanese would occupy Thailand as a base for the third drive—an invasion of Burma. At the outset of the war, smaller forces would quickly seize British Hong Kong and U.S. Guam and Wake Island.

However, the first and most important single operation of the initial phase of the war plan was an attack to destroy or neutralize the U.S. fleet at Pearl Harbor, Hawaii. The second phase of the Japanese strategy would be a period of consolidation—the organizing of efficient military control over the conquered territories and establishing a strong defensive perimeter around the Japanese Empire from the Kurils through Wake Island and the Marshall, Gilbert, and Bismarck island groups, thence westward through northern New Guinea, Timor, and Java, and northward through Sumatra, Malaya, and Burma. The third phase of the Japanese strategy would be defensive—to intercept and destroy any Allied attacking force that might attempt to penetrate the defensive perimeter.

As the Japanese prepared to launch their grand design, British ground forces in Malaya under Lieutenant General A. E. Percival consisted of three divisions and numerous supporting troops. This force, numbering about a hundred thousand men, was very short of equipment and weapons. In addition, many of the British troops had only recently arrived, and they were not yet accustomed to the tropical climate. The major British deficiency was a leadership, civilian and military, that could at best be classed as mediocre.

The Japanese plan for attacking Malaya called for Japanese forces to sweep down from Thailand. Japan already held Indochina, which had been occupied in 1941 with the virtual acquiescence of Vicky France. This provided the Japanese with the naval and air bases they needed to carry out the invasion of Malaya. Using Indochina as a staging area, Japanese troops would make amphibious landings and drive down the Malay Peninsula to capture the British stronghold at Singapore. At the same time, massive Japanese air and naval forces would launch a major assault against the oil-rich Dutch East Indies. Then the Japanese would drive the British out of Burma.

The Japanese force was led by Lieutenant General Tomoyuki Yamashita, commander of Japan's Twenty-fifth Army, which consisted of three infantry divisions, four tank regiments, and numerous supporting artillery units. These troops were well equipped veterans of fighting in China and recently had undergone extensive jungle training in preparation for the campaign.

The attack began at dawn on December 8, 1941, with a surprise air attack against British airfields in Malaya and Singapore. Soon afterward Japanese troops poured ashore at Singora (Songkhla) and Pattani in southern Thailand, and then near Kota Bharu in northeastern Malaya. The amphibious force had embarked from the island of Hainan off the southern coast of China. The convoy of transports was to steam 1,100 miles across the South China Sea to rendezvous with an escort of Japanese warships off the tip of Indochina. The combined force would then enter the Gulf of Siam, veering sharply to the west and south as it arrived at the projected invasion beaches on the far side of the gulf.

As the rendezvous was being effected on December 6, a British Hudson bomber on a reconnaissance patrol from the British airbase at Kota Bharu in northern Malaya saw the force. Because he was low on fuel, the pilot turned for home. Upon returning to base, he reported a number of Japanese merchant ships accompanied by cruisers and destroyers traveling northwest, west, and southward. The British Far East Command headquarters in Singapore received the report and ascertained that the Japanese were on the move. The question was where. There were three possible targets: Bangkok, Singora (a port in southern Thailand not far from the border with Malaya), or northern Malaya itself. Or possibly all three. If the target were

Thailand, the British would be faced with a delicate situation. Thailand had managed to avoid becoming an appendage of Japanese imperial power. The British in Malaya had worked out a plan, under the code name Matador, for the sending of troops to the defense of Singora if a Japanese invasion of southern Thailand appeared imminent. London, however, had repeatedly urged restraint, and the high command in Malaya was reluctant to make the move.

Sir Arthur Brooke-Popham, supreme head of the Far East Command, making no reference to Matador, issued orders that brought all forces in Malaya to "the first degree of readiness" and increased the number of reconnaissance flights over the Gulf of Siam. The weather the next day favored Yamashita because squalls and pelting rains severely hampered visibility. Nevertheless, by evening, Japanese vessels had been spotted heading toward Singora, as well as others nearing Pattani, another southern Thai port closer to the Malayan border, and Kota Bharu. Although this revealed Yamashita's invasion strategy, word of the sightings did not reach Singapore until 2100 hours—just three hours before the Japanese transports began to anchor off Singora, Pattani, and Kota Bharu.

Nothing seemed to go right for the British from the start. Although Royal Air Force (RAF) planes attacked the transports off Singora, setting two afire and sinking a third, this action had little impact on the invasion because 5,300 Japanese troops had already debarked. Brooke-Popham delayed his decision about putting Matador into effect until it was too late. Even then, he settled on a half measure, sending a battalion of infantry to seize a commanding ridge 30 miles inside Thailand on the road to Pattani. However, the battalion, late in starting, was held up at the frontier by the Thai constabulary, and was driven out of Thailand by the Japanese before reaching the ridge. Therefore, Pattani fell without a fight, and at Singora the Thai troops put up only token resistance.

Yamashita was off to an auspicious start. This was essential, because he had only 60,000 troops at his disposal, as opposed to 88,000 British. However, the numerical superiority did not reflect reality, because the British army in Malaya was a hastily assembled hodgepodge of British, Australian, Indian, and Malay recruits, some of whom were undependable, as was demonstrated at Kota Bharu. The two Indian divisions lacked leadership because many of their junior officers and noncoms had been sent to India to train new units of recruits. In addition, the British army in Malaya was desperately short of tanks, artillery, communications equipment, tools, and spare parts. This situation was a result of London's absorption in other theaters of war, and its resultant giving of a low priority to Malaya's requests for materiel. The Japanese soldiers, on the other hand, were well equipped for the climate and well trained in jungle operations (rehearsed on similar terrain on Hainan and in Indochina). In addition, many of them had fought in China.

Having gained a foothold on the peninsula, the Japanese strategy for the campaign in Malaya was simple: from Singora and Pattani, Japanese troops would strike westward across the Isthmus of Kra—less than a hundred miles wide at that point—then move southward into Malaya and down its western coast, thus bypassing the mountain range in the center of the peninsula. At the same time, a secondary drive would be made from Kota Bharu down the east coast. Near the tip of the peninsula, the two forces would converge for an assault on Singapore, the "Gibraltar of the Pacific."

Although the Japanese attack was initially very successful, things went a bit better, at least initially, for the British at Kota Bharu. As the Japanese came ashore, they were pinned down by withering British machine-gun fire from pillboxes behind the beaches. Later, however, for each pillbox a Japanese soldier would dash forward and fling himself across the slit of a pillbox; then his comrades would charge the blinded position with hand grenades and bayonets. Gradually the beach defenses were breached. In addition, long-range Japanese planes flying from Indochina repeatedly bombed and strafed the base. At about 1600 hours, the defenders panicked when a false rumor reported enemy ground troops at the perimeter. A hurried evacuation began; the station staff set fire to the buildings, the operations room, and most of the stores. In their haste, they forgot about the remaining stocks of bombs and fuel, and left the runways in usable condition. Within twenty-four hours of the landings, Kota Bharu and the air base were in Japanese hands.

The powerful British naval squadron at Singapore, commanded by Admiral Sir Tom Phillips, responded as soon as the Japanese began landing on the northeast coast of Malaya. Wanting to strike swiftly, to sink as many of the Japanese troop transports as possible, Phillips steamed out of Singapore on December 8, 1941, with Force Z, which consisted of a battleship, a battle cruiser, and four destroyers. The RAF had suffered too severely from Japanese dawn attacks on its Malayan bases to be able to provide land-based air cover for the squadron. However, no battle cruiser or battleship had ever been sunk by air attack, and Phillips believed that by striking hard and fast, he could inflict great damage on the Japanese invasion force and then get back to Singapore before Japanese planes could cause him serious trouble. He was convinced

that deftly handled, strongly defended capital ships could fight off aerial attacks.

The Japanese convoys off Kota Bahru had moved away before the British squadron arrived, so Phillips and his ships began searching. This was slow work without scouting planes, and as a result his force was for several hours within range of Japanese air bases in southern Indochina. The British ships, with no protecting air cover, were sighted by Japanese submarines and patrol aircraft. Subsequently, in a 2-hour battle, swarms of Japanese naval aircraft based in Indochina attacked and sank battleship HMS *Prince of Wales* and battle cruiser HMS *Repulse* off the east coast of Malaya. The Allies had no more major warships to challenge Japanese offensives in the Indian Ocean, in the China Sea, or in the southwest Pacific. When word of the fate of Task Force Z reached London, Prime Minister Winston Churchill was shocked. He later recalled, "In all the war I never received a more direct shock. As I turned over and twisted in bed, the full horror of the news sank in upon me. Over all this vast expanse of waters Japan was supreme, and we everywhere were weak and naked."

With the sinking of *Repulse* and *Prince of Wales* and the crippling of the British air forces in Malaya, the way was now clear for an all-out Japanese assault down the peninsula. Yamashita had estimated that he could capture Singapore in 100 days. In reality, it would take only 70. In the following weeks, Japanese troops fought their way to the tip of the Malay Peninsula, stunning the British by their ability to work their way through the dense, tangled jungle. The British had expected the jungle to be an impenetrable obstacle that would stop the Japanese. They had not taken the time to reconnoiter the terrain more thoroughly; much of the peninsula was in reality rubber plantations, straight rows of trees that actually provided avenues down which bicycle-mounted troops could pedal. The Japanese also proved adept at moving through dense jungle, infiltrating their way into the center of British positions or working their way around to encircle the defenders, a tactic which worked most of the time against the slow-moving and off-balance British. The Japanese also used captured fishing vessels to conduct a number of small amphibious landings behind the British flank on the west coast of the peninsula.

By early January 1942, the British were in serious trouble. Losses were heavy and the defenders were exhausted by three weeks of continuous fighting in the oppressive heat. By this time, Yamashita's forces controlled two-thirds of the peninsula. The British frequently found themselves cut off from their lines of communications, then harassed from front, flanks, and rear as they tried to fight their way out, continually under fire from Japanese snipers who took their toll, particularly on the officers.

As events unfolded, the Allies had hastily established a combined military organization, the ABDA Command, and British General Sir Archibald P. Wavell was placed in command of all American, British, Dutch, and Australian forces in Southeast Asia and the nearby island groups. Shortly after assuming command, Wavell flew to Singapore and saw that the British defenses in Malaya were collapsing. Although Percival wanted to continue fighting a delaying action down the peninsula, to allow time for reinforcements to reach Singapore, Wavell ordered Percival to fall back to Johore, on the narrow and more easily defended southern portion of the Malay Peninsula.

The British withdrawal gave the Australian division a rare chance to force on the Japanese a dose of their own medicine by setting ambushes and infiltrating enemy lines at night. The Australians joined the withdrawing Indian troops and fought a savage battle against the crack Imperial Guards in the jungle around the Muar River. Despite valiant efforts of the Australian and Indian troops, the superior strength of the attackers prevailed. The victorious Japanese systematically decapitated 200 Australian and Indian wounded soldiers who had been left behind when the main body withdrew. Although the Australian and Indian forces blunted the Japanese advance for nearly two weeks, the retreat further exhausted and demoralized the poorly conditioned troops.

On January 17, the Japanese smashed a hole in the new British line. Two weeks later, with his defenses once again crumbling, Percival withdrew all of his remaining troops back to Singapore Island, which had been extensively fortified. Unfortunately, however, the British never expected an assault from the land side; all the heavy guns pointed out to sea and their power cables were too short to permit these pieces to turn toward the land. Percival hastily began to fortify the island's unprotected northern shore. He ordered engineers to blow a 60-foot gap in the road and railroad causeway that ran over the Strait of Johore to the mainland. The city was now isolated and in a state of siege. Percival spread out his three divisions in defensive positions and rushed a fourth division to the front after it arrived by sea from England. Percival thought he could defend Singapore even against a long siege; the British had plentiful supplies of food and ammunition, and he thought they could hold out until reinforcements arrived from Britain.

Yamashita, however, had no intention of attempting a protracted siege and was, in fact, worried that a street-by-street defense might well swallow up his forces. It took him a week to prepare his forces for the assault on Sin-

gapore. He brought up his artillery and began an extensive bombardment of the British positions; at the same time, Japanese aircraft, operating from captured air bases in Malaya, bombed targets all over Singapore, encountering pitiable RAF opposition. Meanwhile, Yamashita had brought up two hundred collapsible boats that were to ferry his soldiers across the Strait of Johore. After three days of intensive preparation, the Japanese, using the boats and armored landing barges, made a bold, nighttime amphibious assault on the northwest portion of the island, where they had not been expected. At 11 P.M. on February 8, under cover of an artillery bombardment, Yamashita's troops embarked for the mangrove swamps on Singapore's northwest shore. The defenders, two recently arrived Australian battalions with no combat experience, were thrown into disarray by this night attack, and by morning the Japanese had established a firm beach-head on the northwest coast of Singapore Island. By noon nearly twenty-three thousand Japanese troops were moving toward Bukit Timah, a 600-foot hill that dominated the island. Other landings followed, and the attackers drove eastward to reach the southern end of the causeway, permitting tanks to rumble across from the mainland to join the attackers.

The British attempted a desperate counterattack, but it was repulsed by the Japanese, who then advanced to the central portion of the island. A fierce battle ensued for three days, but by February 14 the Japanese had taken the island water reservoirs and the British realized that they were beaten. Yamashita sent Percival a message on the morning of February 13, demanding the British surrender. Percival cabled the contents of Yamashita's note to Wavell in Java and noted that he did not intend to dignify the demand with a reply. However, the next day the British realistically looked at the situation and found their position hopeless. The city was by then ravaged by mobs of looters, many of whom were drunken, demoralized British troops. That afternoon Percival met with Yamashita to discuss terms, but Yamashita said the fighting would go on unless Percival agreed to an immediate surrender.

Ultimately Percival agreed, and at 8:30 P.M. on February 15, the guns fell silent. Singapore had fallen to Yamashita's army and a lethal blow had been dealt to British prestige as much to as to British military power. The contrast between the confused, ineffectual British effort in Malaya and Singapore and the dogged American-Filipino defense of the Bataan Peninsula was obvious and humiliating. It would be another two months before the Americans would surrender. In slightly more than two months, the Japanese had conquered Malaya and captured supposedly impregnable Singapore. In doing so, they had lost approximately 10,000 men killed and wounded; the British had suffered 138,708 casualties (including 70,000 who surrendered when Singapore fell). The capture of Singapore gave Japan absolute control of the Malay Peninsula and its abundant natural resources. Moreover, the victory provided the Japanese with bases for further offensives. It is an indication of the demoralization of the British that not one soldier saw fit even to attempt to continue the struggle by means of guerrilla warfare—again in contrast to the American-Filipino postsurrender resistance in the Philippines.

The fall of Singapore has been called by many the greatest disaster in British military history. It had been caused by an underestimation of the Japanese, lack of aggressive leadership, inadequate armaments, a divided command structure, and improper use of reinforcements. From Singapore the Japanese could advance easily against the Netherlands East Indies (from Singapore, it was only 65 miles to Sumatra, the second largest of the Dutch East Indies and the site of some of the richest oil fields in Asia), and also strike west into the Indian Ocean. At the same time, Malaya and occupied Thailand became Japanese springboards for an invasion of Burma. Nearly four years of struggle, at immense cost, were to elapse before Singapore was recovered.

FURTHER READINGS

Allen, Louis. *Singapore, 1941–1942* (1979).
Dupuy, Trevor N. *Asiatic Land Battles: The Expansion of Japan in Asia* (1963).
Falk, Stanley L. *Seventy Days to Singapore* (1975).
Weinberg, Gerhard L. *A World at Arms* (1994).

James H. Willbanks

SEE ALSO ABDA Command; *Prince of Wales* and *Repulse*, Sinking of

Manchuria

A prime target for exploitation and conquest by the Japanese since the late nineteenth century, Manchuria was a province in northeastern China. Blessed with fertile soil and a wealth of raw materials (including such vital resources as iron ore and oil shale), Manchuria became subject to increasing domination between 1905 and 1933, when the Japanese satellite state of Manchukuo was proclaimed in the province.

Manchuria was first occupied by Russian troops in the wake of the Boxer Rebellion of 1901, but Japan saw Russian control of the province as a grave threat to Japanese control of Korea. In the Russo-Japanese War (1904–1905) most of the land combat took place there, and after Japan's victory Tokyo received important economic concessions in the region, the most important being control over the strategically vital South Manchurian Railway. A quasi-public corporation, the South Manchurian Railway Company, was set up in 1906 to govern its operation.

Responsibility for the protection of the railway was given to an elite division of the Japanese army, which in 1919 was granted independent status as the Kwantung Army. In the 1920s this army became increasingly politicized, and it attracted the most ambitious of a new generation of officers, including Tojo Hideki. The belief grew among the leadership of the Kwantung Army that Japanese interests required the occupation of all Manchuria. If developed industrially, they argued, the region could serve as a prime source of raw materials as well as an outlet for the supposedly overpopulated home islands. Moreover, it would provide a buffer between Japan and the potentially hostile Soviet Union. The Kwantung Army began exacting additional concessions from the compliant ruler of Manchuria, the Chinese warlord Chang Tso-lin. By 1928, however, the growing strength of the Kuomintang in China had begun to stiffen Chang's resistance to Japanese demands. When the Kuomintang leader, Chiang Kai-shek, announced his refusal to recognize any agreement to which he was not a party, Chang nullified an agreement allowing the South Manchurian Railway Company to construct five new lines into northern Manchuria. This act of defiance led to the warlord's assassination by an officer of the Kwantung Army. The army hoped to follow up this murder by occupying the entire region, but the civilian government in Tokyo vetoed this scheme.

Chang Tso-lin was succeeded by his son, Chang Hsueh-liang. Aware of Japanese involvement in the death of his father, he immediately aligned himself with the Kuomintang and began taking a hard line against Japan and the South Manchurian Railway Company. By the late summer of 1931 the situation had grown so intolerable in the eyes of the Kwantung Army that its leadership decided to take matters into their own hands. On the night of September 18, agents of the army blew up a section of the South Manchurian Railway at Mukden, blamed it on Chinese sabotage, and used this incident as a pretext for occupying all of Manchuria. The government in Tokyo was presented with a fait accompli. Although some civilian politicians denounced the move, none dared risk the wrath of the military by demanding withdrawal from Manchuria.

The League of Nations, however, felt differently, the League Council voting 31 to 1 (with only Japan's delegate voting no) to demand that Japanese troops leave Manchuria. The Kwantung Army refused to do so, and in March 1932 it declared the establishment of Manchukuo, a supposedly independent state ruled by Henry Puyi, the last emperor of China. In reality, however, Manchukuo was nothing more than a puppet regime administered by the Kwantung Army. The League of Nations voted 42 to 1 (again, with only Japan dissenting) to refuse recognition to Manchukuo, prompting the Japanese delegation to walk out of the conference hall. Soon afterward Japan withdrew completely from the League.

Manchukuo remained a major source of raw materials for Japan, and the South Manchurian Railway Company played a key role in the development of heavy industry and mining in the region. Economic development, however, was hampered by the continuing war in China, and Japan's oppressive control of the province led to the growth of an indigenous resistance movement after 1937. Meanwhile, the much-feared Kwantung Army, once Japan's most elite ground fighting force, was gradually weakened by the transfer of its most experienced units to other fronts. On August 8, 1945, Soviet forces invaded Manchuria from the north, crushing Japanese resistance and overrunning the province within days. Manchukuo was declared dissolved and the area was returned to China.

FURTHER READINGS

Barnhart, Michael J. *Japan Prepares for Total War: The Search for Economic Security, 1919–1941* (1987).

Morley, James W. *Japan Erupts: The London Naval Conference and the Manchurian Incident, 1928–1932* (1984).

Saburo, Ienaga. *The Pacific War, 1931–1945* (1978).

Thorne, Christopher. *The Limits of Foreign Policy: The West, the League, and the Far Eastern Crisis of 1931–1933* (1973).

Yoshihashi, Takeihiko. *Conspiracy at Mukden: The Rise of the Japanese Military* (1963).

Young, Louise. *Japan's Total Empire: Manchuria and the Culture of Wartime Imperialism* (1998).

John E. Moser

SEE ALSO Mukden Incident

Manila, Fall of

On January 1, 1942, the Japanese 48th Division, supported by two tank regiments, halted 12 miles from Manila's northern outskirts. Elements of the 16th Division approached from the south. Both division commanders

wanted to enter the city that day. Lieutenant General Tsuchibashi of the 48th Division became impatient over the absence of orders to enter Manila, so he sent an urgent message to the Fourteenth Army commander, Lieutenant General Masaharu Homma, recommending immediate entry. The message reached Homma too late for him to react with the urgency suggested.

Instead, Homma ordered a halt. If those two divisions went in simultaneously from the north and south, without proper controls, he believed, anything could happen. He was worried that his men, "flushed with victory," might destroy the city. Homma analyzed two plans: to enter Manila immediately, or to send a military commission into Manila to urge its surrender. For the second option, the Japanese would remain outside the city. Homma decided to enter with his combat forces. There would be no negotiations.

Late that evening, Homma ordered the 48th Division to seize Manila. Three battalions would enter from the north and stop at the Pasig River, the boundary established to separate the two divisions. Before either division could move, however, supplementary orders directed that entry would be delayed until daylight. Homma wanted to make a good impression when his men entered. The troops were to be clean and orderly.

As the Japanese prepared to enter, eight large fires burned across Manila. Fires in the Pandacan oil district, however, dwarfed them all. Dark clouds overhung Manila like the canopy of a dense tree, and from its smoky heights dripped drizzling rain, oil, and soot. Supplies not burned to keep them out of enemy hands were often released by the authorities to the people. Manila's citizens suddenly stared at unbelievably huge piles of riches. The port area became a popular destination. Citizens used cars and trucks to haul off merchandise, including electric refrigerators, lawn mowers, electric motors, diesel engines, and valuable rugs. One truck driver roared off with his vehicle filled to the top with powdered milk. Another loaded up with canned fish, fruit, and corned beef.

Where the authorities did not open the door, mobs did. Red Cross warehouses in the Santa Ana and Santa Mesa districts were looted of medical and hospital supplies as well as of 20,000 bags of cracked wheat. An adjoining army warehouse filled with medical supplies was likewise sacked. Two hundred thousand pesos' worth of materiel was looted or lost in the fires that subsequently burned down the Santa Ana bodega.

Looting was initially orderly, quiet, and purposeful, almost gentlemanly. It began as a pleasant outing by thousands of people. They hauled goods away in horse carts or wooden wheelbarrows, then came back for more. A person would pile his or her loot in a street, search for more, and return to the untouched cache. This good-natured cooperation vanished as merchandise became more scarce, and the looting got out of hand. People stashed their loot, raced back to the waterfront piers, and returned to their stash with new treasures only to find that they, in turn, had been robbed. Ten thousand people swarmed and fought over the mountains of merchandise.

The success of looters at the port area and the excitement of free goods led to attacks on locked stores. Some store owners just shrugged and let the mobs in. It seemed futile to fight one's own countrymen to protect goods that the Japanese would surely steal in another day or two, anyway. Gangs broke into private houses and stole everything in sight. Mobs beat down doors or broke windows, poured into stores, and grabbed what they could carry. Even policemen joined in. Firemen who had been called in to disperse looters instead loaded the fire trucks with goods.

When darkness fell, Manilans had difficulty sleeping. The oil fires at Pandacan lit the sky as if it were day. The big oil-storage tanks boiled and glowed like giant kettles. Pier 7 was on fire, either by accident or as a result of U.S. Army demolition teams. The Manila Fire Department responded, yet at midnight, more than half the pier was burning. Cinders drifted across the city's flickering skies. Throughout the long, tense night, dogs caught the fear of their masters and kept up an all-night howl.

From the beginning of the war to dawn on January 2, more than a third of Manila's population had fled the city. Those still in the city stayed at home, huddled in groups, and spoke softly. The streets had a deserted look. Store owners had boarded up their shops and had stacked sandbags everywhere. Normal delivery services of all kinds had collapsed. Electric streetcars operated irregularly and did not charge fares. Buses, taxicabs, and most of the two-wheeled horse-drawn *carromatas* were gone.

The day the Japanese were to enter Manila dawned dark and chilly with a tragic and foreboding atmosphere. A depressing drizzle of oily rain sprinkled from a hazy, dull red overcast. Fires sent blankets of heavy smoke over the city that the sun could not pierce. The atmosphere was so bad that pet canaries gasped in their cages, then died, gassed by the smoke. Garbage had not been collected for days. The city stank of destruction and fear. Few people could be seen on the streets except those fleeing the fires or prowling through abandoned buildings.

Waiting for the Japanese was proving difficult. The Japanese were already in the city's outskirts. An advance guard had stopped just 4 miles south of Manila's southern limits. Women feared a repetition of Japanese atrocities in China. Would it be another Rape of Nanking? Some women were so afraid that they dared not look out a window. Frantic parents drove single daughters into sudden marriages that were solemnized en masse.

Looters were still active. A mob swarmed over a burning ship and pulled goods out of holds even as the flames grew. Crowds broke into Chinese grocery stores in the fashionable Ermita district. Observers could watch a man walk by with a leg of ham in one hand and a roll of khaki cloth in the other, then spot a truck packed with cigarettes, sardines, and Carnation milk, then see men carrying typewriters and adding machines. A police car drove by, and an officer used a loudspeaker to encourage everyone to return home. No one paid any attention.

The Japanese were slow to arrive. It was not until late afternoon that three battalions from the 48th Division marched into northern Manila. Soldiers drove along Rizal Avenue and Quezon Boulevard tossing out leaflets warning Filipinos not to take any hostile action. The 16th Reconnaissance Regiment and a battalion from the 20th Infantry Regiment entered the southern sector of Manila along Taft Avenue. Japanese civilians released from internment crowded around the soldiers, waved flags, and shouted, "Banzai." They walked about proudly, wore miniature Japanese flags, and acted as guides and interpreters.

Japanese forces from north and south combined at the rotunda in front of City Hall, then dispersed to occupy public buildings. Filipino and U.S. civilians looked on in disbelief. No matter how many Japanese had landed, no matter how few defenders there were, it simply was not possible for the Japanese to win. It was one thing to hear from friends and on the radio about the Japanese advance. Even when they appeared in the flesh, it was just too hard to believe. How could these bandy-legged, shabbily equipped men with such small-bore rifles have defeated the Americans? Almost in mockery, large automobile-agency billboards still extolled the virtues of the 1942-model Pontiacs, Studebakers, and Packards that would never be delivered. In many ways, Manila and Paris shared the unhappy distinction of being the only two modern, consumer-oriented, motorized cities ever to be conquered.

Throughout the night of January 2, trucks loaded with more Japanese soldiers drove into Manila. The men billeted themselves in hotels and public buildings. Units marched down streets singing weird songs (at least to the ears of Manilans). Into the posh Admiral and Bayview Hotels marched the Japanese. A Japanese officer elbowed through guests in the Manila Hotel to the front desk. His aide, quietly and in precise English, ordered all floors above the fourth emptied at once. Japanese soldiers occupied the University of the Philippines and other schools. Soldiers with interpreters set up tables at major intersections and began checking the identity of pedestrians. Japanese riding on trucks waved at Filipinos. Only a few Filipinos waved back.

When January 3 dawned, Manila's populace was quiet and unmoving. Japanese flags flew from the tall flagpole in front of the U.S. high commissioner's residence and over ancient Fort Santiago, Malacanan Palace, the Army and Navy Club, the Manila Hotel, and numerous other public and private buildings. The main body of Japanese troops entered the city at 1000 hours. Cars driving in Manila flew the flags of Japan, Spain, France, Italy, Germany, Portugal, and Thailand.

The Japanese suspended courts, took over the city's utilities, and placed government departments under protective custody. Soldiers stood in pairs at all major road intersections and in front of significant buildings. With the exception of a few servants who were sent to the market only to find everything closed, Manilans dared not leave their houses this day. The Japanese ordered U.S. and British civilians to remain in their quarters.

Initial pronouncements by the first arriving Japanese troops seemed peaceful enough. The Japanese army would not interfere with civilian activities or molest individuals. Japan's aim in the Philippines was to emancipate the islands from oppressive U.S. domination. The Philippines would become part of the Greater East Asia Co-prosperity Sphere. The Japanese stressed the blood brotherhood between their two countries, an approach not especially well received. Educated Filipinos, subjected to Western culture for nearly four hundred years, looked on the Japanese as inferior.

Although Japanese logistics officers were disappointed to find so little gasoline, lubrication oil, and fuel oil left in Manila, there was still great pride in capturing the city. And there were huge quantities of food, drugs, and clothes, as well as the normal machinery and infrastructure of a big city. Cigarettes, liquor, and food lay at the feet of the Japanese. For the next eighteen months, Japanese in Manila would want for nothing.

The Filipinos, however, had just begun their 3-year nightmare. They would awake only after the near-total destruction of their city in 1945, when U.S. troops returned and the Japanese refused to go without a fight.

FURTHER READINGS

Agoncillo, Teodoro A. *The Fateful Years: Japan's Adventure in the Philippines, 1941–45,* 2 vols. (1965).
Brines, Russell. *Until They Eat Stones* (1944).
Hartendorp, A. V. H. *The Japanese Occupation of the Philippines* (1967).
Morton, Louis. *The Fall of the Philippines*. United States Army in World War II: The War in the Pacific. Office of the Chief of Military History (1953).
Swinson, Arthur. *Four Samurai: A Quartet of Japanese Army Commanders in the Second World War* (1968).

John W. Whitman

SEE ALSO MacArthur, Douglas; Philippines, Fall of

Marine Corps, U.S.

Tempered by heavy ground combat during World War I and honed during the subsequent two decades by small-unit actions in the Central American "Banana Wars," the U.S. Marine Corps entered World War II with a new tactical and strategic vision. As early as 1922, Commandant John A. Lejeune embraced a revolutionary combat doctrine for an enlarged and modernized corps eager to contest the Pacific sea-lanes the Japanese coveted. That concept differed radically from the army infantry model the marines had adopted during World War I. Nor did the new model mirror the small-unit concept that proved effective in the jungles of Central America. Rather, Lejeune's concept joined these models, supporting them with an amphibious capability. His vision emphasized infantry-heavy, combined arms forces that could be projected into the front yard of those nations that militarily opposed the United States. The Marine Corps, in Lejeune's words, would become "a mobile . . . force adequate to conduct offensive land operations against hostile naval bases."

Between the world wars, the Marine Corps conceived, explored, and tested the doctrine of amphibious offensive combat. Doubting pundits watched and criticized, emphasizing the lessons of British amphibious failure at Gallipoli during World War I. Despite such criticism, by 1935 the corps had developed a dynamic plan of amphibious warfare, articulated in a benchmark marine publication, *The Landing Operations Manual*. Tangible instruments of the doctrine followed immediately. New landing craft for ship-to-shore movement went into limited production. Additional troop strength swelled the ranks of the corps. With the manpower augmentations came funding for an expanded air wing for each division to strengthen the combined-arms concept.

In late 1941, armed with new purpose and evolving doctrine, 65,000 men served in the corps. Two marine divisions supported by thirteen air-wing squadrons trained for amphibious operations. But the marines found themselves spread thinly. Troop outposts stretched from Iceland to China. Japanese aggression in the Pacific would force the marines to consolidate and test their newly conceived but only partially tested amphibious doctrine. First, however, the corps would fight a series of valiant but unsuccessful delaying actions in the Pacific.

Pearl Harbor and Its Immediate Aftermath

The bombs that fell on Pearl Harbor on December 7, 1941, signaled the beginning of a period of sacrifice and defeat for the marines. The corps found itself under attack from the Japanese offensive that savagely struck the marine outposts from Hawaii to China.

The Japanese attacked Pearl Harbor with the surprise and ruthlessness that characterized their actions early in World War II. Of the 4,500 marines stationed in Hawaii on December 7, 112 died.

Immediately following this attack, small marine detachments on Guam and in China surrendered relatively quickly to overwhelming Japanese forces. But the marines stationed on Wake Island in the central Pacific proved a different story.

A marine fighter squadron and 500 men of the 1st Marine Defense Battalion with 1,000 construction workers defended Wake, which was then being developed as a naval air base. On December 11, the first of the Japanese aerial and naval assaults on the small island began. The marines initially drove off the Japanese task force. But the enemy attacked in force the following day. Despite a desperate effort, the marines on Wake Island surrendered on December 23, 1941.

The Japanese imprisoned 470 Marines and 1,100 civilians. Until they sailed for Shanghai on January 12, the American prisoners hoped for rescue by an ill-managed naval relief force dispatched in December from Honolulu. However, the commander's extreme caution prevented the convoy from reinforcing or rescuing the beleaguered garrison, generating much bitter criticism, not all of it from marines.

The marines surrendered hard at Wake Island. Their performance immediately subsequent on the Bataan and Corregidor in the Philippines mirrored their heroism on Wake. Charged with delaying the Japanese advance on the peninsula of Bataan and the small, fortified island of Corregidor off the tip of the Bataan, the marines, with other U.S. and Philippine personnel, fought on, eventually without the hope of either victory or relief. The Bataan fell on April 9, 1942. One hundred five marines joined 75,000 other U.S. and Filipino troops in the infamous death march to the Japanese prison camps.

The following day the Japanese intensified the siege of Corregidor. Fourteen hundred marines, primarily from the 4th Regiment, joined 2,500 other Allied defenders. The island measured only 3.5 miles in width and 1.5 miles in length. A large central ridge that ran the length of the island dominated the terrain. A massive, fortified bombproof tunnel complex within the ridge provided the U.S. troops with a relatively secure command post, storage, hospital, and so on.

The final Japanese attack came on the night of May 5 and the morning of May 6. With the 4th Marines under Colonel Samuel L. Howard and attached units making the fight, the U.S. troops gave a heroic account of themselves. But Japanese strength of numbers prevailed. Again the marines found themselves laying down their arms. Marine officers and men wept as they surrendered to the Japanese.

During the Corregidor and Bataan campaigns, 600 marines fell either killed or wounded. Another 1,083 became prisoners of war; of these, 209 marines died in captivity. During the confusion of Corregidor's final defense, neither the 2d nor the 4th Battalion of the 4th Marines closed with the enemy.

As the marine defenders of Corregidor struggled to survive their initial and brutal Japanese imprisonment, the balance of power slowly began to tilt toward the Allies. U.S. naval victories at the Battles of the Coral Sea and Midway (May–June 1942) signaled the change in fortunes. During this same period, 49 marines died in the Japanese air bombardment of Midway. The defense of the island marked the beginning of naval success as Admiral Ernest J. King directed the Pacific Fleet to the offensive.

Guadalcanal

The marines of the 1st Division sailed for the Solomon Islands in the South Pacific during late July 1942. The doctrine of amphibious warfare would receive its first severe test on the island of Guadalcanal.

Major General Alexander A. Vandergrift, a veteran of the Central America and China operations, led the 1st Marine Division (reinforced), a total of 19,000 men. The marines had received their movement order unexpectedly in New Zealand during late June 1942. Japanese construction of an airbase on Guadalcanal forced an early invasion on August 7, 1942. With no accurate maps and little credible intelligence, the marines landed on "The Canal." Supported by two battleships and three aircraft carriers carrying 250 aircraft, the concept of amphibious warfare became a reality for the marines.

Although strengthened by the hard sinews of the veteran noncommissioned officer corps, the raw recruits of the 1st Division had only recently graduated from the rigors of marine boot camp. Now they faced their baptism of fire. The arena chosen tested the marines in a cauldron of searing heat, constant rain, bizarre insects, and impenetrable jungle in an area that measured 25 by 90 miles.

The first contact developed on the nearby islands of Gavutu, Florida, and Tanambogo. On the latter, marines landed under a canopy of naval and aerial gunfire. After three days of savage fighting, the marines secured all the islands, killing no fewer than fifteen hundred Japanese. A day earlier, the 1st Battalion of the 1st Marine Regiment had occupied the Japanese airfield under construction on Guadalcanal. Shorthanded because of combat commitments, the marines and sailors on the beach battled with the logistic problems that mounted as the navy continued to off-load men and supplies on five landing beaches. Despite this problem, victory seemed imminent. Then disaster struck.

On August 9, two days after the initial landing, a Japanese naval force sank four U.S. cruisers and a destroyer off Savo Island. Coupled with this defeat and the hurried withdrawal of the U.S. carrier force (by the same commander who had let the marines down at Wake Island, Admiral Frank Jack Fletcher), the remainder of the U.S. amphibious fleet, including loaded troop and supply ships, departed from Guadalcanal. Almost immediately the Japanese seized the initiative and landed 30,000 heavily armed troops. As the air and sea war heated up, the marines ashore found themselves isolated, facing heavy odds.

The marines fought back with a determination characteristic of the corps. Early in the campaign, a false surrender by the Japanese resulted in an ambush during which sixty-five marines died. Subsequently, marine intelligence received few Japanese prisoners to interrogate. The marines' attitude toward their enemy hardened. Contempt replaced earlier grudging respect. The marines adopted a no-quarter attitude that followed them through the Pacific campaigns and beyond.

The climate and environment weighed heavily on the 1st Marine Division. Heat, rain, jungle, and exhaustion stripped 30 pounds from many of the marines. Not until November would the tide of the ground battle turn favorably.

A much-needed naval command change in the Guadalcanal theater of operations galvanized leadership at sea. Under Admiral William "Bull" Halsey, the U.S. Navy struck the Japanese with precision and enthusiasm. But during its first three months on Guadalcanal, the 1st Marine Division struggled to survive.

With the Japanese more or less controlling the surrounding seas, the marines dug in around the airstrip, now called Henderson Field, and began to improve it. By August 20, thirty-one marine planes had arrived to provide some aerial support for the five battalions of infantry. Brigadier General Roy S. Geiger took command of the marine air contingent in early September. Geiger's tough aggressiveness matched the courageous skill of his pilots. In addition, the growing number of planes and supplies tipped the air war to the marines.

On the ground, the marines engaged the Japanese in what General Vandergrift later described as a "war without quarter." On August 18, 1,500 Japanese troops landed near the marine defenses on the shallow Tenaru River. Three days later, the marines fought off a night bayonet attack. The following morning, August 21, marines isolated and killed many of the remaining Japanese on the beach. Thirty-four marines died during the fighting. The Japanese lost 800 men, and their commander committed suicide. Marine pilots destroyed a light carrier and other ships of a Japanese reinforcing convoy on August 31. The Japanese turned back, and the marines continued to hold precariously at Henderson Field.

On Saturday and Sunday, September 12–13, the Japanese struck the exhausted marine defenders along a grassy ridge overlooking the high ground just south of Henderson Field. Japanese air and naval support fell simultaneously on the airstrip. On Bloody Ridge, as the grassy eminence later became known, Captain Merritt A. "Red Mike" Edson, commander of the famed Raider battalion, designed an in-depth defense to offset the numerically superior Japanese. Fighting at close quarters on the moonlit ridge on two consecutive nights, the marines beat off the Japanese. Edson's "cushion" defense bent but never broke. In the morning, the ridge was littered with Japanese dead, and the enemy retreated into the jungle under attack from marine air. The marines had paid a heavy price for their victory. One in every five Americans had been killed. Edson and his executive officer, Major Kenneth D. Bailey, earned the congressional Medal of Honor for their actions.

In late September, the navy succeeded in putting ashore 4,000 men of the 7th Marine Regiment. Led by the legendary Colonel Lewis B. "Chesty" Puller, a decorated hero of the Central America and China campaigns (and future corps commandant), the 1st Battalion of the 7th Marines attacked south to the marine beachhead as Vandergrift went to the offense. However, after initial success, the marines fell back under heavy Japanese attack. The navy and Coast Guard succeeded in efforts to extricate the marines, returning to the marine enclave near Henderson Field. Both the Japanese and the Americans now fed additional troops and supplies into Guadalcanal.

Again on the defensive, the marines sparred with a force of 8,500 Japanese who attacked the defenders of Henderson Field on October 24. After three days of savage hand-to-hand fighting, the marines held. They interred 2,000 Japanese in mass graves. The marines dug in deeper and awaited the next Japanese offensive.

It never came. On Friday, November 13, the navy began a 3-day battle with an approaching Japanese naval convoy. The naval Battle of Guadalcanal resulted in the sinking of seven of the eleven Japanese transports. That Japanese defeat marked a turning point in both the Battle of Guadalcanal and World War II. The marines took the offensive, never again to relinquish it.

During November, Vandergrift attacked with two full divisions along Guadalcanal's western coast. Against diminishing Japanese resistance, the offensive continued as army personnel gradually replaced the marine veterans. By late November, the 1st Marine Division had withdrawn. By late February, the veterans of the 2d Marine Division, now under the command of army General Alexander M. Patch, joined two army divisions in finally clearing Guadalcanal after a desperate six-month campaign. The Americans had their first major offensive ground-combat victory of World War II. The success provided an inspirational home-front morale builder as well as a tactical springboard for U.S. forces in the relentless effort to reach Tokyo and the Japanese heartland. A grateful nation awarded General Vandergrift a congressional Medal of Honor for the sacrifice and courage of his marines during the Guadalcanal campaign, one of the longest of the war.

Victory at Guadalcanal came at a heavy cost. Eleven hundred fifty-two marines lay in fresh graves with more than twice that many wounded. Guadalcanal claimed an additional 400 army dead with a proportionate number of wounded. The climate and jungle also extracted a painful and often lingering price in sick, malarial marines and soldiers.

Casualties for the Japanese were staggering. Nippon lost 23,000 soldiers as well as 600 of its best pilots. The latter represented an irretrievable loss of quality.

Lessons learned for the marines evolved from the confusion and clumsiness of joint U.S. Navy–Marine Corps high command during the operational and logistic nightmare in the early phases of combat. During future landings, the marine ground commander would be subordinate to the amphibious task force commander only during the movement to contact phase of the amphibious operation. Once ashore, the marine ground commander would assume control of the assault elements on the beach. This structural command change would diminish some of the infighting endemic to all joint-service operations, identify accountability, and establish responsibility during the crucial initial stages of amphibious operations.

The marine veterans retired to New Zealand to refit, repair, and gather themselves for the next test of combat. Other larger, fiercer battles loomed in the central Pacific for the soldiers of the sea.

Rabaul and Bougainville

Earlier battles had shown the need for new equipment and improved weaponry. The marines traded their World War I Springfield bolt-action rifles for the new, semiautomatic Garand. Camouflage and herringbone-style dungarees replaced the old leggings and uniforms. The World War I tin helmets disappeared, replaced by the larger "soup pot" type with camouflage covering.

Perhaps most sobering to the veterans, new weapons with great lethality appeared, signaling the next phase of the amphibious war in the Pacific. New and better flamethrowers, hand grenades, and antitank weapons became available for the beginning of the second phase in the Pacific theater.

Because of its massive air base, Rabaul, on the eastern edge of New Britain Island, became the focus of the developing marine Pacific offensive following victory on the ground at Guadalcanal. (Victory in the air took longer because the Japanese continued to contest the skies over Guadalcanal in early 1943.)

The winds of the air war changed with the marines' adoption in the spring of 1943 of a new fighter, the F4U Corsair. This gull-winged aircraft flew faster than any of its Japanese counterparts. This speed matched with superlative marine combat pilots translated into victory. On April 7 alone, the marines flying Corsairs from Henderson Field shot down 76 Japanese planes. On June 16, the air war over Guadalcanal came to a successful climax. The Japanese lost virtually all of a 120-plane armada in their final attack on Henderson Field. The consequences of the loss of so many of their pilots earlier at Guadalcanal was becoming obvious.

On June 21, 1943, marines operating with U.S. Army units drove up the Solomon Island chain. Thirty thousand soldiers and marines landed at the northern tip of New Georgia Island. The poorly planned and cautiously executed offensive resulted in the capture of the strategically important Munda airfield. The cost of victory included 128 dead marines and thrice that wounded in addition to army losses. Significantly, the Japanese lost 358 aircraft defending Munda.

As the marines pressed up the Solomons, command changes evolved in the rapidly expanding corps. General Vandergrift, who had led the 1st Marine Division on Guadalcanal, assumed command of the 1st Marine Amphibious Corps, then the umbrella of command that provided the structure marine units assigned to the Pacific offensive. On November 9, 1943, Major General Geiger replaced Vandergrift, who returned to Washington, D.C., to serve as the Marine Corps commandant, effective in 1944.

As 1943 ended, the corps girded for continued amphibious warfare on three fronts. The 1st Marine Division prepared to assault Cape Gloucester on New Britain Island. Simultaneously, the 2d Marine Division readied itself for an attack on Tarawa in the Gilbert Islands. Finally, the 3d Marine Division coiled to strike the island of Bougainville. Bougainville came first.

The marines had closed on the Japanese air base at Rabaul, the final prize of the Solomons. Bougainville provided the final stepping-stone during the incremental movement on Rabaul. The Japanese air base on that island lay but a scant 210 miles from Bougainville.

To cover their intent, the marines dispatched Lieutenant Colonel Victor H. "Brute" Krulak (another future commandant) and his 2d Parachute Battalion to attack Chosen Island near the real objective, Bougainville. Then, on November 1, 1943, the 3d Marine Division assaulted Bougainville with 17,000 men, landing on a narrow strip of beach on the mountainous and jungled island. The marines found 30,000 entrenched Japanese waiting, in one of the few campaigns in which the defenders outnumbered the attackers—not a promising prospect.

Major General Allen H. Turnage, a veteran commander who had fought through the marines' World War I, Caribbean, and China campaigns, led a now-familiar mix of combat veterans and raw "boots" of the 3d Marine Division. The division's courage and resourcefulness were tested immediately as the Japanese opposed the amphibious landing with point-blank fire from automatic weapons and artillery pieces, firing from pillboxes that skirted the beachhead. Lessons learned at Guadalcanal were immediately and successfully applied as the marines employed infantry, air, and naval gunfire to move off the beach despite strafing runs by Japanese fighters.

By evening, 14,000 marines of the 3d Division ashore had moved off the slender beach into the jungle beyond. That night, the U.S. Navy successfully defended the sea approaches to the beachhead during the U.S. naval victory of Empress Augusta Bay.

The marines rapidly expanded the beachhead and built an airfield under fire. The numerically superior Japanese defenders fought desperately to prevent both objectives. On November 24, in desperate hand-to-hand fighting at Piva Fork, the marines killed 1,071 Japanese soldiers. One hundred fifteen marines died during the fight. Close air support and unrelenting infantry pressure helped the marines inch forward, expanding their constricted perimeter. On December 18, 1943, the marines captured Hellzapoppin Ridge, the final anchor to the perimeter within which they would construct their airfield.

The following month, the 3d Marine Division turned over both its perimeter and the newly constructed airfield to U.S. Army troops. Marine casualties during the Bougainville campaign numbered 423 dead and more than three times that many wounded. But daily flights of marine aircraft now flew from Bougainville in the expanding air war against Rabaul.

Tarawa

The island of Tarawa, more specifically the nearby atoll of Betio, offered Allied Pacific forces both a good land site and a safe naval anchorage in the stepping-stone journey to Japan. But the open, flat terrain, 3 miles in length and 600 yards across at its widest point, made it easily defensible. A dug-in and resolute enemy held the advantage of uncluttered fields of fire and easily mined reef and harbor approaches to deter amphibious assault. Tarawa, encrusted with over two hundred Japanese heavy-caliber guns, presented a target of formidable defensive strength.

U.S. high command decided that Tarawa could not be isolated and bypassed. Thus strategic location overruled caution. That decision had consequences that forever haunted those charged with sending young men into harm's way.

The veteran 2d Marine Division received orders to storm the Betio atoll by amphibious assault. During November 1943, it sailed for the small island of Betio. High command scheduled the amphibious assault, code-named Operation Galvanic, for November 20, 1943.

Elite Japanese marines, or *rikusentai,* defended the atoll. These same *rikusentai* and their warrior brothers were no strangers to the U.S. Marines. They had demonstrated esprit and ferocity on Wake, Tulagi, and Gavutu Islands eighteen months earlier. Tarawa held 2,600 of these elite troops supported by 2,000 laborers.

Fortunately for the Americans, the Japanese defense remained only partially completed on Betio's northern perimeter. Here, a vast lagoon enclosed by a reef from 600 to 1,000 yards offshore provided a natural barrier to the beach approach. Because of the configuration of the reef and the lagoon, the transport ships would off-load the landing force 6 miles from shore. Naval and aerial gunfire required precise timing to fit safely into the logistically complex plan needed to put 12,000 marines ashore.

The marines faced several problems in addition to the motivated and professional Japanese defenders who planned to meet them at water's edge. First, the landing craft required at least 4 feet of water to float across Betio's barrier reef. In the event of a neap, or "dodging," tide, the marines would have to off-load on the reef and either walk ashore or transfer to a limited number of amphibious tractors (amtracs) for the final push for the beach. Second, because of concern over Japanese naval or aerial strikes, the U.S. convoy commanders restricted the pre-assault naval and aerial bombardment of Betio to four hours. Finally, the 2d Marine Division would make the landing without the 6th Marine Regiment, which would be held in reserve for either Betio or a coinciding army landing at nearby Makin Island. The marines would land four battalions on a broad front, hoping that the tide, short preparatory fires, and the limited number of amtracs available would not confound the landing.

At 0900 hours on November 20, three waves of ninety-three amtracs bulging with the lead assault element waddled ashore at Tarawa. They placed their marines into a hornet's nest of flame and violence in what became one of the most savage land battles of World War II. A survivor later described the actions during the subsequent four days as "utmost savagery."

Two factors immediately imperiled the operation and the marines as they braced in their amtracs and crossed the outer reef and approached Betio's northern beach. First, the low tide allowed the amtracs but not the small landing craft in the following assault waves to cross the reef for the final 600- to 800-yard run to the beach. Second, it was painfully obvious from the start that the abbreviated naval and aerial bombardment of Tarawa had done little to soften Japanese defenses. In fact, as the tracked vehicles crawled resolutely across the lagoon toward the coconut-tree seawall on the island's northern shore, Japanese defenders emerged from their fortifications, mounted the seawall, and challenged the amtracs moving on their positions. That bravery proved a harbinger of the Japanese courage and will that followed.

The men of the 2d Marine Division steeled themselves with the confidence of victory on Guadalcanal and the nearly year and a half of training that followed. Major General Julian Smith, the division commander, Colonel "Red Mike" Edson, chief of staff, and Colonel David Shoup, chief of operations, provided solid leadership.

Others such as Major "Jim" Crowe, commanding the 2d Battalion of the 8th Marines, were beacons of raw courage and charismatic leadership for their men during the subsequent four days of travail.

In the end, however, it was the nameless squad leaders and enlisted men who not only endured but prevailed at Betio. To them fell the daunting task of rooting out the 4,600 Japanese defenders who would die almost to the man. These enlisted marines, many not a year removed from civilian life, endured 1,000 casualties each day, proportionately the highest for any U.S. battle in World War II.

That dying began early in the battle. Shoup came ashore with five battalions from the 2d and 8th Marine Regiments. Crouching in an improvised command post on the northwest edge of the island, the blunt-spoken, barrel-chested 39-year-old colonel assessed the situation. The brief 4-hour artillery and aerial bombardment had wiped out some of the Japanese artillery and destroyed much of the enemy's communication. But the Japanese infantrymen had scarcely been touched by the bombardment. They met the attacking marines on the beach with small-arms and automatic-weapons fire.

The first three waves of marines, crowded into the available amtracs, reached the landing area with heavy but tactically acceptable casualties. But the Higgins boats could not cross the reef and off-loaded their troops as the normal battle confusion mounted.

The limited number of amtracs had been scheduled to return to the reef after their initial run to the beach. Amid the maelstrom that erupted in the lagoon, however, few returned as scheduled to the reef. Stranded, the marines began the long wade toward the seawall under intense, almost point-blank fire while struggling through waist- to neck-deep water.

A long pier skirted the lagoon on the east. Japanese gunners situated on this position opened flank fire on the marines in the water. As the reinforcing assault waves inched through the lagoon toward Shoup and the beach, they were surrounded by a cone of withering, interlocking enemy small- and automatic-weapons fire.

Ashore, Shoup fought to break away from the seawall, throwing forward small bands of men to silence the fire from bunkers with flamethrowers, small-arms fire, and grenades. As night fell on the first day at Betio, Shoup found himself precariously ashore with poor communications, heavy resistance, and 50 percent casualties.

With the forces ashore isolated by a 600-yard gap in their lines, the marines dug in for their night on the island. The issue remained gravely in doubt. Unbeknownst to Shoup and his men, an artillery air burst had killed the

Japanese commander, during the initial phase of the battle. The Japanese were leaderless at the very moment circumstance demanded instant reaction and flexibility. Even with tactical opportunity, adequate numbers of men, and a surfeit of courage, the Japanese failed to seize the moment.

Aboard his command ship, General Julian Smith watched events unfold with grave concern. He later said that a concerted Japanese attack on the first night would have driven his marines into the sea. But that attack never came.

In the morning, General Smith was feeding three additional battalions into the fight. During the night, the Japanese had occupied the pier in force and placed numerous snipers among the burned-out hulks of the amtracs and other craft and vehicles now littering the lagoon. Second-day reinforcements found themselves in the all-too-familiar death dance of wading the lagoon enfiladed by enemy fire and awash with the bodies of marines killed the previous day.

Again, casualties mounted, but the marines kept coming. With all marine reserves ashore, Shoup had exhausted his options. With his artillery regiment and tanks now committed, eight battalions of marine infantry began the systematic brutal reduction of Japanese emplacements. The stench of death and cordite rose from the island and the lagoon as the carnage continued, wafting to the naval transports.

Somehow the 2d Marine Division rose above all this. For example, Lieutenant William Deane Hawkins, commander of the scout-sniper platoon and a former enlisted man who had been commissioned for gallantry during the fighting on Guadalcanal, organized and led two assaults on the pillboxes that dominated the beachhead. He personally knocked out pillbox after pillbox with small-arms fire and grenades, refusing medical attention despite his several wounds. At 1030 hours on the second morning of the battle, the Japanese succeeded in shooting Hawkins down.

Such primal courage changed the tide of battle at Tarawa. Four marines, including Hawkins, received the congressional Medal of Honor. Extreme gallantry proved common during the battle. By the end of the second day, the outcome no longer remained in doubt. The evening of the second day, Colonel Shoup, ever the reserved pragmatist, radioed a combat situation report to the command group afloat: "Casualties many; percentage dead not known; combat efficiency: We are winning."

That laconic assessment proved correct. On day three, the marines closed the gap between their two beachheads and began systematically to destroy the remaining Japa-

nese defenders. On the fourth, and final, day of the fight, they cleared and swept the island of all defenders. Almost eleven hundred Marines died in a ninety-six-hour time span. Three times that number suffered wounds. All but 146 of the Japanese defenders died during the battle. The marines had put another stepping-stone in place for the thrust toward Rabaul. But at high cost.

Changing Strategies and the Final Battle in the South Pacific

Initially, U.S. operational strategy in the Pacific focused on a two-pronged approach led by General Douglas MacArthur calling for a convergence in 1944 at the Japanese air, sea, and troop base on the island of Rabaul, northwest of Guadalcanal. With what was perceived as an Allied shortfall in both troops and equipment, this strategy mandated a series of simultaneous rather than surprise attacks. Because of the vast distances involved in the Pacific theater, the always immediate priority of the Allies centered on aircraft landing bases.

But as Japanese military strength ebbed, the U.S. strategic concept changed. In February 1943, U.S. forces seized the unoccupied Russell Islands northwest of Guadalcanal. In November 1943, the army captured Munda, and the marines destroyed the Japanese force on Betio/Tarawa. The importance of Rabaul diminished with the acquisition of these new landing sites. The growing strength of the U.S. amphibious capability became apparent. By mid-January 1944, Japanese resistance in the New Britain Islands ceased. That last Japanese failure provided a cornerstone for a new U.S. strategic concept in the Pacific.

The Japanese gave up the Gilbert, Marshall, and southern Caroline Islands reluctantly but with the realization that strategically these outposts meant little. But the Japanese fortified the Marianas with a renewed spirit of the samurai. Japanese high command understood that the Marianas offered island bases for growing U.S. air and naval power from which to strike the Japanese mainland.

Evolving U.S. strategy divided the nation's growing military power in the Pacific into twin prongs. General MacArthur would lead one force into the southwest Pacific toward the Philippines, his ultimate objective being the Japanese mainland. Simultaneously, Admiral King would coordinate a joint navy-marine assault group in the central Pacific, also with the ultimate goal of reaching Japan.

By that time, the prewar Marine Corps of 25,000 regulars had grown to 478,000. From a traditionally all-volunteer force, the corps now met its increased personnel needs by drawing from the general conscription pool.

Empathetic selective service boards diverted the most physically able and militarily motivated young men to the expanded marine recruit centers on both coasts. The corps, following dictates from President Franklin Delano Roosevelt, had also enlisted a small number of blacks for duty with defense and service units. A few women also entered the corps to fill clerical and administrative posts.

The nature of the marines' war in the Pacific shifted in concert with the new strategic concept. The early battles had been fought essentially in jungle terrain. Small-unit operations had characterized these operations, the centerpiece being Guadalcanal. But Betio/Tarawa (November 20–24, 1943) signaled a new period of more conventional warfare once the amphibious force reached the beach. The Japanese would defend in force and desperation those islands selected in accordance with island size and wind patterns in an effort to defend the Japanese mainland. They would henceforth defend in depth rather than squandering their diminishing resources on the beach during amphibious assaults as they had early in the war.

As veterans supremely confident in their own fighting abilities, the 1st Marine Division headed north toward Cape Gloucester. On December 26, 1943, the victors of Guadalcanal waded ashore unopposed by serious enemy defense. Storm followed the initial calm. Aided by jungle conditions as bad as or worse than any previously encountered, the Japanese flung themselves at the marines with reckless and often suicidal abandon. Marine counterattacks often foundered on well-engineered Japanese bunker systems. Target Hill and Suicide Creek were the sites of benchmark battles as violent as any in which the corps had engaged previously. However, mud, vegetation, and the enemy delayed but did not defeat the marines. By mid-January, Japanese resistance had ceased on Cape Gloucester. For the next three months, the division mopped up New Britain Island, clearing the remaining Japanese survivors. The marines' last effort in the South Pacific ended in April. They listed more than thirteen hundred casualties from that campaign.

Preparation for the Shift to the Central Pacific

As harsh as the South Pacific had proven, even greater trials lay ahead in the central Pacific. Guadalcanal, New Georgia, Bougainville, and New Britain ended the first phase of the marines' war in the South Pacific. Those actions provided the corps with a primer on jungle warfare. Subsequently, the corps entered a new phase of the battle for the Pacific, one that defied in magnitude and violence anything all but the most pessimistic veteran had anticipated. The Marine Corps had grown and matured during the first two years of the war. Now as the battle moved into the central Pacific and closer to the Japanese homeland, the violence intensified dramatically in a no-quarter fight for survival.

As the war had changed, so had the objectives of the United States. After two full years, the wealth and energy of that nation had fielded the most powerful war machine ever devised. A stream of military weapons and supplies flowed from U.S. ports on both coasts. As quantity increased, the quality of weapons continued to improve. The American citizenry that recoiled at the reports and pictures of the carnage in the lagoon at Betio now saw the war in the same uncompromising view as its sons in the Pacific. The demand for unconditional surrender of the enemy meant a dramatic increase in violence for both sides in which quarter was neither asked nor given.

A Marine Corps of nearly six divisions continued to put into effect those lessons learned in the South Pacific. The squad increased in size by one to a total of thirteen men. The extra man served as squad leader of three 4-man fire teams, each trained to fight independently or in concert as circumstances dictated. Each squad carried three Browning automatic rifles (BARs), a superb light machine gun. The added BARs gave a net increase for each battalion of 300 guns. Flamethrowers now became part of some tank armament. Individual flamethrowers in the infantry battalions increased tenfold to approximately two hundred fifty. An amtrac battalion of some five hundred men augmented each division.

The new objectives evolved from another lethal weapon, the long-range B-29 bomber that carried huge strategic bomb payloads great distances. The B-29s needed airfields specifically in the Marianas Islands to the north. Tinian, Guam, Rota, and Saipan offered areas suitable for bases for the long-range bombing effort. From these airfields the Allies could strike the Japanese urban centers.

Mariana Islands

To take the Marianas, Rear Admiral Richard Kelly Turner commanded his fifth Pacific amphibious operation. He directed an armada of 535 ships carrying more than 120,000 marine assault troops. The landing party divided into northern and southern landing forces. Marine Lieutenant General Holland M. "Howlin' Mad" Smith commanded the V Amphibious Corps made up of the 2d and 4th Marine Divisions. Marine Major General Geiger led the III Amphibious Corps composed of the 1st Provisional Marine Brigade and the 3d Marine Division. Two army divisions, the 77th and the 27th, supported the marines as reserve.

Smith, a 38-year corps veteran who had fought in both World War I and the Caribbean Banana Republic Wars, struck first on Saipan with V Corps. On June 15, the marines landed on a two-division front extending 4 miles. In less than a half hour, landing craft and amtracs put 8,000 marines ashore. Lead elements suffered 30 percent casualties as the marines found the Japanese well fortified and heavily armed at beach edge. Despite the fierce Japanese defense, marines continued to land throughout the day. At sundown, 20,000 Americans held a tenuous beachhead against the 32,000 resolute defenders. Having suffered 2,000 casualties on the first day, the marines fought off waves of counterattacking Japanese that first night ashore.

The Japanese concentrated in the island's northern sector. Savage fighting continued as eventually 78,000 marines and army soldiers opposed a smaller Japanese force prepared to fight to the death.

On June 19, 1944, good news blessed the forces ashore. In a naval battle of epic proportions, U.S. naval forces under Vice Admiral Marc A. Mitscher destroyed the Japanese planes based on Guam and, in subsequent action, shot 476 enemy carrier-based aircraft from the skies. Although the Japanese fleet remained operable after this action—termed "The Great Marianas Turkey Shoot"—the victory gave U.S. forces both air and sea superiority.

On June 22, 1944, the marines began the second phase of the Saipan operation. Both 2d and 4th Marine Divisions pivoted northward and attacked. Although the two divisions already had suffered a combined total of more than six thousand casualties, morale and efficiency remained high.

As fighting continued, discord grew within the U.S. command. Marine General Smith criticized what he alleged to be the reluctant and ineffective performance of the army's 27th Division involved in the northern advance with the 2d and 4th Marine Divisions. On June 23, after much acrimony Smith relieved the commander of the 27th Division, Major General Ralph C. Smith. Marine General Smith cited the 27th Division's inability to meet its attack objectives, increasing the normal controversy that simmers during army-marine joint operations.

Still, the argument paled in the face of action by a defiant and resolute enemy. By June 30, U.S. Army and Marine units had reported more than ten thousand combined casualties, but at that point they held central Saipan. The Japanese withdrew behind their final defensive lines. On July 2, U.S. troops launched their final offensive. The Japanese met this effort with a desperate suicidal attack involving 3,000 infantrymen, who flung themselves against the combined army-marine defensive line. Although the army units suffered especially high losses, the Japanese suffered even more grievously. On July 9, the 4th Marine Division reached Saipan's northern coast. Admiral Turner then declared Saipan secured. U.S. casualties totaled more than sixteen thousand killed and wounded; more than thirty-two thousand Japanese soldiers had died. Additionally, hundreds of Japanese civilians, despite the efforts of U.S. psychological warfare troops to reassure them that they would not be harmed, threw themselves off the precipitous northern Saipan beach cliffs as the clamor of battle gave way to yet another tragedy.

Marine Commander "Howlin' Mad" Smith subsequently called Saipan "the decisive battle of the Pacific." The Japanese agreed. When official word of the loss of Saipan reached Tokyo, the imperial cabinet resigned. "Our war was lost with the loss of Saipan," one Japanese admiral later lamented.

Nearby Tinian, with terrain ideal for airfield construction and defended by only 9,000 Japanese, offered the next target for the victors of Saipan. The marines sought to make good use of their Saipan experience to pick off Tinian. The 4th Marine Division attacked on July 24, 1944. Surprising the enemy by attacking on two isolated but narrow beaches, the marines used heavy preinvasion fires, deception, and surprise to offset the difficulties inherent to the landing area. Success followed. The division came ashore with only 300 casualties. The 2d Marine Division followed as the attack continued in the face of a strong Japanese defense, which included desperate banzai attacks. On August 1, 1944, the marines secured Tinian. U.S. casualties had been held to fewer than two thousand marines; the Japanese had suffered 5,000 dead in their defense of Tinian.

One hundred miles south of Saipan and Tinian, the island of Guam provided rugged terrain distributed over approximately 120 square miles of densely volcanic landscape. Geiger's veteran III Amphibious Corps landed without surprise against prepared defenses on the island's northern coast. The beaches abutted coral cliffs that gave way to heavy underbrush and jungle. On July 21, 1944, the marines returned to Guam two and a half years after their defeat there following Pearl Harbor. Heavy fighting developed as the marines fought through the enemy's beach defenses and followed the enemy into the jungle beyond the coral cliffs walling in the beach.

Overextended along a 5-mile front, elements of the 21st and 9th Marines endured the operation's fiercest Japanese counterattack on the night of July 25. Robert E. Cushman's 2d Battalion of the 9th Marines fought off seven counterattacks by sake-fueled Japanese troops. On the morning of July 26, Cushman (yet another future corps commandant) found his unit locked in hand-to-hand combat. At first light, marine tanks smashed the enemy's flank, finally breaking the attack. More than half of Cushman's command became casualties during that night's savage fighting. Marine dead and wounded totaled 600 men. In turn, the marines killed 3,200 Japanese.

From that point, all trails spiraled downward for Guam's defenders. The 77th Army Division joined the 3d Marine Division and the 1st Marine Provisional Brigade in clearing the island. On August 10, General Geiger declared the island secure. Although many Japanese remained hidden in the jungles, U.S. engineers quickly built two large air bases on Guam to support the giant B-29s in their strategic bombing runs over Japan.

Guam supplied the end piece to the vital Marianas campaign. The two marine attack elements, the III and V Corps, had fought magnificently during their advance in the central Pacific. They had destroyed the Japanese bastions at Saipan, Tinian, and Guam. The air bases to leapfrog forward the B-29s for their strategic bombing runs against the Japanese provided one of the final linchpins on the road to U.S. victory in the Pacific.

Victory dramatically affected U.S. strategic intentions. During the Marianas operations, the Japanese lost much of their naval air power. And for the first time, their island homeland became vulnerable to the growing U.S. air fleet. But victory did not come without a severe cost. Seven thousand marines died during the campaign in the Marianas. Three times that total suffered reported wounds.

The Marianas provided the corps with a glowing testament to the effectiveness of amphibious warfare. There remained, as in any military operation, room for improvement.

The campaigns in the Marianas illustrated graphically the need to improve and coordinate supporting arms with the infantry to increase combat power and to diminish friendly casualties. Naval and aerial gunfire had often proved inadequate. Costly firsthand experience had taught marine infantry (and all marines are, at least in theory, infantry) that enough is never enough and that the most effective bombardment immediately precedes and supports the rifle companies during the assault phase.

Tactical and technological problems played a major role in these failures of supporting-arms coordination. Some pilots and commanders needed better training to identify targets more quickly and precisely and to adjust

fires accordingly. But simple command problems could be immediately solved.

On occasion, orders from high command overextended and misdirected subordinate units. During these challenging times, decisions often evolved piecemeal from the top down. As always, the farther from the battle, the more unrealistic the commands. The characteristic "fog of battle" thickened in direct proportion to the intensity of combat. Often, in those situations demanding the most precise and insightful of directives, the exact opposite occurred, as commanders attempted to micromanage the battlefield.

These lessons and a resolute, often fanatical, enemy provided a daunting obstacle for the corps. Although the marines were armed with greater firepower and tactical initiative, the struggle in the Marianas reduced finally to rifle against rifle, man against man. This matchup built forever in the American public's mind the image of the Marine Corps, an image that extended far beyond the bitter fights in the Marianas. Profane, irreverent, and contemptuous of their enemy (as well as of the U.S. Army), the marines swaggered into the Valhalla of U.S. history. They needed all those qualities to persevere in the fights beyond the Marianas: Peleliu, Iwo Jima, and Okinawa.

Peleliu

Five hundred miles east of the Philippine Islands lies Peleliu, a tangled mass of rough terrain that cloaked the fortifications of 10,000 well-trained Japanese defenders. Despite the obvious hazards, the marines received orders to assault the island to protect the flank of army units under General MacArthur preparing to attack the Philippines. After the killing match at Tarawa, many Marine Corps and navy planners saw wisdom in bypassing and isolating Peleliu. MacArthur insisted that Peleliu be taken to relieve the anticipated pressure on his flank from the Japanese. The decision cost the corps 10,000 casualties, including nearly eighteen hundred dead.

The 1st Marine Division (reinforced), some twenty-eight thousand men, drew the assignment for taking the small island in what later would be described, in the words of one expert, as one of the bloodiest battles of the war. Major General William H. Rupertus, commander of the 1st Marine Division, predicted a quick marine victory in only two to three days. However, Rupertus and most of the planning officers proved far too optimistic. Learning from past mistakes, the Japanese decided to surrender the beaches but defend in depth from the island's interior, honeycombed with elaborate fortifications. Along the Umorbrogol Ridge, the island's centerpiece, the Japanese dug in to make their fight. On September 15, 1944, the first assault units of the 1st Marine Division landed on Peleliu.

The assault waves struggled through murderous indirect and enfilade fire on the beach. The Japanese fired cannon and mortars from the high ground on predesignated areas, hammering the men, landing craft, and tanks as they crossed the beach. From each end of the beach, Japanese heavy weapons enfiladed the marines wading ashore. These indirect fires lengthened the already long odds confronting the 1st Marine Division. They attacked with but 9,000 infantry. The Japanese, with 10,000 men, outnumbered the marines and had the additional advantage of fighting from prepared positions. Additionally, the army's 81st Division formed the floating reserve with one battalion from the 7th Marines. The commander of the 1st Marine Division adamantly opposed the introduction of army units into the fight, resurrecting memories of the interservice squabbles and rivalries that beset the assault group on Saipan earlier in the war.

Despite the misgivings of both veteran commanders and seasoned troops, the marines attacked with their usual confidence and aggressiveness. Three highly regarded leaders led the three regiments of the 1st Marine Division ashore. Colonel Lewis B. "Chesty" Puller attacked with the 1st Marines on his left flank, aiming for the Umorbrogol Ridge that bordered Peleliu's airfield on the north. Colonel Herman H. "Haiti" Hanneken led the 7th Marines ashore on the right flank, sweeping the southern portion of the island. Colonel Harold D. "Bucky" Harris waded ashore with his 5th Marines at the center of the assault and headed directly for the Peleliu airfield. The marines met stiff resistance on every front. In the late afternoon, the Japanese counterattacked. The enemy abandoned the banzai tactics the marines had grown accustomed to destroying with superior firepower. Rather, Japanese infantry advanced using cover and concealment, attacking the marines at the vulnerable junction point of the 1st and 5th Marines in the north-central area of the island.

As the sun rose over Peleliu on the second day of battle, the 1st Marine Division already had overcome a variety of obstacles. Friendly fire from artillery and aircraft had slowed the 5th Marines' advance in the island's center. Searing heat with temperatures reaching 110 degrees Fahrenheit reduced the pace of the assault and contributed to marine casualties. Supply troops floated water ashore packaged in improvised oil drums. This aid sickened many of the troops when they replenished their canteens on the beach and drank the tainted water. But the enemy provided the marines with their biggest obstacle.

Using flamethrowers and grenades, the 7th Marines cleared the island's southern end, killing 2,600 of the enemy. By the seventh day of battle, the 5th Marines had secured the island's center after intense fighting. But in Puller's northern sector, the 1st Marines endured some of the most savage combat of the war. The Japanese defended a rocky jumbled landmass, the Umorbrogol Ridge. During the first three days of battle, the 1st Marine Regiment suffered 50 percent casualties, some twelve hundred men. The terrain broke the battle into continuous small-unit actions within the moonscape of coral ridges and heavy vegetation. The Japanese seemed everywhere but nowhere, vulnerable only to attack at extremely close quarters. By the end of the first week's fighting, the marines held the airfield and the southern half of the island. But the enemy remained firmly lodged on the high ground overlooking the airfield. By this time, Puller's men had suffered the highest casualties, 1,600 men killed and wounded, for a single battle of any regiment in the corps' long history.

Doubt grew over the wisdom of the continued frontal assaults on the prepared Japanese positions. Over General Rupertus's objection, Major General Geiger relieved the decimated 1st Marines, replacing them on September 21 with the 321st Regiment of the army's 81st Division. The army unit quickly swept north on Peleliu's western plain and with the 7th Marines continued to assault the ridge's center, isolating the enemy. With the 5th Marines joining in the assault on the ridges, the tide of battle turned. Under orders to proceed cautiously rather than assault aggressively, the 5th Marines made slow but steady progress against the Japanese. Major resistance on the island ended on October 15, 1944. The marines, with army support, had killed 10,200 Japanese and taken 300 prisoners during the battle. But the victory came at a terrible cost.

The marines suffered 1,200 dead and another 6,200 wounded. The army casualties totaled nearly three hundred dead and over a thousand wounded. Not surprisingly, some critics questioned the strategic purpose of assaulting Peleliu, believing the island fortress should have been bypassed and isolated. Others criticized the marine tactics of frontal assault that led to the extraordinarily high casualties in the 1st Marine Regiment. The veteran naval commander Admiral William F. "Bull" Halsey summed up the frustrations years later: "I feared another Tarawa, and I was right."

Both battles, Tarawa and Peleliu, provided bloody crucibles testing the courage and will of the marine infantry involved. After both battles, pundits criticized Marine Corps tactics and strategy. But in neither instance did either the enemy or the critics find the courage and sacrifice of the individual marine rifleman wanting.

During late October 1944, the army under General MacArthur landed in great numbers on the island of Leyte in the Philippines. The army requested only two battalions of marine artillery for the ground operations but requested and received seven marine dive-bomber squadrons. The fliers endeared themselves to the U.S. infantry with characteristically aggressive close air support. Marine air supported the army with distinction in the Luzon campaign in the Philippines. Meanwhile, the planning for the final two marine island conquests began.

Iwo Jima

Black sulfuric ash composed much of Iwo Jima's 7.5-square-mile combination of beach, plain, and hill terrain dominated by the 600-foot-high Mount Suribachi on the island's southern tip. From the beaches on the southern end of the island, the terrain rose to a plateau to the north, where the Japanese had built two airfields. Flying from these bases, Japanese fighter planes had intercepted many of the U.S. B-29 Superfortresses as they reached the halfway point on the 1,200-mile flight between the Mariana Islands and their bombing targets on the Japanese mainland.

Some twenty-one thousand well-trained Japanese troops under Lieutenant General Tadamichi Kuribayashi defended the island. The enemy had labored for eight months on an in-depth cave defense system that surpassed all previous Japanese efforts to defend their island bases. Kuribayashi constructed two defense lines across the plateaued area of Iwo Jima and fortified Mount Suribachi. An elaborate thousand-cave defense system with interconnecting tunnels awaited the marine assault units.

Those units, V Corps, had boarded 800 ships and landing craft in several training and staging areas during late January and early February. The assault on Iwo Jima began on the morning of February 19, 1945. Major General Harry Schmidt led the 3d, 4th, and 5th Marine Divisions onto the soft, black terraced beaches of Iwo Jima to begin the corps' most costly campaign of World War II. Schmidt led a veteran force with increased flame capability at both the infantry and the armor level. Lessons learned in cave warfare on Peleliu led to the addition of another platoon in each infantry battalion equipped with flamethrowers, satchel charges, and handheld shaped-charge bazookas. The tank battalions in each regiment added more flamethrowers.

Characteristically, the pre-landing preparation fires by ship and aircraft fell far short of marine estimates of what was necessary. But stoically, the marines accepted their task, realizing intuitively if reluctantly that only the individual rifleman could destroy the Japanese in their underground defense network. With this in mind, the marine tactical plan proved simple. The marines would land eight infantry battalions abreast on Iwo's eastern shore between Mount Suribachi on the south and the Motoyama Plateau to the north. The 28th Marine Regiment would attack Suribachi. The 4th and 5th Marine Divisions would wheel to the north into the Motoyama Plateau. The 3d Marine Division would be held in reserve.

The marines landed on a clear, windy morning and encountered little initial resistance. But as the landing area clogged with marines, the Japanese artillery and mortar began to fall among the assault force. Chaos followed.

Night finally fell on the black terraced beach across which the marine landing force struggled to survive. During the first day of battle, commanders reported 2,300 casualties to secure a 3,000-meter-wide beachhead that at no point exceeded 1,500 meters. The congestion of the beachhead had contributed to the carnage of the day as indirect enemy fire fell on the assault waves with unerring precision and deadly profusion. During the next four days, the marines met increasing resistance but finally secured their initial objectives. The first enemy airfield fell, and with considerable difficulty the marines reached the first Japanese defensive line fronting the Motoyama Plateau. But the most noteworthy victory took place when the 28th Marines took Mount Suribachi on the island's southern tip. The serendipitous (second) summit flag-raising photograph etched itself into the American consciousness and remained *the* marine icon. When Secretary of the Navy James Forrestal first saw the photo, he exclaimed, "This ensures the Corps for another hundred years!" But even as the American flag rose above Suribachi, the battle continued in its ferocity.

Seven infantry battalions of the 4th and 5th Marine Divisions attacked the first of two Japanese defense lines deployed across the Motoyama Plateau. Reinforced by armor and artillery, the marines fought against an enemy concealed and protected in caves and pillboxes. Progress proved slow, casualties appalling. General Schmidt reinforced the 4th and 5th Divisions with two reinforced regiments of the 3d Marine Division. As the battle continued, deaths and wounds decimated the marines fighting against an often unseen enemy. Some battalions suffered casualties of more than 80 percent. By March 10, 1945, the three marine divisions penetrated the first enemy defensive line, pressed onto the high ground beyond, ruptured the second enemy defensive network, and moved toward the sea.

And the fighting continued. Artillery and aircraft attacked the Japanese defensive positions. Marine infantry followed with flamethrowers and satchel charges to root the enemy out of their caves and bunkers. The cycle tragically repeated itself again and again. As marine infantry advanced on each enemy defensive position, automatic and mortar fire cut through the U.S. ranks. Marine artillery lined nearly hub to hub fired salvo after salvo into the enemy positions, but ultimately success depended on the courage and fortitude of the individual rifleman. On the beach, support units struggled with the soft sand and high tides as well as the enemy, off-loading the supplies that fueled the battle. Enemy mortar and artillery fire randomly fell on all points of the treeless Iwo Jima terrain, leaving no place a sanctuary from the death and wounds that eventually claimed 26,000 marines, nearly 3,000 sailors, and a handful of army personnel.

On March 16, General Schmidt declared Iwo Jima secured. The marines had taken the final piece of the puzzle in the air war against the island of Japan. Dead lay General Kuribayashi and almost all the island's twenty-one thousand resolute defenders. But they had exacted a terrible toll from their U.S. attackers. For the first time in the Pacific theater, marine casualties exceeded the number of Japanese killed and wounded.

At home, Americans voiced their amazement at the courage of the marines while criticizing the number of friendly casualties. Subsequent events, however, vindicated the price paid for Iwo Jima. The island swiftly became a haven for the Superfortresses flying the round-trip from the Marianas to Japan on the daily bombing runs. In fact, even before the island was secured, several warplanes had safely made emergency landings on Iwo. By war's end, the incredible total of 2,500 B-29s had made emergency return landings at Iwo Jima. Additionally, some three thousand air attacks and thirteen hundred fighter sorties against Japan originated from the air bases on Iwo. The individual and collective courage of the marines who fought on Iwo Jima made this aerial success possible. Admiral Chester W. Nimitz paid eloquent tribute to those who had secured the hellish island: "Among the Americans who served on Iwo Island uncommon valor was a common virtue."

Okinawa

Okinawa provided yet another stepping-stone in the journey to the island of Japan. Here the Americans planned to link the army and marines, the campaigns of Admiral Nimitz and General MacArthur, joining at the enemy fortress a mere 350 miles from the enemy's homeland. Some 548,000 Americans in all would attack. Army General Simon Bolivar Buckner Jr. would lead the U.S. Tenth Army. Lieutenant General Mitsuro Ushijima led Japan's Thirty-second Army. Ushijima defended in depth, avoiding the beaches and airfields where U.S. fire superiority gave his enemy an advantage.

To repel the U.S. invaders, the Japanese deployed a force of nearly a hundred thousand men. Okinawa, a slim 80 miles in length, early became the focus of U.S. intentions in the Ryukyu Islands. Just south of the 2-mile-wide Ishikawa Isthmus stood an obstacle to any advance by large military formations, a series of ridges that formed a natural defense line for the Japanese. South of these ridgelines stood the capital city of Naha and Shuri Castle, the ancient Okinawan citadel.

Although U.S. planners anticipated a fierce defense, they believed that the island located so close to the Japanese homeland would provide a base from which to cut the remaining supply lines and attack the enemy. Conversely, this closeness placed the Allies within range of at least one hundred Japanese airfields supporting 4,000 aircraft. The Japanese strategy evolved from the proximity of these airfields. The Thirty-second Japanese Army on Okinawa would engage and delay the U.S. amphibious assault while kamikaze, or suicide, aircraft attacked the U.S. fleet. The Japanese earlier had used this tactic in the Philippines.

The assault force encompassed the Army XXIV Corps and the Marine Corps III Amphibious Corps. Major General Geiger commanded the 1st, 2d, and 6th Marine Divisions for what, unbeknownst to the marines, would be their final amphibious assault of the war. Four marine air groups joined the huge marine contingent that numbered nearly ninety thousand men, or half the assault force. The marines anticipated heavy fighting on the Okinawa beaches as well as in the area surrounding the two prized airfields, Kadena and Yontan. A week of heavy naval and air bombardment would precede the attack.

Amazingly, the Tenth Army went ashore almost without opposition on April 1, 1945—prophetically, All Fools' Day. The marines landed with heavy air and naval gunfire support with the 6th Division on the north and the 1st Division to their south. The 2d Marine Division remained afloat as reserve. By 0900 hours, the eight battalions of the initial marine assault waves signaled that they were ashore, over the seawall on the western beaches, and advancing with virtually no casualties. By April 3, the 6th Marine Division began to wheel to the north and attack toward the Ishikawa Isthmus. The army began a similar movement to the south.

Twelve days ahead of schedule the 6th Division secured the Ishikawa Isthmus. Marines even swam off the pleasant

Okinawan beaches during the initial phase of the operation.

But hope for a bloodless campaign passed quickly. On April 6–7, nearly seven hundred Japanese aircraft attacked the U.S. fleet off Okinawa.

By April 10, 1945, some one hundred-sixty thousand marine and army troops had landed on Okinawa. Because of the easy early going, the marine floating reserve, the 2d Marine Division, was pulled out of the battle and sent back to Saipan. Clearly, U.S. intelligence had misgauged or misinterpreted the enemy's intentions.

However, supplies continued to come ashore in profusion, and the U.S. position seemed secure. A harbinger of the trouble ahead could be seen in the continuing kamikaze raids by the Japanese against U.S. ships off Okinawa. On April 12–13 and 15–16, nearly two hundred Japanese aircraft attacked the U.S. naval fleet in successive raids. As sailors battled these one-way attackers that flew beneath the radar defenses of their ships, the land battle on Okinawa ignited for the marines pushing north from the Ishikawa Isthmus. The 6th Marine Division found the enemy on the west coast lodged in the mountains of the Motobu Peninsula. The 4th and 29th Marine Regiments immediately attacked a heavily fortified cave complex around Mount Yaetake. On April 14, the marines attacked on three sides the 1,200-foot hill mass in terrain so rugged only the infantry could move up the slopes fronting the enemy stronghold. Fighting intensified, and on April 16 Japanese and marine warriors took and relinquished the summit of Mount Yaetake several times in hand-to-hand fighting. Finally, with the support of indirect fires, the marines secured and held the summit. Four days later, organized Japanese resistance ceased on the peninsula. On April 21, the marines reached the northern tip of Okinawa, ending the first phase of the battle.

But as the marines soon learned, the Japanese had concentrated their forces in the south. The primary enemy position screened the town of Naha with Shuri Castle at the center of this defensive barrier. Another heavily defended area circled the town of Yonabaru on the island's south side. The terrain, filled with limestone caves and cliffs with broken ridges and twisting roads, fit the positional defensive concept developed by Japanese General Ushijima. Here the Japanese hoped to fight a delaying action while their aircraft devastated the Americans in suicidal attacks.

The cornerstone of the Japanese defense rested on Shuri Ridge between the towns of Naha and Yonabaru. Three divisions of the army's XXIV Corps with heavy air and artillery support attacked the ridge on April 19. The attack against the massive bunker complex failed. Army General Buckner's frontal-assault tactics received heavy criticism as casualties surpassed the U.S. advance. The marines offered to have the floating reserve, the recalled 2d Marine Division, land behind the enemy fortifications. But Buckner, perhaps caught in the trap of earlier interservice rivalry, declined assistance. Despite the army's reluctance, the 27th Army Division found itself relieved from the fight before Shuri on May 1 by the 1st Marine Division.

That division immediately attacked the Shuri line, driving south in heavy rains along the western side of the island. The Japanese counterattacked on the night of May 3–4 in concert with yet another massive kamikaze raid against the U.S. fleet off Okinawa. The Japanese attempted to move by barge up both coasts, landing behind the marines in the west and the army in the east. The marines quickly destroyed the amphibious landing attempts. The Japanese did envelop the army lines but were finally destroyed. By May 5, the marines had seized the heights above the Asa River and looked down on a front where more than six thousand Japanese lay dead, killed during their counterattack. The enemy also lost fifty artillery pieces during this decisive U.S. victory. By May 8, V-E Day in Europe, the 6th Marine Division had assumed the right flank supporting the 1st Marine Division, the army's 77th Division having replaced the marines in Okinawa's relatively quiet northern area.

Lead elements from the 1st Marine Division inched across the Asa River on May 10. The following day the marines opened a new offensive aimed at dislodging the strongly emplaced enemy defending the Shuri Castle area. The army's 96th and 77th Divisions joined in the fight.

Immediately confronting the marines stood Sugar Loaf, a rectangular hill mass 300 yards in length and rising 50 feet above the open ground that fronted the natural defensive position. On the southeast of Sugar Loaf rose yet another similar hill mass, Half Moon Hill. To the southwest rear of Sugar Loaf stood the Horseshoe, yet another natural defensive position. The triangle of hills formed a natural redoubt honeycombed with caves, with each hill mass capable of supporting the others with direct and indirect fire. The 22d Marines reached Sugar Loaf on May 12.

For five days, the men of the 6th Marine Division assaulted the heavily fortified hills. The battle ebbed and flowed with the only constant the unremitting intensity of the fighting. On May 16, combat reached deep into the reserves of marine courage and sacrifice. The 22d Marines fell to 40 percent effectiveness. The 29th Marines replaced their decimated sister regiment and renewed the attack on Sugar Loaf in concert with simultaneous attacks on Half Moon and Horseshoe Hills. At last, the marines, on May 17, succeeded in taking and holding Sugar Loaf. But the victory came at the sacrifice of 6th Marine Division's 2,662 battle casualties and 1,289 non-battle casualties during nine days of fighting.

While the 6th Marine Division paid its heavy price at Sugar Loaf, the 1st Marine Division fought beneath Shuri heights. The 7th Marines attacked Wana Ridge. The 5th Marines assaulted the Wana gorge immediately below the ridge. Casualties were heavy. On May 19, further casualties resulted in the relief of the 7th Marines engaged on Wana Ridge. As the 5th Marines continued in efforts to penetrate the gorge, the fresh 1st Marine Regiment continued the attack on the heavily fortified ridgeline above. But on May 21, heavy rains swept the area; fighting came to a standstill in a sea of mud. On the marines' left flank, the army's 96th and 77th Divisions made good progress. But by May 22, the rain and mud had halted their efforts as well.

The rains stopped on May 28, and the U.S. advance began immediately. The following day, the 5th Marines assaulted and occupied Shuri Ridge, a cornerstone of the enemy defensive position. Then, much to the consternation of advancing army units, the marines attacked 800 meters out of their area of responsibility and took the Shuri Castle landmark. Interservice rivalry continued both to limit and to drive the performance of army and marine units. As the rains again began, the Japanese fought a ferocious rearguard action as they retreated toward the very southern tip of Okinawa. By this time, more than sixty-two thousand Japanese had been killed. As replacements filled the billets of fallen veterans, the fighting effectiveness of the U.S. units diminished.

On June 4, the battle continued as the 4th Marines assaulted amphibiously the Oruku Peninsula on the southwestern edge of Okinawa, site of the Naha airfield. On June 14, Japanese resistance on the peninsula ended. The marines had killed more than four thousand of the enemy on the peninsula but had suffered more than sixteen hundred dead and wounded.

The marines immediately engaged in a no-quarter fight at Kinishi Ridge, a 1,500-meter-long hill mass heavily fortified by the Japanese on the southern tip of Okinawa. All three infantry regiments of the 1st Marine Division attacked the ridge in a series of assaults that finally brought victory on June 16. The 1st Marine Division reported more than a thousand casualties. But, augmented now by the 6th Marine Division fresh from its victory on the Oruku Peninsula, the marines pressed ahead into yet another enemy-defended hill mass, Me-

zado Ridge. The 22d Marine Regiment attacked and secured the ridge.

At the very edge of their endurance, both marine divisions badly needed relief. The 8th Marines from the 2d Marine Division reserve came ashore on June 18 and supplied a breath of freshness and vigor. The marine units continued to advance to the south and southwest, pinning the enemy against the sea at Okinawa's southern tip. On June 21, marine Major General Geiger, the first of his service to command a field army, declared Okinawa secure. Few of the marines in the surviving rifle companies had been with their units during the invasion on Easter Sunday, but a month previous.

Casualty reports listed more than 20,020 marine casualties during the Okinawa campaign, of which 3,561 were killed in action. The army's X Corps suffered 7,613 dead and another 31,807 wounded. Estimates of Japanese casualties approximated 100,000 soldiers and 42,000 civilians.

Japanese Mainland

Victory at Okinawa presaged preparations during the late spring and early summer of 1945 for the impending final marine strike. Despite their losses, the Japanese defended their mainland with an estimated 1.5 million soldiers. The six veteran marine divisions with their supporting air wings anticipated a massive and costly amphibious assault on Japan during late 1945 or early 1946. The two-pronged strike fronted by the veteran Marine III and V Corps attacking with an equally seasoned army contingent projected an estimated hundred thousand American casualties.

The marines began the cyclic ritual of refitting, replacing, training, and waiting, but now they were more sober than ever, as they reflected on the anticipated costs in light of the casualties on Okinawa, Iwo Jima, and Tarawa. As they prepared, massive air strikes continued against the Japanese mainland. These attacks culminated on August 6 and 9 with the dropping of the atomic bombs, first on Hiroshima and then on Nagasaki. On August 15, 1945, the Japanese agreed to Allied surrender terms. World War II had ended.

Immediately, the 4th Marine Regiment embarked by ship from Guam to Japan. The first marine infantry regiment to fight in World War II now led the U.S. occupation of a defeated Japan.

Conclusion

In 1945, the Marine Corps listed nearly five hundred thousand men and women in its ranks. Half of those served in the Pacific theater. The corps' efforts in the Pacific had helped secure the defeat of the Japanese from a beginning fraught with difficulty. From the smoke and flame of Pearl Harbor and the early defeats on Wake, Guam, and Corregidor emerged grim efforts resulting in the subsequent bloody victories in such epic fights as Guadalcanal, Tarawa, and Iwo Jima. The U.S. Marines had evolved into one of the most powerful fighting forces in military history.

But success came with an expensive price tag. The Marine Corps suffered 91,718 casualties during World War II, nearly 20,000 of which were deaths. Many of the marine veterans who returned to the United States at war's end had seen combat as intense and ferocious as any in the history of warfare.

History would emphasize the role that the Marine Corps amphibious tactics and strategy played in U.S. victory in the Pacific. It was also a time when women and blacks first entered the corps, although complete racial integration would have to wait for another war, in Korea. The hard-earned battle streamers of World War II marine victory and sacrifice now waved against the traditional Marine Corps battle flags backgrounded in red.

FURTHER READINGS

Leckie, Robert. *Helmet for My Pillow* (1957).

Manchester, William. *Goodbye, Darkness: A Memoir of the Pacific War* (1982).

McMillan, George. *The Old Breed: A History of the First Marine Division in World War II* (1949).

Millett, Allan R. *Semper Fidelis: The History of the United States Marine Corps* (1980).

Moskin, J. Robert. *The Story of the U.S. Marine Corps* (1979).

Sherrod, Robert. *History of Marine Corps Aviation in World War II* (1952).

———. *Tarawa: The Story of a Battle* (1944).

Stockman, James R. *The Battle for Tarawa.* U.S. Marine Corps Historical Section (1947).

Toland, John. *The Rising Sun* (1970).

Mike Fisher

SEE ALSO Army, Japanese; Army Ground Forces, U.S.; Navy, U.S.

Marshall, George Catlett (1880–1959)

Called the "Organizer of Victory" in World War II, George Catlett Marshall was one of the foremost soldier-statesmen in U.S. history. Born in Uniontown, Pennsylvania, on December 31, 1880, Marshall graduated from the Virginia Military Institute in 1901. Com-missioned a second lieutenant of infantry in 1902, he served in the Philippines during 1902–1903. He returned to the United States and graduated first in his class from the Infantry and Cavalry School at Fort Leavenworth (1907) and remained there at the staff college (1907–1908). Promoted to first lieutenant in 1907, Marshall was an instructor at Fort Leavenworth (1908–1910) and then held several other brief assignments before returning to the Philippines (1913–1916), where he was aide to General Hunter Liggett.

Marshall was not a transcendent intellect. Success came to him through hard work. Although he was almost always diplomatic in dealing with others, he was known to have a volcanic temper, which occasionally got out of control. Even as a young lieutenant, Marshall was recognized as a superior staff officer. As a first lieutenant, he planned maneuvers involving 17,000 men. Promoted to captain in 1916, he then served as aide to General James E. Bell, first in the Western Department and then in the Eastern Department (1917).

Marshall established his reputation as a brilliant staff officer while serving in France with the American Expeditionary Force (AEF) in World War I. In June 1917, he accompanied the 1st Division to France as a staff officer. He was promoted to temporary colonel in July 1918, joined General John J. Pershing's headquarters in August, and planned the Saint-Mihiel Offensive in September. Marshall won well-deserved praise for his planning of the relocation in only ten days of 600,000 troops and 2,700 guns from the Saint-Mihiel sector to the Meuse-Argonne front. In October 1918, he was named chief of operations for the First Army, and in November he became chief of staff for VIII Corps.

After the armistice, Marshall served with U.S. Army occupation forces in Germany. He reverted to his permanent rank of captain on his return to the United States in September 1919, when he became an aide to army Chief of Staff General Pershing (1919–1924). During this time, he helped Pershing prepare his reports on the war. Marshall was promoted to major in 1920 and to lieutenant colonel in 1923. He then served in Tientsin (Tianjin), China (1924–1927).

Marshall returned to the United States to become assistant commandant of the Infantry School at Fort Benning, Georgia (1927–1932), during which time he worked on developing new doctrines and tactics and identified officers capable of carrying them out. In 1933, he was promoted to colonel while working with the Civilian Conservation Corps. Marshall was then senior instructor to the Illinois National Guard (1933–1936), and in 1936 he was promoted to brigadier general and became commander of the 5th Infantry Brigade (1936–1938). In 1938, he headed the War Plans Division of the Army General Staff in Washington, D.C. That same year he was promoted to major general and became deputy chief of staff.

On September 1, 1939, as German panzers rolled into Poland, President Franklin Delano Roosevelt had Marshall sworn in as army chief of staff. Promoted to temporary full general on assumption of this post, he worked hard at building up the U.S. Army, which at 200,000 men ranked below that of Portugal or Romania. Marshall had to utilize his considerable diplomatic skills to convince Congress of the need for national military preparedness. Three months before the Japanese attack on Pearl Harbor, there was a move in Congress to reduce the size of the army. Under Marshall, the U.S. Army would grow to more than 8 million men. Marshall also reorganized the Army General Staff, and in March 1942 he reorganized the army into three major commands: Army Ground Forces, Army Service Forces, and Army Air Forces.

Marshall was easily the most influential of the World War II Joint Chiefs of Staff. Chief of Naval Operations Ernest King was mainly interested in expanding operations in the Pacific, while Commanding General of Army Air Forces Henry H. Arnold argued that bombers, if enough were provided, could do the job alone. Only Marshall never wavered from the prewar estimates that Germany could win the war without Japan but that Japan could not win without Germany. This meant a Europe-first strategy, and Marshall held that the only way of winning in Europe was through a land invasion of the continent. During the war, Marshall constantly fretted about "localitis" and "theateritis," whereby commanders had only a limited perspective.

FDR relied on Marshall absolutely, and the general attended the principal wartime conferences with him. Certainly he was one of the main Allied strategists of World War II. His matter-of-fact approach to problems and lack of boastfulness contributed to smooth relations with the British, and it was Winston Churchill who bestowed on Marshall the grand title "Organizer of Victory."

Marshall never enjoyed a close relationship with General Douglas MacArthur. The two men had developed a dislike for each other from their early service in the Philippines. In part, this was a matter of personalities: Marshall was not gregarious, whereas MacArthur surrounded his person with those who shared his lofty opinion of himself. During the war, MacArthur complained frequently of personal slights; he also failed to realize that the European theater of operations had to have first claim on scarce resources.

Marshall wanted very much to command the grand coalition of forces that would invade the European continent from the west, but, good soldier that he was, he left that decision up to FDR. The president told Marshall he could have that command if he wanted it but added that he would not sleep easily at night with Marshall out of the country. Marshall refused to press the matter, and the command he had so much wanted went to his protégé General Dwight D. Eisenhower. This decision denied Marshall his rightful place in history. In December 1944, Marshall was promoted general of the army (five stars), the same rank held by his mentor, Pershing.

Marshall has been criticized for not thinking "politically" about military decisions, particularly in Europe. This is true, but it stemmed from his deep conviction that such matters belonged to the political chiefs. At the same time, however, Marshall firmly believed that political leaders should not meddle in military decision making. He kept FDR at arm's length and gave his own field commanders wide latitude. This relationship between political and military leaders was very different elsewhere; in Britain, for example, Churchill exercised political power but also overrode his military chiefs on numerous occasions.

Marshall was an excellent judge of men and chose his field commanders well, although he was not forgiving of error. Unlike many military chiefs, he agonized over the human cost of victory; he saw to it that the president was informed weekly about casualty totals and declared it was essential to remember the sacrifices, "because it is easy to get hardened to them."

Marshall resigned from active service on November 20, 1945. Less than a week later, President Harry S. Truman persuaded him to return to public service as special envoy to China (1945–1947), but after more than a year there, he was unable to heal the rift between Nationalist Party leader Chiang Kai-shek and Communist Party leader Mao Tse-tung. In January 1947, Marshall replaced James Byrnes as secretary of state, a post he held until 1949. This led to his name being forever linked with the Marshall Plan, the single most important factor in the postwar recovery and development of Western Europe. In September 1950, Truman again persuaded Marshall to leave retirement to replace Defense Secretary Louis Johnson and rebuild the U.S. armed forces. Marshall restored morale, increased the size of the military, and restored harmony between the Defense and State Departments. He also established a good working relationship with the Joint Chiefs of Staff. Marshall defended the concept of a limited war in Korea and supported Truman's decision to fire General Douglas MacArthur.

The Truman administration was then under heavy attack, and in June 1951 Senator Joseph McCarthy demanded the resignations of Secretary of State Dean Acheson and Marshall and threatened President Truman with impeachment. McCarthy all but called Marshall a communist. This unjust attack may well have confirmed Marshall's decision to step down from a post he had in any case agreed to hold for only six months to a year. At Truman's request, he stayed in office until September 1, 1951. His final retirement on that date marked the end of fifty years of government service. Surprisingly, General Eisenhower failed to speak out in Marshall's defense. In 1953, Marshall was awarded the Nobel Peace Prize in Oslo, Norway, the first soldier to be so honored. He died in Washington, D.C., on October 16, 1959, at the age of 79.

FURTHER READINGS

Cray, Ed. *General of the Army: George C. Marshall, Soldier and Statesman* (1990).

Dupuy, Trevor N., Curt Johnson, and David L. Bongard. *The Harper Encyclopedia of Military Biography* (1992).

Pogue, Forrest C. *George C. Marshall: Education of a General, 1880–1939* (1963).

———. *George C. Marshall: Ordeal and Hope, 1939–1942* (1966).

———. *George C. Marshall: Organizer of Victory, 1943–1945* (1973).

Spencer C. Tucker

SEE ALSO Army Ground Forces, U.S.

Matsuoka Yosuke (1880–1946)

Matsuoka served as foreign minister in the second cabinet of Prince Konoe Fumimaro and was a major force behind the signing of the Tripartite (Berlin) Pact of 1940 with Germany and Italy.

Born in 1880, at the age of 13 Matsuoka went to sea with his uncle, who dumped him ashore in the United States and told him to fend for himself. He was raised by an American family in Portland, Oregon, where he worked at a variety of jobs while pursuing an education. He received a law degree from the University of Oregon in 1900, and returned to Japan soon thereafter. Matsuoka was a member of the diplomatic service for the next twenty years, holding posts in China, Europe, and the United States, before taking a position as director of the South Manchurian Railway Company. In the 1920s he rose rapidly through that quasi-public company, becoming vice president, then president, making important contacts (among them Tojo Hideki) in the Japanese army and bureaucracy along the way. A strong advocate of an aggressive foreign policy, as early as 1929 Matsuoka was called a "fanatical ideologue of Japanese imperialism" by the Soviet ambassador to Japan.

In 1933, in the wake of the Japanese occupation of Manchuria, Matsuoka was chosen to head Japan's delegation to the League of Nations. When that body refused to recognize Japan's new satellite state of Manchukuo, he led the rest of the delegation in walking out of the conference chamber. Japan formally withdrew from the League soon after, and Matsuoka became a hero to an increasingly nationalistic and chauvinistic Japanese public. In 1936 he was asked to join a cabinet advisory council to assist the government in setting policy toward China.

Four years later Prime Minister Konoe Fumimaro invited Matsuoka into his second cabinet as foreign minister. It was by far Konoe's most controversial appointment, and even the emperor asked the prime minister to reconsider his choice. But Konoe was impressed by Matsuoka's powers of persuasion and forceful manner of speech—qualities most Japanese politicians lacked.

As foreign minister, Matsuoka's first priority was the conclusion of an alliance with Nazi Germany, which had just stunned the world by its rapid conquest of the Low Countries and France. He believed that an alliance with Hitler would place Japan on the winning side in World War II and might help to improve Japanese relations with the Soviet Union, which at the time was acting in partnership with Germany. Moreover, an alliance with Germany would assist in ending the war in China by discouraging the United States from getting involved. After a month of negotiations, the Tripartite Pact was signed on September 27, 1940, by representatives of Germany, Italy, and Japan.

Matsuoka's next priority was to obtain German support for Japanese expansion in Southeast Asia and, if possible, German mediation in the ongoing border disputes between Japan and the Soviet Union. To this end the foreign minister made a much-publicized tour of Europe in March and April 1941, but the results of his visit with Hitler in Berlin fell far short of his expectations. The German leader took the opportunity to demand loudly that Japan attack the British fortress of Singapore at once, and when asked about the Soviet Union, he warned Matsuoka not to get too close to Stalin. Having gained nothing concrete from Germany, the foreign minister stopped in Moscow on his way home. There, to the great dismay of Hitler, he concluded an agreement with Stalin whereby Japan and the Soviet Union each promised to remain neutral in the event of war involving the other country. He then returned to Tokyo, confident that he had pulled off the greatest diplomatic coup of his career.

Upon his arrival, however, Matsuoka was met with news that a "draft understanding" between the United States and Japan had been approved by Washington, and that the Japanese cabinet was waiting for the foreign minister to act on it. Matsuoka was outraged that such an agreement had been negotiated without his knowledge, let alone his approval. He was alone among the cabinet in his suspicion (which proved to be correct) that the draft understanding did not represent the official position of the U.S. government. In a stormy cabinet meeting on May 3, Matsuoka claimed that to negotiate on the basis of the draft understanding would be a violation of the spirit, if not the letter, of the Tripartite Pact. Instead of trying to reach a comprehensive settlement of all outstanding issues between the United States and Japan, he argued, Tokyo should seek to conclude a simple neutrality pact with Washington on the model of the one he had just signed with Stalin. Nearly every cabinet member present at the meeting expressed disagreement, yet no attempt was made to pressure the foreign minister into accepting the draft understanding. Nine days later Matsuoka issued his response—American mediation of the China war would be welcomed, but peace could be concluded only on terms favorable to Japan. Furthermore, he warned the United States not to become involved in the European war, which was as good as won by Hitler.

Matsuoka's reputation in the Japanese government went into steady decline after his return from Europe. His frequent and repeated calls for an attack on Singapore alienated even the military, which preferred to concentrate on Indochina. The German invasion of the Soviet Union in June further eroded his position, having come as a complete surprise to most Japanese. Matsuoka then angered his colleagues by demanding that the neutrality pact with Stalin be abandoned. The military, he argued, should give up its plans to occupy southern Indochina, which would needlessly antagonize the United States, and launch an attack on the Soviet Union as soon as possible. He took his case to the emperor himself, until it became obvious that neither Konoe, nor the military, nor the emperor was interested in such a course of action.

Yet it was Matsuoka's antagonistic posture toward the United States that led most directly to his downfall. Having spent his formative years in the United States, he believed himself to be an expert on the "American mind." The best way to prevent war with the United States, he claimed, was to "stand firm and start hitting back." Only then would Japan gain the respect of the United States.

On June 21 the American secretary of state, Cordell Hull, issued an "oral statement" in which he criticized "some Japanese leaders in influential official positions" who were ideologically committed to Nazi Germany. The statement went on to question Japan's attitude toward further negotiations as long as such leaders remained in power. Matsuoka, realizing that the statement was directed primarily at himself, began to demand that Tokyo break off relations with the United States.

Such talk was more than even the tolerant Konoe could endure, and the cabinet became resolved to remove Matsuoka from the post of foreign minister—even Tojo had become concerned about the damage he was causing to U.S.–Japanese relations. Yet the prime minister was unwilling to fire him, for fear the move would be interpreted as bowing to U.S. pressure. Therefore, on July 16, 1941, Konoe asked for the resignation of his entire cabinet. Two days later he organized a new government with all of the same cabinet members except Matsuoka. The foreign minister's portfolio went to Admiral Toyoda Teijiro, a known moderate.

After his removal from the cabinet, Matsuoka faded into relative obscurity. In 1945, however, he was one of the first Japanese civilians to be arrested by the occupation authorities on charges of war crimes. He died in prison in 1946, before the completion of the war crimes trials in Tokyo.

A brilliant public speaker and domineering personality, Matsuoka's nicknames included "Mr. 50,000 Words" and "The Talking Machine." He was described by one Japanese general as "voluble and unconventional by nature," and an admiral condemned him for "recklessly advancing in the wrong direction." Some, including Hitler and Navy Minister Oikawa Koshiro, suspected that he was insane. Unfortunately, his public eloquence was not accompanied by any particular perspicacity in foreign affairs. Though he cannot be blamed for the ultimate outbreak of war with the United States (which, after all, happened five months after he left office), his failure to appreciate U.S. interests in East Asia were a prime cause of the decline in U.S.–Japanese relations which occurred in 1940–1941.

FURTHER READINGS

Bamhart, Michael E. *Japan Prepares for Total War: The Search for Economic Security, 1919–1941* (1987).

Butow, Robert J. C. *Tojo and the Coming of War* (1961).

Ike, Nobutaka, ed. *Japan's Decision for War: Records of the 1941 Policy Conferences* (1967).

Lu, David J. *From the Marco Polo Bridge to Pearl Harbor* (1961).

Morley, James W., ed. *The Fateful Choice: Japan's Advance into Southeast Asia 1939–1941* (1980).

Schroeder, Paul W. *The Axis Alliance and Japanese–American Relations, 1941* (1958).

John E. Moser

SEE ALSO Hirohito; Home Front, Japanese

Matterhorn, Operation

Operation Matterhorn was the name of the U.S. air operation against Japan. In 1943, the B-29 bomber of the U.S. Army Air Forces (USAAF) went into mass production. Designed as a long-range strategic weapon that could penetrate the very heart of the enemy's homeland and destroy his war machine, it had originally been planned for an air offensive in Europe. But delays in production had so postponed the date of quantity delivery that it was deemed too late to play a major role in the strategic bombing of Germany. As a result, the USAAF turned its attention toward utilizing the B-29 in a war-winning air assault against Japan from bases in China and in the Mariana Islands of the western Pacific. These bases, however, were not expected to be ready before the end of 1944, prompting the USAAF to devise a new plan for the bomber's initiation to combat. Dubbed Matterhorn, the plan called for B-29s to strike vital spots in the Japanese industrial zone beginning in the spring of 1944 from bases in China, the closest base area to Japan then under Allied control. Through their psychological effect, the very heavy bombers would help keep Generalissimo Chiang Kai-shek and his Chinese Nationalist forces in the war at a time when it was possible they might collapse.

To preserve its strategic character, Operation Matterhorn was to function directly under the Joint Chiefs of Staff (JCS), with General Henry H. Arnold, chief of the Army Air Forces, as the executive agent. The JCS would control the deployment, missions, and target selection, although the commander of the China-Burma-India (CBI) theater would be given the right to use the B-29s in a tactical role in case of emergencies. The principal targets were to be coke ovens, Japanese industrial areas, shipping concentrations, and aircraft-assembly plants. Oil refineries in the Netherlands East Indies were a secondary target.

Because the CBI theater already labored under a load of difficult logistic projects that were being handled by a minimum of service units and equipment, Matterhorn was to operate from its own bases and with its own line of communications. Specifically, plans prescribed the construction of airfields in India that would serve as home

bases for the B-29s and the construction of airfields in China that would serve as staging bases for the initial raids against Japan. Also, XX Bomber Command, the USAAF unit charged with carrying out Operation Matterhorn, would be responsible for the supply of all its needs and the transport of its fuel and supplies from India to China by means of the "Hump" route over the Himalaya Mountains, the only supply route to China.

Major General Claire Chennault, commander of the China-based Fourteenth Air Force, and planners in the JCS objected to Operation Matterhorn from its inception, on the grounds that the CBI theater, with its excessively long supply lines and low priority in the Allied global war effort, was hardly the ideal place for a major bomber offensive. But President Franklin Delano Roosevelt, who saw in Operation Matterhorn an opportunity to "do something" for China politically, and Arnold, who viewed Matterhorn as a way of furthering his dream of autonomous strategic air power, were determined to push ahead with the project. Contending that Operation Matterhorn was "bold but entirely feasible," FDR won the support of Chiang and British Prime Minister Winston Churchill at the Sextant Conference in Cairo, Egypt, at the end of November and early December 1943. Approval from the combined chiefs of staff (Great Britain and the United States) and the JCS followed.

Operation Matterhorn began with the construction of bases. In the case of India, southern Bengal—because of its position vis-à-vis China, relative security from Japanese attack, and the port facilities of Calcutta—was chosen as the base area, and eventually XX Bomber Command settled on the use of five airfields located in the flatlands west of Calcutta. All had existing 6,000-foot-long runways made of concrete. These could be lengthened and strengthened to accommodate B-29s, which required 8,500-foot-long runways capable of supporting 70 tons. Work on the airfields began in late November 1943, and at the end of April 1944 there were close to six thousand U.S. troops on the job. They were assisted by 27,000 Indian civilians provided by India's Central Public Works Department. Because many engineer units arrived from the United States without the heavy equipment required for grading the runways, they had to borrow equipment from U.S. units working on other projects in India and Burma. Moreover, instead of the 8,500-foot runways designated in Washington, those in India were constructed only to 7,500 feet to get them in operation as soon as possible. The concrete was produced with the equipment on hand and laid and spread by Indian workers using hand tools. Although all the airfields were not completed until September 1944, XX Bomber Command was able to receive and house the combat groups as they arrived in their B-29s in April and May.

The forward bases were placed in the area of Chengtu, China, in Szechwan Province. While U.S. troops had bases in China closer to Japan, Chengtu was chosen because of its greater security from Japanese air and ground attacks. Under the agreement between Roosevelt and Chiang, the United States was to provide the planning, overall supervision, and funding for the airfields, while the Chinese would supply the labor and materials and direct the construction. Through this arrangement, the size of the U.S. establishment at Chengtu could be kept at a minimum so as to lessen the burden on the local economy. Because it was impractical to fly heavy equipment over the Hump, almost all of the work would have to be done by hand. In January 1944, the Chinese directors and U.S. officers estimated that a labor force of at least 240,000 workers would be required to construct the bomber airfields and three supporting fighter strips. Within two weeks, more than 200,000 were on the job, and later, to catch up with the construction schedule, another 100,000 were put to work. Most of the workers were Chinese peasants conscripted by the governor of Szechwan. To these conscripts were added 75,000 contract workers.

The cost of the airfields quickly became a major source of friction between U.S. and Chinese officials. Chiang demanded that the United States pay for the airfields at the official exchange rate of 20 Chinese dollars to 1 U.S. dollar, even though the black-market rate in early 1944 was 240 to 1. At this rate, U.S. officials estimated the airfields would cost $800 million instead of the approximately $20 million budgeted. The Treasury and State Departments wanted to insist on the black-market rate. But Arnold, fearful the dispute might delay the completion of the airfields, pushed for a compromise. Eventually, Chiang and U.S. officials agreed to a quick fix under which the United States would accept a temporary rate of 100 to 1 pending the outcome of negotiations for a permanent arrangement. These negotiations proceeded at a desultory pace, and in November the U.S. Army finally settled the account for 1944 at $185 million.

Actual work on the airfields began in January 1944. Leveling the ground was a massive task in itself. In some instances, 7 feet of earth had to be excavated to get to solid ground, all of it done by thousands of workers using shovels, shoulder yokes, carts, and wooden wheelbarrows. Because it was impractical to fly in either cement and cement mixers or asphalt, the runways had to be built of rock, gravel, and sand. The base course consisted of stones brought from nearby streams, set with gravel and sand.

The wearing course was made of a native slurry of crushed rock, sand, clay, and water. The rocks were crushed by hand with little hammers. Huge stone rollers drawn by hundreds of men, and sometimes women, compacted the slurry, which had been puddled in pits by barefoot men and boys. The first airfield was available on April 24, and by May 1 all four bomber airfields had opened to traffic, as had the fighter strips.

In the meantime, the USAAF had been moving high-priority personnel and freight to India. The first important movement occurred in January 1944, when Brigadier General Kenneth Wolfe, commander of XX Bomber Command, led twenty C-87s from the United States to India carrying key command personnel and some equipment. Other personnel and freight were sent by sea. The overseas movement of the B-29s was to begin on March 10, 1944. According to the initial plan, 150 B-29s of the 58th Bomb Wing would leave the United States in daily increments of 9 or 10 planes on a five-day trip covering 11,530 miles from Salina, Kansas, to Calcutta by way of Gander Lake, Newfoundland; Marrakech, Morocco; and Cairo. If everything went well, all the bombers would be at their stations in India by March 31. But the problems involved in getting a new type of aircraft prepared for combat in a theater halfway around the world were too many to have the planes ready on time. As a result, the first contingent did not leave Salina until March 26 and did not reach India until April 2. By the second week of May, however, all but 9 of the original 150 B-29s were either on hand in India or momentarily expected. Through the rest of 1944 and into early 1945, 255 additional B-29s were ferried to India, so that by the end of March 1945, when Matterhorn was closed down, 405 B-29s had been committed to the operation.

No aspect of Matterhorn was more demanding than the transport of supplies from India to Chengtu. Using its own transports and the B-29s, XX Bomber Command was to carry all its own cargo over the Hump. Even under the most ideal conditions, a self-sustaining operation was wishful thinking. Lacking sufficient transport capacity, Matterhorn was soon making demands on the Air Transport Command (ATC), creating a very heavy drain on the limited transport resources available for other U.S. operations in China. Moreover, using the gluttonous B-29 as a transport plane was an expensive proposition. At its worst, the B-29 burned twelve gallons of gasoline to put down one gallon in Chengtu; at its best, it was 2 to 1. If that were not enough, it took seven trips back and forth across the Hump for one B-29 to move enough fuel to the Chinese staging bases for one B-29 to participate in one mission against Japan.

Operation Matterhorn's first combat mission was a "shakedown" raid against railway workshops at Bangkok, Thailand, on June 5, 1944. The first mission against Japan itself occurred on the night of June 15 with a raid against the Imperial Iron and Steel Works plant at Yawata on the island of Kyushu. Only one bomb hit any part of the sprawling Yawata works, a power plant nearly thirty-seven hundred feet away from the coke ovens that were the intended target. During the next two months, raids were conducted against targets in Japan, Manchuria, and the Netherlands East India with similar results. These raids represented only a minimum effort, because XX Bomber Command, even with the aid of the ATC, could not bring enough fuel and supplies to China to enable it to meet Arnold's expectations for the number of raids. A typical long-range mission against Japan took four days, with one day to fly from India to China, one day in China to get organized, one day to fly the mission, and one day to return to India. Counting the days that were required to get fuel and supplies to China, this meant that XX Bomber Command could fly at most only one combat mission a week.

Disappointed by these results, Arnold relieved Wolfe in July 1944, leaving Brigadier General LaVerne Saunders in temporary command of XX Bomber Command until Major General Curtis LeMay arrived in late August as Wolfe's replacement. LeMay had orders to produce, but even his driving leadership made little difference in the pace of raids or their effectiveness. At the same time, Matterhorn was cutting into the operations of the Fourteenth Air Force and Chinese forces. Both had their hands full attempting to contain a major offensive the Japanese had launched in eastern China, and there simply was not enough fuel and supplies arriving in China to support them in their defense against the offensive and the B-29s.

XX Bomber Command also undertook a number of missions outside the Matterhorn concept. In October 1944, it flew three missions against targets on Formosa in support of the U.S. invasion of Leyte in the Philippines. A similar mission was carried out in January 1945 in support of the invasion of Luzon. Moreover, on December 18, 1944, the command raided Hankow, China, a major supply center for the Japanese forces engaged in their offensive. About half the designated target area was burned to the ground with incendiary bombs, ending Hankow's value as a major supply base and demonstrating that firebomb raids by low-flying B-29s could be an effective weapon against Japanese cities.

By this time, U.S. forces had captured the Mariana Islands and transformed them into a major base for a massive B-29 assault against Japan. Because it had always been agreed that the main strategic bombing of Japan would come from the Marianas, there no longer seemed any reason to continue Matterhorn. The XX Bomber Command flew its last mission from the advance bases in China in January 1945, although raids against targets in Southeast Asia were carried out from India until the end of March 1945. Beginning in February, XX Bomber Command units were gradually withdrawn from India and sent to the Marianas, and by May all B-29s had left the theater.

Matterhorn had been conceived as an experimental operation to put the B-29s into action against Japan as soon as possible, with the hope that it might shorten the war by crippling key segments of the Japanese economy and prop up Chinese morale. Notwithstanding all the effort, it had little impact in either respect. At a cost of eighty-two B-29s lost in combat, XX Bomber Command flew 3,085 sorties in forty-nine missions and dropped 11,477 tons of bombs. Only half this bomb tonnage was dropped by B-29s flying out of China, and only half this tonnage was expended in the ten strikes against targets within the Matterhorn concept, meager results that did little to justify the lavish expenditures poured out for the operation. Matterhorn may have contributed to the Chinese will to resist the Japanese, but this outcome was at best fleeting. Finally, the burden of Matterhorn on logistics in the CBI was more than the theater could handle. From the outset, Matterhorn competed with the Fourteenth Air Force and Chinese forces for the limited capacity of the Hump airlift, absorbed a goodly portion of the shipping space allotted to the theater, increased congestion at the port of Calcutta, and diverted service troops and supplies from other CBI theater projects. For these reasons, the U.S. Strategic Bombing Survey concluded after the war that Matterhorn was a disappointment and that the "aviation gasoline and supplies used by the B-29s might have been more profitably allocated to an expansion of the tactical and anti-shipping operations of the 14th Air Force."

FURTHER READINGS

Anderton, David. *B-29 Superfortress at War* (1978).

Byrd, Martha. *Chennault: Giving Wings to the Tiger* (1987).

Craven, Wesley Frank, and James Lea Cate, eds. *The Army Air Forces in World War II*, vol. 5, *The Pacific: Matterhorn to Nagasaki, June 1944 to August 1945* (1953).

LeMay, Curtis E., and Bill Yenne. *Superfortress: The Story of the B-29 and American Air Power* (1988).

Romanus, Charles F., and Riley Sunderland. *Stilwell's Command Problems* (1956).

Rust, Kenn C. *Twentieth Air Force Story in World War II* (1979).

                    John Kennedy Ohl

SEE ALSO Air Offensive, Japan; Army Air Corps/Air Forces, U.S.; China-Burma-India Theater of Operations; LeMay, Curtis

Merrill's Marauders (Galahad)

"Merrill's Marauders" were a special long-range penetration force originally patterned after Major General Orde Wingate's Chindits. When the force went into action in Burma in early 1944, it was the only U.S. ground combat unit operating on the Asian continent. The name "Merrill's Marauders" was coined by the U.S. war correspondent James Shepley. Their official name was the decidedly uninspired 5307th Composite Unit (Provisional). The Allied code name for the force was Galahad.

The idea for Galahad was born at the Quadrant Conference in Quebec in August 1943. At that conference, Wingate gave the top Allied leaders a briefing on the long-range penetration methods he had been employing with his Chindit force in Burma. President Franklin Delano Roosevelt was sufficiently impressed to agree to provide a similar U.S. force of a size comparable to that of the Chindits. The training and organization of the Galahad force were to be supervised by Wingate. Under the original plan, Wingate was to command Galahad. That did not sit well with Lieutenant General Joseph Stilwell, the commander of the U.S. China-Burma-India theater. Before Galahad actually was committed to operations, Stilwell managed to have it placed under his own command.

Wingate's ideas of deep penetration were not universally accepted among the top Allied military leaders. General Sir Alan Brooke, chief of the British Imperial General Staff, thought that rather than making dramatic and deep penetrations into Burma, the special penetration forces should work in closer coordination with the main Allied forces in contact with the Japanese main forces. Stilwell agreed with this, and under his command Galahad was used for a series of short hooks into the Japanese immediate rear areas.

The original formation of Galahad consisted of some 2,830 volunteers—950 were combat-experienced troops from the South and southwest Pacific, and 1,900 came from jungle-training centers in the Caribbean and the United States. The force started to form in San Francisco in September 1943 under the temporary command of Colonel Charles H. Hunter. In October, it sailed for Bombay, India, on commercial liner *Lurline,* stopping at Nouméa and Brisbane to pick up veterans of the Pacific fighting.

On arriving in India, Galahad was met by Colonel Francis G. Brink, who had been appointed officer in charge of training the force. Hunter, however, still remained in acting command. On January 1, 1944, the 5307th Composite Regiment (Provisional) came officially into existence. That same day Hunter was formally appointed its first commander. The odd command arrangement between Brink and Hunter continued until January 4, 1944, when Brigadier General Frank Merrill assumed command of Galahad. The day before, the name of the unit had been changed to the 5307th Composite Unit (Provisional), because a regiment was deemed beneath the command level of a general officer. Merrill dismissed Brink but retained Hunter as second in command.

The combat elements of Galahad were organized into three battalions. The first was commanded by Lieutenant Colonel William L. Osborne; the second by Lieutenant Colonel George A. McGee; and the third by Lieutenant Colonel Charles E. Beach. The 3d Battalion consisted mostly of the Pacific veterans. Rounding out the force were the 31st and 33d Quartermaster Pack Troops, a detachment of the 835th Signal Service Battalion, and a platoon of the 502d Military Police Battalion.

The Quartermaster Pack Troops were particularly important because the primary source of motive power for Galahad was animal transport. Originally the force was supposed to have 700 pack mules. It received only 360 because the second half of the contingent was lost when the ship bringing them was torpedoed in the Arabian Sea. The shortfall was made up with 340 horses—almost none of which survived the campaign.

Galahad had an unusual internal organization. Based on guidance from Wingate, each of its three battalions was organized into two combat teams—which were much different from the usual U.S. form of a combat team. The teams were designated by color codes: red and white (1st Battalion); blue and green (2d Battalion); and khaki and orange (3d Battalion). Each team consisted of a rifle company, a heavy-weapons platoon, a pioneer and demolition platoon, a reconnaissance platoon, and a medical detachment. Each team had a combined strength of 16 officers and 456 enlisted men.

In late January and early February 1944, Galahad moved from its training sites in India to Ningbyen in northern Burma in preparation for the Allies' 1944 offensive. The original plan called for Chinese forces under Stilwell to drive south, up the Hukawng Valley toward the north Burmese town of Myitkyina, a major transportation center. Simultaneously, two British corps would move into Burma from India, while another Chinese force would attack from China into eastern Burma. The Chindits would support these drives with raids on the Japanese lines of communications. Seizing Myitkyina would move the Allies closer to the old Burma Road, as well as deny the Japanese the use of a key airfield from which their fighters were able to attack Allied aerial supply routes over "the Hump" to China.

Before the start of the Allied offensive, the British came under pressure from a new Japanese drive toward India and were forced to postpone their Burma offensive. Then the Chinese backed out of the agreement to attack into eastern Burma from China. Stilwell nonetheless decided to carry out his part of the plan, hoping to make as much progress as possible before the start of the monsoon season in June.

On February 24, two U.S.-trained Chinese divisions under Stilwell advanced slowly up the Hukawng. Simultaneously, Galahad moved around the flank of the Japanese 18th Division and set up a pair of blocking positions near Walawbum, astride the enemy's expected main line of withdrawal. The Chinese relief force, which included a tank group, was slow in arriving, leaving Galahad to face the Japanese with only small arms and mortars. By March 7, the U.S. troops had inflicted some eight hundred casualties, while sustaining about two hundred themselves. Concerned about the high casualties, Merrill withdrew his troops from the blocking positions. By that time, the Japanese had bypassed the roadblocks and fallen back to the Jambu Bum mountain range.

Wishing to secure the Jambu Bum before the start of the monsoons, Stilwell sent Galahad's 1st Battalion, along with the Chinese 113th Regiment, around the Japanese right flank to establish blocking positions south of Shaduzup. He sent the other two battalions even deeper to cut off the Japanese farther to the south. After the operation started, however, Stilwell's staff ordered the 2d and 3d Battalions to stop a Japanese counterthrust against the left flank of the Allied main force.

With this change, the mission became one of static defense, rather than one of holding temporary blocking positions after flanking movements. It was not the sort of mission for which Galahad was trained or organized. The 2d Battalion established a defensive position along the isolated Nhpum Ga ridgeline and held it against repeated attacks for eleven days. Merrill, meanwhile, led the 1st and 3d Battalions south to relieve the 2d. In the middle of the operation, Merrill suffered a heart attack and was evacuated. Under Colonel Hunter's command, the relief force finally linked up with the 2d Battalion on April 9. The Japanese withdrew to the south.

The Galahad force was now down to about fourteen hundred effectives and desperately needed a rest. Stilwell, under pressure from the Joint Chiefs of Staff, wanted to take Myitkyina before the start of the monsoons. On April 27, he sent what was left of Galahad, along with two Chinese regiments, 65 miles to the southeast over the 6,000-foot Kumon Range. On May 17, the Allies achieved total surprise and captured the Myitkyina airstrip.

Once the Allied task force seized the airfield, however, the drive on the city itself faltered as the Japanese defenses stiffened. Merrill had returned to the field to resume command and shortly thereafter suffered a second heart attack and was again evacuated. At that point, Galahad was a totally spent force and should have been relieved. Politically, however, Stilwell felt he could not withdraw the only U.S. infantry force operating between Italy and New Guinea. Stilwell once again ordered Galahad into the type of set-piece battle for which it was neither trained, equipped, nor organized.

By the end of May, Galahad was rapidly losing what little cohesion it had left. The soldiers were racked with malaria, typhus, and dysentery. Medical evacuations averaged between seventy-five and a hundred per day. Because the War Department had designed Galahad to last for only a single mission of three months, there was no replacement or convalescent system for the unit. The Joint Chiefs of Staff had, however, sent personnel to India to form a new Galahad-type force.

In order to keep Galahad from bleeding to death, overzealous staff officers cleared out the hospitals and sent every Galahad soldier capable of walking back into the battle. Galahad's remaining effectives were re-formed into a single battalion. Desperate for manpower, Stilwell's headquarters formed the inadequately trained new personnel into a two-battalion force called "New Galahad" and threw it into the battle. The troops suffered heavy casualties. When Hunter protested over the treatment of his troops, he was relieved. His relief came on August 3—the day Myitkyina finally fell.

The capture of Myitkyina was a major victory. It enabled the expansion of the Hump airlift into China, and it gave the Allies access to the road and rail network of Burma. Without Galahad's unique penetration capabilities, Stilwell never could have accomplished the mission. When the treatment of Galahad leaked out in the United States, however, it caused an uproar. The press blamed Stilwell and his staff for the disintegration of an elite unit, and the chairman of the Senate Military Affairs Committee launched an official investigation.

Galahad accomplished much in its very short life. In a little more than five months, it marched almost seven hundred fifty miles through thick jungles and over the hills of northern Burma in what is arguably the world's worst terrain. It fought in five major and seventeen minor engagements in a campaign that drove the Japanese out of an area the size of Connecticut. Galahad's troops endured some of the harshest fighting conditions of any U.S. soldiers in World War II, subsisting largely on K rations and sometimes going without food or water for up to thirty-six hours. Galahad received the Presidential Unit Citation (the unit equivalent of a Distinguished Service Cross) for its actions at Myitkyina.

In August 1944, the survivors of Galahad were organized into the 475th Infantry Regiment. They were then combined with the 124th Cavalry to form a new long-range penetration unit, the Mars Task Force. The 475th Infantry was inactivated in China on July 1, 1945. In June 1954, the 475th Infantry was reactivated on Okinawa and designated the 75th Infantry. It was inactivated two years later. The 75th Infantry was reactivated again in January 1969, this time as the parent regiment for all Ranger units in the U.S. Army. The regiment's current coat of arms is closely patterned after the original—but unofficial—shoulder patch of Merrill's Marauders.

FURTHER READINGS

Baker, Alan. *Merrill's Marauders* (1972).
Hogan, David, Jr. *U.S. Army Special Operations in World War II.* U.S. Army Center of Military History (1992).
Hoyt, Edwin P. *Merrill's Marauders* (1980).
Hunter, Charles N. *Galahad* (1963).
Ogburn, Charlton, Jr. *The Marauders* (1959).
Peers, William R. "Guerrilla Operations in Northern Burma," *Military Review* (June–July 1948).
Romanus, Charles F., and Riley Sunderland. *Stilwell's Command Problems* (1956).
U.S. War Department, U.S. Army Center of Military History. *Merrill's Marauders* (1945, 1990).

David T. Zabecki

SEE ALSO China-Burma-India Theater of Operations; Stillwell, Joseph Warren; Wingate, Orde C.

Midway, Battle of

The Battle of Midway can be considered the turning point of the Pacific war. In early 1942, after the Japanese had secured their planned defensive ring, leaders in Tokyo debated their next move. The ease of the initial conquests, and fears that morale might suffer if they were simply to stand on the defensive, prompted them to continue offensive operations. The navy favored thrusts against Australia and the Hawaiian Islands. The army, with its attention focused on China and Manchuria, was unwilling to release the troops required for such expeditions.

Japanese navy leaders hoped that further successful strikes in either direction might overcome the army's opposition and induce it to provide the troops necessary for one of these expeditions. The navy itself, however, was divided about the best direction. Admiral Yamamoto Isoroku and the Combined Fleet staff wanted to take Midway Island, 1,100 miles west of Pearl Harbor, Hawaii, as bait to draw the U.S. Pacific Fleet into action and crush it. The naval staff preferred a push through the Solomon Islands to take New Caledonia and Samoa, in order to sever the sea routes between the United States and Australia.

Debate over the alternative plans was interrupted and diverted by a series of U.S. carrier raids during the period February–May 1942, the most famous of which was the April 18 (Doolittle) raid on Tokyo. These attacks were extremely embarrassing to the Japanese leadership and influenced Tokyo's decision to go on the offensive in order to lure U.S. carriers into a trap. The Japanese reasoned that a thrust at U.S. territory would force the navy to commit its carriers. Their destruction would lead to a decisive fleet action, which would shorten the war. The Tokyo raid in particular produced approval both for Yamamoto's Midway plan and the effort to expand the outer defense ring further, so as to cut off Australia. The decision to try to do both was detrimental to concentration of effort and strength, and the plan itself was probably too complicated to promise a reasonable chance of success.

The Japanese effort to cut off Australia led to the decision to advance deeper into the Solomon Islands in order to seize Tulagi as a seaplane base to cover a further move southeastward, as well as to the plan to capture Port Moresby, on the south coast of New Guinea. The latter produced the May 7–8 Battle of the Coral Sea, in which U.S. Navy forces sank the Japanese light carrier *Shoho* and caused the invasion force to turn back. The Americans lost the giant carrier *Lexington,* and carrier *Yorktown* was damaged. The Japanese believed both U.S. carriers had been sunk, but, in an astonishing development, the Americans were able to repair *Yorktown* in just two days instead of the expected ninety, just in time for the next fight. The Japanese, however, were unable to repair carrier *Shokaku* in time. The battle hurt the Japanese for the next clash in another way as well. Japan kept all its best naval aviators on the carriers, rather than rotating them and using their knowledge to train replacements. As a result there was no combat-ready reserve to replace the losses sustained in the battle. This was the reason carrier *Zuikaku* could not participate in the Midway clash.

As the Battle of the Coral Sea was occurring, Imperial General Headquarters in Japan had already set the next confrontation in motion. The Combined Fleet staff produced the plan that would result in the Battle of Midway. The plan was comprehensive; it was also too elaborate and polycentric. Like so much of Japanese planning during the Pacific war, it also lacked flexibility.

The Japanese committed almost their entire navy to the operation. In all, the Battle of Midway involved some two hundred ships of the Imperial Navy, including eight carriers, eleven battleships, twenty-two cruisers, sixty-five destroyers, and twenty-one submarines. These were assisted by more than six hundred aircraft. U.S. Pacific Fleet commander Admiral Chester Nimitz, on the other hand, could put to sea just seventy-six ships, and of this number, a third—those in the north Pacific force—never entered the battle.

The Japanese plan at Midway was twofold. First, they would take Midway and the islands of Attu and Kiska in the Aleutian chain, to expand their defensive perimeter and block a supposed invasion route toward Japan. Midway Island, although quite small, could be important as a forward base in any future Japanese operation against Hawaii, if the U.S. fleet were destroyed. If not, it would still be an important base for surveillance of the U.S. fleet. Second, and more important, they sought to draw the U.S. fleet, especially the carriers, out of Hawaii and force it into the defense of Midway, thus providing the opportunity for its destruction.

Yamamoto's plan for the Midway battle was extremely complicated. Japanese ships were divided into eight task forces. Close to Pearl Harbor, where Yamamoto assumed the Pacific Fleet would be located, a line of Japanese submarines would be posted. Then, before the actual blow against Midway, he would mount a diversionary attack against several of the U.S. Aleutian Islands and take some of them. His major goal was to draw the U.S. fleet northward and out of position to defend Midway. If U.S. forces went north, they would meet Yamamoto's Second Mobile Force, centered on carriers *Ryujo* and *Junyo*. If they went toward Midway, they would face Vice Admiral Nagumo Chuichi's First Carrier Force of *Hiryu, Soryu, Kaga,* and *Akagi.*

Given their belief that they had sunk at least two U.S. carriers in the Battle of the Coral Sea, the Japanese thought the Americans would have only one carrier, at the most two, at Midway. Before U.S. carriers (*Enterprise,*

Hornet, and *Yorktown*—the latter hastily repaired at Pearl Harbor just in time for the battle) could reach Midway, Yamamoto expected his picket line of submarines to exact their toll. Thus, no matter the U.S. move, Yamamoto was confident of victory.

The Japanese force bound for Midway consisted of (1) the line of submarines, arrayed in three cordons, to cripple U.S. movements; (2) an invasion force, commanded by Vice Admiral Kondo Nobutake, of twelve escorted transports carrying 5,000 troops, with close support by four heavy cruisers, and a more distant covering force of two battleships, a light carrier, and four heavy cruisers; (3) Nagumo's First Carrier Force of four fleet carriers, carrying more than two hundred fifty planes and escorted by two battleships, two heavy cruisers, and a destroyer screen; (4) the main battle fleet under Yamamoto's command, with three battleships (including the giant 70,000-ton *Yamamoto* with nine 18-inch guns), a destroyer screen, and a light carrier. One of Yamamoto's mistakes in the Midway fight was to keep his battleships well back; they might have been brought up to bombard Midway. As it was, the battleships did not even participate.

The Japanese force headed for the Aleutians consisted of (1) an invasion force of three escorted transports carrying 2,400 troops and a support group of two heavy cruisers; (2) a carrier force of two light carriers; (3) a covering force of four older battleships.

The Japanese planned for the battle to begin in the Aleutians. They would initiate it with air strikes on June 3, followed by landings on June 6. On June 4, Nagumo's aircraft would attack Midway. The next day they would strike an atoll 60 miles to the west, occupying it for a seaplane base. On June 6 the Japanese cruisers would bombard Midway itself. Once the island was sufficiently softened up, Japanese troops would go ashore, covered by Kondo's battleships.

Yamamoto counted on the element of surprise. He did not expect any U.S. ships to make for the Midway area until after they were alerted by the attack there, and he did not expect them to reach the island until after the landing. He assumed any U.S. warships in the area would hurry north on news of the opening air strike in the Aleutians.

But in his planning to cover all eventualities, Yamamoto diluted his effort at Midway. Of eight carriers committed to the operation, he sent two to the Aleutians; two others were with the accompanying battle groups, and their movements were tied to the slow-moving transports. Because his main objective was destruction of the U.S.

carriers, Yamamoto should have concentrated his air assets at Midway.

Nonetheless, Nimitz and the Americans faced daunting odds. As a result of the Pearl Harbor attack, Nimitz had no battleships and only three carriers. He did have one great advantage, however. Thanks to superior U.S. intelligence operations, he had an accurate picture of the Japanese order of battle and plans. In contrast, the Japanese had virtually no accurate information on U.S. assets and their location. Through U.S. code breaking, Nimitz had learned that Midway was the Japanese destination. In their plans, the Japanese repeatedly referred to a location known only as "RF." To confirm that "RF" was indeed Midway, headquarters in Pearl Harbor ordered the commander on the island to broadcast that his water pump was out of order. When the Japanese relayed the message by radio that the water pump was out at "RF," Nimitz had his proof. Certainly his one great, and offsetting, advantage was the superiority of his information.

There was one important leadership change on the U.S. side. Vice Admiral William F. Halsey, Jr., commander of the U.S. carriers under Nimitz, fell ill. At his suggestion, Rear Admiral Raymond A. Spruance replaced the temporarily incapacitated Halsey. This was probably fortunate, because Spruance, a "poker player" like Yamamoto, was unlikely to be drawn into a trap. Given his moves in the 1944 Battle of Leyte Gulf, Halsey might have gone too far at Midway.

Before the battle, the Japanese, especially the flyers, were supremely confident. Commander Fuchida Mitsuo noted, "We were so sure of our own strength that we thought we could smash the enemy fleet single-handed, even if the battleship groups did nothing to support us." Later he would cite "arrogance" as one of the key factors in the Japanese defeat. The cautious Admiral Nagumo was not so certain; he had no idea of the whereabouts of the U.S. carriers. If he had possessed the detailed knowledge available to Rear Admirals Spruance and Frank Fletcher, commanding the two U.S. carrier task forces, this critically important battle might have ended in a Japanese victory.

Nimitz, meanwhile, loaded Midway with B-26 and B-17 bombers and laid an ambush position with the U.S. carriers. The three carriers with their 233 planes were to be located some three hundred miles northeast of the island. The Americans would hope for a surprise attack, trying to catch the Japanese carriers with their planes on their decks while avoiding this situation themselves. It was hoped that the carriers would be out of sight of Japanese reconnaissance planes, yet could count on getting early word of Japanese movements from long-range PBY Cat-alina aircraft flying from Midway. In the actual battle there were eighty-six Japanese ships against twenty-seven U.S. The Japanese pitted 325 planes against 348 (including 115 land-based aircraft) for the United States.

On June 3, the day after the U.S. carriers were in position (they had sailed from Pearl Harbor just before the Japanese submarines had reached their intercept position), air reconnaissance detected the slow-moving Japanese transports some six hundred miles west of Midway. On the other hand, gaps in search patterns flown by the Japanese allowed the U.S. carriers to remain undetected. Deployment of seaplanes on Japanese cruiser *Tone* was held up by catapult trouble, and one of cruiser *Chikuma*'s seaplanes had an engine problem. The latter, which would have flown directly over the U.S. ships, had been forced to turn back because of mechanical problems and foul weather. In any case, Yamamoto and Nagumo did not expect the U.S. Pacific Fleet to be at sea.

Early on June 4 Nagumo launched a strike by 108 aircraft against Midway while keeping another wave of similar size ready to attack any U.S. warships sighted. The first attack wave inflicted serious damage on installations, with little loss to itself, but its pilots reported to Nagumo that there was need for a second attack. Nagumo's own carriers were then being bombed by land aircraft from Midway, but the B-17 bombers, which had been "sold" to Congress by the U.S. Army Air Corps as a coastal defense weapon, failed to score any hits. Nonetheless, Nagumo concurred in the need to neutralize the island's airfields, and he ordered his second wave of planes to change from torpedoes to bombs for that purpose. There was still no sign of U.S. carriers.

Shortly afterward, a group of U.S. ships was spotted about two hundred miles away by the belated *Tone* plane, but was first thought to consist only of cruisers and destroyers. But at 0820 hours there came a precise report identifying a carrier. This was an awkward moment for Nagumo; most of his torpedo-bombers were now equipped with bombs, and most of his fighters were on patrol. He also had to recover the first wave of aircraft returning from Midway.

On receiving the news of the U.S. ships, Nagumo ordered a change of course northeastward toward them. This helped him avoid the first wave of dive-bombers from the U.S. carriers. And when three successive waves of slow-moving torpedo-bombers attacked between 0930 and 1024, Japanese fighters or antiaircraft guns downed forty-seven of fifty-one. The Japanese now believed they were victorious.

But two minutes later, thirty-seven American dive-bombers from carrier *Enterprise,* almost out of fuel from searching for the Japanese ships, swooped down on the Japanese carriers from an altitude of 19,000 feet. The attack caught the Japanese by surprise and was without opposition because the Japanese fighters that had shot down the third wave of U.S. torpedo-bombers were all down low and had no chance to climb and counterattack.

The Japanese carriers had ordnance on their decks, and Nagumo's flagship *Akagi* was hit by bombs that exploded many of the torpedoes topside. Soon the crew was forced to abandon ship. Carrier *Kaga* suffered bomb hits that caused it to sink that evening. A third carrier, *Soryu*, sustained three hits by half-ton bombs from *Yorktown*'s dive-bombers that had just arrived on the scene, and was abandoned within twenty minutes.

Thus the final debacle was the result of good fortune on the American side, the uncoordinated concentration of the dive-bombers hitting the Japanese carriers at just the right moment. Except for those six minutes, Nagumo and the Japanese would have won the battle.

The only intact Japanese fleet carrier in Nagumo's force, *Hiryu*, now struck back at *Yorktown*, damaging it so badly that it eventually had to be abandoned. *Yorktown* was already weakened by the hastily repaired damage sustained in the Battle of the Coral Sea. But twenty-four U.S. dive-bombers, ten of them from *Yorktown*, caught the fourth Japanese carrier in the late afternoon and damaged it to the point that it was abandoned early the next day.

Spruance and Nimitz were the men most responsible for the victory. Yamamoto was the Japanese commander most responsible for the defeat. As with Pearl Harbor, he had conceived the idea and forced it on the naval general staff. On learning of the disaster, he brought up his battleships and recalled the two light carriers from the Aleutians in hopes of a more conventional sea fight. But the loss of the fourth carrier and Nagumo's gloomy reports caused him to break off the battle. He still hoped to trap the Americans by drawing their ships westward, but Spruance refused to take the bait, although he did launch further air attacks.

Meanwhile, the Japanese attack on the Aleutians had gone forward as planned on June 3, but did little damage, thanks to clouds obscuring the ground at Dutch Harbor. A second attack the next day was slightly more successful. Then on June 5 the carriers were called southward. On June 7, however, the small Japanese invasion force landed on Kiska and Attu. Although Japanese propaganda made much of this success, the islands were barren and entirely unsuited for air or naval bases.

Ironically, the attack on Dutch Harbor provided an intelligence bonanza for the United States. A Japanese Zero aircraft that had crash-landed on a small island east of Dutch Harbor on June 3 was later discovered by the Americans virtually intact, its pilot dead. The plane was then repaired, studied, and put through flight tests that revealed its strengths and weaknesses. The Grumman F6F Hellcat, about to come on line, outclassed the Zero in almost every respect.

Midway, a crushing defeat, was kept secret from the Japanese people. Japan lost four fleet carriers—*Akagi, Kaga, Hiryu, Soryu*—and some 332 aircraft, most of which went down with the carriers, as well as heavy cruiser *Mikuma*. Several other ships were damaged. The Japanese had also lost 5,000 men. The Americans lost only carrier *Yorktown* and destroyer *Hammann*, 179 aircraft, and some three hundred men; there was also some bomb damage to Midway and Dutch Harbor.

The original flaws of the Japanese strategic plan were multiplied by tactical errors: the failure to fly enough search planes to look for the U.S. carriers; the lack of sufficient fighter cover at high altitude; poor fire precautions; striking with planes from all four carriers, which meant that all would have to rearm and refit at the same time, a period in which they would all be especially vulnerable. The loss of so many highly trained aircrews was a body blow for Japan. The Imperial Japanese Navy would never regain its ascendancy. Once the Japanese had lost four fleet carriers and their well-trained aircrews, their preponderance in battleships and cruisers counted for little. These ships could safely venture only where they could be covered by land-based aircraft. The subsequent Japanese defeat in the long struggle for Guadalcanal was principally due to lack of air control. The Battle of Midway provided the Americans an invaluable breathing space until, at the end of 1942, the new *Essex*-class fleet carriers began to enter the fleet.

Thus it can be reasonably said that the Battle of Midway was the turning point in the Pacific war and spelled the ultimate doom of Japan. In Nimitz's words, "Midway was the most crucial battle of the Pacific War, the engagement that made everything else possible."

FURTHER READINGS
Barker, A. J. *Midway: The Turning Point* (1971).

Fuchida Mitsuo, and Masatake Okumiya. *Midway, the Battle That Doomed Japan: The Japanese Navy's Story* (1955).

Morison, Samuel Eliot. *History of United States Naval Operations in World War II*. Vol. 4, *Coral Sea, Midway, and Submarine Actions* (1949).

Prange, Gordon W., with Donald M. Goldstein and
Katherine V. Dillon. *Miracle at Midway* (1982).

Spencer C. Tucker

SEE ALSO Coral Sea, Battle of the; Nagumo Chuichi;
Spruance, Raymond Ames; Yamamoto Isoroku

Mikawa Gunichi

This "gentle and soft-spoken" admiral was best known as
the victor of the Battle of Savo Island. During the surprise
attack on Pearl Harbor he commanded Japan's support
force, which consisted of the 3d Battleship Division (*Hiei,
Kirishima*) and the Eighth Cruiser Division (*Abukuma,
Chikuma, Tone*).

In mid-1942 Mikawa commanded the Eighth Fleet,
which consisted of five heavy cruisers (*Aoba, Chokai, Furutaka, Kako, Kinugasa*), two light cruisers (*Tenryu, Yubari*), and one destroyer (*Yunagi*) operating out of Rabaul.
At Savo Island he sortied for Guadalcanal the same day
the Americans landed there—August 7, 1942. He led his
troops from his flagship *Chokai*, rather from shore as his
superiors urged. Mikawa spent August 8 under way, planning a night attack in order to avoid U.S. carrier-based
aircraft and to play to Japanese strength in that tactic.
Unknown to him, the overall Allied commander, Admiral
Frank Fletcher, had withdrawn his carriers earlier that day.
Although spotted three times before closing with the Allied warships covering the landing, Mikawa was able to
close with the enemy unmolested.

The Allied force of cruisers and destroyers protecting
the landing, under Admiral V. A. C. Crutchley of the
Royal Navy, suffered from severe disorganization. Just after midnight on August 9, Mikawa slipped into the Allies'
midst unnoticed. At 0136 hours he gave the order to
commence fire. With the Allied ships silhouetted by flares
dropped by their float planes, the Japanese ships let loose
with torpedo and gun fire. At one point Mikawa's force
was split in two by a navigational error. But what in any
other circumstance would have been a tactical mistake
proved only to make matters worse for the U.S. ships
flanked on both sides. In quick succession cruisers HMAS
Canberra, USS *Astoria*, USS *Quincy*, and USS *Vincennes*
were all hit and in various stages of sinking. Cruiser USS
Chicago was also hit, and although it did not sink, the
captain committed suicide.

By 0220 hours, Mikawa, understandably satisfied with
his forty minutes' work, ordered the Eighth Fleet to regroup northwest of Savo Island. There he prepared for
the final assault on the now defenseless transports. At
0240 hours Mikawa, fearing that U.S. carrier planes
would attack at daylight, decided to return to Rabaul in-

stead. His only loss occurred on the return trip, when the
U.S. submarine S-44 torpedoed and sank *Kako* the day
after the battle. However, Savo Island represented the
U.S. Navy's worst defeat in its history in anything close
to a fair fight. And if Mikawa had known that Fletcher
had pulled out his carriers, he could have massacred the
unprotected transports, endangering the Guadalcanal
landing in its infancy.

Mikawa later led the Eighth Fleet in bombardment
raids against the U.S. ground troops on Guadalcanal and
Henderson Field. He also commanded a poorly planned
and undersized assault against 7,500 Australians and
1,300 Americans building an airstrip at Milne Bay in eastern New Guinea. On August 25, the first 1,500 Japanese
marines and naval engineers landed nearby. After being
reinforced by another 800 men, they attacked the Allies
on September 1. These assaults failed, and the Japanese
were pursued by the Australian infantry. Mikawa approved evacuation of the 1,300 remaining troops on September 6. (He was obviously a better commander at sea
than on land.)

Admiral Mikawa also led the Southwest Area Force
during the Battle of Leyte Gulf. His force included units
commanded by Admirals Sakonju and Shima but saw little action. Mikawa survived the war.

FURTHER READINGS

Newcomb, Richard. *Savo: The Incredible Naval Debacle
off Guadalcanal* (1961).

Robert Kirchubel

SEE ALSO Navy, Japanese; Savo Island, Battle of

Miles, Milton E. (1900–1961)

Milton E. Miles was deputy commander of the Sino-
American Cooperative Organization (SACO), a combined intelligence and guerrilla-warfare unit consisting of
3,000 U.S. Navy personnel and 100,000 Chinese. These
forces, ranging from Indochina and the China coast to
the Gobi Desert, provided vital weather and intelligence
data.

Born in Jerome, Arizona, in 1900, Miles graduated in
1922 from the U.S. Naval Academy and was assigned to
the China station at Hong Kong, where he served until
1927. He completed several tours as an electrical engineering officer and in 1939 commanded a destroyer.

In April 1942, Miles was sent to Chungking as a naval
observer, but he had secret orders to establish a system of
coast watchers to support the Pacific Fleet and prepare
for future amphibious landings. He worked with Nationalist Chinese General Tai Li to organize SACO, with Tai

Li as its director and Miles as deputy director. Miles commanded the U.S. Naval Group China, consisting of the American trainers and advisers in SACO. At the beginning of 1943, director of the Office of Strategic Services (OSS) William J. Donovan, who sought a presence in China, placed his organization within SACO and asked Miles to coordinate its activities.

Miles was a close friend and confidant of General Tai Li, who headed Chiang Kai-shek's Bureau of Investigation and Statistics, a huge espionage organization in both free and occupied China. In exchange for Tai Li's help in setting up camps to train Chinese for guerrilla action against the Japanese, Miles shared his portion of the China-Burma-India theater's meager supplies. At war's end, SACO was operating ten training camps with navy instructors and OSS technicians teaching demolition, communications, and close-combat skills.

The OSS charged Tai Li's agents with assassinations, narcotics smuggling, blackmail, and torture and referred to Tai Li as "the Chinese Himmler." OSS officers wanted to use U.S. bargaining power over control of supplies and weapons to force Tai Li to concentrate more on accomplishing Allied war objectives against the Japanese than on eliminating Chiang Kai-shek's enemies. They also demanded authority to act independently in gathering and evaluating intelligence.

Tai Li wanted to keep secret from the Americans matters that might discredit the Nationalist government. Miles accepted the Kuomintang's anticommunist propaganda and stated his satisfaction with Tai Li's work, which the OSS considered obsolete. After a year of troubled collaboration, Donovan relocated his OSS group to General Claire Chennault's Fourteenth Air Force.

Studies done in the late twentieth century suggested that SACO's principal achievement was to help the Nationalist Chinese prepare for civil war—not that it did them much good. But Miles claimed in his memoirs that his guerrillas, in addition to frequently battling Chinese Communist military units, inflicted significant damage on the Japanese, harassing convoys and raiding supply dumps.

In 1943, Miles's Navy Group set up an intelligence network in Indochina. French naval officer Commander Robert Meynier led this effort using his Vietnamese wife's connections. Meynier's agents kept Miles informed regarding fortifications, troop movements, and bombing targets, as well as local political activity.

After the war, Miles, who was promoted to rear admiral, commanded cruiser divisions of the Atlantic Fleet, the Naval Department in the Panama Canal Zone, and the Third Naval District headquarters in New York City.

In 1958, he retired from the navy with the rank of vice admiral. He died of cancer at the Naval Hospital in Bethesda, Maryland, on March 25, 1961.

FURTHER READINGS

Miles, Milton E. *A Different Kind of War: The Little-Known Story of the Combined Guerrilla Forces Created in China by the U.S. Navy and the Chinese during World War II* (1967).

O'Toole, G. J. A. *The Encyclopedia of American Intelligence and Espionage: From the Revolutionary War to the Present* (1988).

Spector, Ronald H. *Eagle against the Sun: The American War with Japan* (1985).

Camille Dean

SEE ALSO Chiang Kai-shek; Chinese Communists versus Nationalists; Office of Strategic Services in the Pacific

Mitscher, Marc Andrew (1887–1947)

One of America's premier fast-carrier leaders and commander of Task Force 58 (38), Marc Andrew "Pete" Mitscher was born in Hillsboro, Wisconsin, on January 26, 1887, and grew up in Washington, D.C. Mitscher received an appointment to the U.S. Naval Academy from Oklahoma, where his father had been an Indian agent. An average student with a penchant for wild escapades that earned him the nickname "Oklahoma Pete," he graduated in 1910. He served aboard armored cruiser *Colorado* in the Pacific, briefly aboard battleship *South Dakota*, and on gunboats *Vicksburg* and *Annapolis* in the Caribbean before being commissioned as an ensign in 1912. Mitscher was then assigned to armored cruiser *California* (1913–1915, renamed *San Diego* in 1914) and briefly served aboard destroyers *Whipple* and *Stewart*.

He reported to Pensacola, Florida, in October 1915 for flight training, received his wings in June 1916, and after additional flight training was made lieutenant (junior grade) in April 1917. He served on convoy escort until October and then spent the rest of World War I at three naval air stations, commanding two of them. He was transferred to the Aviation Section in the Office of the Chief of Naval Operations in February 1919 and received the Navy Cross in 1919 for piloting one of three flying boats across the Atlantic Ocean in the first transatlantic air crossing. He moved to California in the fall of 1919 to serve aboard a converted aircraft tender and in December 1920 became commander of the naval air detachment in San Diego. Promoted to lieutenant commander in

1921, Mitscher commanded the Naval Air Station Anacostia in Washington, D.C. (1922–1925), where he worked on experimental aircraft, and also served with the Plans Division of the Bureau of Aeronautics. He led the navy flight teams at the International Air Races in 1922 and 1923.

After serving aboard the first U.S. Navy aircraft carrier, *Langley*, in the Pacific in 1926, Mitscher later that year helped to prepare the giant new carrier *Saratoga*. When *Saratoga* was commissioned in 1927, he became its air officer and landed the first aircraft on its flight deck. He served briefly back aboard *Langley* as executive officer (1929–1930), before returning with the rank of commander to the Bureau of Aeronautics (1930–1933). Mitscher worked as chief of staff to the Base Force Air Commander aboard seaplane tender *Wright* in the Pacific (1933–1934) and as executive officer of *Saratoga* (1934–1935). He then served again at the Bureau of Aeronautics in charge of the Flight Division (1935–1937). In 1937, Mitscher became skipper of *Wright* and was promoted to captain in 1938. In November 1938, he assumed command of Patrol Wing One at San Diego until his appointment as assistant chief of the Bureau of Aeronautics in June 1939.

Assigned to new carrier *Hornet* in July 1941, Mitscher oversaw its commissioning in October and was promoted to rear admiral just three days before the Japanese attack on Pearl Harbor. James Doolittle's famous raid on Tokyo in April 1942 was launched from Mitscher's *Hornet,* and Mitscher captained the carrier during the pivotal Battle of Midway. Shortly after the battle, Mitscher commanded Patrol Wing Two at naval air station Kaneohe, Hawaii, and in December was made commander of Fleet Air at Nouméa. In April 1943, as air commander at Guadalcanal, he led navy, army, marine, and New Zealand air units in the Solomon Island campaign. He returned to the West Coast in August to command fleet air units.

In January 1944, Mitscher became commander of Carrier Division Three and Fast Carrier Task Force 58 (or 38, depending on whether Admiral Raymond A. Spruance or William F. Halsey was in command). As Task Force commander, he led the attacks on the Marshall, Truk, and Mariana Islands and on New Guinea. Promoted to vice admiral in March 1944, Mitscher in June led U.S. carrier forces to victory in the Battle of the Philippine Sea (also known as the "Great Marianas Turkey Shoot"). During the battle, he saved the lives of numerous air crewmen by turning on his ships' lights at night to guide the planes, low on fuel, home in the dark.

In August, he was named commander of the First Fast Carrier Force Pacific (TF 38) and fought in the Battle of Leyte Gulf in October 1944, destroying the Japanese decoy carrier force. He was on leave from November 1944 to January 1945, when he returned to command TF 58. His force supported the landings on Iwo Jima in February and on Okinawa in April, and he directed the U.S. victory in the Battle of the East China Sea in April, sinking most of the remainder of the Japanese surface fleet. However, his forces suffered heavily in the Japanese kamikaze attacks in April–June 1945.

Mitscher returned to Washington in July 1945 as deputy chief of Naval Operations (Air). Promoted to admiral in March 1946, he commanded Eighth Fleet, Atlantic. In September, he was made commander in chief of the Atlantic Fleet in Norfolk, Virginia, and died there while on active duty on February 3, 1947.

A physically small man who avoided publicity, Mitscher was regarded with great respect, even love, by his men. He was a great tactical and operational carrier commander, one of America's finest. Although he was calm and capable in battle, the strain of the war eroded his health, and he probably suffered a mild heart attack in the spring of 1945.

FURTHER READINGS
Reynolds, Clark G. *The Fast Carriers: The Forging of an Air Navy* (1978).
Taylor, Theodore. *The Magnificent Mitscher* (1954).
Van Deurs, George. *Wings for the Fleet* (1966).
Laura Matysek Wood

SEE ALSO Aircraft Carriers: Japanese, U.S., and British; Navy, U.S.

Mountbatten, Louis (1900–1979)

Louis Francis Albert Victor Nicholas Battenberg was born at Frogmore House, Windsor, on June 25, 1900, to Prince Louis of Battenberg (later Lord Milford Haven) and Princess Victoria of Hesse-Darmstadt, granddaughter of Queen Victoria. He started his naval education as a cadet at Osbourne Naval Training College in 1913–1914 and then continued at Dartmouth and the Royal Naval College at Keyham, from which he graduated first in his class in June 1916. His first posting was to Admiral David Beatty's flagship, *Lion* (1916–1917). He then served as a midshipman aboard battleship *Queen Elizabeth* (1917–1918) and finished World War I as a lieutenant aboard a P-boat (coastal torpedo boat). During World War I, Louis's father, who had achieved high office in the Admiralty, changed the family name to Mountbatten in order to lessen the prejudice against their German heritage but was still forced to resign from the Royal Navy, the victim of a fit of anti-German hysteria. (The royal family also changed its name at this time from Saxe-Coburg to Windsor.)

After the war, Mountbatten attended Cambridge University and was chosen president of the Cambridge Union. He then went on a 2-year tour (1920–1922) of Australia, Japan, and India with the Prince of Wales, who was his cousin and friend. In 1923, he served aboard battle cruiser *Revenge* and in 1925 graduated first in his class from Signals school. Because of his skill with the radio, Mountbatten became assistant fleet wireless officer (1927–1928) and then fleet wireless officer in the Mediterranean (1931–1933). He was promoted to commander in 1932. Mountbatten then commanded destroyers *Daring* (1932–1934) and *Wishart* (1934–1936). His advice was sought by his royal relatives during the crisis over King Edward VIII's abdication, and then he was assigned to the Naval Air Division of the Admiralty in London (1936–1939), where he helped the Admiralty gain control over the Fleet Air Arm, just in time for World War II. For his service, he was promoted to captain in 1937. In 1938, he received command of new destroyer *Kelly* and oversaw its completion and launch in 1939.

After the outbreak of war, Mountbatten, aboard *Kelly*, was named commander of Destroyer Flotilla 5. He oversaw the evacuation of the duke and duchess of Windsor from the Continental mainland that same month. His service aboard *Kelly* was not ideal: The ship nearly capsized early on, came close to ramming another destroyer, and was torpedoed twice and mined once. In June 1940, he earned distinction during the evacuation of Namsos in Norway. *Kelly* was sunk during the evacuation of Crete in May 1941, and Mountbatten subsequently commanded new carrier *Illustrious,* which was in the United States being repaired. He used his time during the repairs to tour the States and make important contacts among the military. In October 1941, he was promoted to commodore and by the end of the month was adviser for Combined Operations to the chiefs of staff back in London. Winston Churchill had pushed hard for Mountbatten's promotion, and the princeling vaulted over many more experienced sailors. As head of Combined Operations Headquarters (COHQ), Mountbatten had control over a broad and ill-defined area; he was responsible for coordinating and overseeing interservice operations, including planning, intelligence, training, and communications. He worked hard to improve Great Britain's amphibious warfare capabilities, particularly in securing landing craft. He also helped develop the "mulberry," or artificial harbors, used so effectively later at Normandy,

and the PLUTO (Pipe-Line Under the Ocean) project. COHQ carried out a variety of raids on the European mainland and helped lay the groundwork for the future invasion. Unfortunately, in April 1942, COHQ was urged to launch an operation against the French coastline. The raid on Dieppe showed the numerous problems that could plague a large amphibious operation against the mainland of Europe. Mountbatten made mistakes (which he always denied), but much of the problem lay in the chiefs of staff's inability to decide whether the operation was a raid or an invasion; in addition, he had little control over the air support or composition of his forces.

In August 1943, Mountbatten attended the Quebec Conference with Churchill and soon afterward was promoted, again over senior officers, to be supreme Allied commander for Southeast Asia, the only theater during the war with a Brit in overall command. Mountbatten directed Allied operations in the China-Burma-India area, and he faced a tough dilemma, because U.S. and British interests in the area were not always the same, particularly in relation to the liberation of China. Mountbatten, responsible to both governments, had to try to balance operations to please the needs of both nations. This job was made more difficult by the fact that Mountbatten's deputy supreme commander was the acerbic U.S. General Joseph Stilwell. With General Sir William Slim, Mountbatten oversaw the liberation of Burma. He also accepted the Japanese surrender in Southeast Asia, liberated prisoners of war, and revealed the awful conditions to which they had been subjected.

In the immediate postwar period, Mountbatten was in charge of reestablishing British colonial authority in Southeast Asia and was given expanded responsibility for Indochina and Indonesia. Personally, Mountbatten believed that British colonial rights were anachronistic, as well as doomed (for which opinions he was considered in some more conservative quarters as "something of a Bolshie"), but he used his personal prestige and familial ties to the royal family to help maintain a dignified and respected British presence. He hoped that by being open to local leaders, Britain might gain allies for the future.

Mountbatten's command in Southeast Asia ended in 1946, and he hoped to return to service in the navy. He became a viscount in 1946. Prime Minister Clement Attlee, however, asked Mountbatten to serve as viceroy to India in 1947. Reluctantly, Mountbatten agreed; he was the perfect choice because he not only had experience in Southeast Asia but also was a relative of the king-emperor of India and the Indian princes felt they could relate to this aristocrat. Mountbatten would encourage and oversee the withdrawal of Great Britain from the Subcontinent in 1947, thus serving as the last viceroy. He was made Earl Mountbatten of Burma in 1947. From September 1947 until June 1948, he served as governor-general of newly independent India and helped to divide the Subcontinent into India and Pakistan by settling disputes between Muslims and Hindus. He served as fourth sea lord (1950–1952) and commander in chief of the Mediterranean fleet (1952–1954). In 1953, he was promoted to admiral and in 1954 worked within the North Atlantic Treaty Organization. Mountbatten then reached the pinnacle of his naval career when in 1955 he became first sea lord (a post his father had been denied during World War I because of anti-German sentiments) and in 1956 was promoted to admiral of the fleet. In July 1959, he became chief of the United Kingdom Defence Staff and chairman of the Chiefs of Staff Committee and served until his retirement in 1965. He then was appointed to the largely ceremonial post of governor of the Isle of Wight, and in 1974 he was made lord lieutenant of the island. After his retirement from the service, Mountbatten became a roving ambassador for Great Britain and a good one; with his prestige, royal blood, large network of friends, and ability to think and act independently, he proved a great asset for the government. He also acted as an unofficial adviser to the royal family, since he had helped to raise Prince Philip and then introduced him to the future queen. On August 27, 1979, Mountbatten, along with his grandson Nicholas, was killed by an Irish Republican Army bomb planted aboard his yacht in Donegal Bay, Ireland.

Charming, generous, warmhearted, tolerant, resilient, courageous, and absolutely self-assured, "Dicky" Mountbatten relished responsibility and proved capable of gaining results in almost any job he held. Although not a great thinker, Mountbatten had a great ability to set a goal, figure out what he needed to do to achieve it, and then drive relentlessly until he had.

FURTHER READINGS

Donnison, F. S. V. *British Military Administration in the Far East* (1956).

Ziegler, Philip. *Mountbatten* (1985).

Laura Matysek Wood

SEE ALSO Burma; Navy, Royal

Mukden Incident

On the night of September 18, 1931, a bomb explosion destroyed 3 feet of rail on the South Manchuria Railway just outside the Manchurian city of Mukden. A patrol of soldiers under Lieutenant Kawamoto Suemori of Japan's Kwantung Army then claimed to have been ambushed while investigating the explosion; under this pretext, 500 Japanese troops quickly attacked and overran a nearby barracks compound housing 10,000 Chinese soldiers. Fighting did not end there. By noon of the next day, the Japanese army had seized all military installations around Mukden and several other Manchurian towns and cities besides.

Japanese Prime Minister Wakatsuki Reijiro and Foreign Minister Shidehara Kijuro were taken by surprise and pressed the Japanese military and the Kwantung Army to take no further aggressive actions. The military leadership followed a completely different course, giving the Kwantung Army full authority to take whatever action it believed necessary. As a result, with the help of the Japanese Korean army moving into Manchuria to assist, and with the Mukden Incident as a justification, the Kwantung Army defeated local Manchurian forces many times their number, quickly conquering the vast provinces of Manchuria. By February 5, 1932, Japanese troops had reached all the way to Harbin, near the Soviet border. Once military control had been established, the Kwantung Army engineered the creation of Manchukuo, a Japanese puppet state. Spiriting Henry Pu-yi, former heir to the Chinese throne, out of the Chinese city of Tientsin, the Japanese proclaimed the founding of Manchukuo on March 9, 1932, with Henry Pu-yi as its purely ceremonial head of state. Manchukuo was to form with Japan "a self-sufficient economic unit," in other words, a colony.

The entire incident—from the rapid defeat of Chinese forces in the region to the creation of a Manchurian state under Japanese control—was the handiwork of a group of the Kwantung Army's junior officers, led by Colonel Itagaki Seishiro and Lieutenant Colonel Ishihara Kanji. Carefully crafting an elaborate and audacious plan to conquer all of Manchuria, these men worked, it appears, without the knowledge or participation of their commanding officer, Honjo Shigeru, and the Japanese government, which intended to take a much more moderate line with China in Manchuria.

Despite this, the officers of the Kwantung Army were encouraged by the reception their decisive action in Mukden received in Japan after the fact. They had hoped through their coup to replace Japan's relatively liberal, internationalist foreign policy of the 1920s with one much more confrontational and expansionist, regardless of the objections of world opinion. In this, they succeeded completely. Under the twin pressures of the Great Depression and the growth of radical, militarist nationalism, the Japanese civilian government was incapable of reining in the Kwantung Army's belligerent junior officers. Sensationalist newspaper and newsreel coverage of Japanese military successes electrified public opinion, and the principle of civilian control over the armed forces was seriously undermined.

World reaction to the Japanese conquest of Manchuria was passively disapproving. The Chinese public was outraged by Japanese actions, but the Chinese government was too weak and China itself too divided to resist effectively. The Chinese government did not even break off diplomatic relations with Japan, let alone declare war, despite fierce fighting between Chinese and Japanese troops far to the south in Shanghai. Instead, China appealed for assistance to the League of Nations, which would prove unable to act quickly or decisively.

The Soviet Union was the state besides China most threatened by the Japanese occupation of Manchuria. In addition to beginning a massive military buildup, strengthening its defenses in the Far East, and creating a new Pacific fleet on April 21, 1932, the Soviet government worked simultaneously to appease Japan and to avoid any cause for conflict. Offering a nonaggression pact to Japan, the Soviet Union would eventually sell its stake in the Chinese Eastern Railway; running through Manchuria, it was a constant irritant in Soviet-Japanese relations.

The United States and Great Britain, also disturbed by Japanese expansionism, were unwilling and unable to do much to stop it, letting the League of Nations (of which the United States was not a member) investigate the matter as a means of avoiding action. U.S. President Herbert Hoover and Secretary of State Henry Stimson considered imposing economic sanctions on Japan but had to be satisfied with the League of Nations' October 1931 condemnation of Japanese conduct. Though not recognizing the formation of Manchukuo, the United States did not attempt military pressure to curb Japanese expansionism. Great Britain, fearing for its colonies in the Pacific, ventured little more than diplomatic protests against the Japanese actions.

In Japan itself, the Mukden Incident and its consequences were another fateful step on the road away from civilian control of the military and toward the solution of foreign-policy problems by force, as Japan withdrew from the League of Nations and found itself diplomatically isolated. Wakatsuki's government collapsed in December 1931; his replacement, Inukai Tsuyoshi, was assassinated by military extremists on May 15, 1932, marking the end of party government in Imperial Japan.

FURTHER READINGS

Iriye, Akira. *The Origins of the Second World War in Asia and the Pacific* (1987).

Thorne, Christopher. *The Limits of Foreign Policy: The West, the League, and the Far Eastern Crisis of 1931–1933* (1972).

Yoshihashi, Takehiko. *Conspiracy at Mukden: The Rise of the Japanese Military* (1963).

David Stone

SEE ALSO Army, Japanese; Chiang Kai-shek

N

Nagasaki

See Atomic Bomb, Decision to Use against Japan

Nagumo Chuichi (1887–1944)

A Japanese naval officer who played a major role in Japanese naval air operations from 1941 through late 1942, Chuichi Nagumo was commander in chief of the Japanese navy's elite carrier striking force. In that capacity, he commanded the carrier task force that attacked Pearl Harbor and participated in the Japanese navy's Southern Operations, the Battle of Midway, and the Guadalcanal campaign. In 1944, he was assigned to command the Fourth Fleet in the defense of the Mariana Islands. On July 6, 1944, he died on Saipan, during the closing phase of the invasion of that island by U.S. amphibious forces.

Nagumo graduated from Japan's Naval Academy in 1908. He was recognized as an expert in torpedo warfare, having been both a student and a teacher of the subject (he was appointed president of the Naval Torpedo College in 1937). Although Nagumo had no prior training or experience in aviation, he was appointed commander in chief of the newly organized First Air Fleet in April 1941. The First Air Fleet at that time consisted of five aircraft carriers, with their air groups and escort destroyers. It was significantly strengthened toward the close of 1941 with the addition of new fleet carriers *Shokaku* and *Zuikaku.*

At the opening of hostilities, Nagumo commanded the carrier task force that attacked the U.S. Pacific Fleet based at Pearl Harbor on the Hawaiian island of Oahu. During the planning and preparations for the attack, the commander in chief of the Combined Fleet, Admiral Isoroku Yamamoto, had considered the possibility of withdrawing Nagumo from this operation because the latter showed little confidence in its success and often voiced his reservations. Although Nagumo carried out the operation ac-

cording to plan, he was criticized for failing to exploit the surprise attack by not launching a follow-up air strike to destroy Pearl Harbor's naval facilities and do further damage to the Pacific Fleet. Admiral Matome Ugaki, the Combined Fleet's chief of staff, in commenting on Nagumo's actions in the Hawaiian operation stated, "He was like a robber fleeing the scene, happy with small booty."

During the remainder of the first phase of the Japanese offensive, Nagumo participated in the Southern Operations. His carriers launched large air strikes against air bases and ports in New Guinea, the Netherlands, East Indies, Australia, and Ceylon. His striking force inflicted considerable damage on shipping and port facilities and sank a number of Allied warships, including elderly British aircraft carrier *Hermes* and heavy cruisers *Cornwall* and *Dorsetshire.*

Twice during the Southern Operations, Nagumo was compelled to divert his task force in an effort to intercept U.S. carrier task forces that had attacked the Japanese-held Marshall Islands (February 1942) and the Japanese home islands (the Doolittle raid in April 1942). In each instance, his efforts proved futile.

As commander in chief of the First Air Fleet and, later, the Third Fleet, Nagumo participated in three carrier-versus-carrier battles. In the first, the Battle of Midway, Nagumo's striking force was soundly defeated. All four of the fleet carriers under his command were sunk by U.S. Navy carrier dive-bombers. Nagumo was criticized as being indecisive and having made judgmental errors at critical points in this battle. Admiral Yamamoto did not relieve Nagumo of his command, even though the defeat at Midway had severely and irreparably weakened the Combined Fleet's naval air arm. Nagumo continued to command the Combined Fleet's carrier striking force, which was reorganized and redesignated the Third Fleet in July 1942.

In the second carrier battle in which he participated, the Battle of the Eastern Solomons, Nagumo was again defeated. His carrier striking force failed to destroy or significantly weaken U.S. air and naval power in the vicinity of Guadalcanal Island. His carrier air groups had only moderately damaged carrier *Enterprise,* while U.S. troops sank light carrier *Ryujo* and prevented a Japanese troop convoy from landing reinforcements on Guadalcanal.

In the third carrier battle, the Battle of the Santa Cruz Islands, Nagumo won a tactical victory when his carrier air groups sank carrier *Hornet* and seriously damaged carrier *Enterprise.* Yet his carrier forces were substantially weakened: Two carriers were badly damaged, and his air groups suffered heavy losses. Furthermore, he drew criticism for departing from the operational plan in his effort to avoid detection by Allied reconnaissance aircraft.

Soon after the close of the Battle of the Santa Cruz Islands, Nagumo was replaced by Vice Admiral Jisaburo Ozawa as commander in chief of the Third Fleet. Nagumo was appointed commandant of the Sasebo Naval District. In 1944, he was appointed commander in chief of the Fourth Fleet, a small area fleet charged with defending the Mariana Islands. When the Allies launched an amphibious assault on the Marianas, Nagumo was headquartered on the island of Saipan. As the invasion of that island was nearing its conclusion, Nagumo took his own life.

Admiral Nagumo became a tragic and ironic figure in his role as commander in chief of Japan's carrier forces during the first year of the war. Several of his colleagues contended that he lacked aggressiveness and was overly cautious and indecisive. They even questioned his courage and competence and showed little sympathy that he was put into a command position for which he was ill prepared and, probably, ill suited. Furthermore, they gave him little credit for his carrier forces' accomplishments during the first five months of the war, accomplishments that made Nagumo, for all his faults, the most successful admiral in Japan's World War II navy.

FURTHER READINGS

Fuchida, Mitsuo. *Midway: The Battle That Doomed Japan* (1955).
Lundstrom, John B. *The First Team and the Guadalcanal Campaign* (1994).
Prange, Gordon W. *At Dawn We Slept* (1981).

George H. Curtis

SEE ALSO Coral Sea, Battle of the; Midway, Battle of; Navy, Japanese; Pearl Harbor, Japanese Attack on

Nanking, "Rape" of

One of the most appalling atrocities of the Sino-Japanese War (1937–1945), the "rape" of Nanking came in the course of Japan's drive into the interior of China in the fall of 1937. Having taken the port city of Shanghai, the Imperial Japanese Army drove on to the Nationalist capital that December. Despite assertions by Nationalist President Chiang Kai-shek's generals that the city would be defended "to the last man," a Chinese army of 100,000 was routed in only four days; the city was in Japanese hands by December. The events that followed galvanized anti-Japanese sentiment in most of the world and ignited a historical controversy that continues today.

The horrors that subsequently befell the civilian population of Nanking were evidently sanctioned by Lieutenant General Prince Asaka Yasuhiko. Because of the Chinese refusal to heed Japanese leaflets demanding complete submission, orders were issued demanding "harsh and relentless" treatment of all Chinese. An atmosphere conducive to brutality had developed even as Imperial troops advanced into the city. Among the war news carried by Japanese newspapers was the story of two junior officers who had begun a contest to be the first to kill 100 Chinese. One of the contestants described the killing as "fun" but conceded that "one must indulge in a hearty massacre to be satisfied." Follow-up stories the next week reported that because neither of the two officers was certain who had first reached the goal of 100 kills, the goal had been extended to 150. It was not a good omen for the people of Nanking.

Some fifty thousand triumphant Japanese troops entered the city behind General Matsui Iwane, a figure associated with the traditional restraint expected of the Imperial Army. Also prominent in the victory parade, however, was Colonel Hashimoto Kingoro, an officer with connections to the younger "superpatriots" who were not averse to more savage methods. As the Japanese victory celebration inside the city continued, several dozen foreign residents organized what they hoped to designate as a "safety zone" for refugees. This hope went unmet, though a Japanese diplomat later conceded that the presence of foreign neutrals may have served to ameliorate somewhat the slaughter that followed. The "rape" of the city proceeded initially as a consequence of specific orders, which directed Japanese soldiers to secure the city, find food and shelter, destroy any industrial or commercial concerns, and eliminate fugitive Chinese soldiers. Accordingly, the first executions were ostensibly grounded in military necessity, but the killings rapidly got out of control as civilians likewise became targets. As the city began to burn as a result of Japanese arson, drunkenness became more commonplace. On December 16, as mass executions accelerated, the first rapes were reported.

The events that transpired over the next several weeks shocked a still relatively naive world. Falling on the helpless populace of Nanking, Japanese troops indulged in an orgy of bloodshed and rape. Making no discrimination as to age or gender, Imperial troops massacred Chinese by means as varied as they were cruel. Western observers reported that hapless victims were murdered individually and in groups, by bullet, bayonet, sword, hand grenades, flaming gasoline, industrial acid, drowning, strangling, live burial, and myriad other savage means. It was reported that even observers from Nazi Germany were appalled at Japanese conduct.

The rape of the city's female population continued unabated until December 31. Though reliable statistics are difficult to come by, contemporary estimates put the number of victims as between eight thousand and twenty thousand. Many were killed after being raped. A final accounting of Chinese deaths in the course of the "rape" of Nanking is also problematic. Chinese authorities numbered the dead at two hundred fifty thousand. Late-twentieth-century research suggested that in Nanking and the immediate environs, upwards of thirty thousand were killed. Physical destruction in and around the city was also extensive.

The most immediate consequence of the "rape" of Nanking was shock and outrage worldwide. More expressions of revulsion came in response to Japanese General Homma Masaharu's description of the conduct of Japanese troops as "not notably inferior" to that of the armies of World War I. Premier Konoe Fumimaro's observation that events in Nanking reflected the "loyalty and courage of the Japanese soldiers" was met with similar disdain. In the United States, Japanese savagery at Nanking was the subject of countless newspaper and periodical-press articles over the next year. The episode did much to catalyze anti-Japanese sentiment in the United States, where the public was already incensed over the Japanese sinking of gunboat USS *Panay* on the Yangtze River in early December 1937. The terrible fate of Nanking made the distant war in China much more immediate for those for whom it had been an abstraction. The *Time-Life-Fortune* journalistic empire of Henry Luce, born to American missionaries in China, was particularly scathing in its depiction of Japanese bestiality in China.

The behavior of Japanese troops at Nanking was a topic of controversy at the time and in later years. There is some evidence that a policy of unrestrained terror and destruction was intentional, with the object of disrupting China's political and industrial development, or at least

shaping such development to correspond to Japan's imperial design. There was, for example, little destruction of industrial resources in north China, which Japan hoped to exploit more directly. In the south, however, especially in the Yangtze basin, destruction and plundering of industrial resources were widespread. The Japanese policy of executing all Chinese prisoners also may have served more immediate military needs, because General Matsui's army could not afford to guard and care for prisoners. Late-twentieth-century studies also noted that this same force was not trained for urban warfare of the type that occurred at Nanking, the result being that the Imperial Army's discipline rapidly broke down in unfamiliar circumstances. Cultural anthropologists suggested that Japanese soldiers, bound by strict social conventions and behavioral codes in Japan, found themselves bereft of moral or ethical guideposts in alien situations and acted without restraint. But none of these explanations could account for the fact that Japanese behavior toward prisoners of war in the Russo-Japanese War and World War I was nearly impeccable.

Following Japan's defeat, the International Military Tribunal for the Far East gave little weight to Japanese justifications for the atrocities in Nanking. Among those sentenced to death for war crimes was General Matsui, who had led the assault on the city.

FURTHER READINGS

Chang, Iris. *The Rape of Nanking: The Forgotten Holocaust of World War II* (1997).

Harries, Meirion, and Susie Harries. *Soldiers of the Sun: The Rise and Fall of the Imperial Japanese Army* (1991).

Ienaga, Saburo. *The Pacific War, 1931–1945* (1978).

Tuchman, Barbara. *Stilwell and the American Experience in China, 1911–45* (1971).

Wilson, Dick. *When Tigers Fight: The Story of the Sino-Japanese War, 1937–1945* (1983).

Blaine T. Browne

SEE ALSO Army, Japanese

National Guard of the United States

During World War II, much of the National Guard of the United States was deployed to the Pacific, where it played a significant role from the first day of the war. By the end of the war, nine of eighteen mobilized Guard divisions had deployed to the Pacific, and a tenth had been created there, mainly from existing Guard units. The Guard also contributed two cavalry regiments; eleven infantry regiments (including the African American multistate 372d Infantry), fifteen nondivisional artillery battalions and three corps artillery headquarters, four engineer regiments and thirteen nondivisional engineer battalions, thirteen coast artillery regiments and twenty-seven coast artillery and antiaircraft battalions, five tank destroyer battalions, and three tank battalions and one tank company. The Guard also was a significant source of officers for non–Guard units, both from prewar officers and from Guard enlisted men commissioned during the war; the most notable in the Pacific was Kenneth Cramer, colonel of Connecticut's 169th Infantry in 1940 and for most of the war a brigadier general and assistant division commander of the regular army's 24th Infantry Division.

The National Guard was called to active duty in late 1940 and early 1941 as part of the U.S. prewar mobilization effort. The Guard had never been funded for full-strength units, it lacked modern equipment, its pre-mobilization training varied widely in quality among units, and many of its officers were too old or unprepared for wartime duties. The Guard shared these characteristics with the regular army, and units of both spent much of 1941 working to overcome these problems. In 1942, Guard units underwent extensive changes as the army adopted new equipment and tactical organizations; these changes split many Guard units into separate battalions and regiments, and greatly changed the structure of the infantry divisions. In addition, many individual Guardsmen left their units to provide cadre for new units, to join the air force, or to accept commissions. These changes, along with the use of draftees in early 1941 to bring units to full strength, often diluted the Guard character of units, but many still retained a strong sense of themselves as a state unit and usually were viewed as such by others. Regular army officers often found themselves replacing Guard officers, especially senior ones, and this did much to inflame traditional Guard–regular army tensions; regular army officers doubted Guardsmen's skills, and Guardsmen resented their condescension.

As American–Japanese relations deteriorated during 1941, the Guard provided a pool of units readily available to reinforce positions in the Pacific. Hawaii's two infantry regiments were assigned to regular army divisions on Oahu; in 1942 these regiments were replaced because of fears that their large numbers of Japanese Americans would prove unreliable. An infantry regiment and two coast artillery regiments were sent to Alaska. New Mexico's 200th Coast Artillery Regiment and two tank battalions (created from Guard divisions' tank companies) were sent to the Philippines, where they played crucial roles in the Bataan campaign—and were lost to a man. Other, more fortunate units en route to the Philippines

on December 7, 1941, were diverted to Australia; a battalion of Texas's 131st Field Artillery was sent to Java, where it was lost, in March 1942.

During 1942, Guard units remained an important source of units available for deployment to the Pacific; a number of units scheduled to go to Great Britain instead found themselves sailing across the Pacific. Three coast artillery and two infantry regiments reinforced Alaska. Guard units deployed to build up U.S. strength in the South Pacific included five infantry divisions—the 32d (Wisconsin/Michigan), 37th (Ohio), 40th (California), 41st (Washington/Oregon/Idaho/Montana), and 43d (New England)—and a number of regiments and battalions of combat and engineer troops. A sixth infantry division, the Americal, was formed in May 1942 on New Caledonia, mainly from Guard units. (The Americal remains the only U.S. Army division never assigned a number.)

These units provided much of the personnel for early army operations, beginning in October 1942 with Washington's 164th Infantry Regiment reinforcing marines on Guadalcanal and the start of the 32d Infantry Division's effort to capture Buna, New Guinea. The battle for Buna dragged on for four months because of terrible terrain, tough Japanese defenses, and inadequate U.S. preparation and leadership at all levels. This leadership failure included a reluctance early in the battle by the 32d's regular army commander, fired during the battle, to relieve senior Guard officers unequal to the task for fear of increasing Guard–regular army tensions.

Some Guard units faced problems similar to the 32d's during their first battles; others, like the 37th Infantry Division, performed well from the start. The 37th's commander, Robert Beightler, was the only Guard division commander to lead his division from mobilization to demobilization, and one of only two prewar Guard generals given general officer commissions in the postwar regular army. In their first battle performances and in subsequent battles, Guard units did not differ much from other components of the army: some units excelled, a few remained problematic, and most developed into solid campaigners. Guard units formed a significant portion of army combat forces in the Solomons and on New Guinea through 1944, and played major roles in the liberation of the Philippines; half of the divisions and many of the nondivisional units used there were Guard.

Though Guard units operated in all parts of the Pacific (including Burma, where Texas's 124th Cavalry Regiment deployed in 1944), most served in either Alaska or the South Pacific because they were available early in the war to fill pressing needs in those areas. The major exception was New York's 27th Infantry Division, which fought across the central Pacific to Okinawa in 1945. Along the way it became entangled not only in the usual Guard–regular army tensions but also in army–marine frictions because this was primarily a navy/marine theater. These frictions first heated up over marine displeasure at the 27th's performance at Makin (1943), and exploded on Saipan (1944) when the V Amphibious Corps commander (a marine) relieved the 27th's commander (a regular army officer) because of what the marine general believed was the poor performance of the 27th. This incident quickly escalated into a major interservice controversy and, thanks to pro–Marine press reports, an ugly public argument that involved marine–army doctrinal differences and questions about the fitness of Guard units for modern war.

The National Guard played a major role in the U.S. war effort in the Pacific. Crucial to U.S. mobilization in 1940–1941, the Guard provided a readily available source of units with which the army could stop the Japanese advance, regain the initiative, and then begin the march to victory. Because of their early heavy use in the Pacific and because the Pacific was a smaller theater than Europe for the army, Guard units played a proportionally greater role in the Pacific than they did in Europe.

FURTHER READINGS

Frankel, Stanley. *The 37th Infantry Division in World War II* (1948).

Goldstein, Donald M. and Katherine V. Dillon. *The Williwaw War* (1992).

Jacobs, Bruce. "Tensions Between the Army National Guard and the Regular Army." *Military Review* (1993).

Kaune, Charles S. "The National Guard in War: An Historical Analysis of the 27th Infantry Division in World War II" (Thesis, U.S. Army Command and General Staff College, 1990).

U.S. Army Office of the Chief of Military History/Center of Military History, *United States Army in World War II*, War in the Pacific volumes.

William M. Donnelly

SEE ALSO Army, U.S.

Nationalist Army, Chinese

The history of the Chinese Nationalist Army began with the Whampoa military academy, which was organized in 1924 near Canton with Soviet funds and was staffed by Soviet advisers. Chiang Kai-shek, the first commandant of the academy, used his personal power base at Wham-

poa to take charge of the Nationalist Army. Following the death of Sun Yat-sen on 12 March 1925, Chiang took a leading role in the Nationalist Party and on June 9, 1926, he officially became the commander in chief of the Nationalist forces. Under Chiang's command, the Northern Expedition was launched on July 7, 1926 to reunite China. By the spring of 1927 all of southern China was under Nationalist military control; in particular, the capture of Shanghai on March 21, 1927, by the Nationalist Army was hailed as a major victory for the Northern Expedition. Tensions rapidly increased between the Nationalists and their Communist allies and on April 5, 1927, Chiang order his troops to disarm all militia in Shanghai who were not members of the Nationalist Army, including many Shanghai Communists. By April 12, this action increased into a full-blown purge that resulted in the massacre of thousands of Communists. With his Soviet advisers ousted and former Chinese Communist allies either killed, imprisoned, or in hiding, Chiang once again began the Northern Expedition in early 1928 and declared the unification of China from his new capital in Nanking on October 10, 1928.

In the 1930s, Chiang turned to Germany for help in training the Nationalist Army. During the course of four major "bandit suppression campaigns," beginning in December 1930 and lasting until 1932, the Nationalists failed to push the Communists from their rural base and exterminate them. During 1933, the Nationalists began their fifth, and final, anti-Communist campaign. With a combined force of sixty divisions—700,000 men—the Nationalist troops began in October 1933 to encircle gradually the Communist-controlled areas, building pillboxes and fortresses as they advanced to establish a blockade. Coordinated with the help of Chiang's German advisers—most notably the military strategist General Hans von Seeckt—the Nationalists forced the Chinese Communists from their base in southern China, and they undertook the "Long March," a 6,000-mile journey, to their new base at Yenan. In January 1935, Mao Tse-tung was made a member of the Politburo Standing Committee, and by the end of Long March he was the unchallenged leader of the Communist Party.

Meanwhile, tensions increased with Japan and on January 28, 1932, Japanese troops engaged Chinese troops from the Nationalist's Nineteenth Route Army in Shanghai. Although the Japanese met stiff resistance from the Nineteenth Army, as well as later from Nanking's modern Fifth Army, after only a month the Chinese forces were dispersed. The Nanking government, fearing a Japanese advance on the capital city, quickly retreated to the inland city of Loyang. An armistice was signed in May 1932, which required Chinese troops to withdraw from Shanghai, and a neutral zone was created around the city. Meanwhile, the Japanese consolidated their control throughout Northern China by creating the puppet state of Manchukuo (Manchuria).

The Nationalists' unexpected reverses once again pushed them into allying with the Communists. Following the "Sian Incident" in December 1936, during which Chiang was kidnapped and temporarily held captive by one of his warlord supporters, talks opened between the Communists and the Nationalists and a second United Front aimed at repelling Japanese aggression was established. Chiang was released on December 25, 1936. The immediate effect of this new alliance was that Chiang called off the sixth anti-Communist suppression campaign, and the attention of the Nationalist army was redirected against Japan.

Japan did not take the renewal of Nationalist-Communist relations lightly. Beginning in July 1937, with the so-called "Marco Polo Bridge Incident," Japanese troops invaded northern China, quickly securing control over Peiping and Tientsin. The Japanese continued to push west and southward, taking Tatung in September, Taiyuan in November, and Tsinan in December 1937. On August 14, 1937, hostilities also erupted in Shanghai, where Chinese troops outnumbered the Japanese ten to one. Chiang helped exacerbate this confrontation when he ordered the Chinese air force to bomb Japanese warships in Shanghai harbor. This aerial attack proved not only to be ineffectual—most of the bombs missed the Japanese ships and hit local civilian areas instead—but it annoyed the Japanese and prompted Tokyo to expand operations into central China.

In Shanghai, Chiang had at his disposal his best troops, the German-trained 87th and 88th divisions. They successfully surrounded and contained the Japanese for three months. But Tokyo sent a total of fifteen divisions to China, and in early November 1937, the Japanese used an amphibious landing at Hangchow Bay, south of Shanghai, to outflank the Nationalist army. The Chinese troops were forced to retreat, and were in such a panic that they failed to hold the defenses at Wuhsi, thus leaving the road to Nanking unguarded. The Nanking government was forced to abandon its capital once again and fled to the inland city of Chungking.

The fall of Nanking in mid-December 1937 led to the massacre of more than two hundred thousand fugitive soldiers and civilians in the aptly named "Rape of Nanking." Following the occupation of Nanking, the Japanese forces controlled all traffic along the Yangtse River. In the midst of their retreat, the Nationalist forces broke the dikes along the Yellow River during June 1938 to slow the Japanese advance. This strategy, while temporarily successful, destroyed thousands of Chinese villages and inflicted incalculable hardship on the Chinese population throughout northern China.

The final events that marked the end of the first phase of the Sino-Japanese war were the fall of Canton on October 21 and the fall of Wuhan on October 25, 1938. During the summer of 1938, the Japanese assembled an enormous assault force, composed of tanks, airplanes, and artillery, and during five brutal months they pounded the Wuhan area. After sustaining an estimated two hundred thousand casualties and the loss of more than a hundred aircraft, the Japanese controlled virtually all of eastern China. Japan's victory was almost exactly two years after Chiang had agreed at Sian to form a second United Front with the Communists.

Throughout the period from 1937 to 1945, the Nationalist and Communist anti-Japanese resistance continued, but they were hampered by their inland locations, which interfered with the transport of weapons, ammunition, and other military supplies. As soon as Chiang reestablished his capital in Chungking, efforts were made to reorganize the Nationalist Army. But Chungking's only link with the outside was the Burma Road, a 715-mile track cut through the steep mountains and gorges of southwest China. Opened in December 1938, this road allowed supplies to be shipped to China from Rangoon, Burma.

In addition to remaining commander in chief of the army and air force, Chiang was made "director-general" of the Kuomintang party during 1938. This move gave him supreme power over the Nationalist government.

In the midst of the Nationalists' forced retreat, the United Front was temporarily strengthened, but by the late 1930s relations between the Nationalists and the Chinese Communist Party began to deteriorate. Because the Nationalists were too weak to undertake an effective counteroffensive against the Japanese, they began to restrict the political activities of the Communists instead. Soon, Chungking outlawed Communist-sponsored organizations and criticized them for not allowing direct Nationalist command over the Communist armies.

Increasing military friction culminated in the "New Fourth Army Incident" of January 1941, when Nationalist and Communist armies clashed. In a week of fighting in early January 1941, an estimated three thousand Communist troops were killed and many others were captured and imprisoned. Although the Nationalists ordered the New Fourth Army to be disbanded, and arrested its commander to be court martialed, the Chinese Communists ignored this order and placed another Communist commander in charge.

With the United State's entry into the Pacific war in late 1941, American military advisers, weapons, and ammunition became more abundant. American economic support for China was most notable, with lend-lease aid increasing from $26 million before the attack on Pearl Harbor (1941) to a total of $1.3 billion by the end of the war; in addition, American credit to China was significant, reaching $500 million. Although China continued to resist Japan, Chiang's forces were still hesitant to fight, because an outright defeat might throw the balance of power toward the Chinese Communists. This situation created tensions between Chiang and his American military adviser, General Joseph Stilwell, who argued that Chiang should end his embargo of the Communist areas and allow the Eighteenth Route Army to fight the Japanese; at any one time, Chiang had 400,000 of his best troops blockading the Communists instead of fighting the Japanese.

At Chiang's insistence, Stilwell was relieved of his command in October 1944 and was replaced by General Albert Wedemeyer. The Nationalist Army, trained and led by American advisers, finally mounted an offensive in the spring and summer of 1945. General Wedemeyer commanded the training and arming of thirty-nine divisions of the Nationalist Army, and by early August 1945 they had retaken Kweilin and were preparing to head southward toward Canton.

Another important American military adviser was Claire Lee Chennault of the U.S. Army Air Forces, who became famous during World War II as the leader of the so-called "Flying Tigers." In August 1941, Chennault organized the American Volunteer Group in China. On July 4, 1942, his Flying Tigers, after inflicting impressive losses on the Japanese with their inferior P-40B fighters, were incorporated into Fourteenth U.S. Air Force. Once the Burma Road was cut, the Flying Tigers provided a vital link with the outside world, ferrying in much needed military supplies and fuel.

Chennault was also in charge of air operations in China. The first American bomber attack against Japan, the famous Doolittle carrier strike, was launched in April 1942. This raid prompted the Japanese to open the East China Campaign to destroy all Nationalist airfields. Thereafter, during the summer of 1943, the Japanese continued to put pressure on southeast China. By early June 1944, however, new airfields east of Chungking were ready and a B-29 raid on Bangkok, Thailand, was their first mission. On June 15, the Allies carried out a large raid on the southern Japanese island of Kyushu and bombed vital Japanese industries. In response to these heavy bomber attacks, the Japanese began a new offensive, called "Operation Ichigo" (Operation Number One). This campaign besieged and destroyed the city of Changsha, which had successfully fought off Japanese troops since 1941. Although the Nationalist forces resisted valiantly, Changsha fell in August 1944. By November 1944, Japanese troops had destroyed the B-29 airfields near Kweilin. The end of the year, however, saw Japan begin withdrawing troops to fight U.S. forces elsewhere in the Pacific.

Arguably only the United States' entry into the Pacific war in late 1941 allowed the Nationalists merely to retain their military position in central China, much less attack and eventually help defeat the Japanese army. At the time of Japan's surrender in August 1945, China was still divided by the Nationalist-Communist fissure, and Nationalist-Communist hostilities were soon renewed. For the remainder of the decade, the Communists, through their People's Liberation Army (PLA), were victorious over the Nationalists. By the fall of 1949, Mao Tse-tung had led the PLA to victory, forcing Chiang to retreat to Taiwan. Mao officially declared a new national government in Peking on October 1, 1949.

FURTHER READINGS
Ayling, Keith. *Old Leatherface of the Flying Tigers: The Story of General Chennault* (1945).
Chang, Iris. *The Rape of Nanking: The Forgotten Holocaust of World War II* (1997).
Chi, Hsi-sheng. *Nationalist China at War: Military Defeats and Political Collapse, 1937–45* (1982).
Dreyer, Edward L. *China at War, 1901–1949* (1995).
Scott, Robert Lee, Jr. *Flying Tiger: Chennault of China* (1959).
Tuchman, Barbara. *Stilwell and the American Experience in China, 1911–45* (1971).
Van Slyke, Lyman P. *Enemies and Friends: The United Front in Chinese Communist History* (1967).
Wilson, Dick. *When Tigers Fight: The Story of the Sino-Japanese War, 1937–1945* (1982).

Bruce A. Elleman

SEE ALSO Burma; Burma Road; Chennault, Claire Lee; Chiang Kai-shek; People's Liberation Army; Stilwell, Joseph Warren; Wedemeyer, Albert Coady

Natives, Pacific Islands

The Pacific war reached many islands and island groups that were strategically located for military purposes. Such locations had been recognized, documented, and written into strategies and tactics years before by planners of the major powers. Some of these islands were deserted, even under water part of the year. Others were inhabited by peoples who had nothing to do with the origins of the Pacific war and did not participate in its course. Caught up in the fight when it came to their homes, they suffered, fought, coped, and persisted through their time in the forward area. They were changed by the war, and they helped to change it as well. Although certain characteristics and experiences were unique to specific groups and places, those of the people of the Solomon Islands, northeast of Australia, may serve to illustrate how the war and the inhabitants of such lands interacted.

Numbering perhaps in the hundreds, the Solomon Islands chain—including the islands of Guadalcanal, Bougainville, Vella Lavella, Santa Isabel, New Georgia, Choiseul, Kolombangara, and Rendova—stretches in a crescent northeast of Australia. Until recently the interiors of some had not been mapped by outsiders. Peoples native to them speak dozens, if not hundreds, of dialects. Unusually insulated by their location, they had little, if any, contact with outsiders until the 1940s: missionaries, adventurers, British colonial residents, miners, treasure hunters, and loners were what they knew of the outside world.

People native to the Solomon Islands have a rich culture, living in harmony with, rather than exploiting, the land and its resources. This led outsiders to believe that the area was ripe for development. Well before World War II, foreign companies established plantations for rubber, copra, and other local products; missionaries established churches; and other ventures, such as mining, began. As the 1930s wore on, the Coastwatchers, a group of observers who were to warn Australian military officials of possible Japanese military moves in the area, joined them. Locals adjusted to outsiders' presence by learning to communicate through a dialect, known as pidgin English, that combined elements of English and native languages; guiding outsiders through the dense jungle; furnishing assistance in the movement of baggage and equipment, overland and by sea; and becoming converts of religious missionaries. Some even joined local constabularies established by British colonial officials. It was a quiet, isolated world almost unknown to the outside, with its own rules, culture, and customs.

The Japanese approach in 1942 changed everything. Most persons not native to the area left as soon as they could, although a few planters and missionaries stayed. Coastwatchers concealed themselves in the jungle. Local inhabitants, unaware of Japanese or Allied military and political goals, served as jungle guides and carried equipment for the Japanese. By thus becoming involved with outsiders, they gained the ability to observe outside forces and keep apprised of their intentions. Living on the front lines, they suffered proportionately; people were killed by ground, air, and sea attacks, both intentionally and unintentionally; villages were wrecked; food supplies and sources were damaged or destroyed; economies and ways of life were shattered.

Both sides vied for the loyalty of local inhabitants. The latter in many cases favored the Allies because of their established relationship and familiarity with the British colonial officials who had been there for years and had exercised a relatively benign "indirect" rule. They furnished intelligence, recovered and returned downed aviators and sailors, and hid Coastwatchers and missionaries. Coastwatchers taught them skills to preserve their effectiveness behind the lines: messages were written in local languages, not English, in case the enemy captured and attempted to read them. Documents carried by canoe were put at the bottom of a basket of stones that could be thrown overboard if the canoe was captured.

Mobilized by Coastwatchers and other Allied behind-the-lines personnel, local inhabitants participated in the fighting, attacking Japanese outposts or taking Japanese fliers prisoner. Such loyalty was linked to the length of Japanese occupation of each particular island. The Allies did not advance to such Solomon Islands at the northwest of the chain as Bougainville, which the Japanese made a determined effort to bring under their control, until November 1943. Japanese commanders there had a much longer time to indoctrinate locals than did those in areas to the southeast, such as Guadalcanal, invaded by the United States a few weeks after the Japanese arrived. Weighing their alternatives, locals in some cases threw in their lot with the Japanese, turning in Coastwatchers and furnishing intelligence to the Japanese, as did some natives on Choiseul (the population of which nonetheless remained largely friendly to the Allies) in October 1942, or attacking villages friendly to the Allies, as some did on Bougainville.

Notable cases in which local inhabitants assisted the Allies or the Japanese were the rescue of the crew of light cruiser USS *Helena,* torpedoed on July 6, 1943, in the Kula Gulf off the coast of Kolombangara; the rescue of Lieutenant J. G. John F. Kennedy's PT-109, sunk August 1 in the Blackett Strait, also off Kolombangara; and the evacuation, by submarine, of a group of Catholic nuns from Bougainville on December 31, 1942. Yet just six months later, the Bougainville populace, despairing of Allied assistance, helped the Japanese drive out the Coast-watchers.

Local inhabitants demonstrated fierce loyalty and stamina in the fight for the Solomons. Sergeant Major Jacob Vouza, a retired police constable, worked with famous Coastwatcher Martin Clemens on Guadalcanal, advising him of Japanese positions and moves. Captured and interrogated, he refused to give away Allied intelligence. Bayoneted, Vouza struggled back to marine positions, where he refused medical treatment until he had given his report. He survived to command a group of locals who guided U.S. Marines through the jungle to attack Japanese units.

Geoffrey Kuper, whose mother had married a German planter on Santa Ana island, ran a Coastwatchers' station on Santa Isabel. Eventually he mobilized the entire island—strategically located almost in the center of The Slot, the body of water between New Guinea and the Solomons, over which numerous air and naval battles were fought—to recover, hide, and return to Allied positions pilots downed in combat.

Serving as executive officer to famous Coastwatcher Donald Kennedy on Segi, New Georgia, William Bennett led a local militia against Japanese outposts and patrols. Their efforts assisted the United States in securing the area and establishing a fighter strip in June 1943.

Another member of the local police force, Sergeant Yauwika, proved invaluable to Bougainville Coastwatchers in rescuing fliers, evacuating noncombatants, and communicating with and obtaining assistance from numerous villages, deep in the interior, that even in 1943 were unaware of the war.

Hiding him in the bottom of his canoe under some palm fronds, Ben Kevu, cheerfully waving at prowling Japanese patrol planes, brought Lieutenant John F. Kennedy to Coastwatcher Reg Evans, who notified the U.S. forces of Kennedy's crew's location. Only recently has recognition come to inhabitants of these lands who participated in the war.

Soon the war moved on. The southwest Pacific offensive moved up The Slot. Locals rebuilt shattered villages; the jungle healed quickly. Aside from obvious physical and mental traumas, the war left an indelible imprint on the peoples of the lands northeast of Australia. Colonialism gradually ended, and peoples of such new nations became self-governing. Indigenous culture and religion proved remarkably durable, absorbing elements of outside influences while retaining their integrity. Western missionaries converted a number of islanders, adding another dimension to local culture. Locals earned money, at first as contract laborers hauled to distant places by

ship; later, for the British and other Westerns; and then, during the war, for the Americans. They were able to replace clothing made of local materials with purchased cloth garments.

As bad as it was, World War II could have been harder for the inhabitants of the South Pacific. In most places the Japanese occupation, relatively speaking, was mercifully short, especially in such places to the east as Guadalcanal. Experience in areas occupied far longer demonstrated the difficulties and tragedy it brought. Nonetheless, the war continued a gradual process, begun with the Solomons' discovery by Álvaro de Mendaña in 1567 and accelerated by the imposition of British rule in 1893, of Westernizing the inhabitants of the South Pacific lands. In a frontier land viewed by outsiders as a place of opportunity and exploitation, both inhabitants and outsiders became aware of that land's place in the world.

Fairly familiar with Westerners by the outbreak of World War II, peoples of the Solomons easily incorporated such influences as technology into their culture. Sudden exposure to them sometimes led inhabitants of such other areas as New Guinea and the New Hebrides to establish "cargo cults," which persisted until the local culture and society could adjust. "Cargo cults" were objects or activities brought by outsiders that, observed out of context by natives unfamiliar with their cultural, economic, or industrial origins, manifested themselves as veins of outside influence in unusual ways. An often told example is that of the refrigerator. Having observed U.S. Navy and Seabee personnel remove food from refrigerators, locals built a box and painted it white, then checked inside it occasionally, awaiting the magical appearance of good things to eat.

Experiences of the Solomons inhabitants typified in some ways typified those of the peoples of other Pacific lands. Fighting was more intense in such areas of New Guinea as Buna, Lae, and Salamaua, with locals regularly fighting in unit strength and suffering to a correspondingly higher degree. A few dozen men acting as porters was considered a large number in the Solomons. On the other hand, 3,900 locals assisted the 2d Battalion of the 32d Infantry Division in the move overland from Port Moresby to Wanigela over the infamous Kokoda Track, from October to December 1942, to open the offensive against the Japanese in New Guinea.

The end of Western colonialism has brought a greater recognition of the contributions of formerly marginalized people. The peoples of these lands endured hardships in a fight which they did not provoke, in which they had no stake, which they did not understand, and to which they ended up contributing admirably.

FURTHER READINGS

Coggins, Jack. *The Campaign for Guadalcanal* (1972).

Craven, Wesley F., and James Lea Cate, eds. *The Army Air Forces in World War II.* Vol. 4, *The Pacific: Guadalcanal to Saipan, August 1942 to July 1944* (1950; 1983).

Donovan, Robert J. *PT-109: John F. Kennedy in World War II* (1961).

Feldt, Eric A. *The Coastwatchers* (1959).

Keesing, Roger M. *Kwaio Religion: The Living and the Dead in a Solomon Island Society* (1982).

Lord, Walter. *Lonely Vigil: Coastwatchers of the Solomons* (1977).

Mayo, Lida. *Bloody Buna* (1974).

Spector, Ronald. *Eagle Against the Sun: The American War with Japan* (1985).

Van der Vat, Dan. *The Pacific Campaign: The U.S.–Japanese Naval War, 1941–1945* (1991).

Steven Agoratus

SEE ALSO Coastwatchers

Nauru

The tiny island (now nation) of Nauru has a unique World War II history, in that it was attacked by Nazi Germany and invaded by imperial Japan. Situated in the central Pacific, Nauru lies near the equator, approximately twenty-five hundred miles southwest of Hawaii. Discovered by the British in 1798, Nauru was annexed by Germany in 1888. The rich deposits of high-grade phosphate on the island were soon exploited, although the outbreak of World War I saw ownership of the island change with the arrival of an Australian occupation force. In 1919 the League of Nations awarded a joint mandate over the island to Australia, New Zealand, and Great Britain. Phosphate mining operations quickly expanded, with some 4.3 million metric tons exported between 1933 and 1939.

On the morning of December 8, 1940, the German navy's Far East Squadron, comprising auxiliary cruisers *Orion* and *Komet,* together with supply ship *Kumerland,* arrived off Nauru, disguised as Japanese merchant ships. A planned raid on the island to destroy the phosphate works and capture any shipping was abandoned because of high seas. Turning their attention to the shipping in the area, the heavily armed converted merchantmen managed to sink five Allied merchant ships with a combined tonnage exceeding twenty-five thousand tons. The German vessels returned on December 15 for another attempted landing, which was likewise canceled because of bad weather. *Komet* revisited Nauru on December 27, draped the Nazi battle flag over its Japanese markings, and proceeded to shell the shore installations for more than an hour. These very minor attacks were the most successful German actions in the Pacific during the war. In response, the Australian government established a small garrison on Nauru of fifty soldiers and two field guns.

The next year, on the opening day of the Pacific war, December 8, 1941, a Japanese flying boat circled Nauru. As Japan began to sweep ever closer to the island, the Australian garrison was evacuated on February 23, 1942, leaving behind the administrator, six other Europeans, and the native population. A Japanese invasion of Nauru had been proposed as part of Operation MO (abbreviated from Port Moresby in New Guinea). This complex undertaking, coordinated by Vice Admiral Inouye Shigiyoshi, commander of the Japanese Fourth Fleet, involved the establishment of a seaplane base at Tulagi, off Guadalcanal; an amphibious assault on Port Moresby; and the occupation of Nauru and Ocean Island. The defeat of the Japanese navy at the Battle of the Coral Sea, however, led Inouye to cancel the Nauru landing. He subsequently dispatched a force to seize Nauru and Ocean Island (Banaba) on May 10, 1942, but the sinking of fleet flagship *Okinoshima* by a U.S. submarine prompted the cautious Inouye to cancel the mission and retire to Truk.

The Japanese eventually attacked Nauru on the night of August 23-24 with a naval bombardment, followed three days later by the landing of Japanese marines. Representatives of the (Japanese) South Seas Development Company who arrived soon after to investigate the resumption of phosphate mining declared it impractical. The island was subsequently fortified as part of Japan's Pacific Island Defensive Chain, in preparation against an Allied attack. On March 25, 1943, aircraft from the U.S. Seventh Air Force bombed the newly completed airbase. Those Europeans who had chosen to remain on the island were executed in retaliation. Additional atrocities committed by the Japanese included the extermination of the native leper colony.

After a joint U.S. and British chiefs of staff meeting at Washington in May 1943, it was decided to begin offensive operations against the Japanese through the central Pacific region. After investigating possible options, Admiral Chester W. Nimitz announced plans for Operation Galvanic, the seizure of the Gilbert Islands and Nauru. Assigned to the invasion of Nauru was the U.S. 27th Infantry Division, a former New York National Guard unit. Preliminary plans for the operation called for the entire division to be involved, with two regiments landing on the northwest coast and the third remaining offshore in reserve.

The decision to occupy Nauru was not universally approved, however. The rocky atoll lacked sheltered waters, and the newly built Japanese airfield was relatively small. Because Nauru was riddled with caves, it was doubted that the division alone would be able to capture it. Any strategic benefit in taking the little island would be offset by potentially high casualties. The distance of 390 miles between Nauru and the western Gilbert Islands would place a major strain on the available shipping and would disperse the U.S. fleet, which then faced the possibility of Japanese attack.

On September 24 Admiral Chester Nimitz received a recommendation from Admiral Raymond A. Spruance that the landing on Nauru be canceled. Instead, Spruance proposed that Makin atoll be invaded because of its superior beaches, smaller Japanese garrison, and greater potential for airstrip construction. The next month a revised plan for Operation Galvanic detailed the scheduled landings on Tarawa, Apamama (Abemama), and Makin. The threat posed by Nauru was to be removed by carrier strikes, naval bombardment, submarine patrols, and bombing missions flown by the Seventh Air Force.

With the increasing isolation of Nauru and insufficient food supplies, the Japanese shipped 1,200 natives to the Caroline Islands. Of the Japanese who remained, more than three hundred soldiers died from starvation, with some troops resorting to cannibalism for survival. The capitulation of Nazi Germany in May 1945 brought forth renewed demands by the Australian and New Zealand governments for the reoccupation of the island and the resumption of vital phosphate mining. The British forces were, however, unwilling to expend lives on such an undertaking, and the focus of the Americans was the forthcoming invasion of the Japanese homeland.

With the dropping of the atomic bomb and the surrender of Japan, the U.S. chiefs of staff decreed that Nauru surrender to Australian military forces. On September 13, 1945, Brigadier J. R. Stevenson, aboard HMAS *Diamantina,* formally accepted the surrender of Captain Soeda Hisayuki. The Japanese garrison on the island at the time of surrender consisted of the 67th Naval Guard Unit and the Yokosuka Special No. 2 Landing Party. These three battalions plus assorted units totaled 2,681 men; there also were 54 Korean laborers and 513 Japanese civilians. The Japanese POWs were transferred to Bougainville before repatriation.

FURTHER READINGS
Muggenthaler, K. *German Raiders of World War II* (1977).
Pacific Islands Yearbook, 16th ed. (1989).

Williams, Maslyn, and Barrie Macdonald. *The Phosphateers: A History of the British Phosphate Commissioners and the Christmas Island Phosphate Commission* (1985).
David M. Green

Navajo Code Talkers

More than four hundred Navajo Native Americans participated in World War II as members of the U.S. Marine Corps's secret Navajo code talkers. They were instrumental in the American island-hopping campaign against Japan, using a military communications code based on the Navajo language. Throughout the war the Navajo code resisted all attempts by the enemy to break it. Some experts think the Navajo code talkers appreciably shortened the war because they enabled the U.S. military, which had broken the Japanese Purple Code, to communicate secretly while simultaneously knowing the intentions and thinking of the opposing commanders.

Due to the lack of exact equivalents for military terms, the use of Native American languages in combat situations often proved problematic. Nevertheless, the U.S. armed forces used such communication on a limited basis. During World War I, Comanches and Choctaws transmitted and received military messages over telephones, secure from German eavesdropping. Company D of the 141st Infantry, for example, had eight Choctaw who served as signal corpsmen. Also, during World War II the American forces transmitted messages in the Comanche, Choctaw, Creek, Menominee, Ojibwa, and Hopi languages, using Native Americans to do the communicating. None of those groups matched the Navajo contribution in the Pacific.

The Navajo code talkers program was established in 1942, after Philip Johnston, a civil engineer for the city of Los Angeles, convinced Major General Clayton B. Vogel that the Navajo language could be utilized as a communications code in the war. Johnston, the son of Presbyterian missionaries, had grown up among the Navajo people, and was fluent in their language. He believed that Navajo had great potential for military use because it was a tone language, making it difficult for adults to learn. Also, it had not been put into written form, making it virtually impossible for linguists in Germany and Japan to have any knowledge of it. In 1940 only thirty people outside the tribe knew Navajo. Johnston suggested, in addition to Navajo translations of U.S. military messages, the building up of a code of Navajo words that could be memorized. The subsequent code was so ingenious that nontrained Navajo were unable to decipher it.

During the war in the Pacific, the U.S. signal corpsmen used the words "New Mexico" and "Arizona" to signify that the incoming message was in the Navajo code. In such cases only code talkers, always Navajo, manned the radios. The code word for "dive-bomber" was "sparrow hawk," *gini* in Navajo. Bombs were "eggs," *ay-yay-gee*. A battleship was a "whale," *so-tso*. An amphibious assault was called "frog," *cha-ita*. The United States was referred to as "our mother," *ne-he-mah*. When it was necessary to spell out words, a special alphabet code was used. Each letter of the English alphabet was given a name, usually after an animal (e.g., A for ant, *wol-la-chee;* B for bear, *shush*). As the war progressed and new weapons were introduced, it was necessary to expand the original 211-word code and the alphabet code.

The Navajo code talkers participated in many of the bloody campaigns of the Pacific: Guadalcanal, Tarawa, Tinian, Saipan, Iwo Jima, Okinawa. During the fighting on Guadalcanal and in the Marshall Islands, many of the marines hearing the code on their radios for the first time thought that Japanese were broadcasting on their frequency. In person, the Navajo code talkers experienced dangers from confused Americans who mistook them for Japanese because of their seemingly Asiatic appearance, a situation prompting many marine units to assign bodyguards for their Indian compatriots. If some of the Americans were initially unhappy with the Navajo presence, their attitudes changed when it became apparent how valuable the code talkers were to the war effort. Until the code talkers took over communications, it had been impossible for the United States to neutralize Rabaul, New Britain, because the Japanese were reading American naval orders and knew when each air attack was coming. After the November 1943 departure of the Japanese warships from Rabaul harbor, the Navajo were more appreciated by their superiors and comrades.

The Battle of Iwo Jima proved to be the code talkers' greatest moment. In the first forty-eight hours of the attack, the Navajo transmitted 800 messages. During that invasion, the code talkers handled all of the radio traffic to and from the sea-based command center to the three division headquarters ashore. Also, the Navajo directed all of the naval gunfire and close air support. Major Howard Conner, signal officer with the 5th Marine Division, stated flatly, "Were it not for the Navajo code talkers, the marines never would have taken Iwo Jima."

Several code talkers were part of the American occupation force in Japan. Paul Blatchford and Rex Malone, for example, relayed messages to San Francisco in which there were descriptions of the devastation of Nagasaki after the dropping of the second atomic bomb. Also, some of the code talkers were sent to China during the early fighting between Nationalist and Communists forces.

In all, during the Pacific war the U.S. Marine Corps deployed some five hundred forty Navajo code talkers, of whom about thirty became casualties.

Not until many years after the war did the Navajo code talkers come to the public's attention. During the reunion of the 4th Marine Division Association in 1969, the code talkers received their first national recognition. In 1971 President Richard Nixon awarded the group a special certificate, citing its "patriotism, resourcefulness, and courage." The U.S. Senate, at the insistence of Arizona Senator Dennis DeConcini, decreed August 14, 1982, as National Code Talkers Day. "Since the Code Talkers' work required absolute secrecy, they never enjoyed the national acclaim they so much deserved," explained DeConcini. "I do not want this illustrious yet unassuming group of Navajo marines to fade into history without notice."

FURTHER READINGS

Aaseng, Nathan. *Navajo Code Talkers* (1992).
Bernstein, Alison. *American Indians and World War II* (1991).
Bixler, Margaret T. *Winds of Freedom: The Story of the Navajo Code Talkers of World War II* (1992).
Hafford, William E. "The Navajo Code Talkers." *Arizona Highways* (February 1989).
Kawano, Kenji. *Warriors: Talkers* (1990).
Paul, Doris A. *The Navajo Code Talkers* (1973).

Roger Chapman

SEE ALSO Iwo Jima, Battle of

Navy, Japanese

The Japanese navy that confronted the United States at the opening of the Pacific war was, in many ways, the most powerful fleet in the world. Though inferior to the U.S. Navy in number of ships and aggregate tonnage, the Imperial Japanese Navy nevertheless held important advantages over the U.S. and British navies. Japan possessed the largest group of fleet carriers in the world, and the naval aviators who flew from them were unquestionably the finest anywhere. As a result, Japan was well ahead of both the U.S. and British navies in the ability to project naval power. Also, Japan's surface forces were highly trained and heavily armed, and possessed a sound tactical doctrine. In the areas of night fighting and torpedo warfare, in particular, they had no equals.

The first six months of the war seemed to validate Japan's position as a first-rank naval power. The imperial fleet struck at the major U.S. naval base at Pearl Harbor, Hawaii, with devastating effect, and humbled the Royal Navy two days later by quickly dispatching battlecruiser *Repulse* and new battleship *Prince of Wales*. Within the first four months of the war, Japan's carrier task forces launched destructive raids across the breadth of the Pacific, from Hawaii to Australia and as far as the Indian Ocean. Within that time span, the Japanese swept the Allied naval forces out of the whole of the southwest Pacific with contemptuous ease.

Yet within three and a half years, the Imperial Japanese Navy was completely destroyed as a fighting force. Why did the Japanese lose? The superficial answer is that Japan was simply outbuilt by the United States. However, the truth is more complex and requires an understanding of the origins of the Imperial Japanese Navy, how it intended to fight a major war, and the force structure that resulted from this doctrine.

The imperial navy, like the modern Japanese state, arose from Japan's collapsed feudal order in the mid-1860s. Transforming an agrarian/mercantile economy into an industrial state almost overnight, Japan developed essentially all of the military trappings of a modern European nation-state by the early 1900s. It did so through the confluence of several important factors: the vision of its leaders, the unstinting productive efforts of its people, and a shrewd ability to adopt the best Western military practices and adapt them to meet Japanese ends.

From the beginning, Japan was determined to develop itself along Western lines. Logically enough, the imperial army had shaped its forces along the lines of the German army, then the foremost land power in Europe. By the same token, the imperial navy modeled itself after the world's leading navy, that of Great Britain. Japan purchased its warships from prominent British yards such as Vickers and Yarrow. The Japanese naval academy at Etajima (near Hiroshima), modeled itself after British naval schools, and taught a curriculum built on Royal Navy practice. English was the language used in ship-handling and naval communications. The result was a navy that from the outset focused on achieving the very highest standards of professionalism.

Japan also methodically developed the ability to support its naval ambitions. Industries that directly supported the navy were given government financial support and expanded as rapidly as possible. Japan imported large quantities of naval materiel, and quickly developed the capability not only to replicate existing Western designs but also to produce its own. The launch of battle cruiser *Kongo* by Vickers in 1911 marked the final Japanese capital ship built by a foreign supplier. *Kongo*'s three sister ships were built in Japanese yards. Thenceforth, Japan was essentially self-sufficient in the production of naval power plants, armor plate, heavy ordnance, fire-control systems, and optics. By this time, too, Japan was well along in developing its unique naval doctrine.

Japanese naval doctrine is often described as Mahanian (after Alfred Thayer Mahan, a naval officer and historian), in that it supposedly advocated control of the seas and the primacy of the battle fleet in securing that control. Imperial Japanese naval doctrine certainly contained elements of Mahan's thesis; however, Japan's doctrine as a whole was based upon its own experiences as a modern state, and as such it aimed at different (and generally less ambitious) goals than the naval policies of colonial maritime states like Great Britain.

Modern Japanese naval doctrine had its roots in the wars fought against China in 1894–1895, and against Russia during 1904–1905. In both of these conflicts, Japan sought to advance limited military goals on the Asian mainland. It was the navy's supporting role to prevent enemy naval forces from interfering with the army's campaign ashore. In both wars, the imperial navy performed this role adequately, and in some cases brilliantly. By the end of the Russo–Japanese War, capped by the stunning victory at the Battle of Tsushima, Japan was clearly established as an important second-rank naval power.

Yet Japan drew some dangerously flawed lessons from its victories. The first was a belief that the outcome of future wars would be determined by a single decisive naval battle, on the order of Tsushima. The second was a belief that quality could overcome quantity, as had been the case in each of the naval duels against Japan's larger foes.

Unfortunately, Japan failed to apprehend two important countervailing arguments. The first was that although Tsushima had indeed been decisive to *its* war, naval combat historically has been characterized by longer conflicts and attritional warfare. And although being able to win named naval battles has always been important in judging a navy's effectiveness, the ability to perform economic blockading, scouting, amphibious assault, and pro- and anticommerce missions must also factor into the equation. On the basis of Tsushima, the Japanese navy largely lost sight of these other important naval roles and devoted itself almost exclusively to the pursuit of victory in a decisive surface battle.

Second, although Japan had prevailed against larger opponents in its first two wars, both of these opponents had suffered from serious internal weaknesses. Neither had particularly competent military forces, and both lacked the domestic political will to fight a protracted war. Yet Japan believed that its victories validated its ability to create naval wars that were short-lived and limited in both geographic and tactical scope.

At the end of World War I, the Japanese navy built on these concepts as it began shifting its attention to its newest potential foe, the United States. To any dispassionate observer, the United States represented an entirely different opponent than the decrepit imperial regimes Japan had bested previously. The United States was a vibrant nation, bustling economically, and with a long tradition of maritime excellence. Preparing for war against the United States necessitated not only an entirely new Japanese naval strategy but also a new national strategy. Nevertheless, although Japanese military leaders paid lip service to the economic might of the United States, they failed to comprehend what fighting such an opponent might mean. Coupled with the chronic squabbling between the army and navy, Japanese strategy and doctrine in the 1920s and 1930s became increasingly dogmatic at the very time that it needed to be far more innovative. As a result, as one writer has noted, "The Japanese navy neither understood nor prepared for *war* at all. Rather, it believed in and prepared for *battle*." This created, in the words of the same author, "a fighting force that was both one-dimensional and brittle" (Evans and Peattie, p. 515).

The doctrine and tactics with which Japan fought the Pacific war were essentially a baroque construction (something like the "pagoda" structures piled layer upon layer on Japanese battleships) atop the central theme of how to conduct the "decisive battle" against the United States, a battle that never occurred. The imperial navy knew that its battle line would inevitably be outnumbered in any decisive encounter with the U.S. Navy, and spent much of the 1920s and 1930s searching for answers to this problem. The solution that emerged rested on a two-pronged approach: massed torpedo attacks delivered at night against the main U.S. fleet, to whittle down its numbers, and long-range heavy gunfire during the day against the (presumably) disorganized remnants of the enemy fleet. Both forms of attack depended on the ability of the Japanese to outrange the enemy's comparable gun and torpedo weapons systems. These requirements played an important role in determining the characteristics of Japan's warships.

In a sense, warships can be viewed as physical manifestations of the naval doctrine they serve. In other words, warships should be designed to fight in the fashion in which a navy as a whole intends to fight. Budgetary pressure and politics being what they are, however, most ship designs are usually modified away from purely doctrinal

requirements. However, the warships of the Japanese navy as a whole represented a fairly congruent implementation of the navy's intended approach to fighting a war. They emphasized speed and offensive firepower while placing less importance on structural strength, stability, protection, and range.

The quality of the onboard equipment was in general very good, although certain disparities did exist between Japanese and Western equipment. Japan's optics, torpedoes, and flashless gunpowder were world-class. Its naval guns, propulsion systems, and aircraft (at least at the outbreak of the Pacific war) were broadly comparable with their Western counterparts. However, Japan lagged in the development of the newer naval and aerial technologies, such as radar, sonar, the combat information center, and supercharged aircraft engines. These shortcomings would have disastrous consequences as the war progressed.

As stated above, an important factor in Japan's approach to defeating the U.S. battle fleet was having the ability to outrange it in combat. In keeping with that tenet, Japanese battleships were designed to be qualitatively superior, with a larger caliber (and hence longer range) main battery. This trend culminated in the creation of the giant *Yamato*-class battleships, the first of which was laid down in 1937. These 63,000-ton behemoths, the largest ever built, mounted the largest main battery ever placed aboard a warship; nine 18.1-inch naval rifles capable of hurling a 3,220-pound shell more than twenty-five miles. In addition, Japan had modernized its older battleships with upgraded turrets (allowing higher gun elevation and corresponding longer range), better fire-control systems, and enhanced protection, thereby ensuring that all ten of its older capital ships could be in the line of battle.

After the signing of the Washington Naval Treaty in 1922, battleship construction worldwide was halted. This "battleship holiday" shifted the emphasis in warship construction toward cruisers, particularly the larger "Treaty" cruisers (which subsequently became known in most navies as "heavy cruisers"). Japanese heavy cruisers as a rule were large, fast, and powerful. They mounted as many as ten 8-inch guns, in comparison to the six to nine barrels carried by foreign contemporaries. More important, they also mounted up to sixteen 24-inch torpedo tubes, each of which was capable of launching the exceptional Type 93 Long Lance torpedo, giving them a punch unmatched by any foreign cruiser design.

Japan, alone among the world's navies, gave a place of doctrinal primacy to fleet destroyers. Anxious to offset their numerical weakness against the U.S. battle fleet, the Imperial Japanese Navy charged its fleet destroyers with attacking the U.S. fleet at night, using massed torpedo volleys. To implement these tactics, and carry a powerful torpedo load, Japanese destroyers of necessity had to be large and fast. With the introduction of the revolutionary *Fubuki* class in 1928, the Japanese created the archetypal World War II fleet destroyer—a 2,000-ton warship armed with 5-inch guns in weatherproof, power-operated mounts, carrying a powerful torpedo load, and capable of better than thirty-five knots per hour. In its time, *Fubuki* was the most powerful destroyer in the world, and its many descendants were similarly formidable.

Japanese submarines also supported the "decisive battle" concept in that they were developed primarily with warships, rather than merchant shipping, as their main prey. Japanese submarines were expected to serve as advance scouts for the fleet. Thus fleet submarines tended to be large, with a long cruising range and a high surface speed in order to reach distant patrol points. They also carried numerous torpedo tubes and reloads, the more effectively to engage fast, heavily protected warships. However, Japanese submarines tended to eschew such niceties as deep diving and good underwater handling characteristics. This eventually left them vulnerable to Allied antisubmarine warfare, especially as Allied tactics were honed in the fight against German U-boats.

Naval Aviation

The Japanese navy followed its standard formula for entering the new field of aviation technology—acquire technology and practices from leading foreign innovators (in this case Great Britain and the United States), begin limited licensed production of important aircraft components, then move fully to indigenous designs. In late 1921, the arrival of a British mission in Japan that was equipped with the latest aviation technologies (including aircraft, weapons, and communications gear) greatly elevated the professionalism of the imperial navy's fledgling aviation arm. The following year, Japan's first aircraft carrier, *Hosho*, was delivered to the fleet. By this time, too, the major Japanese aircraft manufacturers, Nakajima, Mitsubishi, Kawasaki, and Aichi, were well established.

By the 1930s the Japanese aircraft industry was beginning to produce its own designs, initially derivative but eventually taking on unique characteristics. By the end of the decade, domestic Japanese designs were equal, and in some cases superior, to their Western counterparts. With the opening of the Pacific war, the Allies discovered to their surprise that aircraft like the much-feared A6M2 Zero fighter, the G4M Betty bomber, and the D3A Val dive-bomber were eminently suited to the offensive war Japan intended to fight. The A6M2 in particular gained

a reputation for near invincibility in the opening stages of the conflict.

With the completion of Japan's first large aircraft carrier, *Akagi,* in 1927, the imperial navy could begin experimenting in earnest with a true fleet carrier. *Akagi* and the equally large *Kaga* (which joined the fleet in 1930) were the platforms for testing Japan's rapidly emerging naval aviation doctrine. By the mid-1930s, the Japanese navy was the equal of the British and U.S. navies in this new mode of naval warfare, having developed both the requisite shipboard technology—hangar design and operations, arresting gear, landing lights—and the domestic industrial base to support large air units. This trend culminated in April 1941 with the formal establishment of the First Air Fleet.

The First Air Fleet, composed of Japan's four large fleet carriers—*Akagi, Kaga, Soryu,* and *Hiryu*—was organized to operate as a single unit. In the fall of 1941, the four original ships were augmented by newly commissioned *Shokaku* and *Zuikaku*, making Japan's carrier fleet the finest in the world. Establishing this unit was a truly revolutionary development. For the first time in history there existed an agglomeration of naval air assets (ships, planes, pilots, and air doctrine) that had the potential to create strategically meaningful results on the battlefield. The British and U.S. navies had clearly influenced this agglomeration (the Japanese were keenly aware of the very successful British carrier operation against the Italian fleet at Taranto, for instance), but the Japanese navy was the first to establish a "critical mass" of naval air power at an operational level. By doing so, it moved naval aviation out of its scouting/raiding role, and transformed it into a decisive arm of battle. The age of the battleship had now ended.

When the imperial navy entered the Pacific war, it possessed a potent naval aviation force. Its six large fleet carriers (and their air wings) outnumbered and outclassed the U.S. and Royal Navy inventories. The quality of the men flying them was superb—actually too good, as the course of the Pacific war would show. Many of Japan's naval pilots had gained experience in operations over China since 1937, and as a result, the navy possessed a large number of veteran fliers. Again, however, in China the Japanese were not fighting a first-class military power. They had developed effective carrier-borne torpedo and dive-bombing techniques, and the navy's numerous land-based medium bomber squadrons were proficient in both level bombing and torpedo attacks. All in all, the Japanese naval aviation force was the finest on the planet in late 1941.

As with the naval aviation arm, training levels in the navy as a whole were very high. The imperial navy had a tradition of realistic training. It was standard practice to conduct exercises in the foul weather conditions prevalent in the north Pacific, and many were conducted at high speed, in formation, and at night. Losses of personnel were commonplace, as were collisions and damage to the ships involved. But the Japanese motto in this regard was "train hard; fight easy." The result was a force that at the outset of hostilities was at a razor's edge of performance.

As the Pacific war wore on, the Japanese navy began to suffer heavy losses of experienced crews, and the operational efficiency of its vessels deteriorated. Yet even in its most desperate hours, it never collapsed as a fighting force. It is a tribute to the professionalism and dedication of the navy's personnel that it carried on to the bitter end despite the annihilating blows being rained upon it by the vastly more powerful Allied forces.

The general history of the Pacific war, and the specifics of the campaigns and battles, are described and analyzed elsewhere in this volume. Certain battles and campaigns, however, merit comment for their importance in regard to the fate of the Japanese navy.

Japan's naval operations from December 7, 1941, to April 1942 produced an almost unbroken string of tactical victories. In each of the major operations of the early war period—the attack against Pearl Harbor, the sinking of the *Prince of Wales* and *Repulse,* the four separate engagements around Java, and the operations in the Indian Ocean in April 1942—Japanese forces emerged victorious and inflicted heavy losses on Allied forces. In the process, they destroyed the Allied naval position in the area.

In this stage of the conflict, Japan was able to shape a war that concealed its weaknesses while playing to all its military strengths. The navy fought with sound, flexible tactics. The ships were well designed to implement naval doctrine, were heavily armed, and were equal or superior to their opponents in offensive power. The fighting crews were superbly trained, and the ships could work cohesively under almost any circumstances. Armed with such advantages, the imperial navy justly reaped the rewards of its prewar labors.

Yet at the Battle of Midway, the Japanese navy, with overall numerical superiority in the theater of action, failed to deploy its forces to ensure decisive superiority at the point of attack. The U.S. Navy, possessing the decisive advantage of superior intelligence, managed (with a good deal of luck) to sink four large carriers—*Akagi, Kaga, Soryu,* and *Hiryu*—against the loss of one of its own. The remainder of the Japanese forces not being within supporting distance of the beaten First Air Fleet, the Japanese

were forced to retreat, thus handing the U.S. Navy its first clear-cut victory of the war.

The importance of the Japanese defeat at Midway is both difficult to underestimate, yet prone to overemphasis. Although the strategic offensive power of the imperial navy had been badly mauled by the destruction of First Air Fleet, Midway did not portend the end of the war. The Japanese navy still possessed adequate offensive capabilities in its remaining carriers and surface forces to initiate offensive operations elsewhere. Indeed, in the upper ranks of the Japanese navy the mood (rightly or wrongly) was hardly one of abject defeat.

Yet the Battle of Midway did bare for the first time some of the key weaknesses that would plague the imperial navy for the rest of the war. The Japanese had clearly failed in their approach to aerial scouting. Their ships were inadequately protected with antiaircraft weapons. Japanese aircraft carriers were poorly armored, and their designs made them vulnerable to hangar explosions and fires. Exacerbating these problems, damage-control technique was far behind that of the U.S. Navy. In sum, the Japanese navy had been shown for what it was—a first-class force whose ships and tactics were skewed toward the offensive, and that had difficulty avoiding and recovering from battle damage.

If the Battle of Midway was notable for its stunning impact, the Solomon Islands campaign was an entirely different affair. Grinding, brutal, and primarily attritional in character, the fighting around Guadalcanal and then up "The Slot" toward Rabaul on New Britain effectively destroyed the imperial navy's balance as a fighting force. It also crushed the flimsy logistical underpinnings of Japan's defensive positions in the South Pacific.

The fighting in and around the Solomons was conducted primarily at night between surface forces. Although there were two important carrier battles (the Battle of the Eastern Solomons and the Battle of Santa Cruz), it was the frequent sharp night clashes between the cruiser and destroyer forces that set the tone of the naval campaign as a whole. In these engagements, the imperial navy frequently emerged as the victor, at least in a tactical sense. The Battle of Savo Island in particular showed the Japanese mastery of night combat. In a single 30-minute action, Admiral Gunichi Mikawa's force of five heavy cruisers, two light cruisers, and one destroyer sank four Allied heavy cruisers outright, at negligible cost to themselves, in the worst at sea defeat in U.S. Navy history. The raw results of this encounter were impressive enough, but what is often overlooked is that Admiral Mikawa was able to defeat U.S. Navy forces with an odd-lot force of mostly older ships that had never exercised together. The Savo

Island action speaks volumes about the cohesiveness of Japanese tactics and training.

Yet despite brilliant tactical victories like Savo, the fact remained that Japan was never able to translate them into strategic advantage. The United States remained well in the fight. Not only that, but the U.S. Navy was learning valuable tactical lessons, and was slowly beginning to bring its powerful economic advantages into play. Even though its losses were heavier, the U.S. Navy was inflicting serious damage on the Japanese navy, and the Japanese could not make these losses good. As sinkings increased, the remaining vessels in the Japanese inventory were called upon to do more, meaning delays of scheduled maintenance and of rest and rehabilitation for their crews. The fighting effectiveness of the Japanese forces remaining in the Solomons was increasingly sucked into a downward spiral. Meanwhile, in the Japanese home islands, shipyards were jammed with damaged ships requiring refit and repair. This hampered Japan's ability to replace losses with fresh construction.

At the conclusion of the Solomons campaign, the imperial navy had so many cruisers and escort vessels sunk or damaged that it was no longer capable of supplying its outlying garrisons, of conducting patrolling operations, or of providing sufficient escorts to its remaining carrier forces. As a result, Japan's ability to protect its early gains was fatally weakened. Equally important, the termination of the campaign left the Allies not only with an expanding numerical superiority but also in possession of the tactical acumen to fight the Japanese on an even basis. The Americans proved to be fast learners, certainly much more willing and quick to learn from their mistakes and losses then were the Japanese.

During the latter half of 1943, both sides took time to rebuild their carrier forces and prepare for the struggle ahead. For the Americans, the respite afforded time to assemble the first true carrier task forces. The U.S. Navy now possessed three critical advantages. First, it had enough fleet carriers to deploy as many as a dozen at a time, escorted by new fast battleships, cruisers, and destroyers. Second, the Americans had vastly increased the number and quality of their antiaircraft weapons. Many of the U.S. Navy's antiaircraft weapons were now controlled by radar, and the heavier mounts employed the new VT radar-fused ammunition, which improved their lethalness by three to five times. As a result, U.S. task forces were now almost impossible to attack from the air without suffering heavy losses. Third, the U.S. Navy had perfected the art of underway replenishment, and had the logistic assets to support naval forces at sea almost indefinitely. The Americans had taken the Japanese task force concept—originally embodied in the First Air Fleet—to its logical conclusion. Whereas the Japanese carrier group that opened the war was essentially a raiding force, the U.S. Navy now possessed the ability to maneuver offshore for weeks at a time and batter the most powerful island bastions into impotence.

While the Americans were thus transforming the entire basis of carrier warfare, the Japanese were struggling to rebuild their shattered air groups, train new recruits, and re-create a semblance of the naval airpower they possessed before the Battle of Midway. By early 1944, Japan had regained a reasonable mass of fleet carriers. However, carrier pilot training was suffering from a lack of both time and petroleum. In contrast, U.S. programs were now churning out well-trained pilots in staggering numbers, and they were flying aircraft superior to the Japanese models. These dynamics had grim consequences for the Japanese during the battle that developed during June 19–20, 1944.

The Japanese battle plan anticipated the need to use both land-based and carrier-based aircraft to defeat the Americans. By employing longer-range carrier aircraft, and using bases in the Marianas as refueling points, the Japanese hoped to keep their ships out of range of U.S. aircraft. With this advantage, as well as the formidable number of land-based aircraft present on Guam and Saipan (nearly twelve hundred), they expected that their new carrier force would be able to defeat its American counterpart decisively.

In the event, Japanese meticulous battle planning went for naught. During the opening of the battle, U.S. air strikes largely eliminated Japanese land-based airpower in the Marianas. (The Japanese fleet was not informed of this development.) As a result, when the Japanese attempted to shuttle aircraft from their carriers to Guam and Saipan, they found the supposedly secure land bases dominated by U.S. warplanes. Worse yet, the Japanese attackers had to run a gauntlet of antiaircraft weapons and combat information center-directed screening fighters surrounding the American task force, and suffered hideous losses.

Furthermore, the Japanese still had not remedied their deficiencies in antisubmarine warfare, radar location, fighter direction, and damage control. U.S. submarines sank the large carriers *Shokaku* and *Taiho* during the afternoon of June 19. *Taiho*, after receiving a single torpedo hit abreast the forward aviation gasoline storage, fell victim to faulty damage-control efforts and was gutted by a gasoline vapor explosion. U.S. carrier aircraft also dispatched carrier *Hiyo* and damaged several other vessels.

The battle was a disaster of the first order, and demonstrated just how far the imperial navy had fallen behind the U.S. Navy, not only in numbers but also in technique, across every aspect of the new mode of naval warfare. The battle also marked the end of Japanese naval aviation. The imperial navy's carrier force still existed, but it lacked sufficient aircraft and trained pilots to fight. From this point on, the only role the Japanese carriers could play would be to act as a bait force. This was precisely their fate during the final great naval battle of the war.

The Battle of Leyte Gulf represented Japan's last desperate attempt to translate its one remaining significant naval asset—its heavy surface units—into a victory over the U.S. forces preparing for an invasion of the Philippines. The Japanese battle plan was extremely complex, with several surface groups converging on Leyte while a bait force of Japanese carriers was used to draw the U.S. Navy's carriers and fast battleships northward, out of the fight. This might give the Japanese the tactical advantage when they descended on the invasion beaches. The result was the largest naval battle in history.

Japan's plans very nearly came to fruition, despite the mauling of its surface units during their approach to the beaches. Admiral Jisaburo Ozawa's carrier "bait" force did indeed succeed in luring Admiral William F. ("Bull") Halsey northward and out of the way. This deceptive maneuver, combined with an undetected move back toward the invasion beaches by Admiral Takeo Kurita's northern attack force, presented the Japanese navy with what appeared to be a golden opportunity.

At dawn on October 25, 1944, the powerful Japanese surface force sighted the masts of U.S. carriers. They belonged to a group of small escort carriers, destroyers, and destroyer escorts covering the landing beaches. The Japanese opened fire at once, and bore down on their smaller, slower opponents. Yet despite the apparent odds against them, the lightly armed U.S. escorts charged the Japanese main body while the escort carriers quickly launched several hundred aircraft in their own defense. In the melee, the Japanese fell into confusion and eventually retired after inflicting only moderate damage. During that day and the next, U.S. carrier warplanes badly mauled Japan's retreating main body and its bait force. The imperial navy had, for all intents and purposes, ceased to exist. Its remaining heavy combatants were hounded back to the home islands, where they languished for lack of fuel, and eventually fell victim to carrier raids.

By the time of Japan's surrender in August 1945, the Imperial Japanese Navy had been all but annihilated. Japan had only one battleship still afloat, no serviceable aircraft carriers, and a handful of battered cruisers, destroyers, and other combatants left, many of them damaged and crippled by a lack of fuel oil. Japan had lost 334 major warships and more than 150 submarines, and had suffered more than three hundred thousand fatalities in battle.

It was Japan's misfortune to be pitted against a foe that was not merely huge but also adaptable, grimly determined to win, and adroit at translating economic might into the sinews of war. The United States quickly transformed the short-lived, limited war Japan had hoped for into a total war of unlimited scope. The fact that Japan's forces often performed brilliantly at a tactical level in no way negated the long-term consequences of its bankruptcy at the level of grand strategy. By failing to recognize that attacking the United States meant not just fighting a single "decisive battle," but waging total war, Japan doomed itself to a conflict it could not win in the long term. Eventually, it was overwhelmed by the Allies on so many levels that it could not react effectively on any one of them. In short, Japan's fate after 1942 was to be outfought in every aspect of the war it had created.

At another level, Japan's basic failure in grand strategy led to the creation of a naval doctrine that was fatally flawed. It is no wonder that under such conditions the naval force's structure was badly warped in terms of its ability to fight a protracted naval conflict. The navy's inability to effectively protect the nation's shipping, its lack of emphasis on developing sound antisubmarine warfare techniques, its misuse of its submarine force, its failure to create a viable pilot replacement program, and its eschewing of almost every sort of defensively oriented advantage—from effective ship damage-control techniques to the simple provision of armor protection for fighter aircraft—meant that the navy's men and ships suffered disproportionate casualties for little long-term gain.

Japan also suffered from a dearth of decisive naval leadership. In a war against an opponent like the United States, the Japanese navy had zero margin for error. It had to use its assets audaciously, avoid squandering them, and learn from its mistakes. Yet throughout the war, the Japanese navy showed a remarkable inability to come to grips with its challenges. Examples of this mental blind spot include its failure to quickly fortify its outlying defensive perimeter while it still retained naval superiority, its lethargic expansion of wartime pilot training programs, and its neglect of convoying and antisubmarine warfare until U.S. submarines had already fatally damaged the Japanese merchant marine. (Certainly in the latter case, the Japanese had ample precedent at hand in the "bridge of ships" between the United States and Great Britain in both world wars—a bridge made possible almost solely by convoying.) Equally disastrously, Japanese naval planners blindly persisted in looking for the "decisive battle," preferably battleship against battleship, until the navy had ceased to exist. Locked into a doctrine that recognized only a single type of warfare, the Japanese leadership often seemed to operate by rote. In the final analysis, the Imperial Japanese Navy was an impressive, but inflexible, instrument of war. When used in the mode of battle for which it was intended, it performed superbly. But the navy was ill-adapted to fighting in ways for which it had not been designed, and in the end it failed in almost every conceivable fashion.

Just as its early victories in the Pacific war had been fairly bought with the coin of careful staff work, hard training, and fighting spirit, so its catastrophic final defeat was purchased by its lack of foresight, its utter failure to grasp the strategic realities of the war it had initiated, and its inability to adapt to a multidimensional battlefield.

FURTHER READINGS

Dull, Paul S. *A Battle History of the Imperial Japanese Navy, 1941–1945* (1978).

Evans, David C., ed. *The Imperial Japanese Navy in World War II: In the Words of Former Japanese Naval Officers* (1986).

Evans, David C., and Mark R. Peattie. *Kaigun: Strategy, Tactics and Technology in the Imperial Japanese Navy, 1877–1941* (1997).

Jentschura, Hansgeorg, Dieter Jung, and Peter Mickel. *Warships of the Imperial Japanese Navy, 1869–1945* (1977).

Jon Parshall

SEE ALSO Aircraft Carriers: Japanese, U.S., and British; Leyte Gulf, Battle of; Midway, Battle of; Ozawa Jisaburo; *Prince of Wales* and *Repulse*, Sinking of; Savo Island, Battle of; Torpedo, Long Lance (Japanese)

Navy, Royal

The growing tension between the United States and Japan in 1941 was a source of great concern for the British, who were in their third year of war against Nazi Germany. Senior officials in the British government realized that few resources were available to defend their Far Eastern interests if the Japanese embarked on a war of expansion. The British did, however, have a defense plan created during the interwar years. In 1921 Great Britain, in response to pressure from the Pacific dominions for protection against Japanese expansionism, pledged to New Zealand and Australia that it would send a fleet ninety days after the outbreak of war. To this end, the Admiralty constructed a new naval dockyard in Singapore, which was operational by February 1938. By 1941 Prime Minister Winston Churchill wanted to send a naval force to Singapore as a deterrent to Japanese aggression in the Far East, despite the low level of available military resources.

Unfortunately, lack of resources was not the only problem that dogged British plans for the defense of the Far East. The majority of the vessels of the Royal Navy were obsolete by World War II, many of the capital ships having seen service in World War I. Compounding this problem was Churchill's underestimation of the value of the aircraft carrier to war at sea. These factors in combination resulted in the British dispatching a fleet to the Far East that was incapable of matching the strength of the more modern Imperial Japanese Navy, which possessed far more aircraft carriers than did the Royal Navy. The ships of the newly designated Eastern Fleet, commanded by Admiral Tom Phillips, arrived in Singapore on December 2, 1941. It consisted of new battleship *Prince of Wales,* World War I battle cruiser *Repulse,* three ancient cruisers, and an escort of destroyers. The fact that there was no air cover (the covering carrier had run aground and would be permanently delayed) for the fleet cost the British dearly at the outbreak of war. In accordance with their war plans, the Japanese embarked on the conquest of Malaya and its island fortress of Singapore on December 7, 1941. A portion of the Eastern Fleet, code-named Force Z and including *Prince of Wales* and *Repulse* under Phillips, tried to defend Malaya against invasion, but was overwhelmed and sunk by Japanese carrier-based planes on December 10. The destruction of Force Z and the death of Admiral Phillips was the first of several disasters for the Royal Navy in the early years of the war against Japan. It also clearly revealed the inadequacy of Britain's defense policy in the East.

Following the loss of Force Z, the Royal Navy was pushed out of the Pacific after the loss of all of Britain's possessions in the region. Most important were the losses of Singapore, which fell on February 15, 1942, and that of Hong Kong on December 25, 1941. The only Royal Navy presence in the theater following these defeats consisted of naval units attached to the ABDA Command in the South Pacific, which was established January 3, 1942, and comprised American, British, Dutch, and Australian warships. Despite the severe blows to their prestige, their empire, and their navy, the British endeavored to build an effective resistance at sea against Japan. Responsibility for this rested with the new commander in chief of the remnants of the Eastern Fleet, Vice Admiral Sir James Somerville.

The British immediately set to work building defenses on their island possession of Ceylon (now Sri Lanka), which served as the new base for the Eastern Fleet. The island's two major ports, Colombo and Trincomalee, had excellent harbors. Meanwhile, the Japanese had turned their attention to the Dutch East Indies (now Indonesia), whose oil was vital to the imperial war effort. The Japanese attacked these islands on February 3, 1942. The naval forces of the ABDA command tried to defend the islands, but suffered from the same lack of airpower that had doomed Force Z of the Eastern Fleet. Of the five cruisers and ten destroyers of the force, only four U.S. destroyers survived. Following this crushing defeat and the subsequent disintegration of the ABDA Command, the only remaining forces of the Royal Navy or the British Commonwealth in the Pacific theater were in either Ceylon or Australia.

Somerville had a daunting task following these Japanese successes. The Admiralty entrusted him with the defense of Ceylon and the eastern seaboard of the Indian subcontinent, but Somerville knew that such defense was impossible because of overwhelming Japanese naval power. As a result the admiral had to accept the fact that the Eastern Fleet was in reality only a "fleet in being" whose existence alone would, it was hoped, deter further Japanese attacks. No one could realistically expect the force to do much else. The nucleus of the reconstituted Eastern Fleet was the old battleship *Warspite* and the "R" class *Resolution, Revenge, Royal Sovereign,* and *Ramillies.* Only the *Warspite* had been modernized; the others were World War I design. The fleet also had three aircraft carriers, but one of these was *Hermes,* built in 1924 and far too slow for modern naval warfare. Another of the carriers, *Formidable,* was brand new and not ready for combat duty. Escorting this dubious force were fourteen cruisers and sixteen destroyers.

The first test for the new Eastern Fleet came in April 1942 with the arrival of Vice Admiral Chuichi Nagumo's carrier strike force with orders to attack Ceylon. His fleet of five carriers, four battleships, and escorting vessels was far too powerful for the Eastern Fleet to contest. Somerville and his advisers agreed that Ceylon could not be defended in the face of such great Japanese naval strength. They decided to evacuate the Eastern Fleet from Ceylon, the four "R" class battleships being dispatched to Mombasa, Kenya, to protect shipping lanes while the remainder of the fleet sailed to Bombay, India. The wisdom of Somerville's decision, despite its angering Churchill, was quite evident following the events of April 9, 1942, when *Hermes* and its accompanying destroyer, which had failed to escape Ceylon, were destroyed in a little over twenty minutes by Nagumo's carrier-based air force. Somerville saved the bulk of the Eastern Fleet, but its retreat resulted in the surrender of the eastern Indian Ocean to the Japanese. The power of the Eastern Fleet after this humiliating retreat was greatly diminished by the assault on Vichy French Madagascar, code-named Operation Ironclad. The end of this operation saw the Eastern Fleet based at Kilindini, Kenya, where it was assigned to protect trade routes.

Somerville decided to return to Ceylon on May 29, 1942, but this was largely a symbolic gesture. Increasing pressures for additional ships in other theaters of war further weakened the Eastern Fleet. One carrier and three destroyers were sent to the Mediterranean, and the Americans requested a diversionary strike by the Eastern Fleet to distract the Japanese from U.S. preparations for the attack on Guadalcanal. This led to Operation Stab (August 1–10, 1942), a sortie of debatable success toward the Andaman Islands in the Bay of Bengal.

Yet another British defeat overshadowed this operation. Ships of the Royal Navy Commonwealth were operating as escorts for the U.S. landing forces at Guadalcanal in the central Pacific. One such force, under the Rear Admiral Victor Crutchley, met with disaster in the Battle of Savo Island on August 9, 1942. Of the force's three Australian cruisers, five U.S. cruisers, and fifteen destroyers, the Japanese destroyed four of the cruisers in a daring night attack. Three of the lost ships were American, and as a result, the decision was made that any British admiral who had U.S. ships under his command would be subject to the control of a senior U.S. naval officer. This was a great blow to British prestige in the theater. The U.S. loss of confidence colored relations between the two allies throughout the war in the Pacific. From the debacle at Savo Island through 1943, no Royal Navy or Commonwealth squadron operated with the Americans in the Pacific war. This does not mean that the British were totally absent from the theater, however; individual British ships took part in the struggle. The most significant of these instances was the loan of aircraft carrier *Victorious* to the United States in May 1943, an unusual reversal of the flow of weapons from the United States to Great Britain.

The Savo Island disaster was not the last for the Royal Navy; the fortunes of the Eastern Fleet were yet to hit their lowest ebb. The Indian Ocean diminished in strategic importance, and the demands of other theaters of war, particularly the Mediterranean, systematically whittled away at Somerville's command until the Eastern Fleet virtually ceased to exist as a fighting force by the end of 1943.

The dire situation of the Royal Navy in the Pacific war changed by the beginning of 1944, thanks to the establishment of a new command in the Far East. Deep disagreements between Somerville and other members of the British Far Eastern command structure over a planned amphibious assault to reoccupy Burma led to the appointment of a supreme commander Southeast Asia (SEAC). The energetic, wellborn new commander, Lord Louis Mountbatten, confirmed on November 15, 1943, wasted little time increasing Royal Navy operations in the Far East. In January 1944, the fleet received reinforcements, and by April the Eastern Fleet comprised four battleships, two aircraft carriers, two escort carriers, and escorting forces. Somerville led the fleet first in Operation Cockpit, an attack on the oil refineries at Sabang off northern Sumatra, on April 19, 1944. Operation Transom, on May 17, 1944, was against Japanese air bases at Surabaja, Java. It was clear after these operations that the British suffered from two major problems: lack of training in aircraft carrier operations, and supply. The supply problem was particularly vexing, and dogged the Royal Navy's efforts throughout the remainder of the Pacific war. Somerville's final action was Operation Crimson, beginning July 25, 1944. The admiral by this time was sixty-two years old, and the Admiralty began to fear for his health. On August 23, 1944, Admiral Sir Bruce Fraser took command of the fleet.

Fraser quickly became involved in events that completely changed the Royal Navy's status in the Pacific. Prime Minister Churchill offered the Americans the services of the British fleet in the Pacific, which President Franklin Roosevelt accepted, partly to avoid damaging relations between the Allies. The acceptance ended the existence of the Eastern Fleet by dividing it into two forces on November 22, 1944. The first was the East Indies Fleet, commanded by Admiral Sir Arthur Power, which remained under the operational control of SEAC. The second force was the British Pacific Fleet, under Admiral Fraser. The most pressing consideration for the British was the assurance that the British Pacific Fleet would serve under U.S. Admiral Chester Nimitz's control in the central Pacific and not in the southwest Pacific, because the eventual capture of the Philippines would make the latter theater less important. The British government wanted to regain the prestige the Royal Navy had lost and also to have a claim to the restoration of its empire in the Pacific after the war.

Having the British Pacific Fleet in the thick of the fighting was vital to the country's imperial interests, because it would give the appearance of Britain's liberating its possessions from the Japanese. Admiral Fraser met with

Nimitz at Pearl Harbor in December 1944 with these concerns in mind. The result of the conference was the Pearl Harbor Agreement (N/F 1). Under the agreement the British Pacific Fleet, if needed, was subject to U.S. orders; the British task force commander would have the status of his U.S. equivalent; and Admiral Ernest King would decide where to employ the British fleet. This last stipulation was problematic because King was greatly against having the British Pacific Fleet serve in any substantial capacity. Admiral King's objection stemmed mainly from his opposition to revived British influence in the Pacific, but he also believed that the British Pacific Fleet was not sufficiently trained in carrier operations to participate in a U.S. force. (The irascible King also seemed to possess an unexplained anti–British animus.)

The British Pacific Fleet arrived in Sydney, Australia, on February 10, 1945. It comprised one battleship, four aircraft carriers, three cruisers, and nine destroyers under the command of Vice Admiral Sir Bernard Rawlings. Admiral Fraser remained in Sydney as overall commander. Even after the arrival of the British Pacific Fleet in Sydney, Fraser did not know where or under whose command it would operate. The admiral wanted his force to take part in the upcoming invasion of Okinawa, code-named Operation Iceberg. Much to his delight, Fraser learned that king had assented, partly after being pressured by Nimitz, to the inclusion of the British Pacific Fleet in the U.S. Fifth Fleet under Nimitz's command, and it would therefore participate in the invasion. The Americans designated the British force as Task Force 57, under the operational command of American Admiral Raymond Spruance.

Despite its being included in the invasion force, the Americans did not consider the British fleet sufficiently experienced to take part in the main assault on Okinawa. Spruance consequently assigned Admiral Rawlings's command the task of destroying the airfields on Sakishima Gunto, the islands between Formosa (now Taiwan) and Okinawa. Rawlings felt confident with his force of two battleships, four carriers, seven cruisers, and eleven destroyers, and began the operation on March 26, 1945. The British encountered little resistance until April 1, when the fleet endured Japanese kamikaze attacks in defense of the islands. The Japanese scored hits on the British carriers, but very little damage was done thanks to their armored flight decks. Although this feature decreased their complement of planes in comparison with their U.S. counterparts, it proved invaluable against the kamikaze, who had far greater success against the wooden flight decks of the U.S. carriers. With the exception of a short respite for refueling, Task Force 57 continued to bomb the airfields of Sakishima Gunto until April 20, when it withdrew to Leyte, the Philippines.

The last assignment for the British force during Operation Iceberg was additional attacks against the airfields of Sakishima Gunto, which continued to offer some resistance. These final attacks took place May 4–25, 1945, and were a further tribute to the armored flight decks of the British carriers. All the carriers of the task force were hit by kamikazes or bombs, but all remained operational and on station. Overall, the British were successful in their mission. During Operation Iceberg the fleet conducted 5,335 sorties that dropped 958 tons of bombs on the airfields of Sakishima Gunto. The heavy surface units of the force added to the destruction with 200 tons of shells. No ships were lost, but the operations did cost the British about 150 aircraft.

While the ships of Task Force 57 engaged the Japanese at Okinawa, the forces of the East Indies Fleet had one final noteworthy engagement. On May 16, 1945, destroyers of the 26th Flotilla engaged and sank the Japanese cruiser *Haguro* near Panang, Malaya. *Haguro* was the last Japanese warship of any significance operational in the Indian Ocean. Following its sinking, the ships of the East Indies Fleet concentrated on the destruction of Japanese merchant shipping for the remainder of the war.

The final engagement for the ships of the British Pacific Fleet was air strikes on the Japanese mainland in preparation for the Allied invasion. Code-named Operation Olympic, the ships of the Royal Navy struck the Japanese between July 17 and August 10, 1945. Significantly, the ships of the Royal Navy were not allowed to strike at the remaining surface units of the Japanese navy. This was largely due to a political decision by senior American officials to let only U.S. ships attack them in revenge for the assault on Pearl Harbor, Hawaii, in December 1941.

The sterling service provided by the Royal Navy met an abrupt and poor end; the majority of the fleet was forced to return to base because of low fuel supplies, a problem for the fleet throughout the Pacific war. Admiral Rawlings was somewhat comforted by the fact that the United States agreed to allow a token British force to attend the surrender ceremonies in Tokyo Bay, which were set for September 2, 1945. On August 27, 1945, the British Pacific Fleet steamed into Tokyo Bay with one battleship, one aircraft carrier, two cruisers, and nine destroyers. Admiral Fraser accompanied this force on battleship *Duke of York* and attended the surrender ceremonies on board battleship *Missouri*. General Douglas MacArthur signed the instrument of Japan's surrender in the name of the Allied powers.

The Royal Navy endured a series of humiliating defeats in the opening stages of the Pacific war, but survived and provided great aid in the Indian and Pacific oceans. Despite its record, however, the fleet could never overcome the blow dealt by the Japanese to Britain's empire and prestige in the Far East in 1941. The victory over the Japanese was in this respect a hollow one for the Royal Navy.

FURTHER READINGS

Barnett, Correlli. *Engage the Enemy More Closely: The Royal Navy in the Second World War* (1991).
Gray, Edwin. *Operation Pacific: The Royal Navy's War Against Japan, 1941–1945* (1990).
Roskill, Stephen. *The War at Sea, 1939–1945* (HMSO, 1954).
Winton, John. *The Forgotten Fleet: The British Navy in the Pacific, 1944–1945* (1970).

Eric W. Osborne

SEE ALSO ABDA Command; Aircraft Carriers: Japanese, U.S., and British; Dutch East Indies; Fraser, Bruce A.; Pearl Harbor Conference; *Prince of Wales* and *Repulse*, Sinking of; Savo Island, Battle of

Navy, U.S.

The U.S. Navy was ill equipped for the possibility of fighting Japan when war broke out between that nation and China in July 1937. The composition of the navy at that time was largely the result of the interwar policies of isolationism and disarmament. Battleship construction was suspended following the signing of treaties at the Washington Naval Conference of 1922, which limited capital ship construction by the major maritime powers in an attempt to prevent a naval arms race. In 1937 the navy possessed 15 battleships, 3 aircraft carriers, 17 heavy cruisers, 10 light cruisers, and 196 destroyers. Senior American officials realized the inadequacy of this fleet for the defense of both the Atlantic and the Pacific oceans. President Franklin D. Roosevelt consequently called on Congress on January 28, 1938, to authorize a 20 percent increase in the overall tonnage of the navy. The naval expansion bill, passed on May 7, 1938, called for the construction of three battleships, two aircraft carriers, nine light cruisers, and twenty-three destroyers. It was meant to strengthen the U.S. position in the Pacific and also was intended as a warning to Japan against further imperial conquest.

This gesture, however, went unheeded by the Japanese, who continued their expansionist policies. Added to this failure was the outbreak of war in Europe in September 1939 and the string of Allied defeats by Nazi Germany in the first half of 1940. The dire position of the Allied powers led to a much larger naval expansion bill in 1940. Many American politicians believed a further increase in naval construction was necessary because of the distinct possibility that the United States might shortly stand alone against German and Japanese aggression. The new expansion bill, presented to Congress on June 18, 1940, called for the creation of a two-ocean navy. The $4 billion plan called for a 70 percent increase in naval tonnage: 7 battleships, 18 aircraft carriers, 27 cruisers, 115 destroyers, and 43 submarines. Congress passed this bill on June 20, as France was tottering toward defeat at the hands of Nazi Germany. Although the completion date of this program was 1946, the construction it authorized was crucial to the U.S. war effort in the coming struggle against Japan. The industrial might of the United States made this plan possible, and the ships it yielded would eventually overwhelm the lesser resources of the Japanese.

Despite this huge program and the obvious concern that Americans had regarding Japanese intentions in the Pacific, the focus of attention until the second half of 1941 was the Atlantic theater. This changed after U.S. intelligence received information on July 8, 1941, that Japan planned to ignore the warnings of the United States and Great Britain, and expand into Southwest Asia. Diplomatic negotiations between the United States and Japan collapsed by the end of November 1941. Following on the heels of this breakdown, on December 1, 1941, the Japanese decided to go to war against the United States.

The subsequent attack by Japanese carrier-based planes on the U.S. naval base of Pearl Harbor, Hawaii, on December 7, 1941, was the greatest disaster by far for the U.S. Navy in the Pacific. The assault, however, did not achieve everything hoped for by the Japanese. The Japanese sank four of the eight battleships moored there and damaged all the others (one only slightly), but of the eight only two were beyond repair. The attackers failed to find the U.S. aircraft carriers in port, which left the navy with its real striking force intact. Finally, the Japanese did not destroy the huge oil depots and machine shops at the base. Consequently, Pearl Harbor remained operational. This attack, far more than any presidential exhortation or government propaganda, galvanized the American people in their determination to defeat Japan utterly. Almost of equal importance, the loss of the battleships at Pearl Harbor forced the U.S. Navy to embrace the concept of a carrier task force. The aircraft carrier replaced the battleship as the capital warship of the navy.

The U.S. Navy was quickly put on a war footing following President Roosevelt's declaration of war against Japan on December 8, 1941. The most immediate step for the navy was the removal of Admiral Husband E. Kimmel, the commander in chief of the Pacific Fleet, on the charge of negligence concerning the defense of Pearl Harbor. Roosevelt chose the prewar commander of the U.S. Atlantic Fleet, Admiral Ernest J. King, to replace Kimmel not only as commander of the U.S. Pacific Fleet, but also, by March 1942, as commander in chief of the entire U.S. Navy. King, for all his abrasiveness, was a good choice because of his vast experience as both a sailor and a bureaucrat.

Following this change in leadership, the most pressing question was how best to pursue the defeat of Japan. The task was indeed daunting because of the distance between the two countries. In order to attack Japan, the United States would have to project its naval strength across the Pacific Ocean. This problem became all the more vexing after the string of Japanese successes following Pearl Harbor. The Japanese captured Guam on December 11 and Wake Island on December 23. They invaded the Philippines on December 22, 1941; all organized U.S. forces surrendered by May 6, 1942. The British also suffered heavily, with the destruction of battleship *Prince of Wales* and battle cruiser *Repulse* in the defense of Singapore on December 8, 1941; the loss of Hong Kong on December 25, 1941, and the loss of Singapore and the entire Malay Peninsula in February 1942. Added to these losses was the destruction of the ABDA Command, a collection of Allied warships, in February 1942 during the defense of the Dutch East Indies (now Indonesia) that practically removed the Royal Navy from the Pacific.

Amid these disasters the top military officials of the United States and Britain met in early 1942 and decided that for purposes of naval operations during the war, the world would be divided into strategic theaters. The British were made responsible for the Middle East, Indian Ocean, and eastern Atlantic; the United States concentrated on the Pacific. In order to project U.S. naval strength across the Pacific, American strategists recognized the necessity of recapturing lost American possessions and conquering Japanese Pacific holdings as forward bases for fleet operations. The command of the Pacific was divided into two theaters to achieve this end. The first was under the command of General Douglas MacArthur and comprised the southwest Pacific. Admiral Chester Nimitz commanded the second, consisting of the North, central, and South Pacific.

The establishment of the two theaters of command did little to resolve the question of how best to pursue the defeat of Japan. MacArthur envisioned an advance of army and ground-based air units from Australia through the large islands of the Dutch East Indies toward the Philippines. This did not sit well with the Navy Department, which argued vehemently for the execution of Plan Orange, a strategy formulated during the interwar years for the possibility of a future conflict against Japan. It called for a protracted war in which U.S. naval forces would advance through the central Pacific, seizing Japanese island possessions by means of amphibious operations. The plan also called for offensive engagements against Japanese naval forces. The overall vision was to isolate and exhaust Japan by crossing the Pacific and blockading the home islands, thereby cutting off overseas trade and economically destroying the country. The joint chiefs of staff (JCS) endorsed both theater commanders' plans, but the navy was primarily engaged in the execution of Plan Orange because Nimitz commanded the bulk of the navy in his theater.

During the first months of the war, the navy had few resources with which to pursue this grand strategy. At the beginning of 1942 the U.S. Pacific Fleet comprised four aircraft carriers, some prewar cruisers, a destroyer force, and some submarines. Admiral King, knowing that the Pacific Fleet could not face the Japanese in a surface action after Pearl Harbor, had ordered Nimitz on the afternoon of December 7, 1941, to deploy the submarines of the fleet for a blockade of Japan. This order roughly corresponded to the stipulations of Plan Orange with its vision of a blockade of Japan. Although the initial results were not great, due to poor or obsolete equipment and too many U.S. Navy officers still following peacetime routines, the submarine campaign proved increasingly vital to the U.S. offensive in the Pacific. Japan neglected the defense of its merchant shipping in the belief that such a campaign would be too difficult for the Americans, owing to the tremendous distances involved. This reasoning was extremely shortsighted, considering that the Japanese depended completely on overseas resources for their economic survival. At the beginning of the war, the Japanese possessed 6 million tons of merchant shipping and built another 2 million during the conflict. U.S. submarines sank almost 5 million tons of this shipping, a feat that went far toward the Plan Orange vision of starving out Japan.

The order for submarine warfare, however, did not address the initial U.S. problem. The navy's building program held much promise for the future, but in early 1942 the question was how to stop further Japanese expansion with the few resources at hand. Admirals King and Nimitz and the JCS recognized the threat that Japanese aggression

posed to Australia. Intelligence information indicated that the Japanese were planning to expand their defensive perimeter farther into the southwest Pacific by seizing the islands around Australia, thereby isolating it. The possibility of the loss of Australia was serious because the country was vital as a naval base and an area to station troops. Its loss would be a body blow to Allied morale, already at a low ebb because of Japanese victories. King was determined to blunt the Japanese advance despite the navy's limited means. In March 1942 he unveiled his Pacific plan to Roosevelt. The navy would defend Hawaii against further attack while helping Australia in any way possible. In addition, King proposed a limited naval offensive using the aircraft carriers for hit-and-run raids against the Japanese. Roosevelt approved the plan and King immediately ordered Nimitz to institute it, although Nimitz preferred to keep the carriers in the central Pacific for defense rather than risk them in small raids that held little strategic importance.

Nimitz's view of the purpose of these raids missed the point envisioned by King. Although these raids did little damage to the Imperial Japanese Navy or to Japan's war effort, they disrupted Japanese planning and boosted Allied morale. The most dramatic of these was the April 18, 1942, Doolittle raid that bombed Tokyo. A carrier task force comprised of carriers *Hornet* and *Enterprise* and commanded by Admiral William Halsey launched sixteen medium Mitchell bombers against the Japanese capital. The attack inflicted little damage, but it shook Japanese confidence while raising American morale. More important, it ended all opposition among Japanese naval officials to the plan for forcing a decisive fleet engagement with the United States at Midway Island.

At the time of the Doolittle raid, intelligence reports indicated that the Japanese were poised to execute the first stage of their plans for the isolation of Australia: an invasion of Port Moresby on the southern coast of New Guinea. Nimitz sent the bulk of his available forces to the Coral Sea to resist the impending assault; the United States could still act only defensively in the Pacific at this stage of the conflict. U.S. hopes for stopping the Japanese advance rested on a force comprising only two aircraft carriers, *Yorktown* and *Lexington*, three cruisers, and a few destroyers. The resulting clash, the Battle of the Coral Sea in May 1942, was the first in history where the opposing warships never came within sight of each other, and achieved mixed tactical results. The U.S. Navy lost *Lexington*, *Yorktown* was badly damaged, and one destroyer was sunk. The imperial navy lost a light carrier and sustained damage to the two heavy carriers of its force. Despite the fairly even losses, the battle was a strategic victory for the United States. The U.S. Navy had halted Japanese expansion in the Pacific. Equally important was the fact that the two Japanese heavy carriers were too badly damaged to participate in the next major battle in the Pacific, at Midway Island.

Following the Doolittle raid on Tokyo, the commander in chief of the imperial navy, Admiral Yamamoto Isoroku, won the acceptance of his plan to force a major fleet engagement with the U.S. Navy by attacking the U.S. base at Midway Island. Yamamoto knew that such a move would force action because the Japanese occupation of Midway would give them a submarine base and a fuel depot, and would provide a stepping-stone for an invasion of Hawaii. The United States could not afford this because it threatened the safety of Hawaii, which King had pledged to defend.

The task of defending Midway was indeed a daunting one. The Japanese force comprised 162 ships with 4 aircraft carriers, 8 battleships, and 8 heavy cruisers. Facing it was a much smaller American force built around the three carriers *Enterprise, Hornet,* and *Yorktown* and a collection of prewar cruisers. The Battle of Midway on June 3–6, 1942, was a triumph for the U.S. Navy, which was victorious in large measure due to the codebreaking by U.S. intelligence that predicted the attack and provided the element of surprise against the Japanese. The imperial navy lost all four of its carriers, a cruiser, and 275 planes with their pilots, whereas the U.S. Navy suffered the destruction of *Yorktown,* a destroyer, and 150 planes. The defeat at Midway was devastating for the Japanese. They lost four of their finest carriers and many of their highly trained pilots. The lack of well-trained pilots became an increasingly dire problem and vastly reduced the effectiveness of future imperial navy carrier striking forces. After Midway the Japanese did not have the naval strength to move any farther into the South Pacific. The balance of sea power began shifting toward the United States.

In the wake of the victory at Midway, the JCS approved an offensive against Rabaul, New Britain, one of the two principal Japanese bases in the South Pacific and a strong point in their defensive perimeter. Nimitz was to approach Rabaul through an assault on the southern Solomon islands, particularly Guadalcanal, while the forces under MacArthur advanced in New Guinea. The initial landing in Guadalcanal, on August 7, 1942, went forward with little resistance from the Japanese, who were surprised by the assault, and the U.S. Marines gained a foothold on the island. The imperial navy, however, vigorously resisted any further U.S. advances and launched numerous naval attacks against U.S. forces in the region. The conflict proved costly to the naval and land forces of

both sides and continued until mid–November 1942, when Allied forces finally gained the advantage on Guadalcanal (Rabaul remained operational). The cost of the operation led to changes in U.S. objectives in the Pacific. In the wake of the Casablanca Conference of January 1943, which called for a continuation of U.S. offensives in the Pacific, MacArthur and Nimitz agreed that their forces did not have the resources to conquer Rabaul in 1943. This realization sparked debate about the course of the Pacific war.

The lack of a concrete plan for the defeat of Japan hampered Allied progress in the Pacific war until mid–1943. The two theater commanders, MacArthur and Nimitz, held vastly different ideas concerning the advance across the Pacific. Allied leaders began to address this problem in May 1943 when Roosevelt and Churchill met at the Trident Conference in Washington; there they agreed, with the knowledge that the campaign against Rabaul had stalled, to the opening of a new front into the central Pacific. This suited the navy well because it was entirely in keeping with the Plan Orange vision of an advance through that area. The islands in this region were crucial to the Japanese defense of the Pacific, because from them the U.S. Navy could strike northward at Japan. The idea of a new front took a more concrete form following the Quebec Conference of August 1943, at which a JCS plan was presented that called for a two-pronged offensive against the Japanese. Under this plan MacArthur would advance northwest through the Solomons while Nimitz's forces attacked the Marshall and Caroline island chains in an island-hopping campaign toward the Marianas Islands in the central Pacific. Although the conference did not attach priority to either of the two advances, the acceptance of the plan provided a more concrete approach to the question of how to pursue the Pacific war.

Before Nimitz could begin his advance through the Marshalls and Carolines, he had to capture the Gilbert Islands (now Kiribati), which were part of Japan's defensive perimeter and contained the island fortresses of Makin and Tarawa. Makin succumbed quickly to U.S. forces, but the attack on Tarawa, November 20–24, 1943, the first large-scale American amphibious attack in the Pacific, was a bloody struggle. The assault force of 5,000 troops suffered 991 dead and 2,311 wounded. These heavy losses seemed prove the case of MacArthur and his supporters that the cost of the central Pacific advance was prohibitive. King and Nimitz were distressed at the high casualties on Tarawa, but stood by their belief that their plan was the best course of action. The conquest of the Gilberts positioned the U.S. Navy for a strike against the Marshall Islands.

Operations against the Marshall Islands proved the value of the leap-frogging strategy in the central Pacific campaign. Instead of attacking some of the more heavily defended islands in the eastern portion of the group, the USN advanced to the Japanese communications center at Kwajalein, conquering it on February 4, 1944. Nimitz followed up this success with an attack against the island of Eniwetok, which fell on February 22, 1944. The other islands' garrisons were left to wither away as their supply lines were cut by the loss of Kwajalein and Eniwetok. Japanese power in the area was further damaged during this campaign when U.S. carrier-based planes struck the fortress island of Truk in the Carolines to preclude the possibility of the Japanese launching air strikes to defend the Marshall Islands. While attacking Truk, the Americans realized that the Japanese fleet was no longer stationed there. The imperial navy had withdrawn to the Palau Islands because it no longer had the strength to fight the U.S. fleet. The building programs instituted during the prewar years had greatly augmented the strength of the U.S. Navy by this time. Not only did it have new, modern battleships at its disposal, but it also had several of the new *Essex* class mass-produced heavy carriers that would serve as the backbone of U.S. naval power in the Pacific. The retreat of the imperial navy and the devastation inflicted upon Truk during the Marshall Islands campaign led to the decision to bypass the base and the rest of the Carolines because they no longer posed a major strategic threat.

By mid-1944 the Japanese position in the Pacific was precarious. The two-pronged U.S. offensive had split the weakened imperial navy, and hampered the protection of Japan's shrinking defensive perimeter. For the Japanese it was crucial to prevent the success of the next stage of the central Pacific advance: the invasion of the Marianas Islands. These islands, which include Saipan, Tinian, and Guam, lie about fifteen hundred miles from Japan. America's giant long-range B-29 bombers could use the islands, particularly Saipan and Tinian, as airfields from which to launch strikes against Japan. The Japanese reaction to the invasion of the Marianas, beginning in June 1944, was exactly as King had foreseen. The imperial navy sortied against the U.S. Navy for the first time since the Guadalcanal invasion in the fall of 1942. Commanded by Admiral Toyoda Soemu, the force consisted of nine carriers and eighteen battleships and cruisers. Facing Toyoda was a much stronger force under Admiral Raymond Spruance that included fifteen aircraft carriers. These forces clashed in the Battle of the Philippine Sea (June 19–20, 1944), between the Marianas and the Philippine Islands. The attack was a disaster for the Japanese, who found them-

selves overwhelmed by the tremendous striking power of the U.S. carriers. The imperial navy retreated after the loss of 476 planes and 445 pilots. The battle also resulted in the destruction of three of their aircraft carriers and damage to three others. Spruance's force lost thirty planes and sustained damage to one battleship. The lost carriers were a serious blow for the Japanese, but far more important was the loss of the dwindling supply of trained pilots. The U.S. victory and the subsequent conquests of Saipan (July 9, 1944), Tinian (July 31, 1944), and Guam (August 10, 1944) ushered the Pacific war into its final phase. War Plan Orange was reaching fruition with the loss of these islands. Bombing raids against Japan were now possible, as was implementation of the blockade that would lead to its defeat.

The conquest of the Marianas completed the list of concrete plans that the JCS had presented in 1943 and raised the question of where to attack next. By July 1944 MacArthur had conquered New Guinea, and Nimitz the Palau Islands after the Marianas campaign, in order to cover MacArthur's right flank for his advance to the Philippines. The JCS now debated the next goal in the Pacific war. MacArthur strongly maintained that the next target should be the Philippine Islands, whereas King argued for bypassing them and attacking Formosa (now Taiwan). MacArthur's plan won out largely because of logistical questions, although the recovery of a lost U.S. possession was also appealing. The Allies lacked both the manpower and the materiel to attack Formosa in 1944. In October 1944 the JCS decided on the Philippines as the next target and ordered Nimitz to support the amphibious invasion, to take place at the island of Leyte on October 20, 1944, with the Pacific Fleet. The navy would follow up the invasion in early 1945 by extending the central Pacific campaign to Iwo Jima, in the Volcano Islands, and to Okinawa, in the Ryukyu chain.

By the time of the Leyte landing, the U.S. Navy was nothing like the navy that had faced the Japanese almost three years earlier. The tremendous industrial strength of the United States had produced the great number of vessels called for in the prewar naval expansion plans, plus additional warships and support craft. The size of the naval force that Nimitz employed for the invasion was staggering: seventeen heavy aircraft carriers, eighteen light escort carriers, eighteen battleships, seven cruisers, seven light cruisers, and ninety-five destroyers. These ships were organized into two fleets. The first was the Seventh Fleet, under Vice Admiral Thomas Kincaid, whose mission was to protect the landing of more than two hundred thousand troops of the Sixth Army on Leyte. The second was the Third Fleet, under Admiral Halsey, accompanied by the smaller Task Group 77.4, under Rear Admiral Thomas Sprague. Their mission was to carry out air strikes against Japanese forces on Formosa and the large Philippine island of Luzon in order to protect the landing force and guard against sorties by the imperial navy.

The invasion of the Philippines presented a crucial situation on which the fate of Japan hinged. The loss of the islands would cut the trade routes for vital raw materials between Japan and the Dutch East Indies. The Japanese high command decided to sortie the bulk of their Combined Fleet to a successful Allied landing at Leyte. Their plan called for three forces to take part in the operation. The first, commanded by Vice Admiral Kurita Takeo and known as the Center Force, would approach Leyte from the north, through San Bernardino Strait. The force comprised two superbattleships *Yamato* and *Musashi,* three other battleships, ten heavy cruisers, two light cruisers, and fifteen destroyers. Approaching Leyte from the south, through Surigao Strait, would be the Southern Force under Vice Admiral Shoji Nishimura, which comprised two battleships, three heavy cruisers, and eleven destroyers. The third force, under Vice Admiral Jisaburo Ozawa, would sail to a position north of the Leyte landing site. This force was a diversion to lure the supporting U.S. naval forces away from the landing zone, leaving it unprotected against Kurita and Nishimura's forces. Ozawa's fleet consisted of four aircraft carriers, two battleships, two light cruisers, and a small destroyer escort force. The offensive potential of this fleet was virtually nonexistent because the tremendous loss of pilots meant that none of the carriers had a full complement of aircraft. Ozawa's mission was basically one of sacrifice, in the hope of inflicting a crushing defeat on the U.S. landing force at Leyte.

The U.S. landing at Leyte Gulf on October 20, 1944, led the Japanese to implement their plan. The Battle of Leyte Gulf, October 23–26, 1944, was a complete disaster for the imperial navy. The great preponderance of U.S. carrier-based air power and the sheer weight of numbers in warships led to crushing losses for the Japanese. By the end of the battle the U.S. Navy had sunk sixty-eight Japanese warships, including three battleships (one of them superbattleship *Musashi*), all four of Ozawa's aircraft carriers, ten cruisers, and nine destroyers. The U.S. Navy lost only one light carrier, two escort carriers, and three destroyers. The Battle of Leyte Gulf destroyed the remaining offensive power of the imperial navy and ruined it as a fighting force. It was also the greatest naval battle of modern history. The Japanese never sortied their combined fleet again. Coupled with this tremendous loss was the failure of Japanese efforts to hold the Philippines

against the U.S. invasion. The Japanese garrison defending the Philippines had no chance after the defeat of the imperial navy. The Americans gained absolute air superiority over the Japanese and cut their supply lines following the Battle of Leyte Gulf. U.S. ground forces fought against stubborn Japanese defenders in the Philippines for the rest of the war, but the issue was never in doubt and the islands were under U.S. control by mid–March 1945. Their loss signaled the end of Japanese hopes for achieving even a stalemate in the Pacific war.

The U.S. Navy, however, did not come away from the Battle of Leyte Gulf with a completely unblemished record. The Japanese plan nearly succeeded, owing to the decision of Admiral Halsey to pursue Ozawa's decoy force. This decision became one of the most controversial of the war because the admiral left the Leyte beachhead undefended and vulnerable. Although Nishimura's Southern Force was destroyed before it reached Leyte, the Center Force under Kurita got through and approached the undefended Leyte landing zone. Disaster was averted only by a combination of bravery and luck. Kurita's ships met a small U.S. force of six escort carriers, three destroyers, and four destroyer escorts under the command of Rear Admiral Clifton Sprague. Despite being hopelessly outgunned, Sprague ordered his three destroyers to attack Kurita's force. This daring shock tactic succeeded because of Kurita's lack of intelligence information. He mistakenly believed that he faced Halsey's much larger and more powerful Third Fleet, not realizing that Ozawa's decoy mission had succeeded. Kurita decided to retreat while only 40 miles from the uncovered Leyte beachhead.

The retreat of Kurita's Center Force meant that Japanese naval strategy had failed, and the end of the Pacific war was now in sight. In accordance with the October 1944 JCS decision on fleet operations, King and Nimitz refocused the attention of the U.S. Navy to the central Pacific campaign. The last two objectives of the island-hopping campaign were Iwo Jima, some 750 miles from Japan, and Okinawa, only 350 miles from the home islands. The U.S. Navy bombarded Iwo Jima and provided valuable air support during the invasion (February 19–March 26, 1945). Although the cost of taking Iwo Jima was high, with the Marines suffering 18,070 wounded and 6,891 killed, the prize was invaluable. Iwo Jima helped to fulfill the vision of Plan Orange by becoming a base from which B-29 bombers could attack the Japanese home islands at will. From March to August 1945 almost two thousand bombers used Iwo Jima as their base in the bombing campaign against Japan.

The campaign for Okinawa, in the Ryuku Islands, proved much more taxing on the U.S. Navy than that for

Iwo Jima. On April 1, 1945, a U.S. invasion fleet of 1,213 ships landed 183,000 troops on Okinawa. Supporting this force was the Fifth Fleet under Spruance, comprised of 40 aircraft carriers of differing types, 18 battleships, and nearly 200 destroyers. The force at Okinawa was different from those deployed during the majority of the Pacific war because it was an Allied rather than solely a U.S. naval force. The British had returned to the Pacific theater a short while before the Okinawa campaign. Four of the aircraft carriers and 2 of the battleships were from the British Pacific Fleet, commanded by Vice Admiral Sir Bernard Rawlings.

Despite their now desperate strategic situation, the Japanese planned to defend the island. One of the defense elements would be land-based planes flown by Japanese kamikaze pilots. The kamikaze suicide method of attack, although very costly in planes and pilots, was the best use of the dwindling airpower of Japan because at this stage in the war its pilots had very little training. During the Okinawa campaign the kamikaze pilots flew a total of ten attacks of 1,465 suicide planes against the Allied invasion fleet. These strikes inflicted heavy damage on the naval forces, which had no real defense against such desperate tactics. The kamikaze attacks resulted in the deaths of 4,907 American sailors and 26 ships sunk, with damage to an additional 164 vessels.

Added to the kamikaze attacks was an attempted sortie by some of the remaining surface units of the imperial navy. The imperial navy task force that sailed for Okinawa comprised a light cruiser, eight destroyers, and super-battleship *Yamato. Yamato,* with nine 18.1-inch guns, was, like the kamikaze aircraft defending Okinawa, on a suicide mission. The task force had only enough fuel to reach the island; once there, its orders were to beach the super-battleship and use its massive guns to shell U.S. positions. This mission was doomed from the start, owing to the tremendous carrier-based air strength of the Allied fleet at Okinawa. On April 7, 1945, *Yamato,* its attendant cruiser, and four destroyers, were sunk in the East China Sea by U.S. carrier-based aircraft. This was the last attack of major imperial navy surface units during the Pacific war. Okinawa was under American control by June 21, 1945, and by July 2 the campaign in the Ryuku Islands was over. The loss of Okinawa virtually completed the U.S. Navy Plan Orange goal of blockading Japan and destroying its economy. Regular bombing missions from Saipan, Guam, Tinian, Iwo Jima, and Okinawa laid waste Japan's industrial centers, which were starved for raw materials because of the supremacy of the U.S. Navy at sea. Allied battleships ranged boldly off the coast of Japan to pound industrial targets with their heavy guns. The final act of the war, the invasion of Japan, was now in sight.

In May 1945 the JCS decided on an invasion of Japan following a period of naval blockade and bombing. The navy would control the amphibious portion of the invasion and maintain the blockade. King supported the plan, which seemed al the more feasible with the surrender of Germany on May 8, 1945. Resources were now being directed entirely to the Pacific, and by mid–August almost all of the U.S. Navy was in the Pacific theater of operations, poised for the greatest invasion in history. While these resources slowly accumulated, the navy executed its orders for a blockade of Japan and destroyed the remaining surface units of the imperial navy in their home island ports. (It was also roughly at this time that the U.S. Navy suffered its final loss in the Pacific, the submarine sinking of USS *Indianapolis,* the last American warship to be sunk by enemy action.) These preliminary operations, however, did not lead to the invasion envisioned by King and the U.S. Navy. Following the atomic bomb blasts at Hiroshima and Nagasaki, Japan formally surrendered on the deck of battleship *Missouri* in Tokyo Bay on September 2, 1945. The fact that the surrender ceremony took place on a U.S. warship was a strong symbol that the U.S. Navy was the principal tool of Japan's defeat in World War II.

FURTHER READINGS

Baer, George. *One Hundred Years of Sea Power: The U.S. Navy, 1890–1990* (1994).

Hagan, Kenneth J., ed. *In Peace and War: Interpretations of American Naval History, 1775–1984* (1984).

Howarth, Stephen. *To Shining Sea: A History of the United States Navy, 1775–1991* (1991).

Morison, Samuel Eliot. *A History of United States Naval Operations in World War II,* vols. 3–8, 12–14 (1948–1960).

Morison, Samuel Eliot. *The Two Ocean War: A Short History of the United States Navy in the Second World War* (1963).

Pratt, Fletcher. *The Compact History of the United States Navy* (1975).

Eric W. Osborne

SEE ALSO ABDA Command; Aircraft Carrier Raids, U.S. Navy (1942); Aircraft Carriers, Japanese, U.S. and British; Amphibious Operations; Bismarck Sea, Battle of the; Coral Sea, Battle of the; Eastern Solomons, Battle of; Eniwetok; Gilbert Islands; Guadalcanal, Battle for; Halsey, William Frederick, Jr.; Island-Hopping and Leapfrogging, U.S. Strategies; Kamikazes; Kimmel,

Husband Edward; Leyte Gulf, Battle of; Logistics, U.S.; Makin Atoll; Midway, Battle of; Navy, Japanese; Nimitz, Chester William; Okinawa, Battle for; Palau; Pearl Harbor Conference; Savo Island, Battle of; Shipbuilding, U.S.; Shō-Go Plan; Spruance, Raymond Ames; Submarines, U.S.; Tarawa, Capture of; Tinian, Battle for; Truk; Washington Naval Treaty (1922) and Japan; Yamamoto Isoruku

Netherlands East Indies

See Dutch East Indies

New Britain

The beginning of World War II had little initial effect on people of New Britain, a British possession in the Solomon Islands. Though the Solomon Islands Defense Force (SIDF) had been organized, the islanders were convinced that no German troops would ever come to the Pacific. The situation changed in December 1941, when Japan declared war on the British Commonwealth and the United States. On January 23, 1942, Japanese troops invaded New Britain and the other Solomon Islands. The units of the SIDF on each island retreated into the mountains to begin a guerrilla war rather than attempt to fight the vastly superior Japanese forces. (This was one of the very few occasions when British Empire/Commonwealth troops fought an irregular campaign in the first few years of the Pacific war.) The SIDF members had been informed that their most valuable contribution to the war effort would be to maintain radio contact and to relay information regarding the numbers and distribution of Japanese forces on the islands.

The Allied offensive to recapture the Solomon Islands began with the U.S. invasion of Guadalcanal, the most southeastern of the Solomon Islands. The U.S. plan was to use island-hopping and leapfrogging in the recapture of the Solomon Islands. Islands deemed essential would be captured, then used as staging areas for the taking of the next essential island. Islands not deemed essential would be isolated and cut off from resupply while they were bombed, in order to prevent the Japanese forces from being used offensively.

Through the island-hopping and leapfrogging system, the Allies advanced through the Solomon Islands until they reached New Britain. By mid-1943 the port of Rabaul, on the eastern peninsula of New Britain, had been developed as a core of Japan's base system and was supported by two carrier air groups based on Truk. Rabaul, which was defended by the Japanese 17th Division and

the 39th and 65th Brigades, was deemed too heavily fortified to recapture by amphibious assault, whereas the remainder of the island was only lightly defended. As a result, in December 1943, the U.S. 112th Cavalry Regiment, the 40th Infantry Division, and the 1st Marine Division invaded the island. Meanwhile, American aircraft flew almost thirty thousand sorties over Rabaul in order to neutralize the Japanese garrison and prevent it from engaging in offensive operations.

With the assistance of Australian ground forces, the Americans completed the isolation of the Rabaul garrison. The Allies then allowed starvation and disease, along with continued air raids, to take a heavy toll on the Japanese defenders. By the time the Japanese surrendered in August 1945, New Britain had cost the Allies 200 Australian and 2,000 American casualties; the Japanese had lost 20,000 dead. In addition, the Allies had trapped 69,000 Japanese troops and 20,000 civilian workers in Rabaul for almost two years. This was one of the most intelligent and effective uses of the island-hopping strategy.

FURTHER READINGS

Hoyt, Edwin P. *Glory of the Solomons* (1983).

Miller, John, Jr. *Cartwheel: The Reduction of Rabaul* (1959).

Morison, Samuel Eliot. *History of United States Naval Operations in World War II*. Vol. 6, *Breaking the Bismarcks Barrier, 22 July 1942–1 May 1944* (1950).

Shaw, Henry I., Jr., and Douglas T. Kane. *History of U.S. Marine Corps Operations in World War II*. Vol. 2, *Isolation of Rabaul* (1963).

Spector, Ronald H. *Eagle Against the Sun: The American War with Japan* (1985).

Alexander M. Bielakowski

SEE ALSO Island-Hopping and Leapfrogging, U.S. Strategies

New Caledonia

The beginning of World War II had little effect on France's colonial possessions in the Pacific. After the fall of metropolitan France to Germany in 1940, however, many of the French Polynesian islanders transferred their loyalty from the Vichy government under Marshal Henri Pétain to the Free French government under General Charles de Gaulle. In some of the islands, plebiscites were held to determine whom the islanders wished to support. On the island of New Caledonia, the presence of a French warship, whose crew was loyal to Pétain, prevented such a plebiscite.

Because New Caledonia was strategically important for both its geographical position and its mineral resources, the Allies could not allow it to remain in the Axis camp. In September 1940, therefore, the arrival of Australian heavy cruiser HMAS *Adelaide* at the chief New Caledonian port of Nouméa caused the Vichy French warship to leave and allowed the island's government to support De Gaulle's Free French government in exile.

For almost two years the New Caledonians worried that the Australians might annex the island out of military necessity. After all, New Caledonia was on the routes from Australia to the United States, and from Japan to New Zealand. The island also was large enough for major airstrips to be built, and it could easily accommodate thousands of troops. Equally important, its ports were deep and it possessed significant deposits of nickel. The fears of the New Caledonians were eased on March 12, 1942, with the arrival of U.S. Task Force 6814. For most islanders the American presence represented a defense against both the Japanese and the Australians.

Through agreements between the Free French government and the United States, the Americans were allowed extensive use of New Caledonia and the New Hebrides in exchange for a guarantee of French control over the islands. In practice, however, it was American generals and admirals, rather than the civilian French officials, whose policies affected almost every critical sphere of life in wartime New Caledonia. For two months after its arrival, Task Force 6814 garrisoned and defended both New Caledonia and the New Hebrides. On May 27, 1942, the Americans organized an infantry division from the units assigned to Task Force 6814. Because U.S. troops had received such a warm welcome in New Caledonia, the new division was named "Americal" (America-Caledonia), in honor of the island.

From June 19, 1942, until June 15, 1944, New Caledonia was the headquarters of the U.S. South Pacific Force, under the command of Vice Admiral Robert L. Ghormley, and then of Vice Admiral William F. Halsey, Jr. As the war moved closer to the Japanese home islands, however, New Caledonia became less important as a base of operations. After the war ended, the island regained brief importance when excess U.S. supplies were processed through New Caledonia between September 1945 and February 1946.

The islanders benefited both economically and socially from the U.S. presence on the island. Mineral exports soared, all the meat and vegetables that the islanders could produce were purchased at high prices to feed the American troops, and the troops freely spent their money in shops and bars throughout the island. Perhaps more im-

portant, the native Polynesians received decent wages for the first time, to the disgust of the French elite, who worried that the unheard-of payments would "spoil" their islanders.

After the war the islanders benefited from the roads and airfields that had been built by American engineers and by the equipment, worth $3 million in 1945, that the United States left behind. The only significant military contribution made by the New Caledonians during World War II was as part of the Bataillon Pacifique, composed of islanders from all of French Polynesia. The battalion was part of the Free French Brigade that successfully defended Bir Hacheim, Libya, against attacks by one Italian and two German divisions in May 1942.

FURTHER READINGS
Dornoy, Myriam. *Politics in New Caledonia* (1984).
Levine, Alan J. *Pacific War: Japan Versus the Allies* (1995).
Alexander M. Bielakowski

SEE ALSO Americal Division

New Georgia

In the summer of 1943, Allied forces in the South Pacific, commanded by Admiral William F. Halsey, were driving northwest through the Solomon Islands as part of Operation Cartwheel, the Allied operation to envelop and isolate the major Japanese base at Rabaul, New Britain. Halsey's chief objective in this phase of Cartwheel was the seizure of the New Georgia island group. Defended by approximately 10,500 troops, it was considered vital because of the airfield at Munda Point, on the northwest coast of the main island of New Georgia. Because a long barrier reef made Munda Point inaccessible to large vessels, the plan of operations, designated Toenails, called for the initial seizure of Rendova Island, three miles away, to serve as a jumping-off point for the principal invasion as well as for the occupation of three other strategic places: Sengi Point on New Georgia Island, to serve as a fighter base, and Viru Harbour on New Georgia Island and Wickham Anchorage on Vangunu Island, to serve as staging areas for supplies and reinforcements. These actions were to be followed by a major landing on New Georgia Island at Zanana, 5 miles east of Munda Point, and a secondary landing at Rice Anchorage, on the northwest coast of New Georgia, to prevent the Japanese from sending reinforcements from nearby Kolombangara Island.

Operation Toenails was assigned to Rear Admiral Richmond Kelly Turner's III Amphibious Force, with the assault to be carried out primarily by the army's 43d Division, under the command of Major General John H. Hester. Hester was also in charge of the New Georgia Occupation Force (NGOF), the command responsible for all ground forces participating in the operation. Thus, he had to manage administrative and logistical aspects of the operation as well as fight his division, a double duty for which he had neither the experience nor the staff.

The New Georgia landings began on June 21, 1943, when a U.S. Marine battalion seized Segi. On June 30 U.S. troops landed at Viru, Wickham Anchorage, and Rendova; on July 2, they landed at Zanana; and on July 5, at Rice Anchorage. Hester began his advance against Munda Point on July 5, and from the outset things went badly. Poor leadership and inexperience in the 43d Division, heat, constant rain, tangled undergrowth, a shortage of supplies, and determined Japanese resistance under the direction of Major General Noboru Sasaki slowed the division. When it reached the main Japanese defense line on the high ground east of Munda, it was forced to halt. At the same time, the troops who had landed at Rice Anchorage were unable to prevent the Japanese from reinforcing their troops on New Georgia. As the U.S. advance sputtered, the army's 37th and 25th divisions were committed to the battle. In addition, Major General Oscar W. Griswold, commander of the XIV Corps, replaced Hester as commander of the NGOF and took control of ground operations.

The New Georgia landings precipitated several naval battles. Early on the morning of July 6, a U.S. task force tangled with a Japanese squadron bringing reinforcements to New Georgia Island; and in the Battle of Kula Gulf (July 13), the Americans lost a light cruiser, and the Japanese, two destroyers. A U.S. task force encountered another Japanese squadron carrying reinforcements to New Georgia Island on July 12–13; and in the Battle of Kolombangara the Japanese lost a light cruiser, and the Americans, a destroyer. Three weeks later, on August 6–7, another U.S. task force smashed a Japanese squadron bringing reinforcements to Kolombangara in the Battle of Vella Gulf, sinking three destroyers that were carrying more than a thousand troops and ending any Japanese hope of expelling the Americans from New Georgia.

On July 25, Griswold launched a major offensive against Munda Point, supported by heavy air, artillery, and naval bombardment. The going was tough, however, especially for the tired 43d Division. Hester, who had carried too much of a load during the first days of the campaign, when he was in charge of the division and the NGOF, was exhausted, and on July 29 he was relieved of command of the 43d Division. His relief coincided with a Japanese decision to fall back because of heavy casualties,

and on August 5 the 43d Division captured Munda airfield.

Despite an aggressive U.S. pursuit over the next two weeks, most of the remaining Japanese defenders escaped to the nearby islands of Arundel, Baanga, and Kolombangara. Both Baanga and Arundel were captured by the end of September, but Halsey decided to bypass Kolombangara, which was heavily defended, and moved 15 miles to the northwest, to the weakly held island of Vella Lavella, invading it on August 15. By the end of September it was in Allied hands, rendering Kolombangara useless to the Japanese. Between September 28 and October 3, they evacuated more than nine thousand of its defenders to Bougainville, 100 miles to the northwest, ending the campaign for New Georgia.

The New Georgia operation provided Halsey with several good airfields and brought the Allies one step closer to Rabaul. It was, however, more costly and more involved than originally anticipated. Designed to be a one-division affair, it ultimately required three army divisions, elements of a fourth, and several marine battalions to defeat the greatly outnumbered Japanese. Army and marine losses were 1,094 dead and 3,873 wounded, along with several thousand nonbattle casualties due to disease and battle fatigue. Japanese casualties are not known, although XIV Corps reported 2,483 dead exclusive of Vella Lavella.

FURTHER READINGS
Hamel, Eric. *Munda Trail* (1989).
Lofgren, Stephen J. *Northern Solomons* (1993).
Miller, John, Jr. *Cartwheel: The Reduction of Rabaul* (1959).
Morison, Samuel Eliot. *History of United States Naval Operations in World War II.* Vol. 6, *Breaking the Bismarcks Barrier* (1950).
Morton, Louis. *Strategy and Command: The First Two Years* (1962).

John Kennedy Ohl

New Guinea

On July 2, 1942, the U.S. joint chiefs of staff ordered General Douglas MacArthur, commander of the Southwest Pacific Area, to begin a limited offensive to clear the Japanese from New Guinea. New Guinea had nothing either side wanted, nor did anyone want the terrain for terrain's sake. The island, however, was a staging area for offensives either to the north or to the south, as well as a defensive barrier.

For the Allies—the Australians and Americans—a series of advances would extend their air umbrella to cover the Bismarck Archipelago and isolate Japanese air bases and the port of Rabaul, New Britain. MacArthur wanted to gather all the forces he needed for an advance on Rabaul before starting his offensive, but European priorities, logistics, and Japanese thrusts prevented him from doing so.

The Japanese New Guinea offensive was one of two prongs (the other was the Solomons) reaching south toward Australia and U.S. communications sustaining that advanced base. Their first landings took place at Lae and Salamaua in February and March 1942. The Japanese had set their sights on Port Moresby, on the southeast coast of Papua New Guinea. That port and air base formed the key to Papua (an Australian territory that covered southeastern New Guinea) and to northern Australia. Port Moresby would give Japan either a base for attacks against Australia or an outpost to protect Rabaul. However, the Battle of the Coral Sea in early May 1942 turned back the Japanese task force headed for Port Moresby.

The Coral Sea repulse did not totally stop the Japanese. On July 21–22, they landed 4,400 men of the South Seas Detachment at Gona, on the northern coast of Papua. The newly activated Seventeenth Army initially directed New Guinea operations from Rabaul. (It would also assume responsibility for Guadalcanal in the near future.) An air campaign was already in progress over New Guinea. Disappointing results led to the assignment of Major General George C. Kenney as Allied air force commander. Kenney immediately invigorated his airmen and started to seize control of New Guinea's skies.

Once 11,000 Japanese were ashore, Major General Horii Tomitaro sent 1,800 men and 1,300 laborers overland toward Port Moresby on August 13; they were soon followed by many more. However, no one had properly reconnoitered the route. Imperial general headquarters had used only aerial photographs. As a result, Horii committed his men to a march over the 8,000-foot-high Owen Stanley Range along a jungle trail that was unsuitable for either fighting or supply.

Imperial general headquarters had not massed sufficient naval, air, or ground forces for what they hoped to do both at New Guinea and in the Solomons. They had the men and the ships; they just did not believe that significant forces would be needed. Contrary to legend, the Japanese were no more innately capable of operating in a jungle than were Western troops. (Japan has no jungle, and the Japanese army had no wartime jungle experience in China.) Lacking the logistical, engineering, and medical "tail" that followed the Americans, the Japanese were less capable of sustained jungle efforts. Yet for speed

marches over impossible terrain and for daily endurance, no army could match them.

Horii's men advanced south along the Kokoda Trail, slipping down deep gorges and struggling up dizzying ridges. They drove an Australian militia battalion and native constabulary out of Kokoda. The arrival of more Australian regulars slowed the Japanese and finally stopped them at Imita Ridge, 32 miles from Port Moresby, on September 14. The close fighting had been bitter. Few prisoners were taken. Maps were poor. Weather changed quickly. Combat was at point-blank range over ground and in vegetation of extreme difficulty. Japanese logistics broke down under the difficult terrain, shortage of porters, and air attacks from the U.S. Fifth Air Force.

Still confident in the ability of their light infantry to drive all before them, the Japanese landed 2,000 Special Naval Landing Force troops at Milne Bay the night of August 25–26. They needed a naval, air, and logistics base here, at the eastern tip of Papua, for the advance against Port Moresby. The Allies also wanted Milne Bay for its airstrip and as a logistics base. The Australians, warned by Ultra code breakers, reinforced their garrison of one militia brigade at Milne Bay with a regular brigade just before the Japanese landed. Nearly nine thousand Australians and Americans opposed the Japanese. A landing of 600 Japanese reinforcements on August 29 did not bring victory. Hard-fighting Australian infantry and Royal Australian Air Force P-40s drove the Japanese back to their beachheads. On September 4, the Japanese navy evacuated 1,200 of the 2,600 Japanese who had landed.

At the Kokoda Trail, the exhausted and famished Japanese had been ordered back north. Japanese priorities had shifted to Guadalcanal. The Japanese withdrew on September 24, and the Australians pursued. Along the Kokoda Trail there developed one of the most vicious and physically demanding battles of the Pacific war. The weather was hideous; the steep, jungle-covered slopes of the Owen Stanleys defied description; and for both pursuer and pursued, supplies were more important than tactics. Often supplied by airdrop, the Australians harried, outmaneuvered, and in the first half of November nearly annihilated General Horii's troops. Horii drowned while attempting to escape.

Surviving Japanese reached Papua's north coast at Gona, Sanananda, and Buna, and dug in. Most of the 8,000 Japanese now along the coast had not participated in the Owen Stanley march, and they were fresh. Their engineers had developed defenses from which the infantry would try to deny the Allies the Buna airfield. The Americans wanted the field to cover subsequent air attacks against points farther west (Lae and Salamaua).

Into the buzz saw of Buna marched the fresh, confident, inadequately trained U.S. National Guardsmen of the 32d Division. November 19, 1942, was the debut of U.S. infantry in the southwest Pacific, and MacArthur had great hopes for their performance. He had criticized supposedly poor Australian performance, so he had more than a purely tactical interest in the upcoming battle. Unfortunately, the unacclimated Americans, lacking artillery, tanks, and their normally munificent logistical tail, and faced with many more Japanese than their intelligence had estimated, failed ignominiously in their first attempts against the Buna defenses.

The Australian 7th Division closed in on the Japanese at Gona and Sanananda to the west and was repulsed, and the U.S. 32d Division at Buna was stymied. Disease (scrub typhus, dysentery, dengue fever, and malaria, to name a few), lack of supporting weapons, and uncertain leadership all but immobilized the U.S. division. One of its regiments entered the nearby Sanananda battle (mainly an Australian effort) with 1,199 officers and men, and walked out with only 165.

Yet the Americans, reinforced by a few light tanks, finally crushed the fortified Japanese defenses. Small parties crawled through dense jungle underbrush, pushed through thick mud, and reduced one bunker at a time. They proved that Americans could defeat the Japanese, in the jungle, on ground of Japanese choosing. The Americans concluded the Buna fight on January 20, 1943.

Three thousand Australians and Americans had died, as had 12,000 Japanese. The 45-day fight had been so hard on the U.S. 32d Division that it took nearly a year to rehabilitate the organization. The Australian 7th Division also suffered badly. It took until January 22, 1943, to finish the Japanese at Sanananda, during which time another 3,500 Australians and Americans became casualties. Australia and the lines of communication to the United States were now safe. But Buna-Sanananda proved to be one of the costliest ground campaigns of the Pacific war, with nearly twice the casualties of the much better known Guadalcanal.

In early January 1943, the Japanese reinforced Lae and Salamaua (which lay on northeast New Guinea's Solomon Sea coast). Guadalcanal had ended in defeat for the Japanese, so they now concentrated their efforts on New Guinea. A new army, the Eighteenth, for the moment headquartered on Rabaul, now controlled Japanese forces on New Guinea. In mid–January it ordered an offensive targeted against Wau, from which it was hoped to launch another trans–Owen Stanley effort against Port Moresby. The Australians reinforced Wau with air-landed infantry just in time to repulse that attempt. They then pushed the Japanese back toward Salamaua, ending their offensive hopes.

Allied airpower in Papua had grown to 207 bombers and 129 fighters by the end of February 1943, and these aircraft greatly hampered resupply of Japanese forces. From now on, Japan defended New Guinea in hopes that Allied casualties would be so great that the Americans and Australians would weary of military action and negotiate for an end to the war. Allied strength, although growing, remained too low to force a quick end to the campaign.

U.S. and Australian aircraft stopped reinforcements headed for Lae and Salamaua at the Battle of the Bismarck Sea (March 1–4, 1943) and destroyed most of the Japanese 51st Division's 115th Infantry. No more large convoys would attempt the trip to Lae; small coastal vessels would shuttle Japanese down New Guinea's coastline. Submarines and high-speed ships would deliver high-priority supplies. Troops would be landed beyond Allied air coverage and march to Lae.

Lieutenant General Hatazo Adachi's Eighteenth Army headquarters moved from Rabual to Lae in March 1943, and assumed command of forces on New Guinea's northeast coast. The Fourth Air Army took control of aerial operations. The 41st Division arrived from China and joined the 20th and 51st Divisions. The Japanese army was slow to reinforce its air forces on New Guinea; it took the intervention of Admiral Isoroku Yamamoto for aircraft to be sent from his Third Fleet carriers at Truk. The Japanese launched several unsuccessful air attacks in early April. A large-scale June raid also failed to bring worthwhile results. Only after June did the Japanese army's 7th Air Division move into eastern New Guinea to join the 6th Air Division.

MacArthur commenced the New Guinea portion of Operation Cartwheel on June 30, 1943. He sent elements of the U.S. 41st Division ashore at Nassau Bay to establish a logistics base that would support U.S. forces and the Australian New Guinea Force in the planned attack against Lae and Salamaua. It was a small operation, but it provided valuable amphibious experience on which to build, and it gave the Allies an airfield and a base for seaborne supplies.

On August 17 a surprise raid by 200 U.S. Fifth Air Force aircraft on Japan's four airstrips at Wewak (which the Japanese believed was beyond U.S. fighter range) caught aircraft on the ground and inflicted serious losses. After another Allied raid the next day, Japanese air strength in the Fourth Air Army averaged only 100 planes.

MacArthur planned an early September regimental parachute assault on Nadzab, inland and behind Lae. Immediately thereafter, the 7th Australian Division would be flown to Nadzab and head for Lae. The 3d Australian Division would launch a diversionary attack toward Salamaua. The 9th Australian Division would approach Lae from the sea. The operation worked well. The 9th Australian Division began landing east of Lae on September 4, the American 503d Parachute Infantry Regiment jumped into Nadzab the next day, and the 7th Australian Division began landing on September 7. The thoroughly outmaneuvered Japanese abandoned Lae.

The Japanese loss of Lae and Salamaua, combined with defeats in the central Solomons and trouble in the Aleutians, caused imperial general headquarters to decide that their forces were overextended. Western New Guinea would be the next defensive line. Japanese troops on New Guinea and even at Rabaul, New Britain, were no longer expected to defeat the Allies, only to hold out as long as possible.

The Americans, on the other hand, were becoming proficient in amphibious landings, land- and sea-based air operations, and all the elements that make up ground tactics: leadership, soldier health, civil affairs, and supporting arms. They learned that tanks could be used to great effect in the jungle. A quickening pace meant that while one operation was being planned, another was in progress and earlier operations were winding down.

In August 1943, the U.S. joint chiefs of staff decided to bypass Rabaul (MacArthur had desired to capture it). MacArthur did not originate the island-hopping/leapfrogging technique, but he quickly adapted it and became brilliant at it. He bypassed strong areas and crushed weak ones. In the absence of aircraft carriers, relatively short hops became the rule. The range of Allied land-based fighters proved to be a determining factor in selecting objectives. Allied airpower immobilized the Japanese. The Japanese could not introduce fresh ground forces against U.S. landings, nor could they supply the men already in place. Neither could bypassed Japanese be recovered or moved to active fronts.

By late January 1944, MacArthur had five U.S. divisions, three U.S. regimental combat teams, and five Australian divisions. Three more U.S. divisions were en route. Kenney's efficient Fifth Air Force, now with 1,000 combat aircraft, wrecked the Japanese 6th Air Division at Hollandia (now Djajapura) in a series of raids between March 30 and April 3. His warplanes destroyed over three hundred Japanese aircraft.

On March 24, 1944, imperial general headquarters wrote off eastern New Guinea and ordered a strategic withdrawal to a new line beginning at Hollandia. Unfortunately for the Japanese in eastern New Guinea, the Eighteenth Army was unable to move west to become part of the new line. Numerous Japanese troops died from disease and starvation after the Allied front passed them. Those who tried to retreat northwest suffered severe privations. Stragglers and lost soldiers died at the hands of New Guinea natives. Some units lost half their men to disease and exhaustion. Japanese tactical dispositions were soon entirely dependent upon where units could find food.

The troops of Lieutenant General Walter Krueger's Sixth Army landed near Hollandia on April 22, surprised the Japanese, and developed the area into a major base with docks and airfields. The Japanese Eighteenth Army was once again cut off, and the Japanese lost their best air bases. Local Japanese garrisons also retreated westward, cross-country. Ninety-three percent of these men died in New Guinea's "green desert."

A new phase in New Guinea operations began in March 1944 when the U.S. joint chiefs of staff started to move Allied forces in the southwest Pacific toward the Philippines. MacArthur planned to seize air bases along New Guinea's north coast in order to advance his air coverage toward the Philippines. The joint chiefs simultaneously wanted to get B-29s within range of the Japanese home islands and placed priority on Admiral Nimitz's drive through the central Pacific. MacArthur's attack along New Guinea's coast would confuse the Japanese and require them to defend against two U.S. drives.

From April through August 1944, U.S. and Australian air, ground, and sea forces launched seven major offenses, bypassed the major Japanese base at Wewak, and advanced 1,300 miles, from the Huon Peninsula west to the northwest tip of New Guinea. Where they did land, the Americans built huge logistics bases and airfields. Docks, supply dumps, and pipelines sprang up to service the combat forces.

MacArthur was now in position to attack the Philippines. In October 1944, Australian troops started to assume responsibility for the remaining fighting on New Guinea, so as to release U.S. troops for the invasion of the Philippines. The Australians continued the campaign into May 1945 with the capture of Wewak, now completely behind the "front lines." From the start of the campaign until its conclusion, Australia committed six divisions and their air forces to the New Guinea campaign. Until January 1944, the Australian infantrymen had engaged in more combat and had suffered more losses than the Americans. The New Guinea campaign never quite ended, for there were still 13,500 Japanese resisting when Japan surrendered.

New Guinea had proved to be a test for the reduction of fortified areas, for air-sea coordination, and for low-level air attacks against shipping. Company grade, field grade, and general officers, as well as their soldiers, had developed into competent, confident veterans. Crews of PT boats learned the art of barge destruction. Pilots refined close air support, air resupply, and troop transport. Logisticians and engineers gained experience on leap-frogging airfields to extend coverage to the next objective, supplying forces, and building bases. Amphibious doctrine and techniques improved. Air-ground-sea coordination became routine. The Japanese were on the receiving end of this instruction.

The time it would take to develop air bases, roads, and ports became a major issue and constrained tactical plans. Dock space, port facilities, longshoremen, lighters, trucks, warehouses, cargo-handling equipment, engineers, and amphibious shipping availability became even more important than the availability of combat troops. The medical establishment overcame disease—or at least kept it in check. Intelligence from Ultra usually allowed American planners to land at weakly defended points. The principal lesson was the ascendancy of air power and its pivotal role in every stage of warfare.

New Guinea was a lingering disaster for the Japanese. "No one returns alive from New Guinea" was the terrible rumor. All told, the Japanese lost nine divisions, three army headquarters (Second, Eighteenth, Nineteenth), an area army headquarters (Second), an air army of two air divisions, and all their support troops—either destroyed or cut off. Other Japanese forces perished trying to reinforce New Guinea. Japanese naval air forces also suffered heavily. Japanese offensives against U.S. landings always failed. But the 1944 campaign was also costly to the Allies. They suffered 20,000 battle casualties, including over 3,600 dead. At Aitape alone, the Allies lost as many men as did the marines at Tarawa—but, again, Tarawa was the more publicized battle.

Japanese troops fought with a determination that defied their shortages of food, air cover, and medicine. But it was in vain. They failed to stop the Allied march toward Japan. New Guinea's jungles killed many more Japanese than did the Americans and Australians. The Japanese never knew where the next air attack might fall or when the next amphibious assault might land, and they were surprised time and again. They could hold only those pieces of ground the Allies did not want. Once a garrison's supply lines were cut, the men were doomed. On New Guinea 148,000 Japanese died, the vast majority through disease and starvation.

FURTHER READINGS

Bergerud, Eric. *Touched with Fire: The Land War in the South Pacific* (1996).

Miller, John, Jr. *CARTWHEEL: The Reduction of Rabaul* (1959).

Prefer, Nathan. *MacArthur's New Guinea Campaign* (1995).

Smith, Robert Ross. *Approach to the Philippines* (1971).

U.S. War Department. *Papuan Campaign: The Buna–Sanananda Operation, 16 November 1942–23 January 1943* (1990).

John W. Whitman

SEE ALSO Bismarck Sea, Battle of the; Buna, Operations at; Hollandia; Kenney, George C.; National Guard of the United States

New Zealand

Geographically New Zealand was a Pacific dominion, and politically New Zealand has always taken a close interest in the island territories and micro states of the South Pacific. During World War II, however, New Zealand's war effort was firmly oriented toward the European and Mediterranean theaters. Although the war against Japan was certainly not ignored, the New Zealand government chose to maintain its emphasis on the war against Germany.

As early as 1936 the New Zealand government had considered the measures necessary to strengthen the defenses of Fiji in the event of war, and in July 1940 the chiefs of staff decided to send troops to garrison the island. The 8th Brigade was duly dispatched in November. After New Zealand declared war against Japan on December 8, 1941 (local time), this garrison force was greatly increased in strength with the addition of the 14th Brigade, which arrived in January 1942. The force was then designated B-Force, 2d New Zealand Expeditionary Force (2NZEF) and given divisional status. Relieved by the U.S. 37th Division in June, the New Zealanders, now designated the 3d New Zealand Division, returned home for reorganization and training in jungle warfare techniques. In late 1942–early 1943 detachments from the New Zealand army were deployed to Norfolk Island (N-Force) and the kingdom of Tonga (T-Force).

Command of 2NZEF in the Pacific (2NZEF IP) was invested in Major General H. E. Barrowclough, who had earlier commanded a brigade in North Africa, and the 3d Division was moved to New Caledonia in late 1942, to continue its training. In August 1943 it was finally assigned a combat role, and was deployed to Guadalcanal to prepare for the operations to clear the island of Vella Lavella in the central Solomons. This task was assigned to the 14th Brigade, which commenced operations in September. In late October the 8th Brigade landed on Mono in the Treasuries group, supported by aircraft from the Royal New Zealand Air Force. Vella Lavella was cleared of the Japanese by October 9, and organized enemy resistance ceased on Mono on November 12. The 3d Division's last operation was in February 1944, when, in concert with U.S. troops, it landed on Nissan, northwest of Bougainville. The division was gradually reduced in strength to provide reinforcements for the 2d Division in Italy, and to meet the manpower needs of New Zealand industry. It was officially disbanded in October 1944. At its peak there were 17,891 men serving in 2NZEF IP. The force suffered 203 dead, 213 wounded, and 26 POWs.

The other New Zealand services made small contributions to the war against Japan. A squadron from the Royal New Zealand Air Force flew against the Japanese during the Malayan campaign and the Allied retreat through the Netherlands East Indies. New Zealand bomber, fighter, and reconnaissance squadrons operated from Guadalcanal, on antishipping and antisubmarine operations in the Bismarck and Solomons groups, and against Japanese positions at Rabaul, New Britain. However, because it was a party to the Empire Air Training Scheme, New Zealand's major aerial effort was made in Europe, as part of the Royal Air Force.

Ships of the Royal New Zealand Navy, under U.S. operational control, provided escorts to convoys plying between the United States and the South Pacific and took part in the battle of Kolombangara in July 1943, in which the cruiser HMNZS *Leander* was lost. Toward the war's end New Zealand ships joined the British Pacific Fleet and took part in the screening operations that covered the U.S. landings on Okinawa and against Truk. The 25th Minesweeping Flotilla, composed of New Zealand corvettes, operated under the commander, South Pacific Area.

New Zealand industry and agriculture supported the Allied war effort in both Europe and the Pacific; New Zealand food production actually increased in the course of the war, despite the heavy demands of the services on the country's manpower. Home defense had been placed in the hands of the Home Guard, raised in August 1940, and after the beginning of the Pacific war, registration in the Home Guard was made compulsory for men of military age not already in the services, and for all men aged between 46 and 50. The Home Guard was placed in reserve in December 1943. New Zealand also functioned

as a leave destination for U.S. forces in the South Pacific, especially during the protracted fighting for the Solomons.

Despite a small population base, New Zealand's war effort overall was one of the greatest of any of the Allies. Although the Australians brought their forces home from the Mediterranean in 1942 in order to meet the threat from Japan, the New Zealanders acceded to the wishes of the British and Americans that they maintain their forces in Europe, a decision explained as much by geography as by sentiment. In the Pacific war, New Zealand's most important function was as a base of supply for the forces operating in the South Pacific.

FURTHER READINGS
Crawford, John, ed. *Kia Kaha: New Zealand in the Second World War* (2000).

Jeffrey Grey

SEE ALSO Australia

Nimitz, Chester William (1885–1966)

Commander of the U.S. Pacific Fleet during World War II, Chester William Nimitz was born February 24, 1885, in Fredericksburg, Texas. Although he was the grandson of a sea captain, he first applied to the U.S. Military Academy before entering the U.S. Naval Academy at age 15. In 1905 he graduated seventh in a class of 114.

Nimitz's first sea experiences were unpromising. He suffered seasickness on his first cruise, and he ran his second command, destroyer *Decatur*, aground. Despite being court-martialed and reprimanded, by World War I Nimitz had risen to chief of staff to the commander of the Submarine Division, Atlantic Fleet. Between the wars he taught naval science at the University of California and acquired extensive sea experience. He served on cruisers and battleships, and gained a reputation as an expert submariner.

Chief of the Bureau of Navigation at the time of the Japanese attack on Pearl Harbor, Hawaii (December 7, 1941), Nimitz had been considered in 1940 for the position of commander of the Pacific Fleet, a post that went instead to Admiral Husband E. Kimmel. Kimmel's career was a casualty of the Japanese attack on Pearl Harbor; and although he preferred sea duty, Nimitz replaced Kimmel on December 17, 1941.

As commander in chief of the Pacific Fleet, Nimitz was responsible for operations in the immense Pacific Ocean Area, subdivided into the North Pacific Area, Central Pacific Area, and South Pacific Area. He shared Pacific command with General Douglas MacArthur, who commanded forces in the Southwest Pacific Area. The joint chiefs of staff had overall command of the Pacific theater; Admiral Ernest J. King was Nimitz's immediate superior, and General George C. Marshall was MacArthur's.

Faced with protecting U.S. Pacific interests and rebuilding his badly weakened and demoralized fleet, Nimitz soon displayed his considerable talents. As repair crews desperately worked to put his battleships into action after the Pearl Harbor attack, Nimitz struck back with his submarines and aircraft carriers, which had not been touched by the Pearl Harbor disaster. Moving quickly to throw the Japanese off balance, he ordered unrestricted submarine warfare (a strategy that had brought an indignant United States into World War I against Germany) and a series of limited carrier attacks on Japanese targets, including the bomber raid on Tokyo, led by James Doolittle, on (April 18, 1942). Although of little strategic importance, these actions proved invaluable in boosting American morale and providing combat experience for crews.

In early May 1942, prompted by intercepted and decoded Japanese radio communications, Nimitz ordered a carrier force under Rear Admiral Frank Jack Fletcher to the Coral Sea. In a series of engagements, Fletcher's command inflicted serious losses on Admiral Inouye Shigeyoshi's Fourth Fleet, sinking light carrier *Shoho* and destroying seventy-seven aircraft. U.S. losses included giant aircraft carrier *Lexington* and sixty-six warplanes. Although the results of the Battle of the Coral Sea were somewhat ambiguous, the U.S. fleet did prevent Inouye from landing an invasion force on the island of Tulagi and at Port Moresby, New Guinea, thus providing a propaganda victory.

On June 3, Admiral Isoroku Yamamoto dispatched the Japanese Combined Fleet to seize strategic Midway Island in the central Pacific. Again informed of Japanese intentions by intelligence intercepts, Nimitz deployed two carrier groups under Raymond Spruance and Frank Fletcher to intercept Yamamoto's fleet. By June 6, U.S. forces, at the cost of aircraft carrier *Yorktown,* had sunk five Japanese aircraft carriers and decisively halted the Japanese advance. The November victory of Admiral William Halsey's fleet over Japanese forces at Guadalcanal signaled a new offensive policy in Nimitz's strategy.

MacArthur and Nimitz, smoothing over earlier differences, worked well together as the Americans went on the offensive in the Pacific, beginning in 1944. Aided by a rapid buildup of reinforcements and materiel, Nimitz's units swept across the central Pacific as MacArthur's forces moved toward the Philippines and Japan from New Guinea. Relying on the newly developed and less costly "island-hopping" technique, the two commanders avoided strongly defended Japanese-held islands, neutralizing them by blockade and aerial bombardment. Nimitz directed the successful battles in the Solomon Islands in late 1942 and early 1943, and in the Gilberts in 1943. In 1944 he oversaw operations in the Marshall Islands, the Marianas, Palau, and the Philippines.

On December 19, 1944, Nimitz was promoted fleet admiral, the naval equivalent of MacArthur's army rank. The year 1945 was marked by cooperation between the two commanders as Nimitz's forces took Iwo Jima and Okinawa. On September 2, 1945, hostilities officially ended when a Japanese delegation signed the formal surrender on battleship *Missouri* in Tokyo Bay.

After the surrender Nimitz succeeded Admiral Ernest King as chief of naval operations (1945–1947). In this capacity he directed the demobilization of the wartime fleet and successfully opposed the proposed consolidation of the army and navy.

In December 1947 the immensely popular Nimitz retired from the navy. He held decorations from the United States and eleven foreign countries as well as honorary degrees from fifteen universities. During his retirement he acted as a goodwill ambassador, for the United Nations (1949–1952), and in 1960, with E. B. Potter, he edited *Sea Power: A Naval History.* Nimitz died on February 20, 1966.

FURTHER READINGS

Admiral Nimitz Command Summary: Running Estimate and Survey, 1941–1945, 3 reels (Commander in Chief, Pacific Fleet, USN, n.d. (microfilm)

Potter, E. B. *Nimitz* (1976).

———, and Chester Nimitz, eds. *Sea Power: A Naval History* (1980).

Jeff Kinard

SEE ALSO Coral Sea, Battle of the; Doolittle (Tokyo) Raid; Eastern Solomons, Battle of; Iwo Jima; Okinawa, Battle for; Palau; Spruance, Raymond Ames

Noemfoor Island

The Japanese began fortifying Noemfoor (Numfoor) Island in late 1943 as part of their western New Guinea defense network. They hoped that their forces on this flat, jungle-covered, circular island in Geelvink Bay, north of New Guinea, would stop or at least delay General Douglas MacArthur's Southwest Pacific Area (SWPA) offensive drive toward the China–Formosa–Luzon region. By June 1944 Japanese commander Colonel Shimizu Suesada and his 2,000 troops were hard at work on three airfields: Kamiri and Kornasoren in the north and Namber on the west coast.

MacArthur wanted Noemfoor for a number of reasons. Seizing the island would move his offensive farther along the New Guinea coast, and he could use its airfields to deploy the growing number of aircraft at his disposal. Once the island was in U.S. hands, MacArthur's Noemfoor-based air forces could reach all the way along New Guinea's northern coast to threaten Japanese positions on the Vogelkop (Bird's Head) Peninsula. In addition, many in SWPA suspected (correctly) that the Japanese were using Noemfoor as a conduit to infiltrate reinforcements and equipment to the island of Biak, 45 miles to the east, thereby prolonging the struggle that began when the Americans landed there in late May. Finally, an American–held Noemfoor could alert SWPA of any Japanese naval offensive in the region.

MacArthur's general headquarters estimated that there were some seventeen hundred Japanese soldiers on Noemfoor, but the SWPA ground forces commander, Lieutenant General Walter Krueger, suspected that the Japanese might reinforce the island at any time. To play it safe, he decided to use Brigadier General Edwin Patrick's 158th Regimental Combat Team (RCT) for the assault, then reinforce it with Colonel George Jones's 503d Parachute Infantry Regiment. Both units were veterans; the 503d had jumped at Nadzab, New Guinea, the year before, and the 158th had recently seen action at Wakde–Sarmi.

On July 2, 1944, two battalions from the 158th RCT landed at Kamiri airfield after a heavy air and naval bombardment. They met little resistance, and quickly seized the airstrip. The only real problem, in fact, was the thick coral reef that surrounded the island and made the landing of equipment difficult. Even so, Patrick worried about conflicting interrogation reports, one of which placed Japanese strength as high as seven thousand men. He asked Krueger to deploy the 503d as soon as possible, and Krueger agreed. Because SWPA lacked ships to transport personnel, Krueger decided to parachute the unit onto Kamiri airstrip a battalion at a time, one a day, starting on July 3. Unfortunately, miscommunications, scattered debris and wreckage on the airfield, overhanging smoke, and the low altitude from which the paratroopers were dropped caused many injuries among the first two battalions, so Krueger scraped together ships to transport the last battalion.

As it was, the 503d was not really needed. The 158th occupied Kornasoren on July 4, and Namber two days later, without significant losses. On the night of July 4–5 the 158th's 1st Battalion fought the operation's only major engagement at Hill 201, beating off a strong but poorly coordinated Japanese attack. Mopping up continued for the remainder of the month, with the 158th clearing the southern half of the island and the 503d concentrating on the north. Troop interest in the task was sparked by rumors that the Japanese commander, Colonel Shimizu, possessed a jeweled sword ripe for the taking by any GI who could pry it from his dead hand. Although the Americans skirmished with the retreating Japanese at hills 670 and 380, they never found Shimizu or his sword.

The Noemfoor operation cost the Americans 66 killed and 343 wounded. The Japanese lost 1,730 men killed and 186 captured. Although the airfields were in terrible condition, American engineers had them ready in time to support the Sansapor–Mar operation on the Vogelkop Peninsula in late July. In addition, the operation put an end to Japanese infiltration efforts to Biak, and moved MacArthur's offensive farther westward.

Steven Taafe

SEE ALSO Biak, Battle for; Krueger, Walter; New Guinea

Nomura Kichisaburo (1877–1964)

An accomplished former naval officer, Nomura served as naval attaché in Washington, D.C., during World War I, Japan's foreign minister in 1939, and ambassador to the United States in 1941.

As naval attaché Nomura developed a friendly acquaintance with Assistant Secretary of the Navy Franklin D. Roosevelt. This relationship would serve him well in Japanese politics, because he was selected for positions in which good relations with the United States were deemed important. In September 1939 he was chosen foreign minister in the cabinet of General Abe Noboyuki, but the Abe government lasted less than six months.

Near the end of 1940, Nomura was asked by Prime Minister Konoe Fumimaro to serve as ambassador to the United States. The admiral accepted, but only on the condition that the Konoe cabinet would be willing to rethink its policies in China and Southeast Asia. He arrived in Washington early in 1941, and immediately began talks with Secretary of State Cordell Hull. His command of the English language was weak, however, which led to serious diplomatic bungling over the "Draft Understanding" concluded at New York in April. That document was drawn up by unofficial negotiators and was passed on by Hull, on the understanding that it represented no more than a starting point for future discussions. Nomura, however, sent it on to Tokyo, believing that it was a serious offer by Washington.

In the summer of 1941, Nomura was instrumental in trying to arrange a meeting between Prime Minister Konoe and President Roosevelt, but these efforts came to nothing. When the third Konoe cabinet resigned in October, the ambassador became so discouraged by the likely course of U.S.–Japanese relations that he offered his resignation. However, the new prime minister, Tojo Hideki, refused to accept his resignation, telling Nomura that the emperor had commanded that talks with the United States continue.

In November, Nomura was joined in Washington by special envoy Kurusu Saburo, and the two of them set out to draft a modus vivendi, a last-ditch effort to avert war in the Pacific. Their efforts, however, proved irrelevant, because the Tojo cabinet had already decided to attack the United States. Nevertheless, Nomura continued to warn Tokyo of the dangers of a war with the United States to the very end. On December 7, 1941, as Japanese aircraft were attacking the U.S. Pacific fleet at Pearl Harbor, Hawaii, Nomura personally handed Secretary of State Hull the Japanese declaration of war.

After his repatriation to Japan, Nomura resigned from the diplomatic service and lived in relative obscurity until his death in 1964. A capable diplomat and an individual of great common sense, he had, despite his problems with the English language, a far deeper understanding of the American mind than did his superiors in Tokyo.

FURTHER READINGS

Barnhart, Michael J. *Japan Prepares for Total War: The Search for Economic Security, 1919–1941* (1987).

Morley, James W. *The Fateful Choice: Japan's Advance into Southeast Asia, 1939–1941* (1980).

Schroeder, Paul W. *The Axis Alliance and Japanese–American Relations* (1958).

Lu, David J. *From the Marco Polo Bridge to Pearl Harbor* (1961).

John E. Moser

SEE ALSO Drought, Father James M.; Iwakuro Hideo

Nurses

During World War II, 350,000 women joined the U.S. armed forces—approximately two percent of the military who served. Of these, 76,000 were nurses serving in the Army Nurse Corps and the Navy Nurse Corps. Nursing was a long-standing role for women in the military, the Army Nurse Corps having been founded in 1901 and the Navy Nurse Corps in 1908.

At the start of World War II only 1,000 nurses were in the military, and they served ably in the Pacific during the attack on Pearl Harbor and in the Philippines in late 1941. Eighty-two army nurses were serving in Hawaii when the Japanese bombed Pearl Harbor. Army and navy nurses, as well as all other medical personnel in the area, cared for the huge numbers of casualties from the bombing attack. Medical supplies gave out quickly and conditions were grim. Thirteen navy nurses were serving on navy hospital ship *Solace* at the time of the bombing. *Solace,* unscathed, became an emergency ward for the casualties who were carried aboard and treated by doctors, nurses, and medical corpsmen. With enemy bombers overhead, nurses cared for the wounded and charred men who were often covered in oily fuel.

Within hours the same appalling scene was played anew in the Philippines, where nearly one hundred army and navy nurses were stationed. The day before the Japanese attack, the nurses were serving in what seemed like a paradise, with tropical palms, sandy beaches, and lush golf courses.

That all changed on December 8, 1941, when the Japanese commenced bombing. Hospitals were inundated with casualties in desperate condition. The nurses worked long hours caring for the wounded, some of whom were severely burned. After the air war ended and the Japanese invaded Luzon, General Douglas MacArthur, the U.S. commander, ordered his troops, including the army nurses, to the Bataan Peninsula, opposite Manila, while he moved to the nearly island of Corregidor. All the army nurses had left Manila by December 31, but eleven navy nurses were captured when the Japanese took the city on January 2, 1942. In early March the navy nurses were interned at Santo Tomas University in Manila. The university was to serve as a notorious internment camp throughout the war.

Army personnel at Bataan had a plan to set up a provisional hospital close to the battle lines to care for the wounded. Nurses arrived on Christmas Eve, 1941. They had to put together their own beds that night and then the next day began to assemble hospital equipment. After a long hard day the nurses and doctors sat down to Christmas dinner but were interrupted by the arrival of wounded soldiers at their barely functional hospital. General Hospital #1 at Limay had shedlike buildings with a large operating room containing seven or eight operating tables. In one month 1,200 patients were admitted for surgery. On January 16, 1942, 187 surgical procedures were carried out in twenty-four hours. As the Japanese closed in on Limay, Hospital #1 was relocated to a site called "Little Baguio." A large Red Cross sign was painted on the roof of one of the buildings. It turned out to be useless; the Japanese bombed the facility anyway.

Nurses helped set up General Hospital #2 for non-surgical patients. Beds were out in the open, covered from view by the forest canopy. In late February there was a lull in the bombing, but at the end of March the Japanese struck again, even making direct hits on the hospitals. More than a hundred patients were killed or seriously wounded. After the bombing raids, nurses were caring for thousands of patients at both hospitals. In addition to the wounded, the nurses also ministered to the victims of tropical disease, especially malaria. Supplies, including food, were cut off. Though at first some of the military men resented the arrival of the women in a combat zone, the demeanor and hard work of the nurses won them the title of "Angels of Bataan." When the capture of Bataan was imminent, MacArthur, who was now safely in Australia, ordered the nurses to Corregidor, where they arrived on April 9, 1942.

At Corregidor, an underground tunnel system called the Malinta Tunnel was home to the hospital and the army headquarters and stores. But conditions deteriorated rapidly. Food was scant, supplies were running out, and even fresh air became a luxury. The concussion of bombs made the tunnels tremble, dislodging dust and dirt.

MacArthur had left Major General Jonathan Wainwright in charge, and he ordered the evacuation of as many nurses as possible to Australia. On April 29, twenty nurses were flown out on two planes. One of the planes hit a rock that disabled it and the ten nurses from that plane were eventually captured, but the other plane made it. On May 3, submarine *Spearfish* succeeded in carrying eleven army nurses and one navy nurse out of Corregidor.

When the nurses returned to the United States for family visits they received a tremendous outpouring of public sentiment for their service. Although weak and undernourished, they participated in recruiting campaigns for more nurses to volunteer.

Fifty-four Army nurses remained on Corregidor in the Malinta Tunnel. When Corregidor was captured on May 6, 1942, the nurses feared the worst, having read of Japanese atrocities toward conquered women, but with the exception of one incident, they were left unmolested. The army nurses were allowed to keep on with their hospital work for a time, but as U.S. troops were placed in prisoner of war camps and medical supplies were removed by the Japanese, their usefulness ended. On July 2, they were moved to a Japanese troop ship and taken to Manila. Much to their dismay, the nurses were separated from the

army and put into prison with civilians at Santo Tomas. They did not suspect that they would be imprisoned for nearly three more years.

At Santo Tomas the nurses took over the hospital duties of the camp, relieving the civilians who had been administering to the patients. They kept working until the end of their captivity in 1945. Over the years, conditions in Santo Tomas worsened.

In April 1943, when Santo Tomas became extremely overcrowded, a new camp was set up at Los Baños. The camp executive committee was told to choose 800 able-bodied men to be transferred. The eleven navy nurses asked to be sent to Los Baños because they chafed at being dominated by the more numerous army nurses. Their request was granted, and they moved to the Agricultural College, where they created a useful 25-bed hospital from the ill-used college infirmary. Los Banos eventually contained more than three thousand prisoners.

While the nurses in the Philippines suffered captivity, army and navy nurses were stationed throughout the Pacific theater. Navy nurses were more likely to serve on hospital ships than were the army nurses. Nurses served as administrators and educators, teaching medical corpsmen; they also served in noncombat zones on hospital ships that were one step behind the ships in battle. The few women on the ships shared close quarters with hundreds and sometimes even thousands of men.

Army nurses served in hospitals in Hawaii, Australia, New Zealand, Fiji, New Caledonia, and the New Hebrides. As the military island-hopped, and new islands came under U.S. control, the nurses moved forward. They were to stay behind the forces yet be as close as possible for evacuees to reach them quickly. Evacuation was carried out by hospital ships and aircraft on which army nurses served. Six nurses were killed when USS *Comfort* was bombed by the Japanese in Leyte Gulf in April 1945.

A new role proved crucial in World War II—that of the flight nurse. Flight nurses were particularly important in certain terrains the Pacific, where mountains and islands often made ground transport of the injured difficult or impossible. Usually one nurse and one medical corpsman flew in the planes, which could not be marked by the Red Cross because they might also carry troops or cargo. Nurses faced traumatized patients who had just been wounded or were victims of battle fatigue so severe they had to be restrained during the flight. Nurses made decisions that under normal conditions would be made by physicians and that were complicated by the fact that medical procedures had to be adapted to high altitudes. Hospital planes sometimes crashed and nurses had to minister to their patients while stranded and waiting for rescue. The 500 army flight nurses worldwide lost only 47 patients out of 1,176,048 during the flight. Seventeen of the flight nurses lost their lives during the war.

As the Allies took control of the Solomons, Marianas, and Marshall Islands, nurses served in hospitals at each location. Battle casualties from the long Okinawa campaign in 1945 were overwhelming. From April to June, 50,000 U.S. soldiers, sailors, and marines were wounded. Nurses worked twelve hours a day, seven days a week. Patients suffered from blood loss, severe shock, and shattering wounds. When Japanese suicide bombers hit ships, burn patients severely taxed nurses' abilities. Much of the medical care that nurses provided was for disease—malaria, dengue fever, dysentery, and beriberi were the diseases that were most common in the Pacific theater.

Army nurses were also assigned to hospitals in Burma, China, and India. In the still-segregated army, African American nurses were sent to Burma to care for the African American troops who were building the Ledo Road. African American nurses also served in the Southwest Pacific, where they were assigned to the 268th Station Hospital, which was an all-black hospital.

Probably the most well known event of the Pacific theater involving nurses occurred in 1945 when the army and navy nurses in captivity in the Philippines were liberated after years of imprisonment. During the last year, conditions had become ever more dangerous. Rations were cut; supplies from outside were not allowed; and the Japanese were growing more unpredictable by the day. Toward the end, the nurses subsisted on 700 calories a day and suffered severely from maladies associated with malnutrition. Remarkably, they all survived. They were fortunate to have been imprisoned in a civilian internment camp where conditions were better than in a prisoner of war camp, where the death rate was 50 percent. MacArthur knew that conditions were execrable, so he fought to liberate Luzon before the prisoners were all dead from hunger.

On February 3, 1945, American troops broke through the fence at Santo Tomas. Food was on the mind of most of the internees, and the kidney beans and soybeans that the soldiers served at their first meals after liberation seemed like feasts. But the joy was short-lived when the Japanese began shelling Santo Tomas. Sadly, after surviving years in captivity, many prisoners were killed and hundreds were wounded. The nurses, gaunt from malnutrition, were taken to a convalescent hospital in Leyte. On February 5, 100 fresh army nurses arrived to take their places. The liberation of Los Baños came later, on February 23. The American troops burst into the camp and killed all the Japanese guards. The newly liberated navy and army nurses were evacuated to San Francisco for evaluation and released by hospitals in March 1945.

Although nursing had been the most accepted role for women in the military from the early years of the twentieth century, nurses in World War II greatly expanded the parameters of women's roles in the military. Their bravery under fire, their innovation with scarce resources, their sacrifices and their untiring work brought them the gratitude of a nation. Through it all—from battlefield conditions to captivity and sometimes death—nurses acquitted themselves with great courage and discipline.

FURTHER READINGS

Bischoff, Gunter, and Robert L. Dupont. *The Pacific War Revisited* (1997).
Kaminsky, Theresa. *Prisoners in Paradise: American Women in the Wartime South Pacific* (2000).
Norman, Elizabeth M. *We Band Of Angels: The Untold Story of American Nurses Trapped on Bataan by the Japanese* (1999).
Weatherford, Doris. *American Women and World War II* (1990).

Bonnie L. Ford

SEE ALSO Bataan Death March; Corregidor; Manila, Fall of

Office of Strategic Services, Detachment 101

Detachment 101 was the first U.S. Office of Strategic Services (OSS) Special Operations unit sent abroad after formation of the OSS, in June 1942, from the remnants of the Office of the Coordinator of Information (COI). Always a very a small force, Detachment 101 could nonetheless count many notable achievements during the time it operated in northern Burma. The idea of creating a specially trained, jungle-fighting guerrilla force capable of harassing the enemy from behind the lines was first raised in early 1942 in the Philippines, where U.S. forces were besieged by the Japanese on Bataan and Corregidor. Fully aware that a Japanese victory in the Philippines was inevitable, several U.S. Army soldiers began to consider the prospect of infiltrating enemy lines to form guerrilla units and fight until liberation. Before such clandestine units could be raised, however, the Philippines fell.

Elsewhere, the rapid advance of enemy forces through Southeast Asia in early 1942 threatened the only remaining land supply route through Burma to the nearly four million Nationalist Chinese soldiers under Chiang Kaishek fighting the Japanese. Anticipating this crisis, the director of COI, William J. Donovan, began to correspond with General Joseph W. Stilwell, Chiang Kai-shek's American chief of staff and the U.S. Army commander of Sino–American forces then fighting a desperate rearguard action in Burma. Drawing on American experiences and ideas in the Philippines, Donovan asked Stilwell about the possibility of forming a unit to fight behind the lines against the Japanese in northern Burma and possibly even in Tibet. With the Allies needing every available man to stem the enemy advance, Stilwell flatly opposed Donovan's idea of having any American guerrilla units operating in China. He did accept, however, the offer of a special operations team that could conduct intelligence-gathering and guerrilla activities in Burma. He encouraged the COI to send such a unit to India as soon as possible, to set up a base of operations for activities in north Burma, an area of Stilwell's immediate interest and control. Thinking that a small role in north Burma was better than no role in the theater at all, Donovan accepted Stilwell's suggestion.

To lead the proposed irregular group, Donovan selected Colonel Carl Eifler, a former Border Patrol officer, policeman, deputy customs collector in Honolulu, and, most recently, a U.S. Army Reserve officer. Eifler was a major in the 35th Infantry Regiment in Hawaii when the Japanese attacked Pearl Harbor, Hawaii, on December 7, 1941. He joined the COI in March 1942. After several weeks of discussion between Stilwell and Preston Goodfellow of COI, Eifler was notified by Donovan that he was to begin forming a team of American guerrillas to fight in Southeast Asia under his command. In the following weeks, Eifler selected whomever he wanted from within COI, the U.S. Army, and the U.S. Navy to serve in the new detachment. Among the first recruits were two U.S. Army officers, Captain John G. Coughlin, a West Point graduate, and Captain William R. "Ray" Peers.

Because no unit similar to Detachment 101 existed in the U.S. military at the time, Eifler developed new training methods, weapons, tactics, and operational techniques. Looking to America's allies, Eifler relied heavily on the aid and expertise provided by the two British agencies most like the American OSS: the Secret Intelligence Service and the Special Operations Executive. The result of Eifler's efforts was the top-secret Detachment 101, officially formed on April 14, 1942. To mask the group's true purpose and identity, it was named the U.S. Army Experimental Station. (Its "101" designation also meant nothing.)

Throughout World War II, Detachment 101, although under the direct command of OSS, was always subject to the command and control of General Stilwell and U.S. Army authorities at China–Burma–India (CBI) headquarters, rather than to the authority of British officials in either the India theater or the Southeast Asia Command (SEAC). Although initially skeptical of the true value and worth of the small OSS detachment, Stilwell eventually developed a very high regard for the group, believing it far more useful to his operations in the Northern Combat Command Area (NCCA) than the British Special Operations Executive team serving there.

By the time Eifler and the initial Detachment 101 team reached India in October 1942, the COI had been abolished and the new Office of Strategic Services was formed. On arrival, Eifler immediately established his base in Assam, in northeast India, about four hundred miles from Stilwell's Northern Area Combat Command headquarters in Burma. The OSS members in Assam soon discovered, however, that supplies would be a constant problem because of the remoteness of their base, because they were at the very end of the Allied supply chain in Asia, and because CBI was considered of lesser importance than larger U.S. combat theaters in Europe and the Pacific. Even when supplies could be approved, it often took more than six months for them to arrive from the United States. The constant lack of such basics of combat operations as portable radios often hampered Detachment 101's effectiveness.

Nonetheless, operating from its secret base in northern Assam, the 21-member detachment soon raised a significant force of Burmese nationals, primarily Kachin mountain tribesmen who nursed serious grudges against the occupying Japanese. There was never much love lost between the Kachin and the lowland Burmese; the fact that most of the latter were pro–Japanese was all the more reason for the Kachins to fight the invaders.

These "Kachin Scouts" were trained in intelligence collection and internal propaganda, as well as espionage, sabotage, and harassment operations. Detachment 101's reliance on the assistance and manpower provided by Kachin tribesmen proved crucial, because as late as the fall of 1943, due to OSS manpower shortages, the unit still included only twenty-five Americans.

Detachment 101 had several missions to perform in support of Stilwell's more conventional military operations. First, the unit was to disrupt Japanese air defenses in order to secure Allied supply flights over the Himalayas, the famed and fearsome "Hump," and thereby maintain the stability and fighting ability of Chinese Nationalist forces in Burma and China. As part of this mission, De-

tachment 101 was to help rescue downed American airmen. During the war it succeeded in rescuing between 25 and 35 percent of those who had crashed during the very hazardous supply flights over the mountains between India and China, and thus secured U.S. Army Air Forces' strong support. Second, Detachment 101 was to collect intelligence for Stilwell's forces and for other Allied units. It has been estimated that 85 percent of all of the intelligence received by Stilwell's NCCA came from Detachment 101 sources, either American agents or Kachin tribesmen. Third, Detachment 101 was to engage in direct sabotage and guerrilla activities against Japanese military forces, not only to hinder their combat movements and effectiveness but also to make the occupation of Burma more difficult and expensive in terms of manpower, time, and materiel expended. Thus, the majority of Detachment 101 operations involved the destruction of vital Japanese military objectives in the jungle: supply and military bases; railroad rolling stock, locomotives, tracks, switches, and trestles; airstrips; and lines of communication.

By the end of 1942 the unit had succeeded in infiltrating Burma on several occasions, in spite of its limited resources, and within a year it had established six secret bases, staffed by both American and Kachin guerrillas, behind Japanese lines.

In late 1943, Colonel Eifler was injured in an abortive landing on the Burmese coast during an intelligence mission. He was in failing health from repeated bouts of malaria and the daily pressures of command. Suffering from what appeared to many of his comrades to be a nervous breakdown, Eifler was relieved of his command and replaced with Lieutenant Colonel John Coughlin. Within a short time, however, Coughlin was reassigned to direct all OSS operations in CBI, and command of Detachment 101 was passed to the last of the original founders, Lieutenant Colonel William R. Peers.

By the start of 1944, Detachment 101 included about four hundred Americans and was considered to be one of the largest and most important military forces in CBI. Its value became even greater as Stilwell prepared plans for his 1944 Burmese offensive. Peers worked very closely with Stilwell's staff to ensure that Detachment 101 did all it could to assist the Allied forces mounting the February 1944 attack. As conventional units pounded Japanese positions from the front, American and Kachin members of Detachment 101 were fully engaged in guerrilla warfare behind the lines, making life and combat difficult for the Japanese. In March 1944, Detachment 101 guerrillas assisted Orde Wingate's ill-fated Chindit airborne assault in northern Burma, code-named Operation Thursday, and unit activities were crucial in helping to restore the Burma Road link with China by June 1944. Intelligence provided by American and Kachin members of Detachment 101 proved especially valuable in the battle for the Myitkyina airstrip and in the final drive on the Japanese military stronghold of Lashio.

Detachment 101 continued to harass Japanese units behind the lines throughout 1944 and into 1945, playing an especially crucial role during the final Burma offensives in 1945. For its role in the latter operations, Detachment 101 received the coveted presidential unit citation. During operations in March–June 1945, the citation recorded, under the most hazardous jungle conditions the members of Detachment 101 displayed extraordinary heroism in leading coordinated battalions of natives to complete victory over a superior Japanese force. The unit met and routed 10,000 Japanese soldiers in an area of 10,000 square miles; killed 1,247 enemy troops while sustaining losses of only 37 men; demolished or captured four large enemy dumps; destroyed enemy motor transport; and inflicted extensive damage to communications and other facilities. All told, the 566 Americans who served with Detachment 101 during the war, as well as their nearly ten thousand Kachin guerrilla allies, accounted directly for 5,447 enemy confirmed killed and a further 10,000 enemy troops estimated killed and wounded due to their actions. Wartime Detachment 101 losses were 18 Americans and 184 Kachins and lowland Burmese killed.

FURTHER READINGS

Dunlop, Richard. *Behind Japanese Lines with the OSS in Burma* (1991).

Hogan, David, Jr. *U.S. Army Special Operations in World War II* (U.S. Army, Center of Military History, 1992).

Hymoff, Edward. *The OSS in World War II* (1972).

Roosevelt, Kermit. *War Report of the OSS*, 2 vols. (1976).

Clayton D. Laurie

SEE ALSO China-Burma-India Theater of Operations; Intelligence in the Pacific Theater; Office of Strategic Services in the Pacific; Psychological Warfare, U.S.; Stilwell, Joseph Warren

Office of Strategic Services in the Pacific

On June 3, 1942, the U.S. Office of Strategic Services (OSS) was formed as a supporting agency of the U.S. joint chiefs of staff (JCS) from the remnants of the Office of the Coordinator of Information. Its purpose was to provide intelligence, psychological warfare activities, and unconventional warfare in support of conventional U.S. military operations. Wartime operations conducted by the OSS included espionage, research and analysis, subversive propaganda, sabotage teams, and agent support to guerrilla forces in Axis and Axis-occupied countries. By V-J Day (August 14, 1945), the OSS employed more than ten thousand military and civilian personnel worldwide.

In contrast to its relative success in Europe, however, the OSS had a difficult time establishing a significant and secure operational niche in the Pacific and Asian theaters. OSS members at all levels found that they continually had to maneuver among the many Asian and European nationalist, Communist, and imperialist interests in the region, most of which threatened the independence and success of OSS operations. In China, Burma, and elsewhere in Southeast Asia, for example, the OSS was subjected to close control and scrutiny by American, British, French, Australian, Dutch, and Chinese civilian and military authorities. Ironically, agency difficulties were compounded by the reluctance of U.S. military leaders, particularly General Douglas MacArthur and Admirals Chester Nimitz and William F. Halsey, to allow the OSS to operate in their theaters (the Southwest Pacific Area, the Central and North Pacific Ocean Area, and the South Pacific, respectively). As a result, the OSS never gained the autonomy or success it achieved in the European and Mediterranean theaters.

The OSS experience in the Southwest Pacific Area was fairly typical. Its director, William J. Donovan, began efforts to form a niche within MacArthur's general headquarters (GHQ) command shortly after the theater was created in April 1942. Although Donovan had the strong support of President Franklin D. Roosevelt, his initial attempt to establish an OSS office in Australia was rebuffed by MacArthur, who informed the joint chiefs of staff, with War Department support, that the OSS was not needed because the Allied Intelligence Bureau (AIB) was already performing all psychological warfare functions in the theater. Later one OSS man was accepted as a civil adviser to the Philippine Regional Section of G-2 within the AIB at GHQ.

In 1942 MacArthur's grudging acceptance of a token OSS presence prompted Donovan to complain to the Joint Psychological Warfare Committee in Washington, D.C., that the Southwest Pacific Area lacked properly qualified officers familiar with psychological warfare and subversive operations, and could not effectively or vigorously carry out such activities. Furthermore, Donovan claimed, psychological warfare transcended the boundaries of any single theater, as the OSS was already demonstrating in Europe and the Mediterranean, and these activities were certain to affect MacArthur's operations in the southwest Pacific, New Guinea, the Dutch East Indies, and the Philippines.

After being rebuffed in 1942, Donovan attempted to break into the Southwest Pacific Area in midsummer 1943 via the joint chiefs of staff. At this time he set forth the OSS "Basic Military Plan for Psychological Warfare in the Southwest Pacific Theater," describing the special and subversive morale operations and secret intelligence missions he hoped to perform there. The plan called for 62 U.S. Army officers and 273 enlisted men, with some native help, all under OSS control, to conduct operations in the southwest Pacific, Burma, China, and the Dutch East Indies. MacArthur declined to review it. With the strong support of his intelligence officers, MacArthur argued that the OSS was not needed in the Southwest Pacific Area, and that if it were, it would be used only for short-term, specific missions. Donovan persisted, however, and MacArthur again wrote to the JCS that "any OSS base in Australia would create [an] impossible situation and jeopardize [the] existing harmony." All psychological warfare was being handled by general headquarters, Southwest Pacific Area, and "due to security and to avoid political questions," it was "inexpedient to send any organization for [further] participation."

During Donovan's April 1944 visit to the southwest Pacific, MacArthur indicated a willingness to have OSS personnel attached to his staff and to use OSS frogmen, but he insisted that all such personnel be under his direct command rather than remaining under Donovan, a condition that was quickly and flatly rejected. OSS personnel, therefore, were never present in the southwest Pacific in large numbers.

The OSS undertook efforts to create a role in the South Pacific theater beginning in early 1943 when an OSS representative arrived at Admiral William F. Halsey's headquarters with a letter from Donovan describing the many services the OSS could perform. The letter came while U.S. forces were heavily engaged in Munda, New Georgia, and on Vella Lavella, and Donovan's plans, containing what many on Halsey's staff thought were nebulous ideas, were rejected as being wasteful of scarce personnel and material. No significant OSS mission was ever established in the South Pacific.

In the central Pacific, Donovan's plan to deploy a team of some three hundred officers and enlisted men never came to fruition after the joint staff planners noted that the OSS "Basic Military Plan for Psychological Warfare in the Pacific Theater" was impractical, considering the characteristics of warfare as carried out by the U.S. Navy

and U.S. Marine Corps in the Pacific Ocean Area. Admiral Chester Nimitz concurred, and in the summer of 1943 was reported as being "averse to establishing in Oahu an organization [the OSS] whose value at present and for some time to come is not apparent." Even after Donovan visited Nimitz in April 1944, and obtained the subsequent appointment of an OSS liaison officer to Nimitz's staff, and after he had made a second visit to Nimitz in late February 1945, the OSS was still excluded from the theater; Nimitz often referred to the agency as a "superfluous impracticality." OSS activities in the central Pacific remained confined to those of a small liaison office in Hawaii.

The only significant OSS operation in the central Pacific was a Morale Operations Branch clandestine radio unit that arrived on Guam and Saipan in July 1944. However, it was not allowed to operate freely or to go on the air. Finally, after months of negotiations involving the U.S. Navy, the OSS, and the Office of War Information, an OSS team, working with a nisei staff, began medium-wave, nightly clandestine radio broadcasts to the Japanese mainland in April 1945.

Compared with their experiences in the major U.S. theaters in the Pacific, the OSS was relatively successful in the China and China–Burma–India theaters. The first OSS presence in China was established in Chungking in late 1941, under the Office of the Coordinator of Information, and consisted of a Foreign Information Service outpost under a former journalist, E. McCracken Fisher. In early 1942, OSS Secret Intelligence and Research and Analysis Branch units arrived in Chung-king and began limited operations.

Surprisingly, William Donovan encountered the most vocal opposition to his organization from the Nationalist Chinese, particularly Generalissimo Chiang Kai-shek and his chief of intelligence, General Tai Li (sometimes called "The Chinese Himmler"). Both Chinese leaders demanded absolute control of all foreign intelligence and special operations agencies in China, and Chiang's resistance continued even after the well-known and trusted Captain Milton E. Miles, who had operated a U.S. Navy–affiliated intelligence and special operations group in China since December 1941, was appointed chief of the OSS China theater by Donovan on January 1, 1943. Unknown to Donovan, Miles had no desire to see the OSS, a potential competitor to his own operation, succeed in China; he accepted the new post only to hinder the operations of the OSS.

In the attempt to reduce the ongoing political difficulties among the Allies, which were detracting from the war effort against Japan in China, American and Chinese officials negotiated a special technical agreement in May 1942. One section of this agreement granted the OSS permission to operate in China as part of a body known as the Sino–American Cooperative Organization (SACO), under Tai Li's control. However, Tai Li and Miles continued to withhold approval for OSS activities in China throughout 1943, prompting Donovan to make yet another trip to Asia to promote the OSS. Following direct negotiations involving Donovan, Miles, and Tai Li, during which Donovan relieved Miles as chief of OSS China, an agreement was reached on December 9, 1943, whereby the Chinese intelligence chief granted full approval for the commencement of OSS operations in areas under Nationalist Chinese and Japanese control.

By January 1944, a small Morale Operations Branch office was organized in Chungking under U.S. Army lieutenants Gordon Auchincloss and James Withrow, who reported to Major Herbert Little, the OSS Far East area operations officer. By the end of 1944 this single unit had produced and circulated more than thirty-five thousand pieces of literature, printed on native presses, for distribution by Chinese agents behind enemy lines.

Still dissatisfied with the SACO/OSS relationship, and unconvinced that Tai Li would adhere to the agreement made in December 1943, Donovan formed a new partnership with the commander of the U.S. Fourteenth Army Air Force in China, General Claire Chennault, in February 1944, placing a small OSS detachment in Kunming. By agreement with Chennault, this OSS unit became part of a new, exclusively American organization called the 5329th Air and Ground Forces Resources and Technical Staff, ultimately responsible to China and China–Burma–India Theater headquarters through the respective G-5 staffs. Finally, as of August 26, 1944, all OSS branches in China, including a highly useful Research and Analysis team, came under the Air and Ground Forces Resources Technical Staff. Thereafter, the OSS in China enjoyed a higher degree of independence, primarily because Chennault's stature was so great that Chiang Kai-shek and Tai Li could not interfere with the OSS without incurring the general's wrath.

To these continuing OSS activities in southern China was added the multiservice Dixie Mission, a U.S. military detachment stationed with Mao Tse-tung's Communist guerrilla forces after July 1944. The Dixie Mission gathered intelligence, assisted with guerrilla operations against Japanese forces in north China, and maintained a politically delicate liaison with Mao and his forces until the autumn of 1945. Indeed, by the end of the war, several teams of OSS agents were fighting behind the lines, with both Communist and Nationalist Chinese guerrilla units, against Japanese forces throughout China.

The China-Burma-India (CBI) theater, an unusual adjunct to the China theater, was the one clear OSS success story in Asia and the Pacific. As early as April 1942 an OSS Special Operations unit, known as Detachment 101, was formed to support U.S. military objectives, using guerrilla tactics in the China–Burma–India theater, from behind Japanese lines. Almost from the outset, however, the OSS ran into trouble with the British, who wanted supervisory control over all OSS activities in Southeast Asia, including OSS operations and personnel in India, Burma, Thailand, and Indochina. General Joseph Stilwell, the U.S. CBI commander, who tightly controlled all OSS activities in CBI and personally supervised Detachment 101, protested the British action, as did William Donovan and the JCS. In the end, the Americans successfully resisted all attempts to have the OSS placed under British control, a decision that lasted for the duration of the war, even though a liaison arrangement was reached in September 1943. Detachment 101 went on to conduct very successful guerrilla operations against the Japanese in northern Burma.

Later, with Stilwell's approval, Donovan ordered the creation of an OSS Morale Operations (MO) unit to support Detachment 101 in December 1943. In early January 1944, an MO officer arrived in CBI to study the situation, noting in particular what propaganda techniques and media could be employed to undermine Japanese morale and to gain the support of Kachin and Burmese natives. MO lacked the personnel and equipment to mount anything but a small effort, however, and most U.S. Army personnel were indifferent to its work. As a result, MO agents were diverted to interrogation or intelligence work during the Myitikina campaign of 1944. The only notable MO success in CBI was a mission code-named Gold Dust, staged late in the Burma campaign. With native help, a team of eight U.S. Army officers and four enlisted men attached to MO produced subversive leaflets for distribution behind the Japanese lines, although to what effect remains unclear.

The establishment of the Southeast Asia Command (SEAC) in 1943–1944, under Britain's Lord Louis Mountbatten, opened new opportunities for the OSS in Asia under Colonel Richard Heppner. With OSS teams already stationed in Calcutta and New Delhi, India; at Chungking and Kunming, China; at CBI headquarters; and at SEAC headquarters in Kandy, Ceylon (now Sri Lanka), it was decided in mid-1943 to undertake new operations against the pro–Axis government of Thailand. Detachment 404, established in early 1944, was to handle the Thai operations from its secret training and base camp near Kandy. Here a group of Thai students, who had formed the Free Thai Army in 1942, while in the United States, became the core of an army of national liberation. Other OSS branches, in particular the Research and Analysis and Secret Intelligence branches, enlisted Thais as area specialists and espionage agents both in Washington, D.C., and in Ceylon.

Overall, OSS operations in Japanese-occupied Thailand, as elsewhere, were stymied by differences among the Allies over postwar policies in the region and by a deep-seated distrust between the Thais and the Nationalist Chinese, who claimed hegemony over the area south of China proper. Nonetheless, in October 1944, Free Thai Army units began to infiltrate their homeland from OSS bases in China to gather intelligence. Although many agents were immediately killed or captured by the Japanese, an OSS Secret Intelligence post was established in the Thai capital of Bangkok and subsequently fed much useful information to the OSS Research and Analysis Branch in Washington concerning Japanese troop movements and the attitudes of the Thai population toward their pro–Axis rulers and Japanese occupiers. By the time of the Japanese surrender in August 1945, both the OSS and Britain's Special Operations Executive were arming, training, and equipping sizable units of the Free Thai Army and an underground organization in preparation for an anti–Japanese uprising at the end of 1945.

The imminent end of hostilities in Europe prompted the transfer of a considerable number of highly trained OSS personnel, including the legendary Jedburgh teams, to Asia in the early months of 1945. These trained agents established contact with many nationalist and Communist guerrillas in Asia, especially in Indochina. Most notable among these contacts were those with Vietnamese nationalist leader Ho Chi Minh, who met with OSS representatives in Kunming, China, on at least four occasions in late 1944 and early 1945, seeking arms, money, and American support for his anti–Japanese Viet Minh guerrilla movement operating in Vietnam. Ho promised, in return for this aid, to rescue downed American airmen in Indochina and to provide intelligence on Japanese troop movements and dispositions.

Eventually five OSS sabotage, intelligence, and guerrilla support teams operated in cooperation with Ho Chi Minh's forces in Vietnam north of the 16th parallel in the summer prior to the Japanese surrender. One noteworthy success was a combined OSS and Viet Minh raid on a Japanese divisional headquarters at Lang Son, on the Chinese border, in mid–1945. In addition to harassing the Japanese with Ho Chi Minh's assistance, the OSS

established training and guerrilla bases at Cao Bang, Bac Kan, and Lang Son before the end of the war, to train Viet Minh guerrilla forces in the use of modern weapons and explosives. Branching into other areas of Indochina, a ten-man OSS team was earmarked for operations in Laos just prior to the end of hostilities. It did not arrive in Vientiane until October 1945.

As the end of the war against the Japanese in Asia was approaching, the OSS found itself increasingly embroiled in incidents with Communist forces that foreshadowed the start of the cold war in Southeast Asia. Ironically, considering OSS support for Ho Chi Minh, the first American to die at Communist hands was Colonel A. Peter Dewey, the ranking OSS officer in Indochina, who was shot by Viet Minh forces under questionable circumstances in September 1945. In China, at the same time, in spite of the success of the OSS-supported Dixie Mission, another OSS officer, Captain John Birch, was killed by Chinese Communist forces. Birch was later memorialized in the fervently anticommunist John Birch Society.

FURTHER READINGS

Dunlop, Richard. *Behind Japanese Lines with the OSS in Burma* (1979).

Hogan, David, Jr. *U.S. Army Special Operations in World War II.* (U.S. Army Center of Military History, 1992).

Hymoff, Edward. *The OSS in World War II* (1972).

MacDonald, Elizabeth. *Undercover Girl* (1947).

Roosevelt, Kermit. *The War Report of the OSS,* 2 vols. (1976).

Smith, Bradley. *The Shadow Warriors* (1983).

Smith, R. Harris. *The OSS: The Secret History of America's First Central Intelligence Agency* (1972).

Stewart, Richard W. "The Office of Strategic Services (OSS) Operational Group Burma: The 'Arakan' Group.' " In U.S. Army Center of Military History, *The U.S. Army and World War II: Selected Papers from the Army's Commemorative Conferences* (1998).

Clayton D. Laurie

SEE ALSO China–Burma–India Theater of Operations; Intelligence in the Pacific Theater; Office of Strategic Services, Detachment 101; Psychological Warfare, U.S.

Oil, Role of in the Pacific War

The Pacific war, remembered for its huge scope and incredible savagery, was also very much an economic war. The Japanese government wanted to expand its empire to gain resources (living space, rubber, minerals, food) and to become self-sufficient and independent of Western political and economic domination. To become or remain a great power in the modern age required easy and secure access to these resources. But the primary resource that Imperial Japan needed for its modern military economy was oil, of which it had few sources under its direct control. As a vital resource, oil affected the strategy and tactics of both sides.

The Japanese empire in 1941 had access to relatively small oil fields on Sakahlin Island and in Manchuria, both of which were close to the Soviet Union, which was not a friendly neighbor. These supplies did not begin to meet Japan's needs, so it was forced to buy petroleum from the United States and the Dutch East Indies (which operated under a government-in-exile in London after Nazi Germany overran Holland in May 1940). In retaliation for Japan's takeover of French Indochina in July 1941, the United States, United Kingdom, and Dutch East Indies instituted an oil embargo against Japan. This was a direct threat to Japanese military operations and had a corresponding affect on political deliberations in Tokyo. If action were not taken to rectify the situation, the country would be almost out of oil in less than a year. Even though there were other factors that were important in Japanese calculations for war (primarily the weak state of Allied forces in the Pacific due to the preoccupation with Europe), it was the alarming situation with regard to dwindling oil supplies that pushed the Japanese government to opt for war with the Western powers.

While shaping their offensive strategy to seize the oil fields of the Southern Resources Area, Japan did not adequately plan for the effective exploitation and protection of this resource. The Japanese leadership (like that of Germany) was counting on a relatively short war, and the focus was on the fighting forces. There were not enough tankers to fulfill the increased demands and probable losses that would occur in a long war. The economic and industrial bases were not sufficient to fight a long war. Specifically, the shipyards of Japan were not capable of constructing ships quickly. Japan had stockpiled a large amount of oil in preparation for war, but the experts had drastically underestimated the rate of consumption. The multitude of operations at the beginning of the war, especially the big fleet operations in the Indian Ocean and the battles at Coral Sea and Midway, constituted huge drains on the oil stocks that were never replaced. The convoy system was not well organized, nor were there enough modern escorts to protect them from American submarines. The attrition of Japan's supply fleet (along with a shortage of carrier pilots), forced the imperial navy in 1944 to split its fleet, basing many heavy units that consumed the most fuel in Singapore and the Dutch East

Indies, to be near the oil wells. This increased the U.S. Pacific Fleet's operational freedom and meant that no major sea battles were fought from the end of 1942 until June 1944 (the Battle of the Philippine Sea). Flight operations for training purposes were also curtailed, at drastic cost in pilot quality.

Nor did the Japanese direct their tactical military efforts to reduce materially American oil supplies. No attacks were made on the exposed oil tank farms at Pearl Harbor, the loss of which would have forced the U.S. Pacific Fleet to pull back to California to be close to its remaining fuel supplies. This would have probably lengthened the war. The Japanese mounted no serious assaults on the vulnerable oil producing areas along America's west coast. Nor was there a coordinated submarine campaign against American sea lines of communication in the Pacific. The general Japanese naval doctrine, in line with the code of *bushido* (the way of the warrior) was to attack warships rather than auxiliaries, even though the U.S. Navy could not operate for long in the vast Pacific without a long fleet train. An early example of what the Japanese could have achieved had they concentrated on naval auxiliaries was when a submarine sank tanker *Neches* on January 23, 1942, forcing Vice Admiral Wilson Brown to cancel an air strike by *Lexington* on recently captured Wake Island. Similarly, had the battle of the Coral Sea continued past May 8, 1942, the loss of U.S. tanker *Neosho* on the previous day would have seriously restricted carrier *Yorktown's* operations.

In contrast, the Allies operated from a position of strength with respect to oil resources, although this was not necessarily completely understood until later. Their economic and industrial base was immense, and they were able notably to outproduce the Axis powers in war material. The Japanese conquest of the oil fields in the Dutch East Indies in early 1942 was serious and alarming, but not a fatal loss. The continental United States produced vast amounts of oil in the West and Southwest, well protected from any enemy attacks (except for some inconsequential shelling by a Japanese submarine off southern California in January 1942). A large, sophisticated, and well-equipped infrastructure for drilling, refining, and transport already existed by the time the Americans entered the war. There was a huge, protected industrial base to produce new equipment for the Allied oil industry. Experienced personnel were directing its expansion before December 1941. The Allies also had good access to the oil reserves of Latin America and the Middle East. Axis forces in North Africa were a very potent threat to the British oil fields in the Middle East, but could not advance far enough to attack them. Only the undersea warfare carried out by the German navy's skilled U-boat fleet seriously interfered with the shipment of oil across the Atlantic and Mediterranean. Severe losses in these theaters in turn affected tanker availability in the Pacific, but in the latter half of 1943 the Allies were gaining the upper hand in their campaign against enemy submarines. Fortunately for the Allies, there was no coordination of efforts by Tokyo and Berlin.

The Allies formed several national and international committees to coordinate the production and distribution of oil around the world. Despite the normal conflicts over objectives, these boards, such as the U.S. Petroleum Administration for War and the Combined Resources and Products Board, succeeded in effectively rationalizing the Allied oil situation. Although the Allies had to transport their oil over longer distances to reach the operating areas than did the Japanese, the Allies (primarily the Americans) were able to deliver. American shipyards also produced many more new tankers much faster than did those in Japan.

The Allied policy was to protect their existing supplies of oil, and to cut off Japan's access to oil. It was the Allies' understanding of the vital role of oil in the modern military machine that led them to target Japanese oil resources (oil wells, tank farms, refineries, and especially tankers). This led to a consequent restriction of Japanese aerial and naval activities, allowing greater freedom of action for the Allies. It was the Japanese focus on the purely military aspects of the conflict (attacking warships) that led to their neglecting the protection of their oil resources.

The tactical sphere logically blends into the area of logistics. It was here that the Americans proved themselves to be the masters of the field. The U.S. Navy understood underway replenishment, built many tankers, and was very organized. One might speculate that the Americans had perhaps a better understanding of logistics in that they had for some time supported large military forces overseas, in Hawaii and the Philippines, some distance away from home for a longer period than had the Japanese. As it turned out, the loss of so many Allied ships at the beginning of the war, particularly the battleships, actually somewhat reduced demand at a time when oil supplies were not large.

The Allies could not have won the Pacific war without a secure supply of oil, plenty of ships, and an efficient and protected delivery system. They were able to produce and distribute petroleum products in the enormous quantities that allowed them effectively to operate the thousands of ships, planes, and military vehicles that helped defeat the Axis. Japan probably would have gone to war with the Western Allies sooner or later in order to maintain and expand its empire, but the dangerous threat posed by the 1941 oil embargo forced its hand. One can say that Japan went to war for oil, and was defeated by it.

FURTHER READINGS
Carter, Worrall Reed. *Beans, Bullets, and Black Oil: The Story of Fleet Logistics Afloat in the Pacific During World War II.* (Government Printing Office, 1953).
Barnhart, Michael A. *Japan Prepares for Total War: The Search for Economic Security, 1919–1941* (1987).
Goralski, Robert, and Russell W. Freeburg. *Oil and War: How the Deadly Struggle for Fuel in WW II Meant Victory or Defeat* (1987).
Marshall, Jonathan. *To Have and Have Not: Southeast Asian Raw Materials and the Origins of the Pacific War* (1995).
Stoff, Michael B. *Oil, War and American Security: The Search for a National Policy on Foreign Oil, 1941–1947* (1982).
U.S. Strategic Bombing Survey. Pacific War. Oil and Chemical Division, *Oil in Japan's War*, Government Printing Office (1946).
Worth, Roland H., Jr. *No Choice But War: The United States Embargo Against Japan and the Eruption of War in the Pacific* (1995).

Daniel K. Blewett

SEE ALSO Greater East Asia Co-Prosperity Sphere; Navy, Japanese

Okinawa, Battle for

After securing Iwo Jima in March 1945, the Americans looked to Okinawa as the most suitable of the Ryukyu Islands to use as a staging base for the projected invasion of Japan. The bloody fight for Iwo Jima provided an example of what U.S. forces could expect from the Japanese as they neared the Japanese home islands.

Okinawa is about some 70 miles long and 2 to 18 miles wide. It offered air bases, anchorages, and staging grounds suitable for the invasion of Japan. The island is mountainous in the north and south, and level and cultivated in the narrow center. The natives are a mixture of different cultures. Japan had invaded the island in 1875 and had generally treated the natives as an inferior race, confining them to traditional agriculture.

Operation Iceberg, the invasion of Okinawa and the other Ryukyu Islands, began after a weeklong bombardment that included B-29 air strikes. Still stinging from the heavy resistance on Iwo Jima, from March 24 to 31 the Americans conducted the heaviest bombardment yet in the Pacific, expending more than thirty thousand large shells. They planned the landing for Easter Sunday, April 1, 1945. It would be the largest amphibious operation, supported by 1,300 ships (including a small British fleet, forty carriers, eighteen battleships, and hundreds of destroyers and amphibious assault vessels).

Lieutenant General Simon Bolivar Buckner, Jr., son of a Confederate general commanded the U.S. Tenth Army, which led the assault. He had played a dominant role in the 1942–1943 retaking of Attu and Kiska in the Aleutians. Upon the initial landing at the low center of Okinawa, the plan was for the U.S. Marine III Amphibious Corps (1st and 6th Marine divisions) to turn north while the U.S. Army XXIV Corps (7th and 96th Infantry divisions) swung south. As the main landing commenced, the 2d Marine Division would stage an amphibious demonstration on the southern end of the island. The army's 27th Infantry Division and 77th Infantry Division would be held in reserve during the initial landings, then be used to take two small outlying islands.

On April 1 the Americans launched wave after wave of amphibious assault craft at the center of the island. The landings utilized the amphibious warfare techniques perfected during the Pacific war. A total of 16,000 troops were brought ashore in the first hour, and 50,000 were landed by the end of the day. The troops initially encountered almost no resistance. In the past the Japanese had attempted to beat back landings at the beach, then slowly fell back while being annihilated. The Americans were confused at the lack of resistance, which was part of the Japanese plan.

The Japanese had anticipated the invasion, and General Ushijima Mitsuru had withdrawn the majority of his 24th and 62d divisions, composing the 120,000 man Thirty-second Army, to the rugged southern end of the island to make a determined stand on good defensive ground. Ushijima doubted his small force would be able to withstand the onslaught of half a million U.S. troops, but he intended to make a determined stand.

Although Ushijima had doubts about the plan, his superiors in Japan did not. After the Americans were drawn into the island's defenses, the Japanese planned to launch a violent counterattack from sea and air. The Japanese had used kamikazes before the invasion, and they now hoped to drive the U.S. fleet from Okinawa and destroy the invasion force at leisure. As the kamikazes pounded the Americans, venerable battleship *Yamoto,* with several escort vessels, would run up on the beach and destroy the remnants of the U.S. fleet.

The Americans had already had a taste of the kamikazes. On March 18–19 naval Task Force 58 had suffered a heavy Japanese attack. Carrier *Franklin* took two bomb hits on the flight deck that virtually incinerated the upper decks of the ship. The crew saved the vessel after suffering the loss of 724 men, the highest casualty rate of any surviving U.S. Navy vessel in the war. Carrier *Wasp* also took a kamikaze hit, and was saved by the crew's use of new fire-fighting techniques. A civilian firefighter, Lieutenant Thomas A. Kilduff, had introduced a new hose nozzle that produced a fine spray to knock down flames.

On the ground, the Americans had bisected the island by April 4, when the U.S. Marine III Amphibious Corps turned north and the army's XXIV Corps moved south. The 6th Marine Division advanced north up the island and cornered a determined band of 2,000 Japanese defenders on the Motobu Peninsula on April 8. The peninsula was cleared within a week while the 1st Marine Division and a regiment from the 6th Division cleared the rest of the northern part of the island. While marines mopped up the northern part of the island, the army's XXIV Corps met stiff resistance in the south. They found the Japanese well dug in along a series of ridgelines with forward and reverse slope defenses. The Japanese incorporated caves in successive lines of mutually supporting positions. The offensive quickly ground to a bloody halt.

As the ground forces began to slow, the Japanese launched the second part of their defensive plan, a massive counterattack by sea and air. On April 6 the Americans received their largest kamikaze attack yet. At the same time the venerable *Yamoto,* escorted by eight destroyers and a cruiser, left Japan. The Japanese hoped to blast their way through the Allied ships, beach on Okinawa, and destroy the attackers. The plan was foiled when U.S. aircraft spotted the Japanese ships. On April 7, 280 aircraft from Task Force 58 began pounding the battleship and its escorts. After a two-and-one-half-hour assault the great ship finally capsized and sank with most of its 2,300-man crew. *Yamato*'s loss marked the end of Japan's great navy.

The kamikaze assault was more successful. On April 6 the Japanese attacked with 900 aircraft, 300 of which were kamikazes. The Americans shot down 108 planes, and the attackers sank an LST, two destroyers, and an ammunition ship. Japanese attacks continued the next day; a carrier, a battleship, and two destroyers took hits. The Americans then extended their destroyer screen up to 95 miles from Okinawa. The destroyers provided early warning of the attacks, but they also became easy targets for the kamikazes. From April 6 until July 29, the destroyer screen was pounded by suicide attacks, and fourteen destroyers were sunk. Also starting on April 6, and continuing through June 10, the Japanese launched ten mass kamikaze raids of 50 to 300 planes each at the fleet. During the two months the U.S. Navy was off Okinawa, it endured some nineteen hundred kamikaze attacks that sank thirty-eight ships and damaged many others, including carriers *Hancock, Enterprise,* and *Bunker Hill.* The cost was almost unbearable. Suicide warfare, however, inherently depletes resources, and by June the Japanese had run short of both pilots and planes.

On Okinawa the U.S. advance still had problems. On April 22 the 1st Marine Division took up a position on the right of the army's line and was joined later by the 6th Marine Division; they encountered the main Japanese line with the heart of its defense at Shuri Castle. On May 4 the Japanese launched a desperate counterattack that made some headway before the Americans turned it back.

Admiral Chester Nimitz became impatient with the slow land advance and complained that he was losing "a ship and a half a day." But he soon realized that because the Japanese were well entrenched and fighting without quarter, it would be an ugly fight. Japanese defensive lines ran east–west, using ridgelines across the southern part of the island. In places, they had incorporated ancient Okinawan tombs into their defenses, as prefabricated pillboxes.

As the U.S. troops slugged it out in a landscape eerily reminiscent of Europe in World War I, they heard news first of President Franklin Roosevelt's death and later of V.E. Day. Although they were saddened at Roosevelt's death and heartened at the prospect of aid from American forces in Europe, little of it made much difference to men trying to survive one more day on the line. Hampered by rain and mud, the Americans measured gains by yards and inches as they destroyed barricaded Japanese positions. On May 18 the marines took Sugar Loaf Hill, the western portion of the Shuri Line, and four days later the Japanese fell back 7 miles south to a new line.

Criticisms of the campaign continued, especially by the U.S. press, which styled the battle a fiasco. David Lawrence in the Washington *Evening Star* went so far as to call it "a worse example of military incompetence then Pearl Harbor." The critics ridiculed Buckner for placing the marines on the right of his line when he could have used them to make an amphibious assault flanking the Japanese position. This criticism continued even after Secretary of War James Forrestal and admirals Richmond K. Turner and Marc Mitscher stated their public support for the tactics on Okinawa. Finally Admiral Nimitz took the almost unheard-of step of holding a press conference with seventy-six reporters on Guam. He pointed out the impracticality of an amphibious flanking operation, noting that the enemy's lines were equally strong on both sides; he went on to defend Buckner's

tactics and the army's "magnificent performance" on Okinawa. On June 18 General Buckner was killed by enemy artillery fire, becoming the highest-ranking American officer lost to hostile fire in the war. General Roy S. Geiger, commander of the Marine III Amphibious Corps, directed the final days of the fighting, becoming the only U.S. Marine in the war to command a field army.

On June 21, with just a few pockets of resistance remaining, General Geiger declared the island secure. Soon General Ushijima and many of his officers committed ritual suicide as the last of his forces were eliminated. The Americans captured only 7,400 prisoners, many of whom were too sick or too seriously wounded to kill themselves or fight to the death. Japanese losses were frightful—107,539 were killed and another 27,764 were sealed in caves. Okinawa was also the costliest battle for the Americans in the Pacific. The Tenth Army lost 7,374 killed, 31,807 wounded, and 239 missing. The U.S. Navy sustained more casualties than in all previous wars combined: 4,907 men killed and 4,874 wounded; 38 ships sunk and 368 damaged; 763 aircraft were lost.

The grimmest aspect of the fight may have been the fate of civilians on Okinawa. Many who were barricaded in the caves with the army committed suicide; others were killed when the Americans assaulted the strongholds. Of Okinawa's prewar population of 450,000, between 70,000 and 160,000 were killed.

Although the Americans needed Okinawa as a springboard to Japan, the battle seemed a prelude to the fighting to come. As the Americans built up their forces on Okinawa for the invasion of Japan, the dropping of two atomic bombs on Japan brought the war to an end. Rather than being a prelude to a bloody invasion of Japan, Okinawa was the last campaign battle for the Americans in the Pacific theater.

FURTHER READINGS

Appleman, R. E. *Okinawa: The Last Battle* (U.S. Army, Office of the Chief of Military History, 1948).

Feifer, George. *Tennozan: The Battle of Okinawa and the Atomic Bomb* (1992).

Gow, Ian. *Okinawa, 1945: Gateway to Japan* (1985).

Keegan, John. *The Second World War* (1989).

Morison, Samuel Eliot. *History of United States Naval Operations in World War II.* Vol. 14, *Victory in the Pacific, 1945* (1975).

Wheeler, Richard. *A Special Valor: The U.S. Marines and the Pacific War* (1983).

Thomas D. Mays

SEE ALSO Buckner, Simon Bolivar, Jr.; Kamikazes

Osmeña, Sergio (1878–1961)

Filipino politician and second president of the Philippine Commonwealth. Born at Cebu City in 1878, Osmeña, the illegitimate son of Chinese and Filipino parents, attended San Juan de Letran School and the University of Santo Tomás. While working as the editor of a weekly paper, he expressed nationalist sentiments and favored independence from American control. He obtained his law degree by 1903, then served as prosecuting attorney on Cebu. In 1906 became governor of the island. The next year, as a member of the Nacionalista Party, Osmeña attained recognition as a national leader. He was elected to the Philippine Assembly and served as its first president (1907–1922).

Despite a political rivalry with Manuel Quezon, in 1935 Osmeña won nomination for the commonwealth vice presidency on a ticket headed by Quezon, and was elected to that office. In spite of lacking Quezon's flash and charisma, Osmeña was liked by his countrymen for his trustworthiness, prudence, forbearance, and stability.

After Japan invaded the Philippines in 1941, Osmeña accompanied Quezon to Corregidor. On December 30, 1941, on a stand near the entrance to Malinta Tunnel, he and Quezon were sworn in for second terms, to which they had been elected several weeks earlier. When Quezon announced he would notify President Franklin D. Roosevelt of his desire for independence and neutrality, Osmeña prevailed upon him to reconsider the impact of such action. The president, Osmeña reasoned, could be stigmatized as a treasonous coward, and would risk the security of his family at the hands of the Japanese.

Osmeña was evacuated with Quezon to Australia and then, maintaining that Washington, D.C., was the best spot for a Philippine government-in-exile, sailed to the United States. Once in America, Osmeña was assigned the chairmanship of the Postwar Planning Board created by Quezon, but became irritated at the latter's reluctance to decide on a postwar plan. An impersonal relationship, produced by decades of political contention, still existed, and Quezon tried to keep Osmeña from the limelight. Osmeña nevertheless accepted his subordinate position and yielded to the whims of an ill and brooding president. When his presidential term expired, Quezon asked Roosevelt to extend it by executive order. Osmeña, however, urged a vote by the U.S. Congress to retain Quezon. In 1943 Osmeña went along with a bill signed by Roosevelt which provided that both men would continue in office until the ouster of the Japanese.

By 1944 Osmeña had become more animated in public affairs because of Quezon's declining health and recurring absences from Washington. After Quezon's death later that year and his accession to the presidency, Osmeña initiated discussions with U.S. officials, focusing mainly on the necessity of renewing commercial ties between the United States and the Philippines.

Notwithstanding advice to the contrary, Osmeña met General Douglas MacArthur in Hollandia, Dutch New Guinea (now Djajapura, Irian Barat, Indonesia), prior to the U.S. return to the Philippines. Put off by an air of scheming and haughtiness within the general's staff, Osmeña considered returning to Washington. Nevertheless, several hours after the initial landings on Leyte in October 1944, Osmeña stepped ashore with MacArthur. Despite being overshadowed by the general and his fears of a slow return of civilian control, Osmeña's commonwealth government at Tacloban, the provincial capital of Leyte, received authority over all freed Philippine territory. In Manila, on February 27, 1945, MacArthur reinstated complete constitutional administration of the islands.

Osmeña opposed the appointment of an American high commissioner, out of concern for the possible reestablishment of some measure of foreign control, and contended with MacArthur's Department of Civil Affairs. Even though Osmeña was supposedly in control, Philippine Civil Affairs units possessed the capability and exercised the power to clear up daily governmental and administrative questions. To add to his difficulties, MacArthur had empowered Osmeña to announce that Filipino servicemen would receive 50 pesos per month in overdue payment when, in fact, the United States permitted only 8 pesos. Owing to U.S. slowness in providing relief supplies, Osmeña was forced to go through MacArthur for aid, thereby conceding credit for the assistance to MacArthur.

Osmeña's administration was further hindered by MacArthur's preference for Manuel Roxas, a suspected collaborator and now president of the Philippine Senate. Roxas claimed that he was always on the side of the Allies, and had played a double game with the Japanese occupiers in order to ease the sufferings of his compatriots. Osmeña believed the collaboration issue should involve not only occupation of office under the invaders but also the reason for such officeholding and the incumbent's official acts. Soon many individuals, apparently vindicated after release from the custody of the U.S. Army Counterintelligence Corps, received significant posts, giving Osmeña's government a tinge of collaboration. Through the Senate's powerful Commission on Appointments, Roxas influenced Osmeña's choice of many of these officials.

Osmeña was eager for postwar U.S. bases and economic aid. He traveled to Washington in 1945 and 1946, and received promises of assistance from President Harry S.

Truman. In 1946 he ran for reelection and lost to Roxas. Osmeña died on October 19, 1961, of heart and kidney disorders, at Veterans Memorial Hospital in Manila.

FURTHER READINGS
Bernstein, David. *The Philippine Story* (1947).
Friend, Theodore. *Between Two Empires: The Ordeal of the Philippines, 1929–1946* (1965).
Karnow, Stanley. *In Our Image: America's Empire in the Philippines* (1989).
Valencia, Elpidio. *Presidente Sergio Osmeña* (1977).

Rodney J. Ross

SEE ALSO Quezon, Manuel; Roxas, Manuel

Ozawa Jisaburo (1886–1966)

Japanese naval officer who commanded the Southern Expeditionary Fleet in the early months of the war and played a major role in Japanese naval aviation. In 1944 he participated in two major naval engagements, the Battle of the Philippine Sea and the Battle of Leyte Gulf. He served as the last commander in chief of the Imperial Japanese Navy's Combined Fleet.

Ozawa graduated from the Japan Naval Academy in 1909. During World War I he served aboard a destroyer on convoy duty in the Mediterranean. He became a specialist in torpedo warfare, eventually serving as president of the Naval Torpedo College. He also was an enthusiastic supporter of naval aviation. In November 1939, Ozawa was appointed commander of Carrier Division 1, serving in that capacity for a year. In that post he became an outspoken advocate of consolidating all aircraft carriers into one striking force. In April 1940 he submitted his idea to the commander in chief of the Combined Fleet, Admiral Isoroku Yamamoto, who approved the concept and organized the First Air Fleet on April 10, 1941, thereby joining the carriers and air groups of Carrier Divisions 1, 2, and 4.

On October 18, 1941, Ozawa was appointed commander in chief of the Southern Expeditionary Fleet and was given the responsibility of supporting the Japanese landings in Malaya and the Netherlands East Indies. During this operation he initiated the first overt, belligerent act of the war when he ordered the destruction of a British reconnaissance aircraft that was shadowing the Japanese invasion forces sailing toward Malaya. Following the successful conquest of Malaya and the Netherlands East Indies, Ozawa's fleet conducted operations in the Bay of Bengal in support of the Japanese offensive in Burma.

On November 2, 1942, Ozawa was appointed commander in chief of the Third Fleet, which comprised the Japanese navy's carrier striking force. Japan's carrier forces had been considerably weakened, however, following the Coral Sea and Midway carrier battles and operations in support of the Guadalcanal campaign. Ozawa had few aircraft carriers available to him, and carrier air groups had experienced heavy losses of irreplaceable experienced personnel.

Ozawa was given little time to rebuild the Third Fleet. In an effort to halt or delay the Allied offensive in the Solomon Islands and New Guinea, he was repeatedly called upon to transfer his air groups to Rabaul, New Britain, in support of large-scale air operations. The first such operation was A-Go Plan, which began in April 1943. The actions took a steady and heavy toll on Ozawa's air groups. In support of Operation Ro-Go, an air operation directed at the Allied landings on Bougainville, Ozawa lost 70 percent of Carrier Division 1's 173 planes and 44 percent of their air crews.

In anticipation of a new Allied offensive, Ozawa was appointed commander in chief of the Mobile Fleet (which constituted about 90 percent of the Combined Fleet) on March 1, 1944, and was directed to prepare for a decisive battle against the U.S. Navy. In June 1944, Ozawa led the Mobile Fleet as it bore down on the U.S. Navy task forces involved in the invasion of the Mariana Islands. He engaged the U.S. Navy's carrier task forces, commanded by Admiral Marc A. Mitscher, on June 19 and 20, launching four air strikes against the U.S. fleet. The engagement, designated the Battle of the Philippine Sea, was a disaster for Ozawa. His air groups were virtually annihilated, and three of his carriers, including flagship *Taiho*, were sunk. Although Ozawa was badly defeated, the eminent historian Samuel E. Morison described him as

. . . one of the ablest admirals in the Imperial Navy; a man with a scientific brain and a flair for trying new expedients, as well as a seaman's innate sense of what can be accomplished with ships. Although himself not an aviator, he was a strategist, and it was he who had initiated the offensive use of aircraft carriers. . . . Altogether, Ozawa was a worthy antagonist to Mitscher.

The following October, Ozawa commanded a carrier task force in Plan Sho-Go, an operation intended to prevent or disrupt the U.S. amphibious landings in the southern Philippines. Ozawa's purpose was to draw Admiral William F. Halsey's Seventh Fleet away from the landings, thereby giving other elements of the Japanese Combined Fleet an opportunity to attack the U.S. landing forces. He succeeded in his mission, but in the ensuing attacks directed against his task force (the Northern Force), designated as the Battle off Cape Engaño, all of his carriers were sunk.

On November 11, 1944, Ozawa was appointed vice chief of the Naval General Staff. In that capacity he played an instrumental role in the naval defense of Okinawa. He later said that he was responsible for the suicide mission of superbattleship *Yamato* in March 1945.

On May 29, 1945, Ozawa was appointed commander in chief of the Combined Fleet and supreme commander of the Imperial Japanese Navy, positions he held until the close of the war.

FURTHER READINGS

Howarth, Stephen (ed.). *Men of War: Great Naval Captains of World War II* (1993).

Morison, Samuel Eliot. *New Guinea and the Marinas.* (1953).

George H. Curtis

SEE ALSO Shō-Go Plan

Pacific War Medicine

More than any previous conflict, the Pacific war taxed the limits of medicine. The chief circumstances that made the conduct of the Pacific war unique were the differences in environment and terrain in theaters of operations, the great distances between bases and the operational units, and the emphasis on naval and amphibious operations. Another important factor was the racist ideological nature of the conflict, which charged the fighting in the Pacific with a level of ferocity that transcended the limits and sensibilities of the participants. Ultimately, Western medicine proved able to meet these challenges, but it was greatly transformed in the process, both in terms of applied science and public perception. After the war's end, medical science acquired a double-edged image—as both a boon to civilization and as a potential danger to humanity.

World War I (1914–1918) demonstrated the value of a well-organized military medical system. New and old technologies alike—heavy artillery, machine gun and rifle fire, poison gas, aerial combat, and submarine warfare—had tested the existing knowledge base of physicians. The limits of men to withstand the pressures of the new warfare were also gauged, leading doctor and officer alike to reconsider the frailty of their charges. In response, new techniques were developed and put into widespread use, including x-rays, anesthesia, blood transfusion, wound debridement, tetanus and typhoid inoculation, and orthopedic and plastic surgery.

The lesson most learned from World War I was the absolute necessity of a well-organized military medical infrastructure. During the interwar years, all the major powers established a chain of evacuation and treatment of those wounded on the battlefield that adhered roughly to the same model. Aid companies attached to battalions administered basic first aid and prepared casualties for evacuation by litter companies and motorized ambulance companies to battalion or regiment casualty clearing stations. From there, wounded personnel were routed, based upon the severity of their injury or illness: regimental hospitals; field divisional hospitals; corps hospitals; and ultimately, base hospitals in the extreme rear. During the war, the most immediate changes to this structure were the expansion of motorized ambulance companies and the creation of forward surgical stations for immediate treatment of those seriously wounded.

The immense scope of the Pacific war tested the limits of Western medicine on land and sea. Each operational theater offered a unique challenge, requiring different approaches and solutions. The steaming jungles of the Southwest Pacific, the Philippines, and Burma were fetid breeding grounds for disease and parasites, including dengue fever, skin infections, and malaria. The frozen, wind-swept rocks of the Aleutians were equally dangerous, where frostbite was the rule and hypothermia as likely to kill a man as his wounds. The atolls and islands of the Central Pacific also had their own dangers. So ferocious was the fighting at Tarawa, Peleliu, and Iwo Jima that evacuation of the wounded required a herculean effort. The equatorial heat not only caused frequent sunstroke and heat exhaustion, but also sped the process of rot and decomposition. The dead might lay unburied for weeks on the narrow confines of the island battlefield. Such unsanitary conditions contributed to the spread of fly-borne disease and gas gangrene.

Naval warfare presented another set of problems. Despite the precautions of damage control measures, modern warships were floating deathtraps, packed with diesel and aviation fuel and ordnance. Fire was the greatest fear for sailors and shipborne aviators. There were two distinct types of burn injuries: flash burns from exploding ordnance, and the more dire third-degree burns from contact with burning fuel oil. Burn cases received lavish attention, first to combat the infection with sulfa drugs, then rehydration with saline, glucose, and plasma, and finally the long process of changing dressings and debridement of any necrotic flesh. Initially tannic acid was used to coat burned areas. After it had proven ineffective, a petroleum distillate gel similar to vaseline, impregnated with antibiotics and topical anesthetic, became the standard. Evacuation of the wounded was another problem. It simply was not possible to transfer the injured from one ship to another during combat. In lengthy engagements, the wounded could remain on board a ship for more than a week before transfer to a hospital ship.

The vast distances of the Pacific exacerbated these difficulties for all participants. Lines of supply and communication were so long that attackers and defenders alike were forced to make due with what supplies were on hand. Shortages were not restricted to medical supplies such as anti-malarials and antibiotics. Depleted food stocks would result in nutritional conditions that rivaled malaria and gangrene as dangers to combat effectiveness. In the first two years of the war these shortages contributed to several tenuous situations for U.S. forces in the Southwest Pacific. The 1st Marine Division and the two army divisions, the American and the 25th Infantry, suffered chronic shortages of food and basic medical supplies throughout the Guadalcanal campaign, as did the ANZAC and U.S. Army forces under General Douglas MacArthur in Papua, New Guinea. Malaria ran unchecked in these units. Raw incident rates often exceeded 90 percent of a unit's strength. Malaria and malnutrition combined to decimate the effectiveness of Allied forces in the theater; it was not uncommon for regiments on the Solomons or New Guinea in 1942 and 1943 to field less than two hundred effectives on any given day.

The problems of malaria, disease, and infection were among the first to receive serious attention. Allied forces would appreciate the benefits from several important developments in medical science during the war, especially from within the United States, where the War Department assumed control of the Office of Scientific Research and Development (OSRD) and the subordinate Committee on Medical Research (CMR). This bureaucracy coordinated and prioritized the research and development efforts of the U.S. (and ultimately, Allied) scientific community in the name of the war effort.

The first success was with the anti-malarials. After the Dutch East Indies were lost to the Allies in 1941, so was their access to the world's chief supply of quinine, the main substance used to fight malaria. When considering the projected paths to both Japan and Germany, it was

determined that a substitute treatment for malaria was of strategic significance. It was recalled that in the 1930s, German chemists developed several synthetic compounds that were successful in treating malaria, but they were dismissed as being too expensive and impractical. Wartime necessity led to a reconsideration of this earlier conclusion. The result was the first mass-produced synthetic anti-malarial drug: Atabrine. However, while more effective than quinine in preventing malaria and suppressing the symptoms of the disease, Atabrine also caused a number of unpleasant side effects, including nausea, headaches, and a jaundice-like discoloration of the skin. These side effects (along with the usual rumors of how the drug caused impotence and infertility), led many initially to resist taking their required daily dosage—resulting in disciplinary measures to ensure full compliance. Once these initial objections were overcome, however, Atabrine proved to be highly successful in both treating and preventing new outbreaks of the disease.

Antibiotics were the next significant chemotherapy development of the war. Developed just before the war, sulfa drugs (sulfadiazine, sulfaguanidine, sulfamezathine, sulfanilamide, and sulfathiazole) offered an effective tool for combating infection. Administered orally or topically, sulfa compounds were especially useful in preventing infections from developing in wounds and burns. Yet as good as the sulfa "wonder drugs" were, they were overshadowed by penicillin. Arguably the most significant medical development of the war, penicillin offered physicians a true "magic bullet" suited for use against virtually any bacterial infection. After entering widespread use in 1944, the drug rescued many who would otherwise had died from infection and gangrene. Penicillin was singly responsible for reducing mortality from infection to almost zero percent in the last two years of the war, and it proved extremely useful in combating bacterial diseases, including syphilis, that had been resistant to the sulfa drugs.

Malaria was not the only disease spread by an insect vector. Dengue fever, dysentery, typhus, typhoid, and others were serious health risks spread through contact with flies, lice, and mosquitoes in the many environments of the Pacific. While each could be treated, the better solution was the elimination of the insect vector. The discovery of DDT in 1943 provided the Allies a universal solution to all insect-borne diseases. Used liberally throughout the Pacific, DDT replaced the existing techniques of insect control and helped eradicate disease wherever it was found.

There were other important developments as well. American physicians had led the way in World War I toward the development of anticoagulant typing that made whole blood transfusion a possibility. However, the distances and environment of the Pacific theater combined with the scale of combat to create chronic shortages of whole blood. The most common solution was the use of blood plasma—the fluid remaining after red and white corpuscles were extracted from whole blood—as a substitute. While plasma was not intended to replace blood, it did stave off blood-loss shock, giving the wounded a much better chance to survive evacuation for additional treatment and surgery.

The task of evacuating casualties was another challenge for American and Commonwealth forces throughout the Pacific theater of operations. Compounding the difficulties of retrieving casualties from the jungle and island battlefield was the perceived need of field commanders to retain as many men as possible. Throughout the crisis period, from 1942 through 1943, many feared that once evacuated to the rear, soldiers would never be replaced. Nonetheless a system was developed that ensured as much as possible a rapid turnaround of wounded and debilitated soldiers from the front to recovery and return to the combat zone. Combat medics and corpsmen offered basic field medicine and sent casualties to aid stations and collection points just behind the front line. From there, the sick and injured were evacuated by stretcher bearers to clearing stations, where if necessary they were taken to field hospitals. The field hospital was the final classification and treatment area in the combat zone. Less serious cases were quickly treated and sent back to the front; those needing more extensive recovery and treatment were evacuated to station and general hospitals in the base areas by C-47 transports, or to hospital ships by landing craft. From there casualties would either recover and return to service or be evacuated back home for rehabilitation and discharge.

Each major combatant developed its own approach to military medicine. Often the response was driven more by necessity than any innate systemic orientation. Overall, Japanese medical services were less technologically oriented than the Allies. This was only partially due to the state of Japanese medical science, which was generally equal to that of the West before the war. More responsible was the combination of Japanese hubris and the American submarine campaign. The Imperial Japanese Army (IJA) had indoctrinated itself into believing that the inherent toughness of the Japanese soldier would triumph over injury or disease. Instead of being a necessary component of warfare, illness and suffering were seen as a weakness, an excuse for malingerers, cowards, and inferiors. In short,

the Japanese were supposed to be tougher than their opponents and not in need of coddling.

This harshness was compounded exponentially by American submariners. Immediately after the attack on Pearl Harbor (1941), the U.S. Navy undertook a sweeping anti-merchant shipping campaign against the Japanese, intended to cut communications between the home islands and their newly conquered possessions. Thus, supply shortages became endemic throughout the Pacific theater. The results were felt even before Allied forces launched operations against Japanese defenders, as nutritional disorders like pellegra and beriberi, and diseases like dengue fever, scrub typhus, tuberculosis, and dysentery took their toll. In the South Pacific and Southeast Asia, malaria was rampant as well. Although their conquest of the Dutch East Indies in 1941 gave the Japanese control world's primary source of quinine, the drug could not be shipped past the submarine blockade. Combat medicine fared no better. Individual Japanese units even practiced what was bitterly known among the troops as "grenade medicine," whereby seriously wounded soldiers were left behind—with a hand grenade. All across the Pacific and Asia, individual Japanese surgeons labored under conditions reminiscent of the pre–Florence Nightingale Crimean War.

This dismal state is particularly ironic considering the history of military medicine in Japan. From 1904 on, Japanese military medicine and sanitation were held in high esteem by Western observers; most especially the evacuation and hospitalization schemes. Equally admired were Japanese attitudes toward captured enemy soldiers. In the Russo-Japanese War (1904–1905) and World War I (1914–1918), Russian and German prisoners were treated as guests of the emperor by the Japanese Red Cross. Such charity toward the enemy did not survive the militarization of Japanese society in the 1920s. In China, Japanese military medical services joined in the brutalization and dehumanizing of the Chinese. The most famous example is seen in the horrendous work of the infamous Unit 731, the Japanese military hospital detachment in the Harbin region that performed experiments on live subjects. This type of brutality pervaded the Kwantung Army and in turn set the tone for Japanese conduct in other theaters.

At the time of Pearl Harbor and the Japanese invasion of the Philippines, American medical services were generally unprepared for the scale of casualties that were received. In Hawaii, both the army and navy medical services were overwhelmed by the wounded—many burn cases—suffering in the surprise attack. Forces in the Philippines fared even worse. Efforts to build up supplies and personnel on Luzon were still incomplete in December 1941, as was a plan to store medical supplies in depots across the island. This state of unpreparedness would make itself felt after December 23, 1941, when General Douglas MacArthur ordered the evacuation of all forces to Bataan and Corregidor, abandoning the base hospitals of Manila and the stockpiles of medical supplies housed there. As a result, the defenders quickly fell victim to malnutrition and disease, which in turn diminished their combat effectiveness.

The U.S. Army and Navy medical departments rapidly absorbed the lessons of these early setbacks, as well as the mistakes made in the Southwest Pacific in 1942 and 1943. Not surprisingly, interservice rivalry and personal egos presented the greatest obstacle for American military medicine. Squabbling between the two chief theater commanders, General Douglas MacArthur and Admiral Chester W. Nimitz, and their subordinates for priority of resources exacerbated the already significant problems of distance and environment that the medical system faced. Nonetheless, a system developed that accommodated both services. Within the army, the size and capability of battalion aid stations were expanded, giving battalions and regiments more autonomy in the field. The navy medical department's mission was twofold: not only was the medical service to provide care in the fleet, but it also had the task of providing combat medical support for the marine corps. Support for the marine divisions was organized along the same lines as that of the army medical department. The chief difference was the use of LCTs and LSTs as amphibious hospitals and evacuation ambulances.

Great Britain's experience mirrored in some ways that of the United States, but in others was even worse. Britain had gathered its resources and summoned the assistance of the dominions in response to the war in Europe. As a result, imperial outposts were understaffed and underequipped throughout Southeast Asia, while the bulk of Australia's and New Zealand's forces were engaged in North Africa. Britain's imperial forces were all in a precarious state in December 1941, not only because of the immediate shortages of supplies and manpower, but also because Britain's resources were already stretched to the breaking point in Europe. Long after the initial disasters of December 1941–January 1942, medical services in Burma, India, and Australia would remain an afterthought, the Pacific theater taking a secondary role after the war in Europe for the British.

Decisions made in London about the respective priorities of the European and Pacific theaters affected the quality of medical services for British, ANZAC, and Indian forces in the Pacific. The experiences of the Austra-

lians and New Zealanders in New Guinea was similar to that of the U.S. Army and marines in the region, save that the ANZACs enjoyed the advantage of relative proximity to base hospitals in Australia. The question of supply shortages for the ANZAC medical services was remedied when General MacArthur assumed overall command of the Southwest Pacific theater (SWPAC) in April 1942, at which point the ANZAC medical services entered the American supply chain. British and Indian forces in Burma were not so fortunate. If anything, the combat environment in the China-Burma-India theater (CBI) was even more extreme than what the Americans and ANZACs faced in New Guinea. Disease, especially malaria, was as serious a factor in the Burmese rainforest as in the SWPAC. The terrain itself was a factor as well. Logistically, Burma was a nightmare. It was a mountainous region with few roads, and evacuation, replacements, and resupply was problematic at best. Still, by 1944 the British and Indian armies had made great strides in remedying the problems of the environment. An anti-malarial campaign featuring DDT and Atabrine had achieved measurable results, while the Royal Air Force (RAF) was committed to air evacuation. Whereas evacuation of casualties could take weeks along what passed for the Burmese road network, by 1945 soldiers were being flown to base hospitals in India within hours of their being wounded.

Despite the many Allied successes in the practice of medicine and public health made during the war, it remains important that the war not be simply portrayed as a period of "great progress" for medical science. Such triumphalism obscures the human element, such as the internal conflicts that arise when the civilian healer dons the military uniform; specifically, which role was more legitimate for the military physician—saving lives or preparing men for war. Also often overlooked in the positivist literature is the interaction between civilian-oriented medicine and the military in wartime, and the broader socioeconomic, cultural, and political contexts of this relationship. Take, for example, the transformations that World War II wrought in the societal perspective of science and medicine in the United States. After 1945, medical science became increasingly bureaucratized, as wartime successes were carried into peacetime, shifting responsibility and sponsorship for private research from private foundations to the state. Thus, American medical science and practice began its great transformation from profession to industry. At the same time, the general public reacted to the paradoxical images of the role played by science in total industrial war. On one hand were the positive contributions: penicillin, Atabrine, blood plasma, and burn therapy. But almost tipping the scale the other way were the images of the worst depravities committed in the name of science, including live human testing. The result was a cautious ambiguity toward medicine following war's end: the promise of medical science as Promethean gift, balanced by a fear of callow and amoral scientists eager to make a Faustian deal with evil men for the sake of knowledge. Ultimately, however, the greatest lesson to be gained from the Pacific war was the discovery that a properly managed human endeavor could overcome the most extreme conditions of nature and the greatest expanses of time and space. In a very real sense, the success of American and British military medicine in the Pacific theater bore witness to the power of industrial management and applied technology over the vicissitudes of the elements.

FURTHER READINGS

Checkland, Olive. *Humanitarianism and the Emperor's Japan, 1877–1977* (1994).

Condon-Rall, Mary Ellen, and Albert E. Cowdrey. *The Medical Department: Medical Service in the War Against Japan* (1998).

Cooter, Roger, Mark Harrison, and Steve Sturdy. *War, Medicine and Modernity* (1998).

Cowdrey, Albert. *Fighting for Life: American Military Medicine in World War II* (1994).

Gabriel, Richard A., and Karen S. Metz. *A History of Military Medicine*, vol. II. *From the Renaissance through Modern Times* (1992).

Herman, Jan K. *Battle Station Sick Bay: Navy Medicine in World War II* (1997).

Raina, B. L., *World War II, Medical Services: India* (1990).

Bobby A. Wintermute

Palau

Lying roughly five hundred miles east of the southern Philippines, in the westernmost portion of the Caroline chain, Palau (Beleu) consists of several large islands and more than one hundred smaller ones. Prior to the Pacific war, the Japanese established airfields in the Palaus, which had been mandated to Japan in 1919. The Japanese used the main air base, located on Peleliu, in the southern portion of the chain, for reconnaissance missions at the outbreak of war. They also used the Palaus as a staging ground for operations mounted against the Philippines, the Dutch East Indies, and New Guinea in December 1941 and the opening months of 1942.

In March 1944, the U.S. joint chiefs of staff, whose responsibilities included planning strategy for the Pacific war, selected the Palaus as an invasion target, explaining that their occupation would extend Allied control over the eastern approaches to the Philippines and Formosa, as well as provide air bases that could support operations against the Philippines, Formosa, and the China coast. Six months later, U.S. forces effected Operation Stalemate, the invasion of the Palaus. Supported by Admiral William F. Halsey's Third Fleet, the U.S. 1st Marine Division, commanded by Major General William H. Rubertus, assaulted Peleliu on September 15 and the U.S. Army's 81st Infantry Division, commanded by Major General Paul J. Mueller, made landings on Angaur, the southernmost of the Palaus, on September 17.

Peleliu proved to be among the most difficult campaigns waged by U.S. forces in the Pacific war. In the amphibious phase of the campaign, the 1st Marines encountered a 600-yard-long reef obstructing the approach to the landing beaches. As at Tarawa in the Gilbert Islands (November 1943), the marines relied upon amphibious tractors (amtracs) to traverse the reef because standard landing craft ran aground in the uncertain tides and became easy targets for enemy guns. Yet, even with an adequate supply of amtracs, the 1st Marines suffered significant casualties as they made their way to the beaches in the face of deadly fire from well concealed Japanese pillboxes.

Once ashore, the marines discovered to their horror that their intelligence information about Peleliu's topography and the extent of Japanese defenses was inaccurate. Aerial reconnaissance, conducted during July and August, indicated that the island was flat and lightly defended. In reality, Peleliu's terrain, especially the coral ridges making up Umurbrogol Mountain (Bloody Nose Ridge) on the western side of the island, was rugged, and a garrison of 10,600 soldiers, commanded by Colonel Kunio Nakagawa, awaited.

Prior to the U.S. landings, Nakagawa's soldiers transformed the numerous caves found in the ridges of Umurbrogol Mountain into mutually supporting fortified positions that proved invulnerable to both the preinvasion bombardment and postlanding artillery. Some of the larger fortified caves contained electric lighting, ventilation systems, and communication equipment, and housed as many as one thousand soldiers. Once the marines had established a beachhead, Nakagawa's troops, rather than conduct suicidal banzai charges, as the Japanese had done in defending other islands, withdrew into their established positions and compelled the Americans to wage a time-consuming, bloody war of attrition in heat that occasionally reached 115 degrees Fahrenheit. Relying on flame-throwers, grenades, demolition charges, and raw courage, the 1st Marines, with the assistance of the 81st Infantry, cleared Peleliu cave by cave and ridge by ridge during two months (September 15 to November 27) of hard fighting. For the 1st Marines, victory on Peleliu carried a heavy price tag: 6,525 casualties (1,250 killed and 5,275 wounded).

On Angaur, a scenario similar to that on Peleliu, though on a smaller scale, unfolded between September 17 and October 21. Although they met no resistance in getting ashore, the 81st Infantry ran into the same tactical problem confronted by the 1st Marines on Peleliu. Major Goto Ushio's 1,600 soldiers responded to the invasion by withdrawing to fortified positions on Ramuldo Hill in the island's northwest corner. Like the 1st Marines on Peleliu, the 81st Infantry found it necessary to eliminate Japanese strongholds almost one by one, suffering heavy casualties in the process. In the Palaus campaign, the 81st suffered 3,278 casualties (542 killed and 2,736 wounded), many of these occurring on Angaur.

Strategically, the capture of the Palau Islands did not prove as valuable as anticipated. Although an airfield constructed on Angaur was an effective heavy bomber base and aircraft staging ground during Allied campaigns in the northern Philippines, especially that on Luzon (January to August 1945), Operation Stalemate was undertaken primarily because Admiral Chester W. Nimitz, commander in chief, U.S. Pacific Fleet; General Douglas MacArthur, commander, Southwest Pacific Area; and the U.S. joint chiefs of staff sincerely believed that the success of the Allied invasion of the southern Philippines, scheduled to begin with Mindanao on October 5, 1944, depended on securing the Palaus. Nimitz, in particular, insisted that the Palaus operation go forward. However, because of changes in Allied plans—the substitution of Leyte for Mindanao and the moving forward of the date of Leyte's invasion to October 20—the Palau Islands played no role in MacArthur's campaigns in the southern Philippines. It is therefore possible that Admiral Halsey, the only high-ranking U.S. commander in the Pacific who consistently opposed Operation Stalemate and who urged that it be scrapped as late as September 13, was correct in his assessment that the Palaus could have been safely bypassed without a detrimental effect on the invasion of the Philippines.

In retrospect, it appears that Allied possession of Peleliu and Angaur had little impact in determining the future course or the final outcome of the Pacific war, and that the only real by-product of the campaigns was to provide a foretaste of what the U.S. Marines and Army would confront on Iwo Jima and Okinawa in early 1945.

FURTHER READINGS
Costell, John. *The Pacific War, 1941–1945* (1982).
Crowl, Philip, and Edmund G. Love. *Seizure of the Gilberts and Marshalls* (Office of the Chief of Military History, Department of the Army, 1955). In the series U.S. Army in World War II.
Morison, Samuel Eliot. *History of United States Naval Operations in World War II*. Vol. 7, *Aleutians, Gilberts, and Marshalls, June 1942–April 1944* (1951).
Spector, Ronald. *Eagle Against the Sun: The American War with Japan* (1985).

Bruce DeHart

Panay

The elderly river gunboat USS *Panay* was at the center of an international incident in December 1937, during the Sino–Japanese War. While escorting three Standard Oil tankers down the Yangtze River, the vessel was attacked and sunk by Japanese naval aviators. The event threatened to worsen already strained relations with Japan, though the U.S. response has since been interpreted as a manifestation of the deep isolationist sentiment that pervaded American public opinion in the late 1930s.

Panay was one of a number U.S. gunboats that were common sights in Chinese waters by the 1930s. The U.S. naval presence in the Far East went back to the turn of the century, when the Boxer Rebellion in China impelled Western intervention. The collapse of the Manchu dynasty in 1911 left China in intermittent turmoil, and by the 1920s the U.S. Asiatic Fleet employed river gunboats to show the flag and offer protection to missionaries and diplomatic personnel. The *Panay* was typical of the type of craft utilized. Brought into service in 1900, the 191-foot-long, twin-engined, shallow-draft ship, named for one of the islands in the Philippine archipelago, carried twin stacks and armament including a 57-millimeter bow gun, half a dozen smaller guns, and several .30-caliber machine guns, the latter mounted for a horizontal rather than a vertical field of fire. The crew of about fifty could seek shade from the often intense sun under extensive canopies fore and aft. In late 1937 the skipper of the trim buff and white ship was Lieutenant Commander James J. Hughes, an Annapolis graduate.

The events leading to *Panay*'s ordeal began on December 11, 1937, with the ship anchored in the Yangtze River off Nanking. With a Japanese army on the verge of surrounding the city, pressure was growing on foreign nationals and warships to depart the area. The decision to do so was made that day. *Panay* weighed anchor and headed upriver with a small group of evacuees, including

Norman Alley, a cameraman for Universal Newsreels, and two Italian journalists, Luigi Barzini and Sandro Sandri. Together with three Standard Oil tankers, *Panay* anchored for the night about 12 miles from Nanking. The situation began to deteriorate the next morning when Japanese artillery, on orders from the local commander, Colonel Kingoro Hashimoto, began shelling traffic on the river, sinking a number of Chinese junks just downstream from *Panay*'s group. The small flotilla moved farther upriver, but halted when Japanese guns were trained on it from the shore. A Japanese army lieutenant came aboard and demanded to inspect the ships; Hughes refused, and ordered him off. Moving on, the ships finally anchored in an apparently quiet spot nearly 30 miles from Nanking.

Unknown to Hughes and his crew, a flight of twenty-four Japanese naval air force bombers was headed in his direction. The Japanese aviators were responding to an army request to intercept a group of Chinese ships reportedly fleeing Nanking with Nationalist troops aboard. The Japanese pilots sighted *Panay* and the tankers at about 1:35 P.M., and their subsequent actions became the source of both contemporary and historical controversy. Though *Panay* was showing extensive identification, including a U.S. flag on the mizzenmast and the national colors painted on the large canopy on the afterdeck, a group of six Japanese aircraft attacked with bombs before strafing the four vessels. *Panay* was not adequately armed to fend off an air attack, and despite valiant efforts by the crew, suffered hits that ruptured a fuel line and blew holes in the hull. As the gunboat was being abandoned, the three tankers, all of which suffered some damage, attempted to ground themselves. Sometime after 3 P.M., *Panay* rolled over and sank. The attack wounded sixteen of the crew and left two dead, the journalist Sandri and a seaman. The survivors huddled on the shore, awaiting rescue.

Panay had been in radio communication with Yangtze Patrol headquarters in Shanghai when the attack interrupted transmission. A party from the Patrol gunboat reached Hohsien and notified their command of the attack, word of which rapidly made its way to Admiral Henry Yarnell, commander of the U.S. Asiatic Fleet, and ultimately to President Franklin D. Roosevelt, whose outrage mirrored that of the American public. Despite Japanese protestations that the attack was a case of mistaken identity, the majority of Americans saw it as a manifestation of Japanese arrogance and duplicity. Norman Alley's film of the attack, which was featured in newsreels throughout the country, showed Japanese aircraft so close to *Panay* that an error in identification seemed most implausible. The "*Panay* Incident" was virtually concurrent

with the "Rape of Nanking," and both did much to strengthen an already formidable anti–Japanese sentiment among Americans.

Nonetheless, there was little popular sentiment in favor of violent retaliatory action for the attack. Japanese officials, including Yamamato Isoroku, were quick to offer apologies, and ultimately the imperial government agreed to pay more than $2.2 million in reparations. Many Americans remained skeptical of Japanese sincerity; the Los Angeles *Times* accompanied its account of Japan's apology with a photo of the cigarette-smoking Japanese ambassador, Hirosi Saito, above the sarcastic caption "So Sorry" (sometimes rendered stereotypically as "So solly"). Ultimately, American outrage was overcome by an almost impervious isolationism. The destruction of *Panay*, however galling, was not worth a major war with Japan.

The debate over Japanese intentions in the *Panay* sinking continued for decades. For many years after the end of the war, it was commonly assumed that the attack was an intentional test of U.S. determination in the Far East. There is, however, considerable evidence to suggest that the attack was indeed a mistake. One of the Japanese aviators involved recounted how later on December 12, his unit began an attack on two other ships on the Yangtze. Only after bombs had been released were the vessels identified as the British gunboats HMS *Cricket* and HMS *Scarab*. The attack was called off after the mistake was realized. Japanese pilots involved in the attack on *Panay* were summoned before superiors and interrogated, after which they received severe written reprimands castigating them for their failure to adequately identify the vessels before attacking. More generally, it would not have served Japan's objectives in China to run the risk of provoking American ire at this juncture; Japan's war machine remained greatly dependent upon crucial American exports such as petroleum. Indeed, it was the embargo of that commodity which led most directly to Japan's decision to go to war against the United States, almost exactly four years after the sinking of *Panay*.

FURTHER READINGS

Hoyt, Edwin P. *The Lonely Ships: The Life and Death of the U.S. Asiatic Fleet* (1976).

Perry, Hamilton D. *The Panay Incident* (1969).

Prados, John. *Combined Fleet Decoded: The Secret history of American Intelligence and the Japanese Navy in World War II* (1995).

Blaine T. Browne

Pearl Harbor, Japanese Attack on

The United States entered World War II at 7:55 A.M. local time on Sunday, December 7, 1941, when 131 Japanese aircraft struck the U.S. naval and air bases on Oahu, Hawaii. The initial raid was followed an hour later by a second wave of attackers. The objective was to cripple the U.S. Pacific Fleet at Naval Station Pearl Harbor and damage nearby air bases. The surprised defenders put up little initial resistance. The result was one of the most costly American defeats in history. Over two thousand Americans died, and every battleship present was either sunk or heavily damaged. Unfortunately for Japan, the Pacific Fleet's three aircraft carriers were absent, and Admiral Chiuchi Nagumo, their Carrier Strike Force commander, failed to follow up his tactical victory by sending a third wave against the naval station's submarine base or its repair and fuel facilities. The combination of misfortune and his mistake came to haunt Japan in the Pacific campaigns's later battles.

The Japanese attack marked the culmination of years of growing friction between the two Pacific Ocean powers. Japan saw the United States as the primary obstacle to its political and economic objectives in Asia. The United States saw Japan's ongoing war in China as a prelude to the conquest of Asia, including the U.S. possessions of Guam and the Philippines. Their bilateral relations had become especially hostile after Japan occupied Vichy French bases in Indochina on July 21, 1941. President Franklin Roosevelt responded five days later by freezing Japan's financial assets in the United States. More significantly, the United States and the European powers in Asia imposed an embargo on shipments of oil and iron ore to Japan. Denied the raw materials needed to sustain its economy and war machine, Japan's military leaders initiated planning to gain those raw materials by conquest.

The Japanese general staff gave some consideration to invading the Soviet Union, but the Soviet victories over the Japanese in 1939 and the vastness of that country's territory led them to drop the idea. Moreover, the Kwantung Army was already heavily engaged in China, and it was recognized that Japan could not afford to take on a second major land power. The Imperial Japanese Navy, on the other hand, had long been considering the seizure of Southeast Asia's European colonies. The problem was the U.S. Pacific Fleet and its bases in the Philippines. From those bases, the Americans could interfere with any attempt to take the European colonies. Japan's commander of the Combined Fleet, Admiral Isoroku Yamamoto, conceived a plan.

Although he was opposed to war with the United States, Yamamoto had recognized the growing tensions between the two countries in 1939. His solution, in the event war became inevitable, was to destroy the U.S. Pacific Fleet in one blow by attacking Pearl Harbor. He had confided his plan to his chief of staff, Admiral Fukodome Shigeru, in December 1940, and had been preparing the Japanese navy for such an operation since taking over as commander in chief of the Combined Fleet on August 30, 1939. A visionary who recognized the importance of sea-based airpower, he had initiated a rigorous training program for Japan's carrier pilots. Forcing them to conduct low-level attacks over mountainous terrain and enclosed harbors, ostensibly to prepare for ground support operations, provided Yamamoto with a carrier force prepared for the mission even before his staff had heard of it. Yamamoto named the Pearl Harbor attack Operation Z, drawing his inspiration from Admiral Togo Heihachiro's "Z" signal, dispatched the night before his famous victory over the Russian fleet in the Tsushima Strait (1905).

Detailed planning was assigned to Rear Admiral Takijuro Onishi, chief of staff of the 11th Naval Air Force, Japan's land-based naval bomber force. As one of the navy's few air-minded officers, Onishi was uniquely qualified for the task. He asked for, and received, permission to consult with a colleague, Commander Minoru Genda, of carrier *Kaga*. A former naval attaché in London who had studied Britain's torpedo-plane attack on the Italian fleet at Taranto (1940), Genda told Onishi the idea was feasible.

Genda's views came to dominate the planning from that point on. He rejected Yamamoto's original idea of making the air strike a one-way affair. Instead, he recommended that the carriers launch from a distance close enough to recover the planes. Such a strike would maximize damage to the U.S. fleet and its supporting infrastructure while preserving Japan's carrier strike force for immediate operations elsewhere. He shifted the strike's target priority from battleships to carriers, arguing that U.S. aircraft carriers posed the greater threat to Japanese interests. He centered the attack force around Japan's six most formidable carriers: *Kaga, Akagi, Hiryu, Soryu, Zuikaku,* and the soon-to-be commissioned *Shokaku*. The combined air wing numbered some three hundred sixty aircraft of all types—the largest sea-based air force up to that time.

The bulk of the plan was ready by the end of March 1941. The carriers would be supported by an advanced screen of twenty I-class and five midget submarines. The I-class submarines were to act as forward reconnaissance units reporting on U.S. movements around the Hawaiian Islands and also as a rear guard to derail any U.S. counterattacks against the strike force. The midget submarines were to enter the harbor just before the attack, to sow confusion among the defenders.

The air strikes were planned with two options, one if surprise was achieved and the second if the defenders were alerted. In both cases, the initial wave consisted of torpedo planes and dive-bombers and level bombers. The first option called for the dive-bombers and torpedo planes to strike the Pacific Fleet first; Commander Mitsuo Fuchida was to lead the level bombers over the harbor, attacking the fleet with armor-piercing bombs once the others were clear. The second option called for the dive bombers to attack Wheeler and Hickam air bases, where the Americans based their fighters and bombers, respectively. The dive-bombing element assigned to Hickam was also to attack the navy airfield on Ford Island. Any planes with bombs remaining were to attack the marine corps air station at Ewa. Both options called for the fighter escort to circle over central Oahu and attack any fighters that rose to intercept. With their aircraft destroyed, the Americans could neither intercept Japan's aerial strike group nor attack its carriers.

Secrecy and operational security was paramount. The two forces were to take different, circuitous routes to the Hawaiian Islands. The special submarine attack force would take a southerly route from Truk to Oahu while the Carrier Strike Force took a northerly route out of Tankan Bay in the Japanese Kurile Islands. Although the air wing's training schedule was intensified that summer, the pilots still believed their training was in preparation for ground and amphibious support operations. Yamamoto had chosen Kogashima Harbor in southern Japan for their training. Its topography, surrounding terrain, and general layout were very similar to those of Pearl Harbor. Interestingly, neither the local residents nor foreign agencies placed any special significance on the pilots' activities.

Technical considerations also affected planning. Genda considered the problem of using torpedoes in Pearl Harbor's relatively shallow 45-foot harbor. Most air-dropped torpedoes plunged 70 to 90 feet underwater before rising to their preset run depth. To prevent that, the Japanese installed an expendable wooden fin on the sterns of their torpedoes, to turn the noses upward shortly after they entered the water, thus ensuring that the torpedoes returned to their running depth of 27 feet before they hit the harbor bottom. Production of the new torpedoes began in September, and the last of them were delivered on November 18, barely in time to be used.

There was also some concern over whether Japan's armor-piercing bombs could penetrate U.S. battleship armor. Therefore, special armor-piercing bombs were improvised from 16-inch gun shells. The modification consisted of adding a tapered body with fins to the shell. Given the shell's 1,600-pound weight, armor-piercing design, and probable velocity when dropped from 10,000 feet, the Japanese rightly believed the new weapon would be highly effective. In fact, the level bombers were included in the strike group because Japan's Val dive-bomber couldn't carry the new bomb.

Intelligence preparation for the attack was extensive. Japan's Oahu consulate had several active agents, and the Japanese navy had used submarines to monitor the Pacific Fleet's activities around the islands for years. Japan's long-range, high-frequency stations in the Marshall and Kurile Islands had monitored the Pacific Fleet's communications since the late 1920s. Nonetheless, Japanese naval intelligence dispatched Yoshikawa Takeo to Honolulu in mid-March 1941. An experienced naval officer supposedly retired for health reasons in 1936, he spoke English fluently but had no espionage training or experience. He did, however, have an outstanding memory and a keen eye for detail. He worked the clubs and establishments around Oahu and toured the island, escaping notice and suspicion while he collected information about the island's defenses and naval activities.

Another agent, a German national named Otto Kuhn, was activated in late November. His task was to establish a signal lamp system to warn the strike force of any fleet sorties or movements that might threaten the task force. Three of the advance force's submarines were stationed off Oahu to watch for his signals. Also, merchant ship *Taiyo Maru* steamed along the strike force's proposed route between Midway and the Aleutian Islands, transmitting weather, sea, and shipping information. *Taiyo Maru* reported sighting no ships during its journey. The ship also acted as a secure courier, returning to Japan with Yoshikawa's reply to Yamamoto's critical question on what day the most ships would be in port: Sunday.

Meanwhile, fleet training and planning continued. Vice Admiral Nagumo was chosen to command the carrier strike group and Commander Fuchida to lead the air wing. An unimaginative and cautious officer, Nagumo was a poor choice; his assignment was based on seniority, not brilliance. Fuchida, however, was an outstanding selection. A charismatic and innovative leader, he was the perfect partner for Genda. The latter was a brilliant planner, and Fuchida was a great commander who converted his plans into reality. Both men emphasized that no bombs or torpedoes were to be wasted. Each pilot was to take as many passes as necessary to ensure a perfect attack.

Contrary to popular myth, the Americans were neither idle nor unaware of the threat during this period. The air threat to Pearl Harbor had been recognized as early as the 1932 fleet maneuvers when 150 aircraft were launched from *Saratoga* and *Lexington* against the naval base. They had achieved total surprise and success. Admiral Husband E. Kimmel, the Commander in Chief of the Pacific forces, took no notice of the Taranto raid's lessons. But Kimmel's superior, Secretary of the Navy Frank Knox, reviewed the navy's report on that raid and ordered the defenses at Pearl Harbor strengthened. Specifically citing the torpedo-bomber threat, Knox ordered additional anti-aircraft guns, radar equipment, antitorpedo nets, and interceptor aircraft. Kimmel objected to the addition of antitorpedo nets, arguing that they would interfere with ship movements in the harbor.

A second opportunity to improve the defenses was lost in March 1941, when Pearl Harbor's air defense commander and Hawaii's army air corps commander issued a joint assessment of the island's vulnerability. In it they accurately predicted the nature, direction, and timing of the Japanese attack. They also identified the forces required to patrol the waters around Hawaii to prevent surprise: 180 B-17Ds—more than the entire inventory of the army air corps at the time. Many of their other recommendations were more reasonable, such as establishing an integrated radar warning network around Oahu. Their report, which reached Washington on August 30, was ignored. Spending money on Far East defenses was not popular in Washington at that time.

General Walter C. Short, the army commander of the Hawaiian Islands, shared Kimmel's concerns about Hawaii's defense. However, unlike General George C. Marshall in Washington, Short did not see Japanese airpower as the most likely threat. He concentrated on repelling a Japanese invasion, even drawing air crews away from maintenance and flying duties to build beach defenses and practice small unit tactics.

Kimmel's threat assessment was similarly misguided. In a letter to Secretary of the Navy Knox in March 1941, he described the most likely threat as "fast Japanese ships" supported by a carrier. Kimmel focused his planners on preparing for a major surface engagement, either near the Hawaiian Islands or in the western Pacific. Little was done in Pearl Harbor itself, but reinforcements were deployed to Wake and Midway islands. America's distant island outposts were considered more likely initial Japanese targets.

Japan's diplomats pressed U.S. Secretary of State Cordell Hull for resumption of oil and scrap metal shipments. Hull refused, stating that the raw material embargo would end only when Japan withdrew from Indochina and halted its war of aggression against China. The negotia-

tions continued throughout the fall, with the Japanese insisting on unfettered access to Southeast Asia's raw materials and markets, and the Americans pressing for Japan's withdrawal from Indochina. Japan's military leaders were becoming impatient. The navy's staff debated the merits of Yamamoto's plan.

Although most of the Japanese navy staff thought war with the United States was inevitable, they opposed Yamamoto's strike plan, objecting primarily to its risks. To resolve the impasse, the annual staff war games were moved up from December to September. The games' first run resulted in two carriers lost, a result unacceptable to the naval staff. The carrier strike force's overwhelming victory in the second run did little to assuage the staff's reservations. In late October, Yamamoto dispatched an emissary, Captain Kameto Kurashima, to the naval staff. Kurashima was directed to resolve the staff's objections and gain approval. However, he was unable to force a decision. He called Yamamoto and returned with a message: Yamamoto and his entire staff would resign if the operation was not approved. After a short discussion, the naval staff authorized the operation on November 3, 1941.

The U.S. intelligence picture of Japan was somewhat unclear at this time. Although the United States had broken Japan's diplomatic codes, the resulting intelligence remained in Washington, D.C. For example, Washington knew that the Japanese negotiators were facing a November 29 deadline to win agreement, after which "events would happen automatically." Also, U.S. signals intelligence was regularly decoding the daily reports emanating from Japan's Oahu consulate. Those reports focused almost exclusively on navy activities in and around the Hawaiian Islands. In October, the reports began to include the exact locations of warships within Pearl Harbor. Washington, placing no significance on this change in emphasis, failed to report the intercepts to the commanders in Hawaii. In fact, Washington-based intelligence services provided little more than vague warnings to Pacific commands in mid–November. The warnings offered no details and expired on November 30, four days before Japan's carrier strike force departed for Hawaii.

On November 30 Japan's senior leaders held a conference in the Imperial Palace to determine if the attack should go forward. The emperor's advisers reported his reservations, but Prime Minister Tojo Hideki insisted war was inevitable. Access to the Far East's raw materials could be assured only by conquest. Moreover, Tojo thought the chances for victory were very great. The destruction of the U.S. fleet would open all of Southeast Asia to Japanese invasion. No other Western country had the naval forces to oppose Japan in the Pacific. Tojo believed the Americans would be so shocked by their defeat that they would negotiate an end to the crisis. His arguments assuaged the emperor's concerns. One change was made to the plan, however. Instead of presenting the Japanese declaration of war at the moment of the Pearl Harbor attack, 1:30 P.M. Washington time, it was decided to present it thirty minutes before—8:00 A.M. Honolulu time. Tojo's advisers felt that would ensure the attack's achieving surprise in Pearl Harbor while preventing President Roosevelt from claiming that the attack was without warning.

Meanwhile, Admiral Nagumo's Carrier Strike Force was steaming through heavy seas toward Hawaii. It refueled at sea on Saturday, December 1 (local time). The tankers then withdrew to the postattack refueling point. At 2130 that night, Admiral Nagumo received the signal *Niitaka-Yama Nahore* (Climb Mount Niitaka), indicating the negotiations had failed. It was followed by a signal indicating the date of the attack, December 8 in Japan, (December 7 in Hawaii).

The submarines arrived on station around Oahu on Friday, December 5. The Pacific Fleet was in port, except for its carriers. They were at sea, on the way to deliver fighters to Midway and Wake Island. Yoshikawa transmitted his final shipping report at 9 P.M. the next day: "nine battleships, three cruisers, three submarine tenders, and seventeen destroyers at anchor. Four cruisers and three destroyers in dock. All carriers and other cruisers at sea." Nine hours later, Nagumo's carrier strike force arrived at its launch point, 230 nautical miles northwest of Pearl Harbor. At 5:15 A.M., he launched two seaplanes to scout Oahu's defenses. Meanwhile, Japan's fourteen-section ultimatum was being transmitted to Washington. Its final section was due to be received at 9:00 A.M. Washington time, for 1 P.M. presentation to Secretary of State Cordell Hull.

Oahu's defenders had several opportunities to awaken before it was too late. The first came at 3:45 A.M., when coastal minesweeper USS *Condor* spotted something following target-towing minesweeper USS *Antares* into Pearl Harbor's outer torpedo net. After careful and patient observation, *Condor*'s watch officer recognized the object as a submarine conning tower, and reported it to nearby destroyer USS *Ward*. A patrolling aircraft also spotted the conning tower, and marked its location with a smoke float. *Ward* then steamed toward the Japanese submarine, opening fire with its forward gun at 100 yards' range—America's first shots of the Pacific campaign, the submarine submerged before it could be hit. *Ward* followed up with a depth charge attack that sank the submarine. *Ward* transmitted a report of the action to CINPACFLT

headquarters at approximately 6:35 A.M., but the fleet's staff duty officer and the assembled duty section were still discussing the report when the Japanese aircraft arrived overhead.

The five midget submarines were supposed to strike the attack's first blow, and *Ward*'s contact is one of three known to have reached the harbor. The second was sunk by destroyer USS *Monaghan* in the harbor during the initial air raid. Its hulk was incorporated in the harbor's seawall, where it remains. Another ran aground on an Oahu beach later in the day, and its crew was captured. A fourth was found in the Pearl Harbor basin in the 1990s. Nothing is known of the fifth submarine's fate.

The weight of the Pearl Harbor attack therefore fell almost solely onto Fuchida's pilots. They had been assembled on their carrier flight decks since 5:30 A.M., awaiting Admiral Nagumo's order to take off. Facing deteriorating weather and hearing nothing from his seaplanes, Nagumo launched the strike thirty minutes early. His decision precluded the ultimatum's delivery taking place before the attack.

Commander Fuchida was the first to launch, lifting off at 6:00. The first wave's 181 aircraft followed him in rapid succession. The last plane was airborne by 6:15. Thirty minutes later, two American radar operators at Opana Point detected a single unidentified aircraft flying toward Oahu. They chose to ignore it, believing it to be a U.S. patrol plane. They were partially correct. It was a patrol plane, but it was Japan's. Pearl Harbor's defenders had missed a second chance to be alerted.

The defenders' third and final opportunity came at 7:00 A.M. when the radar operators detected a large body of aircraft approaching from 130 miles to the northwest. They reported the contacts to the air warning center at Fort Schafter but were ordered to forget it. The duty officer believed it was a dozen B-17s scheduled to arrive from California that morning. At that moment, the first wave was forty minutes from Oahu and nearly fifty minutes from Pearl Harbor. No alarm was raised.

Fuchida's attack group passed Kahuku Point, Oahu's northernmost point, at 7:40 A.M. Seeing the ships and aircraft arrayed below, he couldn't believe his luck. The planes were lined up wingtip to wingtip, and the ships were anchored in nearly perfect straight lines. Rolling back his canopy, Fuchida fired a single flare, a signal to the strike group that surprise had been achieved. Unfortunately, the fighter escort commander did not acknowledge the signal. Fuchida fired a second flare. What followed was one of the war's most insignificant errors: the dive-bomber element commander, Lieutenant Commander (LCDR) Kuichi Takahashi, mistook the second flare to mean the defenders were alerted, and dived on Oahu's airfields. The other elements stuck with the original plan and attacked the fleet.

Takahashi's fifty-one dive-bombers split into two groups, one going after Hickam Airfield and Ford Island while the second went after nearby Wheeler Air Base. LCDR Shigeharu Murata's forty Kate torpedo planes flew directly at Pearl Harbor's battleship row. LCDR Shigeru Itaya led his forty-three Zeros over the center of the island while Fuchida led forty-nine level bombers equipped with 1,600-pound armor-piercing bombs around Oahu's western shore. No antiaircraft fire or other form of resistance greeted the attackers.

Admiral Nagumo and the assembled carrier crews had spent the intervening two hours in nervous anticipation. The second wave had taken off at 7:00, so the ships' crews had been assembled on the now clear flight decks. For morale purposes, the strike group's reporting circuit had been patched to the ships' deck speakers so everyone could monitor the attack. Hearing nothing from the seaplanes, they had no information on the strike group's status or the situation over Oahu as 8:00 approached. Then, shortly after 7:50, came the message *To To To* (Charge, Charge, Charge). The attack was under way. A few minutes later, the flagship received Fuchida's now famous signal *Tora Tora Tora* ("Tiger, Tiger, Tiger," meaning surprise achieved). The crews cheered.

The dive-bombers were the first to reach their targets, dropping their bombs on Hickam Airfield at approximately 7:55. They were ecstatic at the sight before them. The U.S. planes were arrayed in a straight line along the taxiways below, almost wingtip to wingtip. Never again would Japanese pilots see such an easy target. Within minutes virtually every bomber was destroyed. Next came nearby Ford Island airfield with its naval patrol planes and seaplanes, and the pattern of destruction was repeated. It was from Ford Island that Commander Logan C. Ramsey issued the the other famous signal of the day: "Air Raid Pearl Harbor! This is no drill! This is no drill!" It was not yet 8:00.

Hickam and Ford Island suffered heavy damage, but Wheeler Air Base was the priority target. Wheeler's fifty fighters constituted the greatest threat facing the Japanese strike group. Their destruction was critical to the attack's success, particularly for the subsequent strike waves. As at Hickam, the planes were arranged in compact rows, making them easy targets. Although Wheeler had protected parking areas for its fighters, General Short, ignoring the advice of his predecessor, had ordered all planes lined up on their airfields to facilitate guarding against sabotage. Fuchida's fighter escorts joined in the attack, strafing the

U.S. planes. Within minutes, Wheeler became an inferno, its hangars and a third of its aircraft destroyed and several hundred of its personnel killed or wounded.

The torpedo planes reached Pearl Harbor Naval Base five minutes later. They caught the fleet preparing for morning colors. Approaching low and slow, each pilot selected his assigned target. Battleships *California*, *Oklahoma*, and *West Virginia* were the first to be hit, absorbing one to two torpedoes each in the first attack. Heavy cruiser *Helena* was next, followed by heavy cruiser *Raleigh* and target ship *Utah* (which represented a double mistake by the Japanese aviators. *Utah*, an old, demilitarized battleship, was mistaken for an aircraft carrier.) A few of the dive-bombers joined in, attacking the battleships. Battleship *Arizona* suffered a boiler and forward magazine explosion. Over a thousand of her crew died and several hundred more were wounded. It was America's greatest single loss in the attack.

Commander Fuchida and his level bombers circled over Pearl Harbor while he observed the results below. He led the bombers in as the last torpedo plane pulled away. His planes made several passes over the fleet, but only the first one was easy. As the bombers wheeled about for their second pass, the finally alerted fleet met them with heavy flak. Three of his bombers were shot down.

Meanwhile, in Washington, Japan's ambassador, Kichisaburo Nomura, waited frantically for the decoding of the incoming signal from Japan. Not realizing it was a declaration of war, the ambassador's staff painstakingly checked it for accuracy before translating it into English. The U.S. Signals Intelligence Service was actually decoding and translating the Japanese message more quickly than the ambassador's staff. The Americans finished the final section an hour before the Japanese embassy. General Marshall transmitted the warning to General Short just after noon, Washington time. Unfortunately, in one of the war's most colossal blunders, the War Department's communications center sent the message via commercial channels. Hawaii didn't receive it until after the attack. Nomura arrived at the State Department over an hour late. It was 2:00 Washington time, and Secretary Hull, unlike Nomura, knew the Pearl Harbor attack was under way. It was not a cordial meeting.

Nomura entered the State Department just as the second wave arrived over Oahu. Its 170 aircraft, led by LCDR Shigekazu Shimazaki, encountered fiercer resistance than the first wave. Two U.S. fighters rose from Wheeler Air Base to intercept, and antiaircraft fire met them as they approached their targets. Thick black smoke and flak bursts obscured many targets. The eighty dive-bombers went after the battleships because their original targets, the carriers, were absent. Their commander, LCDR Egusa Takeshiki, led them against the ships putting up the most antiaircraft fire. He reasoned that those were the ships most in need of destruction. Shimazaki turned the fifty-four level bombers on Hickam, Ford, and Kaneohe airfields. The thirty-six fighter escorts strafed whatever undamaged airplanes they could find on the ground.

At this point battleship *Nevada* got under way and tried to break for the open sea. Seeing its movements, several Japanese dive-bombers attacked, hoping to sink it in the channel. The already damaged *Nevada* shuddered as five more bombs pierced her armor. Seeing the danger, the battleship's officer of the deck ran it aground at Hospital Point rather than risk blocking the channel. Shimazaki's raiders spent roughly an hour over their now aroused targets. Twelve unarmed American B-17Ds arrived over Hickam in the middle of Shimazaki's attack. Engaged by both the U.S. antiaircraft guns and the Japanese fighters, they suffered heavily. Eighteen dive-bombers from carrier *Enterprise* also arrived during the second raid, landing successfully at Kaneohe Naval Air Station despite the base defenders' intense antiaircraft fire. The last of Shimazaki's wave departed Oahu at 9:45, just fifteen minutes before Fuchida recovered aircraft aboard *Akagi*. They left virtually no undamaged major combatants in their wake. Fuchida recommended another strike, but Nagumo felt they had risked enough. The carrier strike force turned toward Japan as soon as the last aircraft recovered was aboard. For a price of twenty-nine aircraft, they had sunk or crippled eight battleships, three cruisers, three destroyers, and eight auxiliaries. They also had destroyed 96 of the 231 army air corps aircraft on Oahu, and the airfields were devastated.

The Americans rushed to repair the damage and get as many planes in the air as they could. Unfortunately, neither Short nor Kimmel had a clear idea of where the attack originated, and no one thought to ask the radar plotters. They had tracked the raiders outbound to a range of nearly one hundred fifty nautical miles. The Japanese pilots had abandoned their planned indirect deception routes and flown directly back to the carriers because they were running out of fuel. The Americans were too confused to exploit the situation. At noon, Hickam launched six surviving B-17s to search for the Japanese task force south of the islands. Half an hour later, Kaneohe launched nine undamaged *Enterprise* dive-bombers loaded with 500-pound bombs. They flew to the northwest but turned back 150 nautical miles from Oahu. Neither group found anything.

Pearl Harbor cost the United States some 2,403 dead and enraged the nation. Nervous gunners fired on anything that flew for hours afterward, and the fires burned for days. Admiral William F. Halsey, commander of the Pacific Fleet's Carrier Force, was shocked at the destruction when he entered Pearl Harbor with his carriers later in the day. Concerned about his vulnerability in port and eager to take revenge, he refueled his task group quickly and returned to sea.

Operation Z was an overwhelming tactical and operational victory. It inflicted casualties far out of proportion to the Japanese forces engaged and lost. Operationally, it left the U.S. Pacific Fleet crippled and unable to interfere with Japan's conquest of Southeast Asia. For nearly six months, the Imperial Japanese Navy faced no effective resistance in the southern Pacific. But it was a limited victory.

Nagumo's failure to destroy the submarines, fuel farm, and shipyard at Pearl Harbor enabled the Pacific Fleet to strike back. U.S. submarines began to decimate Japanese shipping almost immediately. Of the damaged warships, all but the battleships returned to service within weeks. Except for *Arizona* and *Oklahoma*, the battleships were repaired, and returned to participate in the liberation of the Philippines three years later. Hawaii's irreplaceable fuel depot supported the U.S. forces that fought the Japanese during the early months of the war. Finally, the destruction of the battleships forced the U.S. Navy to embrace the aircraft carrier as naval warfare's new capital ship. If it had not, there would have been no U.S. victories at the battles of the Coral Sea and Midway.

The Pearl Harbor attack also failed in its strategic objective: stunning the American people into accepting Japanese dominance in the Pacific. It did shock the American people. Everyone old enough to remember that day knows where they were and what they were doing when they heard the announcement of the attack. None of that induced a feeling of defeat. In fact, the impact was quite the opposite. The attack's treachery instilled a deep and abiding desire for revenge. President Roosevelt exploited that feeling to rally American public opinion to the war effort.

The Pearl Harbor attack altered America's character and culture. Prior to Pearl Harbor, Americans felt safe behind their oceans, and the majority had little interest in world affairs. Short stories and other forms of fiction dominated the content of American books and magazines, competing with household hints and local events for attention. Within a year of the attack, fiction and short stories gave way to news about the war, world events, and international developments as the central element of

American magazines. News and analysis of world events retained primacy in America's printed media until the final years of the cold war. Pearl Harbor was the catalyst that inspired America to become a world power. In that respect, its impact continues into the twenty-first century.

Pearl Harbor Attack: Losses

	American	Japanese
Killed	2,403	189
Wounded	1,178	0
Aircraft		
Destroyed	188	29*
Damaged	159	?
Ships		
Sunk	5 battleships**	1 I-class submarine
	1 minelayer	5 midget submarines
	1 target ship	
Damaged beyond repair	2 battleships**	0
	2 destroyers	
Severely damaged	2 battleships	0
	1 sub tender	
	1 repair ship	
Damaged	3 battleships	0
	3 heavy cruisers	

*Japanese aircraft losses were nine fighters, fifteen dive bombers and five torpedo bombers. Most were lost in the second wave.

**Arizona and Oklahoma were sunk and damaged beyond repair. Arizona remains in Pearl Harbor as a war memorial. Oklahoma was raised but sank again outside Oahu after the war, while on the way to a Japanese scrap yard. All other ships were repaired and returned to service.

FURTHER READINGS

Barker, A. J. *Pearl Harbor* (1969).

Prange, Gordon W. *At Dawn We Slept* (1981).

———. *Pearl Harbor: The Verdict of History* (1986).

Winton, John. *Air Power at Sea 1939–1945* (1976).

Carl O. Schuster

SEE ALSO Kimmel, Husband E.; Nagumo Chuichi; Nomura Kichisaburo; Short, Walter Campbell; Yamamoto Isoruku

Pearl Harbor Conference

On July 26–27, 1944, United States President Franklin D. Roosevelt met with Admirals Chester W. Nimitz and William D. Leahy and General Douglas MacArthur at Pearl Harbor, Hawaii, to discuss future American moves in the Pacific. Together they decided to forge ahead with an attack to liberate the Philippine Islands.

In the spring of 1944, Nimitz and MacArthur, the two dominant military personalities in the Pacific campaign, were headed for a showdown over upcoming operations.

Chief of Naval Operations Admiral Ernest J. King wanted to bypass the Philippines and move instead on Formosa to create B-29 bases there. MacArthur, largely for reasons of personal prestige and a sentimental attachment to the Philippines, where he and his father had served, wanted to fulfill his promise and return to the Philippines. Roosevelt, Army Chief of Staff General George C. Marshall, and most commanders in the field had not decided one way or the other. The Joint Chiefs of Staff (JCS) mirrored this lack of certainty and resented being left in Washington.

Nimitz initially called for a meeting to coordinate the Central and Southwest theater plans for Morotai, Palau, and Mindanao islands operations. When MacArthur heard of Nimitz's formal proposal he wanted to fly to Washington to sell his own concept directly to the president. Nimitz instead invited the general to Pearl Harbor to discuss the issue. The general refused, saying that now he was too busy to leave his Brisbane, Australia, headquarters.

MacArthur, by reason of personality and seniority, had grown accustomed to independent action. An invasion of the Philippines archipelago—1,000 miles from north to south and possessing a longer coast line than the continental United States—would be such a vast undertaking that he needed the support of most of the U.S. fleet in the Pacific. He couldn't go this one alone. During the U.S. presidential election campaign in 1944, MacArthur represented a direct challenge to Roosevelt, his commander in chief. In fact his name was placed on the ballot as a Republican candidate in the Wisconsin and Illinois primaries, where he picked up a few delegates. Only when a poorly worded letter to a Nebraska congressman backfired and discredited his candidacy did MacArthur discretely pull out of the race. Because he was no longer a political rival, the president agreed to meet the general. At this point, Marshall ordered MacArthur to Hawaii to meet "Mr. Big."

Roosevelt arrived at Pearl Harbor on the July 26 and was to have been honored with appropriate naval fanfare. MacArthur, annoyed over bring summoned from his headquarters for what he dismissed as a "political picture-taking junket," grandiosely upstaged his commander in chief by arriving late in the flashiest convertible in Honolulu, borrowed from a local madame, with police motorcycle escort and sirens blaring. That piece of ego behind them, the four leaders and their staffs met to work out the details of the Pacific campaign.

Nimitz argued for the use of sea and air mobility to avoid a major ground battle like that in New Guinea, and instead go for Formosa. The JCS and Admiral King supported that course of action. MacArthur took over and talked until midnight. His primary argument hung on the "mother country's" duty to the "17 million loyal, Philippine Christians" and 3,700 American POWs left on the Philippine islands. Only after making that moral point did he discuss the military aspects of the operation. After three hours of MacArthur's bombast, Roosevelt told his physician, "Give me an aspirin, in fact give me another aspirin to take in the morning. In all my life nobody has ever talked to me the way MacArthur did."

But the general's preparation, eloquence, and point of view won the day when the leaders reconvened at 10:30 the next morning. Nimitz was at a disadvantage and had nothing to counter the touchy political issues concerning the liberation of the Philippines. Roosevelt adroitly handled the strong personalities present. As Leahy later said, "He tactfully steered the discussion from one point to another and narrowed down the areas of disagreement between MacArthur and Nimitz."

The president worried about high casualties and their effect on opinion at home. MacArthur gave him overly optimistic and ultimately false estimates of expected U.S. losses. In fact, casualties would be substantial. The United States committed more troops to the Philippines than to any other campaign except for western Europe. Despite misgivings, FDR agreed to the Philippine thrust while MacArthur supported his commander's re-election by reporting to the American public how well the Pacific campaign was going.

After the war, Nimitz wrote, "I think the decision was correct." King initially opposed the move to the Philippines, but Nimitz convinced him otherwise in late September. Marshall came around for reasons of national honor and because he thought taking the Philippines would be easier than capturing Formosa. The Combined JCS, interested more in military than moral matters, formally approved the agreement at the Quebec conference.

According to the plan "the Philippines should be recovered with ground and air power then in the western Pacific"; that is, there should be no waiting for the anticipated German defeat. Operational details stated that the Philippine invasion would be pushed back slightly to make way for some preliminary moves each service felt necessary. The Army Air Forces needed the Talaud Islands for airfields to support the assault and Nimitz wanted Yap and Ulithi in the western Carolines. MacArthur agreed to land on Mindanao on November 15 and Leyte on December 20, only after Morotai had been taken on September 15 and the Talauds were secured on October 15. Even this schedule changed as the U.S. Navy discovered that far fewer Japanese defended the Philippines than earlier thought.

The ultimate wisdom of a direct assault on the Philippines aside, the Pearl Harbor conference succeeded masterfully. It proved the primacy of politics in strategic military matters. We can see how relatively easy single-nation decision making is when not hampered with coalition issues as in Europe. Roosevelt, in the role of "the Chairman," demonstrated his undisputed personal leadership. MacArthur showed he could sublimate his vanity as he and Nimitz cooperated wonderfully. Added together, these factors guaranteed the success of the conference and of the Allied war effort.

FURTHER READINGS
Larrabee, Eric. *Commander-in-Chief* (1987).
Manchester, William. *American Caesar.* (1979).
Spector, Ronald. *Eagle Against the Sun* (1984).
Wilmott, H. P. *The Barrier and the Javelin* (1987).

Robert Kirchubel

SEE ALSO Leahy, William D.; MacArthur, Douglas; Nimitz, Chester William; Roosevelt, Franklin Delano

People's Liberation Army

The Chinese Communist People's Liberation Army (PLA) was created on August 1, 1927, when the 24th Division of the Kuomintang's (KMT) Eleventh Army mutinied against the KMT leader, Chiang Kai-shek (Jiang Jieshi). The mutiny, under the command of Chu Teh and Lin Piao (destined to become important Communist leaders), failed because many of the common soldiers refused to participate. The mutineers retreated southward, and in 1928 they linked up with Mao Tsetung in the Chinese Communist Party's (CCP) mountain stronghold on the border of Hunan and Kiangsi provinces. Chu Teh quickly took charge of all of the CCP's forces and reorganized them into the 6-regiment Fourth Red Army.

By 1930 the PLA numbered between sixty thousand and sixty-five thousand men.

Between 1930 and 1934, the KMT forces launched five campaigns against the CCP stronghold. The tactics in the fifth campaign, which enabled the KMT to surround and isolate the PLA, caused the approximately eighty thousand Communist cadres to begin a retreat to northwest China. By 1935 the PLA had completed the 8,000-mile "Long March" from the southeast province of Kiangsi to the northwestern frontier province of Shensi. Of the 80,000 men and women who started the journey, only 20,000 reached the CCP's new headquarters in Yenan as a coherent unit.

During the mid–1930s the Japanese threat to China became apparent. After consolidating control in Manchuria (forming the puppet state of Manchukuo in 1931–1932), Japan began to encroach southward into Chinese territory. In December 1936, one of Chiang Kai-shek's warlord supporters, Chang Hsueh-liang, kidnapped Chiang outside the city of Sian and pressured him to ally with the Communists against Japan. Chiang was released on Christmas Day, 1936, and quickly returned to his capital in Nanking. The incident eventually led to the creation in 1937 of the "second" KMT–CCP United Front (the first had lasted from 1923 to 1927), directed against Japan. However, tensions remained high between the Communists and the Nationalists.

Accounts of the PLA's effectiveness against Japan during World War II are mixed; even sympathetic accounts by the Chinese Communists suggest that they spent as much time (or more) time trying to outmaneuver the KMT as they did fighting Japan. During 1940, the PLA conducted the "Hundred Regiments Campaign" against Japanese strongholds in northern China. Its victories were negligible, and Japanese counterattacks quickly devastated the CCP's base area. The PLA's Eighth Route Army alone reportedly sustained 100,000 casualties.

KMT–CCP tensions escalated into open conflict after the "New Fourth Army Incident" in January 1941. The PLA's New Fourth Army was located in Kiangsi province in south China. During December 1940, Chiang Kai-shek ordered it to move north and cross the Yangtze River. Apparently resisting Chiang's orders, the New Fourth Army remained in Kiangsi, where it was ambushed by Nationalist forces. In a week of fighting (January 7–13, 1941), an estimated three thousand Communist troops were killed, and many others were captured and imprisoned.

After Pearl Harbor, the U.S. island-hopping campaign brought much-needed relief to the Chinese front. Although China continued to resist Japan, both the KMT and the CCP waited to see what the United States would do next.

FURTHER READINGS
Dreyer, Edward L. *China at War, 1901–1949* (1995).
Hsu, Immanuel C. *The Rise of Modern China* (1995).
Liu, F. F. *A Military History of Modern China, 1924–1949* (1956).
Spence, Jonathan D. *The Search for Modern China* (1990).

Bruce A. Elleman

SEE ALSO China-India-Burma Theater of Operations

Philippines, Anti–Japanese Guerrillas in

An extensive resistance movement began to form in all parts of the Philippine Islands within weeks of the Japanese invasion in December 1941. The earliest anti–Japanese groups established contact with General Douglas MacArthur's beleaguered headquarters, and MacArthur, before leaving for Australia in March 1942, sent groups of American and Filipino army officers from Bataan into the interior, to organize and coordinate the activities of these independent resistance units. The officers were soon joined by several score Filipino and American civilians, survivors from sunken ships or downed Allied aircraft, and remnants of Filipino and American units who had taken to the hills rather than surrender during the rapid Japanese advance. Even before the fall of Corregidor in May 1942, about fifty guerrilla groups had emerged among the 17 million inhabitants of the vast Philippine archipelago, consisting of some seventy-one hundred islands spread over 115,000 square miles.

The resistance movement in the Philippines, like such groups elsewhere during World War II, was very diverse in terms of its makeup, military effectiveness, ideology and motivation, and overall usefulness. In addition, the Philippines resistance movement was much less cohesive than similar groups in Europe, in spite of General MacArthur's intense organizational efforts. Besides U.S. and Filipino military officers and enlisted men who had eluded capture or who had infiltrated the lines before the archipelago fell, it included Communists and other radicals, as well as thousands of American and Filipino civilians who were outraged by Japan's heavy-handed and ruthless occupation policies.

The goals of the various anti–Japanese groups, despite postwar claims to the contrary, were equally diverse and often radically dissimilar. Relations between these groups were not always harmonious. Though ostensibly all sought to kill the Japanese invaders/occupiers, some sought only to survive until the liberation rather than to engage in combat. Other groups took the opportunity provided by wartime dislocations of Philippine political and law enforcement institutions to engage in banditry against both the Japanese military and the Filipino peasant population. It is estimated that about 70 percent of Filipinos so greatly feared the Japanese that they did not actively resist; they also clearly resented the activities of alleged resistance groups that in reality were little more than bandits and common criminals. Some groups, however, did fight the Japanese throughout the occupation; but even some of these, such as the Communist Huks, fought primarily to gain popular peasant support and combat experience in order to facilitate a postwar takeover of the country. Many other Filipinos aided the resistance for nationalistic and patriotic reasons, or out of loyalty to the Americans, and others sought to take vengeance on the Japanese for their numerous, senseless acts of brutality. Some other groups, especially on Mindanao, fought for sectarian reasons, such as Muslims and Christians, and resisted the Japanese simply because they were of a different religion—often while fighting among themselves for the very same reasons.

In general, guerrilla groups in the Philippine archipelago were well favored by the mountainous jungles, numerous remote and small islands that could serve as hideouts and bases, and the limited size and relatively concentrated deployment of enemy occupation forces in coastal and urban areas. The forests, mountains, and limited road network, for example, especially in northern Luzon and on Mindanao, greatly facilitated guerrilla movements and their tactical operations, and the numerous remote villages provided a ready source of recruits, food, shelter, water, and supplies.

During the early days of the Japanese occupation, especially in 1942 and 1943, guerrilla units lived off the land and the favors of sympathetic civilians, often making their own weapons, ammunition, equipment, fuel, and even money. What they could not manufacture, they stole from the Japanese military or from enemy dead. The need for mobility, stealth, and security kept these early groups constantly on the move, so most units were initially very lightly equipped both in the field and at their secret, remote bases.

The stunning Japanese victories of early 1942 caught the Allies entirely off guard and left them in great disarray throughout Asia and the Pacific. Until the Allies could regroup, most guerrilla units were completely isolated and out of touch with the outside world, including General MacArthur's Southwest Pacific Area general headquarters in Australia. This situation changed within months, however, and communications between MacArthur's forces in Australia and rebel groups in the Philippines were reestablished by the late fall of 1942. As a result, the various Philippine guerrilla groups began to gather an ever increasing amount of intelligence for Allied military headquarters while engaging in more frequent combat operations against Japanese occupation forces.

MacArthur and his staff quickly realized that anti–Japanese resistance activities in the Philippines were in dire need of strong military leadership, effective countrywide coordination, and competent military control. Initially all resistance groups in the entire Southwest Pacific Area—whether in the Philippines, New Guinea, or the Netherlands East Indies—came under the responsibility of the Allied Intelligence Bureau (AIB) attached to MacArthur's general headquarters (GHQ). In 1943, however, as U.S. forces began preparing for the liberation of the Philippines, command and control of the various island resistance groups was stripped from AIB and turned over to the exclusive control of the Philippine Regional Section, G-2, GHQ, Southwest Pacific Area, under Colonel (later Brigadier General) Courtney Whitney. Overall control of Philippine Regional Section activities was exercised by MacArthur's assistant chief of staff for intelligence, Colonel (later Major General) Charles A. Willoughby.

By late 1943 GHQ had established contact with most of the major resistance groups in the Philippines, either by radio or by agent, and had begun to provide leadership and organizational personnel from Australia to bring some semblance of military order and centralized command to the movement. MacArthur's ultimate goal, never fully realized, was to consolidate the various groups, which continued to operate independently, into one large anti–Japanese irregular force responsive to MacArthur's strategic and tactical needs. In the spring of 1943, for example, Lieutenant Commander Charles Parsons arrived on Mindanao from GHQ, Australia, to arrange and organize an extensive and united guerrilla movement on the island, to set up a system of coastwatcher stations, and to gather intelligence on the Japanese for the immediate use of MacArthur's command. With such guidance, guerrilla forces were slowly unified, starting with Mindanao and the Visayan Islands.

Along with organizational personnel, GHQ formed a relatively regular and secure submarine supply service from Australia to various points in the Philippines. Thus, as the Allied forces became stronger and better supplied, the material support for the guerrilla groups improved as well. Recognizing the guerrillas' dire need for all manner of weapons and supplies, the submarine delivery service, established in late 1943, was soon transporting significant amounts of medicines, money, arms, and equipment, as well as U.S. Army advisers, radio personnel, and technicians. After 1943, two U.S. Navy supply submarines made regular runs from Australia and were permanently attached to MacArthur's command for such missions. Once these regular supply runs became a reality, Philippine guerrilla units received newer arms, explosives, grenades, medicines, and radios. Thus equipped and organized, they became a more potent fighting and intelligence-gathering force. Guerrillas could now be supplied and treated with medicines, and their wounded could be evacuated to Australia. Filipino guerrillas under U.S. control knew that in addition to having a good chance of medical evacuation, they could count on postwar recompense, either for themselves or to their next of kin. They would not be left to die by the side of some jungle trail, forgotten, their families impoverished. Such knowledge assisted in the recruitment of new guerrillas.

The dispatch of U.S. Army officers to coordinate and control the Philippine guerrilla units, and of U.S. Army radio personnel and technicians to set up weather stations and coastwatching posts, improved an extensive system that was already fully functional and operational in many areas. It was soon discovered by the U.S. Army newcomers from GHQ that many Filipino groups had already established their own recruiting stations and shadow governments, were running officer and military basic training schools, and had even begun printing their own currencies. Indeed, organizers from MacArthur's headquarters found hundreds of small guerrilla groups, consisting of Filipinos in the ranks and often led by two or three U.S. Army officers, forming a force estimated to number 175,000 or more armed men operating on a full- or part-time basis. By 1943 these guerrillas were strong enough to attack small Japanese outposts and garrisons, to block roads and otherwise destroy transportation and communication infrastructure, and to aggravate enemy supply problems by attacking depots and destroying supply convoys. In numerous other ways, guerrillas made the occupation of the Philippines more difficult and costly in terms of manpower, already a scarce commodity in the Japanese military. Guerrillas went to great lengths to make the countryside inhospitable by sniping at and ambushing Japanese convoys and patrols, as well as by using tetanus-poisoned bamboo barbs, called *suak*, as booby traps along trails known to be frequented by the enemy.

Although guerrilla groups were formed throughout the archipelago, the largest groups, and therefore the most vigorous anti–Japanese activities, were located on Luzon, the Visayan Islands (particularly on Leyte and Samar), and on Mindanao. Eventually, GHQ, Southwest Pacific Area, established ten military districts to coordinate guerrilla activities in these areas, as well as the operations of smaller resistance groups on the lesser Philippine islands of Panay, Negros, Sulu, Palawan, Mindoro, Masbate, Bohol, and Cebu.

The largest guerrilla organizations existed in central and northern Luzon. The nuclei forming these units came from the remnants of U.S. Army forces overrun during the rapid Japanese advance in late 1941 and early 1942. One of the most famous and long-lived groups was that organized in northern Luzon under a 30-year-old West Pointer, R. W. Volckmann. Promoted to regimental commander during the U.S. Army retreat to Bataan, Volckmann took to the hills and joined one of many small resistance bands. He connected with two other American officers who also were stranded; the three men, with numerous American and Filipino regular troops, formed a sizable a guerrilla army. Dwindling supplies, and a thorough Japanese policing of Luzon in late 1942, resulted in the capture or nearly complete destruction of most of these early groups. One major unit, for example, that under Colonel Claude Thorp, headquartered near Mount Pinatubo, was discovered during a Japanese sweep and splintered, its members fleeing. Thorp was captured in October 1942.

Realizing from the initial sweeps that the countryside was far from pacified, the Japanese conducted a major antiguerrilla operation in northern Luzon in the spring of 1943. Thousands of enemy troops garrisoned villages, conducted 10-day, 200-man patrols throughout the countryside, and razed villages suspected of harboring or supporting guerrillas. Entire areas of Luzon were burned out as a result, and countless civilians were brutalized and killed. The Japanese also hired numerous Filipino spies and informants, then put these collaborators on all roads and trails to watch for and to report guerrilla movements. In addition, sizable cash rewards were offered to individuals willing to turn in Americans or their Filipino collaborators. Such efforts did bring limited success; for instance, a major guerrilla group under Colonel Hugh Straughn was broken up in August 1943.

The overall impact of these Japanese efforts was to impede the growth of the resistance movement in central and northern Luzon and to bring about a substantial decrease in the number of full-time, active guerrillas by mid–1943. In response, General MacArthur ordered the groups on Luzon to "lay low," to concentrate on avoiding capture, to organize combat cadres and intelligence nets, and to conserve ammunition and arms until resupply could come from Australia. Guerrilla forces were to avoid combat in all but the most advantageous circumstances. Farther from Australia than guerrilla units operating in the southern regions of the Philippines, the Luzon forces of necessity had to develop and operate largely on their own.

The remnants of these early Luzon guerrilla groups nonetheless managed to avoid capture, and by mid–1944 had allegedly formed sixteen major guerrilla armies counting hundreds of thousands of armed, full-time members. Volckmann, for example, reestablished direct radio contact with MacArthur's Australian headquarters in August 1944, and informed the Southwest Pacific Area commander that his guerrilla command had grown from 2,000 to 8,000 men with a reserve of another 7,000 part-time guerrillas and 5,000 men organized into service units. After November 1944, following substantial submarine and air resupply, Volckmann went on the offensive in northern Luzon. His guerrillas provided information to General MacArthur that the Japanese army had withdrawn from the Lingayen Gulf area; as a result, it was chosen as the site of the successful U.S. invasion in January 1945.

Once U.S. forces landed, large numbers of guerrillas became active throughout Luzon for the first time, tying down significant numbers of enemy troops in the interior and harassing their movements. When the U.S. Sixth Army landed in January 1945, for example, Volckmann reported for duty to the invading force as the commander of a force of over twenty thousand men with its own supply services. Volckmann had divided Luzon into six military districts, each with its own commander and separate military and civilian organizations. From January to June 1945 his five guerrilla regiments destroyed and disrupted Japanese supply, transportation, and communications lines, intercepted and destroyed scouting and foraging parties, and ambushed numerous troop units. By Volckmann's estimates, his units accounted for more than fifty thousand Japanese casualties during the occupation and liberation.

In addition to the guerrilla units led by former American and Filipino military personnel on Luzon, the Japanese had to contend with the Communist Hukbo ng Bayan Laban sa Hapon (People's Anti–Japanese Army), or Hukbalahap. The Huk resistance drew on longstanding nationalist sentiment—many Filipinos had resisted the Spanish and Americans decades before. Huk groups were organized along quasi-military lines and were commanded by 29-year-old Luis Taruc. Huk units were formed into regiments, battalions, companies, platoons, and squads, and by war's end the Huks had established numerous liberated and semiliberated areas where they harassed what had become virtually besieged Japanese units.

Guerrilla groups emerged in the Visayans, especially on Leyte and Samar, shortly after the Japanese occupation began. Each group, however, maintained a separate and distinct organization for many months, during which time jealousy and strife between the groups were rampant. All groups, however, possessed the same hatred and contempt for the Japanese, and circumstances soon compelled the guerrillas to band together for their mutual protection. As time passed, the stronger groups absorbed the weaker ones by force or conciliation, and gradually they developed a relatively orderly and effective organization recognized by GHQ in Australia. Indeed, by early 1942, seven separate resistance groups were operational on Leyte alone, each commanded by a Filipino or American army officer who had escaped capture during the Japanese conquest. Colonel Ruperto K. Kangleon, a veteran of twenty-seven years in the Philippine army, emerged as the strongest guerrilla leader on Leyte by October 1944, commanding approximately thirty-two hundred men organized into what was designated the 92d Division of the Philippine army. On nearby Samar, six major guerrilla groups, totaling 8,000 men, were eventually unified under Lieutenant Colonel Charles M. Smith, who was sent from GHQ, Australia, for that purpose in September 1944.

The guerrilla movement on Mindanao was dominated mainly by Americans under Colonel Wendell W. Fertig, a prewar mining engineer and reserve officer. Fertig built a guerrilla force of 38,000 from an initial body of 5 officers and 175 enlisted men; its value and size were recognized by GHQ in 1943 when it was designated the 10th Military District. Fertig's guerrilla command was so large and ferocious that the Japanese, who maintained a force of 150,000 troops on Mindanao alone, hesitated to commit troops to antiguerrilla activities. Indeed, when U.S. Army troops landed on Mindanao, 95 percent of the island was under control of the various guerrilla forces led by Fertig. Japanese forces were confined to scattered pockets primarily in the Lanao and Malabang areas.

The Philippine resistance movement, like all such endeavors, had to have mass civilian support and cooperation to succeed, or even survive the Japanese occupation. Ironically, the Japanese helped to provide and ensure this civilian support by their ill-considered occupation policies and atrocious behavior. Throughout the occupation they failed to understand the nature of their target, always believing they were fighting isolated groups of bandits rather than coordinated resistance forces that were relatively well equipped from the outside. Thus the Japanese response to Philippine guerrilla units was rarely appropriate or effective, generally consisting of limited and isolated sweeps of areas suspected of harboring resistance units. The various Japanese headquarters failed to coordinate counterguerrilla operations anywhere in the Philippines, at any time during the war, and launched only local punitive actions. The Japanese high command had no idea that they were fighting almost the entire Filipino population. The harsher the Japanese became toward the local populace in order to root out guerrillas or force peasant cooperation or acquiescence, the more recruits joined anti–Japanese forces or aided guerrilla activities. A peasant whose hut has been burned down and his family tortured to death has little alternative to joining the local resistance.

In late 1943, as guerrilla forces became more organized, better supplied, and thus more active, the Japanese increased antiguerrilla patrols throughout the country, making great sweeps of the smaller islands, sometimes using armor and aircraft. Such sweeps generally produced nothing because the guerrilla intelligence network was extensive and usually warned local resistance forces well before Japanese soldiers reached the area. Indeed, guerrilla units often ambushed frustrated Japanese troops as they wearily returned to their bases at the end of these unsuccessful operations.

The Japanese usually had limited successes when they acted on information provided by collaborators belonging to the "Good Neighbor Association." The use of collaborators became a major threat, and a particular cause for alarm in 1942 and 1943, but many of the spies and collaborators Japan hired, as well as local warlords and bandits, used their association with the Japanese military as an excuse to rob, pillage, and create their own fiefdoms in the countryside, further alienating the peasant population and benefiting the resistance. The Japanese also tried, without success, to turn guerrillas by offers of amnesty, jobs, and the prospect of a return to a more normal, less dangerous lifestyle. In most cases, however, captured guerrillas were summarily executed by the Japanese, often publicly. The guerrillas responded by killing one collaborator for each of their own number lost, often mutilating the bodies as a grim reminder of how traitors were treated. When American troops arrived in the Philippines in late 1944, most Filipinos either were guerrillas or actively supported them. Even if not openly sympathetic to the resistance movement, most peasants did not help the Japanese, whose decline was evident by early 1945.

Although anti–Japanese guerrilla groups in the Philippines never seriously challenged enemy military and political control of the archipelago, they did make the Japanese occupation more difficult and expensive in terms of manpower, materiel, and funds. For three years they furnished General MacArthur's headquarters with strategic intelligence that proved especially valuable when the Americans returned in late 1944. Indeed, when American forces came to liberate the Philippines, they were often greeted on the beaches by the local resistance leader. He had available an intact guide force that knew the terrain and enemy dispositions, and was very ready and willing to help.

Once the U.S. Sixth and Eighth armies took the field, all guerrilla organizations in their zones of operation came under direct military command and control. From that point on, guerrilla units became irregular auxiliary components of regular army units.

Although the final reconquest the Philippines took ten months of hard campaigning by U.S. Army forces between October 1944 and August 1945, in many areas guerrillas already controlled the countryside. By 1945 the Japanese were forced from the interior and had to cluster in coastal towns or in major inland cities for protection. In many areas, Japanese military forces did not venture into the interior for fear of guerrilla ambushes. Throughout the campaigns of 1944–1945, guerrilla units assisted U.S. Army combat units involved in tactical operations by performing scouting and patrolling activities. They also assisted U.S. Army units in conducting sabotage activities, ambushes, and reconnaissance missions. Guerrillas also saved numerous towns from destructive U.S. bombardment and possible civilian casualties when they could demonstrate that such sites held no enemy troops.

Perhaps the most important role of the anti–Japanese guerrillas in the Philippines was their contribution to maintaining the morale of the Filipino people during a long and brutal Japanese occupation. The various units formed a direct link to the Philippine government-in-exile in Washington, D.C., and were proof that the islands had not been permanently conquered and would one day be liberated.

FURTHER READINGS

Asprey, Robert B. *War in the Shadows: The Guerrilla in History* (1975).

Hogan, David, Jr. *U.S. Army Special Operations in World War II* (U.S. Army, Center of Military History, 1992).

Ingham, Travis. *Rendezvous by Submarine: The Story of Charles Parsons and the Guerrilla Soldiers of the Philippines* (1945).

Valeriano, N. D., and C. T. C. Bohannan. *Counter-Guerrilla Operations: The Philippine Experience* (1962).

Villamor, Jesus A. *They Never Surrendered: A True Story of Resistance in World War II* (1982).

Volckmann, R. W. *We Remained* (1954).

Willoughby, Charles A. *The Guerrilla Resistance Movement in the Philippines* (General Headquarters, U.S. Army Forces, Pacific, Military Intelligence Section, General Staff, 1948).

Wolfert, Ira. *American Guerrilla in the Philippines* (1945).

Clayton D. Laurie

SEE ALSO Fertig, Wendell W.; Scouts, Philippine

Philippines, Fall of the

The Japanese army had no interest in attacking the Philippines, nor did the Japanese government have any economic or military reason to seize the islands. The islands would, in fact, be an economic burden on Japan. It was the navy, usually considered the less militaristic of the three Japanese military services, that decided that Japan must take the Philippines, for American air and naval bases there threatened the flank of operations farther south. Although they could bypass and neutralize the Philippines, planners could not ignore the threat of American aircraft reinforcing the islands and U.S. submarines working out of Manila Bay.

Prewar American plans did not envision a serious defense for the Philippines. The U.S. Navy knew it could not quickly relieve a surrounded Philippine garrison, and the army maintained only limited forces in the islands. But on August 16, 1941, the War Department changed its mind. B-17 bombers in sufficient numbers supposedly now offered a quick and inexpensive way of deterring Japanese expansion.

Modest pursuit and bomber assets were dispatched, many more aircraft were scheduled, and thousands of army specialists were sent to reinforce and lead the mobilizing Philippine army. Big luxury liners steamed into Manila Bay packed with American soldiers and filled with supplies and equipment. It was a race to see if adequate forces could be slipped into the Philippines before the Japanese attacked.

The Japanese won that race. They began the war in the Philippines on December 8, 1941. Air strikes launched by the 11th Air Fleet from Formosa resulted in amazing successes at Clark and Iba fields. The Japanese outmaneuvered General Douglas MacArthur's air forces and crippled them.

Even before the war, there had been no U.S. naval presence of significance. Admiral Thomas C. Hart's Asiatic Fleet—only two cruisers and some destroyers—had sailed south for safety. Submarines remained, but poor tactics, some ineffective skippers, and mechanically unreliable torpedoes rendered them impotent. With no navy and in the face of the air losses, the defense of Luzon fell to the nascent Philippine army. The Americans immediately deployed the ill-trained, poorly equipped Filipinos to Luzon's beaches.

Mobilization of the new army had begun in September, and the recruits had hardly started the process that might, some day, result in trained soldiers. On December 8, MacArthur's army (120,000 Filipino draftees and 31,000 regulars) was only slightly better than an armed mob. Eighty-eight thousand men were concentrated on Luzon. The only well-armed regular forces available were the U.S. Army's 26th Cavalry Regiment, the Philippine Division (one infantry regiment of white troops, two of

Philippine Scouts, and regular artillery and engineers), two battalions of light tanks, and five regiments of coast artillerymen (antiaircraft and big seacoast guns). Although the Philippine army also had ten reserve divisions on the books as well as a regular division (cadre only), these men carried old rifles, were short of automatic weapons and artillery, and were led by Filipino officers so junior that a few "third lieutenants" commanded battalions.

The Japanese were better prepared. They had been planning the invasion for months. Air attacks after December 8 had cleared most of the remaining American planes from the skies. Small amphibious landings in north and south Luzon put Japanese elements ashore that secured air strips to support the upcoming main landings. Neither the U.S. Navy nor MacArthur's reduced air forces were able effectively to challenge these landings. The Japanese soon brought army aircraft onto these fields to augment navy aircraft making long flights from Formosa.

By December 17, Japanese warships, transports, and men stood ready at ports on Formosa, the Pescadores, and the Ryukyus. When the order to sail arrived, bugles sounded "Depart Harbor." Crews lined the rails and waved their caps in salute. Soldiers crowded the decks, cheered, and waved Japanese flags and naval ensigns. The soldiers, sailors, and airmen of the empire, long considered amusing underdogs by the West, were on the march. Not a single American aircraft or submarine would challenge their approach.

Late on the night of December 21, the invasion fleet entered Lingayen Gulf, north of Manila along Luzon's west coast. Nine minesweepers on a clearance mission took the lead. Sailors struggled on wet decks in the inky darkness to stream their sweeps. They found no mines, and most of the Japanese vessels were anchored off the invasion beaches by 0210 hours. The seventy-six Army and nine Navy transports carried six regiments of infantry and tanks. Well offshore stood the Second Fleet with its two battleships, two heavy cruisers, and ten destroyers. The Third Fleet, two heavy cruisers, two light cruisers, thirteen destroyers, and sundry smaller craft stood in toward the shore as escort and fire support for the landing forces.

Lieutenant General Masaharu Homma, commander of the Fourteenth Army (roughly equivalent to a U.S. Army corps), had 43,100 men, 34,856 of whom were here at Lingayen Gulf. His 48th Division was reinforced by a regiment of the 16th Division, two tank regiments, and normal support forces. MacArthur had mainly Filipino recruits, the largest collection of which were also at Lingayen, waiting. Unfortunately, most were defending the south end of Lingayen Gulf, and the Japanese landed on beaches farther to the north.

Despite some stinging attacks by one audacious submarine and surviving American P-40s and P-35s, the Japanese landed and brushed aside elements of a single, frightened Filipino regiment. Only the weather seriously threatened landing operations. A baby typhoon had whipped the seas, and waves drove landing craft into the sand. Strong tides further disrupted the landings. Had the defenders been able to counterattack, they might have driven the Japanese back into the sea. But the Filipinos were totally incapable of such an effort, and the Japanese pushed inland. Their forces soon had a solid beachhead.

Major General Jonathan M. Wainwright, commander of North Luzon Force (the 11th, 21st, and 71st Divisions and the 26th Cavalry Regiment), knew his beach defenses had collapsed. He needed someone to delay the Japanese long enough to get his Filipinos away from the Japanese and safely to new positions. He turned to his most elite unit, the famed 26th Cavalry Regiment, Philippine Scouts. These horse cavalrymen, long-service Filipinos serving in the regular army, were well-armed and equipped and had been trained razor sharp. Unlike the Philippine army, the Scouts could fight as a disciplined team.

The Scouts galloped into position next to the town of Damortis, just south of the invasion beaches. They dismounted and took up positions. Machine gunners laced the enemy with fire, and Scout riflemen picked off Japanese with deliberate, aimed fire from their new M-1 rifles. "It was a wonderful thing," recalled the regiment's operations officer, "to watch these little brown soldiers, who had never before seen a gun fired in anger, calmly choosing their positions, adjusting their rifle slings, and proceeding to pick off Japs as though they were silhouette targets on the rifle range."

The Japanese, who until now had faced just scattered, frightened Filipinos, found that they now had a fight on their hands. But a few hundred cavalrymen with light weapons can offer only finite resistance. The Japanese pressed harder and harder, fired artillery and naval guns, and brought in air support. The Scouts found it was time to go. They mounted and rode cross-country to the next delay position. They left the Japanese with the battlefield, but they also left them with casualties and a new respect for the Filipino soldier.

Because of the cavalry's fight, Wainwright gained time to bring more of his corps into action. On the second day of the invasion, elements of the 71st Division deployed at Sison, southeast of the beaches where the coastal mountains open into Luzon's central plain. The Japanese blew

them out of the small town after a five-hour fight. When a regimental combat team of MacArthur's reserve 91st Division moved into the town of Pozorrubio, the Japanese ran them out that night. The results of the day's fight: two Philippine Army divisions committed, two Philippine Army divisions routed. The Japanese were poised for their advance on Manila.

Faced with the collapse of his beach defenses, MacArthur ordered his forces to execute the withdrawal provisions of War Plan Orange 3, a retreat to Bataan. On that rugged peninsula forming the north breakwater for Manila Bay, MacArthur's men would try to block the sea entrance to Manila. If the army could hold out for six months, the U.S. Navy was supposed to arrive with a relief force. Or so everyone hoped.

From December 23 until January 1, 1942, MacArthur pulled his men out of north and south Luzon, removed his headquarters and logistics from Manila, and rushed them toward Bataan. Wainwright's men in north Luzon fell back along five prewar delay lines. They held each line long enough to force the Japanese to deploy and attack, thereby slowing the advance. The Japanese were also slowed by difficulties in bringing their supplies across Lingayen's beaches, then down to the front lines.

On December 24, a second major Japanese landing on Luzon's east coast at Lamon Bay only confirmed MacArthur's decision to withdraw. South of Manila, Brigadier General Albert M. Jones and the South Luzon Force (the 41st and 51st Divisions) effectively delayed the 16th Division's attack northward toward Manila. But in point of fact, the Japanese myopic focus on Manila was more responsible for MacArthur's success in reaching Bataan than any military prowess on the part of the defenders.

Lead Japanese troops entered Manila on January 2, 1942. When they belatedly realized that the army on Bataan and the fortress of Corregidor blocked the entrance to Manila Bay, troops marched off to mop up what they believed were routed and disorganized remnants. The Japanese did not have much strength left with which to do this, for large numbers of Homma's army were already being transferred for campaigns farther south. The entire 48th Division and most of the air forces were marshalling to depart.

On Bataan were nearly eighty thousand Filipinos and Americans, I and II Philippine Corps with ten divisions. Here the Filipinos and Americans had to fight. The first defenders the Japanese faced were Philippine Scouts, hardened, spirited infantrymen of the 57th Infantry Regiment led by American officers. When the Japanese attacked down the East Road the night of January 11 and hit Major General George M. Parker's II Corps, nasty, close combat erupted. Most discouraging to the Japanese was the incredible weight of artillery, 75-mm and 155-mm, that fell on them, often from well-maneuvered half-track mounts. No matter how hard they tried, they could not exploit their initial successes.

Japanese of the 65th Brigade (reinforced to 13,000 men) turned west and probed the Filipino line. The 65th Brigade were the men scheduled to garrison the Philippines after resistance had ended, and they were almost as lightly armed and unprepared for combat as the Filipinos. The Filipino 41st Division had dug in along rough, broken hills, and here the Filipinos fought, died, and refused to run. Japanese and Filipino were equally brave, but the Filipinos' lack of training allowed the Japanese to press them right up to, but not past, the breaking point.

The frustrated Japanese probed farther west and found the 51st Division. Here, in extremely rough and broken ground, they had more success. Despite their own numerical inferiority, they routed the 51st Infantry Regiment, penetrated the division front, and made ready to rupture the entire II Corps line. On January 16, at the very moment of Japanese successes against the 51st Division, the best American troops on Bataan, the all-American 31st Infantry and the Philippine Scout 45th Infantry, rocked them with a counterattack. Like their comrades in the 26th Cavalry and 57th Infantry, these men were professionals, regular army.

The battle for the Abucay Hacienda lasted seven hot, dusty days. The two sides stumbled about in thick shrubs and deep ravines, fought, and died. Because of the jungle, Japanese aircraft support was limited. And because of the jungle, American artillery superiority was rendered nearly useless. It was infantryman against infantryman. And neither side was willing to quit.

As is often the case, the battle was resolved by indirection. Because of the stalemate along II Corps' front on Bataan's east coast, the Japanese launched attacks against Filipinos defending Bataan's west coast, against troops of Wainwright's I Corps. His men had to defend some of the roughest terrain on the peninsula. Mountains dropped directly into the sea, and a single winding road provided the only supply route. Here the Japanese showed their prowess at small unit tactics and their ability to infiltrate large forces behind enemy lines. They established a roadblock across I Corps' main supply route, and a battle developed as the Americans tried to break the stranglehold on their supplies. Unit after unit of Philippine Army moved against the roadblock, but the Japanese stoutly repulsed every attack.

General Parker's corps reserves and MacArthur's army reserves were committed against the 65th Brigade's penetration in II Corps, so no help could be send to Wainwright. Wainwright's men began a cross-country retreat, a movement that resulted in the loss of much of I Corps' artillery. Because I Corps was heading south and exposing II Corps western flank, II Corps was also endangered. Japanese forces would be able to cut behind II Corps. The Americans realized they had to pull II Corps back as well.

II Corps began its effort to break contact. The battle still raged at Abucay, so it would be tricky to get the men out without collapsing the entire line. II Corps' heavy artillery, the very effective 155-mm's, began their march on January 23. Service and support units also pulled out. Hospital Number 2 moved nearly seven hundred patients to safety. Despite Japanese control of the skies, all these moves were made without alerting anyone.

The tactical units withdrew at dusk on January 24. First, a covering force disengaged, moved south, and deployed to cover the withdrawal of the main body. Then a thin shell of troops, one-third of the infantry bolstered by machine guns and some artillery, spread itself across the entire front. Once they were in place, the main body marched south. Confusion was rampant, for most of these units were filled with poorly trained troops. It was dark, officers lost contact with their men, and men could not understand each other's dialects.

At midnight, the Japanese pushed, but the thin covering shell held. Throughout the night, the roads south were jammed with vehicles and men. There was no control, just long lines of individuals pressing south. Confusion and chaos reigned. Units dissolved and came out as hordes, not cohesive organizations. Soldiers packed trails and roads. Considering how poorly II Corps executed its withdrawal, the Japanese must be censured for failing to notice it. Once they did pursue, they ran into American light tanks and self-propelled artillery that beat them back. The rest of the withdrawal went unchallenged.

When MacArthur's army settled into its new lines, now halfway down the length of the peninsula, it was be for a last stand. The best defensive terrain had been farther north, and much barrier material had been expended there. The Filipinos were now poised at their last ditch. There was insufficient maneuver room behind them for another withdrawal.

In late January and early February, the Japanese launched new attacks against II Corps, only to lose men and equipment in futile efforts to penetrate the line. The Philippine army had learned to fight. The Japanese also made several landings in the west behind I Corps' new line, and here the Japanese posed a real threat. But they could not reinforce the landings, and their attempts to link with the isolated amphibious landings by attacks overland failed. So badly handled was this Japanese effort and so strong were American counterattacks (mainly Philippine Scouts) that two entire battalions of the best Japanese troops perished.

By mid-February, a lull settled over the peninsula. Both armies were exhausted. The Japanese had flung themselves against the Filipinos so many times with so little regard for losses that they had been reduced in strength to the equivalent of three battalions of infantry. The Filipinos and Americans were suffering from malnutrition and disease. Because of MacArthur's prewar decision to defend Luzon's beaches rather than immediately retire to Bataan when war began, too little food had been stocked on Bataan and much had been lost in the retreat to Bataan. There would be no relief from the United States, so the army attempted to run the Japanese naval blockade and bring in food. Most of the ships were lost, and only a few small vessels with limited cargoes got through. So although the Filipinos had gained experience as fighting men, they now began to lose the physical strength needed to fight.

The defenders tried to prepare for a new enemy offensive through February and March. The men dug new lines, American instructors gave specialized training to the Filipinos, and officers prepared plans. There were finite assets available to the defenders, and every day brought them closer to starvation. Disease dropped men from the ranks and laid them out in growing numbers at makeshift aid stations and crowded hospitals. Under orders from President Roosevelt, MacArthur left Corregidor for Australia on March 11, Wainwright assumed command of all forces in the Philippines, and the competent and beloved Major General Edward P. King took command of the army on Bataan.

On the Japanese side, reinforcements flowed in. Infantry replacements arrived for the decimated, veteran outfits still facing the Filipinos. New formations also arrived, including the 4th Division from Shanghai and elements of the 21st Division. Most important was the mass of heavy artillery that arrived for Homma's 14th Army, the Kitajima Artillery Group. The Japanese ran their men through hard jungle training, developed new tactics to facilitate fighting in jungles, and smoothed infantry-artillery coordination. They used captured American entrenchments to practice close combat techniques, warned their subordinates against staging reckless attacks, and admitted a new respect for the defenders.

The Japanese were ready by late March. They drove the weakened Filipinos off the outpost line of resistance and moved close to the main line for the big attack. Air attacks and shelling increased. An American infantry instructor with a Filipino unit wrote on March 31: "Terrific bombing all day, Food situation critical. Malaria cannot be controlled. Front of 42nd Infantry evacuated. Outpost line pushed back and not restored." Little time remained to the "Battling Bastards of Bataan." Their slogan was: "No Poppa, no Momma, no Uncle Sam—and nobody gives a damn."

The Japanese attacked II Corps on April 3. They massed six infantry regiments and a regiment of tanks along a narrow front. A heavy, sustained, and stunning artillery preparation opened the door for the ground troops. The well-armed, well-trained, and confident Japanese rolled over shell-shocked Filipinos and dispersed entire regiments simply by advancing. There would be no stopping the Japanese this time. Despite an American counterattack launched on April 6, the Japanese moved south. Filipino units that had fought tenaciously in January and early February fell apart from disease, starvation, and hopelessness. The American 31st Infantry Regiment attacked, was repulsed, and stumbled south in small groups. The famed Philippine Scouts did slightly better, attacking and even stopping the Japanese at a point or two, but the Japanese immediately outflanked them and forced them also to retreat.

By April 8, the entire II Corps line was in full rout. Only a handful of officers and men of a haphazard rear guard stood between the Japanese and what had once been an infantry corps. By April 9, the army had collapsed, and the American commander on Bataan, General King, surrendered. After ninety-three days of siege, the defense of Bataan ended. Into the merciless and brutal hands of the Japanese passed 75,000 Americans and Filipinos.

Now the island fortress of Corregidor stood alone. Its rifled cannon, mortars, and antiaircraft guns lay directly in the sights of Japanese artillery rolling into place along the southern edges of Bataan. No longer did the island garrison have the protection of the field army on Bataan. Built in an earlier day to face an earlier threat, designed to fight warships rather than siege artillery and aircraft, Corregidor's fate was clear, yet it hung on and fought back fiercely for another month.

From April 9 through the beginning of May, the Japanese bombarded Corregidor and its small island companions from the air, from Bataan, and from the southern shores of Manila Bay. Although aircraft attacks were noisy and impressive, it was the artillery that did the major damage. Day after day, shells probed for Corregidor's armament. One after another, casemates, magazines, and guns were crushed, blown up, and overturned. Explosions

---

leveled field fortifications, brushing aside obstacles. The garrison burrowed deep into the ground while 75-mm, 105-mm, 150-mm, and 240-mm shells plowed the surface and literally changed the island's topography. But the "Army's Concrete Battleship," the mighty island emplacement of Fort Drum, remained almost impervious to enemy fire, and its huge dreadnought guns were the largest American weapons in use against the enemy anywhere in the world at the time.

Morale on Corregidor remained steady even as the strain increased. By now, few men expected relief. Only death or captivity remained. Yet the Philippine Scouts and American coast artillerymen, the marines, and a few Bataan survivors defied the Japanese. There would be no surrender of Corregidor until the Japanese came to take down the flag.

The Japanese came on the night of May 5. They were confident that their month-long artillery barrage had reduced the island to rubble, and they expected the landing to go smoothly with few losses. But as landing craft neared Corregidor's northeast coast, the last intact American 12-inch mortar opened up as did the 12-inch mortars on Fort Hughes and Fort Drum's great guns. It seemed to the Japanese that a hundred guns were raining hot steel on them.

Japanese leaders were appalled. It was a horror that surpassed anything they had seen before, especially because it was so unexpected. The lead Japanese battalion reached shore after losing half to three quarters of its men. The second battalion lost even more. American artillery and small arms fire sank or rendered useless half to two-thirds of the landing craft. As few as 800 of 2,000 assault troops survived to scramble ashore. The Japanese who had made it to the beach went to work throughout the morning of May 6. They cut the thin tail of the island in two and facilitated the landing of tanks and artillery. Three American counterattacks failed. A final counterattack, hardly more than 500 sailors carrying rifles, initially drove the Japanese back, but it stalled in the face of a single, obstinate machine gun crew.

The Japanese were also reaching a crisis. If the fighting continued at this pace, their ammunition would be exhausted within a few hours. This was to be no Singapore romp. On Bataan, General Homma was nearly panicked. "I have failed miserably on the assault," he lamented. Actually, it was not that bad. Three Japanese tanks rolled into action and shook American resolve. No antitank guns existed to stop them. Wainwright knew that the Japanese planned another amphibious assault that night, and their artillery could easily resume the barrage. All Wainwright's reserves had been committed and consumed.

Without the ability to influence the action, and fearing a slaughter if the fighting continued into the night, he decided to surrender.

Corregidor fell, and within days, so did the rest of the Philippines. The Japanese had already landed on several of the lesser islands. The defenses and state of training on Mindanao and the small islands were worse than that on Luzon. Filipino troops had been pulled up to Luzon from the southern islands, and supplies needed for mobilization had not reached the men who remained. Wainwright initially tried to limit his surrender to simply Corregidor, but under Japanese pressure, he ordered the southern islands to surrender also.

Japan had received a nasty check on Luzon, but the delays there had not proved serious. Most significant was the realization that the Japanese could be stopped. Even as the Japanese extended their conquests through the Pacific, their aura of invincibility had been pricked. Bataan and Corregidor had heartened Americans and their defense was far more effective than the half-hearted efforts of the British and the Dutch in their Pacific possessions. It was the only glimmer of success the nation had see since the disaster at Pearl Harbor.

FURTHER READINGS

Bell, Walter F. *The Philippines in World War II, 1941–1945: A Chronology and Select Annotated Bibliography of Books and Articles in English* (1999).

Young, Donald J. *The Battle of Bataan: A History of the 90 Day Siege and Eventual Surrender of 75,000 Filipino and United States Troops to the Japanese in World War II* (1992).

John W. Whitman

SEE ALSO MacArthur, Douglas; Manila, Fall of; Scouts, Philippine

Pick, Lewis A. (1890–1956)

U.S. Army chief of engineers who directed construction of the India-to-China Ledo Road. Born in Brookneal, Virginia, Pick graduated from Virginia Polytechnic Institute in 1914 and worked for two years as a civil engineer for the Southern Railway. Upon U.S. entry into World War I, he was commissioned first lieutenant in the U.S. Army Corps of Engineers. Pick served in France as a company commander of engineers and participated in the Meuse–Argonne offensive. After being discharged in 1919, he obtained a regular army commission as captain in the Corps of Engineers in July 1920.

From 1920 to 1923 Pick served in the Philippines, where he commanded a company of the crack Philippine

Scouts and organized the first native engineer regiment. In 1924 he graduated from the Engineer School at Fort Belvoir, Virginia. Pick taught military science and tactics at Alabama Polytechnic Institute (1924–1925), and he served in the New Orleans Engineer District (1925–1928). In 1928 he organized the ROTC unit at Texas A&M College and was commandant of cadets there for four years. He next served at the Command and General Staff School at Fort Leavenworth, Kansas, until 1938. After graduating from the Army War College in 1939, Pick was assigned to the engineer district at Cincinnati.

Promoted colonel when the United States entered World War II, Pick gained national prominence for his flood-control efforts during the ruinous Missouri River floods of 1943 and for his collaboration in the comprehensive 1944 Pick-Sloan plan endorsed by Congress for future flood prevention, irrigation, and hydroelectric power.

In October 1943, Pick was assigned to command Advance Section 3 of the Army Service Forces in the China–Burma–India theater and charged with finishing construction of the Ledo Road, which would connect the old Burma Road with Ledo, India. The Burma Road was the main supply route for Allied troops in Burma and southwestern China.

After the Japanese had driven the British and Americans from Burma in May 1942, General Joseph W. Stilwell had made completing the Ledo Road a major priority. Desiring to reduce reliance on the expensive and dangerous air supply flights over the Himalayas, he authorized logistical support for the road-building effort despite Generalissimo Chiang Kai-shek's opposition.

On October 29, 1942, Stilwell ordered Brigadier General Raymond A. Wheeler to commence the road. The work, under the direction of Colonel John C. Arrowsmith, advanced slowly because the China–Burma–India command structure failed to provide the requisite supplies and equipment. Impatient with delays, Stilwell demanded Arrowsmith's replacement.

When Pick assumed command, monsoon rains and tropical disease had slowed progress to only 42 miles of completed road. Faced with swollen streams and mud, Pick recalled his earlier experiences with flood control. He declared, "The Ledo Road is going to be built—mud, rain, and malaria be damned!" Pick's engineering and command skills, together with his indomitable spirit, provided the leadership necessary to finish the project.

Pick commanded a force of nearly ninety thousand people, including American and Chinese soldiers and Indian and Burmese laborers. To build the 478 miles of road, they cut through dense jungle and bridged ten major rivers and 155 streams. They crossed 100 miles of mountainous terrain so steep that at one point 200 hairpin curves were required within 7 miles. Demanding round-the-clock construction, Pick enforced strict discipline and sanitary measures, and used quinacrine to fight malaria.

Stilwell's victory at Myitkyina in northern Burma (August 3, 1944) opened the way for finishing the road. Pick's engineers, laborers, technicians, and construction crews followed close behind combat troops. They cleared ground for the highway, fuel stations, supply points, and motor shops, and laid two pipelines that would carry aviation and motor fuel directly from India to China. Construction advanced at an impressive average of a mile a day.

In February 1944 Pick was promoted to brigadier general. A year later, on January 12, 1945, he personally led the first convoy over the finished highway from Ledo to Kunming, China.

Once the Ledo Road, nicknamed "Pick's Pike," linked up with the old Burma Road, it was renamed in honor of General Stilwell, who had been recalled from China on October 21, 1944. The $150 million road, considered a landmark achievement in military construction, had cost numerous casualties, including more than eleven hundred American lives.

After the war Pick, as Missouri River division engineer from 1945 to 1949, implemented the Pick-Sloan Plan for flood control. Promoted to major general in 1949 and to lieutenant general in 1951, he served from March 1949 to February 1953 as chief of Army Engineers, and he participated in the massive cold war program that built American bases around the world. After retiring from the army in 1953, Pick settled in Alabama, where he was involved in civic and business activities. He died in Washington, D.C.

FURTHER READINGS

Anders, Dan. *The Ledo Road* (1965).

Dod, Karl C. *The Corps of Engineers: The War Against Japan* (1966).

Spector, Ronald H. *Eagle Against the Sun: The American War with Japan* (1985).

Camille Dean

SEE ALSO Burma Road; Engineers, Allied Services; Stilwell, Joseph Warren

Prince of Wales and *Repulse*, Sinking of

Prince of Wales and *Repulse* were the first capital ships of any nation in history to be sunk solely by air assault while at sea.

Battle cruiser *Repulse* was launched on January 8, 1916, and was completed on August 16 of that same year, having been built in record war time. Her sister ship was *Renown. Repulse* displaced 32,000 tons and was 794 feet long. Her main battery consisted of six 15-inch guns, six 4-inch guns, as well as numerous anti-aircraft and smaller guns. As a class, battle cruisers sacrificed armor for speed, following First Sea Lord Sir John Fisher's unexamined dictum that "Speed is Armor." During World War I (1914–1918), *Repulse* served with the Grand Fleet in the North Sea and was still stationed with the Home Fleet when the World War II began in 1939. Between October 1939 and October 1941, *Repulse* saw action against German naval forces off Norway and convoy duty in the North Atlantic and Mediterranean. In May 1941 it participated in the pursuit of the German battleship *Bismarck,* but did not see action.

Prince of Wales was a much newer vessel, one of five battleships of the King George V class. It was built by the Cammell Laird yards and was launched on May 3, 1939, being placed into service only in March 1941. More than 740 feet long and displacing 36,570 tons, *Prince of Wales* had armament consisting of ten 14-inch guns (note smaller main battery caliber than in the much older *Repulse*) in one twin and two quad turrets, sixteen 5.25-inch guns, and an array of 2-pounder Bofors and Oerlikons guns. Steam turbines could propel the ship at 27.5 knots, making it the fastest vessel in the Royal Navy at that time.

Although not fully operational, and with workmen still on board, *Prince of Wales* was assigned to protect the Denmark Strait in the North Atlantic against German warships. It saw extensive action against German battleship *Bismarck* and heavy cruiser *Prinz Eugen* and was with *Hood* when that ship was blown up on May 24, 1941. *Prince of Wales,* although hit four times by *Bismarck*'s 15-inch guns, managed to fire six salvoes in return, hitting the German ship at least twice, but it had to break off the action. The damage it inflicted, however, helped slow *Bismarck,* leading to its eventual destruction by other British warships.

After undergoing repairs, *Prince of Wales* carried Prime Minister Winston S. Churchill to Placentia Bay, Newfoundland, in August 1941 for the Atlantic Conference with U.S. President Franklin D. Roosevelt. At the close of the meeting, the Atlantic Charter was signed on board. After returning to British waters, *Prince of Wales* was assigned to convoy duty in the Mediterranean.

As Anglo-Japanese relations grew strained in October 1941, the British government, on the suggestion of Foreign Secretary Anthony Eden, backed by Prime Minister Churchill, made the ill-fated political decision to send *Prince of Wales* and *Repulse,* each with two destroyers, to the Indian Ocean to deter Japan from entering the war. The idea of sending one of the Royal Navy's most modern battleships to these waters was against the advice of the Admiralty, the First Sea Lord, and the Commander-in-Chief of the Home Fleet, that is, those who knew the situation. Nonetheless, the ships were ordered to proceed and they rendezvoused on November 28 in Colombo, Ceylon. The entire force, designated the Far East Fleet, was placed under the command of Rear Admiral Sir Tom Phillips, an appointment that raised eyebrows in the Royal Navy, for Phillips was an officer without any sea experience thus far in World War II. Admiral Phillips also believed that well-protected, efficiently handled modern warships could fight off enemy air attacks. This ill-judged consideration would soon cost the admiral his life.

The ships were to have been joined in Ceylon by the modern aircraft carrier *Indomitable,* but that ship was being repaired after having run aground off Jamaica.

Together, *Repulse* and *Prince of Wales,* with their destroyer escorts but minus *Indomitable,* sailed to the Royal Navy base at Singapore, arriving on December 2, 1941. Even though the Admiralty had received intelligence of Japanese naval air, surface, and submarine forces in the region, including the existence of airfields in southern Indochina, both British warships were snugly anchored in Singapore harbor on December 8, 1941.

When the Japanese attacked the U.S. military complex at Pearl Harbor on December 7, 1941 (December 8 in Singapore), *Repulse* and *Prince of Wales* were the only Allied capital ships between Hawaii and the Mediterranean. Early that same afternoon, on the decision of Admiral Phillips, the two British capital ships, accompanied by four destroyers, *Vampire, Tenedos, Electra,* and *Express,* designated Force Z, sortied to attack a landing by the Japanese Twenty-ninth Army reported to be taking place in Thailand and on the Kra Isthmus of Malaya in the Gulf of Siam.

When aircraft could not be provided to support the British ships, and after all hopes of surprising the Japanese were gone, Admiral Phillips, aboard *Prince of Wales,* ordered the ships to turn back to Singapore. Phillips was then informed, however, that another Japanese landing was in progress at Kuantan, closer to his position. Assuming that air cover would be coming, as he was now within range of aircraft flying from both southern Johore and from Singapore, he changed course to investigate while maintaining radio silence so as not to alert the Japanese. Soon it was apparent that the reports of landings were false, but the maintenance of radio silence prevented the

British from learning of Phillip's position and thus providing the promised air cover.

That same day, December 9, the fleet was sighted by a Japanese submarine at 1340 hours. While contact was soon lost by the first vessel, another submarine sighted the fleet during the early morning hours of December 10. This second submarine fired five torpedoes without effect, reported the fleet's position as being 50 miles off the Malayan coast, 150 miles north of Singapore, and then withdrew.

By 1015 hours on December 10, Force Z had been located by Japanese reconnaissance aircraft. Thus alerted, a force of eighty-six twin-engine naval bombers, eighteen high-level bombers, and twenty-five torpedo bombers belonging to Rear Admiral Sadaichi Matsunaga's First Air Force based in French Indochina, was launched. The Japanese airmen found the two capital ships cruising about one-half mile apart and surrounded by the four destroyers.

The attack on *Repulse* started at 1115 as gun crews engaged the approaching aircraft. It was *Repulse's* first and last combat action of World War II. The first attack on the ship was made by nine high-level bombers that dropped twenty-seven bombs from an altitude of 10,000 feet. Survivors recalled that all Japanese attacks were carried out with consummate skill and daring, coming in at sea level to make attacks with torpedoes and low-level strafing attacks of the decks. During the next hour, *Repulse* was hit by at least one 550-pound bomb and five torpedoes. With fire engulfing the vessel, the order to abandon ship was given at 1231. *Repulse* then heeled over to port and sank at 1233, taking with her 327 of the 960 officers and crew. Her commanding officer, Captain William Tennant, survived.

Even after the Japanese aircraft were sighted and had begun their bomb runs, Admiral Phillips continued to maintain radio silence (the final of his ill-judged decisions) and no message was heard from the British ships until 1158 when *Repulse* sent an emergency message to Singapore. While British fighter aircraft were scrambled to provide assistance after hearing that the attack was underway, they were too far distant and arrived too late to help.

The first attacks on *Prince of Wales* were made by torpedo bombers. The ship was hit aft by one or two torpedoes on the first attack, then two or more torpedoes on subsequent runs. The ship was already badly damaged and sinking when a high-level bomber attack finished her off with two direct bomb hits. Only three guns were firing at time of last attack. Survivors recalled that *Prince of Wales* was shattered by one, and possibly two, 1,100-pound bombs, and upwards of six torpedoes. Although

afire, the ship did not explode and valiant efforts were made to save the vessel before Phillips ordered abandon ship at 1315. Five minutes later, *Prince of Wales* rolled over, settled at the stern with the bow rising in the air, before going down at 1320. Of 1,612 crew members, 1,285 were rescued by the accompanying destroyers as were the surviving *Repulse* crew members. Neither Phillips nor Captain J. C. Leach, the captain of *Prince of Wales*, were among the survivors. Both men were thought to have left the bridge too late and were dragged down by the suction of the sinking ship. Only three Japanese aircraft were lost in the battle.

The destruction of *Prince of Wales* and *Repulse* was a major shock to the British government, the Royal Navy, and the British public, and Admiral Phillips's actions during the engagement were the subject of much muted criticism in Royal Navy and government circles. The sinking of these capital ships was a disaster for which no one in Britain was prepared, and it raised grave doubts about the nation's ability to defend its overseas possessions with naval power alone. Prime Minister Churchill later wrote that he had never received more of a direct shock at any other time in the war than that of hearing of the fate of *Prince of Wales* and *Repulse*. But worse was to come, a series of humiliating disasters to Great Britain's Asian forces, brought on as much by British military incompetence and underestimation of the enemy as by Japanese power, and culminating in the surrender of Singapore itself in 1942, the greatest capitulation in modern British history.

FURTHER READINGS

Ash, Bernard. *Someone Has Blundered: The Story of the Repulse and Prince of Wales* (1960).

Barnett, Corelli. *Engage the Enemy More Closely: The Royal Navy in the Second World War* (1991).

Bennett, Geoffrey M. *The Loss of the Prince of Wales and Repulse* (1973).

Franklin, Alan G. C. *One Year of Life: The Story of the HMS Prince of Wales* (1944).

Hough, Richard A. *Death of the Battleship* (1963).

Clayton D. Laurie

SEE ALSO Battleships, Malaya, Japanese Conquest of; Navy, Royal

Prisoners of War

The treatment of Allied prisoners of war (POWs) by Japan was the mirror image of that of the Germans. The Germans treated Western Allied POWs with some "correctness," whereas civilian prisoners endured the full horrors of the concentration camps. The Japanese, on the other hand, were merciless to Allied POWs for their "weakness" in surrendering. Conversely, civilian internees were abused but not, for the most part, subjected to direct brutality.

The first significant numbers of prisoners of the Pacific war were captured within hours of the attack on Pearl Harbor as Allied garrisons across the Pacific capitulated to the Japanese. (The first individual POW of the Pacific war was an officer from a Japanese midget submarine, captured on December 7, 1941.) Guam was the first to fall, on December 11, 1941, putting 134 Americans into captivity. Wake Island was next, on December 23, resulting in the capture of 486 servicemen and no less than 1,100 civilians. On December 25, 1941, the surviving defenders of Hong Kong, numbering roughly twelve thousand British, Canadian, and Chinese troops, fell into Japanese hands. A staggering blow came on February 15, 1942, when General Arthur Percival calmly surrendered Singapore and its 62,000 defenders to a much smaller Japanese force in the greatest and most shameful capitulation in British military history. In March, 93,000 Dutch and native soldiers were captured when the Netherlands East Indies surrendered.

The majority of the 21,000 American POWs were captured in the Philippines: on April 9, 1942, U.S.–Filipino forces on Bataan capitulated, and on May 6, 1942, General Jonathan Wainwright surrendered the 11,000-man garrison of the Corregidor island forts. The capture of smaller groups of prisoners in other Japanese assaults, including the campaign in Burma and air and naval operations in Southeast Asia, brought the total number of Allied prisoners in Japanese hands to roughly 140,000. In addition, some 180,000 Asian troops (mainly Filipinos, Indians, Chinese, and Indonesians) were captured while serving with the American, Commonwealth, and Dutch forces. Thousands of these native auxiliaries died in the first weeks of captivity; most of the survivors were released after a few months.

Although Japan had never ratified the 1929 Geneva Convention Relative to the Treatment of Prisoners of War, Allied governments were not unduly worried about the fate of their soldiers in captivity. The rulers of Meiji Japan was been enthusiastic about embracing Western legal codes, and lost no time in translating and adopting the Geneva Convention of 1864 and the Brussels Declaration. Japan signed and ratified the Hague Conventions of 1907, and had treated its prisoners humanely, even generously, during the First Sino–Japanese War (1894–1895), the Russo–Japanese War (1904–1905), and World War I. In January 1942 the Japanese government stated that it would observe the Geneva Convention mutatis mutandis, which Allied governments took to mean that Japan would observe the spirit, if not the letter, of the convention.

However, there were already indications that the Japanese attitude toward prisoners had changed drastically in the interwar era. A number of the Japanese troops captured during the Russo–Japanese War had experienced profound shame upon their return home, and some were even chased out of their villages because they had disgraced themselves by falling into enemy hands. Attitudes against surrender hardened during World War I; one prominent writer observed that it would be a national disaster if large groups of Japanese soldiers surrendered, as European troops did. In 1932, a Major Kuga, who had been captured when hostilities broke out in Shanghai, returned to the scene of his capture and committed suicide. Kuga became a national hero, cementing in the Japanese public mind the connection between surrender and shame.

Precisely how all this would affect captivity in the Pacific theater was not immediately clear to Allied governments, but their servicemen soon discovered that Japanese soldiers had as little respect for captured enemies as they did for their own men who surrendered. Indeed, from the moment of capture, POWs found that their lives were of little consequence to their captors. After the fall of Hong Kong, Japanese soldiers slaughtered wounded prisoners and their doctors in St. Stephen's Hospital, then raped the nurses who had survived the attack. Similar outrages were committed at Alexandra Hospital in Singapore. None of this, of course, could be seen as connected to the "shame" of surrender; the soldiers were helpless in their beds, and the nurses were simply doing their duty. American soldiers captured in the Philippines endured the Bataan death march, an 85-mile trek from their place of surrender to Camp O'Donnell, a former U.S. Army base where they were first incarcerated. Some seventy-five thousand American and Filipino soldiers began the march; as many as ten thousand never reached their destination.

Some six hundred separate camps housed Allied prisoners in the Far East. Initially they were scattered throughout the occupied territories, including Java, the Philippines, Thailand, Formosa (Taiwan), and Korea, but as the war progressed, the Japanese government began moving prisoners to the Japanese home islands, so that their labor could be used for the war effort. In contrast to Europe, where the majority of camps were standardized, purpose-built facilities, camps in the Far East came in all shapes and sizes. Many of them, like Cabanatuan (the Philippines; later the scene of the only successful POW rescue raid by U.S. Rangers and Alamo Scouts), Bandung (Java), and Shamshuipo (Hong Kong), were set up in former Allied barracks or military installations. Other camps were more makeshift. Fukuoka Camp #6, in southern Japan, was a disused railway shed; prisoners held at Serang, in northern Java, were confined in an old movie theater; Bilibid prison camp in the Philippines was Manila's old municipal jail. Prisoners sent to labor on the Burma–Thailand railway were expected to build their own camps. Their guards provided them with tools and instructions, then left the prisoners to clear the jungle, lay out a compound, and erect huts.

Conditions in these camps varied enormously. The Davao Penal Colony, on the island of Mindanao, housed long-term criminals until a group of 1,100 POWs arrived there in late 1942. They found a pleasant compound surrounded by coconut, citrus, avocado, and banana groves, wild papayas, and fields of corn, sweet potatoes, and rice. A hospital was provided for ailing prisoners, and healthy prisoners performed light agricultural work under Filipino overseers. In January 1943, each prisoner received two 11-pound Red Cross parcels of food and toilet articles; a large shipment of bulk food and medical supplies reached the camp at the same time, and was carefully distributed by camp staff.

Unfortunately, conditions in Davao were entirely untypical of the Japanese prison camp system as a whole, and the vast majority of camps were brutally primitive. Heating was often nonexistent, even during the coldest months; buildings quickly became infested with vermin, and sanitary facilities were primitive at best. North Point camp (Hong Kong), for example, had previously been a veterinary hospital, and prisoners arrived to find the floors covered with animal carcasses and excrement. Prisoners who entered the camp at Koagi, near Nagasaki, Japan, in October 1942 discovered that the buildings had not yet been completed. Throughout the winter of 1942–1943, they lived in unfinished, unheated barracks, with only two wood-fiber blankets for warmth. Narumi camp, near Nagoya, had completed barracks, but the prisoners' sleeping space was restricted to a mat barely eighteen inches wide. Only the deaths of fellow prisoners allowed the survivors to spread out.

In such conditions, it was difficult for even the strongest prisoner to maintain good health. The rations made it doubly difficult. Quite apart from the fact that Western prisoners were not used to a diet based on rice, the quantities provided were barely sufficient to maintain health. At first, the captors provided a mixture of rice, beans, vegetable scrapings, fish, and occasionally meat or citrus fruits, but as the war dragged on, the extras disappeared and prisoners relied more and more on rice alone. Some camp commanders permitted prisoners to grow gardens or to buy food from natives, but generally prisoners had to rely on their wits to scrounge. Starving prisoners quickly discarded their prewar sensibilities and ate anything they could find, including snakes, rats, fish heads, frogs, and grasshoppers.

Allied governments made every effort to supplement these rations with food parcels, but protracted negotiations succeeded only in persuading the Japanese to accept a few thousand tons of relief supplies. The three ships used to exchange civilian internees in August and September 1942 took back to Japan about one hundred thousand parcels for Allied prisoners, and another exchange ship carried about fifty thousand parcels to Singapore, Manila, and Japan in October 1943. In addition, some two thousand tons of food parcels were distributed through a depot in Vladivostok. Distribution of these parcels was uneven, some POWs receiving a dozen or more while others were issued only a single parcel to be shared among ten, twelve, or even seventeen prisoners. Many parcels were stolen by camp guards and sold on the black market, but most were simply stockpiled. When the camps were liberated in 1945, Allied soldiers found thousands of Red Cross food parcels that had been left to rot in Japanese warehouses.

Given the inadequacy of rations, it is hardly surprising that prisoners' health suffered. The imbalance of vitamins in the diet caused a host of deficiency diseases related to malnutrition. In addition, inadequate facilities for purifying water enabled the spread dysentery and cholera in some camps. An absence of adequate mosquito control measures meant that malaria, too, ran rife. Minor cuts and scrapes quickly ulcerated and became septic. To make matters worse, camp doctors had few means to battle disease, despite the efforts of neutral authorities to bring medical supplies into the camps. A sympathetic camp commander might issue medicine or allow a doctor to purchase it from local sources, but more often than not a prisoner had to rely on comrades or his own inner strength to recover. Indeed, many POWs did everything they could to avoid being moved to the camp "hospital"; in some camps, it was not a place to be treated but the place where prisoners who were past hope were taken to die.

Despite the meager rations and poor state of health, prisoners were forced to perform hard labor, often in appalling conditions. The sick were forced to work as well as the healthy. Because the Japanese insisted that a certain percentage of POWs be available for work parties, doctors were placed in the unenviable position to having to select which of the sick would be put to work. Extra incentive was provided by the Japanese philosophy that the prisoner who did not work did not need as much to eat, and therefore had his rations reduced. Contrary to the Geneva Convention, the Japanese had no compunction about forcing prisoners to work for their war effort. Prisoners in camps around Osaka, on Honshu, worked in a factory that manufactured bomb cases. Around Yokohama, prisoners built and repaired Japanese naval and merchant ships; in Hong Kong they dug storage bunkers for gasoline and ammunition, and extended the runway at Kai Tak air base. On Wake Island, ninety-six American civilian construction workers labored for eighteen months to improve Japanese defenses there. In October 1943, when U.S. warships began to bombard the island, the Japanese commander ordered the immediate execution of the entire workforce. The largest and most notorious labor project was the Burma–Thailand railway, commonly known as the Death Railway, which was intended to link Rangoon with the front in Burma. From July 1942 to October 1943, some sixty-one thousand POWs and two hundred seventy thousand native conscripts worked to carve a 260-mile railway line out of the jungle. As many as a hundred thousand of the native laborers may have perished due to a combination of overwork, disease, and lack of food; Allied figures put the POW death toll at approximately twelve thousand.

The Death Railway is the most notorious atrocity committed against Far East prisoners, but subsequent war crimes trials revealed a litany of other horror stories. On December 14, 1944, 139 American POWs at Palawan in the Philippines died when their captors crammed them into air raid shelters, poured in gasoline, and set them on fire. In February 1945, on the Bonin Islands north of Iwo Jima, eight captured airmen were executed and cannibalized by Japanese garrison troops, including the general and admiral commanding the military and naval forces. During that spring and summer, more than two hundred downed B-29 crewmen were executed by their captors, either summarily or after perfunctory court-martial proceedings. No less violent was the fate of 2,500 British and Australian POWs held in Sandakan, in northern Borneo. In January 1945, to keep them from falling into the hands of advancing Allied troops, the Japanese began moving the prisoners inland some two hundred fifty kilometers. They were subjected to such appalling abuses on the march that fewer than half survived to reach their destination, and most of the rest were put to death not long after reaching their new camp. Of the 2,500 prisoners who had left Sandakan, only 6 were alive at the end of the war.

To add to the prisoners' despair, death seemed to offer the only escape. POWs initially believed they would be transferred to Japan, where conditions could not possibly be worse, but their hopes were soon dashed. The journey was a nightmare. Conditions on the transports, known as hell ships, were dreadful, with the weakened prisoners packed into dirty and unventilated holds. A greater hazard, however, was posed by Allied submarines, for the unmarked POW transports were placed among general Japanese convoys. On September 7, 1943, *Shinyo Maru* was sunk by the U.S. submarine *Paddle* west of Mindanao, killing more than six hundred American prisoners. On October 24, *Arisan Maru* was torpedoed east of Hong Kong, probably by USS *Snook,* and sank with hundreds more American POWs. On September 12, 1944, *Kachidoki Maru* and *Rokyu,* carrying over twenty-two hundred British and Australian prisoners from Singapore, were attacked and sunk by U.S. submarines off Hainan, China. Fewer than half of the prisoners survived.

Escape, a reasonable option for prisoners held in Europe, was scarcely considered by POWs in the Far East. Many camps were so isolated that the prospective escapee would have to traverse hundreds of miles of jungle before reaching relative safety, a journey that was beyond the physical capabilities of the weakened prisoners. It was impossible to blend in with the civilian population, nor could the escapee count on receiving assistance from friendly natives. Americans who escaped in the Philippines or Britons who escaped from Hong Kong had a reasonable expectation of receiving aid, but Dutch soldiers in Java were fully aware that they would receive little sympathy from any natives they encountered. Furthermore, all prisoners knew that recaptured escapee would be subject to very harsh punishments that ranged from beatings to summary execution. Four Canadians who escaped from Shamshuipo camp in Hong Kong in August 1942 were executed within hours of their recapture. Shortly afterward, camp officials divided the POWs into groups of five, and announced that if one member of any group attempted to escape, the other four would be executed. The commander of Changi in Singapore ordered all prisoners to sign a statement that they would not attempt escape. When they refused, he ordered the execution of four prisoners who had been recaptured after escaping four months earlier.

The Allied governments learned of this mistreatment through reports from neutral authorities and escaped prisoners, and went to great lengths to ameliorate conditions. Besides the attempts to send food and medical parcels into the camps, Allied officials tried to negotiate an exchange of sick and wounded prisoners with Japan. A number of exchanges were successfully concluded with Germany and Italy, and Allied authorities began sending out feelers to Japan as early as the summer of 1942. Negotiations continued for the rest of the war and saw the Allies offer a number of categories of prisoners, including sick and wounded POWs, civilian internees, and even Japanese combat troops cut off in isolated garrisons, in exchange for Allied POWs. In a last, desperate attempt, the U.S. government even offered to waive Article 74 of the Geneva Convention, which prohibited exchanged prisoners from returning to combat roles, to encourage Japan to come to terms. The response was negative, and no exchange of POWs occurred in the Pacific theater. Surprisingly, the Allies never specifically threatened punishment for those who had abused POWs.

Part of the reason for this failure undoubtedly lay in the fact that Japan did not want its prisoners back. The Japanese forces were by now thoroughly permeated with the notion that it was a disgrace to be captured ("Never live to experience shame as a prisoner," read the Japanese army's 1940 Field Service Code), and the Imperial Japanese Army took the position that the Japanese POW did not exist. For exchange purposes, this was almost literally true: in October 1944, when there were more than 100,000 Allies in Japanese hands, only about 6,000 Japanese soldiers had been captured. By war's end, the total of Japanese prisoners was only 41,000, and the determination of Japanese soldiers to die rather than be captured resulted in incredible casualty rates among Japanese units. When American troops finally overran the island of Saipan, they took only 921 prisoners of the original garrison of 43,000. Of the 135,000 Japanese troops deployed to defend Leyte in the Philippines, only 400 allowed themselves to be captured.

The first permanent camps for Japanese prisoners of war were established in Australia and New Zealand. In September 1942, at the request of American authorities, a former New Zealand army training camp at Featherston was converted into a prison camp. Roughly eight hundred POWs were confined there during the war; the bulk of them were from a labor battalion that had been captured while working on an airfield on Guadalcanal, but there was also a sizable contingent of naval personnel. The camp at Cowra, Australia, had been opened in 1941 to house German and Italian prisoners; the first Japanese prisoners did not arrive until early 1943, when roughly a thousand survivors of the campaign in New Guinea were brought to the camp. Some fifty-four hundred Japanese prisoners were held in camps in the United States, and the majority of the remainder were detained in the Philippines.

Despite the conditions in Japanese camps, Allied governments were scrupulous in their treatment of Japanese prisoners. The 800 Japanese prisoners in Camp Featherston, New Zealand, received medical, dental, and optical care, and were paid for work they performed (this money was converted into Japanese currency and given to the prisoners upon their release). Rations of meat, rice, bread, fresh milk, butter, and fruit brought their daily caloric intake to 2,700, three or four times what Allied POWs subsisted on. One Japanese soldier who was captured on Leyte in October 1944 recalled friends referring to their camp in the Philippines as paradise, and their internment as the best time of their lives.

For some Japanese, however, this beneficent treatment made the sting of captivity more painful, and drove them to desperate attempts to erase the stain of capture. On February 25, 1943, the prisoners at Featherston refused to work and charged the guard company, pelting them with projectiles. The guards immediately opened fire, and the ensuing melee left forty-eight prisoners and one guard dead. In August 1944 there was an even bloodier outbreak. Shortly after midnight in the large camp at Cowra, Australia, more than a thousand Japanese prisoners suddenly poured from their barracks and charged the wire. Armed with homemade weapons, they hoped to take over the camp and attack a nearby infantry training center. The camp guards opened fire, killing 234 of the prisoners, but 334 escaped. All were either killed or recaptured within days. As the war's end approached, Japanese prisoners talked of mass suicide rather than face the shame of returning from captivity. Indeed, more than 10 percent of the Japanese soldiers who died in Australian captivity were suicides.

After the surrender of the Japanese government, recovery teams traveled to the known prison camp locations, but it was some time before they were able to find all of the isolated work camps. Compounds that could not be evacuated immediately were supplied with food, medicines, and clothing (packed into gasoline drums and dropped by Allied bombers). As soon as arrangements could be made, able-bodied prisoners were transported to a staging facility in Hong Kong; from there they went to the Philippines to be processed and examined before returning home. Sick POWs were taken by U.S. hospital ships directly to the Philippines or the Marianas, where they were treated until they were strong enough to begin the journey home. For some men, treatment was a lengthy process, and military doctors were astonished at the physical condition of the survivors, who suffered from beriberi, malaria, dysentery, avitaminosis, and a host of other diseases. Once they began processing and tabulating the liberated prisoners, Allied governments were shocked at how many had not survived: 7,412 of 21,726 Australian, 12,433 of 50,016 British, and 7,107 of 21,580 American POWs did not return from the prison camps of Japan.

By this time, General Douglas MacArthur's Supreme Command of the Allied Powers had begun to assemble evidence against suspected war criminals. In the first major trial, General Tomoyuki Yamashita, commander of the Fourteenth Area Army in the Philippines, was arraigned on 123 individual charges and one general charge: that he failed to prevent his troops from committing crimes against POWs and civilians in the Philippines. He was convicted and sent to the gallows in February 1946, just six weeks before the execution of General Masaharu Homma, who had been convicted on similar charges, including responsibility for the Bataan death march. Both judgments were controversial because it was not proven that the defendants ordered, or even knew about, the atrocities in question, only that they had failed to exercise command responsibility over their troops. The Allied governments convened hundreds of war crimes trials over the next three years, and passed nearly a thousand death sentences against government and military officials, prison camp officers, and guards for their parts in abuses against POWs. In one of the strangest trials, guard Kanao Inouye was tried for abusing Canadian prisoners at Shamshuipo camp. What began as a war crimes trial became a civilian trial when the defense pointed out that Inouye, who had been born in British Columbia, was in fact a Canadian citizen. Prosecutors then shifted their strategy, charged Inouye with treason, and saw him convicted and executed.

Liberated prisoners took cold comfort from these trials, for their own private battles were continuing. A few months of full rations and expert medical care seemed to cure their most acute symptoms, and many former prisoners were determined to return to normal as soon as possible. However, the long-term effects of malnutrition and tropical diseases were not well understood at the time, nor were the psychological effects of captivity (which would later be called post-traumatic stress disorder). Soon, former prisoners began to exhibit a host of physical and psychological ailments, including heart disease, gastrointestinal disorders, optic atrophy, and circulatory problems. Doctors began to study Far East POWs as a group, and their work revealed that the effects of captivity and privation were more serious and long-lasting than anyone had imagined. Studies revealed that the rates of premature death among former Far East prisoners of war far exceeded those of other veterans, or of former prisoners in the European theater. Doctors in Canada dis-

covered that former prisoners from Hong Kong had a life expectancy ten to fifteen years shorter than the national average; tuberculosis alone killed former Far East POWs at a rate that was more than twice the national average.

The survivors' symptoms worsened as the years passed. A major 1987 study revealed the degree to which the health of Far East POWs had been permanently impaired. One out of every nineteen survivors had gone blind since being liberated, and 29 percent suffered from heart disease or hypertension. More than 37 percent of survivors suffered serious neurological disorders directly traceable to captivity. Nearly a third had foot deformities or neuritis due to frostbite, and fully one-third were affected by spinal or paraspinal ailments that worsened with age. Half suffered from psychiatric conditions, and half experienced gastrointestinal ailments; this figure did not represent a great improvement over the first major study in 1948, which found that more than 70 percent of the survivors of one regiment were infested with intestinal parasites. In fact, dysentery, which had been such a killer in the camps, continued to fell former prisoners long after the war. In all, every survivor in the study group suffered from chronic ailments that were directly related to the privations of captivity.

FURTHER READINGS

Daws, Gavan. *Prisoners of the Japanese: POWs of World War II in the Pacific* (1994).

LaForte, Robert, and Ronald E. Marcello, eds. *Building the Death Railway: The Ordeal of American POWs in Burma, 1942–1945* (1993).

Mason, W. Wynne. *Prisoners of War* (New Zealand, Department of Internal Affairs, War History Branch, 1954).

Moore, Bob, and Kent Fodorowich, eds. *Prisoners of War and Their Captors in World War II* (1996).

Piccigallo, Philip R. *The Japanese on Trial: Allied War Crimes Operations in the East, 1945–1951* (1979).

Shohei, Ooka. *Taken Captive: A Japanese POW's Story* (1996).

Vance, Jonathan. *Objects of Concern: Canadian Prisoners of War Through the 20th Century* (1994).

Jonathan F. Vance

Prophets of the Pacific War

In the early 1980s, a congressional investigation into the internment of Japanese Americans during World War II invoked the spirit of Homer Lea. His pre–World War I forecast of a Japanese attack against the Philippines, Hawaii, and the U.S. West Coast, *The Valor of Ignorance,* was, in the opinion of the investigators, an instrument of malice. The committee's final report disclosed that Secretary of War Henry Stimson had mused over Lea's 1909 invasion hypothesis in February 1942. Within a week, he recommended to President Roosevelt that the issei and nisei be evacuated from the Western Military District as a precaution against espionage, sabotage, and collaboration with Japanese naval and amphibious forces. Stimson had met Lea around 1911, during an earlier term as secretary of war, under President William Howard Taft. At that time, he had dismissed Lea's theme as a fantasy. In the dark days following the Japanese attack on Pearl Harbor, as imaginations ran wild, Stimson considered that Lea's apprehension might have been well founded after all.

In 1925 another, more cautious, oracle, Hector Bywater, had mentioned Lea in his own what-if book, *The Great Pacific War, 1931–1933.* Bywater regarded Lea as an alarmist, considering that the likelihood of a successful Japanese invasion of the North American continent was unrealistic in 1925, and all the more so in 1909. Bywater had compiled a book of "docufiction" from the viewpoint of a historian of an imaginary conflict, whereas Lea had written an opinion piece. The two books are the most striking exemplars of what has become known as "Yellow Peril" literature—forecasts and warnings about a coming Japanese onslaught against Western possessions in the Pacific arena.

The form was well established. In 1871, a British colonel of volunteers, George Tomkyns Chesney, had published a serial in *Blackwood's Magazine,* "The Battle of Dorking," which later was issued as a pamphlet. The articles reflected back from the vantage point of 1925 on a successful German invasion of England (the German army had thrashed French armies and besieged Paris). The book stirred parliamentary debates on preparedness—as was intended. The mock-historical approach and the meticulous attention to building a plausible military scenario became the stock-in-trade of a whole generation of "coming war" novelists and essayists who were instrumental in fomenting war jitters in the period before World War I. Similarly, the "Yellow Peril" genre created a climate of apprehension and mutual distrust between the Japanese and American peoples.

The white men of the U.S. West Coast had begun their war on the yellow man in the 1870s, with the arrival of large numbers of Chinese immigrants seeking employment opportunities. Caucasian California settlers anticipated being racially inundated. The perceived threat was demographic rather than military. A few fantasies of a warlike Chinese incursion following the nonviolent migration were circulated in the 1880s and 1890s, but these were the work of romantic visionaries rather than martial Cassandras. In 1880, P. W. Dooner's *The Last Days of the Republic,* for example, predicted that the expansion of cheap Chinese coolie labor, combined with the Chinese tendency to stick together and remain loyal to the homeland, would eventually lure invading yellow hordes to America's shores. It was only with the coming of the Japanese in large numbers that military professionals contemplated the "Yellow Peril"; this attention was due to events abroad.

The first of these momentous developments was Japan's victory in the Sino–Japanese War of 1894–1895, followed by Japan's victory over Russia in 1905. Victory over China surprised Western observers and immediately established Japan as the preeminent rising power in Asia. Japan's astonishing victory in the Russo-Japanese War confirmed this impression of a new world power to be reckoned with—a power, moreover, that was neither "white" nor Christian nor grounded in the so-called humanistic traditions of the West.

Alarmed by these overseas conflicts, along with the flood tide of "yellow" immigrants, military seers conjectured about the nature of an inevitable showdown war between the Caucasian colonial powers, chiefly the United States, and Japan in the Far East. Most such writings were the work of hacks who were more interested in shocking or admonishing than in informing. A few, however, stand out as offering discerning and prescient analyses of the likely shape of the Japanese–American struggle for control of the Pacific.

Between 1906 and 1913, the Germanophile Hearst Publishing Syndicate adopted as its pet project measures to prevent the prospect of a Japanese–American war: the segregation of Asian schoolchildren in the San Francisco school system, denial of land sales to Japanese immigrants, and legislative restrictions on immigration from Asian nations. This attitude reflected the *Gelbgefahr* (Yellow Peril) of Wilhelmine Germany. The sensationalist pulps obligingly fanned Californians' fears of a Japanese "subversive" advance party who would be followed by swarms of predatory "little yellow men" surrounding West Coast metropolises. The "assailants" would work methodically and with great precision, thanks to preparatory reconnaissance by squads of spies posing as waiters and houseboys. News photos of the sunken hulks at Port Arthur, China, lent veracity to these warnings. Pulp publishing mills eagerly snapped up retaliatory Japanese-bred fantasies in which the Land of the Rising Sun would teach the haughty, race-baiting Americans a little respect. In fact, the Japanese tabloids had been inspired by translations from earlier American scare stories.

The coming conflict became common speculation after the startling humiliation of imperial Russia by Japan in 1905, the first modern defeat of a European power by an Asiatic one. Almost at once a flurry of opinion in the professional military press began to foresee a successful Japanese attack on U.S. possessions, if not on the heartland itself. The unanticipated emergence of Japan as a military power with regional, if not worldwide, ambitions caught the attention of media-aware army and navy officers during the war scare of 1907–1908.

The earliest serious media "think pieces" in the United States regarding the vulnerability to overseas attack appeared on the newsstands around 1906. Frederick Louis Huidekoper, a scholar of Napoleonic warfare, dryly assessed the real versus the apparent balance of forces and the shape of a conceivable Japanese effort to take the Philippines ("Is the United States Prepared for War?" *North American Review,* March 1906). Huidekoper noted the difficulty that would attend any counterattack by a U.S. relief expedition dispatched against the 800,000-man Japanese force. The entire Japanese expeditionary army, he claimed, could be landed within a month. Huidekoper estimated that the Americans would have arrived too late to save Manila. Huidekoper also saw the Germans embarking an army corps within three days, and, allowing sixteen days for the crossing, landing more than two hundred thousand trained regulars within the territorial limits of the United States in five weeks.

The following year, *Journal of the Military Services Institution* published a translation of a meticulous analysis of Japanese invasion prospects Captain Ignez Rodic of the Austro-Hungarian general staff. The article opened with an analysis of the potential order of battle at the projected scene of hostilities. Rodic took his cue from a remark by the U.S. military commander of the Pacific coast, General Frederick Funston, who suggested that a single Japanese division landing in the vicinity of San Francisco would suffice to conquer the territory. Rodic contemplated a Japanese amphibious descent that would circumvent seaward-facing artillery at fortified harbors. The gun emplacements could thereafter be taken at leisure from the rear. Rodic deduced that the extent and rapid pace of the Japanese arms buildup indicated a far more ambitious project than seizure of the Philippines or Hawaii. His scenario anticipated that of Homer Lea, with the difference that Rodic's initial landing force was about one-seventh as large as Lea's.

More circumspect was the account of Captain Alfred Bjornstead of the 28th Infantry, "The Military Necessities of the United States and the Best Provisions for Meeting Them," which won the Military Service Institution's gold medal for 1907. After a detailed consideration of troop strengths available to both parties, Bjornstead concluded that Japan could muster and transport an army of 300,000 for use in the Philippines, Alaska, Hawaii, and Panama.

A British naval authority, writing under the nom de plume "Cruiser," attempted to dispute the Rodic/Lea thesis. "Cruiser" published "The Conditions of a Japanese–American War" in *Contemporary Review* (September 1907). He dismissed the possibility of an invasion of the North American continent expedition, as being beyond the capabilities of the Japanese merchant marine. In any event, the numerically larger U.S. battle line would handily dispatch any such cumbersome train of vessels well in advance of a landing. The conflict would normally be a purely naval contest. The complications introduced by the precarious American position in the Philippines would comprise the main problem confounding U.S. war aims in the western Pacific. There is a lucid and careful examination of the naval problems involved in transferring the main battle fleet from the Atlantic to the Pacific via the Strait of Magellan under wartime conditions—if the fleet were stationed in the Atlantic or Caribbean at the opening of hostilities.

Alarmist American service lobbyists sounded the alarm throughout 1908. In May, June, and September, *Cosmopolitan* magazine unfolded a lengthy and detailed prospectus for a Japanese–American war. Navy Captain Richmond P. Hobson, a hero of the Spanish–American War, described the taking of the Philippines and Hawaii as well as the storming of the Pacific Slope with some precision. The key difference from the Rodic analysis is that Hobson assumes British cooperation with Japan in accordance with a mutual assistance pact they had signed in 1903. It would facilitate transport and convoy protection for 250,000 troops on their way to Canadian harbors, from which they could move down through Puget Sound. The naval task force steaming from Vancouver would be augmented by an overland descent to neutralize shore defenses. Simultaneous expeditions south of San Francisco and Los Angeles would cut vital rail links and seal mountain passes.

Army Lieutenant Hugh Johnson (later head of President Franklin Roosevelt's National Recovery Administration) painted a similarly dismal picture in "The Lamb Rampant" (*Everybody's Magazine,* March 1908). Despairing over the gaping holes in the field command left by retiring junior officers, he dramatized his criticism principally through the device of a German menace. In his account homesick German immigrants in Brazil set up a "colony" and wire home for help in confederating with the fatherland, an action leading the U.S. president to invoke the Monroe Doctrine. Germany ignores the threat and proclaims a union with the nationalist cell. War erupts in June 1908 as a German strike force advances up the South American coast to join a transatlantic procession off the Florida Keys and converges upon a landing site at Rockaway Beach, Long Island, from whence New York City would seized. The next segment discusses likely Japanese moves. The U.S. Navy's Asiatic and Philippines squadrons are rapidly crushed by the better-drilled and -motivated Imperial Japanese Navy. The ensuing invasion parrots the Rodic scheme fairly closely. Only 40,000 poorly organized and equipped U.S. troops are deemed to be available on the West Coast, with no possibility of reinforcements for at least three months. The Japanese are able to land four armies: at Bodega Bay, Monterey Bay, and San Pedro, California, and Grays Harbor, Washington.

Brigadier General Thomas MacArthur Anderson reflected upon Johnson's frightful counsel in the May 1908 issue of *The Pacific Monthly* as he contemplated "Our Battle of Dorking." Adopting the familiar Rodic/ Hobson/Johnson scenario, the general provides more precise and up-to-date data on the Pacific coast fortification and manpower lacks.

The May *Literary Digest* presented further ruminations by German geopoliticians in its review of a new book by Graf von Reventlow, naval officer and editor of *Armee und Marine, World Peace or World War: Which Way Is Germany to Turn?* Reventlow, later translator and chief promoter of the German edition of Homer Lea's *The Day of the Saxon,* portrays a Japanese conquest of the Philippines and Hawaii. He stops short of a clash on the Pacific coast, figuring that the loss of its overseas bases would lead the United States to sue for peace on acceptable terms.

Previously, in 1907, Ferdinand Heinrich Grautoff had published a documentary-type novel, *Bansai,* a meticulous "after action" report in the form of news clippings that portrayed a Japanese–American conflict including a successful Japanese incursion as far as the Blue Mountain passes in Oregon and Idaho. The plausibility of Grautoff's well-delineated military account led to an American edition in 1908, issued under the pseudonym "Parabellum." The English translation was soon followed by an American-bred preview of the Japanese drive to the east whose legacy was to resonate through the winter of 1941–1942.

Homer Lea's enduring fame rests upon his two books of geostrategic forecasting, *The Valor of Ignorance* (1909)

and *The Day of the Saxon* (1912). The second book, dealing with German designs upon England's empire and the rise of the Russian menace, is of no concern here. *Valor of Ignorance* received limited contemporary notice in American tabloids and military service professional journals. Its endorsement by high-ranking U.S. Army officers generated protests by Japanese journalists and trade representatives. The book was largely forgotten until, in the Christmas 1942 edition, the *Newsweek* military correspondent recalled that Lea had "foretold" the Pearl Harbor attack more than thirty years earlier.

There was a ripple of attention to the neglected Lea when Clare Boothe Luce had visited Charles Willoughby, Douglas MacArthur's intelligence chief, in the Philippines in 1941 and was dazzled with his intuition about the likely Japanese invasion plan. Willoughby divulged that the whole scheme had been revealed thirty years earlier by Homer Lea. Shortly after the Pearl Harbor attack, Luce's ruminations on Lea and his works appeared in *Harper's* weekly, and later as prefaces to Lea's reissued works.

Homer Lea, a dilettante military critic, was an outsider—essentially today's "military buff." His frail health and hunchback frustrated his desire to serve in the U.S. Army during the Spanish–American War. However, Lea's knowledge of Asian languages and culture, and his impressive book knowledge of military history and modern theory, gained him an assignment as a mercenary officer in one of the Chinese armed gangs troubling the dowager empress just before the Boxer Uprising. His actual role in the anarchic southern provinces at that time is unclear, although he returned to the United States to much fanfare, sporting a self-designed "general's" uniform and rank, and boasting of close ties to Sun Yat-sen, who apparently was impressed by Lea's strategic knowledge. Later, Sun solicited Lea's advice on strategy, much to the chagrin of the indigenous officers on his staff.

The first half of *The Valor of Ignorance* condemns America's moral decay and its consequent lack of the martial spirit necessary to back up its arrogance in a dangerous world. The root of this "effeminacy" was an obsession with accumulating wealth. Lea promotes a calculus of military power applying concepts such as converging spheres of expansion, ratios of relative force, and other asserted, rather than proven, axioms governing international relations. In the second half of his book, he speculates upon the threat that rising Japan will control the Pacific trade routes.

When will Japan strike? Lea doesn't say, simply hinting that the war could come within months. The clash is motivated by Japan's superior grasp of the unavoidable showdown and its comprehension of America's impotence. The presumed operational sequence is implied, inasmuch as Lea does not present a chronological scenario or a recital of a connected chain of events. He begins by dividing the Pacific into six interlocking subsidiary zones of control, each with its "strategic center": Manila, Guam, Pago-Pago, the Hawaiian Islands, the Aleutians, and Alaska. Unopposed Philippine landings would be followed up with twin columns converging on Manila from beachheads at Polillo Bight and Lingayen Gulf, precisely as it happened thirty-two years later.

Hawaii is taken through a fifth-column stratagem by a de factor Japanese army of occupation, which, according to Lea, was clandestinely slipped in between 1904 and 1909 by replacing some forty-two thousand agricultural workers with skilled combatants who had fought at Liao-Yang and Mukden, China.

It appears that the southwestern and southern Pacific key points are taken concurrently with the Philippines operations. Alaska is next to go; a provisional station is set up at Sitka to serve as a depot for the 100,000 men transferred within four weeks of the start of hostilities. This overwhelming force initiates the amphibious assault on Grays Harbor and Willapa Bay, Washington, the only deep-water channels beneficial to a prospective invader on the northern axis. The "strategic centers" of Chehalis and Centralia, Washington, would be taken next. From these points, the Japanese would control rail and road transportation routes. The invaders would next move inland to take up blocking positions at the two bottlenecks through which any relief columns from the east must proceed: passes in the Blue Mountains of eastern Oregon and the Bitterroot Range between Idaho and Montana.

Next, the action moves to southern California, which in 1909 was practically identical with Los Angeles and its surrounding areas. Landings along the open shoreline of Santa Monica Bay a descent by artillery-backed infantry at the unguarded rear of the San Pedro harbor defenses.

The victory is consolidated by Japanese occupation of the crucial San Jacinto and Cajon passes. In the three to four months it would take to assemble 100,000 U.S. Army regulars and militia, the Japanese tighten their grip on Washington/Oregon and southern California. This leaves San Francisco as the only avenue of approach for relief columns approaching from the east. When it finally arrives, the ragtag 100,000-man mob is obliged to split into several isolated groups. Five months after the opening moves, the Japanese land 50,000 seasoned troops at or above Bodega bay, three to five days' march northward

from the likely American defense perimeter at Sausalito. Another 120,000 Japanese land at Monterey Bay, 6 miles south of the American entrenchment bridging the San Francisco Peninsula. The larger army marches north to confront the 70,000 Americans manning the fieldworks at the San Francisco approaches. The smaller Japanese army moves southward to flank the American lines extending westward from San Rafael. Naturally, the Japanese initiatives are all successful.

Bywater's magnum opus, *The Great Pacific War: A History of the Japanese-American Campaign of 1931–1933* (1925; reprinted 1933, 1942, and 1990) has been a boon to war games and counterfactual "history," providing a precise and methodical study of a feasible sequence of events.

During World War I, Bywater had been connected (unofficially) with the British Secret Service, where his fascination with naval technology and facility with the German language helped him to garner valuable information on German naval progress and intentions. This information enhanced his competency in assessing the balance of naval power. In 1921, Bywater published *Sea Power in the Pacific*, a volume of naval analysis that contains the seeds of *The Great Pacific War*. The canvass of relative combat strength, distances, firepower, and logistics that buttress the plot of *The Great Pacific War* are laid out in essay form.

Six years after the period in which *Great Pacific War* was drafted, the Japanese population explosion is causing severe social and political strains that culminate in the assassination of a key minister in the "war party." In order to unite the nation and preserve the imperial dynasty, the Japanese cabinet determines to provoke a war with the United States, with which tensions are already mounting over American immigration limitations and trade competition in China.

The conflict opens with Japanese saboteurs blowing up a ship in the Panama Canal, blocking it for the duration of the war and forcing the U.S. main fleet to take the lengthy passage around Cape Horn. The U.S. "Asiatic Squadron" is destroyed in a surprise attack, and therefore cannot interfere with ensuing Japanese attacks, nor is the main naval force from the Atlantic seaboard able to intervene in time. The attack on the U.S. fleet is followed immediately by an attack on the Philippines, where the tiny U.S. air fleet inflicts much damage on the Japanese landing parties the inadequate land forces cannot keep the Japanese from moving beyond their beachheads. The Japanese invasion of Hawaii is planned to coincide with an uprising among the islands' 140,000 Japanese. Authorities in Tokyo cancel the invasion at the last minute, but imperial army reserve officers in Honolulu proceed with their insurgency. They occupy key depots and barracks before the uprising is crushed. Next, Guam falls after a "heroic and spectacular" defense. Subsequent to these humiliating losses, Japanese submarines and cruisers stifle trade along the U.S. Pacific coast, harassing air raids are dispatched from plane-launching merchant cruisers positioned off Los Angeles and San Francisco, and Japanese navy submarines shell targets of opportunity along the shoreline.

The tide begins to turn in America's favor when the Japanese expedition to seize Samoa is repulsed with heavy losses. Thereupon begins an island-hopping campaign, much as set forth in the official (but then still secret) War Plan Orange. The U.S. battle fleet secures a vital advanced base by evicting the Japanese from Truk in the Carolines. A feint against the Japanese home islands draws attention from the U.S. task force proceeding to Yap, where dummy battleships further divert Japanese units away from the U.S. battle group. The ensuing fleet action off Yap leaves the Americans victorious. Newly united China joins the American war effort, an alliance that assures the defeat of Japan. The latter begins peace negotiations, bringing the war to a close at the end of 1932. However, the Americans enjoy a pyrrhic victory; ocean commerce is in tatters, and the war debt drives up taxes, draining the American economy of all competitive vitality.

Some critics pointed out that the British dominions would hardly have remained neutral. Others felt that the Philippines would have held out for more than a few days. Airpower advocates argued that the Japanese surely would have utilized their superiority in warplanes to hamper the U.S. Navy's unmolested advance across the Pacific. Most agreed that the U.S. deficiency in planes and submarines would make the eventual victory far more costly than it need have been. Many other lessons from Bywater's *Great Pacific War* were recorded in the professional naval journals and in the instructional materials for the Naval War College. Colorful, but barely credible, is the assertion of one recent Bywater biographer that Yamamoto Isoruku, the architect of the Pearl Harbor raid, virtually modeled his opening strategy on information gleaned from Bywater's docufictional account. This assertion is largely based on the fact that Japanese naval writers and authorities often referred to Bywater's works.

Lea and Bywater are by far the most prominent representatives of the "Yellow Peril" clairvoyants. Throughout the period spanning the close of the Russo–Japanese War and the Pearl Harbor attack, there were dozens of less striking attempts to caution citizens and war planners of the dangers ahead. In late 1940, one of the more reflective Japanese works, by a journalist named Matsuo Kinokai, was translated into English as *The Tripartite Alliance and a Japanese–American War* in 1941. Meanwhile, U.S. military and naval affairs journalists such as Sutherland Denlinger and Charles Gary (*War in the Pacific: A Study of Navies, Peoples and Battle Problems* [1936]) continued to estimate how the U.S. air and naval forces might contend with likely Japanese moves against remote U.S. outposts in the western Pacific.

There is little point in quibbling over how much the prognostications of informed amateurs and literary officers "influenced" the drafting of official and secret war planning documents. The strategists on both sides of the Pacific constantly updated a file of plausible scenarios, whatever the source. They also needed to be kept abreast of public opinion in the enemy camp. However, war planning is driven by the exigencies of the government and its diplomatic and economic objectives, not the notions and anxieties of popular journalism or fiction. More consequential than the nebulous effects of the "Yellow Peril" literature—and its Japanese counterpart—on war strategy was its propaganda value in fomenting a climate of mutual mistrust and race hatred.

FURTHER READINGS

Anschel, Eugene. *Homer Lea, Sun Yat Sen, and the Chinese Revolution* (1984).

Bywater, Hector C. *The Great Pacific War: A History of the American-Japanese Campaign of 1931–1933.* (1925; repr. 1942).

Clarke, I. F. *Voices Prophesying War: Future Wars 1763–3749* (2d ed. 1992).

Daniels, Roger. *The Politics of Prejudice: The Anti-Japanese Movement in California and the Struggle for Japanese Exclusion* (1977, 1962).

Dower, John W. *War Without Mercy: Race and Power in the Pacific War* (1986).

Hofstadter, Richard. *Social Darwinism in American Thought* (rev. ed. 1962).

Iriye Akiraa. *Power and Culture: The Japanese-American War, 1941–45* (1981).

Lea, Homer. *The Valor of Ignorance* (1909; repr., with preface by Clare Boothe Luce, 1942).

Vagts, Alfred. *A History of Militarism* (1967).

James Bloom

SEE ALSO Navy, U.S.

Psychological Warfare, Japan

Japanese psychological warfare operations were modeled on campaigns conducted by the British in World War I and the Germans in World War II. The Germans established a branch of their propaganda ministry in Japan, which resulted in close psychological warfare collaboration between these two Axis powers. As a result, their propaganda themes, such as both nations having divine or semidivine rulers and being populated by super races whose destiny was to rule the world, were strikingly parallel.

Psychological warfare served four general goals of the Japanese war effort: to weaken and destroy the morale of the Western powers, to encourage the resistance of friendly forces in territories occupied by the Western powers, to promote dissension between Western government/military forces and their home fronts and allies, and to keep neutrals neutral or to procure their active cooperation against the West. The Japanese conducted three general forms of psychological warfare, which were primarily coordinated by the Cabinet Information Board. However, the headquarters of the Japanese army remained autonomous and conducted its own psychological operations.

Strategic propaganda was directed against the home fronts, political leadership, and status of the Western powers in Asia. The Japanese had defied these Western powers by invading the Chinese territory of Manchuria in 1931 and, as a result, gained a powerful psychological advantage over them. They capitalized upon it with the slogan "Asia for the Asiatics." Although most of the Japanese leadership, both political and military, seemed sincerely to believe in the slogan's sentiments, it was nonetheless used as a pretext for Japan's policy of military expansion. Japan's intent was to be viewed as the liberator of the Asiatic peoples and to show that the rule of the Western powers in Asia was now over.

In the decade preceding their surprise attack on Pearl Harbor, Hawaii, on December 7, 1941, the Japanese preyed upon the split in American public opinion between isolationists and interventionists to further their policies. Ambiguity, threats, and promises of goodwill were elevated to an art form. These made possible the continued provision of strategic resources such as fuel oil and scrap iron to the Japanese economy, as well as the secret fortification of the islands mandated to Japan by the League of Nations.

Operational and tactical propaganda were directed against the military forces of the Western powers. In this regard Pearl Harbor a master stroke at the operational level, but at the same time it was, was a strategic blunder that utterly destroyed ten years of psychological opera-

tions directed toward the United States. Their belief that the "decadent" Americans would crumple at the first blow and meekly turn over most of the Pacific to Japan shows that the Japanese were every bit as "racist" as the Americans.

Operational and tactical Japanese psychological warfare included the broadcasts made by Radio Tokyo, especially those of Tokyo Rose, and the dropping of propaganda leaflets. An example of the latter is the depiction of an Aussie soldier fighting in New Guinea while an American soldier takes liberties with an Australian girl back home. Japanese leaflets directed at U.S. troops invariably depicted the Americans clad in World War I–style uniforms, complete with "soup bowl" helmets, equipment not seen in that army since the fall of the Philippines. The iconography was usually Oriental and the "English" text fractured. American troops eagerly gathered such efforts and traded them like baseball or bubble-gum cards, not for their "political" content but for their graphic pornography and hilarious texts. Surrender appeals ("You will be treated in accordance with the principles of Bushdo") were unlikely to have much appeal to troops who knew about the Bataan death march and the torture-murders of captured Americans on Guadalcanal.

Allied naval personnel were amused by Tokyo Rose's crocodile tears shed for "the poor boys on the _____, sunk last night by our brave submariners." The "poor boys," as likely as not, were enjoying the broadcast aboard the warship supposedly resting on the bottom. On the other hand, Radio Tokyo broadcasters, possibly borrowing a leaf from the Germans, did have the wit to broadcast the latest American popular music. Jazz, big band, bebop, jitterbug—the latest Tommy Dorsey or Glen Miller or Bing Crosby recordings—could be heard on Axis radio well before Allied broadcasts disseminated them. But U.S. sailors were so immune to the political blandishments of the likes of Tokyo Rose that such enemy broadcasts were actually piped through the public address systems of Pacific Fleet ships, both for the humor and for the sailors to catch up on the latest stateside hits. Japanese tactical psywar against Allied troops must be judged a complete failure. Nowhere has there been such great listenership with so little result.

Propaganda directed toward conquered Asian peoples formed the basis for the creation of Japan's envisioned Greater East Asian Co-Prosperity Sphere. All traces of former Western rule were to be eliminated in the regions the Japanese occupied. The Japanese occupiers forbade listening to Allied broadcasts, introduced pro–Japanese textbooks, replaced European language courses with Japanese courses, and trained local protégés for administrative positions. Toward the end of the war such propaganda shifted away from promoting Japanese language and culture to creating feelings of anticolonial nationalism, in an attempt to prevent the Western powers from taking back their former colonies.

The staged spectacle of the once lordly white rulers being forced by their Japanese conquerors to sweep the streets of Singapore was something not to be forgotten by Asian nationalists. The Japanese had staged what Communists termed "the propaganda of the deed"; they had completely outfought the British, the French, the Dutch, and the Americans in a fair fight, using the most modern weapons of Asian manufacture. Even the often bestial behavior of occupying Japanese troops could not obliterate such considerations. When the colonial powers returned in 1945, they found a changed Asia that would no longer tolerate foreign colonial overlordship. This was the one undoubted success of Japanese psychological warfare in World War II.

FURTHER READINGS

De Mendelssohn, Peter. *Japan's Political Warfare* (1944).
Foot, M. R. D., and Havens, T. R. H. "Psychological Warfare." In *The Historical Encyclopedia of World War II* (1980).
Margolin, Leo J. *Paper Bullets: A Brief Story of Psychological Warfare in World War II* (1946).
Sandler, Stanley. *Cease Resistance, It's Good for You: A History of U.S. Army Combat Psychological Operations* (1999).
U.S. Army Special Operations Command, Historical Archives, Civil Affairs and Psychological Operations Collection. Fort Bragg, N.C.
Warburg, James P. *Unwritten Treaty* (1946).

Robert J. Bunker

SEE ALSO Psychological Warfare, U.S.; Tokyo Rose

Psychological Warfare, U.S.

Psychological warfare, as defined by the U.S. joint chiefs of staff during World War II, consisted of the integrated use of all means, moral and physical—other than those of recognized military actions—that would tend to destroy the will of the enemy and to damage his political and economic capacity; that also would tend to deprive the enemy of the support, assistance, or sympathy of his allies or associates or neutrals; or that would tend to maintain, increase, or acquire the support, assistance, and sympathy of neutrals. By 1944 the broader generic term "psy-

chological warfare," and the older and more specific terms "combat propaganda" and "propaganda," had become virtually interchangeable. (There was also some feeling that "propaganda" had been in bad odor as a result of the work of the Nazi propaganda chief, Paul Joseph Goebbels, a man who could give lying a bad name.)

When properly applied, psychological warfare supposedly could bolster morale in one's own forces while so undermining an enemy's fighting spirit that collapse could occur within the first hours of hostilities. Psychological warfare could undermine the enemy's morale and destroy its will to resist, both on the main line of resistance and on the home front. It could destroy alliances, cause civil disorder, divide officers from the enlisted ranks and citizens from their leaders, and create chaos in the enemy's homeland. Psychological warfare required less in terms of personnel than did traditional armed forces, it could enhance the effectiveness of conventional weapons, and it could provide the final push to an already demoralized enemy. In short, its adherents claimed, psychological warfare could shorten wars, save both money and lives, and decrease the overall level of violence.

Psychological warfare was broadly divided into three interdependent classes during World War II: strategic, tactical, and consolidation. Strategic propaganda was directed to enemy and enemy-occupied countries, and had the double task of undermining the will to resist and sustaining the morale of those supporting the Allies over the long term. Tactical or combat propaganda was conducted against enemy forces in the forward areas and sought very specific, short-term goals. Consolidation propaganda was directed toward civilians in rear areas or areas recently occupied by Allied troops, to ensure their cooperation.

The weapons of psychological warfare were those of the civilian media in film, print, or audio form. During World War II, the armed forces relied primarily on the printed leaflet, newspaper, or news sheet. More than eight billion leaflets were dropped by aircraft or delivered by artillery shells worldwide by the Allied powers, the vast majority in Europe. In addition, the Allies used motion pictures and still photographs, and broadcast medium- and shortwave radio programs to the home fronts of their enemies. On the tactical level, U.S. military personnel conducted frontline radio propaganda programs and used loudspeakers and megaphones. Nearly every campaign in the Pacific and Asian theaters during World War II witnessed the use of some form of psychological warfare waged by either a civilian or a military agency.

In contrast to Europe, however, the Pacific war represented a vastly different world for Allied propagandists because of the number of operational theaters in the region, including the Southwest Pacific Area (SWPA) under General Douglas A. MacArthur; the South Pacific under Admiral William F. Halsey; and the Central and North Pacific theaters under Admiral Chester W. Nimitz. These areas at times overlapped the boundaries of the Southeast Asia Command (SEAC) under Britain's Lord Louis Mountbatten, the China theater under Generalissimo Chiang Kai-shek, and the China–Burma–India (CBI) theater under U.S. Army General Joseph W. Stilwell. Psychological warfare activities, as a rule, started much later in Asia and the Pacific than they did in Europe. At no time during the war were such activities coordinated by a single, regional Allied agency.

Other complications faced by propagandists in the Pacific theater included the huge geographic area held by Japanese military forces by mid-1942 and the diversity of the peoples inhabiting it. Reaching all possible targets and gaining the necessary supplies and equipment to mount a massive psychological warfare campaign proved difficult at best. In addition, adequate numbers of personnel familiar with the many Pacific peoples, including the Japanese, and their languages and cultures were always in short supply. Further complicating the task of the propagandists was the pervasive attitude that neither the Japanese soldier nor the Japanese civilian would surrender under any circumstances, and that psychological warfare was thus unlikely to succeed.

Although U.S. forces holding out against the Japanese in the Philippines undertook the initial Allied psychological warfare operations, with minimal success (hardly a surprise; they were losing the battle), the initial U.S. psychological warfare operations in the Pacific were conducted by the civilian Office of War Information (OWI) in New Caledonia and Australia in early 1942. The Foreign Information Service of the Office of the Coordinator of Information established an outpost in Sydney at this time to provide information to Australians about the U.S. war effort, and assisted U.S. Army officials with propaganda campaigns against Japan in the Dutch East Indies and South Pacific. The first step toward creating a military psychological warfare capability, however, came when Section D of the combined Allied Intelligence Bureau was formed on June 19, 1942. This unit was charged with conducting all manner of psychological warfare activities from the Malay States to the Solomons, and was officially known as the Far Eastern Liaison Organization (FELO), under Commander J. C. R. Proud, of the Royal Australian Naval Reserve. FELO consisted primarily of Australian military personnel, but also included British and Dutch nationals. It went from a membership of 5 in June 1942 to 474 by August 1945.

Although FELO was willing to support U.S. Army operations, the Americans did not recognize any interests in the Dutch East Indies or the states of Melanesia, and were hesitant to endorse FELO themes or take advantage of its expertise. Only slight contact was maintained between FELO and general headquarters (GHQ), SWPA, and the former came to see its operations as being outside General MacArthur's command and control. This created a certain tension because many Americans considered FELO to be "primarily [a] British Imperialistic Agency," even if under Australian control. FELO activities were therefore restricted in SWPA, and the U.S. Army did not widely use the group's valuable materials.

Very little combat psychological warfare was used on Guadalcanal or elsewhere in the South Pacific theater, commanded by Admiral William Halsey. Only a few local and entirely spontaneous operations, using leaflets and loudspeakers, were tried, due to the scarcity of resources and people, and lack of command support. FELO did provide propaganda for use on Bougainville, but no staff-level agency controlling psychological warfare existed in Halsey's command, although discussions were held about creating some form of capability in the theater between December 1942 and February 1943. Halsey allegedly regarded "psychological warfare as some impractical plaything of effete civilians."

The idea of creating a psychological warfare unit in the Southwest Pacific Area was considered as early as July 1943, but General MacArthur decided to wait until after the New Guinea campaign, when American forces would be clear of the colonial areas of the region and their political complications, to create such a body. He wanted at all costs to prevent the inclusion of non–Americans in any new psychological warfare branch, thereby avoiding inter–Allied, interservice political disputes. He also sought to avoid practicing the type of psychological warfare the Australians, British, and Dutch would find necessary to reestablish their colonial rule. As the return to the Philippines became more of a reality, MacArthur decided to create a purely American organization, comprised only of U.S. Army personnel and, where necessary, OWI civilians. In early June 1944 the Psychological Warfare Branch (PWB) was founded within SWPA/GHQ. In all respects, PWB was a fully independent, self-sufficient, special staff agency under military control, first under G-1 and then, by late September 1944, G-5. Soon after its founding, the branch was included in the Office of the Military Secretary to the Commander in Chief, and formed combat propaganda teams that later served with armies, corps, and divisions in the Philippines.

The closest the U.S. Navy came to creating a psychological warfare unit prior to 1944 was OP-16-W, the Special Warfare Branch of the Office of Naval Intelligence, formed on October 7, 1942. The five naval officers, one navy yeoman, and five civilians of OP-16-W assisted the OWI with its campaigns. Prior to mid-1944 some leaflet work had been done by a team of fifteen to twenty U.S. Marine Corps language officers who prepared stock surrender leaflets and antimorale materials, but according to one U.S. Marine colonel, "A few early attempts, crude at best, to wage psychological warfare brought negative results," because the attitude and training of the Japanese soldier provided a natural defense.

Psychological warfare in the Pacific included radio operations. In November 1943 the OWI sought JCS approval to erect a 100-kw transmitter in Hawaii to relay Voice of America programs from San Francisco to Japan and the Far East, but it was not until July 1944 that OWI received significant support from U.S. Navy officials (following a visit to Hawaii by President Franklin Roosevelt and OWI director Elmer Davis). OWI eventually established radio transmitters for propaganda purposes in Australia and the Philippines, as well as on Pacific islands including Hawaii, Guam, and Saipan. The efforts of OWI, however, were soon eclipsed by the U.S. Navy and the U.S. Army.

In 1943, within the central Pacific command there existed the Joint Intelligence Center, Pacific Ocean Area (JICPOA), a joint army–navy body. Although this office had filled requests for leaflets in the Gilberts, Marshalls, and Marianas prior to mid-1944, it did not have a formal psychological warfare function. This changed on July 20, 1944, when the Psychological Warfare Service, JICPOA, was created under Colonel Dana Johnson of the U.S. Army. The PWS was a military body that eventually consisted of twelve navy and army officers, twelve nisei (second-generation Japanese Americans), twelve Japanese prisoners, and three navy yeomen. OWI personnel, whose talents were used by the army, were never an official part of the organization because of the military opinion that psychological warfare in combat areas was a function of military command, and should not be entrusted to civilian personnel.

The PWS task was multifaceted and typical of psychological warfare commands in the Pacific. It was to prepare plans; conduct strategic operations against the Japanese home islands and occupied areas; establish, operate, and maintain units for the rapid supply of combat propaganda to forward areas; and train and equip teams for attachment to field units. It was also to conduct consolidation campaigns in cooperation with civil affairs units, and to initiate a course of instruction on psychological warfare for combat units.

Within a month of its creation, the PWS had produced more than three hundred sixty thousand copies of fourteen leaflets and newspapers, using OWI facilities in Hawaii, on the American mainland, and on Saipan. Significant transportation and technical problems, however, hampered production, but by V-J Day (August 1945) more than six million leaflets were being printed per month, 95 percent of them going to Japan for aerial distribution.

Elsewhere, in the Far East, OWI established a China Division in Chungking in late 1941, followed by an OSS Morale Operations unit in early 1944. Both groups provided leaflets and information for Allied military use in China, targeting Chinese military and civilian personnel as well as Japanese audiences. After General Albert C. Wedemeyer replaced General Joseph Stilwell as commander of U.S. forces in China and CBI, he appointed his intelligence officer, Colonel Joseph K. Dickey, to be in charge of psychological warfare operations at theater headquarters, coordinating military needs with the activities of OWI and the OSS in the region.

In early 1945 a theater directive on psychological warfare was issued by Wedemeyer and guided such activities for the remainder of the war, marking a clear division of responsibility among the U.S. Army, the OWI, and the OSS. The order also created the post of theater psychological warfare officer (TPWO) under the theater G-3 (later G-5). Along with eight other U.S. Army officers and twenty-five enlisted men from headquarters, U.S. forces, China theater, he served as the link between the various field agencies and the theater commander. In addition, the TPWO was to assume active control of operations and represent the theater commander in all psychological warfare decisions and activities, as well as review all OWI and OSS printed material, a standard operating procedure throughout the Pacific and Asia.

By July 1945 the average number of leaflets dropped per month in China averaged more than 800,000, and production soon expanded to well in excess of 1 million per month. The total number of leaflets produced and disseminated to Japanese military units and Chinese civilians had grown from 105,000 per month to over 4.2 million in June 1945. Although combat psychological warfare in China always remained strictly a U.S. operation, the units attached to the China theater created well over 200 different leaflets in Japanese, Chinese, and Annamite French, producing nearly 54 million units between December 3, 1944, and September 5, 1945. Over

75 percent of these leaflets were dropped between June 22 and August 1945.

There was need for a unit to operate in Assam, north Burma, and Thailand. As a result, on October 6, 1943, the Assam Psychological Warfare Team was created. Within a year, it numbered some fifty people, the majority stationed at the forward headquarters, CBI, with additional personnel at leaflet printing centers in Ledo and Calcutta. Between late 1943 and late 1944, the team produced and disseminated some 1.5 million leaflets in the Northern Combat Area Command (NCAC), 900,000 of sixty-six different types to Japanese targets and 400,000 of forty types to Burmese groups. More than 500,000 were delivered in September and October 1944 alone.

After the fall of Myitkyina, in northern Burma, in 1944, combat psychological warfare was increasingly accepted. With the cooperation of OWI/India, a psychological warfare section consisting of five U.S. Army officers and four enlisted men was officially established as an independent staff section at NCAC headquarters on September 23, 1944. It formed part of a larger theater psychological warfare section at CBI/GHQ, established on the same date.

Significant political differences between the United States and Great Britain concerning what psychological warfare themes and messages should be used in Southeast Asia delayed the start of a comprehensive campaign in this region. After months of negotiations, on April 29, 1944, SEAC headquarters issued a directive creating the combined Psychological Warfare Division, SEAC, under Lord Louis Mountbatten. It included representatives from Britain's Political Warfare Executive and Special Operations Executive, as well as members of the American OWI and OSS. According to the SEAC directive, the new body would "not deal with controversial political or postwar matters," but direct its activities toward combat, consolidation, and strategic psychological warfare, in order to meet immediate wartime needs. In spite of these assurances, however, the OWI refused to participate in most propaganda activities in SEAC, leaving the U.S. role to the OSS.

Although psychological warfare was practiced against Japanese civilian and military audiences throughout Asia and the Pacific during World War II by a variety of Allied military and civilian agencies, its effect on the outcome of the war was problematic, especially when compared with the much more extensive and seemingly more successful operations of psychological warfare agencies in the European and Mediterranean theaters.

One area of U.S. psychological warfare did enjoy undoubted success, however. This was the well-known "city" leaflets showered on Japanese cities. These instruments showed the U.S. Air Force's B-29 heavy bomber and listed Japanese cities, with the exact dates on which they would be bombed by those B-29s. Postwar interrogation reports indicate that the Japanese were influenced by these leaflets to the extent that production in targeted cities dropped by as much as one-fourth just before such bombings. Civilians also noted that those officials who went on the most about "last-ditch" fighting seemed to be the first to pile family and belongings into a truck and head for the country. The emperor of Japan admitted to his interrogator that he had found such a leaflet in the Imperial Palace garden and became depressed regarding Japan's prospects for victory. Although the success of U.S. psychological operations against the Japanese military was problemmatical, against the Japanese civilian population it can be judged a success, albeit very late in the war.

FURTHER READINGS

Laurie, Clayton D. "Simply One More Weapon of War: The U.S. Army and Psychological Warfare Operations, 1918–1945" (unpublished manuscript, U.S. Army Center of Military History, 1992).

———. "The Ultimate Dilemma of Psychological Warfare in the Pacific: Enemies Who Don't Take Surrender and GIs Who Don't Take Prisoners." In U.S. Army Center of Military History, *The U.S. Army and World War II. Selected Papers from the Army's Commemorative Conferences* (1998).

Paddock, Alfred, Jr. *United States Army Special Warfare, Its Origins: Psychological and Unconventional Warfare, 1941–1962.*

Sandler, Stanley. *Cease Resistance; It's good for You: A History of U.S. Army Combat Psychological Operations* (1999).

Clayton D. Laurie

SEE ALSO Office of Strategic Services, Detachment 101; Office of Strategic Services in the Pacific; Psychological Warfare, Japanese

Quezon, Manuel (1878–1944)

Filipino politician and first president of the Philippine commonwealth. Born at Baler in Tayabas (now Quezon) Province on August 19, 1878, Quezon came from a humble background. Ancestrally a mestizo, he spoke with an Iberian accent and looked more European than Malay. Quezon graduated from the College of San Juan de Letran, participated in uprisings against Spain and the United States, and, following a short incarceration, pursued a law degree at Manila's University of Santo Tomas. A onetime prosecuting attorney in Mindoro and Tayabas Provinces as well as the latter's governor, he served in the Philippine Assembly, led the Nacionalista Party, acted as Resident Commissioner to the United States, and presided over the Philippine Senate before his election in 1935 as chief executive of the commonwealth government.

Quezon, an intelligent and intuitive politician, detested minutiae but persisted in operating the commonwealth in a very personal manner. More an extemporizer than methodical designer of programs, he was an impressive orator, conceited about his looks and attire, charming around women, and a frank and amusing talker. As commonwealth president, Quezon believed security was the prime and critical necessity of the Philippines. He favored a defensive policy complemented by League of Nations membership and the archipelago's neutralization. Filipinos should be trained for military service; however, he opposed the establishment and support of expensive military installations when not at war. In late 1934, Quezon asked the Roosevelt administration to request Congress that legislation enacted in 1926 furnishing military advisers to Latin America be revised to embrace the commonwealth. Once the law was amended, he selected his friend and compadre General Douglas MacArthur, the retiring chief of staff of the U.S. Army, as his principle

military adviser. The National Defense Act, passed by the Philippine National Assembly on December 21, 1935, provided for an army, with the constabulary of no more than ten thousand enlistees, augmented by motor torpedo boats and army air units whose principal mission was seacoast protection. Critics of Quezon's plan complained of the navy's inadequate size, the financial strain on the budget, the threat of military dictatorship, and the retention of an American presence in the Philippines.

Quezon and MacArthur had become fast friends during the latter's tour as major general and commanding officer of the Philippine Department between 1928 and 1930. Quezon had recommended MacArthur's appointment as Philippine governor general. As military adviser, the general convinced the commonwealth president that the islands could be defended prior to independence with a 19,000-man permanent army and a citizen reserve of 400,000 at a complete expenditure of $80 million.

But by 1939, Quezon had become disillusioned with MacArthur's advice. Chinese military defeats at the hands of Japan and the outbreak of war in Europe persuaded Quezon that the Philippines were vulnerable. Feeling he had been misled by MacArthur's assurances in the face of a growing Japanese threat, Quezon favored immediate independence and neutrality. He created a department of defense, which diminished the significance of MacArthur's position. He also terminated public school military instruction and slowly curtailed the Reserve Officers Training Corps (ROTC). Quezon even asked the U.S. High Commissioner for the Philippines, Francis B. Sayre, to return MacArthur to Washington. However, when President Roosevelt selected MacArthur to command the U.S. Army Forces in the Far East (USAFFE), making the Filipino army a component of the American military, Quezon quickly reversed his attitude and warmed once again to the general.

On December 8, 1941, Japanese aircraft raided the Philippines and, among other places, bombed targets at Baguio, the commonwealth's summer capital. Once the Japanese invaded and the situation became critical, Quezon assigned Jorge Vargas, his executive secretary, and Josè Laurel to stay behind and deal with the enemy while he withdrew to the island fortress of Corregidor on December 24. Six days later he was inaugurated for a second term as commonwealth chief executive. Demonstrating his endorsement of MacArthur, on January 3, 1942, Quezon ordered a payment of $640,000 to the general and certain members of his staff, a largesse that was kept secret for decades. Ten days later he transmitted a message to Washington by way of the general lamenting Roosevelt's failure to fulfill a promise to dispatch assistance to the archipelago. He pressed the president to throw the whole might of the United States against Japan immediately. Quezon was angered by the Allies' Europe-first policy and disturbed by growing antagonism between Filipino and American troops on Bataan. He considered surrendering himself to the Japanese and declaring independence and neutrality (another high-level proposal that remained a secret for years after the war). Once reassured by Roosevelt that Washington would never forsake its Philippine ally, Quezon recanted.

In February, Quezon departed Corregidor in U.S. submarine *Swordfish* for Panay and then via B-17 bomber to Australia. He later established a Philippine government-in-exile in Washington. His primary concerns were to explain publicly the commonwealth's part in the conflict and to make the United States mindful of the distinct national interest of Filipinos. He established a cabinet, accepted membership in the United Nations, and attended sessions of the Pacific War Council. Upon the expiration of his second term, the U.S. Congress voted to keep him in office. Terminally ill with tuberculosis, Quezon died at Saranac Lake, New York, on August 1, 1944, only a few month short of the liberation of his homeland. His remains were returned to the Philippines in 1946.

FURTHER READINGS

Friend, Theodore. *Between Two Empires: The Ordeal of the Philippines 1929–1946* (1965).

Gopinath, Aruna. *Manuel L. Quezon: The Tutelary Democrat* (1987).

Karnow, Stanley. *In Our Image: America's Empire in the Philippines* (1989).

Petillo, Carol Morris. *Douglas MacArthur: The Philippine Years* (1981).

Rodney J. Ross

SEE ALSO MacArthur, Douglas; Philippines, Fall of the; Roxas, Manuel; Romulo, Carlos P.

R

Rangers

The U.S. 6th Ranger Battalion was born of the desire of Lieutenant General Walter Krueger to build upon the accomplishments of the Alamo Scouts, small strike-reconnaissance teams, in the Southwest Pacific Area. While planning for the forthcoming invasion of the Philippines, General Krueger realized that a battalion-sized unit of highly trained infantrymen would be useful in the defeat of Japan. In 1944, Krueger authorized the formation of a Ranger battalion. The new outfit took its organizational lineage from the U.S. 98th Field Artillery Battalion stationed in Port Moresby, New Guinea. The 98th had a brief, but unique, history. In response to the start of World War II in Europe, President Franklin D. Roosevelt authorized the expansion of the peacetime American military through the National Defense Program. In January 1941, the U.S. Army federalized the U.S. 98th Field Artillery Battalion at Fort Lewis, Washington. After the attack on Pearl Harbor in December 1941, the battalion was transferred to the Southwest Pacific Area. In 1944, the U.S. Sixth Army absorbed the artillery unit.

Turning an artillery battalion into an elite fighting unit was a difficult task, and General Krueger selected Lieutenant Colonel Henry A. Mucci, known for his leadership capabilities and toughness, as the commander of the newly formed U.S. 6th Ranger Battalion. Mucci was graduated in 1936 from United States Military Academy at West Point. He later attended the Infantry School at Fort Benning, Georgia. Before the attack on Pearl Harbor, he was stationed at Fort Warren, Wyoming, as a company commander. When war broke out in 1941, Mucci was reassigned to the Hawaiian Islands, where he trained in jungle warfare.

Before training of the new unit could start, Colonel Mucci had to make some organizational changes to the battalion. Because he wanted an all-volunteer outfit, Mucci allowed transfers to other units. Then he divided the battalion into six companies consisting of two platoons. Each platoon was separated into two 11-man assault teams. Mucci's insistence on an all-volunteer unit and the rigorous training for Rangers thinned the ranks. Training for Ranger candidates included physical conditioning, weapons firing, small-unit tactics, hand-to-hand combat, jungle warfare, and amphibious training. In the end, the short, pipe-smoking, Mucci put his men through the toughest infantry training course in the Pacific. Mucci, however, was not just an observer. Known for his inspirational leadership and commitment to his soldiers, Mucci trained along with the enlisted men and officers.

In October 1944, the U.S. Army invaded the Philippines. General Douglas MacArthur's first target was the island of Leyte. The task of seizing Leyte was given to the U.S. Sixth Army commanded by General Krueger. The Leyte invasion plan called for the landing of two corps consisting of four infantry divisions on the east coast of the island. Sixth Army planners were concerned that several small islands that guarded the approaches to the assault beaches created navigational dangers that could cause naval vessels to run aground.

Krueger tapped the U.S. 6th Ranger Battalion to seize the islands of Dinagot, Homonhon, and Suluan from the Japanese and place navigation lights near the shores to provide guidance for the task force steaming into Philippine waters. On October 17, after being delayed for several hours by rough seas, Rangers landed unopposed on Suluan. They immediately moved inland and assaulted four buildings. A small group of Japanese soldiers counterattacked, killing one U.S. soldier, but when the Americans returned fire, the enemy troops melted into the jungles. Inside the building, the Rangers smashed a radio and seized documents. Unfortunately, none of the documents were the coveted coastal mining charts. The same day, Rangers landed on Dinagot. Encountering no resistance, they placed a navigation beacon. On October 18, the Rangers, delayed for a day by rough seas, landed on Homonhon, where they met no resistance and placed a channel beacon light. With the help of these navigational beacons, the American invasion fleet entered the waters off of Leyte with little difficulty.

In January 1945, the U.S. Army invaded the main Philippine island of Luzon. As U.S. soldiers fought toward Manila, Filipino guerilla leaders told American officials that around five hundred U.S. prisoners of war were being held in a prison camp near Cabanatuan City. General Douglas MacArthur and Krueger feared that the Japanese might kill the POWs, many of them survivors of the Bataan death march. Krueger called for a daring rescue mission of these sick and wounded prisoners and charged the U.S. 6th Ranger Battalion with the task. On January 27, 1945, Colonel Mucci began to plan for the raid with all available information from army intelligence, Alamo Scouts, and Filipino guerillas. Mucci was able to secure air cover from P-61 Black Widows night fighters and assistance in the countryside from Filipino resistance leaders.

On January 28, the rescue force, which consisted of 128 Rangers, Alamo Scouts, and Filipino guerillas, left for Guimba 20 miles away. From Guimba, the group moved 5 miles closer to the village of Balincarin. For the next day and a half the Ranger force continued to gather information on the prison encampment and update the plan of attack. On the January 29, 200 more soldiers coincidentally reinforced the 223-man guard detail. The raid began at nightfall the next day at 7:44 P.M. The Rangers charged forward killing the perimeter guards and opening the main gate. Once inside the compound the Rangers systematically killed the remaining guards and troops while rounding up the confused prisoners. In all, the Japanese suffered more than four hundred casualties. After the raid, the Ranger force and the 512 liberated prisoners began their long 25-mile return trip in the night to American lines. Many of the sick and wounded prisoners needed assistance along the way. Rangers commandeered carts from local villagers to carry the incapacitated. The next day, as the tired group neared Sibul, Mucci radioed for assistance. In a short time, trucks and ambulances arrived to transport the men back to safety. Ultimately, the successful Cabanatuan raid was the zenith of the U.S. 6th Ranger Battalion's activity in the Pacific war.

In June 1945, Rangers played a small part in the destruction of the Shobu Group in the mountains of northern Luzon. The Sixth Army plan to defeat the Japanese army in the Cagayuan Valley region consisted of a main thrust over mountainous terrain on Route 5. While this attack was conducted, Krueger wanted to maintain pressure on the Shobu Group with limited attacks along Route 11. To accomplish this task, I Corps created a small detachment of infantry companies from the 32d and 33d Infantry Divisions, one company of Rangers, and artillery units into a combat team named Task Force Connolly. Commanded by Major Robert V. Connolly, Task Force Connolly was sent into the region around the town of Apparri and helped to attack Japanese troops in the area.

For the final part of the war, the U.S. 6th Ranger Battalion was assigned tasks unbecoming of an elite unit. Army Rangers guarded Sixth Army headquarters, hunted for bypassed Japanese soldiers, and preformed minor reconnaissance patrols. On September 15, 1945, the battalion was transferred to Japan as part of the American occupation force. For its brief but spectacular history, the 6th Ranger Battalion was awarded the Presidential Unit Citation and the Philippine Presidential Unit Citation. In December, the battalion was deactivated and sent back to the United States.

FURTHER READINGS

Breuer, William. *Retaking the Philippines: America's Return to Corregidor and Bataan, October 1944–March 1945* (1985.)

Cannon, M., Hamlin. *The United States Army in World War II War in the Pacific: Leyte: Return to the Philippines* (1954).

Krueger, Walter. *From Down Under to Nippon: The Story of the Sixth Army in World War II* (1979).

Lock, John D. *To Fight With Intrepidity: The Complete History of the U.S. Army Rangers, 1622 to the Present* (1998).

McRaven, William H. *Spec Ops Case Studies in Special Operations Warfare: Theory and Practice* (1995).

Smith, Robert R. *The United States Army in World War II War in the Pacific: Triumph in the Philippines* (1963, 1984).

Erik D. Carlson

SEE ALSO Alamo Scouts; Philippines, Anti-Japanese Guerillas in

Romulo, Carlos P. (1899–1985)

"People of the Philippines! This is the Voice of Freedom! I am speaking to you from the Tunnel of Corregidor, from the front lines of Bataan. . . . " With those words, Major

Carlos P. Romulo began another radio address to the Japanese-occupied Philippines.

Just before the war, in early December 1941, Romulo, a brilliant, articulate reporter, editor-in-chief, and part owner of the DMHM chain of newspapers, and a Columbia University graduate, was one of the leading citizens of Manila. He was an unfailing supporter of Philippine President Manuel Quezon and an outspoken champion of autonomy and freedom for the Philippines.

He had a deep hatred of imperialism, a hatred that grew when he toured the Far East just before the war. Yet he loved democracy and understood the telling differences between American imperialism and that brand practiced by the French, British, and Dutch. Romulo warned that the subject peoples of Southeast Asia (other than the Filipinos) would not only submit to the Japanese and not fight, they would welcome them.

War broke out in the Philippines on December 8. Romulo, a personal friend of General Douglas MacArthur, the principle American military leader in the Philippines, received a call on December 16 bringing him to active duty in his reserve rank as a major. Romulo had already written the articles that would win him a Pulitzer Prize for his reporting (articles that warned of the Japanese threat), and now MacArthur placed him in charge of press and radio. His task was to keep the citizens of the Philippines alert yet calm. The Americans wanted to prevent the dislocation and impediment to military maneuvers caused by panicked, displaced civilians.

MacArthur told Romulo, "Keep 'em warned, but don't panic them. Always tell them the truth. People can stand the truth." Romulo operated at first from Manila with its active press and numerous radio stations. He issued press releases and helped editors select headlines that would simultaneously soothe and inform. Hardly more than a week later, however, the Japanese drove the Americans and Romulo from the city to the fortress island of Corregidor. Cut off from normal communications, President Quezon needed to reach his people with words of hope and truth. So he called on Romulo to establish a radio station. MacArthur selected its name, "The Voice of Freedom."

Romulo wrote radio programs designed to alert public opinion to the dangers facing the Philippines. His Corregidor station played comforting music and whatever good news that could be found: "Don't listen to the Japanese, don't believe their lies, the Japanese victory is temporary. Keep your faith in America. America will return and liberate the islands." The fight was not *for* America, it was *with* America and *for* freedom.

Three times a day, Romulo spoke to the Filipinos and Americans fighting on Bataan and to the civilians under enemy occupation. He toured the Bataan battlefields to talk to the soldiers there. Romulo served MacArthur on Corregidor both as press coordinator and as an aide-de-camp. He remained on the island when MacArthur was ordered out in March 1942.

The Bataan army was collapsing in early April. MacArthur and Quezon agreed that Romulo must get out of the Philippines. He was a wanted man by the Japanese, a "traitor" with a price on his head. Romulo left Corregidor for Bataan late on April 8. After some wild driving through the rear areas of the defeated army, Romulo caught a ride in the last aircraft to fly out, a salvaged, patched, navy biplane. He was literally the last man out of Bataan.

MacArthur sent Romulo to the United States with orders to tell the Philippine story to the American people. Romulo reported to both President Quezon and to President Franklin D. Roosevelt. Then he was off on a lecture tour that would cover every state in the Union. He met with relatives of the men trapped in the Philippines, he gave interviews, and he lectured at banquets. He spoke to factory workers, and he spoke to Congress. "Remember Bataan!" He brought the Philippine resistance alive to the people in America. He told them of the small bands of poorly-armed guerrillas, men who were keeping the faith. Because of Romulo's efforts, the Philippines were no longer a distant country. Romulo was the embodiment of the country. He was its representative, its chronicler who told everyone about the fight on Bataan and Corregidor. He became a celebrity.

MacArthur called now–Brigadier General Romulo back to the Pacific in late 1944. Romulo and the new Philippine President, Sergio Osmeña (Quezon had died in the United States), joined MacArthur on October 20, 1944, in USS *Nashville*'s motor whaler as it carried them to Red Beach on Leyte, the Philippines. The party disembarked into knee-deep water and waded ashore. MacArthur addressed the Filipino people over a portable radio transmitter, Osmeña spoke to his countrymen, and Romulo closed by announcing restoration of his 1942 radio program.

"People of the Philippines, after two years of silence you are again hearing the Voice of Freedom. It was a voice that first cried out to you in the anguish of war. It speaks to you again in exhilaration. For this is liberation that brings us home."

Romulo's stay in the Philippines was short, however, for MacArthur ordered him back to Washington. Once again, Romulo addressed Congress. He told them of Mac-

Arthur's return to Leyte and of the loyalty of the Filipinos. In an amazing feat of guerrilla organization, Romulo's family, hiding for the past two years on Luzon, listened on a radio to Romulo address Congress.

Romulo returned to Luzon and joined the march on Manila. He was with MacArthur when the American flag was raised over Corregidor. Even now, his stay in his homeland was to be brief. President Osmeña sent Romulo to San Francisco in April 1945 as the chairman of the Philippine delegation to the newly organizing United Nations. It was an inspired choice. Romulo became an impassioned champion of the small nations of Asia.

Romulo returned to the Philippines to witness and record the celebrations marking Philippine independence on July 4, 1946.

After the Japanese surrender, Romulo continued his fervent opposition to imperialism. He was instrumental in ensuring that the word "independence" rather than "self-governing" would apply in the United Nation's charter in referring to that international body's goal for former colonies and protectorates.

Romulo remained in the United States for seventeen years as Philippine ambassador and as fourth U.N. General Assembly president, the first Asian to hold that post. However, Romulo's long stay in the United States did leave him open to the unfounded charge that he was merely a spokesman for that superpower, and he did seem a remote figure to the average poverty-stricken Filipino, to whom Romulo's eighty-four honorary degrees (mostly from U.S. institutions) and almost one hundred special medals and citations meant little.

Romulo returned to his homeland to serve as president of the University of the Philippines and later as Philippine foreign minister. He died in December 1985.

FURTHER READINGS

James, D. Clayton. *The Years of MacArthur*, 3 vols. (1970–1985).

Romulo, Carlos P. *I Saw the Fall of the Philippines* (1942).

Wells, Evelyn. *Carlos P. Romulo: Voice of Freedom* (1964).

John W. Whitman

SEE ALSO MacArthur, Douglas; Philippines, Fall of the

Roosevelt, Franklin Delano (1882–1945)

Franklin Delano Roosevelt, thirty-second President of the United States (1933–1945), was born into an aristocratic New York family in 1882. He attended Groton, Harvard, and Columbia law school, and briefly practiced law with

a prominent Wall Street firm. He was a distant cousin of Theodore Roosevelt, who became the twenty-sixth President of the United States. In 1905, Franklin married Theodore's niece, Eleanor Roosevelt. Always imbued with the ideals of public service, Roosevelt was elected to the New York state senate in 1910 and was appointed assistant secretary of the navy in 1913 in the Wilson administration. In the navy department Roosevelt pushed for American involvement in World War I and championed American membership in the League of Nations after that war.

Roosevelt, a rising star in politics, was nominated for the vice-presidency in 1920 by the Democratic Party. The Republicans won a landslide victory that year, but Roosevelt emerged as a Democratic heir-apparent. He contracted polio in 1921, which led to immense suffering, permanent paralysis of his legs, and the seeming end of his political career. But he struggled back, and in 1924 took an active role in the Democratic campaign, continuing to advance the cause of the League and Wilsonian internationalism. In 1928 he was elected governor of New York. In the wake of the Great Depression, Roosevelt was elected president in 1932 in a landslide victory.

Roosevelt's top priority in his first two terms was to alleviate the depression by means of government programs—the so-called New Deal. In the realm of foreign affairs, he was handicapped by the isolationist mood that gripped the country. One of his first major acts was to recognize the U.S.S.R., which the Soviets hoped would deter Japanese aggression and which ultimately established the basis for wartime U.S.-Soviet cooperation. FDR, as he was universally known, also improved U.S. relations with Latin America, renouncing the use of force in the region in 1933. This led to more extensive hemispheric defense cooperation after 1939. Finally, in his first term he sought to lower tariffs in order to stimulate trade and promote economic recovery.

The mid and late 1930s were marked by the rise of Fascist aggression in Europe and Asia. Congress feared that this aggression might lead to a new world war, and reflecting the general American mood that World War I had been an unnecessary tragedy, passed legislation designed to prevent any American involvement. The Neutrality Acts of 1935, 1936, and 1937 required the president to place an arms embargo on both aggressor and victim. Further, belligerents had to pay for nonmilitary goods in cash and ship the purchases themselves. FDR was reluctant to challenge the stranglehold of the isolationists on American foreign policy. For example, after Japan invaded China in 1937, Roosevelt called for the "quarantine" of the aggressors, but drew back after public opinion reacted strongly against this speech.

The outbreak of World War II in 1939 enabled Roosevelt to secure a revision of the Neutrality Acts so that belligerents could buy arms on a cash-and-carry basis. In practice, this favored Britain, whose navy controlled the Atlantic. The fall of France to Nazi invasion in June 1940 shocked American public opinion. Roosevelt obtained $1.7 billion in additional defense spending (including funds for a 2-ocean navy), transferred fifty obsolete destroyers to Britain in exchange for Caribbean bases, and instituted the first peacetime draft in American history. Despite the urgency of the situation, Roosevelt moved relatively cautiously, because his top priority in 1940 was to secure re-election. Once this was achieved, he had much greater freedom to aid the opponents of Germany and Japan.

At the end of 1940, for example, the British could no longer pay cash for war purchases, so FDR devised the concept of "lend-lease." Lend-lease empowered FDR to transfer war materiel to any country deemed "vital to the defense of the United States," with the understanding that such materiel would, in theory, be returned after the war. Also in 1940, at Roosevelt's urging, the United States began the first peacetime draft of its young men, and the war production program was accelerated. In early 1941, FDR agreed to repair British ships in U.S. shipyards, and extended U.S. naval patrols as far as Iceland. Furthermore, Roosevelt aided China in order to tie down Japanese forces, and thus prevent Japan from attacking British, French, or Dutch possessions in the Far East. In addition to financial aid, American military personnel were transferred to China in the guise of a "volunteer group"—the so-called Flying Tigers.

Historians have long debated FDR's wartime leadership. He was clearly one of the most significant presidents—the effects of his decisions are still felt today—but at the same time he was a highly enigmatic figure. This was deliberate—subtle and devious (his successor, Harry S. Truman, termed him, "cold, cold to the bone"), he often acted through surrogates, and he disliked having his policy deliberations documented. His actions are therefore subject to wide interpretation. For example, William Langer denies that FDR had a strategy and argues that he simply reacted to events. Robert Dallek claims FDR was a prisoner of public opinion. Stephen Ambrose considers that FDR's wartime policies were "dictated by military necessity." Many conservatives, like Robert Nisbet, view FDR as a naïf, swindled by the crafty Stalin. Conspiratorialists insist that FDR feverishly schemed to enter the war at Britain's side, and "sold out"

Eastern Europe during the war. Some even claim that FDR maneuvered Japan into attacking Pearl Harbor, and knew the attack was coming, but let it happen in order to unite the country. Presumably, the crafty FDR could even see into the future, and foresaw that Hitler would declare war on the United States after a *Japanese* attack on the Hawaiian base. George Morgenstern, Charles Beard, and Harry Elmer Barnes exemplify this school of thought. Finally, Warren F. Kimball, Waldo Heinrichs, and Keith Sainsbury make a convincing case that FDR had a long-term strategy not driven by the immediate needs of public opinion or the military situation. They show that FDR participated in the planning of major operations, closely followed their unfolding, and overruled his military advisers when necessary. In short, he ran the war.

In *Threshold of War,* Heinrichs demonstrates that Hitler's attack on Russia in June 1941 fundamentally changed the U.S. strategic situation worldwide. From that moment on, FDR's central concern was to ensure the survival of the Soviet Union, for the defeat of the Soviet Union would mean a Nazi-dominated Eurasia. FDR particularly wanted to deter Japan from attacking Siberia. From deciphered Japanese diplomatic cables, he knew that the Japanese were debating whether to attack Siberia or Southeast Asia, and that the Germans were naturally encouraging Japan to choose the former. In response, FDR's strategy from July to December 1941 was to contain Japan by building positions of strength in Southeast Asia. This presented the Japanese with a dilemma—they could hardly move north into Siberia while leaving a large and growing American threat behind them in the south. This strategy, of course, ran the risk that Japan would attack the United States before the containment structure was complete.

The first step was to shut off the supply of oil to Japan from the United States. Sanctions had been contemplated for some time, and were finally imposed on July 26, 1941. Japan's occupation of southern Indochina provided the pretext for the sanctions, but a more compelling reason was to inhibit Japan from attacking Russia, which Japan could not do without an assured supply of oil.

FDR moved to strengthen the Philippines, ordering hundreds of B-17s and P-40s to the islands, and approved MacArthur's plan to train a 120,000-man Filipino army/militia. FDR thought that the B-17s would be especially effective in deterring Japan from attacking Russia, because from the Philippines the bombers could strike Japan and land in Siberia, if Japan and Russia were at war. FDR met Churchill at Argentia Bay, Newfoundland, in August 1941 and there encouraged the British to increase their strength in Malaya. FDR agreed to permit the U.S. Navy to escort convoys in the western Atlantic, which released British naval assets for the Far East. Churchill agitated for an explicit U.S. guarantee for Malaya and the Dutch East Indies against Japanese aggression, but FDR would not go this far.

Parallel to the effort to deter Japan from attacking was the search for a diplomatic solution. FDR wanted to avoid war with Japan if he could do so honorably in order to concentrate on what he and high U.S. policymakers felt was the more important European theater. On November 20, the Japanese presented a plan for a modus vivendi, which entailed a relaxation of trade restrictions (especially oil) in exchange for a withdrawal of Japanese troops from southern Indochina. However, the Japanese also wanted the Americans to cease aiding China during projected Sino-Japanese peace negotiations, a condition that was unacceptable to FDR. Furthermore, the world situation was not conducive to conciliation—Japanese troopships were sailing, and the Nazis were at the gates of Moscow. Thus, on November 26, Secretary of State Cordell Hull presented the Ten Point Note, which demanded that the Japanese withdraw all forces from China and Indochina. These conditions were anathema to the Japanese, and they unleashed their assaults on Hawaii, the Philippines, and Southeast Asia on December 7–8, 1941.

FDR's goals in 1942 were to keep Russia in the war, to keep the anti-Axis alliance together, and to maintain unity on the home front. Allied strategy was to crush Germany first, but the question was how. Stalin demanded a second front in France, but Churchill adamantly opposed this. FDR insisted that American troops had to engage the Germans in combat somewhere in 1942, and in July, Churchill agreed to an Anglo-American invasion of French North Africa in November. Meanwhile, FDR rushed troops to the Pacific to stem the Japanese advance, and the naval victory at the battle of Midway in June was followed by an amphibious assault on the island of Guadalcanal.

In January 1943, FDR met Churchill at Casablanca in Morocco. Stalin was invited to attend but claimed that the military situation did not permit his leaving the U.S.S.R. Here FDR announced the war demand of the "unconditional surrender" of Germany, Italy, and Japan. He thereby sought to keep the anti-Axis coalition together. FDR feared that Stalin might negotiate a separate peace with Hitler, and hoped that the "unconditional surrender" formula would discourage Stalin from doing so. At Casablanca, FDR and Churchill agreed to conduct a combined bomber offensive against Germany and to attack Sicily in the summer of 1943. The future of France

was a contentious issue at this conference. Churchill backed General Charles de Gaulle as the leader of the Free French, but FDR wanted to subordinate De Gaulle to General Alphonse Giraud. After a brief show of amity, De Gaulle worked relentlessly and ultimately successfully to expel Giraud from the leadership of the Free French movement.

The Allied victories at Stalingrad, Tunisia, and Guadalcanal in early 1943 required the Allies to decide the organization of the postwar world. In *The Juggler,* Warren F. Kimball argues that FDR formulated a vision of the postwar world sometime in 1942. FDR thought the postwar political system should consist of the Big Four—the United States, Britain, the Soviet Union, and China—as guarantors of the peace, while colonial empires would be dismantled, and the United States would fund postwar reconstruction. In particular, the "disturbers of the peace"—Germany and Japan—would have to be disarmed, and Germany broken up into a number of independent states. FDR's vision could only be realized with Soviet cooperation, which he believed would be possible once Stalin's demands for the U.S.S.R.'s 1941 frontiers and for the dismemberment of Germany were satisfied. Roosevelt zealously pursued this dream of postwar U.S.-Soviet cooperation for the remainder of his life, and this political goal decisively influenced American military strategy during that period.

The surrender of Italy in September 1943 finally induced Stalin to meet Roosevelt at Teheran. However, Stalin insisted on a meeting of the British, American, and Soviet foreign ministers in Moscow prior to Teheran. In Moscow, British foreign secretary Anthony Eden advanced proposals designed to limit Soviet influence in Eastern Europe—which would, of course, open the way for British influence. The Soviet foreign minister, Vyacheslav Molotov, argued that the U.S.S.R. should have no restrictions in the region. Cordell Hull, acting on FDR's instructions, sided with Molotov, and the issue was settled.

FDR met Churchill and Chiang Kai-shek in Cairo immediately prior to Teheran. Chiang desired an amphibious assault in the Bay of Bengal to coincide with a Chinese offensive in Burma, but Churchill opposed him. FDR supported Chiang, though the operation was later canceled. At Cairo, FDR, Churchill, and Chiang agreed that Japan should be stripped of all territories conquered since 1914, and that lands stolen from China (such as Manchuria and Taiwan) should be returned. This promise conflicted with Stalin's plans for the Far East, as FDR would soon learn.

Teheran was unquestionably the most important wartime conference. At Teheran, FDR laid out the possible Anglo-American courses of action and allowed Stalin to choose between them. Thus, Stalin decided Anglo-American strategy in 1944–1945. The main question was whether the Anglo-Americans should pursue additional operations in the Mediterranean before Operation Overlord, the Allied invasion of Western Europe, was launched. Churchill agitated for the clearing of northern Italy and an invasion of the Balkans, even if this meant delaying Overlord. Stalin, however, asserted that Overlord must not be delayed, and that the only Mediterranean operation should be an invasion of southern France. After prolonged argument, the British agreed to the mounting of Overlord in May 1944 in conjunction with an invasion of southern France.

FDR met Stalin privately at Teheran and advanced a plan for postwar U.S.-Soviet cooperation. They discussed the elimination of Germany and Japan as major powers and the dismantling of the European empires. FDR proposed a postwar peacekeeping body (the United Nations), ruled by an executive body which would include the Big Four. FDR assured Stalin of his willingness to meet Soviet security needs, particularly with respect to Eastern Europe. Poland would be moved to the West, and the U.S.S.R. would control the Baltic states. FDR truly believed that the Soviets would cooperate after the war if their territorial sources of insecurity were removed.

In the spring of 1944, FDR resisted continued pressure from Churchill to commit Anglo-American forces to the Balkans. Such adventures could only jeopardize Overlord and would also arouse Soviet suspicions. The issue was not finally settled until August 1944, when the invasion of southern France committed the only forces that could have been used in the Balkans. In the first half of 1944, FDR made strenuous efforts to limit the influence of Charles de Gaulle, whom FDR saw as an obstacle to his plan to strip France of her overseas empire after the war. De Gaulle's difficult personality did not make matters any easier.

In November 1944, FDR was elected to an unprecedented fourth presidential term. Roosevelt's health, however, was declining, and some historians assert that he was too sick to deal effectively with Stalin at the Yalta conference in February 1945. Those closest to him, however, believed he was mentally alert. In fact, the major agreements reached at Yalta were simply the realization of plans that had been developing since Teheran.

The military context for this conference was most unfavorable for the Anglo-Americans—the Soviet armies were only 40 miles from Berlin, while the Anglo-American armies were still on the Rhine River. German and Polish questions dominated the conference. Agreement was reached on the organization for the occupation of Germany, and the occupation zones were delineated. FDR asserted that American troops would depart within two years, and France was given an occupation zone carved out of the American zone. FDR, Churchill, and Stalin also reached agreement on voting rights in the United Nations.

Stalin insisted that the U.S.S.R. should have the post–World War I Curzon line as her new western frontier, and that Poland should be compensated at German expense. Neither FDR nor Churchill challenged this demand strongly, though they argued for the inclusion of "democratic elements" in the new Polish government. FDR and Stalin also discussed Soviet entry into the Pacific war. The Americans desired a Soviet declaration of war in order to ensure the defeat of Japanese forces in Manchuria and to provide Siberian bases for U.S. air attacks on Japan. Stalin agreed to attack Japan three months after the surrender of Germany. In return, the U.S.S.R. would receive the Kurile Islands, southern Sakhalin Island, control of the Manchurian railways, and use of a warm-water port on the Kwantung peninsula. Moreover, the status quo in Mongolia (a pro-Soviet government) would be preserved. Although this agreement affected China, Chiang Kai-shek was neither consulted nor informed.

Roosevelt lived only a few months after Yalta. During this period, he maintained his policy of U.S.-Soviet cooperation, despite Churchill's repeated complaints about Soviet behavior in Eastern Europe. Churchill agitated for Anglo-American thrusts on Berlin and into Czechoslovakia, but Roosevelt rejected these pleas. Up to the moment of his death, FDR believed that postwar cooperation with Stalin would be possible—in his last letter, he told Churchill that he tended to "minimize the general Soviet problem as much as possible." A sharp change in American policy came quickly after Roosevelt's death; Harry S. Truman did not share FDR's optimistic assumptions.

Franklin Roosevelt's greatest contributions to the Allied victory in World War II lay in his support to the British in the teeth of substantial disapproval across the American opinion spectrum, his mobilization of the American home front, a process begun well before Pearl Harbor, and his tireless work for Allied unity.

FURTHER READINGS

Heinrichs, Waldo. *Threshold of War: Franklin D. Roosevelt & the American Entry into World War II* (1989).

Kimball, Warren F. *The Juggler: Franklin Roosevelt as Wartime Statesman* (1991).

Sainsbury, Keith. *Churchill and Roosevelt at War: The War They Fought and the Peace They Hoped to Make* (1994).

James Perry

SEE ALSO Home Front, U.S.

Roxas, Manuel (1892–)

First president of the independent postwar Philippines (1946–1948). Born at Capiz (now Roxas City), Panay, on January 1, 1892, Roxas studied law, receiving a degree from the University of the Philippines. He began his political career as governor of Capiz Province between 1919–1921 prior to serving in the Philippine house of representatives between 1921–1933 and as speaker for a term. After participation in the constitutional convention of 1934, he held office in the national assembly between 1935 and 1937 and appointment as secretary of finance the next year. In 1941 he was elected senator.

The slender, intelligent but irascible Roxas became the protégé of Manuel Quezon, the leading Filipino political figure of the time. Dispatched by his benefactor to the United States in 1930 to discuss the independence question, he endorsed U.S. legislation that would extend commonwealth status to the Philippines.

Although Quezon actually favored Roxas over Sergio Osmeña for commonwealth vice president, it was the latter who achieved the office. As a senator at the time of Japan's invasion, Roxas served on the council of state in December 1941, and, the same month, General Douglas MacArthur, also a patron, commissioned him a lieutenant colonel in the U.S. Army to act as his contact with President Quezon.

Roxas fled to the Corregidor island forts with Quezon and other Filipino officials after the Japanese invasion in December 1941. There, like Osmeña, he protested the Quezon's proposed initiative to declare the Philippines neutral. Before Quezon was evacuated from Corregidor, he delegated to Roxas wide-ranging authority to act in his (Quezon's) name. One of his responsibilities prior to his own departure was the clandestine submerging of Philippine gold bullion in Manila Bay near Corregidor. On March 5, 1942, Quezon appointed Roxas his successor if he and Osmeña failed to live through the hazardous flight from the archipelago to Australia. Once the president's entourage made its escape, Roxas remained as the highest ranking Philippine official.

Roxas escaped from Corregidor before the stronghold capitulated. Reaching Mindanao, he was seized by the Japanese but saved from execution by a local Japanese officer. Brought back to Manila, he went into seclusion,

and, when pressed to collaborate, he resisted, claiming he had a heart problem. Meanwhile, President Quezon's intelligence sources discovered that the Japanese were considering Roxas as their first choice to head a puppet government. As a consequence, he and General MacArthur wanted to attempt a submarine rescue of Roxas and his family; however, the scheme was dropped because of the risk. The Japanese authorities' pressure on Roxas to cooperate peaked in the spring of 1943, at which time they determined that he had no intention of aiding them. Discontinuing their attempt, they turned to Jose P. Laurel.

Roxas eventually did serve in the Japanese-installed regime, participating as the vice chairman of the inauguration committee for President-elect Laurel and for a short time presiding over the economic planning board. In April 1944, Laurel appointed him chief of the Bigasang Bayan (BIBA), a food agency under the board. Roxas claimed he assumed the position because he believed no patriot should refrain from using his prestige or influence to mitigate his people's sufferings. The agency proved to be ineffective, Laurel eliminated the post, and Roxas went back into retirement. When the Philippine republic considered a declaration of war against the Allies, Roxas disapproved of that move and of the creation of a puppet army. Once the conflict turned against the Japanese by February 1945, he indicated no interest in evacuation to Japan, and he was not pressured by the Japanese to leave.

By the time Roxas eluded the Japanese and entered the U.S. Sixth Army's lines, General MacArthur had already cleared him of responsibility for aiding the enemy. MacArthur brought Roxas to Manila, openly embraced him, and reinstated him as a general on his staff. He vouched for Roxas's patriotism, contending that he was guiltless of collaboration and had actually assisted the guerrilla underground. MacArthur's preferential handling of his friend caused a chorus of complaint. President Sergio Osmeña's temporary secretary of national defense, Tomas Cabili, a possible Roxas competitor for the presidency, published a general order in March that questioned his restored rank. The decree miscarried because Roxas's ally, Chief of Staff Basilio Valdes, quickly placed him on inactive duty, meaning he was constitutionally accountable to official action solely for the commission of a grave crime.

In fact, Roxas's cooperation with the enemy and his underground espionage links were both not substantial. Because of contacts with Allied intelligence, he claimed absolute exoneration from any culpability for heading puppet-government agencies. Actually, the Japanese had their suspicions of him, and, at the beginning of the occupation, Laurel had promised their command he would be answerable for Roxas's conduct. Yet Roxas soon touched base with a Manila guerrilla unit that communicated Japanese military activity to MacArthur's base. Protected from the Kempeitai (the secret police) by Laurel and evading detention, he made infrequent and circuitous contacts with Australia and took into his house on one occasion an operative sent by the exiled President Quezon. On the other hand, for all of their suspicions of Roxas, he was never arrested or suffered physical duress at their hands.

With the summoning of the Philippine congress near the end of the war, Roxas was selected president of the senate and chairperson of the committee on appointments. He decided to run against Osmeña in the forthcoming presidential election. By July Roxas had gained control of the Liberal party, using it to divide the opposing Nacionalistas. After his nomination, in an acceptance speech before the assembled Liberals the following January, he referred to himself as an affirmed foe of wartime collaborators, not a particularly brave stand to take in the postwar Philippines. Roxas won the presidency in April and brought most of his party's candidates into office with him despite a narrow margin of victory. He died two years later, on April 15, 1948, while delivering an address at Clark Field.

FURTHER READINGS

Bustos, Felixberto. *And Now Comes Roxas (The Story of the First President of the Republic of the Philippines and the Occupation)* (1946).

Friend, Theodore. *The Blue-Eye Enemy: Japan Against the West in Java and Luzon, 1942–1945* (1988).

Lichauco, Marcial P. *Roxas: The Story of a Great Filipino and of the Political Era in Which He Lived* (1952).

Steinberg, David Joel. *Philippine Collaboration in World War II* (1967).

Rodney J. Ross

SEE ALSO Osmeña, Sergio; Philippines, Fall of the; Quezon, Manuel

Russell Islands

Situated less than fifty miles north of Guadalcanal, the Russell Islands served an important, if obscure, role in World War II. Following the Japanese defeat and evacuation from Guadalcanal in February 1943, U.S. military planners immediately turned to their next target, the Russell Islands. Known for their coconut plantations prior to the war, the islands, under U.S. occupation, would offer Guadalcanal protection from Japanese counterattacks, air-

fields for attacks farther north in the Solomon Islands, supply bases for future operations, and rest areas for soldiers after battles. Though overshadowed by other operations in the Solomons, the occupation and use of the Russells created lasting and sometimes bitter memories for those soldiers who were there.

Admiral Chester Nimitz gave Admiral William Halsey permission to proceed with Operation Cleanslate, the invasion and occupation of the Russell Islands, in late January 1943. Halsey envisioned using the two main islands in the Russell chain, Pavuvu and Banika, for airfields, PT boat bases, supply depots, and staging areas for future operations. He feared that if the islands were left unoccupied, the Japanese might use them to stage surprise attacks against Guadalcanal. Reconnaissance of Pavuvu and Banika in early February revealed that the Japanese had withdrawn their forces. Even with this information, Halsey decided to move forward with the operation for the reasons already mentioned, and also to give some very necessary training in amphibious landings to his raw troops.

Halsey placed Rear Admiral Richmond K. Turner as the overall commander of Operation Cleanslate. Turner commanded a hodgepodge force of soldiers, marines, and sailors. Men from the 43d Army Infantry Division and the 3d Marine Raider Battalion comprised the main invasion force, with support from the 11th Marine Defense Battalion, 10th Marine Defense Battalion, and 35th Naval Construction Battalion. Task Force 61, consisting of six destroyers, four destroyer-type transports, four minesweepers, one tanker, eight PT boats, and twelve landing craft-tanks, transported the invasion force from Koli Point on Guadalcanal to the Russell Islands on February 21. Although the landings occurred without opposition, they provided valuable training for future operations. In particular, Operation Cleanslate marked the first use of landing craft-tanks and radar-equipped airplanes in the Pacific theater.

Within a week of the invasion over 9,000 troops were on Pavuvu and Banika, and the numbers increased until there were 16,000 in mid–April. These men were given the unenviable task of turning these very primitive islands into bases for future operations. The first task was to construct a base for PT boats. Second, airfields had to be built on Banika to handle both fighters and bombers. Finally, construction had to be completed on sites to serve as staging areas for other operations, supply depots, and rest areas. PT boats began operating out of the Russells on February 25, the first airfield was completed by mid–April, and the other facilities soon followed.

In 1943 the Russell Islands served two major functions: as air bases for operations in the Solomons and as the staging area for Operation Toenails, the occupation of the New Georgia Islands. One of the first air operations involving the Russells occurred accidentally. On April 18, a squadron of U.S. P-38s from Guadalcanal made a successful surprise attack on Japanese Admiral Yamamoto Isoroku's plane. One P-38 was damaged and had to make an emergency landing in Banika. Once the airfields were fully operational, pilots based at Banika flew F4F Wildcats, F6F Hellcats, F4U Corsairs, TBF Avenger torpedo bombers, SBD Dauntless dive-bombers, PV-1 Venturas with onboard radar, and B-25 bombers. The planes offered valuable support for operations in the central and northern Solomons.

In addition to providing airbases, the Russells served as a staging area for Operation Toenails from June to August 1943. The 43rd Infantry Division, which had occupied the Russells in February, trained on Pavuvu and Banika for operations in the New Georgia Islands. Specifically, they practiced amphibious landings, jungle fighting, and attacking bunkers like the ones the Japanese had built on Guadalcanal. Once the operation began, bases on the Russell Islands provided planes for constant daylight support, served as the debarkation point for parts of the invasion force, and operated a supply depot.

After the Japanese were cleared from the Solomons, Pavuvu was turned into a rest/training area for the 1st Marine Division, and Banika served as a major supply depot and hospital. To say that the Russells, and in particular Pavuvu, left something to be desired is an understatement. Over fifty years after the war, marines who passed through Pavuvu remembered it as their worst station of World War II. In 1944 the 1st Marine Division used Pavuvu as a rest area and training ground before its invasion of Peleiu. Unfortunately, the island was not ready for over fifteen thousand marines. It was too small for divisional training. Almost constant rain left knee-deep mud in places, and the marines always wet. Many of them suffered from jungle rot as painful sores developed on their skin. To compound the hardships caused by the weather, falling coconuts, rats, and crabs plagued the marines. Their miseries did not end there; Pavuvu also lacked mess halls or recreation buildings during most of the marines' stay.

There were a few bright spots for the troops stationed in the Russells. When the weather permitted, they could swim, play baseball or basketball, or go walking. Also, if very lucky, a marine could visit Banika, where women served as nurses and Red Cross volunteers. For men stationed in the Pacific this was a rare treat. Finally, right before the 1st Division left for the invasion of Peleiu, Bob Hope and his troupe visited both Banika and Pavuvu. Hope remembered his trip to Pavuvu as the most exciting moment in his tour of the South Pacific.

Caught between operations in Guadalcanal and New Georgia, the Russell Islands have been virtually forgotten in the study of Pacific theater of World War II. This is unfortunate, because the islands played important supporting roles in several operations. Although the war would have been won without the Russells, the occupation of the strategic Solomon Islands would have been much more difficult.

FURTHER READINGS

Dyer, George Carroll. *The Amphibians Came to Conquer: The Story of Richmond Kelly Turner* (1991).

Hoyt, Edwin P. *The Glory of the Solomons* (1983).

Jones, William D., Jr. *Gyrene: The World War II United States Marine* (1998).

Shaw, Henry I., Jr., and Douglas T. Kane. *Isolation of Rabaul.* History of the U.S. Marine Corps, Operations in World War II, vol. 2 (1963).

Zimmer, Joseph E. *The History of the 43d Infantry Division, 1941–45* (1945;1982).

David L. Snead

Saipan, Battle of

The Mariana Islands were the next U.S. target after the Marshalls. Some three thousand miles from Pearl Harbor and one thousand miles from Eniwetok, the Marianas were a key element in Japan's inner defenses. In U.S. hands, they could be used as bases for long-range B-29 bombers to strike Japan.

Saipan was the principal objective of the campaign and the first to be taken. Tinian, only 3.5 miles south of Saipan, was next. Not only was it close to Saipan, but it was mostly level terrain and thus suitable for airfields. Guam, about 150 miles southwest of Saipan, had to be taken largely as a matter of national pride. It had been U.S. territory from 1898 until 1941, when Japan seized it by force.

For the Marianas operation, Vice Admiral Richmond Kelly Turner had some five hundred thirty warships and auxiliaries in his 5th Amphibious Force. The force was divided into a Northern Attack Force, commanded by Turner, for Saipan and Tinian and a Southern Attack Force, commanded by Rear Admiral Richard L. Conolloy, for Guam. The V Amphibious Corps, numbering approximately 127,000 men commanded by Marine Lieutenant General Holland McTyeire ("Howlin' Mad") Smith, would make the land assaults.

Saipan was some seventy square miles in size. A refueling base for the Imperial Navy, it also had a seaplane base and two airfields. The assault force for Saipan would number about fifty thousand men: the 2d Marine Division (Major General Thomas E. "Terrible Tommy" Watson), 4th Marine Division (Major General Harry "The Dutchman" Smith), and attached elements. The army's 27th Division (Major General Ralph Smith) was the floating reserve.

Overall defense of the Marianas fell to Vice Admiral Chuichi Nagumo, who had his headquarters on Saipan.

His Central Pacific Fleet had no major warships. Nagumo's naval shore component was the 5th Base Force. Saipan was also headquarters for Hideyoshi Obata's Thirty-first Army. Lieutenant General Yoshitsugo Saito was the island's army commander. Saito and Nagumo were not on good terms, because the admiral had been unable to stop depredations by U.S. submarines, which were sinking one out of every three supply and transport vessels bound for the Marianas; another third of the vessels were being damaged. Slowly the Japanese were being starved of reinforcements, supplies, and fortification materials. In all, the Japanese had 30,000 army and navy troops on the island, and there was a substantial civilian population.

Turner's invasion force sallied to the Marianas from Eniwetok. Prior to their arrival, Admiral Marc Mitscher's Task Force 58 softened up the islands. During June 11–12, fighter and bomber attacks cost the Japanese 200 aircraft and a dozen or more cargo ships. The next day Mitscher's battleships and destroyers began pounding Saipan with naval gunfire, but this was not very effective because few Japanese installations were precisely identified.

For the assault, the marines had greatly increased their firepower. On Saipan, each marine rifle squad had three Browning automatic rifles (as opposed to one earlier), increasing the division's automatic-rifle strength from 558 to 853. Each platoon also had a special assault squad with a bazooka, demolitions, and two flamethrowers. The number of flamethrowers per division had increased from 25 to 245, and there were also 24 long-range flamethrowers for mounting on light tanks. The number of medium tanks had also increased. Each tank battalion now had forty-six Shermans. The marines were also given additional pack howitzers and mortars.

The landings began on the morning of June 15. After a feint to the north of Saipan, the main landing got under way on a 4-mile front on eight beaches on the island's southern coast. The 2d and 4th Marine Divisions met immediate resistance from General Saito's garrison and Admiral Nagumo's 6,000 shore-borne sailors. Nagumo surveyed the invasion fleet through binoculars and noted with some admiration that several of the battleships his pilots had sunk at Pearl Harbor were back in action. By nightfall, the marines were secure ashore.

On June 17, Mitscher's carriers departed. Later, all his warships left the Marianas, the result of the Japanese A-Go Plan. This plan called for Nagumo and Saito to destroy U.S. troops on Saipan, while the Combined Fleet, commanded by Admiral Soemu Toyoda, would sally forth and attack U.S. Navy forces in what many knowledgeable Japanese regarded as their last hope of turning the tide of war in the Pacific. The A-Go Plan resulted in the Battle of the Philippine Sea. This battle, June 19–21, the first fleet engagement between Japanese and U.S. troops in two years, destroyed the Japanese fleet; but it also deprived U.S. ground elements on Saipan of valuable naval gunfire and air support.

The Japanese defense of Saipan was conducted by first-rate troops and was well executed; U.S. advances, while sure, were slow and costly. On June 18, U.S. troops secured the airfield. Heavy Japanese resistance, however, prompted the commitment on June 19 of the 27th Division. Slow progress by this division angered "Howlin' Mad" Smith, who on June 24 relieved General Ralph Smith from command of the 27th Division. This matter, largely the result of different tactical doctrines, remained a subject of controversy between the army and navy into the twenty-first century.

Generally, the Japanese fought to the death, and it was not until July 9, after a last-ditch banzai charge by 3,000 survivors, that organized resistance came to an end. Saipan was pronounced secure on July 13, although mopping-up operations continued for weeks afterward against enemy troops in caves and pillboxes. In taking the island, the United States sustained casualties of 3,126 killed, 13,160 wounded, and 326 missing. Japanese losses were approximately 27,000 killed, including several hundred civilians who leaped to their deaths from the island's cliffs. Only about 2,000 Japanese were taken prisoner; both Nagumo and Saito committed suicide.

The fall of Saipan brought General Hideki Tojo's resignation as premier on July 20. The island had become Japanese in 1920 as a consequence of World War I and was considered a part of Japan. Guam was secured from July 21 to August 10 and Tinian from July 25 to August 2.

Having the Marianas under its control was militarily valuable to the United States. Even as the islands were being cleared of their last defenders, navy Seabees were working under Japanese fire to build runways for air bases from which long-range B-29 bombers could strike Japan.

FURTHER READINGS

Hoffman, Carl W. *Saipan: The Beginning of the End.* U.S. Marine, Corps Historical Branch (1950).

Isely, Jeter A., and Philip A. Crowl. *The U.S. Marines and Amphibious War* (1951).

Love, Edmund G. *The 27th Infantry Division in World War II* (1982).

Morison, Samuel Eliot. *History of United States Naval Operations in World War II,* vol. 3 (1961).

Smith, Stanley E., ed. *The United States Marine Corps in World War II* (1969).

Wheeler, Richard. *A Special Valor: The U.S. Marines and the Pacific War* (1983).

Spencer C. Tucker

SEE ALSO Army, Japanese; Nagumo Chuichi; Navy, U.S.; Tinian, Battle for

Santa Cruz Islands, Battle of

The Battle of Santa Cruz Islands was the fourth carrier-versus-carrier battle of the Pacific war. Designated by the Japanese "the Naval Battle of the South Pacific," this naval air engagement was fought in late October 1942 in the vicinity of the Stewart and Santa Cruz Islands, located, respectively, to the northeast and east of Guadalcanal Island.

During the fourth week of October, Japanese troops launched a major offensive on Guadalcanal in an effort to gain control of U.S.-held Henderson Field, the only operational airfield on the island. Anxious to provide greater support to the beleaguered U.S. troops on Guadalcanal, Vice Admiral William F. Halsey, commander of the South Pacific Force and Area, ordered his carrier task forces to redeploy. They were directed to sweep north of the Santa Cruz Islands and proceed southwesterly east of San Cristobal Island to a position in the Coral Sea where they could intercept Japanese forces approaching Guadalcanal.

Halsey's carrier forces consisted of Task Force 16 (TF 16) and Task Force 17 (TF 17). U.S. carrier *Hornet,* four cruisers, and a destroyer screen made up TF 17, which was commanded by Rear Admiral George D. Murray. TF 16, which had arrived on station on October 24, consisted of U.S. carrier *Enterprise,* new battleship *South Dakota,* two cruisers, and a destroyer screen. Its commander was Rear Admiral Thomas C. Kinkaid, who would also serve as overall tactical commander of these two task forces. Combined, the two forces were designated Task Force 61 (TF 61). The two carriers had a total of 137 aircraft. Task Force 64, under the command of Rear Admiral Willis A. Lee, was ordered to continue to operate south of Guadalcanal. It consisted of new battleship *Washington,* three cruisers, and six destroyers.

Well to the north of Guadalcanal and Halsey's task forces, major elements of the Japanese navy's Combined Fleet had been maneuvering for days awaiting the capture of Henderson Field. They were anxious to advance south to take up a position where they could intercept and destroy any Allied naval forces attempting to provide support to U.S. troops on Guadalcanal. U.S. aircraft operating from Henderson Field had kept the Japanese fleet far to the north.

The Japanese had estimated that the Sendai Division of the Japanese Seventeenth Army would capture Henderson Field on October 22. By October 25, however, the Japanese offensive had yet to succeed, and the main body of the Japanese fleet, designated the Support Force, continued to linger well to the north of Guadalcanal.

The Japanese Support Force, under the overall tactical command of Vice Admiral Nobutake Kondo, was formidable, especially in terms of air power. It included the three carriers of Carrier Division 1 (*Shokaku, Zuikaku,* and *Zuiho*) and one carrier (*Junyo*) of Carrier Division 2 (carrier *Hiyo,* also of Carrier Division 2, had withdrawn from the operation on October 22, crippled by a fire in its engine room). They were accompanied by a sizable portion of the Combined Fleet, including four battleships and ten cruisers.

Although both sides were aware of the presence of substantial enemy naval forces in the area, neither knew the composition and current location of its opponent. Kondo's forces had withdrawn to the north on October 24, beyond the range of U.S. search planes, while Kinkaid's TF 61 was advancing north to the Santa Cruz Islands. On the night of October 24–25, Kondo's Support Force again advanced south, anticipating that Henderson Field would soon be captured.

During the morning of October 25, U.S. long-range aircraft sighted and reported the location of various elements of Kondo's Support Force. On receiving the search reports, Halsey ordered his task forces to engage the enemy. At that time, TF 61 was east of the Santa Cruz Islands. Beginning at 1336 hours, an air search was launched from *Enterprise,* and, at 1408 hours, that carrier

began launching an air strike. Neither air group, however, sighted the Japanese forces. The latter had reversed course on learning that they had been detected.

On the night of October 25–26, the Japanese Support Force once again turned south in anticipation that Henderson Field would be captured. The course of the Japanese ships would take them east of Malaita Island, which lay a short distance northeast of Guadalcanal, approaching TF 61 head-on.

The disposition of the Support Force at that time was as follows: a striking force of carriers from Carrier Division 1, a heavy cruiser, and a destroyer screen, under the command of Vice Admiral Chuichi Nagumo; a vanguard force, about sixty to eighty miles ahead of the carriers, consisting of two battleships, four cruisers, and a destroyer screen, under the command of Rear Admiral Hiroaki Abe. Approximately eighty miles to the west was the advance force of two battleships, five cruisers, and a destroyer screen under the direct command of Admiral Kondo. About twenty miles farther to the west of the advance force was carrier *Junyo* and two destroyers under the command of Rear Admiral Kakuji Kakuta. Aboard the four Japanese carriers were 194 operational aircraft.

Early in the morning of October 26, U.S. long-range aircraft once again sighted the Japanese fleet, but the reports on the Japanese carriers were delayed in reaching Admiral Kinkaid. He received more timely reports from the 16-plane armed air search that *Enterprise* had launched around 0500 hours. One 2-plane element of the morning air search reported at about 0650 hours the location of Nagumo's carriers, which were in the vicinity of the Stewart Islands.

The Japanese learned of TF 61's location from a sighting report *Hornet* made at about 0630 hours. Admiral Nagumo's striking force received a second sighting report at 0658 hours from one of *Shokaku*'s aircraft. At that point, TF 61 was a short distance north of the Santa Cruz Islands.

In response to the sighting reports, Nagumo launched a 64-plane air strike (twenty-one dive-bombers and twenty torpedo bombers, escorted by twenty-one fighters and two contact/report aircraft) at 0710 hours. A second strike of forty-five planes (nineteen dive-bombers and sixteen torpedo bombers, escorted by nine fighters and one contact/report plane) was launched about an hour later; the dive-bombers departed first, followed about fifty minutes later by the torpedo bombers.

At 0730 hours (that is, a short time after Nagumo's carriers began launching their air strikes), *Hornet* launched fifteen dive-bombers, six torpedo bombers, and eight escort fighters under the command of Lieutenant

Commander William J. Widhelm. Twenty minutes later *Enterprise* launched three dive-bombers, nine torpedo bombers, and eight fighters under the command of Commander Richard K. Gaines. At 0815 hours, *Hornet* launched a second strike, consisting of nine dive-bombers, nine torpedo bombers, and seven fighters led by Commander Walter F. Rodee.

The first successful air attack of the battle occurred around the time that the opposing carrier forces were launching their air strikes. At 0740 hours, a 2-plane element of Kinkaid's morning air search bombed *Zuiho*, damaging the light carrier's deck and plane-arresting gear, rendering it incapable of receiving aircraft.

Approximately one hour later, Nagumo's first air strike, commanded by Lieutenant Commander Shigeharu Murata, encountered the three air strikes launched by TF 61. Nine of the Japanese escort fighters broke formation to attack Commander Gaines's torpedo bombers from *Enterprise*. In the ensuing fight, the Japanese shot down two torpedo bombers and three escort fighters and damaged several other aircraft from *Enterprise*. Lieutenant Commander Murata's air strike, less the nine fighter aircraft that attacked the *Enterprise* air strike, continued to the southeast, where it located TF 17. His air group began its attack on *Hornet* at 0910 hours, scoring many bomb hits and near misses on the carrier, as well as two torpedo hits.

Soon thereafter the three air strikes launched by TF 61 made contact with elements of Kondo's Support Force. The fifteen dive-bombers in *Hornet*'s first air strike succeeded in attacking *Shokaku*. Beginning their attack at 0927 hours, they scored six 1,000-pound bomb hits on the Japanese carrier. Other elements of the U.S. air strikes attacked two of the cruisers in Admiral Abe's vanguard force, scoring two direct hits and two near misses on cruiser *Chikuma*.

The Japanese did not know until around 0930 hours that TF 61 included a second carrier. Consequently, Nagumo's second air strike, commanded by Lieutenant Commander Mamoru Seki, was redirected toward the *Enterprise* task force. Seki's dive-bombers began their attack at about 1015 hours, scoring two direct hits and one near miss on *Enterprise*, resulting in seventy-five wounded and forty-four fatalities. The torpedo bombers failed, however, to score a hit on *Enterprise*, although one of them crashed into destroyer *Smith*. At 1121 hours, the *Enterprise* task force was again attacked, this time by a 29-plane air strike (twelve fighters and seventeen dive-bombers) led by Lieutenant Yoshio Shiga that had been launched from *Junyo* at 0914 hours. This air group scored a near miss on *Enterprise* and one direct hit each on battleship *South Dakota* and antiaircraft cruiser *San Juan*.

The Japanese then redirected their attention to *Hornet*. At 1515 hours, seven torpedo bombers from *Junyo* attacked *Hornet*, scoring one torpedo hit, which prompted the decision to abandon the carrier. At 1540 hours, the wounded *Hornet* was attacked by a 13-plane strike from *Zuikaku*, led by Lieutenant Ichiro Tanaka, making one direct bomb hit on the carrier. At 1702 hours, *Hornet* was subjected to a dive-bomb attack by ten aircraft from *Junyo*, receiving one more direct hit.

With one U.S. carrier sinking and the other damaged, TF 61 withdrew to the south in an effort to avoid a night surface engagement with Admiral Kondo's Support Force, which was rapidly approaching from the northwest. Kinkaid's destroyers were unsuccessful, however, in scuttling *Hornet* before the arrival of Admiral Abe's vanguard force (which makes one wonder as to the seriousness of its damage). The carrier was eventually torpedoed by the Japanese, who withdrew to the north in the early morning of October 27.

Although the Japanese could confirm the destruction of *Hornet*, they were uncertain as to the amount of destruction of other elements of TF 61. They had received reports that their air groups had left three U.S. carriers ablaze.

TF 61 had been badly mauled in this battle. It had lost a carrier and a destroyer (USS *Porter*, which had to be abandoned due to a "friendly" torpedo hit). Four other ships, including *Enterprise*, were damaged. But Japan's carrier forces had been substantially weakened. They had lost ninety-nine carrier aircraft and 145 aviators, many of whom were seasoned veterans, such as commanders Murata and Seki. As for their carriers, neither *Zuiho* nor *Shokaku* would be operational during the remainder of the Guadalcanal campaign, whereas *Enterprise* would be operational and present for the next major sea battle of that campaign: the Battle of Guadalcanal (November 12–15, 1942). For the Japanese navy, the carrier battle of October 26, 1942, proved both a tactical and a Pyrrhic victory.

FURTHER READINGS

Frank, Richard B. *Guadalcanal* (1990).
Hammel, Eric. *Guadalcanal: The Carrier Battles* (1987).
Lundstrom, John B. *The First Team and the Guadalcanal Campaign* (1994).
Morison, Samuel Eliot. *The Struggle for Guadalcanal* (1954).
Rose, Lisle A. *The Ship That Held the Line* (1995).

George Curtis

SEE ALSO Guadalcanal, Battle for; Nagumo Chuichi; Navy, Japanese; Navy, U.S.

Sato Naotake (b. 1882)

The Japanese career diplomat Naotake Sato served as ambassador to Great Britain and later as foreign minister. During much of World War II, he was posted to the Soviet Union, where he worked diligently to maintain the precarious neutrality between Japan and the U.S.S.R.

As ambassador to London, Sato emerged as a strong advocate of a pro-Western foreign policy. He was appointed foreign minister in 1937 as part of the cabinet of General Hayashi Senjuro, a moderate who within four months was forced into retirement. During his short period in charge of Japanese foreign affairs, however, Sato repeatedly criticized Tokyo's policy toward China and called for renewed recognition of the Open Door policy for that nation.

In August 1942, Sato was chosen to represent Japan in the Soviet Union, largely on the basis of his experience with the Soviet leadership—early in his career, he had spent nine years at the Japanese consulate in Leningrad. In Moscow, he stressed the need for the Japanese military to do nothing that might encourage Joseph Stalin to abandon the 1941 neutrality pact that he had signed with then–foreign minister Mastuoka Yosuke. One early sore point was Japanese interference with U.S. ships, reflagged with Soviet colors and carrying Lend-Lease materials across the Pacific to Vladivostok. Though Japan's Axis partner Germany demanded greater efforts to disrupt the flow of supplies to the Soviet Union, Sato warned that seizures or sinkings of such reflagged vessels would lead to war. Reluctantly, and to Adolf Hitler's chagrin, Tokyo heeded these warnings.

In April 1944, Sato spoke with Soviet Foreign Minister Vyacheslav Molotov about the possibility of extending the neutrality pact and offering Japanese help in mediating the war with Germany in exchange for Soviet help in ending the war in China. Molotov rejected this offer, however, because he knew that Hitler did not share the Japanese desire for peace between Germany and the U.S.S.R.

On April 5, 1945, with the war in Europe practically over and an invasion of the Japanese home islands by British and U.S. troops appearing increasingly likely, Stalin announced that the 1941 neutrality agreement would be allowed to expire. Sato was immediately instructed to ask the Soviet government to mediate peace between Japan and the Western Allies. The ambassador, however, was skeptical; he had spent enough time in the Soviet Union to know that Stalin was primarily interested in what he could get out of any diplomatic maneuver and was certain that the Soviets had been promised far more by the British and Americans to enter the war than Tokyo

would be willing to offer to keep them neutral. He boldly recommended instead that Japan accept any terms that the Allies were willing to offer, as long as the emperor could be allowed to remain on the throne.

Yet the Japanese government, even at this late stage of the war, refused to countenance an unconditional surrender and ordered Sato to arrange for a meeting in Moscow between Stalin and former prime minister Prince Konoe Fumimaro. The ambassador dutifully requested such a meeting but received no answer; instead, on August 8, Molotov handed him the Soviet declaration of war on Japan. On the following day, the Red Army invaded Manchuria, quickly overcoming the resistance of the Kwantung army.

Sato was, by all accounts, a capable diplomat with a far better understanding of the Soviet leadership than any of the political and military leaders in Tokyo. He was in an especially precarious situation from 1943 to 1945, when the tide of war on the eastern front had clearly turned in Stalin's favor. It is difficult to imagine how a different Japanese policy might have avoided an eventual war with the U.S.S.R.; indeed, it is a testimony to Sato's diplomatic skills that, given Japan's alliance with Hitler, a war did not occur sooner.

FURTHER READINGS

Barnhart, Michael A. *Japan Prepares for Total War: The Search for Economic Security, 1919–1941* (1987).
Butow, Robert J. C. *Japan's Decision to Surrender* (1954).
Weinberg, Gerhard. *A World at Arms: A Global History of World War II* (1994).

John E. Moser

SEE ALSO Soviet Operations Against Japan

Savo Island, Battle of

It would be difficult to dispute the conclusion of naval historian Samuel Eliot Morison that the August 9, 1942, Battle of Savo Island off Guadalcanal was "probably the worst defeat ever inflicted on the United States Navy in a fair fight." It was inarguably the worst defeat in a fleet action that the U.S. Navy has ever suffered.

The struggle on land for Guadalcanal prompted the battle. In July 1942, Washington authorized a Solomon Islands campaign (Operation Watchtower) to roll back the Japanese advance in the southeast Pacific. Task One involved landing 20,000 marines, a massive operation involving seventy ships under the overall command of Vice Admiral Frank Jack Fletcher. On July 26 during a planning conference, Fletcher shocked his subordinates Rear

Admiral Richmond K. Turner and Major General A. A. Vandegrift by announcing he would minimize the risk to his carriers of land-based Japanese aircraft by keeping them off Guadalcanal for no more than forty-eight hours. Turner pleaded that he would need four days to unload his transports, during which time they would need air cover, but he failed to move Fletcher.

On August 7, 1942, U.S. landings began on Tulagi and Guadalcanal. The news reached Vice Admiral Mikawa Gunichi on Rabaul the same morning. He immediately made plans to reinforce the Japanese garrison on Guadalcanal and to attack the ships at the landing site.

Mikawa's troop reinforcement consisted of only a few hundred men from Rabaul sent out aboard transport *Meiyo Maru.* Shortly before midnight on August 8 the transport was sunk by U.S. submarine *S-38* off Cape St. George.

Mikawa's naval reaction would have a different result. He quickly assembled a task force from Kavieng and Rabaul. At 1900 hours on August 7, heavy cruisers *Chokai* (flagship), *Aoba, Kako, Kinugasa,* and *Furutaka,* light cruisers *Tenryu* and *Yubari,* and destroyer *Yunagi* rendezvoused in St. George Channel and then steamed for Guadalcanal. Mikawa's plan of attack, signaled under radio silence by hooded blinker, was to enter in the early hours of August 9 what would aptly become known as "Ironbottom Sound," attack the warships protecting the invasion force, destroy the transports, and then retire—all before daylight. The operation was risky. Chances were great that U.S. forces would detect the Japanese because they would be steaming down the "Slot" of the central Solomons in daylight.

The Japanese had the advantage of concentration of force and surprise. Although Mikawa's ships were on average about ten years older than those he would encounter and had not before operated together as a task force, their crews were well trained in night-fighting techniques, and they had the superb Long Lance torpedo (U.S. and Australian cruisers did not carry torpedoes). U.S. and Australian crews not only were inexperienced at night fighting but were exhausted from having been at general quarters for nearly two days.

At noon on August 7, B-17 crews sighted "six unidentified ships." Later a submarine reported two destroyers and three larger ships moving southeast. The next day, August 8, U.S. air reconnaissance was inadequate to cover the Slot, in part because of bad weather.

At 1016 hours local time on August 8, an Australian Hudson pilot spotted Mikawa's force and trailed it briefly. The Japanese were then some 350 miles from Savo Island, but the report was so badly processed that Admiral Turner

did not receive it for eight hours. The pilot, kept at bay by heavy antiaircraft fire, identified two of the cruisers as "seaplane tenders or gunboats." Turner concluded that with only three cruisers the Japanese force was too small to be headed to Savo and that it probably was headed to Santa Isabel Island, 150 miles short of Savo, in order to establish a seaplane base.

Rear Admiral Victor Crutchley, a Royal Navy officer serving in the Australian navy, commanded the screening forces, which were divided into three groups to guard all possible approaches to Ironbottom Sound. A small force under Rear Admiral Norman Scott, consisting of two light cruisers and two destroyers, was sent to patrol between Tulagi and Guadalcanal. This group, which was too far removed to be involved in the battle, included thin-skinned antiaircraft light cruiser *San Juan.* Had it been to the west, its new SG radar probably would have detected Mikawa's force.

Crutchley assigned defense of the two western approaches on either side of Savo Island to six heavy cruisers and four destroyers. Two other destroyers, *Blue* and *Ralph Talbot,* had new SC radars and were set up as pickets to patrol to the west. Crutchley took command of the southern group consisting of HMAS *Australia* (flag) and *Canberra,* USS *Chicago,* and two destroyers. Captain Frederick Riefkohl commanded the northern approach force of three cruisers—USS *Vincennes* (flag), *Astoria,* and *Quincy*—and two destroyers. Crutchley neither conferred with his cruiser captains before the battle nor issued a battle plan.

At about 1810 hours on August 8, Admiral Fletcher began withdrawing his three-carrier task force from its covering position, depriving the landing force of air cover. He did so with the explanations that two days of operations had reduced his fighter strength by 21 percent and that the carriers were short of fuel. The real reason was that the unlucky Fletcher, who had already lost *Lexington* and *Yorktown,* did not intend to lose another carrier. Fletcher did not consult with Turner beforehand. This was why Turner, convinced there would be no Japanese attack that night, called a sudden meeting at about 2020 hours with General Vandegrift and Crutchley aboard his flagship *McCawley.* Crutchley pulled *Australia* out of formation, signaling to Captain Bode of *Chicago,* "Take charge of patrol." Bode did not alter his position, keeping his ship at the end of the column (Morison wrote that he "acted as if dazed"). Crutchley and *Australia* did not return in time for the battle.

Mikawa's task force, streaming at high speed in radio silence, escaped detection visually or by radar by the two U.S. destroyer pickets, both of which were spotted by

Japanese lookouts. The Japanese warships passed silently by. *Blue* was the closest of the two destroyers; its captain had been told not to expect a night attack, and Condition II was set in order to give half the crew some needed rest. Its radars were manned by inexperienced operators, and the Japanese were aided in that the night was overcast and squally.

Beginning at 2345 hours, Mikawa's cruiser-launched floatplanes made several flights over the transports and Allied warships, passing back valuable information on Allied dispositions. The Japanese aircraft elicited no response from observers, who assumed the planes were friendly.

As Admiral Mikawa's lead cruiser made its way down the 7-mile passage between Savo Island and Guadalcanal, his lookouts identified the southern-force warships. Mikawa ordered his one destroyer, *Yunagi*—at the rear of his column—to reverse course and protect his rear from the two U.S. picket destroyers; the rest of the task force then moved to attack first the southern force and then the northern force behind Savo Island. Mikawa ordered a turn to port to train weapons and, at 0133 hours, "All ships attack." Within five minutes, his cruisers had fired off torpedoes. The first alarm came at 0143 hours, when Commander Frank Walker of destroyer *Patterson* broadcast: "Warning, warning, strange ships entering harbor." Simultaneously, the Japanese floatplanes dropped flares to silhouette the U.S. ships, and the Japanese cruisers opened gunfire.

Canberra was the first to be hit, by two torpedoes. At a range of less than a mile, it was literally torn apart by Japanese gunfire—twenty-four hits in less than a minute. Soon abandoned, it was eventually scuttled. *Chicago* was similarly surprised. It took one shell hit and a torpedo forward. Instead of engaging the Japanese cruisers, Bode ordered *Chicago* to make for Mikawa's lone destroyer; this in effect took the U.S. cruiser out of the battle. After having dealt with the southern force, Mikawa's cruisers steamed for the second western defense group, which was on a northern track and—thanks to a rain squall—unable to see what was going on to the south. Cruiser *Astoria* was pounded by Japanese gunfire and sank the next day. *Quincy* was next, although it at least put up a gallant fight. Mortally wounded by shells and torpedoes, it sank at 0235 hours. Leading the northern group and last to come under fire was *Vincennes*. It, too, was destroyed by gunfire and torpedoes and sank a few minutes after *Quincy*.

Mikawa now committed his only, but key, mistake. His ships had become separated, and at 0220 hours he signaled them to regroup northwest of Savo Island, apparently before attacking the almost-unprotected transports.

At 0240 hours, however, he ordered his ships to return to Rabaul. The reason, he confessed later, was that he feared a daylight air attack on his ships from Fletcher's carriers, then steaming away from the battle!

In the 32-minute Battle of Savo Island, the Japanese sank four Allied heavy cruisers and one destroyer. Three other ships were heavily damaged. Some 1,270 officers and men were killed, and another 709 were wounded. Mikawa's ships sustained negligible damage, and only 35 men were killed and 57 wounded. On the return trip to Rabaul, however, a U.S. submarine, *S-44*, exacted some revenge by sinking cruiser *Kako*.

So fearful were the Allies that the Japanese would return the next day to finish the job that all transports and supply ships were quickly unloaded and withdrawn to Nouméa, leaving the marines ashore with scant ammunition for their heavy guns and only slightly more than a month's supply of food.

Although the Allies had paid heavily for failing to concentrate all military and naval assets, especially aircraft, before the Battle of Savo Island, an after-action investigation apportioned blame so evenly that nobody was punished (although Captain Bode later committed suicide). The report cited failure to anticipate a night attack, failure to recognize the implication of Japanese planes, and misplaced confidence in the new destroyer radars. Admiral Chester Nimitz summed it up succinctly in attributing the defeat to "lack of battle mindedness."

One change following the battle was the removal of superfluous inflammable materials aboard ship. Also, improved fire-fighting techniques, including the "fog nozzle" for spraying water, were instituted.

In not striking at the amphibious force, Mikawa lost an opportunity to alter the strategic balance. The result was a protracted and desperate campaign for an island that neither side really wanted but that each was unwilling to abandon to enemy control.

FURTHER READINGS

Lacouture, John. "Disaster at Savo Island," *Naval History*, 6, no. 3 (Fall 1992).

Morison, Samuel Eliot. *History of United States Naval Operations in World War II*, vol. 5, *The Struggle for Guadalcanal* (1989).

———. *The Two-Ocean War: A Short History of the United States Navy in the Second World War* (1963).

Spencer C. Tucker

SEE ALSO Mikawa Gunichi; Navy, Japanese; Navy, U.S.

Scouts, Philippine

A mixed bag of military forces in the Philippine Islands fought the Japanese from December 1941 until May 1942: U.S. Army regulars, Philippine army regulars and draftees, Philippine Scouts, grounded naval aviators and crewmen, grounded Army Air Corps personnel, Philippine constabulary, and civilians. As the war progressed, the situation grew bleaker. Yet a unique force of 12,000 Philippine Scouts repulsed the Japanese attack with calm, confidence, and discipline, despite heavy losses.

The U.S. Congress had organized Filipino soldiers into the Philippine Scouts in 1901. Scout organizations had grown to include units in the elite, 10,400-man Philippine Division, a regular-army force stationed in the Philippines. It had three well-trained and well-equipped infantry regiments: the 31st Infantry, composed exclusively of U.S. officers and enlisted men, and the 45th Infantry and the 57th Infantry, officered by Americans and manned by Filipino enlisted men called Philippine Scouts. Scouts were equipped with the same gear standard to U.S. infantry and were well known throughout the army for their superb marksmanship and love of soldiering. Scout units were filled with physically fit, alert men, who cut a fine appearance in their starched khakis, polished brass, and shiny boots.

The two Scout infantry regiments were famous for their soldierly qualities. Filipinos considered selection to the Scouts a great honor, and entry standards were strict. Long lists to enter Scout units were common, and instances of waiting ten years were not unknown. One U.S. officer interviewed 1,500 candidates for 100 openings and was able to insist that each applicant be a college graduate. Athletes were always in demand, partly because they made excellent soldiers but also to fill regimental sports teams with quality contenders.

Divisional artillery consisted of the 2-battalion 24th Artillery, with British truck-drawn 75-mm guns and mule-packed 2.95-inch mountain howitzers; and the 1-battalion 23d Artillery, with a single battery of 2.95-inch mountain howitzers and two batteries of 75-mm guns. The division was supported by the 12th Quartermaster Regiment, 12th Ordnance Company, 12th Military Police Company, 12th Medical Regiment, 12th Signal Regiment, 14th Engineer Regiment, and 4th Veterinary Company.

Enlisted men had between six months' and twenty years' service. The average Scout had been in the army for seven and a half years. "They had all signed up for life," remembered an American, "regardless of what the enlistment oath said." Most Scouts were high school graduates, and all spoke a reasonable dialect of English, although not all were fluent.

As with any military unit, the Scouts had their weaknesses. Because they were reluctant to say no and to admit they did not understand something, their answers were sometimes suspect. Most men generally understood English, but some U.S. commanders gave their orders in English and then let the Scout first sergeant give the order again in his own version of English. Then everyone understood.

Many Scouts came from villages without modern amenities such as electricity, telephones, and running water, so they viewed machinery and heavy equipment with suspicion and fear. Trucks were perceived as uncertain animals that needed feedings of grease, oil, and gasoline. Speed limits and vehicle loads were often seriously exceeded. Scouts also had a general aversion to making decisions and accepting responsibility. They were wonderful soldiers, yet the Americans found it difficult to build in them a sense of initiative. If an American counseled a Scout sergeant about neglect of duty, the Scout would answer that he had done nothing wrong, for he had done nothing at all. A Scout who took his own initiative ran a serious risk of doing the wrong thing. The loss of face would be humiliating.

Language was part of the problem. If a Scout did not understand his U.S. officer, he rarely asked for clarification. Instead, he would firmly say, "Yes sir," and march off without the least idea of what he was supposed to do. Initiative and independent thinking were not Scout strong points. It required constant pressure from the U.S. leaders to develop initiative in the soldiers. Successes were limited, but through no fault of American or Filipino. Whatever faults the elite Scouts might have had, they were still without peer in the world of soldiers.

They carried M1 rifles and the new gas masks. Each rifle company had three 60-mm mortars (unfortunately, there was no ammunition), and each heavy-weapons company had one or two 81-mm mortars. (In comparison, a regiment in the United States was authorized eighteen of these new mortars.) There was a shortage of light machine guns, 60-mm and 81-mm mortars, .50-caliber machine guns, and the new 37-mm antitank guns. The Scouts had the latest infantry web gear, bedrolls, and unlimited small-arms ammunition. They wore fine leather shoes made specially for them in the United States, woolen olive-drab clothing in winter, khaki in summer, and steel helmets. Their morale was excellent.

The Philippine Scout 26th Cavalry, stationed at Fort Stotsenburg, was a regular-army horse cavalry regiment. These Scouts were thoroughly imbued with a spirit to take the offensive, a spirit traditional to U.S. cavalry. If a cavalryman's son was physically fit, naturally he would attempt to join the regiment. The cavalry, like the Philippine Division, was well trained and professional. Training in the field for several days at a time and up to two weeks straight was common. Riding from dawn to dusk, the Scout cavalryman imperturbably roasted in the sun or shivered under pouring rains.

Unfortunately, the regiment operated on a much reduced organizational level and fielded two squadrons instead of three like standard cavalry regiments. It also lacked mortars, antitank guns, and other modern equipment. Although each squadron had three troops, the troops were smaller than those stateside, and the regiment lacked the newest equipment. Regardless of their equipment, Scout cavalrymen were second to none in military prowess. The older sergeants knew troop tactics as well as any officer. Serving as a Scout in the 26th Cavalry was the most significant fact in their lives. They were alert when in the field, able to ride and shoot, and soldiered superbly.

Their post at Fort Stotsenburg had lovely frame officers' houses beneath large tropical trees and bordered by shrubs and flowers. Troop barracks consisted of large, square one-story wooden buildings standing on stilts four feet above the ground. The barracks had large wooden windows, hinged at the top and able to open wide to allow breezes to flow through. Also stationed here were two small Scout artillery regiments, the 86th Artillery and 88th Artillery, along with the Philippine Division's organic cannon, the 23d and 24th Artillery Regiments.

The second-largest collection of trained Americans and Philippine Scouts on Luzon (after the Philippine Division) was the Philippine Coast Artillery Command, an organization that manned the harbor defenses of Manila and Subic Bays. Harbor defenses consisted of the U.S. 59th and 60th Coast Artillery Regiments and the Philippine Scouts' 91st and 92d Coast Artillery Regiments. They manned the big coast artillery cannon of the Manila and Subic Bay forts. Like their Philippine Division counterparts, coast artillery Scouts were superb soldiers.

The Philippines offered a good tour for coast artillerymen, and service here attracted the best of that branch's officers and men. The largest combination of coast artillery units anywhere else totaled just three battalions. On Luzon were four regiments armed with all kinds of weapons: 12-inch mortars and 12-inch guns; 10-inch, 8-inch, and 6-inch guns; 155-mm cannon; and 3-inch and .50-caliber antiaircraft guns. There were fifty-six seacoast pieces and seventy-six antiaircraft weapons. Twenty-three batteries of seacoast weapons dotted Corregidor Island.

The coast artillerymen were in regular-army outfits filled with soldiers who knew what they were doing. They were proud of their expertise and considered themselves a cut above field artillerymen. They were mathematicians and brain-proud, for they could not just fire a salvo at a stationary target, they could see where it hit, and then adjust. They also had to track targets moving at 20 knots, take into consideration winds, muzzle velocity, and the rotation of the earth, and then drop their huge rounds 20 miles away within a dozen yards of the target.

Scout units, be they infantry, cavalry, field artillery, or coast artillery, were as close as regular families. Their backgrounds were similar because they were often recruited from the same village. Someone in the unit always knew the applicant. There were few surprises or "bad apples." Prospective recruits served an apprenticeship with the unit they wanted to join. They worked as houseboys, janitors, gardeners, painters, or kitchen help. Only after they had satisfied the unit's sergeants, and in particular the first sergeant, did their names go on the waiting list.

Father-son combinations seldom drew comments. It was a matter of pride and honor to serve with the Scouts. Although many Scouts were the sons of the men who had fought in the Philippine insurrection against U.S. rule early in the century, they were intensely loyal to the United States, well trained, and deeply proud of their regiments—the most important structure in their world to which they devoted their lives. Scouts had served in the U.S. armed forces even before World War I, and no finer soldier could be found in the Philippines, or perhaps anywhere else. They were in the tradition of other crack indigenous levies raised by imperial powers, such as Britain's Asian Gurkhas and Germany's African Askaris.

An American privileged to work with Scouts learned to avoid slang and sarcasm, address only one subject at a time, and confirm oral orders in writing. Long-term Scout first sergeants were always concerned that a new company commander might do something to cause the unit to lose face, so they would politely review the commander's orders and point out possible problems, explain the intricacies of tribal customs, and educate the American on family relationships.

Recruits were often weak and sickly but a few months of Scout routine and rations would give them an excellent carriage and endurance. After just four months of training and discipline, it was hard to tell the long-service Scout from the new recruit. The new men were motivated and eager to learn, for they knew that highly qualified applicants stood ready to replace them if they faltered. Scouts were confident and self-reliant. They were enthusiastic about their jobs, followed instructions literally, and were proud of being Scouts.

Rank was slow to attain and earned when achieved. It could take a perfectly acceptable Scout twenty years to make private first class before prewar expansion. During Scout expansion in early 1941, units took in many new recruits, often the sons of Scouts already in the unit. They enlisted for extended periods with pay and benefits similar to civilian scales, and when they retired, they settled in their native villages as honored men. They often became the town's police chief or fire chief. A retired Scout's home was easy to spot. It was tidy, had a picket fence around the front, and exuded achievement.

The average Filipino was devoted to his family, and Scout training strengthened that devotion. The Scouts led uncomplicated, God-fearing lives and gave their U.S. officers few disciplinary problems. Officers in the U.S. 31st Infantry frequently participated as members of courts-martial for their white soldiers. Few officers serving with Scouts ever had to prefer charges, and even fewer ever sat on a court-martial.

As soon as war broke out, Scout units deployed. It was quickly evident that the recently mobilized Philippine army of ten divisions could not repulse the enemy. Simply surviving would be difficult. Scout cavalry rode to the Japanese landing and bought time for the army to retreat to Bataan. Scout infantry and artillery repulsed the first Japanese attacks on Bataan, destroyed hostile landings along the west coast, and formed the last, disciplined rear guard until the Bataan army collapsed on April 9, 1942. Scout coast artillerymen serviced their guns when Corregidor Island came under siege. They held off the Japanese despite unrelenting aerial and artillery bombardment. Even after the Philippines fell, Scouts took to the hills and organized guerrilla bands.

Their battle performance—whether as cavalrymen during the withdrawal from the beaches, as infantrymen on Bataan, or as artillerymen on Corregidor—was outstanding. All who saw them admired their discipline and bravery. Sadly, these proud Scout units were expended in a short, 5-month campaign. The Japanese triumphed, but Scout battle history has lived longer than the fleeting gains of the Japanese invaders.

FURTHER READINGS

Chandler, William E. "26th Cavalry (PS) Battles to Glory," *Armored Cavalry Journal* (March–April 1947).

Harrison, Thomas R. *Survivor: Memoir of Defeat and Captivity Bataan, 1942* (1989).

Mellnik, Stephen. *Philippine War Diary, 1939–1945* (1981).

Morton, Louis. *The Fall of the Philippines.* United States Army in World War II: The War in the Pacific. Office of the Chief of Military History, United States Army (1953).

Olson, John E., and Frank O. Anders. *Anywhere, Anytime: The History of the Fifty-seventh Infantry (PS)* (1991).

Whitehead, Arthur K. *Odyssey of a Philippine Scout* (1989).

John W. Whitman

SEE ALSO MacArthur, Douglas; Philippines, Fall of

Shepherd, Lemuel C., Jr. (1896–1990)

A general and a postwar commandant of the Marine Corps, Lemuel C. Shepherd Jr. was born on February 10, 1896, in Norfolk, Virginia. His father was a doctor whose family roots in Virginia's Tidewater society dated to 1652. During the Civil War, most male members of the family fought for the Confederacy. Indeed, Shepherd was named for an uncle, Lemuel Cornick, who was killed at the Battle of Chancellorsville in 1863. His mother was a schoolteacher from Massachusetts who had moved from Nantucket to Norfolk in search of a job. As a boy, Shepherd was fascinated by both horses and electricity; he rode daily and assembled his own radio set. Years later, he would recall a night in 1912 when he monitored radio traffic heralding the sinking of *Titanic*. In 1913, Shepherd entered the Virginia Military Institute (VMI) with hopes of studying electrical engineering. The next four years were relatively undistinguished, except for one overexuberant New Year's celebration that saw the newly made cadet corporal firing skyrockets out his barracks window. Caught in the act, Shepherd never again held cadet rank. But when the United States entered World War I in April 1917, Shepherd was filled with martial enthusiasm and applied immediately for a commission in the newly expanded Marine Corps. His request granted, he graduated from VMI early, on May 3.

Second Lieutenant Shepherd then joined the 5th Regiment of marines. After an extended period of training in both the United States and France, the 5th Regiment entered combat in late May 1918. As a platoon leader and then company commander, Shepherd established a heroic record. Wounded three times, he would be awarded the Distinguished Service Cross, the Navy Cross, and the Silver Star for actions at Belleau Wood and Mont Blanc.

Following the war, Shepherd remained in the Marine Corps. He occupied a variety of billets that mixed the mundane with the unusual. While he attended the standard professional schools and commanded his share of shipborne marines, Shepherd also mapped European battlefields, commanded the marine detachment at Franklin Roosevelt's Warm Springs, Georgia, retreat, and served as aide-de-camp to a commandant of the Marine Corps, Major General John A. Lejeune. Other assignments included staff and troop commands in China and Haiti and field-testing the Marine Corps' newly developed amphibious warfare doctrine. By the time the United States entered World War II in 1941, Shepherd had become a colonel and assistant commandant of Marine Corps schools. The wartime expansion of the corps would bring him rapid advancement and continued success.

Shepherd, like many marines, asked immediately to be assigned a combat unit. In March 1942, he got his wish when the Marine Corps sent him to command the newly created 9th Regiment at San Diego, California. Shepherd trained the regiment rigorously and led it eventually to Guadalcanal in August 1943. There, the regiment continued to train as a part of the 3d Marine Division. However, Shepherd did not remain long. Promoted to brigadier general, he was made assistant divisional commander of the 1st Marine Division, then resting and retraining in Australia after its exhausting conquest of Guadalcanal. Shepherd would not have much time to adjust to the new position. On December 26, the 1st Division waded ashore at Cape Gloucester in New Britain. In this operation, General Douglas MacArthur, the theater commander, wanted the marines to secure the northern coast of New Britain and prevent the Japanese from reinforcing and supporting their operations in New Guinea. In the 3-week campaign to follow, Shepherd played a critical role. As a sector commander, he was responsible for pushing the Seventh Marines and its supporting units deep into the jungle to seize a series of prominent hills anchoring the Japanese position. The combat was brutal, because the marines had to fight not only the Japanese but probably the thickest jungle and deepest mud in the South Pacific. Nevertheless, by the middle of January, western New Britain had been secured.

Owing no small amount to his performance at Cape Gloucester, Shepherd was ordered in March 1944 to assume command of the 1st Provisional Brigade. Created out of two regiments filled with combat veterans, the Twenty-second and Fourth Marines, the brigade moved to attack Guam on July 21, 1944. Guam was to be the last objective in the U.S. campaign against the Mariana Islands. Joining the 1st Provisional Brigade were the 3d Marine Division and the 77th Infantry Division, which was to act as a corps reserve. The initial amphibious assault was unusual in that Shepherd's brigade and the 3d Division landed at two widely separated beachheads. Although the navy provided an excellent preinvasion bombardment, the initial landings occurred at great cost. After establishing the beachhead and securing points inland, Shepherd turned his brigade north to clear out the Orote Peninsula so as to secure an airfield and Apra Harbor. In the heavy combat to follow, which included a highly effective Japanese nighttime counterattack on July 25–26, Shepherd could be seen in the forward areas exhorting and leading his troops. He always emphasized the necessity of getting forward in combat, as reflected in a comment he had made to a reporter during World War I: "You can't find out how a battle is going sitting in a command post." By July 29, Japanese resistance on the peninsula had been crushed. All that remained for Shepherd and the brigade was to bury the dead and conduct extensive long-range patrolling over the remainder of the island.

After the success at Guam, this most visible of marines was promoted to major general and given command of the then–organizing 6th Division. Assigned to the III Amphibious Corps and training for the attack on Okinawa, the 6th would combine Shepherd's 1st Provisional Brigade and the Twenty-ninth Marines. With an extended period to prepare for the invasion, Shepherd trained his division hard. By this time, his marines had nicknamed him "the Driver." While he certainly pushed his men, Shepherd drove himself no less, prompting even his chief of staff to wonder if the short and thin general would break down physically. He never did.

When the invasion of Okinawa began on April 1, 1945, the 6th Division occupied the northern-most, or left, flank of the amphibious landing. Like the rest of the landing force, Shepherd's troops faced little opposition. Over the next few weeks, that opposition stiffened appreciably as the 6th Division moved north and conquered the Motobu Peninsula. Almost simultaneously, other units in the attack force began to experience heavy Japanese resistance to the south. Tenth Army commander Lieutenant General Simon Bolivar Buckner now reversed the 6th Division and fed it into the western, or right, flank of the attack. Beginning May 11, a general U.S. advance clawed its way south. The torturous phase of the Battle of Okinawa had started.

While Lieutenant General Buckner ordered the 1st Division to reduce the Shuri Castle in the Japanese center, Shepherd's division drew the coastal capital city of Naha as its objectives. Chief among the obstacles facing the 6th Division was a series of hills, including one nicknamed

Sugarloaf. After two weeks of heavy fighting made more difficult by rain and mud, the division seized Sugarloaf and punctured the Shuri line. The division's trials were not yet finished. The Japanese retained strong points on the Oroku Peninsula. Rather than engage frontally, Shepherd decided to go around the enemy by using an amphibious landing on June 4. The operation was a brilliant success. Less than three weeks later, Okinawa was taken.

Shepherd left Okinawa with his reputation enhanced. Not only had the division accomplished its difficult mission, but Shepherd had cemented his standing as a front-line commander. Aggressive, and a firm believer in always maintaining the offensive, the general continued to lead by example. According to one observer, the future Lieutenant General Victor H. Krulak, each morning Shepherd determined where the day's hottest activity would be. He then went there and remained as long as possible. Krulak even went so far as to state that Shepherd logged more frontline time than any private. While this may be stretching the truth, Shepherd did leave most of his marines with the impression that he was ever present at the front. It was an impression indispensable to Shepherd's ability to motivate marines and win battles.

Immediately after concluding the campaign in Okinawa, Shepherd and the 6th Division departed for Guam, where they began training for the expected invasion of the Japanese home islands. The dropping of the atomic bombs made the attack unnecessary, but the war was not quite over for Shepherd. On October 10, he moved his division to north China, where it supervised the surrender of Japanese forces. Shepherd remained in north China until December 26, when he departed for the United States and a resumption of peacetime marine duties. A succession of important billets followed, including assistant to the commandant of the Marine Corps, commandant of Marine Corps schools at Quantico, Virginia, and commander of the Fleet Marine Force, Pacific. This last position gave Shepherd one more taste of combat. Now a lieutenant general, he assumed his duties in June 1950 just as the Korean War broke out. As commander of Fleet Marines, Shepherd worked closely with General MacArthur, commander in chief of the Far East. With Shepherd acting as his amphibious warfare adviser, MacArthur mounted his brilliant Inchon landings. This attack temporarily reversed the tide of the Korean War and broke U.S. forces out of the cramped and deadly Pusan Perimeter. Repeating a career-long pattern, Shepherd made sure that he got to the front as soon, and often, as possible. He did this following the landings and then again at the near disaster that was the evacuation of the 1st Marine Division from the Chosin Reservoir in December.

Strategic stalemate in Korea did not stop the general's advancement. On January 1, 1952, Shepherd became a four-star general and commandant of the Marine Corps. It was a promotion that President Harry Truman had promised four years earlier when the more senior Clifton Cates edged out Shepherd for the job. The new commandant made the most of his tour of duty. Beyond becoming the first marine to sit with the Joint Chiefs of Staff—an event beyond his making—Shepherd molded the corps for the remainder of the twentieth century. First, he reorganized marine headquarters in the manner of a general staff. Second, he emphasized the development of the helicopter and high-speed naval transport. Third, he convinced the secretary of the navy to codify in law the status of the Marine Corps within the navy. Fourth, and no less important, Shepherd paid meticulous attention to preserving the history, traditions, and public-relations symbols of the modern Marine Corps. Accordingly, he ordered formal mess and parade proceedings, which were still in use at the beginning of the twenty-first century; he created the Marine Corps Museum and the official Marine Corps seal; and, finally, he drove to completion the Iwo Jima statue in Washington, D.C.

Shepherd retired in early 1956 only to be recalled to active duty by President Dwight Eisenhower. This time, he would serve as chairman of the Inter-American Defense Board. The board was a cold-war product created to organize hemispheric defense. Although faced with often insuperable difficulties bred of bringing twenty-one nations into some kind of military alliance, Shepherd operated with force and tact. After serving almost four years, he retired permanently in 1959, leaving a legacy of improved relations and closer ties among the forces of the U.S. military.

The general enjoyed a long and productive retirement, first in Virginia and later in California. He sat on corporate boards, supervised international policy forums, became active in his church, and worked hard on behalf of his alma mater, VMI. Shepherd died on August 6, 1990, to the end the personal symbol of the values of the U.S. Marine Corps. He was buried at Arlington National Cemetery next to his wife, Virginia.

FURTHER READINGS

Krulak, Victor H. "Lemuel Cornick Shepherd, Jr., 1896–1990," *Marine Corps Gazette* (October 1990).

Simmons, Edwin H. "Remembering General Shepherd," *Fortitudine: Bulletin of the Marine Corps Historical Program* (Fall 1990).

Thompson, P. L. "General Shepherd," *Alumni Review,* Virginia Military Institute (Winter 1983).

Kyle S. Sinisi

SEE ALSO Island-Hopping and Leapfrogging, U.S. Strategies; Marine Corps, U.S.

Shipbuilding, U.S.

Maritime resources determined the ability of the United States to move men and materiel, contest control of sealanes, and open offensives against the enemy in World War II. Such sea power depended on ships of a quantity and quality never before planned or produced. The building of these ships to meet the challenges of World War II transformed an industry with technical, political, economic, and social changes.

Pressing requirements to staff ship-construction jobs eventually pushed aside established social norms. The expansion of shipyard employment swelled the number of female workers to as much as 10–20 percent of the workforce. At first reluctantly accepted, women faced down male insecurity and hostility, in part by compiling a superb labor record.

The antecedents of World War II's shipbuilding program lay in the prewar shipbuilding recession. A post–World War I glut of civil shipping, plus the economic recession of the early 1920s, left most civil yards without shipbuilding orders. The Washington Naval Treaty of 1922 imposed a tonnage ratio of 5:5:3 on the three principal signatories—the United States, the United Kingdom, and Japan, respectively—and a 10-year capital-shipbuilding "holiday." The follow-up London Naval Treaty of 1930 extended the holiday another five years. The two treaties halted capital shipbuilding, idling not only yards but also such industries as steel mills that made armor plate. The teams of skilled ship designers and engineers painstakingly assembled over the previous two decades broke up. Economy-minded national administrations canceled much treaty-permitted construction, aside from ten heavy cruisers and carrier *Ranger.*

Even while yards were quiet however, detailed industrial mobilization plans, called for by the National Defense Act of 1920, were being devised. These plans—formulated as the Industrial Mobilization Basic Plan in 1924—were refined repeatedly over the next fifteen years to form the bedrock of the industrial base that built the navy's ships for World War II.

The ascension of naval advocate Representative Carl Vinson (Dem., Ga.) to the chair of the House Naval Affairs Committee in 1932 and the election of Franklin D. Roosevelt, a former assistant secretary of the navy, to the presidency changed the picture. Primarily as a means of fostering economic recovery, the Roosevelt administration began a naval shipbuilding program under treaty terms, reviving the industry. On June 16, 1933, the $3.3 billion National Industrial Recovery Act provided funding for the first substantial naval shipbuilding in more than a decade, turning out carriers *Yorktown* and *Enterprise,* as well as four cruisers, twenty destroyers, four submarines, and two gunboats. This was only a start; on March 27, 1934, the Vinson-Trammel Act funded seventy new ships—cruisers, destroyers, and submarines.

The gradual deterioration of international relations during the 1930s encouraged shipbuilding, increasing yard capacity and building the industrial base and a body of skilled workers, despite the American public's isolationist sentiment. In 1934, preparatory talks took place among the United States, the United Kingdom, and Japan for the projected London Conference of 1936, which would replace the expiring London Treaty of 1930. Failing to gain parity with the United States and the United Kingdom in capital-ship tonnage, Japan delivered the required 2-year notification that it intended to drop out of the treaty, potentially triggering an arms race. A series of expansionist moves by Japan, as well as Japanese bombing of USS *Panay* in 1937, focused the attention of the navy, President Roosevelt, and the House Naval Affairs Committee on the fleet.

Congress established the Maritime Commission in 1936 to rebuild the civil shipbuilding industry. The outbreak of war in Europe brought British contracts to the commission, including a modified freighter design eventually dubbed the "Liberty" ship, enabling the commission to begin building an infrastructure, reactivating existing yards, and hiring contractors to build new ones. The first Liberty, SS *Patrick Henry,* was launched in September 1941 in Baltimore, Maryland.

On June 18, 1935, Germany signed a treaty with Great Britain agreeing that its navy would not exceed 35 percent of the United Kingdom's. Germany's occupation of Austria and ambitions for Czechoslovakia provoked increased shipbuilding. On May 7, 1938, President Roosevelt signed the Second Vinson Act, bringing just over $1 billion for three battleships, two aircraft carriers, nine light aircraft carriers, twenty-three destroyers, and nine submarines. Providing for an increase in the navy by about a fifth, it became known as the 20 Percent Increase Act. Indicative of the increased activity, the navy signed contracts to reactivate steel plants for armor plate closed in 1922.

The debate over the extent of U.S. involvement in the war in Europe gripping Congress through late 1939 delayed the passage of this bill and cut from 25 percent to 11 percent a bill calling for an increase in aircraft carriers, escorts, and antisubmarine patrol vessels to fight U-boats. The German blitz of France in May and June 1940, however, caused enough alarm not only to pass the bill but also to make the 11 percent increase seem insufficient. Another bill calling for a far larger increase of 70 percent quickly passed on July 19, 1940. This bill, which became known as the Two-Ocean Navy Bill, or the 70 Percent Increase Act, called for 13 battleships, 6 aircraft carriers, 32 cruisers, 101 destroyers, and 39 submarines.

Determining which ships to build was not easy. Battleships, the pre–World War I naval-arms centerpiece, figured prominently in plans for war with Japan. Despite mounting evidence on the potential of aircraft carriers, the navy's shipbuilding blueprint, the Victory Program, gave pride of place to battleships. As World War II approached, convoy escorts—corvettes, light aircraft carriers, and destroyer escorts—were added to fight German submarines. The dominance of aircraft carriers in the Battles of the Coral Sea and Midway changed long-held assumptions. The navy canceled or slowed battleship construction and used the resources for other, more urgently needed vessels such as aircraft carriers and invasion craft. Lighter ships turned out to be more flexible than heavy ones, and the Maritime Commission completed fifty freighters as escort aircraft carriers.

Wartime needs quickly occupied the almost 80 shipbuilding ways in the navy's yards and those of its major contractors. The navy added capacity in its own yards and, through tax breaks, induced industry to expand existing yards and to create new ones, known as "emergency" or "Victory" yards. In 1944, approximately 855 building ways operated in both navy and commercial yards. The Maritime Commission started the war with 53 building ways in nineteen yards; at war's end, the commission's successor, the War Shipping Administration, had more than 500 ways in eighty yards.

More difficult than improvements to facilities was the re-creation of the superb corps of naval designers and engineers assembled during the naval armaments race of the first twenty years of the century. The Washington and London treaties' 15-year capital-shipbuilding holiday dispersed this group to the extent that the navy and its contractors were at first sharing such resources when work recommended on battleship designs in the mid-1930s.

Shipyard employment climbed rapidly. Yards that had been on one shift soon tripled their employment and went to three shifts. In mid-1943, 650,000 people were working in Maritime Commission yards, and 966,000 were building, overhauling, or repairing combatant ships, up from 70,000 total in 1939. A congressional study found that contractors and subcontractors employed between two and three persons for every one actually building ships, to total almost 3 million persons in the industry.

As a result of their distinctive contributions, a few individuals became well known among the millions who participated in the shipbuilding effort. At a critical time, Andrew Jackson Higgins of New Orleans came up with a landing-barge design so successful it was named after him. Henry J. Kaiser, an industrialist new to shipbuilding, built ten yards whose ways in 1943 contributed almost a third of the nation's total shipbuilding output, including freighters, destroyer escorts, escort aircraft carriers, troopships, and tankers, at a rate, by 1945, of more than one per day. (Kaiser apparently knew so little about ships that he habitually referred to their "fronts" and "rears.") Rear Admirals Emory S. Land and Howard Vickery built the Maritime Commission, and later the War Shipping Administration, into a production juggernaut.

The goal of World War II shipbuilding was to deliver as many ships as possible in the shortest amount of time. Capacity increases—construction of new yards and ways—diligent management by the U.S. Navy, industry contractors, the Maritime Commission, and, of course, superb efforts by the workers themselves contributed substantially to the industry's success in doing so. Innovation in the design and building of ships accounted for much of the rest. Welding, rather than riveting, speed up production. Prefabrication of components that did not have to be built on the ways, or even in the shipyard, enabled mass production of standardized designs. Foremost, ships needed in large numbers, such as destroyer escorts and freighters, were designed with simplicity, strength, and flexibility in mind, for speed and ease of construction as well as operation. Common structures and a limited number of simple shapes were used, especially for hull plates. Parts were interchangeable. Liberty ships were equipped with durable vertical triple expansion (VTE) engines so simple that machine shops, rather than marine engine builders, could construct them. Destroyer escorts could mount any of four types of engines, whichever was available when needed. Not all innovation was technological; the Maritime Commission encouraged improved building times by offering bonuses for ships completed ahead of schedule.

Innovation inevitably brought problems. Delays in ship launchings, as well as lack of availability of those already delivered, resulted when welded components cracked, rendering ships structurally unsound in some cases. New welding methods and materials and component redesign reduced the problem. In some areas, production delays resulted because workers jumped from yard to yard, seeking higher wages, until stopped by a 1943 federal order. Mass-production methods broke down when prefabricated components did not arrive in time for installation on waiting vessels. The armed forces, industry, and the Maritime Commission competed for resources, delaying completion of some ships. Consistent attention by a succession of agencies and programs—notably, the War Production Board, the Materials Control Agency, and the Controlled Materials Plan—eventually enabled the wartime production system to function, although such high-demand items as machine tools and steel remained in tight supply.

By the war's end, U.S. shipbuilding had increased the U.S. Navy from 400 to 10,000 vessels and put 60 percent of the world's merchant tonnage in Maritime Commission–built hulls. Navy and contractor yards turned out 10 battleships; 2 large cruisers; 48 heavy and light cruisers; 29 fleet-type aircraft carriers, primarily *Essex* class; 102 escort and light carriers, built on freighter or cruiser hulls; 361 destroyers; 505 destroyer escorts; and 206 submarines. Maritime Commission yards turned out 2,708 Liberty and Victory ships; 1,026 landing ship tanks (LSTs); almost 1,500 oil tankers, ammunition ships, attack cargo ships (AKAs), attack troop transports (APAs); hundreds of such auxiliaries as oilers, replenishment and repair ships, tenders; 3,073 landing craft of various types; and more than 3,000 small craft. Some measurements had shipbuilding consuming 20 percent of total U.S. steel output. Together, ship construction added up to almost 25 percent of all wartime-produced U.S. munitions, costing the Maritime Commission $13 billion and the navy $18 billion.

Despite these successes, experts realized that the creation of a robust shipbuilding program after Pearl Harbor absorbed resources and workers needed elsewhere, prolonging the war. Shipbuilding predictions (fortunately) were conservative, resulting in charges that the navy had overbuilt its fleet. But such supposed overbuilding was certainly preferable to the alternative.

FURTHER READINGS

Bailey, Ronald H. *The Home Front: U.S.A.* World War II (1977).

Brown, T. J. "Ain't No Way to Mobilize," *Proceedings,* U.S. Naval Institute (September 1998).

Davidson, Joel R. *The Unsinkable Fleet: The Politics of U.S. Navy Expansion in World War II* (1996).

Dorn, David R. "Ships for Victory," *Proceedings,* U.S. Naval Institute (February 1984).

Friedman, Norman. *U.S. Submarines through 1945: An Illustrated Design History* (1995).

Garzke, William H., Jr., and Robert O. Dulin Jr. *Battleships: United States Battleships, 1935–1992* (1995).

Hagan, Kenneth J. *This People's Navy: The Making of American Sea Power* (1991).

MacCutcheon, Edward M. "World War II Development & Expansion." In Randolph W. King, ed., *Naval Engineering and American Seapower* (1989).

McCoy, James L., Virgil W. Rinehart, and Prescott Palmer. "The Roosevelt Resurgence." In Randolph W. King, ed., *Naval Engineering and American Seapower* (1989).

Meyer, J. J., Jr. "Our Nation's Shipyards," *Proceedings,* U.S. Naval Institute (November 1964).

Steven Agoratus

SEE ALSO Home Front, U.S.; Navy, U.S.

Shō-Go Plan

The Shō-Go Plan (short for *Shō-Itchi-Go,* Operation Victory One) marked the last attempt of the combined Imperial Japanese Navy to defend its empire during the war in the Pacific. Japan's strategy at the dawn of war in the Pacific had called for the occupation of all areas west of a perimeter extending to Marcus Island, Wake Island, and the Marshall and Gilbert Islands. Strong garrisons would defend these islands, and the imperial fleet would defend any threatened areas from its forward base at Truk. The Japanese hoped this defensive arrangement would make any invasion by the United States costly and force a compromise peace through war weariness. A critical requirement to the success of the Japanese strategy was an early decisive fleet action to destroy the U.S. fleet and negate the industrial superiority of the United States.

Events in the Pacific war soon dictated a change in this strategy. Japan's failure to win the decisive battle at Midway (June 4–6, 1942) compromised its war plans and badly damaged its navy, particularly the carrier air arm. The campaign for the Solomons from August 1942 to the end of 1943 further weakened Japanese naval strength. Added to these setbacks were the late but devastating effects of the Allied submarine offensive against Japanese merchant shipping, particularly the loss of tanker tonnage that exacerbated Japan's oil shortages. Japan would lose 8 million tons of merchant shipping during the war, 60 percent of which was destroyed by submarines. Consequently, the Japanese navy in early 1944 had a striking distance of only 2,500 miles due to oil shortages. The combination of these factors forced the Japanese to abandon their prewar strategy. The U.S. invasion of the Marshall Islands in late 1943 heralded this change with the withdrawal of the fleet from Truk to the Caroline Islands.

By mid-1944, the U.S. Pacific offensive had confined Japanese commerce to the areas behind an island screen consisting of the Philippines, Formosa, and the Ryukyu Islands. The Japanese war effort depended on the defense of this perimeter. The loss of any one of these islands would cut off the home islands from the oil resources of the southwest Pacific and starve the Japanese war machine.

Following the invasion of the Marianas (June 1944), the Japanese implemented a strategy to concentrate all military resources to counter a U.S. invasion of one of these vital strategic points. On July 26, 1944, the Naval General Staff informed the commander of the Japanese Combined Fleet, Admiral Soemu Toyoda, that the code name for these schemes was *Shō*, the character *Shō* meaning "to conquer." From July 24 to August 1, the Naval General Staff created four Shō plans to deal with assaults on the vital island perimeter that guarded Japanese commerce: Shō-1 (*Shō-Itchi-Go*), for an invasion of the Philippines; Shō-2 (*Shō-Ni-Go*), for an attack on Formosa and the Ryukyu island chain; Shō-3 (*Shō-San-Go*), for defense of the home islands; and Shō-4 (*Shō-Yan-Go*), in case of an invasion of Hokkaido.

On March 1, 1944, the Japanese established the First Mobile Fleet, commanded by Vice Admiral Jisaburo Ozawa, as the means to execute these plans. It incorporated the Second Fleet under Vice Admiral Takeo Kurita containing the majority of battleships and cruisers of the Imperial navy. Its core consisted of the two most powerful battleships ever built, *Yamato* and *Musashi* (18.1-inch guns), and *Nagato* (16-inch guns). The First Mobile Fleet also incorporated the Third Fleet under Admiral Ozawa, which contained the carrier air strength of the task force. All light cruisers and destroyers not participating in antisubmarine duty supplemented these powerful sections of the fleet. In effect, Toyoda combined all remaining forces of the Japanese navy into one large strike fleet capable of concentrating on any area designated by the Shō plans. Each plan envisioned the use of land-based aircraft combined with carrier air forces to attack and decoy U.S. carrier groups as the surface forces destroyed U.S. warships and troop transports and supporting vessels for the amphibious assault. The Japanese hoped to employ their superiority in night fighting to crush the enemy, as they had done in the Battle of Savo Island (August 9, 1942), where

they sank four Allied heavy cruisers and one destroyer at no cost to their own force.

The Shō operations were reactionary plans. The Japanese could implement none of them until they learned where the United States would next attack. U.S. strikes in the western Carolines at Yap and Palau, the occupation of Morotai on September 15, 1944, and especially subsequent bombings of the Philippines convinced the Japanese that the Philippines were the next target for amphibious assault. On September 21, Toyoda received a communiqué from Imperial Headquarters that it "anticipates carrying out the Shō operation sometime during or after the last part of October in the Philippines area." It ordered Toyoda to prepare accordingly. On the same day that Toyoda received this communiqué, Japanese intelligence warned of an impending U.S. attack on Formosa to destroy Japanese bases north of the Philippines and isolate the islands. Toyoda reacted immediately and ordered an alert for the implementation of Shō-2, the defense of Formosa, and eventually amassed 600 carrier-based airplanes there at the expense of Ozawa's carrier air force. The subsequent loss of no fewer than 650 planes during U.S. air attacks on Formosa (October 13–16) devastated the Japanese fleet air arm so recently and painfully rebuilt after the Battle of the Philippines Sea (June 19–21, 1944), a battle that had crippled Ozawa's carrier-based air force. A further, and major, problem was the lack of time to train new pilots for service.

On October 17, Japanese coastal watchers east of Leyte Gulf spotted U.S. warships off Suluan Island. The following day Toyoda activated Shō-1 and ordered Kurita to sail the Combined Fleet from its base at Lingga Roads near Singapore to Brunei in Borneo. Toyoda gave Kurita operational command on Ozawa's suggestion despite Kurita's being a subordinate. Ozawa's carrier force was in port in Japan taking on new carrier air groups and could not effectively command from such a distance. Ozawa was isolated from the rest of the First Mobile Fleet because the Japanese did not believe U.S. forces would attack the Philippines until November. Because the Japanese failed to concentrate their forces in time, the fleet had no chance of conducting operations as a unified force. On October 21, Toyoda ordered Kurita to sortie to the Tacloban area in the northwestern corner of Leyte Gulf. Once there, he was to destroy the U.S. surface fleet and then inflict as many losses as possible on the U.S. landing forces.

Kurita issued his battle plan for Shō-1 that night, ordering the main force to sortie from Brunei on the morning of October 22, to travel eastward through the San Bernardino Strait, and to arrive in the vicinity of Suluan Island in the early morning of October 25, X-Day, the scheduled day of attack. The main portion of Kurita's force, known as the First Diversion Attack Force (Center Force), consisted of super battleships *Yamato* and *Musashi*; older battleships *Nagato*, *Kongo*, and *Haruna*; twelve cruisers; and fifteen destroyers. The remaining portion of Kurita's command, under Vice Admiral Shoji Nishimura, consisted of old battleships *Yamashiro* and *Fuso*, supported by one heavy cruiser and four destroyers. Kurita ordered Nishimura to depart Brunei during the afternoon of October 22, sail through Surigao Strait, and meet him at the mouth of Leyte Gulf for a combined attack on U.S. forces on the morning of X-Day. Speed dictated the composition of Nishimura's force (Southern Force). The top speed of aging *Yamashiro* and *Fuso* was only 21 knots. Kurita feared their inclusion in the First Diversion Attack Force would compromise the effectiveness of his force, the maximum speed of which without the two older battleships was 26 knots. His decision to detach Nishimura undermined the Shō-Go Plan by creating a weak task force ripe for destruction at the hands of superior U.S. forces. An additional force of two heavy cruisers, one light cruiser, and seven destroyers under the command of Vice Admiral Kiyohide Shima would sail from the Calamian Islands west of Mindoro and follow Nishimura's force through Surigao Strait.

Japanese success depended on Admiral Ozawa's carriers, the main force of the First Mobile Fleet. Ozawa possessed a formidable force on paper, his fleet consisting of carrier *Zuikaku*, three light carriers, two battleships, three light cruisers, and eight destroyers. However, his fleet was a paper shark. Because of heavy aircraft losses incurred in the defense of Formosa, most of the hangars on his carriers were empty. The combined air strength of all four carriers was only 116 planes, the pilots of which were woefully inexperienced. These weaknesses, combined with Ozawa's force's separation from Kurita's force, led the Japanese to commit his carriers solely to a decoy mission. The main force of the First Mobile Fleet would sail south from Japan, maneuver east of Luzon, and bait the U.S. carrier forces away from Leyte to remove the threat of carrier-based air attacks on Kurita's forces. All depended on the success of this decoy.

The Shō-Go Plan also called for heavy reliance on land-based planes to protect Kurita's warships as they approached and to attack U.S. naval forces, especially since Ozawa could no longer provide meaningful air support. The dependence on land-based air forces was a serious weakness in all the Shō plans but especially in Shō-1. The Japanese had in all only some three hundred fifty planes with ill-trained pilots based in Luzon. The Battle of Leyte Gulf clearly showed the uselessness of these planes: U.S. air strikes mauled the First Diversion Force (Center Force) with little opposition from Japanese warplanes. The condition of this land-based air force also undermined the Shō-Go Plan. The original plan, in which land-based air power played a critical role, was impossible given the strength of these forces.

The Shō-Go Plan had a number of flaws that made its success improbable. It was a complicated strategy that produced a lack of coordination of the many fleets. (Japan's planners had a weakness for complicated operations that after 1941 never came off.) Nishimura's Southern Force had a maximum speed of 21 knots, while Kurita's force could steam at 26 knots. This difference made it difficult for the two forces to coordinate an attack. Nishimura's force was also too weak to defend itself against the massive U.S. attack in Surigao Strait. Kurita's dispersal of the forces at his disposal compromised the Shō-Go Plan from the start.

The Shō-Go Plan also had a more fundamental flaw. Ozawa's First Mobile Fleet acted successfully as a decoy to give Kurita time to attack Leyte Gulf. However, even had the double envelopment of Kurita and Nishimura worked, the overall plan still would have failed. Once the U.S. carrier forces had destroyed Ozawa, they would have turned on Kurita, who had virtually no air cover. Undoubtedly the Americans would have then annihilated his fleet. Even if the Japanese had destroyed the U.S. force, the imperial navy would have paid a heavy price. The Japanese were prepared to accept such loss, however. The near success of this plan is important to remember. Kurita had the chance to destroy a portion of the U.S. fleet and landing force in the battle off Samar, but he lost heart and withdrew before he achieved a victory. Kurita abandoned the endeavor after sustaining heavy losses on his approach to the gulf and because he believed, incorrectly, that he faced a much stronger force than his own.

The failure of the Shō-Go Plan in the Battle of Leyte Gulf sounded the death knell for the Japanese war effort on two counts. First, it ensured U.S. success in cutting off the home islands from the rich oil resources of the South Pacific, consequently starving the Japanese war machine. Second, the Japanese after Leyte had no means with which to reverse their defeat in the Philippines. They lost all four carriers of Ozawa's force, three battleships, six heavy and three light cruisers, and eleven destroyers. They also lost 500 aircraft and an estimated 10,500 sailors and airmen. The Shō-Go Plan was the last operation for the Imperial Japanese Navy as a coherent fighting force. It also marked the end of any Japanese chance of defending their empire.

FURTHER READINGS

Andrieu d'Albas, Emmanuel Marie Auguste. *Death of a Navy* (1957).

Dull, Paul S. *A Battle History of the Imperial Japanese Navy, 1941–1945* (1978).

Evans, David C., ed. *The Japanese Navy in World War II* (1986).

Field, James A., Jr. *The Japanese at Leyte Gulf: The Shō Operation* (1947).

Jentschura, Hansgeorg, et al. *Warships of the Imperial Japanese Navy, 1869–1945* (1977).

Morison, Samuel Eliot. *History of United States Naval Operations in World War II,* vol. 12, *Leyte* (1975).

Eric W. Osborne

SEE ALSO Leyte Gulf, Battle of; Navy, Japanese

Short, Walter Campbell (1880–1949)

A U.S. Army officer, born in Fillmore, Illinois, Walter Campbell Short graduated from the University of Illinois in 1901 with a B.A. After teaching mathematics at Western Military Academy, he accepted an appointment as a second lieutenant in the U.S. Army in March 1902. Following duty at the Presidio in San Francisco, Short served with the 25th Infantry at Fort Reno, Oklahoma, in the Philippines, and with the 16th Infantry in Nebraska and Alaska. After a brief tour in California, in early 1913 Short was appointed secretary of the School of Musketry at Fort Sill, Oklahoma, where he also commanded a detachment in the 12th Infantry. Promoted to captain in July 1916, Short participated, as a member of the 16th Infantry, in the punitive expedition into Mexico in pursuit of Pancho Villa.

During World War I, Short earned an outstanding record for training troops. After a brief tour as a small-arms training officer at an officers' training camp in Georgia, he went to France in the summer of 1917. There Short taught in the 1st Division school and directed the I Corps automatic weapons school and the II Corps infantry weapons school. From April to November 1918, Short, holding the temporary rank of lieutenant colonel, was assigned to the training section of the General Staff of the American Expeditionary Forces. In this assignment, he directed the training of machine-gun crews. After the armistice, he served as assistant chief of staff in charge of training for the Third Army in Germany before returning to the United States in June 1919.

Over the next two decades, Short rose in rank from major to major general, a most unusual progression in those peacetime years of agonizingly slow promotion,

while holding a variety of staff and troop assignments. These assignments included a tour as an instructor at the General Service Schools at Fort Leavenworth, Kansas, during which he attended the School of the Line; service with the Far East Section of the Military Intelligence Division of the War Department General Staff; attendance at the Army War College; service Puerto Rico with the 65th Infantry; an instructorship at the Command and General Staff College at Fort Leavenworth; a stint as assistant to the chief of the Bureau of Insular Affairs; command of the 6th Infantry; assistant command of the Infantry School at Fort Benning, Georgia; and command of the 2d Infantry Brigade, the 1st Infantry Brigade, the 1st Division, and the I Corps. In February 1941, War Department Chief of Staff General George C. Marshall, impressed with Short's excellent record with troops in World War I and his work at Fort Benning, promoted him to the temporary rank of lieutenant general and gave him command of the Hawaii Department, the army's largest overseas command. Short had made all the right career moves.

During the next months, Short worked to strengthen the defenses of Hawaii as U.S. relations with Japan worsened. Like his superiors in Washington, however, Short expected that if war broke out between Japan and the United States, it would occur in Southeast Asia. As a result, he focused his attention on training his troops and on anti-sabotage measures. Short irritably dismissed those, including his immediate predecessor, who warned him of the possibility of a Japanese carrier-borne sneak attack. He would pay heavily for his shortsightedness.

When the Japanese launched their surprise carrier-based air attack against Pearl Harbor on December 7, 1941, Short and his naval counterparts, despite warnings from Washington over the last months that war with Japan was likely, were caught off guard and suffered a severe blow. On December 17, Short was relieved of his command, and in January 1942 a special commission headed by Associate Supreme Court Justice Owen Roberts charged Short and Admiral Husband Kimmel, commander of the U.S. Pacific Fleet, with dereliction of duty for failing to take adequate joint measures in protecting Hawaii against air attack. Under pressure from his superiors, Short retired from the army with the rank of major general on February 18, 1942, subject to possible court-martial proceedings. He then worked with the Ford Motor Company in Dallas, Texas, as a traffic manager until ill health forced his retirement in 1946.

Short never faced a court-martial, although inquiries into the Pearl Harbor fiasco subsequent to his retirement were critical of him. The most notable was a joint congressional investigation in 1945–1946, whose majority report judged that Short and Kimmel, while not guilty of dereliction of duty, bore major responsibility for the defeat because of "errors of judgment," including failure to respond to adequate warnings from Washington, to prepare a unified defense system, to conduct adequate air reconnaissance, and to anticipate all possible attacks. In his defense, Short argued that he had acted in accordance with his instructions from Washington, that he was denied adequate materiel and intelligence to carry out his duties, that the war warnings from Washington were incomplete and misleading, and that he was made a scapegoat to protect higher-ups in Washington. Judged in hindsight, Short, like most U.S. leaders, miscalculated the probability of a Japanese attack on Hawaii (even though carrier-borne war-game attacks had been made successfully at least twice before the Japanese carried out the real thing in 1941), and he was not well served by Washington in the weeks before the attack. His failing was that he did not have his forces at a full state of readiness at a time when war was imminent. He was yet another example of a high-ranking officer with a good record in World War I who failed to measure up in the early days of World War II. Short died in Dallas, Texas, in 1949.

FURTHER READINGS

Beach, Edward L. *Scapegoats: A Defense of Kimmel and Short at Pearl Harbor* (1995).

Conn, Stetson, Byron Fairchild, and Rose C. Engelman. *Guarding the United States and Its Outposts.* The United States Army in World War II (1964).

Pogue, Forrest C. *George C. Marshall: Ordeal and Hope, 1939–1942* (1966).

Prange, Gordon. *At Dawn We Slept* (1981).

John Kennedy Ohl

SEE ALSO Navy, U.S.; Pearl Harbor, Japanese Attack on

Singapore, Fall of

Singapore is a small island situated at the base of the Malay Peninsula, in the bottleneck of the strategic shipping lane that forms the shortest route between the Indian and Pacific oceans. This strategic location made Singapore the most important naval/military base in Asia for the British Empire in the years before World War II. It was thus a principal target for the Japanese offensive that began the war in the Pacific. The fall of Singapore in February 1942 was a humiliating defeat for the British. It drove them to the periphery for the rest of the war against Japan, leaving the brunt to the United States. It also accelerated the

eventual collapse of the British Empire in the postwar years. The loss of Singapore was all but guaranteed by events and decisions that occurred before the war started. But the manner of that defeat, and thus to a large degree its consequences, were aggravated by how the campaign was fought.

Singapore came into prominence shortly after World War I. The war left the British battered physically and economically, still depending on their vast overseas empire to maintain their place in the world. To make matters worse, because of international politics, especially the desire not to clash in any way with the United States, the British allowed their military alliance with Japan to lapse and accepted agreements that drastically reduced the size of the Royal Navy. Yet in the long run Japan now loomed as the most likely threat to the empire in Asia. Somehow, the British Empire and its Commonwealth had to be protected with smaller forces and with less money. The compromise eventually implemented became known as the "Singapore Strategy."

From the mid–1920s on, the British constructed a major naval base in Singapore. The idea was that because any threat from Japan must come in the first instance from the sea, the Royal Navy should carry the load in any war against Japan. Because the navy was too small to station forces everywhere, the base would enable the "main fleet" to sail to Asia if need be, draw on its facilities, then repel any Japanese attack on the empire. However, there were holes in this strategy that looked possibly fatal. It was unclear what the fleet would do once it arrived: Exactly how would it smash the Japanese? Worse, to some it seemed unlikely that the fleet would be available. Perceptive critics argued the Japanese were unlikely to risk attacking the British unless the latter were already at war closer to home, which very likely would leave the navy unable to spare a fleet to operate from Singapore. With no real alternative, by default the "Singapore Strategy" stood. Instead of reconsidering the strategy, most attention was paid to the problem of how to defend the base, to make sure it was available to the fleet if needed. Military planners called the problem the "period before relief," the time the base must be held against any Japanese attack while the fleet was on its way from Europe. Before the war this time of peril was periodically increased as the situation changed, rising from forty-two to ninety days. When the British first decided to build the base, the problem did not seem unmanageable. Singapore is separated from the mainland only by the narrow Strait of Johore, which is as narrow as 700 yards at some points. But in the early 1920s Malaya was not very developed. Few good roads penetrated what was then dense jungle; nature itself seemed the best defense against any attack from the north.

That left an attack from the sea, the direct route, as the most likely threat. The base was therefore sited on the northern coast of the island, protected in due course by a combination of heavy coastal artillery—eventually including five 15-inch guns, capable of taking on the largest battleships—backed up by beach defenses, plus four air bases, meant to house bomber aircraft able to intercept an invader well out to sea. Unfortunately, things changed for the worse in the 1930s, and the plans and deployments of the defenders did not keep pace.

Perhaps paradoxically, prosperity and development opened up the west and south of Malaya enough to make it possible for an invader to advance down the peninsula and attack Singapore from the north. The defenders took these changed circumstances into consideration when rethinking their plans, assuming from 1938 that in order to defend Singapore and hold the naval base, it was necessary to defend all of Malaya, to keep an invader out of striking range. But the resulting decisions only made matters worse. The Royal Air Force hoped to prevent an invasion altogether, by intercepting any invader far out to sea. Thus it built air bases along the east coast and in the north of the peninsula. But due to the strain of events in Europe, it could not deploy the modern technology needed to use the bases effectively. Yet now the bases were there, and an invader could not be allowed to seize them, for that would allow him to bring his own aircraft close enough to cut Singapore off from all reinforcement. Therefore, on the eve of war the British army found itself in a terrible situation—required to defend a naval base for a fleet which might never arrive, and forced to spread out in order to protect an air force which was not there.

The decisive year was 1940. First, the Germans forced France to surrender. That left the British Empire fighting for survival at home, without any major allies. It also allowed the Japanese to move forces into northern Vietnam, then a French colony, bringing them within striking distance of Singapore. The British government was forced to admit there was now little chance the fleet could be spared to meet any Japanese threat, which all but killed the "Singapore Strategy." London had to concentrate on the fight for survival and take a calculated risk with the safety of the empire in Asia. It gambled that in any clash with Japan, powerful assistance from the United States would be available from the start, which would prevent the Japanese from concentrating their forces against Singapore. Singapore must be held, to help deny the resource-rich territories of Southeast Asia to the Japanese and, of course, to keep the tin and rubber flowing to the

beleaguered Home Islands. But the main responsibility for Singapore's defense was shifted to the Royal Air Force (RAF). Unfortunately, the RAF was in no position to spare enough forces to secure Singapore, fighting as it was to prevent a German invasion of the United Kingdom. In practice that left the brunt to the army.

Reinforcements were received during 1941 by all three services. But none was strong enough to face any attack with confidence, and the "period before relief" (sometimes with grim humor termed "the period beyond belief") now stood at an intimidating *180 days*. The army remained spread out to hold air bases without enough planes, in order to hold a naval base with no battle fleet. It was built up piecemeal by whatever formations could be spared from several different parts of the empire, none with any combat experience. Time ran out before it could either train to fight well in the jungle or build the defenses needed to hold such a large area. And there was one final complication. Planners expected the Japanese to land in neutral southern Thailand, to avoid initial opposition, then move into northern Malaya. Local commanders devised a plan to launch a preemptive strike into southern Thailand if the Japanese moved toward the Malay Peninsula, to keep them at bay. But until the very eve of war the British government refused to allow local commanders to trigger the plan if the Japanese moved. It was feared that if the British violated Thai neutrality, this could ignite a debate in the United States which might jeopardize U.S. intervention. That left the defenders unsure what defense plan they might implement, as well as feeling too weak to hold the area against a serious attack.

The attack on Singapore was rated second behind only the strike against the U.S. Navy's Pacific Fleet in Pearl Harbor, Hawaii, in the plan for the grand Japanese offensive designed to knock the Western Powers out of the way and seize the rich territories of Southeast Asia. Three of the best divisions in the Imperial Japanese Army were allotted to the attack, specially and intensively trained and equipped for jungle warfare. The Japanese were also supported by powerful air and naval forces. When the invasion fleet set sail in early December 1941, the Japanese were in a very good position. Although they faced larger ground forces, their troops were more experienced, better trained, better led, and more homogeneous, and had far stronger air support. Even though they invaded at the very places expected by the defenders, the fall of Singapore was all but a foregone conclusion from the start. But the speed and ease of that fall need not have been, and in the long run did much damage.

The Japanese allotted 100 days for the fall of Singapore. They took it in 70, and captured some 130,000

British Empire troops, double their own number. In addition to the gravely compromised position from which the defenders started, three factors accounted for the disastrous outcome. The Japanese outfought and outgeneraled their enemy. And the defenders helped finish themselves off by taking a bad hand and playing it badly. The first setback for the defenders was the successful neutralization of the U.S. Pacific Fleet by the Japanese strike at Pearl Harbor on December 7, 1941. This exploded the British assumption that powerful U.S. Navy forces would compel the Japanese to divide their strength, helping buy time to reinforce Singapore, before the main battle in Malaya was even joined. The bold Japanese advance pushed British forces from their main positions in the north, and into headlong retreat, in less than four days. Determined Japanese air attacks gained dominance of the air in three days. A Royal Navy squadron sent out to Singapore to deter the Japanese was, on the third day of the war, caught without air cover at sea and destroyed; this was the first successful attack by air forces on capital ships at sea. All this left the defenders, after only 100 hours, without any hope of help from the Pacific, and facing an enemy with the initiative on the ground, dominance in the air, and command of the sea. The fate of Singapore now rested on a race between the Japanese advance and the ability of the British command to dispatch reinforcements from afar; meanwhile, the forces on the spot must hold fast. The gap in the "Singapore Strategy" now blew up in its authors' faces.

In command of the Japanese Twenty-fifth Army was Lieutenant General Yamashita Tomoyuki, arguably the best army commander they had throughout the war. Yamashita was well aware that the campaign hinged on a race, and acted accordingly. Taking bold, calculated risks with his supplies and the fitness of his units, Yamashita drove his army forward in a relentless advance, aiming to keep the defenders off balance and to chew them up before they could regroup. Unfortunately, the strategy pursued by his counterpart, Lieutenant General Arthur E. Percival, arguably the British army's worst commander of the war, played into Yamashita's hands. After the prewar plans fell apart, Percival could not bring himself to take any calculated risks to try to stem the onslaught. In order to keep the Japanese as far from the naval base as possible, and to deny the air bases, he tried to stand and fight in the north. But to prevent the Japanese from landing again closer to Singapore, now that they dominated the sea, he kept his army divided, to cover too many threats at once. That strategy allowed the Japanese to defeat his less experienced troops one formation at a time—helped by several landings from the sea to turn defensive positions, and

by strong air support. The defenders were driven onto the now isolated island of Singapore on the last day of January 1942.

The siege of Singapore itself was an anticlimax. Although some reinforcements did arrive, they were too late and too weak to turn the tide. One Australian division arrived only four days before the British capitulation, and regained its land legs only to march into POW cages. The island was crammed with refugees who drained its stocks of food and water. Singapore's defenses were not designed to withstand a land attack from the north; the attacker was to have been kept at bay. Most of the great guns could be, and were, brought to bear on the attackers, and the Japanese stretched their supplies very thin by their rapid advance. But they also had the island surrounded, and could bomb and shell it at will; they had the advantage of landing where they chose on an all but unfortified northern coast; and they were riding high on the euphoria of their victories. The final invasion began on the night of February 8. The fighting was sometimes intense in places, but confused, and again the defenders failed to concentrate effectively or to show any real boldness. After only a week Percival's army unraveled, and the vaunted "impregnable fortress" collapsed. On February 15, Percival surrendered the largest British-led force lost in any war, under a white flag flying next to the Union Jack.

The contrast between the public boasting about "Fortress Singapore" and the speed and disarray with which its large garrison fell was stark. This debacle made more of an impression on the world, then and later, than the many reasons which made the outcome not all that surprising. British forces were soon pushed out of the entire region and back to India, leaving them on the defensive and marginalized. The sight of British weakness and humiliation at the hands of an Asian power, plus resentment at being made to suffer a cruel occupation under that same power, fueled the rise of nationalism in the lost European colonies. Even when they returned to Singapore in 1945, the British came back, largely due to U.S. successes elsewhere, to a region no longer dominated by the impression of European superiority. The rapid fall of Singapore in 1942 not only left the British a secondary ally in the war against Japan, it also exposed the fact they could no longer hold the empire they had built. Their day as a first-rate power in Asia was clearly over.

FURTHER READINGS

Allen, Louis. *Singapore 1941–1942* (1977).

Barber, Noel. *Sinister Twilight: The Fall of Singapore* (1968).

Elphick, Peter. *Singapore: The Pregnable Fortress* (1995).

Falk, Stanley. *Seventy Days to Singapore* (1975).

Kirby, S. W. *Singapore: The Chain of Disaster* (1971).

Leasor, James. *Singapore: The Battle That Changed the World* (1968).

Murfett, M. H., B. P. Farrell, et al. *Between Two Oceans: A Military History of Singapore* (1999).

Percival, A. E. *The War in Malaya* (1949).

Tsuji Masanobu. *Singapore 1941–1942* (1960).

Wigmore, Lionel. *The Japanese Thrust* (1957).

Brian P. Farrell

SEE ALSO Malaya, Japanese Conquest of;

Slim, William Joseph (1891–1970)

One of Great Britain's most successful military commanders of World War II, William Slim (later 1st Viscount Slim) came from a lower-middle-class background. For a person from such a background, a career as an officer in the British army would have been almost impossible. But World War I gave Slim the opportunity to enlist and serve with distinction in the Middle East, for which service he was rewarded with a commission from the ranks. But lack of opportunity for advancement in the class-oriented British officer corps amid the retrenchment of the interwar period led Slim to transfer to the Indian army, where he assumed a regular commission in the 6th Gurkhas. By the outbreak of World War II in September 1939, he had risen to the rank of brigadier and served again with distinction, leading his brigade in the Abyssinian campaign of 1941. Thereafter, he was given command of a division, which he led in the occupation of Iraq to displace its pro-Nazi rulers and secure access to Iraqi oil.

In the spring of 1942, Slim was sent to command I Corps in Burma at the very moment that the Japanese launched a massive invasion of the country. In Burma, he found British forces woefully unprepared, both materially and psychologically, to fight the Japanese. As a result, between March and May 1942, Slim had to conduct a grueling and demoralizing 900-mile retreat with shattered forces from Rangoon, Burma, to Imphal, India, before the Japanese onslaught ran out of strength in northern Burma.

At Imphal, Slim's weak forces remained on the defensive until December 1943. During this period, he tackled the difficult task of rebuilding the morale and fighting capabilities of his troops with few resources and little support from a British government that viewed the China-Burma-India theater as a backwater of defeat. Nonetheless, Slim laid down a clear, farsighted offensive theater strategy that aimed to retake Burma and that emphasized the need to use surprise and deception to compensate for the numerical and material weaknesses of his forces. During 1942–1943, Slim retrained his troops to a standard unparalleled in the British army of World War II and restored their morale. In particular, he stressed that troops must not undertake demoralizing retreats, like those of 1942, if the Japanese ever again cut their lines of communication. Instead, Slim demanded that his soldiers stand and fight, even if this meant encirclement, and promised to use aerial resupply to sustain any such isolated forces until he could organize relief operations.

Lacking resources, the British were able to mount only limited counteroffensive operations from India into Burma during the 1942–1943 dry season before the arrival of the summer monsoon. The Japanese defeated an attack into the Arakan, and deep penetration operations by Chindit irregulars, while enjoying initial good results, suffered heavily and absorbed enormous quantities of precious resources and supplies. These initiatives thus failed to change the strategic balance in the theater.

Late in 1943, however, a promoted Lieutenant General Slim assumed command of a newly designated Fourteenth Army and energetically prepared his command for counteroffensive operations to be carried out during the spring of 1944 before the monsoon. He developed an excellent working knowledge of Japanese doctrine and tactics and inculcated his troops with logical counters to the enemy's techniques. He also developed close cooperation with the Third Tactical Air Force, which was slated to support his ground forces. During November 1943, Slim appreciated Japanese intentions to launch an offensive into northern India to capture Assam and secure a more defensible front. He thus quickly launched his own counterattack into the Arakan in January 1944 to forestall and disrupt this imminent Japanese attack, to gain a better defensive position himself, and to protect his lines of communications and forward airfields in East Bengal. By late January, he had gained most of his limited objectives and so assumed the defensive. Even so, it had taken 180,000 British and Indian troops with an overwhelming superiority in aircraft, artillery, and armor to defeat a single Japanese division of 8,000 men.

At the same time, the success of Slim's preemptive strike compelled the Japanese to launch their planned counteroffensive prematurely and piecemeal as a counterattack. Nonetheless, the Japanese offensive, when it came in late January, upset Slim's well-laid plans for a general counteroffensive later that spring as the Japanese struck in strength for the Imphal Plain. Slim was forced to stand and fight on flat, open terrain against an enemy superior in strength. Forbidden to withdraw by Slim, the 5th and 7th Indian Divisions found themselves isolated by the Japanese advance. Slim demanded that they stand fast, and he put into effect the aerial resupply operation he had promised. He also energetically launched relief operations that rescued the beleaguered troops and hammered the Japanese Fifteenth Army. Caught between the two forces, the Japanese were forced to withdraw in tatters through the jungle back into Burma. Slim's success demonstrated the efficacy of his operational approach, silenced his critics, and greatly boosted troop morale.

However, these reverses led Japan to reinforce its forces in Burma, and it launched a renewed major invasion of India via Imphal and Kohima between March and July 1944 that again sorely tested Slim's troops and their morale. In the face of superior strength, Slim's forces were compelled to make a fighting withdrawal on Imphal, during which a lightning Japanese advance surrounded the 17th Indian Division. Slim had to do an about-face and rescue the division before it could withdraw into the defensive perimeter British and Indian forces established outside Imphal in early April. Aided by the arrival of much needed reinforcements from India, Slim's troops brought the Japanese offensive to a grinding halt during May 1944 in a protracted battle of attrition.

After thwarting the Japanese offensive, in early 1945 Slim prepared to launch an ambitious counteroffensive aimed at recapturing Burma. During the summer of 1944, he exploited his success by capturing crossings over the Chindwin River at Sittang and Kalewa, despite atrocious monsoon conditions, to acquire jumping-off points for future offensive action. He then developed lines of supply via Tamu through the Kalew Valley to Kalewa to provide the logistic base for a renewal of offensive operations. During the late summer of 1944, Slim prepared to engage and destroy the enemy on the Shwebo Plain during the winter of 1944–1945 via an encirclement operation on Mandalay. But mounting signs of Japanese intentions to effect a general withdrawal behind the highly defensible barrier of the Irrawaddy River compelled Slim to scrap these plans.

Instead, he now planned to make a deep penetration into Burma to capture Meiktila, the key base and communications center of the Japanese Burma Area Command. Such a bold and deep advance through the jungle into the Japanese rear could only succeed if Slim managed to confuse the enemy as to his intentions. Using elaborate security and deception measures, he transferred the IV Corps from Tamu to Pokokku on the Irrawaddy, within striking distance of Meiktila, unseen by the enemy. At the same time, the XXXIII Corps frontally attacked across the Irrawaddy River toward Mandalay to draw Japanese reserves there. When the enemy had fully committed all its available reserves, IV Corps struck across the Irrawaddy and captured Meiktila on March 3, 1945. The Japanese were thrown off balance by this daring, lightning strike, and as a result, XXXIII Corps also captured Mandalay during late March.

The Japanese reacted violently to the British crossing of the Irrawaddy and launched numerous counterattacks to eliminate the British bridgehead but suffered crippling losses in the process. Slim's forces then decisively defeated the Japanese at Meiktila during March 15–31, 1945. Making use of aerial resupply again, Slim kept his forces moving forward rapidly to storm Rangoon on May 2, 1945, as the first monsoon rains began to fall. The recapture of Rangoon brought to a conclusion one of the best-conceived and most boldly enacted British ground campaigns of World War II.

Slim took demoralized and badly beaten troops and restored them to a standard of proficiency unmatched in the British army of World War II. He also became the only Allied general of the war decisively to defeat the Japanese army on the Asian mainland and to prevail over the enemy with limited air support. His battlefield achievements showed him to be a great soldier of sharp intelligence and shrewd judgment. In the opinion of many authorities, Slim was the best commander produced by Great Britain during World War II.

FURTHER READINGS
Calvert, Michael. *Slim* (1973).
Lewin, Ronald. *Slim, the Standardbearer: A Biography of Field-Marshal the Viscount Slim, KG, GCB, GCMG, GCVO, GBE, DSO, MC* (1976).
Slim, William J. Viscount. *Defeat into Victory* (1956).
Russell A. Hart

SEE ALSO Army, Japanese; China-Burma-India Theater of Operations

Small Arms, Japanese

Japanese army and naval-infantry forces relied on a standard assortment of small arms in World War II. These arms can be grouped into rifles and carbines, pistols, light machine guns, and submachine guns. Heavy machine guns, while not normally considered small arms, will also be covered under this topical heading. Japanese small-arms ammunition could be identified, in many instances, by the following colored bands: pink (ball), black (armor-piercing), and green (tracer).

The two basic rifle models in service by the Japanese were the 38 and the 99. The Model 38 (1905) 6.5-mm rifle, also known as the Arisaka, was based on the German Mauser bolt-action design and fitted to take the Model 30 (1897) bayonet. A carbine version of this rifle, the Model 38 (1905) carbine, which was shorter and lighter than the original model, was also manufactured. A carbine variant, the Model 44 (1911) carbine, was slightly longer than the Model 38 carbine and came with a folding spike bayonet. A sniper's version of the Model 38 rifle, the Model 91 (1931), was essentially the same as the original except for the inclusion of a telescopic sight. Some Italian-made 6.5-mm rifles were also used by the Japanese.

The Model 99 (1939) 7.7-mm rifle succeeded the Model 38 as the need arose during the war for a more powerful service rifle. It was basically the same as the Model 38 except it was shorter and had a larger caliber. A long variant of the Model 99, a sniper variant, and an experimental model reworked to use light-machine-gun magazines were also produced. Both the Model 38 and the Model 99 rifle could be fitted with spigot, rifled, and cup-type grenade launchers, which fired fragmentation, smoke, and high-explosive antipersonnel grenades. Toward the end of the war, a few Japanese 7.7-mm semiautomatic rifles, based on captured U.S. Garands, were also manufactured.

The standard Japanese pistol design was based on the Nambu (1914) 8-mm pistol. Modeled in appearance after the German Luger yet different in its internal functioning, this semiautomatic pistol is named after its Japanese inventor, Colonel Kijiro Nambu. A wooden combination shoulder-stock-holster was developed to turn this pistol into a carbine but was obsolete prior to the war in the Pacific. The Nambu was superseded by the Model 14 (1925) 8-mm pistol, a significantly modified version. The Model 14 was mass-produced and became the major Japanese pistol used in World War II. A rare 7-mm version, reserved solely for the use of staff officers, was also manufactured.

Two other Japanese pistols were also in service. The Model 94 (1934) 8-mm pistol was of poor design and initially produced for export, mostly to Japanese living in South America. It was supplied to aircraft crews and infantry forces during the war. The model 26 (1893) 9-mm revolver was based on a hinged-frame Smith & Wesson model. It was the only revolver ever produced in quantity by the Japanese. The Model 11 (1922) 6.5-mm light machine gun was based on the French Hotchkiss yet was hampered by its reliance on 5-round ammunition clips fed into a hopper instead of a more standard feed system. At one time standard to the Japanese infantry squad, this weapon was replaced by the Model 96 (1936) 6.5-mm light machine gun. Although the Model 96 externally resembled the British Bren gun, with its magazine feed and carrying handle, it was based on French and Czech internal designs. This light machine gun had a bipod mount and was fitted to take the Model 30 (1897) bayonet.

The Japanese also used other machine-gun models during World War II. The Model 99 (1939) 7.7-mm light machine gun was basically the same as the Model 96 except that it was based on a larger caliber. The BRNO, ZB (1925) 7.92-mm light machine gun also saw considerable service. Originally of Czech manufacture, it was purchased by the Japanese prior to the war, looted from the Chinese, and produced in their captured arsenals. Because of the large quantities of British ammunition seized by the Japanese, attempts were made to produce imitations of Allied weapons.

The Japanese used very few submachine guns in the war because they did not appreciate their value until well into the conflict. Those machine weapons that were encountered were mostly German Bergmanns, Swiss-made Solothurns, or captured Allied models. Still, three Japanese submachine-gun designs were manufactured either in small quantities or as prototypes. The Type 0 (1940) 8-mm submachine gun was used by Japanese naval infantry and by paratroopers at Leyte in 1944. The experimental 6.5-mm light machine gun was a cheap, easy-to-make weapon produced during the final Japanese emergency and is notable for its blowback operation. The experimental 8-mm machine gun, which was very compact and had a special rate-of-fire selector, was never placed in production.

The Model 92 (1932) 7.7-mm heavy machine gun represented the standard Japanese heavy machine gun. It was a modified Hotchkiss-type weapon and was mounted on a tripod for use against ground targets; however, an adapter allowed it to be used against aircraft. A Model 92 variant based on the Lewis-type machine gun, which was drum-fed rather than strip-fed, also existed. Another variant, known as the Type 0 heavy machine gun, was lighter than the standard Model 92 and simpler in design, making it one of the best heavy-machine-gun designs of the war.

The Model 93 (1933) 13-mm twin heavy machine gun, which was tripod-mounted and had a steel chair for the gunner, was used against both tanks and aircraft. Model 93 ammunition has a different colored-band system than standard small-arms ammunition: black (ball), white (armor-piercing), and red (tracer). A single-barreled version of this heavy machine gun was also produced.

FURTHER READINGS

Chamberlain, Peter, and Terry Gander. *Axis Pistols, Rifles, and Grenades* (1976).

Smith, W. H. B. *Small Arms of the World: The Basic Manual of Military Small Arms* (1948).

U.S. War Department. *Handbook on Japanese Military Forces*, TM-E 30-480. U.S. Government Printing Office, 1 October 1944 (1991 reprint).

U.S. War Department. *Japanese Infantry Weapons*, special series, no. 19, U.S. Government Printing Office, 31 December 1943.

Robert J. Bunker

SEE ALSO Army, Japanese; Small Arms, U.S.

Small Arms, U.S.

According to the U.S. Army's somewhat imprecise definition, "small arms" included any weapon that foot soldiers carried and fired by hand, from the shoulder, or from some small structure. For the most part, U.S. forces enjoyed a significant advantage over the Japanese in small arms. U.S. infantry weapons surpassed their Japanese counterparts in reliability and stopping power as well as capacity and rate of fire. Although they had some flaws, small arms served U.S. soldiers, sailors, and marines well.

During World War II, the U.S. military designated its types of small-arms ammunition by caliber. For example, a .30-caliber, or .30-cal, was a bullet, or "round," with a 0.3-inch diameter. Later in the twentieth century, bullet diameters were denoted in metric values so that .30-cal and .45-cal became approximately 7.62-mm and 11.43-mm.

The U.S. military issued several pistols to troops in the Pacific. The M1911A1, known as the .45, became the U.S. military's most widely used pistol in World War II. More than 1.85 million M1911A1s were manufactured during the war years. The .45 had a 5-inch barrel, held seven rounds in a detachable box magazine, and weighed approximately 2.5 pounds. These pistols had legendary stopping power and superior reliability, though there were at least two drawbacks: They were difficult to shoot accurately without practice, and they had a maximum effective range of 50 yards. Some .45-cal and .38-cal revolvers by Colt and Smith & Wesson also saw limited service with military police, aviators, and support personnel.

The 1903 Springfield and the Garand rifles served as basic weapons for U.S. forces during World War II. Earlier versions of the 1903 Springfield, such as the M1903 and M1903A1, were used in World War I, and many of these returned to war in 1941. In 1942, the M1903A3 was introduced in an attempt to increase wartime production. Some 1903 Springfields were fitted with telescopic sights and used as sniper rifles; others served as grenade launchers. These weapons fired the .30-cal round, held five rounds in a charger-loaded box magazine, and weighed approximately 9 pounds. With superior accuracy at 600 yards and the reliability of a bolt-action, the 1903 Springfield remained popular among U.S. troops throughout World War II. In fact, because of the Marine Corps' emphasis on marksmanship and its assumption that every marine was a rifleman, the "leathernecks" particularly liked this rifle. Major General Thomas Holcomb, who started the corps' rifle team, won the national championship in 1911, and later served as commandant of the Marine Corps from 1936 to 1943, actually preferred the 1903 Springfield over its replacement, the Garand.

Although it was originally produced in 1937, the .30-cal M1 Garand began to appear in the Pacific only in early 1943. The M1 was nicknamed after John Garand, its inventor. Early models received numerous modifications to correct design and operation problems. The rifle held eight rounds from a top-loaded clip and weighed 9.5 pounds. With a semiautomatic rate of fire of twenty rounds per minute (rpm) and a 600-yard effective range, the Garand boasted impressive firepower. More than 5.5 million Garands had been manufactured by 1945, and they were utilized in all theaters. Despite disparaging remarks by marines and soldiers who still favored the 1903 Springfield, the M1 Garand had all the hallmarks of U.S. small arms: It was potent, rugged, accurate, and easy to maintain. Its strong combat performance soon won over most of its critics.

In addition to rifles, the army and Marine Corps issued the M1 and M2 carbines to U.S. troops as replacements for pistols and submachine guns, respectively. They were neither as heavy (at less than 5.5 pounds) nor as bulky (with an 18-inch barrel) as the Garand or 1903 Springfield (both with 24-inch barrels). Yet the M1 surpassed all pistols in offensive capability because it had a magazine capacity of fifteen rounds and an effective range of 230 yards. Introduced in 1945, the M2 carbine offered a fully automatic option with an impressive 750-rpm rate of fire and an enlarged 30-round magazine; however, the M2's effective range fell to 150 yards. Although it never supplanted the submachine gun, the M2 did provide a viable alternative. Both the M1 and M2 fired 0.3-inch-diameter pistol-type rounds. Some U.S. troops griped about their insufficient stopping power compared with the Garand, yet both carbines did achieve a large following among U.S.

troops. Six million carbines were manufactured—more than any other U.S. military firearm in World War II.

To increase an infantryman's short-range firepower, the Thompson and M3 submachine guns were issued to U.S. troops. Troops carried several models of the Thompson (supposedly the weapon of choice of Prohibition-era Chicago gangsters), such as the M1928A1, the M1, and the M1A1. They all weighed about 11 pounds, held 20- or 30-round detachable box magazines, and had a maximum effective range of 300 yards. Thompsons proved unwieldy because they fired the .45-cal at a rate of 700 rpm; in addition, they were expensive to manufacture. Some complaints also arose over their lack of penetrating power in jungles and against armor. However, the combination of the large caliber and the high rate of fire gave the Thompson devastating firepower at close range against enemy infantry.

Like the Thompson, the M3 submachine gun fired the potent .45-cal round and carried thirty rounds in its magazine. The M3, commonly known as the "grease gun," had strengths that made it often preferable to the Thompson. With a lower rate of fire at 400 rpm, the M3 could be more easily controlled for accurate automatic fire. Despite being ugly, its simple design was lighter, cheaper, more reliable, and easier to maintain than that of the Thompson.

To provide more substantial fire support to squads of infantry, the army adopted the M1918 Browning automatic rifle, or BAR. This fully automatic rifle offered increased firepower with .30-cal rounds, a 500–600-rpm rate of fire, and a 600-yard effective range. In addition, because the BAR's stopping and penetrating power surpassed that of submachine guns, it remained a very popular weapon throughout World War II. Finally, the Japanese army did not have a weapon similar to the BAR in its arsenal. Yet the BAR did have some drawbacks: It was too heavy at 20 pounds; it had a barrel that overheated too often; and its 20-round detachable box magazine was not large enough fully to exploit automatic fire.

Although U.S. forces carried a variety of small arms capable of automatic fire, none could maintain such fire for sustained periods. To accomplish this task, the U.S. military developed the .30-cal M1919A4 air-cooled, the .30-cal M1917A1 water-cooled, and the .50-cal HB-M2 air-cooled machine guns during World War I or shortly thereafter. Of the two .30-cal weapons, the air-cooled light machine gun was the more versatile because of its relatively light weight at 30 pounds. Typically, this weapon covered infantry advances or bolstered defensive positions. Owing to its heavier weight at 80 pounds, the water-cooled .30-cal usually served in defensive roles.

Both light machine guns were very popular among U.S. troops. The .50-cal and its variants were the most widely used machine guns in World War II. The more than two million .50-cals were used in all branches of the U.S. military by infantry, on vehicles, in aircraft, and as antiaircraft weapons. These heavy machine guns earned a legendary reputation for formidable firepower and outstanding reliability. They boasted a maximum effective range of 1,800 yards, or about one mile. The .30-cal and the .50-cal machine guns shared similar rates of fire at 450–600 rpm and were fed by belts of ammunition with 100–250 rounds.

In addition to the above small arms, U.S. infantrymen also needed projectile weapons that combined the firepower of artillery with the compactness of infantry arms. The mortar fulfilled this tactical niche. This muzzle-loaded weapon fired high-explosive, illuminating chemical or gas rounds in a high trajectory—not unlike a very light howitzer. The mortars could be placed in the front lines and provide intense fire support for offensive or defensive movements. Two types saw action: the M2 60-mm mortar and the M1 81-mm mortar. Weighing a mere 38.5 pounds, the 60-mm mortar had an 18-rpm rate of fire and a maximum effective range of 1,985 yards. The M1 81-mm mortar was heavier at 136 pounds, but it had an 18-rpm rate of fire and a longer maximum effective range of 3,290 yards. Both weapons could be carried by two or three men.

Mortars were not the only portable weapons with the firepower of light artillery. The U.S. infantry also utilized M1A1 and M9A1 bazookas when increased firepower was needed to destroy enemy tanks or emplacements. These weapons launched rockets with several pounds of high explosives through 4- or 5-foot tubes. Two-man teams operated the bazookas: One aimed and fired the weapon, while the other loaded the rockets into the tube. Weighing 13.1 pounds, the M1A1 had a maximum effective range of 250 yards and a 4–5-rpm rate of fire. It exhibited deficiencies such as electrical ignition malfunctions and tube corrosion, the latter being exacerbated in the Pacific's tropical climate. The M9A1 made significant changes to solve these problems. Although at 15.9 pounds it weighed slightly more than its predecessor, the M9A1 had a tube that could be dismantled into two sections and was thus less cumbersome. In addition, its tube was aluminum to prevent rusting. The M9 had a longer maximum effective range of 300 yards yet still had a 4–5-rpm rate of fire. Bazookas proved effective antitank weapons—especially in the Pacific against the lighter Japanese tanks.

Among the more potent weapons in the U.S. arsenal, portable flamethrowers were capable of directing jets of flaming liquid against targets at ranges from 25 to 60 yards for eight to ten seconds. Developed for the U.S. armed forces by the Army Chemical Warfare Corps, the M1A1 and the modified M2-2 flamethrowers saw action primarily in the Pacific and not in the European theater, against Caucasians. A flamethrower's firing mechanism worked in the following way: One infantryman carried three pressurized containers weighing 70 pounds on his back, and a second infantryman adjusted the valves on the containers. Nitrogen from one container forced the jellied gasoline from the other container through a hand-held tube. Flamethrowers had two triggers on this tube. One was used to adjust the amount of liquid in the tube, and the other sparked the ignition of the liquid. As the jellied gasoline emerged from the tube, it became a stream of flaming liquid, which burned incessantly and stuck to any surface. Although temperamental and limited in range, the flamethrower was one of the most effective—and most horrendous—Allied weapons against Japanese forces in hardened positions, such as pillboxes or caves, and could turn enemy soldiers into human torches to die an agonizing death.

U.S. soldiers are probably the most caustic critics of their own weapons, but this was not the case in the Pacific war.

FURTHER READINGS

Canfield, Bruce N. *U.S. Infantry Weapons of World War II* (1994).

Forty, George. *US Army Handbook, 1939–1945*, 2d ed. (1995).

Rottman, Gordon L. *U.S. Marine Corps World War II Divisions, Brigades, and Regiments* (1995).

Sledge, E. B. *With the Old Breed at Peleliu and Okinawa* (1981).

Thompson, Henry C., and Lida Mayo. *The Ordnance Department: Procurement and Supply* (1960).

David Ulbrich

SEE ALSO Army Ground Forces, U.S.; Marine Corps, U.S.; Small Arms, Japanese

Smith, Holland McTyeire (1882–1967)

A marine general, Holland McTyeire Smith pioneered amphibious warfare techniques used in the South Pacific during World War II. Born at Hatchachubbee, Alabama, on April 20, 1882, Smith grew up in nearby Seale then attended the Alabama Polytechnic Institute (later Auburn University). Bored by mandatory drills, Cadet Smith read books on Napoleon and military leaders to learn basic

tactics. When he graduated in 1901, he was offered an appointment to the United States Naval Academy, but his father, a noted criminal attorney, insisted that he pursue a law degree from the University of Alabama. Smith joined his family's law firm in 1903 but disliked the courtroom.

Smith retained his military ambitions. Congressman Ariosto A. Wiley informed him there were no vacancies in the army and suggested he enlist in the marines. Smith passed the examinations and was commissioned a second lieutenant in the Marine Corps in March 1905. After completing the Annapolis School of Application, Smith served in overseas assignments, including a 1916 expedition to Santo Domingo, where he first came under fire. That year, he initiated experiments with amphibious landings in the Dominican Republic.

Soon after the United States entered World War I, Smith accompanied U.S. troops to France. He was the first marine officer to complete the Army General Staff College at Langres. As adjutant of the newly established Marine Brigade of the army's Second Division, Smith served with distinction. He received the Croix de Guerre for courage at the Battle of Belleau Wood and was promoted to the rank of major, later serving in the occupation of Germany.

During the interwar years, Smith developed amphibious assault equipment and tactics that later proved effective in the World War II Pacific theater. In 1920 at the Naval War College, he declared that the traditional naval doctrine being taught was obsolete, promoting amphibious tactics instead. Smith predicted that future battles in the Pacific would require troops on ships attacking land posts, but conservative naval officers, wedded to Mahanite visions of great dreadnought clashes on the high seas, dismissed his views. Smith insisted that ships would be crucial in transporting troops and supplies to land in addition to bombarding positions, impressing a few high-ranking more progressively minded officers who invited him to be the first marine on the Joint Army-Navy Planning Committee.

Smith improved his amphibious warfare techniques in the Caribbean, particularly while training troops in Haiti. In 1939, he was a brigadier general and in command of the First Marine Brigade at Quantico, Virginia, and took his troops to Cuba to practice his amphibious tactics. The major obstacle was the lack of suitable craft to land, unload cargo, and leave quickly. Smith tested shallow draft boats similar to those used by rumrunners during Prohibition. He and boatbuilder Andrew Jackson Higgins designed a useful boat and an amphibian tractor based on craft used in the Everglades. Smith gained the rank of major general, and Admiral Ernest King selected him to command I Corps. Smith directed army and marine divisions in amphibious training exercises in North Carolina, preparing the troops for future landings in both Pacific and Atlantic theaters.

Tired of training, Smith yearned for battle. In June 1943, he met Admiral Chester William Nimitz at a conference and asked to be appointed amphibious commander. Nimitz placed Smith in command of the Joint Army-Marine V Amphibious Corps in the central Pacific. Allied forces effectively utilized his amphibious strategies during island-hopping campaigns in the Pacific. Smith's troops had taken two Japanese-held atolls, Makin and Tarawa, in the Gilbert Islands by November 1943. At the assault on Tarawa, Smith was angered that landing craft were caught in coral, ensuring easy targets, which he called a "futile sacrifice of Marines." He demanded that more amphibious tractors be utilized, a crucial order for victory. Smith constantly sought better boats and weapons and increased naval bombardment to expedite landings.

Interservice rivalry resulted in bitterness between commanders. Smith argued with navy colleagues about how to conduct amphibious operations and stressed that once troops landed, naval officers lacking training in land warfare should transfer command to more experienced marine leaders. Often labeled arrogant, Smith believed that controlled anger was a useful leadership technique; he also occasionally disregarded protocol in order to achieve goals and objectives. He aggressively promoted himself, bluntly saying older generals should retire. One uncharitable officer remembered, "General Smith was a sorehead, indignant and griping about everything."

Smith's supporters attempted to soften his image, depicting him as a compassionate leader to counter his "sulphurous" manner. Relentlessly, Smith pushed his troops to assault swiftly, believing that speed would save lives. He was intolerant of cautious, deliberate commanders. One reporter described him in battle as "clad in a green-spotted jacket, grasping a carbine, jumping up and down, alternately swearing and beaming over his silver-rimmed spectacles." Contemporaries credited Smith's temper for inspiring his nickname, "Howlin' Mad," but Smith steadfastly claimed it was a mere mispronunciation of his name.

Smith was featured on the cover of *Time* magazine in February 1944, with an article lauding his mastery of amphibious attack. In 1944, he directed the successful capture of atolls in the Marshalls and Marianas, securing Kwajalein, Eniwetok, Saipan, Tinian, and Guam. At Saipan, Smith relieved the commander of the army's 27th

Division for not attacking, in his opinion, aggressively enough. This dismissal of an army officer by a marine officer was unprecedented and upset interservice cooperation in the theater; Smith was accused of prejudice against the army. He noted, in response, that many military leaders thought his actions were justified. "The Army is extremely jealous and is forever making faulty and specious claims," he argued, insisting that he had "leaned over backwards to assuage their feelings." The press also now seemed to turn against Smith, blaming him for heavy casualties and labeling him a "reckless butcher."

Despite this controversy, Smith, who had recently been promoted to lieutenant general, was named commander of the Fleet Marine Force, Pacific, established in August 1944. In other assaults, Smith was praised for his acute tactical instincts. Admiral Raymond A. Spruance called Tinian "the most brilliantly conceived and executed amphibious operation of the war," noting it was a "classic for which Holland Smith and his Marines deserve full credit." During the war, Smith received the navy Distinguished Service Medal with four gold stars, recognizing his "high caliber of combat leadership and conceptual brilliance." Marines respectfully called him the "Old Man of the Atolls."

In 1945, Smith commanded three marine divisions at the assault of Iwo Jima. He had unsuccessfully requested a lengthier period of preinvasion bombing, and the result was heavy casualties. Feeling disappointed and betrayed, Smith relinquished command in July to General Roy Geiger and accepted the position of commanding general of the Marine Training and Replacement Command in San Diego. He remained there until May 1946. After promotion to full general (the third marine to receive four stars), he retired in August 1946.

Moving to La Jolla, California, "Mr. Marine Corps," as Smith was called, published a serialized account of how he developed amphibious warfare in the *Marine Corps Gazette*. His autobiography, *Coral and Brass,* was published in 1949. This controversial tome was Smith's attempt to vindicate and protect himself and the Marine Corps from continued attacks, mostly focusing on Saipan, in popular magazines and military journals. Unfortunately, Smith criticized many of his colleagues, included errors, and accepted credit for others' accomplishments. His reputation suffered, overshadowing his role in the deployment of amphibious warfare to secure victory in the Pacific.

In 1950, he hosted the television program *Uncommon Valor* and portrayed himself in the movie *Sands of Iwo Jima*. Smith was honored by the establishment of Camp H. M. Smith, the headquarters of the Fleet Marine Force, at Halawa Heights on Oahu, Hawaii, in 1956. "Saddened and distressed" by war casualties, he volunteered to help underprivileged and fatherless children because "I lost a lot of fathers in the war. So I decided I would spend the rest of my life helping their children." Smith also assisted the founding of the Marine Military Academy in Harlingen, Texas.

While dedicating the Marine Corps Memorial Building in Texas, Smith suffered a heart attack and later died in the San Diego naval hospital on January 12, 1967; he was buried at Fort Rosecrans National Cemetery and eulogized as the "father of amphibious warfare."

FURTHER READINGS

Cooper, Norman V. *A Fighting General: The Biography of Gen. Holland M. "Howlin' Mad" Smith* (1987).

Draughon, Ralph B. "General Holland M. Smith, U.S.M.C.," *Alabama Review* (1968).

Gailey, Harry A. *Howlin' Mad vs. the Army: Conflict in Command, Saipan, 1944* (1986).

Smith, Holland McTyeire. *Coral and Brass* (1991).

———. *The Development of Amphibious Tactics in the U.S. Navy* (1992).

Elizabeth D. Schafer

SEE ALSO Marine Corps, U.S.

Sorge, Richard (1895–1944)

One of the Soviet Union's most effective espionage agents, Richard Sorge (Rikhard Zorge) was born in Baku to a Russian mother and a German father who had come to Russia as an engineer for the Baku oil industry. While Sorge was still quite young, the family moved to Berlin. After serving in the German Army during World War I (1914–1918) and being wounded three times, he embraced Marxism. Sorge quickly became an active member of the newly formed German Communist Party, organizing communist cells while teaching political science. His talents attracted the attention of the leadership of the Communist International (Comintern), the Soviet-dominated body linking the world communist parties, and he was invited to Moscow in 1924 for a new career as a Comintern agent.

Sorge's first assignments abroad took him to Scandinavia and later to the United Kingdom. His international experience and considerable facility for languages made him a natural candidate for intelligence work—despite his weaknesses for liquor and women. By 1929, as part of his new assignment in China, he had been transferred from the Comintern to Soviet military intelligence.

Under cover as a journalist in Shanghai, Sorge was assigned to gather political and military intelligence on China and the foreign community there. While in China, he met his most valuable contact for his subsequent work in Japan: the well-connected Japanese journalist Hotsumi Ozaki, who would become one of Japan's most prominent China specialists. When Sorge returned to Moscow in 1933, he was told his next assignment would be Tokyo.

Traveling first to Nazi Germany to establish his cover as a journalist, this true believer communist joined the Nazi party and became the Tokyo correspondent for the *Frankfurter Zeitung* and the *Täglishche Rundschau*. Sorge arrived in Tokyo in September 1933 and quickly ingratiated himself among Japan's German expatriates. He became a leading member of Tokyo's German community, rapidly establishing solid ties with the German ambassador, Herbert von Dirksen, and the military attaché, Eugen Ott, while reactivating his connection to Hotsumi Ozaki. The spy network that Sorge established, together with his unmatched access to the German embassy and the journalistic community, proved invaluable for gathering intelligence for Moscow. For a time, Sorge himself actually wrote the German military attaché's reports back to Berlin.

Though the steady intelligence Sorge provided was valuable, including advance notice of the creation of Germany and Japan's Anti-Comintern Pact, his fame today as a spy rests on two feats. First, Sorge gave ample warning of Operation Barbarossa, the German attack on the Soviet Union in June 1941. Charming the German officers who regularly passed through Tokyo, he was able to obtain a remarkably accurate picture of Hitler's intentions. One officer on his way to Thailand had special secret instructions for Ott and happily repeated the same information to Sorge: Germany would attack the Soviet Union on June 20, 1941, with some one hundred eighty divisions. Though Sorge's valuable data was to some degree sabotaged by the unreliable agent he had transmitting his messages, the Soviet Union received clear advance notice of Hitler's invasion, which actually began on June 22. What Stalin did with this information was an entirely different matter.

The Soviet dictator ignored Sorge's warning, along with other signs of the impending attack, but paid more attention to the next piece of vital information Sorge passed on. With German divisions racing ever closer to Moscow, the Soviet high command dared not pull troops from the Soviet Far East for fear of imminent Japanese attack. Conflict indeed raged within Japan's army and navy over whether Japan should take advantage of Germany's success to attack a distracted Soviet Union or turn toward Western colonies in southeast Asia. Through Ozaki's connections in elite Japanese political and business circles, and a careful account of Japan's desperate need for the resources of the southeast Asia, by Sorge could report by September 1941 that the Soviet Far East was safe until at least the spring 1942, and he repeated that message more forcefully the next month in his very last transmission. The Japanese intended to move against American, British, and Dutch possessions, not against the Soviet Union. Sorge's intelligence allowed Moscow to transfer hardened Siberian divisions west to turn back the German drive on Moscow in December 1941.

Sorge's ring began to unravel when a German investigation of his leftist past led the Japanese military police (the Kempeitei) and secret police to place him under surveillance in 1941. The real break in the case came, however, through interrogations of Japanese communists. That trail led first to Ozaki, then to Sorge. He was arrested on October 18, 1941, and gave a full confession in under a week. Finally put on trial in 1943, he was convicted and sentenced to death. He and Ozaki were hanged on November 7, 1944.

FURTHER READINGS

Andrew, Christopher, and Oleg Gordievsky. *KGB: The Inside Story* (1990).

Johnson, Chalmers. *An Instance of Treason: Ozaka Hotsumi and the Sorge Spy Ring* (1964)

Prange, Gordon W. *Target Tokyo: The Story of the Sorge Spy Ring* (1984).

David Stone

Soviet Operations against Japan

Although actual Soviet combat operations against Japan in the Pacific theater were minimal in terms of time, the overall presence of Russian forces on the Asian mainland had enormous implications for the struggle in the Pacific. To begin with, Soviet troop deployments into the Far Eastern Command kept hundreds of thousands of Japanese soldiers from being deployed to face the American onslaught and advance from the east.

In order to avoid just such a predicament that a two-front war presented, the Soviet Union signed a non-aggression treaty with Japan in April 1941. Nonetheless, during the Teheran Conference in November of 1943, Stalin agreed to renounce the treaty and attack Japan once the allies had defeated Nazi Germany. On April 5, 1945, the Kremlin officially renounced the accord with Tokyo and commenced the build-up of forces in the Far East. As the Third Reich collapsed, Moscow began redeploying

fully operational divisions eastward to the Pacific area. By the end of July the U.S.S.R. had assembled more than 1.5 million troops organized into three army groups (fronts) under the Soviet Far East Command. Led by Marshal Aleksandr M. Vasilevsky, these forces were arrayed in eleven armies, including three air armies, three air defense armies, and one tank army. In theater, the Soviets had also deployed 3,800 aircraft, 26,000 guns and mortars, and 5,000 tanks.

The Japanese forces were centered in Manchuria around Japan's Kwantung Army, which in July 1945, had an officially reported strength of 950,000 troops. The actual figure was closer to 700,000, of which approximately 300,000 were Manchukuoan puppet units. Though forced to defend in East Asia, the Kwantung's operational capability was further degraded as a substantial number of combat veteran units were redeployed during 1944–1945 to defend against the approach of U.S. forces in the Pacific. The Japanese commander in Manchuria, General Otaza Yamada, was forced to stand by and watch as the Soviets reinforced their armies surrounding him during the period from April through July 1945.

By May, Tokyo was forced to respond to these developments and ordered the Kwantung Army reinforced. These efforts were severely hampered by Chinese counter-operations, which by late June had severely degraded Japanese capabilities in moving through the Indo-China corridor. By July 1, more than 100,000 Japanese troops were isolated in the Canton area, while another 100,000 had retreated back into northern China after being thoroughly harassed by the 14th and 15th U.S. Army Air Forces.

The Soviet Union declared war on Japan on August 8, 1945, and commenced offensive military operations on August 9 in Manchuria, Sakhalin, and the Kurile Islands. Stormy weather contributed to the shock and surprise of the Soviet attacks in Manchuria. The 3d Far Eastern Army Group (FEAG), Commanded by Marshal Radion Y. Malinkovsky, attacked Yamada's left while Marshal Kirill A. Meretzkov's 1st FEAG attacked on the right. From the north, at Blagoveschensk, the 2d FEAG descended south across the Amur River. Each area proceeded forward with three lines of advance, searching for opportunity and moving in pincerlike attack. Yamada was faced with attack from nine lines of offensive operations all descending upon his army from three sides. The 1st and 2d Soviet FEAGs moved against Harbin, linked up, and attacked southward toward Korea. In the northeast, the Soviet Trans-Baikal Army (attached to the 3d FEAG) moved eastward against Hsinking and Mukden.

The viability of the Japanese defense in Manchuria was pierced by advance elements of Malinovsky's group.

While the Japanese had put up stiff resistance all across the front, they were caught unprepared as Malinovsky's 6th Guards Tank Army made an uncontested transit through the near trackless Kinghan Mountains. Exploiting this success, Malinovsky pushed additional divisions through the passage. By August, Soviet forces had penetrated the Central Manchurian Plain and had completed their envelopment of the Kwantung Army. By August 14 the Japanese faced total annihilation by the Soviet army. This destruction was forestalled by surrender of Japan on August 14, 1945. The Russians accepted the surrender of 590,000 troops and had inflicted 80,000 casualties on Yamada's forces while suffering 30,000 casualties of their own.

Simultaneously with the commencement of action in Manchuria, the Soviets attacked the Japanese 88th Division in southern Sakhalin with an amphibious assault. They also struck in the Kurile Islands. Fighting also continued south across the Yalu River into Korea, were the U.S.S.R. launched concurrent land and amphibious operations which continued until August 23, 1945. Soviet combat operations against Japan officially ceased on August 31, after the successful invasion and occupation of the Kurile Islands. With the Soviet Union now the dominant military power on the Asian mainland, it can be argued that no four days of military operations in modern time ever yielded so much.

FURTHER READINGS

Dupuy, R. Ernest, and Trevor N. Dupuy. *The Harper Encyclopedia of Military History: From 3500 B.C. to the Present,* 4th ed. (1993).

Glanz, David. *August Storm: The Soviet 1945 Strategic Offensive in Manchuria.* (1984).

Isby, David C. *Weapons and Tactics of the Soviet Army* (1981).

Keegan, John. *The Second World War* (1990).

ROTC Manual, No. 145020. *American Military History: 1607–1958* (July 17, 1956).

Smurthwaite, David. *The Pacific War Atlas: 1941–1945* (1995).

Sidorenko, A. A. *The Offensive: A Soviet View* (1970).

James McNabb

SEE ALSO Army, Japanese

Spruance, Raymond Ames (1886–1969)

One of the U.S. Navy's most prominent and successful commanders, Raymond Ames Spruance was born in Baltimore, Maryland, on July 3, 1886. He graduated from the U.S. Naval Academy in 1906 and participated in the global voyage of the Great White Fleet in 1907 aboard battleship *Minnesota.* He was commissioned an ensign in 1908 and in 1909 studied electrical engineering at General Electric in New York. He served with the Atlantic Fleet aboard battleship *Connecticut* (1910–1911) and then with the Asiatic Fleet aboard cruiser *Cincinnati.* As a lieutenant (j.g.) Spruance commanded old destroyer *Bainbridge* in 1913–1914; promoted to lieutenant in 1914, he served as an inspector at the Newport News Shipbuilding and Dry Dock Company. He became electrical officer on new battleship *Pennsylvania* (1916–1917) and in August 1917, shortly after the United States entered World War I, Lieutenant Commander Spruance was assistant engineering officer at the New York Navy Yard. In 1918, Commander Spruance served as executive officer of troop transport *Agamemnon.*

From 1919 to 1921 he successively commanded destroyers, *Aaron Ward* and *Percival.* Spruance then headed the Electrical Division at the Bureau of Engineering (1921–1924) before serving on board cruiser *Pittsburgh* (1924–1925) as assistant chief of staff to the commander of U.S. naval forces in the Mediterranean. Spruance commanded destroyer *Osborne* (1925–1926) before attending the Naval War College (1926–1927). He served at the Office of Naval Intelligence (1927–1929) and subsequently became executive officer of battleship *Mississippi* (1929–1931). In 1931 he returned to the Naval War College to head the correspondence courses until 1933 and earned promotion to captain in 1932. He next served aboard cruiser *Raleigh* (1933–1935) as chief of staff to Commander Destroyer Scouting Force before returning for an uncommon third tour of duty at the Naval War College. In 1938 he took command of *Mississippi* and was promoted to rear admiral in 1939. He next headed the new Tenth Naval District at San Juan, Puerto Rico (1940–1941).

In July 1941, shortly before the United States's entry into World War II, Spruance became commander of Cruiser Squadron Five at Pearl Harbor, Hawaii, with his flagship, heavy cruiser *Northhampton.* As surface screen commander for Admiral William Halsey's carrier forces, Spruance took part in the raids on the Gilbert, Marshall, Wake, and Marcus Islands in February and March 1942. He also served in this capacity for Halsey's fleet as it launched the Doolittle Raid on Tokyo in April.

In May 1942, Spruance relieved Halsey as commander of Task Force 16 on board the carrier *Enterprise.* He was junior admiral under Frank Jack Fletcher at the Battle of Midway but emerged as the victorious commander during the course of the battle. His brilliant disposition of his ships and the use of available aircraft, despite the fact that he was not an aviator, proved decisive in the sinking of four Japanese carriers—a disaster from which the Japanese never recovered.

Two weeks later Spruance became chief of staff, and in September also deputy to Pacific Fleet Commander Admiral Chester W. Nimitz. In May 1943 he received promotion to vice admiral and in August was given command of the Central Pacific offensive that he had helped to plan. In November he oversaw the invasion of the Gilbert Islands and the Marshalls in 1944. He led the air raid on the Japanese base at Truk later in February. In March 1944, Spruance became a full admiral and in April was redesignated commander of Fifth Fleet and led the air strike on the Palaus. During the summer of 1944 Spruance directed the invasion of the Marianas and in June prevailed in the Battle of the Philippine Sea, including the "Great Marianas Turkey Shoot," which destroyed most of the Japanese carrier-based aircraft.

Spruance returned to Pearl Harbor from August 1944 to January 1945 while he planned the invasions of Iwo Jima and Okinawa. He subsequently commanded these operations in February and March–May 1945. Spruance helped to prepare the proposed plans for invasion of the Japanese home islands, which proved unnecessary because of Japan's surrender in August 1945. In November 1945, Spruance became commander in chief of the Pacific Fleet, and he served in that capacity until his appointment in February 1946 as president of the Naval War College. Spruance retired from the navy in July 1948 but was later appointed U.S. ambassador to the Philippines.

Admiral Spruance is considered by many historians to be the most brilliant fleet commander of World War II. A superb combination of fighter and intellectual, he relied on his intelligence and not on emotions during battle, and he maintained a healthy respect for the Japanese throughout the war. He encouraged initiative among subordinates, and as overall commander, he avoided getting mired in details. He was always eager for battle and was willing to press on until victory. Spruance was known for his integrity and during the war spoke out against internment of Japanese Americans. Throughout his career Spruance avoided publicity. As a result, he remains an enigma—a quiet man of great courage and a master of naval warfare who suffered with periodic bouts of seasickness—and a relative unknown among the great Commanders of World War II. He died at Pebble Beach, California, on December 13, 1969.

FURTHER READINGS

Buell, Thomas B. *The Quiet Warrior: A Biography of Admiral Raymond A. Spruance* (1974).

Forrestal, Emmet P. *Admiral Raymond A. Spruance, USN: A Study in Command* (1966).

Laura Matysek Wood

SEE ALSO Midway, Battle of; Navy, U.S.

Stereotypes, Japanese and American

Toward the end of the twentieth century, historians began to acknowledge a significant racial dimension to the Pacific war that did much to shape perceptions of that conflict and may well have affected the strategy and tactics of both Japan and the United States. Americans and Japanese more often than not viewed each other through the distorting lens of racial and/or cultural prejudice, and well-developed racial stereotypes existed in both countries at the outbreak of war. War acted as a catalyst, energizing preexisting images and providing a negative context in which these stereotypes could be further defined. As a consequence, racial hatreds and national stereotypes played a significant role in the conflict.

American Perceptions of the Japanese

In April 1945, as he joined U.S. forces in the Pacific, the famous war correspondent Ernie Pyle noted very quickly among U.S. forces a "different attitude toward the enemy" from that evident in the European theater. Pyle observed that U.S. servicemen "looked upon the Japanese as something subhuman and repulsive, the way some people feel about cockroaches or mice." Pyle was not alone in noting the discrepancy in the way that Americans perceived their Axis enemies. A wartime study of American popular opinion concluded that "from the beginning of our participation in the war, Americans have hated the Japanese more than the Germans." Indeed, Americans did view these two enemies very differently. Contemporaries and historians alike have suggested that hatred of the Japanese was evident in the conduct of the Pacific war, transforming the conflict, in one scholar's words, into a "war without mercy."

Americans had little contact with the Japanese until around the turn of the century, when significant numbers of Japanese immigrants began to arrive on the West Coast of the United States in pursuit of jobs and a better life. Almost immediately, these immigrants inherited the negative racial stereotype previously applied to Chinese immigrants. Though the hapless Chinese had been barred from further immigration by the Exclusion Act of 1882, many West Coast Americans had formed complex impressions of Asians. Most of the associations were negative; Americans had quickly defined the Chinese as "inscrutable," backward, filthy, treacherous, superstitious, overly fecund, and, ultimately, racially alien to the point of incomprehensibility. Because few Americans were inclined to differentiate between Chinese and Japanese, the same traits were easily projected onto the latter, especially as Californians began to complain about unfair economic competition from the Asian newcomers.

Despite these initially negative impressions, the bulk of American popular opinion sided with Japan during the Russo-Japanese War (1904–1905). The clear lesson seemed to be that, unlike the Chinese, the Japanese had modernized and Westernized many aspects of their national life and hence easily defeated the decaying, autocratic Russian empire. Much contemporary evidence suggests that many Americans hailed the Japanese "David's" defeat of the tsarist "Goliath."

These positive associations were short-lived, however, as Japanese suspicions about U.S. designs in the Pacific surfaced following President Theodore Roosevelt's successful negotiation of the Treaty of Portsmouth. The result was a decade of worsening relations marked by frequent war scares and immigration controversies. Japan's role on the Allied side in World War I did little to improve American images of the Japanese, because Japan's demands on China seemed to mark increased aggressive tendencies. Although the 1920s brought somewhat better relations with and, concomitantly, better impressions of the Japanese, the onset of the world depression and the collapse of democratic government in Japan heralded the beginnings of a decade in which American images of the Japanese would be more sharply and negatively defined by international events.

During the 1930s, Japan's expansion in Asia and its escalating war against China were the primary determinants of a rapidly polarizing Japanese stereotype. During the first surge of Japanese aggression between 1931 and 1933, Americans began to view the Japanese as an aggressive, ruthless people, based largely on the conduct of the Japanese military in China. These same Japanese depredations brought a much closer media scrutiny of Japan, as evidenced by the many reportorial assessments of the country that began to appear in the periodical press. The composite picture that emerged did little to ameliorate American apprehensions about the Japanese. Japan was inevitably described as a bizarre, insular, and xenophobic land, almost schizophrenic in its paradoxes. The Japanese were portrayed as governed by inconceivable superstitions and a medieval warrior code, all fanatically devoted and racially bound to a god-emperor whose divinity made the Japanese a superior race. The outbreak of the Sino-Japanese War in the summer of 1937 provided a context in which this negative image could be more

clearly defined. Press coverage of Japanese atrocities in China went far toward convincing Americans that the Japanese were indeed a race of warrior-fanatics, thoroughly regimented in the service of the Japanese empire and completely devoid of any moral system that might serve as a brake on their innate cruelty. All that was needed to activate this stereotype was a catalyst; the Japanese "sneak attack" on Pearl Harbor provided that.

As the Pacific war opened, most Americans held a clearly defined image of the Japanese enemy—one that was almost universally negative. The events of the next four years further enhanced and polarized that image. During the war years, the American image of the Japanese was largely defined by the actions of Japanese soldiers, which most often served to build a picture of a ruthless and dangerous enemy. Gone were the prewar suggestions that the Japanese were childlike, imitative, and physically incompetent soldiers. Events in the first six months of the war quickly disabused Americans of such inaccurate notions. In fact, now Americans tended to perceive the Japanese enemy as a "superman," physically hardy, inured to privation and pain, and virtually invincible, especially in jungle terrain. Although immediate apprehensions about a superhuman enemy subsided, the common image of Japan's fighting man was a fearful one, emphasizing cruelty, treachery, fanaticism, and incomprehensibility.

As U.S. forces in the far Pacific were overwhelmed in the first six months of 1942, stories of wanton murder, calculated brutality, and casual torture punctuated such infamous events as the Bataan death march and the Japanese occupation of former Western enclaves in Asia, such as Hong Kong. U.S. press reports brought frightening evidence of Japanese rapacity against helpless civilians and captured Allied soldiers. Later in the war, Japanese brutality toward downed U.S. aviators strengthened this image. In wartime films depicting the Japanese, cruelty was one of the most frequently emphasized characteristics. Japanese treachery quickly assumed a similarly potent quality in the stereotype. As U.S. forces began the long, arduous task of retaking the many island groups of the Pacific, reports began to filter into the U.S. press of incredible treachery. Japanese soldiers were, according to reports from the field, willing to engage in any form of deception, including feigning surrender or death and then turning on unsuspecting GIs and marines. This reputation for duplicity led U.S. soldiers to take fewer chances and fewer prisoners. One GI lamented that the Japanese even mined the bodies of their dead comrades, thus ensuring that "even a dead Jap isn't a good Jap."

The nature of the Pacific campaign and the Japanese response in an increasingly defensive war enhanced American belief in Japanese fanaticism. In virtually every island campaign, U.S. troops remarked on the fanaticism of the enemy, who seemed to prefer death by any means rather than surrender, even in the most hopeless situations. Suicide by bullet, sword, grenade, or jumping from cliffs, as well as mass suicide, seemed proof of the enemy's irrational fanaticism. The use of kamikaze tactics late in the war confirmed that the mentality of the hopeless banzai charge was innate in the Japanese mind. All of these traits combined made the enemy incomprehensible to many fighting the Pacific war. As a consequence, many Americans, combatants and noncombatants alike, tended to dismiss the Japanese as either an animallike "ape in khaki" or a member of a race too alien in its values and beliefs to be comprehended by the rational West.

Not surprisingly, the Japanese enemy was dehumanized, and in the summer of 1945, as U.S. policy makers discussed what might be required for Japan's final defeat, some cautioned that Japan was willing to commit national suicide rather than accept defeat. Such admonitions may have played a role in the decision to use the atomic bomb against Japan. Certainly, most American attitudes had irreducibly hardened by this point. One of the most comprehensive pictures of the Japanese in the American mind was presented in Frank Capra's *Know Your Enemy—Japan,* an "informational film" produced under the guidance of the Office of War Information. Though never released for public viewing, the film provides a more precise portrait of American perceptions of the Japanese as of 1945 than of the Japanese themselves. Cruel and fanatic, a believer in Japanese racial superiority, the Japanese was said to be a willing and dedicated cog in the imperial war machine, ready to visit any savagery on those who stood in the way of Japan's divine mission to rule. He was unrestrained by any recognizable ethical code other than that of merciless Bushido, embedded in "his little brain." This was the enemy, the film's narrator warned, who "must be shot down like the mad dog in your neighborhood."

Japanese Perceptions of the Americans

Japanese perceptions of Americans were shaped in large part by the same historical developments that determined American views between 1900 and 1941. Few Americans were attuned to the inequities that many Japanese saw in changing relations between their two nations. Whereas many Americans warily eyed Japanese expansion in the far Pacific and Asia, to many Japanese it was only reasonable that Japan should become the Far Eastern imperial power. Japanese policy makers saw hypocrisy in Western criticism of Japanese inroads onto the Asian mainland,

believing that the rules had been changed after Western imperial powers had sated their colonial appetites. Likewise, Japanese civilian and military officials perceived Japanese activities in China as part of an effort to impose imperial "order" on a chaotic land. A second inflammatory issue was that of race. Japanese were understandably offended by anti-Japanese campaigns on the Pacific coast of the United States and insulted by the egregious racism inherent in the 1924 National Origins Act, which prohibited further Japanese immigration to the United States.

The issue of whether the Japanese subscribed to a belief in their own racial superiority is controversial and has been addressed by the historian John W. Dower in *War without Mercy: Race and Power in the Pacific War.* Dower contends that the Japanese did not define themselves as racially superior in the same way that many Anglo-Saxons did. Japanese superiority was not contingent on race per se but rather was couched in terms of Japanese uniqueness. The Japanese, Dower suggests, defined their uniqueness as a consequence of a historical purity. This concept had both genetic and moral dimensions, both of which did, at times, lend themselves to attitudes that appear much akin to Western racism. The difference, Dower maintains, is that the Japanese built their conception of their own superiority not by denigrating others but by elevating themselves. The distinction is a subtle one and rests largely on the centrality of such important dichotomies to Japanese national life as "purity versus pollution" and "insiders versus outsiders."

Historically, Westerners, and especially Americans, had been perceived as outsiders whose purity was questionable. Not surprisingly, as relations between Japan and the United States deteriorated throughout the 1930s, militant Japanese nationalists increasingly attacked Western influences in Japan as threatening to Japanese purity, thus further distinguishing insider from outsider and stressing the danger posed by impurity. By the late 1930s, many Japanese military officials had come to accept images of Americans founded in this context. Impure and ignoble as they were, Americans, it was believed, lacked the qualities that would make them a dangerous foe. Materialistic, timid, and obsessed with self-gratification, Americans did not seem likely to oppose Japanese aspirations in the Far East effectively. Such stereotyped assessments may well have played a role in the Japanese decision to attack the U.S. Pacific Fleet in Hawaii. There is little question but that the nature of the attack (a "sneak attack," as enraged Americans would see it) demonstrated a deep misunderstanding of the American psyche. As much as anything else, the manner in which the Pacific war was initiated led Americans to dedicate themselves to the complete defeat of Japan.

The early months of the war seemed to confirm Japan's belief in the superiority of the "pure Self." As Allied forces suffered defeat after defeat, the inferiority of the "barbarians" appeared self-evident. Even after the tide turned in favor of the Allied effort, however, the Japanese press continued to define the Americans in essentially the same terms. Often this meant depicting them as animals, brutes, or beasts. The bestial nature of Americans, it was claimed, was evident in their obsession with sex, creature comforts, and race hatred. Not only were Americans brutal in their treatment of their own African American population, they now promoted race hatred of the Japanese even among children, enjoining them to "kill Japs." Lacking the positive traits of filial piety, gratitude, and goodwill, the Americans were uncivilized beasts whose rapacious behavior was clear proof of their degradation. There was no infamy to which the American beasts would refuse to stoop. As was reported in a *Reader's Digest* article during the war, one Japanese writer informed his readers that each U.S. marine recruit had to prove, prior to induction, that he had murdered one of his parents.

As the intensity of combat grew during the island-hopping campaign, more proof of the savagery of the American "demons" was presented. U.S. soldiers, it was reported, laughingly killed Japanese POWs, grinding them into the dust under tank treads, wrapping them in barbed wire, and drowning them and desecrating the remains of the dead. Ironically, these were all atrocities identical to those which Americans accused, with somewhat more veracity, Japanese of perpetrating. As the war wore on and Japanese victories came less often, the continued denigration of Americans as demons and barbarians was attended by depictions of the valorous qualities of Japanese soldiers. Most often these were described as a product of Japanese purity. The willingness to sacrifice and die for a pure and idealistic cause was an increasingly common topic by the later years of the war. Inevitably, this was contrasted with the crude and hateful behavior of the American enemy. By 1945, it had become obvious that Japanese purity, as exemplified by the samurai spirit, the code of Bushido, or selfless dedication to the emperor, was not adequate to overcome U.S. material superiority and offensive capabilities. All that remained for Japan was the consolation of purification through sacrifice and suffering: "Our will against their steel."

Conclusion

In retrospect, Americans and Japanese alike viewed each other through the same distorted lens of stereotype during the war years. Before 1941, this led Americans to dismiss the Japanese as cruel though technologically incompetent fanatics, a perspective that may have led U.S. policy makers to underestimate Japanese capabilities prior to the debacle at Pearl Harbor. Combat conditions in the Pacific did much to confirm American beliefs about Japanese savagery, duplicity, and irrational fanaticism. The result was a willingness to consider the Japanese as only marginally human.

The Japanese acceptance of stereotypical misconceptions about Americans proved catastrophic. Nippon's leaders made the decision for war against the United States in the fall of 1941 believing that Americans lacked the will and determination to fight a long and distant war of attrition in the Pacific. It was a fatal miscalculation.

FURTHER READINGS

Dower, John W. *War without Mercy: Race and Power in the Pacific War* (1986).

Iriye, Akira. *Power and Culture: The Japanese-American War, 1941–1945* (1981).

Shillony, Ben-Ami. *Politics and Culture in Wartime Japan* (1981).

Spector, Ronald H. *Eagle against the Sun: The American War with Japan* (1985).

Blaine T. Browne

SEE ALSO Psychological Warfare, Japanese; Psychological Warfare, U.S.

Stilwell, Joseph Warren (1883–1946)

Commander of U.S. and Chinese forces in the China-Burma-India theater and Generalissimo Chiang Kai-shek's chief of staff from 1942 to 1944, Joseph Warren Stilwell oversaw completion of the Ledo Road and led Chinese troops in retaking north Burma.

As a result of three tours of duty in China between 1920 and 1939, Stilwell knew the Chinese language and people. Based on his observation of Japanese troops invading China, he believed that the Chinese, properly equipped and trained, could defeat them.

On March 10, 1942, Stilwell, a highly regarded officer originally slated after Pearl Harbor to command a proposed invasion of North Africa, accepted the complicated China assignment. With limited resources and direction, he carried out multiple command responsibilities. Stilwell had to serve two masters, the Chinese and U.S. governments. When Chinese Nationalist leader Chiang Kai-shek was invited by the British and Americans to command a United Nations Allied China theater, he asked for an

American chief of staff and accepted Stilwell in that role. Stilwell's other major responsibility as commanding general of U.S. Army Forces in China, Burma, and India (CBI) was directing U.S. assistance to the Chinese war effort and improving the Chinese army's combat efficiency.

In addition to these tasks, Stilwell supervised U.S. Lend-Lease to China and commanded Chinese armies in India and Burma. In 1943, when the Allies established the Anglo-American Southeast Asia Command and appointed Stilwell deputy supreme Allied commander under the British Admiral Lord Louis Mountbatten, he again faced conflicting policy, strategy, and chains of command.

President Franklin Roosevelt instructed Stilwell to treat China like a great power; he wanted it to fill the power vacuum that would be left by a defeated Japan. Because U.S. wartime strategy prioritized European victory, the CBI theater received relatively few supplies. Five years of war had nearly exhausted China, and U.S. policy makers feared that the Chinese government might negotiate a separate peace that would release more Japanese forces to fight in the Pacific. Washington hoped that a reinvigorated Chinese army could tie down Japanese troops and that China might provide the base for a final assault on Japan.

In the spring of 1942, when Stilwell arrived at the Nationalist Chinese capital in Chungking, the Japanese had already taken Rangoon and cut the Burma Road, China's lifeline. Chiang sent Stilwell to Burma with the Fifth and Sixth Chinese armies to help the British stop the Japanese advance. A determined fighter and an able, courageous commander, Stilwell prodded his dispirited, undernourished Chinese units to fight vigorously and personally led a counterattack that prevented their encirclement. Stilwell later learned that Chiang was husbanding his resources to fight Chinese Communists and secretly instructing his commanders not to attack or decisively engage the Japanese.

Stilwell declined evacuation for himself by air when British and Chinese armies retreated. With the enemy only 20 miles away, the 60-year-old general chose to lead his isolated remnant of 114 men on a 150-mile march across mountainous terrain to India. Accusing the British of defeatism and incompetence in Burma, he mocked their claims of "a heroic, voluntary withdrawal." Stilwell delighted the U.S. press by candidly admitting "we took a hell of a beating" and resolving to retake Burma.

On the walkout from Burma, Stilwell formulated the plan he pursued for the next eighteen months to reopen China's lines of communication. Immediately after Japan took almost all of Burma, the Allies began a stopgap mea-

sure of "flying the Hump" over the Himalayas, but these flights were dangerous and costly and could not adequately supply China's wartime needs.

Stilwell aimed to reform and reorganize the Chinese army, consolidating its 300-plus divisions into about 100 and training and equipping them under U.S. direction. With Chiang Kai-shek's permission, he took the two divisions he commanded in Burma to India and set up a training base at Ramgarh. Many of these troops had not been paid or received proper food, clothing, or medical treatment since being impressed into the army. Stilwell was a strict disciplinarian. At Fort Benning, Georgia, he had acquired the name "Vinegar Joe" for his tough training techniques. Adapting German World War I infantry tactics for Chinese troops, "Stilwell-corps" training stressed simplicity, common sense, and improvisation.

Stilwell had ambitious plans. In addition to training Chinese troops in India that were designated X Force, he hoped to train a Y Force within China at Kunming. A Z Force based in eastern China at Kweilin, though less well trained and equipped than the others, could play a role in driving the Japanese from China. All the while, Stilwell pressed the laborious and hazardous construction of the Ledo Road, dubbed "Pick's Pike" after its chief engineer, General Lewis A. Pick. When connected with the Burma Road, it would provide a land supply route supplementing air flights over the Himalayas.

Several obstacles besides Japanese opposition impeded Stilwell's plans. The British, faced with nationalistic turmoil in India and with strained resources and priorities in other theaters, did not share the U.S. government's high estimate of China's value. Fearing that Chinese assistance in defending Burma might kindle Asian nationalism, they preferred to reclaim it with an impressive British imperial force.

Chiang Kai-shek presented a more serious problem. Stilwell disliked Chiang not only because of the Nationalist government's inefficiency and corruption but because of his failure to pursue an all-out effort against the Japanese. Throughout the war, Chiang tended to hold his armies back to fight Mao Tse-tung's Chinese Communist forces once U.S. forces had defeated the Japanese, and he tied up many of his best troops blockading the Communists. Chiang often threatened to stop fighting and attempted several times to have Stilwell removed. He opposed Stilwell's plans to reform the Chinese army, fearing that dismissing incompetent commanders might also remove loyal supporters. By stressing his status as a major ally and renewing his promise to fight the Japanese, Chiang could stockpile supplies for the future conflict.

Stilwell's frustrations led him to abandon tact and diplomacy. He made no secret of his disdain for the self-important Chiang Kai-shek, whom he nicknamed "Peanut." Stilwell preferred soldiering and building roads with Chinese peasants to dealing with British imperialists and upper-class Chinese bureaucrats.

Chiang depended on U.S. General Claire L. Chennault's promise to drive the Japanese out of China almost solely by using air power instead of allowing Stilwell to build an army that could beat the Japanese and perhaps stand up later to the Communists. At the May 1943 Trident Conference, Chiang convinced Roosevelt, over War Department objections, to give Chennault's air power priority in the meager supply tonnage reaching China via the Hump. This hurt Stilwell's programs to build the Ledo Road and train Chinese armies. Stilwell accurately predicted that Chennault's air offensive would provoke the Japanese to seize the east China air bases and that Chiang would lack the forces needed to defend them.

Chiang's supporters were successful in gaining strong political support in the United States. Instead of trusting Stilwell's military judgment and his extensive knowledge of China, Roosevelt sent special emissaries with little understanding of the situation to determine U.S. policy in China. Stilwell's abrasive personality also alienated those whose support he needed.

Although the mid-1943 U.S. Pacific victories lessened the likelihood that operations on the Chinese mainland would be needed to defeat Japan, it did seem that China might provide a base from which B-29 bombers could attack the Japanese home islands. But this would require greater tonnage than airlifts over the Hump could deliver. With Chennault's plan having failed, completing the road through Burma and establishing a safer and shorter, more southerly, air route assumed priority.

At the Cairo Conference in late 1943, which both Chiang and Stilwell attended, Allied leaders endorsed a limited campaign to free north Burma. Following Stilwell's suggested plan of attack, the British would land on the southern coast while Chinese troops attacked in a pincers movement from northern Burma and across the Salween River. When the Allies met at Tehran and committed to an invasion of Western Europe, the British could not spare landing craft for southern Burma. Chiang took this opportunity to announce that he would not let Chinese troops cross the Salween.

In December 1943, Stilwell arrived at the Ledo front to join the Chinese X Force that was already advancing into north Burma; he remained there until July 1944. He intended to capture the all-weather airstrip at Myitkyina before monsoon season. From there the Ledo Road could connect with the existing Burma Road.

British Major General Orde C. Wingate's Chindits supported Stilwell. The only U.S. component of the Chindits was the 5307th Composite Unit (Provisional), better known as Merrill's Marauders and code-named Galahad; it fought under Stilwell's direct command. The plan called for the British commandos to penetrate the area while the 5307th enveloped the Japanese and set up blocks in the rear and the Chinese attacked from the front. On the eve of the campaign, Stilwell upset the complex Southeast Asia command system by placing himself under British General William J. Slim, whom he knew to be a fighter.

Under Allied attack, Japanese troops began to withdraw. With the monsoons approaching, Stilwell struck boldly to seize the airstrip at Myitkyina. On May 17, 1944, after a grueling march, his combined force of Marauders and Chinese took the airfield, but the Japanese reinforced the town, which did not fall until August 3. By capturing Myitkyina—a feat the British high command considered impossible—Stilwell reopened land access to China. Although he demonstrated that Chinese soldiers could be successful against the Japanese, their effort wore out the Chindit and Galahad units, who blamed Stilwell for sacrificing them in favor of his Chinese troops.

While Stilwell was fighting in Burma, a Japanese operation overran U.S. air bases in east China, advanced on the Kweilin base, and threatened Chungking itself. With China demoralized by conscription, extortionate taxes, and famine, Stilwell increasingly prodded Chiang Kai-shek to employ Communist troops, probably the best Chinese fighting units. Chiang's failure to keep his promise and contribute to his own defense by letting Y Force join the Burma campaign disappointed Roosevelt. Further alarmed by the crisis in eastern China, the U.S. president promoted Stilwell to four-star general and demanded in early July 1944 that Chiang recall Stilwell from Burma and put him in full command of Chinese troops.

Chiang Kai-shek feared that putting a foreigner in control of his army would allow the Communists to portray him as a weak ruler. Embattled for years by the Communists and the Japanese, many in the Nationalist Chinese government resented U.S. interference, though they remained eager to receive Lend-Lease aid. Stilwell pushed the Chinese to take the offensive against the Japanese, but the Chinese preferred their traditional strategy, defense in depth and scorched earth, which was hell on the Chinese masses. They criticized Stilwell for using the best troops and most valuable resources in the Burma endeavor. In their eyes, Stilwell, who trained and led soldiers himself, lacked the aloof demeanor of a commanding general.

In August 1944, Roosevelt sent the wealthy Oklahoma politician Patrick J. Hurley as his personal emissary to resolve tensions between Chiang Kai-shek and Stilwell. In addition to their antagonism and disagreements over policy, Chiang now bitterly held Stilwell responsible for Roosevelt's sterner treatment. Chiang resolutely demanded Stilwell's dismissal; Hurley advised the president that the conflict was insurmountable. On October 21, 1944, Stilwell left China with orders not to discuss the situation.

In early 1945, after Stilwell's departure, the Ledo Road—renamed the Stilwell Road in his honor—reached China. Stilwell assumed command of the Tenth Army in Okinawa, preparing to lead the final invasion of the Japanese home islands. After Japan surrendered, Chiang Kai-shek insisted that Stilwell not participate in the liberation forces being prepared for China. Following the war, Stilwell was named commander of the Sixth Army, with headquarters in San Francisco; he died on October 12, 1946, of cancer.

FURTHER READINGS

Haiti, Michael E. " 'I'll Go Where I'm Sent': 'Vinegar Joe' Stilwell in the CBI," *Military Review,* 72 (May 1992).

Liang, Ching-ch'un. *General Stilwell in China, 1942–1944: The Full Story* (1972).

Romanus, Charles, and Riley Sunderland. *Stilwell's Command Problems.* U.S. Army in World War II (1956).

———. *Stilwell's Mission to China.* U.S. Army in World War II (1953).

———. *Time Runs Out in CBI.* U.S. Army in World War II (1959).

Spector, Ronald H. *Eagle against the Sun: The American War with Japan* (1985).

Stilwell, Joseph W. *The Stilwell Papers.* Edited by Theodore H. White (1948).

Tuchman, Barbara W. *Stilwell and the American Experience in China, 1911–45* (1971).

White, Theodore H., and Annalee Jacoby. *Thunder out of China* (1946).

Camille Dean

SEE ALSO Chiang Kai-shek; China-Burma-India Theater of Operation; Merrill's Marauders (Galahad); Wingate, Orde C.

Stimson, Henry Lewis (1867–1950)

Henry L. Stimson was U.S. secretary of war from 1940 until 1945. Although a life-long Republican who had served as both secretary of war under President William Howard Taft and secretary of state under President Herbert Hoover, Stimson joined Democratic President Franklin D. Roosevelt's cabinet in 1940 and oversaw the massive expansion of American military power and its deployment through World War II.

Stimson headed the greatest buildup in military history of both the U.S. Army and its air component, the U.S. Army Air Forces. He coordinated competing demands for military personnel, raw materials, weapons, manufacturing facilities, and mobilization of the civilian population with the U.S. Navy, civilian war agencies, and industry. Stimson was one of the advisers on whom Roosevelt leaned heavily for military advice, a group that also included U.S. Army Chief of Staff George C. Marshall, Secretary of the Navy Frank Knox, head of the Office of War Mobilization James F. Byrnes, and presidential adviser Harry Hopkins. Stimson also regularly participated in discussions with Congressional committees, executive agencies, and the joint chiefs of staff to determine and balance military priorities, and to provide personnel, weapons, and materiel to meet those priorities.

In politics, Stimson could be considered a member of the Republican "Eastern Establishment." Characterized by a sense of duty to the state, rectitude, honesty, and straightforwardness, the careers of this ruling class typically gave them experiences in running large organizations and in dealing with leaders in and out of government on a national and international level.

A Yale graduate (1888), Stimson received his LL.B from Harvard (1890). A protégé of Republican statesman and attorney Elihu Root, he became involved in politics while practicing law in Root's firm. After President Theodore Roosevelt appointed Root Secretary of War in 1905, Root circulated Stimson's name among Roosevelt and other leading Republicans. Roosevelt appointed Stimson as U.S. Attorney for the Southern District of New York in 1906. Assembling a talented staff that included future Supreme Court Justice Felix Frankfurter, Stimson successfully prosecuted companies that were evading the Sherman Antitrust Act. Root and Roosevelt convinced him to run, unsuccessfully, for governor of New York in 1910.

Once again recommended by Root, Stimson served as secretary of war for President Taft from 1911 to 1913. When Stimson took office, the U.S. Army, numbering 4,300 officers and 70,250 enlisted men, was organized and trained to fight the Indian wars of the past half century. During his brief tenure, Stimson reorganized the army and its training for modern warfare. His efforts gave the permanent cadre some preparation for eventual U.S.

involvement in World War I, although the army still had a long way to go to achieve a full combat-ready status.

When the United States finally entered World War I in 1917, Stimson, true to the sense of obligation of his class, enlisted in the army and served as a colonel with the artillery in France. When, as President Calvin Coolidge's special envoy in 1927, he brokered an end to civil strife in Nicaragua, he began a steady service of statesmanship that would last until 1945. Appointed by Coolidge as Governor General of the Philippines from 1927–1929, Stimson began to gain the experience in Pacific affairs that later would serve him well. Between stints of service to presidential administrations, Stimson practiced law and honed his political and social connections by hosting gatherings at his Long Island estate.

President Herbert Hoover appointed Stimson secretary of state in 1929. During his tenure in this administration, Stimson dealt with the roots of the foreign policy problems that came to a head ten years later. The United States emerged from World War I as a global creditor. The deteriorating worldwide economic situation caused Hoover and Stimson to devise various unsuccessful methods of debt and reparations restructuring. Stimson headed the U.S. delegations to the critical London Naval Conference in 1930 (successor to the Washington Treaty of 1922) in which the naval disarmament treaties that balanced the relationships among the five powers—the United States, Great Britain, France, Italy and Japan—were negotiated. Stimson gained experience and insight in dealing with the military policies and representatives of Japan at this conference. He served a similar role at the less successful Geneva Disarmament Conference in 1932.

Japan's occupation of Manchuria in 1931, another step on the road to confrontation that characterized U.S.-Japanese relations since early in the century, provoked Stimson to announce what came to be known as the "Stimson Doctrine," which proposed international non-recognition of the conquest. As was the case at home, however, the international community was preoccupied with the economic turbulence of the 1930s, and little notice was taken of his initiative.

Leaving his office to Cordell Hull in 1933, Stimson served as a liaison between Hoover and President-elect Roosevelt. Although out of office during FDR's first term, Stimson continued to contribute to domestic and foreign policy. He backed some New Deal policies and even, to the dismay of some Republican senators, supported a bill in 1934 to give tariff-bargaining powers to the president. Eventually his statements on domestic and foreign policy caused dissension between Stimson and the Republican Party.

Arguments as to the extent of U.S. international involvement gradually came to dominate the American political scene during the 1930s as dictators in Germany and Italy came to power and as Japan prosecuted its war in China. These debates grew heated as war approached. Those favoring little or no involvement, the isolationists, included many prominent Republicans, while those favoring a leading international role for the United States were regarded as interventionists, especially after the war in Europe started.

One of the few internationalists during these years, Stimson advocated a leading role for the United States in foreign relations, particularly with regard to the relationship between the United States and Japan. He supported policies advocated by FDR and Hull, called for firmer measures toward Hitler and Mussolini, and advocated an end to U.S. trade in strategic materials to Japan in the face of continued Japanese aggression in China. As war grew closer, Stimson waded deeper into the isolationist-interventionist debate, supporting the controversial policy of "cash-and-carry" aid to Britain and France. All the while, the rift between Stimson and the Republican Party grew wider.

As the 1940 election grew near, and as the war overseas worsened, FDR took steps both to balance his administration politically and to prepare it to arm America and aid Britain. FDR decided to fill two key cabinet positions, the war and navy departments, with Republicans. He settled on Stimson for war and Frank Knox—of convictions similar to Stimson's, and one of Theodore Roosevelt's Rough Riders—for navy. Stimson's public support of the New Deal and his reputation as an interventionist peaked on June 18, 1940, when he advocated a military draft and all-out aid to Great Britain in a speech at his strongly isolationist alma mater, Yale. At that point FDR appointed him secretary of war. Infuriated Republican Party leaders formally asked that he depart their ranks.

Stimson found the war department with a sudden bounty of money and people, (both conditions to which it was not accustomed), and accompanying confusion and waste. Within a year and a half, a time in which every day was critical to preparations for the rapidly approaching war, Stimson brought order and direction to mobilization. As he had decades before in New York, Stimson employed such extraordinarily talented assistants as Robert Patterson, John McCloy, and Robert Lovett. These men figured importantly in the successful prosecution of the war and subsequently served in influential unelected posts in future administrations. He established a smooth working relationship between the civil and military sides of the department, particularly with Army Chief of Staff George C. Marshall.

As FDR had hoped, Stimson (and Knox) blunted some of the partisanship in Roosevelt's cabinet. Seventy-two when he took office for the last time, he was proud of his World War I combat service, preferring to be addressed as "colonel." Stimson was aware of the edge his seniority, class, and lack of partisanship gave him; he was one of the few people (besides the First Lady) who could take FDR to task and get away with it. Reflecting the experience of his decades of foreign policy experience, Stimson became involved in the key policy discussions of the Roosevelt administration. His longstanding experience with international law came to the fore in hearings on the destroyers-for-bases deal and Lend-Lease. He also did not hesitate to give FDR personal advice. In the contentious days before Pearl Harbor, he pushed FDR for stepped-up aid to Britain and for a military draft. As isolationist debate swirled about the administration, he urged FDR to be more decisive and to lead public thought. After the Japanese attack on Pearl Harbor (1941), he urged a declaration of war on Germany. (Hitler, however, forestalled Stimson with his own, inexplicable declaration.) Along with other U.S. advisers, Stimson (unsuccessfully) disagreed with Churchill's "soft underbelly" policy, urging a direct cross-Channel invasion rather than the invasion of North Africa. Stimson sometimes became so closely involved with policy that his name is mentioned in the debates regarding the appropriateness and accuracy of information given to Admiral Husband E. Kimmel and General Walter C. Short, the navy and army commanders in Hawaii at the time of the Pearl Harbor attack.

FDR further confirmed Stimson's value when he appointed him to the Manhattan project advisory committee, bringing him into the limited circle of people who knew about the top-secret program to develop the atomic bomb. Stimson prospered in this role to the extent that FDR made him his senior adviser on the use of nuclear weapons in May of 1943. Stimson subsequently fended off investigations of the project by Senator Harry S. Truman, who, with his Special Committee Investigating National Defense, was trying to ensure that public money was not being wasted. With General Marshall, he carefully arranged with Congressional leaders for continued financing of the Manhattan Project, without revealing the nature of its mission. Truman was not to know of the atomic bomb until he became president on the death of Roosevelt in April 1945.

Stimson's role in the atomic bomb project expanded when President Truman took office. New to the global responsibilities of his role, Truman was thunderstruck by Stimson's briefing on the atomic bomb. At the president's request, Stimson subsequently formed the interim committee, composed of civilian and military members, to advise Truman on the use of nuclear weapons. The committee recommended on June 1, 1945, that the bombs be used, although Stimson urged that the target list not include the Japanese religious center of Kyoto, and that the Japanese be clearly warned of the nature of the bomb. In discussions of surrender terms for Japan, Stimson advised Truman that the Japanese be permitted to keep the emperor as a condition of surrender. Feeling that the war's end had been bought at a terrible price, Stimson hoped to extend the peace by stabilizing the postwar world. He advocated international control of the atomic bomb, and opposed the Morgenthau plan for turning postwar Germany into an impoverished agricultural country.

The war challenged the forthrightness and honesty typical of Stimson's class. An early harbinger of the new era came during his tenure as secretary of state, when Stimson, lecturing that "gentlemen do not read other gentlemen's mail," tried to cancel a U.S. Army project to break Japanese codes. In 1942, California officials and West Coast congressional delegations demanded approval of a plan to place Japanese Americans in internment camps. Although he realized such a move directed at American citizens was unconstitutional, Stimson reluctantly approved the plan on the grounds of military necessity and safety. Similarly, although he admitted that racism was at fault when advised of misuse of and discrimination against African American soldiers and airmen, Stimson's recommendations extended only as far as increasing the effectiveness of African American units. Stimson also did support emergency refugee shelters in the United States for Jews rescued from the Nazis.

After a lifetime of service to his country, Stimson retired on September 21, 1945, his 78th birthday, to his home on Long Island, where he died on October 20, 1950.

FURTHER READINGS

Burns, James MacGregor. *Roosevelt: The Lion and the Fox* (1956).

———. *Roosevelt: The Soldier of Freedom* (1970).

McCullough, David. *Truman* (1992).

Morison, Elting. *Turmoil and Tradition: The Life and Times of Henry L. Stimson* (1960).

Stimson, Henry L., and McGeorge Bundy. *On Active Service in Peace and War* (1948).

Steven Agoratus

SEE ALSO Marshall, George Catlett; Roosevelt, Franklin Delano; Knox, Frank

Submarines, Japanese

The performance of the Imperial Japanese Navy's submarine force in World War II fell far short of prewar expectations. The Japanese naval high command inaccurately predicted the type of war it would embark on in 1941, and the submarine force in particular quickly became a victim of unrealistic military planning and preparation. First designed to weaken a U.S. fleet of 21-knot battleships en route to an anticipated massive clash with Japanese dreadnoughts in the western Pacific, the submarine force was from the outset of the war confronted by much faster U.S. aircraft carriers and new battleships after the successful Japanese carrier air attack on battleship row in Pearl Harbor. The submarine force was left groping for an effective strategic and operational plan of action, while a sophisticated U.S. Navy undersea force quickly hardened to the reality of wartime conditions.

Despite significant changes in the international balance of power by the eve of World War II, the basic strategy of the imperial navy did not change after 1907. A decisive battle with a weakened U.S. fleet in Asian waters, as in the Battle of Tsushima (1905), remained the goal. Fulfillment of this goal became the imperial navy's obsession.

Modern long-range submarines received crucial and complex assignments. Submarines were to reconnoiter U.S. naval bases and anchorages. Then they were to track and pursue the U.S. fleet after its sortie, radio news of the enemy's activities to the Japanese fleet commander, and repeatedly ambush and torpedo the enemy's main force while it sailed westward to the Marianas, as the plan eventually developed from the late 1920s into the 1930s. Japanese occupation and use of U.S. bases in the Philippines and on Guam was also intended to weaken the U.S. fleet while it was steaming westward by denying it support from those bases. The chief innovation came in the 1940 plan when the site of the projected decisive battle between Japanese and U.S. dreadnoughts was moved nearly two thousand miles eastward from the Marianas to the Marshalls. Submarines were expected to have far more direct contact with U.S. naval forces over a longer period than any other type of Japanese warship, and this expectation heightened the sense of the importance of submarines in the Japanese scheme for action.

Japanese long-range prewar strategy was suddenly upset on the eve of the Pearl Harbor attack. An entirely new role for submarines was hammered out. The new terms of war were not ideal for the submarine force, although there had been several decades of painstaking development of submarine materiel, personnel, institutions, and strategic and tactical doctrines. In general, more than twenty submarines were to precede the carrier strike force to Hawaiian waters and there check on possible U.S. fleet movements. If warships were sighted, the submarines were to track, but not fire on, the enemy warships until the start of the air strike. Thereafter, the submarines were to lurk outside Pearl Harbor and between the Hawaiian Islands and the U.S. mainland to attack any warships attempting to escape from the air strike, to finish off any damaged ships trying to limp back to mainland ports, and to prevent any reinforcements from reaching Oahu.

Japanese submarines in Hawaiian waters were plagued by mishaps and failure. Naval planners anticipated that the nine fleet-type submarines of the 3d Submarine Group would have the best chance to attack the enemy. With their vantage point some forty miles from Pearl Harbor, these submarines formed a dense line capable of concentrated attack on U.S. warships off Oahu.

However, U.S. Navy antisubmarine warfare (ASW) forces were effective against the Japanese in about the only good news from Pearl Harbor on December 7. For example, *I-68*, some thirty miles from the entrance to Pearl Harbor, came under heavy depth-charge attack and suffered some damage. *I-69*, after launching an unsuccessful torpedo attack against a cargo ship on the night of December 7, was near Barbers Point in southern Oahu when it got caught in what the Japanese thought was an antisubmarine net. (*I-69* probably became entangled in a stray U.S. towline or a harmless drill minefield used by U.S. Navy minesweepers for practice.) The submarine was also heavily depth-charged. Captain Nobuki Nakaoka, commander of Submarine Division 12, on board *I-69*, recalled later that a depth-charge explosion under the hull produced a very hard shock and the boat had to dive as deeply as possible. Leaks were dangerous, and it was impossible to use the ejection pump at such great depths. The Japanese sailors were determined to fight to the end, but they also abhorred defeat. Thus, they armed demolition explosives before making a final attempt to escape from their entanglement. At a depth of 250 feet (245 feet was this submarine's safe maximum diving depth), *I-69* slipped out of the net by going full astern and blowing its main tanks. *I-69* was lucky to escape undetected on the surface after some forty hours of struggle.

Several other submarines of the 3d Submarine Group were also depth-charged and had little success. *I-72*, for example, sank a small cargo vessel some 250 miles south of Oahu on December 8, and *I-75* made a similar claim 100 miles south of Kauai on December 17. Having caused no damage to U.S. warships, plagued by failures and missed opportunities, the remaining submarines of the group left Hawaiian waters on December 17 to return to Kwajalein.

Some of these submarines later returned. *I-72,* for example, left Kwajalein for Hawaiian waters on January 12, 1942. After a few days of patrolling, *I-72* sank oil tanker *Neches* (AO-5) south of Niihau Island on January 23. The incident was not without consequence, for *Neches* was the sole source of fuel at sea for aircraft carrier *Lexington* and its escorts. Because no other tanker was available, *Lexington*'s plans to attack Japanese forces on Wake Island were called off.

Some fourteen other Japanese submarines continued to patrol in Hawaiian waters after the air strike on Pearl Harbor. The three submarines assigned originally as an advance screening unit for the Carrier Strike Force joined four ocean-cruising submarines of the 1st Submarine Group to continue patrol operations in Hawaiian waters. Of these seven submarines, *I-9,* the flag submarine of Rear Admiral Tsutomu Sato, Commander Submarine Squadron 1, made a modest attack—it sank U.S. steamer SS *Lahaina* (5,645 tons) several hundred miles northeast of Oahu on December 11. The seven older ocean-cruising submarines of the 2d Submarine Group also continued patrols in Hawaiian waters until January 11, 1942. The flag submarine, *I-7,* launched its seaplane for a completely successful dawn reconnaissance flight to Pearl Harbor on December 17, despite the tightened defenses of Pearl Harbor. Thus the high command in Tokyo received a full report of the damage caused by its air attack.

The failure of the I-boats in Hawaiian waters in December resulted in part from directing operations from afar. The commander of the Sixth Fleet (the submarine fleet), Vice Admiral Mitsumi Shimizu, filled the air each night shortly before the attack on Pearl Harbor with radio messages from Kwajalein to his submarines around the Hawaiian Islands. Naval authorities in Hawaii were thus made aware of the number and, to some extent, location of the Japanese submarines. Consequently, U.S. ships and various merchantmen were routed carefully to avoid the Japanese submarine menace.

Five ocean-cruising submarines, each with a piggyback midget submarine Type A Target (*Ko-hyoteki*), did not become part of the grand plan to attack U.S. forces until the fall of 1941. The five submarines were on their assigned stations near the entrance to Pearl Harbor on the night of December 6 (Hawaii time). Despite trouble with the gyro compass of *I-24*'s two-man midget submarine, its commanding officer, Ensign Kazuo Sakamaki, was determined to disembark in his little submarine as scheduled. In the end, Sakamaki's mission was a failure, and his little submarine drifted beyond Diamond Head to

become stranded on a reef near Bellows Army Air Field. He was washed ashore unconscious and captured on December 8, 1941, as the first prisoner of war; his stalwart crewman died in the heavy surf. The other four midget submarines were more easily launched before dawn on the day of the air attack. Nevertheless, almost no information was received from any of them after they sortied. Only Lieutenant (junior grade) Masaji Yokoyama in *I-16*'s midget submarine sent a message—he reported, "*Tora, tora, tora*" (meaning surprise attack succeeded), at 2241 hours on December 7. Thus Japanese submariners believed that an explosion sighted near midnight was caused by a torpedo launched from Yokoyama's midget submarine. But this is not confirmed by U.S. Navy evidence; moreover, it is obvious that the error-riddled operation was poorly executed and that reports of success were often based on modest evidence.

All five midget submarines were lost despite the efforts of the parent submarines. The five large I-boats patrolled the waters south of Oahu during the day of the air attack on Pearl Harbor; then they shifted to the south of Lanai, which was the designated area for recovery of the midget submarines. The area was searched in vain before the parent submarines left Hawaiian waters en route to Kwajalein on the night of December 11.

In January 1942, there were only four U.S. Navy fast heavy carriers in the Pacific—*Lexington* (CV-2), *Saratoga* (CV-3), *Yorktown* (CV-5), and *Enterprise* (CV-6). *Hornet* (CV-8) reached the Pacific in March, and *Wasp* (CV-7) arrived in June. U.S. carrier strength in the Pacific was weakened considerably by the temporary removal of *Saratoga* when *I-6* badly damaged the big carrier in an attack about two hundred seventy miles from Johnston Island on January 11. *Saratoga* did not complete repairs in Bremerton, Washington, and get back into action in the South Pacific until August 1942. Indeed, the strategic balance early in the Pacific war remained precarious with the loss of *Lexington* in early May in the Battle of the Coral Sea. A month later *I-168* sank *Yorktown* and destroyer *Hammann,* tied alongside the severely damaged carrier. The strategic balance of carriers was barely maintained because the Japanese also suffered heavy losses of aircraft carriers, particularly at Midway.

During this time, hundreds of U.S. warships—including aircraft carriers *Enterprise, Lexington, Saratoga,* and *Yorktown* and their cruiser and destroyer escorts—steamed in and out of Pearl Harbor, but only *Saratoga* was hit by a Japanese submarine-launched torpedo. A few minor cargo vessels were sunk and no warships. Otherwise, some night bombardments of islands—Maui, Hawaii, and Kauai, for example—were carried out, an indication that the submarines were about to conclude their patrols and start homeward. (On an I-boat's return to home port, a depleted supply of deck-gun ammunition was viewed as evidence of warlike prowess.) None of these bombardments caused much damage, and U.S. intelligence officers, who knew that a bombardment was a fairly reliable indication that the submarine was departing the area, used this information for routing ships, as already noted. Thus Japanese submarines were a nuisance in Hawaiian waters, to be taken seriously, but in their operations they pretty well unmasked themselves and caused no strategic damage to the ability of the United States to respond to Japan's attack on U.S. territory.

The formidable undersea arm of the imperial navy operated aimlessly and without a coherent strategy in the opening months of 1942. Inflexible prewar battle objectives usually held sway, and any new ones were often ill conceived and incomplete. Moreover, in the Battles of the Coral Sea and Midway, the Japanese submarine force again failed to measure up to prewar expectations, but opinion of the navy high command continued to hold that submarines should be used chiefly to assist in the decisive battle of capital ships. Then came the surprise U.S. offensive at Guadalcanal in August 1942, when the imperial navy was about to launch a major offensive in the western reaches of the Indian Ocean. The operation was immediately canceled, and much of that naval force was then concentrated in the lower Solomons.

U.S. carriers remained highly valued prey for Japanese submarines at the outset of the Guadalcanal campaign. At the end of August, near San Cristobal Island, a torpedo fired by I-26 struck Saratoga. The veteran carrier was again temporarily withdrawn for repairs, although the damage this time was less than that caused by I-6's attack some eight months earlier.

The biggest independent blow to U.S. carrier strength in 1942 came on the afternoon of September 15, when three torpedoes fired by Commander Takaichi Kinashi in I-19 tore gaping holes in the starboard side of Wasp. Halfway between the New Hebrides and the Solomons, the fleet carrier was abandoned after an hour, and later, after dark, it was sunk by U.S. torpedoes. Moreover, two other U.S. warships were also hit during Kinashi's remarkable six-torpedo salvo. Three kerosene-and-oxygen-fed Type 95 torpedoes sped on past Wasp to approach another carrier group built around USS Hornet some twelve miles away—one torpedo hit and slightly damaged battleship USS North Carolina (BB-55). (The slight damage nonetheless knocked the new fast battleship out of the war for two months for repairs.) Then another torpedo hit destroyer USS O'Brien (DD-415), causing the ship later to

break in two and sink on October 19 while en route to the United States for refitting. Only the sixth torpedo from I-19 ran its long course without hitting any ships. This surely was a record for a "one-shot" submarine attack during World War II, one of the most successful for the Japanese submarine service. Although the element of chance, always present in war, favored Kinashi's hits on North Carolina and O'Brien, this remarkable salvo offers ample evidence of the superiority of Japanese torpedoes.

Two additional U.S. Navy warships were effectively attacked by I-boats in October and November before the Japanese submarine operational patterns changed decidedly. Heavy cruiser USS Chester (CA-27) was damaged during an attack by I-176 on October 20; it withdrew from the Pacific for repairs in Norfolk, Virginia, and rejoined the Pacific Fleet several months later in 1943. However, I-26's attack on USS Juneau (CL-52) on November 13 was disastrous. Damaged badly earlier in the first battle of Guadalcanal, the light cruiser was hit by the submarine's torpedoes on the port side under the bridge. An enormous explosion caused the warship to disintegrate and sink almost immediately. Nearly seven hundred men, including the five Sullivan brothers, went down with Juneau or died in the open sea, in one of the worst single-ship disasters in U.S. naval history. (As a result of this sinking, the U.S. Navy issued regulations forbidding close relatives from serving in the same ship.)

Nonetheless, the struggle for Guadalcanal was costly for the Japanese submarine force. Nine submarines were lost in the campaign between the U.S. landings in August and the Japanese withdrawal in February 1943. These losses were serious, if not devastating, to the future of the Japanese submarine force. During the same period, submarines were responsible for sinking Wasp, Juneau, and O'Brien; and Saratoga, North Carolina, and Chester were damaged by submarine torpedoes. These warships represented no inconsiderable loss to the Allies at a crucial stage in the Pacific war. Yet when one considers the large number of Japanese submarines committed to the strategically critical Guadalcanal campaign, one could reasonably expect that many more U.S. naval ships ought to have been sunk.

The crisis situation after late 1942 required the use of submarines in dangerous supply and evacuation missions. The fate of the Japanese submarine force was thus sealed.

After major Japanese counterattacks in August and September failed to capture the crucially important Henderson Air Field, Imperial Headquarters still refused to give up the struggle for Guadalcanal. The 38th Division, conqueror of Hong Kong, was ordered to "Starvation Island," as Guadalcanal was soon to be called, but transport and supply of Japanese troops were made extremely difficult by growing U.S. air strength. Combined Fleet Headquarters conducted November's campaign for Guadalcanal as it had the previous month. Reinforcements were run in to the island by fast destroyers, and naval strength was enhanced by the big guns of Japanese battleships. By November 15, two major battles had taken place off Guadalcanal, with the Japanese losing two battleships, *Hiei* and *Kirishima*, and the United States losing two light cruisers. A critically important Japanese convoy was annihilated on November 13 (9,000 of the 14,000 reinforcing troops failed to reach the island), and Guadalcanal started to become a desperate island for the poorly supplied Japanese soldiers there.

The ordeal of the Japanese submarine fleet was further intensified less than a year after the attack on Pearl Harbor, when many boats were assigned transport duty. On November 16, 1942, Admiral Isoroku Yamamoto, commander in chief of the Combined Fleet, ordered the use of submarines for transportation missions because of the critical conditions faced by Japanese forces, particularly on Guadalcanal but also at Buna in eastern New Guinea. Thirteen large submarines were initially assigned to participate in these dangerous missions.

These submarines transported about 1,115 tons of cargo to Guadalcanal and evacuated more than two thousand troops (several thousand more soldiers were evacuated by fast destroyers); however, the submarine force suffered badly. As with the fast destroyers of the so-called Tokyo Express, the place and hour of arrival of I-boats were often known in advance through U.S. cryptologic intelligence. *I-3* was lost on December 9 when attacked by *PT-59* near Cape Esperance, Guadalcanal; *I-4* was lost soon after its final communication was received on December 20; and *I-1*, after being badly damaged in an attack by two New Zealand corvettes, was successfully beached in Kamimbo Bay at the northwestern end of Guadalcanal and abandoned on January 29, 1943. *I-1* yielded valuable code books. *I-18* was lost in early February after completing its supply mission to Guadalcanal. Because of these overwhelming casualties and the continued deterioration of Japanese positions on the island, in mid-February 1943 submarines were finally withdrawn from the transportation operations at Guadalcanal. It is perhaps too easy to suggest that Japanese submarines were misused during the supply and evacuation operations at Guadalcanal; nevertheless, the strength and determination of the Allied armed forces and the tradition of Japanese armed forces never to surrender left Japanese submariners with no alternatives.

Guadalcanal was a turning point for the Japanese submarine force, and by 1943 its losses had started to increase markedly while the sinking of U.S. warships, its primary target, had decreased drastically. The table demonstrates this change.

	12/1941	1942	1943	1944	1–8/1945
U.S. warships sunk by Japanese submarines	0	5	3	2	2
U.S. warships damaged (not sunk) by Japanese submarines	0	4*	0	2	0
Japanese submarines lost	3	17	27	54	26

*ISN carrier *Saratoga* was damaged twice by submarine-launched torpedoes in 1942.

No small combatant ships or naval auxiliaries are included in the table's statistics, only submarines, destroyers, cruisers, aircraft carriers, and battleships. Also excluded are the very few warships from U.S. allies that were victims of Japanese submarine attacks. For example, one Dutch and one Russian submarine (probably by mistake; Russia was neutral until the last two weeks of the war) were sunk by Japanese submarines, and the old British battleship *Ramillies* was damaged in an attack by the *I-20*'s midget submarine.

The year 1944 was disastrous for the Japanese submarine force. Its demise was, of course, symptomatic of the destruction of the navy as a whole. Nevertheless, the threadbare plans for the decisive battle were particularly feeble in 1944, when the elusive set-piece confrontation was expected to occur in the so-called zone of absolute national defense, near the Philippines. If the Japanese had failed to bring about this decisive battle at the beginning of the war when the imperial navy was an estimated 70 percent of the strength of the U.S. Navy in the Pacific, what likelihood was there in 1944 that a vastly superior U.S. Navy could be tricked into fighting a largely contrived decisive battle? The Allies would choose the most advantageous circumstances in which to bring to bear their overwhelming forces, and inevitably the site drew closer to the Japanese home islands.

The Japanese submarine force often operated helter-skelter, being constantly obligated to commit submarines in unanticipated and ever-increasing and dangerous crises. Submarines undertook a wide variety of assignments in addition to supply and evacuation operations with by-passed Japanese island garrisons. For example, they were deployed along picket lines in an attempt to ambush and pursue enemy naval forces, only to be ordered and sometimes reordered to dash elsewhere when enemy forces were discovered beyond the original picket lines. Submarines were assigned to reconnoiter heavily guarded enemy ports and advance anchorages. There they sometimes launched midget submarines, human-piloted torpedoes, and aircraft, with minimal results. Submarine aircraft also dropped a few incendiary bombs on Oregon forests, and submarine deck guns fired on other minor targets on the U.S. mainland and various islands. Submarines also transported highly explosive gasoline for refueling seaplanes. On the other side of the globe, the Japanese undertook dangerous submarine transport operations with their German allies, with whom they exchanged personnel and small amounts of strategic goods, such as quinine and tungsten, and blueprints and prototypes of war machinery. Of the five large I-boats that attempted the trip to German-occupied France and back to Japan, only one was fully successful. There were also forays into the Indian Ocean, but crises in the Pacific usually resulted in a concentration of submarines there in an effort to combat strong and rapidly advancing Allied forces. These highly dispersed operations characterized much of Japanese submarine strategic and operational activity throughout the war. The occasional entreaty to concentrate against enemy sea communications and extended U.S. supply lines, particularly to the South Pacific and Australia, was always played down and usually rejected.

The failure of the submarine force may also be explained by shortcomings in Japanese naval doctrine. The Imperial Navy's neglect of ASW before the war proved deadly to the wartime Japanese merchant marine, but the Japanese submarine force was also adversely affected. Japanese submarines were poorly prepared to cope with U.S. Navy ASW operations.

During months of work against German U-boats in the Atlantic before the attack on Pearl Harbor, the U.S. Navy had gained the experience of escorting convoys, experience that sharpened ASW skills. The Japanese navy had no such wartime experience. When war came, Japanese submariners were unaware that they could be so effectively and systematically pursued on the surface by enemy radar and beneath the sea by sonar. Japanese submarines made little effort to avoid detection by such sophisticated sensors. Even late in the war, after ample opportunity to sharpen their skills and to observe U.S. ASW operations, Japanese submariners often seemed oblivious to new and dangerous conditions. For example, I-52 (discovered in May 1995 west of the Cape Verde Islands, more than three miles deep, on the Atlantic floor) was en route to Lorient, France, with 2 metric tons of gold when it came under attack and was soon sunk just

after midnight on June 24, 1944. A U.S. aircraft missed the surfaced Japanese submarine in an initial bomb attack. During the following thirty minutes, acoustic buoys were dropped over a mile of sea, and soon the noise of the churning propellers was radioed by the buoys to the aircraft circling above. A homing Mark 24 torpedo, also known as Fido, was dropped, and, as an action report claimed, it fatally struck I-52's starboard side and exploded. Other than crash-diving on the initial attack, apparently I-52 did not make use of any special evasive maneuvers. The Japanese submarine might have rigged for silent running and escaped with a very slow speed that produced little propeller noise. Or escape would have been guaranteed if I-52 had dived to its safe maximum depth of 330 feet, somewhat below that of the little Fido with its 92-pound explosive charge.

With no significant ASW doctrine, Japanese submariners, unlike their U.S. and German counterparts, had little understanding of the theories of sound promulgation in relation to temperature layers or water stratification. Careful maneuvering while submerged could reduce the chance of detection, but deeply submerged Japanese submarines usually ascended directly to periscope depth to reconnoiter in a quick 360-degree sweep and then surfaced, fearing only the possibility of being spotted directly and visually by an enemy patrol. In some respects, Japanese submarines were superior to Western submarines. They were usually large, powerfully armed, and fast on the surface for effective operation in the vast Pacific Ocean. But once detected, they often made good targets because of their poor submerged speed, limited maneuverability, and shallow diving depth (330 feet was the maximum, whereas a comparable U.S. Navy submarine could easily operate at 400 feet). Finally, Japanese submarine designs failed until late in the war to emphasize noise-reduction features. The 5,223-ton I-400, first of a new class completed in December 1944, had an anechoic coating to impede sonar detection. Also at that time, Japanese submarine-borne radar and active sonar were first used, but they were primitive by U.S. Navy standards and of little consequence. However, the I-400 class was fitted with a snorkel, a device for supplying air to a submerged submarine, unlike any U.S. Navy submarine in World War II.

Enormous hardships and losses were suffered by Japanese submariners (127 of about 160 large submarines in service during the war were lost—79 percent—usually with all hands), but their spirit never faltered. (The much larger German U-boat fleet suffered even heavier losses: Out of 842 U-boats assigned to battle duty, 783 were lost, an incredible 93 percent. Of a total of 248 U.S. Navy fleet submarines in commission during the war years, 52 were lost from all causes, that is, 21 percent.) Loyalty and unit cohesion remained strong among the elite members of the Japanese submarine force. Many of them, especially enlisted men, came from poor farm families; these young men frequently volunteered for submarine duty—in part, for the extra pay submariners received. They were thus able to send more money home to help their families; the special pay made submariners the envy among surface sailors. These circumstances and the prestige associated with submarine service reinforced Japanese submariners' sense of pride and commitment to their service and fellow undersea comrades. Japanese submariners, like submariners in the U.S. and German navies during the war, were loyal and dedicated sailors who functioned courageously and competently in the most trying of circumstances.

Epilogue

By the beginning of 1945, the Japanese submarine force, like the rest of the imperial navy, had fallen into a shambles. Submarine policy had not been effectively focused since the outset of the war; therefore, nothing could be saved near the end.

The Japanese submarine force made prewar training as realistic as possible, but the realities of the war increasingly surpassed the capacity of the force to adapt. The mindset and command structure in the imperial navy prevented complete identification of the problems that plagued the submarine force. Moreover, rapidly changing circumstances of the war, in which the powerful U.S. Navy was the pacesetter, inhibited the implementation of fresh and crucial alternatives. Thus the Japanese were prisoners of their past, and the legacy of prewar thinking offered only a grim fate for the Japanese submarine force after 1941.

Japanese submarine operations were frequently widely scattered. When they were concentrated to take part in major Combined Fleet operations early in the war—at Pearl Harbor and Midway, for example—submarines failed to live up to the expectations of Japanese operation planners.

Submarine effectiveness against U.S. warships during the Guadalcanal campaign, particularly in September 1942, was quite distinguished. Yet submarines did not inflict enough damage to force a U.S. withdrawal from Guadalcanal; nor were the Japanese air and surface naval forces capable of accomplishing the high command's goal.

Immediately after the Pearl Harbor attack, the Japanese navy should have concentrated *all* oceangoing and fleet-type submarines in Hawaiian waters and off the U.S. mainland. Operations like those of *I-25* in October 1942, including actions more aggressive than the incendiary bombing of Oregon forests, ought to have been emphasized. The large submarines ought to have been rotated systematically, and these two war patrol areas (Hawaii and the U.S. west coast) should have been maintained at least through 1942. That is, one-third of the available submarines should have been on station, one-third en route, and one-third undergoing refitting. Only Japanese submarines could chance operations around the Hawaiian Islands and eastward after December 7, 1941. While manning these two patrol areas, the submarines could have obstructed quite effectively the flow of U.S. reinforcements being rushed westward, and at least in the early part of 1942 they would have been ideally situated to attack U.S. warships en route to the U.S. mainland for permanent repairs after damage during the Pearl Harbor attack.

As a corollary to submarine operations on the Hawaiian and California coasts, *I-25*–like operations should have included a large tanker I-boat for refueling in order to continue I-boat–aircraft operations in the Panama Canal area. Bombing the canal locks would have been the goal, and even if there were no hits on the vital waterway, such an attack would have alarmed the American public. Thus the U.S. Congress would have voted more enormous defense expenditures, funds that would not have been available for the U.S. buildup in the South Pacific in 1942.

After the Pearl Harbor attack, Japanese air and surface naval forces should have focused exclusively on the southern and westward areas of expansion *without* demanding the heavy involvement of the submarine fleet. The major enemy capital ships in those areas, HMS *Prince of Wales* and *Repulse*, for example, were sunk by air power in early December 1941. Other available British battleships of the Eastern Fleet were the four old World War I R-class slow battleships and faster *Warspite*. These capital ships, with the much newer fleet aircraft carriers HMS *Indomitable* and *Formidable*, were incapable of effective opposition to Japanese expansion. And surely the Japanese air and surface naval forces could have overwhelmed the ABDA (American, British, Dutch, and Australian) cruisers and lesser warships without the, as it turned out, modest aid of the submarine force. At a minimum, the medium-range RO-class submarines could have served as an arm of Combined Fleet operations in southern and westward expansion during the first thirteen months of the war. As it turned out, Japan's submarine force never had a chance to prove itself as a strategic arm because it was always subordinated to local needs and tactical situations.

FURTHER READINGS

Boyd, Carl. "American Naval Intelligence of Japanese Submarine Operations Early in the Pacific War," *Journal of Military History,* 53 (April 1989).

Boyd, Carl, and Akihiko Yoshida. *The Japanese Submarine Force and World War II* (1995).

Carpenter, Dorr, and Norman Polmar. *Submarines of the Imperial Japanese Navy* (1986).

Fukaya, Hajime. "Three Japanese Submarine Developments," *Proceedings,* U.S. Naval Institute (August 1952).

Goldingham, C. S. "Japanese Submarines in the Second World War," *Journal of the Royal United Service Institution* (February 1951).

Hirama, Yoichi. "Sensuikan sensenka zoshin ni kansuru ikensho" (A paper on the effective use of submarines), *Gunji shigaku* (Journal of military history) (December 1993).

Holmes, W. J. *Undersea Victory: The Influence of Submarine Operations on the War in the Pacific* (1966).

Japan. Boeicho Boeikenshujo Senshibu (Defense Ministry, Defense Research Institute, War History Branch), ed. *Sensuikan shi* (History of submarines). Senshi Sosho (War history series), vol. 98 (1979).

Lind, L. J. *Toku-tai: Japanese Submarine Operations in Australian Waters* (1992).

Torisu, Kennosuke. *Kaiten* (Human torpedo) (1981).

Torisu, Kennosuke, and Masataka Chihaya. "Japanese Submarine Tactics," *Proceedings,* U.S. Naval Institute (February 1969).

Webber, Bert. *Retaliation: Japanese Attacks and Allied Countermeasures on the Pacific Coast in World War II* (1975).

Carl Boyd

SEE ALSO Navy, Japanese

Submarines, U.S.

American submariners were, and still are, the unsung heroes of the Pacific war. Their tiny force, only around fifty thousand men, waged overwhelmingly effective warfare against Japan. By early 1945, U.S. Navy submarines had almost completely curtailed Japan's shipping of food, fuel, munitions, and personnel to its far-flung empire in East Asia and the Pacific, as well as the importation of vital supplies, including food, to the home islands. At war's end, U.S. submarines had sunk 5.3 million tons, representing more than thirteen hundred ships (about 55 percent of all Japanese shipping losses). Less than 2 percent of the navy's men, then, were responsible for more than

half of all Japanese shipping losses during the war. U.S. submarine casualty rates were, however, the highest of the war. During the Pacific war the U.S. Navy lost fifty-two submarines and 3,500 officers and men. Proportionally, U.S. submariners paid the greatest price and exacted the greatest toll against the enemy of any American military service in the Pacific war.

A significant portion of the credit for the submariners' kills must be given to U.S. code breakers. Throughout all of the Pacific war American code breakers were, unknown to the Japanese, able to intercept and decipher Japanese radio transmissions with relative ease. Code-breaking intelligence provided the U.S. Navy with detailed information about the movements of enemy warships and merchant vessels. U.S. submarines were very frequently vectored to large convoys by naval intelligence, and it has been estimated that the code breakers contributed to approximately half of all sinkings of Japanese ships by the U.S. Submarine Service.

Command of the U.S. submarine forces in the Pacific war was divided. Soon after Pearl Harbor, U.S. submarines of the Asiatic Fleet headquartered in the Philippines fled and took up new station in Australia, where there would be two submarine bases during the war: Brisbane, in eastern Australia, and the remote port of Freemantle, in western Australia, south of Perth. These early craft managed a few sinkings, including destroyer *Natsushio,* but for the most part their usefulness was quite limited. Later in the war, as U.S. submarines were produced in massive numbers, the Australian bases serviced submarines for the U.S. Seventh Fleet (which was sometimes called "MacArthur's Navy"). The larger Pacific Fleet of submarines, based at Pearl Harbor, was ultimately answerable to Admiral Chester W. Nimitz. This unfortunate division of U.S. submarine command reflected the conflict between the Nimitz and MacArthur commands.

Submarine Types

Fortunately for the U.S. Navy, the Japanese sneak attack on Pearl Harbor, Hawaii, on December 7, 1941, did not inflict significant damage on U.S. submarines. On December 8, 1941, the U.S. Navy in the Pacific had fifty-one submarines at its disposal: twenty-two at Pearl Harbor and twenty-nine in the Philippines (including six ancient S-class boats). This total represented a motley and outdated assortment of models. Immediately after Pearl Harbor the navy began placing orders for large numbers of new and improved submarines, but modern submarines up to the task of devastating enemy shipping did not come on the scene in large numbers until early 1943, when the *Gato*-class craft were starting to become the workhorse of the U.S. submarine forces. Until then, the Americans had to make do with what they had.

S-class. The oldest submarines were the S-class, built during World War I and the 1920s. These craft had speeds of 14.5 knots surfaced and 11 knots submerged (11 knots was, by the standards of the day, a very fast submerged speed; it reflected U.S. interwar doctrine that submarines needed fast submerged speeds to escape depth charges fired by enemy antisubmarine vessels). They were armed with one 4-inch gun and five torpedo tubes (four forward and one aft), with a carrying capacity of twelve torpedoes. These small submarines displaced 903 tons surfaced, were 265 feet long, and had test depths of only 200 feet. Before the war they were the favorite training boats for submariners. The *S-44* was the last S-class submarine to see action in the Pacific war; it was sunk by a Japanese destroyer in October 1943.

P-class. These submarines became the basic model upon which all subsequent submarine improvements during the Pacific war were made. Their speeds were 19 knots surfaced and 8 knots submerged. Armament consisted of one 4-inch gun on the deck and six torpedo tubes (four forward, two aft), with a carrying capacity of sixteen torpedoes. Displacing 1,330 tons surfaced, they were 300 feet long and had test depths of 250 feet.

Salmon/Sargo class. The main advantages of these boats over the P-class craft were their greater number of torpedo tubes (four forward, four aft) and total torpedo carrying capacity (twenty). Otherwise, their specifications were not remarkably different from the P-class craft: 20 knots surfaced and 9 submerged; one 4-inch gun on deck; displacement of 1,449 tons surfaced; 310 feet in length; and test depth of 258 feet.

T-class (Tambor-class). T-class subs were derived from the *Salmon/Sargo* class, but had a larger number of torpedo tubes and increased torpedo-carrying capacity that remained constant throughout the Pacific War: ten tubes (six forward, four aft) and a complement of twenty-four torpedoes. Their top speeds were 20 knots surfaced and 8.75 knots submerged, and the deck armament was one 5-inch gun. They displaced 1,475 tons surfaced, were 307 feet long, and had test depths of 275 feet. One such T-class submarine, *Tautog,* scored the highest number of kills for the war: twenty-six ships sunk.

Gato-class. The *Gato*-class submarine, named for the first craft of this class produced, eventually became the standard U.S. submarine during the Pacific war. Capable of traveling at 20.75 knots surfaced and 8.75 knots submerged, these subs had one 4-inch gun on deck and the standard number of torpedo tubes established by the T-class boats: twenty-four, with six tubes forward and four

aft. Also like the T-class craft, they carried a full load of twenty-four torpedoes. They displaced 1,825 tons surfaced, were 312 feet long, and had test depths of 300 feet. They went into battle in increasing numbers starting around January 1943.

Balao-class. The *Balao* boats, named for the first submarine of their class produced, were improved versions of the *Gato* craft. Their surfaced and submerged speeds, torpedo tubes and capacities, displacements, and lengths were essentially identical to the *Gato* boats; what distinguished them from the former was the prefabrication used in part of their manufacturing process, the slightly larger 5-inch deck gun, and the significantly deeper test depth of 400 feet. *Balao*-class subs began appearing in battle around January 1944.

Submarine Warfare Strategy

U.S. submarine warfare strategy differed significantly from Japanese strategy. From early in the war, unlike their Japanese counterparts, American submariners did their best to disrupt Japanese merchant shipping and slowly reduce the Japanese empire's ability to wage war. Tankers were high-priority targets because they carried the fuel and oil necessary to keep Japan's war machine running. The Japanese, on the other hand, thought of submarines mainly as assets to be deployed along with surface warships against large U.S. warships, and as intelligence and reconnaissance vessels.

By late 1943 the war of attrition against the economic foundations of the Japanese empire was beginning to tell. In September 1943 the Japanese militarists were startled to learn that because of the U.S. submarine warfare against Japanese commerce, Japanese shipping was reduced to just over 5 million tons, a million less than needed for successful prosecution of the war. U.S. submarines fired a total of 14,748 torpedoes at 4,112 Japanese merchant ships during the war and greatly contributed to the grand wartime total of 8,141,591 tons of Japanese shipping sunk. In 1942 Japan lost 952,965 tons of merchant shipping to all causes and built only 260,059 tons of replacement shipping. Japanese shipbuilding never kept pace with shipping losses: in 1943, 1,803,409 tons were sunk but only 769,085 were built; the totals for 1944 were 3,834,377 tons sunk and 1,699,203 built; and by war's end in August 1945, the totals, reflecting Japan's greatly weakened economy, were 1,607,678 tons sunk and only 503,162 built.

The road to such final and devastating victory against the Japanese foe was not a smooth one. It was fraught with inexperience, equipment malfunctions, petty jealousies, and simple bureaucratic incompetence. Arguably, chief among all of the submariners' problems were the unreliable torpedoes they had to use until midway through the war.

More often than not in the Pacific war, American submariners hunted Japanese shipping as lone wolves or solitary snipers—unlike their Nazi counterparts in the Atlantic, who frequently hunted in wolf packs and engaged in constant radio chatter with one another, thus giving away their positions to Allied antisubmarine warships, American submariners were concerned about maintaining as much radio silence as possible. By mid-1943 the Japanese did in fact possess sophisticated radio transmission detection equipment that allowed them to locate submarines. (By mid-1944, even the minimal radio traffic between U.S. submarines in wolf packs had revealed much information to the Japanese about the diving capabilities of submarines, and the Japanese consequently improved their antisubmarine efforts.) Further, the German wolf pack strategy worked well in the North Atlantic, where shipping lanes between North America and Britain were fairly well defined, but it would never have been effective in the vast Pacific. The Americans did not begin experimenting with wolf pack patrols until late 1943. Most skippers feared sinking a friendly submarine within a pack and had reservations about having a senior commander on board giving orders and trying to coordinate the attacks. They also disliked patrolling in packs, and the results of such patrols were often disappointing. Nevertheless, they did increase in 1944 and 1945, and in June 1945 the daring wolf pack raid by nine U.S. submarines into the Sea of Japan became one of the high points of the naval war.

Torpedoes

"*Damn* those exploders . . . damn them all to *hell!*" exclaimed the skipper of submarine *Jack,* Lieutenant Commander Thomas Michael Dykers, on June 20, 1943, as he watched through the periscope and saw a torpedo, fired from an excellent position and at the optimal range of 1,000 yards, "premature" (explode before reaching its intended target), a 1,500-ton trawler. "Son of a bitch from *Baghdad!*" Dykers roared as the other two torpedoes he fired also failed to reach their target, either missing or failing to detonate.

This flawlessly executed attack, the premier combat for both the *Jack* and its skipper, failed because of faulty torpedoes. Very unfortunately for the U.S. war effort in the Pacific, its submarine campaigns were plagued for fully the first half of the war with torpedo problems. These problems included premature detonation, running depths deeper than specified, and failure to explode upon contact

with a ship's hull. Often one of these problems masked another, with the solution of one problem seemingly leading to the emergence of another, unanticipated one. The full extent of the torpedo problems was not known or completely remedied until the fall of 1943.

But, as if to compensate for this American failing, the Japanese committed an equal or greater strategic blunder of their own: they chose not to make extensive use of submarine warfare against U.S. shipping. Throughout most of the war, Japanese submarines and torpedoes were superior to their U.S. counterparts. Japanese submarines, or I-boats, were bigger than the U.S. submarines, and their torpedoes were vastly superior. Even after it was perfected, the U.S. Mark-14 torpedo had a range of 4,500 yards, a warhead of 668 pounds of Torpex (a specially designed mixture of TNT, other explosive compounds, and beeswax), and a speed of 46 knots. (Fired at 31 knots, the Mark-14 theoretically had a range of 9,000 yards, but this setting was seldom used, except against anchored ships.) The electrical Mark-18-1 torpedo, which came into increasing use toward the end of the war, had a range of 3,500 yards, a top speed of only 33 knots, and a warhead of 500 pounds. By contrast, the typical Japanese submarine torpedo, the Type 95, had a range of 10,000 yards, a speed of 49 knots, and a warhead of 900 pounds. It took only three such torpedoes, fired from Japanese submarine *I-19* on September 15, 1942, in the Coral Sea, to fatally cripple aircraft carrier *Wasp.* On the same day a Japanese torpedo blew a 32-foot hole in the hull of battleship *North Carolina.*

The Mark-14. The standard Mark-14, the torpedo most commonly used by U.S. submarines in World War II, had three problems: running too deep, exploding prematurely because of faulty magnetic detonation devices, and not detonating at all upon contact with a ship's hull, because of poorly designed mechanical detonators. The first fault to be detected and corrected was running below set depths. When this problem was solved, the issue of premature detonations came next, and when this in turn was resolved, faulty mechanical detonators had to be reworked until they performed satisfactorily.

In June 1942 navy technical personnel placed a large fishnet across a bay in western Australia and then fired three torpedoes at it. Two torpedoes set to run at 10 feet tore through the net at 18 feet and 25 feet, respectively, and a third, set to run on the surface, pierced the net at 11 feet. The U.S. Bureau of Ordnance (BuOrd) questioned the unsophisticated protocols of this test, but its own more careful tests confirmed that the torpedoes were indeed running deep. The reasons involved, among other things, weight differences between live and dummy torpedoes tested, improperly calibrated equipment, and inaccurate recordkeeping. Instead of addressing all of these problems, submariners simply set torpedo depths for 10 feet less than they needed.

The next major problem with the Mark-14 torpedoes was the Mark-6 magnetic exploder, a device copied from captured German U-boat torpedoes and designed, at least in theory, to detonate the torpedo's warhead just as it passed through the magnetic field beneath the keel, usually the most vulnerable and least armored part of a ship. Unknown to the Americans, the Nazis had encountered so many problems with their own magnetic exploder device that they eventually abandoned it as unreliable.

The Mark-6 Exploder. The most infuriating quirk with the Mark-14 torpedo equipped with the Mark-6 exploder was not that it *never* worked, but that it worked *unpredictably.* When this torpedo/exploder combination did perform as designed, it was devastatingly effective, and severely damaged or sank any vessel unfortunate enough to be its target because it broke up the ship exactly at its most vulnerable part, the keel. These successes happened with just enough frequency to convince BuOrd that the torpedoes were largely problem-free.

Predictably, skippers very quietly deactivated the magnetic exploders on their torpedoes and set them to detonate on contact only. Most did not reveal that they had done so, because tampering with the government's ordnance was, technically, a serious offense that could get them court-martialed. Admiral Charles A. Lockwood, commander of the Pacific Fleet submarines, eventually learned of this practice and sided with the skippers. He also decided to take his case against the faulty magnetic exploder to the commander of the Pacific fleet, Admiral Chester Nimitz. After hearing Lockwood's grievances, Nimitz directed Lockwood to issue orders for the deactivation of the faulty devices, and this Lockwood did in June 1943.

Disabling the magnetic exploders did greatly reduce the premature explosion problem, but an equally serious fault emerged: dud torpedoes. Instead of exploding prematurely, many torpedoes did not explode at all, even when they hit an enemy hull with a solid thud.

On July 24, 1943, Dan Daspit, skipper of *Tinosa*, was on the trail of a huge tanker of 19,000 tons, *Tonan Maru III.* Two of the first four torpedoes he fired at the vessel were solid hits, and smoke began billowing from the tanker. Finding no surface or air escorts for the tanker, Daspit had a matchless opportunity to send it to the bottom. In all, he fired fifteen torpedoes, the last against a Japanese destroyer. All failed to detonate. Daspit saved his last torpedo to take back to Pearl Harbor as proof that

something was drastically wrong with U.S. torpedoes. At Pearl Harbor, Lockwood and others soon concluded that the contact detonators were malfunctioning, and a team of investigators was soon looking into the problem. Dummy warheads fitted with the defective exploders were dropped 90 feet from a crane onto a thick steel plate. When the warheads hit the plate at the perfect angle of 90 degrees, the contact detonators were crushed by the impact before they could strike the fulminate caps. But when the warheads were dropped onto a plate angled at 45 degrees, only about half were duds. It was clear that the detonators were poorly designed, and torpedo experts at Pearl Harbor immediately began reworking them. (Ironically, the new and improved detonator devices were fashioned out of very tough metal obtained from Japanese aircraft propellers found in the Hawaiian Islands.) Lockwood directed that all Mark-14 torpedoes thereafter be equipped with the new detonators, and told submarines still at sea to try for angled shots instead of the ideal 90 degree approaches.

By the late summer of 1943, all of the torpedo problems were remedied. Only now could submariners confront the enemy with full confidence in their ordnance. The reworked torpedoes soon led to dramatic increases in submarine sinkings of Japanese shipping, and by the first quarter of 1944, more than 1,750,000 tons of Japanese shipping were destroyed, which nearly equaled the figure of 1,803,409 sunk for all of 1943. By the end of 1944, the destruction of Japanese shipping was truly devastating: more than 3.8 million tons sunk.

The Mark-18. Early in 1942 the Allies had captured a German electric torpedo, and eventually Westinghouse was producing copies. One of the main advantages of the electric torpedo was its wakeless track, which made it much more difficult to spot. Westinghouse's Mark-18 electric torpedo also proved to have none of the depth control or detonation problems of the Mark-14s, and its production costs were less. Its main immediately discernible drawback was its slower speed of about 30 knots.

But as the Mark-18 was taken into combat situations, problems emerged. For one thing, it ran slower in cold water because the cold reduced the power of its batteries. Hydrogen leaks from its batteries led to several fires and explosions, and ventilating the torpedoes of hydrogen became a frequent precaution. (Later, hydrogen-burning technology right inside the torpedo itself made this unnecessary.) Torpedo technicians at Pearl Harbor quickly identified and remedied these and other problems, and by 1944 the Mark-18 was gradually gaining acceptance from submariners. Gradually a consensus arose: they would use the electric Mark-18s by day and the now reliable Mark-14s by night. Some 30 percent of the torpedoes fired from U.S. submarines in 1944 were electric, and by war's end the figure had risen to 65 percent. By the end of the war, the Mark-18 had definitely proven its worth: it had sunk nearly a million tons, about one-fifth of the total sent to the bottom by U.S. submarines.

The torpedo was the submariner's main tool of war, and its improvement was the single most important technological development in U.S. submarine warfare during World War II. But other items of equipment and improvements in them also contributed to the stealth and deadliness of the U.S. submarine.

The TDC

In the 1930s, P-class and *Salmon*-class subs were equipped with Mark 1 torpedo data computers (TDCs), manufactured by the Arma Corporation. When submariners fed data on an enemy ship's bearing, range, and angle on the bow (relative bearing) into the TDC, the device automatically computed and displayed on dials the enemy ship's relative course and gave the proper gyro angle settings for the torpedoes. In the late 1930s Admiral Thomas Hart, chairman of the navy's General Board and an arch-conservative who seemed to despise any submarine equipment he had not known in his youth, disliked the TDC "gadgets" and the "luxuries" (air-conditioning) by then aboard submarines, and he tried to have them disapproved. Lockwood, who chaired the Submarine Officers' Conference in 1938, resisted Hart's technophobia and ultimately won the day, securing approval for installing TDCs and air-conditioning aboard the T and all future classes of submarines. During the Pacific war, a superior TDC called the Mark 3 was developed by the Arma Corporation.

The TBT was installed on all submarines that saw action in the Pacific war. Essentially a large binocular telescope that fed data to the TDC for setting the proper gyroscope angles on torpedoes, it was used primarily for night surface attacks.

Radar

By August 1942, many U.S. submarines were using both surface and air radar. Some skippers, concerned that extensive radar use would be detected by the enemy and give away their positions, limited its use. At war's end, however, it was revealed that these concerns were unwarranted; the Japanese never did develop effective radar detection technology.

By January 1942 the simple SD radar device was available for submarines to use in detecting enemy aircraft. The SD radar was nondirectional, meaning that it gave

an aircraft's range but no bearing. Its range was limited to about six to ten miles. Later in the war, Japanese antisubmarine aircraft learned to surprise U.S. submarines by approaching them at low altitudes, literally flying under radar. Submarines did not rely solely on SD radar for detecting enemy aircraft and constantly had sharp-eyed crewmen on deck, on the lookout for aircraft whenever the submarine was running on the surface.

Surface (SJ) radar was first used aboard U.S. submarines in late July 1942. It searched the surface of the sea for enemy ships and could detect them at a range of up to thirteen miles. Later improvements increased its effectiveness. In June 1943 the plan position indicator (PPI) positioned the submarine at the center of the submarine's SJ radar sweep and located "pips," or radar contacts, relative to the submarine's position. This was a significant improvement over the simple "A-scope" of the original SJ radar, which, like the SD radar, gave range but no relative bearing. The next month, an improved SJ radar (SJ-1) became available. It used a perforated parabolic antenna that increased the effective range of the surface radar to over thirty miles.

The Bathythermograph

In March 1943 a new technology became available that contributed significantly to a submarine's stealth. The bathythermograph was a device that made two measurements for a submerged submarine: the sub's depth and the temperature of the surrounding water. Thermoclines, or layers of cold water, very often deflected the "pinging" of surface sound equipment and thus foiled the efforts of enemy antisubmarine vessels to locate the submerged submarine. If a submarine skipper could get his craft beneath such a layer, chances were very good that he could escape detection. Sharp submarine commanders who managed to maneuver into firing position against enemy convoys with time to spare would sometimes take their boats down to see if they had such protective layers of water beneath them.

The Mark-27

The Mark-27, a small electrical homing torpedo, became available in the summer of 1944 and was used aboard a few submarines. Copied from a German design (possibly the *Zaunkönig*) and manufactured by Westinghouse, it was designed to home in acoustically on the sounds of an enemy craft's screws, but its combat performance was spotty. Apparently the "Cutie," as it was called, was ineffective when used against craft traveling faster than about 8 knots. Nonetheless, 106 "Cuties" were fired at Japanese ships, with a 31 percent hit rate; twenty-four ships sunk and nine damaged.

FM Sonar

A device that made its debut in late 1944 was the FM sonar, designed to help a submarine detect and avoid anti-submarine mines. Several U.S. submarines had been destroyed when they attempted to pass through mined waters. The year 1944 produced a bumper crop of U.S. submarine sinkings of Japanese shipping, and by early 1945 the Pacific Ocean had more or less been swept clean of large Japanese warships and merchant vessels.

Hungry for more targets, in June 1945 nine U.S. submarines equipped with FM sonar managed to thread their craft through the mined waters of the Tsushima Strait and entered the Sea of Japan, an area where Japanese naval commanders had vowed U.S. submarines would never go. Some of the submarines contacted mine cables, but none of the mines were dragged down far enough to touch the submarines and be detonated. In two weeks the nine submarines sank twenty-eight ships (including a submarine, *I-122*) for a total of 54,784 tons. One of the subs, *Bonefish,* was lost with all hands after Japanese antisubmarine forces spotted and fatally depth-charged it. On the foggy night of June 24–25, the eight remaining submarines dashed out of the La Pérouse (Soya) Strait on the surface at 18 knots. They all made it out safely, without a shot being fired at them.

Other Technology

By the fall of 1944, American technicians were coming up with all sorts of new devices for enhancing submarine warfare. One example was a decoy "noisemaker" device fired from a submarine undergoing depth-charge attacks. This device sometimes managed to fool enemy sonar and allow the submarine to slip away without fatal damage. A night periscope designed to let in much more light also came on the scene.

The primary objective of U.S. submarines in the Pacific war was, of course, to sink as much Japanese shipping as possible. But submarines did occasionally perform other functions, including reconnaissance, mine-laying in enemy waters, covert resupply missions, rescues of civilian populations, and especially "lifeguarding," or standing ready to rescue American pilots whose planes had been shot down over the Pacific. By war's end, eighty-six submarines on "lifeguard" duty had rescued 504 American airmen. The record for such rescues was held by *Tigrone,* which snatched thirty-one downed American flyers from the Pacific. Among the rescued airmen was George Herbert Walker Bush, who later became the forty-first president of the United States.

FURTHER READINGS

Blair, Clay, Jr., *Silent Victory: The U.S. Submarine War Against Japan* (1975).

Calvert, James F. *Silent Running: My Years on a World War II Attack Submarine* (1995).

Gannon, Robert. *Hellions of the Deep: The Development of American Torpedoes in World War II* (1996).

Harris, Brayton. *The Navy Times Book of Submarines: A Political, Social, and Military History* (1997).

Hoyt, Edwin P. *Bowfin: The Story of One of America's Fabled Fleet Submarines in World War II* (1983).

Hoyt, Edwin P. *Submarines at War: The History of the American Silent Service* (1983).

Lockwood, Charles A. *Sink 'em All: Submarine Warfare in the Pacific* (1951).

Roscoe, Theodore. *United States Submarine Operations in World War II* (1949).

David C. Wright

SEE ALSO Navy, U.S.

Sutherland, Richard K.

The driving force in Douglas MacArthur's staff during World War II was Richard K. Sutherland, "The Power before the Throne," a veteran of World War I in France, a man with considerable troop time, and a graduate of Leavenworth and the Army War College. As MacArthur's chief of staff, Sutherland set a furious pace and poured scorn on inefficiency. He knew that someone at MacArthur's headquarters had to be a hard-driving disciplinarian who was not concerned with being personally popular, and he did not think that MacArthur was the one to be it. Sutherland took up that role. He was not then, and would not later become, easily approachable. Starting as a lieutenant colonel and ending as a lieutenant general, he was abrupt, serious, and efficient but never warm.

Sutherland ran staff meetings that were called models of group thinking. His powers of concentration were amazing. He defined problems, broke them into key elements, and drew forth contributions from attendees. MacArthur described him as invaluable in clarifying and crystallizing a situation. Sutherland became especially adept at anticipating and understanding what MacArthur wanted, then executing it. MacArthur could afford to be gracious to his subordinates, for behind his composure was Sutherland's figurative whip. Sutherland was a hard man with a temper, had a commanding, even arrogant voice, and was not concerned about hurting feelings.

Sutherland acted as more than just a chief of staff. He was a deputy commander. MacArthur, of course, made policy, but Sutherland had worked with MacArthur to originate and define that policy. MacArthur gave general directions for operations and left Sutherland to fill in the details. In Manila and later on Bataan, Sutherland was closely involved in tactical decisions—probably more so than MacArthur. He called the corps commanders on Bataan and issued orders in MacArthur's name.

He could do this only because he and MacArthur were of the same mind. Yet Sutherland did not have the personality or warmth to be MacArthur's friend. He was MacArthur's chief adviser and sounding board, but not a friend. They respected and understood each other. That mutual respect was such that Sutherland was the only man on the staff who could, and did, confront MacArthur's verbal eloquence and exuberance with sharp, unemotional logic that brought MacArthur back to earth.

Sutherland would develop a reputation for shielding MacArthur from his commanders. That trait ran him into trouble on December 8, 1941, when the Japanese attacked the Philippines. MacArthur's air commander, Major General Lewis H. Brereton, tried to get permission to launch an air attack against Formosa. Sutherland intercepted Brereton and carried the request to MacArthur. Delays ensued, and the Japanese caught the U.S. bombers on the ground. The true sequence of events in this case will never be known. Whether or not Brereton asked for permission to strike Formosa, whether or not Sutherland agreed or disagreed, and what role MacArthur played cannot now be learned. Suffice it to say Sutherland played a key role, and the results were disastrous.

Sutherland closely coordinated with the field commanders during the defense of the Philippines, passed MacArthur's orders, and responded to questions from the commanders. (MacArthur himself only visited the Bataan front once, early in the campaign.) He developed the plan to spirit Philippine President Manuel Quezon out of the country. Sutherland then convinced MacArthur that he should comply with the president's orders sending him to Australia. Sutherland argued that MacArthur would be more valuable to the war effort commanding the new southwest Pacific theater than as a volunteer on Bataan, and he personally selected the fortunate few (which included himself; if MacArthur were indispensable to the Pacific war effort, so was his chief of staff) who made the daring PT boat dash to safety.

Sutherland rebuilt MacArthur's staff in Australia. It would now be much larger than that left on Corregidor. New officers arrived, and Sutherland integrated them into the cadre from the Philippines. Unfortunately for Sutherland, he met a young married Australian woman in Melbourne. The attraction between the two was obvious, and the affair became gossip within headquarters. This relationship would lead to serious difficulties with MacArthur.

In late 1942, MacArthur sent Sutherland to Buna on New Guinea to see why the fighting there was so slow. MacArthur gave Sutherland authority to relieve General Robert L. Eichelberger if Sutherland thought that such a drastic step was necessary. Had Sutherland done so, he would have assumed command of I Corps and would have taken the first big step toward command of an army. But Sutherland placed the good of the service above his own ambitions. Eichelberger stayed.

Sutherland's position began to change in January 1943. No longer would he be intimately involved with tactical operations. Instead, MacArthur began to use him for strategic planning and liaison with the Joint Chiefs of Staff. This did not bode well for army-navy relations, for Sutherland was tactless and hostile toward the navy.

A chief of staff's relationship with his boss's subordinate commanders can be tricky. Most of MacArthur's commanders would come to dislike Sutherland. General Walter Krueger, Sixth Army commander, loathed him. Krueger made a point of ignoring Sutherland and striding past him directly into MacArthur's office.

When Major General George C. Kenney, MacArthur's new air boss, first arrived, Sutherland sent him a detailed air operations order. Kenney challenged Sutherland. He took a piece of blank paper from Sutherland's desk, penciled in a tiny dot, and told Sutherland that the dot represented what Sutherland knew about air matters and the rest of the page represented what Kenney knew. Sutherland, nonplussed, calmed down and let Kenney run his airmen as he desired.

But Sutherland won his share of battles as well. In another argument with Kenney, Sutherland conceded that yes, Kenney was correct, Kenney was an air force commander and Sutherland was only MacArthur's chief of staff. As a staff officer, Sutherland could not give an order to Kenney. But Sutherland could draft an order and sign it Richard K. Sutherland, By Command of General Douglas MacArthur. Then it became an order Kenney had to obey. And that is what Sutherland did.

Sutherland flew to Washington in March 1943 to represent MacArthur at discussions about operations scheduled for 1943–1944. There he met with Philippine President Quezon as well as with Franklin Roosevelt. Sutherland, sure of his standing with and understanding of MacArthur, began acting on his own initiative and informing MacArthur after the fact, a dangerous procedure for anyone under MacArthur.

While preparing for another conference, Sutherland sent a message under MacArthur's signature stating that he, Sutherland, was completely familiar with the Pacific situation and was authorized to speak with MacArthur's full authority. That message, whether or not seen by MacArthur, was simply a reaffirmation of what had been written before and what would be written again. By October 1943, Sutherland had begun to consider himself MacArthur's equal in planning and executing the Pacific war. He was not only MacArthur's agent; he considered himself MacArthur's equal in exercising power.

Sutherland had grown a bit too large, however, for he ignored direct, unequivocal orders MacArthur had given him about not bringing his Australian mistress to the Philippines. Twice! And MacArthur found out both times.

The first time, in September 1944, Sutherland threatened to resign or take sick leave over the issue, but MacArthur refused him either option. The second occasion was much more explosive. MacArthur stormed up to Sutherland in a towering rage and shouted that Sutherland had disobeyed his orders. MacArthur relieved Sutherland and placed him under arrest. Everyone figured that he would be shipped home. Even Sutherland wanted to go. But within a day, MacArthur had him back at work, still chief of staff. The Australian woman, however, was decidedly gone.

Sutherland had hoped that MacArthur would give him command of an army, appropriate recognition of his masterful services. But the trouble over the Australian woman killed those chances. MacArthur now took other favored officers with him on trips and left Sutherland behind to mind the store. Sutherland, who had stood nearly as MacArthur's equal, was now just one of many multi-starred officers, preeminent to some but no longer his own man.

Sutherland's standing with MacArthur improved with time, but Sutherland was now disgusted with MacArthur. He had lost credibility with MacArthur's commanders, some of whom were pleased to be able to settle old insults. Sutherland became tired and unenthusiastic. By February 1945, he was performing his duties robotically and without interest. Everyone—the navy, the War Department, and most of the staff—thought he was finished. Only MacArthur believed otherwise. MacArthur needed him and kept him on the job.

By late summer 1945, Sutherland had so deteriorated that MacArthur allowed him to take leave in the States. MacArthur wanted a rested chief of staff for the invasion of Japan. Sutherland had been home less than a week when Japan surrendered. MacArthur called him back. Sutherland arrived just in time to rescue the headquarters from the chaos involved in the surrender and in getting an occupation force to Japan. Once again, Sutherland imposed order in MacArthur's headquarters.

Sutherland stayed with MacArthur for the first three months in Japan. Then he returned to Washington, D.C., and was released from active duty. His war ended in bitterness and broken hopes. Regardless, he had proved indispensable to MacArthur, and his work through the entire Pacific war was remarkably successful. He made no friends, nor did he garner glory, but his service had been professional, honorable, and essential.

FURTHER READINGS

James, D. Clayton. *The Years of MacArthur,* 3 vols. (1970–1985).

Mellnik, Stephen. *Philippine War Diary: 1939–1945* (1981).

Rogers, Paul P. *The Bitter Years: MacArthur and Sutherland* (1991).

———. *The Good Years: MacArthur and Sutherland* (1990).

Willoughby, Charles A., and John Chamberlain. *MacArthur, 1941–1951* (1954).

John W. Whitman

SEE ALSO Army, U.S.-Filipino; MacArthur, Douglas

Taiwan (Formosa)

A large island (some 14,000 square miles, with almost 6 million inhabitants in 1941) located 115 miles off the east coast of China, and given the name Formosa (Portuguese for "beautiful") in 1590 by Portuguese sailors. The capital city is Taipei. Formosa had been ceded to Japan by China in 1895 after the Chinese defeat in the Sino-Japanese War of 1894–1895. The Japanese proceeded to colonize the island and strengthen its military bases. During World War II they began work to produce fuel from the sugar crop on Formosa. Imperial Japan used Formosa as a base to launch attacks against the Chinese mainland and to control the Chinese coast. In December 1941, Formosa was used as a base by Japan's Eleventh Naval Air Fleet and the Fifth Army Air Force to attack U.S. forces in the Philippines.

Recognizing the threat, General Douglas MacArthur and his staff had drawn up plans to attack Japanese bases there with B-17 long range bombers. However, most of the planes were destroyed or damaged on the ground in the first Japanese air attacks on the Philippines December 8.

Many in the U.S. armed forces considered that the capture of Formosa would be necessary for the final invasion of the Japanese home islands. The taking of Formosa would disrupt Japanese communication lines to southern China and the oil fields of Southeast Asia. The China-based 20th Bomber Command carried out aerial attacks on Formosa in 1944, but they were hindered by attenuated logistical lines stretching back to India.

A heated argument on the strategic direction of the American offensive in the Pacific culminated in a meeting in July 1944 at Pearl Harbor between the two chief Pacific leaders, Admiral Chester W. Nimitz and General Douglas MacArthur, President Franklin D. Roosevelt. MacArthur (in charge of the Southwest Pacific offensive) wanted to attack the Philippines, while Nimitz (directing the Central Pacific offensive and supported by Chief of Naval Operations Admiral Ernest J. King) argued for an attack on Formosa and the China coast. Eventually the president chose the Philippine operation. To destroy Japanese air power before the invasion at Leyte by the U.S. Sixth Army, the aircraft carriers of Admiral William F. Halsey's Third Fleet started attacking Formosa's many airfields on October 9, 1944, and were joined by B-29 Superfortresses flying from China. These attacks reduced the amount of Japanese land-based airpower that could participate in the Battle of Leyte Gulf (October 1944), and they were repeated in January 1945 in support of the American invasion of Luzon. The British Pacific Fleet carriers (Task Force 57) attacked Formosa in April 1945 in order to reduce the number of planes conducting kamikaze attacks on Allied task forces operating off Okinawa.

In hindsight, it is probably just as well for the Allies that the heavily defended island was not assaulted; its conquest would have entailed a long and costly campaign that would not have advanced the American forces as much as the bloody Okinawa campaign did. In addition, the American logistical forces were not strong enough to do everything.

In November 1943, in the official communiqué of the Cairo conference, Allied leaders declared that Formosa would be returned to China after the war. Oddly, the Formosans/Taiwanese did not have the bitter hatred for their former Japanese occupiers that was so much a part of Korean nationalism. The formal Formosa surrender ceremony took place on October 25, 1945. Four years later the island became the haven for the Nationalist Chinese government, fleeing from the victorious Communists at the end of the long Chinese civil war. Today, Taiwan is the seat of the Republic of China, but it is considered a renegade province by the People's Republic of China.

FURTHER READINGS

Craven, Wesley Frank, and James Lea Cate, eds. *The Army Air Forces in World War II*: vol. V, *The Pacific: Matterhorn to Nagasaki, June 1944 to August 1945* (1983).

Ka, Chih-ming. *Japanese Colonialism in Taiwan: Land Tenure, Development, and Dependency, 1895–1945* (1995).

Lamley, Harry J. "Taiwan Under Japanese Rule, 1895–1945" in Rubinstein, Murray A., ed. *Taiwan: A New History* (1999).

U.S. Army. Far East Command. *Formosa Area Operations Record (Mar. 1944–Aug. 1945): Operation Arrangement and Record of the 10th Regional Army (Formosa and South Western Islands)* (1946).

Daniel K. Blewett

SEE ALSO Army, Japanese

Tarawa, Capture of

The capture of Tarawa (Operation Galvanic) in the Gilbert Islands by U.S. forces in November 1943 was, in term of percentage of casualties, one of the bloodiest battles in U.S. military history. The first major amphibious landing against a heavily defended coast since Gallipoli during World War I, it also provided valuable lessons for subsequent amphibious operations.

The long battle on Guadalcanal (August 1942 to February 1943) had ended in U.S. victory. As General Douglas MacArthur's forces made leapfrog advances through the Solomons, Admiral Chester Nimitz readied Fifth Fleet for a strike in the Central Pacific. He assembled at Hawaii, the New Hebrides, and the Fijis the largest task force in U.S. Navy history. Commanded by Vice Admiral Raymond A. Spruance, it numbered eight carriers, seven battleships, ten cruisers (seven heavy and three light), and thirty-four destroyers. Nimitz had the 5th Amphibious Force (Admiral Richmond K. Turner) carrying more than one hundred thousand troops, and the V Amphibious Corps, commanded by Marine General Holland McTyeire ("Howlin' Mad") Smith. In addition to carrier-based naval aircraft, Nimitz had the support of Seventh Army Air Force (Major General Willis A. Hale) from the Ellice Islands.

The Gilbert Islands were then Japan's farthest eastern outpost. They consist of about sixteen atolls straddling the equator, just across the international date line. Japanese defense of the Gilberts centered on the two atolls of Tarawa and Makin; about a hundred miles apart, they are ringed with coral reefs. On August 17, 1942, a Marine Raider Battalion had mounted a spectacular raid on Makin from two submarines. A sop to morale at the time, the raid had unfortunate effects in that caused the Japanese immediately to strengthen defenses in the Gilberts. They increased the garrisons there from several hundred to several thousand men. On May 20, 1943, the U.S. submarine *Pollack* deprived the Tarawa garrison of another 1,200 men when it sank the 5,350-ton Japanese transport *Bangkok Maru*.

Makin had already been used as a seaplane base, and the Japanese buildup led to the construction in January 1943 on Betio, Tarawa's biggest island, of a small airfield. From it Japanese aircraft could threaten vital Allied shipping lanes between the United States and Australia. Conversely, U.S. airfields in the Gilberts would ease the capture of Nimitz's next target, the Marshall Islands. For the invasion, 7,000 army troops were allocated to Makin and 18,000 Marines to Tarawa.

Beginning in mid-November 1943, an armada of U.S. Navy warships converged on the islands. From November 13–17, Army Air Forces bombers struck the islands. Navy aircraft also flew more than two thousand sorties. Battleships and cruisers then moved in for heavy shellfire. Reconnaissance flights on November 19 suggested that the bombardment had been successful and that Japanese defenses had been smashed. Unfortunately for the attackers, this was not the case on Tarawa.

On the morning of November 20 the 165th Infantry Regiment of the Army's inexperienced 27th Division, a National Guard unit, went ashore against Butaritari Island of Makin Atoll. The troops had little trouble defeating 250 Japanese army defenders and several hundred workers on the island; the 27th lost only 66 killed and 152 wounded. Most of the prisoners taken were Korean workers. Still, the four days it took the 27th Division to secure the island, despite a crushing superiority in manpower, was too slow for General Smith.

The capture of Makin turned out to be quite costly for the U.S. Navy, however. The delay in taking the atoll forced the Navy task force to stay close to the islands and remain vulnerable to attack from nine Japanese submarines rushed there from Truk. *I-175* sank escort carrier *Liscome Bay*, which went down with 640 men. All Japanese air attacks against the fleet, however, were thwarted by U.S. Navy carrier aircraft.

The capture of Tarawa was quite a different assault from that on Makin. The citadel of the Tarawa defenses was Betio Island, only 2 miles long and several hundred yards across (perhaps three hundred acres in all) but heavily defended. During the naval and air bombardment the Japanese had sought refuge in some four hundred concrete pillboxes, bunkers, and strong points, all covered with coconut logs and thick sand and impervious to anything but direct hits. These fortifications had been constructed after U.S. air attacks in September. Defending artillery also included 8-inch guns brought from Singapore. (The British in their haste to surrender Singapore early in 1942 had obviously neglected to spike their artillery.) The Japanese also had placed submarine mines in the gaps in the coral reefs and had the island ringed with barbed wire.

On the morning of November 20, 1943, marines of the 2d Division began their assault. As they did so most of the 4,700 Japanese troops defending the island and commanded by Rear Admiral Keiji Shibasaki opened a withering fire.

An inadequate U.S. reconnaissance had failed to discover inner coral reefs just below the surface of the water. This meant that marine landing craft could not make it all the way to shore. Although the amphibious tractors (amtraks) carrying the first wave of assaulting troops could cross the reefs and most reached the beach, boats carrying the rest of the force could not; they hung up on the coral reefs and the marines in them were forced to wade through several hundred yards of waist-deep water with their rifles over their heads. These men came under immediate and heavy enemy crossfire. There was virtually no naval gunfire support at the time for fear that the attackers would also be hit.

Those marines reaching the shore had nowhere to go. Betio was ringed with a log seawall about four feet high. Many marines sought protection behind the seawall; those who tried to storm over it were shot down. Some marines did manage to bring small artillery pieces ashore. Colonel David Shoup, commander of the assault force (and a future Marine Corps commandant), set up his command post in a hole at the rear of a bunker with the Japanese still on the other side. With most units both shattered and scattered, the marines fought more as individuals. Of 5,000 marines landed the first day, 1,500 were killed and wounded, a casualty rate of 30 percent.

By nightfall the marines had established two small beachheads ashore. During the night they were able to move ammunition and some tanks and guns ashore. Shoup asked that the reserve be released for help on Betio. He concluded his message with the sobering and, for the U.S. Marines, unprecedented, words, "Issue in doubt." The next day the divisional reserve landed and met the same withering fire, losing 344 men. With no possibility of maneuver in such a small area, the advance ashore was

an inch-by-inch frontal assault. More equipment meant, however, that the marines could fire artillery point-blank at the enemy bunkers and pillboxes. Observers ashore coordinated air and naval gunfire support. Gradually, the marines drove the defenders into the eastern part of the island. That afternoon Shoup sent a message that ended with the words, "We are winning." Most of the Japanese survivors were killed in a suicidal night attack on November 22–23 that was shattered by marine artillery and naval gunfire. By 1:00 P.M., seventy-six hours after it had begun, the battle to take Betio was over. The Japanese lost 4,690 men on Tarawa; the marines took only 17 prisoners, along with 129 Korean laborers. The marines suffered 985 killed and 2,193 wounded. By far the costliest three days of the war to date for the United States, the battle of Tarawa shocked America. Writers referred to it as "tragic Tarawa" or "terrible Tarawa" and compared it to the Crimean War charge of the Light Brigade. There were even demands for a Congressional investigation.

From the capture of Tarawa the Americans learned important lessons for future amphibious assaults. These included the need for better reconnaissance, more effective naval gunfire support (especially plunging fire to destroy fortifications), flamethrowers, demolition charges, and more amphibious tractors. Infantry firepower was also augmented. Within six months the number of Browning Automatic Rifles (BARs) went from one per squad to three; each platoon was given a special assault squad armed with a bazooka, demolition charges, and two flamethrowers. The number of long-range flamethrowers per division also went from 24 to 243 and each division had 24 tank-mounted flamethrowers. The number of medium tanks was also increased. In the months ahead the Marines would fight more costly battles in terms of total casualties, but Tarawa became a symbol of Marine Corps fortitude and gallantry.

FURTHER READINGS
Gregg, Charles T. *Tarawa* (1984).
Johnston, Richard. *Follow Me: The Story of the Second Marine Division in World War II* (1948).
Morison, Samuel Eliot. *The United States Navy in World War II*, vol. 7, *Aleutians, Gilberts, and Marshalls* (1951).
Sherrod, Robert. *Tarawa: The Story of a Battle* (1944).
Stockman, James R. *The Battle for Tarawa*, USMC Historical Section (1947).
Wilson, E. J. et al. *Betio Beachhead* (1945).

Spencer C. Tucker

SEE ALSO Makin Atoll

Terauchi Hisaichi (d. 1946)

As commander-in-chief of the Southern Army, Field Marshal Count Hisaichi Terauchi directed most of the land operations against the British and Americans during the Pacific war.

Born the son of Count Masatake Terauchi, field marshal, former governor-general of Korea, and one-time prime minister, young Terauchi seemed destined for an illustrious military career. As was the case with most of the Japanese army's senior officers, Terauchi spent several years in Europe, first as military attaché to Austria-Hungary (1911–1913), then as a student in Germany (1913–1914). On the outbreak of World War I (1914) he was recalled to Japan where he served in a number of staff positions until being granted his own command—the 5th Division—in August 1930. He went on to serve as commander-in-chief of the Formosa army in 1934.

As a rising senior officer in the interwar period (major-general in 1924, lieutenant-general in 1929, general in 1935), Terauchi became an outspoken advocate of "army purification," which meant that the army should remain aloof from politics and completely loyal to the emperor. He was horrified, for instance, by the so-called 2-26 Insurrection of February 1936, in which extremists in the army attempted a coup d'état against the civil government. This attitude gained him the reputation of a "political innocent," and he was thus asked to serve as war minister in the cabinet of Koki Hirota in 1936. Contrary to Hirota's expectations, however, Terauchi insisted on exercising veto power over all of the prime minister's other cabinet appointments, giving the military virtual control over Hirota's government.

After Terauchi was forced to resign with the fall of the Hirota cabinet in 1937, he received the post of inspector-general of military training, one of the top three offices in the army's hierarchy. When hostilities with China resumed that summer, he took command of the North China Area army but was recalled to Tokyo to serve as military councillor in December 1938. It was during that time that a strong personal rivalry developed between him and another rising star in the army, General Hideki Tojo. Although he respected the count's military abilities, Tojo viewed him as a threat to his political ambitions and sought an opportunity to get him out of Tokyo.

Tojo got his opportunity in the autumn of 1941 when, as prime minister, he appointed Terauchi commander-in-chief of the newly formed Southern Army, headquartered in Saigon, Vietnam, and with responsibility for all imperial army forces in Southeast Asia and the South Pacific. It was in this capacity that Terauchi directed the enormously successful invasions of Burma, the Dutch East Indies, New Guinea, the Philippines, and Malaya; after the fall of Singapore (1942) he moved his headquarters there. The success of these operations rested not so much on his own strategic abilities but rather in his willingness to give free rein to his talented subordinate commanders and staff officers, particularly generals Masaharu Homma and Tomoyuki Yamashita.

In 1942, Imperial General Headquarters ordered Terauchi to oversee construction of a 265-mile railroad connecting the Thai and Burmese rail systems, a line that was intended to carry reinforcements and supplies more quickly to the army in Burma. Although the chosen route passed through some of the most hostile terrain in Southeast Asia, Terauchi managed to complete the project in just eighteen months, thanks to his use of nearly a quarter of a million native laborers plus about sixty thousand Allied prisoners-of-war. The project, however, had a tremendous cost in lives; nearly 20 percent of the POWs, and as many as eighty thousand native laborers died in the construction of the Thai-Burma Railroad.

Terauchi's successes in these endeavors did not go unrecognized. In June 1943 he was promoted to the rank of field marshal. In the following summer, when the *jushin* (senior statesmen) forced Tojo to resign as prime minister, Terauchi was their first choice to succeed him. In a last-ditch effort to prevent his rival from taking power, however, Tojo successfully convinced the *jushin* that removing this popular and effective commander from the field would be detrimental to morale.

In May 1944, Imperial General Headquarters ordered Terauchi to relocate his headquarters to Manila, where he would be closer to the action in the South Pacific. This move, however, proved much too little, and far too late, to reverse the fortunes of war; when American troops landed in the Philippines, Terauchi quickly transferred his headquarters to Dalat, 140 miles northeast of Saigon, where he would remain for the rest of the war. In April 1945 he suffered a cerebral hemorrhage, but since his staff refused to report this fact to Imperial General Headquarters in Tokyo, he was able to retain his command.

Terauchi accepted the emperor's surrender orders in August 1945, but because of his fragile health he was unable to attend the formal surrender ceremonies in Saigon; one of his subordinates, General Seishiro Itagaki, went in his place. At a smaller ceremony on November 30, Terauchi personally surrendered to Lord Louis Mountbatten, the commander of the Allied forces in Southeast Asia. Although many in the Allied leadership wanted to try Terauchi for war crimes because of his role in the forced construction of the infamous Thai-Burma railroad, Mountbatten knew that Terauchi was very ill and could die at any moment. He also feared that the former enemy commander might commit suicide if forced to stand trial. Instead, Mountbatten ordered that Terauchi be moved to Malaya, where he remained under Mountbatten's personal care. The former Japanese field marshal died of a second cerebral hemorrhage in 1946 at the age of 67 and was cremated at the Japanese cemetery at Singapore.

FURTHER READINGS

Allen, Louis. *Burma: The Longest War* (1984).

Fuller, Richard. *Shokan: Hirohito's Samurai* (1992).

Shillony, Ben-Ami. *Politics and Culture in Wartime Japan* (1981).

Spector, Ronald H. *Eagle Against the Sun: The American War with Japan* (1985).

Taya, Haruko, and Theodore F. Cook. *Japan at War: An Oral History* (1992).

John E. Moser

SEE ALSO Army, Japanese; Malaya, Japanese Conquest of; Prisoners of War

Thailand

Thailand is probably most remembered in reference to World War II in the Pacific because the "Death Railway" made famous by the book and movie *Bridge over the River Kwai* was located there. Before the war Thailand had some 15 million people occupying some two hundred thousand square miles, and was the only independent nation in the area, (a constitutional monarchy since December 10, 1932). It (along with Indochina) was a target for Japanese expansion because of its natural resources (tin, rubber, rice) and, especially, its strategic position next to British-controlled Burma and Malaya. Thus the government of Prime Minister Luang Phibun Songkhram (1938–1944) had to be very realistic in its analysis of the dangerous situation, and worked for the best deal it could get. On December 5, 1941, Thailand asked Britain to declare war on Japan just as soon as the Japanese attacked. But the already overcommitted British could promise only very limited assistance, and only after the attack had actually occurred. The U.S. government concurred with the British. The main issue for the Allies was that they had no forces to send to Thailand, thus leaving the Thais with no option but to side with the Japanese. After some limited skirmishes (at Pattani, Songkhla [Singora], Ko Samui, and the mouth of the Chao Phraya River) with the Imperial Japanese Army, the Thais had to agree (December 8) to allow free access to the much stronger Japanese.

On January 20, 1941, the Japanese 33d and 55th Infantry Divisions attacked Burma from staging areas in Thailand.

Under Japanese pressure, the Bangkok government signed a mutual defense pact (December 14, 1941), and actually declared war on the United States and the United Kingdom (January 25, 1942), a move that was unpopular with the people. Great Britain considered this a serious matter, feeling that His Majesty's Government had been pro–Thai in the prewar years, and that Thailand had not resisted enough. M. R. Seni Pramoj, the ambassador to the United States, did not deliver the declaration, so the U.S. government chose to ignore Thailand's action. During and immediately after the war, Thailand was seen by many as actively siding with the Axis, but more recent interpretations have been kinder, recognizing that a weaker state was doing what it could to survive. In compensation for its support, Japan let Thailand take over parts of Burma's Shan states (Kengtung and Mongpan, with 15,000 square miles and more than 256,000 inhabitants), along with the four northernmost Malayan states (Perlis, Kedah, Kelantan, and Trengganu, with almost 15,000 square miles and 1.1 million people). Thailand had long desired to be the most important state in the region, and had even fought a successful border war with French forces in Indochina between October 1940 and January 1941, so these rewards coincided with its expansionist dreams.

Generalissimo Chiang Kai-shek considered that Southeast Asia traditionally fell under China's sphere of influence, but China never had the capability to send forces to operate in Thailand. There were some engagements between Chinese and the Japanese/Thai forces along the Yunan border, but they were minor. Chiang became agitated in late 1943 when the Allied high command considered moving the responsibility for Thailand from the China theater into the new Southeast Asia Command, which was under British Admiral Louis Mountbatten. It was eventually decided to allow both theater commands to operate in the region. The American Office of Strategic Services did train units to operate in Thailand, but infiltrating these agents was difficult. The native organization that was established did not conduct guerrilla warfare, but instead was concerned with administrative and intelligence operations. The country's regent, Prince Luang Pridit Manudharm, was its secret leader. In the United States there existed a Free Thai Movement, led by the Thai ambassador, Seni (who became the postwar prime minister).

The Japanese occupation force (150,000 men at its height) was soon a burden on the country. Rationing and forced labor drafts became common. Several important rail yards and bridges were badly damaged in raids by Allied bombers operating from India and China. Bangkok had the dubious honor of being the first operational target of the long-range Boeing B-29 Superfortresses of the U.S. Army Air Forces' 20th Bomber Command (June 5, 1944), although the government had evacuated to Phetchabun in January 1944. The Thais also resented Tokyo's cultural program that was designed to further incorporate their country into the Greater East Asia Co-Prosperity Sphere. Japanese Premier Tojo Hideki's visit of July 3–4, 1943, did not improve matters. In an atmosphere of possible coups and civil war, Premier Phibun was replaced by Khuang Aphaiwong at the beginning of August 1944. By 1945 the Japanese were retreating across Asia, and British and Indian troops crossed the Thai border with Burma on June 19.

After the war, the United States did not treat Thailand as an enemy country, because there had been no formal recognition by the United States of Thailand's declaration of war. However, other countries were not so lenient. Great Britain demanded that the country send reparations in the form of 1.5 million tons (later adjusted downward) of rice to Malaya (which Thailand took two years to deliver). An official agreement ending the state of war between the two countries was signed on January 1, 1946.

FURTHER READINGS

Aldrich, Richard J. *The Key to the South: Britain, the United States, and Thailand During the Approach of the Pacific War, 1929–1942* (1993).

Haseman, John B. *The Thai Resistance Movement During the Second World War* (1978).

Reynolds, E. Bruce. "Imperial Japan's Cultural Program in Thailand." In Grant K. Goodman, ed., *Japanese Cultural Policies in Southeast Asia During World War II* (1991).

———. *Thailand and Japan's Southern Advance, 1940–1945* (1994).

Daniel K. Blewett

SEE ALSO Mountbatten, Louis

Tinian, Battle for

U.S. conquest of the Mariana islands of Saipan, Guam, and Tinian was the next step after the Marshalls. The United States planned to use these islands as bases for army bombers to strike the Japanese home islands. Saipan was the principal objective of the campaign and the first to be taken. Tinian, only 3.5 miles south of Saipan, was next. Roughly diamond shaped, the island is about 12 miles from north to south and 6 miles across. Not only is it close to Saipan but it is mostly level and thus suitable for airfields. Guam, located about 150 miles southwest of Saipan, was retaken largely as a matter of national pride. It had been U.S. territory from 1898 until 1941, when Japan seized it.

The close proximity of U.S. forces on Saipan eliminated many of the problems that had been present in the invasion of Saipan and speeded the conquest of Tinian. Shore and air bombardments were plentiful and precise, and aerial reconnaissance information was available almost immediately. Supplies were readily transported from Saipan to Tinian.

But Tinian posed special problems. Its shoreline was largely coral ledges and cliffs, and there were few landing beaches. The most desirable of these—in the northwest, which had been used by the Japanese—were less than 600 yards wide, and of that distance, only 200 yards could be used by amphibious tractors or trucks. This raised problems not encountered thus far in the U.S. Pacific amphibious operations, and forced revision of normal shore party and supply procedures. These changes were easily accomplished. Jeter Isely and Philip Crowl noted, "As a study in pure technical skill and amphibious virtuosity, the assault on Tinian excels any other landing in the history of the war."

Plans for the invasion of Tinian began in late April 1944 but were modified in late July as the fighting on Saipan was drawing to a close. U.S. reconnaissance teams surveyed the beach areas on the nights of July 11 and 12, and Tinian came under intense sea-, air-, and land-based artillery attack from July 11 onward. Three battleships, six cruisers (three heavy and three light), sixteen destroyers, and thirty gunboats bombarded the island while some 244 navy and army planes strafed and bombed it. From Saipan 156 artillery pieces added supporting fire.

Some nine thousand Japanese defended Tinian. Colonel Keishi Ogata commanded the defenses, and Vice Admiral Kakuji Kakuta had charge of the naval forces. The two men had a number of disagreements, and Kakuda tried to leave the island by submarine. When that proved impossible, he simply disappeared and the naval command went to Captain Goichi Oya.

Fortunately for the Americans, Colonel Ogata assumed the Americans would attack Tinian Town harbor, which had the island's best beaches, and he positioned most of his defenses there. Ogata thought it extremely unlikely that the Americans would attempt to land on the small northwestern beaches, and as a result he left these lightly defended. Admiral Richmond Kelly Turner had in fact wanted the landing at Tinian Town harbor, but was overruled by Marine Lieutenant General Holland Smith, who pointed out revelations from aerial reconnaissance of Ogata's defensive dispositions.

On the morning of July 24 the Marines stormed ashore. The 4th Marine Division, commanded by Major General Clifton B. Cates, bore the brunt of the beach assault. The 2d Marine Division (under Major General Thomas E. "Terrible Tommy" Watson) carried out a feint against Tinian Town and then landed on the same beaches used by the 4th Marine Division. The 27th Infantry Division (under Major General George W. Griner), minus the 105th Infantry Regiment, made up the corps reserve.

While U.S. Navy vessels lay off Tinian Town on the morning of the assault, they were subjected to an intense enemy bombardment. Before these Japanese guns were silenced, they killed or wounded 241 Americans, 42 of them marines.

Fighting on Tinian lasted until August 2. The initial assault achieved tactical surprise, and by the end of the first day of fighting, the marines had secured a beachhead approximately four thousand yards wide and fifteen hundred yards deep, at the incredibly low cost of 15 killed and 225 wounded, only about one-eighth the number of casualties in the first day of the Saipan invasion. At 2 A.M. the next day the Japanese counterattacked in force with tanks. This attack, which was repulsed, cost the Japanese 1,200 dead and five tanks destroyed.

The remainder of the operation saw steady advances by the marines against a now demoralized enemy. Most of the 2d Marine Division came ashore on July 25. Heavier opposition developed as the marines pressed in on Tinian Town and the enemy's final defenses. July 31 and August 1 saw the heaviest fighting since the initial landing, as the marines beat back several banzai charges. On the evening of August 1, Major General Harry Schmidt, commander of V Amphibious Corps, pronounced Tinian secure, although mopping up continued against remaining pockets of enemy soldiers.

U.S. casualties in the conquest of Tinian were relatively light: 389 dead and 1,816 wounded. Only 25 Japanese were captured of the 9,000 that had manned the island. Some nine thousand civilians also were rounded up.

Tinian was an important victory for the United States. Soon B-29 long-range bombers would use it as a base from which to assault Japan.

FURTHER READINGS

Hoffman, Carl W. *The Seizure of Tinian* (USMC Historical Branch, 1951).

Isely, Jeter A., and Philip A. Crowl. *The U.S. Marines and Amphibious War* (1951).

Smith, S. E., ed. *The United States Marine Corps in World War II* (1969).

Wheeler, Richard. *A Special Valor: The U.S. Marines and the Pacific War* (1996).

Spencer C. Tucker

SEE ALSO Island-Hopping and Leapfrogging, U.S. Strategies; Saipan, Battle of

Tokyo Fire Raid

The fire-bomb raid on Tokyo on March 9–10, 1945, was the single most destructive bombing raid in history.

U.S. Army Air Force B-29 bombers had operated from India and China but with the capture of Saipan, Guam, and Tinian, in the Summer of 1944, the U.S. government placed great hopes on B-29 bombing raids from the Marianas against the home islands of Japan, targeting especially the aircraft industry in and around Tokyo.

The first B-29 Superfortress to land in the Marianas arrived on Saipan on October 12, 1944, piloted by Brigadier General Heywood S. Hansell, Jr., commander of 21st Bomber Command. On October 28, Hansell led twenty B-29s in the first mission from the island; only eighteen took off and four, including Hansell's plane, were forced to turn back; the remainder bombed the island of Truk.

Hansell's B-29s began the battle for Tokyo on November 25, 1944, when they carried out the first U.S. attack on the Japanese capital since the U.S. Doolittle raid of April 1942. A total of 110 Superfortresses were sent against the Nakajima aircraft engine manufacturing plant in the Tokyo suburbs. Seventeen B-29s aborted because of mechanical troubles and six more were unable to drop their bombs. Only twenty-four of the remaining planes bombed the primary target. Two were lost (one rammed by a Japanese fighter) and eleven others were damaged (eight from fighter attacks and three from friendly fire). It was hardly an auspicious beginning.

The B-29 was a superb aircraft, but to carry three tons of bombs 1,200 miles to Tokyo and back (sixteen hours in the air), consumed twenty-three *tons* of gasoline. Plans called for precision bombing (hardly possible from 30,000 feet) but high-altitude jet streams (sometimes above 200 miles per hour) caused the bomb crews more problems than did the defending Japanese aircraft. Crosswinds could cause the bombers to drift off target; flying downwind the B-29s could be over the target at speeds in excess of 500 miles per hour, too fast for precision bombing; and upwinds could reduce ground speed to 125 mph, which made the bombers vulnerable to anti-aircraft fire.

The B-29s also had major engine problems. They often blew cylinder heads on starting and were plagued with poor ignition, leaking oil, and troublesome fuel transfer systems. The engines also had a short life at high altitudes. Gun sighting blisters occasionally blew out at high altitudes of frosted so that it was impossible to see through them. Although such problems were common in a new aircraft, the U.S. government was unsympathetic and wanted the raids to go on. B-29s were also harassed on the ground and in the air by Japanese fighters from Iwo Jima, 700 miles north and on the route to and from Tokyo.

Although the early B-29 raids had an impact on Japan (the frequent air raids affected worker morale and forced the Japanese to disperse industrial activity), the loss rate was running at an unacceptable 6 percent per mission, and USAAF Chief of Staff, General Henry H. "Hap" Arnold, was not pleased with the results. Hansell, a proponent of high-altitude bombing, was himself displeased with bombing accuracy and the too-frequent aborts, ditchings, and indications of poor maintenance; but Arnold ran out of patience and decided to replace Hansell with 39-year-old Major General Curtis LeMay, who had commanded the B-29s of the 20th Bomber Command in India and China. Ironically, on January 18, 1945, the day before LeMay arrived on Guam, Hansell's B-29s had their most successful mission. A total of seventy-seven planes attacked the Kawasaki Aircraft Industries at Akashi, cutting its production by 90 percent.

Controversial throughout his air force career, LeMay was a determined professional and a consummate tactician. Tough, practical, and laconic, his men referred to him as "Iron Ass." Although he immediately instituted a training program, LeMay continued for several weeks to send out the bombers on raids similar to those planned by Hansell. They achieved the same mixed results.

It was a raid on Tokyo on February 25, 1945, that led LeMay to develop new tactics. The U.S. government had ordered a "maximum effort," and LeMay sent up 231 bombers. Each carried one 500-pound general purpose bomb; the rest were incendiaries. Weather again played a role, but 172 of the bombers dropped their loads over Tokyo. Subsequent reconnaissance photography revealed that a square mile of the Japanese capital had been burned out, with 27,970 buildings destroyed.

Japanese industry was widely dispersed (almost two-thirds of production was from small factories of thirty or fewer persons or in homes, which were clustered around the factories) but within five major cities. LeMay decided to send the B-29s in low at night, stripped of their defensive armament save the tail gun. As most Japanese structures were of wood, LeMay proposed to use M-47 and M-69 fire bombs rather than demolition bombs.

Inside its chemical bomb casing the M-47 had a jelly-like mixture of rubber, lye, and coconut oil, all blended with gasoline. The bomb was four feet long and eight inches in diameter. Weighing about one hundred pounds, it was capable of penetrating reinforced structures. After the bomb struck, a delayed bursting charge exploded the casing and spread its contents. A second bomb, ultimately designated the M-69, weighed only 6.2 pounds and looked like an elongated tin can three inches in diameter and twenty inches long. M-69s were held in clusters in the bomb bay but broke free on being dropped, after which a 3-foot cloth streamer stabilized its fall. After the bomb passed through the roof of a house or factory, a delayed fuse exploded magnesium particles, which ignited a gasoline gel that shot out of the rear of the can as far as one hundred feet, starting an intense fire. Although not capable of penetrating reinforced structures, the M-69 worked well against the lightly constructed wooden structures of Tokyo.

LeMay ordered the planes to bomb from altitudes between five thousand and eight thousand feet. Removing machine guns, ammunition, and gunners more than doubled the bomb load. LeMay's orders astonished the crews, however; they believed they would be slaughtered (some people warned LeMay to expect 70 percent losses). As LeMay knew, however, the Japanese did not have radar or flak defenses comparable to those over Berlin. They would have to locate the fast-flying B-29s with searchlights.

On the evening of March 9 a total of 334 B-29s carrying nearly two thousand tons of bombs (average bombload, 6.6 tons) took off from airfields on Guam, Saipan, and Tinian to bomb four designated aiming points in Tokyo about four thousand to six thousand feet apart. Planners estimated that half the bombs would fall within a two thousand-foot radius of the aiming points.

During the long flight to Tokyo astonished crews heard Radio Tokyo play such songs as "Smoke Gets in Your Eyes," "My Old Flame," and "I Don't Want to Set the World on Fire." Although there were some aborts, 325 B-29s reached their target.

Shortly after midnight on March 10, the first pathfinder aircraft dropped their loads of M-47s. Over the next three hours the remaining B-29s dropped 1,667 tons of M-69s. Each bomber carried forty clusters, set to release its individual bombs at 2,000 feet.

Forty Japanese fighters closed to engage but inflicted no damage. Forty-two B-29s were hit by moderate anti-aircraft fire, which was blamed for the loss of fourteen of the bombers (a loss rate of 4.5 percent). Nine crews were lost; the other five were saved by air-sea rescue.

Vast firestorms exceeding 1,800 degrees Fahrenheit (subsequently given by the Japanese the poetic name of "the flowers of Edo") soon raged throughout the capital. Later B-29 crews reported tremendous heat turbulence. One B-29 was actually flipped on its back in an updraft and fell thousands of feet before the crew managed to regain control.

In these circumstances fire-fighting equipment on the ground was totally useless. Some was consumed by flames or melted, and 125 firemen died fighting the firestorms. It was not until about 8 A.M. that the fires burned out on their own. Over fifteen square miles of Tokyo had been devastated. Official Japanese figures list 83,793 dead and 40,918 injured but the actual total was probably much higher (Radio Tokyo called it a "slaughter bombing"). The intense heat caused some people to be consumed by spontaneous combustion, but more than half the fatalities were from suffocation as the atmosphere was drained of oxygen by the flames. Many people drowned or were trampled in the rush to the Sumida River and canals. The destruction of 267,171 buildings left a million people homeless. Most important for the war effort, 18 percent of Tokyo's industry was gone.

The fire bombing of Tokyo was subsequently repeated over other Japanese cities. On March 11, Nagoya, Japan's third largest city, was hit by 313 B-29s and more incendiaries than those dropped on Tokyo two nights earlier. Then came the turns of Kobe, Osaka, Yokohama, and dozens of smaller cities. In all, B-29s fire-bombed some sixty Japanese cities, destroyed 3.1 million homes, killed a million people, and made 14 million more homeless.

Subsequent B-29 losses dropped to only 1.4 percent. This was because the Japanese lacked an efficient night fighter, and the capture of Iwo Jima allowed the island to be used as an emergency landing field/fighter base for U.S. bombers on their way to and from the Marianas. At the end of March 1945 long-range P-47 Thunderbolts and P-51 Mustangs began to operate out of Iwo Jima as escorts for the B-29s, which now mixed medium-altitude daylight bombing with low-level night bombing.

The fire bombing of Tokyo and other Japanese cities did not by itself bring the Japanese surrender that LeMay had sought (he protested the decision to divert some B-29s to mine laying operations, even though these sank a half million tons of Japanese shipping), but the B-29s destroyed Japan's war-making capacity, had a devastating effect on Japanese morale, and weighed heavily in the leadership's decision to sue for peace. After the Tokyo raid of March 10, there could be little doubt that Japan had lost the war.

FURTHER READINGS
Coffey, Thomas M. *Iron Eagle: The Turbulent Life of General Curtis LeMay* (1986).
Jablonski, Edward. *Airwar,* vol. IV, *Wings of Fire* (1971).
Kerr, E. Bartlett. *Flames over Tokyo: The U.S. Army Air Forces' Incendiary Campaign Against Japan, 1944–1945* (1991).

Spender C. Tucker

SEE ALSO Air Offensive, Japan; Army Air Corps/Air Forces, U.S.; LeMay, Curtis

Tokyo Rose

Tokyo Rose was the pseudonym American GIs gave to more than one female Japanese propaganda broadcaster in the Pacific. After the war, Iva Ikuko Toguri D'Aquino, a California Nisei (American born, of Japanese descent), was the primary person identified as Tokyo Rose. Broadcasting in English, such broadcasters tried to discourage and demoralize Allied troops. The legendary Tokyo Rose has symbolized treason ever since World War II. Tokyo Rose, was in reality a mythical figure, but the prosecution of D'Aquino revealed prejudices and lasting wartime intolerance.

In 1943, Radio Tokyo began broadcasting a nightly shortwave program known as the "Zero Hour" to American soldiers throughout the Pacific. Every night at 7:00, broadcasters played music and read scripted propaganda designed to dissuade troops from fighting or simply to lower their morale. These "vocal pinup girls," approximately forty English-speaking women throughout Japanese-occupied cities in the Pacific, attempted to ridicule GIs but, in fact, mostly relieved the troops' tensions.

Entertained and amused by the propaganda, American soldiers did not consider the programs to be sinister, nor did they allow the propaganda to effect the Pacific war effort. As noted, GIs called all of the broadcasters by one name, Tokyo Rose, because the women's voices sounded similar. The moniker, "Tokyo Rose," was actually American invention; none of the announcers introduced herself by that name. Many soldiers looked forward to the evening programs, featuring the most up-to-date American music, conversation, and humorous descriptions of life in America and the Pacific. Troops even openly expressed admiration and support for Tokyo Rose, explaining that her harmless broadcasts healed homesickness and eased boredom. When announcers apologized for repeatedly playing the same records, stating that they were the only ones the station owned, General Robert Eichelberger, Commander of the Eighth U.S. Army, arranged to have a box of records air-dropped to Tokyo Rose during a bombing raid. So convinced were U.S. Navy authorities of the harmlessness of Tokyo Rose that her broadcasts were piped through the public-address systems of ships.

Some Tokyo Rose broadcasts could be unnerving, however. The pilot of the aircraft that dropped the second atomic bomb on Japan recalled how a Tokyo Rose had "welcomed" his top-secret unit to Tinian island, even referring specifically to that unit's distinctive arrowhead-within-a-circle tail emblem.

Iva Toguri, an American citizen, had arrived in Japan shortly before Pearl Harbor (1941) to nurse an ill aunt. A zoology graduate of the University of California at Los Angeles, Toguri was stranded in Japan after war erupted between Japan and the United States on December 7, 1941. Refusing to surrender her American citizenship, she became an outcast; constantly under surveillance by the *Kempei Tai,* the Japanese secret military police, Toguri was monitored and harassed for retaining American dress and customs. Suffering culture shock and speaking minimal Japanese, she quickly exhausted her finances and even went hungry. Lacking money to return home, Toguri applied for a position as an English typist at Radio Tokyo.

Hired for her English-speaking ability, Toguri was promoted to broadcaster; she read scripts penned by prisoners of war who worked for the station. These men primarily wrote entertaining programs, although Australian Major Charles Cousens incorporated anti-Japanese statements whenever possible. Toguri befriended him, and she smuggled food, pharmaceuticals, and blankets to needy allied prisoners. Considering her frequent broadcasts a benign means to support herself, she identified herself as "Orphan Ann," "Orphan Annie," "Your Favorite Enemy Ann," and "Your Favorite Playmate." Introducing records ranging "from Bach to jive," she abstained from taunting troops about their families at home and issuing demoralizing statements about sunken ship and battle losses. She was aware that her parents had been placed in internment camps, where her mother died, but she steadfastly supported the American cause. Toguri married Filipe D'Aquino in Japan in April 1945.

Four months later, after Japan's surrender, the War Crimes Branch of the South West Pacific Theater sought to identify and apprehend Tokyo Rose. At the same time, American reporters desperately competed to print the first interview with this legendary figure. Tokyo Rose was one of the most sought-after occupation interviews. She rivaled Emperor Hirohito, General Hideko Tojo, and General Douglas MacArthur for reporters' attention. Authorities experienced difficulty in pinpointing which broadcaster was the real Tokyo Rose because captured Japanese radio personnel were unfamiliar with a name that had been circulated only by GIs.

U.S. Military Police eventually located D'Aquino, who admitted that she had broadcast for Radio Tokyo. Clark Lee, a reporter for *Cosmopolitan* magazine and an employee of the wealthy publisher William Randolph Hearst, and colleague Harry Brundidge offered D'Aquino $2,000 for an exclusive interview as *the* Tokyo Rose. She was tempted by the money Lee offered her and naively thought she would be revered and celebrated by Americans because she had patriotically boosted morale and helped prisoners. Suffering the privations of postwar Japan, D'Aquino negotiated with Lee and agreed to adopt the name Tokyo Rose. Ironically, she was never paid, and this interview created evidence later used against her.

Meanwhile, military authorities were trying to determine which broadcaster had Tokyo Rose's distinctive "girlish" voice. Tokyo Rose, however, was a composite of several women, and D'Aquino was designated "Tokyo Rose No. 5" by authorities. Broadcasters Ruth Hayakawa and June Suyama were also scrutinized. Several of D'Aquino's radio colleagues who disliked her and wanted to shift the blame from themselves told officials that D'Aquino had issued inflammatory anti-American propaganda. In October 1945 she was arrested, incarcerated in Sugamo Prison, and interrogated. During her year-long imprisonment, D'Aquino suffered dysentery and the discomforts of prison life while the legal section tried to document treason charges against her. She was released when neither military officers nor Justice Department attorneys could substantiate their claims.

D'Aquino, however, was not cleared by the American public. The Los Angeles City Council passed a resolution opposing her return to her home town. Radio commentator Walter Winchell pressured American authorities to reexamine D'Aquino's war activities and punish her for what he defined as treasonous war crimes; in a self-serving, sensationalized campaign, he labeled her a "seductive siren," spewing "venomous" propaganda. Winchell served as a catalyst to fuel mass media hysteria that prevented D'Aquino leaving Tokyo for her American home.

Needing a public scapegoat, American officials pursued their vendetta against D'Aquino. Politicians, wooing voters, used "Tokyo Rose" as a means to reinforce their images of "toughness" toward traitors. Federal Bureau of Investigations Director J. Edgar Hoover, worried that Winchell would portray him as being sympathetic to suspected spies, feared professional repercussions if he did not pursue prosecution of D'Aquino. Fueled by unrelenting media pressure, Hoover ordered D'Aquino to be forcibly taken to the United States. Her trial on charges of treason began in San Francisco in July 1949.

D'Aquino was declared guilty after a trial that included perjured testimony and rigged evidence. Hoover and the FBI cooperated with legal authorities to achieve the desired court verdict. D'Aquino protested that she had never broadcast propaganda and would only admit the obvious: that she had been in Tokyo during the war. Convicted on only one of eight charges (broadcasting the loss of an allied ship), D'Aquino was fined $10,000 and sentenced to a ten-year prison term.

The only Radio Tokyo broadcaster tried and convicted for war crimes, D'Aquino appealed her sentence from a West Virginia women's reformatory. Released in 1956, she was stripped of her citizenship and threatened with deportation. D'Aquino moved to Chicago, where she found work in a family business. She continued to contest her conviction and was assisted by civil rights groups and U.S. Senator S. I. Hayakawa of California.

Finally, in March 1976, President Gerald Ford granted her a full and unconditional presidential pardon, restoring her citizenship. D'Aquino's life, however, had been irreparably altered by the false treason charges. Her husband had been forced to sign an agreement never to enter the United States, and they never saw each other after her trial. The Japanese-American community shunned her, accusing her of damaging the reputation of Nisei soldiers who had fought for the United States. A tragic war victim herself, D'Aquino was a naive person caught up in most of the circumstances of war.

FURTHER READINGS
Duus, M. *Tokyo Rose: Orphan of the Pacific* (1979).
Howe, R. *The Hunt for "Tokyo Rose"* (1990).
Sandler, S. *Cease Resistance—It's Good for You: A History of U.S. Army Combat Psychological Operations* (1999).
Elizabeth D. Schafer

SEE ALSO Psychological Warfare, Japanese

Tongan Army Self Defense Forces

The British colony of Tonga's Self-Defense Forces, numbering a mere two thousand men, was one of the smallest armies to participate in the Pacific campaign. The Tongan Self-Defense Forces were formed initially to defend the small island kingdom against Japan's seemingly irresistible offensive in the Southwest Pacific. By the time its two combat battalions were ready, however, the Japanese offensive had been blunted and the momentum shifted to the Allies. As a result, the forces joined the British Commonwealth units that participated in the Bougainville campaign in 1943. Tongan units fought well in that campaign, demonstrating good fieldcraft and combat cohesion. The army was disbanded after the war and briefly raised again to join Commonwealth forces in Korea in the early 1950s. The Tongan Self-Defense Forces benefitted from the early decision to concentrate on training good noncommissioned and junior officers. That tradition continues today in the two battalions Tonga has raised for United Nations peacekeeping missions, one of which they successfully concluded in Bougainville in 1992.

FURTHER READINGS
Gailey, Harry A., *Bougainville, 1943–1945* (1991).
Morrison, Samuel E., *History of United States Naval Operations in World War II,* vols. 5 and 6 (1959, 1960).
Carl O. Schuster

SEE ALSO Bougainville, U.S. Operations against

Torpedo, Long Lance (Japanese)

The Japanese *Shiki Sanso Gyorai* Type 93 torpedo, known as the "Long Lance" for its more than 40,000-yard range, was one of the most effective torpedoes in history. Developed in 1933 and built through 1945 at the naval arsenal at Kure, the Long Lance was the apex of Japanese naval technology; at the beginning of World War II it was superior to those of any other nation. The surface warfare version was twenty-four inches in diameter, 29 feet, four inches in length, and weighed 6,107 pounds. Powered by liquid oxygen, the Long Lance had a range of 24,000 yards (almost fourteen miles) at 48 knots; at 36 knots its range was a phenomenal 43,744 yards (nearly twenty-five miles). Its warhead weighed 1,100 lbs. By way of contrast, the American 21-inch torpedo had a 780-pound warhead and range of 16,000 yards.

The Long Lance was an improvement on a British design discarded in the 1920s because of technical problems (twists in the oxygen lines resulted in premature explosions). The Japanese solved the problem by reducing turns in the oxygen lines and by keeping them perfectly clean. The imperial navy, unlike the U.S. Navy, also fired torpedoes freely in practice and on maneuvers, thereby constantly improving them.

In 1934, the Japanese developed a smaller 21-inch version of the Long Lance for naval aircraft. Known as the

Type 94, it weighed 3,245 pounds. It had a maximum speed of 41 knots and range of 4,900 yards. On December 7, 1941, Japan attacked the U.S. naval base at Pearl Harbor, Hawaii. In that attack, Nakajima B5N (Kate) torpedo bombers carried the earlier (c. 1931) Type 91 torpedo; considerably lighter than the 21-inch Long Lance, it weighed only 1,764 lbs.

In 1935, a submarine version of Long Lance appeared. Also twenty-one inches in diameter, it was fueled by an enriched oxygen propellant. It had a speed of 50 knots, maximum range of 13,000 yards, and a warhead of 900 pounds. An improved 21-inch submarine model had a maximum range of 8,200 yards and warhead of 1,210 pounds.

American torpedoes in World War II were initially turbine powered and left a wake. The Long Lance, which did not leave a wake, also had a reliable firing system. Not so for the U.S. torpedoes. Early in the war one U.S. submarine fired fifteen torpedoes at a Japanese tanker off Truk; all hit and all were duds. U.S. submariners also discovered that their Mark XIV torpedo ran eleven feet deeper than set (testing had not taken into account warhead weight, an oversight that took six months to correct).

The Long Lance figured prominently in Japanese naval planning. Designed to be carried by destroyers and cruisers, it was to be a key element in the Japanese naval strategy to weaken the American battle line prior to the climactic fleet battle that each side anticipated would be fought in the western Pacific. While the U.S. Navy planned for a daylight clash fought primarily by long-range naval gunfire (torpedoes were in fact removed from U.S. cruiser armament), the Japanese hoped to savage the American battle fleet through close attacks at night that made considerable use of torpedoes. In order to conserve expenditure of these important weapons, Tokyo imposed strict guidelines governing targets against which they might be launched and the number that could be fired.

The Long Lance played a key role in the Solomons battles in 1942 and 1943: Savo Island (August 9, 1942), Tassafaronga (November 30, 1942), Kula Gulf (July 5–6, 1943), and Kolombangara (July 12–13, 1943). U.S. historian Samuel Eliot Morison has noted that the U.S. Navy was deficient in only two techniques in comparison to the Japanese: in long-range search and in torpedo attack. The Americans did not deploy a reliable torpedo until late 1943. Such a deficiency was inexcusable and cost the lives of many U.S. servicemen.

FURTHER READINGS

Blair, Clay, Jr. *Silent Victory: The U.S. Submarine War Against Japan* (1975).

Gray, Edwyn. *The Devil's Device: Robert Whitehead and the History of the Torpedo,* rev. ed. (1991).

Morison, Samuel Eliot. *History of United States Naval Operations in World War II,* vols. 3, 5, and 6 (1989).
Spender C. Tucker

SEE ALSO Navy, Japanese; Navy, U.S.

Tripartite Pact of 1940

Signed on September 27, 1940, the Tripartite Pact was the written agreement that cemented the Axis alliance of Germany, Italy, and Japan. Under its provisions, Germany was to have a free hand in setting up a new order in Europe, while Japan would be free to establish its Greater East Asia Co-Prosperity Sphere. Each of the three signatories pledged political, economic, and military assistance if any of the others were attacked by any power not yet involved in the European war or in the war between China and Japan.

The origins of the Tripartite Pact lay in the Anti-Comintern Pact, a largely symbolic agreement concluded between Germany and Japan in November 1936. Both sides made moves during 1938 and 1939 to strengthen the Anti-Comintern Pact into something resembling a formal alliance, but the Germans and Japanese differed greatly in what they expected from such an arrangement. Hitler sought an alliance directed primarily at Great Britain and the United States, while the Japanese leadership wanted an anti-Soviet agreement. In any event, all discussion of an alliance between Germany and Japan came to an abrupt halt in August 1939, when Hitler concluded his nonaggression pact with the Soviet Union. The Japanese government thereafter treated the Anti-Comintern Pact as a dead issue.

By the summer of 1940, however, the situation had changed dramatically. The rapid German conquests of Poland, Denmark, Norway, the Low Countries, and France suddenly rekindled Japanese interest in an agreement. The leadership in Tokyo believed that Hitler was on the verge of winning the war, and they very much wanted to associate themselves with the winning side. There was also a growing fear amongst Japanese leaders that the German government, having conquered the Netherlands and France, would try to gain control over French Indochina and the Dutch East Indies—colonies that the Japanese wanted for themselves. Therefore, in July the army, navy, and foreign ministry decided to seek some sort of accommodation with Hitler whereby Japan would put pressure on the British in the Far East in return to a free hand in Southeast Asia.

Soon after this decision had been reached, however, the army engineered the fall of the cabinet of Yonai Mitsumasa, who was believed to be too friendly to the United States and Great Britain. His successor, Prince Fumimaro Konoe, appointed the ardently pro-German Yosuke Matsuoka as foreign minister. Matsuoka refused to settle for the limited agreement envisioned by the military, and immediately made known his willingness to conclude a formal alliance that included plans for joint action against Great Britain and, if necessary, the United States. The German government sent an envoy, Heinrich Stahmer, to Tokyo to negotiate the pact at the beginning of September, and the final draft was signed in Berlin before the end of the month.

Both Hitler and Matsuoka had high expectations for the Tripartite Pact, expectations that were in some ways contradictory. Hitler hoped that it would divert the attention of the United States away from the war in Europe and thus slow the pace of American aid to Great Britain. Matsuoka and the rest of the cabinet, on the other hand, believed that it would turn U.S. attention away from the war in Asia, thereby leading to a reduction in American assistance to China. The Japanese saw other benefits in an alliance with Germany as well. It would secure German support for the creation of the Japanese Greater East Asia Co-Prosperity Sphere and might intimidate the United States into looking the other way. It could also lead to a settlement of the China war on terms favorable to Japan. Finally, the Japanese hoped that an alliance with Germany might restrain the Soviet Union in East Asia and encourage Stalin to look toward the Middle East.

Nevertheless, there were some in the cabinet who had grave reservations about the pact. Most Japanese leaders had little love or trust for Nazi Germany, and the navy in particular was apprehensive about any agreement that might oblige Japan to go to war with the United States. In the end, however, they were swayed by the simple fact that Japan's diplomatic isolation could not continue. Ever since 1921—when Great Britain terminated the Anglo-Japanese Alliance of 1902—Japan had remained friendless in the international arena, and in late 1940 Germany was the only nation extending a hand in friendship. It was an opportunity, the cabinet realized, that could simply not be passed up.

The conclusion of the Tripartite Pact had an immediate impact on Japan's relations with the United States. Despite Konoe's demands that the pact be accompanied by new efforts to improve relations with the United States, the Roosevelt administration interpreted it as a decidedly unfriendly gesture and retaliated by placing an embargo on scrap metal to Japan. Japanese negotiators tried to assure their American counterparts that the pact was strictly defensive; Konoe frequently denied that the pact obliged Japan to declare war on the United States even if the United States attacked Germany. Yet for the Roosevelt administration the Tripartite Pact was proof of a global fascist conspiracy, and only by repudiating the pact altogether could Japan prove its good faith.

After Pearl Harbor and the German declaration of war on the United States in December 1941, the Tripartite Pact ceased to function in any effective way, leading one historian to call it a "hollow alliance." There was little willingness on the part of the German or Japanese governments to engage in any joint strategic planning, and there was not even any real discussion of postwar plans. Hitler repeatedly called upon the Japanese to pay closer attention to India and the war on Allied shipping in the Indian Ocean in 1942 and 1943, but the Japanese were far more interested in fighting the Americans in the Central and South Pacific. Conversely, the Japanese government urged Berlin to seek some sort of compromise peace with the Soviet Union, which Hitler steadfastly refused to consider. In the final analysis, both Germany and Japan viewed the Tripartite Pact as a diplomatic tool and not a military alliance of the sort that existed between the United States, Great Britain, and the Soviet Union. It was an agreement designed, above all, to keep the United States out of the war; therefore, the events of December 1941 rendered the Tripartite Pact all but irrelevant.

Though the Japanese cabinet had understandable reasons for entering into the Tripartite Pact, in retrospect the alliance was one of the greatest diplomatic blunders of the twentieth century. Of all the grand expectations that the Japanese leadership had for it, only one—improved relations with the Soviet Union—was ever realized, and even this achievement was fleeting in nature. It had no measurable effects on the China war, and it completely backfired in keeping the United States uninvolved. The Tripartite Pact did not intimidate Washington; it only strengthened in the public mind the association between Japan and Nazi Germany, and it encouraged Americans to view the war in Europe and Asia in terms of a single global conflict against fascism.

FURTHER READINGS

Butow, R. *Tojo and the Coming of the War* (1961).
Ike, N., ed. *Japan's Decision for War: Records of the 1941 Policy Conferences* (1961).
Meskill, J. *Hitler and Japan: The Hollow Alliance* (1966).
Schroeder, P. *The Axis Alliance and Japanese-American Relations* (1958).

Weinberg, G. "Global Conflict: The Interaction between the European and Pacific Theaters of War in World War II," in G. Weinberg, ed., *Germany, Hitler, and World War II: Essays in Modern German and World History* (1995).

Truk is one of the major atolls in the Caroline Islands of Micronesia, a collection of islands whose strategic location dominates the western Pacific between Hawaii and the Philippines. Truk was best known just before and during the Pacific war as the strongly fortified main anchorage of the Japanese position in Micronesia until 1944, when events began to reveal that the strength of the position was largely a myth.

Truk is located 1,200 miles west of the Marshall Islands and consists of fourteen high volcanic islands that surround a huge lagoon, the anchorage that has given the atoll its naval significance. Most of the islands are less than one square mile in area and have surrounding reefs, sandy beaches, swampy areas, and high volcanic uplands. Temperature is on average about 80 degrees Fahrenheit the year round, with rain attaining at least forty to fifty inches accumulation annually.

The Trukese are a fairly homogenous culture, largely descended from groups of southeast Asian migrants whom anthropologists call "Austronesians." With a population of about fourteen thousand in the mid-1940s, the Trukese had contact with Europeans since the 1560s but not significantly until European whalers and missionaries came on the scene in the early 1800s. Spanish sovereignty was claimed over the islands in the 1880s and German occupation actually took place in the 1890s, followed by intensive economic exploitation of copra, fish, and lumber.

Japanese conquest and administration after 1914 brought even more intensive exploitation of fishing resources, as well as Japanese and Okinawan immigrants to supervise and partake in that exploitation. During the Japanese navy's occupation of Micronesia (1914–1922), Truk served as the headquarters for the naval administration, while during the civilian League of Nations mandate, the atoll became the administrative center for the Caroline's section of *Nan'yo,* or the Japanese "South Seas" colony.

Truk took on a mysterious air in the 1920s and 1930s, as did most of Japanese Micronesia. Increasing tensions between Japan and the other Pacific imperial powers (the United States, Great Britain, France, the Netherlands, Australia, and New Zealand) over the future of the Pacific and East Asia caused each side to grow increasingly suspicious of the other's military intentions. Although the major naval powers in the region—the United States, Great Britain, and Japan—had signed naval limitations treaties and nonfortification agreements for the western Pacific in 1922, the Washington treaty system did not bring an end to intelligence operations by the Japanese and the Americans against each other. Nor did the treaty system alleviate suspicions each side had of the other about violations of the agreements and designs for dominating the region.

Accordingly, these two most powerful naval nations in the western Pacific began to suspect that each was fortifying their island possessions in the regions. Actually, neither nation violated the nonfortification clauses of the Washington Treaty during the 1920s or even the early 1930s, at least until after the Japanese withdrew from the League of Nations in 1933 because of its Manchurian–North China policies. Recent investigation of Japanese naval documents has demonstrated, in fact, that Truk was not fortified at all before 1934 and was not heavily fortified until after 1940. Japanese documents even indicate that the navy and army were still rushing to develop Truk and other major islands in Micronesia into viable defense posts when the United States began bombing Micronesia in 1943. Nevertheless, U.S. naval intelligence believed until 1944 that Truk was not only the major anchorage of the Combined Fleet but that it was defended by 100,000 troops.

In fact, the Japanese had only about 40,000 military personnel on Truk at the height of its strength, and though it was the headquarters of the Japanese Fourth Fleet during the war and the Japanese Combined Fleet's main anchorage for a short time between late 1942 and early 1944, Truk can rightly be remembered less for its strength than for its weakness in the face of growing American naval power. The Combined Fleet commanders at this time, Isoroku Yamamoto and then Mineichi Koga, hoped to use Truk as a base from which to give battle to the U.S. Pacific Fleet, but instead it merely became first a staging point for Japanese naval units on their way to the attrition battles in the Solomons and then an exposed forward region after the United States conquered bases in the Marshalls. In fact, most of Truk's airpower was expended defending the great Japanese base at Rabaul, and by late 1943 the Combined Fleet was withdrawing major naval units, such as the Yamato-class superbattleships, to the safer Belau (formerly Palau) Islands.

By early 1944, Truk became a model target for Vice Admiral Marc Mitscher's Task Force 58. In February,

Mitscher's task force used the technique of the fighter sweep, or preliminary fighter attacks, to clear Truk of its air defense before dive and torpedo bombers assaulted the shore installation and ships. The tactic worked wonderfully for the Americans. They succeeded in shooting down more than half of the defending fighters and in just two days of action more than six hundred military personnel had been killed, more than two hundred seventy aircraft had been destroyed, thirty-one merchant vessels and ten warships sunk, and significant amounts of damage inflicted on facilities such as hangers, warehouses, ammunition depots, and dry docks. Truk continued to suffer periodic attacks by U.S. and even British naval forces late in the war as the Allies adopted a strategy of letting it "die on the vine," but it had lost any real military potential by the end of February 1944. In many ways, the near-legendary status of Truk represented a startling failure of U.S. naval intelligence.

FURTHER READINGS

Coulter, John Wesley. *The Pacific Dependencies of the United States* (1957).

Peattie, Mark R. *Nan'yo: The Rise and Fall of the Japanese in Micronesia* (1988).

Reynolds, Clark G. *The Fast Carriers: The Forging of an Air Navy* (1992).

Hal M. Friedman

SEE ALSO Island-Hopping and Leapfrogging, U.S. Strategies

Truman, Harry S. (1884–1972)

Harry S. Truman, 33rd president of the United States (1945–1953), assumed office on the death of Franklin D. Roosevelt on April 12, 1945, after having served as vice president for only eighty-three days. The war against Nazi Germany in Europe was a few weeks short of ending. But the Pacific war still raged, and Truman's first five months in office were consumed with major decisions involving the military and diplomatic moves necessary to win the war against Japan and to bring to an end the most destructive conflict in human history.

Truman was an unlikely figure to arrive on the world stage at such a climactic moment. Nothing in his past had suggested that he would rise to the highest office in the land. The son of farmers from Missouri, Truman grew up in rural and small-town middle America. Early in life he learned the virtues of hard work, personal honesty, and love of country—traits that served him well throughout his political career, especially in the turmoil of his acces-

sion to the presidency. After working as a farmer and a small business owner and serving with an artillery unit in France during World War I, Truman entered Missouri state politics in 1922 as the patron of the powerful machine boss Thomas J. Pendergast. As the chief executive of Jackson County, he gained a reputation for directness, competence, and scrupulous honesty in an environment in which politicians routinely lined their pockets with public funds. He also became noted as a leader who was capable of compromise and who vigorously used all the powers of his office.

Truman's character and ability made him an ideal candidate for higher office, and in 1934 he was elected to the U.S. Senate from Missouri. As a staunch supporter of Roosevelt's New Deal, he carved out a reputation as an independent progressive. From 1941 until mid-1944, Truman led a Senate oversight committee examining waste and mismanagement in the national defense program. His work on this ongoing investigation gave him national exposure and was the basis for his vice presidential nomination as Roosevelt's running mate in 1944.

The sudden death of FDR elevated Truman to the presidency only days after the beginning of the battle for Okinawa, in the Ryukyu Islands. The Ryukyus, southwest of the Japanese home islands, were administered as part of metropolitan Japan. Their conquest by the Americans would mean that the enemy was camped, literally, at the doorstep. The Okinawa campaign was one of the bloodiest engagements of the Pacific war, with more than forty-five thousand American casualties and hundreds of thousands of Japanese military and civilian deaths. It took the Americans more than two months to subdue Okinawa, which served a grim prelude of the ferocious fighting that lay ahead when American forces attempted to invade the main islands of Japan.

The exact course to pursue against Japan, however, was still the subject of debate within the administration at the time Truman assumed the presidency. As the battle for Okinawa progressed and American B-29 bombers ranged freely over Japan fire bombing one city after another, Truman dealt with the collapse of Germany in Europe. On May 8, 1945, Germany surrendered, and the war in Europe was over. In July 1945, Truman sailed to Europe for a meeting in Potsdam, Germany, with British prime minister Winston Churchill and Soviet leader Joseph Stalin. Among the decisions reached during the Potsdam Conference was the agreement on the part of the Soviets to declare war on Japan ninety days after the surrender of Germany—that is, on August 8, 1945. A communique issued at the conclusion of the meeting, the so-called Potsdam Declaration, called on the Japanese to surrender unconditionally or face, as Truman would say in a later address to the American people, "a rain of ruin" unlike that ever witnessed in history.

The Japanese government issued a statement that seemed to reject the Potsdam Declaration, although the exact meaning of certain terminology in their response is the subject of dispute. Depending on how one translates and interprets a key phrase, the response might also be seen not as an outright rejection of the Allies' demand but as an appeal for time.

What is known is that the Japanese government had been trying to appeal to the Soviets, who were still officially neutral in the Pacific war, to act as intermediaries with the United States to find a way to end the war. The government in Japan, however, was walking a difficult line because of strong opposition within the Japanese military to ending the conflict. But Stalin and his foreign minister, Vachyslav Molotov, steadfastly refused to speak with the frantic Japanese ambassador to the USSR, knowing as they did that the Russians would soon be going to war against Japan.

In the face of the apparent Japanese rejection of the Potsdam Declaration, Truman, while sailing back to the United States, gave approval for the air force to drop atomic bombs on Japan whenever it was ready. The bomb, the details of whose development Truman was unaware of until he assumed the presidency, had been successfully tested on July 29, 1945 while Truman was in Potsdam. On receiving news of the test's success, Truman informed Stalin of the existence of a powerful new weapon, but Stalin merely nodded and showed no strong reaction. In fact, Soviet spies had infiltrated the Manhattan Project, which had developed the bomb, and he knew about of the bomb before it was tested.

Truman maintained that dropping the bomb had one goal—to end the war as quickly as possible and prevent millions of American casualties that would have occurred had the United States launched a ground invasion of the main Japanese islands. On August 6, 1945 a B-29 Superfortress named "Enola Gay" flew over the city of Hiroshima and released one atomic bomb. In the explosion that followed, the city was destroyed and more than seventy thousand people were killed. Three days later, on August 9, another B-29 headed for the city of Kokura, the designated target. Clouds shielded the city, however, and the aircraft headed instead for the backup target, Nagasaki, where the second atomic bomb was dropped.

More than twenty-five thousand people died in the initial blast and more than forty-five thousand succumbed later to radiation poisoning.

The atomic bomb attacks were a bewildering shock to the Japanese government, which was still trying to sort out exactly what had happened when on August 9 came the devastating news that the Soviet Union had declared war on Japan and attacked its army in Manchuria. Five days later, on August 14, 1945, Japan surrendered unconditionally. The war in the Pacific was over.

Some historians argue that the Soviet declaration of war was the determining factor in Japan's decision to surrender. The Japanese, they contend, understood that an American occupation, onerous was to accept, would at least end one day, whereas the Soviets would bring communism and a total overthrow of the system. Truman, however, maintained throughout his life that the dropping of the bombs caused the Japanese to surrender. More important for him, he stoutly defended his decision on the basis that he had aborted the war and saved untold numbers of American lives.

Truman's public statements about the use of the bomb are consistent, although he would rarely discuss the subject in public in the twenty years he lived after leaving the presidency. While there is no reason to doubt his publicly stated beliefs that the atomic bombing of Japan saved lives and ended the war, his private feelings about the use of such devastating weapons are less certain. As far as is known, he never expressed any reservations, although he was clearly shocked by the extent of devastation caused by the atomic blasts.

Truman was placed on the world stage by the death of his predecessor. Within five months of assuming office, he received the surrender of the Allies' enemies in Europe and of the Japanese in the Pacific. His part in the Pacific war was brief, but momentous.

FURTHER READINGS
Donovan, Robert J. *Conflict and Crisis: The Presidency of Harry S. Truman, 1945–1948* (1972).
Hamby, Alonzo L. *Man of the People: A Life of Harry S. Truman* (1995).
McCullough, David. *Truman* (1992).
Truman, Harry S. *Memoirs,* 2 vols. (1955–1956).

Richard Steins

SEE ALSO Atomic Bomb, Decision to Use against Japan

U-Boats in the Pacific

To Germany's Admiral Karl Doenitz, the naval war was a chess game in which he deployed his U-boats far and wide in an effort to sink as many ships as possible at the lowest potential risks to his own forces. In late 1942, he sent U-boats into the Indian and Pacific Oceans and established the only effective element of cooperation between Germany and Japan in World War II. Fortunately for the democracies, logistics problems precluded this force achieving anything like its full potential. Those U-boats that operated in the Pacific fell prey to American submarines before they could gain any significant success there. Despite these problems, Germany's second leading U-boat ace, Helmut Luth, scored over a third of his 228,000 tons of shipping sunk while serving in the Far East. Moreover, some of the boats returned to Germany with vital war supplies (tungsten, rubber, and quinine) at a time when surface blockade runners could not make it through.

The first group of U-boats left occupied France on August 1, 1942. Consisting of four long-range Type IXC U-boats supported by a U-boat tanker, it operated off South Africa, sinking over 40,000 tons of shipping without loss before returning to France. The second group departed in September. Using larger and more capable boats that could operate farther afield and remain on station longer, it patrolled the area between South Africa's east coast and Mauritius. This group sank more than twenty-four ships totaling 126,000 tons before running out of torpedoes in December and returning safely to France.

All subsequent groups consisted primarily of the longest-ranged boats and were supported by supply boats or a supply ship. Using new tactics, combined with better intelligence support from an India-based German spy ring reporting out of the Portuguese colony of Goa, they ini-tially enjoyed significant success. One group destroyed thirty-one Allied ships displacing over 168,000 tons at the cost of only one U-boat (*U-197*). Five of the boats then returned to Bordeaux while one, *U-178,* was ordered to Penang, Malaya, in May 1943.

The Japanese had offered Penang and Sebang, Sumatra, as U-boat bases in December 1942, but Doenitz had not seen the need until U-boat losses in the Atlantic and his boats' successes in the Indian Ocean forced him to reconsider. However, Allied antisubmarine (ASW) forces destroyed the majority of the boats despatched after May of 1943. For example, of the three groups Doenitz ordered to the Far East between January 1944 and February 1945, thirteen of the twenty-three boats never made it. Once on station, the survivors found their effectiveness limited by maintenance and supply problems.

Meanwhile, the Allies began stationing their own submarines off Penang and Sumatra, ambushing the U-boats as they entered or departed. Four U-boats went down in quick succession in late October and early November 1944. Two others, *U-537* and *U-183,* moved to the waters north of Australia, where they fell to American submarines in March 1945. The two remaining operational U-boats fled to Germany one month later, carrying tungsten, quinine, and rubber, but they surrendered to Allied forces in France when their fuel ran low.

Japanese naval authorities seized the last five U-boats when Germany surrendered in May 1945, but the boats' poor material condition prevented their becoming operational before Japan's surrender in August. It was an inglorious end to what could have been a potentially successful naval deployment. More than half of the boats despatched were lost en route and the survivors had their effectiveness impeded by poor maintenance and logistics support.

Germany's Far East deployment was another example of too little, too late. Had those units been deployed in greater numbers in late 1942, they would have arrived to face limited Allied ASW defenses and much denser shipping patterns. Moreover, by mid-1943, the Axis would have been better served if the U-boats had been employed against Allied shipping south or east of the Solomons. The U.S. Navy did not escort its convoys in the Eastern and Central Pacific because Japanese submarines were not employed against shipping. By operating in the Indian Ocean at a time when the Allies no longer sailed around Africa, the U-boats found fewer targets and faced stronger opposition. More significantly, Doenitz made no effort to build up his logistics base in the Far East prior to deploying his forces there.

Penang was completely inadequate as a base, having no dockyard and very limited fueling facilities. Worse, the crew members of former German surface raider *Thor* were the only available skilled labor, and they could do little without proper tools and equipment. Admiral Doenitz would have done better had he arranged for tools, equipment and more skilled personnel to precede his U-boats into the base. As it was, by the time units arrived in Penang in force, the Allies were ready, both along the route and in the Indian Ocean itself.

Admiral Doenitz saw the Indian Ocean as a vast expanse of water far from Germany. The distances dictated long transit times followed by short patrols and extensive maintenance periods. He therefore deployed his U-boats there only on an ad hoc basis or as a last resort. The Pacific Ocean was even farther out and seemingly offered no contribution to Doenitz's war in Europe. Still, the Far Eastern U-boats sank more ships for lighter losses than did those in the Atlantic during the war's final year.

FURTHER READINGS

Hessler, Gunther, *The U-Boat War in the Atlantic* (1989).
Piekalkiewicz, Janusz, *Sea War, 1939–1945* (1987).
Roskill, Stephen W., *The War at Sea,* vols. 2 and 3 (1958–60).

Carl O. Schuster

SEE ALSO Navy, Royal; Navy, U.S.

United Nations

The United Nations, an international body founded in 1945 to maintain world peace and security, originated in World War II. Although its forerunner, the League of Nations, had failed to prevent the war, its member states desired a new forum for the discussion of world security

issues. This general support solidified under the direction of the Allied powers, chiefly the United States. Secretary of State Cordell Hull created a planning group in the opening months of the war to put forth governing principles for such a body. The Roosevelt administration made known its desire for a new world body in the Atlantic Charter, published on August 14, 1941. The document was mainly a declaration of basic human rights and the war aims of the Allied powers. It did not make a direct reference to the creation of an international organization, but it did call for the possible future establishment of a permanent system of general security.

This general statement found international support in the Declaration by United Nations (January 1, 1942), signed initially by twenty-six governments. It incorporated the Atlantic Charter and also put forth governing principles of international law. The main purpose of the declaration was to create a wartime alliance against the Axis powers. Even so, this wartime coalition represented a new family of nations that subscribed to the basic principles of international law that governed the League of Nations. The framework was set for future discussions on a new international body. The signatories of the declaration never met as a whole, but the great powers of the group, generally known as "The Allies," met in wartime conferences throughout the duration of the conflict. It was in this environment and under their direction that plans for the United Nations moved forward.

The first step took place at a meeting of Allied foreign ministers at Moscow in October 1943, a preliminary to the Tehran Conference planned for the end of the year. Representatives of the United States, Great Britain, the Soviet Union, and China signed the Declaration of Four Nations on General Security. The declaration called for the creation of a postwar international organization, but it did not contain any concrete proposals for its operation.

This changed in late 1944 when Washington used the Declaration of Four Nations on General Security as an incentive for the Dumbarton Oaks Conference (held in New Hampshire) that met from August to October 1944. The representatives there called for a new, permanent international organization to be known as the United Nations. Its primary goal would be the maintenance of international peace and security. A secondary function would be to serve as a forum to solve world economic, social, and humanitarian problems. The proposed administrative organs of the United Nations were the same as the League of Nations. The first was a General Assembly, composed of all member states, for the discussion and debate of international issues. Executive power was placed in the Security Council, made up of eleven members. Five of these—the permanent members—would be the major Allied powers: the United States, Great Britain, China, France, and the Soviet Union. The remaining six would be nonpermanent positions that rotated to different countries for the sake of fair representation. The proposal also provided for an international court of justice and a secretariat.

The Yalta conference in February 1945 produced additions and some alterations to the scheme. One of the major topics for discussion was a veto where any one member of the security council could block U.N. legislation. Soviet premier Joseph Stalin insisted on this provision because he suspected that the West might use the new organization to further its interests over those of the Soviet Union. Stalin also demanded that the Ukraine and Byelorussia count as separate votes in the General Assembly, although they were integral parts of the Soviet Union. Roosevelt and Churchill gave way on both these issues out of their desire for Soviet entry into the war against Japan.

The Big Three at Yalta also corrected an omission at the Dumbarton Oaks Conference, which had not set up an administration to govern former League of Nation mandate territories. The Allies provided for a trustee system to oversee these as well as lands seized from the Axis powers at the conclusion of the war. This system also would have the power to administer any colonies that imperial nations wished to relinquish.

The final step taken at Yalta was the decision to issue invitations for a conference to take place in San Francisco on April 25, 1945, with the object of creating a charter for the United Nations. These went out to all those nations who had signed the 1942 Declaration by United Nations as well as those countries affiliated with them. Fifty nations answered and attended the San Francisco conference from April 25 to June 26, 1945. The charter

it produced adhered to the administrative structure already outlined by the Allied powers, but with some changes that gave greater authority to smaller states in order to stave off the total domination of the United Nations by the great powers. The United States ratified the charter on September 20, 1945, and it went into effect on October 24, 1945. The governments of all states involved in the San Francisco conference had ratified the charter by December 27, 1945, and the body first met in London in 1946. The following year it moved to temporary facilities in Lake Success, New York, pending the completion of its permanent administrative buildings in New York City.

The United Nations continues to act as the voice of international opinion in the present day. Although criticized for having little real authority over the affairs of sovereign powers, the United Nations has the important role of mediator and sounding board for world affairs from the perspective of international law. It has often been pointed out that much of the best work of the U.N. occurs in the delegates lounges, where unpublicized informal discussions take place between representatives of nations that, on the record, are often bitterly opposed. But perhaps the best argument for the value of the United Nation is the fact that the world has seen no major war since its founding.

FURTHER READINGS

Hoopes, Townsend. *FDR and the Creation of the United Nations* (1997).
Schild, Georg. *Bretton Woods and Dumbarton Oaks: American Economic and Political Postwar Planning in the Summer of 1944.* (1995).

Eric W. Osborne

SEE ALSO Yalta Conference

Vandegrift, Alexander A. (1887–1973)

Born in Charlottesville, Virginia, on March 13, 1887, the talented Alexander A. "Archie" Vandegrift steadily rose through the ranks to become the eighteenth commandant of the United States Marine Corps (1944–1947). After attending the University of Virginia, he received his commission as a second lieutenant in the Marine Corps in 1909. For the next fourteen years, he spent most of his time in Panama, Nicaragua, Mexico, and Haiti. From 1925 until 1935, Vandegrift served in various key staff capacities with the bureau of the budget, the fleet marine force, and the Marine Corps barracks in San Diego, California. In 1934, he was attached to the Marine Corps schools at Quantico, Virginia. As part of his duties, he helped compile the *Tentative Manual of Landing Operations,* a document which laid out marine amphibious assault doctrine for more than a decade thereafter. This educational assignment gave Vandegrift firsthand theoretical knowledge of amphibious warfare that would serve him well later in the Pacific war.

From 1935 until 1937, he was executive officer and later commanding officer of the marine detachment at the American embassy in Peking, China. In 1937, Vandegrift, then a colonel, assumed the position of military secretary to Marine Corps Commandant, Major General Thomas Holcomb. By 1940, Vandegrift was promoted to brigadier general and appointed assistant to the major general commandant. Such diverse staff and command opportunities provided Vandegrift with invaluable training that helped make him an effective leader in the Pacific from 1941 to 1944 and later as commandant.

As assistant to Holcomb in 1940 and 1941, Vandegrift performed the duties of a chief of staff by handling the corps's internal management. An overarching problem facing the corps in the 1920s and 1930s was how to do more with fewer resources. The amphibious assault and base defense—not to mention aviation, ship, and shore—missions hopelessly stretched the Corps's limited resources. Some of the internal difficulties included command structure, training, and promotion stagnation.

Vandegrift tried to reform the fleet marine force's command structure by localizing control under the marine and navy officers on-site. He therefore attempted to eliminate the inherent communication and administration difficulties caused by exercising leadership from several thousand miles away. He also introduced some important reforms within the marine divisions of the fleet marine force. After their training, competent officers would form "a tactical command" made up of the commanding officer and a small tactical staff.

Vandegrift also tried to reconcile rank with competency in an inverse bottleneck caused by the corps's accelerated expansion in the two years before Pearl Harbor. Determining the truly competent leaders, whether younger or older, took time. Officers and senior noncommissioned officers had to be tested under stress to prove their mettle. If an error in assignment were to occur, experienced noncommissioned officers would accompany less-experienced officers. Vandegrift thus hoped to avoid the mistakes made when the United States entered World War I in 1917, when experienced officers led inexperienced noncommissioned officers.

Vandegrift served as Holcomb's assistant until late 1941, at which point he took command of the reinforced 1st Marine Division and advanced to the rank of major general. Within six months of the attack on Pearl Harbor in December 1941, Vandegrift and his marines landed on Guadalcanal and established themselves at Henderson Airfield. Although successful in this first phase, problems occurred because Vice Admiral Frank Jack Fletcher, commander of Task Force 62, withdrew his combat vessels and Rear Admiral Richmond K. Turner pulled back his cargo vessels from the battle area for fear of Japanese air or naval attacks. Their withdrawals left the marines on Guadalcanal stranded and ill-prepared to meet repeated Japanese attempts to dislodge them from Henderson field. Lacking total air superiority and equally important logistical support, the 1st Marine Division endured a long siege. Life on Guadalcanal was miserable because of weather and disease, not to mention tenacious Japanese counterattacks. Only through the able leadership of Vandegrift and his staff did the 1st Marine Division survive and eventually triumph. Throughout the ensuing battle of attrition on Guadalcanal, the stubborn marine defenders earned their often-used nickname "leathernecks" by repelling repeated Japanese ground and air attacks.

Turner and Vandegrift also quarreled over the chain of command. Turner clearly exercised overall operational command of the Guadalcanal landing; however, unity of command under him did not make for a successful campaign. Turner tried to direct the land campaign despite Vandegrift's position as marine commander. This made for an inefficient decision-making structure and thus an less-than-effective campaign. Vandegrift appealed back to Commandant Holcomb in Washington for help in reforming the chain of command. To help solve this dilemma, Holcomb proposed that marine commanders have equal status with navy commanders during the planning and the subsequent tactical operation on land. Navy commanders would exercise undisputed command only during an actual landing operation. In theory, unity of command existed at a higher level with the theater commander.

Even with the command structure reform, Vandegrift still could not obtain the supplies he desperately needed to survive on Guadalcanal. After Vandegrift's numerous pleas to Turner, to Admiral Chester W. Nimitz at Pearl Harbor, and to Washington, President Franklin D. Roosevelt finally intervened and ordered that supplies be sent to Guadalcanal in November 1942.

With an influx of logistical and manpower relief, the 1st Marine Division went on the offensive against the Japanese. Vandegrift was awarded both the Navy Cross and the Congressional Medal of Honor for his outstanding leadership in the Guadalcanal campaign.

In 1943, Vandegrift advanced to the rank of lieutenant general and was given command of the 1st Marine Amphibious Corps in General Douglas MacArthur's South Pacific command. Under Vandegrift's direction, this force engaged in landing operations in Bougainville in late 1944.

On December 1, 1944, Vandegrift took charge of the corps as commandant. He picked up where Holcomb had stopped in supervising the corps' continued growth and success. Vandegrift added another 125,000 men and women to the marines, thus raising the total strength to more than 450,000 by late 1944. He also became the first active duty marine to attain the rank of full general. As commandant, Vandegrift spent much of World War II smoothing over controversies that included interservice rivalries and battlefield casualties. As American forces drove across the Pacific, unity of command remained confusing both at the battlefield and theater levels. Tensions developed once again between marine commanders and their army and navy counterparts on Saipan (1944) and Okinawa (1945); disagreements arose over when or where to land, reinforce, expand, or resupply. Walking a tightrope in Washington, Vandegrift often compromised or found some other less-than-satisfactory arrangement to push the operations forward.

Vandegrift also constantly worked to ensure that the corps' public image remained untainted. Marine units suffered grievously in the Pacific. As American forces approached the Japan's home islands, Japanese soldiers became increasingly desperate to make the invaders pay as a high price as possible for their advance. In February 1945, 21,000 Japanese soldiers on Iwo Jima inflicted 26,000 casualties and some 6,000 dead on three marine divisions. Such losses caused great distress among the American people and Congress. In fact, some media even questioned the marines' capabilities. Reacting quickly to calm the American public and government, Vandegrift argued that fighting a fanatical enemy like the Japanese from cave to cave was inevitably costly in men and material. The high casualties merely testified to the horrific nature of the Pacific war.

When the war in the Pacific ended in August 1945, Vandegrift faced the challenges of demobilization and the threat of unification with other service branches. Traditionally, America's armed forces suffered severe downsizing at the end of a war. World War II was no exception; the corps' strength fell from approximately 450,000 marines in 1945 to 76,000 in 1948. For the corps and Vandegrift, trying to maintain preparedness and fulfill its missions proved to be almost impossible. In addition to demobilization, Vandegrift also faced a second challenge which threatened the corps' continued existence. President Harry S. Truman (who had privately referred to the marines as "Fancy Dans" and publicly said that they had "the world's second-biggest propaganda machine.") wanted to streamline America's military by creating a single unified service. According to Truman's plan, the corps would have been swallowed by the land-based forces, losing its uniqueness and autonomy. There was also talk of absorbing the corps into the army. Vandegrift successfully resisted this proposal by going before the House Naval Affairs Committee chaired by Carl Vinson (Demo-Ga.), a man who had actively supported the seaborne services for decades. In the end, a compromise was struck in which the corps retained its status as a separate service within the department of the navy.

After nearly forty years in the corps, Vandegrift left active service in December 1947 and was subsequently retired in 1949. He died on May 8, 1973, in Bethesda, Maryland.

FURTHER READINGS

Foster, John T. *Guadalcanal General: The Story of A. A. Vandegrift, USMC* (1966).

Millett, Allan R. *Semper Fidelis: The History of the United States Marine Corps,* rev. ed. (1991).

U. S. Marine Corps. *History of U. S. Marine Corps Operations in World War II.* 5 vols. (1958–1968).

Vandegrift, Alexander A., and Robert B. Asprey. *Once a Marine: The Memoirs of General A. A. Vandegrift, USMC* (1964).

Wheeler, Richard. *A Special Valor: The U. S. Marines and the Pacific War* (1996).

David Ulbrich

SEE ALSO Army Ground Forces, U.S.; Guadalcanal, Battle for; Holcomb, Thomas; Navy, U.S.

Wakde-Sarmi

In late 1943 the Japanese began to fortify the Wakde-Sarmi region on New Guinea's northern coast as part of their effort to stop General Douglas MacArthur's Southwest Pacific Area (SWPA) offensive. Although they already possessed a coral-surfaced airstrip on Wakde, the Japanese started construction on two new airfields at Sawar and Maffin Bay on the New Guinea mainland around Sarmi. To defend the area, the Japanese deployed from northern China two regiments of about eleven thousand men from the veteran 36th Division under Lieutenant General Hachiro Tagami. After MacArthur's forces seized the vital Japanese base at Hollandia, 125 miles to the southeast, in late April 1944, the Japanese decided to abandon Wakde-Sarmi and its defenders to their fate. The Japanese hoped that the 36th Division could delay the Americans long enough for the emperor's forces to build a new defensive line in western New Guinea capable of resisting MacArthur's juggernaut.

MacArthur wanted to capture the Wakde-Sarmi area not only to propel his offensive westward toward the China-Formosa-Luzon area, but also to provide bases for his bombers. SWPA had discovered that Hollandia's airfields could not handle bombers anytime soon, but MacArthur needed such airfields to support both his operations westward and the navy's Central Pacific offensive to the north. Unfortunately, reconnaissance photos indicated that the land at Sawar and Maffin Bay was too boggy to deploy bombers, so SWPA focused its attention westward to airfields on Biak Island in Geelvink Bay. To provide fighter-plane support for the planned Biak assault, SWPA decided to seize Wakde's airstrip first.

On May 17, 1944, Brigadier General Jens Doe's 163rd Regimental Combat Team (RCT) from the 41st Infantry Division, veterans of the recent Hollandia-Aitape operation, landed unopposed at Arara on the New Guinea mainland southwest of Wakde. The next morning its 1st Battalion stormed Wakde and its 800 Japanese defenders. Fighting raged for several days, but by May 20, the 163d secured the island at the cost of 40 killed and 107 wounded. All but four Japanese perished in the assault. Engineers moved in soon after the first combat troops hit the beach, and the airstrip was ready in time to provide fighter plane support for the Biak landing on May 27.

Seizing Wakde, however, did not end the operation. SWPA ground forces commander Lieutenant General Walter Krueger worried that the Japanese could threaten the American's mainland beachhead positions from the hills to the west. A Japanese attack could disrupt SWPA logistics and slow down MacArthur's fast-moving offensive, so Krueger wanted to clear the enemy out as soon as possible. Because the 163d RCT was slated for operations farther westward, Krueger ordered in Brigadier General Edwin Patrick's untested 158th RCT to do the job. The 158th moved out on May 23, but it quickly ran into heavy opposition centered on Lone Tree Hill. Lone Tree Hill derived its name from a headquarters map that showed a solitary tree on it, but it was actually covered by dense jungle and full of coral caves and outcroppings. The 158th tried for several days to pry the Japanese from the hill, but it failed and on May 28, Patrick ordered the unit withdrawn to the east. The unsuccessful assault cost the 158th 70 killed and 257 wounded. By way of compensation, the Americans claimed to have killed more than 900 Japanese.

Patrick hoped to renew the offensive, but Krueger needed his unit for the upcoming Noemfoor operation, so he instead ordered in Major General Franklin Sibert's inexperienced 6th Infantry Division to finish the job. Sibert wanted to mount an amphibious assault behind Lone Tree Hill, but Krueger thought that would take too long, so he ordered an immediate attack. The 6th Division began its offensive on June 18, and soon ran into heavy opposition around Lone Tree Hill. The 6th cleared the position on June 24, but only after much of one RCT had been trapped on the summit for two days. Sibert's men spent the next several weeks prying the Japanese from other nearby strongpoints such as Hill 225, Hill 265, and Mount Saksin. American casualties in the last ten days of June alone were 114 killed, 284 wounded, and some 400 evacuated for noncombat injuries. Japanese losses were as high as 1,000.

In late July, Krueger pulled out the 6th Division for operations on New Guinea's Vogelkop Peninsula, and he sent in two RCTs from Major General John Person's inexperienced 31st Infantry Division to keep an eye on what was left of the Japanese 36th Division. Persons used the opportunity to acclimate his men for combat, and after they left in September, Krueger deployed the 33d Infantry Division there for the same purposes. Eventually the Americans abandoned the mainland and relegated Wakde to an emergency airstrip. The remnants of the Japanese troops remained in the Sarmi area for the rest of the war.

The Wakde-Sarmi operation cost the Americans 630 killed, 1,742 wounded, and 41 missing. The Wakde part of the operation yielded SWPA significant strategic results. Wakde's airstrip provided SWPA with the fighter plane support it needed to conduct the Biak landings, and it further protected all-important Hollandia. On the other hand, while attacking Japanese mainland positions did secure the American beachhead in and around Arara, it is debatable that the Japanese there were much of a threat, or that jarring them loose was worth the casualties sustained. For Wakde-Sarmi's Japanese defenders, they managed to delay SWPA's offensive, but not for long.

FURTHER READINGS

"Historical Report: The Battle of Lone Tree Hill," Washington National Records Center, RG 407, Box 7010.

Kreuger, W. *From Down Under to Nippon* (1953).

"Operations Report, Toem Wakde Operation, Tornado Task Force," 163d Infantry Regiment, 41st Infantry Division Journal," Washington National Records Center, RG 407, Box 10634.

Smith, Robert Ross. *Approach to the Philippines: The United States Army in World War II* (1953).

Taafe, S. *MacArthur's Jungle War: The 1944 New Guinea Campaign* (1998).

"158th RCT, Operations Report, Sarmi-Wakdi Campaign", Washington National Records Center, RG 407, Box 21182.

6th Army Headquarters. "Wakdi-Sarmi Operation," Walter Kreuger Papers, United States Military Academy, box 24.

Steven Taafe

SEE ALSO New Guinea

Wake Island, Battle of

Wake is a lonely atoll in the middle of the Pacific Ocean, consisting of three small islands: Wake, Wilkes, and Peale. Annexed by the United States in 1899, it remained virtually ignored until airpower became important. Situated about halfway between Midway and Guam, it was an important link in the San Francisco-Pearl Harbor-Guam-Manila air route. In the mid-1930s, Pan American Airways began using Wake as a refueling base and overnight stop on its transpacific seaplane route. In 1939, President Franklin D. Roosevelt placed Wake under the jurisdiction of the U.S. Navy and authorized the building of an airstrip on the islands. In late spring 1941 the navy dispatched the 1st Defense Battalion, Fleet Marine Force, consisting of six officers and 173 enlisted men, commanded by Major James Devereux; additional Marines would arrive in the fall. Some eleven hundred civilian workers were sent to Wake in 1941 to dredge a small channel in the lagoon and to construct the airstrip. In late November, Navy Commander Winfield Cunningham and a handful of navy officers arrived to prepare the future naval air station; Cunningham was senior officer on the island. In addition, the marine corps provided air protection with Major Paul Putnam's Fighter Squadron VMF-211, consisting of twelve semi-obsolete Grumman F4F-3S Wildcats. By December 1941, there were 27 marine officers, 422 marines, 10 naval officers, 58 enlisted naval personnel, an army communications unit (with one officer and four men), 70 Pan American employees, and 1,146 civilian contract workers on the atoll. Wake's defenders lacked radar, and the observation post had been placed on the highest spot on the islands, atop the water tower. But the continual crashing of waves against the outer reef made it impossible to hear approaching aircraft.

On Monday, December 8, 1941, the base on Wake learned that war with Japan had begun. That same day, from their base at Roi, the Japanese launched their first air raid on Wake, destroying the Pan American facilities and the radio transmitter and wounding a number of the marine aviators. The passenger seaplane *Philippine Clipper* loaded with the Pan American employees took off for Midway at 1330 hours that afternoon. On December 9 and 10, Japanese aircraft again attacked the islands, demolishing the hospital, damaging a warehouse, metal shop, and ammunition supplies; marine aviators from Wake damaged twelve Japanese aircraft and Captain Henry Elrod shot down two. These air raids were designed to soften up Wake's defenses for the Japanese landings.

Shortly after midnight on December 11, marines reported seeing blinking lights offshore and realized that the Japanese were attempting to land. The Japanese invasion convoy, led by Rear Admiral Sadamichi Kajioka consisted of light cruiser *Yubari*, six destroyers, two patrol boats, two armed merchantmen, and two more light cruisers; their aim was to land 150 men on Wilkes Island and another 300 on Wake. Early in the morning Cunningham radioed Pearl Harbor asking that the civilians being evacuated immediately. When the Japanese ships began to shell Wake and move in closer, Major Devereux's marines, using their 3- and 5-inch coastal defense guns, surprisingly damaged *Yubari,* sank destroyer *Hayate,* and damaged destroyers *Oite* and *Mochizuki.* Marine aviators also sank destroyer *Kisaragi* and downed two Japanese aircraft. The results of this abortive Japanese landing was about the only good news the American public had heard or would hear again for months—the Americans had sunk two destroyers and killed at least 500 Japanese while losing only one American. This was also the last time that coast defense guns would beat off an amphibious landing attempt.

Over the next few days the Japanese would continue to pound the Wake defenders with air raids, and by December 14 only two marine planes remained flyable. Back at Pearl Harbor, Admiral Husband E. Kimmel had wanted to relieve Wake as soon as the war began, but he feared risking his carriers when he was unsure of the position of the Japanese fleet. Rescue efforts were also delayed by slow refueling. Not until December 15 did the relief effort (Rear Admiral Frank Jack Fletcher's Task Force 14) finally set sail to bring reinforcements to Wake and remove the civilians. This force would never arrive. On December 13 the marines on Wake had picked up American band leader Kay Kyser's radio broadcast in which commentators claimed the Wake defenders had sent a signal stating "Send us more Japs." The garrison and the civilians now began to realize that there was no help coming.

On December 16, Vice Admiral Shigeyoshe Inouye, commander of the Japanese South Seas Force, dispatched reinforcements to Admiral Kajioka. In addition to the remnants of the original invasion force, Kajioka was given three destroyers, a transport, a minelayer, a seaplane tender carrying special naval landing forces, four heavy

cruisers, and air support from Rear Admiral Hiroaki Abe's carriers, *Hiryu* and *Soryu.* These forces were to attempt another landing on December 23.

On December 17, Admiral Kimmel was relieved of his command and replaced by Vice Admiral William Pye, who would be acting commander until the permanent new commander, Admiral Chester W. Nimitz, arrived. On December 21, Cunningham reported that Wake had been attacked by carrier planes and the last of his marine aircraft had been destroyed. News of the carrier planes over Wake worried Pye, and he ordered Task Force 14 not to sail closer to the atoll.

Shortly after midnight on December 23, marines at Wake again observed flashing lights offshore. Soon the Japanese began landing about 1,000 men on Wake and Wilkes islands. At 0250 hours Cunningham radioed Pearl Harbor, "Island under gunfire. Enemy apparently landing." The defenders resisted valiantly against great odds. By 0500 hours Cunningham sent another message to Pearl Harbor, "Enemy on island. Issue in doubt." Communications broke down between the defenders as the Japanese spread out among the islands; small pockets of defenders slowed the Japanese advance and a few launched effective counterattacks, but without outside relief they were doomed. At 0652 hours Cunningham sent out his last message, "Enemy on Island. Several ships plus transport moving in." Japanese carrier planes were wreaking havoc on the defenders as the sun rose. Pye decided on a general withdrawal of American naval forces in the vicinity of Wake, since he did not know the strength of the enemy, and he so informed Cunningham.

At 0730 hours, after being informed by Devereux that resistance could not be continued much longer, Cunningham decided to end the fighting in order to stop further loss of life. He agreed to unconditional surrender (the marines' first surrender), and Devereux spent the next several hours persuading the remaining pockets of defenders that the fight was ended. The Japanese took 470 American military personnel and 1,146 civilians as prisoners; 122 Americans had lost their lives. The Japanese lost over 800 killed and 300 wounded at Wake. All of the defenders except for 100 of the civilian workers were removed in January 1942 to prisoner of war camps. After an American raid on the atoll in October 1943, these 100 civilians were executed on the orders of the Japanese commander, Rear Admiral Shigematsu Sakaibara, who himself would be hanged for this crime after the war. Wake would not be recaptured by the United States during the course of Pacific hostilities, but its valiant defense became a rallying cry and symbol of

American heroism during the early, dark days of World War II.

FURTHER READINGS
Cunningham, Winfield. *Wake Island Command* (1961).
Devereux, James P. S. *The Story of Wake Island* (1947).
Heinl, Colonel Robert D., Jr. *The Defense of Wake* (1947).
Morison, Samuel Eliot. *History of U.S. Naval Operations in World War II,* vol. III. *Rising Sun in the Pacific, 1931 to April 1942* (1957).

Laura Matysek Wood

SEE ALSO Marine Corps, U.S.

War Artists

Artists served in all the belligerent forces during the Pacific war during one time or another, either in an official capacity or as amateurs sketching in their spare moments. The rationale for using artists was that while the modern camera was very versatile, it had limitations particularly during night action, in foul weather, or for battles that take place over wide expanses of sea, sky, and land. The artist, however, could overcome these obstacles and capture the dramatic intensity of action, making scenes and activity more vivid and poignant, while at the same time integrating important elements and omitting unimportant or classified details.

The U.S. Navy was the first of the American armed services to employ artists, commencing in October 1942. Five serving officers were initially recruited by the office of public relations in the art and poster section to "bring home to the American people a vivid picture of battles and other naval actions." Some of these artists saw action in the South Pacific in late 1942, including Lieutenant Dwight C. Shepler, who served as a junior officer on board a cruiser during several engagements in the campaign for the Solomons. His cruiser was in the midst of the battle of Santa Cruz and he observed Japanese planes dive-bombing his ship. For three weeks he was on Guadalcanal, where he saw the horrific fighting in the tropics; later he covered the Okinawa campaign. His Atlanta-class cruiser series of paintings captured scenes on board the ships, particularly the weaponry. His colleague, Lieutenant Commander Griffith Bailey Coale, depicted the attack on Pearl Harbor and the battle of Midway in a series of murals and paintings, one example being a canvas portraying anti-aircraft gunners in action on board PT boats at Midway, while another large mural represented one of the Japanese carriers being attacked. Coale used his pictures of this battle in a book entitled *Victory at Midway.*

Lieutenant William F. Draper covered the Aleutian campaign in 1942 and 1943, sketching camp scenes and anti-aircraft defenses, Liberty ships in Adak Harbor, as well as the Japanese air raid on Amchitka. Many of the naval paintings done in the first two years of the war were reproduced in *The Navy at War: Paintings and Drawings by Combat Artists,* published in 1943. Later, Lieutenant Mitchell Jamieson, who had previously covered the North African campaign, was present during the invasions of Iwo Jima and Okinawa.

Undoubtedly, the establishment of a naval art program had a strong effect in pushing the army to create a similar program. From an early plan developed by the corps of engineers emerged a full-fledged war art program in early 1943 under the guidance of the war department art advisory committee (WDAAC), which hoped to send correspondents to accompany the artists. The idea was to dispatch thirteen teams of three artists each to the various theaters of the war to record the events. The resulting work would be exhibited around the country and used for public relations purposes in magazines, newspapers, and books. Even before the WDAAC had been formed, the office of assistant chief of staff for operations had sent a classified message to the commander in chief, South Pacific Area, on February 8, 1943, stating that the secretary of war desired to obtain a historical and pictorial record of the war in the form of oil paintings, water colors, drawings, and other graphic media, and proposed to send in April a small art unit composed of approximately six selected individuals for the purpose. A similar message went in April to General Dwight D. Eisenhower, commander of Allied forces in North Africa.

Selected artists began to receive letters of recommendation in February and March 1943, and the these included the following statement from one of the committee members, Henry Poor: "The United States must take the lead and find some way of getting our finest artists and writers the things they alone can give—a deeply, passionately felt, but profoundly reflective interpretation of the spirit and essence of the war." One of the units, consisting of Howard Cook, Aaron Bohrod, and Charles Shannon, was sent to the South Pacific and headquartered at Noumea, although the first group to actually take to the field was the Southwest Pacific Unit made up of Frede Vidar, Barse Miller, and Sidney Simon. They were sent to the headquarters of the Southwest Pacific Defense Command at Brisbane, Australia, arriving in early May 1943. They were joined later by David Fredenthal as well as a navy artist, McClelland Barclay. For the next few months, a steady stream of drawings and paintings arrived back in the States. Many of these depicted the tedium of life behind the front lines. Occasionally the South Pacific unit held exhibitions of their work, one such show being at Camp Barnes, New Caledonia, in June 1943. The members of this unit were frustrated that they had seen little action but eventually were allowed to witness the amphibious assault at Rendova off Munda in the New Georgia islands. In contrast, the Southwest Pacific team was more fortunate and were able to record the allied advance to the Philippines. Fredenthal alone witnessed three island invasions.

The war art program came to an abrupt halt in the summer of 1943 when Congress cut off the funding, leaving the artists literally stranded, although a combat war art program was reactivated in June 1944. Upon hearing of these discouraging developments, Daniel Longwell, executive editor of *Life* magazine, approached Assistant Secretary of War John J. McCloy with an offer to absorb the contracts, and seventeen artists were taken on, although the army was to continue providing transportation and billeting. General MacArthur retained the Southwest Pacific unit with the exception of Fredenthal, who joined *Life,* and its members were able to record the New Guinea campaign; an exhibition of sixty-seven pictures of this campaign was held in various Australian cities in late 1944 and early 1945. One painting by Barse Miller depicted Japanese planes attacking American troops after their surprise landing on Arawe, New Britain, on December 15, 1943. In addition some of these pictures appeared in *Life.* Now headquartered in Manila, the Southwest Pacific unit covered the final campaigns in the Philippines, China, Japan, and Korea until it was deactivated in 1946.

Life magazine had been devoting extensive pictorial coverage of the war in its pages, and one of its earliest war artists was Tom Lea, an alternate for the Southwest Pacific art unit. During August 1942 he was billeted on board USS *Hornet* while that aircraft carrier participated in Allied operations in the South Pacific. Later he covered marine operations at Peleliu. Artists were to be found also on the staff of the semi-official *Yank* magazine, including Howard Brodie who witnessed the Guadalcanal campaign. Besides *Life,* another independent agency employing artists in the region was the Abbott Laboratories of Chicago. As early 1942, Abbott had sent artists to various naval air stations to record naval aviation. Later, it sent twelve artists to the various fronts to cover the work of the army medical department. Robert Benney worked on both projects, and in 1944 experienced the conquest of Saipan, which he portrayed in a series of vivid paintings. Franklin Boggs was an accredited war artist-correspondent for Abbott in the Southwest Pacific including operations in New Guinea and Los Negros and

Manus Islands in the Admiralties. A compilation of pictures drawn from the 250 paintings of army medicine appeared in the 1945 publication *Men without Guns.* Another artist-correspondent who worked for Abbott was Kerr Eby, who had been an official artist in World War I. In a series of thirty drawings and water colors, he depicted the marines fighting on Tarawa and Bougainville. Abbott also contracted several artists to depict amphibious operations in conjunction with the navy, marine corps, and army, and in 1945 circulated an exhibition showing scenes of training, production and transportation, battle action at Saipan, Tinian, Tarawa, Bougainville and the Philippines. Many of the paintings produced for Abbott were exhibited around the United States during the war and in 1945 were presented to the nation.

Unlike the army and navy, the U.S. Marine Corps did not have a formal art program but commissioned several artists serving in the corps to record images of the campaigns in the Pacific for public relations purposes. However, each artist had to pass the rigid entrance requirements of the corps. A 1943 publication entitled *Marines at War,* reproduced works by nineteen marine corps artists including scenes of Guadalcanal. One contemporary writer noted, that marine artists on Guadalcanal lived in tents; ate what and when the marines ate, huddled in soaking foxholes, had to stand ready to repel enemy land attacks, dodged enemy bombs and shells, plodded through the swampy, malarial jungle where snipers lurked—and went to work with their pens, brushes, and paint. One artist was wounded during an enemy bombing raid at Empress Augusta Bay on Bougainville. Later, marine artists such as Harry Reeks covered the Iwo Jima campaign although many of his pictures were considered too violent for use by the corps' public relations department. A number of paintings of the fighting in the South Pacific were shown at New York's Museum of Modern Art during the war.

The Australian artist Geoffrey Mainwaring served with Australian forces in Malaya, Singapore, and New Guinea including the fighting at Buna; his colleagues in the Australian war art program, William Dargie and George Browning, were also present in New Guinea and created some striking paintings of the events; while Russell Clark and Harold Abbott saw action in the Solomons. Many of these pictures were exhibited in Australia in 1944, and one commentator criticized the artists for sacrificing realism for decorativeness. The paintings are now in the Australian War Memorial in Canberra. Like the majority of war artists, the Australian artists made quick sketches and took photographs for reference, only later working up their material into full canvases. The humid and damp conditions in the Pacific were however not conducive to paper, and many of the artists had difficulty working in water color and similar mediums.

In Japan, art school graduates were drafted into the armed forces and directed to paint the war activities emphasizing spirit over materialism. Japanese artists accompanied their armed forces from 1941 until the end of the war, while others painted at home. The representation of war had always been popular in Japan and artists had accompanied the Imperial forces in earlier wars against China and Russia. Arai Shori accompanied the naval task force dispatched to attack Pearl Harbor, and he painted scenes on board the carriers and the departing fighter bombers. His paintings reflected the tradition of the wood-block print so popular in the earlier wars. On land, the early operations in Malaya and Hong Kong were depicted by Usaburo Ihara, Konosuke Tamura, and others. Paintings included the capitulation of Hong Kong, General Jonathan Wainwright surrendering the Philippines to General Masaharu Homma in which the artist showed a Japanese army film unit recording the formal surrender, and a painting by Mukai Junikichi entitled "Record of April 9th (Bataan Peninsula General Attack)," in which large numbers of American and Filipino prisoners trudge past a Japanese officer standing on an American command car at what was the beginning of the Bataan death march. A later artist, Usaburo Ihara, painted kamikaze pilots departing from the airfield in Honshu toward the end of the war; kamikaze pilots awaiting orders at their base at Tachikawa were also the subject of a painting by Iwata Sentaro. As the war began to turn against Japan, defeats were glorified in images of sacrifice and heroism. A large volume of reproductions of war art was published in Tokyo during the war to complement a similar volume containing color and monochrome reproductions of pictures depicting the campaign in China in the late 1930s.

By war's end, the combined works of the various war artists in the Pacific numbered in the thousands. For America, they became the property of the war paintings office in the bureau of public relations, and by May 1945, more than 1,300 paintings had been received and a further 700 more were expected to arrive from the field. Shortly thereafter, ownership passed to the office of the army headquarters commandant. Plans to build a national war museum never materialized, and today the U.S. war paintings can be found in the collections of the various branches of the armed services. Many of the Japanese paintings were confiscated by the occupying forces and brought to the United States, but they were later repatriated and most of them are now in the National Modern Art Museum in Tokyo.

Whatever the merits of these war paintings, it cannot be denied that they provided an important visual representation of war and offered the only images of the fighting then available in color, particularly as much of the color film and photographs have only recently been widely circulated. Their vividness and freshness provided the necessary contrast to the monochromatic tedium of the hundreds of thousands of black-and-white photographs. The paintings and drawings covered the whole range of artistic expression, from the anecdotal and the sensational to the prosaic, but almost always with a steady dose of the drudgery and minutiae of daily life of the soldier. Artists were often able to capture the tensions and fear of life in the Pacific war, topics that elude most photographs.

FURTHER READINGS

Crane, Aimée. *Art in the Armed Forces* (1944).
McCormick, Ken, and Hamilton Darby Perry. *Images of War. The Artist's Vision of World War II* (1990).
———. *Portrait of an Army* (1991).

Peter Harrington

Washington Naval Treaty (1922) and Japan

Three years after the armistice that ended World War I, representatives of nine nations gathered in Washington, D.C. for the conference on naval disarmament and other salient issues. Among the invited were the five acknowledged premier naval powers: the United States, Great Britain, Japan, France, and Italy. Other participants were China, the Netherlands, Belgium, and Portugal, invited in order that imperial and territorial issues might be comprehensively addressed.

American sponsorship of the conference was impelled by several motives, but paramount was the belief that disarmament would greatly reduce the likelihood of world conflict. Secondarily, Republican foreign policy makers in the Harding administration hoped to lessen the Japanese threat in the Pacific by obviating the Anglo-Japanese naval alliance of 1902 and by limiting Japanese imperialism in China and Siberia. Major issues for discussion and possible solutions were initially presented by Charles E. Hughes, the U.S. secretary of state.

Japan was at best a reluctant participant. The only nation to question the parameters of discussion before the conference began, Japan hoped to limit or avoid consideration of such issues as its Twenty-One Demands on China and possession of Shantung. Nonetheless, the scope of the conference included not only these issues but also the China "Open Door" policy, the territorial integrity of Russia and China, the Anglo-Japanese treaty, the status of former German colonial possessions in the Pacific, the Pacific communications cable, narcotics traffic, and, of course, naval arms reduction.

Representatives of the nine powers came together in November 1921 and deliberations lasted until February of the following year. While the conference ultimately produced seven treaties and twelve resolutions, the most compelling issues were addressed early. Secretary Hughes, alarmed by Japan's wartime gains in the Pacific, proposed dramatic steps aimed at reducing international tensions and a burgeoning naval race between the United States, Great Britain, and Japan. In opening remarks that stunned the listening delegates, Hughes suggested strict limitations on the number of capital ships (battleships and battle cruisers) that each of the five major powers might possess. To this end, the secretary proposed a 10-year moratorium on capital-ship construction and the scrapping of sixty-six capital ships already afloat or under construction. Hughes went on to suggest that the major naval powers agree to a ratio that would fix the strength of their fleets.

The Japanese delegates were especially aghast at the U.S. proposals. If implemented, the scheme would cost Japan seventeen capital ships. To some in the imperial navy, it was a thinly disguised American scheme to deprive Japan of its growing naval predominance in the Pacific. Rumors of an end to the Anglo-Japanese naval alliance were cause for further worry. Such limitations of Japanese naval strength would be acceptable only if the security of the empire's Pacific bases were guaranteed. That requirement could be met by Anglo-American agreements to maintain the Pacific status quo and not fortify their Pacific bases. Japan's chief delegate, Admiral Kato Tomosaburo, made such a proposal, which Britain and the United States found acceptable as long as it did not apply to either Singapore or the Hawaiian Islands. The next hurdle for the Japanese delegation was the capital ship ratio to be imposed on Japan. The proposed ratio for Great Britain, the United States, Japan, France, and Italy respectively was 5:5:3:1.75:1.75. The numbers reflected the maximum tonnage allowable to each nation in hundreds of thousands of tons. Not surprisingly, some Japanese delegates perceived the formula as a means by which the two major Western powers in the Pacific could reduce Japan to second-class status without the risk of a confrontation. Despite the protestations of Japanese navy men, moderate counsels prevailed and Japan agreed to the ratio formula. Other provisions limited the displace-ment of capital ships to 35,000 tons and gun size to 16 inches.

Other thorny issues awaited resolution. China's status was a concern for a number of powers, and not all of the related issues were conducive to multilateral accord. The question of Japan's "special rights" in Shantung, acknowledged in the Versailles Treaty, was settled by the Sino-Japanese Treaty of 1922. Here Japan promised the full restoration of Shantung and the withdrawal of Japanese troops. The broader issue of China's relations with the imperial powers was addressed by Hughes, who hoped to redefine America's Open Door policy as meaning equal opportunity for the powers involved in China. The Japanese objected mainly to proposals for a Board of Reference, which Japan feared would become a tool for western interests in China and Asia. These concerns were resolved by the Nine-Power Treaty, which required the signatories to respect China's integrity, refrain from interference in the development of a stable government, and avoid obstructing equal economic opportunities for involved parties. Remaining issues were dealt with in the Four-Power Pact, by which Britain, the United States, Japan, and France agreed to maintain the colonial status quo in the Pacific. The pact also rescinded the Anglo-Japanese naval alliance of 1902.

The apparently successful pursuit of Secretary Hughes's agenda at the Washington Conference won considerable praise for the Harding administration. The American public applauded the initiative toward world peace through disarmament, which had the additional benefit of lower taxes if naval spending were to be reduced. The defects and deficiencies in this approach to peace became evident only in the next decade. Few could have understood in 1922 that the focus on capital-ship limitation was misdirected. Whatever allure that battleships might have held for admirals everywhere, they were increasingly obsolete. Even as the conference proceeded, U.S. Army Colonel Billy Mitchell was busily demonstrating that undefended dreadnoughts were vulnerable to aerial assault by his bombing and sinking of the captured German battleship *Ostfriesland*. (Air power enthusiasts usually failed to note that the bombing was against an undefended warship.) As the next world war would prove, the vessels far more crucial to naval victory were aircraft carriers, cruisers, destroyers, and submarines. The Washington treaties imposed fewer restrictions on aircraft carriers, which gradually gained the attention of naval planners. Faced with scrapping the battleships *Kaga* and *Akagi,* the imperial navy instead converted the two ships to carriers that played critical roles in Japan's war in the Pacific in the 1940s. Similarly, the United States ultimately converted half-built battlecruisers *Lexington* and *Saratoga* into prototype fast carriers. Submarines, objects of almost universal loathing because of their "inhumane" activities in World War I, were initially targeted for abolition by British delegates to the conference. However, objections on the part of the French ended this possibility. Instead, conferees turned to the unlikely instrument of a code of conduct for submarine warfare. Penned by former U.S. secretary of war Elihu Root, the guidelines naively proscribed all but the most polite of submarine attacks on merchant shipping. As the French ultimately refused to ratify Root's document, submarines were left untamed. In the next war, both the United States and Germany would utilize submarine warfare with tremendous success. The delegates meeting in Washington imposed no restrictions on cruisers or destroyers.

The Washington Conference was, at best, a laudable effort to reduce international tensions by limiting what was perceived as the preeminent weapon of naval warfare, the capital ship. The conferees did succeed in imposing significant restrictions that eased taxpayers' burdens. Probably the most lasting result of the Washington Conference was its fostering of the fast aircraft carrier. *Lexington* and *Saratoga* in World War II proved far more valuable than if they had been completed as battle cruisers—but then again, so did *Kaga* and *Akagi*.

If the conference delegates are to be faulted, it is for their lack of prescience about the decline of the battleship and the ascendancy of the aircraft carrier and submarine. It might also be noted that there was few deterrents in the approach taken in Washington. There was little if any threat of retaliation should any of the signatories move beyond the treaties' restrictions, nor was there any international instrument through which retaliatory action could be directed. These omissions were no doubt noted by revisionist powers like Japan, which later disavowed the provisions of the treaties when circumstances and opportunities presented themselves. By the 1930s, the imperial navy was expanded with no further regard for the Washington treaties.

FURTHER READINGS

Griswold, A. Whitney. *The Far Eastern Policy of the United States* (1966).

Iriye, Akira. *Imperialism: the Search for a New Order in the Far East, 1921–1931* (1968)

Neu, Charles E. *The Troubled Encounter: the United States and Japan* (1975).

O'Connell, Robert L. *Sacred Vessels: the Cult of the Battleship and the Rise of the U.S. Navy* (1991).

Wheeler, Gerald E. *Prelude to Pearl Harbor: the United States Navy and the Far East, 1921–1931* (1968).

Blaine T. Browne

SEE ALSO Aircraft Carriers: Japanese, U.S., and British; Battleships; Navy, Japanese; Navy, U.S.

Wedemeyer, Albert Coady (1897–1989)

A prominent U.S. Army officer, Albert Wedemeyer was born in Omaha, Nebraska, on July 9, 1897. He entered West Point in 1916 and two years later graduated as a member of one of the classes abbreviated by U.S. entry into World War I (1917). Commissioned a second lieutenant in the infantry, Wedemeyer graduated from the Infantry School in 1920, and until 1934, holding the rank of first lieutenant, he served with infantry regiments in the United States, the Philippines, and China and as an aid to generals in the United States and the Philippines. In 1925 he married Elizabeth Dade Embick, the daughter of Colonel Stanley Embick, who became his professional mentor and excited his interest in strategic issues and the economic aspects of warfare. From 1934 to 1936 Wedemeyer, promoted to the rank of captain in 1935, attended the Command and General Staff College, and from 1936 to 1938 he served a 2-year stint at the *Kriegsakademie,* the German War College. During the next three years, Wedemeyer was assigned to the 29th Infantry Regiment and later, now with the rank of major, the training section of the office of the chief of infantry.

In 1941, Army Chief of Staff Gen. George C. Marshall, who had been impressed by a lengthy report Wedemeyer had prepared in 1938 on German military doctrine and organization, assigned Wedemeyer to the War Plans Division of War Department General Staff. There he played a central role in the development of the "Victory Plan," which functioned as the basic planning document in mobilizing the manpower and material resources the United States would need to defeat the Axis after it entered World War II in December 1941. As a member of the War Department's Operations Division in 1942–1943, Wedemeyer, now with the rank of brigadier general, was a fervent advocate of an early cross-channel invasion of Hitler's Fortress Europe and, convinced that British strategy was dictated more by postwar political considerations than the early defeat of Germany, spoke out in high-level conferences against British Prime Minister Winston Churchill's proposals for Mediterranean operations. Late in the fall of 1943, Wedemeyer, now holding the rank of major general, was named deputy chief of staff of the newly created Southeast Asia Command. During the next year he grappled with the problems of building up forces in a theater that had a low priority in the Allied war effort, helped plan potential offensives in Sumatra and Malaya, and attempted to reconcile differences between Generalissimo Chiang Kai-shek of China and General Joseph W. Stilwell, commander of U.S. Army forces in the China-Burma-India theater and Chiang's chief of staff.

When Stilwell was relieved of his command in October 1944, Wedemeyer was appointed commander of American forces in China and Chiang's chief of staff. At the time, the Chinese war effort against Japan was flagging, and Sino-American relations were at a low ebb because of the hostility between Stilwell and Chiang. More tactful than Stilwell, Wedemeyer established a good working relationship with Chiang, yet like Stilwell he was also critical of the motives and abilities of Chinese Nationalist leaders and their failure to conduct an effective war. Promoted to the rank of lieutenant general in early 1945, Wedemeyer devoted considerable energy to reorganizing and reequipping the Nationalist army, pressed for increased aid to the Nationalists and lobbied against assistance to the Chinese Communists, and drew up plans for a Chinese offensive to recapture the south China coast from the Japanese. By the end of the war in August 1945, Wedemeyer had notably improved Nationalist morale and fighting capabilities and eased the strain in Sino-American relations.

Wedemeyer remained in his China post until April 1946, helping to oversee the demobilization of Japanese troops in China and assisting in the movement of Chiang's troops into areas previously occupied by the Japanese. As civil war broke out between Chiang's Nationalists and the Communists in the winter of 1945–1946, Wedemeyer steadfastly favored continued American support for the Nationalists and expressed doubts about the efforts of General Marshall, President Harry S. Truman's special emissary, to end the conflict through the creation of a coalition government. At the same time, he warned that Chiang was not strong enough to secure all of China in the face of Communist power and criticized the Nationalist government's corruption and ineptitude.

In July 1947, Marshall, now secretary of state, sent Wedemeyer, who was serving as commander of the Second Army, on a fact-finding mission to China and Korea. Wedemeyer spent a month in China appraising the political, economic, psychological, and military situation. Before leaving he met with Chinese Nationalist leaders and emphasized the need for wide-ranging reforms if they were to triumph over the Communists and secure large-scale aid from the United States. He also criticized the

apathy, lethargy, and abject defeatism he saw in many Nationalist quarters. Wedemeyer's strong words failed to convince the Nationalists to undertake the drastic reforms he suggested. Yet in his final report to Marshall in September 1947, Wedemeyer called for an expansion of American military and economic aid to the Nationalists in the belief that a Communist victory would be disastrous to the American position in the Cold War. The Truman administration, unwilling to undertake a major commitment to the Nationalists, rejected his recommendations and suppressed his report for two years on the grounds that it was politically too sensitive.

Following his China assignment, Wedemeyer served with the War Department General Staff and as commander of the Sixth Army before retiring in 1951. Thereafter he was an executive with the Avco Manufacturing Company and later the Rheem Manufacturing Company and was active in the conservative wing of the Republican Party. His memoir, *Wedemeyer Reports!* published in 1958, strongly criticized aspects of Allied strategy in the war against Germany, and castigated the Truman administration for failing to do more to prevent the Communist victory in China. A tall, imposing individual whose military reputation rested on his strengths in planning and administration, Wedemeyer died at Fort Belvoir, Virginia, on December 17, 1989.

FURTHER READINGS

Cline, R. *Washington Command Post: The Operations Division* (1951);

Kirkpatrick, C. *Unknown Future and a Doubtful Present: Writing the Victory Plan of 1941* (1990).

Romanus, C., and R. Sunderland. *Time Runs Out in CBI, U. S. Army in World War II* (1959).

Stueck, W. *The Wedemeyer Mission: American Politics and Foreign Policy during the Cold War* (1984).

U.S. Department of State. *United States Relations with China, with Special Reference to the Period 1944–1949* (1949).

Wedemeyer, A. *Wedemeyer Reports!* (1958).

John Kennedy Ohl

SEE ALSO China-Burma-India Theater of Operations; Stilwell, Joseph Warren

Wingate, Orde C. (1903–1944)

A British major-general, Orde C. Wingate was one of the most unconventional and controversial military commanders of World War II. He captured the imagination of the Allies as the organizer of the long-range penetration group known as the Chindits. Although almost everyone agreed that his tactics were indeed dramatic, not all were convinced that they were effective, particularly in the long run. Wingate also was perhaps the only British military commander ever to commit the heresy of criticizing the Gurkhas—which in turn earned him much criticism from the Gurkhas' legions of admirers. He may well have also been the last Allied commander personally to have killed enemy troops.

Wingate was born in Naini Tal, India, on February 26, 1903. His father, Colonel George Wingate, served more than thirty years in the Indian Army. Orde Wingate's parents were adherents to the Plymouth Brethren Protestant denomination, and he was brought up in a strictly puritan household, characterized by deep and thorough study of the Bible.

Wingate attended Charterhouse school and the Royal Military Academy at Woolwich. He was commissioned in the Royal Artillery in 1923. Although he was an excellent horseman, he had an intellectual inclination unusual for a regular British officer of the interwar period. He studied Arabic at the School of Oriental Studies in London, and in 1927 he went to the Anglo-Egyptian Sudan to further his studies of the language. While in the Sudan he managed to have himself seconded to the Sudan Defense Force and served on the Ethiopian border until 1933.

After serving several years with artillery units back in England, Wingate was assigned in 1936 as an intelligence officer in Palestine. Considering his religious upbringing, it is not surprising that he became a fervent Zionist and learned Hebrew, to the disgust of his fellow officers, most of whom were anti-Semitic. Wingate received the Distinguished Service Order for his services during the Arab Rebellion, but he also helped the Jewish settlers organize special night squads and led many of their patrols. He found himself in considerable trouble with British authorities when he advised the Hagana (the Zionist underground organization) that they would have to fight the British to establish a Jewish state.

In 1940 the British commander-in-chief of Middle East, General Sir Archibald Wavell, summoned Wingate and assigned him to organize and lead the guerrilla campaign in Ethiopia. By May 5, 1941, Wingate's small force, codenamed Gideon, had returned Emperor Haile Selassie, who had been exiled after the Italian invasion, to his throne in Addis Ababa. Wingate's Gideon force of only 2,000 managed to kill almost fifteen hundred of the enemy and wound more than two thousand. Operating largely by maneuver and bluff, they also captured more than a thousand Italian soldiers and 14,500 colonial

troops. Gideon force operated without fixed bases and relied on radio and aircraft for communication and supply. It was the prototype of Wingate's long-range penetration force concept.

About this time Wingate sent a scathing report to Wavell's headquarters complaining of their lack of support for his operation. He actually had some two hundred fifty copies of the report mimeographed for wide distribution. Members of Wavell's staff flew into a rage and confiscated and burned all the copies. Wingate, in turn, took a room at the Continental Hotel in Cairo and cut his throat in an almost-successful suicide attempt. After Wavell was transferred to India, he once more sent for Wingate, who arrived in India just prior to the completion of the British retreat from Burma. After making a study of the Japanese tactics and operational methods, Wingate developed a proposal for a long-range penetration group patterned on the experiences of his Gideon force. Wavell accepted the proposal.

In June 1942, Wingate was promoted to brigadier and given command of a mixed force of some 3,000 British, Gurkhas, and Burmese. Officially, the force was designated 77 Indian Brigade. Wingate named the force after the Chinthe, the mythical Burmese lion. This soon was corrupted to "Chindit."

The first Chindit operation started in February 1943. Crossing the Chindwin River, the force pushed 200 miles into Japanese-occupied territory and blew up bridges, cut railway lines, and otherwise disrupted Japanese lines of communication. The Chindits returned to India three months later, after suffering one-third casualties. Wingate declared that the lessons learned from the operation, could "if properly used . . . be worth the loss of many brigades." Although the mission was described as a great success by the press, in truth, it fell far short of its claims. Nonetheless, it did help to dispel the myth of Japanese invincibility in the jungle. Wingate, meanwhile, became an instant hero with the British public. In August 1943, Churchill brought Wingate to the Quadrant Conference in Quebec to brief the top Allied leaders. The following month Wingate returned to India as a major-general in charge of Special Force, which included an enlarged Chindit element.

Wingate trained his now division-sized force in the winter of 1943–1944, during which time he suffered a severe bout of typhoid. The second Chindit mission started in early March 1944. In contrast to the first operation, a larger part of the force landed behind enemy lines by glider and transport aircraft. Only one brigade entered on foot. On March 24, 1944, Wingate was flying in a bomber over the Naga jungles north of Assam on a visit to one of his units. In the middle of a tropical storm, the plane crashed in the jungle, killing all on board. A few months after his death, Wingate's only son was born.

The second Chindit mission was badly planned and failed to achieve the grand objectives Wingate had laid out. Whether or not Wingate would have made a difference had he lived remains a topic of debate. Wingate is a difficult commander to assess. He was an innovator in his use of radio and air power, but was he the man of genius Churchill and many other political leaders claimed he was? He also was insubordinate, ruthlessly ambitious, and emotionally unstable. He went out of his way to affect an air of eccentricity, wearing an old-style jungle pith helmet that Lord Mountbatten (Wavell's successor in Southeast Asia) once surmised must have come from some museum. He enjoyed being alone, sitting naked, scrubbing his body with a toothbrush, and sucking on a lemon. Occasionally he practiced all of these attributes simultaneously. Wingate was also a master practitioner of calculated rudeness when it suited his purposes. According to one of his biographers, Leonard Mosley, Wingate had "a special grease-stained uniform to wear when meeting important personages as a mark of his indifference to them."

FURTHER READINGS
Calvert, M. *Chindits: Long Range Penetration* (1973).
Mosley, L. *Gideon Goes to War* (1955).
Role, C. *Wingate's Raiders* (1944).
Sakes, C. *Orde Wingate: A Biography* (1959).

David T. Zabecki

SEE ALSO China-Burma-India Theater of Operations; Chindits; Stilwell, Joseph Warren

Women's Army Corps

Congress established the Women's Army Auxiliary Corps (WAAC) in May 1942 when it became obvious that the United States faced a shortage of able-bodied men to fight a war that was spreading into five continents. Women exceeded all expectations in their joining the new organization. In the first and in each succeeding year, the corps enrolled and trained more than fifty thousand women. By January 1943 many were serving in their volunteer status in North Africa and England. The women performed so well during their first year that Congress discarded its former misgivings about women serving in the army and, in 1943, awarded the women full military status by dropping the demeaning "Auxiliary," giving the organization the new title, the Women's Army Corps (WAC).

Between May and December 1944, more than five thousand WAC officers and enlisted women arrived in Australia and New Guinea for duty in General Douglas MacArthur's major commands in the Southwest Pacific. By October, only a few remained in Australia. The majority had moved on to New Guinea and were adapting to working and living under primitive conditions in a jungle environment.

At Port Moresby and Oro Bay, New Guinea, the women lived within a barbed wire compound in wooden barracks. They slept on cots without mattresses or sheets, but at least with mosquito netting to protect against malaria-carrying mosquitos and other insects. Their showers and toilet areas, without plumbing, were in another building.

The women felt imprisoned within their compounds, guarded by armed soldiers day and night and escorted to work daily by armed guards. They were not being protected from Japanese or native soldiers but from U.S. male troops who had not seen American women in eighteen months. The women thought the guards were unnecessary but the command insisted they remain. The WACs had to wear uncomfortable heavy twill slacks and shirts which, together with the heat and humidity, caused rashes and harbored insects even after washing. Their WAC summer cotton slacks and shirts never arrived, so when possible they borrowed cotton slacks from the nurses or male soldiers.

The New Guinea natives were friendly, and the WACs gave them cigarettes, candy, and items of clothing they could spare. After a few months, it was not unusual to see a native wearing a WAC hat. Some natives sported scarlet red hair; they dyed their black hair with the WACs' peroxide because red hair was a mark of prestige within their tribe.

The oppressive heat and humidity were not eased by frequent heavy rains that combined to make living and working conditions almost unbearable. Both men's and women's diet lacked fresh eggs, fruit, and vegetables, and meat was either dehydrated or in packaged cans. Both men and women suffered from amoebic diseases, dehydration, malaria, skin rashes, and malnutrition, not to mention homesickness. Nonetheless, they kept working, helping each other and waiting for the war to end.

A large WAC postal directory group was located at John's Gully near the base at Port Moresby. There, more than one hundred WAC officers replaced male officers whose duty it was to read and censor mail written home by the soldiers, deleting anything that would disclose their location or other unauthorized information. The group included some two hundred enlisted women who sorted, checked, readdressed, and forwarded soldiers' mail.

Hundreds of other WACs and male soldiers worked together in huge supply depots, receiving, storing, and keeping track of signal, quartermaster, engineer, transportation, and ordnance items.

All these equipment services were needed by the combat troops as they fought their way up the coast of New Guinea on their way to retaking the Philippine Islands from the Japanese. The women kept records on data processing machines, did stenography and typing, operated the switchboards, drove trucks, and cooked. Some women worked as intelligence analysts and decoders, defining the location of Japanese troop transports and supply ships, and their radio codes.

The WAC units moved forward in large groups as Allied combat troops pushed back the enemy. Most were flown some eight hundred miles up the New Guinea coast to Hollandia. Japanese aircraft strafed the landing zone as the first group arrived, but the planes were soon driven away. The climate was even worse here than at the earlier WAC unit locations. The next major move came in November to the island of Leyte, part of the Philippine Islands, where they continued their work in whatever office space was available.

In March 1945, four days after most fighting had ended in the Philippine Islands, the WACs arrived in the outskirts of the devastated city of Manila, where they lived in abandoned schools, colleges, and even a race track. Initially, they had no running water, electricity, or pre- pared food, living instead on K rations for days until additional supplies arrived. The women could hear sounds of combat coming from the city and the women themselves captured some Japanese intruders in their area.

Once again, they resumed their jobs wherever they could find space to work. After the Japanese surrender in August 1945, the WACs gradually departed Manila by ship between September 1945 and January 1946.

Some of the WAC units that served in the Southwest Pacific Area (SWPA) were: U.S. Army Services of Supply (SWPA) WAC Detachment (5200 Army Service Unit-ASU), Central Postal Directory WAC Detachment (5203d ASU), GHQ USAFFE WAC Detachment (5205th ASU), Far East Air Forces WAC Detachment, and the Office of the WAC Staff Director, U.S. Armed Forces Far East, General Headquarters, SWPA.

In praising the WACs performance of duty, General MacArthur termed them "my best soldiers," saying they worked harder, complained less, and were better disciplined than the men. After more than a year of service under great hardships, the women considered this their most prized accolade.

FURTHER READINGS

Treadwell, M. *The Women's Army Corps in World War II* (1954).
Strzelcyyk, H. "Oro Bay—New Guinea," *WAC Journal* (1971).

Bettie J. Morden

Yalta Conference

Meeting held in February 1945 in the Crimea, U.S.S.R. The Yalta Conference was the second and last meeting of the "Big Three"—Churchill, Roosevelt, and Stalin. Much of the actual business of the meeting concerned itself with the impending defeat of Germany and the nature of postwar Europe. The participants reaffirmed their pledge to seek nothing less than the unconditional surrender of Germany. The Western allies accepted that the Soviet Union would dominate in Poland and the rest of eastern Europe, a recognition of the fact that the Red Army would occupy virtually the entire area by the end of the war. Plans were also made for postwar Germany; the Oder and Neisse rivers would make up its eastern border, and the country would be divided into four zones of occupation (Roosevelt insisted on, and Stalin eventually acquiesced in, a French zone of occupation in addition to those of the United States, Great Britain, and the Soviet Union.).

It was only four days into the conference that the participants began to address matters pertaining to Asia and the Pacific. Stalin repeated his offer, first made at the 1943 Tehran Conference, to assist Britain and the United States in the defeat of Japan after Germany had been defeated. His price for intervention, however, was considerable. Not only did he demand the return of the territories lost by Russia in the Russo-Japanese War of 1904–1905 (Port Arthur and the southern half of Sakhalin Island), but he also asked for the Kurile Islands and western recognition of a Soviet satellite regime in Mongolia. In return the Soviet dictator promised to enter the war three months after the surrender of Germany, agreed to provide economic and military aid to the Chinese Nationalists, and pledged to return Manchuria to Chinese sovereignty once the Red Army had cleared it of Japanese troops. Roosevelt and Churchill readily agreed to all this, the former having been advised by his joint chiefs of staff just before the conference that Soviet entry into the war against Japan was absolutely necessary for victory.

Some historical accounts of Yalta in the immediate postwar years claimed that the conference amounted nothing more than a complete sellout to Soviet demands by an enfeebled Roosevelt (he died in April 1945), handing Stalin an impregnable position in both Europe and Asia. The truth, however, is somewhat more complex. Most of the points discussed at Yalta—the fate of Poland and southeast Europe, and the general principle of concessions to the Soviet Union in return for a declaration of war against Japan—had been agreed to at Tehran in 1943.

Furthermore, if the territorial prizes offered to Stalin seem excessive, given that the Soviet contribution to the war in Asia lasted less than a week, this should be viewed in light of the circumstances of the time. After all, in February 1945 even those few who knew of the existence of the atomic bomb project had no idea if it would ever work, let alone be ready for use against Japan. The Allies were making progress against the Japanese—the British in Burma and the Americans in the Southwest and Central Pacific—but the fighting so far had been intense and the casualties high; the Japanese certainly showed no signs of capitulating in the near future. Even more frightening for the Allies was the success of Japan's *Ichigo* offensive of 1944, which had all but shattered the military strength of the Chinese Nationalists. If a new front were not opened in Manchuria, it was feared, the Japanese might be able to transfer large numbers of troops to Burma and the Philippines. Little wonder, then, that the Joint Chiefs urged Roosevelt to secure Soviet involvement at any reasonable cost.

FURTHER READINGS

Gaddis, J. *The United States and the Origins of the Cold War, 1941–1947* (1972).

MacNeill, W. *America, Britain, and Russia: Their Co-operation and Conflict, 1941–1946* (1953).

Snell, J. *Illusion and Necessity: The Diplomacy of Global War, 1939–1945* (1963).

Weinberg, G. *A World At Arms: A Global History of World War II* (1994).

John E. Moser

SEE ALSO Roosevelt, Franklin Delano

Yamamoto Isoroku (1884–1943)

Commander in Chief of the Japanese Combined Fleet, Admiral Isoroku Yamamoto was born April 4, 1884 in Nagaoka, Niigata Prefecture. His father, Sadayoshi Takano, an impoverished former samurai, married into and was adopted by the Takano family. His first marriage produced four sons, and after his wife died he married her sister, Mine. Isoroku was the couple's third and last child. As a youth, Isoroku attended a Christian missionary school. Although he never converted to Christianity, he often kept a Bible in his desk, prompting arguments with Buddhist and Shinto acquaintances.

In 1901, Yamamoto entered the naval academy at Etajima, graduating in 1904. The next year, during the Russo-Japanese War, he served as a cadet aboard cruiser, *Nisshin*. He was promoted ensign on board the warship after being severely wounded and losing two fingers on his left hand when an 8-inch gun burst during combat.

In 1908, Yamamoto enrolled in the basic course in naval gunnery school and completed the advanced course in 1911. A promising officer, he rose rapidly in rank and entered the navy staff college in 1915. Promoted to lieutenant commander in 1916, he graduated from the staff college the same year. At that time he registered as the adoptive son of the late Tatewaki Yamamoto, a former ally of his father in the 1868–1869 Boshin War. Two years later he married a relative of Admiral Gentaro Yamashita. His wife, Reiko, bore him four children, but Yamamoto apparently preferred the company of geishas.

From 1919 until 1921 Yamamoto was posted to the United States as a naval representative and language officer. Promoted to captain, he attended an English language class at Harvard and developed an appreciation for American culture and history, recommending Carl Sandburg's *Lincoln* to colleagues. During his American tour, Yamamoto also made a side trip to Mexico in order to study oil production. A complex personality, Yamamoto eschewed alcohol but was passionately fond of poetry, tobacco, female companionship, and gambling. He was a master of Japanese games of chance such as *shogi* and *go*, as well as poker, billiards, and bridge.

Yamamoto returned to the United States in 1923, accompanying Admiral Ide Kenji. The two officers toured the United States, England, France, Germany, Austria and Italy. Yamamoto was most impressed by America's economic strength, but more important, he developed a profound international perspective that most Japanese officers lacked.

On his return to Japan in September 1924, Yamamoto was appointed to the new Kasumigaura Aviation Corps where, three months later, he became second-in-command and director of studies. This assignment was a turning point in his career, shifting his focus from gunnery to aviation. He also won the respect of younger officers for his technical expertise and willingness to undergo pilot training.

From 1926 to 1928, Yamamoto served once again in the United States as naval attaché at the Japanese embassy in Washington. Again immersing himself in western social life, including a visit to Havana (paradise for this officer, given his love of cigars, gambling, and ladies of the evening), he also made a detailed study of American aviation development.

On his return to Japan in March 1928, Yamamoto was briefly assigned to the naval general staff before assuming command of training cruiser *Isuzu*. He next commanded large aircraft carrier *Akagi,* from which he soon was transferred to the navy ministry. In 1930 he served as an assistant to the Japanese delegation at the London Naval Disarmament Conference.

Promoted to rear admiral in 1930, Yamamoto took over the technical division of the navy's aeronautics department. During his 3-year tenure he successfully pushed for original Japanese aircraft designs, rather than the usual production of copies of foreign prototypes. He was instrumental in the development of the twin-engine Mitsubishi Type 1 Betty attack bomber and the Type 96 Nell.

From October 1933 to June 1934 Yamamoto commanded the 1st Carrier Division from his flagship *Akagi*. His next posting was ashore, with the naval general staff and navy ministry. Promoted to vice-admiral in 1934, he was a delegate at the London Naval Conference of 1935, where he successfully resisted limitations on Japanese naval expansion.

After a brief stint as head of the navy's aeronautics department, Yamamoto reluctantly accepted a political post as navy vice-minister under Admiral Osami Nagano, whom he personally disliked. Nevertheless, he served for nearly three years in the successive Hirota, Hayashi, first Konoe, and Hiranuma cabinets. Although he referred to this position as a "high grade office boy," Yamamoto significantly strengthened the navy's position against militant army factions. In addition, he offended right-wing elements in the army by openly criticizing escalation of the war in China and Japan's proposed entry into the Tripartite Pact.

On August 30, 1939, Yamamoto was appointed commander in chief of the Japanese Combined Fleet. On his first day of duty on board the flagship, battleship *Nagato*, he learned of the German invasion of Poland. Aware of the implications of the escalating European war, he was enraged when the Japanese navy endorsed the Tripartite Pact, which he viewed as a step toward a disastrous war with the United States. Yamamoto's warnings of inadequate Japanese preparations for war and his anti-Tripartite stance alienated many younger officers, who considered him overly sympathetic to England and the United States.

Still, as a professional naval officer, Yamamoto saw no alternative but to perform his duties to the best of his abilities. Although limited by fuel shortages, he initiated intense training throughout the fleet. His crews practiced gunnery, torpedo warfare, and night maneuvers on an unprecedented scale. The truly progressive Yamamoto considered battleships outmoded and gave precedence to carrier operations.

Promoted to full admiral November 15, 1940, Yamamoto began planning the operation that he fervently hoped would destroy America's Pacific Fleet and force an immediate negotiated settlement. Although most hypothetical Japanese strategies against the United States had focused on the Philippines, a Pearl Harbor attack plan had existed since the 1920s. On January 7, 1941, he submitted his 9-page "Views on Preparations for War" to Navy Minister Koshiro Oikawa.

On August 1, 1941, after freezing Japan's American assets, Washington imposed a ban on exports to Japan. This was prompted by the latter's continued aggression in China and Indochina. In response to the deteriorating situation, Yamamoto ordered intensified carrier training operations. Lieutenant-Commander Mitsuno Fuchida, *Akagi* flight commander and leader of the attack force, led his pilots in repeated practice runs over Kagoshima harbor, which closely resembled Pearl Harbor. On November 5, 1941, the chief of the naval general staff, Osami Nagano, issued an order for Yamamoto to begin hostilities against the United States within the first ten days of December.

On November 18, the attack force under Vice-Admiral Chuichi Nagumo on *Akagi* departed for the southern Kurile Islands; and on November 26, Nagumo's task force of six carriers with supporting vessels set sail in heavy seas for Hawaii. On December 2, Yamamoto sent Nagumo the portentous message, "Climb Mt. Niitaka 1208," the go-ahead code for the attack. The first bombs struck Wheeler Field at 7:55 A.M., December 7, 1941. The advance wave of 183 aircraft was followed an hour later by a second wave of 170 that continued the destruction.

Yamamoto received preliminary reports aboard his flagship *Nagato* in the Hashirajima anchorage while playing *shogi*. Upon hearing of the sinking of four American battleships and severe damage to three others, his staff and crew erupted in jubilation despite Nagumo's failure to order a second strike. Although his own losses amounted to just twenty-nine aircraft, Yamamoto appeared depressed; the war he had never wanted was a reality. On December 10 his staff did note his obvious elation upon hearing of the sinking of modern British battleship *Prince of Wales* and aged battlecruiser *Repulse*. Yamamoto had long predicted the obsolescence of capital ships and had also helped develop the types of planes used in the attack.

Ironically, on February 12, 1942, Yamamoto transferred his flag to *Yamato*, which, along with its sister ship, *Musashi*, were the largest battleships in history. Weighing more than seventy-two thousand tons and mounting nine 18.1-inch guns, the two ships were designed to dominate surface sea warfare. Yamamoto had opposed their construction in favor of aircraft carriers.

Yamamoto was determined to finish the job begun at Pearl Harbor. His major goal was to lure the American fleet, and especially its carriers, into battle and defeat it before America's industrial might could be brought to bear. His first attempt, coupled with amphibious assaults on Port Moresby, Tulagi, and Guadalcanal, was thwarted in the Battle of the Coral Sea in May 1942.

The Battle of the Coral Sea signalled the end of strictly surface-to-surface fleet actions. For the first time in history, carrier-based planes alone had decided a major battle; the major units of each fleet had never sighted each other, a trend which Yamamoto had predicted years before. Although a Japanese tactical victory, the Battle of the Coral Sea denied Yamamoto the use of lost carrier *Shoho*, in addition to carriers *Shokaku* and *Zuikaku*, which required repairs and refitting.

In late May, Yamamoto launched his most ambitious effort to destroy the American Pacific Fleet. In early June, as carriers and transports carried out a diversionary attack on the Aleutian Islands, his main force under Admiral Nagumo moved to attack Midway Island in the Central Pacific.

Nagumo's main fleet included *Akagi, Kaga, Hiryu,* and *Soryu,* as well as supporting vessels. Yamamoto, aboard *Yamato* with a battleship force northwest of Midway, directed the probably too-elaborate operation. In Hawaii, Admiral Chester W. Nimitz directed a combined carrier force including *Yorktown, Enterprise,* and *Hornet,* under the command of Admiral Raymond A. Spruance. Again advised of the Japanese plans by intercepted intelligence, Nimitz ordered Spruance to confront the divided Japanese fleet.

On the morning of June 4, Nagumo's bombers inflicted extensive damage on Midway's installations. American dive-bombers, however, sank *Akagi, Kaga, Soryu,* and *Hiryu.* In all, Yamamoto lost four of his six modern fleet-carriers and scores of irreplaceable pilots. His greatest defeat again proved his earlier pronouncements on the value of naval air power. After Midway, Yamamoto knew the war was lost.

Defeats at Midway and Guadalcanal forced Japan into a defensive posture. In the meantime, in February 1943, Yamamoto transferred his flag from *Yamato* to *Musashi* at Truk. Later he shifted his headquarters again to the base at Rabaul on eastern New Britain. In early April his staff announced he would make a 1-day tour of bases in the Solomon Islands. The transmission was once again intercepted by American intelligence, which forwarded it to Nimitz. Nimitz concluded the elimination of his Japanese counterpart merited the risk of compromising American intelligence and, with final approval from President Roosevelt, ordered the interception of Yamamoto's aircraft. On April 18, 1943, as Yamamoto and his staff were flying over Bougainville in two Betty bombers, they were attacked by a flight of American P-38 fighters sent expressly for the purpose. Both Japanese planes were shot down and Yamamoto was killed. Admiral Yamamoto's body was recovered and his ashes returned to Tokyo, where a state funeral was held June 5, 1943. Yamamoto's death cost Japan its most capable strategist.

FURTHER READINGS

Age, Hayrack. *The Reluctant Admiral: Yamamoto and the Imperial Navy* (1979).

Griess, Thomas E., ed. *The Second World War: Asia and the Pacific* (1984).

Liddell Hart, B. H. *History of the Second World War* (1970).

Okumiya, Masatake, Jiro Horikoshi, and Caidin Martin. *Zero!* (1956).

Toland, John. *But Not in Shame: The Six Months After Pearl Harbor* (1971).

Jeff Kinard

SEE ALSO Coral Sea, Battle of the; Midway, Battle of; Navy, Japanese

Yamashita Tomoyuki (1885–1946)

Dubbed "the Tiger of Malaya," Tomoyuki Yamashita often has been ranked as the best Japanese general of World War II. Isolated from the other Japanese leaders, he was a complex and somewhat fatalistic character. He fought in only two campaigns, Malaya from 1941 to 1942 and the Philippines from 1944 to 1945. But his performance in these two campaigns was exceptional, demonstrating in the face of difficult odds an ability to conduct both lightning offensives and staunch defensives. However, Yamashita's fame largely derives from his unjust execution in 1946 after being tried for war crimes by a U.S. military commission. Nevertheless, Yamashita's behavior during the war was not outstandingly moral. Saddened by the futility of the war, his true greatness lay in his determination to disobey his superiors in order to preserve his army and delay the defeat of Japan as long as possible.

The son of a doctor, Tomoyuki Yamashita was born on November 8, 1885 in Osugi Mura, a village on Shikoku Island. He graduated from the military academy at Hiroshima in 1908 and entered the infantry. He rose quickly in the ranks and was known to be highly intelligent. From 1919 to 1935, he served successively as the Japanese military attaché in Switzerland, Germany, and Austria.

Unfortunately, Yamashita became embroiled in the factional fighting within the Japanese army in the late 1930s. He sympathized with the Imperial Way (Kodoka), one of the two factions within the Japanese army vying for political power. This led to bitter antipathy between him and Hideki Tojo, who was a leader in the opposing Control Faction (Toseiha). In 1935, Yamashita, a major general, became head of the investigations board of the war ministry. Thus, Yamashita was in Tokyo when several junior officers, supporters of the Imperial Way, launched a coup known as the Young Officers Revolt against the civilian government. Yamashita had been a mentor for two of the coup's leaders but had not been directly involved in its planning. During the coup, Yamashita served as mediator between the general headquarters and the rebellious officers. In that capacity, Yamashita sympathized with the young officers until the emperor directly ordered the rebellious soldiers to return to their barracks. Faced with his duty to obey the emperor, Yamashita then told the officers to back down and commit *seppuku,* ritual suicide, to save face. Remanded for his involvement in the coup, Yamashita was given a command in Korea, where he would see little action. Furthermore, his actions in the coup earned him powerful enemies, making him suspicious of his peers for the remainder of his career.

Nevertheless, in 1939, Yamashita was promoted to lieutenant general and sent on a military mission to Germany and Italy. On the mission, Yamashita met Hitler, whom he described as "an unimpressive little man." He also snored through a lecture by Herman Goering, the head of the Luftwaffe. Hitler tried to bully Yamashita, to no avail, into agreeing that Japan should declare war against Great Britain and the United States. Yamashita also believed that Germany would lose the Battle of Britain. Nevertheless, his tour of Germany convinced him that air forces were now the paramount arm in modern warfare.

When Yamashita returned to Japan, he reported his conviction that Japan should not go to war with the United States and Great Britain. Instead of extending its power, he thought that Japan should consolidate its political influence. He believed that Japan required time to prepare for war, especially against Russia. The air force needed to be expanded and the equipment of the Japanese army, which lagged behind the German army, needed to be updated. Yamashita called for the mechanization of the army, the development of a stronger tank arm, and the training of airborne troops. He predicted that two years would be required to modernize the Japanese military. Tojo disagreed with Yamashita and most of the report's advice was disregarded.

On November 6, 1941, as Japan was preparing for war against the United States and Great Britain, Yamashita was appointed to command Twenty-fifth Army in the invasion of Malaya. The plan to attack Malaya was devised by Lieutenant Colonel Masanobu Tsuji, Twenty-fifth Army Chief of Operations and Planning Staff, who realized that Singapore was vulnerable to an attack across the Johore Straits. Previously, Tsuji had been part of a special tropical warfare research unit in Taiwan. Yamashita readily utilized Tsuji's knowledge. The British had nearly twice as many men as the Japanese in Malaya but lacked air superiority. The main roads ran along the western coast of Malaya where all of the major population centers were located. Expecting the British to cling to these roads, Yamashita planned to use repeated flanking movements through the jungle and the rubber plantations to dislodge and dislocate the defending British and Indian formations. Because of foreseeable logistical difficulties, Yamashita employed only three divisions in the assault: Lieutenant General Takuo Matsui's 5th Japanese Division, Lieutenant General Renya Mutaguchi's 18th Japanese Division, and Lieutenant General Takuma Nishimura's Imperial Guards Division, plus 3d Japanese Tank Brigade. He was also supported by 459 aircraft of 3d Air Division and 159 naval aircraft.

On December 8, 1941, the Twenty-fifth Army landed at Singora and Patani, on the east coast of Thailand. A brigade group of 18th Japanese Division also landed at Kota Bahru in Malaya to secure the Japanese flank against the 8th Indian Infantry Brigade. Yamashita insisted on landing with the lead convoy at Singora. Only the landings at Kota Bahru faced serious opposition, which was nevertheless overcome. From Thailand, the 5th Japanese Division, with Tsuji in the van, moved quickly into Malaya and attacked the British defensive line at Jitra. The British had spent six months fortifying the Jitra Line, which was expected to hold the Japanese for three months. On December 11, Yamashita conducted a night attack with tank support along the main road combined with a flanking movement to the east. Despite stiff fighting, the defending 11th Indian Infantry Division fell back in disorder. Thousands of British and Indian troops surrendered. Captured supplies fed and fueled the Twenty-fifth Army for the remainder of the campaign. Jitra was the decisive battle of the campaign. Thereafter, Yamashita drove straight down the peninsula exploiting his victory. Abandoning caution, he believed that sustained momentum would preempt and overcome enemy resistance. Repeated flanking movements, often including minor amphibious landings against the enemy rear, drove the British back. On January 11, 1942, he captured Kuala Lumpur and large stocks of supplies. Only on the crucial line of the Muar River was Twenty-fifth Army's advance momentarily held when it confronted elements of 8th Australian Infantry Division. Nevertheless, by the end of January, Yamashita had reached the Straits of Johore and was preparing to assault Singapore.

During the advance, Japanese soldiers and prisoners periodically committed atrocities. Yamashita's orders that prisoners of war to be treated well were not widely obeyed. The Imperial Guards Division beheaded 200 wounded men near the Muar River. In Singapore, Japanese troops butchered wounded men in the hospitals. Yamashita sentenced one officer to thirty days close arrest because three of his subordinates had looted and raped during the advance through Malaya. This is one of the few instances where Yamashita took action against atrocities, although he was never directly involved in any of them.

Yamashita guided the assault on Singapore from the palace of the Sultan of Johore, which had a clear view of the whole battle line. His plan was that, on February 7, Imperial Guards Division would make active feints to draw the enemy to the eastern end of Singapore Island. One night later, 18th and 5th Japanese Divisions would cross onto the western end of Singapore Island, followed by Imperial Guards Division the following evening. Then the divisions would attack under heavy air and artillery support. Yamashita needed to expedite the attack because he was already being burdened by his supply line, which extended all the way back to Thailand. With some hitches, the operation went as planned. The British, despite their numerical superiority, crumbled as the Japanese troops boldly advanced. On February 15, Yamashita accepted the British surrender.

After the victory, Prime Minister Tojo, probably jealous, swiftly and secretly sent Yamashita to command the Japanese army in Manchuria. Facing the Soviet Union, it was a vital post but kept Yamashita away from the fighting front. Over the next two years, the situation in the Pacific deteriorated for the Japanese. On September 25, 1944, Yamashita, now a full general, was appointed to command the Fourteenth Area Army in the Philippines. Imperial General Headquarters (IGHQ) implemented a plan, known as *Sho-1,* to fight the decisive battle of the Pacific war in the Philippines. Yamashita's object in the Philippines, according to IGHQ, was to stage a delaying action on Leyte Island and then fight a decisive battle on Luzon Island, the main island of the Philippines and the location of the capital city of Manila. Privately, Yamashita did not believe that the Philippines could be successfully defended. Moreover, at this point, Yamashita was certain that Japan would lose the war. Indeed, he personally had become very fatalistic and expected to die in the Philippines. However, Count Hisaichi Terauchi, commander of the Southern Army and Yamashita's superior, had a different view of operations. He wanted a decisive battle fought at the point of the initial American landings, which was likely to be Leyte.

Yamashita's position in the Philippines was very weak. His troops were poorly trained and too few to mount an adequate defense. He lacked supplies, and ground defenses were incomplete despite more than two years of Japanese occupation. Yamashita had been in the Philippines for less than a week when the Americans landed at Leyte. His chief of staff, Lieutenant General Akira Muto, would not arrive until October 20, a day after the American landings. Additionally, an increasingly effective guerrilla war plagued the Japanese rear. Yamashita implemented a harsh antiguerrilla policy that would later haunt

him at his war crimes trial. Ironically, Yamashita opposed the policy of having the Japanese army provide for the administration of the Filipino civil population. Yamashita later lamented Japan's failure to assist and cooperate with occupied foreign populations.

Lieutenant General Sasaku Suzuki, Yamashita's chief of staff in Malaya, commanded Thirty-fifth Army defending Leyte Island. Although Yamashita had ordered Suzuki to fight a delaying action, Terauchi ordered that the decisive battle be fought out on Leyte when the Americans landed on October 19. Without adequate shipping to sustain an intense battle on Leyte, Yamashita objected strongly to Terauchi's order, but to no avail. By November, Yamashita believed that the battle for Leyte was lost. The Americans were pushing steadily forward and reinforcements sent to Leyte were being consumed in the battle, weakening the defense of Luzon. Yamashita wanted to pull out, but Lieutenant General Jo Iimura, Chief of Staff of the Southern army, demanded that everything be staked on Leyte. Despite Yamashita's personal protests, Terauchi and Iimura would not abandon the doomed battle. Finally, on December 13, Yamashita directly disobeyed orders and refused to send any more troops to Leyte. On December 22, he told Suzuki to abandon decisive warfare and conduct "self-sufficient" combat. Suzuki would hold out until April 1945 on Leyte before dying in an attempt to pull his army off of the island.

Yamashita had deployed his forces on Luzon in three groups. The Shobu Group, under Yamashita's personal command, consisted of 150,000 men and was located in the mountainous north of the island and defended the expected American point of landing, Lingayen Gulf. The Kembu Group, 30,000 men strong, defended Clark Field and the Bataan Peninsula. The Shimbu Group, with 80,000 men, defended the south of the island, including Manila. Yamashita intended to create an in-depth defense of Luzon and endorsed an operational strategy of protracted action. This entailed a concerted effort to check the breakthrough of the American forces into central Luzon as long as possible and, thereby, delay and contain the American advance against Japan. He withdrew his headquarters north to Baguio, 5,400 feet high in the mountains. There would be no last-ditch defense of the beaches or the central plain of Luzon, where U.S. firepower, airpower, and mobility would place his forces at a distinct disadvantage. He also told Yokoyama to fight a protracted action in his area of operations. Yamashita planned to abandon Manila over the protests of Vice Admiral Mikawa who had 25,000 naval troops of 31st Naval Defense Force deployed in the city. Yamashita also wanted to surrender the 4,000 U.S. prisoners of war in his possession immediately upon MacArthur's landing.

MacArthur landed at Lingayen Gulf on January 9, 1945, and quickly advanced. Yamashita's limited counteroffensives were mauled by U.S. airpower before they could reach the front. Additionally, the defensive line through San Jose was prematurely abandoned. Bolstered by overwhelming superiority in armor and artillery, MacArthur pressed through the central plain and isolated Yamashita to the north. With U.S. forces encircling Manila, 31st Naval Defense Force was unable, as well as unwilling, to withdraw. Cut off in the mountains of northern Luzon, Yamashita was not cognizant of the situation at Manila. He even wanted Yokoyama to counterattack into Manila in order pull out the naval troops. This never occurred. In the ensuing battle for Manila, 100,000 civilians were killed, many by Japanese troops, who resorted to rape and murder in the face of inevitable death. Yamashita was unaware of these atrocities and had no control over the naval troops in Manila.

In the north, Yamashita strengthened his in-depth defensive position ensconced in the mountains around Baguio and the rice-producing Cagayan Valley. In February 1945, MacArthur began attacking Yamashita's forces. The Japanese disputed every inch of ground and the Americans did not break through until April 1945, by which time Yamashita had already prepared a withdrawal further into the mountains. In a continuous delaying action that exacted a heavy toll on the Americans, Yamashita retired to a defensive redoubt deeper in the mountains, near Kianyon and Mount Prog. Still intent on confining U.S. troops to Luzon, Yamashita intended to preserve his forces and continue fighting as long as possible. Therefore, he instructed his troops to abandon the traditional Japanese emphasis on a quick death. He told the soldiers that holding out for days, in order to contain and wear down the Americans, would be a much more difficult task than simply dying quickly with honor. As planned, U.S. forces were tied down and suffered heavy casualties unsuccessfully trying to reduce Yamashita's stronghold.

Nonetheless, by July, Yamashita's army was in a perilous condition. His last artillery ammunition had been expended and his troops were ravaged by disease and starvation. But Yamashita would not allow a final suicide charge. Instead, he planned to break out of the Allied encirclement in September and then disperse his forces into guerrilla bands to continue the war. However, the dropping of the atomic bombs and the surrender of Japan ended this plan. Despite his fatalism, Yamashita refused to commit *seppuku,* expecting to die as punishment for his involvement in the war. He also forbid his troops from

doing so, instructing them that it was their duty to go home and rebuild Japan. Intent on ensuring that the remaining 50,000 men of the Shobu Group did not die of starvation, on September 2, 1945, Yamashita walked down from the mountains and surrendered. He wrote:

My men have been gathered from the mountains
Like wildflowers
Now it is my turn to go
And I go gladly

Shortly after signing the surrender document, Yamashita was placed under arrest for war crimes.

Yamashita's trial by an American military commission in Manila, which set a legal precedent regarding the responsibility of commanders in preventing war crimes, is infamous. Yamashita was accused of having unlawfully failed to discharge his duty to control the brutality of his subordinates. The tribunal brought 123 charges against him, including responsibility for the deaths of 57,000 civilians. Most of these deaths had occurred in Manila. Additionally, Yamashita was accused of having systematically killed 25,000 civilians as reprisals for guerrilla warfare and having ordered the deaths of 151 U.S. POWs. None of the atrocities were the direct result of orders from Yamashita, although his harsh policy against guerrilla warfare was indirectly relevant. As noted above, Yamashita had no control over the actions of the naval troops in Manila and had been physically disconnected from Manila by the success of the MacArthur's advance. Furthermore, only 135 civilian deaths were counted in the Shobu Group area of operations, hardly constituting the alleged systematic campaign of murder and destruction. Nevertheless, the prosecution insisted that a commander was always responsible for the actions of his subordinates. The trial did not meet the usual standards of Western justice. For example, there were few restrictions on the submission of evidence by the prosecution. Even perjured testimony was tacitly permitted. The commission, pressed by MacArthur to expedite a verdict, found Yamashita guilty.

The defense submitted an appeal to the U.S. Supreme Court. The Supreme Court upheld the verdict. However, Justices Rutledge and Murphy drafted dissenting opinions. In particular, Murphy stated that evidence had been improperly admitted in the trial, a sentence had been delivered summarily, and there had been no attempt to prove that Yamashita had violated any laws of war. Moreover, the trial was unprecedented in convicting an enemy general, not merely for committing an illegal act, but for failing to take action to prevent illegal acts. Murphy wrote: "In short, we charge you with the crime of inefficiency in controlling your troops. We will judge the discharge of your duties by the disorganization which we ourselves created in large part. Our standards are whatever we wish to make them." MacArthur personally ordered Yamashita to be executed by hanging, which the Japanese considered a dishonorable way to die. He ignored a petition by 86,000 Japanese requesting that Yamashita be permitted to die by ritual suicide or a firing squad. Amidst demonstrations in Tokyo, Yamashita was hanged on February 23, 1946. The unjustness of the trial and MacArthur's vengeful behavior made Yamashita into a martyr of sorts among the Japanese and many other sympathetic people. Before his execution he wrote:

The world I know is a shameful place
There will never come a better time
For me to die

However, Yamashita should not be considered a martyr. The fact that he was unjustly executed does not obscure the fact that he also never pressed for greater morality in the behavior of the Japanese army. Rather, admiration for Yamashita should derive from his determination, in the Philippines, to disregard the orders of his superiors in order to preserve the lives of his men and delay the invasion of his homeland. He generated unusually strong loyalty and affection from his men, personally sharing in the hardships of the Philippines campaign. And Yamashita had the intellectual acumen to abandon the futile dogma of decisive battle and develop his own, albeit unglamorous, method of waging an unwinnable war.

FURTHER READINGS

Richard Lael. *The Yamashita Precedent: War Crimes and Command Responsibility* (1982).
John Deane Potter. *A Soldier Must Hang* (1963).
Arthur Swinson. *Four Samurai* (1968).
Masanobu Tsuji. *Japan's Greatest Victory, Britain's Worst Defeat,* trans. Margaret Lake (1997).

Carter Malkasian

SEE ALSO Army, Japanese

Yank

Yank was the U.S. Army's weekly illustrated magazine of news, feature stories and viewpoints of World War II. It was an innovative contribution to military journalism in that it was established by the War Department as an organ of the enlisted man, written, edited, managed and published by ordinary soldiers. Commissioned officers at-

tached to *Yank* performed only administrative functions. They had no influence or power over editorial policy. *Yank's* competition was *Stars and Stripes,* an Army-produced newspaper that was created during World War I to provide current news to the soldiers. *Stars and Stripes* was revived during World War II as a major component of informative military journalism, but it was governed by strict military protocol. All major editorial and policy-making positions were held by commissioned officers who served the purposes and philosophies of their superior officers. *Yank,* by contrast, was run by—and for—enlisted men, an unprecedented development in the history of military journalism.

Yank began operations in May 1942 in an office at 205 East 42d Street in New York City, with a $50,000 loan from the War Department, under the direction of the Army Information and Education Division of Army Service Forces. The publication was to be distributed to all servicemen, to contain no advertising, and was to sell for 5 cents per copy.

The first issue of 250,000 copies was printed and released on June 17, 1942. The cover carried the banner "Why We Fight" and a photo depicting a U.S. Army artillery crew in Australia firing practice rounds. The domestic edition of *Yank* was supplemented in November 1942 with a British edition published in London and intended for distribution in North Africa and eventually on the continent of Europe. Each weekly edition consisted of sixteen to twenty-four pages of news, commentary, letters to the editor, cartoons, and photos of currently popular pin-up girls such as Betty Grable and Rita Hayworth. In addition, six to eight pages of material with a local interest would be added by the various local editors in the regions that the magazine would be distributed. Eventually, twenty-one separate editions were printed on seventeen presses in the various theaters of the war.

Sergeant Joseph McCarthy became managing editor in New York in November 1942, and he and his staff oversaw each edition throughout the remaining years of the war. Outstanding contributors to *Yank* during its publication life were Andrew (Andy) Rooney, Merle Miller, William Saroyan, George Baker (whose cartoon "The Sad Sack" continues to amuse readers), the artist Howard Brodie, and many others. Four *Yank* correspondents were killed in action and sixteen were awarded purple hearts for wounds received covering battlefield action.

Eventually *Yank* had a paid circulation of over 2 million copies and a probable readership of six to seven times that number, as enlisted men passed the weekly editions around to each other. By the end of its run after V-J Day in 1945, *Yank* had accumulated a surplus of over $2 million, which was subsequently given over to the U.S. Treasury.

Often controversial in its editorial policy, *Yank's* one major concession to the the sensibilities of its military and political superiors was a tendency to avoid depicting American casualties or photos of dead GIs. Top Army officers such as General George C. Marshall openly supported *Yank,* while others, notably General George Patton, often criticized it. Throughout the war, in the face of opposition and controversy, *Yank* steadfastly maintained the singular viewpoint of the enlisted man. *Yank* published its final edition on October 5, 1945.

FURTHER READINGS

The Editors of *Yank, Yank: The Story of World War II as Written by the Soldiers* (1984).

Kluger, Steve, *Yank: World War II from the Guys Who Brought You Victory* (1991).

Topping, Ira, ed. *The Best of Yank, the Army Weekly, 1942–1945* (1980).

Weithas, Art, ed., *Close to Glory: The Untold Stories of World War II by the GI's Who Saw and Reported the War—Yank Magazine Correspondents* (1991).

James R. Belpedio

Zhukov, Georgii Konstantinovich (1896–1974)

The premier Soviet commander of World War II, Georgii Konstantinovich Zhukov was born in 1896, the son of a peasant shoemaker. Apprenticed to a furrier at the age of twelve, he was drafted into the Russian army in 1915, and during his World War I service was awarded two St. George's Crosses for bravery. When his unit dissolved itself shortly after the Bolsheviks seized power in the Russian Revolution of October 1917, Zhukov quickly volunteered for the newly formed Red Army. He served on several fronts during the Russian Civil War against the anticommunist White Russian forces, including in the famous First Cavalry Army, a unit closely linked to Joseph Stalin and that would provide much of the future leadership of the Soviet army.

Serving chiefly in the Soviet cavalry, Zhukov rose quickly through the ranks, aided by his own natural talents, his ties to old comrades from the First Cavalry Army, and the Great Purges of 1937–1938, which eliminated thousands of the most talented Soviet officers and accelerated the careers of the thousands of younger officers brought in to replace them. In June 1939, Zhukov was sent to command the 57th Special Corps, later reorganized into the 1st Army Group, to drive Japanese troops off Mongolian territory.

Tensions with Japan had run high for years before serious border fighting broke out over the Japanese seizure of hills at Lake Khasan in the summer of 1938. Soviet troops managed to drive Japanese troops away from the disputed border territory, but hostilities resumed the next summer. Though the Japanese high command ordered caution, belligerent officers on the scene took a more aggressive stance.

On May 11, 1939, a small number of Japanese troops seized a stretch of Mongolian territory on the east bank of the Khalkin-Gol River. Under the Soviet Union's mutual defense treaty with the Mongolian People's Republic, the U.S.S.R. dispatched troops to restore the frontier. A renewed Japanese assault on May 28 was repulsed by a counterattack that drove the Japanese from the Khalkin-Gol's east bank and restored the previous frontier, but it was clear this test of strength was not yet complete.

Zhukov arrived in the east in June. A new Japanese offensive beginning on July 2 managed to retake the strip of territory on the Khalkin-Gol's east bank and continued to advance across the river farther into Mongolian territory. Zhukov's counterattack contained and then reversed the Japanese advance, but still left control of the eastern bank in Japanese hands. Over the next two months, Zhukov was put in command of all Soviet and Mongolian troops in the theater and provided with vast amounts of war material. Both sides continued to escalate the clash's importance by shipping more and more men and equipment to the area.

While engaging in active measures to conceal his preparations and mislead the Japanese into believing he was remaining on the defensive, Zhukov assembled overwhelming force and drew up a plan to envelop and annihilate the Japanese and Manchurian troops that remained on Mongolian territory. Zhukov gathered a potent striking force of more than 50,000 men, along with 500 tanks and an equal number of fighter aircraft. Preempting the planned Japanese offensive by four days, Zhukov's troops attacked on August 20. Zhukov skillfully coordinated combined massed infantry, air, and armored assaults to quickly surround and cut off the Japanese forces, inflicting heavy losses on them and crushing all resistance by the end of August. Soviet and Mongolian troops quickly began fortifying what they claimed was the proper boundary between Mongolia and Manchuria. For his work, Zhukov was awarded his first Hero of the Soviet Union decoration upon his return to Moscow.

The decisive Soviet victory at Khalkin-Gol, also known as under the name of Nomonhan, together with the signing of the Molotov-Ribbentrop Pact of August 1939 that gave Japan little hope of aid from Hitler, forced Japan to give up on its attempts to seize Mongolian territory. Japan signed a cease-fire agreement in Moscow on September 15, 1939, and agreed to a commission to settle disputed sections of the Mongolian-Manchurian border.

Zhukov's generalship during the battle of Khalkin-Gol displayed in detail many of the traits of his future command in the Soviet war against Nazi Germany. In particular, Zhukov always attached a great deal of importance to the careful assembly and preparation of overwhelming strength to encircle and destroy enemy forces. Likewise, his masterful use of combined arms tactics, jointly employing infantry, armor, and air power to best advantage, presaged his later successful campaigns.

Zhukov's victories in the east improved his credentials with Stalin, and when Nazi Germany invaded the U.S.S.R. on June 22, 1941, Zhukov was the Red Army's chief of staff. His contribution to the Soviet Union's final victory over Nazi Germany is difficult to overstate. Dispatched to troublespots both to shore up sagging Soviet defenses, especially in the early stages of the war, and to organize the massive Soviet offensives of later years, Zhukov was involved in all of the eastern front's key campaigns: the defense of Leningrad and Moscow (1941), the counteroffensives at Stalingrad (1942–1943) and Kursk (1943), and the final campaigns in Belorussia (1944) and against Berlin (1945).

Zhukov's postwar career rose and fell with the political tides. After final victory over Nazi Germany, Stalin feared Zhukov's power and popularity. After commanding the Soviet occupation forces in Germany, Zhukov was recalled to the Soviet Union in 1946 and sent to languish in a series of lackluster military postings. After Stalin's death in March 1953, Zhukov returned to favor first as deputy and then as full defense minister. Zhukov threw his influence behind Nikita Khrushchev in the political struggles following Stalin's death, earning his fourth Hero of the Soviet Union decoration, but once Khrushchev had a solid grip on power, he had no more use for a possible rival than Stalin did. Zhukov was forced into anonymous retirement in 1957, and was only allowed to return to the public eye and publish his surprisingly interesting memoirs after Khrushchev himself had been removed from power by a Kremlin coup. Zhukov died in 1974.

FURTHER READINGS

Coox, Algin. *Nomonhan: Japan against Russia, 1939* (1985).

Haslam, Jonathan. *The Soviet Union and the Threat from the East, 1933–1941* (1992).

Spahr, William. *Zhukov: Rise and Fall of a Great Captain* (1993).

Zhukov, Georgii. *Memoirs* (1971).

David Stone

Epilogue

Results of the Great Pacific War

World War II in the Pacific ended with the American military and economic colossus bestriding a prostrate Japan as well as the non-Communist world. The most significant, the most consequential event of the twentieth century, World War II, had concluded. Nothing in the preceding forty-five years and nothing through the end of the millennium approaches the changes wrought by the that conflict. Time itself had been redefined into prewar and postwar eras. "Before the war" and "after the war," something like B.C. and A.D., soon became common informal dating methods.

The Pacific war had indeed taken its toll: Manila, capital of the Philippines was as destroyed as Warsaw, Poland. The Japanese lost more than one million battle dead on all fronts, the Americans nearly 60,000, and the Australians around 2,000, not to mention the millions of noncombatant and civilian casualties. As always, the fatalities as well as the wounded and prisoners of war fell by far the most heavily on the infantry, the leading edge of the battle. One major change from earlier wars was that for the first time, except on the Western front in World War I (1914–18), disease did not claim more lives than did enemy action, although tens of thousands of Japanese troops died of tropical diseases in the closing months of the British reconquest of Burma.

In the postwar Pacific, the rapacious economic and militaristic engine that had been Imperial Japan was gone, driven out by American, British, and Australian armies and navies. Slave labor, deportations, and officially sanctioned mass murder (200,000 at Nanking, scores of thousands in prisoner of war camps, and literally millions in China), for a short moment, ended. Japan's fraudulent Greater East Asia Co-Prosperity Sphere had meant, in truth, prosperity—and actually only the potential of prosperity—solely for Japanese. A new economy slowly began to sort itself out from the Pacific war's wreckage.

Japan, the major military and political force in the Far East since the 1930s, had seen its once-vast empire reduced to the bombed, burned, and broken wreckage of the home islands, a result of ruthless U.S. air and naval bombardment. (Japan was the only major power to surrender without an enemy's invasion.) Tokyo's population had fallen from seven to three million. Japan's voracious, live-off-the-land armies, still 5.5 million strong at war's end in 1945, no longer scoured Asia's countries, in itself an inestimable blessing. Its sleek, well-trained navy lay on the bottom of various oceans and seas, and an air force made famous by the dreaded Mitsubishi Zero had been shot from the skies. At least 1.1 million Japanese soldiers had died, as had 670,000 civilians. Some estimates range as high as 2.3 million if one counts from 1937 to 1945.

Fleets of futuristic, silvery B-29 Superfortresses (boldly left uncamouflaged as a mark of U.S. air superiority over Japan) had destroyed Japan's cities and had cut its lines of communication and commerce. The nation's merchant fleet, its colonies and conquests, and its imports of food, fuel, and raw materials were gone. Flocks and herds had been eaten or reduced through neglect. Home island railroads had collapsed from overuse, deferred maintenance, and from the inadequate ministrations of untrained operators. The very productivity of the soil had waned from the absence of fertilizer, farm workers, and machinery. Inflation raged, unemployment awaited returning servicemen, and barter and black markets were about the only commerce that flourished.

About 6.6 million Japanese—military, administrators, colonists, and businessmen—were scattered about Asia at war's end. The Americans forcibly repatriated them to Japan, even those who had lived peaceably in their adopted countries for decades. Another 1.2 million non-

618 Epilogue: Results of the Great Pacific War

Japanese in the home islands, whom the Japanese had brought there by force, wanted to leave and return home. Those movements were the largest mass water-borne migrations in history.

Yet Japan's losses had been small compared to those of its victims, in particular, China. For eight years, China had been battled over and stripped of its resources. The Japanese had fought in China under the "Three Alls" principle: take all, burn all, and kill all. Some 1.3 million Nationalist Chinese soldiers had died as had, by very rough estimate, some 22 million Chinese civilians, mostly from starvation and privation rather than direct combat losses. These losses, very difficult to document as they are, may well have exceeded those of the Soviet Union in World War II.

Those alive were in turmoil, with Nationalist fighting Communist and bandits infesting the countryside. Prices were 2,000 times higher than in 1937. The war had been an economic catastrophe and an inflationary disaster. China's middle class had been nearly wiped out, except for war profiteers. Corruption, incompetence, and inflation had ruined Chiang Kai-shek's government and destroyed its popular appeal. Industry barely functioned, hardly assisted by the Soviet's "Treatment of Manchuria, where factories were carried off in wholesale lots in the last weeks of the war by China's "ally." The Nationalists were stumbling their way to defeat, yet the Communists had not yet developed into the fearsome threat they would one day become.

And here was the most important, unintended, postwar event of the Pacific War: the rise of Communist China. China's entry into the Communist ranks swung the balance of power against the democracies of the Free World. The Pacific war had created the conditions for the Communist triumph. The Communists could concentrate on the collapsing Nationalists, an opponent already weakened physically by the war with Japan, without having to simultaneously fight the Japanese.

The postwar Pacific also changed militarily. The U.S. Navy assumed worldwide the mantle worn for so long and so well by Britain's Royal Navy. By 1945 the Pacific was an American lake. But what now was America's mission? The Japanese fleet was gone, and the Soviets did not have a blue-water navy. The U.S. Navy had trouble developing a coherent postwar strategy. It eventually identified the Soviets as the premier threat and shifted its focus from the Pacific to the Atlantic.

The great naval war in the Pacific confirmed the aircraft carrier as the new capital ship. Aircraft carrier and naval aircraft design dominated the postwar British and U.S. navies. The first question American presidents (and

British prime ministers) would ask in times of crisis was, "Where are the carriers?" Atomic power, first used by the Americans in the Pacific war, would be put to use in submarines to give the U.S. Navy terrifying strategic power.

The U.S. Air Force, too, entered the postwar period with strategy and organization in flux. Air leaders in the newly independent service believed that air forces had replaced the Navy as America's first line of defense. The Pacific war had given strategic bombers the perfect stage to demonstrate their devastating power, both actual and potential. Strategic air power's place in warfare had seemingly been fully proved.

Tactical air power, from afloat and from ashore, and close air support of ground troops, had developed into an important arm of offense and defense. The jet-powered aircraft's roots were in the war experience. Strategic air power had passed through its formative years and had flown full grown into the postwar period. Strategic bombing successes against Germany and Japan and the U.S. nuclear potential against future enemies led to the construction of peacetime U.S. bomber fleets that were unmatched, at least in numbers, in the postwar world. The Air Transport Command had developed an amazing reach and usefulness during the Pacific war, and air transports were a new and growing piece of the newly created Defense Department's budget.

The Pacific had seen the first and only use of nuclear weapons, from actual employment against the enemy's cities to the planned tactical use in support of ground forces for the invasion of the home islands. Nuclear weapons, along with conventional bombing, made a conventional invasion of Japan unnecessary. Without the war, nuclear power—including its nonmilitary uses—would have taken much longer to reach fruition. Nonetheless, the atomic bombing of Hiroshima and Nagasaki was, not surprisingly, in later decades the subject of intense debate, with opponents attempting to show that the two bombings were unnecessary and that they were mounted to overawe the Soviets or simply from sheer racism. Proponents responded to the effect that if the Japanese were "already defeated" military leaders on both sides were hardly aware of this fact *at the time*.

As a result of the Pacific war, amphibious warfare had developed into an art and on such a scale that would never again be seen. Technological advances, especially atomic weapons, made mass landings on a Pacific war scale dangerous even as logistics and technology made them more feasible. However, smaller battalion amphibious task forces would become often-used arrows in the American postwar quiver. Airborne assaults at the division and corps level were also a fading art. Atomic weapons, improved air defenses, and the cost of maintaining huge transport fleets militated against mass drops.

Rockets fired from aircraft and ships had proved their value and would increase in effectiveness and usefulness in the postwar world. Experiences in air-sea rescue would carry over into the postwar military and Coast Guard. Weather forecasting benefited from new war-built observation stations and from an understanding of the newly discovered jet stream. Huge areas of the Pacific had been mapped and charted, ports built, and airfields laid down in support of military operations. Those maps, charts, and facilities would expedite postwar oil and mineral exploration.

Most important for the postwar period was the unification of the U.S. armed forces under the National Security Act of 1947. The Pacific war, in the failure of the Americans to execute true service unification, helped make the very case for unification. A Secretary of Defense would soon preside over departments of the Army, Navy, and Air Force. No longer would the American military have to depend on fortuitous personal interactions of Army and Navy flag officers to ensure coordination of ground and sea operations.

The great strides in military aircraft range, endurance, and reliability, all driven by pressures of military necessity, had laid the groundwork for an upcoming era of air transportation. Thousands of demobilized aircraft, from single-engine trainers to four-engine transports, entered the civilian market. Airlines grew like weeds after a rain, although most faded sooner or later. Men who had flown those very aircraft during the war joined the airlines and pioneered new air routes throughout the Pacific. That new aviation era would bring about the demise of the romantic flying boat. The hundreds of airfields built throughout the Pacific meant that land-based aircraft could hop from island to island. Protected bays and harbors were no longer needed, and the flying boat soon disappeared.

New communications, new cryptography and code breaking, and new military tactics grew out of the Pacific's battlefields. Warfare itself was changing, fragmenting into national struggles against colonial powers. Guerrilla warfare launched by the Americans in the Philippines had led the American Army into the role of insurgency. Guerrilla warfare launched against the Japanese in French Indochina would lead France and the United States into the role of counterinsurgency. The Dutch East Indies, soon to become the independent nation of Indonesia, were in ferment. Anti-Japanese resistance movements translated easily into anti-colonial, nationalist wars of liberation.

The entire political, military, and economic foundation of the Pacific basin had been overturned. Insurgency and counterinsurgency would grip Pacific rim nations for the next thirty years, interrupted only by the conventional Korean War (1950–1953). Counterinsurgency would lead to the development of entirely new strategic, tactical, and political doctrine. The Pacific war had broken the status quo. Asia's populace knew full well that the white man could be defeated—the Japanese had demonstrated that. Peoples with age-old aspirations for independence fought with whatever tools they could acquire, most often with the tools of the guerrilla.

Conventional weapons from destroyed and surrendered Japanese armies glutted local resistance movements. The quality and quantity of war materials available was astounding. At the start of the war, Britain had lost a garrison of some 12,000 men at Hong Kong, almost 140,000 British, Australians, and Indians in Malaya and Singapore, and almost 16,000 in the Dutch East Indies, while the Americans lost 120,000 in the Philippines. Many of the weapons and munitions of these defeated forces still existed. On top of that now came the weapons of the recently defeated Japanese armies. Chinese Communists acquired Japanese arms by "attacking" depots "guarded" by Soviet troops.

With captured weapons came a flood of men, including Japanese, who had spent the last five or more years learning the arts of war, and who found the ways of peace alien or boring. In Saigon, Vietnam, the British occupation commander retained nearly 70,000 armed Japanese troops to suppress "civil disturbance" and hold the country until the French arrived. The French then joined the British and Japanese in clearing Saigon of Viet Minh guerrillas. There is no small irony that the British used Japanese troops (who had ousted the French) to restore the French by fighting Vietnamese (the Viet Minh) who had fought the Japanese in support of the West.

Guerrillas, demobilized soldiers, and regulars, all looked for new martial horizons. And they had weapons. Many resistance movements had been supplied and trained by the Allies, and with the war's end, they were unwilling to beat sword into plowshare. They had developed organization and discipline during their struggles against the common enemy, and the Japanese humiliation of the white man in 1941–1942 had made a lasting impression.

Ho Chi Minh led Vietnam's Viet Minh. Vietnam, north and south, threw off French control and then sank into a protracted civil war. Malaya had a Communist party as well as the Malayan People's Anti-British Army. Luckily for Britain—for it needed the dollars produced by rubber and tin exports—nationalism and Communist insurgency had a slow start in Malaya. Only in 1948 did insurgency explode, and again luckily for Britain, it did not succeed. The British succeeded in their military and political response, and their defeat of insurgency in Malaya provided a model (not often followed) for others so afflicted.

The Philippines lay in ruins, with Manila nearly destroyed. More than a million Filipinos had died. The economy was wrecked, transportation seriously impaired, and infrastructure shattered. The large U.S. force in the Philippines when war ended probably forestalled an Communist-led uprising. The American promise of independence in 1946 as well as an influx of aid enhanced American popularity. Yet it was not long before the Hukbalahap Communist guerrilla forces, under the slogan "land for the landless," rose against a corrupt Manila government and the established social order.

Burma had paid the price for being a battlefield. Its inland towns were in ruins, Rangoon's port was unusable, and railroads and bridges were wrecked from RAF bombing. The people were split into two camps, those who had supported the Japanese (the majority), and those who had opposed them. Burma was spared major anti-colonial guerrilla warfare when the British, in their wisdom, granted the colony independence in 1947.

Korea had been exploited by the Japanese since 1905. Its men had been massively conscripted into Japan's armies during World War II, the very names of its people and cities changed and dictated by the Japanese, and Japanese colonists and administrators imposed on the populace. The World War II victors imperiously divided Korea along the 38th parallel in a political split that would start one of the first hot battles of the Cold War. Postwar American politics ignored Korea, much to everyone's regret in June 1950, when the Communist North invaded the anti-Communist South, igniting the Korean War.

In Indonesia, an independence movement was firmly entrenched after the war. The Dutch were too weak to regain their prewar control, although, as in many such counterinsurgencies, the guerrillas won at the conference table what they could not seize on the battlefield. Japan's wartime promise of independence to the Dutch East Indies—as duplicitous and faithless as were similar offers elsewhere—had, in this case, worked and turned the Indonesian people in a direction the Dutch could not change. Japanese use of Indonesian functionaries during the war and the creation of a national militia had left in place a de facto government and an army armed with Japanese weapons. The use of British and Japanese troops, as in Indochina, to reclaim cities held by local forces led

to major battles. It took until 1949, but the Dutch were on the way out.

Australia emerged as a winner in the postwar world. More than a half million Australians had served overseas, and Australia had developed, for the first time, its own foreign policy distinct from Britain's lead. Its armies had fought in the Pacific, and its economy had mobilized to provide vast quantities of food and support services to the Americans as they moved across the Pacific toward Japan. Japan had frightened Australia. Australia's early, postwar interest was more in protection from, rather than involvement in, Asia. Nevertheless, Australians would find unprecedented prosperity in their postwar world.

A new entity emerged from the war, the Trust Territories of the Pacific Islands (the post–World War II Japanese Mandated Islands). They became a United Nations trusteeship administered by the United States. Island groups made famous during the war as the scenes of horrific fighting—the Palaus, the Carolines, the Marshalls, and the Marianas as well as the individual islands such as Truk, Tinian, and Saipan—were transferred from Japanese to American protection. Separate from the Trust Territory was Taiwan, once Chinese, then Japanese Formosa, and by 1949 the be the last stronghold of the Nationalist Chinese, who retreated there after the Communist victory on the mainland.

Closely tied to military strength is political power. The Pacific war transformed America's position west of California. No longer was America a chiding, unheeded voice railing ineffectively against Japanese militarism. When America spoke, people listened. America was *the* dominant power in the Pacific after the war. The Soviets were poised to become a minor Pacific player, but mainly as a result of their power in Europe. Britain was enfeebled. France was a weak colonial power on its bloody, sad way out in Indochina.

America had learned to work with and lead allies. Isolationist sentiment still existed, but America had entered a new era of world politics and global influence. The war made Americans look more closely at international relations. America's postwar foreign policy would be built on regional alliances, both military and economic. American power had shifted from a continental-based center to the fringes of a brand new, but sometimes poorly defined, defense perimeter. The United States had big economic carrots and sticks with which to support its diplomacy. The economy would expand through links to the Pacific's raw materials and burgeoning population.

America's anti-colonial bent caused conflict with the British, French, and Dutch, the Pacific's "old" colonial powers. But the U.S. anti-Communist foreign policy would link it, sometimes quite unhappily, with foreign colonialism. A series of overseas military bases and forward deployed forces would grow to a level and permanence unimagined before the war. The need for transit bases and services to support the new forward-deployed military tied the United States to nations around the Pacific. The United States began a policy of acquiring bases in the Pacific and denying bases to Communist powers, and there was not much the latter could do about it.

The Pacific war unleashed economic changes that would redefine some of the very foundations of economic thought and theory. The "Asian Tigers," lands of no particular economic significance before the war and for about two decades following, developed enormous industrial and monetary power, defying the conventional wisdom that a nation needed natural resources to advance economically. Hong Kong, Singapore, South Korea, and Taiwan had few if any tangible resources. Cut off from their traditional sources of raw materials by postwar turmoil and then by the Cold War, these small entities had to look inward to their own personal resources, and their postwar economic success challenged prevailing geopolitical constructions. (Of course, Japan had been a strong industrial power before the war, but afterward it was about in the same situation as South Korea or Taiwan.) This development, of course, took practically all economists by surprise. Had anyone foreseen that Taiwan would someday hold more foreign exchange than that of the United States, that South Korean automobiles would carve a respectable niche in the U.S. market, that Hong Kong banks would become major competitors to Chase Manhattan, or that Asian television sets would drive their last U.S. manufacturer from the field, he would have been hooted out of the profession and serious doubts cast on his sanity. Conversely, China and the Soviet Union lagged in economic development, for all their natural resources, including oil.

The war guaranteed social changes throughout the Pacific basin. Even Japan was remade socially. The Japanese military had been filled with violent officers and men. Their code of *bushido* and their bloody application of that code was incomprehensible to most Westerners. The war, however, had so thoroughly overwhelmed and bloodied Japan that the old social order collapsed, and with it, militarism and bushido.

The American occupation was peaceful and benevolent. Manpower losses and the economic destruction in Japan had been immense. The militarists who had led Japan had been thoroughly defeated, disgraced, and repudiated. Demilitarization and democratization, peace and democracy, became the rallying cries. Without a military empire on which to waste its passions, vigor, and manpower, Japan turned its energies to commerce and industry and became an economic and democratic powerhouse and a dutiful ally of the United States.

Japanese women, tightly controlled and until the war subservient to men and tradition, had entered the workforce during the war and were now, after the war, unwilling to return to the home (oddly, unlike most American female defense workers). The role of Japanese men, that of master, militarist, and provider, had been broken. They would not go quietly, of course, or completely, as more than fifty years of postwar history and society have shown. But women gained the vote, joined labor unions, and began to enter politics and business as a direct result of Japan's total defeat.

Not everything in Japan changed. Although land reform abolished the absentee landlords and handed out land to two million small farmers, and although the old zaibatsu, the big business groups, were initially dissolved, the zaibatsu went underground and grew in power and influence as the economy slowly improved. Japanese politicians fought quiet delaying actions against many reforms, such as that of education in the American mode. The prewar elite generally emerged as the postwar elite. Regardless, Japan became fundamentally more democratic, peaceful, and egalitarian than could have occurred or even been imagined by any means other than total and catastrophic military defeat.

America, in contrast to Japan, Britain, France, the Netherlands, and China, stood at an incomparable pinnacle of power—military, political, and economic. The United States was now a oceanic and world power possessing a worldwide amphibious, aerial, and, for a time, unchallenged atomic reach. The United States was and remains the one and the only postwar Pacific power.

Its word was literally law in Japan. The new shogun, Douglas MacArthur, ruled the home islands. America's economic strength was overwhelming, in part because of the collapse of counterbalancing economies of European colonial powers and native economies such as the exhausted Philippines. Its industrial base was intact and undamaged, and, in fact, greatly expanded. Ruined Asian markets lay empty and unprotected before American production that was gearing down from war goods and up for consumer goods.

American criminal law, modified for the purpose into a "victor's law," searched out war criminals and punished them. China, Malaya, Singapore, and the Netherlands also hosted trials and executions, some of the latter more the result of the defendants simply having defeated the Allies in the earlier stages of the war than to any war crimes they were supposed to have condoned. The clear culpability of the accused and the desire to close the door on that part of their nation's failed history led the Japanese quietly to accept the executions. The new Japanese constitution was basically an American product. The American colonial experience in the Philippines had already set the structure for that commonwealth's independence, and America's easy, ungrudging release of the Filipinos contrasted sharply and gratifyingly with British, French, and Dutch attitudes and actions.

American culture stood poised for an incursion into Asian societies as peaceful, beneficial, and long-lasting as Japan's military invasions had been violent, debilitating, and short-lived. American soldiers and sailors had met Asia's inhabitants and, on the whole and by example, showed America's unique culture, its democracy, and its compassion. It was a potent mix. It would take time, but American culture would conquer the Far East more completely than had American arms.

Industrial strides forced by the Pacific war would carry over into the postwar world. Government control of the economy had been necessary for the war and would continue to some degree in the postwar world. Synthetic rubber, plastics, advances in medicine in general and tropical, trauma, and aviation medicine in particular would benefit peoples of the Pacific basin. Malaria control, animal husbandry, crop-yield increases, hospital construction, drug discoveries, and education began to increase average life expectancy.

Changes were by no means limited to the peoples of the Pacific basin. The Pacific war altered American views of the world, of Asia, and of other peoples. Having seen the Pacific, American views of the hometown would be forever changed. Social changes forced by war had moved women into the workforce, had brought African Americans north to the big cities, and had plucked rural inhabitants from their isolation, comfortable or otherwise, and thrown them into a totally new world. Black troops proved, again, they were as capable as whites, although true integration into the military would require another war (Korea). Women had entered the American labor force in huge numbers (roughly 5 million) and into the military in smaller numbers. But American women were forced back to their hearthside as wives and mothers, where the majority would remain for the next three decades.

A huge number of American veterans—more than 12 million in all services—demobilized and flooded the workforce. They came to industry and commerce with experience and confidence gained by doing big things, impossible things. These men had built harbors, airfields, entire industries, had transported cargo and armies and had girdled the Pacific with communications. They had mobilized a nation and sent its armed strength to every corner of the Pacific. They had unleashed the power of the sun on two Japanese cities. They had remembered—and avenged—Pearl Harbor. All this expertise and hitherto untapped talent would explode into economic growth unrivaled anywhere in the world. The American people, in spite of the usual political infighting, strikes, and inflation, looked at a future holding great expectations, unlimited potential, and new frontiers.

The postwar Veteran's Administration administered a home loan program that led, in large part, to two-thirds of Americans owning their own homes. Electricity and running water overlaid the nation. The June 1944 Veterans Act, also known as the GI Bill, gave demobilized military personnel educational grants, loans for businesses and for homes, and hiring preferences. As students, GIs not only greatly expanded American higher education, with their unwontedly serious pursuit of learning, but they transformed it, at least for a decade. Veterans became governors, senators, congressmen, and presidents. Interestingly, after Dwight Eisenhower, all the World War II veterans who became Presidents served in the Pacific: John F. Kennedy, Lyndon B. Johnson, Richard M. Nixon, Gerald Ford, and George Bush. Their personal experiences of war would color their official duties.

The Pacific war was the defining event of the twentieth century for the Pacific basin. No other event and no other period made so many decisive changes to political boundaries and to societies. The rise of Communist China has yet to play out. Japan's vigorous economic reintegration into the Pacific world as *the* industrial competitor to the United States, and into its old empire continues, while American influence—military, economic, and cultural—grows to new heights.

So great and so lasting was the shift in power in the Pacific basin that had occurred by 1945 ("Year Zero"), that it would be almost impossible to imagine the nature of that area of the world had the war not occurred.

FURTHER READINGS

Gilbert, James. *Another Chance: Postwar America, 1945–1985* (1986).

Jackson, J. Hampden. *The World in the Postwar Decade, 1945–1955* (1956).

James, D. Clayton. *The Years of MacArthur*, vol 3 (1985).

Palmer, Michael A. *Origins of the Maritime Strategy: American Naval Strategy in the First Postwar Decade* (1988).

Smith, Bradley F. *The War's Long Shadow: The Second World War and Its Aftermath—China, Russia, Britain, America* (1986).

John W. Whitman

Index

Page numbers set in **bold** indicate the page where the main entry for the topic appears.